REDFERN AND HUNTER
ON INTERNATIONAL ARBITRATION

REDFERN AND HUNTER ON INTERNATIONAL ARBITRATION

SEVENTH EDITION

Nigel Blackaby KC
Constantine Partasides KC
WITH
Alan Redfern

OXFORD
UNIVERSITY PRESS

Great Clarendon Street, Oxford, OX2 6DP,
United Kingdom

Oxford University Press is a department of the University of Oxford.
It furthers the University's objective of excellence in research, scholarship,
and education by publishing worldwide. Oxford is a registered trade mark of
Oxford University Press in the UK and in certain other countries

Sixth Edition published in 2015
Seventh Edition published in 2022
Impression: 1

Published in the United States of America by Oxford University Press
198 Madison Avenue, New York, NY 10016, United States of America

British Library Cataloguing in Publication Data

Data available

Library of Congress Control Number: 2022938193

ISBN 978–0–19–286990–6 (hbk.)

DOI: 10.1093/law/9780192869906.001.0001

Printed and bound in the UK by
TJ Books Limited

FOREWORD BY ALAN REDFERN

A tribute to Martin Hunter; and a personal note.

Redfern and Hunter on International Arbitration is now a well-known treatise. It is read and cited by international lawyers, arbitrators, and judges, and it is taught and studied by teachers, students, and potential arbitrators across the world. But it would not have been written without Martin Hunter.

I first met Martin in the 1960s, when we were both young lawyers at Freshfields. It was then an old-established firm in the City of London, with sixteen or so partners, and it proudly traced its origins to its association with the Bank of England in the early eighteenth century. It is now a global law firm.

After training at Freshfields as a law graduate, I was appointed in 1963 as the firm's first litigation partner. My main task was to establish a litigation department, at a time when litigation was perceived as a somewhat dubious activity for a respectable City law firm. My introduction to the more acceptable world of arbitration began when I was instructed to act for a British company in a construction dispute that eventually led to an international arbitration at the Peace Palace at The Hague.

At about the same time, I was also asked to assist my firm's senior partner, Sir Charles Whishaw, in an international arbitration for the government of Kuwait, for whom Sir Charles had previously acted in the negotiation of oil concessions. I said that if I was to do this, I would need a good, qualified assistant. I was told that I could 'borrow' Martin Hunter, a newly-qualified solicitor who had just joined the firm's corporate department, on 'a short-term loan'. It was a loan that was never repaid; and it was the beginning of a long and memorable friendship between Martin and his wife Linda, and myself and my late wife, Marie-Louise.

Martin joined me as a litigation partner in 1967; and naturally he began to build his own litigation and arbitration practice within the firm. However, we still worked together from time to time, most notably in the well-known Aminoil arbitration in the late 1970s.[1] As the lead partner in that case, I was fortunate to have Martin helping me to prepare and present the case for the Kuwait government.

But what about Martin's life as a lawyer? It seems to me to have moved seamlessly through three different stages. First, there was Martin's role as a partner in what became an international law firm. Secondly, after Martin had retired from that firm in 1993, there was his practice as a counsel and arbitrator at the English bar. Finally (and this is probably what excited him most, and where his true legacy lies) Martin became an inspiring teacher of

---

[1] *Aminoil v Government of Kuwait* (1982) XXI ILM 976. Anyone who is interested can read about the case in The British Year Book of International Law: see Redfern, 'The Arbitration between the Government of Kuwait and *Aminoil*' (Oxford University Press, 1984), pp. 65–110.

international arbitration to young lawyers, not only in England but in other parts of the world, including India and Brazil.

As many readers will know, Martin died at his home at Walton-on-Thames in England, on 9 October 2021, after a long and debilitating illness. Throughout this agonising period, Martin was tirelessly and steadfastly supported by Linda, in sickness as in health.

Since his death, there have been many tributes to Martin, from his friends and colleagues around the world. They have highlighted his achievements and his friendships, and his unceasing contribution to the development and teaching of the law and practice of international arbitration. Amongst the most touching tributes are those from Martin's former students, with heart-warming and affectionate memories of someone whom they were proud to call their friend, their guide, and their mentor.

Martin had no children of his own, but he had a large and devoted following amongst his students and assistants. This included a coterie of young lawyers who were known as 'the M's'. One of them has written:[2]

> Of Martin's many fascinating quirks, my favourites were the 'Friday clinic' and the community of M's he created. The clinic was a unique gathering centre where his past protégés, who had recently started careers in international arbitration, shared experience and lessons learned with a new generation of aspiring practitioners over a gin and tonic at a pub in Covent Garden. The first stop of the Friday clinic was always the local barber shop owned by Martin's good friend. The M's was a naming tradition (MII–MXXVIII) for his research assistants—of which I had the privilege of being one—which came from the fact that his first two research assistants shared his first name.

I should explain why *Redfern and Hunter* would not have been written without Martin. In the early 1980s, Martin was asked if he would be interested in writing a book on international arbitration. He said yes, but not without me. I was very reluctant, and told Martin so. I said that as partners in Freshfields, we already had enough to do to develop the firm's practice in litigation and arbitration, without writing a book. Martin insisted. He persuaded me that we could write the book in our spare time, drafting and exchanging drafts with each other at weekends and holidays; and so, I agreed to do it.

Our first edition was published in 1986. This was at a time when international arbitration was undergoing a major transformation. From being 'a cottage industry, permeated by the culture of French and Swiss legal artisans, or specialists working in particular fields such as insurance or construction,'[3] international arbitration was becoming the leading method of resolving transnational disputes. In doing so, it was greatly helped by the fact that an ambitious project to create a worldwide law on international arbitration was moving nearer to fulfilment. In December 1985, the General Assembly of the United Nations adopted the Model Law on International Commercial Arbitration, as a code of law to be recommended to all member states. The Model Law now stands, with the New York Convention of 1958, as one of the twin pillars of international arbitration.

---

[2] Živa Filipič, 'In Memoriam Professor J. Martin Hunter' (2021) 3 ICC Dispute Resolution Bulletin 11–12.
[3] William Park, in a tribute to Johnny Veeder KC, in (2021) 37(2) Arb Intl 417.

In the closing chapter of the first edition of this book,[4] Martin and I suggested that the Model Law would accelerate the transformation of international arbitration. We thought that lawyers and arbitrators who were working under the Model Law, in whatever country they were based, would benefit greatly from being able to operate under an internationally accepted and harmonised legal system. We also thought that recognition and enforcement of awards by local or national courts would be treated with greater uniformity; and that this would enhance both the popularity and the effectiveness of international arbitration in the peaceful resolution of cross-frontier disputes.

As we then saw it, international arbitration was poised to become truly international. It would be broadly based, with less dependence on the existing major centres of arbitration. Applications to local or national courts in support of arbitrations would be dealt with on a uniform basis, in conformity with modern standards. Above all, arbitral tribunals would be entitled to adopt flexible procedures, designed by parties and arbitrators to meet the particular needs of each individual arbitration, without fear that awards would be nullified for failure to follow particular local or national rules of procedure.

As for the parties to an international arbitration, they would have the power to determine the procedure to be followed in their arbitration. They would also know that arbitrators were legally required to be independent and impartial, even if chosen by the parties themselves. Finally, the parties would know that they would be treated with equality; that each party would be given a proper opportunity to present its case; and that, if required, courts of law across the world would do their best to ensure that international arbitral awards were carried into effect.

That, more or less, was how Martin and I saw the future of international arbitration when we wrote the first edition of this book. It will be for our readers to decide to what extent our vision has come true.

The first edition was published more than a generation ago. Since then, there has been a vast expansion in the nature, scope, and practice of international arbitration. In working on this seventh edition, and in hoping to make it a worthy memorial to Martin, my co-authors and I have not simply updated the text, by adding new references and deleting the old. Instead, we have stood back and taken a fresh look at international arbitration. As practitioners and arbitrators, we have learnt much about it over the past years. We are conscious of the importance of its legal and historical background, and we reflect on this; but we have also done our best to portray international arbitration as it is today, not as it was when the first edition was written.

I have suggested that Martin's working life reached fulfilment as a teacher. My own professional life was centred firmly on my partnership in Freshfields Bruckhuas Deringer, as the firm had become known. But as we learn from Shakespeare, 'that old common arbitrator, Time, will one day end it',[5] and relentlessly, retirement drew near. Some people look forward with eager anticipation to their retirement as an opportunity to pursue new interests or hobbies. For my part, I dreaded the prospect of leaving my practice as a lawyer.

---

[4] Redfern and Hunter, *Law and Practice of International Commercial Arbitration* (Sweet & Maxwell, 1986), p. 404.

[5] *The Folio Shakespeare, Vol. IV, Troilus and Cressida* (1602) (The Folio Society, 1988), act 4.sc.7, pp. 108–110.

As it happened, Tony (later Lord) Grabiner KC, with whom I had worked on cases for Eurotunnel[6] when the Channel Tunnel between France and England was being constructed, suggested that when I retired, I might qualify as a member of the English Bar and join his chambers at One Essex Court, to help establish an international arbitration practice. I did this and I was subsequently joined by two other former solicitors from leading City firms, Andrew Foyle and Christopher Styles KC, and by former members of the judiciary, including Lord Neuberger, who retired from his position as the President of the United Kingdom Supreme Court in 2017, and who then started practising as an arbitrator from One Essex Court.

My membership of chambers brought me into contact with many lawyers, seniors and juniors, from whom I learnt much. They included Liz (later Lady) Gloster, Ian Glick KC, Anna Boase KC, and Peter Leaver KC, who, as well as acting as an international arbitrator, was for a time the Chairman of the Board of Directors of the London Court of International Arbitration (LCIA).

I myself was a non-executive Director of the LCIA for several years; and from July 2002 to December 2014, I was a member of the Court of Arbitration of the International Chamber of Commerce (ICC), first as the UK representative and then as a Vice-President of the ICC Court. This appointment involved preparing for and attending the monthly meetings of the Court in Paris which, in the words of one of my US colleagues, we did 'on our own dime'.

It also involved occasionally chairing meetings of the Comité Restraint which, for a lawyer, was the 'engine room' of the ICC Court. In this context, I would particularly like to express my thanks to Professor Anne Marie Whitesell, who was Secretary-General of the Court from 2001 until 2007 and with whom I later had the pleasure of sitting as an arbitrator; to my friend John Beechey CBE, who was President of the ICC Court in challenging times, from January 2009 to June 2015; to another friend, Jeffrey Hertzfeld, an American lawyer in Paris with whom I sat in several arbitrations; and to the young, talented, and multilingual counsel at the ICC Court, including Dr. Maria Hauser-Morel who, during her time at the ICC, headed a case management team with which I worked in my last case as President of an ICC tribunal.

Finally, I must thank Simon Weber, a research assistant and a good and loyal friend to Martin. Simon had carried out research for Martin which was intended for the first chapter of this book and he then greatly assisted me when I was obliged to take over responsibility for that chapter.

The lawyers to whom I have referred, and others that are too numerous to mention, have all contributed in one way or another to my knowledge of international arbitration. The essence of much of that knowledge is distilled in my contribution to this new edition of *Redfern and Hunter*.

Alan Redfern
London, 2022

---

[6] There were a series of disputes between Eurotunnel, the owner of the Channel Tunnel, and TML, the Anglo-French consortium that was responsible for its construction, including two international arbitrations and a case in the House of Lords, as the UK Supreme Court was then called.

PREFACE

We dedicate this seventh edition to the memory of one of the two great men whose name it bears, Professor Martin Hunter, whom the arbitration world lost in 2021.

Martin Hunter was one of a kind. He was a genuine arbitration visionary, who imagined earlier than anyone else that international arbitration could be a specialist area of commercial legal practice. Together with his extraordinary friend Alan Redfern, he built the first such specialist team at their old firm of Freshfields, and they hired a talented young fellow called Jan Paulsson to lead that practice internationally. After law firm life, Martin developed a career as a leading international arbitrator, who applied his energy, and his legal and commercial acumen, to dispense arbitral justice at the very highest level. He believed in the importance of international arbitration, which he would declare with total conviction was critical to world peace and progress. Of course he would say this with a twinkle in his eye that was a clue that he took what he said much less seriously than he wanted you to take it.

But Martin was so much more than a world-class international arbitrator. Above all else, he was an extraordinarily kind and generous mentor, long before the term mentoring had become fashionable. His father was a teacher, and Martin loved to teach arbitration. But it wasn't just arbitration that he liked to teach; he was passionate in helping young lawyers more generally to find the right path. And so, for the last two decades of his life, he combined the practice of arbitration with extensive teaching at universities around the world; not just at arbitration's traditional centres in the United Kingdom and the United States, but at the frontiers of arbitration's future, in places like Orissa State in India, and universities throughout Brazil, where he introduced generations of lawyers to the law and practice of arbitration. And he didn't just limit his teaching to arbitration or the lecture hall. With the unfailing help and constant support of his partner in life, Linda Hunter, Martin introduced an extraordinary number of young lawyers from all over the world to the Hunters' enthusiastic philosophy of life, and gave them a push that changed numerous destinies.

For us, over the last fifteen years, Martin was a brilliant co-author, with encyclopaedic knowledge of our field, a powerfully simple writing prose, and the kind of personality that would not allow co-authors to get away with missed deadlines! But above all, he was a friend, who gave us the example of his limitless enthusiasm for life.

Just as we began work on the seventh edition with Martin, so we completed it thinking of him. With his and Alan's help, we have attempted to stay faithful to the original genius of *Redfern and Hunter* as an elegantly written, easily comprehensible synthesis of arbitration law and practice. The task of synthesis has become both more difficult and more important over time. Today, there are far more voices in the world of arbitration producing much more noise, and any modern commentary on the field must take that into account. But *Redfern and Hunter* was not intended to be an exhaustive encyclopaedia of arbitral sources or precedents. And the heart of the arbitral process, despite the growing number of accoutrements, remains as true today as it was in 1986 when the first edition was published: an independent dispute resolution process to assist international business and states in which private individuals selected by the parties would hear their disputes and render a binding decision enforceable throughout the world. So whilst we take care to address the proliferating novelties in the arbitration world—whether the ever stronger influence of investment arbitration, the arrival of the emergency arbitrator, the development of soft law on conflicts, ethics, and evidence, or the growing jurisprudence on arbitrator challenges—we have sought to ensure that these novelties do not overshadow the essence of the arbitral process. This, in turn, has allowed us to keep our promise of a single-volume work.

The product of our approach involves much that is new, combined with an essence that will be immediately recognisable to those of you familiar with earlier editions. As Alan and Martin have always demanded, our work on the seventh edition has involved much more than mere updating. To stay alive, this book, like any living organism, must regenerate. And so, whole passages have gone and new ones have appeared. But our structure remains untouched. It follows an international arbitration chronologically through its life with a brief parenthesis to look at the influence of arbitration pursuant to investment treaties. As befits a work whose authors learned their trade as advocates and arbitrators, it has a strong practical focus. For this, it draws on the authors' cumulative century of experience in international arbitration. And this edition expands further its international scope, drawing more deeply from arbitration's new centres: from China to Canada, from Singapore to Brazil, and from the Middle East to Sub-Saharan Africa.

Finding the time for a work of this scope is a challenging task for busy practitioners and those challenges appear only to grow over time. We have been particularly grateful that Alan has continued to play a critical lead role, maintaining the pen on two key chapters and reviewing all others to make sure we undertook a comprehensive review and didn't sit on our laurels. Alan has made sure that stale authorities have been unceremoniously abandoned in favour of fresher examples whilst maintaining an eagle eye for inconsistencies and inelegance of expression. He is also singlehandedly responsible for keeping the pressure on us to finish the book. Alan's lifetime of experience and wisdom, together with other lasting legacies such as the Redfern Schedule, were deservedly recognised when he was awarded the GAR Lifetime Achievement Award in 2021. He was always supported in his work and so much else, particularly when perfect French language skills were required to dissect the complexities of French case law, by his wife Marie-Louise, who—like Linda Hunter—was always very generous with both of us. One of the greatest pleasures of producing this seventh edition has been the excuse to retain frequent contact with Alan who has generously hosted us on several occasions at his home in London for editorial meetings to isolate us from the cares of the office. As all who know him will attest, he combines insight and experience with humour and humility in equal doses, and has been a dear friend and mentor to both of us through most of our careers.

Our ability to ensure we were fully briefed on developments before putting pen to paper is due to the assistance of many talented international arbitration practitioners we have come to know and respect throughout the world, in addition to a pool of young and talented lawyers who gave us a great deal of their free time to participate with enthusiasm for the research for this project. First and foremost, we are particularly grateful to the last of Martin's mentees, Simon Weber, who worked tirelessly to ensure we received Martin's comments and insights during very difficult times. There are too many names from our own teams to mention but they include (in alphabetical order) Alex Alonso, Matheus Bastos Oliveira, Yosr Bouassida, Mihir Chattopadhyay, Oscar Collins, Zara Desai, Rosario Galardi, Santiago Gatica, Brianna Gorence, Maanas Jain, Kimberley Larkin, Virginie Lassez, Maria Paz Lestido, Elliot Luke, Rodrigo Millan, Nicola Peart, Laura França Pereira, Diego Perez, Pedro Ramirez, Julian Rotenberg, Diego Rueda, Luiza Saldanha, Madeline Snider, Joe Spadafore, Ezequiel Vetulli, Paige von Mehren, Geoff Watt, and Jeff Yiu.

Finally, we thank our families for their unfailing support. This book is not written in place of our professional demands, but in hundreds of hours stolen from other parts of our lives. Without the support of Maria and Patricia, Nayeli, Artemis (and Perla), we wouldn't have advanced beyond our first edition as an author team and yet we are now proud to have completed our seventh edition.

A traditional book format relies on a production process that is less immediate than we have come to expect in an internet world. As a consequence, we had to put pens down by a certain date. The date for this edition is April 2022.

Nigel Blackaby KC and Constantine Partasides KC\
April 2022

SUMMARY CONTENTS

CONTENTS

TABLE OF CASES

TABLE OF LEGISLATION

TABLE OF STATUTORY INSTRUMENTS

OTHER LEGISLATION

Argentina

Australia

Austria

Belgium

Brazil

TABLE OF ARBITRATION AWARDS

LIST OF ABBREVIATIONS

AAA	American Arbitration Association, New York (Established 1926)
AAA Rules	AAA Commercial Arbitration Rules and Mediation Procedures, in force 1 October 2013
ABA	American Bar Association, Chicago (Established 1878)
ABQB	Alberta Court of Queen's Bench (Canada)
AC	*Law Reports Appeal Cases*, published by the Incorporated Council of Law Reporting for England and Wales
ACICA	Australian Centre for International Commercial Arbitration, Sydney (Established 1985)
AD	*New York Supreme Court Appellate Division Reports*
ADGM	Abu Dhabi Global Market
ADR	alternative dispute resolution
ADRLJ	*Arbitration and Dispute Resolution Law Journal*, published by Sweet & Maxwell
ALI	American Law Institute, Philadelphia, PA (Established 1923)
All ER	*All England Law Reports*, published by LexisNexis
Am J Comp L	*American Journal of Comparative Law*, published by University of Michigan Law School
Am Rev Intl Arb	*American Review of International Arbitration*, published by Juris
Arab League Investment Agreement	Unified Agreement for the Investment of Arab Capital in the Arab States, Arab League
Arb Intl	*Arbitration International*, published by the LCIA
Arb LM	*Arbitration Law Monthly*, published by Sweet & Maxwell
Arb LR	*Arbitration Law Reports and Review*, published by Oxford University Press
ARIAS	Aida Reinsurance and Insurance Arbitration Society, Mount Vernon, NY (Established 1994)
art./Art.	article (domestic)/Article (supranational)
ASA	Association Suisse de l'Arbitrage [Swiss Arbitration Association], Basel (Established 1974)
ASA Bulletin	*Bulletin of the Swiss Arbitration Association*, published by Kluwer Law International
ASEAN	Association of Southeast Asian Nations, Bangkok (Established 1967)
Asian Intl Arb J	*Asian International Arbitration Journal*, published by Kluwer Law International
BGHZ	*Entscheidungen des Bundesgerichtshofes in Zivilsachen*, published by Carl Heymanns Verlag
Bing	*Bingham's Common Pleas Reports*, published in English Reports
BIT	bilateral investment treaty
BJIL	*Berkeley Journal of International Law*, published by University of California, Berkeley, School of Law
BR	*Bankruptcy Reporter* (US), published by West Publishing

Brussels Convention	Brussels Convention on Jurisdiction and the Enforcement of Judgments in Civil and Commercial Matters 1968
Brussels Regulation	Council Regulation (EC) No. 44/2001 on Jurisdiction and the Enforcement of Judgments in Civil and Commercial disputes
Bus L Intl	*Business Law International*, published by the IBA
BVerfGE	*Entscheidungen des Bundesverfassungsgerichts*, published by Mohr Siebeck
BYIL	*British Yearbook of International Law*, published by Oxford University Press
CA	Court of Appeal
Cal.	California
CANACO	Cámara Nacional de Comercio de la Ciudad de México [Mexican National Chamber of Commerce], Mexico City (Established 1874)
CAS	Court of Arbitration for Sport (of ICAS)
CAS Arbitration Rules	CAS Code of Sports-related Arbitration: Procedural Rules, in force 1 July 2020
Cass. Civ.	Cour de Cassation (Chambre Civil) [Supreme Court, Civil Chamber], Paris
CCA	College of Commercial Arbitrators (US), Austin, TX (Established 2001)
CCBE	Conseil des Barreaux de la Communauté Européene [Council of Bars and Law Societies of Europe], Brussels (Established 1960)
CEDR	Centre for Effective Dispute Resolution, London (Established 1990)
CEPANI	Belgian Centre for Arbitration and Mediation, Brussels (Established 1969)
CETA	European Union–Canada Comprehensive Economic and Trade Agreement, signed 30 October 2016
ch./Ch.	chapter (bibliographical); Chapter (legislative)
CIArb	Chartered Institute of Arbitrators (UK), London (Established 1915)
CIETAC	China International Economic and Trade Arbitration Commission, Beijing (Established 1956)
CIETAC Rules	CIETAC Arbitration Rules, revised 2014, in force 2015
Cir.	Circuit (US Federal)
CISG	United Nations Convention on Contracts for the International Sale of Goods, signed 11 April 1980
CJEU	Court of Justice of the European Union, Luxembourg (Established 1952); formerly (and still informally) known as the ECJ
CLR	*Commonwealth Law Reports*, published by Lawbook Company
CMEA	Council for Mutual Economic Assistance (Comecon), dissolved 1991
Co Rep	*Correspondents' Reports*
CPR	Center for Public Resources, New York (Established 1979)
CPTPP	Comprehensive and Progressive Agreement for Trans-Pacific Partnership, signed 8 March 2018
CRCICA	Cairo Regional Centre for International Commercial Arbitration, Cairo (Established 1979)
DAC	Departmental Advisory Committee
DCF	discounted cash flow
Delvolvé Report	Commission on International Arbitration, *Final Report on Multi-Party Arbitrations* (ICC, 1994)

DIAC	Dubai International Arbitration Centre, Dubai (Established 1995)
DIFC	Dubai International Financial Centre
DIS	*Deutsche Institution für Scheidsgerichtsbarkeit* [German Arbitration Institute], Cologne (Established 1920)
Disp Res Intl	*Dispute Resolution International*, published by the IBA
Disp Res J	*Dispute Resolution Journal*, published by the AAA
DLR	*Dominion Law Reports*, published by Canada Law Book
DNJ	District Court of New Jersey
DR-CAFTA	Dominican Republic and Central America–United States Free Trade Agreement, signed 5 August 2004
DS	*Recueil Dalloz et Sirey*, published by Editions Dalloz
ECHR	Convention for the Protection of Human Rights and Fundamental Freedoms (European Convention on Human Rights), signed 4 November 1950
ECJ	(formerly and informally) European Court of Justice, Luxembourg (Established 1952); now CJEU
ECR	*European Court Reports*, published by Court of Justice of the European Union
ECT	Energy Charter Treaty 1994
ECtHR	European Court of Human Rights, Strasbourg (Established 1959)
EDI	electronic data interchange
edn	edition
EFTA	European Free Trade (Established 1960)
ESI	electronically stored information
European Convention of 1961	European Convention on International Commercial Arbitration, signed 21 April 1961
EWCA	Court of Appeal (England and Wales)
EWHC	High Court (England and Wales)
F, F.2d, F.3d	*Federal Reporter* (US) 1st, 2nd, and 3rd Series, published by West Publishing
FAA	US Federal Arbitration Act of 1925
FCA	Federal Court of Australia
FCN treaty	treaty of friendship, commerce and navigation
Fed. Appx	*Federal Appendix*, published by West Publishing
FET	fair and equitable treatment
FIA	Fédération Internationale de l'Automobile [International Automobile Federation], Paris (Established 1904)
FIDIC	Fédération Internationale des Ingénieurs-Conseils [International Federation of Consulting Engineers], Geneva (Established 1913)
FRCP	US Federal Rules of Civil Procedure
FRD	*Federal Rules Decisions*, published by West Publishing
FTA	free trade agreement
GAFTA	Grain and Feed Trade Association, London (Established 1878)
GCC Convention	1995 Agreement on the Execution of Rulings, Requests of Legal Assistance and Judicial Notices, Gulf Co-operation Council
Geneva Convention	Geneva Convention for the Execution of Foreign Arbitral Awards, signed 26 September 1927

Geneva Protocol	Geneva Protocol on Arbitration Clauses of 1923, signed 24 September 1923
Global Arb Rev	*Global Arbitration Review*, published by Law Business Research Ltd
Hague Convention 1899	Hague Convention for the Pacific Settlement of International Disputes of 1899
Hague Convention 1907	Hague Convention for the Pacific Settlement of International Disputes
Hague Convention 1970	Hague Convention on the Taking of Evidence Abroad in Civil or Commercial Matters
Hague Convention 2005	Hague Convention on Choice of Court Agreements, signed 30 June 2005
Harv L Rev	*Harvard Law Review*, published by the Harvard Law Review Association
Harv Negotiation L Rev	*Harvard Negotiation Law Review*, published by the Harvard Law Review Association
HIPCs	heavily indebted poor countries
HKC	*Hong Kong Cases*, published by Butterworths Asia
HKIAC	Hong Kong International Arbitration Centre, Hong Kong (Established 1985)
HL	House of Lords
HMSO	Her Majesty's Stationery Office (UK)
Holocaust Tribunals	Claims Resolution Tribunal for Dormant Accounts in Switzerland
IACAC	Inter-American Commercial Arbitration Commission (Established 1934); Inter-American Convention against Corruption, signed 29 March 1996
IBA	International Bar Association, London (Established 1947)
IBA Guidelines	IBA Guidelines on Conflicts of Interest in International Arbitration, adopted 23 October 2014
IBA Guidelines on Party Representation	IBA Guidelines on Party Representation in International Arbitration, adopted 25 May 2013
IBA Rules	IBA Rules on the Taking of Evidence in International Commercial Arbitration, adopted 17 December 2020
ICANN	Internet Corporation for Assigned Names and Numbers, Los Angeles, CA (Established 1998)
ICAS	International Council of Arbitration for Sport, Lausanne
ICC	International Chamber of Commerce, Paris (Established 1919)
ICC Court	International Court of Arbitration of the ICC, Paris (Established 1923)
ICC Rules	ICC Rules of Arbitration, revised in and in force 2021
ICCA	International Council for Commercial Arbitration, The Hague (Established 2014)
ICDR	International Centre for Dispute Resolution, London (Established 1996)
ICDR Canadian Rules	ICDR Canadian Dispute Resolution Procedures, in force 1 January 2015
ICDR Rules	ICDR International Dispute Resolution Procedures, revised and in force 2021
ICJ	International Court of Justice, The Hague (Established 1945)
ICLQ	*International and Comparative Law Quarterly*, published by Cambridge University Press
ICSID	International Centre for the Settlement of Investment Disputes, Washington DC (Established 1965)
ICSID Additional Facility Rules	ICSID Additional Facility Arbitration Rules, in force 1 July 2022

ICSID Convention	Convention on the Settlement of Investment Disputes between States and Nationals of Other States, in force 14 October 1966
ICSID Institution Rules	ICSID Institution Rules, in force 1 July 2022
ICSID Rev—Foreign Investment LJ	*ICSID Review—Foreign Investment Law Journal*, published by the ICSID
ICSID Rules	ICSID Rules of Procedure for Arbitration Proceedings, 2022
ICSID Rules 2006	ICSID Rules of Procedure for Arbitration Proceedings, 2006
IELTR	*International Energy Law and Taxation Review*, published by Sweet and Maxwell
IIC	*International Review of Intellectual Property and Competition Law*, published by Max Planck Institute for Intellectual Property, Competition and Tax Law
ILA	International Law Association, Brussels (Established 1873)
ILM	*International Legal Materials*, published by American Society of International Law
ILO	International Labour Organization, Geneva (Established 1919)
ILR	*International Law Reports*, published by Cambridge University Press
IMF	International Monetary Fund, Washington DC (Established 1944)
Incoterms	ICC International Rules for the Interpretation of Trade Terms
Intl Arb L Rev	*International Arbitration Law Review*, published by Sweet & Maxwell
Intl Construction L Rev	*International Construction Law Review*, published by Informa
Intl News	*International News*
Iran–US CTR	*Iran–United States Claims Tribunal Reports*, published by Grotius
ISDA	International Swaps and Derivatives Association, Inc., New York (Established 1985)
J CIArb	*Journal of the Chartered Institute of Arbitrators*, published by CIArb
J du Droit Intl	*Journal du Droit International* ('Clunet'), published by JurisClasseur
J Intl Arb	*Journal of International Arbitration*, published by Kluwer
J Intl Disp Settlement	*Journal of International Dispute Settlement*, published by Oxford University Press
J Priv Intl L	*Journal of Private International Law*, published by Hart
J World Energy L & Bus	*Journal of World Energy Law and Business*, published by Oxford University Press
Jay Treaty	General Treaty of Friendship, Commerce and Navigation, 1794
JBL	*Journal of Business Law*, published by Sweet and Maxwell
JCAA	Japanese Commercial Arbitration Association, Tokyo (Established 1950)
JWIT	*Journal of World Investment & Trade*, published by Brill
KLRCA	Kuala Lumpur Regional Centre for Arbitration, Kuala Lumpur (Established 1978)
L.Ed.	*United States Supreme Court Reports*, Lawyers' Edition, published by LexisNexis
Lando Principles	1998 Principles of European Contract Law
LCIA	London Court of International Arbitration, London (Established 1892)
LCIA Rules	LCIA Arbitration Rules, revised and in force 2020
LMAA	London Maritime Arbitration Association, London (Established 1960)
LNG	liquefied natural gas
LQR	*Law Quarterly Review*, published by Sweet & Maxwell

MAT	Muslim Arbitration Tribunals (England & Wales)
Mauritius Convention	United Nations Convention on Transparency in Treaty-based Investor–State Arbitration, signed 10 December 2014
MD Tenn.	US District Court for the Middle District of Tennessee
Mealey's Intl Arb Rep	*Mealey's International Arbitration Report*, published by LexisNexis
med/arb	mediation/arbitration
Mercosur	Mercado Común del Sur [Common Market of the South]
MFN	most-favoured nation
Milan Chamber of Arbitration Rules	Milan Chamber of Arbitration, Arbitration Rules, in force 1 July 2020
Model Law	Model Law on International Commercial Arbitration, 21 June 1985, with amendments as adopted in 2006
Montevideo Convention	Treaty concerning the Union of South American States in respect of Procedural Law, signed 11 January 1889
Moscow Convention of 1972	Convention on the Settlement of Arbitration of Civil Law Disputes Arising from Relations of Economic, Scientific and Technical Co-operation, signed May 1972
MST	minimum standard of treatment
NAFTA	North American Free Trade Agreement, signed 17 December 1992
NAI	Netherlands Arbitration Institute, Rotterdam (Established 1949)
NAI Rules	NAI Arbitration Rules, in force 1 January 2015
NC App.	*North Carolina Appellate Reporter*
NE	*North Eastern Reporter*, published by West Publishing
NED	non-executive director
New York Convention	Convention on the Recognition and Enforcement of Foreign Arbitral Awards, signed 10 June 1958
New York LJ	*New York Law Journal*, published by the Journal
NILR	*Netherlands International Law Review*, published by Cambridge University Press
NIPR	*Nederlands Internationaal Privaatrecht* [*Netherlands International Private Law*], published by TMC Asser
NJW	*Neue Juristische Wochenschrift*, published by C.H. Beck Verlag
n.p.	no pinpoint (page/paragraph) available
NPV	net present value
NSWLR	*New South Wales Law Reports*, published by Lexis Nexis
NTIR	*Nordisk Tidsskrift for International Ret* [*Nordic Journal of International Law*], published by Martinus Nijhoff
NW	*North Western Reporter*, published by West Publishing
NY	*New York Reports*, published by West Publishing
NYL Sch J Intl Comp L	*New York Law School Journal of International and Comparative Law*, published by New York Law School
NYS	*New York Supplement*, published by West Publishing
OECD	Organisation for Economic Co-operation and Development, Paris (Established 1961)
OGEL	*Oil, Gas, & Energy Law*, published online at https://www.ogel.org/
OGEMID	Oil Gas Energy Mining Infrastructure Dispute Management email list
OGLTR	*Oil and Gas Law and Taxation Review*, published by Sweet and Maxwell

OIC Agreement	Agreement for Promotion, Protection and Guarantee of Investments, Organisation of Islamic Cooperation
OJ L	*Official Journal of the European Union*, L Series
p.	page
Panama Convention of 1975	Inter-American Convention on International Commercial Arbitration, signed 30 January 1975
para.	paragraph
PCA	Permanent Court of Arbitration, The Hague (Established 1899)
PCA Rules	PCA Arbitration Rules, in force 17 December 2012
PCIJ	(former) Permanent Court of International Justice; now the ICJ
PRC	People's Republic of China
QB	*Law Reports, Queen's Bench*, published by the Incorporated Council of Law Reporting for England and Wales
QDR	*Queensland Reports*, published by Supreme Court of Queensland
r.	rule
RDAI	*Revue de Droit des Affaires Internationales*, published by Thomson Reuters/Sweet & Maxwell
Rev Arb	*Revue de l'Arbitrage* [*Arbitration Review*], published by Kluwer
RF CCI	Chamber of Commerce and Industry (Russian Federation), Moscow (Established 1993)
RICO	Racketeer Influenced and Corrupt Organizations Act of 1970 (US)
Riv di Dir Internaz, Priv e Proc	*Rivista di Diritto Internazionale Privato e Processuale* [*Journal of Private International Law and Procedure*], published by CEDAM
Riyadh Convention	Riyadh Arab Agreement on Judicial Cooperation, entered into force in 1985
Rome Convention	Rome Convention on the Law Applicable to Contractual Obligations, signed 19 June 1980
Rome I	Rome Regulation on the Law Applicable to Contractual Obligations, in force 17 December 2009
s.	section
SCC	Stockholm Chamber of Commerce, Stockholm (Established 1917); *Supreme Court Cases* (India), published by Eastern Book Co.
SCC Rules	SCC Arbitration Rules, revised and in force 2017
SchiedsVZ	*Zeitschrift für Schiedsverfahren* [*German Arbitration Journal*], published by Verlag CH Beck
SCIA	Shenzhen Court of International Arbitration
SCR	*Supreme Court Reports*, published by Canadian Government
S.Ct.	*Supreme Court Reporter*, published by West Publishing
SD	Southern District
SDNY	Southern District of New York (US District Court)
SEC	Securities and Exchange Commission (US), Washington, DC (Established 1934)
Sedona Principles	*Best Practices, Recommendations and Principles for Addressing Electronic Document Production* (2nd edn, 2007)
SGHC	Singapore High Court

SHIAC	Shanghai International Arbitration Centre
SIAC	Singapore International Arbitration Centre, Singapore (Established 1991)
SIAC Rules	Arbitration Rules of the SIAC, in force 1 August 2016
SIAR	*Stockholm International Arbitration Review*, published by SCC
SJIL	*Stanford Journal of International Law*, published by Stanford Law School
SLR	*Singapore Law Reports*, published by Justis
Spain Arb Rev	*Spain Arbitration Review*, published by Kluwer Arbitration
SPC	Supreme People's Court (China)
Strasbourg Uniform Law	European Convention providing a Uniform Law on Arbitration, signed 20 January 1966
Swiss PIL	Swiss Private International Law Act 1987
Swiss Rules	Swiss Rules of International Arbitration, revised and in force 2021
TCC	Technology and Construction Court (England and Wales)
TDM	*Trade Dispute Management*, published by MARIS
Tex Intl LJ	*Texas International Law Journal*, published by University of Texas School of Law
TFEU	Treaty on the Functioning of the European Union
U Penn JIL	*University of Pennsylvania Journal of International Law*, published by the University of Pennsylvania
UAA	Uniform Arbitration Act of 2000 (US)
UAE	United Arab Emirates
UCC	Uniform Commercial Code (US)
UCC Rep Serv	*Uniform Commercial Code Reporting Service* (US), published by West Publishing
UCP	ICC Uniform Customs and Practice for Documentary Credits
UKHL	House of Lords (United Kingdom)
UKPC	Privy Council (United Kingdom)
UKSC	Supreme Court (United Kingdom)
UNCC	United Nations Compensation Commission, Geneva (Established 1991)
UNCITRAL	United Nations Commission on International Trade Law, Vienna (Established 1996)
UNCITRAL Model Law	*See* Model Law; revised Model Law
UNCITRAL Notes	UNCITRAL Notes on Organizing Arbitral Proceedings
UNCITRAL Rules	UNCITRAL Arbitration Rules, revised and in force 2021
UNCITRAL Transparency Rules	UNCITRAL Rules on Transparency in Treaty-based Investor–State Arbitration, Resolution 68/109, adopted 16 December 2013
UNCLOS	United Nations Convention on the Law of the Sea, signed 10 December 1982
UNCTAD	United Nations Conference on Trade and Development, Geneva (Established 1964)
UNECE	United Nations Economic Commission for Europe, Geneva (Established 1947)
UNESCO	United Nations Educational, Scientific and Cultural Organization, Geneva (Established 1945)

UNIDROIT Principles	UNIDROIT Principles of International Commercial Contracts, revised and in force 2016
US	*United States Supreme Court Reports*, published by LexisNexis
USMCA	United States–Mexico–Canada Agreement, signed 30 November 2018
Vanderbilt J Transl L	*Vanderbilt Journal of Transnational Law*, published by Vanderbilt University Law School, Nashville, TN
VIAC	Vienna International Arbitration Centre, Vienna (Established 1975)
VJIL	*Virginia Journal of International Law*, published by University of Virginia School of Law
VSC	Supreme Court of Victoria (Australia)
WIPO	World Intellectual Property Organization, Geneva (Established 1967)
WIPO Rules	WIPO Arbitration Rules, revised and in force 2021
WLR	*Weekly Law Reports*, published by Justis
World Arb & Med Rev	*World Arbitration and Mediation Review*, published by Juris
World Court	*See* ICJ
YBCA	*Yearbook of Commercial Arbitration*, published by ICCA
ZPO	*Zivilprozessordnung* [German Code of Civil Procedure]

1

INTRODUCTION

A. Global Dispute Resolution

If international arbitration did not exist, it would be necessary to invent it. As investment, trade, and commerce continue to expand worldwide, agreements that cross national frontiers are a vital part of business and commercial life. Inevitably some of these transnational transactions and investments, whether they involve states, corporations, or individuals, will give rise to disputes. The most immediate solution is for the disputants to try to settle their differences by negotiation. No sensible business person, corporation, or state wants to spend time and money on legal proceedings if this can be avoided. Yet if the dispute cannot be settled, it is important that there should be a fair, reliable, and peaceful method of resolving it and enforcing the result, according to the provisions of the parties' agreement and the applicable legal framework.

1.01

When a dispute arises between parties who are based in the same country, those parties generally have a choice. They may take their dispute to their own national law courts. Or they may agree to resolve the dispute in private by incorporating an arbitration agreement into their contract. Such an arbitration would be a national or 'domestic' arbitration, governed by the rules agreed by the parties and by any mandatory provisions of the local law.

1.02

The situation is very different when the dispute arises out of a cross-frontier (or transnational) business relationship. Unless there is an agreement to arbitrate, the aggrieved party will be obliged to take its dispute to a court of law. In that case, it will be necessary to identify the court that has jurisdiction over the potential defendant. This will usually be the national court in which the defendant has its place of residence or business—that is to say, the defendant's home court, which immediately undermines the idea of a level playing field for the foreign claimant. That claimant may also find that the language of the defendant's court is not the language of the contract, that its long-established domestic procedures are not suitable for international disputes, and that the judges themselves have little or no experience of handling such disputes. It makes sense to avoid such risks by providing that any disputes arising out of or in connection with such an international contract be referred to international arbitration. Indeed, in order to ensure an efficient and enforceable dispute

1.03

resolution process in the transnational environment, international arbitration has been referred to as 'the only game in town'.[1]

(a) The concept of arbitration

1.04   International arbitration is a legal process in which parties to a dispute agree to refer that dispute to a tribunal of one or more independent and impartial arbitrators chosen by or on behalf of the parties to the exclusion of the domestic courts. The task of that tribunal is to give equal consideration to the claims and defences of the parties and to arrive at a decision on the dispute pursuant to the applicable legal framework. That decision is given in writing in the form of a binding award which the parties are obliged to perform without delay and which, in the absence of voluntary compliance, is underpinned by an international system of recognition and enforcement through local courts.

1.05   Arbitration, as a method of settling trade and commercial disputes, has a very long history. In its early days, it was a simple and relatively informal process undertaken without the presence of lawyers. Two merchants or traders in dispute over the price or quality of goods delivered would agree to refer their dispute to a third merchant or trader, whose independence and judgement they trusted. The parties would abide by the decision of this honest and usually unpaid 'arbitrator', not because of any legal order or sanction, but because this was what was expected of them in the community in which they carried on their trade or business.[2] The decision itself would almost certainly take account of any relevant usages or customs of the particular trade concerned; and the arbitrator might well temper his decision in order to avoid undue hardship, if this seemed appropriate in all the circumstances of the case. In this sense, arbitration was indeed, as one author has noted, a 'system of justice, born of merchants, which brings together law and respect for trade usage'.[3]

1.06   As international trade and commerce developed, arbitration inevitably became more formalised. Nevertheless, respect for trade usages remained.[4] The influence of chambers of trade and commerce in developing and promoting arbitration to resolve trade and commercial disputes was (and remains) important. In his classic treatise on 'Arbitration in International Trade',[5] Professor René David refers to the standard form of contract of the

---

[1]   Toby Landau KC used this analogy in 'Arbitral lifelines: The protection of jurisdiction by arbitrators', in van den Berg (ed.) *International Arbitration 2006: Back to Basics?* (Kluwer Law International, 2007), pp. 282–287; and so did Jan Paulsson when he said: 'In the transnational environment, international arbitration is the only game. It is a *de facto* monopoly.' (Paulsson, *International Arbitration is not Arbitration*, Vol. 2 (Stockholm International Arbitration Review, 2008), p. 2.

[2]   After referring to 'the dispute resolution mechanisms of the post-classical mercantile world' that were adopted in particular trades or trading centres, Lord Mustill comments: 'Within such communities, external sanctions would have been largely redundant, even if a legal framework had been available to bring them into play, which in the main it was not.' See Mustill, 'Is it a bird . . .', in Reymond (ed.) *Liber Amicorum* (Litec, 2004), p. 209. To similar effect, see Paulsson, *The Idea of Arbitration* (Oxford University Press, 2013), p. 1, where he says: 'The idea of arbitration is that of the binding resolution of disputes accepted with serenity by those who bear its consequences because of their special trust in chosen decision-makers.'

[3]   Serge Lazareff used this illuminating phrase, which describes how arbitration was seen as a way of settling disputes by reconciling legal principle with equity. See Lazareff, 'L'arbitre singe ou comment assassiner l'arbitrage', in Aksen (ed.) *Global Reflections in International Law, Commerce and Dispute Resolution: Liber Amicorum in Honour of Robert Briner* (ICC, 2005), p. 478.

[4]   Indeed, the present Rules of Arbitration of the ICC still require an arbitral tribunal to take account 'of any relevant trade usages': see the ICC Rules, Art. 21.

[5]   See David, *Arbitration in International Trade* (Kluwer, 1985), p. 38.

Liverpool Cotton Association which included an arbitration clause since 1863. This was undoubtedly a masterstroke. It meant that parties who entered into the standard form contract expressly agreed that if any disputes arose under that contract, those disputes would not be dealt with by the courts of law but by arbitration under the aegis of the Cotton Association itself. According to Professor David, the example set by the Liverpool Cotton Association was quickly followed by the London Corn Trade Association and in Germany by the Cotton Exchange of Bremen, which began to administer arbitrations in 1872.

Following these developments, the London Chamber of Arbitration was founded on 23 November 1892.[6] At the time it was said with an almost evangelical zeal that: **1.07**

> The Chamber is to have all the virtues that the law lacks. It is to be expeditious where the law is slow, cheap where the law is costly, simple where the law is technical, a peacemaker instead of a stirrer-up of strife.[7]

The close association between chambers of commerce and international commercial arbitration has endured, and helps to ensure that international arbitration, and perhaps more importantly international commercial arbitrators, remain firmly connected to the realities of international trade and commerce.   **1.08**

(b) The standard form clause

The International Chamber of Commerce (ICC) in Paris[8] was the first chamber to concentrate solely on *international* commercial disputes. The story is best told by Johnny Veeder, a distinguished counsel and arbitrator with a passion for arbitral history. In an article[9] quizzically entitled '1922: The Birth of the ICC Arbitration Clause and the Demise of the Anglo-Soviet Urquart Concession', Veeder refers to the 'creation of ICC Arbitration in 1922'. This was the year in which the ICC's Rules for Arbitration and Conciliation were first published. Veeder says: 'If international commercial arbitration has a birthday, its year was undoubtedly 1922'; and he adds that in practice 'the most significant advance was the standard form ICC arbitration clause incorporating by reference ICC arbitration rules as a near-comprehensive transnational procedural code'.   **1.09**

Veeder's comment is perceptive. It is a simple matter for parties to put an 'oven-ready' arbitration clause into their contract. The clause itself is usually a simple one. For example, the standard ICC Arbitration Clause reads: **1.10**

> All disputes arising out of or in connection with the present contract shall be finally settled under the Rules of Arbitration of the International Chamber of Commerce by one or more arbitrators appointed in accordance with the said Rules.

It is a simple clause; but it ensures that if there is an arbitration, it will be administered by the ICC and conducted in accordance with the set of procedural rules drawn up and

---

[6] The London Chamber of Arbitration was the predecessor of the LCIA, one of the leading international arbitral institutions.

[7] Manson (1893) IXLQR, cited in Veeder and Dye, 'Lord Bramwell's Arbitration Code' (1992) 8 Arb Intl 330.

[8] Arbitral institutions, including the ICC, are discussed later in this chapter.

[9] See 'Global Reflections in Law, Commerce and Dispute Resolution' ICC Publication 693, at pp. 881–901.

promulgated by that organisation. These basic rules address how to commence and pursue an international arbitration and apply to the tribunal and the parties, who will not need to spend time and money at the outset of the arbitration in drawing up their own basic arbitral rules, as would happen in pure ad hoc arbitrations.

1.11 The creation of a simple arbitration clause, together with procedural codes drawn up and adapted by arbitral institutions in light of their practical experience, has been a major driving force in making international arbitration attractive, as a dispute-resolution process that is in tune with evolving practice and technology. This is one of our themes in this chapter.

(c) The business perspective

1.12 Nation-states have quickly recognised the increased importance of international arbitration as the servant of international investment, business, and commerce. Countries around the world have either modernised their existing laws of arbitration or established new laws to govern and assist the conduct of international arbitrations on their territory. These new laws are often based on or incorporate the 1985 Model Law on International Commercial Arbitration of the United Nations Commission on International Trade Law (the 'Model Law')[10] which reflects arbitral best practice. A country that adopts the Model Law is generally seen as a country that is 'arbitration friendly' although it is important to review how the Model Law is in fact applied in practice through that country's court system.

1.13 The adoption by a country of a modern international arbitration law helps to reassure investors and to attract potentially profitable business, not least the business of arbitration itself.[11] Like a stone thrown into a pond, the ripples of an international arbitration spread in ever-widening circles. A former President of the Arbitration Committee of the ICC, in one of the first articles on the sociology of international arbitration,[12] referred to 'the broad spectrum of persons who may be involved in arbitration proceedings'. In addition to the tribunal, the parties, and their representatives, he included the witnesses, the experts, the secretary, the translator-interpreter, and the relevant arbitral institution. Almost twenty years later, when Professor Emmanuel Gaillard gave his Freshfields lecture on the 'Sociology of International Arbitration',[13] he added to this cast-list third-party funders,

---

[10] The Model Law has been highly successful and has now been adopted by over eighty-five states worldwide. Even countries that have not explicitly adopted the Model Law have been careful to take full account of it. In England, e.g., the departmental committee that advised on what became the Arbitration Act 1996 explicitly stated that any new statute should 'so far as possible have the same language and structure as the Model Law, so as to enhance its accessibility to those who are familiar with the Model Law': see the report of the Departmental Committee on the Arbitration Bill 1996, at para. 1(7).

[11] In a tribute to Johnny Veeder, Professor Park as General Editor referred to the foundation of the journal *Arbitration International* in 1984 by Veeder and others and said: 'At that moment, for better or for worse, international arbitration found itself moving into the realm of serious big business, leaving behind its earlier status as a "cottage industry" permeated by the culture of French and Swiss legal artisans or specialists working in particular fields such as insurance or construction' (2020) 36 Arb Intl 1.

[12] Glossner, 'Sociological aspects of international commercial arbitration', in Schultz and van den Berg (eds) *The Art of Arbitration* (Kluwer, 1982), pp. 143–152.

[13] Gaillard, 'Sociology of international arbitration' (2015) 31 Arb Intl 1.

publishers, and even public relations advisers. He also referred to the nation-states that enforce arbitral awards, courts that in their judgments help to set international standards, and organisations such as the International Bar Association (IBA) which, with its published rules and guidelines, helps both to formulate and to promote the 'soft law' of international arbitration.

(d) Investment arbitration

The growth of international arbitration in recent decades was primarily driven by disputes arising under contracts containing arbitration agreements. But, two decades ago, it was said that 'explorers had set out to discover a new continent for international arbitration'.[14] This 'new continent' permitted a qualifying investor with a qualifying investment to commence an international arbitration against a sovereign state even if it did not have a contract with that sovereign. It was labelled 'arbitration without privity'. The principal means to arrive at this new continent was via a network of bilateral and multilateral treaties[15] for the promotion and protection of investment (including investment chapters in free trade agreements). These treaties revolutionised international law. They empowered an aggrieved investor to claim directly against a host state (without the intervention of that investor's home state) if the investor considered that the host state was in breach of the substantive protections contained in the relevant investment treaty.

1.14

The number of arbitrations against states under investment treaties (known generally as 'investment arbitration') has grown extraordinarily.[16] Many of these cases raise issues of public importance and are not subject to the same presumptions of privacy and confidentiality as 'commercial' or 'contractual' arbitration. They have also led to procedural developments that are having an impact on the law and practice of international arbitration more generally, including the admission of *amicus curiae* briefs and increased transparency. In the light of the importance of investment arbitration in the world of international arbitration, it is addressed as a separate topic in Chapter 8.

1.15

(e) Other specialist forms of arbitration

The success of international arbitration as a method of neutral international dispute resolution away from national courts has led to its adoption in a growing number of specialist areas. One notable expansion took place in June 1984 when the Court of Arbitration for Sport (CAS) was established in Lausanne, Switzerland. The idea was to provide a means for the resolution of disputes related to sport and in particular to offer where necessary (for instance, during the Olympic Games) a rapid and relatively inexpensive procedure for

1.16

---

[14] J. Paulsson, 'Arbitration Without Privity' (1995) 10(2) ICSID Review Foreign Investment Law Journal 232.

[15] One example of a multilateral investment treaty is the Energy Charter Treaty which has been ratified by over fifty countries.

[16] Statistics reported by ICSID show that 469 cases were registered under the ICSID Convention and Additional Facility Rules between 2012 and 30 June 2021, compared to 274 cases registered between 2002 and 2011. See *ICSID Caseload—Statistics* (ICSID, 2021), p. 7.

resolving disputes on such issues as that of an athlete's entitlement to compete. The work of the CAS has expanded to include commercial disputes (including, for example, those arising from licensing agreements with television companies).

1.17   The expansion of international arbitration continues. Another example of its prospective future use is in the resolution of disputes under Bilateral Tax Treaties. For example, 'The Multilateral Convention to Implement Tax Treaty Related Measures to Prevent Base Erosion and Profit Shifting' includes an optional 'Mandatory Binding Arbitration' process for resolving disputes.[17] This option is intended to bring a neutral determinative end to the current unsatisfactory Mutual Assistance Process, which requires the agreement of the tax authorities of the contracting states for a dispute to be resolved.

(f) An arbitration bar

1.18   A final indication of the way in which international arbitration has developed and expanded is that there is now a large and growing 'arbitration bar' of specialist arbitration lawyers and advocates located throughout the world, whether in São Paolo, Moscow, or Washington. Each of these practitioners is regulated by their own national professional code of behaviour. There is not at present a universally binding international code governing the practice of international arbitration, nor is there any international governing body. Nevertheless, the existence of a specialist set of lawyers, whether as part of the dispute resolution group of a major law firm or as a specialist 'boutique' law firm dealing only with international arbitration, is testimony to the growth of international arbitration.

B. Outline of an International Arbitration

1.19   There is no such thing as a typical international arbitration. There are so many arbitral institutions, so many parties, tribunals, and lawyers of different legal and cultural backgrounds and nationalities and such a range of possible disputes that there would be little point in trying to give a detailed description of a particular dispute and claiming that it was in some way 'typical'. What seems to the authors to be more helpful is to set out briefly the key elements of any international arbitration, all of which are developed more fully in later chapters. These are:

- the agreement to arbitrate
- the place of arbitration
- the commencement of an arbitration
- the appointment of the arbitral tribunal
- arbitral proceedings
- the award of the tribunal
- the enforcement of the award.

---

[17]   See Mooij, 'Tax treaty arbitration' (2019) 35 Arb Intl 195.

(a) The agreement to arbitrate

The foundation stone of modern international arbitration is consent. Such consent must be reflected by a valid agreement between the parties to submit any disputes or differences to arbitration.[18] This is recognised both by national laws and by international treaties. Under both the New York Convention on the Recognition and Enforcement of Foreign Arbitral Awards (the 'New York Convention')[19] and the Model Law,[20] recognition and enforcement of an arbitral award may be refused if the parties to the arbitration agreement were under some incapacity or if the agreement was not valid under its own governing law.[21] **1.20**

An 'agreement to arbitrate' is usually (but not exclusively) expressed in an *arbitration clause* in a contract. Arbitration clauses make it clear that any dispute that arises out of, or in connection with, the contract will be referred to arbitration to the exclusion of the courts. Arbitration clauses are drawn up and agreed as part of the contract *before* any dispute has arisen, and so they necessarily look to the future. Naturally, the parties hope that no dispute will arise but they agree that if it does, it will be resolved by arbitration and not by the courts. **1.21**

There is a second, less common type of agreement to arbitrate, where the parties agree to submit an existing dispute to arbitration. This is generally known as a 'submission agreement'. It will often be more detailed than an arbitration clause, because if a dispute has already arisen, it is possible to nominate a tribunal and to describe in detail the dispute and how the parties propose to deal with it. **1.22**

As already indicated, these two types of arbitration agreement have been joined by a third—namely, the agreement to arbitrate that arises under international instruments, such as an investment treaty. A feature of such treaties is that each state party to the treaty agrees to submit to international arbitration any dispute that *might* arise in the future between itself and a qualifying 'investor'.[22] This 'investor' is *not* a party to the treaty. Indeed, the investor's identity is unknown when the treaty is made. Hence this 'agreement to arbitrate' in effect constitutes a 'standing offer' by the state concerned to resolve any 'investment' disputes by arbitration; and a qualifying investor may 'accept' this offer by an unequivocal act, such as the dispatch of a letter or by taking a step pursuant to the dispute resolution process, for instance, by sending to the state concerned a Notice of Dispute or a Request for Arbitration.[23] **1.23**

There are other important matters to consider, including the enforcement of arbitration agreements, the need for a dispute, and the concept of arbitrability. These and other topics are more fully considered in Chapter 2. **1.24**

---

[18] Once there is a valid agreement to arbitrate, the scope of any resulting arbitration may be enlarged, e.g. to cover so-called 'non-signatories', whose consent to arbitrate is a 'deemed' or 'implied' consent. The issues of non-signatories, consolidation of arbitrations, and third-party involvement are discussed in more detail in Chapter 2.

[19] New York Convention, Art. V.

[20] Model Law, Art. 35.

[21] New York Convention, Art. V(1)(a); Model Law, Art. 36(1)(a)(i).

[22] Investment arbitrations are discussed in Chapter 8.

[23] See Dolzer, Kriebaum and Schreuer, *Principles of International Investment Law* (3rd edn, Oxford University Press, 2022), p. 365.

(b) The place of arbitration

1.25   Parties to an arbitration agreement may select the seat (or legal place) of arbitration in that agreement or they may leave the choice until an arbitration is commenced. The selection of a 'place of arbitration' is an important matter. It is not simply (or necessarily at all) a matter of geographical convenience. The place chosen will establish the jurisdiction of the local courts of that place regarding any review of the arbitral award; and it has other consequences that are considered in Chapter 2. The chosen place should be in a state that is 'arbitration friendly'[24] (that is, a state where there will be no undue or inappropriate interference with the arbitral process by the local courts and where the state has adhered to the New York Convention, in order to provide a straightforward and effective method for the recognition and enforcement of the arbitral tribunal's award if enforcement becomes necessary). It is noteworthy that the selection of the seat (or legal place) of arbitration does not require hearings to take place there, as the parties and the arbitrators usually have discretion to hold hearings at a location other than the place of arbitration for reasons of convenience and efficiency.

(c) Commencement of an arbitration

1.26   A formal notice must be given in order to start an arbitration. In ad hoc arbitrations, this notice will be sent or delivered to the opposing party.

1.27   For example, Article 3 of the UNCITRAL Arbitration Rules provides that:

1. The party or parties initiating recourse to arbitration (hereinafter called the 'claimant') shall communicate to the other party or parties (hereinafter called the 'respondent') a notice of arbitration.
2. Arbitration proceedings shall be deemed to commence on the date on which the notice of arbitration is received by the respondent.

1.28   The UNCITRAL Rules then state what should be set out in the notice of arbitration. This includes a reference to the arbitration clause in the contract (or to any other form of arbitration agreement), a brief description of the claim, an indication of the amount involved in the dispute, and a statement of the relief or remedy sought. The notice of arbitration may also include proposals for the appointment of a sole arbitrator or the appointment of the arbitral tribunal.

1.29   In an arbitration governed by the rules of an arbitral institution it is usual for the notice to be given to that institution by a 'request for arbitration' or similar document. The institution

---

[24] In a thoughtful analysis, Professor Bermann argues that it is not enough that a particular state should be 'arbitration friendly'. It is in the long-term interest of international arbitrations that extrinsic values to which the international legal system as a whole attaches importance should be taken into account: 'The point is that the international arbitration community must strive to ensure that, in addressing the concerns and pursuing the values most closely associated with arbitration practice and its efficacy, it does not fall out of step with extrinsic values to which the legal system as a whole attaches fundamental importance': Bermann, 'What does it mean to be 'pro-arbitration?' (2018) 34 Arb Intl 341–353, at 352.

then notifies the respondent or respondents. For example, Article 4.1 of the ICC Rules provides that:

> A party wishing to have recourse to arbitration under the Rules shall submit its Request for Arbitration (the 'Request') to the Secretariat at any of the offices specified in the Internal Rules. The Secretariat shall notify the claimant and respondent of the receipt of the Request and the date of such receipt.

Similar provisions are found in the rules of other arbitral institutions.[25]   **1.30**

(d) Appointment of the arbitral tribunal

The ability of the parties to participate in the selection of the tribunal that will be responsible   **1.31** for deciding their dispute is a fundamental difference between international arbitration and judicial resolution and is likely to give the parties confidence in the dispute resolution process in which they are about to take part.[26]

Considerable time and effort is usually spent by parties in identifying independent and im-   **1.32** partial candidates who would be well suited to the resolution of their particular dispute (for example, because of their arbitral experience, or their legal or cultural background, linguistic abilities, or technical knowledge). Making the right choice of arbitrator is one of the most important decisions in any case. As Professor Pierre Lalive wrote: '[t]he choice of the persons who compose the arbitral tribunal is vital and often the most decisive step in an arbitration. It has rightly been said that arbitration is only as good as the arbitrators.'[27] Indeed, a skilled, experienced, and impartial arbitrator selected from the full pool of suitable candidates is essential for a fair and effective arbitration.[28]

It is important to recognise that an international arbitration demands different qualities in   **1.33** an arbitrator from those required for a domestic arbitration. In an international arbitration, different rules and different systems of law will apply; the parties will almost certainly be

---

[25] The LCIA Rules, Art. 1.1 provides that '[a]ny party wishing to commence arbitration under the LCIA Rules ("the Claimant") shall deliver to the Registrar of the LCIA Court (the "Registrar") a written request for arbitration', and prescribes the relevant content of the request; the ICDR International Arbitration Rules, Art. 2.1 provides that '[t]he party initiating arbitration ("Claimant") shall, in compliance with Article 11, give written Notice of Arbitration to the Administrator and at the same time to the party against whom a claim is being made ("Respondent")'; the ICSID Convention, Art. 36(1) provides that '[a]ny Contracting State or any national of a Contracting State wishing to institute arbitration proceedings shall address a request to that effect in writing to the Secretary-General who shall send a copy of the request to the other party'; and the SIAC Rules, r. 3 provides that '[a] party wishing to commence an arbitration under these Rules (the "Claimant") shall file with the Registrar a Notice of Arbitration' and prescribes the necessary contents of the notice.

[26] For a discussion of the different roles of arbitrator and judge see Lazareff, 'L'arbitre est-il un juge?', in Reymond (ed.) *Liber Amicorum* (Litec, 2004), p. 173; Rubino-Sammartano, 'The decision-making mechanism of the arbitrator vis-à-vis the judge' (2008) 25 J Intl Arb 167; Ancel, 'L'arbitre juge' (2012) 4 Rev Arb 717. The judgment of the UK Supreme Court in *Halliburton Company v Chubb Bermuda Insurance Ltd.* [2020] UKSC 48 also provides an insight into this issue, at [56]–[62].

[27] Lalive, 'Mélanges en l'honneur de Nicolas Valticos', in Dupuy (ed.) *Droit et Justice: Mélanges en l'honneur de Nicolas Valticos* (CEPANI, 1989), p. 289; see also, e.g., Derains and Levy (eds) *Is Arbitration Only as Good as the Arbitrator? Status, Powers and Role of the Arbitrator* (ICC Institute of World Business Law, 2011); Park, 'Arbitrators and accuracy' (2010) 1 J Intl Disp Settlement 25.

[28] See Chapter 4 for more discussion of these considerations.

of different nationalities; and the arbitration itself will usually take place in a third neutral country. Indeed, the place of arbitration will usually have been chosen precisely because it *is* neutral, so that no party has the advantage of 'playing at home'.

1.34   There is a risk that in identifying possible candidates, parties and their counsel revert to candidates with whom they are already familiar, which has tended to result in repeat appointments and a lack of diversity in such appointments.[29] In order to ensure the renovation of the pool of arbitrators and to provide multiple perspectives on a tribunal, it is important to ensure that candidates are considered from diverse backgrounds and that female arbitrators feature prominently in such consideration with a view to moving towards equality between the number of male and female appointments. To help achieve this goal, in 2015 a group of practitioners launched the 'Equal Representation in Arbitration Pledge' which seeks to rectify the under-representation of women on arbitral tribunals by requiring signatories to consider female arbitrators on an equal opportunity basis. In simple terms, amongst other commitments, most arbitral institutions, practitioners, and many frequent users of arbitration have committed to ensure a fair representation of women on lists of arbitrator candidates.[30]

1.35   Ensuring equal gender representation is only part of this discussion. It is equally important to provide opportunities to younger arbitrators and to ethnic minorities who are also under-represented. The first step in any such process is recognition of the need for action. The hope for the future is to see a corps of international arbitrators that reflects all the perspectives of the international commercial community that it serves.

1.36   The fact that a party may choose an arbitrator does not give it a *carte blanche* to choose whoever it pleases. In particular, all arbitrators (including party appointed arbitrators) must be independent and impartial of the parties to the dispute.[31] In general terms, independence refers to the connections that an arbitrator might have with the parties or their counsel, whereas impartiality focuses on an arbitrator's ability to analyse the dispute without prejudgement (for instance, if an arbitrator has already decided the same point of law in another case and so could arguably be held to have prejudged the issue). The leading arbitral institutions, as well as national laws based on the Model Law, confront this problem with provisions for disclosure by a prospective arbitrator of any circumstances likely to give rise to justifiable doubts as to his or her independence or impartiality.[32]

---

[29] See Winkle and Schinazi, 'No Longer "Pale, Male, and Stale"? Approaching Diversity and Inclusiveness in International Arbitration, (31 January 2021) in *Liber Amicorum Guillermo Aguilar Alvarez*, available at SSRN: https://ssrn.com/abstract=3776738 or http://dx.doi.org/10.2139/ssrn.3776738.

[30] See http://www.arbitrationpledge.com/. There are currently nearly 5,000 institutional and individual signatories which has resulted in material improvements in the percentage of female appointments.

[31] Virtually all institutional rules include provisions to this effect. For example, the LCIA Rules, Art. 5.3 provides that '[a]ll arbitrators shall be and remain at all times impartial and independent of the parties; and none shall act in the arbitration as advocate for or authorised representative of any party'; the ICC Rules, Art. 11.1 provides that '[e]very arbitrator must be and remain impartial and independent of the parties involved in the arbitration'; the ICDR Rules, Art. 14.1 provides that '[a]rbitrators acting under these Rules shall be impartial and independent and shall act in accordance with these Rules, the terms of the Notice of Appointment provided by the Administrator, and with The Code of Ethics for Arbitrators in Commercial Disputes'; and the SIAC Rules, r. 13.1 provides that '[a]ny arbitrator appointed in an arbitration under these Rules, whether or not nominated by the parties, shall be and remain at all times independent and impartial'.

[32] Article 12(1) of the Model Law provides that '[w]hen a person is approached in connection with his possible appointment as an arbitrator, he shall disclose any circumstances likely to give rise to justifiable doubts as to his impartiality or independence. An arbitrator, from the time of his appointment and throughout the arbitral proceedings, shall without delay disclose any such circumstances to the parties unless they have already been informed of them by him.' By way of example of provisions in institutional rules, the LCIA Rules provide at Article

Historically, there was a risk that lawyers trained in different jurisdictions would have a   **1.37**
different concept of independence and impartiality. The perception that different standards were being applied led the IBA to create a committee of arbitration specialists representing major legal cultures and traditions in order to reach a consensus as to the proper
practice in international arbitration. The result was the IBA Guidelines on Conflicts of
Interest in International Arbitration, the first edition of which was published in 2004.
They establish general guidelines and a non-exhaustive 'traffic light' system of situations
where a potential arbitrator should decline appointment (red list), only accept with the
express waiver of all parties (waivable red list), only accept with disclosure (orange list),
or accept unconditionally (green list). Although not hard law, the Guidelines are an example of the growing body of 'soft law'; they are almost universally accepted as an appropriate standard and they are followed by the vast majority of parties and tribunals. Their
popularity is reflected by revised versions published in 2014 and 2020. They will be addressed in detail in Chapter 4.

Having looked briefly at the qualities that an arbitrator must possess (a topic that is also   **1.38**
discussed in more detail in Chapter 4) what is the process for establishment of the arbitral
tribunal?

(i) A sole arbitrator

If the dispute is to be referred to a sole arbitrator, the selection of that arbitrator will gen-   **1.39**
erally be left to the parties, with a 'fall-back' or 'default' provision in case they are unable to
agree. The ICC Rules, for example, provide at Article 12.3 that:

> Where the parties have agreed that the dispute shall be resolved by a sole arbitrator, they
> may, by agreement, nominate the sole arbitrator for confirmation.[33]

This is followed by a default provision, so that if the parties fail to agree on an arbitrator, the
ICC Court will itself select and appoint a suitable person.

If the parties are able to agree upon the selection of a sole arbitrator (and this is not always   **1.40**
easy), they will be able to go forward with the proceedings in the knowledge that they
have jointly chosen someone in whose impartiality and judgement they are prepared to
trust to resolve their dispute. If the parties are not able to agree, they will have to rely upon
an 'appointing authority' to make the designation. This appointing authority may be the
institution under whose rules the arbitration is to proceed (as under the ICC Rules) or
it may be the relevant domestic court in a pure ad hoc arbitration (as under the Model
Law). At the moment of drafting the arbitration agreement, a reputable arbitral institution is to be preferred over a court (or some other non-arbitral body, such as the local bar

---

5.4 that a prospective arbitrator shall sign a written declaration stating 'whether there are any circumstances
currently known to the candidate which are likely to give rise in the mind of any party to any justifiable doubts
as to his or her impartiality or independence and, if so, specifying in full such circumstances', while Article 11(2)
of the ICC Rules provides that '[t]he prospective arbitrator shall disclose in writing to the Secretariat any facts
or circumstances which might be of such a nature as to call into question the arbitrator's independence in the
eyes of the parties, as well as any circumstances that could give rise to reasonable doubts as to the arbitrator's
impartiality'.

[33] The practice of the ICC and of other arbitral institutions is that it is the institution that formally *appoints* an
arbitrator, although in doing so they will almost invariably confirm the person nominated by the parties.

association). This is because the institution and its secretariat are likely to be far more aware than a court of the available pool of suitably qualified arbitrators. They are also likely to be more attuned to the qualifications needed in the arbitrator, the need to ensure a diverse panel, and to the types of conflicts of interest that might lead to the challenge of the chosen arbitrator.[34]

(ii) A tribunal of three arbitrators

1.41 If the dispute is to be referred to a tribunal of three arbitrators, it is usual for each party to be given the right to nominate one arbitrator. The parties will often refer to this person as 'their arbitrator'. However, this arbitrator is under the same duty of independence and impartiality, and under the same duty to disclose possible conflicts of interest, as the other members of the tribunal.

1.42 Sometimes the parties are able to agree upon the nomination of the third arbitrator. They may do this either directly, by discussions between themselves, or by delegating the task to the nominated co-arbitrators. If the parties choose the latter course, the nominated co-arbitrators will discuss between themselves possible choices and try to agree on a potential third (presiding) arbitrator. When the co-arbitrators have made a decision, the convention is that they may inform the party that appointed them of their prospective choice. This is not intended to give the parties a veto on that choice, but simply to ensure that there is nothing (such as previous conflicts) which would make it genuinely difficult for a party to accept that candidate. Agreement on the choice of a presiding arbitrator is the ideal. It enables the parties to proceed confidently with the arbitration given their participation, whether directly or by delegation, in the appointment of the presiding arbitrator, who will rank as 'first amongst equals'.

1.43 Various default provisions are available for selection of the third arbitrator if the parties are unable to reach agreement upon a suitable candidate. One option is for the co-arbitrators to agree between themselves (which would require an express agreement). Otherwise, in an institutional arbitration, the supervising institution will make the appointment.[35] In an UNCITRAL ad hoc arbitration, the designation will be made by the 'Appointing Authority' agreed by the parties or (in the absence of agreement) designated by the Secretary General of the Permanent Court of Arbitration.[36]

1.44 The system of party-nominated arbitrators is not without its critics. One of the authors, in a Freshfields lecture[37] about dissenting opinions in international arbitration, noted that they

---

[34] The difficulties resulting from court appointments are amply illustrated in the UK Supreme Court case of *Halliburton v Chubb*. In that case, the High Court appointed an arbitrator who had previously been appointed by one of the parties and then confirmed that appointment despite objections, leading to many years of litigation. See *Halliburton Company v Chubb Bermuda Insurance Ltd.* [2020] UKSC 48.

[35] For example, the ICC Rules, Art. 12.5 provides that '[w]here the dispute is to be referred to three arbitrators, the third arbitrator, who will act as president of the arbitral tribunal, shall be appointed by the Court, unless the parties have agreed upon another procedure for such appointment, in which case the nomination will be subject to confirmation'.

[36] See UNCITRAL Rules, Art. 6.

[37] Redfern, 'Dissenting opinions in international commercial arbitration: The good, the bad and the ugly' (2004) 20 Arb Intl 223.

were almost invariably given by a party-nominated arbitrator in favour of the party that had nominated that arbitrator. A later study (focusing on investment arbitration where there is publicity of awards) reached the disappointing conclusion that:

> The practice of dissent in investment arbitrations may even have reached the point where a party-appointed arbitrator is now expected to dissent if a party that appoints him or her has lost the case entirely or in part.[38]

As discussed later in Chapter 4, it is sometimes suggested that the system of party-appointed arbitrators, although greatly favoured by users, should be abandoned in favour of selection by an exchange of lists, an algorithm, or some other method.   **1.45**

(e) The arbitral proceedings

There are no compulsory rules of procedure in international arbitration and no volumes containing 'the rules of court' to govern the conduct of the arbitration. Litigators who produce their own country's rulebook or code of civil procedure as a 'helpful guideline' will be told to put it to one side and forget it!   **1.46**

The rules that govern an international arbitration are first, the mandatory provisions of the *lex arbitri* (the law of the place of arbitration) which are usually cast in very broad terms;[39] and secondly the arbitration rules that the parties themselves may have chosen, such as the rules of the ICC or UNCITRAL. Under the heading of 'General Provisions', Article 17 of the UNCITRAL Rules states: **1.47**

> Subject to these Rules, the arbitral tribunal may conduct the arbitration in such manner as it considers appropriate, provided that the parties are treated with equality and that at an appropriate stage of the proceedings each party is given a reasonable opportunity of presenting his case. The arbitral tribunal, in exercising its discretion, shall conduct the proceedings so as to avoid unnecessary delay and expense and to provide a fair and efficient process for resolving the parties' dispute.

Within the broad outline of any applicable rules, parties to an international arbitration are free to design a procedure suitable for their particular dispute. This is another of the attractions of international arbitration. It is (or should be) a flexible method of dispute resolution. The procedure to be followed can be tailored by the parties and the arbitral tribunal to meet the law and facts of the dispute. It is not a Procrustean bed, enforcing conformity without regard to individual variation.   **1.48**

---

[38] van den Berg, 'Dissenting opinions by party-appointed arbitrators in investment arbitration', in Arsanjani, Katz Cogan, Sloane, and Wiessner (eds) *Looking to the Future: Essays in Honor of W Michael Reisman* (Koninklijke Brill, 2010), p. 821.

[39] For example, the Model Law, Art. 18, simply states: 'The parties shall be treated with equality and each party shall be given a full opportunity of presenting his case.'

(f) Ending the dispute: settlement or arbitral award

1.49   In the course of the arbitral proceedings, a settlement is frequently reached between the parties. Rules of arbitration usually make provision for this. Article 36.1 of the UNCITRAL Rules, for example, states:

> If, before the award is made, the parties agree on a settlement of the dispute, the arbitral tribunal shall either issue an order for the termination of the arbitral proceedings or, if requested by both parties and accepted by the arbitral tribunal, record the settlement in the form of an arbitral award on agreed terms. The arbitral tribunal is not obliged to give reasons for such an award.

1.50   If the parties themselves cannot resolve their dispute, the power and duty of the arbitral tribunal is to resolve it for them by making a binding decision, in the form of a written award.

1.51   The power (and the duty) of an arbitral tribunal to make binding decisions distinguishes arbitration as a method of resolving disputes from other procedures, such as mediation and conciliation, which aim to arrive at a negotiated *settlement*. The *procedure* to be followed in arbitration to arrive at a binding decision is flexible and adaptable to the circumstances of each particular case. Nevertheless, it is a *judicial* procedure. Any failure by a tribunal to act judicially (that is, respecting the equality of the parties with each party given an opportunity to present its case) may be sanctioned by annulment or non-enforcement of that tribunal's award.[40] No similar enforceable requirement governs the procedures to be followed where parties are assisted in arriving at a negotiated settlement by mediation, conciliation, or some other process of this kind.[41]

1.52   How an arbitral tribunal reaches its decision is a complex process.[42] For a sole arbitrator, the task of decision-making is a solitary one: impressions as to the honesty and reliability of the witnesses; opinions on the merits that may have swayed from one side to the other as the arbitral process unfolds; points that have seemed compelling under the eloquence of counsel, will all have to be reviewed and re-considered once the hearing is over and any post-hearing briefs are received. Justice, money, and reputations depend on the arbitrator's verdict.

1.53   If the arbitral tribunal consists of three arbitrators, the task may be easier in one sense and more difficult in another. It is easier because the decision does not depend upon one person alone. The arguments of the parties can be reviewed, the opinions of each arbitrator can be tested and the facts of the case and the relevant law can be freely discussed. It is at the same

---

[40] For example, the English Arbitration Act 1996, s. 33(1)(a) states that the tribunal shall 'act fairly and impartially as between the parties, giving each party a reasonable opportunity of putting his case and dealing with that of his opponent'. This requirement mirrors Model Law, Art. 18, and is found in most developed arbitral systems.

[41] The arbitral process also produces a different *result* from that which might have been reached by the parties through negotiation, with or without the help of a mediator, since a negotiated agreement will usually result in a compromise acceptable to both parties.

[42] See, e.g., Lowenfeld, 'The party-appointed arbitrator: Further reflections', in Newman and Hill (eds) *The Leading Arbitrators' Guide to International Arbitration* (2nd edn, JurisNet, 2008), pp. 46–48; Fortier, 'The tribunal's deliberations', in Newman and Hill (eds) *The Leading Arbitrators' Guide to International Arbitration* (2nd edn, JurisNet, 2008), pp. 477–482; Puig, 'Deliberation and drafting awards in international arbitration', in Fernández-Ballesteros and Arias (eds) *Liber Amicorum Bernardo Cremades* (La Ley, 2010), pp. 131–158. On the importance of the tribunal's deliberations, see Bredin, 'Retour au délibéré arbitral', in Bernardini et al. (eds) *Liber Amicorum Claude Reymond* (Litec, 2004), p. 50; Derains, 'La pratique du délibéré arbitral', in Aksen (ed.) *Global Reflections in International Law, Commerce and Dispute Resolution: Liber Amicorum in Honour of Robert Briner* (ICC, 2005), pp. 221–224.

time more difficult, because three different opinions may well emerge during the course of the tribunal's deliberations. It will then be necessary for the presiding arbitrator to try to reconcile those differences, rather than face the unwelcome prospect of a dissenting opinion.

Experienced commentators remain divided on the question of whether or not dissenting opinions are of any benefit in international arbitration. Some see them as beneficial, allowing each arbitrator freedom of expression and demonstrating that the parties' arguments have been fully considered.[43] Others, whilst recognising that there are good dissenting opinions, just as there are good dissenting judgments,[44] are concerned that a dissenting opinion may undermine the authority of the tribunal's award.[45] Indeed, a dissenting opinion 'may provide a platform for challenge to the award'.[46]   **1.54**

The debate about dissenting opinions has inevitably spilled over from commercial arbitration, in which awards are generally not publicly available, to investment arbitration, in which a dissenting opinion may have more impact because it is publicly available. It is to be expected that a party-nominated arbitrator will usually have some sympathy with the party that appointed him or her (not least because they have been selected because of the party's perception of their likely conclusions on the issues in light of past writings or awards). However, this should not prevent that arbitrator behaving impartially, as he or she is required to do.[47]   **1.55**

(g) Enforcement of an award

Once an arbitral tribunal has made its final award, it has done what it was established to do. It has fulfilled its function.[48] The award itself, however, gives rise to important, lasting, and potentially public legal consequences. Although the award is typically the result of a private process of dispute resolution and is made by a private arbitral tribunal, it nevertheless constitutes a binding decision on the dispute between the parties. If the award is not carried out voluntarily, it may be enforced by legal proceedings, both locally (that is, by the courts at the place where it was made) and internationally under such international conventions as the New York Convention.   **1.56**

An agreement to arbitrate is not only an agreement to take part in arbitral proceedings. It is also an agreement to comply voluntarily with any resulting arbitral award. This   **1.57**

---

[43] Rees and Rohn, 'Dissenting opinions: Can they fulfill a beneficial role?' (2009) 25 Arb Intl 329.

[44] In the well-known English case of *Liversidge v Anderson* [1941] 3 All ER 336, Lord Atkin gave a dissenting speech in which he argued against the power of arbitrary arrest, even in times of war. Almost four years later, Lord Diplock said that the time had come to acknowledge that the majority were 'expediently and, at that time, perhaps excusably wrong and the dissenting speech of Lord Atkin was right': *Inland Revenue Commissioners v Rossminster* [1980] AC 952, at 1008.

[45] Redfern, 'Dissenting opinions in international commercial arbitration: The good, the bad and the ugly' (2004) 20 Arb Intl 223.

[46] Baker and Greenwood, 'Dissent—but only if you really feel you must: Why dissenting opinions in international commercial arbitration should only appear in exceptional circumstances' (2013) 7 Disp Res Intl 31.

[47] A response to the criticism of both party-appointed arbitrators and arbitrators dissenting in favour of their appointing party is offered in Brower and Rosenberg, 'The death of the two-headed nightingale: Why the Paulsson–van den Berg presumption that party-appointed arbitrators are untrustworthy is wrong' (2013) 29 Arb Intl 7; van den Berg, 'Charles Brower's problem with 10%: Dissenting opinions by party-appointed arbitrators in investment arbitration' (2015) 31 Arb Intl 381.

[48] Save for incidental matters such as the interpretation of the award or correction of obvious errors for which the tribunal remains in being for a limited period of time, and save also for those rare cases in which the tribunal may be required by a court to reconsider its decision: see Chapter 9.

commitment is set out expressly in many rules of arbitration. Article 35.6 of the ICC Rules, for example, states that:

> Every award shall be binding on the parties. By submitting the dispute to arbitration under the Rules, the parties undertake to carry out any award without delay and shall be deemed to have waived their right to any form of recourse insofar as such waiver can validly be made.

1.58   Most arbitral awards are voluntarily carried out by the losing party or parties without the need to refer to any formal legal compulsion. But when they are not complied with, it may be necessary to seek enforcement by a court of law.

1.59   But which court of law? This is something that the winning party will need to consider. The usual method for enforcing an award is to obtain judgment on it. This will generally mean commencing recognition and enforcement proceedings either (a) in the court of the country in which the losing party resides or has its place of business and/ or (b) in the court of the country in which the losing party otherwise has assets that may be seized in satisfaction of the award.

1.60   It follows that in order to have an effective system of international arbitration it is necessary to have a supporting system of national legal systems, so that the courts of country A will enforce an arbitration agreement or an arbitral award made in country B. For this to happen, there must be international treaties or conventions providing for the recognition and enforcement of *both* arbitration agreements and arbitral awards by the courts of those countries that are party to that treaty or convention.[49]

C. The Legal Framework of International Arbitration

1.61   Before turning to the legal framework of international arbitration, we first examine briefly the object of international arbitration and then go on to consider the meaning that should be attributed to the key words 'international' and 'commercial'.

(a) The object of international arbitration

1.62   The object of international arbitration is briefly stated. It is to obtain the fair resolution of a dispute by an independent and impartial tribunal without undue delay or expense. This is easily said, but far less easily done. In fact, it raises a host of questions to which we will revert in subsequent chapters. For example, is an arbitral tribunal bound to apply a specific applicable law or an identified set of legal rules or does it, unlike the judge in a court of law, have discretion to award what seems to be 'fair' rather than what is legally correct? If an arbitral tribunal has such 'discretion', how far does it extend? For instance, does it permit an arbitral tribunal to complete a contract that will not work on its existing wording? To take another example, how do the concepts of 'independence' and 'impartiality' work in practice? Is an arbitrator who is regularly appointed by investors in investment arbitrations genuinely independent or is he or she likely to have a bias in favour of investors? If the arbitrator

---

[49]   These conventions are reviewed in more detail later in this chapter.

nominated by the law firm of one of the parties was the senior partner of that law firm until four years ago, can he or she be regarded as genuinely impartial? These and other important questions will be considered in later chapters.

(b) What is meant by the word 'international'?

The reader of a book on international arbitration is entitled to be told at some stage what the authors mean by the word 'international'—and for this to be followed by being told what is meant by the word 'commercial', since much of the book is about disputes that in the international community are considered to be 'commercial'. The problem is that there is no generally agreed meaning of either term.   **1.63**

'When I use a word, it means just what I choose it to mean—neither more nor less' said Humpty Dumpty, in a rather scornful tone in Lewis Carroll's *Through the Looking Glass*;[50] and in the wonderland of international arbitration no less than three definitions of the word 'international' are to be found. These are set out below.   **1.64**

(i) The international character of the dispute

The ICC, influenced by French law, adopted the *nature* of the dispute as its criterion for deciding whether or not an arbitration was an '*international* arbitration'. At first, the ICC considered business disputes to be 'international' only if they involved nationals of different countries, but it altered its Rules in 1927 to cover disputes that contained a 'foreign element', even if the parties were nationals of the same country. An explanatory booklet issued by the ICC used to explain that: **1.65**

> [T]he international nature of the arbitration does not mean that the parties must necessarily be of different nationalities. By virtue of its object, the contract can nevertheless extend beyond national borders, when for example a contract is concluded between two nationals of the same State for performance in another country, or when it is concluded between a State and a subsidiary of a foreign company doing business in that State.[51]

(ii) Nationality of the parties

The second approach is to focus attention not on the *nature* of the dispute but on the *parties to it*. This involves reviewing the nationality, place of residence, or place of business of the parties to the arbitration agreement. It is an approach that was adopted in the European Convention of 1961,[52] which although little used, contains several useful definitions, including a definition of the agreements to which it applies as: **1.66**

> arbitration agreements concluded for the purpose of settling disputes arising from international trade between physical or legal persons having, when concluding the agreement, *their habitual place of residence or their seat in different Contracting States* [...][53]

---

[50] Lewis Carroll, *Through the Looking Glass* (Macmillan & Co, 1872), ch. 6.
[51] ICC, 'The International Solution to International Business Disputes: ICC Arbitration', ICC Publication No. 301 (ICC, 1977), p. 19. (This useful booklet is no longer in print.)
[52] European Convention on International Commercial Arbitration, signed at Geneva on 21 April 1961: United Nations Treaty Series (1963–64), Vol. 484, p. 364, No. 7041.
[53] European Convention of 1961, Art. I(1)(a) (emphasis added).

1.67   Switzerland is one of the states in which the *nationality* of the parties determines whether or not an arbitration is 'international'. In Swiss law, an arbitration is 'international' if, at the time when the arbitration agreement was concluded, at least one of the parties was not domiciled or habitually resident in Switzerland.[54] The 'nationality' test is also used in part by the United States for the purposes of the New York Convention, with arbitration agreements between US citizens or corporations excluded from the scope of the Convention unless their relationship 'involves property located abroad, envisages performance or enforcement abroad or has some reasonable relation with one or more foreign states.'[55]

(iii) The Model Law

1.68   The lack of an internationally agreed definition of 'international' may create problems. Each state has its own test for determining whether an arbitration award is 'international' or in the language of the New York Convention, 'foreign'. The Convention defines 'foreign awards' as awards made in the territory of a state *other* than that in which recognition and enforcement are sought, which is clear enough; but the Convention then complicates matters by including in the category of 'foreign awards' those that are 'not considered as domestic awards' by the enforcement state.[56] In consequence, whilst the state in which an award is made may consider that award to be 'domestic' (because it involves parties who are nationals of that state), the enforcement state might consider it to be 'foreign' (for instance, because it involves the interests of international trade).

1.69   The Model Law, which was specifically designed to apply to *international commercial* arbitration, recognised that some definition of the term 'international' was essential. The Model Law states, in Article 1(3):

> An arbitration is international if:
>
> (a) the parties to an arbitration agreement have, at the time of the conclusion of that agreement, their places of business in different States; or
> (b) one of the following places is situated outside the State in which the parties have their places of business:
>   (i) the place of arbitration if determined in, or pursuant to, the arbitration agreement;
>   (ii) any place where a substantial part of the obligations of the commercial relationship is to be performed or the place with which the subject-matter of the dispute is most closely connected; or
> (c) the parties have expressly agreed that the subject matter of the arbitration agreement relates to more than one country.

1.70   This definition combines the two criteria mentioned earlier and, for good measure, adds others, so that a dispute is 'international' if:

> (i) the parties are of different nationalities—Article 1(3)(a);
> (ii) the business is of an international character—Article 1(3)(b)(ii);
> (iii) the parties have agreed that the subject matter of the arbitration agreement relates to more than one country—Article 1(3)(c); or

---

[54] See the Swiss Private International Law Act 1987, as amended in 2021, Ch. 12, Art. 176(1).
[55] US Code, Title 9 ('Arbitration') § 202.
[56] New York Convention, Art. 1(1).

(iv) the agreed place of arbitration is outside the states in which the parties are situated—Article 1(3)(b)(i).

For the purposes of this book, the authors adopt this wide definition of the term 'international'. An arbitration is considered to be 'international' (in the sense of the Model Law) if it involves parties of different nationalities, or if it takes place in a country that is 'foreign' to the parties, or if it involves business of an international character, or if the parties have agreed that it is international.[57] Nonetheless, a caveat must be entered to the effect that such arbitrations will not necessarily be universally regarded as international. If a question arises as to whether or not a particular arbitration is 'international', the answer will depend upon the provisions of the relevant national law.   **1.71**

(c) What is meant by the word 'commercial'?

It used to be customary to refer to the 'commercial' character of arbitrations, such as those to which much of this book is devoted. This reflects the distinction made in some countries between contracts that are considered to be 'commercial' and those that are not. This distinction was very important at a time when certain states only allowed disputes under 'commercial' contracts to be submitted to arbitration; and this is still the position in some states.[58] Under the law of that state, it would (for example) be permissible to hold an arbitration between two business people over a contract made in the course of their business, but not in respect of a contract for the allocation of property on the marriage of their children.   **1.72**

The forerunner of the New York Convention, the 1923 Geneva Protocol, distinguished in Article 1 between 'commercial matters' and 'any other matters capable of settlement by arbitration'. This distinction carried with it the implication that 'commercial matters' would *necessarily* be capable of being settled (or resolved) by arbitration under the law of the state concerned, whilst certain matters that the state considered to be 'non-commercial' could *not* be resolved in that manner.   **1.73**

Further emphasis was added to the distinction between 'commercial matters' and 'any other matters' by the stipulation in the Geneva Protocol that each contracting state was free to limit its obligations under the Protocol 'to contracts that are considered as commercial under its national law'.[59] This is the so-called 'commercial reservation'. It remains important because the same reservation by states is allowed under the New York Convention.[60]   **1.74**

---

[57] Spain is one of the countries that has adopted this wide definition in the Spanish Arbitration Act 2003, as amended by the Arbitration Amendment Act 2011, s. 3.

[58] For example, China is one major state that adopted the 'commercial reservation' when it ratified the New York Convention in 1987, and in India, for instance, an 'international commercial arbitration' is defined to mean an arbitration relating to legal relationships that are considered to be commercial under the law in force in India: Indian Arbitration and Conciliation Act 1996, s. 2(1)(f).

[59] Geneva Protocol of 1923, Art. 1.

[60] New York Convention, Art. I(3). It may be important to know whether the legal relationship out of which the arbitration arose was or was not a commercial relationship. If, e.g., it becomes necessary to seek recognition or enforcement of a foreign arbitral award in a state that has adhered to the New York Convention but has entered the commercial reservation, it will be necessary to look at the law of the state concerned to see what definition it adopts of the term 'commercial'.

1.75   The drafters of the Model Law considered defining the word 'commercial',[61] but found it too difficult. Instead, they settled for a footnote saying:

> The term 'commercial' should be given a wide interpretation so as to cover matters arising from all relationships of a commercial nature, whether contractual or not. Relationships of a commercial nature include, but are not limited to, the following transactions: any trade transaction for the supply or exchange of goods or services; distribution agreement; commercial representation or agency; factoring; leasing; construction of works; consulting; engineering; licensing; investment; financing; banking; insurance; exploitation agreement or concession; joint venture and other forms of industrial or business co-operation; carriage of goods or passengers by air, sea, rail or road.

The first four editions of this book were concerned principally with 'commercial' arbitrations, using 'commercial' in the wide sense used in the Model Law. However, given the increased number and importance of investment disputes resolved by arbitration, the authors deleted the reference to 'commercial' in subsequent editions.[62] In doing so, they noted that they were following the practice of the arbitral community that distinguishes 'commercial' arbitration (which arises from a contractual arbitration agreement) from 'investment' arbitration (which arises from consent in a bilateral or multilateral investment treaty) although in most investment arbitrations, commercial interests are usually at stake.

(d) The legal rules applicable to international arbitration

1.76   It would be reasonable to assume that an international arbitration is conducted under the relevant principles of international law; and that the awards of international arbitral tribunals are based upon the substantive rules and principles of international law. However, that is only the position for a small category of arbitrations. So far as any system of law is concerned, most international arbitrations are governed *procedurally* by the laws of the country of the seat where the arbitration is deemed to take place and *substantively* by the applicable national law selected by the parties in the underlying agreement.

1.77   The limited category of international arbitrations governed by international law are, historically, inter-state disputes subject to a specific arbitration agreement; and more recently, investment arbitrations conducted pursuant to state consent in a bilateral or multilateral investment treaty.

1.78   In the first category, states that were in dispute with each other, whether over frontiers or fishing rights, were historically accustomed to refer their dispute to ad hoc tribunals composed (nominally, at least) of heads of state,[63] or to 'mixed claims commissions' whose members were appointed by or on behalf of heads of state.

---

[61] Which neither the Geneva Protocol nor the New York Convention had done.

[62] The definition appears as a footnote to Art. 1(1), which states that the Model Law applies to 'international commercial arbitration'. It is interesting to see that the Model Law includes 'investment' within the definition of the term 'commercial', since in practice a separate regime for investment disputes has tended to develop, particularly where a state or state entity is concerned. See Chapter 8 on investment arbitration.

[63] For instance, President Grant of the United States was sole arbitrator in the *Bulama Island* case and Queen Victoria was sole arbitrator in a dispute between France and Mexico: see Simpson and Fox, *International Arbitration* (Stevens & Sons Limited, 1969), pp. 1–41.

The celebrated Alabama Claims arbitrations of 1872, which arose out of the US Civil War, **1.79** marked a break with this practice. It established a mechanism for appointing neutral arbitrators (one member of the tribunal being appointed by each party and the 'neutral' members being appointed by the King of Italy, the Emperor of Brazil, and the President of the Swiss Confederation).[64]

The role of international arbitration in the peaceful resolution of disputes between states **1.80** was an important feature of the Peace Conferences that took place at The Hague, on the initiative of Tsar Nicholas II of Russia, in 1899 and 1907. The Hague Convention of 1899 that resulted from the First Peace Conference proclaimed arbitration to be 'the most effective and at the same time the most equitable means of settling disputes which diplomacy has failed to settle'. This led to the establishment at The Hague of the Permanent Court of Arbitration (PCA) and then to the Permanent Court of International Justice (which subsequently became the International Court of Justice). Disputes between states have been and continue to be referred to arbitration at the PCA where there is a specific agreement for such reference between the affected states.[65]

However, except for these examples, the vast majority of international arbitrations take **1.81** place between private parties and are governed *procedurally* by the agreed rules of arbitration and the arbitration laws of the seat of the arbitration and *substantively* by the system of applicable law agreed by the parties or, in default of agreement, determined by the tribunal. They are nevertheless enforceable abroad pursuant to an international convention, the New York Convention. The hybrid nature of such cases made them difficult to categorise. Sir Robert Jennings, former President of the International Court of Justice, noted this challenge in his preface to the first edition of this book:

> International commercial disputes do not fit into orthodox moulds of dispute procedures. They lie astraddle the frontiers of foreign and domestic law and raise questions that do not fit into the categories of private international law either. Not least they raise peculiar problems of enforcement.

(e) Is international arbitration autonomous?

In contrast to litigants in a court of law, parties to an international arbitration enjoy a con- **1.82** siderable degree of freedom in the way in which that arbitration is conducted. They are free to select a sole arbitrator or the members of the arbitral tribunal; they are free to select the place of arbitration and the rules that are to govern that arbitration; they are free to select the law that governs the matters in issue and the procedures to be followed in considering

---

[64] The basis of the claims was an alleged breach of the international laws on neutrality in time of war by the British government, which had failed to prevent the *Alabama* and her supply ship *Georgia* (built in British yards), from setting sail to join the Confederacy during the US civil war. The British government was ordered to pay compensation in the sum of $15.5 million, a considerable amount at that time: see Simpson and Fox, *International Arbitration* (Stevens & Sons Limited, 1959), p. 8; Brownlie, *Principles of Public International Law* (7th edn, Oxford University Press), p. 702, fn. 6. Brownlie notes that: 'The popularity of arbitration increased considerably after the successful *Alabama Claims* arbitration of 1872 between the United States and Great Britain' (ibid., at p. 702).

[65] The PCA also administers disputes involving private parties. The first such arbitration was *Radio Corporation of America v China* (1941) 8 ILR 26; for current cases see the official PCA website.

those issues; and they are free to put an end to the entire arbitral process if they reach a settlement during the course of the proceedings.

1.83   Arbitration, whether international or domestic, is essentially a private system of justice depending on the consent of the parties. It stands in contrast to the public system of a country's courts of law. Its procedures are judicial or quasi-judicial, but its arbitrators are private individuals. Unlike judges, international arbitrators do not have the powers and authority of the state behind them.

1.84   There is much learned discussion in the literature, dating back over many years, as to the correct legal characterisation of this essentially private system of justice. Initially, it was argued that international arbitration was 'jurisdictional' in nature. Even if the parties to an arbitration were of different nationalities or had their places of business in different states, there would only be one country that was the 'seat' of the arbitration. That arbitration would be subject to the jurisdiction of the courts of that country and would be dependent on, and gain its authority from, that country's national law. On this basis, an arbitration in London between a German shipowner and a Dutch shipbuilder would be an English arbitration, subject to and dependent upon the law of England; and the tribunal's award would be an English award. It would not be a stateless, 'international' award; and if it became necessary to enforce the award in another country, it would be enforceable as a 'foreign' award under the New York Convention, the title of which states explicitly that it is concerned with the recognition and enforcement of 'foreign arbitral awards'.

1.85   This view, in which an award acquired the nationality of the country of the seat of the arbitration, did not commend itself to more internationally minded lawyers such as Professor Phillippe Fouchard[66] who drew a clear distinction between domestic arbitration and international arbitration. For Professor Fouchard, and for many others, international arbitration was a different creature to the national or domestic variety. An international arbitration was based on the will of the parties (referred to in French as 'l'autonomie de la volonte') who chose to arbitrate in a neutral country that generally had no connection with them or with their dispute. There was thus no need to envisage a juridical link between that country and the award of the tribunal that determined the dispute. Such awards should not be treated as national awards of the place of arbitration. Consistent with the choice of the parties, they were not 'national' awards, but 'international' awards. To summarise, the argument was that the place or seat of the arbitration and the national laws of that place were of no relevance, given:

(i) the participation of parties who had no national or other connection with the seat (or place) of the arbitration, which could be anywhere;

(ii) the existence of rules of arbitration such as those of the ICC that made it possible for an arbitration to be conducted from beginning to end without any reference to any national court or system of law; and

(iii) the existence of international treaties such as the New York Convention that provided for the recognition and enforcement of arbitration agreements and arbitral awards;

---

[66] See in particular Fouchard, *L'Arbitrage Commerciale International* (Dalloz, 1965).

In short, it was argued that international arbitration should properly be regarded as a wholly 'autonomous' and self-contained institution. Its only point of contact with national systems of law would occur if and when a party sought recognition and enforcement of the arbitral tribunal's award.

It is true to say that, in most cases, international arbitrations do proceed 'autonomously' from start to finish, as a driverless car is intended to do. There is no need for a touch on the driving wheel or the brake. There is no need for a reference to a court of law, whether on the challenge of an arbitrator, an application for interim relief, or indeed any other interlocutory matter. In practice, the relevant rules of arbitration are usually adequate to cover such situations, without assistance or intervention from the courts.   **1.86**

One of the high points in the argument for the autonomy of international arbitration came with the 2007 *Putrabali* decision of the French Court of Cassation. This decision and its successors are considered more fully in Chapter 3 but put briefly, the French court held that an international arbitral award set aside by the English High Court could nevertheless be enforced in France. In the view of the French court, the award was not anchored to any particular national legal order, including that of the seat of the arbitration. The court said: '[A]n international arbitral award, which does not belong to any state legal system, is a decision of international justice, whose validity must be ascertained with regard to the applicable rules of the country where its recognition and enforcement are sought'.[67]   **1.87**

This decision has been criticised by many lawyers and commentators who regard any arbitration, whether national or international, as having a necessary juridical connection with the courts of the seat of that arbitration. However, whilst an enforcing court will usually not enforce an award 'set aside' by the courts of the place of arbitration when asked to do so,[68] it retains a discretion to do so under the New York Convention since the grounds for refusing enforcement under the New York Convention (and the Model Law) are not mandatory.[69]   **1.88**

Leaving aside these arguments, there is a very real concern that international arbitration, which already enjoys considerably freedom under most national laws, should be careful not to over-reach itself by asserting complete autonomy. The point was strongly made by Lord Mance, a former judge of the UK Supreme Court when he said:[70]   **1.89**

> Arbitration already offers those engaging in it very substantial autonomy. Siren calls for complete or yet further autonomy should be viewed with scepticism. We—judges, arbitrators and lawyers—are engaged in a common exercise, the administration of justice for the benefit of litigants and society. A degree of order, coordination and interdependence is necessary and desirable if this exercise is to be conducted efficiently and economically in a globalised world.

---

[67] *Societe PT Putrabali Adyamulia v Societe Rena Holding et Societe Mnugotia Est Epices* [2007] Rev Arb 507, at 514.
[68] See New York Convention, Art. V.1(e).
[69] See the discussion of the New York Convention, Art. V.1(e) and the Model Law, Art. 36(1)(v) in Chapters 10 and 11.
[70] Mance, 'Arbitration: A Law unto Itself?' (2016) 32 Arb Intl 223.

1.90   In his judgment in *Bank Mellatt v Hellinki Teckniki*, Sir Michael Kerr also warned against arbitration as an entirely autonomous process:

> Despite suggestions to the contrary by some learned writers under other systems, our jurisdiction does not recognise the concept of arbitral procedures floating in the transnational firmament, unconnected with any system of law.

This was a statement of the position in English law, but it is a position generally adopted by many other legal systems that accept that an international arbitration is anchored to the law of the country which (actually or notionally) is the place or 'seat' of the arbitration; and that there is a juridical link between an international arbitration and the law of that seat. The need for that link becomes apparent when issues such as the review of the award fall to be considered.

1.91   The proponents of arbitration without nationality ('delocalised' arbitration) dream of a world in which there is no intervention, or at most very limited intervention, by national courts in international arbitration.[71] The problem remains that there is no international court of arbitration with the power to enforce agreements to arbitrate or the orders of arbitral tribunals or arbitral awards themselves. If enforcement is needed, it can only come from national courts of law possessed of powers of punishment and sanction that are not available to arbitrators or arbitral institutions.

(f) National law and international conventions

1.92   An understanding of the interplay between the private arbitral process and the different national systems of law that may impinge upon that process is fundamental to a proper understanding of international arbitration. This interplay may take place at almost any phase of the arbitral process. For example, it may be necessary at the outset of an arbitration for the claimant to ask the relevant national (or local) court to enforce an agreement to arbitrate which the adverse party is seeking to circumvent by commencing court proceedings; or it may be necessary to ask the relevant court to appoint the arbitral tribunal (if this cannot be done under the arbitration agreement). During the course of the arbitration, it may become necessary for a party to apply to the relevant court for interim measures that it is empowered to give, for example the blocking of a bank account or the seizure of assets to prevent their disappearance.

1.93   When an award has been made, the losing party may seek to challenge it before the courts of the seat of the arbitration on the basis that the arbitral tribunal exceeded its jurisdiction, failed to respect due process, or on some other legally recognised ground. If that challenge succeeds, the award will either be amended or set aside completely.[72] By contrast, the winning party may need to apply to a national court for recognition and enforcement of the award[73] in a state (or states) in which the losing party has (or is believed to have) assets that can be sequestrated.

---

[71] We return to this discussion in Chapter 3. For a helpful, concise, and informative introduction to the topic see Lew, 'Achieving the dream: Autonomous arbitration', in Lew and Mistelis (eds) *Arbitration Insights: Twenty Years of the Annual Lecture of the School of Arbitration* (Kluwer Law International, 2007), pp. 454–485. For a note emphasising the importance of the seat of arbitration 'at all stages of an arbitration's life-span' see, for instance, Ferrari, 'Plures leges faciunt arbitrum' (2012) 37(3) Arb Intl 579–599, at 596.
[72] See Chapter 10.
[73] See Chapter 11.

States that recognise international arbitration as a valid method of resolving international **1.94** disputes are generally ready to give their assistance to the arbitral process. Indeed, in many cases, they are bound to do so by the international conventions to which they are parties. In return, it is to be expected that they will seek to exercise a measure of control over the arbitral process. Such control is usually exercised on a territorial basis: first, over arbitrations conducted in the territory of the state concerned and secondly, over awards brought into the territory of the state concerned for the purpose of recognition and enforcement.

As to the first proposition, it would be unusual for a state to support arbitral tribunals op- **1.95** erating within its jurisdiction *without* claiming some degree of control over the conduct of those arbitral tribunals—if only to ensure that minimum standards of justice are met, particularly in procedural matters.[74]

As to the second proposition, it is generally accepted that states that may be called upon to **1.96** recognise and enforce a foreign arbitral award are entitled to ensure that minimum standards of due process have been observed in the making of that award, that the subject matter of the award is 'arbitrable' in terms of their own laws, and that the award itself does not offend public policy.[75]

The dependence of the international arbitral process upon national systems of law should **1.97** be recognised, but not exaggerated. Across the world, there is a growing harmonisation of the national laws that govern both the conduct of international arbitrations, and the recognition and enforcement of international awards. This process of harmonisation was inspired by the New York Convention and was then given fresh impetus by the Model Law. Additionally, the importance of international arbitration, in terms both of its contribution to global trade and of the economic benefit that arbitrations can bring to the host country, is increasingly recognised, with new arbitration centres being established in different parts of the world. Some may have only a nominal existence but taken as a whole they represent a potential source of revenue (and perhaps of prestige) to a country.[76]

(g) The role of international conventions and the Model Law

The most effective method of creating a 'universal' system of law governing international **1.98** arbitration has been through international conventions (and, more recently, through the Model Law). International conventions have helped to link national systems of law into

---

[74] See Kerr, 'Arbitration and the courts: The UNCITRAL Model Law' (1984) 50 Arbitration 3, at 14:

> [T]here is virtually no body, tribunal, authority or individual in this country whose acts or decisions give rise to binding legal consequences for others, but who are altogether immune from judicial review in the event of improper conduct, breaches of the principles of natural justice, or decisions which clearly transcend any standard of objective reasonableness.

[75] For further discussion of 'arbitrability' and public policy, see Chapter 2.

[76] Mustill, 'The history of international commercial arbitration: A sketch', in Newman and Hill (eds) *The Leading Arbitrators' Guide to International Arbitration* (2nd edn, JurisNet, 2008), p. 17: 'National governments have also sought to gain economic advantage from the promotion of local arbitration by backing the establishment of arbitration or dispute resolution centres, the idea being that if there is in one's own country a focus of intellectual and practical activity in this field, with facilities for the conduct and study of arbitrations, contracting parties will choose to conclude agreements for arbitration there [...].'

a network of laws that, while they may differ in their wording, have as their common objective the international enforcement of arbitration agreements and of arbitral awards.

1.99   The first such convention, in modern times, was the Montevideo Convention.[77] This was established in 1889 and provided for the recognition and enforcement of arbitration agreements between certain Latin American states.[78] It was therefore essentially a regional convention. The first modern and genuinely *international* convention was the 1923 Geneva Protocol, which was drawn up on the initiative of the ICC and under the auspices of the League of Nations. It was quickly followed by the Geneva Convention of 1927.

(i) The Geneva Protocol of 1923

1.100   The 1923 Geneva Protocol was concerned with both arbitration clauses and arbitral awards. Its main objective was to ensure that arbitration *clauses* were enforceable *internationally*, so that parties to an arbitration agreement could be compelled to resolve their dispute by arbitration rather than through the courts. This was done by requiring national courts to refuse to entertain legal proceedings brought in breach of an agreement to arbitrate. The second and subsidiary objective of the 1923 Geneva Protocol was to ensure that *arbitration awards* made pursuant to such arbitration agreements would be enforced in the territory of the states in which they were made.

1.101   The Geneva Protocol is now a spent force. It is still worthy of note, however, since the enforcement of arbitration agreements remains an objective of both the New York Convention and the Model Law.

(ii) The Geneva Convention of 1927

1.102   The 1927 Geneva Convention[79] was intended to widen the scope of the Geneva Protocol by providing for the recognition and enforcement of Protocol awards made within the territory of *any* of the contracting states (and not merely within the territory of the state in which the award was made).[80] However, a party seeking enforcement of an award under the 1927 Geneva Convention had to *prove* the conditions necessary for enforcement. This led to what became known as the problem of 'double exequatur'. To show that the award had become final in its country of origin, the successful party was often obliged (i) to seek a declaration (an 'exequatur') in the courts of the country in which the arbitration took place to the effect that the award was enforceable in that country before (ii) it could go ahead and enforce the award (a second exequatur) in the courts of the place of enforcement.

(iii) The New York Convention of 1958

1.103   The New York Convention is one of the cornerstones of international arbitration.[81] It has been described as 'the single most important pillar on which the edifice of international

---

[77] Treaty concerning the Union of South American States in respect of Procedural Law, signed at Montevideo on 11 January 1889. The Treaty is published, in an English translation, in United Nations, *Register of Texts of Conventions and Other Instruments Concerning International Trade Law, Vol. II* (UN, 1973), p. 5.

[78] Montevideo Convention, Arts 5–7.

[79] Convention for the Execution of Foreign Arbitral Awards, signed at Geneva on 26 September 1927.

[80] The states that have adhered to the Geneva Convention are substantially those that adhered to the Geneva Protocol (with some notable omissions, such as Brazil, Norway, and Poland).

[81] In 1953, the ICC proposed a new treaty to govern international arbitration. The draft document produced by the ICC gave an early indication of the debate that has continued ever since, concerning the feasibility of a truly *international* award. The ICC's proposal for such an award, which would *not* be subject to control by the law of the

arbitration rests',[82] and one that 'perhaps could lay claim to be the most effective instance of international legislation in the entire history of commercial law'.[83] Indeed, it is principally because of the New York Convention that international arbitration has become the established method of resolving international disputes. The major trading nations of the world have become parties to the New York Convention. At the time of writing, the Convention has 168 state parties on every continent.

The New York Convention provides a simpler and more effective method of obtaining rec- **1.104** ognition and enforcement of foreign arbitral awards than was available under the 1927 Geneva Convention.[84] The title of the New York Convention suggests that it is concerned *only* with the recognition and enforcement of foreign arbitral *awards*, but this is misleading. The Convention is also concerned with the recognition of arbitration agreements.

In order to enforce arbitration agreements, the New York Convention adopts the technique **1.105** found in the 1923 Geneva Protocol. The courts of contracting states are required to refuse to allow a case to proceed if the dispute in question is subject to an arbitration agreement and raised by any party to that agreement.[85]

Courts of different countries have differed (and continue to differ) in their interpretation **1.106** of the New York Convention.[86] However, even if it has provisions that are obsolete,[87] it has stood the test of time and remains a cornerstone of international arbitration.

(iv) Conventions After 1958

The New York Convention[88] represents a vital achievement in the shaping of modern inter- **1.107** national arbitration. No convention since 1958 has had the same impact. There are, however, other treaties and conventions, which may enable recognition and enforcement of arbitral awards in appropriate cases including the 1966 ICSID Convention for arbitrations that take place under the auspices of the ICSID system. These conventions are discussed in Chapter 11 and ICSID arbitration in Chapter 8.

(v) Investment treaties

In the context of international treaties and conventions, a brief mention should be made of **1.108** investment treaties. Historically, states doing business with each other often entered into 'treaties of friendship, commerce, and navigation'. In order to encourage trade and investment, the states concerned would grant each other favourable trading conditions and agree

---

place in which it was made, was unacceptable to the majority of states. It has also proved to be equally unacceptable in more modern times, when the Model Law was formulated.

[82]   Wetter, 'The present status of the International Court of Arbitration of the ICC: An appraisal' (1990) 1 Am Rev Intl Arb 91, at 93.

[83]   Mustill, 'Arbitration: History and background' (1989) 6 J Intl Arb 43, at 49. See also Schwebel, 'A celebration of the United Nations' New York Convention' (1996) 12 Arb Intl 83.

[84]   The New York Convention replaces the 1923 Geneva Protocol and the 1927 Geneva Convention as between states that are parties to both: see Art. VII(2).

[85]   New York Convention, Art. 11(3).

[86]   The ICCA's *Yearbook of Commercial Arbitration* (YBCA) reports, each year, court decisions made in different countries on the interpretation and application of the New York Convention, translated into English where necessary.

[87]   Such as in the 'writing requirement', discussed in Chapter 2.

[88]   The recognition and enforcement of awards under the New York Convention, and the grounds for refusal of such recognition and enforcement, are discussed in Chapters 10 and 11.

that any (inter-state) disputes would be resolved by arbitration. Such treaties have now given way to investment treaties, either bilateral (BITs) or multilateral (MITs), or as investment chapters in free trade agreements.[89] The Energy Treaty Charter, for example, provides for disputes between a contracting state and the energy investor of another contracting state to be referred to international arbitration.[90] Free trade agreements, such as the United States–Mexico–Canada Agreement (USMCA) (which has replaced the North American Free Trade Agreement or NAFTA) also contain similar investor protection and arbitration clauses.

(vi) The Model Law

1.109   The Model Law began with a proposal to reform the New York Convention. This led to a report from UNCITRAL[91] to the effect that harmonisation of the arbitration laws of the different countries of the world could be achieved more effectively by a model or uniform law. The final text of the Model Law was adopted by resolution of UNCITRAL at its session in Vienna in June 1985, as a law to govern international commercial arbitration. A recommendation of the General Assembly of the United Nations commending the Model Law to member states was adopted in December 1985.[92]

1.110   The Model Law has been a major success. The text goes through the arbitral process from beginning to end in a simple and readily understandable form. It is a text that many states have adopted as their own law, either as it stands or with minor changes. So far eighty-five states have adopted legislation based on the Model Law, with some states choosing to modernise their laws on arbitration without adopting the Model Law, whilst being careful to follow its format and to have close regard to its provisions.[93]

1.111   It may be said that if the New York Convention put international arbitration on the world stage, it was the Model Law that made it a star, with appearances in states across the world. Even so, the Model Law, which was enacted in 1985, has been overtaken by a fast-moving world in at least two respects. The first was the requirement for an arbitration agreement to be in writing, which was outdated; the second centred on the provisions governing the power of an arbitral tribunal to order interim measures of relief. To address these concerns, UNCITRAL established a working group in 2000 to consider revisions to the Model Law. This working group produced proposals that were adopted as revisions to the Model Law and approved by the United Nations in December 2006.[94]

---

[89]   According to UNCTAD, there are now more than 2,850 BITs and more than 400 'other' international investment agreements (such as free trade agreements, economic partnership agreements, or framework agreements with an investment element): available online at https://investmentpolicy.unctad.org/international-investment-agreements.

[90]   See, e.g., Huber, 'Investment arbitration and the Energy Charter Treaties' (2010) 1(1) J Intl Disp Settlement 153–190.

[91]   UNCITRAL, *Study on the Application and Interpretation of the Convention on the Recognition and Enforcement of Foreign Arbitral Awards*, UN Doc A/CN9/168 (UN, 1958).

[92]   For a full account of the origins and aims of the Model Law, see the second edition of this book, pp. 508*ff*.

[93]   The advisory committee established in the United Kingdom to report on the Bill that became the English Arbitration Act 1996 stated in Departmental Advisory Committee on Arbitration Law, *Report on the Arbitration Bill* (HMSO, 1996) (known as the 'DAC Report'), at para. 4: '[a]t every stage in preparing a new draft Bill, very close regard was paid to the Model Law, and it will be seen that both the structure and the content of the July draft bill, and the final bill, owe much to this model.'

[94]   Resolution 61/33 adopted by the General Assembly on 4 December 2006, available at https:/undocs.org/en/A/Res/61/33. (Discussion of relevant provisions of the Model law, including the provisions governing interim relief, takes place in the following chapters of this book.)

D. ADR, Litigation, and Arbitration

When parties are negotiating an international agreement, the last thing on their minds is **1.112** probably the question of how to resolve any potential disputes. It is nonetheless a question that needs to be addressed; and it is probably best addressed by the parties during the contract negotiations, whilst relations are good and the prospect of any dispute appears remote.

There are a variety of options to be considered, starting with those that come under the gen- **1.113** eral heading of ADR, the acronym for Alternative Dispute Resolution.[95]

(a) Mediation

One of the most effective forms of ADR is mediation. A mediator is someone who has no **1.114** connection with the parties or their contract, but who is engaged to help them to resolve their differences. To do this in an international commercial dispute, the mediator will usually study the relevant evidence and documents and listen to the parties' complaints and arguments, including their commercial objectives. The mediator will then, as an observer with an objective understanding of what is in issue, attempt to persuade the parties to reach an amicable settlement of their dispute by focusing on their real commercial interests, rather than on what they perceive to be their legal entitlement. Unlike an arbitrator, a mediator cannot issue a binding decision but merely acts as a facilitator with a view to promoting an agreement between the parties and, for that reason, has complete flexibility with regard to procedure. Indeed, unlike an arbitration, in mediation it is common for mediators to meet with each party separately (as well as together) in order to try and broker an acceptable agreement.

In the past, the terms 'mediator' and 'conciliator' were frequently used as if they were **1.115** interchangeable (as evidenced by the 2002 UNCITRAL 'Model Law on International Conciliation'). However, the term 'mediator' has now prevailed in general use and practice.

The time taken by an international arbitration and its expense have led to a renewed **1.116** interest in the development of mediation as a tool for dispute resolution in international contracts. In that context, UNCITRAL updated its 2002 'Model Law on International Conciliation' with the 2018 'UNCITRAL Model Law on International Commercial Mediation and International Settlement Agreements Resulting from Mediation'. In its own terms, 'The Model Law is designed to assist States in reforming and modernizing their laws on mediation procedure. It provides uniform rules in respect of the mediation process and aims at encouraging the use of mediation and ensuring greater predictability and certainty in its use.'

Contemporaneously with the publication of the 2018 Model Law, UNCITRAL Working **1.117** Group II (dispute resolution) developed the Convention on International Settlement Agreements resulting from Mediation, which was adopted on 20 December 2018 by the General Assembly of the United Nations and entered into force on 12 September 2020. As

---

[95] A clear and concise guide to the various forms of ADR is provided in Jenkins, *International Construction Arbitration Law* (3rd edn, Wolters Kluwer, 2021), pp. 141–165.

of April 2022, the Convention (referred to as the Singapore Convention) has been signed by fifty-five states and ratified by only nine states.[96] The Convention requires states to recognise and enforce international settlement agreements resulting from mediation that have been concluded in writing. It deliberately excludes any settlement agreement enforceable as an arbitral award (which would usually be a consent award) to avoid overlap with the New York Convention. As a consequence, covered settlement agreements no longer have to be enforced in member states as a simple contract in accordance with domestic court procedures but are rather directly recognised and enforced.

1.118   If parties wish to include mediation as a preliminary tool in the dispute resolution provision of their international contract, then it would be appropriate to incorporate language noting that they will first attempt to resolve any dispute for a fixed period (perhaps sixty or ninety days) by good faith negotiations, if necessary with the assistance of a neutral mediator to be selected by the parties (with a fallback institutional nomination), failing which the dispute will be referred to binding arbitration under a set of institutional rules.[97]

(b) Multi-tiered dispute resolution provisions

1.119   Many international agreements are for long-term projects. There might, for instance, be an agreement between a state and a major engineering company for the construction of a dam or a motorway; or a long-term agreement for the production and shipping of LNG from the gas supplier to a power plant several hundred miles away. It is important that if a dispute arises it should not hold up the work of construction, with perhaps hundreds of workers on site, or the delivery of the cargoes of liquid gas, with gas tankers at sea. What is needed is a dispute resolution provision that allows the work or transport to continue whilst the dispute is resolved.

1.120   Many standard form contracts used on major engineering or construction contracts now contain provisions for some form of multi-tiered resolution of the dispute.[98] These include 'mandatory negotiation', which obliges the senior management of the disputants to meet and try to negotiate a settlement by taking an overall view of the case, rather than by adhering to an entrenched position that was perhaps adopted by the participants at site level. They also include provisions for the interim determination of the dispute by a 'Disputes Resolution Board'[99] or a 'Panel of Experts', who will act in a quasi-judicial role and whose decision will be binding on the parties, unless it is reversed by an agreement between the parties or by a subsequent reference to a national court or to international arbitration. For example, the 'World Bank Standard Bidding Documents for the Procurement of Works' generally follows the provisions of the FIDIC Red Book providing that any dispute, including a dispute as to the engineer's evaluation of the work, is to be referred for decision to a Dispute Avoidance/

---

[96] As of April 2022, the states who have ratified the Convention are Singapore, Fiji, Qatar, Saudi Arabia, Belarus, Ecuador, Honduras, Georgia and Turkey.

[97] Model clauses for the appointment of a mediator are provided by various institutions, including arbitral institutions such as the ICC and specialist institutions such as the 'Centre for Effective Dispute Resolution' (CEDR), which focuses on mediation for the resolution of commercial disputes and also runs training courses for potential mediators.

[98] 'Tiered Dispute Resolution Precedents' are fully and helpfully discussed in Jenkins, *International Construction Arbitration Law* (3rd edn, Wolters Kluwer, 2021), pp. 66–99 under the title of 'Dispute Avoidance and Resolution'.

[99] See ibid., at pp. 121–140.

Adjudication Board (DAAB) constituted by the parties themselves.[100] That decision will be binding on the parties unless revised by a subsequent amicable settlement by the parties, which should take place before any reference to arbitration. If any party is still dissatisfied, the dispute will be referred to arbitration under the rules of arbitration agreed by the parties or, if there is no agreement, under the ICC Rules of Arbitration.

The use of ADR provisions in standard form or model contracts promoted by multilateral financial institutions and professional organisations is an indication of their success in the resolution of disputes. However, parties may go through the ADR process and still remain persuaded that their evidence or their arguments have not received the attention they deserve or that insufficient attention has been paid to the facts or the law. If so, the next decision for the aggrieved party is (depending on its contract) whether to take its grievance to the national courts or to international arbitration.   **1.121**

(c) The advantage of arbitration

(i) 'The only game in town'
The model and the standard forms of international contract to which reference has been made above provide for international arbitration as the final part of the dispute resolution process. They do so for good reason. International arbitration gives the parties the opportunity of resolving their dispute: (i) in a neutral place of arbitration; (ii) by a tribunal of experienced, independent, and impartial arbitrators; (iii) selected by or on behalf of the parties themselves for their suitability for the task; (iv) working in the language of the contract and of the frequently voluminous documents that form part of that contract; and (v) in a manner which will result in a binding decision that is internationally enforceable. In the international context, there is really no competition from the local courts. International arbitration may well be described, as stated earlier, as 'the only game in town'.   **1.122**

In addition to the points already made about neutrality, and the ability of the parties to select a tribunal of arbitrators who are skilled in their work as well as being independent and impartial, there are other advantages to international arbitration that should be briefly touched upon.   **1.123**

(ii) Enforcement
First and foremost is the fact that the awards of international arbitral tribunals are enforceable by courts worldwide because of a network of international treaties and conventions, of which the New York Convention is still the most important. These treaties and conventions have greater acceptance internationally than treaties for the reciprocal enforcement of judgments.[101]   **1.124**

---

[100] See *Standard Bidding Documents, Procurement of Works* (World Bank, 2020), p. 145; *Conditions of Contract for Construction for Building and Engineering Works Designed by the Employer* (2nd edn, FIDIC, 2017), pp. 100–107.

[101] There is a multilateral treaty for the recognition and enforcement of court judgments made in the EU member states and Switzerland: Council Regulation (EC) No. 44/2001 of 22 December 2000 on jurisdiction and the recognition and enforcement of judgment in civil and commercial matters, OJ L 12/1, 16 January 2001 (formerly the Brussels and Lugano Conventions). The Common Market of the South (Mercado Común del Sur, or

(iii) Privacy and confidentiality

1.125   A distinction needs to be made between privacy and confidentiality. Proceedings in an international arbitration are usually private. There is no public gallery for spectators, no journalists or reporters publishing details of the proceedings in the public press. It used to be possible to say that arbitrations were also confidential such that the evidence, the arguments, the submissions of the parties, and the awards of the arbitrators were only made known if the parties agreed or if there was some public duty to disclose them. This once general principle of confidentiality has been partially eroded in the quest for transparency, although the evidence is that where confidentiality exists it is still greatly valued by the parties, particularly in international commercial arbitrations. In international investment arbitrations, transparency has gained most traction since the matters at issue usually involve reviewing the legality of state measures and the possible payment of damages from the public purse. In those circumstances, there has been great pressure to open up the system to the public (and the taxpayer) who have an interest in calling their governments to account and in seeing the operation of a process where their taxpayer funds are employed. The consequence of this increased demand for transparency in the field of investment arbitration is addressed in detail in Chapter 8.

1.126   An important question is to what extent the move for transparency is likely to 'spill-over' from investment arbitration to international commercial arbitration, which is based on private contracts rather than on public treaties and does not involve the disbursement of public funds. At present, the demarcation line between the two types of arbitration seems to be observed. For example, in 2010 Australia adopted a rule that proceedings would not be confidential unless the parties 'opted in' to such confidentiality.[102] This rule proved so unpopular that it was reversed by legislation in 2015. Now confidentiality is once again the rule in Australia, with the parties free to 'opt out' of that rule if they wish to do so.[103] It has been clear for some years that the privacy and confidentiality of arbitral proceedings, which together were regarded as considerable advantages of international commercial arbitration, can no longer be taken for granted. The debate as to privacy and confidentiality is one of increasing importance. It is more fully explored in the next chapter.

(iv) Adaptability

1.127   Arbitration is an extremely adaptable process, as its history shows. Arbitration can equally well resolve the value of a piece of jewellery in a dispute between two merchants as it can a billion-dollar dispute between two multinational corporations. There are certain basic principles to be followed in the course of an arbitration (for instance that of treating the parties equally and giving them an opportunity to state their case) but there is no code of

---

Mercosur), comprising Argentina, Brazil, Paraguay, and Uruguay, has also established the Las Leñas Protocol for the mutual recognition and enforcement of judgments from Mercosur states within the region. The Hague Conference on Private International Law has drawn up a Convention on Choice of Court Agreements, under which a judgment by the court of a contracting state designated in an exclusive 'choice of court agreement' would be recognised and enforced in other contracting states. At time of writing, the Convention has been signed by the European Union (EU), China, Israel, Montenegro, the Republic of North-Macedonia, Singapore, Ukraine, and the United States, and entered into force on 1 October 2015 (see https://www.hcch.net/en/instruments/conventions/status-table/?cid=98).

[102] See the International Arbitration Amendment Act 2010, s. 22(3).
[103] See the International Arbitration Amendment Act 1947, as amended, ss. 22–23.

civil procedure to be followed. In short, an arbitration can be tailored to meet the specific requirements of the dispute, rather than being treated as if 'one-size-fits-all'.[104] It has been said that every arbitration is a 'microcosm of potential procedural reform'.

(v) Finality of the award

The decision of a court of law may be subject to an appeal first to a court of appeal and then   **1.128**
to a supreme court. This is no doubt good for the development of a country's legal system (as well as for its lawyers). It helps to build a known and reasonably predictable code of law. It is less useful for the individual corporations or individuals who have to finance the process and wait, possibly for years, for its final outcome. Subject to very limited grounds for review of an arbitral award discussed in Chapter 10, the award marks the end of the dispute. There is usually no ladder of appeals to be climbed.

(d) Disadvantages of international arbitration

(i) Multiparty arbitrations, joinder, and consolidation

There are inevitably disadvantages to international arbitration. For a start, any arbitration,   **1.129**
whether national or international, is based on the consent of the parties. Without consent, there is no valid arbitration.

There are cases, for example, where the parties to an arbitration may wish to add (or   **1.130**
join) a third party who is in some way involved in the dispute, such as a parent company, a subcontractor or an insurer. It may often make sense to add (or join) this third party, so as to resolve all outstanding disputes consistently in the same forum. However, in arbitration there may be problems in doing so absent demonstration of consent by the third party.

Alternatively, there may be two arbitrations between the same parties based on essen-   **1.131**
tially the same facts, but with the claimant in the first arbitration being named as the respondent in the second. It would make sense to consolidate the two arbitrations (that is, to bring them before the same arbitral tribunal) but, again, there may be problems in doing this.

Problems such as these (multiparty arbitrations, the joinder of additional parties, the con-   **1.132**
solidation of arbitrations, and so forth) have troubled the users of arbitration for many years. In the celebrated *Dutco* case,[105] there were two respondents who each wanted to nominate an arbitrator. Under the former ICC Rules, they could not do this. They were instead required to nominate one arbitrator between them. They did so under protest—but a complaint was made to the French court, which said that the right of each party to nominate an arbitrator was part of French public policy and could not be waived. As a consequence, the ICC had to devise new rules to deal with such a situation. These new Rules state that where there are multiple claimants or multiple respondents and the parties are unable to agree on

---

[104] Chapter 6, which deals amongst other things with the use of fast-track procedures, has more to say on this topic.
[105] *BKMI and Siemens v Dutco*, French Cass. Civ. 1ere, 7 January 1992, [1992] Bull Civ 1. This case is discussed more fully in Chapter 2.

a method for the constitution of the arbitral tribunal, the ICC Court itself may appoint each member of the tribunal and designate one as president.[106]

1.133 As international trade, commerce, and investment become more complex and global, there are an increasing number of multiparty disputes. For example, a car manufacturer based in Germany may have contracts with suppliers in other countries for the manufacture and supply of components. Any defects in the final product may mean that the German manufacturer will have claims against several suppliers in different locations and subject to different contracts, as it seeks to establish liability for the defects and compensation for its losses.

1.134 The leading arbitral institutions are well aware of the different problems that might arise and they have taken (or are taking) action to address them, so far as this is possible within the limits of 'party consent'.[107] For example, the ICC Rules give the arbitral tribunal (in Article 7.5) the authority to decide (under certain conditions) whether or not a party should be joined to the proceedings in response to a request for joinder. Similarly, the LCIA Rules contain provisions (in Article 22A) that give an arbitral tribunal (under certain conditions and subject to the approval of the LCIA Court) the power to consolidate any other arbitrations that are subject to the LCIA Rules. These provisions, and other developments of the powers of the arbitral institutions to consolidate, are considered in Chapter 2.

(ii) Non-signatories

1.135 The problem of the so-called non-signatory occurs when a claimant wishes to include a person or a legal entity that is not formally a signatory to the arbitration agreement as a co-respondent or (less commonly) where an entity wishes to start a claim pursuant to a contract in which it has an interest but has not signed. A common example is that of a claimant with a dispute under a contract between itself and a thinly capitalised local subsidiary of a major international corporation. The contract contains an arbitration clause and so arbitration can be compelled against the subsidiary company—but the claimant would like to add the *parent* company to the arbitration, so as to improve its chances of being paid if it succeeds in its claim. Is it possible to do this, if the parent company is not a signatory to the contract?

1.136 At this point it is sufficient to say (in very general terms) that the key issue is whether there is any 'deemed' or 'assumed', consent to arbitration. Various legal theories or doctrines have been developed to try to establish such assumed consent, including the 'group of companies' doctrine, the 'reliance' theory, the concept of agency, and the US concept of 'piercing the corporate veil' (so that, for example, a parent company may be taken to be responsible for the actions of a subsidiary that is a mere shell and, accordingly, be treated as if it were a party to any contract made by that subsidiary).[108] This problem is discussed in more detail later, in Chapter 2.

---

[106] This provision of the ICC Rules, first adopted in 1998, works reasonably well in practice, although it removes the right of the parties to nominate an arbitrator if they are unable to agree how this should be done. Interestingly, this is the very issue on which the French court took its stand, the 'fundamental' right of a party to nominate its own arbitrator! Other institutional rules contain similar provisions.

[107] Problems of multi-party arbitrations, joinder, and consolidation are considered in more detail in Chapter 2.

[108] See Hanotiau, *Complex Arbitrations: Multi-party, Multi-contract, Multi-issue—A Comparative Study* (2nd edn, International Law Library, 2020), pp. 95–196.

(iii) Conflicting awards

There is no system of binding precedent in international arbitration—that is, there is no rule **1.137** that an award on a particular issue, or a particular set of facts, is binding on different parties or arbitrators confronted with similar issues or similar facts.[109] Each award stands on its own. An arbitral tribunal that is required (for example) to interpret a particular reinsurance policy may arrive at a different conclusion from that of another tribunal faced with the same question. If the award of the first tribunal is known (and it may not be known, because of confidentiality), it may be of persuasive effect, but no more. The issue is even more acute in investment arbitration where two tribunals constituted to hear the claims of two share-holders in the same company subject to the same state measures may reach diametrically opposed solutions.[110]

The problem of conflicting decisions is a real one. One proposed solution is to create a new **1.138** international court for resolving disputes over the *enforcement* of arbitral awards. But this has been described as 'the impossible dream'.[111] Proposals for a broader appeal mechanism have been made in relation to investment arbitration to ensure consistency between deci-sions.[112] Indeed, the EU has incorporated arbitral appeal mechanisms into some Investment Protection Agreements.[113] This may suit lawyers and arbitrators, who might welcome con-sistency of decisions, but it might not suit business people who are looking for a rapid solu-tion to their dispute, rather than for the opportunity to contribute at their own expense to the development of the law.

(iv) Judicialisation

There has been for many years a continuing discussion about the increasing 'judicialisation' **1.139** of international arbitration:

> meaning both that arbitrations tend to be conducted more frequently with the procedural intricacy and formality more native to litigation in national courts and that they are more often subjected to judicial intervention and control.[114]

---

[109] See Kaufmann-Kohler, 'Arbitral precedent: Dream, necessity or excuse? The 2006 Freshfields Lecture' (2007) 23 Arb Intl 357.

[110] For instance, in *Ronald Lauder v Czech Republic*, Final Award, UNCITRAL, 3 September 2001 and in *CME v Czech Republic*, Final Award, UNCITRAL, 14 March 2003, two claims brought in respect of a single dis-pute, involving virtually undisputed facts, produced conflicting awards from arbitral tribunals in London and Stockholm, as well as giving rise to litigation in the Czech Republic, the United States, and Sweden: see Brower, Brower II, and Sharpe, 'The coming crisis in the global adjudication system' (2003) 19 Arb Intl 424; Cremades and Madalena, 'Parallel proceedings in international arbitration' (2008) 24 Arb Intl 507. See also Professor Kaj Hobér's review: Hobér, '*Res judicata* and *lis pendens* in international arbitration', in Hague Academy of International Law, *Collected Courses of the Hague Academy of International Law*, Vol. 366 (Martinus Nijhoff, 2014), pp. 99–406.

[111] Howard M. Holtzmann, cited in Brower, Brower II, and Sharpe, 'The coming crisis in the global adjudication system' (2003) 19 Arb Intl 424, at 435.

[112] See, e.g., Potesta and Kaufmann-Kohler, 'Can the Mauritius Convention serve as a model for the reform of investor-state arbitration in connection with the introduction of a permanent investment tribunal or an appeal mechanism?—Analysis and roadmap, (3 June 2016). Available at SSRN: https://ssrn.com/abstract=3455511 or http://dx.doi.org/10.2139/ssrn.3455511. The issue is also discussed in Platt, 'The appeal of appeal mechanisms in international arbitration: Fairness over finality?' (2013) 30(5) J Intl Arb 531.

[113] See Chapter Three of the EU–Vietnam Investment Protection Agreement which entered into force on 1 August 2020 and incorporates an arbitration appeal provision for investment arbitrations at Art. 3.39.

[114] Brower, 'W(h)ither international commercial arbitration?' (2008) 24 Arb Intl 181, at 183.

1.140 The problem is most evident in the United States,[115] where there is a tradition of broad-ranging 'discovery' in civil litigation. The US practice of 'discovery' describes seeking out and collecting pre-trial evidence. Such evidence takes two forms: witness testimony and the production of documents.

1.141 If US-style witness depositions are ordered in an arbitration, witnesses may be required to give oral testimony and to be cross-examined on oath by the parties' counsel. Their responses are recorded in a transcript which is then made available for use in the arbitration proceedings as a 'pre-trial deposition'. So far as the production of documents is concerned,[116] the parties to an arbitration may be ordered to disclose generally documents that are relevant and material to the issues in dispute, even if the party that has possession, custody, or control of the documents does not wish to produce them. In a major arbitration, the task of tracing and assembling these documents may take months and cost considerable sums of money, with phrases such as 'warehouse discovery' only palely reflecting the scope of the work to be done. Since the term 'documents' includes emails and other electronically stored information (ESI), the time and costs involved in tracing and assembling the relevant material has increased dramatically.[117] One US lawyer summed up the position in an article, whose title says it all: 'How the creep of United States litigation-style discovery and appellate rights affects the efficiency and cost-efficacy of arbitration in the United States'.[118]

1.142 This trend towards 'judicialisation' is not confined to the United States. The artisanal approach of the arbitration practitioner as master craftsman has undergone something of an industrial revolution. As previously stated, arbitration has become big business undertaken by large teams of lawyers who produce voluminous work product. Inevitably, this increases the workload of the arbitral tribunal: in reaching its decision, the tribunal must give proper consideration to the documents and evidence before it, as part of its duty to proceed judicially—giving each party a proper opportunity to present its case and treating each party equally, on pain of having the arbitral award set aside for procedural irregularity.[119]

1.143 Various ways of dealing with the resulting growth in complexity, cost, and procedural schedules have been canvassed. For example, there has been a proposal for a return to 'first principles', so that the arbitral tribunal would ask in respect of each particular arbitration:

(i) what is the best way of dealing with this case?
(ii) do the parties want a full trial of their dispute whatever it costs? or

---

[115] See, e.g., Seidenberg, 'International arbitration loses its grip: Are US lawyers to blame?' (2010) ABA Journal 51: 'Arbitration was supposed to be the solution for international companies seeking to resolve disputes without expensive and drawn-out court battles. But it is starting to look more like the problem [...] Arbitration of international commercial disputes has taken on many of the characteristics of litigation in US Courts. And this has upset many companies that rely on arbitration to resolve cross-border business disputes.'

[116] In English High Court litigation, the term 'Discovery' is used to cover only the production of documents.

[117] The problem posed by ESI has been addressed, amongst many others, by the British Chartered Institute of Arbitrators (CIArb), with its 2008 Protocol for E-Disclosure in Arbitration. The 2020 IBA Rules on the Taking of Evidence in International Arbitration provide for targeted disclosure of documents, rather than warehouse discovery.

[118] Rievman, Paper presented at a conference sponsored by the Centre for International Legal Studies, February 2005; see also Baker, 'At what price perfect justice?', Presented as part of a coursebook for the 2009 Annual Meeting of the International Institute for Conflict Prevention and Resolution, New York, 15–16 January 2009.

See, e.g., Redfern, 'Stemming the tide of judicialisation in international arbitration' (2008) 2 World Arb & Med Rev 21, at 24: 'It would be comforting, at least for non US lawyers, if it could be assumed that the blight of increasing expense and delay in international arbitration is unique to the United States. It would be wrong, however, to make this assumption.'

[119] For instance, under New York Convention, Art. V, or Model Law, Art. 36.

(iii) to save time and money would they be prepared to accept a shortened procedure, recognising that this would limit their opportunity to develop their respective cases as meticulously as they might wish?[120]

(v) Costs

International arbitration was once a relatively inexpensive method of dispute resolution. It is no longer so. First, the fees and expenses of the arbitrators (unlike the salary of a judge) must be paid by the parties—and in international arbitrations of any significance, these charges are likely to be substantial. Secondly, it may be necessary to pay the administrative fees and expenses of an arbitral institution—and these too may be substantial (and it may also be necessary to appoint a secretary or 'administrative assistant' to administer the proceedings). Finally, in the event of physical hearings it will be necessary to hire rooms and associated facilities rather than make use of the public facilities of the courts of law. In the event of virtual hearings, IT specialists will usually have to be hired to manage the complexities of conducting a hearing virtually from multiple countries through a single platform.

1.144

But the fees of the arbitrators and of the arbitral institutions, the charges for room hire, the costs of court reporters and IT specialists, and other such expenses are usually a drop in the ocean compared with the fees and expenses of the parties' legal advisers and expert witnesses. In a major arbitration, these may easily run into several million dollars.[121] This means that international arbitration is not likely to be cheaper than proceedings in domestic courts, unless there is a very conscious effort to make it so.[122]

1.145

One point that should not be forgotten in considering the cost of arbitration, however, is that it is a form of 'one-stop shopping'. Although the initial cost may not be less than that of proceedings in court, the award of the arbitrators is unlikely to be followed by a series of costly appeals to superior local courts.

1.146

(vi) Delay

Finally, a major complaint is that of delay, particularly at the beginning and at the end of the arbitral process. At the beginning, the complaint is of the time that it may take to constitute an arbitral tribunal, so that the arbitral process can start to move forward.[123] At the end of the arbitration, the complaint is of the time that some arbitral tribunals take to issue their award, with months (and sometimes a year or more) passing between the submission of post-hearing briefs and the delivery of the long-awaited decision.[124]

1.147

---

[120] See, e.g., Rivkin, 'Towards a new paradigm in international arbitration: The town elder model revisited' (2008) 24 Arb Intl 3, at 378.

[121] There are many reasons for this, including (i) the considerable sums of money that are often at stake; (ii) the increasing professionalism of lawyers, accountants, and others engaged in the arbitral process, with a determination to leave no stone unturned (which may lead to excessively lengthy and repetitive submissions); and (iii) the increasing 'judicialisation' of international arbitration, which has been discussed earlier.

[122] One of the objectives of this book is to show how this can be achieved by skilled and effective case management.

[123] For example, under the ICDR Rules, forty-five days may elapse after receipt of the notice of arbitration before the administrator is requested to appoint the arbitrator(s) and designate the presiding arbitrator, and this process may take further time, with the need to find suitable candidates who have no conflict of interest: see ICDR Rules 2021, Art. 13.3.

[124] One of the reasons for delay is the workload of the chosen arbitrators, particularly if they have other professional commitments, e.g. as counsel or as university professors. Ever more frequent challenges to arbitral awards

(vii) Summary

1.148   As the debate about costs and delay continues, it is important to remember that the aim of international arbitration is not simply to determine a dispute as quickly and cheaply as possible. If the parties agreed, that could be done with the spin of a coin. The aim of international arbitration is to arrive at a fair and reasoned decision on a dispute, based on a proper evaluation of the relevant contract, the facts, and the law. As Professor Park has written:

> Much of the criticism of arbitration's costs and delay thus tells only half the story, often with subtexts portending a cure worse than the disease. An arbitrator's main duty lies not in dictating a peace treaty, but in delivery of an accurate award that rests on a reasonable view of what happened and what the law says. Finding that reality in a fair manner does not always run quickly or smoothly. Although good case management values speed and economy, it does so with respect for the parties' interest in correct decisions. The parties have no less interest in correct decisions than in efficient proceedings. An arbitrator who makes the effort to listen before deciding will enhance both the prospect of accuracy and satisfaction of the litigant's taste for fairness. In the long run, little satisfaction will come from awards that are quick and cheap at the price of being systematically wrong.[125]

1.149   At one time, the comparative advantages and disadvantages of international arbitration versus litigation were much debated.[126] That debate should now be over. Opinion has moved strongly in favour of international arbitration for the resolution of international disputes.

E. Ad hoc Arbitration and Institutional Arbitration

1.150   There are broadly two types of international arbitration. The first is an ad hoc arbitration, the second is an institutional arbitration.

1.151   Any arbitration, wherever it is conducted, is subject to the mandatory rules of the *lex arbitri*: that is, the law of the place of arbitration. Generally, these rules will be broad and non-specific. They will say, for instance, that the parties must be treated with equality,[127] but they will not set out the way in which this is to be achieved. For this, more specific rules will be required. Here, the parties have a choice. Should the arbitration be conducted ad hoc, that is, pursuant to a set of rules agreed between the parties without the involvement of an arbitral institution, or should it be conducted according to the rules of one of the established arbitral institutions?

---

have also provoked extreme caution from arbitrators resulting in ever more detailed reasoning and description of the steps taken in the arbitral process. Where awards have to be simultaneously issued in more than one language is also a source of delay.

[125] Park, 'Arbitration and accuracy' (2010) 1 J Intl Disp Settlement 27.
[126] For one of the most effective, and certainly the most entertaining, critiques of arbitration see Kerr, 'Arbitration v litigation: The *Macao Sardine* case', in Kerr, *As Far As I Remember* (Hart Publishing, 2002), Annex.
[127] See, e.g., the Model Law, Art. 18.

(a) Ad hoc arbitration

Parties to an ad hoc arbitration may establish their own rules of procedure (so long as   **1.152**
these rules treat the parties fairly and allow each party a reasonable opportunity to present its case).[128] Alternatively, the parties may agree that the arbitration will be conducted without involving an arbitral institution, but according to an established set of
rules, such as the UNCITRAL Rules. These provide a tried and tested framework for the
proceedings, to which the tribunal and the parties may of course add other provisions,
if they so wish.

In practice, ad hoc arbitrations are now almost universally conducted on the basis of the   **1.153**
UNCITRAL Rules, which the parties agree to accept as a convenient and up-to-date set of
rules.[129] States in particular are likely to regard the UNCITRAL Rules as a preferred option,
since they do not derive their authority from an arbitral organisation based in a particular
country or designed to serve the interests of commerce, but from a broad international consensus reflected in a set of rules designed and adapted under the auspices of the United
Nations.

The principal disadvantage of ad hoc arbitration is that it depends for its full effectiveness on   **1.154**
cooperation between the parties and their lawyers, supported by an adequate legal system
in the place of arbitration. It is not difficult to delay arbitral proceedings, for example by refusing at the outset to appoint an arbitrator with the consequence that there is no arbitral
tribunal in existence and no agreed book of rules to say what is to be done.[130] It will then be
necessary to rely on such provisions of law as may be available to offer the necessary support.[131] It is only when an arbitral tribunal is in existence and a set of rules has been established that an ad hoc arbitration will be able to proceed if one of the parties fails or refuses
to play its part in the proceedings. This is one of the reasons why UNCITRAL arbitration is
often seen as the best of both worlds: in addition to dispensing with the services of arbitral
institutions (which state parties sometimes prefer), the UNCITRAL Rules (by providing
for the designation of an appointing authority to constitute the arbitral tribunal) prevent a
reluctant respondent from blocking the proceedings by refusing to take part in the appointment of a tribunal.

---

[128] Many important arbitrations, e.g. reinsurance disputes under the so-called Bermuda Form, are regularly
conducted ad hoc.

[129] It is not advisable to try to adopt or adapt institutional rules (such as those of the ICC) for use in an ad hoc
arbitration, since such rules make repeated references to the institution concerned and are unlikely to work properly or effectively without it. It seems however (although it is not a practice that the authors would recommend)
that it may be possible to involve two arbitral institutions in what would otherwise be an ad hoc arbitration (although quite why this should be done is another matter). The court in Singapore was faced with an arbitration
clause stating that disputes should be resolved by arbitration before SIAC in accordance with the ICC Rules. The
Singapore International Arbitration Centre was prepared to administer the arbitration under its rules, applying the
ICC Rules to the 'essential features the parties would like to see' and the arbitration proceeded on this basis. The
Singapore court upheld this arrangement: see *Insigma Technology Co. Ltd v Alstom Technology Ltd* [2008] SGHC
134, at 26. For its part, the ICC Court is unwilling to administer proceedings fundamentally different from its own
basic concepts: see Craig, Park, and Paulsson, *International Chamber of Commerce Arbitration* (3rd edn, Oceana,
2000), para. 715.

[130] Unless it has already been agreed that the UNCITRAL Rules are to govern the proceedings.

[131] See Chapter 3.

(b) Institutional arbitration

1.155   An 'institutional' arbitration is one that is administered by a specialist arbitral institution under its own rules of arbitration. These rules cover the progress of the arbitration from commencement to final award, but with differences of approach and emphasis. Some rules reflect the influence of the civil law, whereas others derive greater inspiration from the common law. What is common to all sets of rules is that they are formulated *specifically* for arbitrations that are to be administered by the institution concerned; and they are usually incorporated into the main contract between the parties by means of an arbitration clause. The clause recommended by the LCIA, for instance, states:

> Any dispute arising out of or in connection with this contract, including any question regarding its existence, validity or termination, shall be referred to and finally resolved by arbitration under the LCIA Rules, which Rules are deemed to be incorporated into this clause.[132]

1.156   An arbitration clause is a convenient way of incorporating a set of broad procedural rules, as well as an institution to police the process, into the parties' contract. If at some future date the defending party or parties are unwilling to go ahead with an arbitration, it will nevertheless be possible for the claimant to do so effectively, since there will be a set of rules and an institution to regulate the way in which the arbitral tribunal is to be appointed and the way in which the arbitration is to be conducted and carried through to its conclusion.

(i) Advantages

1.157   Rules laid down by the established arbitral institutions will usually have been proven to work effectively in practice. They also will generally have undergone periodic revision in consultation with experienced practitioners, to take account of new developments in the law and practice of international arbitration. The rules themselves are generally set out in a small booklet and parties who agree to submit any dispute to arbitration in accordance with the rules of a named institution effectively incorporate that institution's 'rulebook' into their arbitration agreement.

1.158   This automatic incorporation of an established 'rulebook' is one of the principal advantages of institutional arbitration. If, for example, there is a challenge to an arbitrator on the grounds of lack of independence or impartiality, or if the defending party is unwilling to arbitrate and fails to appoint an arbitrator, the rulebook will provide a solution to enable the arbitration to proceed and for an award to be issued.

1.159   A further advantage of institutional arbitration is that most arbitral institutions provide specialist staff to administer the arbitration. They will ensure that the arbitral tribunal is appointed, that advance payments are made in respect of the fees and expenses of the arbitrators, that time limits are observed, and generally that the arbitration is run as smoothly as possible.

---

[132] The parties may go on, if they wish, to specify the number of arbitrations, the seat of the arbitration, the language to be used, and the governing law of the contract and it would usually be sensible to do this.

Finally, the assistance that an arbitral institution can give to the parties and their counsel in the course of the arbitral proceedings is appreciable. Even lawyers who are experienced in the conduct of arbitrations may run into problems that they may find it useful to discuss with the institution's secretariat.   **1.160**

(ii) Disadvantages

There are two principal disadvantages of institutional arbitration as opposed to ad hoc arbitration. First, there are the fees of the arbitral institution which will add, some-times considerably, to the cost of the proceedings. Secondly, there is an additional tier of 'management' of the proceedings, in the shape of the staff of the arbitral institution. Experienced counsel and arbitrators may regard this as unnecessary. However, since the tasks performed by the staff of the institution usually need to be performed in any event, and in the absence of an institution would need to be performed by the tribunal itself (or by the tribunal's secretary, if there is one), excluding an institution may prove to be a false economy.   **1.161**

(iii) Selecting an arbitral institution

In recent years, arbitral institutions have moved to centre-stage in the world of international arbitration. Their continued proliferation indicates an increasing demand for the services they offer, although some fall by the wayside. The best of them will offer a full range of serv-ices. First, they will have rules of arbitration, which have either been tested over time and proved to work effectively or which are based on a recognised and trusted model, such as the UNCITRAL Rules. This will save the parties and their lawyers the time and money that would otherwise be spent, as in non-institutional (or ad hoc) arbitrations, in drawing up a tailor-made set of rules.   **1.162**

Secondly, if the parties are unable to agree upon a sole arbitrator, or upon the presiding arbitrator of a three-member tribunal, the selection of a suitably qualified individual will be made by the arbitral institution itself. Thirdly, if an arbitrator is challenged for lack of in-dependence or impartiality, that challenge will not be determined by the court at the place of arbitration but by the arbitral institution itself, exercising a quasi-judicial role. Fourthly, once the arbitration is under way, the institution's secretariat will usually monitor its pro-gress and deal with any enquiries that the parties or the tribunal may have.   **1.163**

Finally, at the end of the arbitral proceedings, and when the award is ready to be issued, it may be reviewed by the arbitral institution, who will refer back to the arbitrators with any minor corrections; and once the award has been signed and dated by the tribunal, it will usually be issued to the parties by that institution. It may even be referred to by the name of the institution, being described in the arbitration journals and reviews as, for instance, an 'ICC Award'. Nevertheless, it is and remains the award of the arbitral tribunal and not of the institution that issues it.   **1.164**

There are so many arbitral institutions or centres in the world that it is not practicable, nor would it be useful, simply to list them all in this book. We therefore propose to assist in the selection of the 'right' arbitral institution for a particular case by setting out some general considerations that might be helpful.   **1.165**

(c) General considerations

1.166   First, if the arbitral institution is relatively new or unknown, steps should be taken to ensure (i) that it is a genuine arbitral institution and (ii) that it has credible premises with staff who are suitably qualified to offer the services that are advertised. As to the first point, although it seems unlikely, fraudulent arbitral institutions are not unknown. For instance, customers of Citibank who had a complaint about credit card debts were invited to submit that complaint to arbitration under the rules of the National Arbitration Council (NAC). Those who did so received an 'award' for the amount of their debt, plus the fee of the NAC. It was not a genuine operation and Citibank eventually obtained an injunction to stop it happening.[133] As to the second point, the staff of a good arbitral institution should be capable of giving advice on potentially sensitive matters, such as the appointment or challenge of arbitrators, unreasonable delay in the conduct of the proceedings, extension of time limits, and so forth.

1.167   Secondly, it is necessary to make a distinction between 'arbitral institutions' and 'arbitration centres'. The titles may cause some confusion. An arbitral institution, properly so called, will administer arbitrations, either under its own rules or under established rules such as those of UNCITRAL. An arbitration centre may in fact be an arbitral institution, like the Cairo Regional Centre for International Commercial Arbitration (CRCICA), which administers arbitrations under a slightly modified version of the UNCITRAL Rules. Alternatively, an arbitration centre may in fact be a business enterprise such as the International Dispute Resolution Centre (IDRC) in London, which offers 'high-tech' facilities for arbitrations, mediations, and conferences but does not itself administer arbitrations.

1.168   Thirdly, there is the question of location. Regional arbitral institutions have grown in importance and it is now possible to look for a reputable regional institution, rather than one based in Europe or the United States. For example, if the parties are based in Africa, consideration should certainly be given to the selection of one of the institutions or centres that are based there.[134] Some institutions that have started regionally now operate internationally. One example is the Singapore International Arbitration Centre which now has representative offices in India, Korea, the United States, and China.

1.169   Finally, there is the question of the *quality* of the arbitrators appointed and the awards rendered under the rules of a given institution. Arbitral institutions compete on accessibility, price, speed of service, and other factors, but the quality of the tribunal should also be taken into account. The way an arbitral institution selects arbitrators is thus a very important factor.

1.170   A good award, made by a tribunal of quality under the auspices of a reputable arbitral institution, should be capable of standing up to most challenges. An award is, of course, the award of the tribunal and not of the arbitral institution, but it nevertheless carries to a greater or lesser extent the imprimatur of that institution. This raises the question of the extent to which an arbitral institution should review an award before it is issued to the parties (and the rules should be reviewed with that question in mind.)

---

[133] See Rau, 'Arbitral Jurisdiction and the Dimensions of "Consent"' (2008) 24 Arb Intl 204 at fn. 19.
[134] See the '2020 SOAS Arbitration in Africa Survey Report' by the School of Oriental and African Studies, University of London.

At one time, it was assumed that parties would comply voluntarily with international arbitral awards, however reluctant they might be to do so. This is no longer the position, as indicated in Chapters 11 and 12. Attempts to challenge (or 'set-aside') international awards at the place of arbitration, and actions in foreign courts to try to enforce such awards, are becoming noticeably more frequent as the amounts in dispute grow larger.   **1.171**

(d) Selection of arbitrators by the institution

The qualities required of international arbitrators are considered in Chapter 4 of this book. In the present context, the focus is simply on the *selection* of arbitrators by an arbitral institution. The ideal situation is no doubt one in which the parties themselves agree on the selection of the arbitrator or arbitrators who are to constitute the arbitral tribunal. However, if the parties cannot agree, it will be for the court or if there is one, the relevant arbitral institution, to make the necessary selection.   **1.172**

In circumstances in which an arbitral institution may be required to select one or more arbitrators for a particular arbitration, it is important to know what method of selection that institution uses. Does it have a list of favourite arbitrators that it appoints in turn, in a contemporary version of 'Hobson's Choice'?[135] Or does it employ a list system on the lines of that in the UNCITRAL Rules, where parties are given a list of possible arbitrators from which they are invited to choose? If so, what are the criteria for inclusion on that list and how often is it revised? Or again, is the choice referred to a committee and, if so, who are the members of that committee and what selection criteria do they use? In effect, is there a genuine list of diverse, skilled, and effective arbitrators or is it a members' club? In general terms, the choice of arbitrators will depend heavily on the nature of the dispute and the skills required to resolve it and so any list system may unnecessarily constrain that choice.   **1.173**

It is not always easy to find the answer to questions on how an institution selects arbitrators for its panel, even by a careful scrutiny of its rules and any accompanying publicity. In an age in which increasing importance is attached to 'transparency', it would be helpful if the answers were more readily available. If parties are to have confidence in arbitrators appointed by an institution on their behalf, it is only right that they should know on what basis those arbitrators are selected.   **1.174**

(e) Costs

An arbitral institution, like any business in the service sector, will charge fees in order to cover its own costs and expenses and, in the case of some institutions, to make a profit that it will pass on to its parent company or owners. There are in general two bases on which these fees are calculated.   **1.175**

---

[135] T. Hobson (1544–1631) owned livery stables in Cambridge, the English university town. He hired out horses to students and visitors in strict order, giving customers the option to take the horse they were offered or none at all.

1.176   They may be calculated *ad valorem*, which is to say as a set proportion of the amount in dispute; or they may be calculated on the basis of time spent on the arbitration by the staff of the institution and the tribunal. The parties to the arbitration will then be required to make an advance payment, based either on the amount in dispute or on an estimate of the time likely to be spent on the case. These payments will add to the overall costs of the arbitral proceedings, sometimes quite substantially, and the parties and their lawyers will want to know that they are receiving value for money.

1.177   The advantage of the *ad valorem* approach is that it means that the parties know from the outset what the arbitration is going to cost, in terms of payments to the tribunal and the institution concerned (although further advances on account of costs may be required if the arbitration turns out to take longer than expected—for example, because of the need for an interim award on jurisdiction). The advantage of the time/cost method, which is the method generally used by professional firms such as accountants and lawyers, is that there is a correlation between the work done (or at least, the time recorded as being spent) and the fees charged.

F. Differentiating the Institutions

1.178   Arbitral institutions that administer international arbitrations are in competition with each other. For some commentators, this should ensure that they strive to maintain high standards and stay ahead of the game—'a race to the top', as it has been described.[136] It might also lead to increased involvement[137] by arbitral institutions in the conduct of arbitrations since they will be judged on the speed and quality of awards made under their auspices.

1.179   Given the large number of important arbitral institutions, it would be of limited use to seek to differentiate them in an introductory chapter. Suffice to say that the leading institutions operating internationally (with their principal seat of operations) are:

- the ICC Court of Arbitration (Paris)
- the LCIA (London)
- the ICDR (New York)
- the SIAC (Singapore)
- the HKIAC (Hong Kong)
- ICSID (Washington DC) (for disputes between investors and states only)

These are all well-respected institutions with an excellent track record. The choice by the parties of a particular institution will often depend on the location of the parties themselves, the place of the dispute, and the experience of counsel. As rule revisions become ever more frequent, and institutions set up offices outside their seat of origin,[138] each institution is seeking to differentiate itself and to take a greater share of the market for international

---

[136] By Professor Catherine Rogers, at http://arbitrationblog.kluwerarbitration.com/2018/03/15_is-internati onalarbitration-in-a-race-to-the-top/.

[137] Or 'intervention' as the critics might say.

[138] For example, the ICC has offices in New York, São Paulo, Singapore, and Abu Dhabi and the SIAC has offices in India, China, and New York.

arbitrations. An entire book could be dedicated to the differences in the rules of these institutions. We simply note here that there is one institution that operates differently from the others and therefore merits particular attention.

The ICC has three distinguishing factors that are rarely replicated in other institutional rules. The first is the requirement for 'Terms of Reference' to be established by the tribunal and signed by the parties.[139] These set out the arbitral tribunal's mission in some detail after the initial exchange of introductory documents. They will contain a statement of the respective claims (and any counterclaims) of the parties and a note of the amounts in dispute, together with a list of issues, unless (as frequently happens) the tribunal considers that it is too early to draft such a list at the opening stage of the proceedings. It is against these Terms of Reference that any eventual award will be measured. The concept of 'Terms of Reference' is a relic of the former French Code of Civil Procedure, which discouraged arbitration of future disputes under an arbitration clause and insisted that a special submission to arbitration, or *compromis*, had to be entered into by the parties *after* the dispute had arisen.[140] The requirement for Terms of Reference has been retained by the ICC, even though the need for a *compromis* has been abolished. Terms of Reference oblige the parties and the tribunal to focus on the issues in dispute at an early stage to establish a clear platform for the future conduct of the case. **1.180**

The second distinguishing factor is the requirement for the tribunal to submit a draft version of its proposed award for scrutiny and approval by the ICC Court. Article 34 of the ICC Rules, entitled 'Scrutiny of Award by the Court', states that the ICC Court 'may lay down modifications as to the form of the award and, without affecting the tribunal's liberty of decision, may also draw its attention to points of substance'. In practice, the procedure is as follows: **1.181**

(i) Counsel in charge of the case reviews the draft award and prepares a draft Report for the Court.
(ii) This draft Report is reviewed by the Management of the Secretariat and becomes the Secretariat's Report.
(iii) The draft award is then formally scrutinised by the ICC Court at one of its weekly sessions, with the Court looking at the draft award, Terms of Reference (if they exist), and the Secretariat's Report.
(iv) For more complex cases involving states or state entities and/or with dissenting opinions, the draft award is scrutinised at the Court's extended committee where there is a report by a member of the Court in addition to the Secretariat's Report.
(v) The ICC Court decide whether to approve the draft award or send it back to the tribunal.
(vi) If the draft award is sent back to the tribunal, it will have to be revised and the revised version will have to be re-submitted and go through the same procedure.

This careful scrutiny of awards is intended to add an extra *imprimatur* of quality to an ICC award with a correspondingly lower risk of the award being challenged or set aside. Most **1.182**

---

[139] Terms of Reference are not needed in expedited procedures: ICC Rules, App. VI, Art. 3.
[140] See Craig, Park, and Paulsson, *International Chamber of Commerce Arbitration* (3rd edn, Oceana, 2000), pp. 273–274.

other institutions engage in a less formal review of the final award to pick up formatting and typographical errors, but do not seek to raise questions of substance with the tribunal.

1.183   The third distinguishing factor is that the ICC (in common with other European arbitral institutions) will assess its own fees and those of the tribunal on the *ad valorem* basis that has already been discussed, whilst other institutions adopt the more modern time/cost approach.

G. The Future of International Arbitration

1.184   It is often said that it is dangerous to make predictions, especially about the future. But there are some predictions that it is safe to make, because, as William Gibson[141] said, 'The future is already here'. So here are some predictions that we can confidently make because we are already seeing part of this future today.

1.185   International arbitration has amply demonstrated its flexibility and adaptability in the way in which it is used to resolve all manner of international disputes, from the athlete who is barred from competing in the Olympic games to the multinational corporation awarded millions of dollars in compensation for the unlawful confiscation of its assets.

1.186   As international arbitration has become the principal means of resolving international disputes, the leading arbitral institutions will continue to search for ways of increasing both the scope of arbitration and their own relevance, and they will seek to do this by exercising more broadly the kind of powers normally reserved to the courts of law, including the power to consolidate arbitrations and the power to impose sanctions on parties and arbitrators.

1.187   As arbitration becomes a more prominent feature of business and public life, governments may be moved to intervene to prevent or regulate certain activities, looking again at what kind of disputes should be 'arbitrable', in the sense of being suitable for resolution by arbitration.

1.188   Technology is likely to have its own transformative effect. The global pandemic of 2019 and 2020 accelerated the move to virtual meetings and hearings; artificial intelligence is being used to assist in responding to requests for disclosure of documents on the Redfern Schedule, as well as to search for documents to support the parties' cases; and there is even talk of 'arbitration by algorithm'.[142]

1.189   The search for greater transparency and for public access to hearings may extend beyond the present ambit of investment arbitrations, unless (as some commentators have suggested)[143] investment arbitrations are treated as a special category of disputes, with their own standing tribunals and a high-level appeal tribunal to ensure consistency of decisions and to build up a corpus of known and well-publicised body of law.

---

[141] William Gibson is an American–Canadian author who is known as the father of the cyberpunk sub-genre of science fiction.

[142] See the discussion in Scherer, 'Artificial intelligence and legal decision-making: The wide open?' (2019) 36(5) J Intl Arb 539–574.

[143] See Redfern, 'A bridge too far', in 'Global Reflections on International Law, Commerce and Dispute Resolution', ICC Publication 693, November 2005, at 665.

There is no doubt that international arbitration is proving to be an adaptable and effective   **1.190**
method of dispute resolution. But it would be wrong to assume that this state of affairs is
bound to continue. There are indications that international arbitration has been used in
areas where it might have been wiser to leave matters (for instance, labour relations and
consumer disputes) to specially constituted tribunals, with appeal procedures to correct
mistakes and to ensure consistency of decisions.

There are also indications of dissatisfaction with the growing judicialisation, cost, delay,   **1.191**
and complexity of international arbitration. If international arbitration strays too far from
its roots as a relatively simple, friendly, and effective method of resolving international disputes, there is a risk that users may return to the national courts or prioritise early mediation
and settlement. It is therefore important that participants in the system such as counsel and
arbitrators do not lose sight of the need to respond to the needs of the end-users (the parties)
who want to see a process of efficiency and finality to assist in making future business decisions. In this context, more frequent use should be made of the many new tools available,
including early dismissal of claims (a type of arbitral 'strike-out' proceeding), Emergency
Arbitrators for early interim relief, and fast-track arbitration. By maintaining its flexibility
and its ability to respond in an agile manner to evolving disputes, international arbitration
will guarantee its own future.

2

AGREEMENT TO ARBITRATE

A. Overview

(a) Introduction

The agreement to arbitrate is the foundation stone of international arbitration.[1] It records the consent of the parties to submit to arbitration—a consent that is indispensable to any process of dispute resolution outside national courts.[2] Such processes depend for their very existence upon the agreement of the parties. As already discussed, many lawyers and commentators attach great importance to the wishes of the parties—to *l'autonomie de la volonté*. Indeed, some go so far as to suggest that this consent, together with an appropriate set of rules, is sufficient to turn international arbitration into an autonomous, delocalised process that takes place independently of national law. For most, this goes too far.[3] It attaches too much importance to the wishes of the parties and not sufficient to the framework of national laws and international treaties within which the international arbitral process must take place. Nevertheless, the consent of the parties remains the essential basis of a voluntary system of international arbitration.[4]

2.01

---

[1] See Chapter 1, paragraph 1.20.

[2] As discussed later in this chapter, consent can be deemed by conduct or found in more than one document.

[3] Except for arbitrations conducted under the ICSID Convention. For further discussion of delocalised arbitration, see Chapter 3, paragraphs 3.83–3.101.

[4] Compulsory arbitration does exist. Nationally, it is used as a supposedly cheap and informal method of resolving disputes in particular areas. Internationally, the most striking example of compulsory arbitration was in the socialist countries of Central and Eastern Europe, where it was employed as the method of settling disputes under the provisions of the Convention on the Settlement of Arbitration of Civil Law Disputes Arising from Relations of Economic, Scientific and Technical Co-operation (Moscow Convention) of 1972. However, compulsory arbitration is outside the scope of this book, which is concerned with the mainstream of international arbitration—that is, with arbitration as a consensual process, taking place pursuant to the parties' voluntary agreement to arbitrate.

(b) Categories of arbitration agreement

2.02   There are two basic types of arbitration agreement, as already indicated, namely the arbitration clause and the submission agreement. An arbitration clause looks to the future, whereas a submission agreement looks to the past. An arbitration clause, which is now the most common, and is usually contained in the principal agreement between the parties, is an agreement to submit to arbitration any *future* disputes. The second is an agreement to submit *existing* disputes to arbitration.

In this book, the terms 'arbitration clause' and 'submission agreement' are used according to these descriptions.

(i) Arbitration clauses
2.03   An arbitration clause that deals with disputes that may arise in the future is usually brief, since when it is agreed the parties do not know what kind of dispute (if any) may possibly arise and if it does, how it should best be handled.[5] Accordingly, parties insert a short model clause, recommended by an arbitral institution.[6]

2.04   These clauses were often barely discussed and were often referred to as 'midnight clauses'— that is, the last clauses to be considered in contract negotiations, sometimes late at night or in the early hours of the morning. Insufficient thought was given to how disputes were to be resolved (possibly because the parties were reluctant to contemplate divorce as they prepared to walk up the proverbial aisle). In consequence, an inappropriate and unwieldy compromise was often adopted[7]—for example, the wrong choice (or no choice at all) of the substantive law or of the place of arbitration. Such neglect is increasingly a thing of the past. Increasingly, parties recognise that all rights under a contract may ultimately be dependent upon an effective dispute resolution clause.

(ii) Submission agreements
2.05   In contrast to arbitration clauses, submission agreements tend to be longer. A submission agreement deals with a dispute that *has* in fact already arisen—and so it should contain many, if not all, of the provisions required to fit precisely the circumstances of the particular dispute. In addition to indicating the place of arbitration and the substantive law, a submission agreement will often name the arbitrators, contain a definition, or at least an outline, of the disputes that are to be arbitrated, and even (if thought appropriate) address procedural

---

[5] In some Latin American states (for instance, Argentina and Uruguay) a clause to submit future disputes to arbitration was *not* operative until a submission agreement (or *compromiso*) had also been executed. In any such jurisdictions, the ICC Rules may be preferred. They provide for a functional equivalent of the *compromiso* (the terms of reference), which are not included in other institutional rules. However, the requirement for an additional *compromise* is now increasingly rare. In 2018, both Argentina and Uruguay enacted new legislation governing international commercial arbitration (Law No. 27,449 on International Commercial Arbitration, published in Argentina's Official Gazette on 26 July 2018; and Law No. 19.636, published on 26 July 2018), neither of which contain a requirement for a submission agreement. In Brazil, there is similarly no requirement for a submission agreement to be executed, but to be valid an arbitration agreement must make provision for the procedure to be adopted in the arbitration, which it may do by reference to a set of institutional rules.

[6] By contrast, in some contexts (e.g. in an ad hoc arbitration) it is possible for parties to agree an arbitration clause that identifies the procedure to be followed in detail, as well as the means of establishing the arbitral tribunal, filling vacancies, and so forth.

[7] For a step-by-step guide to drafting arbitration clauses, see Paulsson, Rawding, and Reed (eds) *The Freshfields Guide to Arbitration Clauses in International Contracts* (3rd edn, Kluwer Law International, 2010).

arrangements, such as the production of documents, the exchange of written submissions and witness statements, and the timetable to be followed.[8]

The position of the parties and their advisers in dealing with a submission agreement is radically different from that of agreeing an arbitration clause. First, as a dispute has actually arisen, this usually means that there will be an adversarial element in the relationship. Secondly, the parties and their legal advisers will know what kind of dispute they are facing, and each side will wish to structure the arbitral procedure in a manner that suits its own case, which may well lead to conflicting positions. Thirdly, the fundamental interests of the parties may conflict, in that the claimant usually wants a speedy resolution of the dispute, whereas the respondent may consider that it would be advantageous to create delay.[9] For these reasons, the negotiation of a submission agreement may be a lengthy and difficult process. It is less advisable than inclusion of an arbitration clause in the underlying agreement and, as a consequence, has become much rarer. **2.06**

Irrespective of whether the parties agree to settle their dispute pursuant to an arbitration agreement contained in an arbitration clause or to one set out in a submission agreement, the following general observations regarding the international conventions governing arbitration, and the international standards derived therefrom, apply. **2.07**

(c) International conventions

As noted in Chapter 1, the 1923 Geneva Protocol and the 1927 Geneva Convention dealt with the recognition and enforcement of international arbitration agreements and the execution of arbitral awards. These were then followed by various regional conventions,[10] until eventually the most important convention in the field of international commercial arbitration, the New York Convention, was promulgated in 1958. **2.08**

The New York Convention continued where the Geneva treaties left off.[11] Its title as a 'Convention on the Recognition and Enforcement of Foreign Arbitral Awards' is a partial misnomer. The Convention's starting point is in fact the recognition and enforcement of arbitration *agreements*.[12] Having first provided for recognition of the validity and enforceability of arbitration agreements, the Convention then provides for the international enforcement of awards that arise from such agreements and comply with the specified criteria.[13] **2.09**

---

[8] This is not a universal rule. A submission agreement may take the form of a brief agreement to submit an existing dispute to the procedures of an arbitral institution. On balance, it is probably better to deal with detailed procedural questions in a separate document, perhaps with the assistance of the arbitral tribunal once the arbitration has commenced.

[9] Although it should, of course, be borne in mind that the claimant may be compensated for the delay by an award of interest and that delay is usually achieved only by the expenditure of costs, e.g. the determination of a preliminary issue. Ultimately, the respondent may be directed to pay the costs of the arbitration, particularly if it is considered that its conduct has contributed to the delay. See Chapter 9.

[10] See, e.g., the Bustamante Code of 1928 and the European Convention of 1961.

[11] The New York Convention replaces the Geneva treaties between states that have become bound by it: Art. VII(2).

[12] New York Convention, Arts II(1) and II(3).

[13] The Model Law follows a similar pattern.

2.10   Closely modelled[14] on the New York Convention, the 1975 Panama Convention[15] was signed by the United States and a significant number of Latin American states, and marked another step forward in the recognition of arbitration as an established method of resolving disputes in a regional context. It has somewhat fallen into disuse as the signatory states have now all ratified the New York Convention.

(d) International standards

2.11   What is important about these and other conventions on arbitration,[16] whether international or regional, is that they establish the requirements for a valid international arbitration agreement and they indicate the parameters within which such an agreement will operate.

2.12   These conventions reflect the provisions to be found in developed arbitration laws and in the practice of arbitral institutions. In turn, together with the Model Law, they have played an important part in modernising and harmonising state laws governing arbitration. An arbitration agreement that provides for international arbitration must take account of these international requirements. If it fails to do so, the arbitration agreement, and any award made under it, may not qualify for international recognition and enforcement.

2.13   In seeking to establish the 'international requirements', the starting point has to be the New York Convention. Under the Convention, each contracting state undertakes to recognise and give effect to an arbitration agreement when the following requirements are fulfilled:

- the agreement is in writing;
- it deals with existing or future disputes;
- these disputes arise in respect of a defined legal relationship, whether contractual or not; and
- they concern a subject matter capable of settlement by arbitration.

2.14   These are the four positive requirements of a valid arbitration agreement, laid down in Article II(1) of the New York Convention.[17] A further two requirements are, in effect, added by the provisions of Article V(1)(a),[18] which stipulates that recognition or enforcement of an award may be refused if the party requesting refusal is able to prove that the arbitration

---

[14]   It too recognises the validity of an agreement that submits existing and future disputes to arbitration: Panama Convention, Art. 1.

[15]   Its formal title is 'The Convention on the Settlement of Civil Law Disputes Resulting from Economic, Scientific and Technological Cooperation'. The text of the Convention appears in (1978) III YBCA 15.

[16]   Such as the European Convention of 1961 and the ICSID Convention.

[17]   The first three are also contained in the Model Law, Art. 7(1) and (2), and the fourth in Arts 34(2)(b) and 36(2)(b)(i). More recently, however, the UN Commission on International Trade Law (UNCITRAL) formulated and adopted a recommendation regarding the interpretation of Arts II(2) and VII(1) of the New York Convention on 7 July 2006, by which it recognised that Art. II(2), which defines the way in which the 'writing' requirement must be fulfilled, must be applied 'recognizing that the circumstances described therein are not exhaustive'. The International Council for Commercial Arbitration (ICCA)'s Guide to the Interpretation of the 1958 New York Convention (2011) acknowledges this recommendation, noting that 'an inflexible application of the Convention's writing requirement would contradict current and widespread business usages and be contrary to the pro-enforcement thrust of the Convention'. See paragraphs 2.15–2.26.

[18]   They are also to be found in the Model Law, Arts 34(2)(a) and 36(1)(a)(i).

agreement was made by a person under incapacity or that the agreement was invalid under the applicable law. Expressed positively,[19] these represent additional requirements to the effect that:

- the parties to the arbitration agreement must have legal capacity under the law applicable to them;
- the arbitration agreement must be valid under the law to which the parties have subjected it or, failing any indication thereon, under the law of the country where the award was made. (In the words used earlier in the New York Convention, in Article II(3), the agreement must not be 'null and void, inoperative or incapable of being performed'.)

Each of these requirements is now considered in turn.

B. Validity of an Arbitration Agreement

(a) Formal validity—need for writing

All the international conventions on arbitration discussed above, as well as the Model Law, require that an agreement to arbitrate shall be 'in writing'. The historical reason for imposing this requirement is not difficult to divine. A valid agreement to arbitrate excludes the jurisdiction of the national courts,[20] and means that any dispute between the parties must be resolved by a private method of dispute resolution—namely, arbitration. This was a serious step to take, albeit one that has become increasingly commonplace in today's world of international commerce. Good reasons therefore existed for ensuring that the existence of such an agreement should be clearly established. This was best done by producing evidence in writing, although, as already noted in Chapter 1, the trend in modern national legislation has moved towards the relaxation of this formal requirement.[21]   **2.15**

Article II(2) of the New York Convention defines 'writing' as follows: 'The term "agreement in writing" shall include an arbitral clause in a contract or an arbitration agreement, signed by the parties or contained in an exchange of letters or telegrams.'   **2.16**

The requirement for signature by the parties has given rise to problems in some states,[22] but the general view today is that a signature is not necessary, provided that the arbitration agreement is in writing.[23]   **2.17**

---

[19] Although it should be noted that the burden of proof is on the party opposing recognition or enforcement, who must prove lack of capacity or invalidity.

[20] See the discussion in Chapter 1, paragraphs 1.20ff.

[21] In this regard, see Landau, 'The requirement of a written form for an arbitration agreement: When "written" means "oral"', Sixteenth ICCA Congress, London, 12–15 May 2002.

[22] See, e.g., the cases cited in Cohen, 'Agreements in writing: Notes in the margin of the Sixth Goff Lecture' (1997) 13 Arb Intl 273. This article was a response to the earlier Kaplan, 'Is the need for writing as expressed in the New York Convention and Model Law out of step with commercial practice?' (1996) 12 Arb Intl 27. More recently, see also *Kanematsu USA Inc. v ATS—Advanced Telecommunications Systems do Brasil Ltda*, SEC 885, 18 April 2012, in which the Brazilian Supreme Court of Justice held that a signature is required where a party seeks to incorporate into a contract an arbitration clause contained in a set of standard terms and conditions.

[23] By way of modern example, see *Jiangsu Overseas Group Co Ltd v Concord Energy Pte Ltd* [2016] 4 SLR 1336 (in which the Singapore High Court held that an arbitration agreement recorded only in draft, unsigned contracts was valid in the light of the parties' conduct and correspondence). See also *Sphere Drake Ins. PLC v Marine Towing,*

2.18   There has, however, been a revolution in communications since the New York Convention was drawn up in 1958. Telegrams are today an archaic curiosity. They have been replaced by various forms of written electronic communication. These changes have been reflected in the Model Law, which goes much further than the New York Convention in its definition of 'writing' and has itself been the subject of important recommended interpretations and revisions.[24]

2.19   The 2006 version of the Model Law contains both a long and a short form option for establishing the writing requirement. Option 1 provides as follows:[25]

[...]

(3)   An agreement is in writing if its content is recorded in any form, whether or not the arbitration agreement or contract has been concluded orally, by conduct, or by other means.

(4)   The requirement that an arbitration agreement be in writing is met by an electronic communication if the information contained therein is accessible so as to be useable for subsequent reference; 'electronic communication' means any communication that the parties make by means of data messages; 'data message' means information generated, sent, received or stored by electronic, magnetic, optical or similar means, including, but not limited to, electronic data interchange (EDI), electronic mail, telegram, telex or telecopy.

(5)   Furthermore, an arbitration agreement is in writing if it is contained in an exchange of statements of claim and defence in which the existence of an agreement is alleged by one party and not denied by the other.

(6)   The reference in a contract to any document containing an arbitration clause constitutes an arbitration agreement in writing, provided that the reference is such as to make that clause part of the contract.

2.20   Option 1 has brought the Model Law into line with modern commercial life, as reflected by national legislation and repeated court decisions in recent decades. For instance, as long ago as the 1980s an exchange of telexes between two firms of brokers in Paris containing the simple statement 'English law—arbitration, if any, London according ICC Rules' was held to be a valid arbitration agreement, providing for arbitration in London under the ICC Rules, with English law as the substantive law of the contract.[26]

Inc., 16 F.3d 666, 669–670 (5th Cir. 1994) (in which the US Court of Appeals for the Fifth Circuit held that an arbitration clause was valid even though the underlying contract was not signed).

[24]   On 7 July 2006, UNCITRAL issued a recommendation that Art. II (2) of the New York Convention be applied 'recognizing that the circumstances described therein are not exhaustive'. Subsequently, on 4 December 2006, the Model Law was amended pursuant to General Assembly Resolution 61/33 to include notable changes to Art. 7 on the writing requirement.

[25]   The options are contained in Art. 7 of the Model Law. By way of example, Option 1 was adopted by Singapore in its 2012 revision to the Singapore International Arbitration Act, s. 2A.

[26]   *Arab African Energy Corporation Ltd v Olieprodukten Nederland BV* [1983] 2 Lloyd's Rep 419. More recently, see *AQZ v ARA* [2015] SGHC 49, in which the Singapore High Court held that an arbitration agreement was valid notwithstanding that it was recorded by one party only and was not signed by the other party at all. See also *Jiangsu Overseas Group Co Ltd v Concord Energy Pte Ltd* [2016] 4 SLR 1336, in which the Singapore High Court held that an arbitration agreement that was recorded only in draft, unsigned contracts was valid in the light of the parties' conduct and correspondence.

However, whilst the formal requirements may have been relaxed, there remains a minimum **2.21** requirement for a permanent record ('useable for subsequent reference' in the terms of the Model Law) from which a written transcription can be made. For example, the Netherlands Arbitration Act 1986 requires that the arbitration agreement shall be proven by an instrument in writing expressly or impliedly accepted by the parties.[27] For its part, as mentioned in Chapter 1, Swiss law requires an agreement to be made in writing or by means of communication that allows it to be evidenced by a text. Section 178(1) of the Swiss Private International Law Act (as amended in January 2021) states simply: 'The arbitration agreement must be made in writing or any other means of communication allowing it to be evidenced by text.'[28]

Thus, for the purposes of the Model Law Option 1, the requirement for writing may now **2.22** be satisfied where there is a record 'in any form' of the content of the arbitration agreement.

Moreover, where a party takes part in an arbitration without denying the existence of an **2.23** arbitration agreement,[29] it will, in the normal course, be deemed to have granted implied consent. In some systems of law, an oral agreement to arbitrate will be regarded as being 'in writing' if it is made 'by reference to terms which are in writing', or if an oral agreement 'is recorded by one of the parties, or by a third party, with the authority of the parties to the agreement'.[30] In these modern arbitration laws, there has, in effect, been a triumph of substance over form: as long as there is some written evidence of an agreement to arbitrate, the form in which that agreement is recorded is immaterial.[31]

Option 2 of the 2006 Model Law goes a step further. It does not refer to a writing require- **2.24** ment at all, but rather provides that it is sufficient to show 'agreement by the parties to submit to arbitration all or certain disputes'.[32] This reflects the latest position under some systems of law that arbitration agreements are not subject to any requirements of form. For instance, Article 1507 of the French Code of Civil Procedure (as modified by Article 2 of Decree 2011-48) provides that 'an arbitration agreement shall not be subject to any requirements as to its form'.[33]

However, a degree of caution is necessary. First, even courts in jurisdictions familiar with **2.25** international arbitration still may refuse to enforce arbitration agreements that are not in

---

[27] Netherlands Arbitration Act 1986, s. 1021; see the commentary on this article in Sanders and van den Berg, *The Netherlands Arbitration Act 1986: Text and Notes, English* (Kluwer, 1987), p. 12, where it is said that the Act abolishes the possibility, which existed under the old Act, that an arbitration agreement could be concluded orally, but that an arbitration agreement is deemed to be concluded if the parties appear before the arbitral tribunal without invoking the lack of an agreement prior to raising any defence.

[28] Similar wording is contained in the Indian Arbitration and Conciliation Act 1996, s. 7. See *Great Offshore Ltd v Iranian Offshore Engineering and Construction Co.* (2008) 14 SCC 240 for an analysis of the Indian law position.

[29] See Sanders, 'Arbitration', in Cappelletti (ed.) *Encyclopedia of International and Comparative Law, Vol. XVI* (Brill, 1987), ch. 12, para. 106.

[30] See, e.g., the English Arbitration Act 1996, ss. 5(43)*ff*. The 'implied consent' provisions of the Model Law are also to be found in s. 5(5). In *Heifer International Inc. v Christiansen* [2007] EWHC 3015 (TCC), the court held that an arbitration agreement was validly concluded by reference to a written arbitration clause contained in another contract.

[31] See, e.g., Liebscher, 'Interpretation of the written form requirement Art. 7(2) UNCITRAL Model Law' (2005) 8 Intl Arb L Rev 164 and the cases cited therein.

[32] In their respective arbitration laws, Belgium and Scotland have adopted the Option 2 wording. See the Code Judiciaire, Art. 1681 and the Arbitration (Scotland) Act 2010, s. 4, respectively.

[33] See also the New Zealand Arbitration Act 1996, s. 7(1), which provides that 'an arbitration agreement may be made orally or in writing'.

a written document signed by the parties or otherwise contained in an exchange of com-munications between the parties.[34] Secondly, an arbitration agreement that is regarded as valid by an arbitral tribunal or court in one country may not be so regarded by the courts of the country in which the award falls to be enforced.[35] By way of example, the Norwegian Court of Appeal refused recognition of an award rendered in London because an exchange of emails did not, in its view, satisfy the writing requirement of Article II(2) of the New York Convention. Although such an electronic exchange was valid and sufficient to evidence the existence of an arbitration agreement as a matter of the law of the place of arbitration—that is, English law—the Court held that the validity of the arbitration agreement was to be sep-arately assessed by the local enforcement authority and that 'it should not be sufficient for enforcement that the arbitral award is valid according to the law of the country in ques-tion' (in this case, England, the place of arbitration).[36] While the authors might expect the Norwegian courts today to reach a different decision on the same question, this judgment shows the risks that are run in some jurisdictions (in the place of enforcement if not in the place of arbitration) if requirements as to form are not satisfied.

2.26   Finally, there are still states in which special requirements of form *are* imposed in respect of agreements to arbitrate.[37] Accordingly, the relevant national law must be examined if there is reason to believe that the formal validity of an arbitration agreement is likely to be ques-tioned under that law.

(b) A defined legal relationship

2.27   Almost all international arbitrations arise out of contractual relationships between the parties. However, for the purposes of both the New York Convention and the Model Law, it is sufficient that there should be a 'defined legal relationship' between the parties, whether contractual or not. Plainly, there has to be some contractual relationship (real or implied) between the parties, since there must be an agreement to arbitrate to form the basis of the arbitral proceedings.[38] Given the existence of such an agreement, the dispute

---

[34] See, e.g., the decision of the US Second Circuit Court of Appeals in *Kahn Lucas Lancaster Inc. v Lark International Ltd*, 186 F.3d 210 (2d Cir. 1999). This decision has been applied by a number of other US courts, which have arrived at varying interpretations (some liberal; others less so) of an 'exchange of letters and telegrams'. See, e.g., the US District Court of the Southern District of California decision in *Chloe Z Fishing Co. Inc. v Odyssey Re (London) Ltd*, 109 F.Supp.2d 1048 (SD Cal. 2000); the US District Court of the Western District of Washington decision in *Bothell v Hitachi Zosen Corporation*, 97 F.Supp.2d 1048 (WD Wash. 2000); the Third Circuit Court of Appeals decision in *Standard Bent Glass Corporation v Glassrobots Oy*, 333 F.3d 440, 449 (3d Cir. 2003). Most recently, the District Court of the Southern District of New York has affirmed the *Kahn Lucas* approach, but found that email exchanges between the parties 'comfortably satisf[ied] the standard set by the [New York] Convention': *Glencore Ltd v Degussa Engineered Carbons LP*, 848 F.Supp.2d 410 (SDNY 2012). See also *TransAsia Lawyers v EcoNova, Inc*, Not Reported in F.Supp.3d (2014).

[35] See the discussion in Chapter 3 on the law governing the arbitration agreement.

[36] Decision of the Halogaland Court of Appeal (Norway), 16 August 1999, (2002) XXVII YBCA 519.

[37] Including, particularly, the requirement in some jurisdictions (e.g. Brazil) that an arbitration clause is not op-erative unless it provides for the procedure to be adopted in the arbitration: see fn. 5.

[38] For an example see *D v U (ASBL) UR*, Court of Appeal, Brussels, Case No. 2016/AR/2048, 29 August 2018. In that case the court found that the requisite defined legal relationship did not exist. The arbitration agreement in question was found in the statutes of FIFA and UEFA, to which the plaintiff had adhered through its own stat-utes. The arbitration clause provided broadly that all disputes between FIFA or UEFA and football clubs would be submitted to CAS arbitration, without further specification. The Belgian Court of Appeal found that this 'general clause did not contain any reference to a defined legal relationship', and that '[t]he intention of the drafters of the clause is visibly to cover any type of dispute between the parties indicated; this makes the clause a general clause,

submitted to arbitration may be governed by principles of delictual or tortious liability rather than (as is usually the case) by the law of contract.

In *Kaverit Steel Crane Ltd v Kone Corporation*,[39] Kaverit commenced court proceedings al-   **2.28** leging that Kone had breached certain licence and distribution agreements. Kone sought a stay and a reference to arbitration pursuant to the arbitration clause in the agreements. The clause stated that all disputes 'arising out of or in connection with this contract' would be referred to arbitration. The ABQB refused the stay on the grounds that some of the claims by Kaverit contained allegations that went beyond breach of contract, for example conspiracy and inducing breach of contract. The court held that these tort-based claims fell outside the scope of the arbitration clause.

However, the Alberta Court of Appeal held that the wording of the arbitration clause was   **2.29** wide enough to bring within its scope any claim that relied on the existence of a contractual relationship, even if the claim itself was a claim in tort.[40] To give an example: because the claim alleging 'conspiracy by unlawful means to harm [Kaverit]' relied upon a breach of contract as the source of the 'unlawfulness', that dispute should be referred to arbitration. However, it was held that those claims that were not based on the existence of a contract should proceed to trial, not arbitration.

More recently, courts around the world have adopted wider interpretations of similar   **2.30** clauses. For example, the Chinese courts have held that 'all disputes arising out of or in connection with the contract' will capture tortious claims.[41] In Hong Kong, a similar test has been applied, pursuant to which a tortious claim will fall within the scope of an arbitration clause if '(1) the resolution of a contractual issue is necessary for a decision on the tortious claim; or (2) the contractual and tortious disputes are so closely knitted together on the facts that an agreement to arbitrate on one can properly be construed as covering the other'.[42] The decision of the English House of Lords (now the UK Supreme Court) in *Fiona Trust* is a notable example of this practical modern trend. Lord Hoffmann considered the prior case law concerning the construction of arbitration clauses and the precise meaning of wording such as 'arising out of' and opined that

which cannot be applied because it is not an arbitration clause recognized in Belgian law': see Stephan W. Schill (ed.) *Yearbook Commercial Arbitration 2019—Volume XLIV* (ICCA & Kluwer Law International, 2019), pp. 1–9, paras 12, 14.

[39] *Kaverit Steel Crane Ltd v Kone Corporation* (1992) 87 DLR (4th) 129, (1994) XVII YBCA 346.
[40] The Court held that a dispute 'arises out of or in connection with a contract' if the 'existence of the contract is germane either to the claim or the defence': ibid., at 295–297.
[41] See the view of the Supreme People's Court (SPC) in SPC, *The Second National Foreign-related Commercial and Maritime Trial Work Meeting Minutes* (26 December 2005), Art. 7. See also *Empresa Exportadora de Azucar v Industria Azucarera Nacional SA* [1983] 2 Lloyd's Rep 171.
[42] See *Gossip Daily Ltd v Next Media Magazines Ltd and Others* [2018] HKCFI 1951. However, by way of contrast in *Castlemil Infant (HK) Supplies Co Ltd v Care N Love Development Ltd* [2018] HKDC 1419, the Hong Kong District Court found that a claim in tort did not fall within the scope of the parties' agreement to arbitrate 'any dispute, controversy or claim arising out of or relating to [their contract]'. Finally, see also the decision of the FCA in *Walter Rau Neusser Oel Und Fett Ag v Cross Pacific Trading Ltd* [2005] FCA 1102, holding that claims in relation to fraud and misrepresentations that took place before the contract was concluded and which allegedly induced the parties to enter into the contract, did not 'arise out of' the contract and therefore fell outside the arbitration clause in question. The *Walter* case is discussed in Morrison, 'Defining the scope of arbitrable disputes in Australia: Towards a "liberal" approach?' (2005) 22 J Intl Arb 569. These issues are discussed in greater detail in van den Berg, 'Scope of the arbitration agreement' (1996) XXI YBCA 415.

'the distinctions which they make reflect no credit upon English commercial law'. He continued that:

> [T]he construction of an arbitration clause should start from the assumption that the parties, as rational businessmen, are likely to have intended any dispute arising out of the relationship into which they have entered or purported to enter to be decided by the same tribunal. The clause should be construed in accordance with this presumption unless the language makes it clear that certain questions were intended to be excluded from the arbitrator's jurisdiction.[43]

(c) A subject matter capable of settlement by arbitration

2.31   In determining whether a dispute is capable of settlement by arbitration, the question is whether a dispute is 'arbitrable'. As explained in Chapter 1, arbitrability, in the sense in which it is used in this book, involves determining which types of dispute may be resolved by arbitration and which belong exclusively to the domain of the courts. The application of the New York Convention and the Model Law is limited to disputes that are 'capable of settlement by arbitration'.[44]

2.32   This requirement is dealt with in more detail later in this chapter.[45] Suffice to say that, in principle, *any* dispute should be just as capable of being resolved by a private arbitral tribunal as by the judge of a national court. However, it is precisely because arbitration is a private proceeding with public consequences[46] that some types of dispute are reserved for national courts, the proceedings of which are generally in the public domain. It is in this sense that they are not 'capable of settlement by arbitration'. National laws establish the domain of arbitration as opposed to that of the local courts. Each state decides which matters may or may not be resolved by arbitration in accordance with its own political, social, and economic policy.

C. Parties to an Arbitration Agreement

(a) Capacity

2.33   Parties to a contract must have legal capacity to enter into that contract, otherwise it is invalid. The position is no different if the contract in question happens to be an arbitration agreement. The general rule is that any natural or legal person who has the capacity to enter into a valid contract has the capacity to enter into an arbitration agreement. Accordingly, the parties to such agreements include individuals, as well as partnerships, corporations, states, and state agencies.

2.34   If an arbitration agreement is entered into by a party who does not have the capacity to do so, the provisions of the New York Convention (or the Model Law, where applicable) may be

---

[43] *Fiona Trust and Holding Corporation v Privalov* [2007] UKHL 40, at [13].
[44] New York Convention, Arts II(1) and V(2)(a); Model Law, Arts 34(2)(b)(i) and 36(1)(b)(i).
[45] See paragraphs 2.125–2.178.
[46] For example, in the recognition and enforcement of the award.

brought into operation, either at the beginning or at the end of the arbitral process. At the beginning, the requesting party may ask the competent court to stop the arbitration on the basis that the arbitration agreement is void, inoperative, or incapable of being performed.[47] At the end of the arbitral process, the requesting party may ask the competent court to re- fuse recognition and enforcement of the award on the basis that one of the parties to the arbitration agreement is 'under some incapacity'[48] under the applicable law.

The rules governing capacity to contract can be found in the standard textbooks on the law   **2.35** of contract. They vary from state to state. In the context of an arbitration agreement, it is generally necessary to have regard to more than one system of law. Questions that may arise in relation to individuals will be addressed before we consider the position of corporate entities, and lastly the particular situation of states and state entities.

(i) Natural persons

The New York Convention and the Model Law, where applicable, require the parties to an   **2.36** arbitration agreement to have the capacity to enter into that agreement 'under the *law* ap- plicable to them'.[49] More correctly, this should perhaps refer to the 'law or *laws*' applicable to them. The capacity of an individual to enter into a contract within the state of his or her place of domicile and residence will depend upon the law of that state—but, in the con- text of an international contract, it may become necessary to have regard also to the law of the contract. For instance, a person aged 18 may well have the capacity to enter into an agreement under the law of his or her domicile, but not under the law governing the trans- action in question. If that transaction were to turn out badly, that person might rely upon the incapacity as a reason for not carrying out the contract (or any agreement to arbitrate contained within it). However, there may be an applicable rule of law that defeats such in- genuity. For instance, Article 13 of the Rome I Regulation,[50] which applies among European Union (EU) member states, provides:

> In a contract concluded between persons who are in the same country, a natural person who would have capacity under the law of that country may invoke his incapacity resulting from the law of another country, only if the other party to the contract was aware of that incapacity at the time of the conclusion of the contract or was not aware thereof as a result of negligence.

(ii) Corporations

The capacity of a corporation to enter into a contract is governed primarily by its bylaws and   **2.37** the law of its place of incorporation. If a corporation enters into a transaction that goes be- yond its power (in other words, a transaction that is *ultra vires*) and the transaction turns out badly, the corporation could contend that the agreement was invalid and thus not bound by the arbitration clause in the agreement. To guard against this possibility, it is not unusual for states to have specific rules of law or principles that restrict or abrogate the doctrine of *ultra*

---

[47] New York Convention, Art. II(3); Model Law, Art. 8(1).
[48] New York Convention, Art. V(1)(a); Model Law, Art. 36(1)(a).
[49] Otherwise, the agreement will be regarded as invalid and accordingly unenforceable: see the provisions of the New York Convention and the Model Law cited above.
[50] Regulation (EC) No. 593/2008 of the European Parliament and of the Council of 17 June 2008 on the law ap- plicable to contractual obligations (Rome I), OJ L 177/6, 4 July 2008. The uniform rules of this Regulation do not apply to questions involving the status or legal capacity of natural persons, except as stated.

vires, so as to protect persons dealing in good faith with corporations, particularly where the person has confirmed that he or she has full power to execute the relevant contract or has benefited from the application of the contract.[51]

2.38   Counsel acting for banks or financial institutions making loans to corporate entities will be well aware of their duty to make sure that the corporate entity concerned has the capacity to enter into the loan agreement. However if that agreement contains an arbitration clause, Counsel will also need to check for any provisions governing that corporate entity's capacity to enter into an arbitration agreement.

2.39   In addition to such issues of corporate governance, the laws of some states may restrict a corporation from initiating arbitration in certain circumstances relating to the status of the corporate entity itself. For example, a number of states within the United States have statutes that restrict a corporation that is not 'in good standing' under the laws of that state from initiating any type of legal proceeding, including arbitration. Thus the failure of a corporation to maintain its good standing could be the basis of an application (or 'motion', to borrow from the US legal lexicon) to stay or dismiss an international arbitration filed by such corporation.

(iii)   States and state agencies

2.40   It is unusual to encounter a corporation that insists, in its bylaws, that any disputes should be referred to the courts, rather than to arbitration. It is more frequent, however, to find states or state agencies that are not permitted to refer disputes between themselves and a private party to arbitration. In France, for example, under Article 2060 of the Civil Code, disputes concerning public collectives and public establishments, and all matters involving public policy, may not be referred to domestic arbitration.[52] However, certain commercial public entities may be authorised by decree to enter into arbitration agreements. Moreover, disputes arising out of industrial or commercial activities of public entities may be referred to *international* arbitration.[53] In Belgium, public law entities were

---

[51]   See, e.g., within the European Union, Directive 2009/101/EC of the European Parliament and of the Council of 16 September 2009 aims to ensure the protection of shareholders and third parties through requiring legislation to ensure the public availability of the key corporate documents which establish the manner in which a corporation can operate, OJ L 258/11, 1 October 2009. Where a corporation retroactively seeks to escape a contractual obligation by alleging *ultra vires*, doctrines such as estoppel, waiver, and, in Spanish speaking countries *actos propios* and legitimate expectations, come into play.

[52]   In 2007, the Labetoulle Report proposed to abolish the prohibition contained in Art. 2060 and a draft law was prepared in order to 'broaden the possibility for recourse to arbitration for public bodies and to clarify the procedural regime of arbitrations involving public law': Groupe de travail sur l'arbitrage en matière administrative, *Rapport*, 13 March 2007, available online at http://www.justice.gouv.fr/art_pix/Rapport_final.pdf (in French). At the time of writing, no amendments have yet been made to Art. 2060.

[53]   See the decision of the Paris cour d'appel in *INSERM v Fondation F. Saugstad*, Paris cour d'appel, 13 November 2008. See also the decision of the Conseil d'État Libanais, *Etat Libanais v Societe FTML (Cellis) SAL*, 17 July 2001, in which the Lebanese State Council, with reference to French law, held that public entities could submit to international arbitration only those contracts that do not involve the exercise of the state's prerogatives of public power. This ruling was heavily criticised in Lebanon and resulted in a new Law No. 40 being enacted by the Lebanese Parliament establishing the validity of arbitration agreements in all contracts of the state and public entities, with the exception of administrative contracts being effective only after approval of the Council of Ministers. However, it is now generally accepted that, under French law, public entities cannot rely on provisions of French law to evade obligations contained in an international arbitration agreement that they have signed: Hanotiau and Olivier, 'Arbitrability, due process, and public policy under Article V of the New York Convention: Belgian and French perspectives' (2008) 25 J Intl Arb 721, at 724.

at one time prohibited from concluding arbitration agreements. This prohibition has now been abolished, but some restrictions remain.[54] In Brazil, the higher courts have consistently ruled that a state body is not prohibited from agreeing to resolve disputes by arbitration and is bound by any such agreement, and this principle has been enshrined in legislation and by presidential decree.[55] In some other countries, the state or state agency must obtain the approval of the relevant authorities before entering into an agreement for international commercial arbitration.[56]

Although this position is now more the exception than the rule, it is advisable to check that the persons entering into the contract on behalf of the state or state agency have the necessary authority to do so. It is also wise to check that any necessary procedures for obtaining consent to an arbitration agreement have been followed. Indeed, it would be sensible to include a statement to this effect in the contract.[57]   **2.41**

It is plainly unsatisfactory for a state or state agency to be entitled to rely on its own law to defeat an agreement into which it has entered freely. A praiseworthy attempt to deal with this problem was made in the European Convention of 1961. This provided that persons considered by the law applicable to them to be 'legal persons of public law' should have the right to conclude valid arbitration agreements. It also provided that if a state were to wish to limit this facility in some way, it should say so on signing, ratifying, or acceding to the Convention.[58] Although the European Convention has met with only limited success, certain countries have dealt with the problem by adopting a similar approach. Swiss law, for example, provides that: **2.42**

> If a party to the arbitration agreement is a state or enterprise or organisation controlled by it, it cannot rely on its own law in order to contest its capacity to be a party to an arbitration or the arbitrability of a dispute covered by the arbitration agreement.[59]

This is a provision that all states would do well to follow, and there is now, in any event, a growing international consensus to the effect that where a state entity has agreed to resolve disputes by international arbitration, it cannot rely on its own domestic laws in order to   **2.43**

---

[54] The arbitration agreement must relate to the settlement of disputes regarding the formation or the performance of an agreement: see the Belgium Code Judiciaire, art. 1676(3).

[55] See *Companhia Paranaense de Gas ('Compagás') v Carioca Passarelli Consortium ('Consortium')*, Appeal No. 247.646-0, Paraná Court of Appeals, 11 February 2004; *Copel v Energetica Rio Pedrinho S.A.*, Agravo de Instrumento No. 174.874-9, Paraná Court of Appeals, 11 May 2005; *Companhia Estadual de Energia Eléctrica ('CEEE') v AES*, Recurso Especial No. 612.439-RS, Paraná Superior Court of Justice, 14 September 2006; Law No. 13.129/15; Decree 10.025 of 26 September 2019.

[56] For example, in Venezuela, the Commercial Arbitration Act 1998, s. 4 provides that when one of the parties to the arbitration agreement is a state entity (or an entity in which the state holds a stake of at least 50 per cent), the arbitration agreement must be specifically approved by the relevant minister. Similar restrictions are contained in the Iranian Constitution, Art. 139 and the Saudi Arabian Law of Arbitration (Royal Decree No. M/34 of 16 April 2012), s. 10.

[57] It would also be advisable to ensure that, under the relevant state law, the subject matter of the contract is 'arbitrable' in the sense discussed later.

[58] European Convention of 1961, Art. II(1) and (2).

[59] Swiss Private International Law Act (as amended in 2021), s. 177(2). Presumably, however, the state concerned might try to rely on its own law to defeat recognition or enforcement outside Switzerland of any arbitration award against it.

avoid submitting to the arbitral process.[60] Some writers[61] have argued that restrictions imposed by a state on its capacity to enter into an arbitration agreement should not be qualified as issues of capacity, but rather as issues of arbitrability. It is argued that the restriction is self-imposed and could be waived at any time by the state concerned and that it is not a true limitation on capacity, such as the protection of persons under mental disability. Accordingly, it is argued that this issue should be treated as a matter of 'subjective arbitrability' rather than as a matter of capacity.[62] The real point, however, is that whatever legal characterisation is given to the issue, it is something that may need to be taken into account.

2.44   In circumstances where civil conflict, a revolutionary movement, or competing political factions exist within a state, a further issue can arise: whether those who claim authority to represent and bind the state are properly empowered to do so. This issue may arise after the execution of the arbitration agreement itself. For example, a stable government may exist at the time the arbitration agreement is entered into, only later to be the subject of competing claims of authority raised by different factions or regimes within a state. In this context, the prospect of a subsequent, prevailing government disavowing the acts of a former regime, including the arbitration agreement and participation in the arbitration, is a real one.[63]

2.45   The difficulty of this situation is highlighted in the English case of *The Maduro Board of the Central Bank of Venezuela v The Guaidó Board of the Central Bank of Venezuela*.[64] Following the 2018 presidential election in Venezuela, there was a dispute as to the identity of the rightful President of Venezuela, with Nicolás Maduro claiming to be the President on the ground that he won the 2018 election, and Juan Guaidó, the President of the National Assembly of Venezuela, claiming to be the Interim President under the constitution on the ground that the 2018 presidential election was flawed. Both of them, however, sought to give instructions on behalf of the Central Bank of Venezuela to release Venezuela's gold reserves held in the Bank of England. The UK Court of Appeal found that, although the UK government recognised Mr Guaidó as the *de jure* President of Venezuela, as a matter of English law, only the *de facto* President was entitled to exercise the power of sovereignty (and it was unclear who the UK government recognised as the *de facto* President of Venezuela). The Court therefore recommended seeking clarification on this point from the UK government's Foreign and Commonwealth Office and, until then, neither Mr Maduro nor Mr Guaidó could have access to Venezuela's gold reserves held in the Bank of England. As of the time of writing, this case is pending an appeal to the UK Supreme Court.

---

[60] See, e.g., *Benteler v State of Belgium*, Ad Hoc Award, 18 November 1983; Award in ICC Case No. 4381, 113 J du Droit Intl 1102 (1986); *Gatoil International Inc. v National Iranian Oil Co.*, High Court of Justice, Queen's Bench Division, 21 December 1988, (1988) XVII YBCA 587; *Buques Centroamericanos SA v Refinadora Costarricense de Petroleos SA* US Dist. LEXIS 5429 (SDNY 1989). See also the 1989 Resolution of the Institut de Droit International, which provides that '[a] State, a state enterprise, or a state entity cannot invoke incapacity to arbitrate in order to resist arbitration to which it has agreed'.

[61] See, e.g., Paulsson, 'May a state invoke its internal law to repudiate consent to international commercial arbitration?' (1986) 2 Arb Intl 90.

[62] It is interesting to note in this context that the Swiss Private International Law Act, s. 177(2), refers both to 'capacity' and to 'arbitrability', so that—at the very least—the two concepts may merge.

[63] For a general discussion of the issues that may arise in these contexts, and the possible ways in which they may be addressed, see Mohtashami, 'Protecting the legitimacy of the arbitral process: Jurisdictional and procedural challenges in public-private disputes', in Kalicki and Raouf (eds) *Evolution and Adaptation: The Future of International Arbitration*, ICCA Congress Series, Vol. 20 (Kluwer Law International, 2019), pp. 619–638.

[64] *The Maduro Board of the Central Bank of Venezuela v The Guaidó Board of the Central Bank of Venezuela* [2020] EWCA Civ 1249.

(b) Third parties to the arbitration agreement

Party consent is a prerequisite for international arbitration. Such consent is embodied in an **2.46** agreement to arbitrate, which, as discussed earlier,[65] will generally be concluded 'in writing' and signed by the parties.[66] The requirement of a signed agreement in writing, however, does not altogether exclude the possibility that an arbitration agreement concluded in proper form between two or more parties might also bind other parties. Third parties to an arbitration agreement have been held to be bound by (or entitled to rely on) such an agreement in a variety of ways: first, by operation of the 'group of companies' doctrine, pursuant to which the benefits and duties arising from an arbitration agreement may, in certain circumstances, be extended to other members of the same group of companies; and secondly, by operation of general rules of private law—principally those governing assignment, agency, and succession. Thus, by way of example: the affiliate of a signatory to an arbitration clause may find itself a co-respondent in arbitration proceedings; an assignee of an insurance contract may be able to commence arbitration against the insurer of the original insured party; a principal may find itself bound by an arbitration agreement signed by its agent; or a merged entity may continue to prosecute arbitral proceedings commenced by one of its original constituent entities.

(i) The 'group of companies' doctrine

A number of arbitral tribunals and national courts have been called upon to consider **2.47** whether an arbitration agreement concluded by a company may be binding on its group affiliates, by reason of the group being a 'single economic reality'.[67] Such attempts are often motivated by the stated aim of finding the 'true' party in interest—and, of greater practical importance, of targeting a more creditworthy member of the relevant group of companies.

Although an objection of principle may readily be made—namely, that corporate personality **2.48** is created precisely in order to contain liability within a particular corporate entity—in practice much will depend on the construction of the arbitration agreement in question, as well as the circumstances surrounding the entry into, and performance of, the underlying contract.[68]

---

[65] See paragraph 2.15.

[66] See, however, *Warner Bros Feature Productions Pty Ltd v Kennedy Miller Mitchell Films Pty Ltd* [2018] NSWCA 81, in which the parties' agreement did not contain an express arbitration clause, but contained a clause that incorporated the standard terms for companies within the Warner Bros group. The New South Wales Court of Appeal held that, because the standard terms proffered by the companies in the Warner Bros group generally contained an arbitration clause, the arbitration clause was also incorporated into the parties' agreement. The parties were therefore required to refer their dispute to arbitration.

[67] See generally Derains, 'L'extension de la clause d'arbitrage aux non-signatories: La doctrine des groupes de sociétés' (1994) 8 ASA Special Series 241; Jarosson, 'Conventions d'arbitrage et groupes de sociétés' (1994) 8 ASA Special Series 209; Derains and Schaf, 'Clauses d'arbitrage et groupes de sociétés' [1985] RDAI 231; Fadlallah, 'Clauses d'arbitrage et groupes de sociétés' [1984–85] Travaux du Comité Français de Droit International Privé 105; Gaillard and Savage (eds) *Fouchard Gaillard Goldman on International Commercial Arbitration* (Kluwer Law International, 1999), paras 500*ff*.

[68] Sandrock has argued that all of the cases usually discussed in connection with the 'group of companies' theory ought to be regarded (or to have been decided) on theories of agency, such as the theory of the undisclosed principal (or, in some legal systems, indirect representation), the reverse construction of mandat apparent, or principles of good faith and estoppel: Sandrock, 'Arbitration agreements and groups of companies', in Dominice, Patry, and Reymond (eds) *Études Pierre Lalive* (Helbing & Lichtenhahn, 1993), p. 625; Sandrock, 'The extension of arbitration agreements to non-signatories: An enigma still unresolved', in Baums, Hopt, and Hom (eds) *Corporations, Capital Markets and Business in the Law: Liber Amicorum Richard M Buxbaum* (Kluwer Law International, 2000), p. 461.

2.49   The *Dow Chemical* case has been invoked as the leading authority on the 'group of companies' doctrine, which emerged from a particular line of cases decided by ICC tribunals and subsequently considered by the French courts. In *Dow Chemical*, a claim was successfully brought before an ICC tribunal not only by the companies that had signed the relevant agreements, but also by their parent company, a US corporation, and a French subsidiary in the same group. The Paris Court of Appeal confirmed the award.

2.50   However, some have argued that the *Dow Chemical* award and judgment have been misinterpreted, and do not in fact lend support to an independent 'group of companies' doctrine. They note that, on a close reading of the decision, the tribunal's analysis was based simply on an attempt to determine the parties' common intention, and its decision may be explained by reference to the traditional requirement for consent in international arbitration.[69]

2.51   In terms, the *Dow Chemical* tribunal found that:

> [T]he arbitration clause expressly accepted by certain of the companies of the group should bind the other companies which, *by virtue of their role in the conclusion, performance, or termination of the contracts* containing said clauses, and *in accordance with the mutual intention of all parties* to the proceedings, appear to have been veritable parties to these contracts or to have been principally concerned by them and the disputes to which they may give rise.[70]

2.52   The tribunal did refer to the relevant group of companies in that case as 'one and the same economic reality [*une réalité économique unique*]'.[71] However, it reached its decision on the basis of 'the intention common to all companies involved', and referred only 'subsidiarily' to the notion of a 'group of companies'.[72]

2.53   Following *Dow Chemical*, another ICC tribunal ruled that 'there is no general rule in French international arbitration law that would provide that non-signatory party members of the same group of companies would be bound by an arbitration clause.[73] Similarly, some other courts, such as those in England, have also refused to accept that a third party may be bound by an arbitration agreement merely because it has a legal or commercial connection to one of the parties.[74] In jurisdictions that have recognised the group of companies doctrine, case law confirms that where a court or tribunal is tasked to determine whether a third party

---

[69]   Hanotiau, 'Consent to arbitration: Do we share a common vision?', 2010 Freshfields Lecture, London, 21 October 2010. See also Ferrario, 'The group of companies doctrine in international commercial arbitration: Is there any reason for this doctrine to exist?' (2009) 26 J Intl Arb 647. Indeed, subsequent French decisions such as *Société Korsnas Marma v Société Durand-Auzias* (Paris cour d'appel, 30 November 1988), *Société Ofer Brothers v The Tokyo Marine and Fire Insurance Co Ltd* (Paris cour d'appel, 14 February 1989), and *Société ABS v Amkor* (Cass. Civ., 27 March 2007) did not determine the application of an arbitration agreement to non-signatories on the basis of a single economic reality of a corporate group. Rather, these decisions considered the participation of the non-signatory in the substantive transaction, its awareness of the scope of the arbitration clause, and the need for there to be a single forum or jurisdiction to deal with all aspects of any interconnected claims.

[70]   ICC Case No. 4131/1982 (Interim Award) in *Dow Chemical France v ISOVER Saint Gobain (France)* (1983) 110 J du Droit Intl 899, noted by Derains in (1984) IX YBCA 131, at 135 (emphasis added)..

[71]   ICC Case No. 4131/1982 (Interim Award) in *Dow Chemical France v ISOVER Saint Gobain (France)* (1983) 110 J du Droit Intl 899, at 904. The tribunal looked carefully at the parties' intentions in concluding the relevant arbitration clauses and said that the negotiating record showed that 'neither the "Sellers" nor the "Distributors" attached the slightest importance to the choice of the company within the Dow Group that would sign the contracts'.

[72]   *Société Isover-Saint-Gobain v Société Dow Chemical France*, Paris cour d'appel, 22 October 1983, [1984] Rev Arb 98, at 100–101, n. Chapelle.

[73]   ICC Case No. 11405/2001.

[74]   *Peterson Farms Inc. v C & M Farming Ltd* [2004] EWHC 121; *City of London v Sancheti* [2008] EWCA Civ 1283.

is bound by an arbitration agreement, it will focus on the parties' common intention.[75] It could be said that consent will often be presumed[76] on the basis of a variety of factors,[77] including: (a) whether the non-signatory actively participated in the conclusion and execution of the contract containing the arbitration agreement;[78] (b) whether the non-signatory has a clear interest in the outcome of the dispute;[79] and (c) whether the non-signatory is party to a contract that is 'intrinsically inter-twined' with the contract under which the dispute has arisen.[80]

Accordingly, the *Dow Chemical* case may perhaps be best characterised as authority for the proposition that 'conduct can be an expression of consent and that among all the factual elements [...] the existence of a group of companies may be relevant'.[81]   **2.54**

(ii) 'Piercing the corporate veil'

A court or tribunal may conclude that a third party is bound by an arbitration agreement where there is evidence that the party to the agreement is being used as 'a device or façade' in order to avoid or conceal liability.[82] In such circumstances, a party may also seek to rely on the 'alter ego' principle,[83] which permits a court or arbitral tribunal to look beyond the   **2.55**

---

[75] See, e.g., *Chloro Controls (I) P Ltd v Severn Trent Water Purification Inc. and ors*, Supreme Court of India, 28 September 2012. The Court referred repeatedly to 'the real intention of the parties' to support its conclusion that an arbitration clause contained in a shareholders' agreement should be extended to a non-signatory company. See also *Cheran Properties Ltd v Kasturi and Sons Ltd*, Supreme Court of India, 24 April 2018. In *Mahangar Telephone Nigam Ltd v Canara Bank*, Supreme Court of India, 8 August 2019, the Court clarified that the group of companies doctrine could be invoked to bind the non-signatory affiliate of a company where: there is a direct relationship between the party which is signatory to the arbitration agreement; a direct commonality of the subject matter; or the transaction between the parties is of a composite nature.

[76] See, e.g., *Orri v Société des Lubrifiants Elf Aquitaine*, Paris cour d'appel, 11 January 1990.

[77] See, e.g., *Kout Food Group v Kabab-Ji Sal,* Paris cour d'appel, 26 June 2020, in which the Court ruled that an arbitration clause should be extended to the parties involved in the performance of the contract and in any disputes arising out of the contract, provided that it can be presumed that they consented to the arbitration clause based on their contractual situation and their activities. The Court focused on the participation of the parent company in the performance, termination, and renegotiation of the relevant agreements to hold that it was bound by the arbitration agreement.

[78] See, e.g., *Sponsor AB v Lestrade*, Court of Appeal of Pau, 26 November 1986, [1988] Rev Arb 153 (the Court emphasised that Sponsor AB played an important role in the conclusion and execution of the contract, and in fact was 'the soul, inspirer and, in a word, the brains of the contracting party'); ICC Case No. 5103/1988 [1988] J du Droit Intl 1206; *Société Orthopaedic Hellas v Société Amplitude*, No. 11-25.891, Cass. Civ. 1ere, 7 November 2012. See also *X et al. v Z*, no. 4P 115/2003, Swiss Federal Tribunal, 16 October 2003. However, it appears that conduct subsequent to the negotiation, performance, and termination of the contract may not, in certain circumstances, be sufficient to substantiate or presume an intention to arbitrate. See, e.g., *Reckitt Benckiser (India) Pvt. Ltd. v Reynders Label Printing India Private Limited*, Supreme Court of India, 1 July 2019.

[79] See, e.g., *Trelleborg do Brasil Ltda v Anel Empreendimentos Participações e Agropecuária Ltda*, Apelação Cível No. 267.450.4/6-00, 7th Private Chamber of São Paulo Court of Appeals, 24 May 2004.

[80] *Khatib Petroleum Services International Co. v Care Construction Co. and Care Service Co.*, Case No. 4729 of the Judicial Year 72, Egypt's Court of Cassation, June 2004; *Chaval v Liebherr*, Recurso Especial No. 653.733, Brazilian Superior Court of Justice, 3 August 2006. See also *New Europe Corporate Advisory Ltd and Epic Financial Consulting v Innova 5 CA* Paris, 18 December 2018, Case No. 16/24924, in which the Paris Court of Appeal ruled that where non-signatories are directly concerned by the performance of the underlying contract, and where the facts suggest that they were familiar with the existence and scope of the arbitration clause, then they may be bound by the arbitration agreement.

[81] Hanotiau, 'Consent to arbitration: Do we share a common vision?' 2010 Annual Freshfields Lecture, London, 21 October 2010.

[82] See *Prest v Petrodel* [2013] UKSC 34, at [22] *per* Lord Sumption.

[83] See, e.g., *Wm Passalacqua Builders v Resnick Developers*, 933 F.2d 131 (2d Cir. 1991). The alter ego doctrine has also been successfully applied in respect of states and state entities: see *Bridas SAPIC, Bridas Energy International Ltd et al. v Government of Turkmenistan and Turkmennneft* 345 F.3d 347 (5th Cir. 2006), discussed in the news section of [2006] Intl Arb L Rev N3334; cf. ICC Case No. 9151, *Joint Venture Yashlar and Bridas SAPIC v Government of Turkmenistan*, Interim Award of 8 June 1999.

formalities of a corporate form where it is being abused in order to attribute liability to the individual (or corporation) hiding behind that form.[84]

(iii) Third-party beneficiaries of rights under a contract

2.56   Under some systems of law, a third party may also enforce rights conferred under the terms of a contract in certain circumstances. The English Contracts (Rights of Third Parties) Act 1999 provides that a third party ('A') may enforce a contractual term where the contract expressly provides that A may do so or purports to confer a benefit on A.[85] Where the contract contains an arbitration agreement, the third party is bound by the agreement and constrained to follow the arbitral process.[86] A similar principle exists in France. The Court of Cassation has held that where a contract conferring a benefit on a third party (*stipulation pour autrui*) contains an arbitration clause, the third party is obliged to refer any claim to arbitration. Moreover, that party is precluded from objecting to the tribunal's jurisdiction if it is joined to an action as a respondent.[87] The Italian courts have also confirmed that, in certain circumstances, once a third party decides to take the benefit of a contract, it can be bound to abide by all of the terms of the contract, including any arbitration agreement.[88] The US courts have invoked the principle of estoppel to similar effect.[89]

(iv) Beneficiaries under a trust

2.57   A deed of trust is not normally considered to be a contract. Where a deed contains a dispute resolution clause providing for arbitration, the question therefore arises whether a dispute between a trustee and a beneficiary under that deed is governed by an arbitration agreement at all.[90] To complicate matters further, a deed of trust is not typically signed by the

---

[84] See, e.g., *Wm Passalacqua Builders v Resnick Developers*, 933 F.2d 131 (2d Cir. 1991). The alter ego doctrine has also been successfully applied in respect of states and state entities: see *Bridas SAPIC, Bridas Energy International Ltd et al. v Government of Turkmenistan and Turkmennneft* 345 F.3d 347 (5th Cir. 2006), discussed in the news section of [2006] Intl Arb L Rev N3334; cf. ICC Case No. 9151, *Joint Venture Yashlar and Bridas SAPIC v Government of Turkmenistan*, Interim Award of 8 June 1999.

[85] Contracts (Rights of Third Parties) Act 1999, s. 1.

[86] See Contracts (Rights of Third Parties) Act 1999, s. 8. See also *Nisshin Shipping Co. Ltd v Cleaves & Co. Ltd* [2003] EWHC 2602 (Comm), in which the English High Court held that brokers seeking to enforce the terms of charterparties that conferred benefits on them (the payment of commissions) were bound by the arbitration clause therein. However, see *Fortress Value Recovery Fund I LLC v Blue Skye Special Opportunities Fund LP* [2013] EWCA Civ 367, in which the English Court of Appeal held that a third party joined as *defendant* in a contract claim in the English courts could not invoke the arbitration clause in the contract to obtain a stay of proceedings under s. 9 of the English Arbitration Act 1996.

[87] *Banque populaire Loire et Iyonnais v Société Sangar*, Cass. Civ. (1ere Ch. Civ.), 11 July 2006.

[88] See, e.g., *Assicurazioni Generali SpA v Tassinari*, Judgment No. 2384, Corte di Cassazione, 18 March 1997; *Polisuole Srl v Pietrella*, Judgment No. 13474, Corte di Cassazione, 10 October 2000; *Consorzio Cooperative Costruzioni-CCC Società Cooperativa v Punta Gradelle SCARL*, Judgment No. 2568, Tribunale di Milano, 24 April 2020.

[89] See *Cargill International SA v M/T Pavel Dybenko*, 991 F.2d 1012, 1019 (2d Cir. 1993); *American Bureau of Shipping v Société Jet Flint SA*, 170 F.3d 349, 353 (2d Cir. 1999); *Avila Group Inc. v Norma J of California* 426 F.Supp. 537, 542 (DCNY 1977) ('To allow [a plaintiff] to claim the benefit of the contract and simultaneously avoid its burdens would both disregard equity and contravene the purpose underlying enactment of the Arbitration Act'); *Astra Oil Co. Inc. v Rover Navigation, Ltd*, 344 F.3d 276, 279, n. 2 (2d Cir. 2003); *Birmingham Associates Ltd v Abbott Laboratories* 547 F.Supp.2d 295 (SDNY 2008), 2008 US Dist LEXIS 30321; *GE Energy Power Conversion France SAS, Corp v Outokumpu Stainless USA, LLC*, U.S. Supreme Court Case No. 18-1048, Slip. Op. 590 U. S. (June 1, 2020), p. 6 ('The text of the New York Convention does not address whether nonsignatories may enforce arbitration agreements under domestic doctrines such as equitable estoppel [...] nothing in the text of the Convention could be read to otherwise prohibit the application of domestic equitable estoppel doctrines').

[90] Strong, 'Arbitration of internal trust disputes: The next frontier for international commercial arbitration?', in Kalicki and Raouf (eds) *Evolution and Adaptation: The Future of International Arbitration* ICCA Congress Series, Vol. 20 (Kluwer Law International, 2019).

beneficiaries. It could therefore be argued in such circumstances that the beneficiaries have not consented to arbitration, and that as a consequence any dispute resolution clause in the deed that purports to compel the beneficiaries to arbitrate does not, in fact, bind them.

In order to address this problem, English law has developed the doctrine of 'deemed ac- **2.58** quiescence', which provides that, by accepting the gifts or rights conferred to them pursuant to a trust deed, beneficiaries of a trust are deemed to have agreed to settle any dispute arising thereunder in accordance with the arbitration agreement contained in the deed.[91] The US courts have adopted a similar approach, based on what is known as the 'conditional transfer' theory: '[a] beneficiary takes only by benevolence of the testator, who may attach lawful conditions to the receipt of the gift'.[92] This concept is similarly recognised in the ICC's 'Clause for Trust Disputes'.[93]

(v) Assignment, agency, and succession

Assignment   The effect of an assignment of a contract on an arbitration clause con- **2.59** tained therein will be determined principally by reference to the law governing the assignment in question, as well as the law governing the arbitration agreement. If the arbitration agreement is assignable under the relevant laws, there will be a further question as to the particular form, if any, which the assignment must take. This requirement must not be confused with the writing requirement that applies to the arbitration agreement itself.

Different laws take differing positions on whether an arbitration agreement should be pre- **2.60** sumed as having been assigned along with the main contract. The law of some jurisdictions, for example German, French, English, and Greek law, makes this presumption.[94] New York law also adopts this general presumption, albeit with certain limited exceptions.[95]

---

[91] The alternative concept is known as 'conditional transfer'.

[92] See *American Cancer Soc., St. Louis Division v Hammerstein*, 631 S.W. 2d 858, 864 (Mo. App. 1981), cited in Strong, 'Arbitration of internal trust disputes: The next frontier for international commercial arbitration?', in Kalicki and Raouf (eds) *Evolution and Adaptation: The Future of International Arbitration* ICCA Congress Series, Vol. 20 (Kluwer Law International, 2019). As discussed in paragraphs 2.172–2.174 below in the context of the arbitrability of trust disputes, a number of states in the United States have enacted legislation that expressly recognises the enforceability of binding arbitration clauses in wills and trusts. Similarly, New Zealand's Trusts Act 2019 expressly recognises the courts' power to enforce any provision in a trust that requires an internal matter to be subject to an ADR process, including arbitration.

[93] See ICC Commission on Arbitration and ADR, *ICC Arbitration Clause for Trust Disputes, 2018*, p. 7. The Commission notes that '[t]he ICC Arbitration Clause for Trust Disputes is formulated as an agreement which is binding on the original parties to the trust by virtue of their executing the trust instrument, and on all others by virtue of their having acted under, or claimed or accepted benefits under, the trust'. The ICC further explains that '[b]eneficiaries are deemed to have agreed to the arbitration clause when they obtain benefit or otherwise derive advantage from the trust'.

[94] See Bundesgerichtshof decision (1978) 71 BGHZ 162, 164–165, and (2000) 53 NJW 2346. The French Code Civil, Art. 2061 provides that transfer of the arbitration agreement is automatic on assignment of the main contract. However, Arts 1341-1, 1337, and 1338 of the Code Civil make a distinction between perfect and imperfect assignments, of which only the former discharges the original debtor of its obligations through novation, but requires the original creditor's consent to that effect. For the English law position, see *West Tankers Inc. v RAS Riunione Adriatica di Sicurta SpA (The Front Comor)* [2005] 2 All ER (Comm) 240. For the Greek law position, see Greek Supreme Court, Case No. 176/1976 ('Under articles 471 and 472 of [the Greek] Civil Code, the person who assumes per agreement with the creditor the debt of another person is obligated vis-à-vis the creditor also as regards the ancillary obligations of the debtor, including the arbitration agreement existing between the creditor and the debtor').

[95] There was a common law principle in New York law that arbitration was an 'obligation' not assumed by an assignee of a contract: see *United States v Panhandle Eastern Corporation et al.* 672 F.Supp. 149 (D. Del. 1987); *Gruntal & Co., Inc. v Ronald Steinberg et al.* 854 F.Supp. 324 (DNJ 1994); *Lachmar v Trunkline LNG Co.*, 753 F.2d 8, 9–10 (2d Cir. 1985); cf. *Banque de Paris v Amoco Oil* 573 F.Supp. 1465, 1472 (SDNY 1983). However, according to *GMAC Commer Credit LLC v Springs Indus* 171 F.Supp.2d 209 (SDNY 2001), 2001 US Dist LEXIS 5152, 44

The Swedish Supreme Court appears to have adopted a middle position—namely, that an arbitration clause will be presumed to be assignable if the parties have not expressly agreed otherwise, but that, once assigned, it will operate vis-à-vis the assignee only if that party has actual or constructive knowledge of the arbitration clause.[96]

2.61   **Arbitration agreements concluded by agents**   The binding effect of an arbitration agreement concluded by an agent on behalf of a principal involves questions of authority (that is, the agent's ability to bind the principal to such agreements) and allied questions of necessary form.[97] Thus an ICC tribunal invited to determine whether a principal was bound by an arbitration agreement concluded by its agent distinguished between the law governing the arbitration agreement (in that case, the law of the seat of the arbitration), the laws that governed the agent's capacity to conclude an arbitration agreement on behalf of the principal (the law of the principal's registered office), and the form in which such capacity should have been conferred on the agent (the law of the jurisdiction in which the agreement between the agent and the principal was concluded).[98]

2.62   National laws feature substantial differences on questions of necessary form (that is, whether the principal's written authorisation is required) and content (that is, whether the principal's authorisation need expressly envisage the conclusion of an arbitration agreement). For example, Swiss, Austrian, and Italian law requires the principal expressly to authorise an agent to enter into an arbitration agreement on its behalf in order for that principal to be bound by such an agreement, but only Austrian and Italian law requires such express authorisation to be in writing.[99] Under French,[100] and German[101] law, no particular form of authorisation is required.

UCC Rep. Serv. 2d 708 (6th Cir. 2001), this principle was superseded by New York's adoption of the Uniform Commercial Code (UCC) § 9-318 in 1964 (now § 9-404 after the UCC was revised in 2000). In *GMAC*, the Court held that 'the adoption of the Article 9 of the U.C.C. means that a finance assignee suing on an assigned contract is bound by that contract's arbitration clause unless it secured a waiver from the signatory seeking to arbitrate': *GMAC*, at 215.

[96] *Ms Emja Braack Shiffahrts KG v Wärtsilä Diesel AB*, Supreme Court of Sweden, 15 October 1997, [1998] Rev Arb 431, at 433, n. Hansson, Lecoanet, and Jarvin.

[97] See Reiner, 'The form of the agent's power to sign an arbitration agreement and Art. II(2) of the New York Convention' (1999) 9 ICCA Congress Series 82.

[98] ICC Case No. 5832/1988 (1988) 115 J du Droit Intl 1198. Applying Austrian law, which requires authorisation to be given in writing by a principal to an agent in order for the latter validly to conclude an arbitration agreement ('to provide clear and simple evidence and to protect the parties against the waiver of procedural guarantees'), the tribunal refused to regard the principal as bound by the purported arbitration agreement. The conflict-of-laws rules on these different aspects of agency are notoriously complex. See further Dicey, Morris, and Collins, *The Conflict of Laws* (15th edn, Sweet & Maxwell, 2012), pp. 2109ff.

[99] On Austrian law, see the Civil Code, s. 1008 and fn. 88; on Swiss law, see the Swiss Federal Code of Obligations, Art. 396(3); on Italian law, see the Italian Civil Code, Art. 1392 and the Italian Code of Civil Procedure, Arts 807 and 808, discussed in *De Maio v Ferraro* Judgment No. 3109, Corte Suprema di Cassazione, 24 March 1998.

[100] See Code Civil, Art. 1985; Code de Commerce, Art. L110-3 (in respect of the contract of mandate or mandat); *Total v Achille Lauro*, Judgment No. 361, Corte di Cassazione, 25 January 1977, (1977) 17 Rassegna dell'Arbitrato 94, at 95. However, under Art. 1989 of the Code Civil, the conclusion of an arbitration agreement requires specific authorisation.

[101] See Landesgericht Hamburg, Judgment of 19 December 1967, [1968] Arbitrale Rechtspraak 138, at 140 (in respect of a commercial broker or *Handelsmakler*, under the German Commercial Code, s. 75h(2)). In Sandrock, 'The extension of arbitration agreements to non-signatories: An enigma still unresolved', in Baums, Hopt, and Hom (eds) *Corporations, Capital Markets and Business in the Law: Liber Amicorum Richard M Buxbaum* (Kluwer Law International, 2000), p. 467, the author expresses a belief that an arbitration agreement concluded by an agent or representative without the principal's written authorisation would bind that principal only if, in the circumstances, third parties' legitimate expectations were to require protection.

It is not only private parties, but also state entities, which can be bound to an arbitration **2.63** agreement by way of agency. In the recent case of *Egiazaryan v OJSC OEK Finance*,[102] the English Commercial Court held that the City of Moscow, although not a signatory to the arbitration agreement, was nevertheless bound by it, on the basis that, pursuant to English conflict of laws rules (English law being the proper law of the contract), the question of whether a parent is liable to perform an agreement entered into by its subsidiary is one that should be resolved in accordance with the law of the signatory's place of incorporation (in this case, Russia).[103] The contracts in question had been entered into by OJSC OEK Finance (a company owned by the City of Moscow) and, pursuant to Article 105 of the Russian Civil Code, the City of Moscow was found to be bound by the relevant contracts as a whole, and thus also bound to the arbitration agreement.[104]

Succession and novation   Questions of succession in international arbitration arise most **2.64** often in connection with companies, rather than natural persons.[105] The general rule is that arbitration agreements, like other contracts, enure to the benefit of universal successors of companies[106]—that is, the entities that succeed them as a result, for example, of a voluntary merger,[107] or by operation of law. Such questions involve the status of a company and are thus generally to be resolved by reference to the law of its incorporation (or, in respect of natural persons, by reference to the law of succession).[108]

(c) Joinder and intervention

Unlike litigation in state courts, in which third parties can often be joined to proceed- **2.65** ings, the jurisdiction of an arbitral tribunal to allow for the joinder or intervention of third parties to an arbitration is limited. The tribunal's jurisdiction derives from the will of the parties to the arbitration agreement and therefore joinder or intervention is generally only possible with the consent of all parties concerned.[109] As between the original parties to the arbitration agreement, such consent may be either express, implied, or by

---

[102] *Egiazaryan v OJSC OEK Finance* [2015] EWHC 3532 (Comm).

[103] Ibid., at [6(ii)], [10], [18], and [21].

[104] Ibid.

[105] On natural persons, see the English Arbitration Act 1996, s. 8(1): 'Unless otherwise agreed by the parties, an arbitration agreement is not discharged by the death of a party and may be enforced by or against the personal representatives of that party.'

[106] See, e.g., Interim Award in ICC Case No. 7337 (1999) 24 YBCA 149; *Fyrnetics Ltd v Quantum Group Inc.* 293 F.3d 1023 (7th Cir. 2002).

[107] See Award in ICC Case No. 6223/1991 (1997) 8 ICC Bulletin 69. See also *AT&S Transportation LLC v Odyssey Logistics & Technology Corporation* 803 NYS 2d 118 (2005), in which the US courts held that the sale of substantially all of the assets of company A to company B constituted a *de facto* merger and bound company B to an arbitration agreement signed by company A.

[108] See the section on insolvency at paragraphs 2.143–2.148.

[109] See, e.g., the Privy Council (Turks and Caicos Islands) decision in *The Bay Hotel and Resort Ltd v Cavalier Construction Co. Ltd* [2001] UKPC 34, discussed in Melnyk, 'The extent to which non-contracting parties can be encouraged or compelled to take part in arbitral proceedings: The English (Arbitration Act 1996) perspective' (2003) 6 Intl Arb L Rev 59, at 63. On the issue of joinder generally, see Hanotiau, *Complex Arbitrations: Multiparty, Multicontract, Multi-issue and Class Actions* (2nd edn, Kluwer Law International, 2020), ch. IV; Voser, 'Multiparty disputes and joinder of third parties', Presented at the ICCA Congress, Dublin, 9 June 2008. Note, however, Judgment No. 21/2017 of the Belgian Constitutional Court dated 16 February 2017, in which the Belgian Constitutional Court ruled that third parties whose rights were prejudiced by an arbitral award should be afforded the opportunity to file third-party opposition to the award.

reference to a particular set of arbitration rules agreed to by the parties that provide for joinder.[110]

2.66   Following recent revisions to many of the main institutional rules, most now contain a specific provision for joinder of third parties to an arbitration.[111] For example, Article 7.1 of the ICC Rules provides that:

> A party wishing to join an additional party to the arbitration shall submit its request for arbitration against the additional party (the 'Request for Joinder') to the Secretariat. The date on which the Request for Joinder is received by the Secretariat shall, for all purposes, be deemed to be the date of the commencement of arbitration against the additional party. [...] No additional party may be joined after the confirmation or appointment of any arbitrator, unless all parties, including the additional party, otherwise agree. The Secretariat may fix a time limit for the submission of a Request for Joinder.

2.67   Some rules now set out a detailed procedural framework for joinder applications.[112] By way of example, the SIAC Rules provide as follows:

> The party or non-party applying for joinder [...] shall, at the same time as it files an application for joinder with the Registrar, send a copy of the application to all parties, including the additional party to be joined, and shall notify the Registrar that it has done so, specifying the mode of service employed and the date of service.[113]

2.68   The SIAC Rules, the Swiss Rules, and the Rules of the Hong Kong International Arbitration Centre (HKIAC) also allow for intervention—that is, a third party may, of its own initiative, request to participate in the arbitration.[114] The Swiss Rules provide:

> A party asserting a claim against another party other than a claim in the Notice of Arbitration or a counterclaim in the Answer to the Notice of Arbitration (cross-claim), or a party asserting a claim against an additional party (joinder), or an additional party asserting a claim against an existing party (intervention), shall do so by submitting a notice of claim.[115]

2.69   Subject to the particular rules of arbitration applicable, parties should be mindful that joining a third party to arbitration proceedings may be problematic if the tribunal has already been constituted. It is important to ensure that all parties are treated equally and, if relevant, that the procedure for participation in the appointment of the tribunal is respected.[116]

---

[110]   See Platte, 'When should an arbitrator join cases?' (2002) 18 Arb Intl 67; Mohan and Teck, 'Some contractual approaches to the problem of inconsistent awards in multi-party, multi-contract arbitration proceedings' (2005) 1 Asian Intl Arb J 161, at 164.

[111]   Besides the UNCITRAL Rules, see also: HKIAC Rules, Art. 27; ICC Rules 2017, Art. 7; LCIA Rules 2020, Art. 22.1.x; SIAC Rules 2016, r. 7; Swiss Rules, Art. 4.2.

[112]   The ICC, the HKIAC, and the SIAC Rules contain detailed provisions on joinder procedure, including the required contents of the request for joinder.

[113]   SIAC Rules, r. 7.3.

[114]   Swiss Rules, Art. 6.1; SIAC Rules, r. 7.1; HKIAC Rules, Art. 27.9.

[115]   Swiss Rules, Art. 6.1.

[116]   See Voser, 'Multiparty disputes and joinder of third parties', presented at the ICCA Congress, Dublin, 9 June 2008, at 46–49.

D. Analysis of an Arbitration Agreement

An arbitration agreement confers a mandate upon an arbitral tribunal to decide any and all **2.70** of the disputes that come within the ambit of that agreement. It is important that an arbitral tribunal should not go beyond this mandate.[117] If that happens, there is a risk that the award will be refused recognition and enforcement under the provisions of the New York Convention. Article V(1)(c) provides that recognition and enforcement may be refused: 'If the award deals with a difference not contemplated by or not falling within the terms of the submission to arbitration, or if it contains decisions on matters beyond the scope of the submission to arbitration [...].' The Model Law contains an almost identical provision to the effect that an award may be set aside by the competent court, as well as refused recognition and enforcement, if it 'deals with a dispute not contemplated by or not falling within the terms of the submission to arbitration or contains decisions on matters beyond the scope of the submission to arbitration'.[118]

There are, in general, three categories of claim that are potentially within the scope of an ar- **2.71** bitration agreement. These are:

- contractual claims (including claims incidental to the contract, such as *quantum meruit*);
- claims in tort; and
- statutory claims.

The first two are self-explanatory. The third relates to those claims that arise out of legis- **2.72** lation that might bind the parties, such as securities and antitrust legislation. In all three categories of claim, it is necessary to determine whether a particular claim or defence has a sufficient connection with the contract to be covered by the arbitration agreement on its terms.[119] Likewise, in relation to statutory claims, the arbitral tribunal or a judge may need to examine a claim or defence in relation to the wording of the arbitration agreement in order to decide whether there is a sufficiently close connection. In all such cases, the form of words used in the arbitration agreement will be important.

It is important to ensure that the wording adopted in an arbitration agreement is adequate **2.73** to fulfil the intentions of the parties. Usually, when parties agree to resolve any disputes between them by arbitration, they intend such recourse to arbitration to be mandatory, rather than optional. Accordingly, the arbitration agreement should be drafted so as to make clear that resolving disputes by arbitration is not only the parties' right, but also their obligation.[120] Similarly, where parties include an arbitration agreement in their contract, they

---

[117] The poet's reflection that 'a man's reach should exceed his grasp, or what's a heaven for?' seems not to be apposite for an international arbitrator: Browning, 'Andrea del Sarto' (1855), line 97.

[118] Model Law, Arts 34(2)(iii) and 36(i)(a)(iii). The reference to a 'submission to arbitration' would include an arbitration clause and, e.g., the terms of reference in an ICC arbitration (as to which, see Chapter 1). There is a saving provision under both the Convention and the Model Law to the effect that if it is possible to separate the matters that *were* submitted to arbitration from those that were not, the award may be saved in respect of the matters that were submitted.

[119] For example, the Austrian Supreme Court held that 'disputes *resulting from* the agreement' does not cover non-contractual claims based on competition law that are connected to the underlying contract in no more than a 'functionally illustrative' way: Decision of the Supreme Court (*Oberster Gerichtshof*) No. 4 Ob. 80/08f, 26 August 2008, discussed in (2009) 12 Intl Arb L Rev 40 (emphasis added).

[120] As a matter of Indian case law, arbitration clauses that stated that 'parties *may* refer disputes to arbitration' have been held in the past to be optional rather than mandatory, thereby requiring the parties to agree afresh (by

usually intend to resolve *all* disputes between them by this method (unless a specific exception is made). Accordingly, the arbitration agreement should be drafted in broad, inclusionary terms, rather than referring only certain categories of dispute to arbitration and leaving others to the jurisdiction of national courts.

2.74   Fortunately, most national courts now regard arbitration as an appropriate way of resolving international commercial disputes and, accordingly, seek to give effect to arbitration agreements wherever possible,[121] rather than seek to narrow the scope of the agreement so as to preserve the court's jurisdiction. Thus the English Court of Appeal referred to a 'presumption of one-stop arbitration' in the interpretation of the arbitration agreement and this approach is increasingly reflected in law and practice around the world.[122] Similarly, the Swiss Federal Tribunal tends to interpret arbitration clauses broadly: a general reference to 'disputes related to the agreement' may extend to claims arising out of ancillary or connected contracts, provided that those contracts do not contain different dispute resolution clauses.[123]

2.75   General words such as 'claims', 'differences', and 'disputes' have been held by the English courts to encompass a wide jurisdiction in the context of the particular agreement in question.[124] In the United States, the words 'controversies or claims' have similarly been held to have a wide meaning, and if other words are used, it may be considered that the parties intended some limitation on the kind of disputes referred to arbitration.[125]

---

way of a submission agreement) to refer a particular dispute to arbitration: see the judgment of the Indian Supreme Court in *Wellington Associates Ltd v Mr Kirit Mehta* (2000) 4 SCC 272. See also the judgment of the Punjab and Haryana High Court in *Sudarshan Chopra and ors v Company Law Board and ors* (2004) 2 Arb LR 241.

[121]   A striking illustration of this policy can be seen in the decision of the US Federal District Court in *Warnes SA v Harvic International Ltd*, 3 December 1993, summarised in [1994] ADRLJ 65. The arbitration clause referred to the 'New York Commercial Arbitration Association', a non-existent association. The court held that it was clear that the parties intended to arbitrate and that an agreement on a non-existent forum was the equivalent of an agreement to arbitrate that does not specify a forum. Accordingly, the parties were directed to arbitrate in the AAA system. See also *KVC Rice Intertrade Co Ltd v Asian Mineral Resources Pte and another suit* [2017] SGHC 32, in which the Singapore High Court found that two arbitration clauses, in two contracts, evinced a clear intention to settle any disputes 'by arbitration' and were thus valid and binding, notwithstanding the fact that they designated neither the seat nor the governing law nor the rules for the arbitration.

[122]   See *Fiona Trust & Holding Corporation v Yuri Privalov* [2007] EWCA Civ 20, at [19]. This pro-arbitration approach was endorsed by the House of Lords: *Premium Nafta Products Ltd (20th Defendant) and ors v Fili Shipping Co. Ltd and ors* [2007] UKHL 40. Recent English cases confirm that, in circumstances where a dispute involves multiple, inter-related contracts, each containing a different dispute resolution clause, the presumption articulated in *Fiona Trust* provides a useful starting point, but is not decisive. In such circumstances, the English courts will consider which of the contracts pertains to the 'centre of gravity' of the dispute and, similarly, which dispute resolution clause is 'closer to the claim', in order to decide: *Trust Risk Group SpA v Am Trust Europe Ltd* [2015] EWCA Civ 437, at [48], followed in *Costain Ltd v Tarmac Holdings Ltd* [2017] 1 CLC 491 (QB), at [30] and [39]. See also *Deutsche Bank AG v Comune di Savona* [2018] EWCA Civ 1740, at [3].

[123]   See, e.g., Decision No. 4A-103/2011, 20 September 2011, in which an arbitration clause contained in a licence agreement was held to be wide enough to cover a dispute arising out of a connected sale-and-purchase agreement.

[124]   See, e.g., *Woolf v Collis Removal Service* [1948] 1 KB 11, 18; *F & G Sykes (Wessex) Ltd v Fine Fare Ltd* [1967] 1 Lloyd's Rep 53; *The Angelic Grace* [1995] 1 Lloyd's Rep 87 (CA).

[125]   In the case of *Prima Paint Corporation v Conklin Mfg Co.*, 388 US 395, 87 S.Ct. 1801, 18 L.Ed.2d 1270 (1967), the words 'any controversy or claim arising out of or relating to this agreement' were described as a broad arbitration clause; in *Scherk v Alberto-Culver*, 417 US 506 (1974), 'any controversy or claim' was held to include statutory claims under the Securities Exchange Act of 1934.

Linking words such as 'in connection with', 'in relation to', 'in respect of', 'with regard to', **2.76**
'under',[126] and 'arising out of'[127] may also be important in any dispute as to the scope of an
arbitration agreement. However, in *Fiona Trust*,[128] the English courts drew a line under this
debate as a matter of English law. Arriving at a broad interpretation of the arbitration clause
in question, the Court of Appeal held as follows:

> For our part we consider that the time has now come for a line of some sort to be drawn
> and a fresh start made at any rate for cases arising in an international commercial con-
> text. Ordinary businessmen would be surprised at the nice distinctions drawn in the
> cases and the time taken up by argument in debating whether a particular case falls
> within one set of words or another very similar set of words [...] If any businessman
> did want to exclude disputes about the validity of a contract, it would be comparatively
> simple to say so.[129]

Finally, when considering the scope of the arbitration agreement and in addition to the **2.77**
form of words used, the parties, by their conduct in referring a matter to arbitration, may
be taken as impliedly agreeing to confer on the arbitrator jurisdiction beyond that which
would have existed pursuant to the terms of the arbitration clause alone. Accordingly, a
claim in tort that may not be within the scope of the arbitration clause may nevertheless
come within an arbitrator's jurisdiction where the parties address that claim in the arbitral
proceedings, without reservation as to jurisdiction.[130]

There is no shortage of learned commentaries on the drafting of an arbitration agree- **2.78**
ment.[131] However, most international commercial arbitrations usually take place

---

[126] For example, in *Onex Corporation v Ball Corporation*, 24 January 1994, summarised in [1996] ADRLJ 193
and (1995) XX YBCA 275, the Ontario Court of Justice held that a claim for rectification was a dispute arising
'under' the contract.

[127] See *The Angelic Grace* [1995] 1 Lloyd's Rep 87 (CA). In the United States, a decision of the Fifth Circuit Court
of Appeals on 13 May 1998 evidenced an equally broad approach to the construction of a clause that referred to
arbitration 'any dispute, controversy or claim arising out of or in relation to or in connection with "the agreement"': *Pennzoil Exploration and Production Co. v Ramco Energy Ltd* 139 F.3d 1061, 1068 (5th Cir. 1998). The
approach of the German courts appears to be much the same: see Oberlandesgericht, Frankfurt, 24 September
1985, summarised in (1990) XV YBCA 666, concerning the expression 'arising out of'. A similarly wide interpretation was given to the term 'concerning' in *Fletamentos Maritimos SA v Effjohn International BV* [1996] 2 Lloyd's
Rep 304.

[128] *Fiona Trust & Holding Corporation v Yuri Privalov* [2007] EWCA Civ 20.

[129] Ibid., at [17]. This was expressly endorsed by the House of Lords in its rejection of the appeal: *Premium Nafta
Products Ltd (20th Defendant) and ors v Fili Shipping Co. Ltd and ors* [2007] UKHL 40, at [13]. The English courts
have followed this approach in subsequent cases: see, e.g., *Skype Technologies SA v Joltid Ltd* [2009] EWHC 2783
(Ch); *Starlight Shipping Co. v Allianz Marine & Aviation Versicherungs AG* [2011] EWHC 3381 (Comm); *Black
Diamond Offshore Ltd v Fomento DE Construcciones Y Contratas SA* [2015] EWHC 1035 (Ch), at [19] (holding that
jurisdiction clauses must be construed 'widely and generously' with a presumption in favour of 'one-stop shopping' for dispute resolution); *Dreymoor Fertilisers Overseas PTE Ltd v Eurochem Trading GmbH* [2018] EWHC
909 (Comm), at [53] (holding that a clause referring to 'any dispute or claim arising out of this Contract' can refer
to disputes which relate to non-contractual claims, such as pre-contractual misrepresentation or bribery inducing
the contract).

[130] See, e.g., *The Almare Prima* [1989] 2 Lloyd's Rep 376.

[131] See, in particular, Gélinas, 'Arbitration clauses: Achieving effectiveness' (1998) 9 ICCA Congress Series
47. See also Paulsson, Rawding, and Reed (eds) *The Freshfields Guide to Arbitration* (Kluwer Law International,
2010); Park, 'When and why arbitration matters', in Hartswell (ed.) *The Commercial Way to Justice* (Kluwer Law
International, 1997), pp. 73–99, at p. 96; Derains, 'Rédaction de la clause d'arbitrage', in Desbois (ed.) *Le Droites
Affaires Propriété Intellectuelle* (Librairies Techniques, 1987), p. 15. Also worth mentioning is Bernadini, 'The arbitration clause of an international contract' (1992) 9 J Intl Arb 45; Ball, 'Just do it: Drafting the arbitration clause in
an international agreement' (1993) 10 J Intl Arb 29; Debevoise and Plimpton, *Annotated Model Arbitration Clauses
for International Contracts* (Debevoise & Plimpton, 1996).

pursuant to a standard form arbitration clause, recommended either by the arbitral institution to which they refer, such as the ICC, the LCIA and the SIAC, or by UNCITRAL. Any subsequent arbitration will then take place according to the rules of the institution concerned or of UNCITRAL, and these rules will generally be adequate to guide the arbitral process from beginning to end, including (if necessary) the constitution of the arbitral tribunal, the filling of any vacancies, the exchange of written submissions, and the holding of hearings. Where the parties wish to provide for ad hoc arbitration, but not to make use of the UNCITRAL Rules, it will generally be sufficient to adopt a clause that makes it clear that all disputes are to be referred to arbitration. Also, the clause should specify that the arbitration will have a seat in a state that has a modern law of arbitration, which, if necessary, will provide the necessary support for the arbitral tribunal. In France, for example, a simple clause such as 'Resolution of disputes: arbitration, Paris', whilst not recommended, would be held to be a valid submission to arbitration in an international commercial contract.[132] The French law on international arbitration would then give such support to the arbitral process as required, including appointment of the arbitral tribunal under Articles 1452 and 1453 of the French Code of Civil Procedure.

2.79 Arbitration clauses are usually drawn in wide terms, to ensure that all disputes that arise out of or in connection with a particular contract or contractual relationship are referred to arbitration. The UNCITRAL model refers to '[a]ny dispute, controversy or claim arising out of or relating to this contract, or the breach, termination or invalidity thereof'. Similar language is used in the ICC, SIAC, and LCIA model forms.

2.80 Where a model clause is used, it is sensible to supplement it including by reference to the number of arbitrators, the legal place or seat of arbitration, and the language of the arbitration. Otherwise any problems that arise in these respects and on which the parties cannot agree will have to be resolved by the relevant arbitral institution or by the arbitral tribunal itself.

(a) Key elements

2.81 There follows a note of the key elements of an arbitration clause, including those that may usefully supplement a model clause. Since these key elements have already been discussed, either in this or the preceding chapter, the note is brief.

(i) A valid arbitration agreement

2.82 First, there must be a valid arbitration agreement. In particular, it must be made clear, as it is in the model clauses, that the parties intend that any and all disputes between them shall be finally *resolved* by *arbitration*. Examples of defective clauses in which such an intention was not made clear are given later in this chapter.

---

[132] Gaillard and Savage (eds) *Fouchard Gaillard Goldman on International Commercial Arbitration* (Kluwer Law International, 1999), para. 486; cf. the decision to similar effect in *Arab African Energy Corporation Ltd v Olieprodukten Nederland BV* [1983] 2 Lloyd's Rep 419.

(ii) Number of arbitrators

In an international arbitration, there should be an uneven number of arbitrators, and it is sug-   **2.83**
gested that, in general, a choice should be made between one or three.[133] The dated system of
appointing only two arbitrators, with an 'umpire' or 'referee' to adjudicate between them if
they cannot agree, may be appropriate for arbitrations within a defined trade or commodity
association, but is almost unheard of in mainstream international arbitration today.

(iii) Constitution of the arbitral tribunal

This important subject is dealt with in Chapter 4.   **2.84**

(iv) Ad hoc or institutional arbitration

Whether the tribunal will be ad hoc or institutional is one of the most important decisions   **2.85**
that has to be taken; and ironically, it is one that has to be taken at the wrong time. In an ideal
world, it would be possible to wait until any disputes had arisen and then decide, according
to their importance and complexity, how they should best be handled. But by that stage the
parties may not be talking to each other—or, at best, will be doing so only through their lawyers. Accordingly, good sense dictates that the agreement to arbitrate should be negotiated
and concluded at the same time as the contract to which it relates. As one commentator has
expressed it: 'The primary objective, in inserting an arbitration clause in a contract, is to ensure that when the time comes—that is, when a dispute parts the parties—neither one will
be able to escape arbitration [...].'[134]

The choice between ad hoc and institutional arbitration has already been considered in   **2.86**
Chapter 1,[135] and need not be repeated here. The criteria by which an arbitral institution
should be judged are also considered in that chapter.[136]

(v) Filling vacancies in the tribunal

During the course of an arbitration, it sometimes becomes necessary to replace an arbi-   **2.87**
trator, whether because his or her appointment has been successfully challenged, or because
he or she has died, has resigned, or become incapacitated. The rules of the established arbitral institutions contain comprehensive provisions to cover such contingencies,[137] as do
modern laws of arbitration.[138] Where there is a submission agreement that is intended, as
far as possible, to be self-contained,[139] provisions for filling any vacancies in the tribunal
must be spelled out in some detail.

(vi) Place of arbitration

The place (or legal seat) of arbitration is another decision of major importance. It is the   **2.88**
law of that place which governs the arbitral proceedings (and any challenge to the ultimate
award). This is fully considered in Chapter 3. It is advisable for the parties themselves to

---

[133] See Chapter 4, paragraph 4.22.
[134] Gélinas, 'Arbitration clauses: Achieving effectiveness' (1998) 9 ICCA Congress Series 47, at 51.
[135] See paragraphs 1.150*ff.*
[136] See paragraphs 1.162*ff.*
[137] See, e.g., the ICC Rules, Art. 15; LCIA Rules, Arts 10 and 11; SIAC Rules, r. 17.
[138] See, e.g., the English Arbitration Act 1996, s. 27.
[139] In the sense that it will not need to be supplemented by the applicable law.

choose a suitable place of arbitration, rather than to leave the choice to others. In doing so, as discussed in Chapter 3, they should locate their arbitration in a state the laws of which are adapted to the needs of modern international commercial arbitration and which is a party to the New York Convention. Insofar as they may be likely to privilege the holding of any physical hearings in the jurisdiction, they should also take account of practical matters, such as distance, availability of adequate hearing rooms, backup services, and so on.

(vii) Governing law

2.89   The parties' contract should contain a choice of law clause and they should also consider making express provision for the governing law of the arbitration agreement.

2.90   In most jurisdictions, where parties have not expressly agreed on a governing law for their arbitration agreement, their choice of law for the *main* contract would be taken as a strong indication that they wished to adopt the same law for the arbitration agreement. Where the contract did not contain a 'choice of law' clause (or where the arbitration agreement was not part of that contract), the court would be likely to turn to the parties' choice of seat, in order to determine the law with which the arbitration agreement had its 'closest and most real connection'. This was the approach adopted, for example, by the English Court of Appeal in *Sulamérica*.[140]

2.91   In the recent case of *Enka Insaat ve Sanayi AS*, the UK Supreme Court revisited this issue and held (by majority) that there were good reasons—namely legal certainty, consistency, coherence, and the avoidance of complexity and artificiality—to favour a rule whereby an agreement on a choice of law to govern the main contract should be construed as applying also to the arbitration agreement, even if a different country or national system of laws has been nominated as the seat.[141] However, where parties have made *no* express or implied decision as to the law that is to govern their contract, the arbitration agreement will be governed by the law with which it is most closely connected, which typically will be the law of the seat.[142]

2.92   In the light of the complexity that may arise from the absence of an explicit designation, it is advisable for parties to agree expressly a governing law not only in relation to the main contract but also in relation to the arbitration agreement itself. This topic is discussed in full in Chapter 3.[143]

---

[140] *Sulamérica CIA Nacional de Seguros SA v Enesa Engenharia SA* [2012] EWCA Civ 638. The Court of Appeal's decision in *Sulamérica* was followed by the High Court in *Habas Sinai Ve Tibbi Gazlar Istihsal Endustrisi AS v VSC Steel Co. Ltd* [2013] EWHC 4071 (Comm).

[141] *Enka Insaat Ve Sanayi AS v OOO Insurance Company Chubb* [2020] UKSC 38, at [54].

[142] *Enka Insaat Ve Sanayi AS v OOO Insurance Company Chubb* [2020] UKSC 38, at [53]. The appeal was dismissed on the facts. See also *Kabib-Ji SAL v Kout Food Group* [2020] EWCA Civ 6. In that case, the parties had expressly chosen English law as the law governing their contract, but had not specified the law governing the arbitration agreement. The English Court of Appeal held that, on a proper interpretation of the parties' governing law clause, the parties had made an express choice that their entire contract, including the arbitration agreement, would be governed by English law, notwithstanding that the seat of the arbitration was Paris. By way of contrast, see the decision by the Paris Court of Appeal pertaining to the same arbitration, in which the Court held that, absent an express choice of English law to govern the arbitration clause, the law of the seat (that is, French law), applied to the arbitration agreement: *Société Kout Food Group v Société Kabib-Ji Sal*, Paris cour d'appel, 23 June 2020, Case No. RG 17/22943.

[143] See paragraphs 3.07*ff*.

(viii) Default clauses

It is important that the failure or refusal of one of the parties to take part should not frustrate an   **2.93**
arbitration. The defaulting party is usually the respondent, who sees that it has nothing to win
and may have much to lose by taking part in proceedings that may lead to an award against it.
Exceptionally, however, a claimant may lose heart in the face of a substantial counterclaim. It may
then be the respondent who wishes to proceed. The rules of the arbitral institutions usually contain adequate default provisions; so too does Article 30 of the UNCITRAL Rules, which provides:

1. If, within the period of time fixed by these Rules or the arbitral tribunal, without showing
   sufficient cause:
   (a) The claimant has failed to communicate its statement of claim, the arbitral tribunal
        shall issue an order for the termination of the arbitral proceedings, unless there are
        remaining matters that may need to be decided and the arbitral tribunal considers
        it appropriate to do so;
   (b) The respondent has failed to communicate its response to the notice of arbitration
        or its statement of defence, the arbitral tribunal shall order that the proceedings
        continue, without treating such failure in itself as an admission of the claimant's
        allegations; the provisions of this subparagraph also apply to a claimant's failure to
        submit a defence to a counterclaim or to a claim for the purpose of a set-off.
2. If a party, duly notified under these Rules, fails to appear at a hearing, without showing
   sufficient cause for such failure, the arbitral tribunal may proceed with the arbitration.
3. If a party, duly invited by the arbitral tribunal to produce documents, exhibits or other
   evidence, fails to do so within the established period of time, without showing sufficient
   cause for such failure, the arbitral tribunal may make the award on the evidence before it.

Where there is no default clause in the relevant rules of arbitration, it is sensible to include
one in the arbitration clause.

(ix) Language

It is both customary and logical for the language of the arbitration to be the language of the   **2.94**
contract. This will be the usual position in an institutional arbitration, although the arbitral
tribunal usually has discretion to direct that other languages may be used or that documents may be admitted in their original language without the need for a translation. Thus,
by way of notable example, Article 20 of the ICC Rules expressly provides that, '[i]n the absence of an agreement by the parties, the arbitral tribunal shall determine the language or
languages of the arbitration, due regard being given to all relevant circumstances, including
the language of the contract'.

Sometimes, a contract is made in two languages, each to be of equal authenticity. In such   **2.95**
cases, an attempt should be made to agree a single language for the arbitration as simultaneous interpretation at the hearing and bilingual transcripts greatly increase costs. However,
it is often the case that the very reason the contract is in two languages is because the parties
speak different languages and have each required a version in their own language. As such,
they are unlikely to renounce their right to proceed in their own language.[144]

---

[144] This is particularly the case with sovereign states or state entities who may be required to operate in the
official language of the state when engaging in international proceedings as far as permitted by the applicable rules.

(x) Multi-tier clauses

2.96 Multi-tier dispute resolution clauses have already been described in Chapter 1. The evidence suggests that they are increasingly used, particularly in long-term contracts, such as construction contracts, where it is important that any disputes should be resolved as quickly as possible and without holding up work under the contract.[145] In pursuance of this objective, procedures have been developed which often produce more tiers than can be found on a modest wedding cake. There may, for instance, be a provision for 'mandatory discussions' which obliges the parties' senior management to talk to each other in order to try to reach a settlement of their dispute. In case this fails, there will then be a provision for some form of Alternative Dispute Resolution (ADR). This may involve, for example, 'early neutral evaluation', whereby an expert is appointed to give an opinion on the dispute which may lead to a settlement. Additionally, or alternatively, there may be provision for the dispute to be referred to mediation, in which a skilled mediator will consider the parties' arguments, discuss the position with them, and endeavour to persuade them to agree to settle their dispute. If this fails, there is generally a provision for the dispute to be referred to arbitration which, unlike mediation, will result in a binding decision.

2.97 This is the key point. Parties are rightly being encouraged to insert dispute resolution procedures into their commercial agreements, particularly for those involving large construction and engineering projects. These will almost inevitably involve some form of ADR, whether it is expert evaluation, mediation, or an interim decision by a Dispute Resolution Board or a Panel of Experts (as in the contract for the construction of the Channel Tunnel between France and England). However, in case a mediation does not succeed, or a party is dissatisfied with the decision of a Dispute Resolution Board, a Panel of Experts, or some other interim adjudicator, there should be provision for final recourse to arbitration. This means that, if necessary, the parties will be able to obtain a final and binding decision on their dispute or disputes by a tribunal that will not be operating under the constraint of being obliged to issue a rapid, interim decision in order to enable work or the flow of supplies to continue.

2.98 To be enforceable, a contractual clause must be reasonably certain. Some ADR clauses have failed this test. In *Tang Chung Wah*,[146] for example, the English High Court refused to enforce a multi-tier clause on the basis that it was 'too equivocal' and 'too nebulous', and contained no 'guidance as to the quality or nature of the attempts to be made to resolve a dispute'.[147] The Swiss courts adopted a similar approach in *X GmbH*,[148] in which the multi-tier clause did not provide any procedural framework for negotiations and did not prescribe a time limit for the initiation of conciliation proceedings.

---

[145] For an expert discussion on multi-tier clauses in international arbitration, see Jenkins, *International Construction Arbitration Law* (3rd edn, Wolters Kluwer, 2021), particularly chs 3 and 5.

[146] *Tang Chung Wah v Grant Thornton International Ltd* [2013] All ER (Comm) 1226. In contrast, in the recent case of *Emirates Trading Agency LLC v Prime Mineral Exports Private Ltd* [2014] EWHC 2104, the English High Court upheld a multi-tier clause that required the parties to seek to resolve any dispute by 'friendly discussion' before referring such dispute to arbitration. The Court's rationale was that the clause was sufficiently certain and complete to be enforceable in that the obligation in question was time-limited, and there was an implied and well-defined standard of good faith by which to judge compliance with it (that is, fair, honest, and genuine discussions).

[147] *Tang Chung Wah*, at [72].

[148] See the decision of the Swiss Federal Tribunal in *X GmbH v Y Sàrl*, Decision No. 4A_46/2011, 16 May 2011.

Courts in other jurisdictions are more readily prepared to give effect to an agreement to   **2.99**
engage in a non-binding ADR process. The Australian courts, for instance, consider that
an agreement to negotiate in good faith entails an undertaking to behave in a particular
manner and is therefore more than a mere 'agreement to agree'.[149] Similarly, the Singapore
High Court has held that a bare agreement to mediate is valid and enforceable, referring to
the traditional Asian value of promoting friendly negotiations and settlement whenever
possible.[150]

Irrespective of the applicable law, care should always be taken when drafting multi-tier   **2.100**
clauses to define the ADR procedure clearly (for example stipulating a specific time period,
such as thirty days, for negotiations between senior management), along with the parties'
respective obligations.[151]

(xi) Sole option clauses

Under 'sole option', or 'unilateral option' clauses, one party has a choice as to whether to   **2.101**
bring a claim in a specified forum other than the dispute resolution forum that binds the
other party.

The English courts have consistently ruled that sole option clauses are valid and enforceable   **2.102**
under English law. In *Law Debenture Trust*,[152] the relevant legal instruments provided that
disputes would be resolved by the English courts but the bondholders would have the right
to refer a claim to arbitration if they so wished. The court said that it was not correct to argue
that the provisions of such a clause 'are somehow less than even handed in any relevant way.
They give an additional advantage to one party, but so do many contractual provisions.'[153] It
may be thought that when a clause in a contract is concerned with access to justice, whether
that of a court or of an arbitral tribunal, it should *not* give an additional advantage to one
party: access to justice would seem to merit a level playing field. Nevertheless, courts in
other jurisdictions have ruled that sole option clauses are valid and enforceable under their
domestic laws.[154]

---

[149] See, e.g., *Hooper Bailie Associated v Natcon Group Pty* (1992) 28 NSWLR 206, in which the Supreme Court
of New South Wales stated that what was enforced was not cooperation and consent, but participation in a process from which cooperation and consent might come. See also *United Group Rail Services v Rail Corporation New
South Wales* [2002] CLC 1324.

[150] *International Research Corporation Plc v Lufthansa Systems Asia Pacific Pte Ltd* [2012] SGHC 226. See also
the Model Law on International Commercial Conciliation, Art. 13 which states that courts and tribunals must give
effect to agreements to attempt conciliation pre-arbitration.

[151] See, e.g., *International Research Corp PLC v Lufthansa Systems Asia Pacific Pte Ltd and anor* [2013] SGCA 55,
in which the Singapore Court of Appeal held that the requirements of a multi-tiered dispute resolution mechanism
had not been complied with, because the parties held only 'random meetings' that did not involve 'the precise
persons required'. See also *Asghar v Legal Services Commission* [2004] EWHC 1803, [2004] Arb LR 43; Stockholm
Institute, Interim Award of 17 July 1992 (1997) XXII YBCA 197, 201; Swiss Federal Tribunal decision of 6 June
2007 (2008) 1 ASA Bulletin 87, discussed in Boog, 'How to deal with multi-tiered dispute resolution clauses: Note
on the Swiss Federal Supreme Court's Decision 4A_18/2007 of 6 June 2007' (2008) 26 ASA Bulletin 103.

[152] *Law Debenture Trust Corporation plc v Elektrim Finance BV* [2005] EWHC 1412 (Ch). See also *NB Three
Shipping Ltd v Harebell Shipping Ltd* [2005] 1 Lloyd's Rep 205.

[153] *Law Debenture Trust*, at [44].

[154] In the United States, see, e.g., *DiMercurio v Sphere Drake Insurance plc* 202 F.3d 71 (1st Cir. 2000); in Italy, see
Astengo v Comune di Genova, Judgment No. 2096, Corte di Cassazione, 22 October 1970; in Singapore, see *Wilson
Taylor Asia Pacific Pte Ltd v Dyna-Jet Pte Ltd* [2017] SGCA 32; in Australia, see *PMT Partners Pty Ltd v Australian
National Parks & Wildlife Service* (1995) 184 CLR 302; in Egypt, see the Court of Cassation Judgment dated 19
April 2017, Docket No. 15530 of Judicial Year 85.

2.103   In France, for example, a sole option clause is valid and enforceable so long as it either identifies the additional forum to which one party may refer a dispute or, in the alternative, specifies criteria by which such forum can be objectively determined.[155]

2.104   In Russia, however, sole option clauses have been held to be unenforceable. In *Russian Telephone Co.*[156] and *Emerging Markets Structured Products*,[157] the Presidium of the Supreme Arbitrazh Court held that arbitration agreements that gave one party the sole option to refer disputes to the courts instead of arbitration violated the principle of procedural equality between litigating parties. Different consequences, however, followed in each case. In the former case, the Court construed the clause so that *both* parties had the choice to either arbitrate or litigate.[158] In the latter case, the Court held that the dispute resolution clause in its entirety was invalid. In the light of these contrasting approaches, the Presidium of the Supreme Arbitrazh Court took the opportunity to clarify the issue in 2018, determining that sole option clauses violate the principle of procedural equality, and as a consequence each party should be deemed to have the same rights to choose the forum agreed in such a clause.[159]

(xii)   Other procedural matters

2.105   In general, other procedural matters only need to be covered in a clause providing for ad hoc arbitration, or where the parties wish to deviate in certain respects from the rules that they have adopted in their arbitration clause. An example is where the parties adopt the UNCITRAL Rules, but wish the presiding arbitrator to make an award as if he or she were sole arbitrator in the event that a majority award is not possible.[160]

2.106   The parties may also wish to confer special powers on the arbitral tribunal that do not normally exist under the law governing the arbitration or under the rules of the relevant arbitral institution, if any.[161] These additional powers may enable the arbitral tribunal to

---

[155]   In *eBizcuss.com v Apple Sales international, Apple Inc. and Apple Retail France* (Cass. Civ. (1ere Ch. Civ.), 7 October 2015, Case No. 14-16.898), the parties' dispute resolution clause provided that 'the parties shall submit to the jurisdiction of the courts of the Republic of Ireland' subject to Apple's 'right to institute proceedings against [eBizcuss] in the courts having jurisdiction in the place where [eBizcuss] has its seat or any jurisdiction where a harm to Apple is occurring'. The cour de cassation held that the clause was valid and enforceable, on the basis that it satisfied the principle of legal predictability given that the courts which ultimately could be seised of a dispute could be identified. See, by contrast, *SCI Saint-Joseph v Dexia banque international* (Cass. Civ. (1ere Ch. Civ.), 3 October 2018, Case No. 17-21.309), in which a dispute resolution clause provided that disputes would be referred to the courts of Luxembourg, subject to the right of Dexia to choose another forum. The cour de cassation held that the clause was invalid, on the basis that the clause did not specify the alternative fora or provide specific, objective criteria by which such potential alternative fora could be ascertained.

[156]   *Russian Telephone Company CJSC v Sony Ericsson Mobile Communications Rus*, Case No. A40-49223/ 11-112-401, 19 June 2012.

[157]   *Emerging Markets Structured Products B.V. v Zhilindustriya LLC and others*, Case No. A40-125181/2013, 14 March 2016.

[158]   The Court did not address the validity of the arbitration agreement as such, but instead based its decision on the jurisprudence of the Russian Constitutional Court and the European Court of Human Rights (ECtHR) concerning the right to a fair trial and the opportunity to present one's case.

[159]   Digest of Cases Related to the Functions of Assistance and Control in Relation to Arbitration and International Commercial Arbitration (Обзор практики рассмотрения судами дел, связанных с выполнением функций содействия и контроля в отношении третейских судов и международных коммерческих арбитражей), 26 December 2018, p. 13. The Digest does not formally have precedential value in the Russian system, but nevertheless is considered to provide useful guidance as to the approach Russian courts may take.

[160]   See the UNCITRAL Rules, Art. 33; only in relation to questions of procedure may the presiding arbitrator decide on his or her own in the absence of a majority.

[161]   For the powers of an arbitral tribunal, see Chapter 5.

grant remedies that otherwise might not be available under the applicable law. For example, power may be given to order a party to provide security in relation to an amount in dispute, either by paying it into a special account established in the name of the arbitral tribunal or into some other blocked escrow account.[162]

(b) Separability

The concept of the separability of the arbitration clause[163] is a convenient fiction, which is both interesting in theory and useful in practice.[164] It means that the arbitration clause in a contract (unlike any other clause) is treated as being independent of the main contract of which (like the other clauses) it forms part and so it survives the termination of that contract. Indeed, it would be self-defeating if a breach of the main contract or a claim that it was void or voidable was sufficient to terminate the arbitration clause as well. This is the type of situation in which the arbitration clause is most needed.

2.107

The concept of the 'separability' of an arbitration clause thus ensures that if, for example, one party claims that there has been a total breach of contract by the other, that contract is not destroyed for all purposes. Instead, in the words of a classic authority on the subject:

2.108

> It survives for the purpose of measuring the claims arising out of the breach, and the arbitration clause survives for determining the mode of their settlement. The purposes of the contract have failed, but the arbitration clause is not one of the purposes of the contract.[165]

A better (and non-fictitious) way of analysing the position is that there are, in fact, two separate contracts. There is the primary, or main contract, which sets out the financial or commercial obligations of the parties; and there is a secondary, or collateral, contract which contains the obligation to resolve by arbitration any disputes arising from that commercial relationship. This secondary contract may never come into operation but if it does, it will form the basis for the appointment of an arbitral tribunal and for the resolution of any dispute arising out of the main contract.

2.109

The doctrine of separability is endorsed by institutional and international rules of arbitration, such as those of UNCITRAL, which state in the context of pleas as to the jurisdiction of an arbitral tribunal that 'an arbitration clause that forms part of a contract shall be treated as an agreement independent of the other terms of the contract'.[166] Following the provisions of the UNCITRAL Rules, Article 16(1) of the Model Law provides that:

2.110

> The arbitral tribunal may rule on its own jurisdiction, including any objections with respect to the existence or validity of the arbitration agreement. For that purpose, an arbitration clause which forms part of a contract shall be treated as an agreement independent of

---

[162] Such an express power is contained, e.g., in the LCIA Rules, Art. 25.1.i.

[163] This concept is known in some systems of law as the autonomy of the arbitration clause (*l'autonomie de la clause compromissoire*).

[164] See Paulsson, 'Separability demystified', in *The Idea of Arbitration* (Oxford University Press, 2013), ch. 3, sec. 1(c).

[165] *Heyman v Darwins Ltd* [1942] AC 356, at 374 *per* Lord MacMillan.

[166] UNCITRAL Rules, Art. 23.1.

the other terms of the contract. A decision by the arbitral tribunal that the contract is null and void shall not entail *ipso jure* the invalidity of the arbitration clause.

2.111 Similarly, Article 23.2 of the LCIA Rules stipulates that, for the purpose of a ruling on jurisdiction:

> [A]n arbitration clause which forms or was intended to form part of another agreement shall be treated as an arbitration agreement independent of that other agreement. A decision by the Arbitral Tribunal that such other agreement is non-existent, invalid or ineffective shall not entail *(of itself)* the non-existence, invalidity or ineffectiveness of the arbitration clause.[167]

2.112 In the *Gosset* case,[168] the French Court of Cassation recognised the doctrine of separability in very broad terms, as follows:

> In international arbitration, the agreement to arbitrate, whether concluded separately or included in the contract to which it relates, is always save in exceptional circumstances [...] completely autonomous in law, which excludes the possibility of it being affected by the possible invalidity of the main contract.

2.113 Five years later, the US Supreme Court also recognised the separability of the arbitration clause in the *Prima Paint* case,[169] and modern laws on arbitration confirm the concept. Swiss law, for example, provides that '[t]he validity of an arbitration agreement cannot be contested on the ground that the main contract may not be valid'.[170]

2.114 More recently, the Chinese courts have also accepted that:

> Where the main contract is not concluded (null) or does not come into effect after conclusion (void), it will not influence the effect of the arbitration clause agreed by the parties, as the arbitration clause is completely separable from the main contract.[171]

2.115 An increasing number of countries[172] have made their position clear by making the separability of the arbitration clause part of their laws on arbitration.[173] Inversely,

---

[167] See also ICC Rules, Art. 6.9 (emphasis added).

[168] Cass. Civ. 1ere, 7 May 1963 (Dalloz, 1963), 545.

[169] *Prima Paint Co. v Flood Conklin Manufacturing Corporation* 388 US 395, 402 (1967). In *Buckeye Check Cashing Inc. v John Cardegna et al.*, 126 S.Ct. 1204 (2006), the US Supreme Court confirmed that the *Prima Paint* separability rule applies equally in state and federal courts. For discussion of the doctrine in the United States, see McDougall and Ioannou, 'Separability saved: U.S. Supreme Court eliminates threat to international arbitration' (2006) 21 Mealey's Intl Arb Rep 15; Samuel, 'Separability and the U.S. Supreme Court decision in *Buckeye v Cardegna*' (2006) 22 Arb Intl 477. See also *Preston v Ferrer* 552 US 346 (2008); *Nitro-Lift Technologies v Howard* 568 US 17 (2012). See also the Forced Arbitration Injustice Repeal Act of 2019, which was referred to the US Senate in September 2019 after passage in the House of Representatives. At the time of writing, it is before the Senate Judiciary Committee. The Act proposes to abolish the presumption of separability in the case of employment, consumer, antitrust, and civil rights disputes.

[170] Swiss Private International Law Act, s. 178(3).

[171] *Interpretation on Certain Issues Relating to the Application of the PRC Arbitration Law*, Supreme People's Court, 23 August 2006; *Jiangsu Materials Group Light Industry and Weaving Co. v Hong Kong Top-Capital Holdings Ltd (Canada) & Prince Development Ltd* (the *Yuyi* case), Supreme People's Court, 1998. The courts of the Dominican Republic and the United Arab Emirates have also upheld the doctrine of separability: see *Bratex Dominicana, C por A v Vanity Fair Inc.*, Supreme Court of Justice of the Dominican Republic, 31 May 2005; Petition No. 353 of 2011, Abu Dhabi Court of Cassation, 24 August 2011.

[172] For instance, the Netherlands, in the Arbitration Act 1986, s. 1053; England, in the Arbitration Act 1996, s. 7; India, in the Arbitration and Conciliation Act 1996, s. 16; Brazil, in the Brazilian Arbitration Act of 1996, s. 8; and states that either adopt the Model Law or adapt their legislation to it.

[173] See Marrella, 'International business law and international commercial arbitration: The Italian approach' [1997] ADRLJ 25; Rogers and Launders, 'Separability: The indestructible arbitration clause' (1994) 10 Arb Intl 71; Svernlou, 'What isn't, ain't: The current status of the doctrine of separability' (1991) 8 J Intl Arb 37.

the number of states in which the concept has not yet been accepted is now much diminished.[174]

An independent (or autonomous) arbitration clause thus gives the arbitral tri-bunal a basis on which to decide on its own jurisdiction, even if it is alleged that the main contract has been terminated by performance or by some intervening event. Some laws and rules go further, to establish that the arbitration clause will survive even if the main contract that contains it proves to be null and void.[175] However, this must depend on the reason for which the contract is found to be null and void (that is, is it a reason that will also affect the 'separate' arbitration agreement?), and whether it is void *ab initio*.   **2.116**

While the doctrine of separability is now accepted in principle in all developed arbitral jurisdictions, application of the doctrine continues to vary (even within jurisdictions) in circumstances in which the main contract is argued never to have come into exist-ence at all.   **2.117**

By way of example, section 7 of the English Arbitration Act 1996 provides that an ar-bitration agreement contained in another agreement 'shall not be regarded as invalid, non-existent or ineffective because that other agreement [...] *did not come into exist-ence*'.[176] The doctrine received approval and confirmation by the English courts in *Fiona Trust*,[177] in which the House of Lords (now the UK Supreme Court), confirming the de-cision of the Court of Appeal, held that the arbitrators, not the courts, should determine whether the underlying contract was void for illegality, unless the illegality was directed at the arbitration clause in particular.[178] By way of comparison, the courts in China also regularly apply the principle in accordance with international practice.[179]   **2.118**

It will be appreciated from what has been said that there is a direct connection between the autonomy of the arbitration clause and the power (or competence) of an arbitral tri-bunal to decide upon its own jurisdiction (or competence). This power (that of 'compe-tence/competence', as it is sometimes known) is discussed in Chapter 5, which deals with jurisdiction and other issues.   **2.119**

---

[174] Even by the late 1980s, this number had already grown small. See Sanders, 'Arbitration', in Cappelletti (ed.) *Encyclopedia of International and Comparative Law, Vol. XVI* (Brill, 1987), ch. 12, paras 106–112.

[175] The UNCITRAL Rules, Art. 23.1 states that a decision by the arbitral tribunal that the contract is null and void 'shall not entail automatically the invalidity of the arbitration clause' and, as has been seen, the Model Law it-self adopts this terminology, in Art. 16(1).

[176] Emphasis added. The doctrine was not recognised by the English courts until 1993, in *Harbour Assurance Co. Ltd v Kansa General International Insurance Co. Ltd* [1993] 1 Lloyd's Rep 455.

[177] *Fiona Trust & Holding Corporation v Yuri Privalov* [2007] UKHL 40.

[178] See Altras, 'Bribery and separability: Who decides, the tribunal or the courts? *Fiona Trust & Holding Corp v Yuri Privalov*' (2007) 73 Arbitration 2; Merkin, 'Separability and illegality in arbitration' (2007) 17 Arb LM 1; Pengelley, 'Separability revisited: Arbitration clauses and bribery—*Fiona Trust & Holding Corp v Privalov*' (2007) 24 J Intl Arb 445; *Lesotho Highlands Development Authority v Impregilo SpA* [2005] UKHL 43, [2005] Arb LR 557, in particular the judgment of Lord Steyn. See also *Beijing Jianlong Heavy Industry Group v Golden Ocean Group Ltd* [2013] EWHC 1063 (Comm), in which the English High Court discussed the relevance of public policy consider-ations when examining the validity of an arbitration agreement.

[179] Arbitration Law of the People's Republic of China, s. 19; CIETAC Rules, Art. 5.4. See Wexia, 'China's search for complete separability of the arbitral agreement' (2007) 3 Asian Intl Arb J 163; Yeoh and Fu, 'The people's courts and arbitration: A snapshot of recent and judicial attitudes on arbitrability and enforcement' (2007) 24 J Intl Arb 635, at 638.

(c) Summary

2.120   As already stated, most arbitrations take place pursuant to an arbitration clause in a 'contract'. Where the parties include the model clause recommended by a particular arbitral institution, any dispute between them will be submitted to arbitration under the rules of that institution. Where the parties decide that the services of an arbitral institution are unlikely to be required, but that they would nevertheless like to adopt an existing set of rules, they should incorporate the recommended UNCITRAL arbitration clause into the contract.

2.121   Where such arbitration clauses are adopted, most national courts will recognise and give effect to the parties' wishes to arbitrate any disputes between them. These model clauses bring with them a set of rules that are self-sufficient, and which should be enough to guide the arbitral tribunal and the parties from the beginning to the end of the arbitral process.

2.122   Nonetheless, it would be advisable to add to the model clause at least three of the basic elements of an arbitration agreement discussed—namely, the number of arbitrators, the place of arbitration, and the governing law of the contract. It may also be, or may become, necessary to identify the law governing the arbitration agreement.[180]

2.123   If the parties do not require the services of an arbitral institution and do not wish to adopt the UNCITRAL Rules, a simple submission to arbitration—adapted from one of the model clauses—would be sufficient in theory. In practice, however, it is sensible not only to provide for the number of arbitrators, the place of arbitration, and the governing law, but also to consider such provisions as those relating to the establishment of the arbitral tribunal, the filling of vacancies, and the failure or refusal of a party to take part in the arbitration.

2.124   That the parties have agreed in their arbitration clause to an arbitration under institutional rules does not prevent them from agreeing, when a dispute has arisen, to a different method of resolving the dispute. Thus they may switch from, say, an ICC arbitration to an ad hoc arbitration or vice versa—but if they do so, a new arbitration agreement should be made, submitting the existing dispute (by way of submission agreement) to arbitration.[181]

E. Arbitrability

(a) Introduction

2.125   As already stated, arbitrability, in the sense in which it is used in this book,[182] involves determining which types of dispute may be resolved by arbitration and which belong

---

[180]   See the discussion in Chapter 3, paragraphs 3.07*ff.*

[181]   See paragraphs 2.05–2.07, above, regarding submission agreements.

[182]   In the United States and some other jurisdictions, there is sometimes discussion by judges and others as to whether a particular dispute is 'arbitrable', in the sense that it falls within the scope of the arbitration agreement. The concern in such cases is with the court's jurisdiction over a particular dispute rather than a more general enquiry as to whether the dispute is of the type that comes within the domain of arbitration. See Zekos, 'Courts' intervention in commercial and maritime arbitration under US law' (1997) 14 J Intl Arb 99. For a general discussion of 'arbitrability' in the sense of 'legally capable of settlement by arbitration', see Sanders, 'The domain of arbitration', in Cappelletti (ed.) *Encyclopedia of International and Comparative Law, Vol. XVI* (Brill, 1987), ch. 12, pp. 113*ff;* see also Hanotiau, 'The law applicable to arbitrability' (1998) 9 ICCA Congress Series 146.

exclusively to the domain of the courts. Both the New York Convention and the Model Law are limited to disputes that are 'capable of settlement by arbitration'.[183] What the authors propose to do in this section is to look at the way in which courts in different jurisdictions apply the concept; and then to look at the various categories of disputes in which the concept may arise.

In principle, *any* dispute should be just as capable of being resolved by a private arbitral tribunal as by the judge of a national court. Article 2059 of the French Civil Code, for example, provides that 'all persons may enter into arbitration agreements relating to the rights that they may freely dispose of'. Although Article 2060 further provides that parties may not agree to arbitrate disputes in a series of particular fields (such as family law) and 'more generally in all matters that have a public interest [*plus généralement dans toutes les matières qui intéressent l'ordre public*]', this limitation has been construed restrictively by French courts. Similarly, section 1 of the Brazilian Arbitration Act of 1996 (Law No. 9.307) states that parties may settle disputes through arbitration as long as the subject matter relates to freely transferable rights.[184]   **2.126**

However, it is precisely because arbitration is a private proceeding with public consequences[185] that some types of dispute are reserved for national courts, the proceedings of which are generally in the public domain. It is in this sense that they are not 'capable of settlement by arbitration'.   **2.127**

National laws establish the domain of arbitration, as opposed to that of the local courts. Each state decides which matters may or may not be resolved by arbitration in accordance with its own political, social, and economic policy. In some Arab states, for example, contracts between a foreign corporation and its local agent are given special protection by law, and, to reinforce this protection, any disputes arising out of such contracts may be resolved only by the local courts.[186] In the United States, the arbitration of certain types of dispute that engage public policy appears to be under legislative attack. At the time of writing, the Forced Arbitration Repeal Act of 2019, which has yet to be voted on in the Senate, proposes to invalidate any pre-dispute arbitration clause in relation to employment, consumer, antitrust, and civil rights disputes on the grounds that the weaker of the parties in reality has little or no meaningful choice as to whether to select arbitration.[187] The legislators and courts in each country must balance the domestic importance of reserving certain matters of public interest to the courts against the more general public interest in allowing people   **2.128**

---

[183] New York Convention, Arts II(1) and V(2)(a); Model Law, Arts 34(2)(b)(i) and 36(1)(b)(i).

[184] See also the German Code of Civil Procedure, Art. 1030(1) and (2) which provides that any claim involving an economic interest (*Vermögensrechtlicher Anspruch*) may be the subject of arbitration, as may claims involving a non-economic interest of which the parties may freely dispose.

[185] For instance, in the recognition and enforcement of the award.

[186] See also Mexico, where disputes concerning the administrative rescission of contracts entered into by a state entity are within the exclusive competence of the administrative courts. For a general discussion of restrictions on the arbitrability of disputes involving Mexican state companies, see Wöss, 'El orden público, derecho público, cosa juzgada e inarbitrabilidad en contratos públicos en México' (2012) 14 Spain Arb Rev 111.

[187] Other jurisdictions have grappled with consumer arbitration as well. Pursuant to the English Arbitration Act 1996, s. 91(1) an arbitration agreement in a consumer contract is deemed unfair under the Unfair Terms in Consumer Contracts Regulations 1999 if it relates to a claim for a pecuniary remedy that does not exceed £5,000. An arbitration agreement with a consumer may also be unenforceable under English law pursuant to the Unfair Terms in Consumer Contracts Regulations 1999. See, e.g., *Mylcrist Builders Ltd v Buck* [2008] EWHC 2172 (TCC), in which the English High Court held that an arbitration clause in a building contract was unenforceable on the basis that it caused a significant imbalance between the parties by denying the consumer access to the courts.

the freedom to arrange their private affairs as they see fit.[188] In the international sphere, the interests of promoting international trade, as well as international comity, have proven important factors in persuading the courts to treat certain types of dispute as arbitrable.[189]

2.129   If the issue of arbitrability arises, it is necessary to have regard to the relevant laws of the different states that are, or may be, concerned. These are likely to include: the law governing the party involved, where the agreement is with a state or state entity; the law governing the arbitration agreement; the law of the seat of arbitration; and the law of the ultimate place of enforcement of the award.

2.130   Whether or not a particular type of dispute is 'arbitrable' under a given law is, in essence, a matter of public policy for that law to determine. Public policy varies from one country to the next, and indeed changes over time.[190] The most that can be done here is to indicate the categories of dispute that may fall outside the domain of arbitration.

2.131   Reference has already been made in passing to contracts of agency, for which special provision may be made in some states as a matter of public policy. More generally, criminal matters and those that affect the status of an individual or a corporate entity (such as bankruptcy or insolvency) are usually considered to be non-arbitrable. In addition, disputes over the grant or validity of patents and trademarks may not be arbitrable under the applicable law. These various categories of dispute are considered in greater detail next.

(b)   Categories of dispute for which questions of arbitrability arise

(i)   Patents, trademarks, and copyright

2.132   The grant of a patent or trademark is plainly a matter for the public authorities of the state concerned, these being monopoly rights that only the state can grant. From this it has traditionally followed that any dispute as to their validity was outside the domain of arbitration. While this remains the case in many jurisdictions,[191] in recent years there appears to be a growing acceptance that such disputes are arbitrable. In the United States and in Hong Kong, by way of example, disputes regarding the validity of patents are arbitrable, and such determinations are binding as between the parties to the arbitration agreement.[192]

---

[188] See Paulsson, *The Idea of Arbitration* (Oxford University Press, 2013), in particular ch. 1 on 'The impulse to arbitrate'.

[189] See *Mitsubishi Motors Corporation v Soler Chrysler Plymouth Inc.*, 473 US 614, 105 S.Ct. 3346 (1985), discussed at paragraphs 2.137–2.138. However, the opposite is often argued in the context of less-developed countries. In that situation, it is suggested that the state should impose very strict limits on arbitrability, especially in respect of disputes involving state entities. The reason for such a policy is that this is the only way in which these states can retain control over foreign trade and investment where more economically powerful traders may have an unfair advantage. See Sornarajah, 'The UNCITRAL Model Law: A third world viewpoint' (1989) 6 J Intl Arb 7, at 16.

[190] The concept of so-called international public policy, which may impose limits on the arbitrability of certain agreements such as an agreement to pay bribes (see paragraphs 2.149–2.153) is considered in Chapter 11, in the context of challenging the recognition and enforcement of arbitral awards.

[191] In China, by way of example, the validity of patents and trademarks is a matter determined exclusively by administrative state organs and courts: see the People's Republic of China Patent Act, Art. 45; the People's Republic of China Trade Mark Act, Arts 41 and 42. See also, in respect of the EU, EC Regulation 44/2001, Art. 22(4); EC Regulation 1215/2012, Art. 24(4).

[192] United States Code, Title 35: Patents, Section 294: Voluntary Arbitration (35 U.S.C. § 294); Hong Kong Arbitration (Amendment) Ordinance 2017. See also, e.g., the Swiss Federal Office for Industrial Property Ruling of 15 December 1975, which stated that the Federal Office will execute awards dealing with intellectual property

In addition to disputes as to the validity of a patent or trademark, disputes pertaining to **2.133** the rights and obligations contained in a licence issued by the owner of such intellectual property rights to one or more corporations or individuals are commonly referred to international arbitration. The advantages offered in this regard are threefold: first, arbitration affords the parties an opportunity to select for themselves a tribunal of arbitrators experienced in such matters; secondly (and perhaps more importantly), such proceedings are confidential, which helps to provide a safeguard for trade secrets; and thirdly, arbitration avoids the difficulties that often arise in connection with the enforcement of judgments resulting from separate litigation proceedings commenced in multiple jurisdictions.[193]

Unlike patents or trademarks, copyright is an intellectual property right that exists inde- **2.134** pendently of any national or international registration and may be freely disposed of by parties. There is therefore generally no doubt that disputes relating to such private rights may be referred to international arbitration.[194]

(ii) Antitrust and competition laws

Adam Smith, writing in the eighteenth century, said: 'People of the same trade seldom **2.135** meet together, even for merriment and diversion, but the conversation ends in a conspiracy against the public, or in some contrivance to raise prices.'[195] This early distrust of monopolies and cartels finds its modern echo in increasingly wide-ranging antitrust (or competition) legislation across the world. Amongst national legislators, the United States has been prominent, beginning with the celebrated Shearman Act in 1890. Similarly, in 1958, the (then) European Community adopted rules of law that were to be directly applicable in all member states, and which prohibit agreements and arrangements having as their object or effect the prevention, restriction, or distortion of competition,[196] as well as any abuse of a dominant position,[197] within what is now the European Union. Articles 101 and 102 of the Treaty on the Functioning of the European Union (TFEU) have historically been enforced primarily by the European Commission, which has the power to investigate, to prohibit behaviours, to impose heavy fines, and also to grant exemptions pursuant to Article 101(3)

---

validity issues. See also *AJA Registrars Limited, Holding Socotec SAS v AJA Europe Limited* [2020] EWHC 883 (Ch), in which the High Court considered that an intellectual property claim could be referred to arbitration even if certain relief sought could only be granted by the Court or the UK Intellectual Property Office, on the basis that the arbitrator could direct the party to make the necessary application as part of the award, and the court would lend its assistance, if necessary. The Paris Court of Appeal has similarly ruled that an arbitral tribunal may rule on the existence of an intellectual property right, provided that this issue is incidental to the dispute and the tribunal's determination will have effect only as between the parties: see *Liv Hidravlika v Diebolt*, Paris cour d'appel, 28 February 2008, Case No. 05-10577.

[193] See generally Lew, *Intellectual Property Disputes and Arbitration: Final Report of the Commission on International Arbitration* (ICC, 1997), esp. pp. 7–15; De Werra 'Arbitrating international intellectual property disputes: Time to think beyond the issue of (non-)arbitrability' (2012) 3 International Business Law Journal 299. For a comparative overview of states' approaches to intellectual property-related arbitration, see Hanotiau, 'L'arbitrabilité des litiges de propriété intellectuelle', in de Werra and Pauwelyn (eds) *La Resolution de Litiges de Propriété Intellectuelle* (Schulthess, 2010).

[194] In *Desputeaux v Éditions Chouette (1987) Inc.* [2003] 1 SCR 178, the Supreme Court of Canada confirmed that disputes over copyright ownership are arbitrable. The Court stated that although a creative work is a manifestation of the personality of the author, 'this issue is very far removed from questions relating to the status and capacity of persons and to family matters': ibid., at 181.

[195] Smith, *The Wealth of Nations* (Methuen, 1776), Bk 1, ch. 10, pt. 2.

[196] Article 101 TFEU.

[197] Article 102 TFEU.

TFEU where appropriate in light of the wider benefits of the activity or agreement that infringes Article 101.[198]

2.136   What can an arbitral tribunal do when confronted with an allegation that the contract under which the arbitration is brought is itself an illegal restraint of trade, or in some other way a breach of antitrust law? For example, in disputes between the licensor of a patent and the licensee, it has become almost standard practice for the licensor to allege (amongst a series of defences) that, in any event, the licence agreement is void for illegality. In general, an allegation of illegality should not prevent an arbitral tribunal from adjudicating on the dispute even if its finding is that the agreement in question is indeed void for illegality. This is because, under the doctrine of separability,[199] the arbitration clause in a contract constitutes a separate agreement and survives the contract of which it forms part. More specifically, it is now widely accepted that antitrust issues are arbitrable. In France, the arbitrability of competition law issues is well established, having been acknowledged in the *Mors/Labinal* case in 1993[200] and reaffirmed by the Court of Cassation in 1999.[201] Likewise, in Switzerland, the arbitrability of EU competition law was recognised by a decision of the Federal Tribunal in 1992,[202] in which the Tribunal found that '[n]either Article 85 of the [EU] Treaty nor Regulation 17 on its application forbids a national court or an arbitral tribunal to examine the validity of that contract'.

2.137   The US Supreme Court had already adopted this approach in the well-known *Mitsubishi* case.[203] At one time, it was held in the United States that claims under the antitrust laws were not capable of being resolved by arbitration, but had to be referred to the courts. In the *American Safety* case,[204] the reaction of the court was that:

> A claim under the antitrust laws is not merely a private matter [...] Antitrust violation can affect hundreds of thousands, perhaps millions, of people and inflict staggering economic damage. We do not believe Congress intended such claims to be resolved elsewhere than the Courts.[205]

---

[198] Agreements that offend against Art. 101 are void under Art. 101(2), unless an exemption is granted under Art. 101(3). Until 1 May 2004, the power to grant exemptions fell to the European Commission alone. Since then, pursuant to Council Regulation (EC) No. 1/2003 of 16 December 2002 on the implementation of the rules on competition laid down in Arts 81 and 82 of the Treaty, OJ L 1/4, 4 January 2003, the power has been extended to national courts and competition authorities. Although the Regulation does not mention arbitral tribunals specifically, it changed the landscape of EU competition law and opened the door to arbitration as an arena for the private enforcement of EU competition rules. In this regard, see Dempegiotis, 'EC competition law and international arbitration in the light of EC Regulation 1/2003: Conceptual conflicts, common ground and corresponding legal issues' (2008) 25 J Intl Arb 365.

[199] Under this doctrine, the arbitration clause in a contract is regarded as separate from, and independent of, the contract of which it forms part: see paragraph 2.107.

[200] See the decision of the Paris Court of Appeal of 19 May 1993, [1993] Rev Arb 645, n. Jarrosson.

[201] See the decision of the cour de cassation of 5 January 1999.

[202] Decision of the Tribunal Fédéral, 28 April 1992, [1992] ASA Bulletin 368. The same court reaffirmed this position in its decision of 13 November 1998, [1999] ASA Bulletin 529 and 455. The English courts have also held that 'there is no realistic doubt that such "competition" and "antitrust" claims are arbitrable': see *ET Plus SA v Jean Paul Welter & The Channel Tunnel Group* [2005] EWHC 2115 (Comm). However, merger control and state aid issues are within the exclusive competence of the European Commission and parties cannot agree to settle such issues by arbitration: see Blanke, 'The application of EU law to arbitration in England', in Lew, Bor, Fullelove, and Greenaway (eds) *Arbitration in England, with Chapters on Scotland and Ireland* (Kluwer Law International, 2013), p. 249.

[203] *Mitsubishi Motors Corporation v Soler Chrysler Plymouth Inc.*, 473 US 614, 105 S.Ct. 3346 (1985). And see generally Institute of International Business Law and Practice, *Competition and Arbitration* (ICC, 1993).

[204] *American Safety Equipment Corporation v JP Maguire Co.*, 391 F.2d 821 (2d Cir. 1968).

[205] Ibid., at 826.

However, in *Mitsubishi*, the US Supreme Court decided, by a majority of five to three, that   **2.138**
antitrust issues arising out of international contracts were arbitrable under the Federal
Arbitration Act. This was so despite the public importance of the antitrust laws, the significance of private parties seeking treble damages as a disincentive to violation of those laws,
and the complexity of such cases. In its judgment, the Court stated:

> [W]e conclude that concerns of international comity, respect for the capacities of foreign
> and transnational tribunals and sensitivity to the need of the international commercial
> system for predictability in the resolution of disputes require that we enforce the parties'
> agreement, even assuming that a contrary result would be forthcoming in a domestic
> context.[206]

The Court went on to point out that the public interest in the enforcement of antitrust legislation could be asserted, if necessary, when it came to enforcement of any award made by
the arbitral tribunal. It stated that:

> Having permitted the arbitration to go forward, the national courts of the United States will
> have the opportunity at the award enforcement stage to ensure that the legitimate interest
> in the enforcement of the antitrust laws has been addressed. The [New York Convention]
> reserves to each signatory country the right to refuse enforcement of an award where the
> 'recognition or enforcement of the award would be contrary to a public policy of that
> country'.[207]

In this way, rather than question whether antitrust issues are arbitrable, later decisions   **2.139**
tend to focus—at least in the European Union and United States—on the extent of a state
court's power to review arbitral awards in relation to disputes that raise competition issues.
In its landmark decision in *Eco Swiss China Time Ltd v Benetton International NV*,[208] the
European Court of Justice (ECJ) identified Article 81 of the EU Treaty (now Article 101
TFEU) as a matter of public policy that would justify the annulment or refusal of enforcement of an award that ignores it. In the context of a challenge to an award that gave effect
to a licence agreement that was alleged, only after the award had been rendered, to violate
Article 81 of the EU Treaty, the ECJ ruled that:

> [A] national court to which application is made for annulment of an arbitration award
> must grant that application if it considers that the award in question is in fact contrary to
> Article 85 of the Treaty [now Article 81 TEU], where its domestic rules of procedure re-
> quire it to grant an application for annulment founded on failure to observe national rules
> of public policy.[209]

Although, in *Eco Swiss*, the ECJ did not explicitly rule on whether arbitrators have a   **2.140**
duty to apply Article 81 EC *ex officio* if the parties themselves made no reference to it,
this decision is generally seen—at the very least—as implying that arbitrators should

---

[206] *Mitsubishi Motors*, at 629.
[207] *Mitsubishi Motors*, at 628. However, see *Baxter International v Abbott Laboratories*, 315 F.3d 163 (2d Cir.
2004), in which the US Court's 'second look' was very limited in scope. In that case, the US Supreme Court limited
its review to ensuring only that 'the tribunal took cognizance of antitrust claims and actually decided them'.
[208] *Eco Swiss China Time Ltd v Benetton International NV*, Case C-126/97 [1999] ECR I–3079, (1999) XXIV
YBCA 629.
[209] Ibid., at [41]. The decision arose from a preliminary reference made to the ECJ under Art. 234 TEU (ex Art.
177 EC) by the Supreme Court of the Netherlands.

do so or risk the annulment of their award on grounds of a violation of public policy.[210] However, some uncertainty remains as to how serious the alleged violation of competition law must be in order to justify the annulment of an award. The view that has historically prevailed is that a 'minimalist' standard of review—under which only a 'flagrant, effective and concrete' violation of public policy justifies the annulment of an award— is appropriate,[211] although recent cases have shown a willingness to depart from this approach.[212]

(iii) Securities transactions

2.141 Prior to its landmark decision in *Mitsubishi*, the US Supreme Court had held in 1953 that disputes under the Securities Act were not arbitrable.[213] In 1974, however, the Court held that such disputes *were* arbitrable in an international commercial arbitration. The case was *Scherk v Alberto-Culver*,[214] in which the Supreme Court said that a 'parochial refusal by the courts of one country to enforce an international arbitration agreement' would not only frustrate the purpose of the agreement, but also 'damage the fabric of international commerce and trade and imperil the willingness and ability of businessmen to enter into international commercial agreements'.[215] In subsequent cases, the Court went on to accept the arbitrability of securities disputes in US domestic arbitration.[216]

2.142 Some other national securities laws, existing as they do to protect vulnerable consumers, still restrict the resolution of some disputes thereunder to the national courts. By way of example, German securities legislation expressly restricts the availability of arbitration for such disputes to commercial cases in which both parties are established businesses or companies.[217]

---

[210] See Pinsolle, 'Note on Cass. Civ. 1ere, 6 July 2005' (2005) 4 Rev Arb 8; Dempegiotis, 'EC competition law and international arbitration in the light of EC Regulation 1/2003: Conceptual conflicts, common ground and corresponding legal issues' (2008) 25 J Intl Arb 365, at 380–386. The Organisation for Economic Co-operation and Development (OECD) has also adopted this view: see OECD, *Hearing Report on Arbitration and Competition* (13 December 2011), p. 12.

[211] *Thalès Air Défence v Euromissile*, Case No. 2002/60932, 18 November 2004. This so-called minimalist approach has also been adopted by courts in Switzerland, in *Tensacciai SpA v Freyssinet Terra Armata Srl*, Case No. 4P_278/2005, Swiss Federal Tribunal, 8 March 2006; in New Zealand, in *Attorney-General v Mobil Oil NZ Ltd*, High Court, Wellington, 1 July 1987; in the United States, in *American Central Eastern Texas Gas Co. v Union Pacific Resources Group*, 2004 US App LEXIS 1216; and in Sweden, in *Republic of Latvia v Latvijas Gaze*, Svea Court of Appeal, 4 May 2005.

[212] In the *Genentech* case, the Advocate General of the CJEU observed that the minimalist approach was 'contrary to the principle of effectiveness of EU law': *Genentech Inc v Hoechst GmbH*, Case C-567/14, Opinion of Advocate General Wathelet, 17 March 2016. See also, e.g., *Marketing Displays International Inc v VR Van Raalte Reclame BV*, Court of Appeal, The Hague, Netherlands, 24 March 2005, XXXI Y.B. COM. ARB. 808 (2006); Blanke, 'The minimalist and maximalist approach to reviewing competition law awards: A neverending saga' (2007) 2 SIAR 51.

[213] *Wilko v Swan* 346 US 427 (1953). See generally McCormack, 'Recent US legal decisions on arbitration law' (1994) 11 J Intl Arb 73.

[214] *Scherk v Alberto-Culver*, 417 US 506 (1974).

[215] Ibid., at 516–517.

[216] See, e.g., *Shearson v McMahon*, 482 US 220, 107 S.Ct. 2332 (1987); *Lipcon v Underwriters at Lloyd's*, 148 F.3d 1285 (11th Cir. 1998). See also McCormack, 'Recent US legal decisions on arbitration law' (1994) 11 J Intl Arb 73; Ebenroth and Dillon, 'Arbitration clauses in international finance agreements' (1993) 10 J Intl Arb 5. In recent years, there has been a significant increase in the use of arbitration as a means of resolving disputes in this sector. In September 2013, the International Swaps and Derivatives Association, Inc. (ISDA) released its Arbitration Guide, which offers guidance on the use of arbitration clauses in the ISDA Master Agreement.

[217] German Securities Trading Act (WpHG), s. 37h.

(iv) Insolvency

Issues of arbitrability arise in respect of insolvency law as a result of the conflict between the pri-   **2.143**
vate nature of arbitration and the public-policy-driven collective procedures provided for under
national insolvency laws.[218] Courts and tribunals in various countries have sought to identify
where the boundary of arbitrability should lie, and which insolvency issues are only suitable for
resolution by a court. A distinction can be made between 'core', or 'pure' insolvency issues, which
may be inherently non-arbitrable (for example matters relating to the adjudication of the insolvency itself or the verification of creditors' claims),[219] and related circumstances that are capable
of private dispute resolution between contracting parties. The precise location of this dividing
line varies between countries and will depend in part on national insolvency laws.

In the United States, the national bankruptcy courts were traditionally reluctant to defer   **2.144**
their jurisdiction to arbitrators except in exceptional circumstances.[220] The approach now is
for the courts to look at the type of dispute before them and to determine whether there are
any core insolvency issues in play that deprive an arbitral tribunal of jurisdiction.[221]

In the European Union,[222] Regulation (EU) 2015/848 establishes a common framework for   **2.145**
insolvency proceedings.[223] The Regulation provides, inter alia, that the law of the country in
which insolvency proceedings are commenced shall determine the effect of those insolvency
proceedings on other proceedings brought by individual creditors, including arbitration
proceedings, with the exception of proceedings that are pending, which shall be determined
by the law of the member state in which the lawsuit is pending or in which the arbitral tribunal has its seat.[224]

In Switzerland, the insolvency of one of the parties will not generally affect the arbitration   **2.146**
agreement and arbitrators retain a wide jurisdiction to decide disputes relating to insolvency issues, including claims made on behalf of the estate itself.[225] German law adopts a

---

[218] See generally Lazic, *Insolvency Proceedings and Commercial Arbitration* (Wolters Kluwer, 1998), esp.
pp. 154–177.
[219] See ibid., at pp. 154–157, and see also p. 155. See also Mantilla-Serrano, 'International arbitration and insolvency proceedings' (1995) 11 Arb Intl 69; Levy, 'Insolvency in arbitration (Swiss Law)' (2005) 23 Intl Arb L Rev 28.
[220] See, e.g., *Zimmerman v Continental Airlines, Inc.*, 712 F.2d 55 (3d Cir. 1983). For a discussion of the development of the relationship between arbitration and insolvency in the United States, see Lazic, *Insolvency Proceedings
and Commercial Arbitration* (Wolters Kluwer, 1998), pp. 165–175.
[221] In *Sonatrach (Algeria) v Distrigas Corp (US District Court) Massachusetts* (1995) XX YBCA 795 the
Bankruptcy Court of Massachusetts held that the claim of damages before it did not implicate any major bankruptcy issue and therefore the dispute was arbitrable. However, in *United States Lines, Inc. et al. (US) v American
Steamship Owners Mutual Protection and Indemnity Association, Inc. et al. (US)* (2000) XXV YBCA 1057, 1065
(2d Cir., 1 November 1999), the Court of Appeal for the Second Circuit denied the arbitrability of the dispute,
which it stated was 'integral to the bankruptcy court's ability to preserve and equitably distribute the Trust's assets'.
See also *Larsen Oil and Gas Pte Ltd v Petroprod Ltd* [2010] 4 SLR 501, 501, in which the Singapore High Court
stated, in relation to claims of unfair preference and transactions at an undervalue, 'the policy underlying the
avoidance provisions [...] would be compromised if their enforcement is [*sic*] subject to private arrangements'.
[222] With the exception of Denmark, which opted out of the Regulation.
[223] Its predecessor, EC Council Regulation 1346/2000, continues to apply to insolvencies that commenced before 26 June 2017.
[224] Articles 7 and 18 of the Regulation.
[225] See the Swiss Federal Tribunal Decision No. 4A_50/2012 of 16 October 2012, in which the Tribunal revisited its decision in *Vivendi v Elektrim*, Decision No. 4A_428_2008, 31 March 2009, and held that as long as the
insolvent entity had legal personality according to the law of the place of incorporation, it was capable of being a
party to foreign arbitral proceedings. See also generally Levy, 'Insolvency in arbitration (Swiss Law)' (2005) 8 Intl
Arb L Rev 23. For a more general discussion on insolvency in international arbitration from a Swiss law perspective, see Kohler and Levy, 'Insolvency and international arbitration', in Peter and Jeandin (eds) *The Challenges of
Insolvency Law Reform in the 21st Century* (Schulthess, 2006), pp. 257–284.

similarly liberal approach to arbitrability in this context, with arbitrators generally having jurisdiction to determine disputes relating to bankruptcy proceedings other than 'pure' insolvency issues, such as the appointment of an administrator, the collection and distribution of assets, and the reorganisation of a business.[226] If a liquidator, however, exercises statutory rights to invalidate contracts entered into by the debtor prior to insolvency, the related arbitration agreements will not bind the liquidator.[227]

2.147   In Argentina, any arbitration agreement to which an insolvent company is party will automatically terminate upon the court entering a bankruptcy decree, unless the arbitral tribunal has already been constituted.[228] In Brazil, bankruptcy procedures are considered to be non-arbitrable.[229] However, a company's bankruptcy will not affect the validity of an arbitration agreement to which the company is party.[230]

2.148   Under English law, it is difficult to enforce an arbitration agreement against an insolvent party in circumstances under which the trustee in bankruptcy does not consent. The Arbitration Act 1996 introduced a specific procedure into the English Insolvency Act 1986, which allows a trustee in bankruptcy to adopt or reject an arbitration agreement. If it elects to reject the arbitration agreement, then arbitral proceedings can be brought only with the consent of the company's creditors and the court, which will look at all of the circumstances of the case to determine whether the dispute in question ought to be referred to arbitration.[231] This apparently reflects the more general rule under English law that allows a trustee to refuse to acknowledge 'unprofitable' contracts. Should the trustee elect to confirm the arbitration agreement in a particular case, it becomes binding and enforceable both by and against the trustee.

(v) Bribery and corruption

2.149   Issues of bribery or corruption in the procurement or performance of a contract raise important questions of public policy. In its final report on public policy as a bar to the enforcement of international arbitral awards, the Committee on International Arbitration of the International Law Association (ILA) reviewed the development of the concept of public policy during the latter part of the twentieth century, and concluded that there was an international consensus that corruption and bribery are contrary to international public policy.[232]

---

[226] Lazic, *Insolvency Proceedings and Commercial Arbitration* (Wolters Kluwer, 1998), pp. 163–164.

[227] See also H. Raeschke-Kessler, *The Arbitrator Nominated by an Insolvency Receiver or Liquidator and Conflicts of Interest*, 34 ASA Bulletin 4/2016 (December), pp. 867–870.

[228] Argentina's Bankruptcy Law, Art. 134. See also *Bear Service SA v Cervecería Modelo SA de CV*, Argentine Federal Supreme Court, 5 April 2005.

[229] See *Jutaí 661 Equipamentos Eletrônicos Ltda v PSI Comércio e Prestação de Serviços em Telefones Celulares Ltda*, Superior Court of Justice, 12 March 2013.

[230] See *KwikasairCargasExpressas SA—Bankrupt Estate v AIG Venture Holdings Ltd*, Special Appeal No. 1.355.831, Superior Court of Justice, 19 March 2013.

[231] See Arbitration Act 1996, s. 107 and Sch. 3; Insolvency Act 1986, s. 349A. For a discussion of issues of insolvency and arbitration in English law, see Burn and Grubb, 'Insolvency and arbitration in English law' (2005) 8 Intl Arb L Rev 124.

[232] ILA Committee on International Commercial Arbitration, *Final Report on Public Policy as a Bar to Enforcement of International Arbitral Awards* (ILA, 2002). More generally on this topic, see Sayed, *Corruption in International Trade and Commercial Arbitration* (Kluwer Law International, 2004).

What is an arbitral tribunal to do if there is a dispute as to the performance of an inter-   **2.150**
national commercial agreement and it is said, as an excuse for non-performance, that the
agreement was tainted by the payment of bribes or some other fraudulent inducement? This
issue is first known to have been raised in 1963 before a distinguished Swedish jurist, Judge
Lagergren, who was acting as sole arbitrator in ICC Arbitration No. 1110.[233]

This landmark arbitration involved a dispute as to whether an agreement entered into in   **2.151**
1950 for the payment to Mr X of a 10 per cent commission on the value of industrial equipment then required for a particular public energy project in Argentina also covered the sale
of equipment in 1958 for another similar project. Testifying before Judge Lagergren, Mr X
stated that he ceded certain 'participations' to 'influential personalities' amongst a 'clique of
people which had a controlling influence upon the Government's economic policy'.

Finding the contract to be 'condemned by public decency and morality' because it 'contem-   **2.152**
plated the bribing of Argentine officials for the purpose of obtaining the hoped-for business', Judge Lagergren declined to continue with the arbitration, finding that such a dispute
was not arbitrable and stating that the parties to such a contract had 'forfeited the right to
ask for assistance of the machinery of justice'.[234]

The modern approach (based on the concept of separability,[235] which has now received   **2.153**
widespread acceptance both nationally and internationally) is that an allegation of illegality
does not in itself deprive the arbitral tribunal of jurisdiction.[236] On the contrary, it is generally held that the arbitral tribunal is entitled to hear the arguments and receive evidence, and
to determine for itself the question of illegality.[237] Thus, in Switzerland, in a case involving
a consultancy agreement, the Swiss Federal Tribunal decided that even if a consultancy
agreement were, in effect, an agreement to pay a bribe (and this was not alleged, still less
proven), the arbitration agreement would survive.[238]

---

[233] Wetter, 'Issues of corruption before international tribunals: The authentic text and true meaning of Judge Gunnar Lagergren's 1963 Award in ICC Case No. 1110' (1994) 10 Arb Intl 277.

[234] Ibid. Early commentators on this award criticised this approach as failing to give effect to the principle of the autonomy of the arbitration clause. However, as Wetter's publication of the award thirty years later revealed, there was no such contractual arbitration clause. The dispute had been the subject of a manifestly autonomous submission agreement. Judge Lagergren's decision was founded simply on the grounds of non-arbitrability. For further discussion on this decision, see Sayed, *Corruption in International Trade and Commercial Arbitration* (Kluwer Law International, 2004), pp. 59–65.

[235] See paragraphs 2.89ff.

[236] See Kreindler, 'Aspects of illegality in the formation and performance of contracts', Presented at the 16th ICCA Congress, London, May 2002. For a more recent review by the same author, see Kreindler, 'Public policy and corruption in international arbitration: A perspective for Russian related disputes' (2006) 72 Arbitration 236. See also Kosheri and Leboulanger, 'L'arbitrage face à la corruption et aux trafics d'influence' [1984] Rev Arb 3; Lalive, 'Ordre public transnational et arbitrage international' [1986] Rev Arb 329; Oppetit, 'Le paradoxe de la corruption à l'épreuve du droit de commerce international' (1987) 114 J du Droit Intl 5, at 5–21. See also Knoepfler, 'Corruption et arbitrage international', in Cherpilled (ed.) *Les Contrats de distribution: Contributions offertesau Professor Dessemontet* (CEDIDAC, 1998), p. 371; Derains, *Les Commissions Illicites* (ICC, 1992), pp. 65–68.

[237] For example, see *Fiona Trust & Holding Corporation v Yuri Privalov* [2007] EWCA Civ 20, in which the English courts confirmed that a claim that a disputed contract was induced by bribery should be decided by the arbitrator, not the courts, unless the allegation of illegality relates to the arbitration clause itself. See also Snodgrass, *'Fiona Trust v Privalov*: The Arbitration Act 1996 Comes of Age' [2007] Intl Arb L Rev 27. For a contrary view, see *Hub Power Co. v Pakistan WAPDA*, Supreme Court of Pakistan, 14 June 2000, in which the Court held that allegations of corruption were not arbitrable, notwithstanding that the allegations did not impeach the arbitration agreement.

[238] Decision of the Tribunal Fédéral, *National Power Corporation (Philippines) v Westinghouse (USA)*, ATF 119 II 380, 2 September 1993.

2.154   Rather than raising questions of arbitrability, allegations of corruption made in an arbitration now raise the rather more substantive (and difficult) questions of proof and, if proven, the consequences of such impropriety under the relevant law.[239]

2.155   In relation to the former, accepting without question the arbitrability of allegations of impropriety, an ad hoc arbitral tribunal acting under the UNCITRAL Rules addressed allegations of corruption put before it thus:

> The members of the Arbitral Tribunal do not live in an ivory tower. Nor do they view the arbitral process as one which operates in a vacuum divorced from reality. The arbitrators are well aware of the allegations that commitments by public sector entities have been made with respect to major projects in Indonesia without adequate heed to their economic contribution to public welfare, simply because they benefited a few influential people. The arbitrators believe that cronyism and other forms of abuse of public trust do indeed exist in many countries, causing great harm to untold millions of ordinary people in a myriad of insidious ways. They would rigorously oppose any attempt to use the arbitral process to give effect to contracts contaminated by corruption.
>
> But such grave accusations must be proven […] Rumours or innuendo will not do.[240]

2.156   More recently, some tribunals and courts, recognising the inherent difficulties involved in proving allegations of corruption, have found such allegations to be made out where a party has adduced evidence of a number of indicators of corruption, or 'red flags'—such as a refusal or inability to explain or produce evidence regarding any legitimate activity or services performed under the impugned contract; a lack of qualifications to perform the services called upon by the contract; a contract's short duration; or an unusually high success fee or commission awarded by the contract.[241]

2.157   As to the consequences of a finding of corruption, this will depend on the governing law of the contract. Many laws recognise a difference between a finding that a contract had as its object the performance of an illegality (this will often lead to the contract being *void ab initio*), and a finding that a contract did not have such an illegal object but was concluded by reason of an illegality (which will only be *voidable*, and require some positive step to avoid by a party that has not already affirmed the contract with relevant knowledge).[242] A finding that a contract is void, or has been effectively avoided, will not necessarily exclude the possibility of a non-contractual restitutionary claim related to the contract, where a party that has successfully claimed avoidance has nevertheless taken a benefit from contractual performance.[243]

---

[239] For an overview of how arbitral tribunals have dealt with allegations of corruption, see ICC, 'Tackling corruption in arbitration' (2013) 24 ICC International Court of Arbitration Bulletin, Supplement. The supplement contains extracts from awards rendered between 2001 and 2009 in ICC cases that involved corruption issues, along with a series of articles on the subject.

[240] *Himpurna California Energy Ltd v PT (Persero) Perusahaan Listruik Negara*, Final Award dated 4 May 1999, extracts of which are published in (2000) XXV YBCA 13. See also Partasides, 'Proving corruption in international arbitration: A balanced standard for the real world' (2010) 25 ICSID Rev 47.

[241] Gaillard, 'The emergence of transnational responses to corruption in international arbitration' (2019) 35 Arb Intl 1–19.

[242] See, e.g., *World Duty Free Co. Ltd. v Republic of Kenya*, ICSID Case No. ARB/00/7, Award, 4 October 2006, at [164], [183].

[243] Gaillard, 'The emergence of transnational responses to corruption in international arbitration' (2019) 35 Arb Intl 1–19. See, however, the 2010 UNIDROIT Principles, Art. 3.3.2 which provides that the parties to a partially performed contract that infringes a 'mandatory rule' may recover what they have rendered in performing

A further issue that can arise is the extent to which a tribunal is obliged to pursue, on its own **2.158** initiative, an investigation into possible corruption. If an allegation of corruption is made in plain language in the course of the arbitration proceedings, the arbitral tribunal is clearly under a duty to consider the allegation and to decide whether or not it is proven.[244] It remains less clear, however, whether an arbitral tribunal has a duty to assume an inquisitorial role and to address the question of corruption on its own initiative where none is alleged. Initiating its own investigation and rendering a decision on the outcome of such a self-initiated investigation might leave a tribunal open to charges of straying into territory that is *ultra petita*.[245] Conversely, a failure to address the existence of such illegality may threaten the enforceability of an award and thus may sit uncomfortably with an arbitral tribunal's duty under some modern rules of arbitration to use its best endeavours to ensure that its award is enforceable.[246] Striking the right balance between these competing considerations may not be easy, and different national courts have adopted different approaches.[247]

For example, in relation to the *Alexander Brothers v Alstom* arbitration, the Swiss, French, **2.159** and English courts arrived at different views as to their respective roles (and thus, implicitly, an arbitral tribunal) in considering allegations of corruption. In annulment proceedings in Switzerland,[248] the Swiss Federal Supreme Court limited itself to an analysis of the facts as found by the arbitral tribunal in the award, observing that, while corruption was indeed prohibited by Swiss public policy, the Court's role was neither to complete nor question the facts as presented by the arbitral tribunal. By contrast, in enforcement proceedings in France,[249] the Court of Appeal observed that its review of the facts was not limited to those established by the arbitral tribunal, and thus the Court could accept new evidence regarding allegations of corruption. The Court found that there were 'serious, precise and consistent indicia' (that is, red flags) that payments made by Alstom had been used to bribe government officials, and on that basis refused to enforce the award. By way of further contrast, in enforcement proceedings in London,[250] the Commercial Court found that Alstom had not 'run an overt and positive case of bribery' in the underlying arbitration, but rather had made a 'tacit' case relying on alleged indicia of bribery. Finding that 'conclusive evidence' of corruption must be adduced to establish such an allegation, the Court concluded

---

the contract 'where this would be reasonable in the circumstances'. The Official Commentary to the UNIDROIT Principles makes clear that Art. 3.3.2 was drafted with instances of corruption in mind. See also *Patel v Mirza* [2016] UKSC 42.

[244] For a notable example of an award in which an international arbitral tribunal discusses the consequences of a finding of bribery, see *World Duty Free v Republic of Kenya*, Award, ICSID Case No. ARB/00/07, IIC 277 (2006), signed 25 September 2006, dispatched 4 October 2006. In that case, the bribery was clearly established and the tribunal held that, as a matter of international public policy, the claims under a contract that had been procured by the payment of a cash bribe to the head of state, President Daniel arap Moi, should be dismissed immediately and in their entirety: see Anon, 'ICSID arbitrators: $2m payment to President Moi was a bribe' (2006) 21 Mealey's Intl Arb Rep 4.

[245] See Kreindler, 'Aspects of illegality in the formation and performance of contracts', Presented at the 16th ICCA Congress, London, May 2002, at fn. 75.

[246] See, e.g., ICC Rules, Art. 42; LCIA Rules, Art. 32.2.

[247] See Kreindler, 'Public policy and corruption in international arbitration: A perspective for Russian related disputes' (2006) 72 Arbitration 236, esp. at 242–245. See also Sayed, *Corruption in International Trade and Commercial Arbitration* (Kluwer Law International, 2004), pp. 33–36, for discussion on an arbitrator's initiative in raising the non-arbitrability of public procurement-related matters in relation to suspected bribery.

[248] Swiss Federal Tribunal, 3 November 2016, No. 4A 136/2016.

[249] *Alstom Transport v Alexander Brothers*, cour d'appel, 28 May 2019.

[250] *Alexander Brothers v Alstom Transport* [2020] EWHC 1584 (Comm).

that Alstom had not met the required standard of proof. On this basis, the Court did not consider that it was appropriate to probe matters of illegality itself, and described Alstom's raising of this issue only during the enforcement phase as an abuse of process.[251]

(vi) Fraud

2.160   Where there are allegations of fraud in the procurement or performance of a contract, there appears to be no reason for the arbitral tribunal to decline jurisdiction.[252] Indeed, in the heat of battle, such allegations are frequently made, although much less frequently proven. Where a claim put forward in the course of an arbitration is found to be fraudulent, it will be for the arbitral tribunal to dismiss it. However, problems may arise if the alleged fraud is not discovered until an award has been made. In the *Fougerolle* case,[253] an ICC tribunal rejected a claim by the subcontractor under a turnkey contract, to the effect that it had encountered unexpected ground conditions and in a partial award, the arbitrators ordered Fougerolle to repay monies to its main contractor. Some months later, the main contractor relied on the same grounds as had been unsuccessfully advanced by Fougerolle (which the main contractor had denied and which the tribunal arbitrators had rejected) in support of its own claims against the engineer. The arbitral tribunal refused to review its award, on the basis that it had been made and could not be reversed at that stage, the award having been approved by the ICC Court. The Paris Court of Appeal stated that the award could be annulled if fraud was proved—but, in the event, it was decided that there had been no fraud.[254]

2.161   Another example is *L'affaire Tapie* case, which became a 'cause célèbre' in France and cast a shadow over the reputation of arbitration in that country.[255] In 1992, Bernard Tapie, a high-profile French businessman, a former minister in the French government, a football club owner, and a television celebrity, decided to sell his majority shareholding in Adidas AG to repay several outstanding loans. He instructed his bank, Crédit Lyonnais (which was at that time the largest state-owned French bank), to carry out the transaction. On 12 February 1993, Crédit Lyonnais and an affiliate sold the shareholding for approximately 218 million euros to a group of investors, who then sold it for considerably more in a pre-arranged transaction completed in December 1994.[256]

---

[251] Ibid, at [135].

[252] In *Ayyasamy v Paramasivam* (2016) 10 SCC 386, the Supreme Court of India ruled that a mere allegation of fraud *simpliciter* is insufficient to find a dispute non-arbitrable; such disputes are non-arbitrable only if they relate to 'very serious allegations of fraud', such as criminal offences, complex fraud, forgery or fabrication of documents, fraud relating to the arbitration agreement itself, or allegations of fraud that permeate the entire contract (at [20]). See also the decision of the Nigerian Court of Appeal in *BJ Export & Chemical Processing Co. v Kaduna Refining and Petrochemical Co.*, 31 October 2002, (2003) 24 WRN 74.

[253] *Fougerolle v Procoface*, Cass. Civ. 1ere, 25 May 1992.

[254] For a fuller account of this case, see de Boisséson, 'L'arbitrage et la fraude' [1993] Rev Arb 3. In the same article, de Boisséson also reviews the unpublished *Beltronic* case, which came before a French court of appeal. This was a somewhat unusual case, in that the arbitral process itself was fraudulent. A fake arbitration centre was set up, with the arbitrator and the fake centre sharing the damages awarded by the arbitrator against the unfortunate Canadian defendant!

[255] Following the judgment of the French cour de cassation annulling the arbitral tribunal's award in Tapie's favour, an article in the Global Arbitration Review referred to 'L'affaire Tapie', which it said 'has scandalised the French population and threatened the reputation of the Paris arbitration bar because of the allegations of fraud and case-rigging': see 'Tapie: the end of the affair?' Global Arbitration Review, 20 May 2017.

[256] For a more detailed account of the background to the case, and of the decision of the French cour de cassation, see Cameron Diver, 'The Adidas arbitration: A cautionary tale on independence and impartiality in the arbitral process' (2016) 5 Intl Arb L Rev 9.

Bernard Tapie and most of his group of companies subsequently went into liquidation, and **2.162** in 1995 the liquidators began proceedings in the French courts against Crédit Lyonnais and an affiliate, alleging fraudulent concealment of the pre-arranged transaction and breach of the mandate it had been given to sell the shares at their proper value. There followed a series of cases in the French courts, with the Paris Court of Appeal giving a judgment in favour of the liquidators for 135 million euros, and the Court of Cassation reversing this judgment in part and referring the case back to the Paris Court of Appeal with a different bench of judges.

In order to bring an end to the various court cases in which they had been involved for more **2.163** than a decade, the parties entered into a submission agreement (or *compromis*) in 2007 in which they agreed to submit *all* the disputes between them to an ad hoc tribunal of three arbitrators, whose mission was to decide all disputes between the parties under French law, with the seat of the arbitration in Paris.

In view of the French government's majority shareholding in Crédit Lyonnais, the parties' **2.164** proposal to enter into the *compromis,* and so refer the disputes to arbitration in order to put an end to the various court cases, was approved by Christine Lagarde, who was at that time the Minister of the Economy and of Finance, Industry and Employment.

The arbitral tribunal issued its award in July 2008. The award represented a considerable **2.165** success for the claimants, including an order for the payment of 45 million euros to Bernard Tapie and his wife for 'moral damages'.[257] The award was paid in full, but the Paris Court of Appeal was subsequently asked to review the case, in what through media reports had become something of a state scandal.

The arbitrator nominated by the claimants, who was alleged to have been very influential **2.166** in the drafting of the award, was found to have had a long-term business relationship with Tapie and a member of his legal team. This relationship had not been disclosed as it should have been; and in consequence, the award was annulled by the Paris Court of Appeal, a decision that was confirmed by the French Court of Cassation.

L'affaire Tapie underlines the importance that courts rightly attach to the requirement for **2.167** arbitrators to be strictly independent and impartial, and for them to disclose any relationships that might throw doubt on this. The case was followed, however, by an unexpected and, it might be thought, unfortunate development. Lagarde herself, who presumably acted upon the advice of her officials, was accused of culpable negligence first, by approving the decision to take the case to arbitration and secondly, by agreeing to payment of the amount awarded by the arbitral tribunal. The case against Lagarde was heard by the Court of Justice of the French Republic, which concluded that she had not been negligent in agreeing to the arbitration but had been so in agreeing to payment of the award, rather than challenging it. However, no punishment was imposed upon her.[258]

---

[257] Usually, an award for moral damages under French law would be for a fairly nominal amount.
[258] The Court of Justice of the French Republic is a special court established to try Ministers and former Ministers accused of dereliction of duty in public office. For a fuller account of the charges against Lagarde, see Redfern, 'The importance of being independent: Laws of arbitration, rules, guidelines—and a disastrous award' (2017) 6(1) Indian Journal of Arbitration Law.

(vii) Corporate governance disputes

2.168 In most jurisdictions, parties are free to submit corporate governance disputes to arbitration. By way of example, the German courts have held that disputes concerning the validity of shareholders' resolutions are in principle arbitrable.[259] In England, the courts have reaffirmed that arbitral tribunals have wide powers to rule on corporate governance matters. In *Fulham Football Club*,[260] shareholder disputes were described as 'essentially internal disputes about alleged breaches of the terms or understandings upon which the parties were intended to co-exist as members of the company'.[261] The Court held that there was no reason why an 'unfair prejudice' claim should be 'inherently unsuitable' for determination by arbitration. The applicable test in each case is whether:

> […] the matters in dispute […] engage third party rights or represent an attempt to delegate to the arbitrators what is a matter of public interest which cannot be determined within the limitations of a private contractual process.[262]

2.169 Similarly, the Singapore courts have affirmed that so-called 'oppression' claims, and claims involving allegations of misconduct by large financial institutions, are arbitrable. In *Tomolugen*, the Singapore Court of Appeal considered a claim brought by a shareholder under section 216 of the Companies Act 1967 alleging that the affairs of the company in which it held a minority interest were conducted in a manner that was oppressive or unfairly prejudicial towards it. The Court of Appeal distinguished the types of claims that engage public policy issues (for example, related to the liquidation of an insolvent company or avoidance claims arising from insolvency) from statutory oppression claims.[263]

2.170 In Australia, the Federal Court in *WDR Delaware* stayed a winding up application of a joint venture company and referred the underlying dispute to arbitration, despite the argument that the winding up of a company is a matter subject to government authority, and therefore non-arbitrable. The Court considered that the winding up dispute in fact related to breaches of contract and wrongful conduct in a corporate governance sense, and ruled that such matters were capable of decision by arbitration. In particular, the Court distinguished the case before it from cases involving insolvency, ruling that the corporate governance dispute was essentially between shareholders, with no substantial public interest element in the determination of the dispute.[264]

2.171 But an acceptance of the arbitrability of corporate governance disputes is not universal. In Russia, a series of decisions by the courts cast doubt on the arbitrability of corporate

---

[259] Case No. II ZR 255/08 of 6 April 2009, in which the German Federal Court of Justice held that disputes over the validity of shareholders' resolutions in German limited liability companies are arbitrable, provided that the arbitration agreement complies with the criteria set out in the judgment. However, see *Groenselect Management NV v Van der Boogaard*, Dutch Supreme Court, NJ 2007, 561, 10 November 2006, in which the Dutch courts held that a dispute concerning the validity of a shareholders' meeting or resolutions is not arbitrable.

[260] *Fulham Football Club (1987) Ltd v Sir David Richards* [2011] EWCA Civ 855.

[261] Ibid., at [58].

[262] Ibid., at [107]. For further discussion of this case, see Lew and Marsden, 'Arbitrability', in Lew, Bor, Fullelove, and Greenaway (eds) *Arbitration in England, with Chapters on Scotland and Ireland* (Kluwer Law International, 2013), p. 410.

[263] *Tomolugen Holdings Ltd and another v Silica Investors Ltd and other appeals* [2015] SGCA 57. See also *TMT Co Ltd v The Royal Bank of Scotland plc (trading as RBS Greenwich Futures) and ors* [2017] SGHC 21, in which the Singapore High Court held that '[t]he mere allegation of abuse or conduct involving a financial institution, even a large one, cannot be grounds to deny arbitration if that is what the parties agreed'.

[264] *WDR Delaware Corporation v Hydrox Holdings Pty Ltd* [2016] FCA 1164, at [161]–[163].

disputes under Russian law. In *Maximov v Novolipetsky Metallurgicheskiy Kombinat*,[265] both the lower courts and the Supreme Arbitrazh Court found that 'corporate' disputes are under the special jurisdiction of the arbitrazh courts pursuant to Articles 33 and 225(1) of the Arbitrazh Procedural Code, and are therefore non-arbitrable.[266] In 2016 and 2019, Russia enacted legislation aimed at reforming certain aspects of its arbitration law, in order to align it more closely with the Model Law. One notable feature of these reforms is that certain corporate disputes involving shareholders should now, in principle, be arbitrable, subject to meeting certain requirements.[267]

(viii) Trusts

It is well established that disputes between a trust and a third party do not raise issues of arbitrability. However, in the context of disputes arising under a trust between a trustee and a beneficiary, questions of arbitrability may arise.   **2.172**

One potential constraint on arbitrability, viewed from a common-law perspective, is that a state's courts maintain an inherent supervisory jurisdiction over the administration of trusts and the conduct of trustees, both of which require close public scrutiny.[268] So, for example, the grant to an arbitrator of the power to remove a trustee, which is traditionally within the purview of the courts, could be considered an impermissible encroachment on the courts' jurisdiction, and therefore a matter incapable of settlement by arbitration.   **2.173**

Some courts have nevertheless acknowledged that there may be valid policy reasons to allow parties to resolve privately such disputes, and that doing so does not necessarily preclude the courts from exercising their inherent supervisory jurisdiction. In Australia, for example, the Court of Appeal of New South Wales concluded that there is nothing inherently contrary to public policy for a trustee and a beneficiary to resolve their disputes by arbitration, provided that the private settlement does not oust entirely the supervisory jurisdiction of the courts.[269] Thus, even if an arbitrator does not possess the same statutory powers as a court, such as the power to remove a trustee, an arbitrator may nevertheless grant relief in relation to a beneficiary's request to remove a trustee—for example by ordering the trustee to resign, to appoint a new trustee, and to convey the trust property to a new person—and such an award will be enforceable.   **2.174**

---

[265] *Maximov v Novolipetsky Metallurgicheskiy Kombinat* Ruling of the Supreme Arbitrazh Court, VAS-15384/11, 30 January 2012.

[266] The Constitutional Court rejected Mr Maximov's challenge to Art. 33 on the basis that it was unconstitutional later that year. The Court stated that the legislature had the right to establish specific procedures for hearing certain categories of disputes, although it did not address the *arbitrability* of corporate governance disputes as such: see Ruling of the Constitutional Court No. 1488-O, 17 July 2012.

[267] Other requirements include that the arbitration agreement was concluded after 1 February 2017, and that the arbitration is seated in Russia and administered by a 'registered' arbitral institution. Some have suggested that the legislative amendments introduced additional, more burdensome requirements for foreign arbitral institutions seeking to be registered (e.g. if a foreign arbitration institution wishes to administer a wide range of corporate disputes, including, e.g., disputes relating to the creation of Russian legal entities or disputes brought by shareholders to recover damages caused to a legal entity, it must deposit special rules for the arbitration of corporate disputes at the time of its registration application). At the time of the 2019 legislative enactment, four institutions were 'registered' (each of which is Russian). HKIAC has since also registered.

[268] *Rinehart v Welker* [2012] NSWCA 95, at [173].

[269] *Rinehart v Welker* [2012] NSWCA 95, at [177]. See also *Fitzpatrick v Emerald Grain Pty Ltd* [2017] WASC 206.

(ix) Public law disputes

2.175   Questions of arbitrability can also sometimes arise in relation to arbitration agreements entered into by, on the one side, a private entity and, on the other, a state entity. The traditional concern is that, having been endowed with a public function, a state entity should not be shielded from public scrutiny in respect of its exercise of that function, including in relation to the resolution of disputes arising from contracts that the public entity has entered into with private parties.

2.176   Today, such concerns are increasingly rare. By way of example, in 2015 Brazil amended its arbitration legislation so as to permit expressly entities of the public administration to arbitrate disputes.[270] In 2019, Brazil's President issued Decree No. 10.025, which provides that disputes regarding 'property rights' (for example, including contractual rights and obligations) arising from contracts entered into by the government in relation to the port, road, rail, waterway, and airport sectors, are arbitrable, subject to certain requirements being met.[271]

2.177   Other jurisdictions that were slow to recognise the general arbitrability of disputes arising under contracts with state entities have been changing their laws in a similar way,[272] and this modern reality is likely to continue.

(c) Summary

2.178   The significance of 'arbitrability' should not be exaggerated. It is important to be aware that it may be an issue, but in broad terms most commercial disputes are now arbitrable under the laws of most countries.[273]

F. Confidentiality

2.179   The confidentiality of arbitral proceedings has traditionally been considered to be one of the important advantages of arbitration. Unlike proceedings in a court of law, where press and public are generally entitled to be present, an international arbitration is not a public proceeding. It is essentially a private process and therefore has the potential for remaining confidential. Increasingly, however, confidentiality cannot generally be relied upon as a clear duty of parties to arbitral proceedings. Parties concerned to ensure the confidentiality of their proceedings would therefore do well to include confidentiality provisions in their agreement to arbitrate, or in a separate confidentiality agreement concluded at the outset of the arbitration.

2.180   In this section, the following issues will be addressed:

- the distinction between privacy and confidentiality;
- the classical position and current trend as far as confidentiality is concerned;

---

[270] Law no. 13.129/15 (amending the Brazilian Arbitration Act, Art. 1).

[271] Such arbitrations must apply Brazilian law, be public, be seated in Brazil, and in general should be institutional (with such institutions to be approved by the Federal Attorney's office).

[272] For example, the Dominican Republic and Mexico.

[273] See Kirry, 'Arbitrability: Current trends in Europe' (1996) 12 Arb Intl 373; van den Berg, 'Arbitrability' (1996) XXI YBCA 450.

- the confidentiality of the award;
- confidentiality in investor–state arbitrations; and
- institutional arbitral rules on confidentiality.

(a) Privacy and confidentiality

As far as the hearing is concerned, the major institutional rules are in agreement: the   **2.181**
hearing is private. Article 26.3 of the ICC Rules states:

> The arbitral tribunal shall be in full charge of the hearings, at which all the parties shall be
> entitled to be present. Save with the approval of the arbitral tribunal and the parties, per-
> sons not involved in the proceedings shall not be admitted.

The rules of the ICDR, LCIA, SIAC, International Centre for the Settlement of Investment
Disputes (ICSID), and World Intellectual Property Organization (WIPO) contain similar
provisions, as do the rules of commercial arbitration organisations such as the Austrian
Federal Economic Chamber, the Swiss Chambers' Arbitration Institution, the China
International Economic and Trade Arbitration Commission (CIETAC), and the Japanese
Commercial Arbitration Association (JCAA).[274]

Article 28.3 of the UNCITRAL Rules spells out the position in similar terms: **2.182**

> Hearings shall be held in camera unless the parties agree otherwise. The arbitral tribunal
> may require the retirement of any witness or witnesses, including expert witnesses, during
> the testimony of such other witnesses, except that a witness, including an expert witness,
> who is a party to the arbitration shall not, in principle, be asked to retire.

The 'privacy' of arbitration hearings is therefore uncontroversial. And if the hearing is to
be held in private, it would seem to follow that the documents disclosed and the evidence
given at that hearing should also be—and should remain—private. In principle, there
would seem to be no point in excluding non-participants from an arbitration hearing if
they can later read all about it in printed articles or on an authorised website. However, a
broader duty of confidentiality in international arbitration is now far from clear.

(b) Confidentiality—classical position

The classical view of confidentiality is based on the existence of an implied duty of confidentiality   **2.183**
as a natural extension of the privacy of the hearing in an international commercial arbitration.
For example, in *Hassneh Insurance Co of Israel v Mew*,[275] the English High Court recognised:

> If it be correct that there is at least an implied term in every agreement to arbitrate that the
> hearing shall be held in private, the requirement of privacy must in principle extend to

---

[274] For research that points towards confidentiality as one of the reasons for choosing arbitration, see the references in Pryles, 'Confidentiality', in Hille and Newman (eds) *The Leading Arbitrators' Guide to International Arbitration* (Juris, 2004), p. 415.
[275] *Hassneh Insurance Co of Israel v Mew* [1993] 2 Lloyd's Rep 243.

documents which are created for the purpose of that hearing. The most obvious example is a note or transcript of the evidence. The disclosure to a third party of such documents would be almost equivalent to opening the door of the arbitration room to that third party. Similarly witness statements, being so closely related to the hearing, must be within the obligation of confidentiality. So also must outline submissions tendered to the arbitrator. If outline submissions, then so must pleadings be included.[276]

2.184   This position was reaffirmed in *Ali Shipping Corporation v 'Shipyard Trogir'*,[277] where the Court of Appeal stated that the confidentiality rule was founded on the privacy of arbitral proceedings and that an implied term as to the confidentiality of arbitration was a term that 'arises as the nature of the contract itself implicitly requires'.[278] The Court acknowledged, however, that 'the boundaries of the obligations of confidence which thereby arise have yet to be delineated'.[279]

2.185   In the case of *John Forster Emmott v Michael Wilson & Partners Ltd*,[280] the Court of Appeal nevertheless noted that the duty of confidentiality in arbitration proceedings was not absolute and noted as follows:

> [T]he content of the obligation may depend on the context in which it arises and on the nature of the information or documents at issue. The limits of that obligation are still in the process of development on a case-by-case basis. On the authorities as they now stand, the principal cases in which disclosure will be permissible are these: the first is where there is consent, express or implied; second, where there is an order, or leave of the court (but that does not mean that the court has a general discretion to lift the obligation of confidentiality); third, where it is reasonably necessary for the protection of the legitimate interests of an arbitrating party; fourth, where the interests of justice require disclosure, and also (perhaps) where the public interest requires disclosure.[281]

2.186   The Singapore courts have adopted a similar approach, accepting the existence of an implied duty of confidentiality, but stipulating that they will impose such a duty 'only to the extent that it is reasonable to do so'.[282]

(c) Confidentiality—the current trend

2.187   In recent years the general trend has been against the assumption of confidentiality for international arbitral proceedings as a whole. This trend seems to have been influenced by arbitrations in which the public interest was at play. For example, in *Esso Australia Resources*

---

[276]   Ibid., at 247 *per* Colman J.
[277]   *Ali Shipping Corporation v 'Shipyard Trogir'* [1998] 1 Lloyd's Rep 643.
[278]   Ibid., at 651.
[279]   Ibid.
[280]   *John Forster Emmott v Michael Wilson & Partners Ltd* [2008] EWCA Civ 184.
[281]   Ibid., at [107].
[282]   *AAY and ors v AAZ (AAY)* [2011] 1 SLR 1093, 1120. The court found that the defendant had legitimate grounds to disclose certain materials to the relevant public authorities because 'there was reasonable cause to suspect criminal conduct' (at 1131). See also *Myanma Taung Chi Oo Co. Ltd v Win Nu* [2003] 2 SLR 945. In the same way, in New Zealand, every arbitration agreement entails a duty of confidentiality unless the parties expressly agree otherwise. An implied duty of confidentiality also applies by default in Scotland and Spain.

Ltd v The Honourable Sidney James Plowman and Ors,[283] the High Court of Australia concluded that whilst the privacy of the hearing should be respected, confidentiality was not an essential attribute of a private arbitration. Specifically, the court found that a requirement to conduct proceedings in camera did not translate into an obligation prohibiting disclosure of documents and information provided in, and for the purpose of, the arbitration. The court then concluded that although a certain degree of confidentiality might arise in certain situations, it was not absolute. In the particular case before the court, 'the public's legitimate interest in obtaining information about the affairs of public authorities' prevailed.[284]

In another Australian case,[285] the appellate court decided that an arbitrator had no power **2.188** to make a procedural direction imposing an obligation of confidentiality that would have had the effect of preventing the government from disclosing to a state agency, or to the public, information and documents generated in the course of the arbitration that ought to be made known to that authority or to the public. It was said that public health and environmental issues were involved:

> Whilst private arbitration will often have the advantage of securing for the parties a high level of confidentiality for their dealing, where one of those parties is a government, or an organ of government, neither the arbitral agreement nor the general procedural powers of the arbitrator will extend so far as to stamp on the governmental litigant a regime of confidentiality or secrecy which effectively destroys or limits the general governmental duty to pursue the public interest.[286]

Notwithstanding the suggestion by the Australian courts that confidentiality is not an es- **2.189** sential feature of arbitration, in recent years Australia has enacted legislative amendments replacing its confidentiality 'opt-in' system with an 'opt-out' system (that is, the arbitration is confidential unless the parties agree otherwise) in respect of contractual arbitrations.[287]

In the United States, neither the Federal Arbitration Act nor the Uniform Arbitration Act **2.190** contain a provision requiring the parties or the arbitrators to keep secret arbitration proceedings in which they are involved. As a consequence, unless the parties' agreement or applicable arbitration rules provide otherwise, the parties are not required by US law to treat as confidential the arbitration proceedings and what transpires in them.[288]

In *United States v Panhandle Eastern Corporation*,[289] Panhandle brought a motion before **2.191** a US federal district court for a protective order, preventing the disclosure of documents relating to arbitration proceedings between it and Sonatrach, the Algerian national oil and

---

[283] *Esso Australia Resources Ltd v The Honourable Sidney James Plowman and Ors* (1995) 193 CLR 10. The case is also set out in (1995) 11 Arb Intl, 3, 235.

[284] Ibid., at 249.

[285] *Commonwealth of Australia v Cockatoo Dockyard Pty Ltd* [1995] 36 NSWLR 662.

[286] Ibid., at 682 *per* Kirby P. See also *Adesa Corporation v Bob Dickenson Auction Service Ltd* 73 OR (3d) 787, [56] (2004), in which the Canadian courts acknowledged that the 'confidentiality of arbitration proceedings should be fostered to maintain the integrity of the arbitration process', but stated that this should be balanced against any wider public interest in disclosure.

[287] Amendments made to the International Arbitration Act 1974 (Cth) by the Civil Law and Justice (Omnibus Amendments) Act 2015 (Cth).

[288] See *Industrotech Constructors Inc. v Duke University* 67 NC App. 741, 314 S.E.2d 272 (1984); *Giacobassi Grandi Vini SpA v Renfield Corporation* US Dist. LEXIS 1783 (1987).

[289] *United States v Panhandle Eastern Corporation* 118 FRD 346 (D. Del. 1988).

gas company. In support of its motion, Panhandle argued that disclosure to third parties of documents related to the arbitration would severely prejudice Panhandle's ongoing business relationship with both Sonatrach and the Algerian government.

2.192 The court denied the motion on the grounds that Panhandle had failed to satisfy the 'good cause' requirements of rule 26(c) of the Federal Rules of Civil Procedure and that the filing was untimely, but it proceeded to address the question of confidentiality and, having rejected the existence of an express confidentiality agreement between the parties, gave no credence to the existence of an implied obligation.[290] This decision has been followed in subsequent US cases in which the courts have refused to find a duty of confidentiality in the absence of an express contractual provision or the adoption of a set of arbitration rules containing such a provision.[291]

2.193 Indeed, the existence of an implied duty of confidentiality is becoming increasingly rare.[292] In Sweden, the Supreme Court has rejected the idea of a general implied duty of confidentiality in arbitration proceedings.[293] The same position prevails in Norway (that is, an 'opt-in' system prevails, in contrast to the Australian approach described above),[294] and France.[295] By contrast, in England, a duty of confidentiality is implied by law (that is, not on the basis that such a term must have been intended by the parties because it is necessary for their arbitration agreement).[296] In Germany, Austria, and Bulgaria, commentators and courts are divided as to whether a duty of confidentiality may be implied into an arbitration agreement.[297]

2.194 The tension between the confidential nature of arbitration and the desirability of transparency where matters of public interest arise was explored by the English courts in the case of *Manchester City Football Club Ltd v The Football Association Premier League & Ors*.[298] In October 2019, the Premier League commenced arbitration against Manchester City Football Club under the Premier League Rules, in relation to Manchester City's alleged failure to provide documents and information in the course of a disciplinary investigation conducted by the Premier League. Manchester City applied to the English High Court to challenge the arbitral tribunal's jurisdiction, but its application was unsuccessful. Moreover,

---

[290] It would seem that the decision of the Court was *obiter*. Moreover, it has been suggested that too much should not be read into this decision. Panhandle was seeking a 'protective order' to shield the arbitration documents from disclosure and the onus of establishing 'good cause' is a heavy one: see Neill, 'Confidentiality in arbitration' (1996) 12 Arb Intl 303.

[291] See, e.g., *Contship Containerlines Ltd v PPG Industries Inc.*, 17 April 2003, 2003 US Dist. 6857.

[292] For a discussion of the implied duty of confidentiality in commercial arbitration, including its historical rationale, costs, and prospects for the future, see Partasides, 'What has been the "spillover" effect of the transparency debate on commercial arbitrations?', in Kalicki and Raouf (eds) *Evolution and Adaptation: The Future of International Arbitration*, ICCA Congress Series, Vol. 20 (Kluwer Law International, 2019), pp. 699–705.

[293] See *AI Trade Finance Inc. v Bulgarian Foreign Trade Bank Ltd*, Supreme Court of Sweden, 27 October 2000, (2000) 15 Mealey's Intl Arb Rep A1.

[294] Norwegian Arbitration Act 2004, s. 5.

[295] Pursuant to Decree No. 2011-48 of 13 January 2011, no express obligation of confidentiality exists in France in relation to international arbitration (in contrast to domestic arbitration).

[296] *Emmott v Michael Wilson Partnership* [2008] EWCA Civ 184.

[297] In Switzerland, arbitrators are bound by an implicit duty of confidentiality with respect to the proceedings, but this does not apply to the parties themselves or to third parties involved in the arbitration. It is, therefore, for the parties to provide for confidentiality in their agreement with third parties or to agree on the general confidentiality of the arbitration, either expressly or by reference to arbitration rules containing confidentiality obligations.

[298] *Manchester City Football Club Ltd v The Football Association Premier League & Ors* [2021] EWHC 628 (Comm).

the High Court decided to publish its judgment, even though both Manchester City and Premier League opposed publication.[299]

Subsequently, the English Court of Appeal upheld the High Court's decision to publish **2.195** the judgment in question. Having weighed the confidential nature of arbitration against the public interest in publication, the Court of Appeal determined that the balance was in favour of the latter. In the Court of Appeal's view, the judgment in question did not contain 'significant confidential information', and disclosure of the existence of the arbitration would not give rise to any prejudice or detriment to the parties in circumstances where the dispute was already widely covered in the press.[300]

(d) Award

Some institutional rules of arbitration provide that the award may be made public only with **2.196** the consent of the parties.[301]

It has always been recognised, however, that there are circumstances in which an award **2.197** may need to be made public, for example for the purpose of enforcement by a national court. In *Hassneh Insurance Co of Israel v Mew*[302] the judge concluded that an award and the reasons contained in that award were different in character from the other elements of the arbitration proceedings (such as notes and transcripts of evidence, witness statements, submissions, and pleadings, all of which were, in his view, covered by the principle of privacy stemming from the fact that arbitration hearings were held in private). He found that the award was potentially a public document for the purposes of supervision by the courts or enforcement in them, and therefore could be disclosed without the consent of the other party or the permission of the court if—but only if—the party seeking disclosure needed to do so in order to assert or protect its legal rights vis-à-vis a third party.[303] This position is now reflected in many of the institutional arbitration rules.

In addition to the disclosure of awards where required by law, disclosure of a kind takes **2.198** place when an arbitral institution—such as the ICC—publishes 'edited and redacted' copies of arbitral awards as a guide for the benefit of lawyers and arbitrators.[304] The ICC has also

---

[299] *Manchester City Football Club Ltd v The Football Association Premier League & Ors* [2021] EWHC 711 (Comm).

[300] *Manchester City Football Club Ltd v The Football Association Premier League & Ors* [2021] EWCA Civ 1110, at [54], [65], and [66].

[301] See, e.g., AAA Rules, Art. 27.4; SIAC Rules, r. 39.2. See also the UNCITRAL Rules 2010, Art. 34.5.

[302] *Hassneh Insurance Co of Israel v Mew* [1993] 2 Lloyd's Rep 243.

[303] The LCIA Rules, Art. 30 mirrors this position, as pointed out by Rawding and Seeger, '*Aegis v European Re* and the confidentiality of arbitration awards' (2003) 19 Arb Intl 484. See also *City of Moscow v International Industrial Bank* [2004] 2 Lloyd's Rep 179, which concerned the publication of a court judgment dismissing a challenge to an arbitral award under the Arbitration Act 1996, s. 68. The court stated that a public judgment was particularly desirable where it involved a point of law that may offer future guidance to practitioners, but emphasised that this must be balanced against the parties' expectations of privacy and confidentiality in arbitration. Ultimately, the court concluded that the judgment should remain private because the party 'had, objectively, no good reason for insisting on [its] publication'.

[304] The ICC has no specific rule as to the confidentiality of awards, although an ICC arbitral tribunal now has an express power under the ICC Rules, Art. 22.3 to make confidentiality orders in relation to arbitration proceedings or other matters in connection with the arbitration. Similarly, the ICSID Arbitration Rules provide that, with the parties' consent, ICSID 'shall publish every Award, supplementary decision on an Award, rectification, interpretation, and revision of an Award' and that, for this purpose, 'the parties may consent to publication of the full text

recently published guidance confirming that any award made from 1 January 2019 'may be published in its entirety no less than two years after the date of [...] notification', subject to any objection by the parties.[305]

2.199   Article 30.3 of the ICDR Rules provides that an award may be made public 'only with the consent of all parties or as required by law'.[306] These Rules further provide that, unless otherwise agreed by the parties, selected awards may be made publicly available, with the names of the parties and other identifying features removed.[307] If the award has become publicly available through enforcement proceedings or otherwise, then the names need not be removed.

2.200   In England, the Privy Council had to consider in *Aegis v European Re*[308] whether an arbitration award in one arbitration under a reinsurance agreement could be relied upon, by the winning party, in another arbitration under the same agreement, despite an express confidentiality agreement in respect of the first arbitration. The case came to the Privy Council on appeal from the Court of Appeal of Bermuda and disclosure of the award was allowed. The Privy Council said that the legitimate use of an earlier award in a later, also private, arbitration between the same parties was not the kind of mischief against which the confidentiality agreement was directed. This decision has been rightly described as:

> [...] eminently sensible in the circumstances of the case. The private and, in theory, confidential nature of arbitration should not mean that the parties can go on arbitrating the same point *ad infinitum* until they get the result they prefer.[309]

2.201   In France, the Paris Court of Appeal ruled, in *Aita v Ojjeh*,[310] that the mere bringing of court proceedings to challenge an arbitration award violated the principle of confidentiality in that it caused 'a public debate of facts which should remain confidential'. The judgment also contains dicta to the effect that it is in 'the very nature of arbitral proceeding that they ensure the highest degree of discretion in the resolution of private disputes, as the two parties had agreed'.[311] More recently, however, and in line with the modern trend, the Paris Court of Appeal in *Nafimco*[312] found that the claimant failed to 'show the existence and foundation of such a duty in French international arbitration law'.

---

or to a jointly redacted text': see ICSID Rules, r. 62(1) and (2). If, however, the parties 'object to publication' or 'disagree on redaction', the ICSID Secretary-General shall 'consider any comments received' from the parties and then proceed to publish 'excerpts' of the award: see ICSID Rules, r. 62(4).

[305] ICC Note to Parties and Arbitral Tribunals on the Conduct of the Arbitration under the ICC Rules of Arbitration, 1 January 2019, at paras 42–43.

[306] Similarly, the SIAC Rules, r. 32(12) states that SIAC may publish, with the consent of the parties and the tribunal, any award with the names of the parties and other identifying information redacted.

[307] The Vienna Rules similarly provide that the VIAC may publish anonymised summaries or extracts of awards, subject to any objection by the parties: Art. 41.

[308] *Associated Electric and Gas Insurance Services Ltd v European Reinsurance Co. of Zurich* [2003] UKPC 11.

[309] Rawding and Seeger, 'Aegis v European Re and the confidentiality of arbitration awards' (2003) 19 Arb Intl 484, at 488–489.

[310] *Aita v Ojjeh* [1986] Rev Arb 583, 583.

[311] Ibid., at 584. Some commentators argue that the reasoning of the French court is unsatisfactory, and that the extreme position advanced must be seen in the context of the court's determination to punish what it evidently viewed as a hopeless and tactically motivated attempt to set aside an English award in the French courts: see Paulsson and Rawding, 'The trouble with confidentiality' (1994) 5 ICC International Court of Arbitration Bulletin 48.

[312] *Nafimco*, Paris cour d'appel, 22 January 2004. Under France's new Decree No. 2011-48, confidentiality obligations apply by default in domestic arbitration proceedings. However, the Decree does not provide for confidentiality in international arbitration proceedings. Accordingly, where parties agree to refer disputes to international

(e) Confidentiality in investor–state arbitrations

In the *Cockatoo Dockyard* case,[313] the Australian court concluded that whilst there was a   **2.202**
'high level of confidentiality' in arbitral proceedings, this should not prevent disclosure
where the public interest was concerned. It is this concern for the public interest—and
for the public's 'right to know'—that has led to the erosion of the principle of confidentiality in arbitral proceedings. The need to balance the private interest in confidentiality
against the possible public interest in disclosure may be seen in arbitrations that have
taken place under the treaty that established the North American Free Trade Agreement
(NAFTA).

In the early 1980s, an international arbitral tribunal applying the ICSID Rules in *Amco v*   **2.203**
Republic of Indonesia[314] held that 'as to the "spirit of confidentiality" of the arbitral procedure, it is right to say that the Convention and the Rules do not prevent the parties from
revealing their case'. Balanced against this finding, the *Amco* tribunal nonetheless referred
to a general duty existing under international law not to exacerbate an ongoing international dispute, and relied on the existence of this duty to recommend to the parties that
they should ensure that their public statements about cases in which they were involved
were both short and accurate.

In the years since *Amco*, tribunals applying the ICSID Rules, including NAFTA tribu-   **2.204**
nals, have striven to achieve the same balance. For example, in *Metalclad Corporation v
United Mexican States*,[315] Mexico made an application for a confidentiality order, pursuant
to Article 1134 of NAFTA ('Interim measures of protection') and Article 28 of the (then)
ICSID Additional Facility Rules ('Procedural orders'). The tribunal dismissed the application, finding that:

> There remains nonetheless a question as to whether there exists any general principle of
> confidentiality that would operate to prohibit discussion of the arbitration proceedings by
> either party. Neither the NAFTA nor the ICSID (Additional Facility) Rules contain any ex-
> press restriction on the freedom of the parties in this respect. Though it is frequently said
> that one of the reasons for recourse to arbitration is to avoid publicity, unless the agree-
> ment between the parties incorporates such a limitation, each of them is still free to speak
> publicly of the arbitration […] Indeed, as has been pointed out by the Claimant in its
> comments, under US security laws, the Claimant, as a public company traded on a public
> stock exchange in the US, is under a positive duty to provide certain information about its
> activities to its shareholders, especially regarding its involvement in a process the outcome
> of which could perhaps significantly affect its share value.
>
> The above having been said, it still appears to the Arbitral Tribunal that it would be of ad-
> vantage to the orderly unfolding of the arbitral process and conducive to the maintenance

---

arbitration, they should make express provision for confidentiality in the contract. See Code of Civil Procedure,
Arts 1464(4) and 1506.

[313] *Commonwealth of Australia v Cockatoo Dockyard Pty Ltd* [1995] 36 NSWLR 662.
[314] *Amco Corporation and ors v Republic of Indonesia*, Decision on Request for Provisional Measures, 9
December 1983, (1983) 1 ICSID Rep 410, at 412.
[315] *Metalclad Corporation v United Mexican States* Award, Ad hoc—ICSID Additional Facility Rules; ICSID
Case No. ARB (AF)/97/1; IIC 161 (2000).

of working relationships between the Parties if during the proceedings they were both to limit public discussion of the case to a minimum, subject only to any externally imposed obligation by which either of them may be legally bound.[316]

2.205   In another NAFTA arbitration, *R Loewen and Loewen Corporation v United States of America*,[317] the US government requested that all filings, as well as the minutes of oral proceedings, be treated as open and available to the public. Loewen did not oppose public disclosure, but requested that the disclosure take place only after the conclusion of the arbitration. The tribunal rejected the US government's request, referring to Article 44.2 of the then ICSID Additional Facility Rules, which provide that minutes of hearings should not be published without the consent of the parties.[318]

2.206   Although the tribunal rejected the US government's request, it did not recognise any general duty of confidentiality; rather, it rejected Loewen's submission that each party is under an obligation of confidentiality in relation to the proceedings. In its award on jurisdiction, the tribunal summarised its conclusions as follows:

> In its Decision the Tribunal rejected the Claimants' submission that each party is under a general obligation of confidentiality in relation to the proceedings. The Tribunal stated that in an arbitration under NAFTA, it is not to be supposed that, in the absence of express provision, the Convention or the Rules and Regulations impose a general obligation on the parties, the effect of which would be to preclude a Government (or the other party) from discussing the case in public, thereby depriving the public of knowledge and information concerning government and public affairs. The decision concluded by repeating the comment made by the *Metalclad* Tribunal, namely that it would be of advantage to the orderly unfolding of the arbitral process if during the proceedings, the parties were to limit public discussion to what is considered necessary.[319]

2.207   The trend towards greater transparency in investor–state arbitration has emerged more clearly in recent years. In *Biwater Gauff (Tanzania) Ltd v United Republic of Tanzania*,[320] the tribunal recognised that the 2006 ICSID Rules reflected this overall trend towards transparency. The tribunal considered the balance between transparency and what it referred to as the integrity of the arbitral process, and concluded that some confidentiality controls were warranted, but ought to be 'carefully and narrowly delimited'.[321] Ultimately, the tribunal did not prevent the parties from discussing the case in public, or from publishing awards and other decisions by the tribunal, but restricted the disclosure of records of hearings, submissions, and witness statements.

---

[316] Ibid., at [13].

[317] *R Loewen and Loewen Corporation v United States of America*, Decision on Hearing of Respondent's Objection to Competence and Jurisdiction, ICSID Case No. ARB(AF)/98/3, IIC 253 (2001), 7 ICSID Rep 425, 128 ILR 339.

[318] Ibid., at [25]. (The current Additional Facility Rules provide that '[u]pon request of a party, the Centre shall publish recordings or transcripts of hearings, unless the other party objects': see r. 75(3).)

[319] Ibid., at [26].

[320] *Biwater Gauff (Tanzania) Ltd v United Republic of Tanzania*, ICSID Case No. ARB/05/22, Procedural Order No. 3, 29 September 2006.

[321] Ibid.

Reflecting this trend towards transparency, UNCITRAL has published the UNCITRAL **2.208**
Transparency Rules already referred to in Chapter 1.[322] The rules provide for the publication of
all documents, including the notice of arbitration, written pleadings, and lists of exhibits (and expert reports and witness statements, if any person so requests). Public access to hearings is guaranteed and interested third parties are entitled to make submissions. However, tribunals have
discretion to order that certain documents should remain confidential if they contain protected
information or if their disclosure would undermine the integrity of the arbitral process. With the
entry into force of the Mauritius Convention on Transparency in Treaty-based Investor–State
Arbitration, in October 2017, the application of the UNCITRAL Transparency Rules has been
extended significantly to all arbitrations arising from an investment treaty concluded before 1
April 2014 where both the host state and investor's home state are parties thereto.[323]

Under the SIAC Investment Rules, the parties are deemed to have given their consent to **2.209**
SIAC to publish certain information regarding a case, including redacted excerpts of the
reasoning of the tribunal.[324]

Under the Stockholm Chamber of Commerce (SCC) Arbitration Rules (2017), third parties **2.210**
may apply to the tribunal to make written submissions in treaty-based investor–state arbitrations.[325] In considering such applications, a tribunal 'shall have regard to: the nature and
significance of the interest of the Third Person in the arbitration; (ii) whether the submission would assist the Arbitral Tribunal in determining a material factual or legal issue in the
arbitration by bringing a perspective, particular knowledge or insight that is distinct from
or broader than that of the disputing parties; and (iii) any other relevant circumstances'.

(f) Revisions to rules of arbitration

The increasing number of arbitrations in which there is a legitimate public interest, such **2.211**
as the investor–state arbitrations discussed in this chapter and in Chapter 11, has led to an
erosion of the concept of confidentiality, with pleadings and awards being publicly available
on the Internet and elsewhere. Some arbitration institutions have therefore amended their
rules to impose an express duty of confidentiality upon the parties, but this may be overridden if it is judged that the public interest so requires.

Article 30 of the LCIA Rules imposes an express duty of confidentiality on the parties to the **2.212**
arbitration as follows:

> 30.1 The parties undertake as a general principle to keep confidential all awards in the
> arbitration, together with all materials in the arbitration created for the purpose of

---

[322] The Rules apply to UNCITRAL arbitrations under investment treaties concluded after 1 April 2014. They
apply to disputes under existing treaties only if the parties so agree. They do not affect commercial or state-to-
state arbitrations. Pro-transparency provisions are now also contained in the US and Canada model BITs, and the
EU trade spokesperson has indicated that the Rules 'set a benchmark for all future EU investment treaties': see
European Commission, 'EU backs new transparency standards for investor-state dispute settlement', Press release (11 February 2013), available online at http://trade.ec.europa.eu/doclib/press/index.cfm?id = 868
[323] United Nations Convention on Transparency in Treaty-based Investor–State Arbitration (New York,
2014) (entry into force 18 October 2017), Arts 1 and 2.
[324] Art. 38.
[325] Appendix III, Art. 3.

the arbitration and all other documents produced by another party in the proceedings not otherwise in the public domain, save and to the extent that disclosure may be required of a party by legal duty, to protect or pursue a legal right, or to enforce or challenge an award in legal proceedings before a state court or other legal authority. The parties shall seek the same undertaking of confidentiality from all those that it involves in the arbitration, including but not limited to any authorised representative, witness of fact, expert or service provider.

30.2   Article 30.1 of the LCIA Rules shall also apply, with necessary changes, to the Arbitral Tribunal, any tribunal secretary and any expert to the Arbitral Tribunal. Notwithstanding any other provision of the LCIA Rules, the deliberations of the Arbitral Tribunal shall remain confidential to its members and if appropriate any tribunal secretary, save as required by any applicable law and to the extent that disclosure of an arbitrator's refusal to participate in the arbitration is required of the other members of the Arbitral Tribunal under Articles 10, 12, 26.6 and 27.5.

30.3   The LCIA does not publish any award or any part of an award without the prior written consent of all parties and the Arbitral Tribunal.

2.213   Similar restrictions are imposed under some other major institutional rules.[326] However, such express confidentiality provisions are no longer widespread. By way of notable example, the ICC Rules only provide that a tribunal 'may make orders concerning the confidentiality of the arbitration proceedings or of any other matters in connection with the arbitration and may take measures for protecting trade secrets and confidential information'.[327] As noted above, once an award has been issued, the ICC may publish the award in a redacted form after two years unless a party objects and will publish such awards for consultation.

2.214   The WIPO Rules carry the protection of 'trade secrets' much further, as might be expected from an organisation concerned with the protection of intellectual property rights. Article 54 of the WIPO Rules defines 'confidential information' as any information, regardless of the medium in which it is expressed:

(a)   [...] which is:
     (i)   in the possession of a party;
     (ii) not accessible to the public;
     (iii) of commercial, financial or industrial significance; and
     (iv) treated as confidential by the person possessing it.
   [...]

2.215   On application by the relevant party, the tribunal may classify such information as 'confidential',[328] effectively restricting its disclosure to the tribunal and the parties. In exceptional circumstances, the tribunal may delegate this duty to a 'confidentiality adviser' who will determine whether the information is to be so classified, and if so, to whom it may be disclosed, in whole or in part.[329] As an additional safeguard, the tribunal may appoint the

---

[326] See, e.g., Swiss Rules, Art. 44; HKIAC Rules, Art. 45. Rule 39.3 of the SIAC Rules specifies that the duty of confidentiality extends to pleadings, evidence, and other materials in the arbitration proceedings, all documents produced by another party, the award, and the very existence of the proceedings.
[327] ICC Rules, Art. 22.3.
[328] WIPO Rules, Art. 54.c.
[329] WIPO Rules, Art. 54.d.

'confidentiality adviser' as an expert to report on specific issues on the basis of the confidential information, without disclosing that information either to the other party or to the tribunal itself.[330]

For completeness, it should be noted that the WIPO Rules extend the protection of confidentiality to the very existence of the arbitration,[331] to disclosures made during the arbitration,[332] and to the award.[333] The duty of confidentiality is also, of course, imposed upon the tribunal and the WIPO centre itself.[334]   **2.216**

(g) Summary

One of the traditional advantages of arbitration was that it is a private proceeding, in which the parties may air their differences and grievances, and discuss their financial circumstances, their proprietary 'know-how', and so forth, without exposure to the gaze of the public and the reporting of the media. That arbitral hearings are held in private still remains a constant feature of arbitration, and this creates the potential for confidentiality. However, many modern laws and rules of arbitration no longer provide that—absent the parties' express agreement—proceedings will be confidential. To ensure the confidentiality of the entire proceedings, it is increasingly necessary to agree this expressly, either by selecting one of those remaining sets of arbitration rules that contain an express provision of the relevant rules (for example those of the LCIA or of WIPO), or to enter into a specific confidentiality agreement as part of the agreement to arbitrate, or at the outset of proceedings.[335]   **2.217**

G. Defective Arbitration Clauses

The principal defects found in arbitration clauses are those of inconsistency, uncertainty, and inoperability. The argument as to whether an arbitration clause suffers from one or more of these defects is likely to be raised where, for example, a party takes action in a national court in relation to a dispute and the defendant seeks a stay of the proceedings on the basis of the existence of the arbitration clause. In such circumstances, the application for a stay may be opposed on the basis that the arbitration agreement was 'inoperative or incapable of being performed'.[336]   **2.218**

---

[330] WIPO Rules, Art. 54.e.
[331] WIPO Rules, Art. 75.
[332] WIPO Rules, Art. 76.
[333] WIPO Rules, Art. 77.
[334] WIPO Rules, Art. 78.
[335] See the concluding comments, which continue to be pertinent, of Rawding and Seeger, '*Aegis v European Re* and the confidentiality of arbitration awards' (2003) 19 Arb Intl 484. The UNCITRAL Notes, paras 31–32, make the very same recommendation. When drafting confidentiality clauses, parties may be aided by the Model Procedural Order on Confidentiality. See also Hwang and Thio, 'A proposed model procedural order on confidentiality in international arbitration: A comprehensive and self-governing code' (2012) 29 J Intl Arb 137.
[336] These terms are used in the New York Convention, Art. II(3), and in the Model Law, Art. 8(1). For a discussion of the approach of national courts to the interpretation of defective arbitration clauses generally, see Auchie, 'The liberal interpretation of defective arbitration clauses in international commercial contracts: A sensible approach?' [2007] Intl Arb L Rev 206. See also Mistelis and Lew, *Pervasive Problems in International Arbitration* (Kluwer Law International, 2006), pp. 163–165.

(a) Inconsistency

2.219 Where there is an apparent inconsistency in the clause, most national courts usually attempt to give a meaning to it, in order to give effect to the general intention of the parties, which was to submit disputes to arbitration. This is the case in England, where the courts uphold a clause and strike out an inconsistent provision if it is clear that the 'surviving clause' carries into effect the real intention of the parties and the 'discarded clause' would defeat the object of the agreement.[337] Of course, much depends on the words chosen by the parties. In *Kruppa v Benedetti*,[338] an English court considered a clause in which the parties agreed that, in the event of a dispute, they would 'endeavour to first resolve the matter through Swiss arbitration' and, '[s]hould a resolution not be forthcoming', the English courts would thereafter possess non-exclusive jurisdiction.[339] The Court observed that '[i]t is logically not possible to have an effective multi-tier clause consisting of one binding tier (i.e. arbitration) followed by another binding tier (i.e. litigation)'[340] and, furthermore, it remained for the parties to agree 'on the number and identity of the arbitrators or upon the [Swiss] cantonal court which would appoint arbitrators in default'.[341] The Court thus construed the clause in such a way so as to avoid an inconsistency: the parties were not bound to resolve disputes by arbitration; rather, they were obliged to 'endeavour' to refer disputes to arbitration—failing which the English courts would have jurisdiction on a non-exclusive basis.[342]

(b) Uncertainty

2.220 Similarly, as regards uncertainty, the courts of most countries have for many years attempted to uphold an arbitration provision[343] unless the uncertainty is such that it is difficult to make sense of it. By way of example, the German courts have shown themselves time and again ready to give effect to clauses that are a long way from certain. In 2006, the Stuttgart court found that a clause referring disputes 'without resource [*sic*] to the ordinary court to Stockholm, Sweden' to be a reference to arbitration under the Stockholm Chamber of Commerce.[344] In the same year, the Oldenburg court held that a reference to

---

[337] See *Central Meat Products Ltd v JV McDaniel Ltd* [1952] 1 Lloyd's Rep 562; note also *EJR Lovelock Ltd v Exportles* [1968] 1 Lloyd's Rep 163, in which inconsistencies and uncertainties were exposed in the clause itself. See too *Mangistaumunaigaz Oil v United World Trade Inc.* [1995] 1 Lloyd's Rep 617, in which the arbitration clause provided for 'arbitration, if any, by ICC Rules in London'. The words 'if any' could be rejected as surplussage. See also *Braes of Doune Wind Farm v Alfred McAlpine* [2008] EWHC 426 (TCC) and the decision of the Swiss Federal Tribunal in Case No. 4A_376/2008 of 5 December 2008, discussed by Scherer, 'Introduction to the case law section' (2009) 4 ASA Bulletin 735.

[338] *Kruppa v Benedetti* [2014] EWHC 1887.

[339] Ibid., at [2].

[340] Ibid., at [12].

[341] Ibid., at [11].

[342] Ibid., at [15].

[343] See *Star Shipping AS v China National Foreign Trade Transportation Corporation* [1993] 2 Lloyd's Rep 445 (CA); *Nokia Maillefer SA v Mosser*, Tribunal Cantonal (Court of Appeal), 30 March 1993, (1996) XXI YBCA 681, (1995) 1 ASA Bulletin 64; *Associated British Ports v Tata Steel UK Ltd* [2017] EWHC 694 (Ch), at [26]–[27], where in the context of upholding an allegedly uncertain arbitration clause, the English High Court observed that, although each case in which a clause is challenged as being void for uncertainty is to be decided on its own facts, many of the cases 'stress that the courts should strive to give some meaning to contractual clauses agreed by the parties if it is at all possible to do so'.

[344] [2006] OLG Report Stuttgart 685.

'the International Court of Arbitration (*Internationales Schiedsgericht*) in Austria' was a reference to the international arbitration centre of the Austrian Federal Economic Chamber.[345] The Singapore courts have recently made sense of and upheld an agreement to refer and resolve disputes 'by arbitration as per Singapore Contract Rules'.[346] In the same way, institutions have generally attempted to give effect to arbitration agreements, notwithstanding a degree of uncertainty arising from the language chosen by the parties. For its part, the ICC has in the past accepted the following vague and imprecise formulations as references to the ICC Court: 'the official Chamber of Commerce in Paris, France', 'the Arbitration Commission of the Chamber of Commerce and Industry of Paris', and 'a Commission of Arbitration of French Chamber of Commerce, Paris'.[347]

From time to time, however, courts and institutions are confronted with clauses that simply fail for lack of certainty.[348] Examples are: **2.221**

(1) 'In the event of any unresolved dispute, the matter will be referred to the International Chamber of Commerce';

(2) 'All disputes arising in connection with the present agreement shall be submitted in the first instance to arbitration. The arbitrator shall be a well-known Chamber of Commerce (like the ICC) designated by mutual agreement between both parties';

(3) 'Any and all disputes arising under the arrangements contemplated hereunder [...] will be referred to mutually agreed mechanisms or procedures of international arbitration, such as the rules of the London Arbitration Association'; and

(4) 'For both parties is a decision of Lloyd or Vienna stock exchange binding and both will subjugate to the International Chamber of Commerce'.

The problem with the first example is that even if the broad reference to the ICC is taken to be a reference to the ICC Court in Paris, the clause by itself does not stipulate whether the unresolved dispute is to be settled by arbitration or by conciliation or by some other procedure. The second example provides for arbitration 'in the first instance', but fails to provide intelligibly for the appointment of an arbitral tribunal. Even if the parties were to agree upon 'a well-known Chamber of Commerce' as arbitrator, this would be of no

---

[345] [2006] Schieds VZ 223 (OLG Oldenburg).

[346] The Singapore High Court held that, notwithstanding the parties' reference to a set of non-existent rules and their failure to designate the seat or governing law of the arbitration, their agreement evinced a clear intention to settle any disputes by arbitration and was therefore binding and enforceable: *KVC Rice Intertrade Co Ltd v Asian Mineral Resources Pte Ltd* [2017] SGHC 32. See also *HKL Group Co. Ltd v Rizq International Holdings Pte Ltd* [2013] SGHC 5, in which the Singapore High Court upheld an agreement to refer disputes to 'the Arbitration Committee at Singapore under the rules of the International Chamber of Commerce', concluding that it was open to the parties to approach any arbitral institution in Singapore to administer the arbitration, applying the ICC Rules. See also, by way of contrast, *TMT v RBS* [2017] SGHC 21, in which the Singapore High Court held that the parties' dispute, which arose from trades of forward freight agreements and options through a clearing house, did not fall within the scope of their agreement to refer any disputes to arbitration under 'the arbitration rules of the relevant exchange or any other organization as the relevant exchange may direct and both parties agree to'.

[347] Derains and Schwartz, *A Guide to the ICC Rules of Arbitration* (2nd edn, Kluwer Law International, 2005), p. 86.

[348] For a recent example, see the Swiss Federal Tribunal's Decision No. 4A_279/2010 of 25 October 2010, in which it refused to uphold an arbitration clause that referred disputes to 'The American Arbitration Association or to any other US court'. The tribunal held that it was impossible to ascertain whether the parties had agreed to arbitrate to the exclusion of the state courts' primary jurisdiction. Another recent example, which is perhaps less easy to comprehend, is a decision by the Russian Supreme Court in Case No. A40-176466/17, in which it held that an arbitration clause was uncertain given that, although it specified the ICC Rules applied, it failed to specify the institution that would administer the arbitration.

avail, since arbitrators must be individuals. The third example requires the future agreement of the parties on 'mutually agreed mechanisms or procedures'. The fourth is simply meaningless.

2.222   Further examples of what have been referred to as 'pathological arbitration clauses' are to be found in Craig, Park, and Paulsson's commentary on ICC arbitration.[349] Two of the more flagrant examples include:

(1) 'In case of dispute (*contestation*), the parties undertake to submit to arbitration but in case of litigation the Tribunal de la Seine shall have exclusive jurisdiction';[350] and

(2) 'Disputes hereunder shall be referred to arbitration, to be carried out by arbitrators named by the International Chamber of Commerce in Geneva in accordance with the arbitration procedure set forth in the Civil Code of Venezuela and in the Civil Code of France, with due regard for the law of the place of arbitration'.[351]

The latter clause is given as an example of a 'disastrous compromise', which might lead to extensive litigation (unrelated to the merits of the dispute) to sort out any contradictions in the various laws stated to be applicable.[352]

(c) Inoperability

2.223   Article II(3) of the New York Convention states that:

The court of a Contracting State, when seized of an action in a matter in respect of which the parties have made an agreement within the meaning of this article, shall, at the request of one of the parties, refer the parties to arbitration, unless it finds that the said agreement is null and void, inoperative or incapable of being performed.[353]

The reference to the agreement being 'null and void' refers to the arbitration agreement itself, since, as seen in the discussion of the principle of separability, in most countries the nullity of the main contract does not necessarily affect the validity of the arbitration agreement. An arbitration agreement is 'null and void' if it is 'devoid of legal effect', for example owing to mistake, duress, or fraud.[354]

2.224   At first sight, it is difficult to see a distinction between the terms 'inoperative' and 'incapable of being performed'. However, an arbitration clause is inoperative where it has 'ceased to have legal effect'[355] as a result, for example, of a failure by the parties to comply with a time limit, or where the parties have repudiated,[356] or by their conduct impliedly revoked,

---

[349] Craig, Park, and Paulsson, *International Chamber of Commerce Arbitration* (3rd edn, Oceana, 2000), pp. 127–135.
[350] Ibid., at p. 128.
[351] Ibid., at pp. 132–133.
[352] Ibid.
[353] Similar words are contained in the Model Law, Art. 8(1).
[354] See, e.g., *Rhone Mediterranee v Achille Lauro*, 712 F.2d 50 (3d Cir.1983); *Albon v Naza Motor Trading Sdn Bhd* [2007] EWHC 665 (Ch). See also ICCA, 'Request for the enforcement of an arbitration agreement', in ICCA (ed.) *ICCA's Guide to the Interpretation of the 1958 New York Convention: A Handbook for Judges* (ICCA, 2011), pp. 51–52.
[355] *Albon v Naza Motor Trading Sdn Bhd* [2007] EWHC 665 (Ch).
[356] *Downing v Al Tameer Establishment* [2002] EWCA Civ 721.

the arbitration agreement.[357] By contrast, the expression 'incapable of being performed' appears to refer to more practical aspects of the prospective arbitration proceedings. It applies, for example, if it is for some reason impossible to establish the arbitral tribunal.[358] Courts tend to construe these provisions narrowly, to avoid offering a 'back door' for a party wishing to escape the arbitration agreement.[359]

An inability to pay advances on the costs of the arbitration,[360] or to make payment of an award,[361]   **2.225** should not mean that an arbitration clause is inoperative or incapable of being performed. However, in India, it has been held in the past that a stay of court proceedings should be refused on the grounds that exchange control regulations would prevent payments in foreign currency to the arbitrators and other overseas expenses of those participating in a foreign arbitration.[362]

H. Waiver of the Right to Arbitrate

In certain circumstances, a party may waive its right under an arbitration agreement to have   **2.226** a dispute finally settled by arbitration. Under most laws, such a waiver will typically require a statement, or conduct, that amounts to a clear and unequivocal renunciation of the right to arbitrate. Such a renunciation can be found in a party's participation in national court proceedings in which the parties, subject matter, and the relief sought[363] are identical to actual or prospective arbitration proceedings.

Article 8(1) of the Model Law provides: **2.227**

> A court before which an action is brought in a matter which is the subject of an arbitration
> agreement shall, *if a party so requests not later than when submitting his first statement on*

---

[357] *Corcoran v Ardra Insurance Co. Ltd*, 842 F.2d 31 (2d Cir. 1988), also reported in (1989) XIV YBCA 773. For the continuation of the saga, see (1991) XVI YBCA 663 and (1992) XVII YBCA 666. See also Pryles, 'Inoperative and operative arbitration agreements: Developments in Australian law' (2006) 23 J Intl Arb 227.

[358] In *Aminoil v Government of Kuwait* (1982) XXI ILM 976, the original arbitration clause provided that the third arbitrator was to be appointed by the 'British Political Resident in the Gulf', an official whose post had ceased to exist at the time that the dispute arose; this defect was, in the event, cured by the conclusion of a new submission agreement. See also *Control Screening LLC v Tech. Application & Prod. Co. (Tecapro)*, 687 F.3d 163 (3d Cir. 2012), where the arbitral institution specified in the arbitration clause ('International Arbitration Center of European Countries') did not exist, and the US District Court held that the arbitration should proceed in New Jersey.

[359] See, e.g., the decision of the Supreme Court of Canada in *Seidel v Telus Communications Inc.* [2011] 1 SCR 531. See also *Bauhinia Corp. v China Nat'l Mach. & Equip. Imp. & Exp. Corp.*, 819 F.2d 247 (9th Cir. 1987), where the US Court of Appeals for the 9th Circuit designated the AAA to administer the arbitration, notwithstanding that the arbitration clause at issue was ambiguous on the choice of forum.

[360] See *El Nasharty v J Sainsbury plc* [2007] EWHC 2618 (Comm), at [4].

[361] See *The Rena K* [1979] QB 377. See also Amparo Directo 465/2005, Tercer Tribunal Colegiado en Materia Civil del Primer Circuito, Servicios Administrativos de Emergencia, 2 September 2005, in which the Mexican courts held that an arbitration agreement cannot be 'inoperative' as a result of external factors that do not pertain to the agreement itself, such as the financial situation of the parties.

[362] See van den Berg, *The New York Arbitration Convention of 1958* (Kluwer Law International, 1981), p. 160.

[363] It is not unusual for parties to bring administrative and court proceedings in parallel to arbitration proceedings in relation to the same underlying subject matter when the relief sought in the administrative and court proceedings is not available from an arbitral tribunal. Such parallel administrative and/or court proceedings would not amount to a waiver of the right to arbitrate. This can happen, e.g., where parties bring administrative and court proceedings to reverse a tax assessment, in parallel to bringing a contractual claim in international arbitration in relation to the consequences of a tax assessment. Whilst an arbitral tribunal can award contractual relief, it cannot take the administrative act of reversing a tax assessment. As a consequence, an administrative or judicial proceeding to reverse the tax assessment could not amount to a waiver of the right to arbitrate a contractual claim. Similarly, as the case of *BEA Hotels NV v Bellway LLC* [2007] EWHC 1363 (Comm) illustrates, if a party commences arbitration, and thereafter commences court proceedings that unequivocally exclude any claims that are subject to the parties' arbitration agreement, such court proceedings do not constitute a waiver.

the substance *of the dispute*, refer the parties to arbitration unless it finds that the agreement is null and void, inoperative or incapable of being performed.[364]

2.228   Under section 9(3) and (4) of the English Arbitration Act 1996, a party wishing to stay court proceedings brought in breach of an arbitration agreement must make its application before taking any step in those proceedings in answer to the other party's substantive claim. In *Eagle Star Insurance*,[365] the House of Lords (now the UK Supreme Court) summarised the position as follows:

> [I]n order to deprive a defendant of his recourse to arbitration a 'step in the proceedings' must be one which impliedly affirms the correctness of the proceedings and the willingness of the defendant to go along with a determination by the Courts of law instead of arbitration.[366]

Applying this test, the Court concluded that an application to strike out a defective statement of claim did not constitute a 'step in the proceedings'.[367]

2.229   A similar approach prevails in Australia. The courts require proof that a party has 'unequivocally abandoned' its right to arbitrate by taking steps that are wholly inconsistent with an intention to have the dispute finally settled by arbitration.[368] An example of such conduct is found in *La Donna v Wolford*,[369] where the Supreme Court of Victoria found that a party had waived its right to arbitrate by applying for security for costs in court proceedings. The Court reasoned as follows:

> [The party] sought an advantage, or at least sought to impose upon La Donna a burden, which was based upon the proposition that the litigation would proceed in this Court, that the defendant would take steps, and that the defendant would incur costs in taking those steps, in that litigation in this Court. This step was an unequivocal abandonment of the alternative course, being an application for a stay and a consequent arbitration.[370]

2.230   In certain circumstances, a party may maintain its right to arbitrate while taking substantive steps in court proceedings, for example by expressly reserving its rights under the arbitration agreement. In *Eisenwerk Hensel Bayreuth GmbH v Australian Granites Ltd*,[371] a party filed a defence in court proceedings and the Australian courts held that there had been no waiver, noting that the party was faced with the immediate threat of a default judgment and

---

[364] Emphasis added.

[365] *Eagle Star Insurance Co. v Yuval Insurance Co.* [1978] 1 Lloyd's Rep 357 (a case decided under the Arbitration Act 1950).

[366] Ibid., at 361. The courts have adopted the same approach under the Arbitration Act 1996: see *Patel v Patel* [2000] QB 551; *Bilta (UK) Ltd (in liquidation) v Nazir* [2010] EWHC 1086 (Ch).

[367] See also *Capital Trust Investments Ltd v Radio Design TJ AB* [2002] EWCA Civ 135, in which a party was held not to have waived its right to arbitrate notwithstanding its application for summary judgment in the court proceedings. The summary judgment application was expressed to be in the alternative to the stay application.

[368] See, e.g., *ACD Tridon Inc. v Tridon Australia Pty Ltd* [2002] NSWSC 896, in which the Supreme Court of New South Wales held that a party had not waived its right to arbitrate although it had consented to directions, obtained an order for document production, and even agreed to be joined as a party to the New South Wales proceedings. The Court considered that the parties were simply 'exploring various ways of resolving the whole or parts of the disputes' (at [75]).

[369] *La Donna Pty Ltd v Wolford AG* [2005] VSC 359.

[370] Ibid., at [26].

[371] *Eisenwerk Hensel Bayreuth GmbH v Australian Granites Ltd* [2001] 1 QDR 461.

had filed a cover letter with its defence, confirming that it had no intention of discontinuing the arbitration proceedings that it had already instituted.

Under Canadian law, a party may waive its right to arbitrate if it files a defence or coun-   **2.231**
terclaim in court proceedings.[372] In Singapore, the filing of an application to strike out a claim, on the basis of alleged technical defects, is not considered a step in the pro-ceeding, but if such an application relates to the merits, it may constitute a waiver.[373] In China, the first court hearing is the final opportunity for any party to raise any objection to the court's jurisdiction on the ground that the dispute is covered by an arbitration agreement.[374]

The US courts have traditionally been reluctant to find that a party has waived its right to   **2.232**
arbitrate unless: (a) the party had knowledge of its right to arbitrate; (b) the party acted inconsistently with that right; and (c) the inconsistency caused prejudice.[375] In *Louisiana Stadium v Merrill Lynch*,[376] this test was satisfied in circumstances under which a party filed and pursued an action in the courts, then waited 11 months to invoke the arbitration agreement.

A party may also lose its right to arbitrate if there is a lengthy delay in the prosecution of   **2.233**
its claim(s). Under the English Arbitration Act 1996, an arbitral tribunal has the power to dismiss a claim on broadly the same grounds as a national court may strike out claims in litigation.[377] The 1996 Act provides that, unless otherwise agreed by the parties, the tribunal may dismiss the claim if it is satisfied that there has been 'inordinate and inex-cusable' delay on the part of the claimant in pursuing its claim, and that the delay either gives rise (or is likely to give rise) to a 'substantial risk' that a fair resolution of the dis-pute is not possible, or that it has caused (or is likely to cause) serious prejudice to the respondent.[378]

---

[372] See, e.g., *Granville Shipping Co. v Pegasus Lines Ltd (TD)* [1996] 2 FC 853, Federal Court of Canada.
[373] *L Capital Jones Ltd v Maniach Pte Ltd* [2017] SGCA 03, at [77]. If a party commences arbitration, and there-after commences court proceedings that unequivocally exclude any claims that are subject to the parties' arbitra-tion agreement, such court proceedings do not constitute a waiver: *BEA Hotels NV v Bellway LLC* [2007] EWHC 1363 (Comm). See also *Amoe Pte Ltd v Otto Marine Ltd* [2013] SGHC 240, in which the plaintiff commenced a court action, and the defendant subsequently served on the plaintiff a request to produce certain documents, namely a copy of the parties' contract (which the defendant did not have in its possession). Because the purpose of the defendant's request was to enable it to ascertain whether the parties' contract provided for arbitration, and it was unable to make an unequivocal election to pursue litigation over arbitration until it was made fully aware of the terms of the contract, the Singapore High Court held that the defendant's conduct did not amount to a waiver (at [19]).
[374] The Arbitration Law of the People's Republic of China, Art. 26.
[375] See, e.g., *Newirth v Aegis Senior Communities, LLC*, 931 F. 3d 935, 940 (9th Cir. 2019) (holding that 'a party acts inconsistently with exercising the right to arbitrate when it (1) makes an intentional decision not to move to compel arbitration and (2) actively litigates the merits of a case for a prolonged period of time in order to take advantage of being in court') (at [941]); *Louisiana Stadium & Exposition Dist. v Merrill Lynch*, 626 F. 3d 156, 159 (2d Cir. 2010); *In re Pharmacy Ben. Managers Antitrust Litigation*, 700 F. 3d 109, 117 (3d Cir. 2012). See also *Airbus SAS v Aviation Partners Inc.*, No. C12-1228JLR, United States District Court, Western District of Washington, 25 October 2012; *Citibank NA v Stok & Associates PA*, No. 09-13556, 11th Circuit, 20 July 2010.
[376] *Louisiana Stadium & Exposition District, State of Louisiana v Merrill Lynch*, No. 10-889-CV, 2d Circuit, 22 November 2010. See also *Great Western Mortgage Corporation v Peacock*, 110 F.3d 222 (3d Cir. 1997).
[377] This provision was incorporated into the Arbitration Act 1950 by the Courts and Legal Services Act 1990. It was later incorporated into the English Arbitration Act 1996, s. 41(3).
[378] The position is similar in Hong Kong. If a claimant has unreasonably delayed in pursuing a claim, it may be dismissed: Arbitration Ordinance, s. 59.

I. Multiparty Arbitrations

(a) Introduction

2.234 When several parties are involved in a dispute, it is usually considered desirable that the issues should be dealt with in the same proceedings, rather than in a series of separate proceedings. In general terms, this saves time and money. More importantly, it avoids the possibility of conflicting decisions on the same issues of law and fact, since all issues are determined by the same tribunal at the same time. In national courts, it is generally possible to join additional parties, or to consolidate separate sets of proceedings. In arbitration, however, it is difficult, and sometimes impossible, to achieve this, because the arbitral process is based upon the agreement of the parties. As a working group of the ICC's Commission on International Arbitration noted in its *Final Report on Multi-party Arbitrations*:

> The difficulties of multi-party arbitrations all result from a single cause. Arbitration has a contractual basis; only the common will of the contracting parties can entitle a person to bring a proceeding before an arbitral tribunal against another person and oblige that other person to appear before it. The greater the number of such persons, the greater the degree of care which should be taken to ensure that none of them is joined in the proceeding against its will.[379]

2.235 Where there is a multiparty arbitration, it may be because there are several parties to one contract, or it may be because there are several contracts with different parties that have a bearing on the matters in dispute. It is helpful to distinguish between the two.

(i) Several parties to one contract

2.236 It is increasingly common—particularly in international trade and commerce—for individuals, corporations, or state agencies to join together in a joint venture, or consortium, or in some other legal relationship of this kind, in order to enter into a contract with another party or parties. Where such a contract contains an arbitration clause and a dispute arises, the members of the consortium or joint venture may decide that they would each like to appoint an arbitrator. This is what happened in *Dutco*.[380] Dutco had entered into a contract with a consortium of two German companies and, when disputes arose, brought arbitral proceedings under the ICC Rules against those two companies. Each of the companies claimed to be entitled to appoint an arbitrator. This created problems, because the ICC Rules do not contemplate an arbitral tribunal of more than three arbitrators.[381] The ICC requested the two German companies to make a joint nomination of an arbitrator. They did so, but

---

[379] Commission on International Arbitration, *Final Report on Multiparty Arbitrations*, Paris, June 1994, published in (1995) 6 ICC Bulletin 26 (the 'Delvolvé Report'), para. 5. See also generally Hanotiau, *Complex Arbitrations: Multiparty, Multicontract, Multi-issue and Class Actions* (Kluwer Law International, 2005). For an illustration of judicial reluctance to order consolidation unless the agreement of all parties is express, see the US courts, e.g. in *Stolt-Nielsen SA v Animal Feeds Intern Corporation*, 2008 WL 4779582 (2d Cir. 4 November 2008); *Glencore Ltd v Schnitzer Steel Products*, 189 F.3d 264, 265–266 (2d Cir. 1999); *Champ v Siegel Trading Co.* 55 F.3d.269 (7th Cir. 1995).

[380] *BKMI and Siemens v Dutco*, French Cass. Civ. 1ere, 7 January 1992, (1992) 1 Bull Civ, (1992) 119 J du Droit Intl 707, 2nd document; commentary by Bellet [1992] Rev Arb 470, at 473–482; excerpts in (1993) XVII YBCA 140.

[381] ICC Rules, Art. 12 (ex Art. 8.4).

reserved their right to challenge the ICC's decision, which they regarded as depriving each of them of the right to nominate an arbitrator. The French Court of Cassation agreed with the German companies: the court regarded the principle of equality in the appointment of arbitrators as a matter of public policy.

Many arbitration rules now make express provision for arbitration proceedings arising under multiparty contracts, so as to avoid the *Dutco* dilemma. For example, Article 12.6 of the ICC Rules states: **2.237**

[…]

Where there are multiple claimants or multiple respondents, and where the dispute is to be referred to three arbitrators, the multiple claimants, jointly, and the multiple respondents, jointly, shall nominate an arbitrator for confirmation

[…]

In the absence of a joint nomination […] and where all parties are unable to agree to a method for the constitution of the arbitral tribunal, the Court may appoint each member of the arbitral tribunal and shall designate one of them to act as president. […]

Article 8 of the LCIA Rules adopts a similar procedure: **2.238**

8.1 Where the Arbitration Agreement entitles each party howsoever to nominate an arbitrator, the parties to the dispute number more than two and such parties have not all agreed in writing that the disputant parties represent collectively two separate 'sides' for the formation of the Arbitral Tribunal (as Claimants on one side and Respondents on the other side, each side nominating a single arbitrator), the LCIA Court shall appoint the Arbitral Tribunal without regard to any party's entitlement or nomination.

8.2 In such circumstances, the Arbitration Agreement shall be treated for all purposes as a written agreement by the parties for the nomination and appointment of the Arbitral Tribunal by the LCIA Court alone.

These and other arbitration rules[382] recognise the right of the parties to nominate a member of the arbitral tribunal if they are able to agree, but takes this right away from all parties equally and vests it in the institution if they cannot do so. This is a sensible solution to the problem of constituting an arbitral tribunal where there are three or more parties who are unable to agree amongst themselves. However, there may be difficulties when it comes to obtaining recognition and enforcement of an award made by a tribunal that has been established *for* the parties, rather than *by* the parties. The New York Convention, in Article V(1)(d), states that recognition and enforcement of an award may be refused on proof that '[t]he composition of the arbitral authority or the arbitral procedure was not in accordance with the agreement of the parties, or, failing such agreement, was not in accordance with the law of the country where the arbitration took place'. The Model Law contains a similar provision.[383]

However, if a losing party in an arbitration were to ask the competent court to refuse recognition or enforcement of an award on these grounds, the party seeking enforcement would   **2.239**

---

[382] See the UNCITRAL Rules, Art. 10; SIAC Rules, r. 12; Swiss Rules, Art. 8; HKIAC Rules, Art. 8.2; SCC Rules, Art. 17.5.

[383] In Model Law, Art. 36(1)(a)(iv).

argue with force that the composition of the arbitral tribunal *was* in accordance with the agreement of the parties, since, by adopting the institutional rules, they had agreed, inter alia, to this particular provision.

2.240   As noted above, many arbitration rules now make express provisions for the joinder of third parties to an arbitration.[384] Some of these rules specify that joinder must be requested before the constitution of the tribunal, in order to protect the new party's right to nominate an arbitrator.[385] Other rules allow the tribunal, having been constituted, to determine the issue of joinder, taking into account whether a joinder in these circumstances will result in any prejudice to the new party.[386]

(ii) Several contracts with different parties

2.241   A different problem arises where there are several contracts with different parties, each of which has a bearing on the issues in dispute. Again, this is a situation that is not uncommon in modern international trade and commerce. A major international construction project is likely to involve not only the employer and the main contractor (which itself may be a consortium of companies), but also a host of specialised suppliers and subcontractors. Each of these parties will be operating under a different contract, often with different choice-of-law and arbitration clauses—and yet any dispute between, say, the employer and the main contractor is likely to involve one or more of the suppliers or subcontractors.[387]

2.242   What happens when a dispute between the employer and the main contractor is referred to arbitration, and the main contractor wishes to join the subcontractor in the proceedings, on the basis that if there is any liability, it is a liability that the main contractor is entitled to pass on to the subcontractor? This was the issue raised in the *Adgas* case.[388] Adgas[389] was the owner of a plant that produced liquefied natural gas in the Arabian Gulf. The company started an arbitration in England against the main contractors under an international construction contract, alleging that one of the huge tanks that had been constructed to store the gas was defective. The main contractor denied liability, but added that if the tank were defective, it would be the fault of the Japanese subcontractor. Adgas brought ad hoc arbitration proceedings against the main contractor before a sole arbitrator in London. The main contractor then brought separate arbitration proceedings, also in London, against the Japanese subcontractor.

---

[384] See paragraphs 2.65–2.69 above.

[385] See, e.g., the ICC Rules, Art. 7, which provides that 'unless all parties, including the additional party, otherwise agree [...], no additional party may be joined after the confirmation or appointment of any arbitrator' and that 'any Request for Joinder made after the confirmation or appointment of any arbitrator shall be decided by the arbitral tribunal once constituted and shall be subject to the additional party accepting the constitution of the arbitral tribunal and agreeing to the Terms of Reference'.

[386] See, e.g., the UNCITRAL Rules, Art. 7.5, which provides that 'the tribunal may [...] allow one or more persons to be joined in the arbitration provided such person is a party to the arbitration agreement, unless the arbitral tribunal finds [...] that joinder should not be permitted because of prejudice to any of those parties'.

[387] Another common situation arises in connection with bank guarantees concluded in connection with the main agreement: see Hanotiau, *Complex Arbitrations: Multiparty, Multicontract, Multi-issue and Class Actions* (Kluwer Law International, 2005), pp. 129–132; Wessel and Gsell, '*ITSA v SATCOM & BBVA*: Spanish court extends an arbitration agreement to guarantor not a party to the contract' [2006] Intl Arb L Rev N16.

[388] *Abu Dhabi Gas Liquefaction Co. Ltd v Eastern Bechtel Corporation* [1982] 2 Lloyd's Rep 425 (CA), (1982) XXI ILM 1057, [1983] Rev Arb 119 (with comment by Paulsson), (1984) IX YBCA 448.

[389] That is, the Abu Dhabi Gas Liquefaction Co. Ltd, which itself was owned by a consortium consisting of the Abu Dhabi National Oil Corporation and several international corporations.

There is little doubt that if the matter had been litigated in an English court, the Japanese   **2.243**
company would have been joined as a party to the action. However, Adgas did not agree that
the Japanese subcontractor should be brought into its arbitration with the main contractor,
since this would have lengthened and complicated the proceedings,[390] nor did the Japanese
subcontractor agree to be joined. It preferred to await the outcome of the main arbitration,
to see whether or not there was a case to answer.

Lord Denning, giving judgment in the English Court of Appeal, plainly wished that an   **2.244**
order could be made consolidating the two sets of arbitral proceedings, so as to save time
and money and to avoid the risk of inconsistent awards:

> As we have often pointed out, there is a danger in having two separate arbitrations in a case
> like this. You might get inconsistent findings if there were two separate arbitrators. This has
> been said in many cases [...] it is most undesirable that there should be inconsistent find-
> ings by two separate arbitrators on virtually the self-same question, such as causation. It is
> very desirable that everything should be done to avoid such a circumstance.[391]

The Court recognised that it was powerless to order consolidation without the consent of
all parties:

> There is no power in this court or any other court to do more upon an application such as
> this than to appoint an arbitrator or arbitrators, as the case may be; we have no powers to
> attach conditions to that appointment, and certainly no power to inform or direct an arbi-
> trator as to how he should thereafter conduct the arbitration or arbitrations.[392]

However, the Court was able to go some way towards meeting the problem of conflicting   **2.245**
decisions. The case had come before the Court on an application for the appointment of
an arbitrator, and the Court decided that it could appoint the *same* arbitrator in each case,
if that arbitrator was ready to accept the appointment (as indeed he was). Lord Denning
said: 'It seems to me that there is ample power in the court to appoint in each arbitration
the same arbitrator. It seems to me highly desirable that this should be done so as to avoid
inconsistent findings.'[393] This was one practical solution to the problem of conflicting decisions—but it still meant that there would be two separate arbitrations arising out of the
same dispute.

(b) Court-ordered consolidation

A different solution that has been adopted in different parts of the world has been to   **2.246**
enact legislation that enables the relevant national court to order consolidation of arbitrations.[394] In the Netherlands, for example, under the 1986 Arbitration Act, the president

---

[390] There was also a different choice-of-law clause in the two contracts.

[391] *Abu Dhabi Gas*, at 427.

[392] *Abu Dhabi Gas*, at 427 *per* Watkins LJ. See also *Hartford Accident and Indemnity Co. v Swiss Reinsurance
America Corporation* 87 F.Supp.2d 300 (SDNY 2000), in which the US courts acknowledged the risk of inconsistent decisions, but stated that this did not give courts 'the authority to reform [...] private contracts'.

[393] *Abu Dhabi Gas*, at 427.

[394] See generally Hanotiau, *Complex Arbitrations: Multiparty, Multicontract, Multi-issue and Class Actions*
(Kluwer Law International, 2005), pp. 179–190.

of the District Court in Amsterdam may order the whole or partial consolidation of two or more connected arbitrations in the Netherlands, unless the parties agree otherwise.[395] Some provinces of Canada also allow for court-ordered consolidation of connected proceedings.[396]

2.247 There is no provision in the Model Law for the consolidation of arbitrations, but nevertheless several states that have adopted it have added a provision providing for court-ordered consolidation. In any given case, it is necessary to consider the relevant legislation of the state concerned to see exactly what provision is made, but two examples illustrate what might be expected. Under the Hong Kong Arbitration Ordinance, the court may consolidate proceedings or order them to be heard concurrently or consecutively if: (a) a common question of law or fact arises in both proceedings; (b) the disputes arise out of the same transaction or series of transactions; or (c) the court considers it desirable to do so for any other reason.[397] In California, the court may order consolidation on such terms as it considers just and necessary. If the parties cannot agree upon the arbitrators, the court will appoint them. The court will also determine any other matters on which the parties cannot agree and which are necessary for the conduct of the arbitration.[398]

2.248 At first sight, court-ordered consolidation seems to be a powerful solution to the problem of ensuring consistent decisions, when the same or similar issues of law and fact would otherwise come before different arbitral tribunals. There are, however, likely to be practical and legal problems. The different arbitration agreements may differ in their provisions as to number and method of appointment of arbitrators, as to the relevant rules of arbitration, as to the power to issue interim awards, and so on. They may also differ as to the law governing the merits of the dispute.[399] Finally, there may be a problem in obtaining recognition and enforcement for such awards. Reference has already been made to the requirement of Article V(1)(d) of the New York Convention to the effect that the composition of the arbitral authority, and the arbitral procedure, must be in accordance with the agreement of the parties. Where an arbitral tribunal that has been imposed upon the parties makes an award, it may be argued that the award should be refused recognition and enforcement under this provision of the Convention.[400] There is strong support, however, for the view that where a court *has* ordered a consolidated arbitration, the award *will* be enforceable under the

[395] Code of Civil Procedure 1986, Art. 1046. Proposals submitted to the Dutch parliament to amend this provision were approved on 27 May 2014. The amended Art. 1046 contains three material differences. First, the parties may now nominate a third party (e.g. an arbitral institution) to decide on a party's request to consolidate arbitration proceedings. This was a power previously held only by the president of the District Court of Amsterdam. Secondly, such a third party's power to consolidate is broader than that of the president (who may order consolidation only where both sets of proceedings are in the Netherlands), in that the third party may also decide on a request to consolidate a Netherlands-seated arbitration with an arbitration seated *outside* of the Netherlands. Thirdly, the requirement that the subject matter of the arbitrations be connected has been removed.
[396] See *Western Oil Sands Inc. v Allianz Insurance Co. of Canada* [2004] ABQB 79.
[397] See the Hong Kong Arbitration Ordinance 2011, Sch. 2, s. 2. However, parties must 'opt in' to this provision: see also *Chun Wo Building Construction v China Merchants Tower Co.* [2000] 2 HKC 255.
[398] California Code of Civil Procedure, § 1297.272. For a note of other states that adopted the Model Law, but added a provision for consolidation of arbitrations, see Sanders, 'Arbitration', in Cappelletti (ed.) *Encyclopedia of International and Comparative Law, Vol. XVI* (Brill, 1987), ch. 12, para. 45. See also Leboulanger, 'Multi-contract arbitrations' (1996) 13 J Intl Arb 43.
[399] As in *Abu Dhabi Gas Liquefaction Co. Ltd v Eastern Bechtel Corporation* [1982] 2 Lloyd's Rep 425 (CA): see paragraph 2.219.
[400] See Hascher, 'Consolidation of arbitration by American courts: Fostering or hampering international commercial arbitration?' (1984) 1 J Intl Arb 127.

New York Convention provided that the parties have at least agreed to arbitration and to the same arbitral jurisdiction.[401]

(c) Consolidation by consent

(i) Under an arbitration agreement

The ICC Commission on International Arbitration's *Final Report on Multi-party Arbitrations* **2.249**
stated that, '[i]n a multilateral relationship, whether involving a single contract or separate related contracts, it may be appropriate or necessary to have a multi-party arbitration clause'.[402]

Drafting such a clause is not easy. It requires a close understanding of the nature of the re- **2.250**
lationship between the different parties and of the type of disputes that may conceivably arise, and it calls for careful and detailed drafting. It is miles away from the standard, or model, form of arbitration clause under which most arbitrations are conducted. The report includes as an annexe examples of multiparty arbitration agreements that have been drawn from various sources.[403]

(ii) Under institutional rules

Neither the Model Law nor the UNCITRAL Rules contain any provision for the consolida- **2.251**
tion of different arbitrations. However, modern sets of institutional rules have developed useful pre-fabricated provisions. Under Article 10 of the ICC Rules, the ICC Court may, at the request of a party, consolidate two or more pending arbitrations where: (a) the parties agree; (b) all claims are made under the same arbitration agreement; or (c) in the case of claims under multiple contracts, the arbitrations are between the same parties, the disputes arise in connection with the same legal relationship, and the Court considers that the terms of the arbitration agreements are compatible.

Article 22A of the LCIA Rules provides that an arbitral tribunal may order the consoli- **2.252**
dation of arbitrations where either (a) all parties to the arbitrations to be consolidated so agree in writing; or (b) the arbitrations to be consolidated were commenced under the same arbitration agreement or compatible arbitration agreements, provided that those arbitrations are between the same parties or arise out of the same transaction or series of related transactions.[404]

Article 4.1 of the Swiss Rules allows for consolidation in the following circumstances: **2.253**

> Where a Notice of Arbitration is submitted between parties already involved in other ar-
> bitral proceedings pending under these Rules, the Court may decide, after consulting with

---

[401] See van den Berg, 'Consolidated arbitrations and the 1958 New York Arbitration Convention' (1986) 2 Arb Intl 367; see also Jarvin, 'Consolidated arbitrations, the New York Arbitration Convention and the Dutch Arbitration Act 1986: A critique of Dr van den Berg' (1987) 3 Arb Intl 254; van den Berg, 'A replique to Mr Jarvin' (1987) 3 Arb Intl 259. See also *Karaha Bodas Co. v Perusahaan Pertambangan Minyak* 364 F.3d 274 (5th Cir. 2004); *Riverstone Ins Ltd v Liquidators of ICD*, Paris cour d'appel, 5 November 2009, Case No. 08/12816.

[402] Delvolvé Report, para. 113.

[403] They are not, however, to be regarded as approved by the Working Group. For further guidance, see Paulsson, Rawding, and Reed (eds) *The Freshfields Guide to Arbitration Clauses in International Contracts* (3rd edn, Kluwer Law International, 2010).

[404] See also the SIAC Rules, r. 8; the CIETAC Rules, Art. 19.

the parties and any confirmed arbitrator in all proceedings, that the new case shall be consolidated with the pending arbitral proceedings. The Court may proceed in the same way where a Notice of Arbitration is submitted between parties that are not identical to the parties in the pending arbitral proceedings. When rendering its decision, the Court shall take into account all relevant circumstances, including the links between the cases and the progress already made in the pending arbitral proceedings. Where the Court decides to consolidate the new case with the pending arbitral proceedings, the parties to all proceedings shall be deemed to have waived their right to designate an arbitrator, and the Court may revoke the appointment and confirmation of arbitrators and apply the provisions of Section II (Composition of the Arbitral Tribunal).[405]

2.254 In an appropriate case, provisions such as these should prove useful in bringing everyone concerned before the same arbitral tribunal. However, the procedure to be followed in the conduct of such a consolidated arbitration would again have to be carefully worked out, so as to ensure that each party is given a proper opportunity to present its case. Otherwise, any resulting award may be refused recognition or enforcement.[406]

(d) Concurrent hearings

2.255 Another practical solution to the problem created by multiparty disputes that are not subject to joinder, consolidation, or class arbitration, is to appoint the same arbitrator to more than one arbitration. If this is to be done, the procedures to be followed need to be considered carefully. Provision should be made for whether, and to what extent, there is confidentiality across the formally different proceedings,[407] and whether the record (and even the transcript of witness testimony) can be used across different proceedings. Such *de facto* consolidation would depend upon the agreement of *all* of the parties concerned and, once again, appropriate procedural rules would have to be worked out.

(e) Class arbitrations

2.256 A 'class', or 'representative', action is a legal proceeding that enables the claims of a number of persons with the same interest (the 'class members') to be brought by one or a number of claimants (the 'representative claimant(s)') against the same respondent. In a class action, only the representative claimant(s) is a party to the action, and although the class members do not take an active part in the proceedings, they are bound by the outcome.

2.257 Although, for many years, class actions were peculiar to the US litigation landscape, variations on the theme have since appeared in other legal systems.[408] Perhaps more surprisingly,

---

[405] See also the Rules of the Belgian Centre for Arbitration and Mediation (CEPANI), Art. 13, which adopts a similar approach.

[406] Under the provisions of the New York Convention, Art. V1(b), or the Model Law, Art. 36(1)(a)(ii).

[407] In this regard, see *Aegis v European Re* [2003] 1 WLR 1041; Rawding and Seeger, '*Aegis v European Re* and the confidentiality of arbitration awards' (2003) 19 Arb Intl 483.

[408] In England, procedural rules of court now exist for collective and representative actions (see the Civil Procedure Rules, Pt. 19). Similar procedural rules exist in Canada and have, since 2003, been introduced for the courts in Sweden, Norway, Finland, Germany, and Italy.

class actions have begun to make an appearance in international arbitration. 'Surprisingly' because one might take the view that a representative action is anathema to the principles of privity and party autonomy that tend to lead to the classic constellation of claimants facing respondents in the same proceedings who are party to the same contract. But US courts, no doubt more comfortable with the concept of class actions than other courts around the world, have seen no reason why class action cannot be exported to international arbitration.

Thus, in the US Supreme Court's 2003 landmark decision in *Green Tree Financial*   **2.258**
Corporation v Bazzle,[409] the plurality of a divided Supreme Court opened the door to class-wide arbitrations. The case involved a lender who had entered into standard-form contracts for home improvement loans with a number of borrowers. As is typical in contracts of this type, the contracts contained an arbitration clause, referring all disputes to 'binding arbitration by one arbitrator selected by us [the lender] with the consent of you'. The matter was commenced by two sets of consumers, who first brought two separate lawsuits before state courts challenging the lender's practices. Both lawsuits were referred to arbitration at the lender's demand, and in both cases the sole arbitrator (who was, in fact, the same individual in both cases) administered the cases as class-wide arbitrations and issued class awards in favour of the borrowers.[410]

The lender challenged the award, submitting that, in 'selecting an' arbitrator that was 'con-   **2.259**
sented to by' one of its customers as required by the express terms of the arbitration agreement, it was not selecting an arbitrator to determine its dispute with its other customers. On this basis, it argued that the terms of the arbitration agreement did not accommodate, but rather forbade, class-wide arbitration.

The South Carolina Supreme Court upheld the class awards, reasoning that there was   **2.260**
nothing in either the contracts or the Federal Arbitration Act to preclude class-wide arbitration. Unable to arrive at a majority opinion, the US Supreme Court nevertheless affirmed the judgment and found in the process that an arbitrator, rather than a court, must determine whether the contracts forbid class arbitration.

The response to *Green Tree* in the United States was immediate. Many companies—   **2.261**
particularly in consumer businesses—modified their standard arbitration clauses to add an express prohibition on class-wide proceedings. This led to another wave of litigation, challenging the enforceability of such class-action waivers. The Californian courts, for instance, have consistently refused to give effect to waivers contained in consumer contracts on the basis that they are unconscionable.[411]

In 2003, US arbitral institutions promulgated new rules that deal with class-action scenarios.   **2.262**
The AAA promulgated Supplementary Rules for Class Actions, which:

- require the arbitrator first to decide whether a class action is permissible under the contract in question and applicable state law;

---

[409] *Green Tree Financial Corporation v Bazzle*, 539 US 444 (2003).
[410] In one of the two cases, the court had certified it as a class action before it was removed to arbitration. In the second case, the arbitrator certified it as a class-wide arbitration himself.
[411] See, in particular, *Discover Bank v Superior Court*, 36 Cal. 4th 148 (2005); *Thibodeau v Comcast Corporation*, 2006 Pa. Super. 306 (2006).

- provide guidance for the arbitrator thereafter in determining whether to 'certify' the existence of a class;[412] and
- in particular, require the arbitrator to set forth his or her ruling on the class-action issues in a 'class construction award' that may itself be enforced or set aside in court.[413]

2.263   As for the courts, until recently there appeared to be a discernible trend towards allowing class treatment of issues that were arbitrable under most standard arbitration clauses, at least where the clause did not explicitly prohibit or restrict class treatment.[414] However, the tide changed following the Supreme Court's decision in *Stolt-Nielsen SA v Animalfeeds International Corporation*.[415] The Court overturned an arbitral award that determined issues on a class basis on the ground that the tribunal had exceeded its powers, stating that:

> An implicit agreement to authorize class-action arbitration [...] is not a term that the arbitrator may infer solely from the fact of the parties' agreement to arbitrate. This is so because class-action arbitration changes the nature of arbitration to such a degree that it cannot be presumed the parties consented to it by simply agreeing to submit their disputes to an arbitrator.[416]

2.264   The Court noted that a shift from an ordinary bilateral or multilateral arbitration to a class-action arbitration involved 'fundamental changes', including a larger number of parties, lack of privacy and confidentiality, the adjudication of rights of absent parties, and the potential for high-value awards that were subject to only minimal judicial review on the merits. It stated that tribunals should therefore not presume that the parties' mere silence on the issue of class arbitration constitutes consent.[417]

2.265   The recent case of *Lamps Plus v Varela*[418] appears—at least for now—to have removed any doubt in the matter. In proceedings before the Court of Appeals for the Ninth Circuit, an employee had successfully argued that an arbitration clause, which was ambiguous as to whether the employee could bring a class arbitration against his employer, should be read *contra proferentum* and was thus enforceable.[419] The Supreme Court, however, appears to have taken its previous findings in the case of *Stolt-Nielsen* a step further. It considered 'whether, consistent with the [Federal Arbitration Act], an ambiguous agreement can provide the necessary "contractual basis" for compelling class arbitration', and concluded that it cannot. In the Court's view, the Federal Arbitration Act requires 'more than ambiguity to ensure that the parties actually agreed to arbitrate on a classwide basis'.[420]

2.266   After much debate, the related question of the validity of class arbitration waivers has also reached the US Supreme Court. In *AT&T Mobility LLC v Concepcion*,[421] it was held that

---

[412] In this regard, the Rules, for the most part, mirror the standards set forth in the Federal Rules of Civil Procedure, r. 23.

[413] Of particular interest for international practitioners, as part of its rules for class arbitrations, the AAA explicitly waived the normal policy of confidentiality.

[414] See the decision of the Southern District of New York in *JSC Surtneftegat v President & Fellows of Harvard College*, SDNY 04 Civ 6069, 11 October 2007.

[415] *Stolt-Nielsen SA v Animalfeeds International Corporation*, 130 S.Ct. 1758 (2010).

[416] Ibid., at 1775.

[417] Ibid.

[418] *Lamps Plus v Varela* 2019 WL 1780275 (2019).

[419] Ibid.

[420] Ibid.

[421] *AT&T Mobility LLC v Concepcion*, 131 S.Ct. 1740 (2011).

such provisions are enforceable. The Court noted the 'liberal federal policy favouring arbitration', and held that arbitration agreements should be placed on an equal footing with other contracts and enforced according to their terms. Most recently, the Supreme Court affirmed in *Epic Systems Corp v Lewis* that 'one-on-one' mandatory arbitration agreements imposed by employers upon their employees are enforceable.[422]

Until recently, the concept of class arbitration found little support outside the United States.[423] This may be changing. Following a number of years of consultation, the European Union recently published the 'Directive on representative actions for the protection of the collective interests of Consumers'.[424] The Directive, which EU member states will have two years to implement (from 4 December 2020) and an additional six months to apply, introduces a right of collective redress across the EU, primarily by requiring member states to establish procedures by which 'qualified entities' will be able to bring representative actions to seek injunctions, damages, and other redress on behalf of a group of consumers against a trader who has allegedly infringed EU law. Although much depends on how the Directive is implemented by member states, there is now the prospect that class arbitration could, in principle, be extended beyond the United States, and the resulting awards enforced internationally.[425]

2.267

---

[422] *Epic Systems Corp v Lewis*, 138 S.Ct. 1612—2018. See also *American Express Co. v Italian Colors Restaurant*, No. 12-133, Supreme Court of the United States, 20 June 2013, in which the Supreme Court refused to carve out an exception to this principle where the cost of pursuing separate arbitrations is prohibitively high.

[423] However, see *Luis Alberto Duran Valencia v Bancolombia*, 24 April 2003, in which a Colombian tribunal allowed a class arbitration to proceed in a post-acquisition dispute involving multiple shareholders.

[424] Directive (EU) 2020/1828 of 25 November 2020 on representative actions for the protection of the collective interests of consumers and repealing Directive 2009/22/EC. The Directive, which was published in the Official Journal on 4 December 2020, was preceded by public consultations on 'collective redress' mechanisms in EU member states, which was launched by the European Commission and resulted in non-binding policy being published on 11 June 2013. In 2017, the Commission issued a Call for Evidence seeking evidence on how the policy was being implemented in practice. In 2018, the Commission issued a report which concluded that, although the policy had achieved its aim of inspiring discussions across the EU regarding collective redress, it had resulted in only limited development of new legislation, and access to collective redress mechanisms remained unevenly distributed across the EU.

[425] Strong, 'Enforcing class arbitration in the international sphere: Due process and public policy concerns' (2008) 30 U Penn JIL 89.

3

APPLICABLE LAWS

A. Overview

(a) Introduction

Many disputes that are referred to arbitration are determined by arbitral tribunals with no more than a passing reference to the law. They turn on matters of fact: what was said and what was not said; what was promised and what was not promised; what was done and what was not done. **3.01**

It would be wrong to deduce from this, however, that international arbitration exists in a legal vacuum. Billions of contracts—most of them made orally, rather than in writing—are made every day throughout the world. They may be as simple as the purchase of a bus ticket or the hire of a taxi, or they may be as complex as the purchase of a company with financing. Most are made, performed—and forgotten. Yet law governs each of these situations. The apparent simplicity of the purchase of a bus ticket or the hire of a taxi is deceptive. They are transactions that involve a contractual relationship and such relationships are underpinned by complex rules of law. These rules may not be referred to expressly, but they exist nonetheless: **3.02**

> It is often said that the parties to a contract make their own law, and it is, of course, true that, subject to the rules of public policy and *ordre public*, the parties are free to agree upon such terms as they may choose. Nevertheless, agreements that are intended to have a legal operation (as opposed to a merely social operation) create legal rights and duties, and legal rights and duties cannot exist in a vacuum but must have a place within a legal system which is available for dealing with such questions as the validity, application and interpretation of contracts, and, generally, for supplementing their express provisions.[1]

Like a contract, an arbitration does not exist in a legal vacuum. It is regulated, first, by any specific rules of procedure that have been agreed or adopted by the parties and the arbitral tribunal; secondly, it is regulated by the law of the place of arbitration. It is important to **3.03**

---

[1] McNair, 'The general principles of law recognised by civilised nations' (1957) 33 BYIL 1, at 7.

recognise at the outset (as even distinguished judges and commentators sometimes fail to do)—that this dualism exists.

3.04   For the most part, modern laws of arbitration are content to leave parties and arbitrators free to decide upon their own specific rules of procedure, so long as the parties are treated equally. Under these modern laws, it is accepted that the courts of law should be slow to intervene in an arbitration, if they intervene at all.[2] Nevertheless, those rules need the sanction of law if they are to be effective and, in this context, the relevant law is the law of the place or seat of the arbitration. This is referred to as the *lex arbitri*. This is an important—and frequently misunderstood—topic, to which it will be necessary to return later in this chapter.

(b) A complex interaction of laws

3.05   International arbitration, unlike its domestic counterpart, usually involves more than one system of law or of legal rules. Indeed, it is possible, without undue sophistication, to identify at least five different systems of law that, in practice, may have a bearing on an international arbitration:

   i.   the law governing the arbitration agreement and the validity, scope, and enforcement of that agreement;
   ii. the law governing the existence and the proceedings of the arbitral tribunal (the *lex arbitri* or, as it is sometimes called, the curial law);
   iii. the law, or the relevant legal rules, governing the substantive issues in dispute (generally described as the 'applicable law', the 'governing law', the substantive law', or 'the proper law of the contract');
   iv. other applicable rules and non-binding guidelines and recommendations;[3] and
   v.   the law governing recognition and enforcement of the award (which may, in practice, prove to be not one law, but two or more systems of law, if recognition and enforcement is sought in more than one country in which the losing party has, or is thought to have, assets).[4]

---

[2] The lead is given by the UNCITRAL Model Law on International Commercial Arbitration Model Law on International Commercial Arbitration 1985 (as amended in 2006) (the Model Law), which states categorically that, '[i]n matters governed by this Law, no court shall intervene except where so provided in this Law'. See Model Law, Art. 5. This judicial deference to pending arbitrations is generally widely applied in practice. Even states that have not adopted the Model Law *per se* have thought it appropriate to make a similar statement. For instance, Swiss law states that its courts will 'decline jurisdiction' where there is an agreement to arbitrate, except in limited circumstances; see Swiss Private International Law Act 1987 (as amended in 2021) (Swiss PIL), s. 7. The Swedish Arbitration Act 2019 (Swedish Arbitration Act) contains a similar provision, at s. 4, although ss. 5 and 6 contain exceptions to this rule. The French Code of Civil Procedure provides for the same at Art. 1458 and the Spanish Arbitration Act 2003, which is based on the Model Law with significant changes, states unequivocally at Art. 7 that, '[i]n matters governed by this Act, no court shall intervene except where so provided in this Act'. Similarly, while the primary federal statute governing arbitration in the United States, the Federal Arbitration Act of 1925 (FAA), pre-dates and is not modelled on the Model Law, US courts have interpreted the FAA's provisions in a manner that is consistent with the Model Law. Thus, in *Stanton v Paine Webber Jackson & Curtis, Inc.*, 685 F.Supp. 1241, 1242 (S.D. Fla. 1988), the US District Court for the Southern District of Florida held that '[n]othing in the [FAA] contemplates interference by the court in an ongoing arbitration proceeding'.

[3] Sometimes referred to as the procedural 'soft law' of international arbitration: see Park, 'The procedural soft law of international arbitration: Nongovernmental instruments', in Mistelis and Lew (eds) *Pervasive Problems in International Arbitration* (Kluwer Law International, 2006), pp. 141–154.

[4] See Chapter 11.

This chapter deals with: the law governing the agreement to arbitrate; the law governing   **3.06**
the arbitration itself (the *lex arbitri*); the law governing the substantive matters in dispute
(the substantive law); the law or rules governing conflicts of law; and certain non-national
guidelines and rules that are increasingly relied upon in international arbitration. Another
relevant law, the law governing the parties' capacity to enter into an arbitration agreement
has been dealt with in Chapter 2, and issues relating to the laws governing the arbitral award
(including challenge, recognition, and enforcement) are dealt with in Chapters 10 and 11.

B. Law Governing the Agreement to Arbitrate

(a) Introduction

An appropriate place to start is the law governing the parties' agreement to arbitrate. The   **3.07**
chosen law is important, because it establishes the rules and norms that will determine any
dispute over the validity, scope, or interpretation of that agreement. The following examples
will illustrate this.

i.   The law of the arbitration agreement will be relevant if there is a dispute over whether
     the tribunal's jurisdiction extends to a particular issue. For example, under English
     law, tort claims related to contractual performance will generally fall within the scope
     of an arbitration agreement drafted appropriately, whereas under Russian law they
     may not.
ii. The law of the arbitration agreement will be relevant to determining whether the ar-
     bitration agreement extends to third parties, such as the parent company of one of
     the parties.
iii. The law of the arbitration agreement will determine the validity of the arbitration
     agreement. Some national laws may invalidate an arbitration agreement, in circum-
     stances where others would find the same arbitration agreement to be enforceable.
iv. The law of the arbitration agreement may also be relevant to deciding the applicable
     method of dispute resolution, where the parties' choice is not clearly set out, or where
     multiple methods are proposed in one arbitration agreement.

An agreement to arbitrate, as discussed in Chapter 2, may be set out in a purpose-made
submission agreement or—as is the case much more frequently—in an arbitration clause.
Both submission agreements and arbitration clauses have been considered in detail in the
previous chapter.

As to the law governing arbitration agreements, it might readily be assumed that this is   **3.08**
the same law as that which the parties chose to govern the substantive issues in dispute—
that is to say, the law governing the broader contractual relationship between the parties.
Commercial parties may be less familiar with the possibility that multiple laws can cover
different aspects of the same contract, and so might reasonably be taken to have assumed
that one law governs all the contractual terms, including the agreement to arbitrate.

However, given the well-established principle of the separability and autonomy of an arbitra-   **3.09**
tion agreement, it is by no means certain that the parties intended that agreement to be treated

just like any other agreement in the contract. Indeed, it is precisely the separability of an arbitration agreement that gives credence to the possibility, at least in principle, that the law governing the contract as a whole and the law governing the arbitration agreement might differ.

3.10   Given the potential that exists for parties to argue, as a preliminary issue, about which law applies to an arbitration agreement, the best course of action is for parties who are entering into an arbitration agreement to make clear what law is to apply to that agreement. This can easily be done, for example by stating the chosen law in the arbitration clause itself. So long as the choice of law is not contrary to public policy, parties are free to choose the law which is to govern their commercial relationship and the law that is to govern their agreement to arbitrate, which may (if they wish) be a different law. However, if there is no express choice of law (a situation that arises more frequently than not[5]), and it becomes necessary to determine the law applicable to the agreement to arbitrate, the question that then arises is: how is a court or an arbitral tribunal to identify the relevant law?

3.11   This is really two questions, because the answer may differ according to whether it is a court or tribunal that has to make the decision. If it is a national court, that court will be expected to decide the question in accordance with its own rules of private international law, which will usually contain binding rules to deal with the choice of law in cases involving a foreign element, and will search for a solution in accordance with those rules. However, if the question is posed to an international arbitral tribunal, the answer is less easy. As will be seen later in this chapter, it is often said that such a tribunal is not bound by any formal 'conflict of law' rules and is free to apply the law that it considers to be appropriate.

(b)   The applicable choice of law rules

3.12   In deciding what law governs or is likely to govern an agreement to arbitrate, a good starting point is the New York Convention of 1958. Article V(1)(a) does not deal directly with the point, but states that if there is a plea before a national court to the effect that an arbitration agreement is invalid, it must be shown that it was invalid 'under the law to which the parties have subjected it or, failing any indication thereon, under the law of the country where the award was made'. What this means, in effect, is that a national court should look first to the parties' express agreement; and if there is no agreement should apply the law of the seat, being the law of the country where the award was made.[6] (While Article V(1)(a) applies specifically in the context of annulment or enforcement of awards, it would, arguably, be illogical to assume that different laws could apply to the validity of a particular award, depending on the timing of the analysis.[7])

---

[5] The UK Supreme Court has observed that '[i]t is rare for the law governing an arbitration clause to be specifically identified (either in the arbitration clause itself or elsewhere in the contract)'. *See Enka Insaat Ve Sanayi AS v OOO Insurance Company Chubb* [2020] UKSC 38, at [43].

[6] New York Convention, Art. V(1)(a). See also Collins (ed.) *Dicey, Morris & Collins on the Conflict of Laws* (15th edn, Sweet & Maxwell, 2018), paragraph 16-014 ('In the light of the pervasive reach of the New York Convention in modern times, this rule, although not itself prescribing a choice of law rule of general application, nevertheless provides a strong indication of one [...].')

[7] This is a view shared by Professor Albert Jan van den Berg in his pre-eminent text, *The New York Arbitration Convention of 1958* (Kluwer Law International, 1981), pp. 126–127 ('A systematic interpretation of the Convention, in principle, permits the application by analogy of the conflict rules of article V(1)(a) to the enforcement of the

Given the wide acceptance of the New York Convention, we might expect to see conformity **3.13** in the approach taken by courts in different jurisdictions to the question of which law applies to an arbitration agreement; and we might also expect international arbitral tribunals to do likewise, even if they are not bound to follow the same rules as national courts. At first glance, it might appear that they do. As discussed in more detail below, national laws and arbitral rules usually accept the parties' choice of appliable law, and some arbitral institutions have a default rule that the law of the seat applies in the absence of the parties' choice. On closer inspection, however, there are significant divergences in the specific approaches taken across different jurisdictions.

Take the national laws of the United Kingdom, France, and the People's Republic of China, **3.14** for example.

    i. English common law looks in the first instance for the parties' express or implied choice of applicable law by reference to principles of English contract law, which establish a presumption that the law applicable to the contract as a whole also applies to the arbitration agreement.[8] Where there is no applicable law clause, an English court will identify the system of law to which the arbitration agreement is 'most closely connected'—a test that, in the absence of strong indications to the contrary, assumes that the 'most closely connected' law is that stipulated by the parties to be the seat of the arbitration.[9]

    ii. French law defers to the express choice of the parties and, in the absence of an express choice, will consider the parties' implied choice. However, unlike English law, in doing so, emphasis is placed on the autonomy of the arbitration agreement, its legal independence from the main contract that contains it, and the absence of any need to refer to a particular national law in seeking to ascertain and respect the intention of the parties.[10]

    iii. Mainland Chinese law looks first for any expressly stated choice by the parties, but, in the absence of any express choice—and unlike English or French law—there is no search for the parties' implied choice. Instead, a court will apply the law of the seat of the arbitration, or, if even that is not stipulated, the law of the place of the relevant arbitral institution.[11]

---

agreement. It would appear inconsistent at the time of the enforcement of the award to apply the Convention's uniform conflict rules and at the time of the enforcement of the agreement to apply possibly different conflict rules of the forum.')

[8] As articulated most recently by the UK Supreme Court in *Enka Insaat Ve Sanayi AS v OOO Insurance Company Chubb* [2020] UKSC 38, at [170(iv)].

[9] Ibid., at [193(iv)].

[10] As stated most recently by the Paris Court of Appeal in *Kabab-Ji (Lebanon) v Kout Food Group (Kuwait)*, cour d'appel de Paris, Pôle 1—chambre 1, 23 June 2020, Case No. 17/22943), pp. 5, 8 ('[e]n vertu d'une règle matérielle du droit international de l'arbitrage, la clause compromissoire est indépendante juridiquement du contrat principal qui la contient directement ou par référence, et son existence et son efficacité s'apprécient, sous réserve des règles impératives du droit français et de l'ordre public international, d'après la commune volonté des parties, sans qu'il soit nécessaire de se référer à une loi étatique').

[11] Interpretation of the SPC Concerning Some Issues on Application of the Arbitration Law 2006, as modified by the Law of the People's Republic of China on the Law Applicable to Foreign-Related Civil Relationships 2010, Art. 16.

3.15   This lack of uniformity among major arbitral jurisdictions can have practical repercussions. The case of *Kabab-Ji v Kout Food Group* is illustrative. The relevant arbitration clause was found in a series of franchise agreements governed by English law and seated in Paris and concluded between a Kuwaiti company, Al Homaizi Foodstuff Company, and a Lebanese company, Kabab-Ji SAL. Al Homaizi was subsequently part of a restructuring that led to the formation of a holding company, Kout Food Group (KFG). A dispute arose under the agreements, and Kabab-Ji initiated arbitration ICC arbitration proceedings against KFG in France. While KFG participated in the arbitration, it contended that it was not a party to the franchise agreements or the arbitration agreements contained in them. This in turn required the tribunal to interpret the arbitration agreement and, in particular, to determine the applicable law. The tribunal found that French law, as the law of the seat, applied to the arbitration agreement and concluded that, under French law, KFG was a party to the arbitration agreements. The tribunal went on to conclude that KFG was in breach of the franchise agreements and awarded damages against the company of around US$6.7 million.[12]

3.16   KFG brought an action in the French courts to annul the award on the grounds that it was not a party to the franchise agreements and not bound by the arbitration agreements. Meanwhile, Kabab-Ji brought enforcement proceedings in England. The Paris Court of Appeal dismissed the annulment action, finding that the arbitration agreement was governed by French law.[13] The English courts reached a different conclusion, finding that the parties' choice of substantive law of their contract, English law, also governed their arbitration agreement.[14] In the view of the English courts, under English law, KFG was not a party to the franchise agreements and not in breach of the franchise agreement.

3.17   This dichotomy between, on the one hand, jurisdictions applying to the arbitration agreement the substantive law of the contract and, on the other hand, jurisdictions applying the law of the seat, and the various rationales for doing so, is the theme to which we turn next.

(c) The law of the contract as the applicable law of the arbitration agreement

(i) The commercial intent of the parties

3.18   As we have already said, it is not unreasonable to ask why, if the parties have expressly chosen a particular law to govern their contract, some other system of law, which the parties have not expressly chosen, should be applied to one of the clauses in that contract, simply because it happens to be an arbitration clause? It might be thought that a better approach would be to assume that an express choice of law by commercial parties was intended to cover all the clauses of the contract. Such an approach would provide the parties with certainty that their 'applicable law' clause would be effective in relation to all the contractual rights and obligations. It would also help to ensure consistency in

---

[12] The arbitration and the findings of the tribunal are described by the UK Supreme Court in *Kabab-Ji SAL v Kout Food Group* [2021] UKSC 48, at [5]–[6].

[13] *Kabab-Ji (Lebanon) v Kout Food Group (Kuwait)*, cour d'appel de Paris, Pôle 1—chambre 1, 23 June 2020, Case No. 17/22943). At the time of writing, the appeal before the Court of Cassation is pending.

[14] *Kabab-Ji SAL v Kout Food Group* [2021] UKSC 48, at [39].

the interpretation of the parties' contract as a whole. Thus, it seems reasonable to say, as Professor Lew has said, that:

> There is a very strong presumption in favour of the law governing the substantive agreement which contains the arbitration clause also governing the arbitration agreement. This principle has been followed in many cases. This could even be *implied* as an agreement of the parties as to the law applicable to the arbitration clause.[15]

A French commentator has offered a similar view:

> The autonomy of the arbitration clause and of the principal contract does not mean that they are totally independent one from the other, as evidenced by the fact that acceptance of the contract entails acceptance of the clause, without any other formality.[16]

The UK Supreme Court has held similarly in relation to circumstances where a contract contains a governing law clause, as well as an arbitration clause:

> [I]t is natural to interpret such a governing law clause, in the absence of good reason to the contrary, as applying to the arbitration clause, for the simple reason that the arbitration clause is part of the contract which the parties have agreed is to be governed by the specified system of law.[17]

Enka v Chubb is now the leading authority on the approach taken under English law to as- **3.19** certain the law of the arbitration agreement. Given its prominence as an authority on the common law relating to this topic, it is worth discussing in more detail.

The underlying dispute concerned a contract under which Enka Insaat Ve Sanayi AS (Enka) **3.20** was to perform works at a power plant in Russia. A Russian company, CJSC Energoproekt, was responsible for the design and construction of the power plant and entered into a subcontract for certain works with Enka. Energoproekt later transferred its rights and obligations under the contract to PSJC Unipro, the owner of the power station. Chubb Russia provided insurance to the owner of Unipro. After a fire caused significant damage to the plant, and Chubb Russia paid out approximately US$400 million, Chubb Russia became subrogated to Unipro's rights to claim compensation from third parties for damage caused by the fire. The contract contained an arbitration clause which provided for disputes to be resolved by arbitration in London under the ICC Rules. Chubb Russia filed a tort claim in the Moscow Arbitrazh Court against Enka (and others), claiming for the damage caused by the fire. Enka, in turn, sought an anti-suit injunction from the English High Court, to restrain Chubb Russia from further pursuing the Russian proceedings against Enka on the

---

[15] Lew, 'The law applicable to the form and substance of the arbitration clause' (1999) 9 ICCA Congress Series 114, at 143 (emphasis added). Other leading commentaries have expressed similar views. See Merkin, 'Arbitration Law', Issue 84 (Informa Subscriptions, 2020), paragraph 7.12 ('[E]ven if there is no express contractual statement to that effect, a choice-of-law clause for the entire agreement is likely to be construed as extending to the arbitration clause. There are numerous decisions to this effect […] However, that presumption may be ousted in appropriate circumstances […]'); Collins (ed.) *Dicey, Morris & Collins on the Conflict of Laws* (15th edn, Sweet & Maxwell, 2018), paragraph 16-017 ('If there is an express choice of law to govern the contract as a whole, the arbitration agreement may also be governed by that law').
[16] Derains, 'The ICC arbitral process, Part VIII: Choice of law applicable to the contract and international arbitration' (2006) 6 ICC International Court of Arbitration Bulletin 10, at 16–17.
[17] *Enka Insaat Ve Sanayi AS v OOO Insurance Company Chubb* [2020] UKSC 38, at [43], citing the sixth edition of this book, paragraph 3.12.

ground that this was in breach of the arbitration agreement. The question arose as to which law applied to the parties' arbitration agreement: under English law, Chubb's tort claim would fall within the scope of the arbitration clause, but under Russian law it would not.

3.21   The High Court rejected Enka's application on the grounds that the most appropriate forum to decide whether the claim fell within the arbitration agreement was the Moscow Arbitrazh Court. This finding was overturned on appeal, and the Court of Appeal issued an anti-suit injunction restraining Chubb from continuing the Russian proceedings. In doing so, it found that there was a strong presumption that the parties had impliedly chosen the law of the seat of the arbitration as the law that governed the agreement to arbitrate.[18] Accordingly, there being no express substantive choice of the law and the place of arbitration having been chosen as London, the arbitration agreement was considered by the Court of Appeal to be governed by English law.

3.22   The UK Supreme Court disagreed with the reasoning of the Court of Appeal but (by a majority) not with their conclusion. Clarifying the position under English common law, the Supreme Court unanimously held that where the parties have made a choice of the law that is to govern their contract, this choice would generally be construed as a choice of the law governing the arbitration agreement as well, unless there was a good reason to conclude otherwise.[19] Where, as in the case before it, there was no express choice of law, the court had to decide what law governed the arbitration agreement. In these circumstances, and contrary to the position taken by the Court of Appeal, the Supreme Court held that there was no presumption that by choosing a seat of arbitration the parties had impliedly chosen the law of that seat to govern the arbitration agreement.[20] What the court had to do, in the absence of any express choice of law, was to look for the law with which the arbitration agreement had 'the closest and most real connection'. This, according to the majority of the Court, was 'the law of the country of the seat, being the place where the arbitration is to be held and which will exercise a supervisory jurisdiction necessary to ensure that the procedure is effective'.[21]

3.23   The presumption that the governing law of a contract applies also to its arbitration agreement is made in other jurisdictions. For example, in *BCY v BCZ*, the Singapore High Court considered the law applicable to a sale and purchase agreement governing the sale of shares of BCY's company to BCZ and a co-purchaser. When BCY decided not to proceed with the sale of the shares, BCZ commenced arbitration. One of the issues in dispute was the existence of an agreement to arbitrate, which would have designated Singapore as the place of arbitration. The arbitrator found there to be a rebuttable presumption that the law of the contract, New York law, governed the arbitration agreement, and that there were no factors displacing that presumption in this instance.[22] Applying New York law, the arbitrator found that the parties' words and conduct established an agreement to arbitrate.

3.24   BCY sought declaratory relief in the Singaporean courts, asserting that the arbitrator had no jurisdiction to hear the claim. That, in turn, required the Singaporean courts to confirm the

---

[18]   *Enka Insaat Ve Sanayi A.S. v OOO Insurance Company Chubb* [2020] EWCA Civ 574, at [91].

[19]   *Enka Insaat Ve Sanayi AS v OOO Insurance Company Chubb* [2020] UKSC 38, at [43].

[20]   Ibid., at [66] and [94].

[21]   Ibid., [101(6)]. The two dissenting judges would have regarded the choice of the seat as being tantamount to a choice of the law of that seat as the law governing the arbitration agreement.

[22]   The arbitration is discussed in the court's judgment. See *BCY v BCZ* [2016] SGHC 249, at 3233.

law governing the arbitration agreement. In doing so, the High Court clarified the choice-of-law approach in Singapore:

> Where the arbitration agreement is a clause forming part of a main contract, it is reason-able to assume that the contracting parties intend their entire relationship to be governed by the same system of law. If the intention is otherwise, I do not think it is unreasonable to expect the parties to specifically provide for a different system of law to govern the ar-bitration agreement. In practice, parties rarely specify the law applicable to the arbitration agreement as distinct from the main contract [...] When a choice of law (such as the one here) stipulates that the 'agreement' is to be governed by one country's system of law, the natural inference should be that parties intend the express choice of law to 'govern and determine the construction of *all* the clauses in the agreement which they signed, *in-cluding the arbitration agreement*' [...] To say that the word 'agreement' contemplates all the clauses in the main contract save for the arbitration clause would in fact be inconsistent with its ordinary meaning.[23]

The High Court proceeded to apply New York law, under which, in its view, there was in fact no agreement to be bound by the arbitration clause.[24]

(ii) Potential conflict with the autonomy of an arbitration clause

3.25 A conceptual difficulty in applying the law of the contract to all terms of the contract is that it arguably runs into conflict with the 'autonomy' of the arbitration clause. As we have previ-ously stated, an arbitration clause is taken to be autonomous and to be separable from other clauses in the agreement.[25] If necessary, it may stand alone. In this respect, it is comparable to a submission agreement. Even if it is presently not customary to find a clause in a commercial agreement which expressly specifies the law applicable to the arbitration clause in that con-tract, it is common for parties to agree on the seat of an arbitration, and this seat may well have its own distinct set of norms, which apply solely to arbitration clauses and not to the rest of a contract.[26] Even those jurisdictions that apply a presumption that the contract and its arbitra-tion agreement are governed by the same law recognise that this is not always the case. The separability of an arbitration clause therefore supports the argument that it is possible for it to be governed by a different law from that which governs the main agreement.

3.26 As noted above, the New York Convention points towards this conclusion.[27] In the provi-sions relating to enforcement, the Convention stipulates that the agreement under which the award is made must be valid 'under the law to which the parties have subjected it', or, failing any indication thereon, 'under the law of the country where the award was made' (which will be the law of the seat of the arbitration).

---

[23] *BCY v BCZ* [2016] SGHC 249, at 59 (emphasis in original).

[24] Ibid., at 97. The Singapore Court of Appeal reached a similar conclusion in *BNA v BNB and BNC* [2019] SGCA 84.

[25] Separability is discussed in Chapter 2. See *Fiona Trust & Holding Corporation and ors v Privalov and ors* [2007] EWCA Civ 20; *Fili Shipping Co. Ltd v Premium Nafta Products Ltd* [2007] UKHL 40 (on appeal from *Fiona Trust*).

[26] The law governing the arbitration, including the law of the seat of an arbitration, is discussed further below at paragraphs 3.42*ff*.

[27] New York Convention, Art. V(1)(a). There is a similar provision in Model Law, Art. 34(2)(a). See discussion above at paragraph 3.12.

(d) Law of the seat of the arbitration

(i) The autonomy of an arbitration agreement

3.27   In those jurisdictions that search for what the parties have impliedly selected, there is division over the emphasis placed on the autonomy of the arbitration agreement. In *Enka v Chubb*, the UK Supreme Court rejected the proposition that the parties could be taken to have selected a governing law of the contract as a whole on the sole basis of their choice of an arbitral seat and found that, in the same way, the law of the seat did not necessarily imply a choice of law of the arbitration agreement.[28] But that is a view not universally held. As two commentators note:

> [T]he consequence of choosing a seat is that many aspects of the arbitration agreement—and not merely the arbitration procedure—will be governed by the law of the seat in any event, regardless of which law applies to the matrix contract. […] In circumstances where many aspects of the arbitration agreement will in any event be governed by the law of the seat in this way, the natural inference is that the parties, by choosing a seat, intended the entirety of that agreement (i.e. the arbitration, not the matrix contract) to be governed by that law.[29]

3.28   Likewise, in *Kabab-Ji (Lebanon) v Kout Food Group (Kuwait),* the Paris Court of Appeal applied French rules of international arbitration law to identify the 'common will of the parties' in the absence of an express choice of law to govern an arbitration agreement. In that case, the parties had agreed a series of franchise agreements governed by English law with arbitration seated in Paris. The Paris Court of Appeal found that the parties had intended to apply French law to their arbitration agreement, in light of their choice of an arbitral seat.[30] The court found further that, given the autonomy of an arbitration clause, it was not possible to infer that the parties intended English law—the law of the contract—to apply.[31]

(ii) The requirements of the law of the seat

3.29   There is also a possibility that the law of the seat itself stipulates that it is to be applied as the law governing the arbitration agreement. Again, in these instances, it might be said that the choice of the law of the seat reflects the parties' implied choice of the law of the arbitration agreement.

3.30   There are institutional and national laws providing that, where applicable as the law of the seat, the same national law will govern the arbitration agreement, absent agreement between the parties to the contrary. For example, the LCIA rules apply the law of the seat of the arbitration, absent the parties' express agreement to the contrary:

> [T]he law applicable to the Arbitration Agreement and the arbitration shall be the law applicable at the seat of the arbitration, unless and to the extent that the parties have agreed in

---

[28]   *Enka Insaat Ve Sanayi AS v OOO Insurance Company Chubb* [2020] UKSC 38, at [116]–[117].

[29]   Glick and Venkatesan, 'Choosing the law governing the arbitration agreement', in Kaplan and Moser (eds) *Jurisdiction, Admissibility and Choice of Law in International Arbitration: Liber Amicorum Michael Pryles* (Kluwer Law International, 2018), ch. 9, at pp. 142–143.

[30]   *Kabab-Ji (Lebanon) v Kout Food Group (Kuwait)*, cour d'appel de Paris, Pôle 1 chambre 1, 23 June 2020, Case No. 17/22943), p. 29.

[31]   Ibid., p. 27. Under Malaysian conflict-of-law rules, in the absence of an express choice of law to govern the law of the arbitration agreement, the designation of a seat of the arbitration is a tacit designation of the law governing the arbitration agreement. See *Thai-Lao Lignite Co Ltd and Anor v Government of the Lao People's Democratic Republic* 6 AMR 219 (2017), at 244.

writing on the application of other laws or rules of law and such agreement is not prohibited by the law applicable at the arbitral seat.[32]

In the *Bulbank* case,[33] the Supreme Court of Sweden confirmed that Swedish courts would   **3.31**
look to the parties' express choice, absent which the Swedish Arbitration Act provides that
the law of the seat will apply to the arbitration agreement.[34] The case concerned a contract
governed by Austrian law, which provided for arbitration seated in Stockholm. In ascertaining the law applicable to the arbitration agreement, the court placed no reliance on the
parties' substantive choice-of-law clause, finding instead that Swedish law governed the
arbitration:

> [N]o particular provision concerning the applicable law for the arbitration agreement itself
> was indicated [by the parties]. In such circumstances the issue of the validity of the arbi-
> tration clause should be determined in accordance with the law of the state in which the
> arbitration proceedings have taken place, that is to say, Swedish law.[35]

In similar fashion, the law of Scotland provides that where parties have agreed to seat their   **3.32**
arbitration in Scotland, but have failed to specify the law governing an arbitration, the arbitration agreement is to be governed by Scottish law.[36] The position is the same under
Turkish law.[37] The US FAA also operates in this way with respect to arbitrations seated in
the United States. The FAA supplies substantive legal rules for any written arbitration agreement that involves inter-state or foreign commerce or that falls within the US courts' ad-
miralty jurisdiction (excluding in the context of employment contracts). For a US-seated
arbitration, the FAA thus constitutes part of the law governing the arbitration agreement
and pre-empts any conflicting rules of the state, or possibly also foreign law, that otherwise
applies to the agreement.[38]

---

[32] LCIA Rules 2020, Art. 16.4. See also Art. 16.5 ('Notwithstanding Article 16.4, the LCIA Rules shall be interpreted in accordance with the laws of England.')

[33] *Bulgarian Foreign Trade Bank Ltd v Al Trade Finance Inc.*, Case No. T1881–99, Swedish Supreme Court, 27
October 2000, (2001) XXVI YBCA 291.

[34] Swedish Arbitration Act, s. 48.

[35] *Bulgarian Foreign Trade Bank Ltd v Al Trade Finance Inc.*, Case No. T1881–99, Swedish Supreme Court, 27
October 2000, (2001) XXVI YBCA 291, p. 293.

[36] Arbitration (Scotland) Act 2010, s. 6 ('Where—(a) the parties to an arbitration agreement agree that an arbitration under that agreement is to be seated in Scotland, but (b) the arbitration agreement does not specify the
law which is to govern it, then, unless the parties otherwise agree, the arbitration agreement is to be governed by
Scots law').

[37] Turkish International Arbitration Law 2001, Art. 4 ('The validity of an arbitration agreement is governed by
the law selected by the parties to be applicable to the arbitration agreement, or failing any choice, by Turkish law').

[38] See, e.g., *Kindred Nursing Centers Limited Partnership v Clark*, 137 S.Ct. 1421, 1426–1429 (2017) (holding a
rule of Kentucky law that disallowed an agent acting under a general power of attorney from entering into an arbitration agreement unless the power of attorney specifically empowered the agent to waive the principal's right
to trial by jury to be pre-empted by the FAA); *Marmet Health Care Center, Inc v Brown*, 565 US 530, 532–533
(2012) (*per curiam*) (holding a rule of West Virginia law which rendered unenforceable any pre-dispute arbitration
agreement insofar as it covered personal injury and wrongful death claims to be pre-empted by the FAA); *AT&T
Mobility LLC v Concepcion*, 563 US 333, 344–352 (2011) (holding a rule of California law which deemed unconscionable an arbitration agreement barring a class arbitration in a consumer contract of adhesion to be pre-empted
by the FAA); see also *Moses H. Cone Memorial Hospital v Mercury Construction Corp*, 460 US 1, 25 n. 32 (1983)
('The effect of [the FAA, s. 2] is to create a body of federal substantive law of arbitrability, applicable to any arbitration agreement within the coverage of the Act'); *Pedcor Mgt Co, Inc Welfare Benefit Plan v Nations Personnel of
Texas, Inc.* 343 F 3d 355 (5th Cir. 2003), 363 ('[I]t is well established that the FAA pre-empts state laws that contradict the purpose of the FAA by "requiring a judicial forum for the resolution of claims which the contracting parties agreed to resolve by arbitration" ').

(iii) The law of the seat as a means to avoid invalidity

3.33   The parties' implied choice of law to govern their arbitration agreement might also be the law of the seat, where the law of the contract as a whole would otherwise invalidate the parties' agreement to arbitrate. As the UK Supreme Court has stated:

> The principle that contracting parties could not reasonably have intended a significant clause in their contract, such as an arbitration clause, to be invalid is a form of purposive interpretation, which seeks to interpret the language of the contract, so far as possible, in a way which will give effect to—rather than defeat—an aim or purpose which the parties can be taken to have had in view.[39]

3.34   *Hamlyn v Talisker* is an early but authoritative example in English law.[40] The case concerned a contract between an English company and a Scottish company, to be performed in Scotland, and provided that disputes would be resolved by arbitration using two members of the London Corn Exchange. The parties' arbitration agreement was valid under English law but not under Scottish law, which required arbitrators to be named. The House of Lords reversed the finding of the Court of Session that the law of the contract as a whole was Scottish law and that the arbitration agreement was invalid. Instead, the House of Lords determined that English law applied to the arbitration agreement, for the following reasons:

> [T]he contract with reference to arbitration would have been absolutely null and voice if it were to be governed by the law of Scotland. That cannot have been the intent of the parties; it is not reasonable to attribute that intention to them if the contract may be otherwise construed [...][41]

and because:

> It is more reasonable to hold that the parties contracted with the common intention of giving entire effect to every clause rather than of mutilating or destroying one of the most important provisions.[42]

3.35   More recently, in *Sulamérica Cia Nacional de Seguros SA and ors v Enesa Engenharia SA and ors*,[43] the English courts were required to consider a contract governed by Brazilian law containing an arbitration agreement that designated London as the seat of any arbitration, without any express choice of law governing the arbitration agreement itself. Under Brazilian law, the arbitration agreement would have been unenforceable, without the consent of the respondent party to submit the specific dispute to arbitration. The Court of Appeal found that the parties could not have intended to apply Brazilian law:

> I do not think that in this case the parties' express choice of Brazilian law to govern the substantive contract is sufficient evidence of an implied choice of Brazilian law to govern the arbitration agreement, because (if the insured are correct) there is at least a serious risk that a choice of Brazilian law would significantly undermine that agreement. [...] this, it seems to me, reflects the fact that although one may start from the assumption that the

---

[39]   *Enka Insaat Ve Sanayi AS v OOO Insurance Company Chubb* [2020] UKSC 38, [106].
[40]   *Hamlyn & Co v Talisker Distillery* [1894] AC 202.
[41]   Ibid., p. 208 (*per* Lord Herschell).
[42]   *Hamlyn & Co v Talisker Distillery* [1894] AC 202, p. 215 (*per* Lord Ashbourne).
[43]   *Sulamérica Cia Nacional de Seguros SA and ors v Enesa Engenharia SA and ors* [2012] EWCA Civ 638.

parties intended the same law to govern the whole of the contract, including the arbitration agreement, specific factors may lead to the conclusion that that cannot in fact have been their intention.[44]

On this basis, the court determined that there was no express or implied agreement between the parties as to the law of the arbitration agreement, and it was necessary for the court to fill the lacuna.

(e) Delocalisation—a French 'third way'

The solutions considered so far have focused on establishing the law governing the arbitration agreement by reference to a national law, whether it is the law of the contract or the law of the seat of arbitration. The French courts, however, have adopted a different approach, whereby the existence and scope of the arbitration agreement is determined exclusively by reference to the parties' discernible common intentions. In this way, the arbitration agreement remains independent of the various national laws that might, in other jurisdictions, be deemed to apply to it. This approach, which fundamentally envisages international arbitration as a truly autonomous system, has the advantage of avoiding the need to have regard to the particular, local 'conflict-of-law' rules developed by different states around the globe. It seeks instead to implement what the court or tribunal finds to be the common intention of the parties.   **3.36**

This French 'third way' was a result of a number of decisions by the Paris Court of Appeal, from the early 1970s through to the early 1990s, which culminated in the Court of Cassation's decision in *Dalico* in 1993:[45]   **3.37**

> [B]y virtue of a substantive rule of international arbitration, the arbitration agreement is legally independent of the main contract containing or referring to it, and the existence and effectiveness of the arbitration agreement are to be assessed, subject to the mandatory rules of French law and international public policy, on the basis of the parties' common intention, there being no need to refer to any national law.[46]

In this context, the reference to the legal independence of the arbitration agreement is a reference to the doctrine of separability of the arbitration agreement, which has already been discussed, and which leads to the arbitration agreement being regarded as being itself autonomous.[47] The French Supreme Court stopped short of a complete delocalisation of the   **3.38**

---

[44] Ibid., at [31].

[45] *Municipalité de Khoms El Mergeb c/Sté Dalico*, Cass. Civ. 1ere, 20 December 1993, [1994] Rev Arb 116. The case was brought by a Libyan municipal authority against a Danish contractor after the latter had initiated arbitration proceedings. The Libyan party argued that the arbitration agreement was governed by Libyan law and that it was invalid under Libyan law. The Paris Court of Appeal rejected these arguments without deciding what law applied.

[46] *Municipalité de Khoms El Mergeb c/Sté Dalico*, Cass. Civ. 1ere, 20 December 1993, [1994] Rev Arb 116, p. 117, as translated by Professor Gaillard in Savage and Gaillard (eds) *Fouchard, Gaillard, Goldman on International Commercial Arbitration* (Kluwer Law International, 1999), p. 437.

[47] Professor Gaillard refers to the 'dual meaning' of 'autonomy' in Savage and Gaillard (eds) *Fouchard, Gaillard, Goldman on International Commercial Arbitration* (Kluwer Law International, 1999), p. 388. See also ibid., pp. 420–421 and pp. 435–451, and in particular p. 441 for an endorsement of the French third way. Regarding the separability of the arbitration agreement from the main contract under French law, see *Sté Omenex c/Hugon*, Cass.

arbitration agreement, by subjecting it to the mandatory provisions of French law and international public policy.[48] Moreover, it remains open to the parties, if such is their common intention, to expressly designate a national legal system or set of conflict laws, as the French Supreme Court clarified in the *Uni-Kod* decision.[49]

3.39   The French approach was examined by the UK Supreme Court in its decision in *Dallah Real Estate and Tourism Holding Co. v Ministry of Religious Affairs, Government of Pakistan*.[50] The decision concerned an agreement between Dallah Real Estate and a Pakistani government trust relating to commercial services for pilgrimages to Saudi Arabia. The agreement included an ICC arbitration clause, with the seat of the arbitration in Paris. Dallah initiated arbitration proceedings against both the government of Pakistan and against the trust. The arbitral tribunal in Paris accepted jurisdiction over Pakistan and rendered an award in favour of Dallah. The award itself was challenged in Paris, the seat of the arbitration; and its enforcement was challenged in the United Kingdom on the basis (among other things) that the tribunal had no jurisdiction over Pakistan, which was not a signatory to the agreement. The UK Supreme Court, applying French law, accepted that, as a starting point, French law (the law of the seat) refers to supranational law:

> [Under French law,] arbitration agreements derive their existence, validity and effect from supra-national law, without it being necessary to refer to any national law. If so, that would not avoid the need to have regard to French law 'as the law of the country where the award was made' under Article V(1)(a) of the [New York] Convention and s. 103(2)(b) of the 1996 [English Arbitration] Act. The Cour de Cassation is, however, a national court, giving a French legal view of international arbitration; and Dallah and the Government agree that the true analysis is that French law recognises transnational principles as potentially applicable to determine the existence, validity and effectiveness of an international arbitration agreement, such principles being part of French law.[51]

(f) Combining several approaches—a Swiss model

3.40   The final approach to determining the law or rules applicable to an arbitration agreement is to combine several approaches, as is the case in Switzerland, under the Swiss PIL which provides:

> As regards its substance, the arbitration agreement shall be valid if it conforms either to the law chosen by the parties, or to the law governing the subject-matter

Civ. 1ère, [2006] Rev Arb 103, in which the court held that an arbitration agreement survives the invalidity of the underlying agreement.

[48] Lew, Mistelis, and Kröll, *Comparative International Commercial Arbitration* (Kluwer Law International, 2003), paragraph 6–66.

[49] *Uni-Kod c/Sté Ouralkali*, Cass. Civ. 1ere, 30 March 2004, [2005] Rev Arb 959.

[50] *Dallah Real Estate and Tourism Holding Co. v Ministry of Religious Affairs, Government of Pakistan* [2010] UKSC 4.

[51] *Dallah Real Estate and Tourism Holding Co. v Ministry of Religious Affairs, Government of Pakistan* [2010] UKSC 4, at [15]. A few months later, the Paris Court of Appeal, in *Gouvernement du Pakistan—Ministère des Affaires Religieuses v Dallah Real Estate and Tourism Holding Co.*, Case No. 09/28533, 17 February 2011, reached a different conclusion as to whether Pakistan, as a non-signatory to the contract, was bound by the arbitration clause.

of the dispute, in particular the law governing the main contract, or if it conforms to Swiss law.[52]

This formulation has the advantage of giving Swiss courts a very considerable opportunity to uphold the validity of an arbitration agreement. **3.41**

C. Law Governing the Arbitration

(a) Introduction

An international arbitration usually takes place in a country that is 'neutral', in the sense **3.42** that none of the parties to the arbitration has a place of business or residence there.[53] This means that, in practice, the procedural law of the country in whose territory the arbitration takes place—that is, the *lex arbitri*—will generally be different from the law that governs the substantive matters in dispute. An arbitral tribunal with a seat in the Netherlands, for example, may be required to decide the substantive issues in dispute between the parties in accordance with the law of Switzerland or the law of New York or some other law, as the case may be. Nevertheless, the arbitration itself, and the way in which it is conducted, will be governed (if only in outline) by the relevant Dutch law on international arbitration.

This difference between the *lex arbitri* (the law of the place, or 'seat', of the arbitration) and **3.43** the law governing the substance of the dispute was part of the juridical tradition of continental Europe, but is now firmly established in international arbitration.[54]

It is right that there should be a distinction between the *lex arbitri* and the substantive law of **3.44** the contract. Where parties to an international arbitration agreement choose for themselves a seat of arbitration, they usually choose a place that has no connection with either themselves or their commercial relationship. They choose a 'neutral' place. By doing so, they do not necessarily intend to choose the law of that place to govern their relationship.[55] Indeed, as well as choosing a place of arbitration, they may well choose a substantive law that has no connection with that place.

---

[52] Swiss PIL, s. 178(2).

[53] A study into corporate attitudes on international arbitration has shown that factors such as 'formal legal infrastructure', including the neutrality and impartiality of its legal system, the national arbitration law, and the place's record in enforcing agreements to arbitrate and arbitral awards are key to parties' choice of the place of arbitration: see White & Case and Queen Mary School of International Arbitration, University of London, 2018, 'International Arbitration Survey: The Evolution of International Arbitration', available online at http://www.arbitration.qmul.ac.uk/media/arbitration/docs/2018-International-Arbitration-Survey---The-Evolution-of-International-Arbitration-(2).PDF. See also dicta by Lord Hoffman in delivering the leading judgment for the House of Lords in *West Tankers v RAS (the Front Comor)* [2007] 1 Lloyd's Rep 391, at [12]: in the case of arbitration, 'the situs and governing law are generally chosen by the parties on grounds of neutrality, availability of legal services and the unobtrusive effectiveness of the supervisory jurisdiction'.

[54] Savage and Gaillard (eds) *Fouchard, Gaillard, Goldman on International Commercial Arbitration* (Kluwer Law International, 1999), p. 1428. Early recognition of this principle in English law may be seen in *Compagnie Tunisienne de Navigation SA v Compagnie d'Armament Maritime SA* [1971] AC 572, at 604.

[55] For choice of law governing the agreement to arbitrate, see paragraphs 3.18*ff*; for choice of law governing the contract, see paragraphs 3.105*ff*.

3.45   If the parties do not make an express choice of the place of arbitration, the choice will have to be made for them, either by the arbitral tribunal itself or by a designated arbitral institution. The UNCITRAL Rules, for instance, state: 'If the parties have not previously agreed on the place of arbitration, the place of arbitration shall be determined by the arbitral tribunal having regard to the circumstances of the case.'[56] Similarly, Article 18.1 of the ICC Rules leaves the choice to the ICC Court.[57]

3.46   In cases of this kind, the place of arbitration will usually be determined by reference to the priority of neutrality as between the parties, and choosing a place that can provide a supportive and reliable supervisory jurisdiction to the arbitration process. In such circumstances, it would be illogical to hold that the *lex arbitri*, as the law of the place of arbitration, was necessarily the law applicable to the issues in dispute.

(b) What is the *lex arbitri*?

3.47   It is appropriate, at this stage, to consider what is meant by the *lex arbitri*. The question was posed rhetorically by a distinguished English judge:

> What then is the law governing the arbitration? It is, as [the present authors] trenchantly explain,[[58]] a body of rules which sets a standard external to the arbitration agreement, and the wishes of the parties, for the conduct of the arbitration. The law governing the arbitration comprises the rules governing interim measures (eg Court orders for the preservation or storage of goods), the rules empowering the exercise by the Court of supportive measures to assist an arbitration which has run into difficulties (eg filling a vacancy in the composition of the arbitral tribunal if there is no other mechanism) and the rules providing for the exercise by the Court of its supervisory jurisdiction over arbitrations (eg removing an arbitrator for misconduct).[59]

(i) The content of the *lex arbitri*

3.48   Each state will decide for itself what laws it wishes to lay down to govern the conduct of arbitrations within its own territory. Some states will wish to build an element of consumer protection into their law, so as to protect private individuals. For example, the Swedish Arbitration Act provides that an arbitration agreement with a consumer involving goods or services for private use is invalid if made before a dispute arises.[60] Similarly, the same Act provides that the arbitral tribunal may order the parties to pay the arbitrators' fees and, if it does so, must set out in its final award its decision as to the fees payable to each of the arbitrators.[61] The arbitral tribunal must also provide clear instruction to the parties of the steps that must be taken to appeal to the district court against this decision.[62]

---

[56] UNCITRAL Rules 2010, Art. 18.1.
[57] ICC Rules 2021, Art. 18.1 ('The place of the arbitration shall be fixed by the Court, unless agreed upon by the parties.')
[58] The reference was to the second edition of this book.
[59] *Smith Ltd v H International* [1991] 2 Lloyd's Rep 127, p. 130.
[60] Swedish Arbitration Act, s. 6.
[61] Swedish Arbitration Act, s. 37.
[62] Swedish Arbitration Act, s. 41. It is an unattractive proposition for arbitrators whose work has been accomplished and whose role is over to face a possible challenge before the local courts in relation to their fees.

In recognition of the distinction between domestic arbitration and international **3.49** arbitration—in which the sums at issue are likely to be larger and the parties better able to look after themselves—some states have (sensibly, it may be thought) introduced a code of law specifically designed for international arbitrations. The French Code of Civil Procedure, for example, includes a specific chapter on international arbitration,[63] Australia has adopted an International Arbitration Act 1974, and Switzerland has adopted the Swiss PIL.

Reference has already been made to the Model Law, which the authors have described as **3.50** the baseline for any state wishing to modernise its law of arbitration.[64] Many jurisdictions incorporate the Model Law into their national arbitration laws. Australia, for example, expressly incorporates the Model Law into Australian law.[65] The provisions of the Model Law are drawn in relatively broad terms. They do not purport to lay down any detailed procedural rules as to the actual conduct of an arbitration—such as rules on the submission and exchange of witness statements, the order in which witnesses are to be called, the time to be allotted for the questioning and cross-questioning of witnesses, and so forth. Indeed, the Model Law expressly provides that:

(1) Subject to the provisions of this Law, the parties are free to agree on the procedure to be followed by the arbitral tribunal in conducting the proceedings.
(2) Failing such agreement, the arbitral tribunal may, subject to the provisions of this Law, conduct the arbitration in such manner as it considers appropriate. The power conferred upon the arbitral tribunal includes the power to determine the admissibility, relevance, materiality and weight of any evidence.[66]

It may be helpful at this point to give examples of the matters with which the *lex arbitri* **3.51** might be expected to deal, although the exact position under the relevant *lex arbitri* should be checked, particularly where these legal provisions are mandatory. With this qualification, the *lex arbitri* is likely to extend to:

i. the definition and form of an agreement to arbitrate;
ii. whether a dispute is capable of being referred to arbitration (that is, whether it is 'arbitrable' under the *lex arbitri*);
iii. the constitution of the arbitral tribunal and any grounds for challenge of that tribunal;
iv. the entitlement of the arbitral tribunal to rule on its own jurisdiction;
v. equal treatment of the parties;
vi. freedom to agree upon detailed rules of procedure;
vii. interim measures of protection;
viii. statements of claim and defence;
ix. hearings, including the permissibility of virtual hearings;
x. default proceedings;
xi. court assistance, if required;

---

[63] French Code of Civil Procedure, Bk IV, Title II ('International arbitration').
[64] See Chapter 1.
[65] Australian International Arbitration Act 1974, Div. 2, Art. 16(1).
[66] Model Law, Art. 19.

xii. the powers of the arbitrators, including any powers to decide as *amiables compositeurs*;

xiii. the form and validity of the arbitration award; and

xiv. the finality of the award, including any right to challenge it in the courts of the place of arbitration.

3.52 These are all important aspects of international arbitration. They may well arise in practice and are all addressed later in this commentary. Three essential points should, however, be made now.

3.53 First, the effective conduct of an international arbitration may depend upon the provisions of the law of the place of arbitration. One way of illustrating this dependence is by reference to any provisions of the local law for judicial assistance in the conduct of the arbitration. Even if the arbitrators have the power to order interim measures of protection, such as orders for the preservation and inspection of property, they are unlikely to have the power to enforce such orders—particularly if the property in question is in the possession of a third party. For this, it is necessary to turn to national courts for assistance.[67]

3.54 Second, the choice of a particular place of arbitration may have important and unintended consequences. This is because the law of that place may confer powers on the courts or on the arbitrators that the parties did not expect, or may deprive an arbitral tribunal of powers that the parties might otherwise have assumed existed.

i. On this latter point, one example is the power to consolidate arbitrations. Whether or not a court or arbitral tribunal has the power to consolidate two or more arbitrations that involve the same basic issues of fact or law is a controversial question. In the present context, it is necessary to note only that such a power may exist under the *lex arbitri* and that this may come as a disagreeable surprise to a party who does not wish to have other parties joined in its arbitration.[68]

ii. Another example arises in the context of sanctions, since it may be that a tribunal is compelled to take into account legal sanctions relevant to the parties' dispute because they form part of the mandatory law of the *lex arbitri*.[69]

3.55 Third, there is an obvious prospect of conflict between the *lex arbitri* and a different system of law that may be equally relevant. Consider, for example, the question of arbitrability—that is, whether or not the subject matter of the dispute is 'capable' of being resolved by

---

[67] See, e.g., Swiss PIL, Ch. 12, Art. 183, which provides that the arbitral tribunal may request the assistance of the court where a party does not voluntarily comply with a protective measure; the English Arbitration Act, s. 44(1) and (2), which gives the court the same powers to order the inspection, photocopying, preservation, custody, or detention of property in relation to an arbitration as it has in relation to litigation; and the Model Law, Art. 9, which allows a party to seek interim measures of protection from a court. It should be noted that while the courts of the seat play the lead role in supporting the arbitral process, *inter alia*, in terms of granting interim relief, it may also be necessary to seek relief from other courts beyond the seat, where, e.g., assets might be located. Various national laws (e.g., Dutch and German law) foresee this possibility, and courts in various other jurisdictions including Hong Kong have intervened in support of arbitrations being conducted overseas: see *The Lady Muriel* [1995] 2 HKC 320 (CA).

[68] British Columbia has adapted the Model Law, in the International Commercial Arbitration Act 1996, s. 27.01, to allow court-ordered consolidation where the parties to two or more arbitration agreements have agreed to consolidate the arbitrations arising out of those agreements. The Belgian Judicial Code 2013 (BJC), art. 1709(3) is unusual in that it provides that where a third party wishes to join proceedings, or is called to join, the arbitral tribunal's decision to allow proceedings in respect of this third party requires unanimity of the arbitrators.

[69] Shahani, 'Impact of Sanctions under the CISG' (2015) 33(4) ASA Bulletin (Kluwer Law International) at 854.

arbitration. The concept of arbitrability, as we have already discussed,[70] is basic to the arbitral process. Both the New York Convention and the Model Law refer explicitly to disputes that are 'capable of being resolved by arbitration'—that is to say, to disputes that are 'arbitrable' in the proper sense of that term.

On the question of arbitrability, it may be said that if a dispute is capable of being resolved **3.56** by litigation in the courts, surely the same dispute is equally 'capable' of being resolved by arbitration? Theoretically, this may well be correct. In practice, however, every state reserves for itself, as a matter of public policy, what might be called a 'state monopoly' over certain types of dispute. Accordingly, whether or not a particular dispute—for example over the disposal of assets belonging to a bankrupt company—is legally 'capable of being resolved by arbitration' is a matter that each state will decide for itself. It is a matter on which states may well differ, with some taking a more restrictive attitude than others. This obviously results in an element of forum shopping; and incidentally may be 'good for business' for those jurisdictions adopting a liberal approach to what disputes are 'arbitrable'. It should be borne in mind, however (and this may be important if it becomes necessary to seek enforcement of an award) that a claim that is arbitrable both under the law governing the arbitration agreement and under the *lex arbitri* may not be regarded as arbitrable under the law of the place of enforcement. An award in such a case, although validly made under the *lex arbitri*, might prove to be unenforceable under the New York Convention.

(ii) Procedural rules and the *lex arbitri*

The preceding discussion about the content of the *lex arbitri* indicates that most, if not **3.57** all, national laws governing arbitration deal with general propositions, such as the need to treat each party equally, rather than with detailed rules of procedure, such as the time for exchange of witness statements or the submission of pre-hearing briefs. The Swiss PIL provides that '[t]he parties may, directly or by reference to arbitration rules, determine the arbitral procedure; they may also submit it to a procedural law of their choice'.[71] Similarly, the English Arbitration Act 1996, provides that 'parties should be free to agree how their disputes are resolved, subject only to such safeguards as are necessary in the public interest'.[72]

At some stage in the conduct of an arbitration—and, indeed, at a fairly early stage—the par- **3.58** ties will need to know where they stand in terms of the detailed procedure to be followed. There are many points to be clarified: will the claimant's statement of claim simply outline the facts supporting the claim, or will it be accompanied by the documents that are relied upon and perhaps by legal submissions? When the respondent has submitted its defence, will the claimant have the right to submit a reply, or is that the end of the written submissions? What about the evidence of witnesses and experts? Will there be opportunities to make document production requests?

It is plainly necessary for the parties and the arbitral tribunal to know what procedural rules **3.59** they are required to follow, particularly in an international arbitration in which the parties

---

[70] See Chapter 1.
[71] Swiss PIL, art. 182(1).
[72] English Arbitration Act, s. 1(b).

will usually come from different backgrounds with a different approach to such questions as the interviewing of witnesses, the production of documents, and so forth. All that needs to be understood at this point is that there is a great difference between the general provisions of the law governing the arbitration (the *lex arbitri*) and the detailed procedural rules that will need to be adopted, or adapted, for the fair and efficient conduct of the proceedings. The rules of the arbitral institutions, such as the ICC and the LCIA, provide an overall framework within which to operate, as do the UNCITRAL Rules. However, it is important to note that even these rules will need to be supplemented by more detailed provisions by the parties or the arbitral tribunal, as discussed in Chapter 6.

3.60   It is therefore often advisable, particularly where parties and their counsel are from different legal backgrounds, to agree such rules at the outset of an arbitration. This may be done by agreement of the parties, or by order of the arbitral tribunal at the first procedural meeting. As part of this process, the parties may agree, or the arbitral tribunal may order, that they adopt or have regard to a pre-existing set of detailed rules, for example the IBA Rules on the Taking of Evidence in International Arbitration.[73] By ensuring that the rules are clearly established early on, the administration of the case will (or at least should) be simplified, and the scope for delay and dilatory tactics reduced.

3.61   The choice of detailed procedural rules raises two issues relevant to this discussion of applicable law. The first is that, as noted in the foregoing, the detailed procedural rules do not displace the *lex arbitri*, rather they apply concurrently. This gives rise to the possibility of a conflict between the two sets of procedural rules and, in these circumstances a tribunal will need to ascertain which law prevails. Where the relevant provision of the *lex arbitri* is mandatory, it will prevail. Some institutional rules pre-empt this scenario: for example, the UNCITRAL Rules provide that the mandatory provisions of the *lex arbitri* shall prevail over the UNCITRAL Rules in the event of any conflict.[74]

3.62   A second issue arises where the institutional rules adopted to govern an arbitration are subject to a requirement that they be interpreted in accordance with a particular national law that differs from the *lex arbitri*. The LCIA Rules, for example, must be interpreted in accordance with the laws of England.[75] This is another source of concurrently applicable laws and, in theory at least, may give rise to conflicts. Thus, in an arbitration governed by LCIA Rules, a tribunal seated in a foreign jurisdiction will be obliged to interpret the LCIA Rules in accordance with the laws of England. As one commentator has noted:

> The highly specific inclusion of the laws of England as the means of interpretation of the LCIA Rules could potentially foreshadow arguments about their implementation in cases where the seat of arbitration is not England, and/or where the parties have chosen a specific law, which is not English law, to govern their Arbitration Agreement. Particularly, Arbitral Tribunals and/or other relevant foreign courts may encounter difficulties in reconciling the new requirements to interpret the LCIA Rules in accordance

---

[73] For a discussion on guidelines and similarly applicable standards, see paragraphs 249*ff*.

[74] UNCITRAL Rules 2010, Art. 1.3 ('These Rules shall govern the arbitration except that where any of these Rules is in conflict with a provision of the law applicable to the arbitration from which the parties cannot derogate, that provision shall prevail.')

[75] LCIA Rules 2020, Art. 16.5 ('[...] the LCIA Rules shall be interpreted in accordance with the laws of England.')

with English law while maintaining their obligations to apply the mandatory procedural law of the arbitral seat.[76]

(c) Seat theory

The concept that an arbitration is governed by the law of the place in which it is held, which is the 'seat' (or 'forum', or *locus arbitri*) of the arbitration, is well established in both the theory and practice of international arbitration.[77] It has influenced the wording of international conventions from the Geneva Protocol of 1923 (the Geneva Protocol) to the New York Convention.

3.63

The Geneva Protocol states: 'The arbitral procedure, including the constitution of the arbitral tribunal, shall be governed *by the will of the parties and by the law of the country* in whose territory the arbitration takes place'.[78] The New York Convention[79] maintains the reference to 'the law of the country where the arbitration took place'[80] and, synonymously, to 'the law of the country where the award is made'.[81] This continues the clear territorial link between the place of arbitration and the law governing that arbitration: the *lex arbitri*. This territorial link is again maintained in the Model Law: 'The provisions of this Law, except articles 8, 9, 35 and 36, apply only *if the place of arbitration is in the territory of this State*.'[82]

3.64

Several modern laws on arbitration are clear on the link between the seat of the arbitration and the *lex arbitri*. Swiss law, for example, states:

3.65

The provisions of this Chapter apply to arbitral tribunals that have their seat in Switzerland if, at the time that the arbitration agreement was concluded, at least one of the parties thereto did not have its domicile, its habitual residence or its seat in Switzerland.[83]

Likewise, a majority of the provisions of German arbitration law apply only to arbitrations which have a place of arbitration in Germany.[84] A similar approach is taken in Belgium,[85] India,[86] and Malaysia.[87] In English law, certain provisions of the Arbitration Act apply only

3.66

[76] Scherer, Richman, and Gerbay, *Seat and Place of Arbitration in Arbitrating under the 2020 LCIA Rules: A User's Guide* (Kluwer Law International, 2021), p. 27.
[77] See, e.g., Park, 'The *lex loci arbitri* and international commercial arbitration' (1983) 32 ICLQ 21; Jarvin, 'Le lieu de l'arbitrage' (1993) 4 ICC Bulletin 7; Born, *International Commercial Arbitration* (2nd edn, Kluwer Law International, 2014), pp. 1530–1531. See also Kaufmann-Kohler, 'Identifying and applying the law governing the arbitral procedure: The role of the law of the place of arbitration' (1999) 9 ICCA Congress Series 336.
[78] The Geneva Protocol, Art. 2 (emphasis added).
[79] Which, by means of Art. VII(2), replaces the Geneva Protocol to the extent that contracting states become bound by the New York Convention.
[80] New York Convention, Art. V(1)(d).
[81] New York Convention, Art. V(1)(a) and (e).
[82] Model Law, Art. 1(2) (emphasis added). Arts 8 and 9 are concerned with enforcing the arbitration agreement and interim measures of protection respectively; Arts 35 and 36 are concerned with recognition and enforcement of the award.
[83] Swiss PIL, Ch. 12, Art. 176(1) (emphasis added).
[84] German Code of Civil Procedure 2005 (as amended in 2021) (German ZPO), bk. 10, s. 1, § 1025(1) ('The provisions of this book [on arbitration] shall apply if the place of arbitration within the meaning of § 1043(1) [i.e., the seat of the arbitration] is Germany.')
[85] BJC, Art. 1676(7).
[86] Indian Arbitration and Conciliation Act 1996 (as amended in 2021) (Indian Arbitration and Conciliation Act), s. 2(2).
[87] Malaysian Arbitration Act 2005 (as amended in 2018), s. 3(3).

where the seat of the arbitration is in England, Wales, or Northern Ireland, whereas other provisions (for example, for the stay of court proceedings commenced in breach of an arbitration agreement) apply even if the seat of the arbitration is not in those countries or if no seat has been designated.[88] The 'seat of the arbitration' is defined as 'the juridical seat of the arbitration' designated by the parties, or by an arbitral institution or the arbitrators themselves, as the case may be.[89] Unless the parties agree otherwise, the seat of the arbitration must be stated in the award of the arbitrators.[90]

3.67 As this introduction tries to make clear, the place, or 'seat', of the arbitration is not merely a matter of geography. It is the territorial link between the arbitration itself and the law of the place in which that arbitration is legally situated:

> When one says that London, Paris or Geneva is the place of arbitration, one does not refer solely to a geographical location. One means that the arbitration is conducted within the framework of the law of arbitration of England, France or Switzerland or, to use an English expression, under the curial law of the relevant country. The geographical place of arbitration is the factual connecting factor between that arbitration law and the arbitration proper, considered as a nexus of contractual and procedural rights and obligations between the parties and the arbitrators.[91]

The seat of an arbitration is thus often intended to be its legal centre of gravity. This does not mean that all of the proceedings of the arbitration have to take place there, although preferably some should do so.[92]

> Although the choice of a 'seat' also indicates the geographical place for the arbitration, this does not mean that the parties have limited themselves to that place. As is pointed out[[93] ...] in a passage approved by the Court of Appeal in *Naviera Amazonia Peruana SA v Compania Internacional de Seguros del Peru* [1988] 1 Lloyd's Rep 116 at 121, it may often be convenient to hold meetings or even hearings in other countries. This does not mean that the 'seat' of the arbitration changes with each change of country. The legal place of the arbitration remains the same even if the physical place changes from time to time, unless of course the parties agree to change it.[94]

3.68 Arbitrators and the parties to an international arbitration often come from different countries. It may not always be convenient for everyone concerned to travel to the country that is the seat of the arbitration for the purpose of a meeting or a hearing. There may be

---

[88] English Arbitration Act, s. 2.

[89] English Arbitration Act, s. 3.

[90] English Arbitration Act, s. 52(5).

[91] Reymond, 'Where is an arbitral award made?' (1992) 108 LQR 1, at 3. There is, however, no such 'curial' law in arbitration proceedings brought pursuant to the International Centre for Settlement of Investment Disputes (ICSID). In accordance with the ICSID Convention, Art. 62, the place of the proceedings is the seat of the Centre unless otherwise agreed, but this does not impose the curial law of Washington, DC.

[92] For the view that at least some hearings and meetings should preferably take place at the seat of the arbitration, see Paulsson and Petrochilos, *UNCITRAL Arbitration* (Kluwer Law International, 2017), pp. 153–154 ('The better view is that tribunals should not be too astute in deciding that various acts, such as hearings, should be outside the agreed seat. That the parties agreed on a seat or [...] the tribunal elected one, connotes an assessment or expectation that the seat has "appropriate" venues').

[93] In the second edition of this book.

[94] *Union of India v McDonnell Douglas Corporation* [1993] 2 Lloyd's Rep 48. (The Peruvian case referred to in this citation is generally known as 'the *Peruvian Insurance* case'.)

limitations on the ability of those involved in an arbitration to travel to a particular location. Alternatively, it may simply be easier and less expensive to meet elsewhere, or the parties and tribunal may be conscious of reducing, where practical and possible, the environmental footprint of their arbitral proceedings. In recognition of this reality, various procedural laws and rules now provide parties with the flexibility to hold meetings and hearings other than in-person and in the place (or seat) of the arbitration. For example, the ICC Rules read as follows:

1) The place of the arbitration shall be fixed by the Court, unless agreed upon by the parties.
2) The arbitral tribunal may, after consulting the parties, conduct hearings and meetings at any location it considers appropriate, unless otherwise agreed by the parties.
3) The arbitral tribunal may deliberate at any location it considers appropriate.[95]

The ICC Rules further state that: **3.69**

The arbitral tribunal may decide, after consulting the parties, and on the basis of the relevant facts and circumstances of the case, that any hearing will be conducted by physical attendance or remotely by videoconference, telephone or other appropriate means of communication.[96]

The UNCITRAL Rules allow arbitrators to meet at any appropriate locations for deliber-   **3.70**
ations, and provides that meetings 'for any other purpose, including hearings may take place in any location, unless agreed otherwise by the parties'.[97] The LCIA has a similar rule:

If any hearing is to be held in person, the Arbitral Tribunal may hold such hearing at any convenient geographical place in consultation with the parties. If the Arbitral Tribunal is to meet in person to hold its deliberations, it may do so at any geographical place of its own choice. If such place(s) should be elsewhere than the seat of the arbitration, or if any hearing or deliberation takes place otherwise than in person (in whole or in part), the arbitration shall nonetheless be treated for all purposes as an arbitration conducted at the arbitral seat and any order or award as having been made at that seat.[98]

The Model Law also allows the arbitral tribunal to meet at any place it considers appropriate for its deliberations or to hear witnesses, unless the parties object.[99]

These are sensible provisions. They recognise the realities of international arbitration, with   **3.71**
parties, lawyers, and arbitrators likely to be based in different parts of the world. They give flexibility to the tribunal and to the parties in selecting a convenient location for procedural meetings, hearings, and deliberations or to decide to hold their proceedings virtually, either

---

[95] ICC Rules 2021, Art. 18.
[96] ICC Rules 2021, Art. 26.1.
[97] UNCITRAL Rules 2010, Art. 18.2.
[98] LCIA Rules 2020, Art. 16.3.
[99] Model Law, Art. 20(2). The Netherlands Arbitration Act 2015 (Netherlands Arbitration Act), s. 1037(3), is to like effect; cf. the law in the United States that requires that hearings be conducted in the place of the arbitration unless the parties agree otherwise: see, e.g., *Spring Hope Rockwool v Industrial Clean Air Inc.* 504 F.Supp. 1385 (EDNC 1981); *Snyder v Smith*, 736 F.2d 409 (7th Cir. 1984), cert. denied, 469 US 1037 (1984); *Jain v de Méré* 51 F.3d 686, 692 (7th Cir. 1995); *National Iranian Oil Co. v Ashland Oil, Inc.*, 817 F.2d 326, 334 (5th Cir. 1987). Under the FAA, where the parties have not agreed on the location of the arbitration, a court may order the parties to conduct the arbitration in its own district: *Clarendon National Insurance Co. v Lan*, 152 F.Supp.2d 506, 524 (SDNY 2001).

in part or in full. It may be, for example, that although the seat of the arbitration is Jakarta, the arbitral tribunal finds it convenient to meet to hold hearings in Singapore.[100] In international construction disputes, it is often necessary for an arbitral tribunal sitting in one country to visit the site of the project in another country to carry out an inspection. Equally, it may be more convenient for an arbitral tribunal sitting in one country to conduct a hearing in another country or continent, for example for the purpose of taking evidence. Virtual proceedings can help avoid delays if one or more arbitrator or party is unable to travel.

3.72   Enabling flexibility in the geographic location of hearings can also avoid practical difficulties created by mandatory provisions of the national law of the seat. As one commentary notes by way of example, local restrictions on who can appear as counsel in court and arbitral proceedings is a 'very important consideration'. In Nigeria, for example, only locally qualified 'legal practitioners' may appear as counsel at hearings.[101]

3.73   An arbitral tribunal that visits another country must, of course, respect the law of that country. For example, if the purpose of the visit is to take evidence from witnesses, the arbitral tribunal should respect any provisions of the local law that govern the taking of evidence.[102] However, each move of the arbitral tribunal does not of itself mean that the seat of the arbitration changes. The seat of the arbitration remains the place initially agreed by, or on behalf of, the parties.[103]

3.74   What is the legal position if, as sometimes happens, the arbitral tribunal—having consulted the parties and perhaps against the objection of one of them—holds all meetings, hearings, and deliberations in a place that is not the seat of the arbitration or entirely remotely? To proceed in this manner reduces the seat of the arbitration to a legal fiction: a place of arbitration in which no physical meetings or hearings take place. In the light of the provisions set out above, and subject to any particular restrictions contained in the *lex arbitri* and the views of the parties,[104] this would seem to be permissible. It conforms with the letter, if not the spirit, of the law or the applicable rules. As aptly stated by the UK Supreme Court:

> [T]he seat of an arbitration is a legal concept rather than a physical one. A choice of place as the seat does not dictate that hearings must be held, or that any award must actually be

---

[100] This was the case in *PT Garuda Indonesia v Birgen Air* [2002] 1 SLR 393 (CA), in which it was held that there was no legal nexus between the arbitration and Singapore simply because hearings were held there.

[101] See discussion in Paulsson and Petrochilos, *UNCITRAL Arbitration* (Kluwer Law International, 2017), p. 154.

[102] For example, the local law may not permit arbitrators to take evidence from witnesses on oath.

[103] The preceding two paragraphs were cited with approval by the court in *Naviera Amazonia Peruana SA v Compania Internacional de Seguros del Peru* [1988] 1 Lloyd's Rep 116.

[104] In ICC Case No. 10623 (2003) 21 ASA Bulletin 60 (including a summary by Professor Crivellaro), the tribunal held all meetings, etc., in Paris, although the seat of the arbitration was in Ethiopia. The Ethiopian government, a party to the arbitration, contested the tribunal's jurisdiction both by challenging it unsuccessfully before the ICC Court and by applying to its local courts, the interference of which the tribunal ignored. Interference by local courts is further discussed at paragraph 3.98. See also the decision of the Svea Court of Appeal in *Titan Corporation v Alcatel CIT SA* (Svea Court of Appeal), RH 2005:1 (T 1038-05) YCA XXX (2005), 139, in which the Court denied jurisdiction to consider an *ex parte* application to set aside an award that stated that the seat of arbitration was Stockholm. The Court based its decision in part on the fact that all of the hearings (in which one of the authors was counsel for the claimant) had taken place in Paris and in London, and not in Stockholm; hence, in its view, the arbitration could not be considered to have any connection to Sweden as required for the Swedish Arbitration Act of 1999 to apply. This decision was subsequently reversed (in relevant part) by the Swedish Supreme Court.

issued, in that place. [...] The point of agreeing to a seat is to agree that the law and courts of a particular country will exercise control over an arbitration which has its seat in that country to the extent provided for by that country's law.[105]

(i) Is the *lex arbitri* a procedural law?

In some countries, the law governing arbitration, including international arbitration, is part **3.75** of a code of civil procedure. This is so, for example, in France and in Germany—and it is sometimes said that the *lex arbitri* is a law of procedure, as if that is all that it is. It is true, of course, that the *lex arbitri* may deal with procedural matters—such as the constitution of an arbitral tribunal where there is no relevant contractual provision—but the authors suggest that the *lex arbitri* is much more than a purely procedural law. Whilst also governing the procedure of the arbitration, it may, in addition, stipulate that a given type of dispute— over patent rights, for instance, or (as in Belgium and some Arab states) over a local agency agreement—is not capable of settlement by arbitration under the local law. This is surely not simply a matter of procedure?[106] Or again, by way of example, an award may be set aside on the basis that it is contrary to the public policy of the *lex arbitri*. Once more, this would not seem to be merely a matter of procedure. One commentary has accordingly described the function of the *lex arbitri* as governing the 'internal' procedure of the arbitration as well as the 'external' oversight of the arbitration by national courts.[107]

It is also sometimes said that parties have selected the procedural law that will govern their **3.76** arbitration by providing for arbitration in a particular country.[108] This is too elliptical and, as an English court itself held in *Braes of Doune Wind Farm*,[109] it does not always hold true. What the parties have done is to choose a place of arbitration. That choice brings with it submission to the laws of that country, including any mandatory provisions of its law on arbitration. To say that the parties have 'chosen' that particular law to govern the arbitration is rather like saying that an English car driver who takes their car to France has 'chosen' French traffic law, which will oblige them to drive on the right-hand side of the road, to give priority to vehicles approaching from the right, and generally to obey traffic laws to which they may not be accustomed.

---

[105] *Enka Insaat Ve Sanayi AS v OOO Insurance Company Chubb* [2020] UKSC 38, at [68].

[106] Another good reason for not labelling the *lex arbitri* 'procedural' is that different countries have different notions of what is a matter of procedure and what is a matter of substance: cf. the treatment of time limits in English law, discussed in Chapter 4, paragraph 4.07.

[107] Collins (ed.) *Dicey, Morris & Collins on the Conflict of Laws* (15th edn, Sweet & Maxwell, 2018), paragraphs 16-009, 16-029 ('In essence, the procedural law of an arbitration deals with two sets of issues: (a) the *internal* procedure of the arbitration itself: commencement of the arbitration, appointment of arbitrators, pleadings, provisional measures, evidence, hearings, and awards; and (b) the *external* intervention of national courts in the arbitral process').

[108] See, e.g., the reference of Lord Diplock to the 'selection' of a particular *lex arbitri* by the choice of a place of arbitration, in *Compagnie Tunisienne de Navigation SA v Compagnie d'Armament Maritime SA* [1971] AC 572, at 604.

[109] The English Technology and Construction Court, in *Braes of Doune Wind Farm (Scotland) v Alfred McAlpine Business Services* [2008] EWHC 426 (TCC), stated that the parties' designation of 'Glasgow, Scotland' as the place of arbitration referred only to the place where it was intended to hold hearings. England was deemed to be the juridical seat owing to the fact that the parties had referred to the application of the English Arbitration Act. This case demonstrates that the parties' choice of procedural law may be determinative of the seat of the arbitration. According to the court, at [17], 'one needs to consider what, in substance, the parties agreed was the law of the country which would juridically control the arbitration'.

3.77   Parties may well choose a particular place of arbitration precisely because its *lex arbitri* is one that they find attractive.[110] Nevertheless, once a place of arbitration has been chosen, it brings with it its own law. If that law contains provisions that are mandatory as far as arbitrations are concerned, those provisions must be obeyed.[111] It is not a matter of choice, any more than the notional motorist is free to choose which local traffic laws to obey and which to disregard.

(ii) Choice of another procedural law

3.78   The concept of subjecting an arbitration in one state to the procedural law of another has been the subject of much theoretical discussion. Thus, for example, an arbitration could be seated in Switzerland, but by agreement between the parties, made subject to the procedural law of Germany. In this regard, Swiss law provides that the parties to an arbitration may 'make the procedure subject to a procedural law of their choice'.[112] Similarly, the French Code of Civil Procedure recognises the possibility that parties may choose a different law to apply to the procedure of arbitrations located in France, and that the French Code of Civil Procedure might apply as the procedural law in arbitrations located abroad.[113]

3.79   It is not easy to understand why parties should wish to complicate the conduct of an arbitration in this way (unless, as is possible, they do not understand what they are doing). It means that the parties and the arbitral tribunal would need to have regard to two procedural laws: that of Germany, as the chosen procedural law; and that of Switzerland, to the extent that the provisions of Swiss law (such as the requirement of equality of treatment of the parties) are mandatory.[114] Nor is this all: if it becomes necessary during the course of the arbitration to have recourse to the courts—for example on a challenge of one of the arbitrators—to which court would the complainant go? The Swiss court would presumably be reluctant to give a ruling on German procedural law; the German court might well prove unwilling to give a ruling on a procedural matter that it could not directly enforce, since the arbitration was not conducted within its territorial jurisdiction.

3.80   It is tempting to suggest that if the procedural law of a particular country is either so attractive or so familiar to the parties that they wish to adopt it, they would do better to locate their arbitration in that country. One needs only to consider the difficulties that a party would face in obtaining a subpoena against a reluctant witness, however, to recognise the problems inherent in a choice of foreign procedural law.[115]

3.81   In a Peruvian insurance case,[116] the English Court of Appeal considered a contract that had been held by the court of first instance to provide for an arbitration to be located in Peru,

---

[110] See Chapter 6.

[111] See, e.g., consolidation under Dutch law and the mandatory provisions of other national laws governing arbitration, such as the mandatory provisions of the English Arbitration Act.

[112] Swiss PIL, Ch. 12, Art. 182; there are provisions in Dutch and Italian law to the same effect, and in the French Code of Civil Procedure, at art. 1509. However, non-compliance with public policy rules would be a ground for setting an award aside even if another procedural law were chosen.

[113] French Code of Civil Procedure, arts 1494–1495.

[114] Swiss PIL, Ch. 12, Art. 182(3).

[115] In many countries, an arbitrator has no power to issue a subpoena and the parties must rely upon the relevant court for such process: see, e.g., Model Law, Art. 27. The United States does allow for an arbitrator to summon a witness to attend and to bring any material documents or evidence, but the local federal district court must be called in to assist in compelling a reluctant witness to attend or to punish a witness who fails to attend: FAA, s. 7. See also Chapter 7.

[116] *Naviera Amazonia Peruana SA v Compania Internacional de Seguros de Peru* [1988] 1 Lloyd's Rep 116.

but subject to English procedural law. The Court of Appeal construed the contract as providing for arbitration in London under English law, but noted that a situation involving a choice of foreign procedural law was theoretically possible. However, practical difficulties were foreseen:

> There is equally no reason in theory which precludes parties to agree that an arbitration shall be held at a place or in country X but subject to the procedural laws of Y. The limits and implications of any such agreement have been much discussed in the literature, but apart from the decision in the instant case there appears to be no reported case where this has happened. This is not surprising when one considers the complexities and inconveniences which such an agreement would involve. Thus, at any rate under the principles of English law, which rest upon the territorially limited jurisdiction of our courts, an agreement to arbitrate in X subject to English procedural law would not empower our courts to exercise jurisdiction over the arbitration in X.[117]

(d) Where an award is made

From time to time, it may become necessary to determine where an award is made. The point is an important one. For example, recognition and enforcement of an award may be refused on the basis that the arbitration agreement was not valid under the law of the country where the award was made, or on the basis that the award itself had been 'set aside or suspended' by a court of the country in which it was made.[118]   **3.82**

In practice, it is rare for parties to stipulate the country in which an award is to be deemed made. Rather, it is more common for parties to identify the place of the arbitration, and for that national law to contain terms that indicate where an award is treated as being made. The English Arbitration Act, for example, provides that: **3.83**

> Unless otherwise agreed by the parties, where the seat of the arbitration is in England and Wales or Northern Ireland, any award in the proceedings shall be treated as made there, regardless of where it was signed, despatched or delivered to any of the parties.[119]

The Model Law contains a similar provision,[120] as does the Netherlands Arbitration Act.[121] Some arbitration rules also deal expressly with the place at which an award is 'made'. For example, the ICC Rules provide that an award is deemed to be made at the place (or seat) of the arbitration and on the date stated therein.[122] The UNCITRAL Rules 2010 state similarly that   **3.84**

---

[117] Ibid., at 120. See also *Union of India v McDonnell Douglas Corp.* [1993] 2 Lloyd's Rep. 48, 50 (QB). In that case, the parties' agreement was to be conducted in accordance with the procedure provided in the Indian Arbitration Act of 1940, while the seat of the arbitration proceedings was to be London. The High Court interpreted the arbitration agreement as requiring the arbitration procedure to accord with Indian law, while the English courts would have jurisdiction to supervise the arbitration. The court acknowledged the 'at least theoretical possibility that the parties are free to choose to hold their arbitration in one country but subject to the procedural laws of another' notwithstanding that this arrangement was 'calculated to give rise to great difficulties and complexities'.

[118] New York Convention, Art. V(1)(e); Model Law, Art. 36(1)(a)(v). Note that these provisions are discretionary: recognition and enforcement may be refused. See also Chapter 10.

[119] English Arbitration Act, s. 53.

[120] Model Law, Art. 31(3).

[121] Netherlands Arbitration Act, Art. 1037(2).

[122] ICC Rules 2021, Art. 32.3.

an award 'shall be deemed to have been made at the place of arbitration'.[123] The 2010 Rules differ from the 1976 Rules, which stated that an award 'shall be made at the place of arbitration', which commentators believed 'could have been construed to require the signing at the place of arbitration', contrary to the drafters' intention to establish a legal framework.[124]

3.85   Automatically equating the place of an arbitration with the place where an award is made avoids the need for arbitrators to be physically present in one particular jurisdiction when signing the award. This is a sensible provision when arbitrators who live in different countries may well have agreed on the final terms of the award by email or other forms of communication. In an international arbitration, with a tribunal of three arbitrators, the award in its final form may well be signed in three different countries, each member of the tribunal adding his or her signature in turn. Even where not specifically provided for in the applicable procedural rules, there is a strong argument that, in such circumstances, the award should be deemed to have been made at the seat of the arbitration:

> The award, it is submitted, is no more than a part, the final and vital part of a procedure which must have a territorial, central point or seat. It would be very odd if, possibly without the knowledge of the parties or even unwittingly, the arbitrators had the power to sever that part from the preceding procedure and thus give a totally different character to the whole.[125]

(e) Delocalisation

(i) Introduction

3.86   An alternative to the 'seat' theory described above is one that delocalises arbitration from any national jurisdiction. As far as international arbitration is concerned, it would save considerable time, trouble, and expense if the laws governing arbitrations were the same throughout the world, so that there were—so to speak—a universal *lex arbitri*. There would then be a 'level playing field' for the conduct of international arbitrations wherever they took place. An arbitral tribunal would not have to enquire whether there were any special provisions governing arbitration that were peculiar to the law of the country that was the seat of the arbitration. On this aspect of the arbitral process, all laws would be the same.

3.87   In practice, however, the idea of a universal *lex arbitri* is as illusory as that of universal peace. Each state has its own national characteristics, its own interests to protect, and its own concepts of how arbitrations should be conducted in its territory. Although the Model Law offers states a simple, yet well-recognised approach to reaching a common standard for the

---

[123] UNCITRAL Rules 2010, Art. 18.1.

[124] See discussion in Paulsson and Petrochilos, *UNCITRAL Arbitration* (Kluwer Law International, 2017), pp. 151–152.

[125] Mann, 'Where is an award "made"?' (1985) 1 Arb Intl 107, at 108. See also *Enka Insaat Ve Sanayi AS v OOO Insurance Company Chubb* [2020] UKSC 38, at [68] ('A choice of place as the seat does not dictate that hearings must be held, or that any award must actually be issued, in that place'). An alternative view is that an award is 'made' at the place where it is signed—a view that may still prevail in some jurisdictions. The question is important and is discussed in more detail in Chapter 9.

practice of international arbitration, certain states that have adopted the Model Law have been unable to resist adding their own particular provisions to it.[126] Also, states with a long history of arbitration, and a highly developed law and practice, are particularly unlikely to adopt simplified models that may, in themselves, create fresh problems.[127] Nevertheless, it is inconvenient (to put it no higher) that the regulation of international arbitration should differ from one country to another—and this has led to the search for an escape route.

In this connection, two separate developments are seen. The first is for the state to relax   **3.88** the control that it seeks to exercise over international arbitrations conducted on its territory. This is the route taken by modern laws of arbitration. These laws take careful note of the theme of the Model Law, which is that their courts should not intervene in arbitrations unless authorised to do so. The role of the courts should be supportive, not interventionist.[128]

The second development is to detach an international arbitration from control by the law   **3.89** of the place in which it is held. This is the so-called delocalisation theory, the idea being that instead of a dual system of control, first by the *lex arbitri* and then by the courts of the place of enforcement of the award, there should be only one point of control: that of the place of enforcement. In this way, the whole world (or most of it) would be available for international arbitrations, and international arbitration itself would be 'supranational', 'a-national', 'transnational', 'delocalised', or even 'expatriate'. More poetically, such an arbitration would be a 'floating arbitration', resulting in a 'floating award'.[129]

---

[126] For example, Egypt has adopted the Model Law, but has added a provision that provides for annulment if the award fails to apply the law agreed by the parties—thus opening the way for the Egyptian courts to review awards on issues of law, which is not permitted under the Model Law. For an authoritative commentary on Egypt's arbitration law, see Atallah, 'The 1994 Egyptian Arbitration Law ten years on' (2003) 14 ICC Bulletin 16. In Latin America, while several states have now adopted the Model Law with limited modifications (Bolivia, Chile, Guatemala, Nicaragua, Paraguay, Peru, and Venezuela), Brazil and Costa Rica chose to tinker with the Model Law's formulation and have added their own customised elements.

[127] This was the view of the Mustill Committee, which recommended that the Model Law should not be adopted, but that the English law of arbitration should nevertheless take careful account of it—as has been done, in the English Arbitration Act.

[128] See, e.g., Mustill and Boyd, 'A survey of the 1996 Act', in *Commercial Arbitration* (2nd edn with 2001 Companion Volume, LexisNexis Butterworths, 2001), pp. 28–30, commenting on the English Arbitration Act. See also Mustill and Boyd, *Commercial Arbitration* (2nd edn with 2001 Companion Volume, LexisNexis Butterworths, 2001), Preface, where it is said that:

> The Act has however given English arbitration law an entirely new face, a new policy, and new foundations. The English judicial authorities [...] have been replaced by the statute as the principal source of law. The influence of foreign and international methods and concepts is apparent in the text and structure of the Act, and has been openly acknowledged as such. Finally, the Act embodies a new balancing of the relationships between parties, advocates, arbitrators and courts which is not only designed to achieve a policy proclaimed within Parliament and outside, but may also have changed their juristic nature.

[129] See in particular Lew, 'Achieving the dream: Autonomous arbitration' (2006) 22 Arb Intl 178, at 202; Fouchard, *L'Arbitrage Commercial International* (Litec, 1965), pp. 22–27; Paulsson, 'Arbitration unbound: Award detached from the law of its country of origin' (1981) 30 ICLQ 358; Paulsson, 'Delocalisation of international commercial arbitration: When and why it matters' (1983) 32 ICLQ 53. For a continuation of the debate, see Nakamura, 'The place of arbitration: Its fictitious nature and *lex arbitri*' (2000) 15 Mealey's Intl Arb Rep 23; Rubins, 'The arbitral seat is no fiction: A brief reply to Tatsuya Nakamura's Commentary, "The place of arbitration: Its fictitious nature and *lex arbitri*"' (2001) 16 Mealey's Intl Arb Rep 23; Pinsolle, 'Parties to an international arbitration with the seat in France are at full liberty to organise the procedure as they see fit: A reply to the article by Noah Rubins' (2001) 16 Mealey's Intl Arb Rep 30; Nakamura, 'The fictitious nature of the place of arbitration may not be denied' (2001) 16 Mealey's Intl Arb Rep 22.

3.90   A judicial manifestation of the delocalisation theory is provided by the French Court of Cassation, which, in enforcing an arbitral award set aside by the English High Court, held that:

> [A]n international arbitral award, *which does not belong to any state legal system*, is an international decision of justice and its validity must be examined according to the applicable rules of the country where its recognition and enforcement are sought.[130]

As noted earlier, this French approach was considered by the UK Supreme Court in *Dallah Real Estate*, in which, without endorsing such an approach under English law, the Court noted that, under French law, 'arbitration agreements derive their existence, validity and effect from supra-national law, without it being necessary to refer to any national law'.[131]

3.91   The delocalisation theory takes as its starting point the autonomy of the parties—the fact that it is their agreement to arbitrate that brings the proceedings into being—and rests upon two basic (yet frequently confused) arguments.[132] The first assumes that international arbitration is sufficiently regulated by its own rules, which are either adopted by the parties (as an expression of their autonomy) or drawn up by the arbitral tribunal itself. The second assumes that control should come only from the law of the place of enforcement of the award. These two arguments are considered in more detail, below.

(ii) Arguments in favour of delocalisation considered

3.92   The first argument is, in effect, that an international arbitration is self-regulating and that this is, or should be, sufficient. This is a view that finds some support in a decision of the Supreme Court of Canada, which has held that:

> The neutrality of arbitration as an institution is one of the fundamental characteristics of this alternative dispute resolution mechanism. Unlike the foreign element, which suggests a possible connection with a foreign state, arbitration is an institution without a forum and without a geographical basis. [...] Arbitration is part of no state's judicial system [...] The arbitrator has no allegiance or connection to any single country [...] In short, arbitration is a creature that owes its existence to the will of the parties alone.[133]

3.93   It is true that the parties to an international arbitration will generally (but not always) have a set of procedural rules to follow, whether they are those of an arbitral institution or are formulated ad hoc. It is also true that the arbitral tribunal will generally (but again, not always) have the power to fill any gaps in these rules by giving procedural directions—and this set of rules, whether agreed by the parties or laid down by the arbitral tribunal, may perhaps be

---

[130] Authors' translation, emphasis added. See *Société PT Putrabali Adyamulia v Société Rena Holding et Société Mnugotia Est Epices* [2007] Rev Arb 507, p. 514 ('[L]a sentence internationale, qui n'est rattachée à aucun ordre juridique étatique, est une décision de justice internationale dont la régularité est examinée au regard des règles applicables dans le pays où sa reconnaissance et son exécution sont demandées [...]').

[131] *Dallah Real Estate and Tourism Holding Co. v Ministry of Religious Affairs, Government of Pakistan* [2010] UKSC 4, at [15].

[132] In this discussion, 'delocalisation' is used (as it was originally) to signify the detachment of international arbitration from control by the law of the place of arbitration. Somewhat confusingly, the term is now sometimes used to indicate not only detachment from the *lex arbitri*, but also the replacement of a national law governing the substance of the dispute by general principles or some other non-national concept: see, e.g., Toope, *Mixed International Arbitration* (Grotius, 1990), p. 19, who states: 'Some [specialists] would preclude the delocalisation of procedure, but allow delocalisation of the substantive law, through the application of "general principles", "a *lex mercatoria*" or international law *per se*.'

[133] *Dell Computer Corp v Union des consommateurs* 2007 SCC 34, (2007) 284 DLR (4th) 577, at 51.

said to constitute 'the law of the arbitration', in the same way as a contract may be said to constitute 'the law of the parties'. Finally, when the arbitration is being administered by an arbitral institution (such as the ICC or LCIA), that institution may be said to have taken over the state's regulatory functions to a large extent, by itself laying down rules for the confirmation or removal of arbitrators, terms of reference, time limits, scrutiny of awards, and so on.[134]

Most arbitrations are conducted without any reference to the law that governs them. **3.94** Nonetheless, to repeat a point that has already been made, this law—the *lex arbitri*— exists.[135] Its support may be needed not only to fill any gaps in the arbitral process (such as the appointment of arbitrators), but also to give the force of law to orders of the arbitral tribunal that reach beyond the parties themselves, for example for the 'freezing' of a bank account or for the detention of goods. More crucially, this law will confer its nationality on the award of the arbitral tribunal, so that it is recognised, for example, as a Swiss award or a Dutch award and may benefit from any international treaties (such as the New York Convention) to which its country of origin is a party.

The second argument in support of the delocalisation theory is that any control of the process **3.95** of international arbitration should come only at the place of enforcement of the award. If this were the position, it would mean that the place of arbitration would be, in legal terms, irrelevant. This may or may not be a desirable solution—but it is significant that one state, Belgium, which had compulsorily 'delocalised' international arbitrations has since changed its mind.[136] For the rest, the prevailing emphasis, both nationally and internationally, is on a necessary connection between the place of arbitration and the law of that place. This may be seen, as has already been demonstrated, in the New York Convention[137] and in the Model Law.[138]

(iii) The position in reality

The delocalisation theory has attracted powerful and eloquent advocates. Professor Gaillard **3.96** described this 'representation' of international arbitration as follows:

> [It] accepts the idea that the juridicity of arbitration is rooted in a distinct, transnational legal order, that could be labelled as the arbitral legal order, and not in a national system, be it that of the country of the seat or that of the place or places of enforcement. This representation corresponds to the international arbitrators' strong perception that they do not administer justice on behalf of any given State, but that they nonetheless play a judicial role for the benefit of the international community.[139]

---

[134] See Fouchard, *L'Arbitrage Commercial International* (Litec, 1965), pp. 22–27.

[135] The point is no doubt so obvious as to need no comment, but the statement of Professor Weil seems particularly apt in this context: 'The principle of *pacta sunt servanda* and that of party autonomy do not float in space; a system of law is necessary to give them legal force and effect.' See Weil, 'Problèmes relatifs aux contrats passés entre un état et un particulier' (1969) 128 Hague Recueil 95, at 181 (authors' translation).

[136] By its law of 27 March 1985, a provision was added to the BJC, Art. 1717 to the effect that a losing party was not permitted to challenge in the Belgian courts an award made in an international arbitration held in Belgium, unless at least one of the parties had a place of business or other connection with Belgium. In the event, however, it appears that this legal provision discouraged parties from choosing Belgium as the seat of the arbitration and the law has since been changed. Belgian law now allows parties to an international arbitration to opt out of local control if they so wish, but no longer provides for compulsory delocalisations. See, BJC, Art. 1676(7) ('Part 6 of this Code [i.e., on arbitration] shall apply and the Belgian courts shall have jurisdiction when the place of arbitration as defined in article 1701, § 1 is located in Belgium or when the parties have so agreed.').

[137] New York Convention, Art. V(1)(a) and (e).

[138] Model Law, Art. 36(1)(a)(i) and (v).

[139] Gaillard, *Legal Theory of International Arbitration* (Martinus Nijhoff, 2010), p. 35.

3.97   Seductive as such theories might be, the reality is that the delocalisation of arbitrations—
other than those, like those of ICSID, which are governed directly by international law—is
possible only if the local law (the *lex arbitri*) permits it. Assessing the theory of 'delocalisation', Professor Paulsson concludes in his treatise *The Idea of Arbitration* as follows:

> [T]he development of international arbitration owes a disproportionately large debt to
> French law and to the conceptual advances of French judges and scholars. Nowhere else
> have the twin lodestars of freedom and internationalization combined in the conception
> of a voluntary process that accommodates the reality of a transnational society, shone so
> bright. Yet the zeal of those who make extravagant claims may do more harm than the re-
> sistance of non-believers and scoffers. The proposition that an effective legal order may be
> built upon diaphanous abstractions like *positive perspectives* or *transnational dynamics* are
> more likely to impede than to facilitate respect for the arbitral process.[140]

(iv) Seat theory and the *lex arbitri*

3.98   The strength of the seat theory is that it gives an established legal framework to an international arbitration, so that instead of 'floating in the transnational firmament, unconnected with any municipal system of law',[141] the arbitration is firmly anchored in a given
legal system. Just as the law of contracts helps to ensure that contracts are performed as they
should be and are not mere social engagements, so the *lex arbitri* helps to ensure that the
arbitral process works as it should. The necessity for such support for (and control of) the
arbitral process is, of course, reflected in the Model Law, which allows for certain functions
(such as the appointment of arbitrators, where there is a vacancy) and for certain sanctions (such as the setting aside of an award) to be exercised by the courts of the place of
arbitration.[142]

3.99   For this reason, the English courts have held that although, under English law and subject
to certain mandatory provisions, parties are free to agree the law and procedure that will
govern how proceedings are conducted, the law chosen must indeed satisfy this function. In
Halpern v Halpern,[143] Jewish law as a religious law was deemed not to be a 'realistic candidate as the law of the arbitration', and in addition was said to lack any supervisory or appellate jurisdiction over arbitrations.

3.100   That different states have different laws governing international arbitration and that some of
these laws may not be well suited to this task has two practical consequences. First, it means
that, wherever an international arbitration is held, the provisions of the local law should be
checked to see whether there are any particular mandatory rules that must be observed in
order to obtain a valid award. Secondly, it means that not every country is a suitable *situs* for
international arbitration and that a certain amount of 'forum shopping' is advisable.

---

[140] Paulsson, *The Idea of Arbitration* (Oxford University Press, 2013), p. 44.
[141] *Bank Mellat v Helliniki Techniki SA* [1984] QB 291, p. 301.
[142] See Model Law, Arts 6 (which allocates various functions to the local courts) and 34 (which allows the local court to set aside awards made in its territory, on certain limited grounds).
[143] *Halpern v Halpern* [2006] EWHC 603 (Comm); affirmed on this point in *Halpern v Halpern* [2007] EWCA Civ 291.

The first point is almost self-evident. For example, if the local law requires an award to be   **3.101**
made within a defined period of time or to be lodged with a local court for it to be valid,
then the necessary action must be taken to conform to this requirement. The second point
is less evident, but equally important. Since the law and practice of international arbitration
differs from one state to the next (and may even differ from place to place within the same
state), care should be taken to choose a place of arbitration in a state that is favourable, rather than in one that is unfavourable. This is a matter of considerable practical importance
and should be considered at the time the parties are drafting their arbitration agreement.[144]

One final comment is necessary before leaving the discussion of delocalisation and the *lex*   **3.102**
arbitri. It seems, for now, that the movement in favour of total delocalisation, in the sense of
freeing an international arbitration from control by the *lex arbitri*, remains aspirational. As
the Belgian experiment showed, delocalisation is possible only to the extent that it is permitted by the *lex arbitri*, and parties to an arbitration may well prefer an arbitral tribunal
that is subject to some rational legal control. However, there is still discontent amongst
practitioners regarding the impact of local laws that are seen to operate unfairly and, at
times, almost arbitrarily, and so there have been cases of what may perhaps be described as
'delocalisation by a side door'.

In *Chromalloy*,[145] for example, the Egyptian court annulled an arbitral tribunal's award   **3.103**
made in Cairo in favour of a US corporation. Despite this annulment by the courts of the
place of arbitration, the award was granted recognition and enforcement by the US District
Court in Washington, DC—'to the advantage of the home team', in the words of certain
distinguished US commentators.[146] And *Chromalloy* is but one example of national courts
enforcing awards that have been annulled by the courts of the place of arbitration.[147]

Then there are the problems caused by local courts that issue injunctions at the seat of the   **3.104**
arbitration to prevent arbitral tribunals from carrying out their task. Some tribunals continue with the arbitral proceedings despite the injunction (even when they are within the
territorial jurisdiction of the court concerned) on the basis that the injunction is not justified.[148] In effect, these arbitrators 'delocalise' their arbitration by refusing to accept the rulings of the local court under the *lex arbitri*.[149]

---

[144] See Chapter 2.
[145] *Chromalloy Aeroservices Inc. v Arab Republic of Egypt*, 939 F.Supp. 907 (DDC 1996), (2003) 19 Arab Intl 424, (2003) 12 Intl Arab Rep 8.
[146] Brower, Brower, II and Sharpe, 'The coming crisis in the global adjudication system' (2003) 19 Arb Intl 415, at 424.
[147] See, e.g., *Corporacion Mexicana de Mantenimiento Integral, S. de R.L. de C.V. v PEMEX- Exploracion y Produccion*, No. 10 Civ 206 (AKH) 2013 WL 4517225 (SDNY, 27 August 2013), in which the district court in the Southern District of New York confirmed a US$400 million arbitral award that had been set aside in the seat in Mexico City. Such examples are considered in greater detail in Chapter 11.
[148] See, e.g., *Himpurna California Energy Ltd v Republic of Indonesia* (2000) XXV YBCA 11, at 176, in which the tribunal, in its interim award dated 26 September 1999, ruled that an injunction (ordered by the Central District Court of Jakarta that arbitral proceedings be suspended) was 'the consequence of the refusal of the Republic of Indonesia to submit to an arbitration to which it [had] previously consented [and] therefore [it did] not, under Art. 28 of the UNCITRAL Rules [on the submission of evidence], excuse the Republic of Indonesia's default'. See also ICC Case No. 10623 (2003) 21 ASA Bulletin 60.
[149] This is discussed in more detail in Chapter 7, especially at paragraphs 7.56–7.62.

D. Law Applicable to the Substance

(a) Introduction

3.105   When questions of procedure have been settled, the principal task of the arbitral tribunal is to establish the material facts of the dispute. It does this by examining the agreement between the parties, by considering other relevant documents (including correspondence, minutes of meetings, and so on), and by hearing witnesses, if necessary. The arbitral tribunal then builds its award on this foundation of facts, making its decision either on the basis of the relevant law or exceptionally, and then only if expressly authorised by the parties, on the basis of what seems to be fair and reasonable in all of the circumstances.

3.106   Once the relevant facts have been established, the arbitral tribunal may not need to go outside the confines of the agreement originally made between the parties in order to determine the dispute. This agreement, particularly in international commercial transactions, will generally be quite detailed. For example, international construction contracts run to many hundreds of closely printed pages, accompanied by detailed drawings and specifications. Properly understood, such an agreement will generally make clear what the parties intended, what duties and responsibilities they each assumed, and therefore which of them must be held liable for any failure of performance that has occurred.

3.107   But, as already stated, an agreement intended to create legal relations does not exist in a legal vacuum. It is supported by a system of law that is generally known as 'the substantive law', 'the applicable law', or 'the governing law' of the contract.[150] These terms all denote the particular system of law that governs the interpretation and validity of the contract, the rights and obligations of the parties, the mode of performance, and the consequences of breaches of the contract.[151]

3.108   Changes in the law applicable to the contract may bring about changes in the contract itself. For instance, a country may enact currency regulations; these regulations will then apply to contracts that are governed by the law of that country. This happened in a case in which the delivery of bearer bonds to their lawful owner was refused because, under the law of then Czechoslovakia, it had become illegal for the bonds to be delivered without the consent of the Central Bank. The Central Bank refused that consent. The owner of the bonds sued for their delivery, but was unsuccessful:

> If the proper law of the contract is the law of Czechoslovakia, that law not merely sustains but, because it sustains, may also modify or dissolve the contractual bond. The currency law is not part of the contract, but the rights and obligations under the contract are part of the legal system to which the currency law belongs.[152]

---

[150] In English private international law, it is also known as the 'proper law' of the contract.
[151] *Compagnie Tunisienne de Navigation SA v Compagnie d'Armement Maritime SA* [1971] AC 572, at 603 *per* Lord Diplock.
[152] *Kahler v Midland Bank Ltd* [1950] AC 24, at 56. Similar problems have arisen in relation to Argentine investments under which obligations payable in foreign currency were forcibly redenominated in Argentine pesos at a rate of one dollar to one peso. This applied only to contracts governed by Argentinian law.

Accordingly, it is not enough to know what agreement the parties have made. It is also essential to know what law is applicable to that agreement. In a purely domestic contract, the applicable law will usually be that of the country concerned. However, where the contract is in respect of an international transaction, the position is more complicated: there may then be two, or more, different national systems of law capable of qualifying as the substantive law of the contract, and—although it is important not to exaggerate the possibilities—these different national systems may contain contradictory rules of law on the particular point or points in issue.

People who cross a national frontier on foot or by car, passport in hand, realise that they are moving from one country to another. The more percipient travellers may also realise that they are moving from one legal system to another—and indeed that what is lawful in one country is not necessarily so in another.   **3.109**

The transition from one legal system to another is less apparent, or at least more easily forgotten, when national frontiers are crossed by electronic signals from telephones or computers. For example, an oil trader in New York may enter into an agreement by telephone to buy crude oil on the spot market in Rotterdam, for shipment to a refinery in Germany. A bullion dealer in London may buy gold by an email from Zurich for delivery to a bank in Italy, on the basis that payment is to be made by an irrevocable letter of credit drawn on a bank in Chicago. These transactions cross national frontiers as unmistakably as travellers by road or train. Although there are no physical frontiers to go through, complex questions of law may still arise because of the crossing of national boundaries. Transactions such as these take place constantly; and rules of law govern each transaction. Yet problems still arise, first, in identifying what law applies, and secondly, in dealing with any conflict between the applicable laws.   **3.110**

(b) Autonomy of the parties

It is generally recognised that parties to an international commercial agreement are free to choose for themselves the law (or the legal rules) applicable to that agreement.[153] The doctrine of party autonomy, which was first developed by academic writers and then adopted by national courts, has gained extensive acceptance in national systems of law:[154]   **3.111**

> [D]espite their differences, common law, civil law and socialist countries have all equally been affected by the movement towards the rule allowing the parties to choose the law to govern their contractual relations. This development has come about independently in every country and without any concerted effort by the nations of the world; it is the result

---

[153] The point as to 'legal rules', by which is meant something other than a national system of law, is developed at paragraphs 3.147–3.224. The Model Law (and the UNCITRAL Rules) allows the parties to choose the 'rules of law' applicable to their contract (which may include, e.g., the *lex mercatoria*), but stipulates that if the parties fail to make such a choice, the arbitral tribunal shall apply 'the law' applicable to the dispute (which would not include the *lex mercatoria*).

[154] See, e.g., Brazilian Arbitration Act 1996 (as amended in 2015), s. 2; English Arbitration Act, s. 46(1); French Code of Civil Procedure, art. 1511; German ZPO, art. 1051(10); Indian Arbitration and Conciliation Act, s. 28(b); Russian International Arbitration Law 1993 (as amended in 2015), s. 28; Swiss PIL, art. 187(1). This approach is not universal, and parties should note that there are some jurisdictions that will not enforce choice-of-law agreements and instead prescribe the applicable law.

of separate, contemporaneous and pragmatic evolutions within the various national systems of conflict of laws.[155]

3.112   The doctrine has also found expression in international conventions, such as the Rome I Regulation.[156] The Rome I Regulation, which is applicable to contractual obligations within the European Union (EU), accepts as a basic principle the right of parties to a contract to choose, expressly or by implication, the law that is to govern their contractual relationship.[157]

3.113   If national courts are prepared (as most of them are) to recognise the principle of party autonomy in the choice of the law applicable to a contract, then, *a fortiori*, arbitral tribunals should also be prepared to do so. An international arbitral tribunal owes its existence to the agreement of the parties and, in applying the law chosen by the parties, an arbitral tribunal is simply carrying out their agreement.

(i) Recognition by international conventions

3.114   Both international conventions and the model rules on international arbitration confirm that the parties are free to choose for themselves the law applicable to their contract. For example, the ICSID Convention provides that '[t]he Tribunal shall decide a dispute in accordance with such rules of law as may be agreed by the parties'.[158] The UNCITRAL Rules provide that '[t]he arbitral tribunal shall apply the rules of law designated by the parties as applicable to the substance of the dispute'.[159] And, amongst the rules of arbitral institutions,[160] the ICC Rules provide that: '[t]he parties shall be free to agree upon the rules of law to be applied by the arbitral tribunal to the merits of the dispute'.[161] As one commentator has stated:

> There are few principles more universally admitted in private international law than that referred to by the standard terms of the 'proper law of the contract'—according to which the law governing the contract is that which has been chosen by the parties, whether expressly or (with certain differences or variations according to the various systems) tacitly.[162]

(ii) Time of choice

3.115   At its origin, the rule of party autonomy related to the freedom of the parties to choose the applicable law at the time of making their contract. It now extends (under the international

---

[155] Lew, *Applicable Law in International Commercial Arbitration* (Oceana/Sigthoff & Noorthoff, 1978), p. 75.

[156] Regulation (EC) No. 593/2008 of the European Parliament and of the Council of 17 June 2008 on the law applicable to contractual obligations, OJ L 177/6, 4 July 2008 (Rome I Regulation).

[157] Rome I Regulation, Art. 3(1). The Regulation does not apply to arbitration agreements, but the subject under discussion here is not that of arbitration agreements, but of the contract between the parties under which a dispute has arisen.

[158] ICSID Convention, Article 42.

[159] UNCITRAL Rules 2010, Art. 35.1.

[160] Other examples include the Rules of the AAA 2013, International Centre for Dispute Resolution (ICDR) 2021, Art. 34.1; LCIA Rules 2020, Art. 22.3; the Rules of the Russian Federation's Chamber of Commerce and Industry 2017, Art. 23.1; the SCC Rules 2017, Art. 22.1; the WIPO Rules, Art. 61.a; the Hague Conference on Private International Law, Principles of Choice of Law in International Commercial Contracts, Art. 2.1.

[161] ICC Rules 2021, Art. 21.1.

[162] Lalive, cited in Lew, *Applicable Law in International Commercial Arbitration* (Oceana/Sigthoff & Noorthoff, 1978), p. 87.

conventions and rules cited) to the right of the parties to choose the law as it is to be applied at the time of the dispute.

It is logical to allow the parties to choose the law that is to govern their contract at the time   **3.116**
when they make it. In their contract, the parties set out the rights and duties that they undertake to uphold towards each other. It is appropriate that they should, at the same time, refer to the system of law by which that contract is to be governed, because that law forms an essential element of the bargain between them.

There is less logic in allowing the parties to choose the applicable law once a dispute has   **3.117**
arisen and yet, in practice, it seems that parties may do so, even if their choice of law differs from that which they had chosen previously. Indeed, the Rome I Regulation makes express provision for this.[163] If any justification for this delayed choice (or even change) of law is sought in legal philosophy, it must lie more generally in the concept of the autonomy of the parties. Parties are generally free to vary the terms of their contract by agreement; in the same way, they should be free to vary by agreement the law applicable to a dispute arising out of that contract.

(iii) Restrictions on party autonomy

For lawyers who practise in the resolution of international trade disputes and who are ac-   **3.118**
customed to wending their way through a maze of national laws, the existence of a general transnational rule of law supporting the autonomy of the parties is almost too good to be true. The natural inclination is to ask whether there are any restrictions on the rule, and if so, what?[164]

The answer is that there may be limited restrictions on the rule, designed to ensure that the   **3.119**
choice of law is *bona fide* and is not contrary to public policy. Thus the Rome I Regulation, for example, does not allow the choice of a foreign law to override the mandatory rules of law of a country towards which all of the factual elements of the contract point—so that, for example, the choice of a foreign law for the purposes of tax evasion or avoiding competition regulation would not be permissible.[165] Thus, in *Soleimany v Soleimany*,[166] the English Court of Appeal refused to enforce an award where the transaction was not illegal under the applicable law, but was illegal under English law.

The case concerned a contract between a father and son, which involved the smuggling of   **3.120**
carpets out of Iran in breach of Iranian revenue laws and export controls. The father and son had agreed to submit their dispute to arbitration by the Beth Din, the Court of the Chief Rabbi in London, which applied Jewish law. Under the applicable Jewish law, the illegal purpose of the contract had no effect on the rights of the parties and the Beth Din proceeded to

---

[163] Rome I Regulation, Art. 3, provides that a choice of law, or a variation of a choice, can be made at any time after the conclusion of the contract by agreement between the parties.

[164] See Moss, 'Can an arbitral tribunal disregard the choice of law made by the parties?' (2005) 1 Stockholm Intl Arb Rev 6.

[165] By way of illustration of the point, the European Court of Justice (ECJ), in *Eco Swiss China Ltd v Benetton International NV* [1999] ECR I–3055, ruled that a breach of EU competition law constitutes a violation of the *ordre public*. In *Marketing Displays International Inc. v VR Van Raalte Reclame BV*, Case Nos 04/694 and 04/695, 24 March 2005, the Dutch Court of Appeal upheld a lower court's refusal to grant exequatur to three US arbitral awards, because the awards were considered incompatible with Art. 81 of the Treaty establishing the European Community of 2002, and thus violated public policy.

[166] *Soleimany v Soleimany* [1999] QB 785.

make an award enforcing the contract. In declining to enforce the award, the English Court of Appeal stated:

> The Court is in our view concerned to preserve the integrity of its process, and to see that it is not abused. The parties cannot override that concern by private agreement. They cannot by procuring an arbitration conceal that they, or rather one of them, is seeking to enforce an illegal contract. Public policy will not allow it.[167]

(c) The choice of applicable substantive law

3.121 Subject only to the qualifications of good faith, legality, and no public policy objection, the conventions and rules on arbitration that have been mentioned make it plain that the parties may choose for themselves the substantive law applicable to the dispute. Parties to an international commercial agreement should make full and proper use of this freedom, inserting a 'choice-of-law' clause into their contract and into any arbitration agreement in that contract.

3.122 If they fail to do so, it will almost certainly be a matter for regret should a dispute arise, since (as will be seen) the search for the proper law can be a long and expensive process. A choice-of-law clause may be drawn in very simple terms. It is usually sufficient to say: 'This agreement shall in all respects be governed by the law of England' (or of Singapore, or of the State of New York, or of any other state that has in place a modern law of contract).

3.123 The question that then arises is: given a free choice, what system of law should the parties choose as the law applicable to the dispute? Is their choice limited to the choice of a national system of law, or may it extend beyond this, perhaps to rules of law such as those of the law merchant (*lex mercatoria*)? Indeed, are the parties limited to a choice of law or of legal rules? May they not, for instance, agree that the dispute should be decided according to considerations of equity and good conscience?

3.124 It is to these questions that attention must now be turned. The choices that may be available to the parties include:

    i. national law;
    ii. public international law (including the general principles of law);
    iii. concurrent laws (and combined laws—the *tronc commun* doctrine);
    iv. transnational law (including international development law, the *lex mercatoria*, codified terms and practices, and trade usages); and
    v. equity and good conscience.

(i) National law

3.125 In most international commercial contracts, including those in which a state or state entity is one of the parties, it is usual for a given system of law to be chosen as the law applicable to the contract itself. There is much sense in such a choice. Parties who choose a law to govern their contract, or any subsequent dispute between them, will generally choose

---

[167] Ibid., p. 800.

an autonomous system of law. Such a system is not merely a set of general principles or of isolated legal rules;[168] rather, it is an interconnecting, interdependent collection of laws, regulations, and ordinances, enacted by or on behalf of the state, and interpreted and applied by the courts. It is a complete legal system, designed to provide an answer to any legal question that might be posed. Furthermore, a national system of law will, in principle, be a known and existing system, capable of reasonably accurate interpretation by experienced practitioners.

In law, as in life, there is no certainty. However, a national system of law provides a known (or at least determinable) legal standard against which the rights and responsibilities of the parties can be measured. In the event of a dispute, the parties can be advised with reasonable confidence as to their legal position—or, at the very least, they can be given a broad indication of their chances of success or failure. If, for example, parties to a dispute that is to be heard in Switzerland agree that the arbitral tribunal shall apply the law of France, then all concerned (arbitrators, parties, and advisers alike) know where they stand. The arbitrators will know to what system of law they have to refer, if such reference becomes necessary. The parties and their advisers will be able to evaluate their prospects of success against the known content of French law. They will know, too, what sort of legal arguments they will have to present and what sort of legal arguments (as to fault, compensation, and so on) they may be required to address.   **3.126**

Choice of a system of national law

The standard arbitration clauses recommended by arbitral institutions, such as the ICC, are usually followed by a note pointing out that, in addition to incorporating the arbitration clause in their agreement, the parties should also add a 'choice-of-law' clause. In-house lawyers and others who are concerned with the drafting of contracts will invariably do this, so that in most commercial contracts, it is usual to find an arbitration clause, in addition to a 'choice-of-law' clause, which should also be expressed to cover that arbitration clause.   **3.127**

Almost invariably, the law chosen is a national law. This may be because of that law's connection with the parties to the contract, or it may simply be because the parties regard it as a system of law that is well suited to governing their commercial relations. Indeed, many contracts incorporate the choice of a particular country's law, although they have no connection with that country. For example, commodity contracts, shipping and freight contracts, and contracts of insurance often contain a choice of English law, because the commercial law of England is considered to reflect, and to be responsive to, the needs of modern international commerce. For similar reasons, many major reinsurance contracts contain a choice of the law of the State of New York.   **3.128**

In an ideal world, almost any national system of law should be suitable, as long as that law has been drawn up, or has developed, in a manner that suits the requirements of modern commerce. In the real world, some national systems of law will be found to contain outdated laws and regulations that make them unsuitable for use in international contracts.   **3.129**

---

[168] Which, in this context, will be referred to as a 'national' system of law, the term being intended to cover not merely a 'national law' properly so-called, such as that of France (and, with it, applicable EU law), but also the law of a 'state' within a federal system, such as New York or California.

3.130   Indeed, even well-developed and modern systems of law are not necessarily best suited to the needs of international (as opposed to purely domestic) commerce. The law of a country reflects the social, economic, and (above all) political environment of that particular country. If a country habitually controls the import and export trade (perhaps permitting such activities only through state corporations), and prohibits the free flow of currency across the exchanges, these restrictions will permeate the national law. This may or may not benefit the country concerned, but it is not an environment in which international trade and commerce is likely to flourish. A national law that does not permit the free flow of goods and services across national frontiers is probably not the most suitable law to govern international commercial contracts and the disputes that may arise from them.

3.131   Parties to an international commercial contract will need to bear these kinds of considerations in mind in choosing a given system of law to govern their contractual relationships. Even in countries that favour international trade and development, problems may arise, particularly where the contract is made with the state itself or with a state agency. The problem, shortly stated, is that the state (as legislator) may change the law and so change the terms of the contract lawfully, but without the agreement of the other party to the contract. The state may, for instance, impose labour or import restrictions, which render performance of the contract more expensive. Unless the contract has been drafted with such possible contingencies in mind—and such contingencies may be difficult to foresee—it is the private party who will suffer from this change in the equilibrium of the contract.

3.132   The problem of protecting a party from changes in the local law was considered in the *Sapphire* arbitration:[169]

> Under the present agreement, the foreign company was bringing financial and technical assistance to Iran, which involved it in investments, responsibilities and considerable risks. It therefore seems normal that they should be protected against any legislative changes which might alter the character of the contract and that they should be assured of some legal security. This would not be guaranteed to them by the outright application of Iranian law, which it is within the power of the Iranian State to change.[170]

Precluding unfair treatment

3.133   Various devices have been borrowed from private law contracts in an attempt to maintain the balance of the contract. Historically, these have included revision clauses, hardship clauses, and *force majeure* clauses, all of which have played a part in helping to maintain the balance of the contractual relationship.[171]

Stabilisation clauses

3.134   One method of maintaining the balance of a contract is by including a 'stabilisation clause', that is, a clause which stabilises (or protects) the agreed terms from subsequent changes in the governing law. Such stability may be particularly important in a long-term government

---

[169] *Sapphire International Petroleum Ltd v The National Iranian Oil Co.* (1964) 13 ICLQ 1011.
[170] Ibid., at 1012.
[171] The UNIDROIT Principles provide examples of such clauses (see Art. 6.2.3 (Effects of Hardship) and Art. 7.1.7 (Force Majeure)).

contract governed by the law of the host state which the government may be in a position unilaterally to change.

The classic type of stability provision was the 'freezing' clause, by which the national law has been 'frozen' by means of the parties agreeing that the law of the state party will be applied as it stood on a given date. Strictly speaking, the state law does not then operate as the applicable law, but as an immutable code of law incorporated into the contract. It will not change no matter what amendments are made to the state law itself. **3.135**

However, stabilisation clauses came under increasing scrutiny on the basis that private investors should not be in a position to limit a host state's ability to modernise its laws. **3.136**

More recently, stabilisation clauses can be divided into broadly two distinct groups— namely, freezing clauses and economic equilibrium clauses, which are becoming more common.[172] **3.137**

As their name implies, 'economic equilibrium', or 'renegotiation', clauses attempt to maintain the original economic equilibrium of the parties at the time of contracting, where subsequent measures might otherwise alter the expected economic benefits to which the parties have subscribed.[173] These clauses do not aim to freeze the law; thus newly enacted laws will apply to the investment. However, they will provide the investor with a contractual entitlement to be compensated for the cost of complying with new laws or, alternatively, may require the parties to negotiate in good faith to restore the original economic equilibrium of the contract. Avoiding any purported restriction on the development of local law, such clauses thereby steer clear of the principal ground of criticism of 'freezing' clauses.[174] **3.138**

Both categories of stabilisation clause therefore present different ways of allocating 'change of law' risk between investors and host states. Moreover, such clauses could support claims by investors pursuant to the 'expropriation', 'fair and equitable treatment', or 'umbrella' provisions in investment treaties. **3.139**

(ii) Mandatory law

Although it is generally recognised that parties to an international commercial agreement are free to choose for themselves the law (or legal rules) applicable to that agreement, there are limits to this freedom. Mandatory rules have been defined as those that 'cannot be derogated from by way of Contract',[175] and may feature in the determination of a contractual dispute in addition to the governing law selected by the parties. **3.140**

---

[172] See Al Faruque, 'Typologies, efficacy, and political economy of stabilisation clauses: A critical appraisal' (2007) 4:5 OGEL 33; Maniruzzaman, 'Damages for breach of stabilisation clauses in international investment law: Where do we stand today?' [2007] IELTR 11; Bernardini, 'Stabilization and adaptation in oil and gas investments' (2008) 1 J World Energy L & Bus 98; Cotula, 'Reconciling regulatory stability and evolution of environmental standards in investment contracts: Towards a rethink of stabilization clauses' (2008) 1 J World Energy L & Bus 158.

[173] Maniruzzaman, in turn, divides economic equilibrium clauses into three categories: stipulated economic balancing provisions, non-specified economic balancing provisions, and negotiated economic balancing provisions. See Maniruzzaman, 'Damages for breach of stabilisation clauses in international investment law: Where do we stand today?' [2007] IELTR 11, at 127ff.

[174] For further discussion of economic equilibrium clauses, see Berger, 'Renegotiation and adaptation of international investment contracts: The role of contract drafters and arbitrators' (2003) 36 Vanderbilt J Transl L 1348; Al Qurashi, 'Renegotiation of international petroleum agreements' (2005) 22 J Intl Arb 261.

[175] Rome I Regulation, Art. 3(3).

3.141   Thus, by way of example, Russian law may feature in the determination of corporate governance issues relating to a Russian company even if the arbitration arises from a shareholders'
agreement governed by Swedish law. In the same way, again by way of example, US-quoted
companies cannot exclude the application of the Foreign Corrupt Practices Act of 1977
from the operations simply by concluding an investment agreement in Kazakhstan that is
subject to Kazakh law. Moreover, in yet another example that the authors have seen in practice in an ICC case in Paris, the commercial export of defence technology from the United
States to the Gulf region will be subject to the US International Trade in Arms Regulations
even if the supply contract in question is governed by the law of the United Arab Emirates.
However, perhaps the most frequently encountered instance of the application of mandatory law is competition, or anti-trust, law, and the authors now proceed to use that as an
illustration.

3.142   As already discussed in Chapter 2,[176] at one time it was widely considered that the private forum of arbitration was not appropriate for the determination of claims under competition law. Landmark judgments such as that of the US Supreme Court in *Mitsubishi
Motor Corporation v Soler Chrysler-Plymouth*,[177] however, have long since confirmed the
arbitrability of competition law issues. A decision of the Court of Justice of the European
Union (CJEU) goes further,[178] and suggests that, in Europe at least, arbitral tribunals may
be duty-bound—or may at least have a discretion—to address issues of European competition law *ex officio* even where they have not been raised by the parties themselves, because
such issues constitute a matter of public policy.[179]

3.143   Another example of the impact of mandatory law is a decision of the CJEU that has called
into question the enforceability of awards rendered by investment treaty tribunals where the
law applicable to their dispute includes EU law. The case of *Slovak Republic v Achmea* concerned a Dutch insurance company that had established a subsidiary in Slovakia that was
detrimentally affected by a change in the regulations concerning private health insurance in
Slovakia. Achmea commenced treaty arbitration under the Czechoslovakia–Netherlands
BIT, which stated that the law applicable to the dispute would include 'the law in force of the
Contracting Party concerned' as well as 'the provisions of […] other relevant Agreements
between the Contracting Parties'.[180]

3.144   Achmea prevailed in the arbitration, and Slovakia sought to annul the award at the seat
of the arbitration, in Germany. Slovakia submitted that the arbitration clause contained
in the Czechoslovakia–Netherlands BIT was contrary to provisions of the Treaty for
the Functioning of the European Union (TFEU), namely: (i) Article 344 TFEU, which
prohibits EU Member States from submitting a dispute concerning the interpretation
or application of EU law to any method of settlement other than those for which the
EU Treaties provide (that is, excluding arbitration); and (ii) Article 267 TFEU, which
provides for a preliminary ruling mechanism that ensures that only the CJEU gives a

---

[176] See Chapter 2, paragraphs 2.135*ff*.
[177] *Mitsubishi Motor Corporation v Soler Chrysler-Plymouth* (1986) XI YBCA 555.
[178] *Eco Swiss China Ltd v Benetton Investment NV* [1999] ECR I–3055.
[179] For a discussion of this subject, see Partasides and Burger, 'The Swiss Federal Tribunal's Decision of 8
March 2006: A deepening of the arbitrator's public policy dilemma?' (2006) 3 Concurrences 26. See also Berman,
'Navigating EU law and the law of international arbitration' (2012) 28 Arb Intl 397.
[180] Czechoslovakia–Netherlands BIT 1991, Art. 8(6).

final, legally binding interpretation of EU law (and which an arbitral tribunal could not request).

The German courts referred these questions to the CJEU for a preliminary ruling, and the CJEU ruled that the arbitration clause in the Czechoslovakia–Netherlands BIT was contrary to Articles 267 and 344 TFEU.[181] Of primary concern to the CJEU was the applicable law clause in the underlying BIT, which directed an arbitral tribunal to interpret and apply the law of the BIT parties (which includes EU law), contrary to the terms of the TFEU.[182] Three years later, the CJEU made a similar ruling in September 2021, in the case of *Komstroy*, ruling that intra-EU arbitrations under the Energy Charter Treaty (ECT) are also incompatible with EU law.[183]   **3.145**

It is important to understand what is behind the rulings of the CJEU, which have understandably caused much disquiet in the world of arbitration. The CJEU is concerned to be and to remain the ultimate authority on the law of the EU. To this end, national courts within the EU can refer a matter of EU law to the CJEU for a preliminary ruling, as the German court did in *Achmea*. This enables the CJEU to have the final word on issues of EU law. But there is no such mechanism of referral so far as arbitral tribunals are concerned, and this has led the CJEU to question whether arbitral tribunals applying EU law threaten the autonomy of the system of EU law, and the CJEU's supervision of that autonomy.   **3.146**

(iii) Public international law, general principles of law, and public policy

Public international law is concerned primarily with states, but not exclusively so.[184] As Dame Rosalyn Higgins, a former president of the International Court of Justice (ICJ) in The Hague, has contended, international law is a dynamic (not static) decision-making process, in which there are a variety of participants: **3.147**

> Now, in this model, there are no 'subjects' and 'objects', but only *participants*. Individuals *are* participants, along with states, international organizations (such as the United Nations, or the International Monetary Fund (IMF) or the [International Labour Organization] ILO) [sic], multinational corporations, and indeed private non-governmental groups.[185]

Amongst the 'participants' to whom President Higgins referred are those individuals and corporations who brought claims before the Iran–United States Claims Tribunal and those 'investors' who seek to protect their investment through the machinery of ICSID.[186] This has brought public international law into sharper focus as far as private individuals and corporations—and their lawyers—are concerned. Increasingly, 'international law' may be specified as the substantive law of a contract, particularly where that contract is with a state or state agency. The reference may be to 'international law' on its own, or it may be used in   **3.148**

---

[181] *Slovak Republic v Achmea B.V.*, CJEU Case No. C-248/16, 6 March 2018, at 60 ('Articles 267 and 344 TFEU must be interpreted as precluding a provision in an international agreement concluded between Member States, such as Article 8 of the BIT, under which an investor from one of those Member States may, in the event of a dispute concerning investments in the other Member State, bring proceedings against the latter Member State before an arbitral tribunal whose jurisdiction that Member State has undertaken to accept').

[182] *Slovak Republic v Achmea B.V.*, CJEU Case No. C-248/16, 6 March 2018, at 40–42.

[183] *Republic of Moldova v Komstroy*, CJEU Case No. C-741/19, 2 September 2021, at 50–66. *Achmea* and *Komstroy* are discussed further in Chapter 8.

[184] Higgins, *Problems Process: International Law and How We Use It* (Clarendon Press, 1994), p. 39.

[185] Ibid., p. 50.

[186] See Chapter 8 in relation to the applicable law in disputes under investment treaties.

conjunction with a national system of law. Commentators have argued that international arbitral tribunals also have an inherent authority to apply general principles of law, and indeed that they routinely do apply non-state law to resolve disputes between private parties, especially where the parties have no agreement on the *lex contractus*.[187]

3.149   Reference has already been made to the freedom that parties (generally) have in selecting the law or the legal rules applicable to their contract. There is no reason, in principle, why they should not select public international law as the law that is to govern their contractual relationship.[188] To quote President Higgins again:

> The increasing importance of international arbitration is an area that we should perhaps be watching. It is now commonplace for a foreign private corporation and a state who have entered into contractual relations to agree to international arbitration in the event of a dispute. (And, in principle, the private party could be an *individual*, though as such he will probably have less leverage than a foreign corporation and may well have to accept the local legal system rather than reference to international arbitration.) The applicable law clause may designate a national legal system, but more usually it will refer to 'general principles of law' or 'the law of country X and the relevant principles of general international law', or some such similar formula. At one bound, therefore, the private party has escaped the need to have his claim brought by his national government, and can invoke international law. Thus, if State X and Mr Y have a contract, State X's ability to vary the terms of that contract will be interpreted by reference to the relevant principles of international law; and compensation due to Mr Y will likewise be appraised by reference to international law [...] Arbitral clauses which refer to international law as the applicable law effectively remove the alleged inability of individuals to be the bearer of rights under international law. This is being done by mutual consent, of course—but the point is that there is *no inherent reason* why the individual should not be able directly to invoke international law and to be the beneficiary of international law.[189]

3.150   There are many sources of public international law, including international conventions and international custom, but probably the most relevant, as far as non-state parties are concerned, are 'the general principles of law recognised by civilised nations'.[190] These have been defined as 'the general principles of municipal jurisprudence, in particular of private law, in so far as they are applicable to relations of States'.[191]

---

[187] See discussion in Kotuby and Sobota, *General Principles of Law and International Due Process: Principles and Norms Applicable in Transnational Disputes* (Oxford University Press, 2017), pp. 36, 44.

[188] Compare the observation of the court in *Orion Compania Espanola de Seguros v Belfort Maatschappij Voor Algemene Verzekgringeen* [1962] 2 Lloyd's Rep 257, at 264, a case brought many years ago:

> Thus, it may be, though perhaps it would be unusual, that the parties could validly agree that a part, or the whole, of their legal relations should be decided by the arbitral tribunal on the basis of a foreign system of law, or perhaps on the basis of principles of international law; *e.g.*, in a contract to which a Sovereign State was a party.

[189] Higgins, *Problems Process: International Law and How We Use It* (Clarendon Press, 1994), p. 54.

[190] Article 38 of the Statute of the ICJ (which was established in 1945 and is generally known as the 'World Court') states that, in applying international law to the disputes before it, the Court is to apply, *inter alia*, those general principles of law.

[191] Jennings and Watts, *Oppenheim's International Law*, Vol. I (9th edn, Oxford University Press, 1992), p. 29, cited with approval in Brownlie, *Principles of Public International Law* (Oxford University Press, 2012), p. 34. Professor Brownlie goes on to add that, in practice, tribunals exercise considerable discretion in how they choose, edit, and adapt elements of municipal jurisprudence: ibid., at p. 35.

However, the problem of adopting public international law as the system of law that is **3.151** to govern a commercial relationship is not a problem of principle, but of practice. Public international law, being concerned primarily with the relationships between states, is not particularly well equipped to deal with detailed contractual issues—such as mistake, misrepresentation, time of performance, the effect of bankruptcy or liquidation, *force majeure*, or the measure of damages, and so forth. The same criticism may be directed at the choice of 'general principles of law' as the governing law of a commercial contract. The problem with the general principles is they are just that: they deal with such topics as the principle of good faith in treaty relations, abuse of rights, and the concept of state and individual responsibility. They are excellent as generalisations (and, in this sense, can, as one commentary puts it, 'isolate the peculiarities of national law that may hinder the fair resolution of an individual case'[192]), but may lack sufficient detail to address all the complexities of contractual relations.[193] That is why the authors suggest that if they are to be used in a contract, they should be used as a concurrent law, rather than on their own.[194]

As another source of concurrently applicable law, some commentators view certain mat- **3.152** ters of international public policy as applying to the interpretation or application of a contract.[195] International public policy considerations may apply, for example, where a tribunal is faced with concerns about a contract being a product of corruption, or where the performance of a contract may comprise part of a corrupt scheme. An illustrative example is the conclusion of the arbitral tribunal in *World Duty Free Company Limited v The Republic of Kenya*, which addressed the argument made by the government of Kenya that a contract with the claimant was tainted with illegality and thus unenforceable, because it was procured by the payment of a bribe from the claimant to the then President of Kenya. The tribunal, having surveyed the near universal condemnation of corruption, concluded that:

> In light of domestic laws and international conventions relating to corruption, and in light of the decisions taken in this matter by courts and arbitral tribunals, this Tribunal is convinced that bribery is contrary to the international public policy of most, if not all, States or, to use another formula, to transnational public policy. Thus, claims based on contracts of corruption or on contracts obtained by corruption cannot be upheld by the Arbitral Tribunal.[196]

The tribunal reached this conclusion, notwithstanding the submission of the claimant that **3.153** 'it was routine practice to make such donations in advance of doing business in Kenya', and

---

[192] Kotuby and Sobota, *General Principles of Law and International Due Process: Principles and Norms Applicable in Transnational Disputes* (Oxford University Press, 2017), pp. 35–36. See also p. 37 ('general principles have been relied upon to guide or even correct the application of otherwise applicable domestic law when that law is underdeveloped, unsuited for a transnational dispute or—in extreme cases—unable to meet minimum standards of propriety and fairness').

[193] For an excellent (and, it must be admitted, detailed) work on this topic, see Cheng, *General Principles of Law as Applied by International Courts and Tribunals* (Cambridge University Press, 1987).

[194] See discussion in Kotuby and Sobota, *General Principles of Law and International Due Process: Principles and Norms Applicable in Transnational Disputes* (Oxford University Press, 2017), p. 39 ('general principles may usefully play an auxiliary role, clarifying ambiguities and filling interstices').

[195] See, e.g., the discussion in Zuberbuhler and Schregenberger, 'Corruption in Arbitration—The Arbitrator's Duty to Investigate', in Muller, Besson, and Rigozzi (eds) *New Developments in International Commercial Arbitration 2016* (Schulthess, 2016), pp. 18–19.

[196] *World Duty Free Company Limited v The Republic of Kenya*, ICSID Case No. ARB/00/7 (Award of 4 October 2006), at [157].

that the payments were 'regarded as a matter of protocol' such that 'domestic public policy' supported upholding the contract notwithstanding the bribe.[197]

3.154   If an award does not adequately address indications of corruption, there is a risk that it may be challenged.[198] This, in turn, suggests that an arbitrator's duty to render an enforceable award may be tied to that arbitrator's consideration, where relevant, of issues of international public policy, regardless (or indeed in furtherance) of a choice of law agreement.

(iv) Multiple applicable laws
Dépeçage

3.155   A single contract may be governed by multiple laws, depending on the parties' choice of law and the context of their agreement. One example is where the parties agree that specific clauses or substantive issues are governed by distinct regimes, known as dépeçage.[199] An example commonly referred to is the 'Bermuda Form' insurance policy, which applies New York law other than where specific issues are governed by English law. The 2019 Guide on the Law Applicable to International Commercial Contracts in the Americas, issued by the Inter-American Judicial Committee of the Organisation of American States (OAS), contains specific provisions on this matter and encourages adjudicators to permit dépeçage when granted discretion to do so.[200]

Concurrent laws, combined laws, and the tronc commun *doctrine*

3.156   In deciding on the 'law' applicable to their agreement, parties may expressly or tacitly adopt multiple laws or rules of law and apply them concurrently to their contractual relationship. As Paulsson and Petrochilos note, the parties' designation of an applicable law may not, on its true construction, cover all of the legal issues that pertain to the substance of a dispute; rather, 'a host of other rules/laws may need to be applied to resolve the substantive dispute'.[201]

3.157   Modern procedural rules provide for this possibility. For example, while the UNCITRAL Rules 1976 provided that a tribunal 'shall apply the law designated by the parties' to their contractual relationship, the subsequently revised UNCITRAL Rules 2010 in Article 35.1 state that the tribunal 'shall apply the *rules of law* designated by the parties'. The reference to the plural 'enables the parties to designate as applicable to their case rules of more than one legal system, including rules of law which have been elaborated on the international level'.[202] Similarly, and as discussed in further detail below,[203] the Model Law provides that

---

[197] Ibid., at [120].

[198] See, e.g., *Alstom v Alexander Brothers*, cour d'appel de Paris, 28 May 2019, Case No. 16/11182 (in which Alstom challenged the enforcement of an arbitral award that ordered Alstom to pay outstanding invoices to Alexander Brothers, on the grounds that the underlying contracts were tainted by illegality. The Paris Court of Appeal refused to enforce the award because to do so would contravene international public policy).

[199] See, e.g., Rome Convention, Art. 3(1) ('By their choice the parties can select the law applicable to the whole or a part only of the contract'); Rome I Regulation, Art. 3(1).

[200] Part XIV of the Inter-American Juridical Committee, Guide on the Law Applicable to International Commercial Contracts in the Americas 2019, Organisation of the American States, available online at http://www.oas.org/en/sla/dil/docs/publications_Guide_Law_Applicable_International_Commercial_Contracts_Americas_2019.pdf.

[201] Paulsson and Petrochilos, *UNCITRAL Arbitration* (Kluwer Law International, 2017), p. 318.

[202] Ibid., p. 315.

[203] See paragraph 3.206 below.

a 'law or legal system' may be designated as the law applicable to the substance of a dispute, while concurrently and '[i]n all cases', a tribunal 'shall take into account the usages of the trade applicable to the transaction' as well as principles of equity where the parties have provided authorisation to do so.[204]

The concurrent application of laws to a commercial dispute involving a state or state party   **3.158** is illustrated by the role of international law. As already indicated in the discussion of contracts to which a state or state entity is a party,[205] one of the main anxieties among commercial organisations engaged in trading or other business relationships with a sovereign state is that, after the bargain has been struck and the contract has been signed, the state may change its own law to the disadvantage of the private party.

One established safeguard against unfair or arbitrary action by the state party to the con-   **3.159** tract is to stipulate that the state's own law will apply only insofar as it accords with either public international law, the general principles of law, or some other system with accepted minimum standards.

The ICSID Convention, which established ICSID,[206] makes use of this system of concur-   **3.160** rent laws. The Convention provides for the resolution of disputes between a state (or a state entity) and a private party;[207] it stipulates that if a dispute arises and there has been no express choice of law by the parties, the arbitral tribunal will apply the law of the contracting state party to the arbitration *and* 'such rules of international law as may be applicable'.[208] Thus honour is satisfied: the state's own law is given proper recognition. Yet some fetter is imposed upon possibly unfair or arbitrary action by means of the reference to public international law.[209]

This is a system of concurrent laws. For example, if a state were to terminate a long-term   **3.161** investment contract by an act of nationalisation, it would presumably do so in a way that would be valid under its own law. However, such an act of nationalisation would not be valid under international law unless it were shown to be non-discriminatory and to serve a public purpose, with proper compensation being offered. In this way, international law would be brought into play to set a minimum standard, which the arbitral tribunal would be empowered to uphold in its award.[210]

Concurrent laws may also apply in circumstances of multiple applicable mandatory laws.   **3.162** This could occur where, for example, economic sanctions are part of mandatory public

---

[204] Model Law, Art. 28.
[205] See paragraphs 3.131*ff.*
[206] See the discussion of this Convention in Chapter 1.
[207] Provided that the state has adopted the ICSID Convention.
[208] ICSID Convention, Art. 42(1).
[209] Rawding, 'Protecting Investments under state contracts: Some legal and ethical issues' (1995) 99 Arb Intl 341 describes this option as subjecting national law to 'international quality control'. The issue of applicable law in cases brought under investment treaties is addressed in Chapter 8. For examples of ICSID cases resolved on the basis of international law (to the extent that there were gaps in the applicable host state law, or where its application would have produced a result inconsistent with international law), see *Klöckner Industrie-Anlagen v Republic of Cameroon*, ICSID Case No. ARB/81/2, Decision of the Ad Hoc Committee, 3 May 1985; *Amco Asia Corporation v Republic of Indonesia*, ICSID Case No. ARB/81/1, Ad Hoc Committee Decision on the Application for Annulment, 16 May 1986; *Wena Hotels Ltd v Arab Republic of Egypt*, ICSID Case No. ARB/98/4, Decision on Annulment Application, 5 February 2002; *Sempra Energy International v Argentine Republic*, ICSID Case No. ARB/02/16, Award, 28 September 2007.
[210] For a discussion of compensation, see Chapter 8.

international law, such as those set by the Security Council of the United Nations, or where an arbitral tribunal applies the mandatory law of a third state. The latter is provided for in the Rome Convention, which provides:

> When applying under this Convention the law of a country, effect may be given to the mandatory rules of the law of another country with which the situation has a close connection, if and in so far as, under the law of the latter country, those rules must be applied whatever the law applicable to the contract. In considering whether to give effect to these mandatory rules, regard shall be had to their nature and purpose and to the consequences of their application or non-application.[211]

Libyan oil nationalisation arbitrations

3.163 The coupling of national law with international law is seen in the three arbitrations that arose out of the Libyan oil nationalisations, the *Texaco*, *BP*, and *Liamco* arbitrations, although it worked effectively in only one of them.[212]

3.164 The choice-of-law clause was identical in the different concession agreements that came before three different arbitrators. It read as follows:

> This concession shall be governed by and interpreted in accordance with the principles of law of Libya common to the principles of international law and, in the absence of such common principles, then by and in accordance with the general principles of law, including such of those principles as may have been applied by international tribunals.[213]

3.165 In the event, this clause was interpreted in three different ways by the three different arbitrators:

  i. in the *Texaco* arbitration, the sole arbitrator held that the clause was primarily a choice of public international law;
  ii. in the *BP* arbitration, the sole arbitrator appears to have regarded it as a choice of the general principles of law;[214] and
  iii. in the *Liamco* arbitration, the sole arbitrator held that the governing law of the contract was the law of Libya, but that the clause excluded any part of that law that was in conflict with the principles of international law.[215]

---

[211] Rome Convention, Art. 7.

[212] *Texaco Overseas Petroleum Co. v Government of Libyan Arab Republic* (1978) 17 ILM 3; *BP Exploration Co. (Libya) Ltd v Government of the Libyan Arab Republic* (1979) 53 ILR 297; *Libyan American Oil Co. (Liamco) v Government of the Libyan Arab Republic* (1981) 20 ILM 1, (1981) VI YBCA 89. See also Greenwood, 'State contracts in international law: The Libyan oil arbitrations' (1982) 17 ILM 14; Rigaux, 'Des dieux et des héros: Réflexions sur une sentence arbitrale' [1978] Revue Critique de Droit International Privé 435; Stern, 'Trois arbitrages, un même problème, trois solutions' [1980] Rev Arb 3.

[213] For this text, see the *Texaco* arbitration, fn. 157.

[214] 'The governing system of law is what that clause expressly provides—namely, in the absence of principles common to the law of Libya and international law, the general principles of law, including such of those principles as may have been applied by international tribunals': *BP*, fn. 240, *per* Judge Lagergren.

[215] *Liamco*, at 143. The fact that three different arbitrators could arrive at three different conclusions on the meaning of the same choice-of-law clause highlights one of the weaknesses of the arbitral system, which is the possibility of conflicting awards on the same basic problem: see Stern, 'Trois arbitrages, un même problème, trois solutions' [1980] Rev Arb 3.

The arbitral tribunal in the *Aminoil* arbitration arrived at a similar conclusion in respect of a **3.166** concession agreement that had been brought to an end by an act of nationalisation, coupled with an offer of 'fair compensation'.[216] Aminoil and the government of Kuwait agreed in the submission agreement that their dispute should be settled by arbitration 'on the basis of law', but left the choice of law to the tribunal, with the stipulation that the tribunal should have regard to 'the quality of the parties, the transnational character of their relations and the principles of law and practice prevailing in the modern world'.[217] On this basis, Aminoil argued that the concession agreement was governed by transnational law, which it equated with the general principles of law, including the principles of *pacta sunt servanda*, reparation for injury, respect for acquired rights, the prohibition of unjust enrichment, and the requirement of good faith (including the prohibition against abuse of rights and estoppel or preclusion). The government, for its part, argued for the application of the law of Kuwait, of which public international law formed part.

It is useful to look at the tribunal's decision on the applicable law for two reasons. First, the **3.167** state of Kuwait actually took part in the *Aminoil* arbitration, unlike Libya which effectively boycotted the Libyan arbitrations; secondly, and more relevantly for current practice, the dramatic increase in the number and importance of ICSID arbitrations has focused attention both on the involvement of national states in international arbitrations and on concurrent law clauses.

The tribunal in *Aminoil* stated that the question of the law applicable to the substantive **3.168** issues in dispute before it was a simple one. The law of Kuwait applied to many matters with which it was directly concerned, but, as the government had argued, established public international law was part of the law of Kuwait and the general principles of law were part of public international law.[218] The tribunal concluded:

> The different sources of the law thus to be applied are not—at least in the present case—in contradiction with one another. Indeed, if, as recalled above, international law constitutes an integral part of the law of Kuwait, the general principles of law correspondingly recognize the rights of the State in its capacity of supreme protector of the general interest. If the different legal elements involved do not always and everywhere blend as successfully as in the present case, it is nevertheless on taking advantage of their resources, and encouraging their trend towards unification, that the future of a truly international economic order in the investment field will depend.[219]

The use of a system of concurrent laws, such as that envisaged by the ICSID Convention **3.169** in the absence of an express choice of law by the parties to the dispute, seems to be the way forward for international contracts to which a state or state entity is a party. The reference to the law of the state concerned gives proper importance to the sovereign position of the state party, yet the reference to international law, or possibly to the general principles of law, provides a measure of protection to the private party to the contract. There is a balance to be

---

[216] *American Independent Oil Co. Inc. (Aminoil) v Government of the State of Kuwait* [1982] 21 ILM 976.
[217] Ibid., at 980.
[218] Ibid., at 1000.
[219] Ibid., at 1001.

struck between state law and international law. It is important that arbitral tribunals should be prepared to give due weight to both.

3.170   While this discussion has shown where the search for a 'neutral' law may lead, particularly in relation to state contracts, the search for such a law is not confined to state contracts. One solution, which has been canvassed in theory and occasionally adopted in practice, is to choose the national laws of both parties and so obtain the best (or possibly the worst) of both worlds. This *tronc commun* doctrine is based on the proposition that, if free to do so, each party to an international commercial transaction would choose its own national law to govern that transaction. If this proves unacceptable, why not go some way towards achieving this objective by identifying the common core of the two different systems of law and applying this to the matters in dispute?[220]

3.171   The *Sapphire* arbitration has already been mentioned as an illustration of the problem of affording protection to the private party to a state contract against changes in the national law enacted by the state party.[221] There was no express choice of law in the contract. There were, however, choice-of-law clauses in similar concession agreements previously made by the respondent, the National Iranian Oil Company, which were in the following terms:

> In view of the diverse nationalities of the parties to this Agreement, it shall be governed by and interpreted and applied in accordance with the principles of law common to Iran and the several nations in which the other parties to this Agreement are incorporated, and in the absence of such common principles then by and in accordance with principles of law recognised by civilised nations in general, including such of those principles as may have been applied by international tribunals.[222]

3.172   This choice-of-law clause appears to be an adoption of the *tronc commun* solution to the choice-of-law problem. It would require the arbitrator to find out what principles existed in the law of Iran, which were also to be found in the national laws of the other parties to the agreement, and to apply those common principles to the matters in dispute before him or her. However, the arbitrator in the case adopted a different approach: he read the clause as entitling him to disregard the law of Iran (although this was specifically mentioned in the choice-of-law clause) and to apply the general principles of law. The arbitrator asserted:

> It is quite clear from the above that the parties intended to exclude the application of Iranian law. But they have not chosen another positive legal system and this omission is on all the evidence deliberate. All the connecting factors cited above point to the fact that the parties therefore intended to submit the interpretation and performance of their contract to principles of law generally recognised by civilised nations, to which article 37 of the agreement refers, being the only clause which contains an express reference to an applicable law.[223]

---

[220] The *tronc commun* doctrine was first elaborated by Rubino-Sammartano in 1987: see Rubino-Sammartano, 'Le tronc commun des lois nationales en presence: Réflexions sur le droit applicable par l'arbitre international' [1987] Rev Arb 133; Rubino-Sammartano, *International Arbitration Law and Practice* (Kluwer Law International, 1990), p. 274.

[221] *Sapphire International Petroleum Ltd v The National Iranian Oil Co.* (1964) 13 ICLQ 1011.

[222] Quoted ibid., at 1014.

[223] Ibid., at 1015.

Many years after the *Sapphire* arbitration, another important example of combined laws **3.173** (or again, more correctly, of combined legal principles) came to be generally reported (and sometimes misreported). In the Channel Tunnel project, the concessionnaire Eurotunnel entered into a construction contract with a group of Anglo–French companies, known as Trans-Manche Link. Surprisingly, this agreement between two private entities referred not to the national law of either party, nor indeed to any national system of law, but instead to the common principles of both systems of law.[224] The relevant clause provided that the contract would:

> in all respects be governed by and interpreted in accordance with the principles common to both English law and French law, and in the absence of such common principles by such general principles of international trade law as have been applied by national and international tribunals.[225]

A dispute under the construction contract went to the English High Court, and this choice- **3.174** of-law clause was considered both by the Court of Appeal and by the highest court in England, the House of Lords (now the UK Supreme Court).[226] In the Court of Appeal, one of the judges said:

> Since both Eurotunnel and the contractors were partly French and partly English, I wonder why they did not choose either English law or French law exclusively—and for that matter why they chose Brussels as the seat of any arbitration. The hybrid system of law which they did choose has a superficial attraction, but I suspect that it will lead to lengthy and expensive dispute.[227]

This comment proved prescient.[228] The search for common principles of English and **3.175** French law meant that, for each dispute that arose under the construction contract—and there were many—teams of French and English lawyers on each side had to determine what the answer was likely to be under the applicable principles of their own law and then work out to what extent, if at all, these principles were common to both systems of law. As one of the construction group's external counsel has commented:

> The main reason for the difficulty in applying a clause providing for the application of common principles between English and French law is that although both systems tend

---

[224] It is surprising in that the *tronc commun* is generally chosen as the 'politically correct' choice of law in cases involving a foreign state, rather than cases involving only private parties.

[225] *Channel Tunnel Group Ltd and France Manche SA v Balfour Beatty Construction Ltd and ors* [1993] AC 334, at [347].

[226] When Eurotunnel sought an injunction to prevent Trans-Manche from carrying out a threat to cease work on part of the project. *Channel Tunnel Group Ltd v Balfour Beatty Construction Ltd* [1992] 1 QB 656, at [675].

[227] *Channel Tunnel Group Ltd v Balfour Beatty Construction Ltd* [1992] 1 QB 656, at [675].

[228] Rubino-Sammartano, 'The Channel Tunnel and the *tronc commun* doctrine' (1993) 10 J Intl Arb 59, at 61, asserts that: 'The Channel Tunnel contract is an example of an express choice by the parties and as such it does not seem to leave the door open to possible argument. The view expressed by Staughton LJ, "I suspect it will lead to lengthy and expensive dispute" cannot consequently be shared.' In fact, as stated above, it was entirely accurate, in that two teams of lawyers, French and English, had to be engaged by each of the parties in order to advise on the many disputes that arose. It is true that the choice-of-law clause was clear; this is not the issue. What was not clear was what were the 'common principles' of French and English law that were applicable to the various different disputes that arose—including, e.g., disputes as to whether a particular claim was or was not barred (or extinguished) by lapse of time.

to produce the same or very similar results, they fall short of providing the set of common principles which is necessary to cover all contractual disputes.[229]

3.176   Although the Court of Appeal was, in passing, critical of this choice-of-law clause—as a hybrid system of law—it did not suggest that it was anything other than a binding and enforceable agreement. This emerges even more strongly in the decision of the House of Lords:

> The parties chose an indeterminate 'law' to govern their substantive rights; an elaborate process for ascertaining those rights; and a location for that purpose outside the territories of the participants. This conspicuously neutral, 'a-national' and extra-judicial structure may well have been the first choice for the special needs of the Channel Tunnel venture. But whether it was right or wrong, it is the choice which the parties have made.[230]

3.177   The Channel Tunnel project was one of the major international construction contracts of the twentieth century.[231] Of course, even if only one system of law had been chosen as the applicable law, both French and English lawyers would have been needed to deal with the financing of the project, as well as 'domestic' issues such as staff accommodation on either side of the Channel, labour relations, and so on—but the dispute resolution process itself would have been simpler, less expensive, and, it is suggested, more predictable.

3.178   There are many large international projects in which lawyers from different countries are likely to be needed. In such major projects, the expense involved in searching for the common principles of two national systems of law, or for 'the common core' of these two national laws, may perhaps be justified (particularly if the two systems are known to have much in common).[232] However, in ordinary trading contracts of the kind that constitute the day-to-day substance of international commerce, it must be doubtful whether the additional trouble and expense can be justified.

3.179   In summary, it is suggested that, in ordinary international commercial contracts, including construction contracts, the parties would do well to try to agree upon a given national law as the law of the contract. It may take time to reach agreement, but it will be time well spent. Where one of the parties to the contract is a state or a state agency, it may be necessary to adopt a system of concurrent laws (which may not be easy to operate, but which will probably be better than a system of combined laws).

---

[229] Duval, 'English and French law: The search for common principles' (1997) 25 Intl Business Lawyer 181, at 182.

[230] *Channel Tunnel Group Ltd v Balfour Beatty Construction Ltd* [1993] AC 334, at 368. In the same judgment, Lord Mustill said, at 353, 'having promised to take their complaints to the experts and if necessary to the arbitrators, that is where the appellants should go'.

[231] For further comment on the House of Lords' decision, see Reymond, 'The Channel Tunnel case and the law of international arbitration' (1993) 109 LQR 337; Veeder, 'L'Arret Channel Tunnel de la Chambre des Lords' (1993) 4 Rev Arb 705.

[232] Rubino-Sammartano, 'The Channel Tunnel and the *tronc commun* doctrine' (1993) 10 J Intl Arb 59, at 61 ('[T]he common part of these two national laws must be treated as that chosen by the parties').

(v) Transnational law (including *lex mercatoria*, the UNIDROIT Principles, trade usages, and *Shari'ah*)

Introduction

The reference to 'such rules of international law as may be agreed by the parties' (as in Article 42 of the ICSID Convention), or to 'the relevant principles of international law' (as in the Channel Tunnel Treaty) serve to remind us that it is not the whole corpus of law, but only certain specific rules of law that are likely to be relevant in any given dispute. For example, an international contract for the sale of goods governed by the law of Austria will usually bring into consideration only those provisions of Austrian law that deal with the sale of goods. An international construction project that is governed by the law of England will principally involve consideration of those particular areas of law that are concerned with construction contracts. This breaking down of the whole body of the law into specific, discrete sections is reflected by increased specialisation within the legal profession itself. Thus, for example, within an association of lawyers such as the IBA, there are specialist groups whose primary expertise is in energy law, or intellectual property, or construction law—and so forth.[233]

3.180

In these circumstances, it seems appropriate to ask whether or not a particular group of bankers, or merchants, or traders may develop their own special rules of conduct that gradually acquire the force of law, either by themselves or by incorporation into national law or international treaty. Experience suggests that the answer to this question is a cautious 'yes'.[234] Indeed, in the past, this is how much of our law developed. Colombos, for example, tells of the early maritime codes such as the Rhodian Sea Law, which dated from the second or third century BC and which was 'of great authority in the Mediterranean, for its principles were accepted by both Greeks and Romans and its memory lasted for a thousand years'.[235] This was an early form of transnational law, as indeed was the celebrated Consolato des Mare which, again according to Colombos, 'throughout the Middle Ages, reigned supreme in the Mediterranean until the advent of sovereign states, national legislation superseding the customary laws of the sea, so often incorporating many of its rules'.[236]

3.181

It is significant that, within time, the 'customary laws of the sea' were superseded by legislation. As states evolve, this is almost inevitable. In the present-day world of sovereign states and complex legislation, it may be questioned whether there is still room for the crystallisation of customary practices into rules of law. Even if there is, it is likely to be confined to particular usages and to particular trades—and to grow, so to speak, in the interstices of existing laws, rather than to form one vast corpus of law.

3.182

There are many different communities carrying on activities that may be as diverse (and have as little in common) as the transport of goods or the establishment of an international

3.183

---

[233] The same division into specialist groups may be seen within law firms from which, increasingly, clients are seeking specialist business sector advice or expertise.

[234] This can be seen in White & Case and Queen Mary School of International Arbitration, University of London, 2010 International Arbitration Survey: Choices in International Arbitration, available online at https://arbitration.qmul.ac.uk/media/arbitration/docs/2010_InternationalArbitrationSurveyReport.pdf, which indicated that 50 per cent of respondents have 'sometimes' used transnational laws and rules to govern contracts.

[235] Colombos, *International Law of the Sea* (6th edn, Prentice Hall Press, 1967).

[236] Ibid.

telecommunications network. The rules of law that are relevant to these different commercial activities are in themselves likely to be very different. They may share certain basic legal concepts—such as the sanctity of contracts (*pacta sunt servanda*)—but even here different considerations are likely to apply. For example, an international contract for the sale of goods will be performed within a comparatively short timescale—but compare this to a major infrastructure project that will take many years to perform and during the course of which the basis upon which the original bargain was struck may change dramatically.

3.184   Given these words of caution, the approach adopted in this book is pragmatic, rather than theoretical. This is probably the most useful approach, since in practice lawyers and arbitrators are concerned with a particular dispute or series of disputes rather than with some 'general theory' of law. In a report on transnational rules, the author referred to the approach adopted by the International Law Association (ILA) formulated as follows:

> The Committee's approach in its continuing study of transnational law has been to step back from the highly contentious issues that arise from any theoretical consideration of transnational law, or *lex mercatoria*, as a discrete body of principles and to examine, in a pragmatic way, the application of individual identifiable principles at least as a phenomenon of international commercial arbitration, which it undoubtedly is.[237]

Lex mercatoria

3.185   One of the more important developments in the field of transnational law has been that of the *lex mercatoria*.

3.186   This modern version of a 'law merchant' is taken to consist of rules and practices that have evolved within the international business communities. Professor Goldman, who named this new 'law' and who contributed greatly to its development,[238] referred to it as having had 'an illustrious precursor in the Roman *jus gentium*',[239] which he described as 'an autonomous source of law proper to the economic relations (*commercium*) between citizens and foreigners (*peregrine*)'.[240]

3.187   The advantage of such a code of law is obvious: it would be adapted to the needs of modern international commerce and it would be of uniform application. The problem is whether such a system of law, which might have existed in Roman times or in the Middle Ages, can today arise spontaneously (as it were)—amongst states that already possess in full measure their own laws, orders, and regulations. Some commentators greeted the new *lex mercatoria*

---

[237] Bowden, 'L'interdiction des se contredire au détriment d'autrui (estoppel) as a Substantive Transnational Rule in International Commercial Arbitration', in Gaillard (ed.) 'Transnational Rules in International Commercial Arbitration', ICC Publication No. 480/4 (ICC, 1993), p. 127.

[238] See Goldman, '*Lex mercatoria*' (1983) 3 Forum Internationale 21. The late Professor Goldman, having referred to the codification of international commercial practices, such as the ICC's Uniform Customs and Practice for Documentary Credits (UCP)and Incoterms, as evidence of the emergence of an *international* business practice (on which, see paragraph 3.201ff), stated, ibid., at 5:

> Commentators in the early 1960s began to take note of this evolution. Clive Schmitthoff was the first in England to salute the new Law Merchant; in France, Philippe Kahn, with respect to international sales, Philippe Fouchard, with respect to international arbitration and Jean Stoufflet, with respect to documentary credits, undertook to study this law. As for myself, I concluded that a place could be acknowledged for the *lex mercatoria*—a name which stuck—within the boundaries of the law.

[239] Ibid., at 3.
[240] Ibid.

with approval.[241] Others were politely sceptical,[242] or (in the context of state contracts) dismissed it as an idea whose time has passed, since more sophisticated laws and rules now exist.[243] Others still were openly hostile.[244] What, then, is this new 'law' that has aroused so much controversy, and which, from time to time, has made its appearance in arbitral awards and in court proceedings?

For Professor Goldman, the distinguishing features of the *lex mercatoria* were its 'customary' and 'spontaneous' nature.[245] It was his view that international commercial relationships: **3.188**

> may perfectly well be governed by a body of specific rules, including transnational custom, general principles of law and arbitral case law. It makes no difference if this body of rules is not part of a legal order[[246]] comporting its own legislative and judicial organs. Within this body of rules, the general principles of law are not only those referred to in Article 38(a) of the Statute of the International Court of Justice; there may be added to it principles progressively established by the general and constant usage of international trade.[247]

It is not difficult to envisage rules developing in a particular area of international trade (such as documentary credits) and eventually being codified, either in national legislation or by international treaty, so as to attain the force of law.[248] But the custom in question is usually that of a particular trade or industry. The point has already been made that international traders do not constitute a homogeneous community. Instead they constitute myriad communities, each with their own different customary rules. How are these very different and specific rules to evolve into universal rules of international trade law? **3.189**

Rather than pose these theoretical questions, it is perhaps more useful to ask: what is this new law? What principles does it embody? What specific rules does it lay down? In short, what is its content? **3.190**

There appear to be two alternative approaches towards assessing the content of the new *lex mercatoria*: the 'list' method and the 'functional' approach. **3.191**

---

[241] Goldman, 'La *lex mercatoria* dans les contrats d'arbitrage internationaux: Réalité et perspectives' (1979) 106 Clunet J du Droit Intl 475; Lalive, 'Transnational (or truly international) public policy and international arbitration' (1986) 3 ICC Congress Series 257; see generally Gaillard (ed.) 'Transnational Rules in International Arbitration 1993', ICC Publication No. 480/4 (ICC, 1993) (a very helpful review of aspects of transnational law by distinguished contributors).

[242] See, e.g., Mustill LJ, 'The new *lex mercatoria*: The first twenty-five years' (1987) 4 Arb Intl 86, at 86, in which he notes that '[t]he *Lex Mercatoria* has sufficient intellectual credentials to merit serious study, and yet is not so generally accepted as to escape the sceptical eye'.

[243] See, e.g., Delaume, 'The proper law of state contracts and the *lex mercatoria*: A reappraisal' (1988) 3 ICSID Rev—Foreign Investments LJ 79, at 106, where this experienced international practitioner suggests that the risk of changes in state law to the detriment of the private party to a state contract may be insured under the Convention Establishing the Multilateral Investment Guarantee Agency (1985) 24 ILM 1589, and that this is far more adapted to the commercial realities 'than the *Lex Mercatoria* which remains, both in scope and in practical significance, an elusive system and a mythical view of a transnational law of State Contracts whose sources are elsewhere'.

[244] See, e.g., Mann, 'The proper law in the conflict of laws' (1987) 36 ICLQ 437, at 448; Toope, *Mixed International Arbitration* (Grotius, 1990), in particular p. 96, where the author concludes: 'It would appear that the so-called *lex mercatoria* is largely an effort to legitimise as "law" the economic interests of Western corporations'.

[245] Goldman, 'La *lex mercatoria* dans les contrats d'arbitrage internationaux: Réalité et perspectives' (1979) 106 Clunet J du Droit Intl 475, at 481.

[246] Although Professor Goldman himself contended that it was part of a legal order.

[247] Goldman, 'La *lex mercatoria* dans les contrats d'arbitrage internationaux: Réalité et perspectives' (1979) 106 Clunet J du Droit Intl 475, at 496.

[248] Both the ICC Rules 2021, Art. 21.2, and the UNCITRAL Rules 2010, Art. 35.3, require arbitrators to take account of relevant trade usages.

3.192   **List method**   As far as the 'list' method is concerned, various lists of rules or principles have been prepared over the past decade,[249] drawing, amongst other things, upon the UNIDROIT Principles and the Principles of European Contract Law 1998, as updated in 2002 (the Lando Principles). The list process has been criticised as lacking flexibility. To counter this criticism, Professor Berger has proposed 'creeping codification':

> Creeping codification is to be distinguished from more formalized techniques for defining the *lex mercatoria* (UNIDROIT and Lando Principles): it is intended to avoid the 'static element' characteristic of other approaches and to provide the openness and flexibility required in order to take account of the rapid development of international trade and commerce.[250]

Creeping codification is intended to ensure that a list of transnational commercial principles is capable of being rapidly, and continually, revised and updated. Professor Berger established a database known as Translex,[251] as the institutional framework within which to develop and update the list on an ongoing basis.[252]

3.193   **Functional approach**   The alternative approach involves identifying particular rules of the *lex mercatoria* as and when specific questions arise. This 'functional' approach regards the *lex mercatoria* as a method for determining the appropriate rule or principle. Professor Gaillard was a leading exponent of this approach,[253] who emphasised that the controversy, which initially focused on the existence of transnational rules, has shifted. He said that it now focused:

> on the establishment in further detail of the *content* of those rules or the more systematic assessment of the means to do so. As a result, very significant differences of opinion on how such goals may be achieved have emerged.[254]

3.194   According to Professor Gaillard, the functional approach presents the advantage that any claim made by a party in a given case would necessarily find an answer, which may not be the position under the list method.[255]

3.195   As a practical matter, when arbitrators seek to identify the content of the *lex mercatoria*, they draw increasingly on the UNIDROIT Principles:

> If the Unidroit Principles embody concepts already in the *lex mercatoria*, [...] these Principles would seem to provide a point of explicit reference for arbitral tribunals. And this is exactly what appears to be happening: the Unidroit Principles have already been

---

[249] See, e.g., Berger, *The Creeping Codification of the New Lex Mercatoria* (Kluwer Law International, 2011). See also Mustill LJ, 'The new *lex mercatoria*: The first twenty-five years' (1987) 4 Arb Intl 86—although the author thought the results 'a modest haul for twenty-five years of international arbitration'. See too Paulsson, 'La *lex mercatoria* dans l'arbitrage de la CCI' [1990] Rev Arb 55; Dalhuisen, 'Legal orders and their manifestation: The operation of the international commercial and financial legal order and its *lex mercatoria*' (2006) 24 BJIL 129, at 179*ff*.

[250] Berger, *The Creeping Codification of Lex Mercatoria* (Kluwer Law International, 1999), p. 192.

[251] Translex is available online at http://www.trans-lex.org

[252] Fortier, 'The new, new *lex mercatoria*, or back to the future' (2001) 17 Arb Intl 121, at 126.

[253] Gaillard, 'Transnational law: A legal system or a method of decision-making?' (2001) 17 Arb Intl 62.

[254] Ibid., at 60; see also Fortier, 'The new, new *lex mercatoria*, or back to the future' (2001) 17 Arb Intl 121, at 126.

[255] Gaillard, 'Transnational law: A legal system or a method of decision-making?' (2001) 17 Arb Intl 62 at 64.

referred to in about thirty ICC cases, it is recently reported, in order to identify general legal principles.[256]

The usefulness of the UNIDROIT Principles and of the Lando Principles (which set out rules common to the main legal systems surveyed) has been recognised by other leading commentators, noting that '[t]he result—a concrete, usable list of principles and rules—addresses head-on the traditional concern of practitioners that the *lex* is too abstract and impractical to be of any use in the real world.'[257] **3.196**

That the UNIDROIT Principles embody concepts within the *lex mercatoria*, but are not a source of it, has similarly been stressed by Professor Mayer in a useful survey of ICC awards on the issue: **3.197**

> Each arbitral award stands on its own. There is no doctrine of precedence or of *stare decisis* as between different awards; and in general there is no appellate court to sort the wheat from the chaff. There is, in this sense, no formal control of the arbitral process.[258] Arbitrators are free to decide as they choose. Conscientious arbitrators will obviously do their utmost to ensure that their decision is made in accordance with the law governing the contract. Their professional conscience will demand no less; and they will not decide *ex aequo et bono* without the express authorisation of the parties. But if the law governing the contract consists of those rules or principles which the arbitrators consider most appropriate, and which may conveniently be labelled as part of the *lex mercatoria*, those arbitrators are in effect free to decide in accordance with what they consider to be just and equitable, whilst purporting to decide in accordance with legal rules.[259]

This is a pertinent observation. Under the guise of applying the *lex mercatoria*, an arbitral tribunal may in effect pick such rules as seem to the tribunal to be just and reasonable—which may or may not be what the parties intended when they made their contract.

The *lex mercatoria* has had some impact upon the law of international arbitration,[260] and has been described by a leading authority as a body of 'substantive and procedural practices which parties and tribunals expect to apply and are applied in international arbitration'.[261] It has also served to remind both the parties to international arbitration and the arbitral tribunals called upon to resolve their disputes that they are operating at an international level, and that different considerations may come into play from those to be found in purely national, or domestic, arbitrations. **3.198**

Where the *lex mercatoria* is said to govern the parties' contract, either by agreement of the parties themselves or by a decision of the tribunal, will a court enforce that choice of law, if **3.199**

---

[256] Molineaux, 'Applicable law in arbitration: The coming convergence of civil and Anglo-Saxon law via Unidroit and *lex mercatoria*' (2000) 1 JWIT 127, at 130.

[257] Fortier, 'The new, new *lex mercatoria*, or back to the future' (2001) 17 Arb Intl 121, at 124–125.

[258] Except on procedural matters, which are not under consideration here.

[259] Mayer, 'The UNIDROIT Principles in contemporary contract practice' (2002) ICC Bulletin (Special Supplement) 111.

[260] For instance, in authorising arbitrators to choose the governing law of the contract, where the parties have not done so, without necessarily following the conflict rules of the place of arbitration.

[261] Lew, 'Is there a "global free-standing body of substantive arbitration law?"', in van den Berg (ed.) *International Arbitration: The Coming of a New Age?* (Kluwer Law International, 2013), pp. 53–61.

called upon to do so? And will such a court enforce an award made in conformity with the *lex mercatoria*, if called upon to do so?

3.200   In principle, the answer to both questions appears to be 'yes'. If the parties have agreed upon a particular method of dispute resolution, the court should be prepared to enforce that agreement following normal contractual principles.[262] Again, if the arbitral tribunal has carried out the mission entrusted to it and has decided the case in accordance with the rules of law chosen by the parties, there would seem to be no reason why a court should refuse to enforce the award. The tribunal has simply done what the parties empowered it to do. As regards enforcement of the award, the ILA expressed the position that should sensibly be taken:[263]

> The fact that an international arbitrator has based an award on transnational rules (general principles of law, principles common to several jurisdictions, international law, usages of trade, etc) rather than on the law of a particular State should not itself affect the validity or enforceability of the award: (i) where the parties have agreed that the arbitrator may apply transnational rules; or (ii) where the parties have remained silent concerning the applicable law.[264]

This position has been adopted by various national courts, including the French Court of Cassation, the Austrian Supreme Court, and the English Court of Appeal.[265]

UNIDROIT Principles

3.201   The influence of codified terms and practices in the concept and development of a new *lex mercatoria* has already been noted. For example, the ICC's Uniform Customs and Practice for Documentary Credits, formulated almost a century ago in 1933,[266] have helped significantly in the move towards a single, uniform international standard for the interpretation of documentary credits—those valuable pieces of paper upon which much of international trade depends. Similarly, the ICC's International Rules for the Interpretation of Trade Terms (known as 'Incoterms') are intended to give a consistent, uniform meaning to terms that are in frequent use in international trade—so that expressions such as 'exw' (meaning 'ex works'), 'cif' (meaning cost, insurance, and freight), and 'fob' (meaning 'free on board') should mean the same to businessmen and traders in São Paulo as they do to those based in Paris or New York.[267]

---

[262] Compare the statement of Lord Mustill in *Channel Tunnel Group Ltd v Balfour Beatty Construction Ltd* [1993] AC 334, at 353 ('[H]aving promised to take their complaints to the experts and if necessary to the arbitrators, that is where the appellants should go').

[263] At its conference in Cairo, April 1992.

[264] Quoted in ICC, Transnational Rules in International Commercial Arbitration, ICC Publication No. 480/4 (ICC, 1993), p. 247. Note, however, that if no choice of law has been made by the parties, the arbitral tribunal may not be free to choose anything other than national law. This is because the relevant rules of arbitration, or the relevant state law, may not allow any other option.

[265] *Banque du Proche-Orient v Société Fougerolle*, Cass. Civ. 2eme, 9 December 1981 (second decision) and Cass. Civ. 1ere, 22 October 1991; Judgment of the Austrian Supreme Court, 18 November 1982, reproduced in (1984) IX YBCA 161; *Deutsche Schachtbau und Tiefbohrgesellschaft GmbH (F/Germ) v R'as Al Khaimah National Oil Co. (R'as Al Khaimah, UAE) Shell International Petroleum Co. Ltd (UK)* [1987] 3 WLR 1023, rev'd on other grounds [1990] 1 AC 295. See also Rivkin, 'Enforceability of awards based on *lex mercatoria*' (1993) 19 Arb Intl 47.

[266] The current version of which is the UCP 600, published in 2007: ICC Publication No. 600.

[267] The latest version of which is the 2020 edition: ICC Publication No. E723E. Both Incoterms and documentary credits are discussed with trade usages at paragraph 3.206.

Reference has already been made to the UNIDROIT Principles,[268] which are, in nature, **3.202** a restatement of the general principles of contract law. The principles are comprehensive,[269] covering not only the interpretation and performance of contractual obligations, but also the conduct of negotiations leading to the formation of a contract. They were developed to include new rules relating to failed contracts, illegality, and conditions, as well as the plurality of obligors and obligees. The emphasis is on good faith and fair dealing.[270] The aim is to establish a neutral set of rules for use throughout the world without any particular bias to one system of law over another. As one experienced commentator has said: 'They were not drafted in the interest of a specific party or lobbying group. They will strike a fair balance between the rights and obligations of all parties to the contract.'[271]

The UNIDROIT Principles 'represent a system of rules of contract law'.[272] They apply **3.203** only when the parties choose to apply them to their contract, or have agreed that their contract will be governed by 'general principles of law', the *lex mercatoria*, or the like.[273] However, in practice, arbitral tribunals may themselves decide to refer to the UNIDROIT Principles as an aid to the interpretation of contract terms and conditions—or even as a standard to be observed, for example in the negotiation of a contract.[274]

In a Swedish arbitration in which a governing law had not been specifically designated in **3.204** the parties' contract, the European claimant argued in favour of Swedish law, basing itself on the choice of Sweden as the place of arbitration. The Chinese party argued in favour of Chinese law because China had the closest connection with the contract. The tribunal relied on Article 24.1 of the Rules of the Arbitration Institute of the Stockholm Chamber of Commerce (SCC Rules),[275] which permitted it to apply 'the law or rules of law which the tribunal considers to be most appropriate'. Having decided that no common intention as to a particular national system of law could be found, the tribunal decided to adopt

---

[268] See paragraphs 3.192, 3.195, and 3.196.

[269] The UNIDROIT Principles were revised in May 2016 and are available online at https://www.unidroit.org/instruments/commercial-contracts/unidroit-principles-2016/

[270] For example, Article 1.7 states: '(1) Each party must act in accordance with good faith and fair dealing in international trade. (2) The parties may not exclude or limit this duty.'

[271] See van Houtte, 'The UNIDROIT Principles of International Commercial Contracts' (1995) 11 Arb Intl 373, at 374.

[272] UNIDROIT has published a commentary on the revised principles entitled *UNIDROIT Principles of International Commercial Contracts, 2016*, available online at https://www.unidroit.org/wp-content/uploads/2021/06/Unidroit-Principles-2016-English-i.pdf.

[273] More precisely, the opening words to the Preamble to the UNIDROIT Principles state:

These Principles set forth general rules for international commercial contracts. They shall be applied when the parties have agreed that their contract be governed by them. They may be applied when the parties have agreed that their contract be governed by general principles of law, the *lex mercatoria* or the like. They may be applied when the parties have not chosen any law to govern their contract. They may be used to interpret or supplement international uniform law instruments. They may be used to interpret or supplement domestic law. They may serve as a model for national and international legislators.

[274] For a review of the application of the UNIDROIT Principles in arbitration practice, see Piers and Erauw, 'Application of the UNIDROIT Principles of International Commercial Contracts in Arbitration' (2012) 8 J Priv Intl L 441.

[275] Now Art. 27.1 of SCC Rules 2017 ('The Arbitral Tribunal shall decide the merits of the dispute on the basis of the law(s) or rules of law agreed upon by the parties. In the absence of such agreement, the Arbitral Tribunal shall apply the law or rules of law that it considers most appropriate').

the only codification of trade law that had the status of an internationally accepted code, namely:

> the UNIDROIT Principles of International Commercial Contracts [...] The Tribunal determines that the rules contained therein shall be the first source employed in reaching a decision on the issues in dispute in the present arbitration.[276]

3.205   An example of how the UNIDROIT Principles are intended to work is its treatment of clauses limiting liability. In many forms of contract, the party that bears the major responsibility for performance will seek either to limit its liability or even to exclude liability altogether. A clause in a construction contract, for example, may state that the contractor has no liability for loss of profit arising out of any breach of the contract, whether caused by negligence or any other breach of duty. The question then arises as to the scope of this clause and, in particular, whether, in specific circumstances, it may be set aside altogether.[277] In relation to such a claim, the UNIDROIT Principles state:

> A clause which limits or excludes one party's liability for non-performance or which permits one party to render performance substantially different from what the other party reasonably expected may not be invoked if it would be grossly unfair to do so, having regard to the purpose of the contract.[278]

The effect of such a clause, in a dispute to which the UNIDROIT Principles are applicable, is to permit an arbitral tribunal to disregard the exemption clause in appropriate circumstances. In each case, it will be for the tribunal to decide what was the purpose of the contract and whether, in all of the circumstances, it would be 'grossly unfair' to apply the exemption clause.

Trade usages

3.206   As already mentioned, institutional rules (such as those of the ICC) and international arbitration rules (such as those of UNCITRAL) require an arbitral tribunal to take account of relevant trade usage.[279] A similar requirement is to be found in the Model Law[280] and in some national legislation, such as the Netherlands Arbitration Act.[281]

3.207   The relevant trade usages will have to be established by evidence in any given case (unless the arbitrators are familiar with them and make this clear to the parties). However, as previously mentioned,[282] organisations such as the ICC have been prominent in attempting to establish a commonly understood meaning for expressions that are in frequent use in international trade contracts and have developed Incoterms, in which the precise meaning and effect of such terms as 'exw', 'cif', and 'fob' are explained. It is obviously important that such terms should have the same meaning worldwide. To this end, the precise extent of these rights and obligations is spelt out in the Incoterms.

---

[276] See Arbitration Institute of the SCC, *Stockholm Arbitration Report* (SCC, 2002), p. 59, with commentary by Fernandez-Armesto.

[277] In the same manner as an exemption clause might be disregarded under domestic legislation to protect consumers.

[278] UNIDROIT Principles, Art. 7.1.6.

[279] ICC Rules 2021, Art. 21.2; UNCITRAL Rules 2010, Art. 35.3.

[280] Model Law, Art. 28(4).

[281] Netherlands Arbitration Act, Art. 1054(4).

[282] See paragraph 3.197 above.

Standard form contracts are commonplace in many fields, including the shipping trade, the **3.208** commodity markets, and the oil and gas industry. The step from the establishment of international terms and conditions to the establishment of uniform rules for the interpretation of these terms and conditions is a small, but important, one. Such uniform rules may apply only within the ambit of a national system of law. But if the same rules are uniformly applied by different national courts, or by arbitral tribunals, the basis is laid for the establishment of a customary law, which will have been created by merchants and traders themselves (rather than by lawyers) and which may achieve international recognition.

Shari'ah *law*

Modern codes of law in Islamic countries take account of *Shari'ah*, often as a principal source **3.209** of law.[283] *Shari'ah* itself contains general principles that are basic to any civilised system of law, such as good faith in the performance of obligations and the observance of due process in the settlement of disputes.[284] Although there are differences from country to country (partly as a result of the different schools of Islamic law and partly because some states are more open to Western influences than others), Islamic law, traditions, and language give these states a common heritage and, to some extent, a common approach to arbitration.[285]

In a case that came before the English High Court, a financial transaction had been struc- **3.210** tured in a manner (an 'Estisna form') that ensured that the transaction conformed with orthodox Islamic banking practice.[286] There was provision for any disputes to be settled by arbitration in London under the ICC Rules and there was a choice-of-law clause that provided for any dispute to be 'governed by the Law of England except to the extent it may conflict with Islamic Shari'ah, which shall prevail'. A dispute arose and the ICC appointed as sole arbitrator Mr Samir Saleh, an experienced lawyer and expert on *Shari'ah* law. The losing party challenged the arbitrator's award, but the English court rejected this challenge, holding that the award was a clear and full evaluation of the issues, and had all the appearances of being right.[287]

According to Professor Fadlallah, however, 'the landscape was clouded'[288] by three well- **3.211** known awards, which, in his view, are not confined to history[289] and continue to have 'harmful effects' on the development of Euro–Arab arbitration.[290] In *Sheikh Abu Dhabi v Petroleum Development Ltd*,[291] *Ruler of Qatar v International Marine Oil Co. Ltd*,[292] and

---

[283] For example, the constitutions of Yemen, Qatar, and Egypt state that *Shari'ah* is a primary source of law.

[284] See Majeed, 'Good faith and due process: Lessons from the Shari'ah' (2004) 20 Arb Intl 97.

[285] See Darwazeh, 'Arbitration in the Arab world: An interview with Professor Ahmed Sadek El-Kosheri' (2008) 25 J Intl Arb 203.

[286] *Sanghi Polyesters Ltd (India) v The International Investor KCFC (Kuwait)* [2000] 1 Lloyd's Rep 480.

[287] See also *Musawi v R E International (UK) Ltd and ors* [2007] EWHC 2981, discussed at paragraph 3.214.

[288] Fadlallah, 'Arbitration facing conflicts of culture: The 2008 Freshfields Lecture' (2009) 25 Arb Intl 303.

[289] See, e.g., *Beximco Pharmaceuticals Ltd and ors v Shamil Bank of Bahrain EC* [2004] EWCA Civ 19, discussed by Fadlallah, ibid. Also of interest is a question posed in the English parliament on 15 December 2008 regarding which 'Islamic tribunals' have authority to act under the English Arbitration Act. The Minister for Business, Enterprise and Regulatory Reform responded that there is 'no specific provision in the Arbitration Act 1996 for "Islamic Tribunals"', but that '[t]he Act allows all parties to have their disputes decided by a set of principles of their choice rather than by national law': HC Deb, 15 December 2008, cols 465–466W. He also referred to the Muslim Arbitration Tribunal (MAT), established in 2007 to provide an alternative route to resolve civil issues in accordance with *Shari'ah* principles. The MAT operates according to the principles of the English Arbitration Act.

[290] Fadlallah, ibid., at fn. 320.

[291] *Sheikh Abu Dhabi v Petroleum Development Ltd* [1952] ICLQ 247.

[292] *Ruler of Qatar v International Marine Oil Co. Ltd* (1956) 20 Int L Rep 534.

Aramco v Government of Saudi Arabia,[293] the tribunals refused to apply *Shari'ah* on the ground that it did not contain a 'body of legal principles applicable to the construction of modern commercial instruments'.[294] Ironically, according to Professor Fadlallah, the outcome in each case would have been the same even if *Shari'ah* had been applied.[295]

Authority to apply non-national law

3.212   The authority of an arbitral tribunal to apply a non-national system of law (such as the general principles of law, or the *lex mercatoria*) will depend upon (a) the agreement of the parties, and (b) the provisions of the applicable law.

3.213   The ICSID Convention, for example, is clear on this point. Article 42 states: 'The Tribunal shall decide a dispute in accordance with such *rules of law* as may be agreed by the parties'.[296] The reference to 'rules of law', rather than to 'law' or 'a system of law', is a coded reference to the applicability of appropriate legal rules even though these may fall short of being an established and autonomous system of law.

3.214   Within different states, different positions are adopted. France and Switzerland, for example, allow arbitrators to decide according to rules of law.[297] By contrast, the Model Law, whilst leaving it to the parties to make an express choice of such 'rules of law' as they wish, requires an arbitral tribunal, if the choice is left to the tribunal, to apply 'the law determined by the conflict of laws rules which it considers applicable'.[298] English law follows this approach: the arbitral tribunal has to decide the dispute (a) in accordance with the law chosen by the parties, or (b) if the parties agree, in accordance with 'such other considerations as are agreed by them or determined by the tribunal'; if there is no choice or agreement by the parties, the tribunal must apply 'the law' determined by the appropriate conflict rules.[299] English courts have considered the meaning of 'such other considerations' under section 46(1)(b) of the English Arbitration Act in the following cases:

    i. in *Musawi v R E International (UK) Ltd and ors*,[300] the court held that section 46(1)(b) of the English Arbitration Act entitled the parties to the arbitration to require the *ayatollah* arbitrator to apply *Shari'ah* law as the applicable law; and

    ii. in *Halpern v Halpern*,[301] which concerned the application of Jewish law, the Court of Appeal ruled that if the seat of arbitration were England, then section 46(1)(b) of the English Arbitration Act would permit the tribunal to apply the parties' choice of some form of rules or non-national law to govern the merits of their dispute.[302]

---

[293] *Aramco v Government of Saudi Arabia* (1963) 27 Int L Rep 117.

[294] *Sheikh Abu Dhabi v Petroleum Development* Ltd [1952] ICLQ 247.

[295] Fadlallah, 'Arbitration facing conflicts of culture: The 2008 Freshfields Lecture' (2009) 25 Arb Intl 303.

[296] Emphasis added.

[297] French Code of Civil Procedure, art. 1496; Swiss PIL, art. 187. The ICC Rules 2021 also now refer to 'the rules of law' (in Art. 21) rather than to 'the law' to be applied.

[298] Model Law, Art. 28(2). Despite the early approach of the common law to require tribunals to apply a fixed and recognisable system of law, the adoption of the Model Law in various common law countries, including Australia, Canada, Hong Kong, and New Zealand, means that there is now growing express recognition of the concept.

[299] English Arbitration Act, s. 46.

[300] *Musawi v R E International (UK) Ltd and ors* [2007] EWHC 2981.

[301] *Halpern v Halpern* [2007] EWCA Civ 291.

[302] As noted earlier, however, an arbitration agreement must be governed by the law of a country (in this case, Swiss or English law—the decision was never made) and cannot be governed by Jewish law.

Nevertheless, the meaning of 'such other considerations' is not yet entirely settled and it is difficult to transpose interpretations from other jurisdictions in which similar concepts may have different meanings. In Switzerland, for instance, *ex aequo et bono* is understood to mean the application of principles other than legal rules, while the concept of *amiable compositeur* requires the application of legal rules, but allows arbitrators to moderate the effect of such rules. In France, meanwhile, the two concepts are given a similar meaning.

The ICC Rules, on the other hand, clearly go further than the Model Law (and the English **3.215** Arbitration Act). They not only allow the parties to choose the application of 'rules of law' to govern the dispute, but also allow the arbitral tribunal, in the absence of an agreement by the parties, to apply 'the rules of law which it determines to be appropriate'.[303] Thus, by confirming their ability to choose rules of law other than those of a single state, the rules confer greater flexibility on both the arbitrators and the parties.[304]

(vi) Equity and good conscience

Arbitrators may, from time to time, be required to settle a dispute by determining it on the basis **3.216** of what is 'fair and reasonable', rather than on the basis of law. Such power is conferred upon them by so-called equity clauses, which state, for example, that the arbitrators shall 'decide according to an equitable rather than a strictly legal interpretation', or, more simply, that they shall decide as *amiables compositeurs*.[305]

This power to decide 'in equity', as it is sometimes expressed, is open to several different inter- **3.217** pretations. It may mean, for instance, that the arbitral tribunal:

   i. should apply relevant rules of law to the dispute, but may ignore any rules that are purely formalistic (for example a requirement that the contract should have been made in some particular form); or

  ii. should apply relevant rules of law to the dispute, but may ignore any rules that appear to operate harshly or unfairly in the particular case before it; or

 iii. should decide according to general principles of law; or

 iv. may ignore completely any rules of law and decide the case on its merits, as these strike the arbitral tribunal.

Commentators generally reject this fourth alternative. To the extent that they do agree, **3.218** commentators seem to suggest that even an arbitral tribunal that decides 'in equity' must act in accordance with some generally accepted legal principles as well as any mandatory law applicable to the arbitration. For example, the Model Law requires that, even when authorised to act as *amiable compositeur*, a tribunal must still 'take into account the rules of the trade applicable to the transaction'.[306] It is also doubtful that a tribunal acting as an *amiable*

---

[303] ICC Rules 2021, Art. 21.1 ('The parties shall be free to agree upon the rules of law to be applied by the arbitral tribunal to the merits of the dispute. In the absence of any such agreement, the arbitral tribunal shall apply the rules of law which it determines to be appropriate.')

[304] For example, they may choose general principles of law, or the *lex mercatoria*, or the UNIDROIT Principles.

[305] Several civil law countries provide for the possibility that an arbitrator can act as an *amiable compositeur*. For example, Italian civil procedure provides for the courts to decide the merits of a dispute *in equita* when the dispute concerns rights which the parties are entitled to waive and the parties jointly request the court to do so. See Codice di Procedura Civile (as amended in 2021), s. 114. The same authority is given to arbitrators in s. 822. There is a similar provision in the Swiss PIL, art. 187(2). Egypt's arbitration law refers to both the power to act as an *amiable compositeur* as well as the power to 'adjudicate the merits of the dispute in conformity with the rules of justice and fairness (ex aequo et bono)'. See Egyptian Arbitration Act, 1994, Art. 39(4).

[306] Model Law, Art. 28(3) and (4).

compositeur can disregard any or all of the express terms of the parties' agreement.[307] Certain procedural rules, for example, may require a tribunal to 'take into account the relevant provisions of the contract, if any',[308] and it seems difficult to conceive of many scenarios in which the draftsmen of a contract intended for an arbitrator to disregard those terms in the event of a dispute.

3.219 This is distinct from the possibility that an arbitrator might act to mitigate the consequences of a proper reading of the parties' contractual terms, for example by adjusting the reparation owed in light of a contractual breach. In ICC Case No. 3344, for example, two state entities entered into a three-year crude oil supply contract running from 1972 to 1974. At the end of 1973, the price of oil increased dramatically and the contract was renegotiated. Under the new terms, the parties agreed a provisional purchase price. The supplier then unilaterally fixed its own, higher price, by telex, to which the buyer did not respond. The tribunal held that on a strict legal analysis the buyer by its silence had accepted the higher price, but that equity allowed the tribunal to adjust the purchase price downward in order to moderate the undesirable effect of the rigid application of national law.[309] This resonates with the approach taken in equity under the common law.[310]

3.220 In many (or perhaps most) cases, an arbitral tribunal will reach its decision based largely on a consideration of the facts and on the provisions of the contract, whilst trying to ensure that these provisions do not operate unfairly to the detriment of one or the other of the parties or are not clearly contrary to the true intent of the parties. French law, for example, allows the arbitrators to act as *amiables compositeurs*, but requires them to satisfy certain standards.[311] The Paris Court of Appeal has held that 'arbitrators acting as *amiables compositeurs* have an obligation to ensure that their decision is equitable or else they would betray their duty and give rise to a cause for annulment'.[312]

3.221 In the case of *Benvenuti & Bonfant v Republic of Congo*, which concerned an alleged expropriation of a joint venture, the parties agreed that the ICSID tribunal could rule *ex aquo et bono*. In a passage illustrative of the boundaries that a tribunal is likely to apply to its powers to act in equity, the tribunal held:

> This principle of compensation in case of nationalization [...] constitutes one of the generally recognized principles of international law as well as of equity. By reason of the above,

---

[307] For the view that such a departure is or ought to be permissible in the interests of fairness and justice, see Kiffer, 'Amiable Composition and ICC Arbitration' (2007) 18(1) ICC Court of Arbitration Bulletin 50. The Court of Appeal of Quebec, Canada, took the opposite view in the case of *Coderre v Coderre* (2008 QCCA 888), Court of Appeal of Quebec, 13 May 2008. In that case, the court found that an arbitrator had exceeded his mandate as *amiable compositeur* under the Model Law by deciding to ignore two provisions of the parties' contractual accounting formula.

[308] ICC Rules 2021, Art. 21.2.

[309] ICC Award No. 3344 of 1981 noted in Jarvin and Derains, *Collection of ICC Arbitral Awards 1974–1985*, Vol. I (Kluwer Law & Taxation/ ICC Publishing, 1990), p. 444.

[310] See, e.g., *Cavendish Square Holding BV v Talal El Makdessi; PakingEye Limited v Beavis* [2015] UKSC 67, at [32] where the UK Supreme Court upheld the common law position that a liquidated damages clause can be struck down as penal where 'the clause imposes a detriment on the contract breaker out of all proportion to any legitimate interest of the innocent party in the enforcement of the primary obligation'.

[311] See Loquin, *L'Amiable Compositeur en Droit Comparé et International: Contribution à l'Étude du Non-Droit dans l'Arbitrage International* (Librairie Techniques, 1980).

[312] Cour d'appel de Paris, 11 January 1996, 351.

the Government must therefore be ordered to pay B&B damages, the quantum of which will be determined *ex aequo et bono*.[313]

In addition to applying equitable principles in the quantification of damages, the tribunal also awarded the claimant moral damages (albeit reducing the amount awarded to one fifth of the amount claimed),[314] and applied a rate of interest that it considered appropriate '[b]y virtue of its power to rule *ex aequo et bono*'.[315]

For an 'equity clause' to be effective, there are, in principle, two basic requirements: first, that the parties have *expressly* agreed to it; and secondly, that it should be permitted by the applicable law. Both requirements are seen in the UNCITRAL Rules 1976, which provides: 'The arbitral tribunal shall decide as *amiable compositeur* or *ex aequo et bono* only if the parties have expressly authorised the arbitral tribunal to do so and if the law applicable to the arbitral procedure permits such arbitration.'[316] (The UNCITRAL Rules 2010 has dropped the second requirement, making reference only to the parties' authorisation as a requirement.)[317] The ICC Rules, LCIA Rules, and SCC Rules all contain a similar provision.[318] **3.222**

It is noteworthy that the UNCITRAL Rules refer to *amiable compositeur* and *ex aequo et bono* as distinct concepts.[319] Although a historical distinction has been drawn between them,[320] the increasing practice of international arbitral tribunals appears to be to view both concepts as granting a discretion to arbitral tribunals to put aside strict legal rules and (subject to what has already been said about the need to take account of trade rules, for instance) decide the dispute by reference to general principles of fairness.[321] **3.223**

The arbitration laws of some states go even further. They assume that the arbitrators will decide in equity unless it is expressly stated that they must decide in law. This recalls a time when arbitration was considered a 'friendly' method of dispute resolution, rather than the law-based process that it has become. If the arbitration is to take place in such a state, parties should take care to specify if they do not want the arbitrators to decide in accordance with principles of equity.[322] **3.224**

---

[313] *Benvenutit and Bonfant SARL v The Government of the People's Republic of Congo*, ICSID Case No. ARB/77/2, Award, 8 August 1980, at [4.65].

[314] Ibid., at [4.96] ('[...] the Tribunal considers it equitable to award [B&B] the sum of CFA 5,000,000 as damages for intangible loss').

[315] Ibid at [4.98].

[316] UNCITRAL Rules 1976, Art. 33.2.

[317] UNCITRAL Rules 2010, Art. 35.2.

[318] ICC Rules 2021, Art. 21.3; LCIA Rules 2020, Art. 22.4; SCC Rules 2017, Art. 27.3.

[319] Paulsson and Petrochilos, *UNCITRAL Arbitration* (Kluwer Law International, 2017), p. 320 ('These terms appear as separate, alternate concepts in both the 1976 and 2010 Rules, because the Working Group hoped to accommodate the different terms existing in various legal systems and literature.')

[320] See Rubino-Sammartano, '*Amiable compositor* (joint mandate to settle) and *ex bono et aequo* (discretional authority to mitigate strict law): Apparent synonyms revisited' (1992) 9 J Intl Arb 5.

[321] See Grierson and van Hooft, *Arbitrating under the 2012 ICC Rules* (Kluwer Law International, 2012), pp. 319–335 (glossary entries for *amiable compositeur* and *ex aequo et bono*); *Halsbury's Laws of England*, Vol. 2 (5th edn, LexisNexis, 2008), footnote to para. 1208; Born, *International Commercial Arbitration* (2nd edn, Kluwer Law International, 2014), pp. 2770–2776.

[322] See, e.g., the Ecuador Arbitration and Mediation Law 1997 (as amended in 2021), Art. 3 ('Las partes indicarán si los árbitros deben decidir en equidad o en derecho, a falta de convenio, el fallo será en equidad', or 'The parties will decide whether the arbitrator shall decide in law or in equity. Unless otherwise agreed, the award shall be in equity' (authors' translation)).

E. Conflict Rules and the Search for the Applicable Law

(a) Introduction

3.225 As the foregoing discussion has endeavoured to make clear, parties to a contract are entitled to choose the law that is to govern their contractual relationship, and parties should exercise this entitlement with proper care and consideration in any international commercial contract into which they may enter. In the event of a dispute, such care and consideration may prove to be very valuable in saving a potentially expensive and time-consuming dispute about what law governs the contract or its arbitration clause.

3.226 The choices generally open to parties have been set out throughout this chapter. If disputes arise and no choice of law has been agreed, it is difficult to make a proper assessment of the rights and obligations of the parties, because there is no known legal framework within which to make this assessment.

3.227 If arbitration proceedings are commenced, one of the first tasks of the arbitral tribunal will be to do what the parties have failed to do—that is, to establish what law is applicable to the contract. In some cases, it might be appropriate for the arbitral tribunal to identify some non-national rule or custom to decide the issue in question, as opposed to a national law.[323] This search for the applicable substantive law may be a time-consuming and unpredictable process. The next section indicates how arbitrators are likely to approach the task if obliged to do so. By way of general introduction, the ILA's Committee for International Commercial Arbitration has recognised the need for guidance and development of best practices for parties, counsel, and arbitrators in ascertaining the contents of the applicable law to an international commercial arbitration. The recommendations made in the report, *Ascertaining of the Content of the Applicable Law in International Commercial Arbitration*, are commended to arbitral tribunals, with a view to facilitating uniformity and consistency in identifying the potentially applicable laws or rules.[324]

(b) Implied or tacit choice

3.228 In the absence of an express choice of law, the arbitral tribunal will usually look first for the law that the parties are presumed to have intended to choose. This is often referred to as a

---

[323] See Mayer, 'Reflections on the international arbitrator's duty to apply the law: The 2000 Freshfields Lecture' (2001) 17 Arb Intl 235, at 237–240, for a discussion of how arbitrators may not be bound to apply the law.

[324] The report issued after the ILA's Seventy-third Conference, held in Rio in August 2008. The Annex Resolution No. 6/2008 contains guidance split into the following sections: general considerations; acquiring information relevant to the ascertainment of the applicable law; interaction with the parties; making use of information about the law's content; and guidance in special circumstances, e.g. where public policy is implicated. Recommendations of particular note are: Recommendation 4, that the rules governing the ascertainment of the contents of law by national courts are not necessarily suitable for arbitration and that arbitrators should not rely on unexpressed presumptions as to the contents of the applicable law, including any presumption that it is the same as the law best known to the tribunal or to any of its members, or even that it is the same as the law of the seat of arbitration; Recommendation 5, that arbitrators should primarily receive information about the contents of the applicable law from the parties; and Recommendation 6, that arbitrators should not introduce legal issues (propositions of law that may bear on the outcome of the dispute) that the parties have not raised.

'tacit' choice of law. It may also be known as an implied, inferred, or implicit choice. There is a certain artificiality involved in selecting a substantive law for the parties and attributing it to their tacit choice, where (as often happens in practice) it is apparent that the parties themselves have given little or no thought to the question of the substantive law applicable to their contract and have not in fact made any choice.

The Rome I Regulation recognises this artificiality when it provides that a choice of law **3.229** must be 'expressed or *demonstrated with reasonable certainty* by the terms of the contract or the circumstances of the case'.[325] The report by Professors Guiliano and Lagarde that was published alongside the Convention has a special status in its interpretation.[326] The report states that the parties may have made a real choice of law, although not expressly stated in their contract, but the court may not be permitted to infer a choice of law that the parties might have made *where they had no clear intention of making a choice*.[327]

Depending on the application of institutional rules, arbitral tribunals may be directed to **3.230** determine the applicable law by applying 'the conflict of law rules it considers applicable'[328] (granting a tribunal wide discretion as to how to determine the governing law), or to apply 'directly' the substantive law that the tribunal deems 'appropriate'[329] (thereby bypassing altogether the need to apply any conflict of laws principles).

In such an event, the court—or the arbitral tribunal— may decide that the contract is to be **3.231** governed by the law of the country with which it is most closely connected.[330] It will be presumed that this is the country that is the place of business or residence of the party that is to effect the performance characteristic of the contract. However, this presumption does not apply if the place of characteristic performance cannot be determined. Indeed, it will be disregarded altogether if it appears that the contract is more closely connected with another country.[331]

In practice, as already indicated, parties to an international commercial contract would do **3.232** well to make a specific choice of law, rather than to leave the matter to be determined by a court or arbitral tribunal.

(c) Choice of forum as choice of law

One criterion for attributing a choice of law to the parties, in the absence of any express **3.233** choice, is that of a choice of forum by the parties. If the parties make no express choice of law, but agree that any disputes between them shall be litigated in a particular country, it may be assumed that they intend the law of that country to apply to the substance of their

---

[325] Rome I Regulation, Art. 3(1) (emphasis added).
[326] Giuliano and Lagarde, Council Report on the Convention on the Law Applicable to Contractual Obligations, OJ C 282/1, 31 October 1980.
[327] Ibid., at p. 17 (emphasis added). See also Collins (ed.) *Dicey, Morris & Collins on the Conflict of Laws* (15th edn, Sweet & Maxwell, 2018), pp. 1809*ff*.
[328] UNCITRAL Rules 1976, Art. 33.1.
[329] UNCITRAL Rules 2010, Art. 35.1; ICC Rules 2021, Art. 21.1.
[330] See, e.g., Swiss PIL, art. 187(1).
[331] Rome I Regulation, Art. 4; see also Collins (ed.) *Dicey, Morris & Collins on the Conflict of Laws* (15th edn, Sweet & Maxwell, 2018), pp. 1818*ff*, for a commentary on this provision of the Convention, which is based on Swiss and, subsequently, Dutch law.

disputes. This assumption is expressed in the maxim *qui elegit iudicem forum elegit ius* ('a choice of forum is a choice of law').

3.234   The assumption makes sense when the reference is to a court of law. For instance, if the parties fail to put a choice-of-law clause into their contract, but provide for the resolution of any disputes by the courts of New York, it would seem to be a reasonable assumption that they intended those courts to apply their own law—that is, the law of the State of New York. The assumption is less compelling, however, when the dispute resolution clause provides for arbitration in a particular country, rather than litigation in the courts of that country. As already discussed, a place of arbitration may be chosen for reasons that are unconnected with the law of that place. It may be chosen because of its geographical convenience to the parties, or because it is a suitably neutral venue, or because of the high reputation of the arbitration services to be found there, or for some other, equally valid reason. In one SCC arbitration, the tribunal highlighted the fallacy of the principle that a choice of forum is a choice of law in the context of arbitration in the following terms:

> [I]t is highly debatable whether a preferred choice of the *situs* of the arbitration is sufficient to indicate a choice of governing law. There has for several years been a distinct tendency in international arbitration to disregard this element, chiefly on the ground that the choice of the place of arbitration may be influenced by a number of practical considerations that have no bearing on the issue of applicable law.[332]

(d) Conflict rules

3.235   In the absence of an express or implied choice by the parties, an arbitral tribunal is faced with the problem of choosing a system of law or a set of legal rules to govern the contract. It must first decide whether it has a free choice, or whether it must follow the conflict-of-law rules of the seat of the arbitration—that is, the conflict rules of the *lex fori*.

3.236   Every developed national system of law contains its own rules for the conflict of laws (sometimes called private international law, in the narrower sense of that phrase). These conflict rules usually serve to indicate what law is to be chosen as the law applicable to a contract.

3.237   To carry out this role, the relevant conflict rules generally select particular criteria that serve to link or connect the contract in question with a given system of law. These criteria are often referred to as 'connecting factors'. However, they differ from country to country; accordingly, the answer to the question 'what is the applicable law?' will also differ from country to country. Some of the rules that are applied to connect a particular contract with a particular national law or set of legal rules now look decidedly out of date. For example, under the conflict rules of some states, the applicable law (in the absence of an express or tacit choice) is likely to be the law of the place where the contract was concluded (the *lex locus contractus*). The place of conclusion of a contract may, at one time, have been a factor of some significance, since it would usually be the place of business or residence of one of the parties and might well also have been the place in which the contract was to be performed. However,

---

[332] See Arbitration Institute of the SCC, *Stockholm Arbitration Report* (SCC, 2002), p. 59, with commentary by Fernandez-Armesto.

with contracts now being concluded by telephone, email, or WhatsApp, or by meetings at an airport or some other location, the place in which the contract is finally concluded is often a matter of little or no significance.

A modern set of conflict rules is that adopted in the Rome I Regulation,[333] which provides   **3.238**
that, in the absence of an express choice by the parties, 'the contract shall be governed by the law of the country with which it is most closely connected'.[334] In this regard, there is a rebuttable presumption that the contract is most closely connected with the country in which the party that is to effect the 'performance characteristic of the contract' has its central administration, principal place of business, or other place of business through which the performance is to be effected.[335]

(e) Does an international arbitral tribunal have a *lex fori*?

As already stated, conflict-of-law rules differ from one country to another. A judge or arbi-   **3.239**
tral tribunal in one country may select the applicable law by reference to the place where the contract was made, whereas in another country it may be selected by reference to the law with which the contract has the closest connection. In short, the same question may produce different answers, depending upon where the judge or arbitral tribunal happens to be sitting.

In the context of international arbitration, this is plainly unsatisfactory. The seat of the   **3.240**
arbitration is invariably chosen for reasons that have nothing to do with the conflict rules of the law of the place of arbitration. This has led to the formulation of a doctrine that has found support in both arbitration statutes and rules—namely, that, unlike the judge of a national court, an international arbitral tribunal is not bound to follow the conflict-of-law rules of the country in which it has its seat. By way of notable example, the Model Law states that:

> Failing any designation by the parties, the arbitral tribunal shall apply the law determined by the conflict of laws rules which it considers applicable.[336]

A leading commentator has spoken of 'the almost total abandonment of the application of   **3.241**
the rules of conflict of the so-called arbitral forum',[337] and the point was emphasised in the *Sapphire* arbitration,[338] in which the tribunal commented that, unlike the judge of a national court, an international arbitral tribunal has no *lex fori*:

> Contrary to a State judge, who is bound to conform to the conflict law rules of the State in whose name he metes out justice, the arbitrator is not bound by such rules. He must look

---

[333] It is worth noting that arbitral agreements are expressly excluded from the scope of the Convention by Art. 1(2)(d), but the discussion in the present section is about contracts as a whole and not about a separate (or separable) agreement to arbitrate.
[334] Rome I Regulation, Art. 4(1).
[335] Rome I Regulation, Art. 4(2).
[336] Model Law, Art. 28.
[337] Goldman, 'La *lex mercatoria* dans les contrats et l'arbitrage internationaux: Réalité et perspectives' [1979] J du Droit Intl 475, at 491.
[338] *Sapphire International Petroleum Ltd v The National Iranian Oil Co.* (1964) 13 ICLQ 1011.

for the common intention of the parties, and use the connecting factors generally used in doctrine and in case law and must disregard national peculiarities.[339]

This was an early enunciation of what has come to be known as the 'direct choice' (*voie directe*) method of choosing the substantive law, which in reality gives arbitrators the freedom to choose as they please.

(f) International conventions, rules of arbitration, and national laws

3.242   The ICSID Convention states that, in the absence of any choice of the applicable or governing law of the contract by the parties, the arbitral tribunal must apply the law of the contracting state that is a party to the dispute, together with such rules of international law as may be applicable.[340] The ICSID Convention, however, is necessarily concerned with states or state entities. Accordingly, it follows the traditional practice of giving weight to the law of the *state* party to a contract, in the absence of any choice of law.

3.243   Other conventions are content to leave the choice to the arbitral tribunal. Article VII of the European Convention of 1961, for instance, provides that '[f]ailing any indication by the parties as to the applicable law, the arbitrators shall apply the proper law under the rules of conflict that the arbitrators deem applicable'. Although the European Convention of 1961 refers to 'rules of conflict', these are *not* necessarily the rules of conflict of the country in which the arbitration has its seat; on the contrary, the reference is to the conflict rules that the arbitrators deem applicable.

3.244   A similar approach is adopted in some institutional rules,[341] as well as the Model Law.[342] The intention is to make it clear that the arbitral tribunal is entitled to choose the governing law of the contract in the absence of any express or implied choice of law by the parties themselves. In doing this, the arbitrators proceed objectively—but should they still be obliged to proceed by way of particular conflict rules? The point may be academic, since in practice an arbitral tribunal will seek to apply the law (or, if permitted, the rules of law) that it considers to be appropriate. Whether this choice is reached through conflict rules or more directly may not matter.

3.245   It should be noted, however, that French law omits any reference to conflict rules. This is both logical and sensible. French law states that: 'The arbitral tribunal shall decide the dispute in accordance with the rules of law chosen by the parties or, where no such choice has been made, in accordance with the rules of law it considers appropriate.'[343] This provision contains two propositions: first, an international arbitral tribunal is not obliged to proceed

---

[339] Ibid.

[340] ICSID Convention, Art. 42(1).

[341] See, e.g., the UNCITRAL Rules 2010, Art. 35.1 ('The arbitral tribunal shall apply the rules of law designated by the parties as applicable to the substance of the dispute. *Failing such designation by the parties, the arbitral tribunal shall apply the law which it determines to be appropriate*' (emphasis added)).

[342] Model Law, Art. 28(2).

[343] French Code of Civil Procedure, art. 1511. The same formulation is now used at Art. 35 of the UNCITRAL Rules 2010.

to its choice of law by the adoption of any national conflict of laws rules; and secondly, it is not obliged to choose a *system* of law as the substantive law of the contract, but may instead choose such *rules* of law as it considers appropriate for the resolution of the dispute.[344] The trail blazed by French law has since been followed by other countries, including Canada, India, Kenya, and the Netherlands.[345]

(g) Conclusion

In reaching its decision on the law to be applied in the absence of any choice by the parties, an arbitral tribunal is entitled (unless otherwise directed by the applicable rules or the *lex arbitri*) to select any of the systems or rules of law upon which the parties themselves might have agreed, had they chosen to do so.

3.246

When it comes to determining how an arbitral tribunal should proceed to its decision, then once again (as so often in international arbitration) no universal rule can be identified. Some systems of law insist that, in making its choice, an arbitral tribunal should follow the rules of conflict of the seat of the arbitration—an attitude that looks increasingly anachronistic. The modern tendency is for international conventions and rules of arbitration to give considerable latitude to arbitral tribunals in making their choice of law, whilst still requiring them to do so by way of appropriate or applicable conflict rules. Some national laws (including the French, the Swiss, and the Dutch) carry the matter to its logical conclusion: by abandoning the reference to conflict rules altogether, they allow an arbitral tribunal to decide for itself what law (or rules of law) the tribunal considers appropriate to settle the dispute.

3.247

This is an approach to be commended. If an arbitral tribunal can be trusted to decide a dispute, so too can it be trusted to determine the set of legal rules by which it will be guided in reaching its decision. If the parties do not wish the arbitral tribunal to have such freedom of action, the remedy is in their own hands: they should agree upon the applicable law or set of legal rules, preferably in their contract, but if not, then at any time after the dispute has arisen. If they do not do so, it will fall to the arbitral tribunal to make a decision that is likely to impact on the outcome of the arbitration. In order to reach this decision (which may be given as a ruling on a preliminary issue by way of an interim or partial award), the arbitral tribunal will usually have to consider detailed arguments of law and fact. This is an expense that could readily have been avoided if the parties had taken the time and the trouble to agree on one of the many choices open to them.

3.248

---

[344] ICC Rules 2021, Art. 21.1; LCIA Rules 2020, Art. 22.3. The SCC Rules 2017, Art. 27.1, and WIPO Rules, Art. 59.a, also endorse the direct approach.

[345] In Canada, by the Ontario International Commercial Arbitration Act 2017, s. 7; in India, the Arbitration and Conciliation Act 1996 (as amended in 2022), s. 28(1)(b)(iii); in Kenya, the Arbitration Act 1995 (as amended in 2010), s. 29(3); in the Netherlands, the Arbitration Act 2015, s. 1054(2). Swiss law also comes close to the same position, in the Swiss PIL, s. 187.

F. Specific Issues, Other Applicable Rules, and Guidelines

(a) Legal privilege

3.249 Issues relating to legal privilege arise most commonly, though not exclusively, in international arbitration in the context of document production, where parties invoke attorney–client privilege or legal privilege as a defence to document production requests. In the context of document production or otherwise, parties are free to agree on the law applicable to legal privilege in their dispute.[346] But in the absence of such a choice, and where there is a dispute as to the proper invocation of legal privilege, it falls to a tribunal to determine the applicable law. In this scenario, tribunals are, more commonly than not, faced with the fact that institutional rules do not provide an answer.[347] Nor do national laws treat the matter uniformly: privilege is, in some jurisdictions, considered a substantive issue (the position adopted in many common law countries), while in others it is a procedural matter (particularly in civil law countries), and tends to be addressed as part of domestic litigation procedure rather than as a specific aspect of international arbitration.[348] If the law of the seat and the law of the contract differ, which law should the tribunal apply?

3.250 The uncertainty resulting from the lack of clarity on this issue can have significant practical repercussions. As one commentator has noted: 'in a dispute involving the United States, France, Iran, and China, each and every party (and their lawyers)—where documents, transactions, and communications transcend borders—it is not necessarily clear which national (or international) norms govern privilege and confidentiality.'[349] Thus, a party may enter into an arbitration assuming that certain in-house communications with another in-house colleague located in another country are protected from privilege, only to learn that, depending on the law governing privilege, those conversations may be discoverable and put into evidence in an arbitration.[350]

3.251 In the absence of explicit or implied choice of law, tribunals may employ a closest connection test, looking at the law that has the closest connection to the relevant attorney–client relationship, such as the law of the country where the attorney–client relationship took place.[351]

3.252 This approach resembles that taken by some courts.[352] Such an approach could, however, result in different legal privileges applying to different parties. This has led some tribunals

---

[346] This may be *ex ante* or *ex post*.

[347] For example, none of the ICC, LCIA, nor UNCITRAL Rules provide any guidance in this respect. One exception is the ICDR Rules 2021, which provide in Art. 25 that the arbitral tribunal should (to the extent possible) give 'preference to the rule that provides the highest level of protection'.

[348] See discussion in Mockesch, *Attorney–Client Privilege in International Arbitration* (Oxford University Press, 2016), at paragraphs 8.16–8.17. See also paragraph 8.28 ('There appears to be no national arbitration legislation which expressly mentions the issue of privilege').

[349] Franck, 'International arbitration and attorney–client privilege: Conflict of laws approach' (2019) 51(3) Arizona State Law Journal 938.

[350] Ibid., at 938–939.

[351] If the client and the attorney live in different countries, this law can be either the client's place of business or the attorney's domicile. See Catelli and Brueggemann, 'Evidentiary objections', in Klaesner, Magal, and Neuhaus (eds) *The Guide to Evidence in International Arbitration* (Global Arbitration Review, 2021), p. 96.

[352] See, e.g., *Wellin v Wellin*, 211 F Supp 3d 793 (DSC 2016), where the US District Court of South Carolina used conflicts principles to determine which US state jurisdiction had the 'most significant relationship' with the legal privilege in question.

to apply a 'most-favoured privilege' rule approach, in which the tribunal adopts the law that grants the parties the highest standard of protection.[353] Given their wide discretion as to which law to apply to the question of privilege, some tribunals have adopted a cumulative approach, applying all laws that might have a close connection to the arbitration and searching for commonalities between them.[354] Other tribunals have adopted their own, autonomous standard.[355]

The IBA set out sensible guidelines for counsel and tribunals concerned with issues of legal professional privilege, in its Rules on the Taking of Evidence in International Arbitration (the IBA Rules). The Rules state that at the request of a party or on its own initiative, an arbitral tribunal may exclude from evidence or production any document, statement, or oral testimony where there is 'legal impediment or privilege under the legal or ethical rules determined by the Arbitral Tribunal to be applicable.'[356] The matters that the tribunal is to take into account in considering pleas of legal privilege include (i) the protection of confidentiality, for the purposes of providing or obtaining legal advice; (ii) the protection of confidentiality for the purposes of settlement negotiations; (iii) 'the expectations of the Parties and their advisors at the time the legal impediment or privilege is said to have arisen'; (iv) possible waiver of privilege by consent, earlier disclosure, use of the relevant information, or otherwise; and (v) the need to maintain fairness and equality between the parties, 'particularly if they are subject to different legal or ethical rules'.[357]   **3.253**

The IBA Rules, as we have said previously, form part of the 'soft law' of international arbitration, but it is increasingly common for experienced counsel and arbitrators to adopt them as part of the procedural rules for arbitrations in which they are engaged. Often, however, rather than make the arbitration subject to another set of rules that have to be obeyed, they will be adopted as guidelines. This avoids the risk of any conflict with other rules to which the arbitration may be subject, such as those of an arbitral institution.   **3.254**

(b) Ethical rules

Much has been said and written about the duties to which arbitrators are subject.[358] But what of arbitration practitioners who appear as counsel in international arbitrations, often outside their home jurisdictions? A lawyer appearing in a court action before his or her own local courts will clearly be subject to the rules of professional ethics of his or her local bar.   **3.255**

---

[353] See, e.g., *Blanco v United Mexican States*, ICISD Case No. UNCT/17/1, Procedural Order No. 5 at [17], [19] (the tribunal was 'concerned that applying different standards on the matters of privilege could affect the balance and equality of treatment of the Parties'). For an in-depth analysis of the advantages and disadvantages of each approach, see Stouten and Jansen, 'Legal privilege issues: At the mercy of the arbitral tribunal', 3 June 2021, International Bar Association, available online at https://www.ibanet.org/legal-privilege-arbitral-tribunal.

[354] See, e.g., ICC Case No. 13054, (2014) 25 ICC ICArb Bull Suppl 14.

[355] See, e.g., *Bank for International Settlements*: Procedural Order No 6 (Order with Respect to the Discovery of Certain Documents for Which Attorney-Client Privilege Has Been Claimed), 11 June 2002, Recueil des Sentences Arbitrales, Vol. XXIII, pp. 169–182 (in which the tribunal defined the scope of legal privilege without reference to any national law).

[356] IBA Rules, Art. 9.2.

[357] IBA Rules, Art. 9.4.

[358] Indeed, this is discussed in Chapter 5.

But what if that lawyer practises outside his or her home jurisdiction? And what if he or she is appearing in an arbitration? And what if that arbitration is taking place in yet another different jurisdiction? Will the lawyer remain subject to his or her local bar rules? Will he or she also be subject to the ethical rules applying to lawyers practising in the jurisdiction in which he or she is now based? Will the lawyer also be subject to the ethical rules applying to lawyers conducting legal proceedings in the place of arbitration, if different?

3.256   The answers to these myriad questions can have a significant impact on the conduct of the arbitration. Let us consider, for example, the question of how much contact a lawyer should have with a witness prior to a hearing. In some jurisdictions, such as England, it is not permissible for a lawyer to 'coach' a witness on the evidence to be given at a hearing.[359] In others, constraints on lawyers appear to be far more limited. In her comparison of standards of professional conduct, one commentator put it thus: 'An Australian lawyer felt that from his perspective it would be unethical to prepare a witness; a Canadian lawyer said it would be illegal; and an American lawyer's view was that not to prepare a witness would be malpractice.'[360] Therein lies the problem: counsel in the same procedure, playing to very different rules, with a possible concrete impact on the substantive outcome of the arbitration.

3.257   Until recently, there had been little alternative for counsel other than to ascertain individually the answers to the following questions.

  i.   'Am I subject to my professional bar rules when I am acting in an arbitration, and even when I am acting in an arbitration abroad?'[361]
  ii. 'If I am practising abroad, am I also subject to the professional ethical rules of the jurisdiction in which I am practising?'[362]
  iii. 'If the seat of the arbitration is in a third jurisdiction, am I also subject to the ethical rules of a third bar?'

3.258   It is a matter of concern that the answers to these questions may not be the same for all counsel participating in the same arbitration proceedings. Commentators have for some time questioned whether professional bar rules might be harmonised to apply to practitioners in international arbitration.[363] The idea is attractive, particularly for those concerned to ensure that the playing field for the participants in international arbitration is level. However, the changes necessary to achieve this should not be underestimated. National bar rules around the world would have to make express exceptions to their general

---

[359] Bar Council of England and Wales Code of Conduct, Pt. VII, s. 705(a). See, e.g., *R v Momdou and anor* [2005] EWCA Crim 177 at [45] ('There is no place for witness training in this country, we do not do it. It is unlawful').

[360] Miller, 'Zip to nil? A comparison of American and English lawyers' standards of professional conduct' (1995) CA 32 ALI-ABA 199, at 204.

[361] van Houtte, 'Counsel–witness relations and professional misconduct in civil law systems' (2003) 19 Arb Intl 457. Professor van Houtte argues that Art. 4 ('Applicable Rules of Conduct in Court') of the Code of Conduct for European Lawyers has the effect that whenever the seat of the arbitration is within the EU, the ethical standards of the seat apply. For standards that should apply to participants in the arbitral process, see Veeder, 'The 2001 Goff Lecture: The lawyer's duty to arbitrate in good faith' (2002) 18 Arb Intl 431.

[362] In many jurisdictions, it is a requirement for foreign lawyers practising in the jurisdiction to register with the local bar.

[363] Paulsson, 'Standards of conduct for counsel in international arbitration' (1992) 3 Am Rev Intl Arb 214. In a similar vein, the Code of Conduct for European Lawyers was originally drawn up and adopted in 1998 by the Conseil des Barreaux de la Communauté Européene (CCBE).

codes for international practitioners.[364] It seems certain that such changes are unlikely to happen quickly, if at all.

An alternative means of harmonisation lies in non-binding guidelines. Again, the IBA has taken a lead on this, publishing its Guidelines on Party Representation in International Arbitration in May 2013. The Guidelines, which are intended to provide practical assistance in dealing with ethical issues that arise in international arbitration, provide useful guidance in relation to some of the most frequent issues encountered by practitioners. **3.259**

The Guidelines address five ethical issues that arise in practice, relating to: **3.260**

    i. conflicts of interest (Guidelines 5 and 6);
    ii. *ex parte* communications with arbitrators (Guidelines 7 and 8);
    iii. misleading submissions to the arbitral tribunal (Guidelines 9–11);
    iv. improper information exchange and disclosure (Guidelines 12–17); and
    v. assistance to witnesses and experts (Guidelines 19–24).

In relation to each, the Guidelines set out best practices and recommended approaches. They also propose certain remedies and sanctions, including admonishing the representative, drawing adverse inferences, and altering the apportionment of costs, as well as a broader reference to any 'other measures' that might ensure the fairness and integrity of proceedings.

The leading international arbitral institutions have also taken their first cautious steps towards regulating the conduct of counsel (and parties) in international arbitration. The ICC, for instance, envisages that an arbitral tribunal may sanction unreasonable conduct in making its award of costs. The ICC Rules provide that, in making a decision on costs, the tribunal shall take account of 'such circumstance as it considers relevant, including the extent to which each party has conducted the arbitration in an expeditious and cost-effective manner'.[365] **3.261**

More boldly, the LCIA Rules set out certain provisions governing a party's legal representatives. These include a provision that each party 'shall ensure that all its authorised representatives appearing by name before the Arbitral Tribunal have agreed to comply with the general guidelines contained in the Annex to the LCIA Rules, as a condition of such representation.'[366] The general guidelines in the Annex are designed to promote 'the good and equal conduct of the parties' authorised representatives of the parties appearing by name within the arbitration', and they provide, for example, that a legal representative should not knowingly make any false statement to the arbitral tribunal, should not conceal or assist in the concealment of any document of which production is ordered, and should not initiate any undisclosed contact with an arbitrator. The LCIA Rules also give an arbitral tribunal the power to order sanctions for the violation of the guidelines, including (broadly) the taking of any measure 'necessary to fulfill within the arbitration the general duties required of the Arbitral Tribunal', as defined elsewhere in the Rules.[367] **3.262**

---

[364] The Brussels Bar Rules contain such express exceptions. For a further discussion of the issue, see van Houtte, 'Counsel–witness relations and professional misconduct in civil law systems' (2003) 19 Arb Intl 457.
[365] ICC Rules 2021, Art. 38.5.
[366] LCIA Rules 2020, Art. 18.5.
[367] LCIA Rules 2020, Art. 18.6.

(c) Guidelines

3.263   Every international arbitration—at least in theory—is a microcosm of potential procedural reform. That potentiality is undoubtedly a quality of the arbitral process, but that quality has a price: procedural unpredictability. And it is a price that many in the expanding constituency of arbitration users are increasingly unwilling to pay. To address this unpredictability, in recent years there has been a steady growth in procedural guidelines and recommendations, which now occupy a prominent place in the practice of international arbitration.

3.264   These many rules and guidelines constitute the so-called 'soft law' of international arbitration. They do not seek to alter any local rules and regulations in relation to the conduct of party representatives, nor do they imbue arbitral tribunals with any of the powers held by national courts, professional societies, or other authorities to enforce such rules and regulations. Instead, they are intended by the parties and by the arbitral tribunal as a useful guide in the conduct of an international arbitration. Many of them feature prominently—side-by-side with the applicable laws—in the conduct of international arbitrations. That is why they are referred to, where appropriate, throughout this book.

4

ESTABLISHMENT AND ORGANISATION OF AN ARBITRAL TRIBUNAL

A. Introduction

In order to start an arbitration, an appropriate form of notice or request for arbitration must be delivered in compliance with the relevant procedural rules. These will usually be the rules of the arbitral institution under which the arbitration is to be conducted or the rules referred to in the agreement to arbitrate (such as the UNCITRAL Rules). If there is no agreed upon set of rules, it will be necessary to comply with the rules of the relevant applicable law, which will be the law of the seat of the arbitration. **4.01**

Once the decision to start an arbitration has been taken and the appropriate form of notice or request for arbitration has been delivered, the next step is to establish the arbitral tribunal. Whilst a national court is a standing body to which an application may be made at almost any time, an arbitral tribunal must be brought into existence before it can exercise jurisdiction. This contrast between an arbitral tribunal and a national court is seen most clearly when a dispute has arisen, attempts at settlement have failed, and one of the parties has decided that the time has come to pursue its legal rights. If the dispute is to be taken to court, the claimant need only initiate whatever form of originating process is appropriate to set the machinery of justice into operation. The parties will have no role to play in the composition of that court. It is different if the dispute is to be referred to arbitration, as there is no permanent standing body of arbitrators and no decisions can be taken or relief sought until the tribunal (or in specific circumstances, a preliminary emergency arbitrator) has been appointed. **4.02**

The establishment of the tribunal may be a relatively lengthy process, especially where one party (almost always the respondent) fails to nominate an arbitrator. Even where the relevant rules provide for an institution to make the remaining appointments in the event of default, this can be especially time-consuming as the institution considers and approaches **4.03** suitable candidates.[1] Except in cases that are expedited, the establishment of the tribunal is likely to take at least two months from the submission of the notice or request for arbitration; and in practice it may well take much longer.

4.04   The question then arises: what can be done pending constitution of the arbitral tribunal, if urgent measures are required? The traditional response was to rely on the relevant national courts for critical relief. Most modern arbitral systems permit an application for interim measures to be sought from national courts pending the formation of the tribunal (or even before the initiation of the arbitration), without such application constituting a waiver of the arbitration agreement.[2] To address the parties' need to obtain a quick decision, most institutions have adopted a specific mechanism in their rules.[3] These rules include summary arbitral proceedings,[4] expedited formation of the tribunal,[5] and (increasingly) the expeditious appointment of an 'emergency arbitrator'.[6]

B. Commencement of an Arbitration

(a) Introduction

4.05   The commencement of an arbitration is a significant step not merely as evidence of a real conflict between the parties, but also in terms of compliance with any applicable limitation period for the presentation of claims.

4.06   Time limits for bringing legal proceedings are imposed by the laws of most countries. The interest of the state is that litigation (or arbitration) should be started within a reasonable time of the events that gave rise to it. As a matter of public policy, potential respondents are protected from stale claims, claimants are obliged to be expeditious, and finality is promoted. Prescriptive time limits may also be imposed by contract (as in many standard forms of contract—whether for the charter of a ship or for the carrying out of a major civil engineering project). Limitation periods in litigation or arbitration must always be considered with care as failure to observe them may be fatal in terms of the jurisdiction of the

---

[1]   For example, the ICC may consult with the relevant national committees regarding suitable candidates and may appoint the presiding arbitrator or make default appointments based on the proposal of that committee. If the Court does not accept the proposal, it may repeat its request or seek a proposal from another national committee or directly appoint any person it deems suitable (ICC Rules, Art. 13.3). The Court also has the power to make direct appointments without consulting national committees in certain prescribed circumstances, including where one or more parties is a state or state entity or where the Court considers that it would be appropriate to appoint an arbitrator from a country where there is no National Committee (ICC Rules, Art. 13.4). The LCIA makes all final appointments, taking into account any written agreement or joint nomination by the parties (LCIA Rules, Art. 5.7) and any particular method or criteria for selection agreed in writing by the parties (LCIA Rules, Art. 5.9). Rule 2 of the ICSID Rules provides for a rather cumbersome process whereby the claimant has to propose an appointment mechanism, which, if not accepted by the other party within sixty days, defaults to an institutional system.

[2]   This principle is generally found in arbitration statutes and institutional rules. See, e.g., Model Law, Art. 9; ICC Rules, Art. 28.2. For more detail on the legitimate support that can be obtained in support of an arbitration from national courts, see Chapter 7.

[3]   See, e.g., LCIA Rules, Art. 9; ICDR Rules, Art. 7; NAI Rules, Arts 35.2–36; ICC Rules, Art. 29 and Appendix V.

[4]   See, e.g., NAI Rules, Arts 35.2–36; ICC Rules, Art. 30.

[5]   See, e.g., LCIA Rules, Art. 9A.

[6]   See, e.g., LCIA Rules, Art. 9B; ICDR Rules, Art. 7; ICC Rules, Art. 29 and Appendix V. See paragraphs 4.11ff for a more detailed discussion on Emergency Arbitrators and how these solutions work in practice.

competent forum. Time usually starts to run from the date on which the cause of action arises. In order to toll the limitation (that is, to 'stop the clock') in a dispute subject to arbitration, it will be necessary to take a step to commence the arbitration, usually through the presentation to the relevant institution (or to the opposing party in an ad hoc arbitration) of a request for arbitration. When considering compliance with limitation periods, it is important that potential claimants take account of any steps that must be completed under the relevant arbitration agreement before proceedings can be launched. For example, if there is an obligation in the agreement to engage in amicable negotiations for thirty days, before commencing a claim which is itself subject to a three-year limitation period, those negotiations must be commenced no later than two years and eleven months after the claim arose. This will ensure that the Request for Arbitration can be served within the limitation period.

There may be a difference in both the length and the nature of the time limits established   **4.07** by different national systems of law. One system of law may classify limitation provisions as matters of procedure, to be governed by the law of the place of arbitration, whilst another system may classify them as matters of substance, governed by the same law as that which governs the other substantive matters in issue. In order to avoid any lack of predictability as to the relevant limitation period, many countries have confirmed that limitation should be governed by the law applicable to the contract; and various countries have passed laws to that effect.[7] However, such laws are not universal and the arbitral tribunal will have to determine the legal nature and consequences of the time limits in each case.

(b) Commencement of an arbitration under institutional rules

In order to stop time running, arbitration proceedings must be commenced in accordance   **4.08** with the arbitration agreement and the relevant applicable law. If there is any difference between this law and any applicable institutional rules of arbitration, the provisions of the applicable law will prevail, unless they are waivable. In most cases, however, national laws permit parties to establish rules for commencement of arbitration by agreement, in which case the claimant need only comply with the relevant institutional rules (or the rules set out in the arbitration clause itself).

By way of example, the ICC Rules require a party wishing to commence arbitration to   **4.09** submit a 'Request for Arbitration', which must contain, inter alia, a description of the nature and circumstances of the dispute, a statement of the relief sought, and any observations or proposals concerning the number of arbitrators and their nomination.[8] Article 4.2 of the ICC Rules states that: 'The date on which the Request is received by the Secretariat shall, for all purposes, be deemed to be the date of the commencement of the arbitration.' Similarly, the LCIA Rules treat the arbitration as having commenced on the date upon which the Request (including all accompanying documents) is received electronically by the Registrar provided that the LCIA has received the registration fee.[9]

---

[7] See, e.g., the English Arbitration Act 1996, s. 13; Foreign Limitation Periods Act 1984, s. 1.
[8] ICC Rules, Art. 4.
[9] LCIA Rules, Art. 1.4.

(c) Commencement of an ad hoc arbitration under the applicable law

4.10   Where the arbitration is ad hoc and not subject to any specific rules (such as the UNCITRAL Rules or specific contractual provisions), the law of the place of arbitration needs to be reviewed to establish how to comply with limitation periods. For example, under English law, time will stop running if and when a request for arbitration is made in conformity with the relevant arbitration clause.[10] Under Swiss law, in the absence of contrary agreement, proceedings are commenced 'when a party initiates the procedure for the constitution of the arbitral tribunal'.[11] In contrast, the Brazilian Arbitration Act 1996 provides that '[t]he arbitration shall be deemed to be commenced when the appointment is accepted by the sole arbitrator or by all of the arbitrators if there is more than one'.[12] The Model Law establishes that an arbitration is commenced when a respondent *receives* a request for arbitration from the claimant.[13]

C. Emergency Arbitrators

4.11   As discussed later in this chapter, it takes time to constitute an arbitral tribunal and a party to the prospective arbitration may be in a position in which it cannot afford to wait. For example, it may need to take urgent action to prevent evidence being concealed or destroyed, or to stop an unjustified call on a bank guarantee or to prevent the transfer of assets out of the jurisdiction in which they are situated. To cater for such situations, if such relief is required prior to an arbitral tribunal being constituted, the main institutional arbitration rules provide for the appointment of Emergency Arbitrators as an alternative to the parties seeking interim relief from national courts. For example, the ICC,[14] the LCIA,[15] the International Centre for Dispute Resolution (ICDR),[16] the Swiss Arbitration Centre,[17] the Stockholm Chamber of Commerce (SCC),[18] the Hong Kong International Arbitration Centre (HKIAC),[19] the Singapore International Arbitration Centre (SIAC),[20] the International Institute for Conflict Prevention and Resolution

---

[10] The English Arbitration Act 1996 provides in art. 14(1) that: 'The parties are free to agree when arbitral proceedings are to be regarded as commenced for the purposes of this Part and for the purposes of the Limitation Acts.'

[11] Swiss PIL, Ch. 12, s. 181. In England, the parties may agree upon when the proceedings are to be regarded as commenced for limitation purposes. Failing agreement, it is when one party gives a written notice to the other party or the appointing authority seeking the establishment of the tribunal, English Arbitration Act 1996, s. 14.

[12] Brazilian Arbitration Act 1996, art. 19.

[13] In this respect, Art. 21 of the Model Law provides that: 'Unless otherwise agreed by the parties, the arbitral proceedings in respect of a particular dispute commence on the date on which a request for that dispute to be referred to arbitration is received by the respondent.'

[14] ICC Rules, Art. 29 and Appendix V.

[15] In addition to providing for the expedited formation of the arbitral tribunal (Art. 9A), the LCIA Rules provide for the appointment of an emergency arbitrator at any time prior to the formation or expedited formation of the arbitral tribunal (Art. 9B). Any such application must set out the specific grounds for requiring the appointment of an emergency arbitrator and the specific claim for emergency relief. Importantly, the Rules provide that any such application will not prejudice a party's right to apply to a national court for interim or conservatory measures before the formation of the arbitral tribunal (Art. 9B.13).

[16] ICDR Rules, Art. 7.

[17] Swiss Rules, Art. 43.

[18] SCC Rules, Appendix II.

[19] HKIAC Rules, Art. 23; Sch. 4.

[20] SIAC Rules, Art. 30.2; Sch. 1.

(CPR) Rules,[21] and the Milan Chamber of Arbitration[22] all provide for Emergency Arbitrator appointments.

Recent changes to these rules ensure that they now apply automatically and do not require a specific opt-in, which had previously limited their scope.   **4.12**

In general, the rules allow parties to appoint an Emergency Arbitrator to determine applications for interim relief as soon as a request for arbitration has been filed or, in some cases, even earlier.[23] Indeed, some institutional rules now give the Emergency Arbitrator the power to order *ex parte* relief, subject to the other party being heard immediately after the preliminary order is granted.[24]   **4.13**

A useful example of the appointment mechanism is set out in the ICC Rules, under which a party may ask the ICC to consider the appointment of an Emergency Arbitrator by sending an application to the Secretariat, together with the relevant supporting documentation and payment of the prescribed fee.[25] If the application is made *before* the applicant files its Request for Arbitration, such a Request must be sent to the Secretariat within ten days to avoid the termination of the emergency proceedings.[26] The Emergency Arbitrator will normally be appointed within two days of the application and must make an order within fifteen days of receiving the file (although this can be extended by the President of the ICC Court pursuant to a reasoned request from the Emergency Arbitrator or if deemed necessary).[27] However, the procedure will not be available if: (a) the arbitration agreement between the parties was concluded *before* the date on which Emergency Arbitrator provisions were introduced into the Rules (January 2012); or (b) the parties have agreed to opt out of these provisions; or (c) the arbitration agreement upon which the application is based arises from a treaty.[28]   **4.14**

Under most rules, including the ICC Rules, the Emergency Arbitrator's decision is interim in nature and will not bind the arbitral tribunal.[29] Although Article 29.2 of the ICC Rules requires the parties to undertake to comply with any order made by the Emergency Arbitrator, the consequences of non-compliance are uncertain. Parties will still need to rely on the support of the national courts to enforce interim measures granted by an Emergency Arbitrator and it is not yet clear whether such enforcement will be granted, given that an interim 'order' is unlikely to qualify as an award and therefore be enforceable under the   **4.15**

---

[21] International Institute for Conflict Prevention and Resolution (CPR) Rules, r. 14.

[22] Milan Chamber of Arbitration Rules, Art. 44. However, because Italian law does not allow arbitrators to issue interim orders (Italian Code of Civil Procedure, art. 818), provisional measures ordered by Emergency Arbitrators have a contractual nature.

[23] The LCIA Rules (Art. 9B), ICC Rules (Art. 29.1), SCC Rules (see Appendix II, Art. 9.4.iii), and the Swiss Rules (Art. 43) permit the appointment of an Emergency Arbitrator before the notice of arbitration is filed. Others, including the SIAC (Sch. 1, Art. 1), ICDR (Art. 7.1 *in fine*), and ACICA Rules (Art. 33; Sch. 1, Art. 1.1.2.b), require that it be filed with or after the notice of arbitration.

[24] For example, Swiss Rules, Arts 43.1 and 26.3.

[25] ICC Rules, Art. 29 and Appendix V, Art. 1.3. The costs of an Emergency Arbitrator Proceeding is set out in Appendix V, Art. 7.1. By the year 2020, the ICC had received more than 140 applications for the appointment of an Emergency Arbitrator.

[26] ICC Rules, Appendix V, Art. 1.6.

[27] ICC Rules, Appendix V, Arts 2.1 and 6.4.

[28] ICC Rules, Art. 29.6.

[29] ICC Rules, Art. 29.3.

New York Convention.[30] However, in some jurisdictions, specific legislative changes have been introduced to ensure that the orders of Emergency Arbitrators are treated in the same way as those of an arbitral tribunal.[31]

D. How Many Arbitrators?

(a) Introduction

4.16   The establishment of an arbitral tribunal involves many considerations. First, should there be more than one arbitrator, and if so, how many more ? Some national laws sensibly provide that the number of arbitrators must be uneven. Clauses providing for two arbitrators and an 'umpire', used historically in shipping and commodities disputes, are now largely relics and in any event unsuitable for contemporary international arbitration.[32] Tribunals of five (or more) arbitrators are best reserved for arbitrations between sovereign states.[33] In commercial cases, the choice is usually between one arbitrator and three, and in investment arbitrations, it is usual for three members to be appointed.

(b) Sole arbitrators

4.17   Article 12.2 of the ICC Rules provides that, where the parties have not agreed upon the number of arbitrators, the Court shall appoint a sole arbitrator unless it appears to the Court that 'the dispute is such as to warrant the appointment of three arbitrators'. Following the same policy, Article 5.8 of the LCIA Rules states: 'A sole arbitrator shall be appointed unless the parties have agreed in writing otherwise or the LCIA Court determines that in the circumstances a three-member tribunal is appropriate (or, exceptionally, more than three).'

4.18   The ICDR Rules adopt a similar approach, with a sole arbitrator being the default solution, although the size and complexity of the case will be taken into account in the decision as to whether or not to constitute a three-member tribunal. Article 12 provides:

---

[30] See Raid Abu-Manneh, 'Emergency Arbitrators: the Case for Enforcement', IBA Arbitration Committee (2021), available online at https://www.ibanet.org/LPD/Dispute_Resolution_Section/Arbitration/Publications. aspx.

[31] For example, the Singapore International Arbitration Act 2012 (art. 2.1) was amended so that the definition of 'arbitral tribunal' included Emergency Arbitrators.

[32] The LMAA still recognises the possibility of two arbitrators and an umpire in its Rules (LMAA Terms 2021, Art. 9) but, absent a specific agreement on the number of arbitrators, three arbitrators will be appointed (LMAA Terms, Art. 8.a).

[33] For example, *Mexico v USA (Cross-Border Trucking)* USA-98–2008–01, 6 February 2001, in which one of the authors was the chair of the tribunal, available online at http://www.nafta-sec-alena.org/. The USMCA, like its predecessor the NAFTA, provides for the appointment of a 'panel' of five members in inter-state disputes without calling them 'arbitrators' (Art. 31.9.1(a)). Other examples may be found online at http://www.pca-cpa.org/, e.g. *Ireland v United Kingdom (Mox Plant)*, an arbitration pursuant to Annex VII of UNCLOS, and *Channel Tunnel Group Ltd and France-Manche SA v United Kingdom and France*, UNCITRAL, PCA, Partial Award, 30 January 2007, IIC 58 (2007), an arbitration brought under a concession agreement between the parties in accordance with Art. 19 of the Treaty of Canterbury between the United Kingdom and France, dated 12 February 1986. A more recent example is *The 'Enrica Lexie' Incident (Italy v India)*, PCA Case No. 2015-28. In 2018, an award was rendered by the first ever five-member ICC tribunal in *PT Ventures v Unitel*, ICC Case No. 21404/ASM.

If the parties have not agreed on the number of arbitrators, one arbitrator shall be appointed unless the Administrator determines that three arbitrators are appropriate because of the size, complexity, or other circumstances of the case.[34]

The advantages of referring a dispute to a sole arbitrator are self-evident. Appointments for meetings or hearings can more easily be arranged. The interests of economy are also served since the parties will have to bear the fees and expenses of only one arbitrator. Moreover, the arbitral proceedings should be completed more quickly, since (obviously) a sole arbitrator does not need to 'deliberate' with colleagues to arrive at an agreed, or majority, decision. If the parties to an international arbitration are able to agree upon the appointment of a sole arbitrator, it makes sense for them to do so, unless the amounts in dispute are so high that it seems more prudent to appoint three arbitrators. The disadvantages of a sole arbitrator include a possibly greater risk of error since sole arbitrators do not benefit from a broader discussion of the case with their co-arbitrators.[35]   **4.19**

Where the agreement provides for a sole arbitrator, and the parties cannot agree on the person to be appointed, an arbitrator will be chosen for them by a national court or by an agreed appointing authority[36] (thus depriving the parties of one of the fundamental benefits of arbitration, namely participating in the choice of the tribunal).   **4.20**

In practice, there is usually a preference for the appointment of three arbitrators in all but the smallest cases. The UNCITRAL Rules reflect this preference by providing that if the parties have not previously agreed otherwise, three arbitrators will be appointed[37] and a similar provision is contained in the Model Law.[38]   **4.21**

(c) Three arbitrators

The preference for international disputes to be referred to three arbitrators has much to commend it. It means that each party will usually be entitled to nominate one arbitrator, leaving the third arbitrator to be chosen either by agreement of the parties, or by the two party-appointed arbitrators, or by an institution. The advantage to a party of being able to nominate an arbitrator is that it gives a sense of investment in the arbitral tribunal. Each party will have at least one 'judge of its choice' to listen to its case.[39] This is particularly important in an international arbitration, where a party may select an arbitrator who will   **4.22**

---

[34] Pursuant to the ICDR Rules, Art. 1.1, the ICDR is the 'administrator' of the rules.

[35] An error in an arbitral award is potentially more serious in arbitration since, unlike the courts where errors by a first instance judge sitting alone can be corrected on appeal, an arbitral award is generally final on the merits.

[36] The procedure for the appointment of arbitrators is discussed at paragraphs 4.25*ff.*

[37] UNCITRAL Rules, Art. 7.1.

[38] Model Law, Art. 10(2).

[39] The expression 'judge of its choice' comes from the Hague Conventions on the Pacific Settlement of International Disputes of 1899 (Art. 15) and 1907 (Art. 37). However, there is a debate as to the pros and cons of party appointments within the arbitral process. See Paulsson, 'Moral hazard in international dispute resolution', Inaugural lecture as holder of Michael R. Klein Distinguished Scholar Chair, University of Miami School of Law, Miami, FL, 29 April 2010; Brower and Rosenberg, 'The death of the two-headed nightingale: Why the Paulsson–van den Berg presumption that party-appointed arbitrators are untrustworthy is wrongheaded' (2013) 29 Arb Intl 43. See also the analysis in Gomez-Acebo, *Party-Appointed Arbitrators in International Commercial Arbitration* (Kluwer Law International, 2016).

be able to explain to the other tribunal members any differences of language, tradition, or culture between the parties. In addition, party-appointed arbitrators can help to clarify the case advanced by their appointing party, whilst remaining independent and impartial, and so fulfil a useful role in ensuring due process.

4.23   A three-member tribunal is inevitably more expensive than one that consists of a sole arbitrator and it will usually take longer to render its award. However, as already stated, the risk of an error of law or fact by a three-member tribunal is likely to be lower than it is with a sole arbitrator.

(d) More than three arbitrators

4.24   Even in a case of major importance, three carefully chosen and appropriately qualified arbitrators should be sufficient to dispose satisfactorily of the issues in dispute. The occasional practice of states in agreeing inter-state arbitral tribunals of five, seven, or more is usually dictated by political, rather than by practical, considerations.

E. Appointment of Arbitrators

4.25   There are several methods of appointing an arbitral tribunal. The most usual are: (i) by agreement of the parties; (ii) by an arbitral institution; (iii) by means of a list system; (iv) by means of the co-arbitrators appointing a presiding arbitrator; (v) by a professional institution or a trade association; (vi) by a national court; or (vii) by an appointing authority. Each method is now considered in turn.

(a) Agreement of the parties

4.26   As we have previously stated (i) a major attraction of arbitration is that it allows parties to submit a dispute to judges of their choice, and (ii) where the arbitral tribunal is to consist of three arbitrators, it is usual for each party to nominate one arbitrator, leaving the third arbitrator to be appointed by one of the methods mentioned above. Where possible, an agreement is always preferable.

4.27   From time to time, a respondent may seek to derail an arbitration which it seems destined to lose, by refusing to appoint an arbitrator. The party-appointed arbitrators may also try but fail to agree on a presiding arbitrator. A reliable arbitral institution will almost invariably have a provision in its rules that will allow it to make the necessary appointment in the event of default.[40] In a situation where such a provision does not exist (for example, in an ad hoc arbitration), it may be necessary to rely on the law of the seat of the arbitration and to ask for the appointment to be made by the competent national courts. However, relying on national courts to appoint is likely to lead to delay and uncertainty, particularly if the relevant court does not have a sufficiently international perspective to make a suitable appointment.

---

[40] See, e.g., ICC Rules, Art. 12.2; LCIA Rules, Art. 7.2.

It is therefore sensible to ensure that there is a provision for the 'default appointment' of an arbitrator in the arbitration agreement itself. This can be done either by choosing an arbitral institution whose rules provide for a default appointment or, in an ad hoc arbitration, by nominating an appointing authority that will make such an appointment.

(b) Appointment by arbitral institutions

4.28 Arbitral institutions each have their own rules for appointing arbitrators. The ICC Rules, for example, provide that where there is to be a sole arbitrator and the parties fail to reach an agreed nomination within thirty days from the communication of the Request for Arbitration, the arbitrator will be appointed by the ICC Court.[41] The Rules also provide that, where there is to be an arbitral tribunal of three arbitrators, the third arbitrator will be appointed by the ICC Court, unless the parties have agreed upon another procedure, in which case the agreed appointment must be made within a limited time.[42] In contrast, the rules of the China International Economic and Trade Arbitration Commission (CIETAC) require the parties to nominate their respective arbitrators from CIETAC's designated panel of arbitrators; alternatively, if they agree to nominate from outside the panel of arbitrators, then that nomination is subject to confirmation by the chair of CIETAC.[43]

4.29 As we indicated earlier, in referring to default appointments in ad hoc arbitrations, many arbitral institutions offer their services as 'appointing authority' for a fee, including the ICC, the ICDR, the LCIA, and the PCA in The Hague.[44] The Secretary-General of ICSID is also prepared to act as 'designating', or appointing, authority for ad hoc arbitration agreements that do not fall within the scope of the ICSID Convention.[45] It is always worth considering the use of these services in an ad hoc arbitration. What the arbitral institutions and international bodies have to offer, compared to national courts or professional societies and trade associations, is their day-to-day involvement in international arbitration and their access to (and knowledge of) a pool of highly qualified arbitrators.

(c) List system

4.30 A 'list system' is often used to assist the parties to reach agreement over the identity of the president of the arbitral tribunal. Typically, the parties will agree on a list of the required criteria (for example, experience, language, nationality) and then each party will compile a list of three or four persons considered to be acceptable as arbitrators who comply with those criteria, perhaps with a brief note of the relevant experience and qualifications of each. The lists are then exchanged simultaneously in an attempt to reach agreement. If there is a

---

[41] ICC Rules, Art. 12.3.
[42] ICC Rules, Art. 12.4 and 12.5.
[43] CIETAC Rules, Art. 26.
[44] The fees for this service are typically £1,250 for the LCIA (Schedule of Costs), €3,000 for the secretary-general of the PCA, US$5,000 for the ICC, and US$2,500–5,000 for ICDR (Canada). These figures are available on each institution's website. See Rules of ICC as Appointing Authority in UNCITRAL or other arbitration proceedings, Appendix, Art. 1; ICDR Canadian Rules, p. 42.
[45] https://icsid.worldbank.org/services/appointments-challenges/appointing-authority.

common candidate, that person is appointed president. Even if this is not the case, the process focuses the thinking of the parties and may help to pave the way towards agreement.[46]

4.31   A variation on this system, used by some arbitral institutions (particularly the ICDR, the SCC, and the Netherlands Arbitration Institute (NAI)), is the dispatch by the institution of the *same* list of names to each party.[47] Each party then returns the list, deleting any name to which it objects and grading the remainder in order of preference. The appointing authority then chooses an arbitrator from the list, in accordance with the order of preference indicated by the parties. The system is slower than that of direct appointment by an arbitral institution but has the advantage of offering an element of choice (even though this choice is restricted to persons initially named by the institution on its list). This procedure may be used to appoint a sole arbitrator as well as to choose the presiding arbitrator.[48]

(d) Appointment by co-arbitrators of the presiding arbitrator

4.32   Where a tribunal of three arbitrators is to be constituted, the arbitration clause or submission agreement often provides that each party is to nominate one arbitrator and that the two arbitrators so nominated will choose the third, who acts as the presiding arbitrator. The same solution is also found in some arbitration rules.[49] This is undoubtedly the most satisfactory way of nominating a third arbitrator, since the party-nominated arbitrators will have confidence in their chosen candidate and their ability to work well together. Before putting forward a possible candidate, it is usual for each of the arbitrators to inform its appointing party of the candidate or candidates that the two co-arbitrators are considering for appointment, so as to ensure that there is not some well-founded objection to that candidate (for instance, a conflict of interest or history of personal animosity). This is considered an acceptable exception to the general rule that there should be 'no *ex parte* communication' in international arbitration.[50] To avoid any misunderstandings, the party-nominated arbitrators should inform each other that they are following this procedure.[51]

---

[46]   One problem that has arisen in practice when the list system has failed and the appointment has been left to a third-party institution, or court, relates to the appointing authority appointing a person who has appeared on one of the party's lists. It is not uncommon for the other party to object to such an appointment on the basis that the candidate has already been discussed by the parties, thereby 'burning' all of those names. To avoid this risk, it is useful to agree in advance that the inclusion of a name on the list will not operate as a bar to the eventual appointment of such a person by the arbitral institution or appointing authority. Another, more tactical, approach is for a party not to nominate the person whom it wants on the first list, but to keep the name in reserve, so that it might emerge in subsequent negotiations. However, such gamesmanship may prove to be self-defeating if the other party agrees to a person named on the first list!

[47]   ICDR Rules, Art. 13.6.

[48]   UNCITRAL Rules, Arts 8.2 and 9.3.

[49]   UNCITRAL Rules, Art. 9.1.

[50]   The IBA Guidelines on Party Representation provide that communications between a party representative and a prospective or party-nominated arbitrator relating to the selection of the presiding arbitrator fall outside the general rule that party representatives should not engage in *ex parte* communications with an arbitrator concerning the arbitration (see Guideline 8(b)).

[51]   As an alternative method to avoid the problem of biased arbitrators, the CPR Rules provide that neither the CPR nor the parties shall advise or otherwise provide any information or indication to any arbitrator candidate or appointed arbitrator as to which party selected either of the party-designated arbitrators ('blind appointments') (r. 5.4).

(e) Professional institution

The president or a senior officer of a professional institution may be named as the appointing authority in arbitration clauses, but before doing this, the parties should ensure that the institution will in fact provide this service, that the person concerned will accept the role, and that the terms (cost and time) of such appointment are understood. In general terms, it is not an option that we would recommend, as it is unlikely that the institution concerned will have a strong knowledge of suitable candidates for an international arbitration; and if there are specialist issues which fall within the knowledge and experience of the members of a particular institution, these can usually be more suitably addressed through expert evidence. More importantly, it is usually impossible to know whether a specific dispute will be of a technical or legal nature before it arises.[52]   **4.33**

(f) National courts

If the parties are unable to reach agreement upon the appointment of an arbitrator and no one is empowered in the arbitration clause or submission agreement to make the appointment for them, the courts of the seat will usually have the power to nominate any remaining members of the tribunal, irrespective of the nationality of the parties or the law governing the substance of the dispute. The relevant rules are usually set out in the arbitration law of the seat (which may be a separate statute or part of a wider code of civil procedure). It is usually sufficient for the claimant (who is invariably the party interested in proceeding speedily) to apply to the relevant court for the appointment. For example, under the English Arbitration Act, the courts have default powers to: **4.34**

- give directions as to the making of any necessary appointments
- direct that the tribunal shall be constituted by such appointments (or any one or more of them) as have been made
- revoke any appointments already made
- make any necessary appointments itself[53]

In making any appointments, a court will often ask the parties' lawyers, or the party-nominated arbitrators, to suggest possible candidates.

In principle, a national court will have jurisdiction where the arbitration is to be conducted on its territory.[54] Accordingly, there should be no problem where the seat of arbitration is specified in the arbitration clause or submission agreement: the party wishing to proceed with the arbitration simply applies to the national courts for the appointment to be made.   **4.35**

---

[52] There may be exceptions, e.g. where the nature of the contract is likely to implicate only the area of expertise of the institution. For example, one author was appointed chair of an ad hoc arbitral tribunal by the President of the Law Society of England and Wales (the governing authority of the solicitors' branch of the profession) acting as the appointing authority in a dispute under a severance agreement between a solicitor who was a partner of a law firm and the firm itself, where issues of solicitors' ethics were concerned. It was thus sensible for a solicitor (which the institution was well-placed to identify) to be appointed as arbitrator.

[53] English Arbitration Act 1996, s. 18(3).

[54] See the discussion concerning the *lex arbitri* in Chapter 3, paragraphs 3.42*ff.*

However, a problem arises if the seat of arbitration has not been specified in the arbitration clause or submission agreement. It may be possible to persuade a court to assume jurisdiction, for example on the basis that the law governing the substantive issues in dispute is the law of the country of that court, or that the respondent is within the jurisdiction of the court (and so capable of being compelled to carry out its orders).[55]

4.36   This situation offers a clear example of the dangers inherent in a defective, or 'pathological', arbitration clause. A clause that fails to provide either for an effective method of constituting the arbitral tribunal or for the place of arbitration risks being inoperable. If a claimant takes its case to a national court, it may be met by an application for a stay of the proceedings on the grounds of the existence of an arbitration clause. At best, there is considerable potential for delay. At worst, there is the possibility that the claimant may be deprived of an effective remedy.

4.37   Countries with developed systems of arbitration law recognise the role that needs to be played by their law and by their courts in assisting the arbitral process. Accordingly, national courts are usually empowered to appoint arbitrators where necessary. Wide powers to appoint arbitrators are contained in most modern national arbitration laws.[56] However, the position under the relevant local law should be checked carefully at the time of selecting the place of arbitration.

(g) Appointing authority

4.38   As we have already emphasised, parties should recognise that in an ad hoc arbitration, it is in their common interest to choose an appointing authority by agreement (such as the PCA)—or, at least, to choose a method of designating an appointing authority. One way of doing this is to adopt the UNCITRAL Rules. Under these Rules, if the parties have not agreed upon an appointing authority, a party may request the Secretary-General of the PCA to designate one.[57]

(h) Designation by the Secretary-General of the PCA

4.39   The UNCITRAL Rules do not specify the information that must be supplied to the Secretary-General of the PCA for the purposes of designating an appointing authority.

---

[55] For example, the English court may appoint an arbitrator where the seat of arbitration has not been designated, provided that the proceedings have sufficient connection with England, English Arbitration Act 1996, ss. 2(4) and 18. Under French law, the French courts may act in support of an international arbitration located abroad if (a) the parties have agreed that French procedural law shall apply to the arbitration; (b) the parties have expressly granted jurisdiction to French courts over disputes relating to the arbitral procedure; or (c) one of the parties is exposed to a risk of a denial of justice (understood as the impossibility to constitute the arbitral tribunal by any other means). See French Code of Civil Procedure, art. 1505. See also Seraglini and Ortscheidt, *Droit de l'Arbitrage Interne et International* (2nd edn, LGDJ, 2019), paras 774–781.

[56] See, e.g., Swiss PIL, Ch. 12, s. 179; French Code of Civil Procedure, art. 1452. Article 11(4) of the Model Law confers upon the appropriate national courts the power to appoint arbitrators where necessary. The English Arbitration Act 1996, s. 18, gives the court the power to make an appointment in the event of a failure of the procedure for the appointment of the arbitral tribunal.

[57] UNCITRAL Rules, Art. 6.2.

However, in practice, the PCA asks for the same documents as are required under Article 6.6 of the UNCITRAL Rules or the appointment of an arbitrator. These documents include the notice of arbitration and the response, if it exists. The Secretary-General will usually also request copies of correspondence indicating that the designation of an appointing authority is necessary because a party has failed to appoint an arbitrator, or that it has been impossible to reach agreement on a sole or presiding arbitrator, or that there is a challenge to an arbitrator.

If the respondent does not participate in making a request, the Secretary-General writes to the respondent to invite comments and specifies a reasonable time for reply. Before designating an appointing authority, the Secretary-General may also ask for the names of potential arbitrators and appointing authorities that have been discussed between the parties and rejected.[58] After reviewing the documents submitted and considering any comments from the parties, the Secretary-General selects the organisation or individual that he or she considers best placed to act as appointing authority.[59] The Secretary-General then enquires whether that organisation or individual is willing to accept the designation. If the answer is in the affirmative, the parties are informed and requested to approach the appointing authority directly for the next steps. The Secretary-General does not give reasons for the decision.[60] **4.40**

F. Qualities Required in International Arbitrators

(a) Introduction

Choosing the right arbitral tribunal is critical to the success of the arbitral process. It is a very important choice, not only for the parties to the dispute, but also for the reputation and standing of the process itself. It is, above all, the quality of the arbitrators that makes or breaks an arbitration. The parties' ability to select a 'judge of their choice'[61] is one of the distinguishing features of arbitration as opposed to proceedings before the courts of law. It is important that this choice should be made wisely. **4.41**

---

[58] Hence the need to be clear, before discussing candidates between the parties, as to whether the candidates rejected may subsequently be appointed by an appointing authority, or if they are excluded or 'burned' as a result. Most parties agree to a 'no burn' rule whereby candidates rejected between the parties may still be appointed by the appointing authority.

[59] The views of the parties, as well as concerns of speed and cost, may influence the Secretary-General's choice of an individual, rather than of an organisation. The Secretary-General's designations of organisations include the ACICA, the AAA, the Arbitral Centre of the Austrian Federal Economic Chamber, the Bombay Incorporated Law Society, the CRCICA, the CIArb, the DIS, the HKIAC, the ICC, ICSID, the KLRCA, the LCIA, SIAC, and the SAA. Examples of designations of individuals include: a former chief justice of New South Wales, Australia, in a dispute between a Korean company and an Asian state entity; an international arbitration practitioner based in the United Kingdom, in a dispute between a French company and the government of a Central European Republic; and an international arbitration practitioner based in the United States, in a dispute between a Dutch company and an African state entity.

[60] In 2019, the PCA received 39 requests to designate an appointing authority or to act directly as the appointing authority. See PCA, *Annual Report of the Permanent Court of Arbitration* (PCA, 2019), p. 10.

[61] See fn. 39.

4.42   In most arbitration systems, any natural person may be chosen to act as an arbitrator, the only general requirements being that the person chosen must have legal capacity and be independent and impartial. Sometimes, however, parties to an arbitration will find that this choice is limited by the restrictions placed on that choice by the clause, the institution, or the applicable statutory rules.

(b) Restrictions imposed by the contract

4.43   Some standard forms of international contracts—particularly those used in the shipping and commodity trades, and the insurance and reinsurance industries—identify the kind of arbitrator to be chosen in the event of a dispute. Some institutional rules require that the arbitrator be nominated from a list held by that institution.[62] In general terms, it is not advisable to fix a list of qualifications, since there may not be someone who both fulfils those criteria and is available to act as an arbitrator at the time that the dispute arises, with the risk that the arbitral clause will be inoperable. For example, one author recalls a clause requiring 'a native English speaker with experience in Brazilian law and the oil and gas industry'. Such detailed qualifications are rarely a good idea: not only are they likely to cause delay in ascertaining whether or not a particular arbitrator comes within the criteria but they may also create unnecessary additional grounds for an obstreperous losing party to challenge an unfavourable award on the basis that the 'composition of the arbitral tribunal or the arbitral procedure was not in accordance with the agreement of the parties'.[63] It is also difficult to choose the qualifications of an arbitrator before the specific nature of the dispute is known. Will a claim be large or small? Is it essentially a legal problem, or does it turn mostly on the facts, the technical aspects of a specific industry, or the quantum of the claim? Is particular expertise required to evaluate the facts quickly and correctly? In which language are the relevant documents? These questions need to be answered before the most suitable arbitrator(s) can be chosen; 'horses for courses' is a rule that applies beyond the race track and is one best applied once the parties know the nature of the dispute. The only restrictions that may be of use are those linked to fluency in the language of the contract (or the likely language of the dispute) and, occasionally, on the residence or nationality of the arbitrators (with the aim of avoiding arbitrators with the same nationality as one of the parties).[64]

4.44   If a potential arbitrator is confronted with specific criteria that have been included in a contract, it is good practice to obtain a clear written confirmation from the parties at the beginning of the arbitral process that the criteria are considered fulfilled, or a clear waiver that a particular requirement is no longer considered necessary. In this way, the arbitrator will avoid the risk of the issue being later deployed by a party in proceedings seeking to annul the award or as a defence to enforcement of the award if it has lost the arbitration.[65]

---

[62] For instance, under the ICSID Convention, if the Chair of the Administrative Council is to appoint the arbitrator(s) he or she must appoint from the Panel of Arbitrators held by the Centre. The parties to the dispute are not subject to such restriction. See ICSID Convention, Art. 40. See also AAA Rules, Arts 3 and 12.

[63] See Model Law, Art. 32(2)(a)(iv).

[64] In this regard, see the discussion of the English courts' decisions in *Jivraj v Hashwani* on the validity of nationality limitations on arbitrator appointments, at paragraph 4.57.

[65] For example, on the basis that the arbitral tribunal was not constituted in accordance with the agreement of the parties: see New York Convention, Art. V(1)(d). See also Model Law, Art. 34(2)(a)(iv).

(c) Restrictions imposed by the applicable law

The most common (and reasonable) requirement imposed by national laws on the choice   **4.45**
of an arbitrator is that of having legal capacity.[66] The number of countries that impose other
restrictions has decreased since the early editions of this work. Spain, for example, repealed
its former rule that the arbitrator must be a qualified lawyer where the dispute involves issues of law.[67] In 2012, Saudi Arabia removed the requirement that all arbitrators be male
and have knowledge of Shari'ah law (although the presiding arbitrator in a panel of three is
still required to hold a university degree in Shari'ah law).[68]

(d) Professional qualifications

International disputes are too varied and numerous for it to be sensible to identify any gen-   **4.46**
eral rule as to the kind of person who should be chosen to act as an arbitrator. Parties must
make up their own minds as to the qualifications that they require. The most that can be
done is to indicate some of the more important considerations.

(i) Sole arbitrator
In international arbitrations before a sole arbitrator, it is usual to appoint a lawyer. Even   **4.47**
where the dispute is relatively simple, difficult problems of procedure and of conflict of laws
may arise. These are problems that a lawyer with suitable procedural and legal experience
is generally better equipped to handle than a person whose expertise lies in another area. In
most international arbitrations, arbitrators are lawyers or professors of law.[69]

(ii) Three arbitrators
Where the arbitral tribunal is to consist of three arbitrators, at least one member of the   **4.48**
arbitral tribunal (preferably the presiding arbitrator) should be a lawyer, or at least a
person who has considerable experience of acting as arbitrator in international disputes,
since someone will need to understand how to manage the arbitration and to drive it
forward.

There is no reason why the other members of the arbitral tribunal should also be lawyers,   **4.49**
unless the issues involved are principally complex issues of law. Part of the attraction of arbitration is the way in which the expertise necessary for the understanding and resolution
of the dispute may be found amongst the arbitrators themselves. For example, in disputes
involving matters of a technical nature, such as construction, quantum, or scientific issues,

---

[66] See for instance the French Code of Civil Procedure, art. 1451.
[67] Spanish Arbitration Act 2003, s. 13, repealing the 1988 Act, s. 12(2).
[68] Saudi Arabia's new arbitration law came into force in July 2012. The new Arbitration Regulation (Royal Decree
No. M/34) is based on the principles of the Model Law and has significantly modernised the pre-existing law in
many respects, including in the requirements of arbitrators: see Harb and Leventhal, 'The new Saudi Arbitration
Law: Modernization to the tune of Shari'a' (2013) 30 J Intl Arb 113.
[69] For a view on the varied profiles of arbitrators in investment arbitration, which regularly includes retired diplomats, migrating commercial arbitrators, and former judges, see van den Berg, 'Qualified investment arbitrators?',
in Wautelet, Kruger, and Coppens (eds) *The Practice of Arbitration: Essays in Honour of Hans van Houtte* (Hart
Publishing, 2012), p. 54.

it may be appropriate that one (or more) of the arbitrators be a civil engineer, an economist, or someone skilled in the technical matters at issue.[70]

4.50   However, if the presiding arbitrator is likely to be a lawyer, a party should consider carefully before nominating a technical arbitrator in cases in which the other party has nominated a lawyer. This combination may result in the arbitral tribunal having two lawyers who communicate fluently between themselves and a technical expert arbitrator with perhaps a more limited interaction.[71] It may therefore be better tactically for the parties to seek to agree that, given the technical nature of a particular dispute, each will appoint, say, an engineer or an economist, with a lawyer as the presiding arbitrator.

(e) Language

4.51   Arbitrators must have an adequate working knowledge of the language in which the arbitration is to be conducted, so that they can manage the procedure, understand the written and oral arguments of the parties, and be competent to draft an award in that working language. Arbitrators should also be able to understand the language in which most of the written and oral evidence is produced. Whilst English has generally been adopted as the working language of international commerce for contracts between parties who speak different languages, the underlying documents and evidence will not always be in that language. If an arbitrator is appointed who does not have a sufficient knowledge of the language of the evidence, it becomes necessary to engage translators and interpreters to translate the evidence of the witnesses and the documents into a language that the arbitrator concerned *can* understand. This circumstance may both affect the efficiency and increase the costs of the arbitration.

(f) Experience, diversity, and outlook

4.52   In addition to choosing an arbitrator with appropriate knowledge of the relevant area of law, it is essential for parties to recognise the importance of experience in international arbitration, particularly for a sole arbitrator or for the presiding arbitrator who is usually solely responsible for the proper and effective control of the proceedings. The sole or presiding arbitrator may have to perform this function against the background of differences of culture and legal training on the part of the parties and particularly of their counsel. At the same time, the proceedings must maintain their momentum and not be allowed to sink into a

---

[70] For instance, in the *Indus Waters Kishenganga (Pakistan v India)* arbitration brought before the PCA, which involved complex hydrogeological issues, one of the arbitrators appointed was Professor Howard S. Wheater FREng, an expert in hydrological science and water resource management (PCA Case No. 2011-01). In this regard, a 2016 survey reports that the commercial understanding of the industry sector is the most important factor in nominating arbitrators for technology, media, and telecoms disputes, followed by knowledge of the law applicable to the contract/arbitration. See Pinsent Masons and Queen Mary University of London, 'Pre-empting and Resolving Technology, Media and Telecoms Disputes', p. 33, available online at http://www.arbitration.qmul.ac.uk/media/arbitration/docs/Fixing_Tech_report_online_singles.pdf.

[71] Even when all of the arbitrators are lawyers, the parties can and should ensure that the technical aspects of the dispute are well understood, by submitting the reports of technical experts.

quagmire of procedural disputes. There may be language problems, both in relation to communications between members of the arbitral tribunal and in the reception of evidence. A timetable and procedure must be set for the various steps of the arbitration (including presentation of submissions, production of documents, exchange of witness statements and expert reports, and rules for the final hearing), as well as dealing with logistical and administrative matters, including the unique challenges of remote hearings, which are becoming more common. These are all tasks that call for skill and, above all, experience in the practice of international arbitration.

Careful thought should therefore be given to the experience or outlook of an arbitrator. Relevant questions to assess whether a particular candidate may be the right choice include: Will the person be organised and efficient? Will the person have enough availability? What is his or her ability to handle procedural issues? Does he or she have sufficient knowledge of the applicable substantive law? Is he or she likely to be a consensus builder? What kind of approach does he or she have to damages calculation issues? What is the candidate's approach to technology (for example, can they work with electronic pleadings and documents) and can they conduct remote virtual hearings efficiently?[72] Many of these questions can be answered only by experienced practitioners familiar with the community of international arbitrators. New data collection platforms also provide useful information on potential candidates, such as their language capabilities, bar admissions, workload, rendered decisions, and publications.[73]   **4.53**

The need to renew the corps of international arbitrators with a more diverse younger generation often creates a tension with the 'tried and tested' group of older white arbitrators. As already noted in Chapter 1,[74] there have been several initiatives focused on ensuring that female arbitrators have an equal opportunity of being nominated including the 'Equal Representation in Arbitration' pledge.[75] The Pledge is a private initiative created by members of the arbitration community in 2015, which seeks to 'increase, on an equal opportunity basis, the number of women appointed as arbitrators in order to achieve a fair representation as soon practically possible, with the ultimate goal of full parity'. The Pledge's website also provides assistance in the search for female arbitrators. Another important initiative has been the establishment of 'Arbitral Women', an international non-governmental organisation (NGO) bringing together female arbitration practitioners.[76] These efforts to encourage female arbitrators were followed by the launch of the non-profit organisation 'Racial Equality for Arbitration Lawyers' (REAL) in 2021.[77] These initiatives were preceded in the 1990s by 'Young Arbitration Practitioner' groups established   **4.54**

---

[72] See Rogers and Brodlija, 'Arbitrator appointments in the age of COVID-19', in Scherer, Bassiri, and Wahab (eds) *International Arbitration and the COVID-19 Revolution* (Kluwer Law International, 2020), pp. 58–59.

[73] See, for instance, the databases offered in the websites of Arbitrator Intelligence, Global Arbitration Review, Jus Mundi, International Arbitration Institute Paris, and the Equal Representation in Arbitration Pledge. See also Rogers and Brodlija, fn. 72, pp. 60–62.

[74] See Chapter 1, paragraphs [1.34–1.35].

[75] More information on the Equal Representation in Arbitration (ERA) Pledge is available online at http://www.arbitrationpledge.com/about-the-pledge. The efforts to achieve diversity in international arbitration should of course include regional and racial considerations.

[76] See https://www.arbitralwomen.org/.

[77] The website of REAL is at https://letsgetrealarbitration.org/.

under the auspices of many of the principal arbitral institutions[78] to enable a younger and more diverse group of arbitrators to be identified. As a consequence, diversity in the nomination and appointment of arbitrators has improved and is likely to continue doing so although it still has a long way to go. But diversity is not simply a box to tick in the consideration of arbitrator candidates. The energy and fresh perspective that such candidates can bring often results in more efficient proceedings and better-prepared arbitrators. It is thus important when considering the identity of potential candidates, to consider carefully suitably qualified female candidates, younger candidates, and those from varying racial backgrounds.

(g) Availability

4.55 Some of the most experienced international arbitrators are also the busiest and their consequent lack of availability can result in significant delays in convening hearings and rendering awards.[79] Indeed, ascertaining a prospective arbitrator's availability before making an appointment may be as important in ensuring an efficient and effective process as establishing his or her experience. The ICC, for example, requires all prospective arbitrators to disclose the number of cases in which they are sitting as co-arbitrator or chairperson, as well as the number of cases in which they are acting as counsel, and to confirm that they have adequate availability to discharge their mandate, when they complete their 'statement of acceptance, availability, impartiality and independence'.[80] This allows either party to make objections based on perceived lack of availability, and the ICC may refuse to confirm appointments on this basis. Additionally, the ICC Rules provide that the ICC Court must take into consideration the diligence and efficiency of the arbitrator, the timeliness of the award, among other factors, in setting the arbitrator's fees.[81] Again by way of example, the LCIA Rules require arbitrator candidates to confirm that they are 'ready, willing and able to devote sufficient time, diligence and industry to ensure the expeditious and efficient conduct of the arbitration'.[82] The ICSID Rules also require arbitrators to disclose their availability.[83]

---

[78] The first 'Young International Arbitration Group' was established by the LCIA in 1997 and was the brainchild of Johnny Veeder KC. Its origins are discussed online at https://www.lcia.org/News/lcia-perspectives-yiag.aspx. This has since been followed by the ICC 'Young Arbitrators Forum', Institute for Transnational Arbitration's 'Young ITA', ICDR's 'Young & International', the Swiss Arbitration Association's 'Below 40' Group, and 'Young ICCA', RAI—Rising Arbitrators Initiative, among others. Also, a recent trend in various jurisdictions is the creation of associations of 'very young arbitration practitioners'.

[79] This is another reason, when appointing arbitrators, to look beyond the 'usual suspects' and towards a younger, more diverse (and usually more available) group of candidates.

[80] The latest version of the statement was introduced in January 2021 and is sent by the ICC to arbitrators to complete when they are appointed. The statement requires arbitrators to confirm their acceptance of the relevant appointment, their ability to 'devote the time necessary to conduct [the] arbitration throughout the entire duration of the case as diligently, efficiently and expeditiously as possible in accordance with the time limits in the Rules', and the number of pending cases in which they are involved as arbitrators and counsel. The arbitral community has highlighted the merits of self-discipline in managing caseload and work. See Reed, 'The David Caron Rule of X' (2019) 37 BJIL 163. In an extreme case, the ICC may remove arbitrators who fail to get on with their task.

[81] ICC Rules, Appendix III, Art. 2.2.

[82] LCIA Rules, Art. 5.4.

[83] ICSID Rules, r. 19(3)(b).

(h) Nationality

In an ideal world, the country in which the arbitrator was born or the passport that he or she **4.56** carries should be irrelevant. The qualifications, experience, and integrity of the arbitrator should be the essential criteria. It ought to be possible to proceed in the spirit of the Model Law which provides simply: 'No person shall be precluded by reason of his nationality from acting as an arbitrator, unless otherwise agreed by the parties.'[84] Nevertheless, in the interests of the perception of neutrality, the usual practice in international arbitration is to appoint a sole arbitrator (or a presiding arbitrator) of a different nationality from that of the parties to the dispute.

The validity of nationality limitations on arbitrator appointments, which are found in most **4.57** institutional rules, was cast into doubt following a ruling of the English Court of Appeal in *Jivraj v Hashwani*.[85] The Court found that arbitrators are 'employed' by the parties and therefore subject to employment equality laws that made 'nationality' restrictions illegal. In a welcome reversal, however, the UK Supreme Court subsequently confirmed that arbitrators are not 'employees' of the parties and therefore not subject to such employment equality laws.[86]

The current practice under most institutional rules is that the sole or presiding arbitrator **4.58** will almost certainly be someone of a different nationality from that of the parties to the dispute. Article 6.7 of the UNCITRAL Rules, for example, provides that:

> The appointing authority shall have regard to such considerations as are likely to secure the appointment of an independent and impartial arbitrator and shall take into account as well the *advisability* of appointing an arbitrator of a nationality other than the nationalities of the parties.[87]

Similarly, Article 30 of the CIETAC Rules lists 'the nationalities of the parties' as one of sev- **4.59** eral considerations for appointment.

Article 12.4 of the ICDR Rules takes a slightly different approach, whilst broadly embracing **4.60** the same principle:

> In making appointments, the Administrator shall, after inviting consultation with the parties, endeavour to appoint suitable arbitrators, taking into account their availability to serve. At the request of any party or on its own initiative, the Administrator may appoint nationals of a country other than that of any of the parties.

Article 13.5 of the ICC Rules goes further and provides that the 'sole arbitrator or presi- **4.61** dent of the arbitral tribunal *shall* be of a nationality other than those of the parties.[88]

---

[84] Model Law, Art. 11(1).
[85] *Jivraj v Hashwani* [2011] 1 WLR 1872.
[86] *Jivraj v Hashwani* [2011] UKSC 40. More generally, this decision upholds the principle of party autonomy in the selection of arbitrators, since the Court refused to use public policy to fetter the parties' freedom to agree what qualities and attributes their arbitrators should have. The judgment is discussed in depth in Style and Cleobury, '*Jivraj v Hashwani*: Public interest and party autonomy' (2012) 27 Arb Intl 563.
[87] Emphasis added.
[88] Emphasis added.

The provision allows an exception 'in suitable circumstances and provided that none of the parties objects'. In a similar vein, Article 6.1 of the LCIA Rules provides:

> Where the parties are of different nationalities, a sole arbitrator or the presiding arbitrator shall not have the same nationality as any party unless the parties who are not of the same nationality as the arbitrator candidate all agree in writing otherwise.

(i) Education and training

4.62   As noted above, the most important qualification for an international arbitrator is experience in the law and practice of arbitration. There is no sense in appointing an experienced lawyer as sole or presiding arbitrator responsible for advancing the process if that experience does not include practical experience of arbitration. The reputation and acceptability of international arbitration depends upon the quality of the arbitrators themselves. The task of presiding over an international arbitral tribunal is no less skilled than that of a surgeon conducting an operation, or a captain in charge of the safe navigation of a ship. It should not be entrusted to someone with no first-hand experience of it.

4.63   It follows that there should be some recognised and effective process by which practitioners can acquire the necessary skills to eventually become arbitrators. Young students sometimes get their first exposure to arbitration by participating in university moot court competitions. In order to ensure that there is continuity between generations, most arbitral institutions and law firms operate internship schemes under which young lawyers and postgraduate students gain practical experience for a period of several months.

4.64   In addition, some arbitral institutions now run training programmes specifically designed for prospective arbitrators.[89] Also, as noted above, many arbitral institutions have established 'young practitioner' groups that enable the younger members of the arbitration practitioner community to meet each other, thus creating a network of future potential arbitrators.[90]

(j) Interviewing prospective arbitrators

4.65   Clients will generally ask their external counsel to suggest arbitrators suitable for the particular dispute. Indeed, this is a key role for external counsel, based on their experience of the candidates. The individuals suggested are then discussed with the client, usually by focusing on the particular skill-set and perspective that each candidate would bring to the dispute. A joint decision is then usually taken as to which arbitrators should be contacted to establish interest, availability, and absence of conflicts of interest.

4.66   Whilst clients tend to trust their external counsel with the selection of suitable candidates, some may wish to meet and interview the individual or individuals concerned.

---

[89] The CIArb, headquartered in London, and other institutions offer specialised programmes to train future arbitrators.
[90] See fn. 78.

This practice is not objectionable, with the caveat that it is engaged in openly and that the scope of the discussion is appropriately restricted. A prospective arbitrator may be asked about potential conflicts of interest and if so, given the names of the parties and counsel involved in the proceedings. It is to be expected that the candidate will be questioned on his or her experience, availability, and knowledge of the business sector. The client and counsel will also take the opportunity to assess the candidate's physical and mental health. However, there should be no attempt to ascertain (directly or indirectly) the prospective arbitrator's views on the substantive or procedural issues that are expected to arise in the case.[91]

In recent years, such interviews have become rarer. They are usually awkward in nature, since external counsel will either know the candidate personally or at least will know about the candidate's experience and ability. In fact, what the client usually wants to know is the candidate's likely opinion on the merits of its case. Indeed, there would be questions as to the impartiality and independence of an arbitrator who, in a pre-appointment interview with a party, expressed views, even hypothetically, on the merits of the case. Experienced counsel thus tend to advise against such interviews; and the client will usually be content to rely on counsel's own knowledge of the group of potential candidates.   **4.67**

If such interviews do take place, one experienced US arbitrator has identified guidelines which are communicated to the interviewers in advance. First, other than in exceptional circumstances, the interviewers must travel to the office of the arbitrator (that is, he will not respond to a 'summons' to the premises of the party concerned or their representatives).[92] Second, the interviewing delegation must be led by an *external* lawyer retained by the party in question (that is, the arbitrator will not see the party's employees alone). Third, the meeting should not be conducted over lunch or other event involving hospitality—regardless of who will pay the bill. Fourth, the arbitrator will take a note of the discussion that he will regard as disclosable to interested parties if appropriate. And fifth, if appointed, the arbitrator will inform the arbitrator nominated by the other party of both the fact and the content of the discussion with the party that appointed him. These are sensible guidelines that should avoid any real risk of impropriety—and prospective arbitrators would be wise to adopt a similar system, or to adapt them in a way that seems appropriate to the circumstances of individual cases.[93] More difficult is the question of interviewing prospective sole or presiding arbitrators in cases in which the arbitration agreement calls for the appointment to be made by agreement between the parties. Again, there can be no objection   **4.68**

---

[91] Parties can agree in advance to adhere to specific guidelines during interviews, e.g. CIArb's Guidelines on Interviews for Prospective Arbitrators (last revised 30 August 2016). The Draft Code of Conduct for Adjudicators in Investor–State Dispute Settlement also contains a rule on pre-appointment interviews, providing that they should be limited to discussion concerning expertise, experience, availability, and absence of conflict (Art. 7). This Draft Code was prepared by the Secretariats of ICSID and UNCITRAL in 2020 (and updated in 2021). The Code is intended to provide applicable principles and provisions addressing matters such as independence and impartiality, and the duty to conduct proceedings with integrity, fairness, and efficiency. The drafters have explained that it is based on a comparative review of standards found in investment treaties, arbitration rules and rules of international courts. See 2020 version, p. 3.

[92] Nowadays, such interviews would rarely be conducted in person and would almost certainly take place by videoconference.

[93] See CIArb's Guidelines on Interviews for Prospective Arbitrators and IBA Guidelines on Party Representation, guidelines 7 and 8. See also Bishop and Reed, 'Practical guidelines for interviewing, selecting and challenging party-appointed arbitrators in international commercial arbitration' (1998) 4 Arb Intl 395.

in principle, provided that both parties' representatives are present and the discussion is carefully controlled.

G. Independence and Impartiality of Arbitrators

(a) Introduction

4.69　It is a fundamental principle of international arbitration that every arbitrator, whether acting as a member of an arbitral tribunal or as a sole arbitrator, must be impartial and independent of the parties not only at the time of accepting the appointment but throughout the entire course of the arbitral proceedings.[94] This raises the question of what is meant by independence and impartiality. 'Independence' is generally considered to be concerned with the relationship or links between an arbitrator and one of the parties, whether financial or otherwise. This is thought to be susceptible to an objective test, as it has nothing to do with an arbitrator's state of mind. By contrast, the concept of 'impartiality' is considered to be connected with actual or apparent bias of an arbitrator—either in favour of one of the parties, or in relation to the issues in dispute. Impartiality is thus a subjective and a more abstract concept than independence, in that it involves primarily a state of mind.[95] In many jurisdictions there is a legal obligation to act with independence and impartiality,[96] and to declare any facts or circumstances likely to cast doubts on their impartiality or independence, so that others may judge whether or not they are truly independent and impartial.[97]

4.70　This duty of disclosure is not a mere formality. An arbitrator may be challenged for lack of independence or impartiality for failure to disclose and if the challenge is upheld, be required to resign. If this happens during the arbitral proceedings, it will cause delay and additional expense as a replacement arbitrator has to be found, nominated, and appointed. If it happens after the tribunal's award has been issued, it may lead to recognition and enforcement of that award being denied.[98] In a situation where the arbitrator knowingly failed to disclose a conflict of interest (and perhaps in a situation where the arbitrator was reckless in failing to do so), that arbitrator might well be held personally liable for the loss and damage caused.[99]

---

[94] See the discussion in Chapter 1. See LCIA Rules, Arts 5.3 and 10.1; ICC Rules, Art. 11.1; UNCITRAL Rules, Arts 11 and 12; ICDR Rules, Art. 14.1; SIAC Rules, Art. 13.1; HKIAC Rules, Art. 11.1; CIETAC Rules, Art. 24.

[95] A comprehensive analysis of challenge and disqualification on grounds of both independence and impartiality under each of the different arbitration rules can be found in Daele, *Challenge and Disqualification of Arbitrators in International Arbitration* (Kluwer Law International, 2012), Chapters 7–8.

[96] See, e.g., Swiss PIL, at art. 180.1.c. (This provision, amended in June 2020 and in force since 1 January 2021, states that a member of the arbitral tribunal may be challenged 'if circumstances exist that give rise to legitimate doubts as to his or her independence or impartiality'.)

[97] In *Halliburton*, the UK Supreme Court stated that the Court of Appeal had 'developed the English law of arbitration' by holding that in addition to the legal duty of independence and impartiality there was also a legal duty upon an arbitrator to disclose circumstances that would render him or her liable to be removed as an arbitrator and that the Court of Appeal was correct to do so: *Halliburton Co. v Chubb Bermuda Insurance Ltd (formerly Ace Bermuda Insurance Ltd.)* [2020] UKSC 48, at [75]–[76].

[98] On the basis that the composition of the tribunal, including as it did someone who was not independent or impartial, was not in accordance with the agreement of the parties: Model Law, Art. 34(2)(a)(iv); New York Convention, Art. V(1)(d).

[99] See, for instance, Art. 21(1) of the Spanish Arbitration Act.

The standard to be met in deciding what needs to be disclosed varies. Under the provisions of the Model Law, and of the many states that have adopted that law, the position is as follows:[100]   **4.71**

> When a person is approached in connection with his possible appointment as an arbitrator, he shall disclose any circumstances likely to give rise to justifiable doubts as to his impartiality or independence. An arbitrator from the time of his appointment and throughout the arbitral proceedings, shall without delay disclose any such circumstances to the parties unless they have already been informed of them by him.

Under what might for convenience be called 'the Model Law test', it is generally accepted   **4.72**
that the standard for disclosure is not what the arbitrator or potential arbitrator considers should be disclosed, but more importantly what a reasonable third person having knowledge of the relevant facts and circumstances would expect to see disclosed.[101] An obvious example would be a substantial financial interest of the prospective arbitrator in the appointing party. Recent trends suggest that arbitrators should be subject to a higher scrutiny and err in favour of disclosure if they have any doubt as to whether a disclosure should be made.[102] For instance, in 2018, the Paris Court of Appeal annulled an award because the sole arbitrator had failed to disclose a previous appointment by one of the parties, even though in the previous arbitration no award was rendered as the parties had settled the dispute.[103] In 2020, the Court of Appeals of the State of São Paulo annulled an ICC award on the grounds that the chair of the tribunal had failed to disclose in a timely manner his appointment by one of the parties to serve as an arbitrator in a non-related case.[104]

Under the influential 'Guidelines on Conflicts of Interest in International Arbitration' is-   **4.73**
sued by the IBA and under the rules of many leading arbitral institutions, the test is a subjective one. The question to be considered by the potential arbitrator is: 'are the facts and circumstances disclosed likely to give rise *in the eyes of the parties* to doubts as to my impartiality or independence'.[105] The difference between this subjective approach, and an objective approach, is important. Suppose, for example, that the tax partner in the prospective arbitrator's law firm has recently acted for the respondent to the arbitration in a case that has no relationship to the arbitration. This may seem to be of no significance to a third-party observer looking at the issue objectively; but from the viewpoint of the claimant, it is likely to be seen as something that at the very least should be explored, if only to test the present (and any possible future) relationship between the respondent and the prospective arbitrator's law firm.

---

[100] Model Law, Art. 12(1).

[101] See *ICS Inspection and Control Services Limited (United Kingdom) v Argentine Republic I*, PCA Case No. 2010-9, Decision on Challenge to Arbitrator, 17 December 2009, at [22.2].

[102] See ICSID and UNCITRAL's Draft Code of Conduct for Adjudicators in Investor–State Dispute Settlement, Art. 10 (the Draft Code also provides that adjudicators should disclose all necessary information throughout the proceedings).

[103] Paris cour d'appel, 29 May 2018, Case No. 15/20168.

[104] *Luiz Henrique de Souza Faria v Alper Consultoria e Corretora de Seguros*, Court of Appeals of the State of São Paulo, Proceeding No. 1056400-47.2019.8.26.0100, 11 August 2020.

[105] See IBA Guidelines, Explanation to General Standard 3, letter (a). See also LCIA Rules, Art. 5.4 where any arbitrator is required to sign a written declaration whether there are any circumstances currently known to the candidate which are likely to give rise *in the mind of any party* to any justifiable doubts as to his or her impartiality or independence (emphasis added).

4.74   When first adopting the subjective standard for disclosure in its 'Guidelines on Conflicts of Interest in International Arbitration' in 2004 (which we shall refer to as the 'IBA Guidelines'), the IBA Working Group observed:[106]

> A purely objective test for disclosure exists in the majority of the jurisdictions analysed and in the UNCITRAL Model Law. Nevertheless, the Working Group recognises that the parties have an interest in being fully informed about any circumstances that may be relevant in their view. Because of the strongly held views of many arbitration institutions (as reflected in their rules and as stated to the Working Group) that the disclosure test should reflect the perspectives of the parties, the Working Group in principle accepted, after much debate, a subjective approach for disclosure. The Working Group has adapted the language of Article 7 (2) of the ICC Rules for this standard.

4.75   Article 7.2 has become Article 11.2 in the 2021 ICC Rules, but the principle has not changed. Article 11.2 makes it clear that the test is both subjective and objective and reads as follows (emphasis added):

> Before appointment or confirmation, a prospective arbitrator shall sign a statement of acceptance, availability, impartiality and independence. The prospective arbitrator shall disclose in writing to the Secretariat any facts or circumstances which might be of such a nature as to call into question the arbitrator's independence *in the eyes of the parties*, as well as any circumstances that could give rise to *reasonable* doubts as to the arbitrator's impartiality. The Secretariat shall provide such information to the parties in writing and fix a time limit for any comments from them.

Article 11.3 of the ICC Rules makes it clear that this obligation of disclosure is a continuing obligation throughout the arbitral proceedings.

4.76   By adopting the practice of the leading arbitral institutions on this issue, rather than simply following the less stringent 'Model Law test', the IBA Working Group showed a commendable understanding of the parties' approach to the issue of bias, including unconscious bias, on the part of the arbitrators who are to stand in judgment on their dispute. For parties who have chosen to submit their dispute to arbitration rather than to the courts, it is 'their' arbitration and 'their' tribunal. When it comes to the appointment of an arbitrator, what matters is how that arbitrator's possible conflict of interest looks *to them*, and not how it might look to a disinterested third party.

4.77   The disclosure by an arbitrator or prospective arbitrator of a *possible* conflict of interest does not necessarily mean that there actually is a conflict. On the contrary, arbitrators who disclose possible conflicts of interest plainly consider themselves to be impartial and independent, despite the facts and circumstances disclosed. If this were not the case, they should not have been prepared to accept the appointment. By making disclosure of what *the parties* might perceive to be possible conflicts of interest, arbitrators give those parties the opportunity: (i) to decide whether they agree with the arbitrators' assessment; (ii) to ask for further, more specific, and detailed information if they think it appropriate to do so; or (iii) to challenge the proposed appointment, if they consider it appropriate to do so.

---

[106] IBA Guidelines, Explanation to General Standard 3.

(b) Disclosure

In the original 2004 IBA Guidelines, it was recognised that when it came to the disclosure of **4.78**
possible conflicts of interest that might throw doubt on the independence or impartiality of a
potential arbitrator, 'parties, arbitrators, institutions and courts face complex decisions about
what to disclose and what standards to apply'. It was also noted that there was a tension between
the parties' right to know of situations that might 'reasonably call into question an arbitrator's
impartiality or independence' and their right 'to select arbitrators of their choosing'. This concern was repeated in the latest revised and updated version of the Guidelines, issued in 2014.[107]

These Guidelines, which apply to both international commercial arbitrations and to invest- **4.79**
ment arbitrations,[108] start by enunciating the general principle that international arbitrators
are required to be both impartial and independent; and they explain that if arbitrators have
doubts as to whether or not they fulfil this requirement, they should simply refuse appointment or, if already appointed, refuse to continue to act.[109] The Guidelines also explain, and
this is important, that the test for *disqualification* of an arbitrator is an *objective* test as to
whether there are *justifiable doubts* as to that arbitrator's independence or impartiality. This
is described as the 'reasonable third person test'. Would a reasonable third person, having
knowledge of the relevant facts and circumstances, reach the conclusion that the arbitrator
was likely to be influenced by factors other than the merits of the case?

It is easy to state the test, but not so easy to apply it. The Guidelines note, for example, the **4.80**
problems that may arise when a partner in a law firm is being considered for appointment
as an arbitrator by a client of that firm. The Guidelines state that a partner must in principle
be considered to bear the identity of his or her law firm, but that the activities of that law
firm should not automatically create a conflict of interest. The suggestion is that the nature,
timing, and scope of the work done by the law firm, and 'the relationship' of the partner to
that law firm, may be such that there is in fact no conflict (a clue as to what exactly is meant
by this is to be found later in the Guidelines, where there is a reference to a law firm rendering services to one of the parties 'without creating a significant commercial relationship
for that law firm and without the involvement of the partner').[110]

---

[107] IBA Guidelines, Introduction at [2]; and the revised version issued in 2014, also at [2] of the Introduction.
The reviewing process of the Guidelines was initiated in 2012 by the IBA Arbitration Committee, conducted by an
expanded Conflicts of Interest Subcommittee composed of 27 individuals from diverse jurisdictions, and included
counsel, arbitrators, and arbitration users. The Subcommittee considered a number of issues that had received
attention in the field since 2004, including 'advance waivers', the so called 'double hatting', 'issue' conflicts, the independence and impartiality of arbitral or administrative secretaries, and third-party funding. See IBA Guidelines,
Preamble.
[108] The 2015 International Arbitration Survey of the Queen Mary University of London showed that 71 per
cent of the respondents had seen the IBA Guidelines used in practice and 60 per cent of them found them to be
effective. However, the *Eiser v Spain* case (in which the ad hoc committee annulled an award against Spain following the claimant's nominated arbitrator's failing to disclose his professional relationship with the claimant's
damages expert) serves as a warning that those lists (which did not cover the scenario that arose in that case)
are not exhaustive and that arbitrators and parties must be proactive in thinking about what scenarios could
create an appearance of bias and/or require disclosure. See *Eiser Infrastructure Limited and Energía Solar
Luxembourg Sarl v Kingdom of Spain*, ICSID Case No. ARB/13/36, Decision of the Ad Hoc Committee, 11
June 2020.
[109] See IBA Guidelines, General Standard 1 and (2)(a).
[110] See IBA Guidelines, Orange List, at [3.2.1]. This sounds a little like special pleading on behalf of the larger
law firms. Arbitral institutions such as the ICC, which have regard to the Guidelines but are not in any way

4.81   The Guidelines go on to describe the 'traffic lights system', devised to help users determine, at least preliminarily, whether a particular situation should be disclosed. There is first a 'Red List', which is divided into (i) relationships that are not waivable and (ii) relationships that may be waived if all the parties to the arbitration agree. The 'Non-Waivable Red List' includes, for instance, cases in which the arbitrator has a significant financial or personal relationship with one of the parties. The basic principle is that no-one should be 'a judge in their own cause'. The Waivable Red List covers situations that are described as being 'serious but not as severe' as those on the non-waivable Red List.[111] The examples given include the case where a close family member of the arbitrator 'has a significant financial interest in the outcome of the dispute'.[112] Such a situation is considered to be waivable, but only if the parties are made aware of the situation and expressly state that they are willing nonetheless to have such a person as arbitrator.

4.82   Next is the Orange List, which is likely to be the most controversial. On the public highways, it is generally accepted (except by cyclists and van drivers) that an orange traffic light means stop—or at least, proceed with caution. In the Guidelines, the Orange List is described as 'a non-exhaustive list of specific situations that, depending on the facts of a given case, may in the eyes of the parties give rise to doubts as to the arbitrator's impartiality or independence'.[113] These are situations that the arbitrator or prospective arbitrator has a duty to disclose, so that the parties have an opportunity to object or to ask for further information, if they wish to do so.

4.83   Many of these duties to disclose are subject to a 'three-year limit'. For example, at paragraph 3.1.4 of the Guidelines, it is said that if an arbitrator's law firm has acted for one of the parties 'within the past three years' in an unrelated matter and without the involvement of the arbitrator, this must be declared. Taken literally, this suggests that after three years, nothing needs to be declared—even if three years and one month ago the arbitrator was a lead adviser to one of the parties. Again, at paragraph 3.3.3, it is said that an arbitrator must disclose the fact that he or she was 'within the past three years, a partner of, or otherwise affiliated with [...] any of the counsel in the arbitration'. Again, this suggests that after three years, there is no conflict of interest. Such a clear cut-off date appears to be somewhat arbitrary; and, when making disclosures, a prospective arbitrator should recall that what is relevant is the *parties'* perception of independence and impartiality and that the Guidelines are simply guidelines and not rules of law.

4.84   Finally, comes the 'Green List'. This is intended to cover cases where there is no real or apparent conflict of interest from an *objective* point of view. There is no duty to disclose such situations. This is because, as the Guidelines state, 'there should be a limit to disclosure, based on reasonableness'.[114] Examples include cases where the arbitrator holds an insignificant number of shares in one of the parties or teaches in the same faculty as counsel to one of the parties.[115]

bound by them, are unlikely to appoint as an arbitrator the partner in a law firm that acts for one of the parties, however remote that partner's connection with the party may be.

[111]   See IBA Guidelines, Part II, at [2].
[112]   Ibid., Waivable Red List, at [2.2.2].
[113]   Ibid., Part II, at [3].
[114]   Ibid. at [7].
[115]   Ibid., Green List, at [4.4.2]–[4.3.3].

The Guidelines do not purport to address every possible conflict of interest that might arise **4.85** in practice. Indeed, they cannot be expected to do so. But the Guidelines do make it clear that the independence and impartiality of international arbitrators is a matter of crucial importance. It is not something that is to be taken lightly or for granted. Prospective arbitrators who consult the Guidelines will be made aware of the need to consider carefully whether there are any possible conflicts of interest that should be declared, so that the parties may see for themselves whether to challenge their appointment. If in doubt about whether a particular situation is caught, an arbitrator should err on the side of caution and disclose it.

The Guidelines are particularly valuable in helping to ensure that arbitrators and pro- **4.86** spective arbitrators think carefully about relationships or situations which might seem perfectly acceptable to them, but which might nevertheless raise reasonable doubts in the minds of one or other of the parties.[116]

In general, the leading arbitral institutions take account of the Guidelines, whilst remaining **4.87** free to make up their own minds when it comes to deciding particular challenges. This is understandable, since the approach taken by the Guidelines may be less rigorous than that adopted by some arbitral institutions. The Guidelines, which were drawn up by an international association of lawyers, offer a more favourable treatment to lawyers and to law firms than the arbitral institutions are likely to do. The ICC, for example, will not appoint as arbitrator a lawyer who is in the same law firm as counsel, even if the prospective arbitrator is in Hong Kong and the counsel in Moscow. Nor will it appoint as arbitrator a barrister who is in the same set of Chambers as counsel for one of the parties, even though it may be argued that they are not partners but self-employed individuals.

(c) Repeat appointments

One of the recurring problems in assessing the independence and impartiality of an arbi- **4.88** trator is that posed by the repeat appointment of an arbitrator by the same party.

The repeat appointment of arbitrators raises two issues. First, does the fact that an arbitrator **4.89** is repeatedly appointed by the same party or law firm mean that the arbitrator's independence is compromised, because an important part of his or her income comes from those appointments? Secondly, does it mean that the arbitrator's impartiality is compromised?

The first issue would seem to be an issue of fact. How much does the arbitrator earn from **4.90** the repeat appointments as opposed to his or her income from other arbitrations or other

---

[116] Whilst the Guidelines may not always be directly cited, they are nonetheless also present in the minds of the authorities when deciding challenges. See for instance the decision of the English Commercial Court in *W Ltd v M SDN BHD* [2016] EWHC 422 (Comm) and the decision by the Colombian Supreme Court in *Tampico Beverages Inc. v Productos Naturales de la Sabana SA Alqueria*, SC9909-2017, Case No. 11001-02-03-000-2014-01927-00. In her Freshfields lecture, Professor van Haersolte-van Hof, the Director-General of the LCIA, referred to the Guidelines as 'not binding, but an important source of soft law'. She also made the point that the situations in which perceived conflicts of interest might arise were 'generally very fact-specific, set in different industry sectors with different customs and practices, and that standards differ depending on the phase of the proceedings and the time and place of review'. Her conclusion was that 'Guidance in codes of conduct and guidelines and case law is incredibly useful, but in my view we should accept that hard and fast, universal rules are not realistic and not likely to be of much use'. Van Haersolte-van Hof, 'Impartiality and independence: Fundamental and fluid' (2021) 37 Arb Intl 599, at 605 and 610.

sources? Or to put it more precisely, is the arbitrator so dependent on repeat appointments by the same client or law firm as to bring his or her independence into question? In one case where an arbitrator had received 18 per cent of his appointments in the last three years, and 25 per cent of his total income as arbitrator in the past three years from cases involving the same party, the English Commercial Court upheld a challenge, considering that a fair-minded observer would conclude that the arbitrator had, or appeared to have, a significant financial dependence or interest in continuing to be appointed.[117]

4.91   The second issue is a more difficult one. Parties who are frequently involved in international arbitrations are likely to become familiar with a particular arbitrator for a variety of reasons—reputation, expertise, familiarity with the relevant contractual terms and conditions, approachability, and so forth—and they are likely to want to re-appoint that arbitrator when possible. The same is true of the law firms who appoint arbitrators. They are likely to know arbitrators for whom they have a high regard, and others that they would not appoint, even if their client pleaded with them with tears in their eyes to do so.

4.92   Accordingly, it is not surprising that there are repeat appointments. But it is reasonable to assume that however much a party might like the style, or the expertise, or the ability of a particular arbitrator, that party would not continue to appoint the same arbitrator if he or she consistently decided against it. Similarly, law firms who value their clients would be unlikely to continue to appoint arbitrators who consistently made awards against them. In short, however upright and honest the arbitrator may be, there is always a real possibility of actual but unconscious bias by that arbitrator in favour of a party or of a law firm that frequently nominates him or her as an arbitrator.

4.93   It follows that when a party or a law firm makes repeated appointments of the same arbitrator, questions are almost certain to be raised as to the independence and impartiality of that arbitrator. This reality is recognised by the IBA Guidelines which require an arbitrator or prospective arbitrator to make a declaration under the Orange List if he or she has been appointed on more than three occasions by the same counsel or by the same law firm in the last three years.[118] Some jurisdictions have taken an even stricter approach. For example, the Paris Court of Appeal has set aside an award on the ground that the tribunal was not properly constituted, due to the non-disclosure by an arbitrator of a single past appointment by one of the parties in a case involving a third party, even though no award was rendered in that case as the parties had settled the dispute.[119]

4.94   The problem of repeat appointments is compounded in international firms where there are a large number of specialist arbitration lawyers, since the pool of qualified arbitrators is not endless and a hard limit would seem to penalise such firms, especially where the nominations are from parties represented by different partners of the firm operating in different continents.[120]

---

[117] *Cofely Limited v Anthony Bingham et al.* [2016] EWHC 240 (Comm).
[118] See IBA Guidelines, Orange List, at [3.3.8].
[119] Fn. 103.
[120] For a discussion of the particular challenges facing international law firms in connection with conflicts of interest for arbitrator appointments, see Fernandez-Perez, 'Conflicts of interests of arbitrators in international law firms' (2018) 34 Arb Intl 105.

There is an added complication in certain business sectors, and notably shipping and com-   **4.95**
modity trading, where it is customary for a party to appoint the same person repeatedly,
from a relatively small group of experienced arbitrators. This issue is recognised in the IBA
Guidelines, which state at footnote 5:

> It may be the practice in certain specific types of arbitration, such as maritime, sports or
> commodities arbitration, to draw arbitrators from a smaller or specialised pool of individ-
> uals. If in such fields it is the custom and practice for parties to frequently appoint the same
> arbitrator in different cases, no disclosure of this fact is required, where all parties in the
> arbitration should be familiar with such custom and practice.

This practice was also recognised by the UK Supreme Court in the *Halliburton* case, which   **4.96**
was concerned with a challenge to an arbitrator who had been appointed more than once
by the same party. The case attracted considerable attention in the international arbitration
community and (somewhat exceptionally) five arbitral institutions intervened to make submissions to the Court.[121] Lord Reed, giving judgment for the court, referred to the interventions by GAFTA and the LMAA at paragraph 43:[122]

> The other interveners are GAFTA, which is concerned with agricultural commodities
> arbitration and which trains and certifies arbitrators who must have extensive practical
> experience in the relevant trades, and LMAA, which is an association of arbitrators con-
> cerned with shipping and trade arbitration and which produces arbitration terms and
> procedures widely used for maritime arbitration in London. GAFTA explains that dis-
> putes often arise in chain or string supply contracts and that arbitrations in such con-
> tracts, which often involve common issues of law or fact, are regularly referred to the same
> arbitrator or arbitrators […].

In *Halliburton*, the UK Supreme Court was concerned with a 'Bermuda Form' arbitration   **4.97**
(a special type of policy developed in Bermuda in the 1980s which usually provides for
London arbitration[123]). One of the issues was the failure of an arbitrator to declare an appointment by the same party, Chubb Bermuda Insurance Ltd in a second related arbitration. The Supreme Court accepted that a Bermuda Form arbitration was a specialist form
of arbitration but held that under English law multiple appointments must be disclosed in
such arbitrations, unless there was an agreement to the contrary by the parties.[124] In short,
Bermuda Form arbitrators were subject to the same rules of disclosure as other arbitrators
in mainstream international arbitrations.

Repeat appointments are particularly problematic where an arbitrator has been appointed   **4.98**
for a second time in relation to two disputes where there is overlapping subject matter. This
raises the potentially difficult issue of whether arbitrators are free to disclose information
about the first arbitration in the second arbitration. The short answer is that they are not free
to do so, without the consent of the parties, if the first arbitration has taken (or is taking)

---

[121] They were the ICC and the LCIA, each represented by external counsel and, with written submissions only,
the CIArb, the LMAA, and the GAFTA.
[122] *Halliburton, fn. 97*, at [43].
[123] See Masters, Range, and Moura, 'The Bermuda Form and arbitration of disputes in London' (2018) 73(1)
Disp Res J 67 *et seq.*
[124] *Halliburton*, fn. 97 at [137].

place on the basis that it was private and confidential. Lord Reed, giving the judgment of the UK Supreme Court in *Halliburton*[125] said:

> Where the information which must be disclosed is subject to an arbitrator's duty of privacy and confidentiality, disclosure can be made only if the parties to whom the obligations are owed give their consent. In such a circumstance, if a person seeking appointment as an arbitrator in a later arbitration does not obtain the consent of the parties to a prior related arbitration to make a necessary disclosure about it, or the parties to a later arbitration do not consent to the arbitrator's disclosure of confidential matters relating to that prospective appointment to the parties to the earlier arbitration, the arbitrator will have to decline the second appointment. Such consent may be express or may be inferred from the arbitration agreement itself in the context of the custom and practice in the relevant field.[126]

Lady Arden concurred in her judgment in the same case, citing with approval the following citation from Julia Dias KC:[127]

> [W]hether there is *in fact* a real possibility of bias depends on matters such as the identity of the parties to the two arbitrations, the nature of the subject-matter, the degree of overlap between the issues and the type of evidence adduced. The problem is that none of this can be explored without disclosing in the first arbitration matters relating to the second arbitration which in principle should be confidential to that arbitration. Indeed, it is impossible to see how the confidentiality of the second arbitration would not be compromised by the need to investigate whether there is an overlap between the two references in relation to subject-matter, issues, etc.

4.99   In addition to concerns about confidentiality, where an arbitrator has been appointed a second time in an arbitration with the same party, arising out of the same event and with the same or similar issues involved, there is an obvious inequality of arms. Specifically, the repeat arbitrator will be privy to information that neither the opposing party in the proceedings nor the other members of the tribunal will know about or are entitled to know about.[128] Lady Arden highlighted this risk in the *Halliburton* case:[129]

> Such an appointment is likely to give rise to a potential inequality of arms and material asymmetry of information. In principle the parties to both the current and proposed arbitration should be given a chance to object to the arbitrator accepting the new appointment. And if there is more than one current arbitration in which the conflict arises, there must if there is to be disclosure be disclosure to the parties in those arbitrations too.

4.100   The same issue has arisen in investment arbitration. In one dispute, the same arbitrator had been nominated by claimant, insurer Liberty Mutual, in two parallel investment

---

[125] Ibid., at [88].
[126] This last sentence presumably refers to the maritime and other arbitrations previously discussed, in which repeat appointments are customary.
[127] *Halliburton*, fn. 97, at [189] quoting Dias, 'Resignation in the face of confidentiality' (2020) TDM 2 .
[128] From experience, it is disconcerting when, as chair of an arbitral tribunal, you realise that one of your fellow arbitrators already knows about the issues, the evidence, and the legal arguments likely to be put forward before you have even been given the opportunity to read the initial pleadings.
[129] *Halliburton*, fn. 97, at [172].

arbitrations against Venezuela, first under the ICSID Additional Facility Rules and then under the UNCITRAL Rules (Venezuela having failed to indicate to the claimant to which set of rules it had agreed under the relevant treaty). Venezuela challenged the arbitrator's appointment in the UNCITRAL arbitration based on 'risk of prejudgment and an information asymmetry with respect to the other co-arbitrators'. The Secretary-General of the Permanent Court of Arbitration (the appointing authority) accepted Venezuela's challenge noting that the arbitrator 'may formulate views on matters of fact and law in deliberations with the ICSID tribunal where his co-arbitrators in the UNCITRAL Arbitration would not participate' and that such situation could lead a reasonable and informed third party to 'hold justifiable doubts regarding the integrity of the proceedings'.[130] In a similar situation, the ICC Court disqualified the respondent's nominee in the ICC case *Anaklia Development Corporation v Georgia*[131] in light of that nominee's appointment to the parallel ICSID arbitration *Bob Meijer v Georgia*.[132] The Court reasoned that the nominee's presence on both tribunals entailed a risk of prejudgment in the ICC case and, again, a risk of asymmetry of information between the co-arbitrators.

This discussion suggests that arbitrators who are offered repeat appointments should consider carefully whether or not to accept. What looks like a precious gift may turn out to be a poisoned chalice.   **4.101**

H. Challenge and Replacement of Arbitrators

(a) Introduction

Challenges to arbitrators were, at one time, a rare event. If a vacancy occurred, it was usually because of the death or resignation of an arbitrator. However, modern international arbitrations often involve vast sums of money and the parties have become more inclined to engage specialist lawyers, who are expert in manoeuvres designed to obtain a tactical advantage, or at least to minimise a potential disadvantage.[133] Statistics on arbitrator challenges are available from most of the main institutions,[134] and some commentators have concluded that the practice has increased to the extent that it might affect the efficiency and   **4.102**

---

[130] *Liberty Seguros, Compañia de Seguros y Reaseguros v Bolivarian Republic of Venezuela*, PCA Case AA809, Decision on challenge of arbitrator, 1 July 2021.

[131] ICC Case No. 25542/HBH, Decision on the Proposal for Disqualification, 25 February 2021.

[132] ICSID Case No. ARB/20/28.

[133] Excessive use of arbitrator challenges as a form of guerrilla tactic has become quite widespread amongst arbitration counsel. See Horvath and Wilske, 'Guerrilla tactics in international arbitration' (2013) 28 IALL (Kluwer Law International) 42. In one extreme case reported by the ICC, a party filed 29 successive challenges against all members of the tribunal, all of which were dismissed. See *ICC Dispute Resolution 2020 Statistics*, ICC Publication No. DRS 895ENG, 2020 (*ICC 2020 Statistics*), p. 13, fn.13 available online at http://www.iccwbo.org/dr-stat.

[134] According to the statistics published by the ICC, the number of challenges to arbitrators filed between 2015 and 2020 has more than doubled. In 2020, there were 92 challenges of which five were accepted by the Court. *ICC Dispute Resolution 2020 Statistics*, fn. 133, p. 13. In 2020, among the 407 cases registered with the LCIA, only six challenges were heard by the LCIA Court (1.5% of these cases) and only one challenge was successful. See LCIA, Annual Casework Report 2020, p. 22, available online at https://www.lcia.org/News/lcia-news-annual-casework-report-2020-and-changes-to-the-lcia-c.aspx. ICSID also reports a very low rate of success for arbitrator challenges: https://icsid.worldbank.org/cases/content/tables-of-decisions/disqualification.

legitimacy of the process.[135] This is particularly noteworthy in investment arbitrations.[136] In short, as the scope of international arbitration widens, and as claims for damages or compensation frequently run into millions of dollars, parties, courts, and arbitral institutions are facing an increasing number of challenges to arbitrators for alleged lack of independence or impartiality.[137]

4.103   Some challenges are undoubtedly meritorious. In other cases, however, challenges are made to obtain a tactical advantage, for example, at the start of an arbitration, to hinder the formation of the tribunal; or, in the course of an arbitration, because the party making the challenge suspects that the arbitrator who is the target of the challenge is not persuaded of the merits of the challenging party's case.[138] Such challenges cause delay and add to expense, since the parties, the challenged arbitrator(s), and the other members of the tribunal will be given time to comment upon the challenges before the relevant institution or individual makes a decision; and indeed, in some institutions the proceedings will be automatically stayed pending resolution.[139]

4.104   Traditionally, institutions have categorised decisions on challenges as administrative in nature and have not provided reasons for their decisions. However, given the important impact such a decision will have on the arbitral process (often affecting the right of one of the parties to have the 'judge of their choice'), there have been ever-stronger demands for institutions to publish and provide reasons for their decisions in order to clarify, both for arbitrators and for parties, the standards applied by the institutions themselves, thus assisting uniformity in the practice of disclosure. This has caused institutions to abandon their traditional reticence and publish the reasons for such decisions. In 2011, the LCIA led the way by publishing its decisions in redacted form.[140] In 2015, the ICC changed its practice to provide reasons, if any party so requested in advance of the decision.[141] The practice of ICSID

---

[135] For a specific and more recent analysis of challenges in both international commercial arbitrations and investment treaty arbitrations, see Ali, Wessel, et al., 'The International Arbitration Rulebook: A guide to arbitral regimes', in Ali, Wessel, et al. (eds) *The Arbitral Tribunal* (Kluwer Law International, 2019), pp. 321–333; Sabahi, Rubins, et al., *Investor-State Arbitration* (2nd edn, Oxford University Press, 2019), pp. 227–288.

[136] By way of example, a respondent state filed six challenges to the same arbitrator in the same arbitration. All were dismissed. In the same arbitration, the respondent state filed a proposal for disqualification of the Annulment Committee, which was also rejected. *ConocoPhillips Petrozuata BV and ors v Bolivarian Republic of Venezuela*, ICSID Case No. ARB/07/30. See the details and relevant decisions of this case at https://www.italaw.com/cases/321. Since most arbitration rules provide for the automatic suspension of the arbitral proceedings whilst the challenge is resolved (irrespective of the merits of the challenge), some challenges are tactically brought on the eve of a long-planned hearing resulting in the necessary abandonment of hearing dates.

[137] See Malintoppi and Carlevaris, 'Challenges to Arbitrators, Lessons from the ICC', in Giorgetti (ed.), *Challenges and Recusals of Judges and Arbitrators in International Tribunals* (Brill, 2015), p. 141; SCC Practice Note: SCC Board Decisions on Challenges to Arbitrators 2016–2018 (2019), p. 9.

[138] *Repsol, SA and Repsol Butano, SA v Argentine Republic*, ICSID Case No. ARB/12/38, Decision on Application for Challenge to the Majority of the Tribunal, 13 December 2013, at [85]–[86]; *Quiborax SA and Non Metallic Minerals SA v Plurinational State of Bolivia*, ICSID Case No. ARB/06/2, Award, 16 September 2015, at [595].

[139] See, e.g., ICSID Rules, r. 22(2) which provide for automatic suspension unless the parties agree otherwise.

[140] The LCIA automatically publishes the challenge decisions online unless the parties agree to the contrary. See https://www.lcia.org/challenge-decision-database.aspx. See, e.g., Challenge to arbitrator's appointment pursuant to Article 10.3 of the LCIA Rules, based on Article 10.1 (justifiable doubts as to arbitrator's independence and impartiality), LCIA Case Reference No. 173566, Decision Rendered 21 July 2017.

[141] See Note to Parties and Arbitral Tribunals on the Conduct of the Arbitration under the 2012 ICC Rules of Arbitration, 8 October 2015, paras 20–22. This change was integrated into the rules from 2017—see, e.g., 2021 ICC Rules, Art. 14 and Appendix II, Art. 5.

has been to publish reasons for decisions on challenges and those decisions have become an important point of reference when considering the scope of independence and impartiality under the ICSID Convention and rules.[142]

(b) Grounds for challenge

Before a challenge can be considered, the applicable rules need to be established. In the event of an arbitration taking place in accordance with institutional rules, the test will be set out in those rules, with a challenge being made to the relevant institution, or (in the case of UNCITRAL) to the appointing authority designated by the parties or, in the absence of such designation, by the appointing authority chosen by the PCA.[143] In the event of a pure ad hoc arbitration (that is, one with no chosen set of rules), the test will be set out in the local arbitration law of the seat of the arbitration. In the absence of any designated appointing authority, a challenge will be decided by the judicial courts of the seat.

4.105

(i) Arbitral rules and the ICSID Convention

In general, the parties may challenge an arbitrator only where they have reasonable doubts as to his or her impartiality or independence. However, the arbitral rules provide their own tests, which may vary from each other.

4.106

For instance, Article 12 of the UNCITRAL Rules provides:

4.107

1. Any arbitrator may be challenged if circumstances exist that give rise to justifiable doubts as to the arbitrator's impartiality or independence.
2. A party may challenge the arbitrator appointed by him only for reasons of which he becomes aware after the appointment has been made. [...]

Commentators on the UNCITRAL Rules note that the inclusion of the word 'justifiable' in Article 12.1 to define the kind of doubt required to sustain a challenge reflects UNCITRAL's clear intention of establishing an objective standard for impartiality and independence.[144]

The relevant case law supports this position.[145] The appointing authority in the challenge decision filed in the UNCITRAL case *Nord Stream 2 v EU* noted that:

4.108

[T]he doubts as to the arbitrator's impartiality or independence must be justifiable pursuant to an analysis of all relevant circumstances from the perspective of an objective, reasonable, and informed third party. Further, a challenge may succeed on the basis of an appearance of bias without requiring proof of actual bias.[146]

---

[142] See, e.g., *Burlington Resources Inc. v Republic of Ecuador*, ICSID Case No. ARB/08/5, Decision on the Proposal for Disqualification of Francisco Orrego Vicuna, 13 December 2013.

[143] See, e.g., *Serafín García Armas and Karina García Gruber v Bolivarian Republic of Venezuela*, PCA Case No. 2013-03, Decision on the Disqualification of the Members of the Tribunal, 5 July 2017.

[144] Caron and Caplan, *The UNCITRAL Arbitration Rules: A Commentary* (2nd edn, Oxford University Press, 2013), p. 208.

[145] *ICS Inspection*, fn. 101, at [22.2].

[146] *Nord Stream 2 v EU*, PCA, Decision on the Challenge to Mr. Peter Rees KC, 9 December 2019, at [30]. See also *Merck Sharpe & Dohme (I.A.) LLC v Republic of Ecuador*, PCA Case No. 2012-10, Decision on Challenge to Arbitrator Judge Stephen M. Schwebel, 8 August 2012.

4.109   The ICC Rules are succinct on the issue. Article 14.1 simply notes that:

> A challenge of an arbitrator, whether for an alleged lack of impartiality, or independ-ence *or otherwise*, shall be made by submission to the Secretariat of a written statement specifying the facts and circumstances on which the challenge is based. [Emphasis added]

4.110   The breadth of this provision is striking. It would appear to grant the ICC Court consider-able discretion to remove an arbitrator.[147] However, as noted above, since 2015 the Court will communicate the reasons for its decision on the challenge to an arbitrator to the parties upon request of any party.[148] This gives the parties an insight into the reasoning behind the decision.

4.111   The LCIA Rules are more explicit. Article 10.1 states that the LCIA Court may revoke any arbitrator's appointment if: 'circumstances exist that give rise to justifiable doubts as to that arbitrator's impartiality or independence'. The ICDR, SCC, SIAC, and HKIAC Arbitration Rules also adopt a 'justifiable doubts' test.[149]

4.112   The ICSID Convention states that:

> A party may propose to a Commission or Tribunal the disqualification of any of its mem-bers on account of any fact indicating a manifest lack of the qualities required by para-graph (1) of Article 14. A party to arbitration proceedings may, in addition, propose the disqualification of an arbitrator on the ground that he was ineligible for appointment to the Tribunal under Section 2 of Chapter IV.[150]

The qualities required by Article 14.1 include the ability to 'exercise independent judg-ment' in the English version, whereas the Spanish version of the same article refers to a person who 'inspires full confidence in their impartiality of judgment'.[151] Since both versions of the ICSID Convention are equally authentic, Article 14.1 has been applied to require arbitrators to be both impartial and independent.[152] As defined by the Chair of the ICSID Administrative Council, 'Impartiality refers to the absence of bias or predis-position towards a party. Independence is characterized by the absence of external con-trol'.[153] The Authoritative Notes to the ICSID Rules explain the effect of the independence provision:

> [A]n arbitrator is to [resign] if, for instance, he may have an interest in the result of the dispute. In fact, in view of the qualities he is required to possess, a candidate is unlikely to

---

[147] The Court can replace an arbitrator on its own initiative 'when it decides that the arbitrator is prevented de jure or de facto from fulfilling the arbitrator's functions, or that the arbitrator is not fulfilling those functions in ac-cordance with the Rules or within the prescribed time limits'. ICC Rules, Art. 15.2. Upon request of any party, the Court will communicate the reasons for its decision. ICC Rules, Appendix II, Art. 5.

[148] ICC Rules, Art. 14 and Appendix II, Art. 5.

[149] See SCC Rules, Art. 19.1; ICDR Rules, Art. 14.1; SIAC Rules, Art. 11.1; HKIAC Rules, Art. 11.6.

[150] ICSID Convention, Art. 57.

[151] The original Spanish text reads: '[…] *inspira plena confianza en su imparcialidad de juicio*'.

[152] *Raiffeisen Bank International AG and Raiffeisenbank Austria d.d. v Republic of Croatia*, ICSID Case No. ARB/17/34, Decision on the Proposal to Disqualify Stanimir Alexandrov, 17 May 2018, at [81]. See also *Repsol*, fn. 138, at [70].

[153] *Raiffeisen Bank International*, fn. 152, at [81].

accept an appointment as arbitrator where his personal interest is involved and, if he realises such involvement after the appointment, he may be trusted to resign. The experience of other international arbitration bodies has, in this respect, apparently been reassuring; it therefore seems unnecessary to particularise grounds for resignation.[154]

The second part of Article 14.1 refers to grounds on which an arbitrator is 'ineligible for appointment'. This refers to the nationality provisions, which are designed to ensure that (unless the parties agree otherwise) the majority of arbitrators are not of the nationality of either of the parties.[155]

As noted by the deciding arbitrators in one case, the ICSID Rules establish an objective standard: **4.113**

> The legal standard applied to a proposal to disqualify an arbitrator is an 'objective standard based on a reasonable evaluation of the evidence by a third party'. As a consequence, the subjective belief of the party requesting the disqualification is not enough to satisfy the requirements of the Convention.[156]

In other words, the challenging party must rely on established facts and 'not on any mere speculation or inference'.[157]

The interpretation of the requirement in Article 57 that the arbitrator must have a 'manifest' lack of the qualities established by Article 14 has been equivocal. To some tribunals, it has referred 'not to the seriousness of the allegation but to the ease with which [the allegation] may be perceived'.[158] Other tribunals have taken the view that 'manifest' must relate to the substance of the conflict itself such that, from the perspective of an informed reasonable person, established facts 'make it obvious and highly probable, not just possible, that the challenged arbitrator is a person who may not be relied upon to exercise independent and impartial judgment'.[159]   **4.114**

(ii) National laws
National laws on arbitration contain tests that operate in the case of a pure ad hoc arbitration with a seat in the country. For example, the Swiss PIL provides that an arbitrator may be   **4.115**

---

[154] ICSID Rules, r. 8, n. C.

[155] ICSID Convention, Arts 38 and 39.

[156] *Raiffeisen Bank International*, fn. 152, at [84]. This objective standard has been applied consistently by ICSID tribunals, e.g. in *ConocoPhillips Petrozuata BV and ors v Bolivarian Republic of Venezuela*, ICSID Case No. ARB/07/30, Decision on the Proposal to Disqualify L. Yves Fortier, KC, Arbitrator, 27 February 2012, at [54]–[56]; *Abaclat and others v Argentine Republic*, Recommendation on Proposal for Disqualification of Prof. Pierre Tercier and Prof. Albert Jan van den Berg, ICSID Case No. ARB/07/05, 19 December 2011, at [54]–[65].

[157] *KS Invest GmbH and TLS Invest GmbH v Kingdom of Spain*, ICSID Case No. ARB/15/25, Decision on the Proposal to Disqualify Gary Born, 30 April 2018, at [44].

[158] *EDF International SA v Argentina*, Challenge Decision regarding Professor Gabrielle Kaufmann-Kohler of 25 June 2008, at [65]–[69].

[159] *Suez, Sociedad General de Aguas de Barcelona SA v Argentine Republic*, ICSID Cases Nos. ARB/03/17 and ARB/03/19, Decision on Second Proposal for Disqualification, at [29]; *Canepa Green Energy Opportunities I, Sarl. and Canepa Green Energy Opportunities II, Sarl v Kingdom of Spain*, ICSID Case No. ARB/19/4, Decision on the Second Proposal to Disqualify Mr. Peter Rees KC, 10 February 2020, at [52].

challenged if circumstances exist that give rise to justifiable doubts as to his or her impartiality or independence.[160]

4.116   Section 24(1) of the English Arbitration Act 1996 is more comprehensive:

(1) A party to arbitral proceedings may (upon notice to the other parties, to the arbitrator concerned and to any other arbitrator) apply to the court to remove an arbitrator on any of the following grounds:

   (a) that circumstances exist that give rise to justifiable doubts as to his impartiality;

   (b) that he or she does not possess the qualifications required by the arbitration agreement;

   (c) that he or she is physically or mentally incapable of conducting the proceedings or there are justifiable doubts as to his capacity to do so;

   (d) that he or she has refused or failed—

      (i) properly to conduct the proceedings, or

      (ii) to use all reasonable despatch in conducting the proceedings or making an award,

      (iii) and that substantial injustice has been or will be caused to the applicant.[161]

The UK Supreme Court considered this standard of disqualification and found that the relevant test is an objective one, namely 'whether the fair-minded and informed observer, having considered the facts, would conclude that there was a real possibility that the tribunal was biased'.[162]

4.117   In the United States, the duty of avoiding evident partiality is established by section 10(a) of the Federal Arbitration Act of 1925 (FAA):

(a) In any of the following cases the United States court in and for the district wherein the award was made may make an order vacating the award upon the application of any party to the arbitration—

[...]

(1) Where the award was procured by corruption, fraud, or undue means;

(2) where there was evident partiality or corruption in the arbitrators, or either of them;

[...]

This section has been interpreted as including a strict duty of disclosure. The US Supreme Court set a high standard in *Commonwealth Coatings* by requiring disclosure of any dealings that might create an impression of bias. In that case, an arbitral award was set aside for failure to disclose business connections with one of the parties, even though the award was unanimous and the Court found that there was no *actual* bias.[163] Yet US courts have been

---

[160] An arbitrator may also be challenged (i) if he or she does not meet the qualifications agreed upon by the parties, or (ii) if a ground for challenge exists under the arbitration rules agreed upon by the parties. See Swiss PIL, art. 180. The same rule is contained in, for instance, the Dutch Arbitration Act 2015, s. 1033.

[161] This has been held to import a 'fair-minded and reasonable observer' test and to require a demonstration of a real possibility of apparent bias, rather than a real possibility of unconscious bias: see *A v B and X* [2011] EWHC 2345 (Comm).

[162] *Halliburton Company v Chubb Bermuda Insurance Ltd & Ors* [2018] EWCA Civ 817, at [52].

[163] However, Justice White noted that an arbitrator, who must not be held to the same standard as a judge, has no duty to disclose 'remote commercial connections [...] He cannot be expected to provide the parties with his complete and unexpurgated business biography': *Commonwealth Coatings Corporation v Continental Casualty Co.*, 393

divided over the precise standard required to show evident partiality. Whereas several circuits have generally held that bias is found where a reasonable person would *have to* conclude that an arbitrator was partial,[164] other circuits have held that a reasonable impression of partiality would suffice.[165]

In France, Article 1456 of the Code of Civil Procedure explicitly states that before accepting appointment an arbitrator shall disclose any circumstance that may affect his or her independence or impartiality'.[166] If one party considers that the arbitrator is not independent or impartial, the issue shall be resolved by the institution administering the arbitration or, where there is no such institution, by the judge acting in support of the arbitration to whom application must be made within one month following the disclosure or the discovery of the fact at issue.[167]   **4.118**

(c) Procedure for challenge

The procedure for challenge of an arbitrator appears in the applicable arbitration rules or, in the event of an ad hoc arbitration, in the arbitration law at the seat of arbitration. Where a challenge falls to be dealt with by the courts, the procedure to be followed is specified in the applicable procedural law. Where the rules of an arbitral institution apply, the procedure is normally that a complaint should be made in the first instance *either* to the arbitral institution *or* to the arbitral tribunal itself.[168]   **4.119**

Most national laws provide for a challenge to an arbitrator to be made promptly during the arbitration.[169] The inevitable delays to the conduct of the arbitration may be minimised by provisions that require the challenge to be made within a specified time of becoming aware of the grounds for that challenge, or by provisions that permit the arbitration to continue whilst the challenge is pending. Such provisions are to be found, for example, in the Model Law and the English Arbitration Act 1996.[170]   **4.120**

U.S. 145, 151 (1968). Lower courts have tended to follow this approach: see, e.g., *Positive Software Solutions, Inc. v New Century Finance Corporation*, 476 F.3d 278, 281–82 (5th Cir. 2007).

[164] See, e.g., *UBS Financial Servs., Inc. v Asociacion de Empleados del Estado Libre Asociado de Puerto Rico*, 997 F.3d 15, 19 (1st Cir. 2021); *JCI Commc'ns, Inc. v Int'l Brotherhood of Elec. Workers, Local*, 103, 324 F.3d 42, 51 (1st Cir. 2003); *Certain Underwriting Members of Lloyds of London v Fla., Dep't of Fin. Servs.*, 892 F.3d 501, 505–06 (2d Cir. 2018); *Morelite Constr. Corp. v N.Y.C. Dist. Council Carpenters Ben. Funds*, 748 F.2d 79, 84 (2d Cir. 1984); *Freeman v Pittsburgh Glass Works, LLC*, 709 F.3d 240, 253 (3d Cir. 2013); *Kaplan v First Options of Chicago, Inc.*, 19 F.3d 1503, 1523 n.30 (3d Cir. 1994); *ANR Coal Co., Inc. v Cogentrix of North Carolina, Inc.*, 173 F.3d 493, 500 (4th Cir. 1999); *Peoples Sec. Life Ins. Co. v Monumental Life Ins. Co.*, 991 F.2d 141, 146 (4th Cir. 1993); *OOGC Am., L.L.C. v Chesapeake Exploration, L.L.C.*, 975 F.3d 449, 453 (5th Cir. 2020); *Positive Software Solutions, Inc. v New Century Mortg. Corp.*, 476 F.3d 278, 282–83 (5th Cir. 2007); *Uhl v Komatsu Forklift Co., Ltd.*, 512 F.3d 294, 306–07 (6th Cir. 2008); *Nationwide Mut. Ins. Co. v Home Ins. Co.*, 429 F.3d 640, 645 (6th Cir. 2005).

[165] See, e.g., *Monster Energy Co. v City Beverages, LLC*, 940 F.3d 1130, 1135–36 (9th Cir. 2019); *Woods v Saturn Distribution Corp.*, 78 F.3d 424, 427 (9th Cir. 1996); *Aviles v Charles Schwav & Co., Inc.*, 435 F. App'x 824, 828–29 (11th Cir. 2011); *Middlesex Mut. Ins. Co. v Levine*, 675 F.2d 1197, 1200–02 (11th Cir. 1982).

[166] French Code of Civil Procedure. See Cohen, 'Indépendence des arbitres et conflits d'intérêts' [2011] Rev Arb 614.

[167] See Art. 1456(3) of the Code of Civil Procedure.

[168] English Arbitration Act 1996, s. 24(2).

[169] English Arbitration Act 1996, s. 24; Model Law, Art. 13; Swiss PIL, Ch. 12, s. 180; Dutch Arbitration Act 2015, s. 1033.

[170] Model Law, Art. 13; English Arbitration Act 1996, s. 24(3).

4.121   A curious gap in the FAA leaves the parties no avenue of judicial review of an arbitrator appointment in an ad hoc arbitration until after an award has been rendered, unless the rules of procedure adopted by the parties provide for earlier review.[171] This means that a party with a valid objection to the composition of the tribunal would have to make an objection 'on the record' and then wait until the end of the case before challenging the award. In *Sussex*, the US Court of Appeals for the Ninth Circuit reasoned that court intervention mid-arbitration should occur only in extreme cases and that the challenge to an arbitrator for an apparent conflict of interest was 'emphatically' not an extreme case.[172]

(i)   ICC challenge procedure

4.122   Article 14 of the ICC Rules provides that a party seeking to challenge an arbitrator must do so within thirty days of the date of notification of the appointment or the date on which that party became aware of the circumstances giving rise to the challenge. The challenge must be made in writing, specifying the facts and circumstances on which it is based. The ICC Court will then decide on the challenge after the Secretariat has afforded an opportunity to the arbitrator concerned, the other party, and the other members of the tribunal to comment.[173] Those comments are to be communicated to the parties and to the arbitrators.

4.123   Article 11.4 of the 2012 ICC Rules expressly stated that the reasons for the challenge decision would not be communicated.[174] As noted above, since 2015, the ICC has changed its practice and now, under Article 5 of Appendix II and upon request of any party, the Court will communicate the reasons for its decisions on challenges to arbitrators.[175]

(ii)   LCIA challenge procedure

4.124   Under the LCIA Rules, a party who intends to challenge an arbitrator must send a written statement of the reasons for challenge to the LCIA Court, the arbitral tribunal, and all other parties, within fourteen days of the establishment of the arbitral tribunal, or within fourteen days of becoming aware of the circumstances justifying the challenge.[176] The LCIA Court will give the other parties and the challenged arbitrator a chance to comment on the challenge. Unless the challenged arbitrator withdraws (or the other party agrees to the challenge) within fourteen days of receipt of the written statement of reasons, the LCIA Court will decide on the challenge.[177] The LCIA Rules expressly require that the decision of the LCIA Court—which, in practice, may be represented by the President, the Vice President, Honorary or former Vice Presidents, or any three members of the LCIA Court—shall be

---

[171] *Gulf Guaranteed Life Insurance Co. v Connecticut General Life Insurance Co.*, 304 F.3d 476, 490 (5th Cir. 2002), in which the court held that 'there is no authorisation under the FAA's express terms for a court to *remove* an arbitrator from service. Rather, even where arbitrator bias is at issue, the FAA does not provide for removal of an arbitrator from service prior to an award, but only for potential vacatur of any award' (emphasis original).

[172] *In re Sussex*, 781 F.3d 1065, 1075 (9th Cir. 2015).

[173] ICC Rules, Art. 14.2 and 14.3.

[174] This rule led to a claim by a respondent state against the ICC in its own courts. Recourse filed by the Argentine Republic against the ICC on 8 February 2006, requesting that the ICC's decision (as appointing authority) be overturned for failure to provide reasons. Two preliminary injunctions were granted by the National Contentious-Administrative Court of Appeals of Argentina in *Estado Nacional—Procuración del Tesoro de la Nación v Cámara de Comercio Internacional*, dated 3 July 2007 and 17 July 2008, available online at http://fallos.diprargentina.com/2009/07/procuracion-del-tesoro-c-camara-de.html.

[175] ICC Rules, Art. 15.2 and Appendix II, Art. 5.

[176] LCIA Rules, Art. 10.3.

[177] LCIA Rules, Art. 10.3–10.6.

made in writing, with reasons.[178] Indeed, if the parties so request, the division may even hold an oral hearing in this regard.

(iii) UNCITRAL challenge procedure

Under the UNCITRAL Rules, any challenge must be notified to the other party and to the members of the arbitral tribunal, including the challenged arbitrator.[179] The time limit for submitting a challenge is fifteen days.[180] The merits of challenges are decided by the appointing authority,[181] and whether reasons will accompany the challenge decision will depend upon the identity of the appointing authority.   **4.125**

(iv) ICSID challenge procedure

Any 'proposal for disqualification' of an arbitrator (terminology used by the ICSID Rules) must be filed with the Secretary-General of ICSID within twenty-one days of either (a) the constitution of the tribunal; or (b) the date on which the party proposing the disqualification first knew or should have known of the facts on which the proposal is based.[182] The party proposing the disqualification of an arbitrator must state the grounds on which it is based and a statement of relevant facts, law, and arguments plus supporting documents.[183] The other party must file its response to the proposal for disqualification within twenty-one days.[184] The challenged arbitrator may make a statement limited to factual information relating to the challenge within a further five day period.[185] Each party is then permitted to file a final simultaneous statement seven days following the arbitrator's statement.[186]   **4.126**

If the challenge is directed against one arbitrator in an arbitral tribunal of three, the decision is taken by the other two arbitrators.[187] If they cannot agree, the decision will be made by the Chair of the ICSID Administrative Council.[188] The decision will also be made by the Chair if the challenge is directed against a sole arbitrator, or against the majority of the arbitral tribunal.[189] The decision will be reasoned.[190] For as long as the constitution of the arbitral   **4.127**

---

[178] LCIA Rules, Arts 3.1 and 10.6. The LCIA was one of the first institutions that started publishing decisions on challenges in a suitably redacted form, since 2006, leading other institutions to then adopt the same approach.

[179] UNCITRAL Rules, Art. 13.

[180] This time limit is applied strictly. For an attempt by a party to challenge facts after expiry of the fifteen-day time limit, see *AWG Group v Argentine Republic*, Challenge Decision of 22 October 2007, at [21], reported as part of the challenge decision in the parallel ICSID case of *Suez and others v Argentine Republic*.

[181] UNCITRAL Rules, Art. 13. If the appointing authority fails to decide on a challenge to an arbitrator within a reasonable time, any party may request the Secretary General of the PCA to designate a substitute appointing authority. UNCITRAL Rules, Art. 6.4.

[182] ICSID Rules, r. 22(1)(a). If the grounds for challenge become known only when the proceedings are closed, then the remedy is a request for an annulment of the award under r. 50.

[183] Ibid, r. 22(1)(b).

[184] ICSID Rules, r. 22(1)(c).

[185] Ibid, r. 22(1)(d).

[186] Ibid, r. 22(1)(e).

[187] Ibid, r. 23(1).

[188] Ibid, r. 23(2)(a) and ICSID Convention, Art. 58.

[189] ICSID Convention, Art. 58.

[190] Although Art. 58 of the ICSID Convention does not explicitly require a challenge decision to state reasons, in practice, these decisions are reasoned. For instance, the annulment committee in *Azurix v Argentina II*, Annulment Decision of 1 September 2009, at [290], held that 'a duty to state reasons for a decision under Article 58 might be considered implicity [sic]'. ICSID challenge decisions are usually published. For recent examples, see *Landesbank Baden-Württemberg and ors v Kingdom of Spain*, ICSID Case No. ARB/15/45, Decision on the Second Proposal to Disqualify All Members of the Tribunal, 15 December 2020; *Vattenfall AB and ors v Federal Republic of Germany II*, ICSID Case No. ARB/12/12, Recommendation on the Second Proposal to Disqualify the Tribunal, 6 July 2020.

tribunal is in doubt because of a challenge to one or more of the arbitrators, the arbitral proceedings are suspended unless the parties agree otherwise.[191] If the challenge is upheld, a vacancy is created in the arbitral tribunal, which must be filled before the proceedings resume. If the challenge is rejected, the arbitration proceeds.

(d) Principal bases for challenge

4.128   In order to understand how challenge decisions are taken, in this section we will consider some of the responses given by the decision-making bodies in contexts such as:

- where there is an alleged connection between the arbitrator and one of the parties;
- where there is an alleged connection between the arbitrator and counsel for one of the parties (which can include, by way of example, where the arbitrator and counsel belong to the same barristers' chambers);
- where the arbitrator acts as counsel for a third party in a dispute involving similar issues, in which he or she is advancing a case contrary to that of one of the parties to the dispute before him or her as arbitrator (the so-called double-hat dilemma); and
- where the arbitrator makes a statement that is alleged to involve a pre-judgment of an issue in the dispute.

(i) Connection with one of the parties

4.129   A connection with one of the parties can arise in different scenarios. The IBA Guidelines provide detailed guidance on a range of specific disqualifying connections. We have already addressed the question of the connection established by repeat appointments by the same party and the risks that such appointments raise.[192] Separately, an arbitrator should not be acting simultaneously as counsel in separate proceedings involving one of the parties. For example, in *ICS Inspection and Control Services Limited v Argentina I*,[193] the appointing authority deemed that a challenged arbitrator who was serving as counsel in an arbitration against the same respondent was in a situation of adversity towards the respondent and that, absent circumstances that would eliminate any justifiable doubts as to the challenged arbitrator's impartiality and independence, the challenge should be sustained.[194]

4.130   If the arbitrator (or a close family member[195]) has a significant financial interest in one of the parties, or in the subject matter in dispute in the arbitration, a challenge would be upheld.[196] In one UNCITRAL case, the respondent challenged the claimant's party-appointed arbitrator due to his connections with a financing partner of the claimant on the project that formed part of the subject matter of the arbitration.[197] It was not disputed

---

[191] ICSID Rules, r. 22(2) .

[192] See paragraphs 4.87–4.100.

[193] *ICS Inspection*, fn. 101, at [22.2].

[194] Ibid., at [22.4].

[195] The IBA Guidelines define 'close family member' as a spouse, sibling, child, parent, or life partner, in addition to any other family member with whom a close relationship exists.

[196] See para. 1.3 of the Non-Waivable Red List (for the arbitrator) and para. 2.2.2 of the Waivable Red List (for close family members) of the IBA Guidelines.

[197] *Nord Stream 2*, fn. 146, at [31]–[35].

that the challenged arbitrator had been the legal director and a member of the executive committee of that financing partner prior to the arbitration (and was expected to receive a pension from the company as a result of his services) nor that he was a shareholder of the company. The Secretary-General of the PCA first determined that the financing partner had a material participation in the project and concluded that the arbitrator's relationship with the financing partner (even though not a party to the arbitration) was enough to give rise to justifiable doubts as to his impartiality or independence in a dispute involving the project. The Secretary-General concluded that these circumstances were enough for an informed and objective third party to find justifiable doubts as to the challenged arbitrator's impartiality and independence. A similar conclusion was reached by the LCIA Court when it concluded that a reasonable and objective third party would have justifiable doubts as to the co-arbitrator's independence based on the following facts: (1) the arbitrator was employed by and taught at a university; (2) the chair of the board of the respondent was a member of the university's Board of Trustees; (3) the university had a cooperation agreement with the respondent; and (4) the claimant in the arbitration expected to refer to decisions approved by members of the board of the respondent in the arbitration.[198]

However, the connection with one of the parties needs to be material. In *Suez et al. v Argentina*, disqualification was sought in an ICSID case by the respondent based on the fact that one arbitrator was a non-executive director of an investment bank that held a small participation in two of the claimant companies, principally as a portfolio investor on behalf of others.[199] The other members of the tribunal considered it to be a remote connection that could not be sufficient in and of itself to justify a disqualification.[200]   **4.131**

As defined by the tribunal in that case, a further step is required: the alleged connection must be evaluated *qualitatively* in order to decide whether it constitutes a fact indicating a manifest lack of independence of judgement and impartiality. This was addressed by means of a four-point test.   **4.132**

- *Proximity* How closely connected is the challenged arbitrator to one of the parties? The closer the connection between the arbitrator and a party, the more likely it is that the relationship may influence an arbitrator's independence and impartiality.
- *Intensity* How intense and frequent are the interactions between the arbitrator and one of the parties? The more frequent and intense the interaction, the more likely it is that the arbitrator's independence and impartiality will be affected.
- *Dependence* To what extent is the challenged arbitrator dependent on one of the parties for benefits? The more dependent the arbitrator is on a relationship for benefits or advantages, the more likely it is that the relationship may influence the arbitrator's independence and impartiality.

---

[198] LCIA Reference No. 142862, 2 June 2015.
[199] *Suez, Sociedad General de Aguas de Barcelona SA, and Vivendi Universal SA v Argentine Republic*, Decision on a Second Proposal for the Disqualification of a Member of the Arbitral Tribunal, ICSID Case No. ARB/03/17, 12 May 2008, at [41]–[44].
[200] Ibid., at [32]. The decision was confirmed by the US District Court for the District of Columbia in 2016. *Republic of Argentina v AWG Grp. LTD.*, 894 F.3d 327, 339 (D.C. Cir. 2018) UNCITRAL, Memorandum Opinion of the US District Court for the District of Columbia, 30 September 2016.

- *Materiality* To what extent are any benefits accruing to the arbitrator as a result of the alleged connection significant? Significant benefits derived from a relationship will be more likely to influence an arbitrator's independence and impartiality than negligible or insignificant benefits.[201]

4.133   A connection can also exist if an arbitrator has acted as counsel on unrelated matters to one of the parties.[202] In a novel UNCITRAL case, the respondent challenged the claimant's party-appointed arbitrator on the basis that the arbitrator had acted as counsel for the challenging party. The appointing authority considered that the challenging party could not demonstrate how the independence of the arbitrator would be in question as he did not have a personal interest in the dispute. However, the appointing authority concluded that an objective observer would have justified doubts as to the arbitrator's impartiality considering the frequency with which the challenged arbitrator had acted as counsel for the respondent (and curiously the challenging party).[203] In a similar vein, the Paris Court of Appeal set aside an ICC award on the basis that the arbitral tribunal was not properly constituted since the arbitrator in question had failed to disclose existing links between his law firm and entities linked to one of the parties during the course of the proceedings. The Court concluded that these circumstances created a reasonable doubt as to the arbitrator's independence and impartiality.[204]

(ii) Connection with counsel or experts

4.134   A connection with counsel can arise in a variety of ways. Unless the parties give their specific agreement, an arbitrator cannot sit in a case in which he or she has a financial relationship with one of the lawyers involved. Most obviously, this will arise if they are colleagues in the same law firm.[205] Similarly, an arbitrator who receives a significant number of repeat appointments from the same law firm could be said to have developed a financial relationship with that firm.[206] Yet, in two recent ICSID cases, the Chair of the Administrative Council dismissed a challenge based on an alleged history of cross-appointments between the

---

[201] *Suez, Sociedad General de Aguas de Barcelona SA, and Vivendi Universal SA v Argentine Republic*, Decision on a Second Proposal for the Disqualification of a Member of the Arbitral Tribunal, ICSID Case No. ARB/03/17, 12 May 2008, at [35].

[202] The fact that an arbitrator regularly advises the appointing party or an affiliate of the appointing party and he or she (or his or her firm) derives significant financial income from such advice is on the Non-Waivable Red List (para. 1.4). Also on the Red List, although capable of being waived by express agreement of the parties, are instances in which an arbitrator has previously given legal advice or provided an expert opinion to one of the parties or an affiliate of one of the parties (para. 2.1.1), or in which he or she is currently representing or advising one of the parties or an affiliate of one of the parties (para. 2.3.1).

[203] *Exeteco International Company S.L. v Republic of Peru*, PCA Case No. AA 535, Decision on Challenge to Arbitrator Mario Castillo Freyre, 28 October 2014, at [83]–[88]. In *Compañía de Aguas del Aconquija SA and Vivendi Universal v Argentina*, ICSID Case No. ARB/97/3, Decision on the Challenge to the President of the Committee, 3 October 2001, at [26], the respondent state challenged the president of an ad hoc annulment committee based on the fact that another partner in his law firm had given limited advice to one of the parties in an unrelated area, which advice was continuing, but nearing completion. The fact had been disclosed by the president, who had no personal involvement in the advice in question. The remaining panel members therefore dismissed the challenge.

[204] See Paris cour d'appel, 27 March 2018, Case No. 16/09386. The cour de cassation confirmed the Paris cour d'appel's decision setting aside the award on 3 October 2019. Cass. Civ. 1, 3 October 2019, Case No. 18-15.756.

[205] The situation of an arbitrator and counsel for one of the parties being at the same law firm is on the Waivable Red List, at para. 2.3.3.

[206] In this regard, as previously stated, para. 3.3.8 of the Orange List encourages arbitrators to disclose if they have 'within the past three years received more than three appointments by the same counsel or the same law firm'.

claimant's counsel and the claimant's party-appointed arbitrator, ruling that 'without some-thing more' the history of cross-appointments was not enough to question the arbitrator's independence and impartiality.[207]

Under the same logic, in *Tecso*,[208] the French courts decided a challenge to an award based **4.135** on an arbitrator's failure to disclose a shared history with the law firm in which a lawyer for one of the parties practised. The arbitrator had left the law firm in question before the lawyer representing the party began working for the firm, although the arbitrator had since provided the firm with two or three legal opinions. The Court of Appeal in Paris set aside the award for the failure of the arbitrator to disclose this connection, but its decision was later reversed by the Court of Cassation.[209]

A similar issue arose in the ICSID case of *Owens-Illinois v Venezuela*. Venezuela challenged **4.136** the claimant-appointed arbitrator on the basis of an alleged connection between the arbi-trator and his former law firm, which had not represented any of the parties to the arbitra-tion, but had acted in several domestic litigations and arbitrations against Venezuela and/ or related state entities. The respondent argued that the challenged arbitrator had relied upon the services of lawyers employed at his former law firm as assistants to tribunals in cases in which he had served as president. The other arbitrators dismissed the challenge, reasoning that the challenged arbitrator had no financial interest in the services rendered by his former law firm and that the lawyers in question had acted as secretaries in cases unrelated to Venezuela. However, the deciding arbitrators also noted their decision would have been different had the challenged arbitrator continued to have a financial interest in the law firm.[210]

England's divided legal profession, comprising solicitors and barristers, poses a particular **4.137** question when it comes to considering an arbitrator's connection with counsel. Unlike partners and associates at law firms, barristers within chambers work as sole practitioners, sharing operating expenses, but not income or case information. For this reason, in English court proceedings, there is no constraint preventing barristers from appearing against each other in the same case nor, indeed, before a former member of their chambers who is now a judge. The situation is less straightforward in international arbitration proceedings, which

---

[207] *Raiffeisen Bank International*, fn. 152, at [93]–[95]; *Ayat Nizar Raja Sumrain and others v State of Kuwait*, ICSID Case No. ARB/19/20, Decision on the Claimants Proposal to Disqualify Prof. Zachary Douglas and Mr V.V. Veeder, 2 January 2020.

[208] *Tecso*, Case No. 11-20.299, Cass. Civ. 1, 10 October 2012.

[209] Professor Thomas Clay has argued that the language used by the cour de cassation simply states that the burden lies with that party which doubts the arbitrator's independence to substantiate such doubts: see Clay, 'Arbitrage et modes alternatifs de règlement des litiges' [2012] Recueil Dalloz 2991. Other scholars, such as Prof. Christophe Seraglini and Laura Weiller, consider that this decision marked a return to a more stringent con-trol on the alleged lack of independence: see Henry, 'Devoir de révélation de l'arbitre: Consécration du critère de l'incidence raisonnable sur l'indépendance et l'impartialité de l'arbitre' (2012) 46 La Semaine Juridique 1675; Weiller, 'Rejet de la prétendue faute de l'arbitre' (2012) 10 Procédures, comm. 284.

[210] *Fábrica de Vidrios Los Andes, CA and Owens-Illinois de Venezuela, CA v Bolivarian Republic of Venezuela*, ICSID Case No. ARB/12/21, Reasoned Decision on the Proposal to Disqualify L Yves Fortier, KC, arbitrator, 28 March 2016. In the same vein, *Universal Compression International Holdings, SLU v Bolivarian Republic of Venezuela*, ICSID Case No. ARB/10/9, Decision on the Proposal to Disqualify Prof. Brigitte Stern and Prof. Guido Santiago Tawil, arbitrators, 20 May 2011, at [52]. See also *Conocophillips Petrozuata BV and ors v Bolivarian Republic of Venezuela*, ICSID Case No. ARB/07/30, Decision on the Proposal to Disqualify L Yves Fortier KC, arbi-trator, 15 March 2016, at [1]–[3].

will generally involve lawyers and parties who are far less familiar with the role and work-ings of barristers' chambers.

4.138   In *Hrvatska Elektroprivreda v Republic of Slovenia*,[211] the respondent state communicated the addition of a barrister to its legal team at a very late stage of the proceedings. The bar-rister in question was a member of the same chambers as the chair of the arbitral tribunal, which led to an objection by the claimant and its non-English legal counsel. Exercising its inherent powers, the tribunal decided that the best way to safeguard the proceedings was to order the counsel in question to withdraw from the respondent's legal team. In so ordering, the tribunal began its discussion by observing that '[b]arristers are sole prac-titioners' and 'chambers are not law firms'—but it observed that '[i]t is, however, equally true that this practice is not universally understood let alone universally agreed, and that Chambers themselves have evolved in the modern market place for professional services with the consequence that they often present themselves with a collective connotation'.[212] Taking into account the fact that the claimant was entirely unfamiliar with the barristers' chambers system of England and Wales, that the respondent had consciously decided not to disclose the identity of the barrister until a very late stage in the proceedings, and that the respondent refused to reveal the extent of that barrister's participation, the tribunal found it necessary for counsel to step down in order to 'dispel' the 'atmosphere of apprehension and mistrust'.[213]

4.139   In *Rompetrol Group NV v Romania*, the tribunal considered an application to exclude claimant's counsel for having been formerly employed at the same law firm as the claimant's party-appointed arbitrator. The tribunal dismissed the challenge applying the standard set by the UK House of Lords (now the UK Supreme Court) in *Porter v Magill*: the facts should raise a 'real possibility that the tribunal was biased'. The tribunal considered that the association between counsel and the arbitrator raised no issue as to either person having a present or future financial or material interest in the other's professional activity. Furthermore, the tribunal concluded that 'the Hrvatska Decision might better be seen as an ad hoc sanction for the failure to make proper disclosure in good time than as a holding of more general scope'.[214]

4.140   In *A and others v B and another*, the English Commercial Court considered an application to remove an arbitrator on the ground that there were justifiable doubts as to his impartial-ity because he was appointed as solicitor by claimant's counsel to defend one of its clients in a local litigation. The Court did not consider that a fair-minded and informed observer, who is presumed to know how the legal profession in the country works, would conclude that there was a real possibility of apparent bias merely because the arbitrator acted as counsel for one of the firms acting in the arbitration. The Court also dismissed the challen-ging party's reliance on the IBA Guidelines and made clear that if there was no apparent or unconscious bias, applying the English common law test, the guidelines could not alter the

---

[211] *Hrvatska Elektroprivreda v Republic of Slovenia*, Tribunal's Ruling on the Participation of Counsel, ICSID Case No. ARB/05/24, 6 May 2008.
[212] Ibid., at [17]–[18].
[213] Ibid.
[214] *Rompetrol Group NV v Romania*, ICSID Case No. ARB/06/3, Decision of the Tribunal on the Participation of a Counsel, 14 January 2010, at [25].

conclusion.[215] Similarly, in *Brescla Calcio SpA v West Ham United FC Plc*,[216] the Board of the International Council of Arbitration for Sport (ICAS) upheld a challenge against the respondent's party-appointed arbitrator because counsel for the respondent was from the same chambers. In the view of the Italian claimant, this circumstance 'cast some doubts, at least in appearance, as to the arbitrator's independence'.[217] The ICAS Board applied an objective test and referred explicitly to the IBA Guidelines, noting that it was convinced that the arbitrator in question was independent and impartial. In 2010, the ICC upheld a challenge to the claimant-appointed arbitrator on the basis that she was a member of the same barristers' chambers as two members of the claimant's counsel.[218] As the IBA Guidelines make clear, it is undoubtedly necessary for disclosure to take place if the arbitrator and another arbitrator, or the counsel for one of the parties, are members of the same barristers' chambers.[219]

It is noteworthy that, following the *Hrvatska* case,[220] English arbitrators began to insert provisions into procedural orders or terms of reference requiring notification of the names of counsel representing the parties and authorising the tribunal to reject counsel to whom there was a reasonable objection in order 'to maintain the integrity of the arbitral process'. An increasing number of arbitration rules now follow this practice by requiring the parties to identify their representatives and authorising the tribunal to dismiss counsel from the case if the tribunal considers this necessary to maintain the integrity of the proceedings. For example, the LCIA has included a provision in Article 18.4 requiring approval of the arbitral panel for changes of legal counsel during the course of the arbitration.[221] Similarly, the IBA Guidelines require a party to disclose the identity of its counsel 'on its own initiative' and 'at the earliest opportunity'.[222] The IBA Rules on Party Representation in International Arbitration provide that, after the constitution of the tribunal, no person should accept representation of a party where there is a conflict of interest with one of the arbitrators and permit the tribunal to take measures necessary to safeguard the integrity of the proceedings, including by excluding the new party representative.[223]

4.141

---

[215] *A and others v B and another* [2011] EWHC 2345 (Comm).
[216] (2012) 3 ISLR 40.
[217] Ibid., at 52.
[218] ICC Case No. 16553/GZ. See Cleis, *The Independence and Impartiality of ICSID Arbitrators*, Nijhoff International Investment Law Series (Brill, 2017), p. 139.
[219] IBA Guidelines , at [3.3.2]. The Bar Council of England and Wales issued an information note regarding barristers in international arbitration and, in so doing, avoided a blanket ban on members of the same chambers appearing in the same case as counsel and arbitrator. According to the Bar Council:

> As a matter of English and Welsh law, there is no prohibition against an advocate appearing before an arbitration tribunal which includes a member of his or her chambers [...] Nevertheless, good practice would dictate that in circumstances where a barrister comes to understand that he or she has been instructed in an arbitration where one or more of the members of the Tribunal are barristers in the same set of chambers, prompt disclosure ought to be made by those instructing the barrister advocate to the legal representatives of the other side. This will ensure as far as possible that the guidance set out in the IBA Guidelines on Conflicts of Interest in International Arbitration is followed (see further below). A failure to make prompt disclosure, could ultimately, lead to a challenge to the independence of the member(s) of the Tribunal in question.

See Bar Council of England and Wales, Information Note Regarding Barristers In International Arbitration, 6 July 2015, pp. 4–5.
[220] See paragraph 4.138.
[221] LCIA Rules, Art. 18.4.
[222] IBA Guidelines, Guideline 7(b).
[223] IBA Guidelines on Party Representation, Guidelines 5 and 6.

4.142   An additional concern has arisen when there is a connection between a member of the arbitral tribunal and the party-appointed experts in the case. In *Eiser v Spain*, an award was annulled for improper constitution of the tribunal and for a serious departure from a fundamental rule of procedure, based on one arbitrator's close ties with a party-appointed valuation expert. Spain challenged the award after it became aware of the relationship between the claimant's party-appointed arbitrator and the claimant's damages experts in that case, which had not been disclosed in a timely manner by the arbitrator. The annulment committee reasoned that there were several past and present professional connections and interactions in various capacities between the arbitrator (as such and formerly as counsel in his prior law firm) and the expert.[224] The annulment committee first determined that the arbitrator had failed to comply with his obligation to disclose the relationship and then concluded that the arbitral tribunal had not been properly constituted.[225]

(iii) Issue conflict

4.143   The notion of issue conflict is not a universal one and does not have a settled definition. Broadly, an issue conflict may arise when (i) an arbitrator has already decided in a previous case an issue arising in a later arbitration; (ii) an arbitrator has previously published views on an issue arising in a later arbitration; and/or (iii) an arbitrator is a member of or is associated with a law firm representing clients facing the same or similar issues as those on which the arbitrator will rule—the so-called 'double-hat' dilemma (see further below at 4.151).[226] In *CC/Devas v India* Judge Peter Tomka, former president of the International Court of Justice, stated his understanding of issue conflict in the following terms:[227]

> The conflict is based on a concern that an arbitrator will not approach an issue impartially, but rather with a desire to conform to his or her own view. In this respect [...] some challenge decisions and commentators have concluded that knowledge of the law or views expressed about the law are not per se sources of conflict that require removal of an arbitrator; likewise, a prior decision in a common area of law does not automatically support a view that an arbitrator may lack impartiality. Thus, to sustain any challenge brought on such a basis requires more than simply having expressed any prior view; rather, I must find, on the basis of the prior view and any other relevant circumstances, that there is an appearance of prejudgment of an issue likely to be relevant to the dispute on which the parties have a reasonable expectation of an open mind.

4.144   The Report of the ASIL-ICCA Joint Task Force on Issue Conflicts in Investor–State Arbitration explained that questions arising under the rubric of 'issue conflict' go to the

---

[224] *Eiser Infrastructure*, fn. 108, at [218] ('the Committee has taken particular note of four instances where [the arbitrator] and [the expert] worked for the same party, as counsel and expert respectively. In two of those cases, [the arbitrator], as counsel, was interacting with [the expert], at the same time that he was acting in this case as an arbitrator and [the expert] as a damages expert of one of the parties. This was in addition to the longstanding relationship between the [the expert's firm] and [the arbitrator]'s then law firm [...], and included another concurrent case—*Bear Creek*—in which [the arbitrator] was working as counsel with [the expert's firm]').

[225] Ibid., at [225], [228], [241]–[242].

[226] Report of the ASIL-ICCA Joint Task Force on Issue Conflicts in Investor–State Arbitration, International Council for Commercial Arbitration, 17 March 2016 (the 'ASIL-ICCA Joint Task Force'), at [8].

[227] *CC/Devas (Mauritius) Ltd. and ors v Republic of India*, PCA Case No. 2013-09, Respondent's Challenge to the Hon. Marc Lalonde as Presiding Arbitrator and Prof. Francisco Orrego Vicuna as Co-Arbitrator, 30 September 2013, at [58].

arbitrator's state of mind, something that is often dependent on context and is not readily susceptible to measurement with mechanical rules, so that 'whatever the precise term used, we must revert to the central question, which is when does a predisposition become inappropriate?'[228]

Challenges in investment arbitrations have been mounted on the basis of prior arbitrations where the challenged arbitrator expressed his or her views on similar legal concepts and/ or publication by an arbitrator of opinions that pertain to an issue in dispute in the arbitration.[229] Generally, challenges based on the arbitrator's past expressions in scholarly or professional writings have not been accepted.[230] The tribunal in *Urbaser v Argentina*[231] set a high threshold for a challenge based on such grounds to succeed: 'there must be a showing that such opinion or position is supported by factors related to and supporting a party to the arbitration (or a party closely related to such party), by a direct or indirect interest of the arbitrator in the outcome of the dispute, or by a relationship with any other individual involved, such as a witness or arbitrator'.[232] In a UNCITRAL case, the respondent challenged the presiding arbitrator and claimant's party-appointed arbitrator, arguing that the challenge was not based on a lack of independence or inappropriate action but on an 'issue conflict'. The respondent alleged that both arbitrators had 'strongly held and articulated positions' on the interpretation of the 'essential security interests' provision in two prior cases in which they had sat together, and that the party-appointed arbitrator had further defended his position in a book chapter he authored. The decision defined the standard for an 'issue conflict' as follows:

> [T]o sustain any challenge brought on such a basis requires more than simply having expressed any prior view; rather, I must find, on the basis of the prior view and any other relevant circumstances, that there is an appearance of pre-judgment of an issue likely to be relevant to the dispute on which the parties have a reasonable expectation of an open mind.[233]

4.145

The appointing authority upheld the challenge against the party-appointed arbitrator and dismissed the challenge against the presiding arbitrator. When applying the above standard, the appointing authority considered decisive that the party-appointed arbitrator had already pronounced his views on the same legal concept in four prior arbitrations and had later defended his position in an article analysing the decision by three different annulment committees which had annulled his decisions on those cases. The appointing authority considered that the respondent was entitled to have its arguments heard and ruled upon

4.146

---

[228] The ASIL-ICCA Joint Task Force, at [17]–[19].

[229] It is questionable, however, if such issue conflicts will exist more broadly in purely commercial cases in which the applicable legal systems, facts, and legal issues are varied, and the ultimate awards rarely published.

[230] The ASIL-ICCA Joint Task Force, at [45]–[52].

[231] *Urbaser SA and others v Argentine Republic*, Decision on Claimants' Proposal to Disqualify Professor Campbell McLachlan, Arbitrator, ICSID Case No. ARB/07/26, 12 August 2010, at [44]–[45]. The tribunal found that the taking of a general position on an issue raised in the arbitration was not sufficient to establish bias, or even the appearance of bias, since a reasonable person would consider that the arbitrator would still give proper consideration to the facts, circumstances, and arguments presented by the parties in the particular case.

[232] *Ibid.* See also *Repsol v Argentine Republic*, ICSID Case No. ARB/12/38, Decision on the Request for Disqualification of the Majority of the Tribunal, at [26]–[30].

[233] *CC/Devas (Mauritius)*, fn. 227, at [58].

by arbitrators with an 'open mind' and that a reasonable observer would not believe that the respondent had a chance to convince the arbitrator to change his mind on that legal concept. On the other hand, the appointing authority considered that the participation of the presiding arbitrator in two of the same cases as the party-appointed arbitrator was not enough to disqualify him, as the presiding arbitrator had not separately expressed his views on this subject and therefore could approach the matter with an open mind and give it full consideration.[234]

4.147 Similarly, in the ICSID arbitration *KS Invest and TLS Invest v Spain,* the Chair of the ICSID Administrative Council reaffirmed that the circumstance that an arbitrator had expressed his views on issues of law or fact common to two or more parallel arbitrations was not enough evidence of partiality or the appearance thereof.[235] The Chair noted that the two cases in which the challenged arbitrator was acting involved different investments by unrelated companies, made at different times, and in different sectors. Further, the Chair affirmed that 'even in cases where issues could be similar, the arguments and the manner in which they are presented by different parties could differ depending on the particularities of each case'.[236] Based on this, and the fact that Spain had not raised concerns about the appointment of the challenged arbitrator at the time of his appointment (when it already knew about his appointment in the parallel arbitration), the Chair dismissed the challenge.[237]

4.148 Similarly, in another ICSID arbitration, the tribunal found that the mere fact that the challenged arbitrator had previously argued the same or similar issues raised by the respondent state in prior arbitrations acting as counsel (for a different respondent state) did not mean that the arbitrator was going to necessarily take the same stance in the present case.[238]

4.149 The situation was different in *Perenco Ecuador Ltd v Ecuador & Empresa Estatal Petróleos del Ecuador,*[239] where the challenge arose out of a published interview with the arbitrator, in which he made various comments about Ecuador's disobedient behaviour, including Ecuador's refusal to comply with orders for provisional measures. The Secretary-General of the PCA found that, although the arbitrator did not specifically refer to the arbitration, his combination of chosen words and the context in which he used them had the overall effect of painting an unfavourable view of Ecuador (which had brought the challenge) in such a way as to give a reasonable and informed third party justifiable doubts as to his impartiality.[240]

4.150 After analysing several challenge decisions based on 'issue-conflicts', the ASIL-ICCA Task Force identified three prongs to analyse whether an arbitrator could be considered impartial: (i) the degree of commitment to the arbitrator's prior views; (ii) the concurrency of the

---

[234] Ibid., at [64]–[66].

[235] *KS Invest GmbH and TLS Invest GmbH v Kingdom of Spain*, ICSID Case No. ARB/15/25, Decision on the Proposal to Disqualify Prof. Kaj Hobér, 15 May 2020, at [89].

[236] Ibid., at [90].

[237] Ibid., at [89]–[93].

[238] *St. Gobain Performance Plastics v Bolivarian Republic of Venezuela*, ICSID Case No. ARB/12/13, Decision on Claimant's Proposal to Disqualify Mr Bottini, 27 February 2013, at [77], [80]–[81].

[239] *Perenco Ecuador Ltd v Republic of Ecuador & Empresa Estatal Petróleos del Ecuador*, ICSID Case No. ARB/08/6, PCA Case No. IR-2009/1, Decision on Challenge to Arbitrator, 8 December 2009.

[240] Ibid., at [48].

arbitrator's position as both counsel and arbitrator in matters involving the same party or otherwise related matters; and (iii) the specificity or proximity to the current case.[241]

(iv) Double-hatting

A particular scenario may arise where a lawyer is sitting in one case as an arbitrator in which **4.151** a point of law is being argued, whilst acting in another case as counsel to a party arguing that same point of law. There is no suggestion of any links with the parties, but rather an allegation that the arbitrator will not be able to be impartial with regard to a decision on a point of law that may be determinative in the case in which he or she is defending the interests of a client as counsel.[242] This scenario—sometimes referred to as the 'double-hat dilemma'—is particularly prevalent in investment arbitration cases, given the discrete number of recurring legal concepts at issue,[243] the publicity of the investment arbitration awards (and sometimes even the pleadings of the parties), and the repeat participation by well-known international lawyers as counsel and arbitrator.

This arose in the *Telekom Malaysia* arbitration[244] where, by reason of the arbitrator's role as **4.152** counsel to an investor in a similar investment arbitration, Ghana challenged his appointment. Ghana argued that, given that the arbitrator was simultaneously acting for an investor in relation to similar points of law, he would be likely to adopt a position favourable to the claimant, Telekom Malaysia. As a result, Ghana argued, the arbitrator lacked independence and impartiality.[245] While the other members of the tribunal and the Secretariat of the PCA rejected the challenge, Ghana brought the matter for review to the Dutch courts, The Hague being the agreed seat of the arbitration. The District Court of The Hague emphasised the 'incompatibility' of the arbitrator's role as attorney and arbitrator, placing much weight on the appearance, rather than the actual existence of bias:[246]

> Even if this arbitrator were able to sufficiently distance himself in chambers from his role as attorney in the reversal proceedings […] account should be taken of the appearance of his not being able to observe the said distance. Since he has to play these two parts, it is in any case impossible for him to avoid the appearance of not being able to keep these two parts strictly separated.[247]

To avoid giving rise to 'justifiable doubts' as to the arbitrator's impartiality and independ- **4.153** ence, the Court permitted him to continue serving on the tribunal, on the condition that he resign as counsel in the other arbitration within ten days.[248]

---

[241] Report of the ASIL-ICCA Joint Task Force, at [65]–[70].
[242] The CAS has amended its rules to prohibit arbitrators from serving as counsel at the same time in CAS cases. See Code of Sports-related Arbitration, s. 18.
[243] International investment law applied as the substantive law in these arbitrations is largely focused on specific legal concepts of expropriation, fair and equitable treatment, and unreasonable or discriminatory measures. See Chapter 8 for more details.
[244] *Telekom Malaysia Berhad v Republic of Ghana*, District Court of The Hague, Decision No. HA/ RK2004.667, 18 October 2004.
[245] Levine, 'Dealing with arbitrator "issue conflicts" in international arbitration' (2006) 3 Disp Res J 60, at 62; Peterson, 'Dutch Court finds arbitrator in conflict due to role of counsel to another investor', Investment Law and Policy Weekly News Bulletin, 17 December 2004.
[246] District Court of The Hague, Civil Law Section, Provisional Measures Judge, Challenge No. 13/2004, Petition No. HA/RK2004/667, Decision of 18 October 2004.
[247] Ibid., at [63].
[248] Similarly, in *ICS v Argentina*, Argentina sought the removal of the investor-appointed arbitrator, who was also acting as counsel for another investor in ICSID annulment proceedings involving Argentina. In

4.154   In *KS Invest and TLS Invest v Spain*,[249] the respondent state challenged the claimant's party-appointed arbitrator on several grounds, including his role as counsel in a parallel arbitration in which respondent's right to regulate was being contested. The Chair of the ICSID Administrative Council dismissed the challenge, noting that the arbitration in which the challenged arbitrator was acting as counsel concerned different claimants, different respondents, different subsectors of the energy industry, and different measures. Given the multiple differences between the two cases, the Chair considered that a reasonable evaluation from a third party could not conclude that the arbitrator manifestly lacked the qualities required under Article 14(1) of the ICSID Convention.

4.155   The issue of double-hatting continues to create concern and is far from settled. In an effort to provide some certainty on the issue, the Draft Code of Conduct for Adjudicators in Investor–State Dispute Settlement, prepared by the Secretariats of ICSID and UNCITRAL, provides a series of options from an outright prohibition to informed consent of the disputing parties.[250] However, some law firms active as counsel in investment arbitrations have been self-policing and adopted internal policies prohibiting lawyers at the firm from acting as arbitrators in investment disputes.

(v) Pre-judgment

4.156   In one UNCITRAL case, the respondent state challenged one of the arbitrators based on comments made during the hearing, alleging that the arbitrator's comments pre-judged one of the issues in the arbitration.[251] During the cross-examination of an expert, the arbitrator had made a comment that could be interpreted as suggesting that the respondent had caused compensable damage to the claimant. The challenge was heard by a division of the LCIA Court, by agreement of the parties. The LCIA admitted that, in isolation, the statement in question could lead a reasonable third person to believe that the arbitrator was pre-judging an issue. However, the LCIA noted that, immediately after the comment in question, the arbitrator clarified that he was posing hypothetical questions to the expert, which from a reasonable point of view eliminated any appearance of pre-judgment.[252]

4.157   Even when comments made by an arbitrator do reveal an evolving thought process, the courts have made it clear that this is a natural result of evaluating evidence. For example, in *Fairchild & Co. Inc. v Richmond*,[253] the DC District Court held that:

> [An arbitrator's] legitimate efforts to move the proceedings along expeditiously may be viewed as abrasive or disruptive to a disappointed party […] such displeasure does

response, ICS argued that the annulment proceedings would soon be completed and that the arbitrator would therefore not be arguing for his investor client at the same time as he would be entertaining the instant arbitration. The appointing authority was unconvinced by such temporal distinctions and, referring to the IBA Guidelines, held that the conflict was 'sufficiently serious to give rise to objectively justifiable doubts as to [the arbitrator's] impartiality and independence'. UNCITRAL, PCA Case No. 2010-9, Challenge Decision, 17 December 2009. See also *Blue Bank International & Trust (Barbados) Ltd v Bolivarian Republic of Venezuela*, ICSID Case No. ARB/12/20, Decision on the Parties' Proposal to Disqualify a Majority of the Tribunal, 12 November 2013.

[249] *KS Invest*, fn. 235, at [83]–[84].
[250] Draft Code of Conduct for Adjudicators in Investor–State Dispute Settlement, Version Three, September 2021, comments by State/Commenter as of 3 November 2021, p. 8.
[251] *National Grid PLC v Argentine Republic*, LCIA Case No. UN7949, Decision on the Challenge dated 3 December 2007, at [38].
[252] Ibid., at [95]–[96].
[253] *Fairchild & Co. Inc. v Richmond F & PR Co.*, 516 F. Supp 1305, 1313 (DDC 1981).

not constitute grounds for vacating an arbitration award […] [E]vident partiality is not demonstrated where an arbitrator consistently relies upon the evidence and reaches the conclusions favourable to one party […] The mere fact that arbitrators are persuaded by one party's arguments and choose to agree with them is not of itself sufficient to raise a question as to the evident partiality of the arbitrators.

Conversely, the LCIA Court upheld a challenge and removed an arbitrator after he pre-   **4.158** maturely expressed his views on the merits of the case. The LCIA Court reasoned that the arbitrator 'conveyed the impression to an objective and informed observer that he had pre-judged the merits of the counterclaims at the jurisdictional phase, creating thereby an appearance of bias'.[254]

(e) Conflict waiver

A question arises concerning the obligation of a party to raise promptly any objection con-   **4.159** cerning the independence or impartiality of an arbitrator (or any other ground of challenge) when the facts upon which the challenge is based come to its attention.

In the ICSID Rules, Rule 28 ('Waiver') states clearly that a party who fails to object promptly   **4.160** to an alleged violation of a relevant rule or a decision of the Tribunal or Secretary-General is deemed to have waived its right to object. Similarly, under Article 40 of the ICC Rules, Article 31 of the ICDR Rules, Article 32.1 of the LCIA Rules,[255] and Article 40.1 of the SIAC Rules,[256] a party who does not promptly raise objections to any non-compliance with such rules will be treated as having waived its right to object.[257] Further, Article 14.2 of the ICC Rules provides that a challenge must be made within the prescribed time limit for it to be admissible.[258] Under Article 13(2) of the Model Law, challenges related to impartiality or independence must be filed with the arbitral tribunal within fifteen days of the party becoming aware of the circumstances giving rise to justifiable doubts.[259] The question then arises if the same objection can be raised later in a challenge to the award or on enforcement proceedings. Whilst this question has not been resolved definitively, the better view is that a failure to comply with the time limits to challenge an arbitrator should bar any attack of the award on this basis.

In common law jurisdictions, the concept of waiver is well established: a party may not 'lie   **4.161** in ambush' with an objection to await the decision of the tribunal. In *A.S.M Shipping Ltd of India v T.T.M.I Ltd of England*, the English Commercial Court ruled that:

It is unacceptable to write making further objections after the hearing was concluded. X KC had made his decision not to recuse himself, rightly or wrongly, at the beginning of the third day. Owners were faced with a straight choice: come to the court and complain and seek his removal as a decision maker or let the matter drop. They could not get themselves into a position whereby if the award was in their favour they would

---

[254] LCIA Reference No. 1322498, 24 December 2014.
[255] ICC Rules, Art. 40.
[256] SIAC Rules, Art. 40.1.
[257] ICDR Rules, Art. 31.
[258] ICC Rules, Art. 14.2.
[259] Model Law, Art. 13(2). See also ICDR Rules, Art. 14.

drop their objection but make it in the event that the award went against them. A 'heads we win and tails you lose' position is not permissible in law as section 73 makes clear. The threat of objection cannot be held over the head of the tribunal until they make their decision and could be seen as an attempt to put unfair and undue pressure upon them.[260]

4.162   Similarly, the United States Court of Appeals for the Third Circuit,[261] considered that a respondent had waived its right to challenge an award based on an arbitrator's alleged insufficient disclosure because it had constructive knowledge of such disclosure at the time of the appointment and failed to challenge the arbitrator at that time. The Court strongly affirmed that:

> This is the paradigmatic case of the 'sore loser', so to speak, trying for a second bite at the apple—and the exact type of case the law disfavors. A party should not be permitted to game the system by rolling the dice on whether to raise the challenge during the proceedings or wait until it loses to seek vacatur on the issue. Nor should a party 'wait[] until [it] los[es] and then almost immediately beg[i]n scouring the internet for anything that might suggest one arbitrator or another was biased against it.' This is all to say, under the constructive knowledge standard, a party may not conduct a background investigation on an arbitrator after the award with the sole motivation to seek vacatur. If it were any other way, arbitrations would cease to have finality and result in endless hearings within hearings.[262]

4.163   The concept of waiver is also known in civil law countries. A challenge to an arbitrator under the Swiss PIL must be brought within thirty days since the requesting party became aware or should have been aware of the ground for challenge and it must be communicated to the other members of the tribunal within the same time limit.[263] Under French law, parties have one month from discovery of the fact at issue to file a challenge.[264] The Court of Cassation has consistently dismissed cases where the facts upon which the challenge was based were publicly accessible and were not brought in a timely manner. For example, in 2016 the Court of Cassation rejected an appeal by the challenging party based on an alleged connection between an arbitrator and the other party's legal expert as it considered that, through simple research on publicly accessible websites, the challenging party could have made itself aware of those relationships. As such, the Court confirmed that parties have a duty to investigate in order to identify publicly available information about the arbitrators that may call into question their independence and impartiality.[265] Similarly, in 2017, the Court of Cassation upheld a decision of the Court of Appeal in Paris not to set aside an award on the ground that the arbitral tribunal had been unlawfully constituted, noting that the documents relied upon by the challenging party had been in the public domain since

---

[260] *ASM Shipping Ltd of India v TTMI Ltd of England*, 2005 WL 3157679, at [49].
[261] *Goldman, Sachs & Co. v Athena Venture Partners, L.P.*, 803 F.3d 144, 150 (3d Cir. 2015). See also *Larison v Magnotti*, 37 NYS.2d 207 (NY Sup Ct 2016).
[262] *Goldman, Sachs & Co. v Athena Venture Partners, L.P.*, 803 F.3d 144, 150 (3d Cir. 2015).
[263] Swiss PIL, art. 180(a). See *Judgment of 30 April 2018*, 37 ASA Bull. 694 (Swiss Fed. Trib.) (2019); Decision 4A_ 14/2012, Swiss Supreme Court, available online at https://www.swissarbitrationdecisions.com. See also *Judgment of 30 April 2018*, 37 ASA Bull. 694, 695 (2019) (Swiss Fed. Trib.).
[264] French Code of Civil Procedure, art. 1456(3).
[265] *NMLK v M.X*, Cass. Civ. (1e chambre civile), 25 May 2016, Case No. 14-20532.

the appointment of the arbitrator and the challenging party could have, but failed, to raise its objection within the 30-day time limit.[266] However, it should be stressed that a party can only be deemed to have waived its rights to challenge based on facts that it was aware of or should have reasonably been aware of.[267]

Finally, it is noteworthy that the community of arbitration specialists recognises the im-   **4.164**
portance of prompt action when a ground for challenge is asserted. In the IBA Guidelines, with the exception of red list conflicts, General Standard 4(a) requires a party to make an explicit objection within thirty days of any disclosure by the arbitrator, or of a party, of facts or circumstances that could constitute a potential conflict of interest, otherwise the party is deemed to have waived the potential conflict.

A discussion of waiver is incomplete without a consideration of the emerging phenomenon   **4.165**
of 'advance' waivers. Since a considerable number of arbitrators work at large law firms, there is a practice whereby such arbitrators send advance waivers to the parties prior to accepting an appointment. Such waivers vary in form, but typically amount to a request for advance clearance from the parties to the effect that the acceptance of the arbitral appointment will not inhibit other lawyers from the same law firm from acting for or against any party involved in the arbitration, as long as such separate mandate is unrelated to the arbitration. Advance waivers raise questions of party autonomy and informed consent. The approach of the leading institutions regarding such waivers is inconsistent. The ICC issued a Note on Conflict Disclosures by Arbitrators in which it expressed that '[a]lthough an advance declaration or waiver in relation to possible conflicts of interest arising from facts and circumstances that may arise in the future may or may not in certain circumstances be taken into account by the Court, such advance declaration or waiver does not discharge an arbitrator from his or her ongoing duty to disclose'.[268] For its part, the IBA Guidelines acknowledge the increasing use of such advanced waivers, and also confirm that they do not discharge an arbitrator's ongoing duty of disclosure, but do not take a position on their validity and effect.[269]

(f) Conclusion on challenges

A prospective arbitrator should carefully consider whether to accept an appointment.   **4.166**
The prospective arbitrator should not accept the appointment if there is reason to believe that either party will genuinely feel that he or she is not independent or impartial. Where

---

[266] Cass. Civ. (1e chambre civile), 15 June 2017, Case No. 16-17108.

[267] Gerbay and Cooper, 'Annulment and enforcement of arbitral awards in England', in *Annulment and Enforcement of Arbitral Awards from a Comparative Law Perspective* (Wolters Kluwer, 2018), pp. 81–106. See also Schwartz and Derains, *Guide to the ICC Rules of Arbitration* (2nd edn, Kluwer Law International, 2005), pp. 375–386.

[268] Note to Parties and Arbitral Tribunals on the conduct of the Arbitration under the ICC Rules of Arbitration, 1 January 2021, available online at https://iccwbo.org/content/uploads/sites/3/2020/12/icc-note-to-parties-and-arbitral-tribunals-on-the-conduct-of-arbitration-english-2021.pdf.

[269] IBA Guidelines, General Standard 3(b). The explanation of General Standard 3(b) provides that the Guidelines 'do not otherwise take a position as to the validity and effect of advance declarations or waivers, because the validity and effect of any advance declaration or waiver must be assessed in view of the specific text of the advance declaration or waiver, the particular circumstances at hand and the applicable law'.

a party objects *after* the arbitrator has been appointed and both parties agree that the arbitrator should resign, then this is determinative—the arbitrator should resign. The arbitrator should also resign if it seems, on reflection, that the objection is, or appears to be, well founded, whether or not the parties agree.[270]

4.167 However, if the objection appears to be without merit, the traditional view is that the arbitrator should not resign but should usually wait for the matter to be resolved through the relevant challenge procedure, in order to discourage unmeritorious disruptive tactics. This is seen as a matter of principle: if a party nominates a perfectly acceptable arbitrator (the 'judge of its choice') and wishes that arbitrator to remain even though an objection has been made, that arbitrator should remain in place unless the appropriate authority rules to the contrary. However, if the issue becomes unnecessarily acrimonious and drawn-out, a challenged arbitrator may decide to resign rather than fight on a matter of principle (particularly where the case is at an early stage).

(g) Filling a vacancy

4.168 A replacement arbitrator must be appointed where a member of a three-person tribunal resigns or is successfully challenged and the other two members do not proceed as a truncated tribunal.[271] If the arbitration is being conducted under institutional rules, in a seat with a sophisticated arbitration law, or under a properly drawn submission agreement, the procedure for replacing an arbitrator will be specified.[272] In general, the new appointment is made in the same way as the original appointment.[273] However, Article 15.4 of the ICC Rules and Article 11.1 of the LCIA Rules, grant discretion to the appointing authority in deciding whether to select a replacement arbitrator following the original procedure.[274]

4.169 Problems are likely to arise in replacing an arbitrator in pure ad hoc arbitrations. The parties themselves may be able to reach an agreement as to the method by which the arbitrator should be replaced and this approach should certainly be attempted first. However, if the parties cannot agree, either on the choice of a replacement arbitrator or on the way of making that choice, then an approach to the relevant national court must be considered. Since an arbitral tribunal is already in existence and the place of arbitration will almost certainly have been decided, the request for the appointment of a replacement arbitrator should be made to the courts at the seat of arbitration. It is necessary to ensure that the court has the power to make the appointment, but most developed national

---

[270] *SolEs Badajoz GmbH v Kingdom of Spain*, ICSID Case No. ARB/15/38, Award, 31 July 2019, at [40]–[41].
[271] Exceptionally, in the case of a three-member arbitral tribunal, the arbitration may proceed with the two remaining members. See the discussion of truncated tribunals at paragraphs 4.170*ff*.
[272] The Model Law, for instance, provides in its Art. 15 that 'a substitute arbitrator shall be appointed according to the rules that were applicable to the appointment of the arbitrator being replaced'.
[273] A notable exception arises under the ICSID Rules, r. 26(3)(a), where, in order to prevent abuse, a party-nominated arbitrator who resigns will be replaced by a person nominated by the chair of the Administrative Council of ICSID rather than by the relevant party, unless the remaining members of the arbitral tribunal have consented to the resignation, under r. 25(2).
[274] ICC Rules, Art. 15.4 ('the Court has discretion to decide whether or not to follow the original nominating process'); LCIA Rules, Art. 11.1 ('the LCIA Court may determine whether or not to follow the original nominating process for such arbitral appointment').

systems of law confer such powers.[275] Nevertheless, it is best not to rely upon recourse to the courts if it can be avoided. To that end, the following guidelines are suggested:

- Where provision is to be made for an arbitration to be conducted according to the rules of an arbitral institution, those rules should be checked to make sure that they contain adequate provision for the filling of a vacancy.
- Where an arbitration is to be conducted ad hoc under the terms of a submission agreement, adequate provisions for the filling of any vacancy should be written into the submission agreement.
- Where an arbitration is to be conducted ad hoc without any formal submission agreement, it should be held only in a country in which the local law contains adequate provision for filling any vacancy that may arise.[276]

(h) Truncated tribunals

Most party-appointed arbitrators act properly and in good faith. It occasionally happens, however, that a party-appointed arbitrator refuses to participate in the arbitration or submits a resignation without sufficient reason. If this happens early in the proceedings or if the case is one in which the interests of justice do not require a quick decision, a replacement may be appointed.[277]   **4.170**

Appointing a new arbitrator may, however, be impractical when the resignation, or refusal to participate, occurs late in the proceedings. Finding and appointing a replacement and allowing the new arbitrator to become familiar with the case, inevitably causes delay. This is particularly aggravated if the arbitrator chooses to resign or refuses to participate at the stage of deliberations. In such cases, and when a quick conclusion to the arbitration is essential, the only sensible course may be for the two remaining arbitrators to continue with the proceedings and to render an award without the participation of the third arbitrator.   **4.171**

A number of celebrated cases provide examples of situations in which arbitral tribunals have continued proceedings and rendered awards as truncated tribunals.[278] Most of these have been pure ad hoc arbitrations, but there have been cases under the UNCITRAL Rules[279] and the ICC Rules.[280]   **4.172**

One US commentator has written: **4.173**

I find it very hard to imagine that, even in the absence of an express rule or agreement, a modern court in a state that otherwise has a public policy of supporting international

---

[275] For example, in English law, the court has wide powers to give directions as to the making of any appointments and, indeed, to make any necessary appointments itself: English Arbitration Act 1996, s. 18.

[276] See Model Law, Art. 15.

[277] In which case, the procedures for filling vacancies would apply as described above.

[278] These cases were discussed at the 1990 ICCA Congress: see Schwebel and Böckstiegel, 'Preventing delay or disruption of arbitration' (1991) 5 ICCA Congress Series 241, at 270–274; Maniruzzaman, 'The authority of a truncated arbitral tribunal—Straight path or puzzle?', Kluwer Arbitration Blog, 15 July 2012.

[279] See, e.g., Order of 17 May 1985, in *Sedco Inc. v National Iranian Oil Co.*, Case No. 129, reprinted in (1985) 8 Iran–US CTR 34, with concurring opinion of Judge Brower at 40; *Uiterwiyk Corporation v Islamic Republic of Iran*, Award No. 375–381–1, 6 July 1988, (1988) 19 Iran–US CTR 107, at 116; also dissenting letter and supplemental opinion in (1988) 19 Iran–US CTR 107, at [161], [169].

[280] See Schwebel and Böckstiegel, fn. 278.

commercial arbitration would invalidate an award issued by a majority of arbitrators because a party-appointed arbitrator, in an effort to frustrate the arbitration, chooses to absent himself at a late stage of the proceedings, or refuses to sign an award. National laws that refer to participation by three arbitrators should be interpreted to have been satisfied, as Professor Gaillard suggests, when all three have had a fair and equal *opportunity* to participate.[281]

4.174   Most of the world's leading international arbitral institutions followed this rule, originally adopted by the AAA.[282] The LCIA has followed the philosophy of leaving the question of whether to proceed on a truncated basis entirely to the discretion of the remaining arbitrators, subject to approval by the LCIA Court.[283] For its part, the ICC adopted a more restrictive approach:

> Subsequent to the closing of the proceedings, instead of replacing an arbitrator who has died or been removed by the Court pursuant to Articles 15(1) and 15(2), the Court may decide, when it considers it appropriate, that the remaining arbitrators shall continue the arbitration. In making such determination, the Court shall take into account the views of the remaining arbitrators and of the parties and such other matters that it considers appropriate in the circumstances.[284]

Thus, not only does the ICC limit the possibility of a truncated tribunal to the deliberations phase, but also it is the ICC Court that makes the decision, rather than the remaining members of the tribunal.

4.175   Several cases in which arbitral tribunals have decided to proceed in truncated form have come into the public domain. The most sensational involved the government of a country in south-east Asia, which exerted considerable pressure to withdraw on the arbitrator whom it had appointed. The final award contains a passage stating comprehensively the relevant facts and analysing the legal consequences. The conclusion of the two remaining arbitrators, relying on the published works of a well-known international jurist, was that it could—and indeed should—proceed in truncated form to render a final award.[285]

4.176   So far as the UNCITRAL Rules are concerned,[286] there is respectable authority supporting the legitimacy of an award issued by a truncated tribunal, where appropriate. In pure ad hoc arbitrations in which the parties have not chosen the UNCITRAL Rules, it is wise for the remaining arbitrators to proceed with caution; at the very least, they should review any relevant provisions of the *lex arbitri* and (if they are aware of it) the law of the place of likely enforcement of the award.

---

[281] See Holtzmann, 'How to prevent delay and disruption of arbitration: Lessons of the 1990 ICCA Stockholm Congress' (1991) 5 ICCA Congress Series 28 (emphasis original).

[282] AAA Rules, r. R-20(b).

[283] LCIA Rules, Art. 12. See also WIPO Rules, Art. 35(a).

[284] ICC Rules, Art. 15.5.

[285] *Himpurna California Energy Ltd v Republic of Indonesia* (2000) XXV YBCA 186, citing Schwebel's Cambridge Lauterpacht lectures, in which he referred to *Republic of Colombia v Cauca Co.*, the *French-Mexican Claims Commission* cases, the *Lena Goldfields* arbitration, the *Sabotage* cases, and the Advisory Opinion of the International Court of Justice (ICJ) in Interpretation of Peace Treaties with Bulgaria, Hungary, and Romania.

[286] UNCITRAL Rules, Art. 14.2. The appointing authority, if the hearings were closed, may authorise the other arbitrators to proceed with the arbitration and make any decision or award.

In sum, the option of proceeding as a truncated tribunal, rather than as a reconstituted full   **4.177**
tribunal, will remain as an exceptional measure to be adopted only when the arbitration is
nearing its end and where there is clear evidence that the arbitrator concerned, voluntarily
or involuntarily, has likely been associated with an abuse of the process.[287]

(i) Procedure following the filling of a vacancy

An important practical question arises when a vacancy in the arbitral tribunal is filled: to   **4.178**
what extent must the newly constituted arbitral tribunal retrace its steps? This will depend
on the applicable institutional rules. The UNCITRAL Rules provide that, where an arbitrator is replaced, 'the proceedings shall resume at the stage where the arbitrator who was
replaced ceased to perform his or her functions, unless the arbitral tribunal decides otherwise'.[288] The ICC Rules provide that the reconstituted tribunal will determine, after having
invited the parties to comment, whether and to what extent any prior proceedings shall be
repeated. However, if the parties agree on a solution, the tribunal will usually follow such
agreement.[289] For its part, Article 34 of the WIPO Rules provides that '[w]henever a substitute arbitrator is appointed, the Tribunal shall, having regard to any observations of the
parties, determine in its sole discretion whether all or part of any prior hearings are to be
repeated'.[290] The 2020 version of the LCIA Rules contains broadly similar provisions.[291]

In national arbitration laws, the approaches vary. The Model Law is silent on this issue, thus   **4.179**
leaving the question to the tribunal's discretion. US courts have abandoned their previous
stance requiring that the proceedings were repeated.[292] However, there is no consensus on
this matter as some national laws require the repetition of all prior proceedings while others
do not.[293]

Given that most rules grant a considerable discretion to the tribunal on the extent of a re-   **4.180**
hearing, how should that discretion be exercised? If the oral hearings have not begun when
the vacancy arises, it is sufficient for the replacement arbitrator to be given time to read the
pleadings and other documents exchanged between the parties, to consider any procedural
directions given by the former arbitral tribunal, and to signify his or her assent to them (in
writing). However, if the vacancy is filled *after* the oral proceedings have begun, the question arises as to whether evidence that has already been heard and legal arguments that
have already been advanced orally should be repeated for the benefit of the replacement
arbitrator. Such repetition is both time-consuming and expensive. It is in the interests of all
parties to try to avoid it, if at all possible.

---

[287] For consideration of the treatment of truncated tribunals by various institutions' rules, see Maniruzzaman,
'The authority of a truncated arbitral tribunal: Straight path or puzzle?' (2012) 90 Amicus Curiae 22.
[288] UNCITRAL Rules, Art. 15.
[289] ICC Rules, Art. 15.4. See also Daele, fn. 95, para. 4.103.
[290] WIPO Rules, Art. 34.
[291] LCIA Rules, Art. 11.3 ('[s]ave for any award rendered, the Arbitral Tribunal (when reconstituted) shall determine whether, and if so to what extent, the previous proceedings in the arbitration shall stand').
[292] *Wellpoint, Inc. v John Hancock Life Ins. Co.*, 576 F.3d 643, 647 (7th Cir. 2009).
[293] Egyptian Arbitration Law, art. 19(3); Indonesian Arbitration and ADR Law, art. 26(4); Dutch Arbitration
Act, art. 1030(3).

4.181 Where a transcript is available, it should be sufficient for the replacement arbitrator to read the transcript and so bring himself or herself up to date with the proceedings. If, as a result of such reading, the replacement arbitrator wishes to have a particular witness recalled, or a particular argument explained in more detail, it may be in the interests of all parties to agree that this should be done in the most economic form possible (for example, by a remote hearing of such witness), rather than run the risk of having to start the oral proceedings again from the beginning. Where there is no transcript of the oral hearing, the extent to which oral evidence and argument already presented needs to be repeated is a question that can be resolved only by discussion between the members of the arbitral tribunal (including the replacement member), the parties, and their legal advisers.

I. Organisation of the Arbitral Tribunal

(a) Introduction

4.182 There is much work to be done behind the scenes to ensure that an international arbitration runs smoothly. The arbitrators are generally of different nationalities, as are the parties, their advisers, and experts. This mixture of nationalities is one of the most intriguing challenges involved in the practice of international arbitration. It needs more careful planning and organisation to bring together such a mixed group of people than it does to arrange a domestic arbitration. Indeed, if a final physical hearing is to take place, its organisation has much in common with the arranging of a series of performances for a band embarking upon an international tour: there is a venue to be arranged, times and dates to be fixed, hotel rooms to be booked, technicians (in the form of interpreters, transcription services, IT support, and so forth) to be engaged. In the context of remote hearings, the work is not greatly reduced. Hearing platforms need to be agreed and tested with the parties, arrangements for witness and expert hearing need to be agreed, decisions need to be taken on the hiring of a specialised company to administer the platform, and cybersecurity concerns need to be addressed. In both cases, the whole performance has to be organised so that, when the time comes, the assembled cast of parties, lawyers, experts, and witnesses are ready to present their offerings to their small, but important, audience—the arbitral tribunal. The work involved in making the administrative arrangements has led to it becoming the established practice in larger and more complex international arbitrations for the arbitral tribunal to appoint a tribunal secretary, whose function includes liaising with the parties to take care of the practical arrangements.[294]

(b) Meetings and hearings

4.183 Where the arbitral tribunal consists of more than a sole arbitrator, it is necessary for the members of the arbitral tribunal to meet from time to time for consultation amongst themselves. There is no reason why such meetings should be held at the seat of the arbitration or

---

[294] For a discussion of the role and functions of a tribunal secretary, see paragraphs 4.208*ff*.

in person and if it is more convenient (or necessary) for the arbitrators to meet elsewhere or by remote means (such as due to travel or sanitary restrictions), they may do so, subject to any provisions to the contrary in the submission agreement or in the applicable rules of arbitration.[295]

(i) Meetings and hearings at which the parties are present

In all but the simplest cases, it is likely that in-person or video conference meetings will take place from time to time between the arbitral tribunal, the parties, and their representatives, so that procedural orders or directions may be considered. Under most applicable laws and institutional rules, the arbitral tribunal may decide to hold meetings with the parties outside of the seat at the most convenient place or by video conference. However, the arbitral tribunal should consult the parties before doing so. If the parties agree to hold all meetings and/or hearings at the place of arbitration, this should guide the tribunal. It is nevertheless noteworthy that, in recent years, with the advances of video conferencing and the radical limitations on travel due to the COVID-19 pandemic, most procedural meetings are held virtually without the need for a physical meeting.[296]   **4.184**

Unless the case is to be decided on the basis of documents only, there is also a final hearing, or a series of hearings, at which the parties and their representatives attend physically or remotely in order to put forward the evidence of witnesses and their legal arguments.[297] Physical witness hearings are generally held at the seat of the arbitration, although provision is sometimes made for the hearing to take place elsewhere.[298] This may be the case, for instance, when another location is closer to where the arbitrators and the parties' representatives are based, or less common, when the evidence of an important witness is required and it is more convenient for the tribunal and the parties to go to the witness than it is for the witness to go to the tribunal.[299] Travel restrictions and other sanitary restrictions linked to the COVID-19 epidemic have obliged parties and tribunals to seek alternatives to final hearings in person such as conducting entire final hearings remotely. The arbitration community adapted rapidly to the complexity of organising such remote hearings which have generally run smoothly if carefully organised in advance. One author recalls a final hearing in an ICC arbitration in Brazil in March 2009 which was suspended halfway through by the tribunal due to the risk of travel bans. The participants returned to their countries of residence and were ordered to make arrangements to resume proceedings remotely two weeks later. In spite of the challenges, a hearing involving parties, counsel, and arbitrators located   **4.185**

---

[295] The UNCITRAL Rules give the arbitral tribunal complete freedom in this respect: see Art. 18.2. So also do the LCIA Rules: see Art. 16.3. See Chapter 3, paragraph 3.57. In the practice of ICSID arbitration, the meetings do not necessarily take place at the seat of the Centre. The 2022 rules provide that the first session 'may be held in person or remotely, by any means that the Tribunal deems appropriate' (r. 29(2)). If the hearing is to be held in person, 'it may be held at any place agreed to by the parties after consulting with the Tribunal and the Secretary-General' (r. 32(3)).The deliberations of the tribunal may be conducted 'at any place and by any means it considers appropriate' (r. 34(2)).

[296] This is to be encouraged where the amounts in dispute are limited and the costs of organising the meeting are considerable.

[297] For a more detailed account of the issues to consider for a final oral hearing, see Chapter 6.

[298] See, e.g., the UNCITRAL Rules 2013, Art. 18.2; LCIA Rules, Art. 16.3.

[299] This may be the case if witnesses are unable to travel for health reasons, if travel restrictions are in place, or if the witnesses are high-ranking government officials or ministers. However, once again, it is now increasingly common for witnesses who, for good reason, cannot be physically present to be heard by video conference. During the COVID-19 pandemic, the use of cameras showing a 360° view of the room where the witness or expert is situated has facilitated the conduct of remote virtual hearings by proving that there are no third parties present.

in ten different jurisdictions was successfully concluded by remote meeting technology. Indeed, in 2020 and 2021 most final hearings have been conducted using such technology. This has led to a great acceleration in the use of technology in arbitrations. Such remote hearings have often improved the efficiency and cost effectiveness of arbitration proceedings and have contributed to a greener process with documents accessed electronically rather than in hard copy and no carbon footprint from travel.[300]

(ii) Fixing dates for hearings

4.186 Where the arbitral tribunal consists of more than a sole arbitrator, the date of the hearing will generally be fixed by the presiding arbitrator, in consultation with the co-arbitrators, the parties, and their advisers. It is inevitably difficult to coordinate the agendas of arbitrators, parties, witnesses, and experts for a period that may be between one to three weeks. It is a useful practice to fix target dates in the procedural calendar at the first procedural meeting, usually annexed to a procedural order, and then to fix actual dates towards the close of pleadings, when both the parties' lawyers and the tribunal will have a better idea of the issues to be tried, the amount of evidence to be considered, the possible need for interpreters, and the number of days to be set aside for the hearing. Once fixed, the target dates will hopefully help to concentrate the minds of counsel and the arbitral tribunal on the need to get on with the case, if the target dates (or anything close to them) are to be met.

4.187 If a reasonable agreement on a date for hearing cannot be reached between the parties and the arbitral tribunal, the tribunal must fix a date without such agreement. There can be little objection to this, as long as the parties are given reasonable notice.

4.188 In fixing this date, the sole or presiding arbitrator should take account of holiday periods in the countries of the participants, and the seat of the arbitration. An arbitrator is unlikely to wish to work during important religious or family holidays in his or her country of residence and should not unreasonably insist that others must do so during such periods in their own countries. This is not a legal obligation; rather, it is a matter of courtesy and respect for the diversity of the other participants. It may also be difficult—or even impossible, in some countries—to provide the necessary infrastructure at the seat for a hearing on a public holiday.

(iii) Length of hearings

4.189 In fixing a date for the start of the hearings, the sole or presiding arbitrator must keep in mind the length of time that the hearing is likely to take. Indeed, this is a question that will be asked repeatedly when making travel and hotel arrangements, when booking rooms in which the hearing is to take place, when making arrangements for the attendance of the parties and their witnesses and when hiring video conference platforms and special equipment for remote hearings.

4.190 It is difficult to estimate accurately how long a case is likely to last, particularly in circumstances where it is unclear if the hearing will be physical or remote. Since participants in a remote hearing are usually located in their own jurisdiction, there are often multiple time

---

[300] In 2019, the Campaign for Greener Arbitrations was launched, an initiative to reduce the carbon footprint of arbitrations through behavioural change. See https://www.greenerarbitrations.com/.

zones to accommodate which can result in hearing days being much shorter than would be the norm for physical hearings.[301] For all of these reasons, it is therefore safer to over-book time at the beginning of a case and then release time later (if it appears that the hearing will not take up all of the allotted days) than it is to try to re-convene the entire proceeding at a later date if insufficient time has been set aside. As in many procedural aspects, it is for the tribunal to strike a balance between affording the parties a reasonable opportunity to present their case and not succumbing to some parties' (or counsel's) tendencies towards procedural excess. One key tool at the arbitrator's disposal to ensure that hearings are 'kept to time' is what is known as the 'chess clock' system whereby the total hearing time is calculated and divided between the parties (after allocating a block of time to the tribunal).[302]

(c) Administrative aspects

(i) Physical hearings

The place of the arbitration is chosen before any hearing is held but, unless the hearing is to   **4.191**
be held remotely, it will be necessary to fix a specific venue in appropriate premises offered by an arbitral institution, conference centre, or other suitable building. In deciding on a venue, the primary consideration must be to find accommodation that is fit for the purpose. Two requirements stand out. First, the venue must provide adequate space, not only for the arbitral tribunal, but also for the parties and their lawyers, for screens, charts, drawings, and other documents, all of which may be voluminous, and for anyone else who is to assist in the conduct of the arbitration, including experts, stenographers, and interpreters (and sometimes even the public in investment arbitrations).[303] Electronic aids of one kind or another will also be deployed and the necessary infrastructure should be available at the proposed venue.[304] Secondly, as far as possible, the facilities chosen must be available for the purposes of the arbitration throughout the whole period of the hearing.

For a physical meeting between the arbitral tribunal and the parties, one large hearing room   **4.192**
will be required sufficient to accommodate all the parties, their counsel, transcript writers, interpreters, and the tribunal and secretary. For a witness hearing—particularly a hearing that is likely to last for more than two or three days—it is important for each party to be assigned a private 'break-out' room in which it can store documents, check transcripts, print material, prepare for the next day's hearings, brief the client, and generally engage in the often frantic activity that goes on behind the scenes in any international arbitration. The arbitral tribunal should also have a room available for its own deliberations, as it is often inconvenient or impracticable to ask the parties to withdraw completely from the hearing

---

[301] By way of example, one of the authors recently participated as counsel in a case from Washington, DC. Opposing counsel were in Paris and the arbitrators were in London, Mexico, and Honolulu. In order to ensure reasonable hearing times, the arbitration took place for four hours each day.

[302] We discuss the 'chess clock' system at paragraph 4.203 below.

[303] Some new free trade agreements and BITs require hearings be open to the public. For instance, in *Gramercy Funds Management LLC and other v Republic of Peru* (ICSID Case No. UNCT/18/2), a public hearing was held pursuant to Art. 10.21(2) of the United States-Peru Free Trade Agreement of 1 February 2009. In *Vattenfall AB and others v Federal Republic of Germany*, ICSID Case No. ARB/12/12, the parties agreed for the hearing to be open to the public.

[304] Such as real-time transcript or another form of recording, and PowerPoint or other software (e.g. Trial Director) to display documents on a screen.

room. In terms of security, the parties (and the tribunal) usually wish to be able to leave documents at the venue without fear that they will be seen by others. Suitable accommodation for a physical hearing, particularly if it is likely to be lengthy is not easy to find. Some of the commonly used alternatives are as follows.

(ii) Remote hearings

4.193   As a result of the COVID-19 pandemic, the entire arbitral community experienced notable developments in the conduct of remote online hearings.[305] Several arbitral institutions prepared protocols or provided guidance on the organisation of remote hearings. For instance, the ICC's Note to Parties and Arbitral Tribunals expressly addresses the organisation of a remote hearing, including the factors that tribunals should consider in order to ensure that parties are treated with equality and that each party is given a full opportunity to present its case.[306] The ICC also issued a checklist for a protocol on remote hearings and suggested clauses for cyber-protocols and procedural orders dealing with the organisation of virtual hearings, from the presentation of documentary evidence and examination of witnesses to online etiquette.[307] If the hearing is to be held remotely, decisions will need to be taken on the preferred IT platform and technology to be used, whether certain equipment is required in each location, and the need to establish a shared document platform containing an electronic hearing bundle. Parties will need to agree on remote break-out rooms that will permit each side and the tribunal to confer privately during the hearing.[308] Nowadays, a number of vendors offer their services to host virtual hearings, which include specialised platforms and even the delivery of specialised equipment to counsel, the tribunal, and witnesses.

(iii) Arbitration centres

4.194   Most major arbitration institutions and centres provide, or at least can recommend, accommodation that is suitable for almost every type of hearing. Where one of the parties is a government or other state enterprises, it is worth considering whether the arbitration can be brought within the facilities of either the PCA at the Peace Palace in The Hague, or of ICSID (that is, the facilities of the World Bank in Washington or Paris). Even where an arbitration does not fall within the PCA Rules, the Secretary-General of the PCA is generally willing to

---

[305] See Bassiri, 'Conducting remote hearings: Issues of planning, preparation and sample procedural orders', in Scherer, Bassiri, and Wahab, fn. 72, Chapter 5.

[306] See ICC, 'Note to Parties and Arbitral Tribunals on the Conduct of the Arbitration under the ICC Rules of Arbitration', 1 January 2021, Section VII(C). See also CIArb, Guidance Note on Remote Dispute Resolution Proceedings; The Seoul Protocol on Video Conferencing in International Arbitration; AAA-ICDR, Virtual Hearing Guide for Arbitrators and Parties; HKIAC, Guidelines for Virtual Hearings; SIAC, Taking Your Arbitration Remote; Vienna International Arbitral Centre, The Vienna Protocol: A Practical Checklist for Remote Hearings.

[307] Available at https://iccwbo.org/content/uploads/sites/3/2020/12/icc-checklist-cyber-protocol-and-clauses-orders-virtual-hearings-english.pdf.

[308] The platform administrator will usually place each individual connected to the hearing into the relevant break-out room at the appropriate time. It is important that each counsel team (and the arbitrators) retain a discipline to make sure that they are in the relevant break-out room before making any comments. This task is facilitated by each participant preceding their name on screen with their affiliation (usually C for claimant, R for respondent, and T for tribunal—e.g. C–John Smith, R–Jane Jones, and T–Rachel Wood). If a participant finds themself in the wrong break-out room, he or she should immediately alert all others present and contact the administrator so that no party conversations are inadvertently overheard.

accommodate arbitrations, even between private parties.[309] Likewise, World Bank rooms may also be available upon request in non-ICSID cases.[310]

Some of the established international arbitral institutions, such as the ICC, ICDR, and LCIA, can also provide hearing rooms. The LCIA has arrangements with the International Dispute Resolution Centre (IDRC) in Central London which has fifteen hearing rooms and over forty break-out rooms available.[311] The ICC also has its own arbitration facilities in Paris at the ICC Hearing Centre, which is separate from the ICC secretariat.[312] The ICDR headquarters in New York can host eight hearings at the same time, and that capacity is supplemented by ICDR's offices in Miami, Houston, and Singapore.[313] The New York International Arbitration Centre also rents rooms for arbitrations in New York.[314] Maxwell Chambers in Singapore can accommodate up to four arbitration cases simultaneously,[315] whilst Arbitration Place in Toronto offers 16 different hearing rooms of varying sizes.[316] Most of these arbitration centres also provide comprehensive support services and technology for remote hearings.[317]   **4.195**

(iv) Hotels

If the seat of the arbitration is not within one of the leading arbitration venues, then it is common to rely on the leading hotels of the city in which the arbitration is to take place for final 'in person' hearings. Such hotels are generally accustomed to looking after business visitors and offering conference or other function rooms, Wi-Fi, photocopying, catering, and other services. Again, a critical concern is to ensure that the same room is available for the duration of the hearing to avoid room changes mid-hearing and that access to it is strictly controlled, so that confidential documents may be left in it overnight or during breaks in the proceedings.   **4.196**

(v) Interpreters

It should be regarded as a fundamental right of a party or a witness to speak at a hearing in his or her mother tongue.[318] Indeed, some witnesses may be unable to express themselves easily, if at all, in the language of the arbitration. In such circumstances, it is necessary to arrange for professional interpreters to be available, so that the witnesses may give testimony in their own language. Arrangements for the engagement of interpreters are usually   **4.197**

---

[309] The PCA has hearing facilities in the Netherlands, Buenos Aires, Mauritius, and Singapore. In addition, the PCA has access to facilities around the world pursuant to its host country agreements with Contracting Parties and cooperation agreements with other institutions (for instance the Inter American Court of Human Rights in San José, Costa Rica, or the Florence Chamber of Commerce in Italy). See https://pca-cpa.org/en/services/hearing-facilities/.

[310] The World Bank room rentals are included in ICSID's administrative fee in cases administered by ICSID under the ICSID, UNCITRAL, or other rules. See https://icsid.worldbank.org/services/hearing-facilities.

[311] See https://www.idrc.co.uk/. The IDRC recently moved to new premises at 1 Paternoster Lane in the City of London.

[312] See https://iccwbo.org/dispute-resolution-services/hearing-centre/.

[313] See http://www.adr.org.

[314] See https://nyiac.org/planning-a-hearing/reservations/.

[315] See https://www.maxwellchambers.com/.

[316] See https://www.arbitrationplace.com/.

[317] See https://icsid.worldbank.org/services/hearing-facilities/virtual-hearings; and https://iccwbo.org/dispute-resolution-services/hearing-centre/icc-virtual-hearings/.

[318] It is not unreasonable, however, for an arbitral tribunal to require a party who wishes to engage lawyers to retain representatives who are able to perform their functions in the working language of the arbitration.

undertaken by the party who requires their services or the arbitral institution. If a witness is to give evidence through an interpreter, it is usual to notify both the arbitral tribunal and the other party of this fact well in advance of the hearing to ensure that necessary arrangements are made.

4.198   The use of an interpreter will almost certainly slow down the proceedings. This is something that the arbitral tribunal should consider when assessing the duration of the hearing. If the witness has some command of the language of the arbitration, then the witness may use the interpreter simply to help him or her to understand the questions and formulate the answers. With modern technology, simultaneous interpretation can work well, particularly where the facilities (such as those of ICSID) are especially designed for its use. Indeed, it is becoming ever more frequent to hold bilingual arbitrations in investment arbitrations, whereby there is interpretation into two of the Centre's official languages simultaneously.[319]

(vi)   Transcripts

4.199   A verbatim transcript, particularly of the evidence, can be of great importance in international arbitrations in which the members of the arbitral tribunal may have different levels of comprehension of the language of the proceedings. Indeed, the experience of the authors is that parties' counsel rely heavily on transcripts of the proceedings, when they are available, for the purposes of preparing closing speeches and post-hearing submissions and that arbitrators refer to them in drafting the award.[320] Transcripts also constitute a permanent record of the proceedings, which may be beneficial later if, for example, a vacancy on the arbitral tribunal has to be filled, or if there are subsequent court proceedings for recourse against, or for enforcement of, the award.

4.200   Transcripts are prepared by means of professional transcript writers. There are wellknown systems, whereby the lawyers' pleadings, the testimony of the witnesses, and the tribunal's interventions are shown instantaneously on laptop computer screens available to the participants in the hearing room. This can be very useful (particularly for counsel during a cross-examination). For most arbitrators, however, the value of the transcript lies in its availability during the deliberations and for reference in drafting the award. In addition to the live transcript, a more refined copy of the transcript is sent electronically to the parties and the tribunal—on the same evening of each hearing day if required (and at an additional cost). This assists both counsel and the tribunal to prepare for the next day's hearing.

---

[319] In such cases, each party may present using its own language with submissions being simultaneously translated into the other language. For example, in a case involving an English-speaking claimant against a Latin American state, the claimant's counsel will present in English (which presentation will be simultaneously interpreted into Spanish) and the respondent's counsel will present in Spanish (which presentation will be simultaneously interpreted into English). Similarly, witnesses can give evidence in either language with simultaneous interpretation into the other language. It is quite common in such cases to have live transcripts in both languages simultaneously.

[320] It is usual to give such references by citing the day, page, and line of the transcript (e.g. 'Day 5, page 70, line 15'). Audio recordings are usually kept as well (and sometimes even video recordings when using online platforms for virtual hearings).

(vii) Hearing hours

In most countries, judges sit in their courts for only a relatively short period each day: per- **4.201** haps no more than five hours. This is sensible in that it allows judges time to read through their notes of the evidence and argument, and to reflect on what they have heard and what they would like to hear. Judges also have other duties to perform. Relatively short working hours also allow the parties and their advisers essential time in which to produce any evidence, information, or data that the court may request, and it also gives them time to prepare for the next session.

This practice is not generally followed by tribunals at final physical hearings where hearing **4.202** days of seven or eight hours are not uncommon. The reason for this is to minimise the multiple costs of the final hearing exercise resulting from lodging and feeding large teams of counsel, witnesses, and experts a long way from home.

In order to ensure that the assigned hearing time is effectively used, the 'chess clock' system **4.203** is frequently adopted. Typically, the first day of the hearing will be dedicated to opening speeches from each party, usually of two to three hours' duration. Similarly, the last day may be reserved specifically for closing speeches (although there has been a tendency to replace closing speeches with post-hearing briefs which allows the physical hearing to be used for what is most useful—the hearing of live witnesses and experts). The total number of hearing hours for the balance of days is then calculated. From that total time assigned breaks (usually 90 minutes a day) and a reasonable estimate of tribunal time must be deducted. Tribunal time (typically one hour per day) would include the time needed to address procedural issues, tribunal questions, and procedural accommodations, for example an early close on one hearing day to avoid a witness testifying over two days. The balance is then divided between the parties[321] to employ in direct examination of their own witnesses and experts and cross examination of the opposing parties' witnesses and experts as each party sees fit. As a consequence, a hearing day of 9am to 5pm (eight hours) would result in party time of 5.5 hours (that is, eight hours minus 1.5 hours for breaks and one hour for tribunal time) which gives 2.75 hours per party. For a five-day hearing, four of which would be dedicated to oral evidence, each party would have eleven hours. At the end of each day, the tribunal secretary (or tribunal) will be asked to provide the parties with an update on how much time they have used so that priorities can be assigned for the remaining period of the hearing. This process is an effective guarantee against hearings overrunning and has the salutary effect of concentrating the minds of counsel as to what is really important in the case and what is peripheral.

The 'chess clock' system also works for remote hearings, albeit based on shorter hearing **4.204** hours (typically four to five hours) to accommodate time differences and the inevitable 'screen fatigue'.[322]

---

[321] A 50:50 split is usual but if the number of witnesses and experts presented by each party is radically different then a 50:50 split may be adjusted accordingly. In any event, each party is made aware of the total number of hours available to it for direct examination and cross examination prior to the hearing commencing.

[322] See ICC, 'Note to Parties and Arbitral Tribunals on the Conduct of the Arbitration under the ICC Rules of Arbitration', 1 January 2021, para. 102.

(d) Other considerations

(i) Relations between the parties and the arbitral tribunal during the hearing

4.205   An international arbitration provides a less formal method of resolving disputes than proceedings before national courts. There are more opportunities for interactions between the parties, their lawyers, and experts on the one hand and the members of the arbitral tribunal on the other. This is something to be encouraged, provided that contacts take place openly. It is perfectly normal and reasonable for the parties and their counsel to converse with the members of the arbitral tribunal in coffee breaks, provided that such conversations are public and do not raise any issue concerning the case (sport, weather, and the quality of the coffee are always safe topics!).

(ii) Functions of the presiding arbitrator

4.206   The presiding arbitrator acts as chairperson of the tribunal and will often be referred to as 'the president' or 'the chair', not only in the established rules of arbitration, but also by the parties and their lawyers during the course of the proceedings.[323] The task of the presiding arbitrator is to take charge of the deliberations of the tribunal, and of the conduct of any meetings and hearings. It is the presiding arbitrator's responsibility to make sure that the proceedings move forward as smoothly and effectively as possible.

4.207   Depending on the rules under which the arbitration is being conducted, the presiding arbitrator may have no more than a voice equal to that of the co-arbitrators when it comes to making decisions, but the presiding arbitrator is nevertheless 'first amongst equals'. If fees are fixed on a lump sum basis, the presiding arbitrator will generally receive a larger fee than the co-arbitrators, because of the greater investment in time involved, including drafting the tribunal's communications with the parties and the initial draft of the award(s).[324] If the arbitrators' fees are based on an hourly rate, the presiding arbitrator is likely to be paid more than the co-arbitrators, because of the additional hours that he or she will be required to dedicate to the case.

(e) The tribunal secretary

4.208   As already indicated, the conduct of an international arbitration will generally involve the sole or presiding arbitrator in a considerable number of administrative tasks, including ensuring that proper arrangements have been made for meetings, interpreters, transcript writers, and so forth.

4.209   It is essential for the smooth running of the arbitration that these arrangements should be made in good time and it has become the practice, particularly in large and complex international arbitrations, for the tribunal to appoint a tribunal secretary both to assist with

---

[323] Usual forms of address may be 'Madame President', 'Madame Chair', 'Mister President', 'Mister Chairman or simply 'Sir' or 'Madame'.

[324] For a comprehensive review of the functions of the presiding arbitrator, see Kaplan and Mills, 'The role of the chair in international commercial arbitration', in Pryles (ed.) *The Asian Leading Arbitrators' Guide to International Arbitration* (JurisNet, 2007), Chapter 6. See also Reymond, 'The president of the arbitral tribunal' (1994) 1 ICSID Rev—Foreign Investment LJ 1.

arrangements that would otherwise fall to be made by the tribunal and to act as a link between the parties and the tribunal.[325] Remote hearings may also create significant administrative work, from the circulation of connection details, to the coordination of break-out
rooms, finalisation of electronic hearing bundles, and verification of the identity of every
person connecting to the online platform.

(i) The role of the tribunal secretary

The tribunal secretary will normally take part in all meetings of the arbitral tribunal as well   **4.210**
as the hearings, to ensure that the various administrative procedures are running smoothly.

The legitimate limits of the role and function of a tribunal secretary have been the subject   **4.211**
of much debate within the arbitral community.[326] Some commentators take the view that
the role of the tribunal secretary should be limited to the purely administrative; others
consider there is nothing wrong in an arbitrator delegating more substantive tasks to a
secretary, in the same way as national judges have, for many years, made use of judicial
clerks.[327] Notwithstanding such differences, there is broad consensus that a tribunal secretary should be appointed only with the knowledge and consent of the parties, and that
it remains the responsibility of the arbitral tribunal to ensure that its decision-making
function is not delegated in any way. The task is to assist the arbitral tribunal, not to usurp
its function.[328]

These considerations, and the increased use of tribunal secretaries, have prompted arbitral   **4.212**
institutions to address their role and duties through their arbitral rules. The LCIA Rules
now contain a specific provision on tribunal secretaries establishing that the arbitral tribunal may obtain assistance from them, as long as the decision-making function is not delegated; moreover, all tasks carried out by a tribunal secretary should be carried out on behalf
of and under the supervision of the arbitral tribunal.[329] The draft rule 34 of the proposed
amendments to the ICSID Rules now clarifies that the secretary may even assist the tribunal
in its deliberation.[330]

Even in an administered arbitration, many detailed arrangements still fall to be made by the   **4.213**
arbitral tribunal itself and the assistance of a tribunal secretary is extremely valuable in this

---

[325] The increased acceptance and use of tribunal secretaries are evidenced in part by recent revisions to leading
arbitral rules. For instance, the LCIA Rules explicitly regulate the appointment, functions, and fees of the tribunal
secretaries in its Art. 14A. A 2015 survey indicates that, overall, arbitral secretaries are used in 53 per cent of
international arbitrations, and 71 per cent of the respondents considered tribunal secretaries to be useful: see the
survey carried out by the school of arbitration of Queen Mary University of London and White and Case LLP,
Improvements and Innovations in International Arbitration (2015), p. 42.

[326] For a more comprehensive analysis, see Jensen, *Tribunal Secretaries in International Arbitration* (Oxford
University Press, 2019).

[327] In 2017, the English Commercial Court considered the issue of the appropriate role of tribunal secretaries.
The judge said: 'An arbitrator who receives the views of a tribunal secretary does not thereby necessarily lose the
ability to exercise full and independent judgement on the issue in question' but he recommended that secretaries
should 'not [...] be tasked with anything which involves expressing a view on the substantive merits of an application or issue'. See *P v Q and others* [2017] EWHC 194 (Comm).

[328] See Partasides, 'Secretaries to arbitral tribunals', in Hanotiau and Mourre (eds) *Players' Interaction in
International Arbitration* (Kluwer Law International, 2012), p. 87. See also ICDR Rules, Art. 17: 'The tribunal may,
with the consent of the parties, appoint an arbitral tribunal secretary, who will serve in accordance with ICDR
guidelines.'

[329] See 2020 LCIA Rules, Art. 14A.

[330] See ICSID, Proposals for Amendments of the ICSID Rules, Working Paper No. 5, 15 June 2021, p. 307.

regard. According to the ICC's Note to the Parties and Arbitral Tribunals on the Conduct of Arbitration (of January 2021), the tasks of the tribunal secretary can include:

- transmitting documents and communications on behalf of the arbitral tribunal;
- organising and maintaining the arbitral tribunal's file and locating documents;
- organising hearings and meetings and liaising with the parties in that respect;
- drafting correspondence to the parties and sending it on behalf of the tribunal;
- preparing for the arbitral tribunal's review drafts of procedural orders as well as factual portions of the award, such as the summary of the proceedings, the chronology of facts, and the summary of the parties' positions;
- attending hearings, meetings, and deliberations; taking notes or keeping time;
- conducting legal or similar research; and
- proof-reading and checking citations, dates, and cross-references in procedural orders and awards, as well as correcting typographical, grammatical, or calculation errors.[331]

4.214   All of these tasks free up the arbitral tribunal to focus on its core role of carefully listening to and reviewing the evidence, and weighing up the arguments, in order to reach a decision on the merits. When a tribunal secretary is appointed, a special arrangement may need to be made to meet the related fees and expenses.[332]

(ii)   Whom to appoint

4.215   The obvious person to appoint as a tribunal secretary is a lawyer with some experience in international arbitration and of the procedural and administrative problems that may arise during the proceedings. The usual practice is for the arbitral tribunal to choose its own secretary, who is generally (although not invariably) a young practising lawyer based in the same city as the presiding arbitrator (and, where the presiding arbitrator works for a firm, often an associate from that firm). A moderate hourly fee is paid appropriate to the nature of the duties.

4.216   It is important to obtain the agreement of the parties before any appointment is made, with a clear explanation to the parties of the nature of the secretary's role and the benefits that such an appointment will give to the process, in terms of efficiency and cost savings. Some arbitral institutions offer clear guidelines on how to appoint arbitral secretaries.[333]

(iii)   Costs of a tribunal secretary

4.217   One of the key reasons for using a tribunal secretary is to save costs for the parties. It is uncontroversial, therefore, for the *Young ICCA Guide on Arbitral Secretaries* to record as 'a general principle' that 'the use of an arbitral secretary should reduce rather than increase the overall costs of the arbitration'.[334]

---

[331] See the duties listed in ICC, 'Note to the Parties and Arbitral Tribunals on the Conduct of Arbitration', 1 January 2021, para. 185. See also *Young ICCA Guide on Arbitral Secretaries* (2014), Art. 2. In what in practice may amount to a limitation on the use of tribunal secretaries, the ICC will require the fees, but not the expenses, of a tribunal secretary to be paid by the tribunal and will not reimburse them.
[332] Note that some arbitration rules contain express provisions on this regard. See, e.g., LCIA Rules, Art. 14A.
[333] See ICC Note, fn. 331, at paras 218–221.
[334] *Young ICCA Guide on Arbitral Secretaries*, fn. 331, at Art. 4(1).

What this means in practice is likely to depend on the applicable arbitration rules. Where **4.218** the arbitral tribunal is remunerated based on the amount in dispute, the fees, and perhaps the expenses, associated with the tribunal secretary are more appropriately borne by the tribunal, rather than the parties. Where the tribunal is remunerated on an hourly basis, the costs and expenses associated with the secretary may be more appropriately borne by the parties, owing to the costs saving achieved by having routine tasks performed at a lower hourly rate by the secretary.

J. Fees and Expenses of the Arbitral Tribunal

(a) Introduction

The cost of bringing or defending a claim before an international arbitral tribunal is likely to **4.219** be considerably higher than that of bringing or defending the same claim before a national court. This is because, in addition to the usual expenses of litigation, it is necessary for the parties to pay the fees and expenses of the arbitral tribunal (including international travel) and the cost of hiring suitable accommodation for physical hearings. In addition, where the arbitration is administered by an arbitral institution, the fees and expenses of that institution must be paid and these are not insignificant. This contrasts sharply with proceedings before a national court, in which the court rooms, the attendants, and the judges themselves are provided and paid for by the state. The parties often make no more than a nominal contribution to the state by way of a registration fee or other levy.[335] The fact that arbitration before a private arbitral tribunal attracts these additional charges makes it more desirable that arbitrations should not be conducted with the time-consuming formalities of proceedings in a national court. The aim should be to make use of the informality and flexibility of the arbitral process, so as to reduce time and costs. Thus, the financial burden on the parties is alleviated, to some extent.

(b) Who fixes the fees?

Where an arbitration is conducted under the auspices of an arbitral institution, it is not **4.220** necessary for the parties to engage in any direct negotiations with the tribunal concerning the basis of its fees. These are generally fixed by the institution, sometimes independently, sometimes after consultation with the sole or presiding arbitrator. The parties have no say in the matter. In an ad hoc arbitration, however, it is necessary for the parties to make their own arrangements. The arbitrators should do this at an early stage in the proceedings to avoid misunderstandings later. The usual practice is for counsel for each party to take part in any discussion with the arbitrators about their fees and expenses, so as to avoid any suggestion of impropriety.

---

[335] Although, in some countries, the court fees are calculated on an *ad valorem* basis and may become substantial when large sums of money are in dispute.

(c) Methods of assessing fees

4.221   No universally established method exists for assessing the fees payable to an arbitrator. At least three methods are usually used:

- the *ad valorem* method, whereby the fee is calculated as a proportion of the amounts in dispute;
- the 'time spent' method, which establishes an hourly or daily rate; and
- the 'fixed fee' method, whereby the sum payable to the arbitrator by way of remuneration is fixed at the outset, without direct reference either to the amounts in dispute or to the time that the arbitrator spends on the case.

(i) *Ad valorem* method

4.222   The *ad valorem* method entails assessing the arbitrators' fees as a percentage of the total amount in dispute (including any counterclaim). It has the merit of being easy to use and capable of uniform application. It is necessary to know only (a) the total amount in dispute, and (b) the percentage figure to be applied. With this information, the parties can work out for themselves what fees they are likely to have to pay, if they take their dispute to arbitration. The ICC is the most prominent amongst the institutions that adopt this method. The ICC Rules contain a 'scale of administrative costs and fees', which shows how the administrative charges of the ICC Secretariat are calculated by applying a different percentage to each successive slice of the sum in dispute.[336] The fees payable to the arbitrators may be calculated on a similar basis, except that the percentages are different and, for each successive slice of the sum in dispute, minimum and maximum percentages are given, to establish a 'range'.[337] In practice, the ICC Court fixes the fees of the arbitrators within the overall range, taking into account the diligence and efficiency of the arbitrators, the time spent, the rapidity of the proceedings, the complexity of the dispute, and the timeliness of the submission of the draft award.[338]

(ii) 'Time spent' method

4.223   The usual method of assessing fees is to establish a rate at which the arbitrators will be paid for the time spent working on the case. This rate is intended to cover not only work done at the hearing, but also any work done outside the hearing. It is usual to establish an hourly or daily rate, or sometimes a combination of both. A lower daily or hourly rate is usually fixed for travelling time, although an arbitrator who works on a train or a flight, for instance, would be justified in charging for the hours actually worked, rather than treating the whole journey as time spent travelling.

4.224   The success of a method of payment based on a time-cost rate depends on the arbitrators keeping an accurate record of the time that they do actually spend on the case. It also depends on the parties being prepared to trust this record, since (apart from time spent at meetings with the parties and at the hearing) it is not something that can easily be checked.

---

[336] ICC Rules, Appendix III, Art. 3.
[337] Where the case is submitted to more than one arbitrator, the ICC Court has discretion to increase the fee up to a maximum of three times the fee payable to a single arbitrator.
[338] ICC Rules, Appendix III, Art. 2.2.

It may be that the presiding arbitrator should consider it to be one of his or her functions to monitor the fee invoices submitted by the co-arbitrators. In an UNCITRAL arbitration, this is inevitable, since Article 40 of the UNCITRAL Rules provides that the arbitrators' fees shall be 'reasonable in amount' and shall be stated separately as to each arbitrator in the award. In general, the hourly and/or daily rate payable is likely to vary according to the status of the arbitrator and to the size, importance, and complexity of the arbitration. It is in this context that the amount in dispute will be taken into account when the time cost method is used.[339] It is right to mention, however, that most international arbitrators with recognised reputations are prepared to accept that smaller cases should be undertaken at a rate lower than their 'normal' rate.

(iii) 'Fixed fee' method

There are cases in which arbitrators ask to be paid on a fixed fee basis. These cases are usu- **4.225**
ally cases of major importance, involving arbitrators of high international standing. Where remuneration is to be paid to the arbitrators on a fixed fee basis, the sum agreed is intended to cover all of the work done by the arbitrators on the case, including time spent at the hearing, however long it may last. The problem is that it is difficult to know at the outset how the case will develop, whether or not it will be settled before it reaches a hearing, and if it is not settled, how long the hearing itself is likely to take. The best that can be done, in such circumstances, is to make an intelligent assessment of the total number of days likely to be spent by the arbitrators on the case, assuming that it runs its full course, and then to multiply this total by an appropriate daily rate, so as to arrive at a figure for the fixed fee. The arbitrators may have done a similar calculation; alternatively, they may have applied a percentage to the total amount in dispute to calculate the fee to which they consider themselves entitled! It may then be necessary for a certain amount of bargaining to take place between the arbitrators, on the one hand, and the parties, on the other, in order to arrive at an agreed figure. In general terms, fixed fees are increasingly rare and most prestigious arbitrators are prepared to work on one of the other two, more reasonable, bases.

(d) Negotiating arbitrators' fees

In an ad hoc arbitration, parties and their legal advisers may find themselves obliged to ne- **4.226**
gotiate with arbitrators concerning their fees and expenses, if they think that the arbitrators are asking for too much. However, no party wants to risk antagonising the arbitrators by criticising their fees, since each party will have it clearly in mind that the same arbitrators will be sitting in judgment on its case.

It may seem foolish to bargain over a few hundred dollars a day if, by doing so, a claim worth **4.227**
many millions of dollars may be put in jeopardy. However, arbitrators of the right calibre

---

[339] The LCIA's schedule of costs provided, as of 1 October 2020, that hourly rates of tribunal's fees shall not exceed £500 per hour, covering both hearings and preparatory work. The ICSID fee scale provides for US$3,000 per day or per eight-hour period of work. The ICDR simply asks individual arbitrators to propose rates in the biographical notes kept by the institution, on the basis that market forces will provide adequate checks and balances. The ICC operates a scale fee system, in which time spent is only one of several factors taken into account when fees are fixed by its Court. Most of the other major arbitral institutions operate a scale based on the amount in dispute.

should not take offence if it is suggested to them that they are proposing to charge rather more than the 'going rate' for the job, as long as the suggestion is made with proper courtesy. However, if such a suggestion is necessary, it should be made by *all* the parties. Often, a reference to the fee rates paid by the leading arbitral institutions can provide a helpful anchor on which to base any discussion.

(e) Commitment or cancellation fees

4.228 A complex international arbitration may involve protracted proceedings in several separate stages. Arbitrators are invariably asked to reserve weeks for hearings in complicated cases. Substantial blocks of time are carved out of the arbitrators' diaries and they must refuse other remunerative work during the reserved period. Three factors may lead to this time being lost to the arbitrator: first, the parties may settle their dispute; second, the parties may terminate the mandate of an arbitrator for some other reason; and third—and most commonly—a procedural schedule may have been fixed that turns out to have been too ambitious, with the result that hearings have to be postponed.

4.229 Courts in England have held that the right to a commitment fee is not an implied term of the contract created when an appointment is accepted, and that it would be misconduct if an arbitrator were to require a commitment fee as a condition of continuing to perform his or her services if the appointment had been accepted without such a reservation.[340] Where the arbitrators were asked to hold available a sixty-day period some two years in the future, it was not improper for the arbitrators to *request* a commitment fee, although 'it did not accord happily with their status to become involved in negotiations about fees' after their appointment.[341] Further, it would be inappropriate if an arbitrator were to conclude an agreement for a commitment fee with one of the parties when the other party had refused to participate in the negotiations. In any event, once the appointment is accepted, the parties are under no obligation to agree to any commitment or cancellation fees.

4.230 It is therefore important for the arbitrators to discuss any commitment or cancellation fee with the parties at the time of accepting the appointment. It is also important to understand that commitment and/or cancellation fees are acceptable in some cultural environments, but so unusual as to be unacceptable in others. It is common for such fees not to represent the full-time cost of the days not used, on the assumption that the arbitrator will be able to undertake some remunerative work during that period; commitment fees ranging between 50 and 75 per cent of blocked time are usual.

(f) Expenses of the arbitral tribunal

4.231 The question of the expenses incurred by the arbitrators will also have to be settled, unless the arbitration is being conducted under the auspices of an arbitral institution, which will

---

[340] *K/S Norjarl A/S v Hyundai Heavy Industries Co. Ltd* [1991] 1 Lloyd's Rep 260; appeal dismissed, [1992] QB 863, [1991] 1 Lloyd's Rep 524.
[341] Ibid., at [268].

collect money from the parties and reimburse the arbitrators. This is usually dealt with at the same time as the question of the arbitrators' fees. The costs of air or train travel are invariably simply reimbursed on an 'as incurred' basis. Two points must be clarified between the arbitral tribunal and the parties: the first concerns the class of travel,[342] which, in order to avoid embarrassment later, should be established at the beginning; the second is whether the arbitrators may claim immediate reimbursement of their travel expenses, rather than wait for the end of the case, or for the next-stage payment date for fees. There is no justification for asking the arbitrators to fund the cash flow for the arbitral process and prompt reimbursement of expenses is reasonable.

On the question of subsistence expenses whilst attending hearings, there are two methods of dealing with arbitrators' subsistence expenses: the first may be described as the 'reimbursement method'; the second, as the '*per diem* method'.   **4.232**

(i) Reimbursement method

If the reimbursement method is adopted, the arbitrators must keep a detailed note of their expenditure, including air fares, hotel expenses, and so on. Then, from time to time, they will arrange to have these expenses reimbursed, by submitting details to the relevant arbitral institution, to a designated member of the arbitral tribunal, to the administrative secretary, or to the parties directly. Sometimes, a limit may be imposed on the amount for which an arbitrator is reimbursed (for example in respect of hotel expenses), and any expenditure over this limit is then for the account of the arbitrator personally.   **4.233**

(ii) *Per diem* method

The alternative method is for the parties to pay an amount fixed at a daily rate. This daily, or *per diem*, rate is fixed at a level sufficient to cover the costs of living away from home at a hotel of good standard in the city where the hearing takes place. It will also cover incidental expenses such as meals, taxis, printing, and so on. It is paid to the arbitrator as a fixed amount of money, calculated on a *per diem* basis by reference to the number of days spent on the case. It is then for the arbitrator to meet the actual expenses out of this fixed allowance and to pay any excess personally. The ICC, for instance, operates a *per diem* rate for reimbursement of subsistence expenses.[343] Of the two methods discussed, this method is preferable as it avoids the detailed clerical work of checking payments against receipts; it also avoids prying into an arbitrator's style of living, so as to decide whether a particular expense was or was not necessary in the interests of the proper conduct of the arbitration.   **4.234**

(iii) ICSID system

Although these methods are the most common in practice for the payment of arbitrators' expenses, variations on these basic themes may be found. For instance, ICSID offers arbitrators some choice in the method of claiming their expenses. An arbitrator in an ICSID   **4.235**

---

[342] The ICC states that the reimbursement of travel expenses is subject to an airfare equivalent to the applicable standard business-class airfare for air travel and the applicable first-class train fare for rail travel. See ICC, 'Note to Parties and Arbitral Tribunals on the Conduct of Arbitration', para. 237. ICSID authorises arbitrators to travel at one class above economy.

[343] The standard ICC *per diem* allowance at time of writing (March 2021) remains US$1,200 for an overnight stay and $400 for a day's expenses if no overnight stay in hotel accommodation is involved.

arbitration is entitled to the following allowances for attending meetings or hearings in connection with the case:

- the actual cost of travel at 'one class above coach', by air, or other means of transport ('coach' being economy class);
- an 'in–out' allowance of a fixed sum, to cover the costs of porterage, taxis, tips, and other expenses of travelling;
- the actual cost of transport within the city where the hearing takes place; and
- a *per diem* allowance, either at the full rate or at the so-called mixed rate.[344]

4.236   The last item on this list merits particular comment. Under the ICSID system, the full *per diem* rate varies from place to place, with different rates being established for different cities, according to whether or not they are 'high-cost cities'. As an alternative to claiming the full *per diem* rate, arbitrators may claim reimbursement under the 'mixed rate'. On this basis, reimbursement may be claimed for the actual cost of a hotel room (plus tax and service charge), together with an allowance of one half of the applicable full *per diem* rate to cover meals, tips, and other expenses. In practice, arbitrators taking part in an ICSID arbitration tend to choose reimbursement on the mixed rate basis unless otherwise agreed, since this comes nearest to covering the expenses likely to be incurred in staying, for instance, at a hotel in Washington, DC, where arbitrations under the ICSID Rules usually take place.

(g) Securing payment of the fees and expenses of the arbitral tribunal

4.237   The question of establishing effective arrangements regarding fees and expenses is as important for the arbitrators as it is for the parties. The fact that arbitrators may become *functus officio* instantly at the joint will of the parties emphasises the importance for the arbitrators of obtaining adequate security for payment of their fees and expenses. The acceptance by the arbitrators of the functions bestowed upon them creates a legal relationship between the parties and the members of the arbitral tribunal. This relationship carries with it an implied undertaking by the parties to compensate the members of the arbitral tribunal fairly in respect of their work and expenses, whether or not an award is issued. However, even under those national systems of law in which this is clear,[345] arbitrators do not usually wish to go to the trouble and cost of suing the parties for their fees and expenses.

4.238   Where the arbitration is being administered by an established arbitral institution, the arbitral tribunal need not concern itself with the collection of payments on account of its fees and expenses. This is handled by the arbitral institution, usually by requesting an advance on costs for the entire proceedings or for every phase of them. In any other case, however, the tribunal should arrange for the parties to make sufficient advance deposits in respect of its fees and expenses.[346] There are two reasons for this: first, it helps the parties to keep a check on expenses as the case proceeds; and second, it is easier to collect payments from the

---

[344] The standard ICSID *per diem* allowance for subsistence expenses (that is, meals, taxis, etc.) still in effect in 2021 is US$115; however, special *per diem* allowances of $135, $170, or $185 apply for certain high-cost cities (e.g. $170 for Washington, DC, which is in the second highest cost category).

[345] See, e.g., English Arbitration Act 1996, s. 28.

[346] The UNCITRAL Rules make provision for this in Art. 43.

parties whilst the arbitration is in progress than when the proceedings are over. In ICSID administered proceedings, when one of the parties fails to make the advance payments, the proceedings may be stayed and even discontinued unless the non-defaulting party pays the other party's share in order to continue with the proceedings.[347]

Where there is no arbitral institution involved to take care of fees and expenses, a bank account should be established for receipt of the deposits made by the parties. This account may then also be used for paying fees and expenses to the members of the arbitral tribunal as and when payments fall due. Any interest earned on the account should be credited to the account (and, accordingly, be accrued for the benefit of the parties). The account is usually opened in the name of the arbitral tribunal, with the sole arbitrator or the presiding arbitrator as signatory on the account. If an administrative secretary or administrative authority has been appointed, the maintenance and operation of the account will usually fall under their responsibilities. As noted, however, some institutions offer this fundholding service irrespective of whether the arbitration is taking place under their rules.[348] This is to be recommended in large cases, since the arbitral institutions are far better equipped to undertake this kind of service than arbitrators and usually do so based on an hourly cost basis far lower than that of the arbitrator.[349] **4.239**

---

[347] ICSID Administrative and Financial Regulations, reg. 14.

[348] The LCIA provides a fundholding service for arbitrations conducted under the UNCITRAL Rules and also for ad hoc arbitrations. Where acting as fundholder, the LCIA sets up a dedicated bank account in either dollars, sterling, or euro, into which advances on costs and other administrative costs should be lodged by the parties. The LCIA will then monitor the account to ensure that it has enough funds to cover the arbitration costs and will make disbursement as determined by the tribunal.

[349] In 2021, the costs of the LCIA fundholding service were £150 per hour.

5

POWERS, DUTIES, AND JURISDICTION
OF AN ARBITRAL TRIBUNAL

A. Background

(a) Introduction

An arbitral tribunal established to determine an international dispute operates in an en-   **5.01**
tirely different context from that of a judge sitting in a national court. Judges sit in a legal
environment that clearly defines the extent of their powers and duties. They are generally
given full immunity in respect of any potential liability arising out of the conduct of their
judicial function. Their jurisdiction, and the extent to which decisions in relation to jurisdiction may be reviewed by an appellate court, are clearly established in the law governing
the proceedings.

The position differs in arbitration—particularly in international arbitration, in which the   **5.02**
powers, duties, and jurisdiction of an arbitral tribunal arise from a complex mixture of
the will of the parties, the law governing the arbitration agreement, the law of the place of
arbitration,[1] and the law of the place in which recognition or enforcement of the award
may be sought.

(b) Practical considerations

A balance must be struck between the sanctions that may be imposed on arbitrators who   **5.03**
carry out their functions in a careless or improper manner and the equally necessary requirement that an arbitral tribunal be free to perform its task without constantly 'looking
over its shoulder' in the fear of being challenged by means of legal process. On one view, it
may be argued that arbitrators should be given virtually unlimited powers, in order to adapt
the process to the dispute in question, and to encourage speed and effectiveness in the arbitral process. However, the requirements of public policy, whether national or international,[2]

---

[1] Or, exceptionally, the law to which the parties have agreed to subject the arbitration. See Chapter 3.
[2] See Chapter 10, paragraphs 10.81*ff*.

make some control necessary, so as to ensure that the parties are not without recourse if the arbitral tribunal acts beyond its jurisdiction,[3] treats the parties unequally, or fails to conduct a fair hearing.

5.04   The system for the protection of parties against excesses on the part of arbitral tribunals is usually contained in the framework for recourse against the award itself, or at the moment of recognition and enforcement.[4] However, arbitrators may be removed for certain types of wrongful conduct during the arbitral process pursuant to the rules of an applicable arbitral institution,[5] or under the law governing the arbitration[6] by an application to the courts of the country in which the arbitration has its seat.

5.05   The powers and duties of an arbitral tribunal are also closely linked to the question of its jurisdiction (particularly in defining the extent of that jurisdiction) and the difficult question of determining the validity of the arbitration agreement. Before turning to the question of the jurisdiction of the arbitral tribunal to decide the particular dispute before it, the powers and duties of the arbitral tribunal will be considered.

B. Powers of Arbitrators

(a) Introduction

5.06   The powers of an arbitral tribunal are those conferred upon it by the parties within the limits allowed by the applicable law,[7] together with any additional powers that may be conferred automatically by operation of law. These powers are established to enable the arbitral tribunal to carry out its task properly and effectively.

5.07   In a well-conducted international arbitration, control of the proceedings moves smoothly from the parties to the arbitral tribunal. At first, the parties are fully in charge. They alone know the issues in dispute, how they intend to set about proving the facts upon which they rely, and the arguments of law that they propose to advance. The case that is to be put to the arbitral tribunal is 'their' case. Indeed, the arbitral tribunal owes its very existence to the parties: it is 'their' tribunal. As the proceedings develop, however, the arbitral tribunal becomes increasingly familiar with the matters in dispute. It begins to decide for itself which facts it regards as relevant and which questions of law it regards as important. It is in a position to start making known its views as to how the case should be presented within the framework of the particular rules that govern the proceedings. The balance of power, in effect, shifts from the parties to the arbitral tribunal. It is right that this should be so: the arbitrators, not the parties, are the final judges of the matters in dispute. However, this shift in

---

[3] See Chapter 10.

[4] For further discussion of this subject, see Chapter 11.

[5] For instance, under the ICC Rules, Art. 15.2, the ICC Court may remove an arbitrator for not fulfilling his or her functions in accordance with the Rules or within the prescribed time limit.

[6] For instance, under the English Arbitration Act 1996, s. 24, the English court may remove an arbitrator for 'justifiable doubts' as to that arbitrator's impartiality.

[7] As far as the tribunal's *powers* are concerned, the applicable law is usually the proper law of the arbitration agreement and the law of the place of arbitration. For discussion of applicable law generally, see Chapter 3.

the balance of power happens only if the arbitrators know when and how to take charge of the proceedings and understand the tools at their disposal.

(b) Sources of arbitrators' powers

(i) Powers conferred by the parties

The parties may confer powers upon the arbitral tribunal directly or indirectly, but only within the limits of the applicable law. Any excess of power (that is, any power granted over and above that allowed by the applicable law) is invalid, even if it is contained in international or institutional rules of arbitration.   **5.08**

A 'direct' conferment of powers takes place when the parties agree expressly upon the powers that they wish the arbitrators to exercise, possibly by setting them out in the terms of appointment or a submission agreement. Such powers are likely to include the powers to order production of documents, to appoint experts, to hold hearings, to require the presence of witnesses, to receive evidence, and to inspect the subject matter of the dispute. The ways in which these powers may be expressly conferred upon the arbitral tribunal in submission agreements have been described in more detail in Chapter 2.[8]   **5.09**

An 'indirect' conferment of powers takes place when the parties have agreed that the arbitration is to be conducted according to pre-established rules of arbitration that set out the powers of the tribunal. In the case of the ICC, some of these powers are conferred on the ICC's International Court of Arbitration itself. For example, the place of arbitration is determined by the ICC Court, unless it has been chosen by agreement of the parties.[9]   **5.10**

(ii) Powers conferred by operation of law

The powers conferred upon an arbitral tribunal by the parties, whether directly or indirectly, fall short of the powers that may be exercised by a national court. Such courts derive their authority from the state, which grants to them formidable coercive powers to ensure obedience to their orders. An arbitral tribunal does not usually possess such powers.[10] The parties cannot confer upon a private tribunal the coercive powers over property and persons that are conferred by the state on a national court. In recognition of this fact, many systems of law supplement the powers of arbitral tribunals by: **5.11**

- giving powers directly to arbitral tribunals;
- authorising national courts to exercise powers on behalf of arbitral tribunals; or
- a combination of these two methods.

---

[8] See Chapter 2, paragraphs 05–2.07.

[9] ICC Rules, Art. 18.1. See also UNCITRAL Rules, Art. 18.1; LCIA Rules, Art. 16.2.

[10] Some Latin American states, such as Colombia and Ecuador, do not follow this rule in domestic arbitrations and grant to arbitrators a degree of *imperium*, such that they can call upon public officers to enforce their orders directly as if they were a court of law. See, e.g., Ecuador's 2006 Arbitration and Mediation Law, s. 9: '[Arbitrators] shall request the aid of public, judicial, police and administrative officers as shall be necessary without having to resort to any ordinary judge at the place where [...] it is necessary to adopt those provisional measures.' See, for a fuller description, Marchan, 'Ecuador', in Newman and Ong (eds) *Interim Measures in International Arbitration* (Juris, 2014), pp. 217*ff*.

5.12   An example of procedural powers being conferred on an international arbitral tribunal by law is provided by the English Arbitration Act 1996. The tribunal is given various powers, including the powers to order a claimant to provide security for costs,[11] to administer oaths to witnesses,[12] and generally to determine procedural matters.[13]

5.13   In practice, the best approach when considering the powers of an arbitral tribunal is to look first at the arbitration agreement (including any applicable institutional rules that may be incorporated within the agreement), then at the law governing the arbitration agreement, and finally at the law governing the arbitration (if different). The arbitration agreement should be considered to establish what powers the parties themselves have agreed to confer on the arbitral tribunal. In general, those powers are set out in the rules to which the arbitration has been subjected. The law governing the arbitration agreement should then be considered to identify how those powers may have been supplemented or restricted. The law of the arbitration agreement, which governs its validity, effect, and interpretation, may confer specific powers (or impose certain limitations) upon the arbitral tribunal.[14] Finally, if different, the law governing the arbitration itself, the *lex arbitri*, should be similarly considered. An example of such a restriction is an arbitration agreement governed by English law, but which provides for the arbitration to take place in Paris. The arbitration agreement might include an express provision that the arbitrator is entitled to administer oaths to any witnesses in the arbitration. French law, however, does not permit a private individual, such as an arbitrator, to administer oaths.[15] This is a mandatory provision of French law which, as the law governing the arbitration, would override the express or implied provisions of the arbitration agreement.

(c) Common powers of arbitral tribunals

(i) Establishing the arbitral procedure

5.14   In general terms, the arbitral tribunal enjoys a very broad power to determine the appropriate procedure. Indeed, this is one of the defining features of arbitration as opposed to courts, in which a fixed procedure exists. It is, however, subject to an overarching respect of due process or natural justice—that is, equality of treatment and an opportunity to be heard. One example of this dichotomy is provided by Article 17.1 of the UNCITRAL Rules which contains a general power for the arbitral tribunal to 'conduct the arbitration in such manner as it considers appropriate, provided that the parties are treated with equality and

---

[11] English Arbitration Act 1996, s. 38(3). The arbitral tribunal can enforce this order by dismissing the claim if it is not complied with: s. 41(6).

[12] Ibid, s. 38(5).

[13] Ibid, s. 34. This power is also granted by Model Law, Art. 19(1).

[14] See, e.g., New Zealand Arbitration Act 1996, s. 12; Swiss PIL, s. 183; Brazilian Arbitration Act 1996, art. 22.

[15] French Code of Civil Procedure, art. 1467: '*Le tribunal arbitral peut entendre toute personne. Cette audition a lieu sans prestation de serment* [The arbitral tribunal may hear any person. This hearing takes place without taking an oath].' By contrast, some jurisdictions require oaths to be taken in a prescribed manner while others adopt a middle ground and grant to the tribunal the power to administer an oath. In the US case *In re Arbitration between International Bechtel Co. Ltd v Department of Civil Aviation of the Government of Dubai* 300 F.Supp.2d 112 (DDC 2005), the US District Court for the District of Columbia refused to enforce an award set aside in Dubai on the basis of the failure properly to administer the oath in accordance with the then current version of the UAE Civil Code.

that at an appropriate stage of the proceedings, each party is given a reasonable opportunity of presenting its case'.[16]

(ii) Determining the applicable law and seat

Parties sometimes fail to address important matters in the arbitration agreement, such as **5.15** the seat of the arbitration or the applicable law. In case this happens, and in order to prevent the parties' agreement to arbitrate becoming inoperative, the arbitral tribunal (and, in some cases, the arbitral institution) is usually provided with the power to determine the seat[17] and the applicable rules of law.[18] Such important decisions will normally be made only once both parties have had an opportunity to be heard on the issue.[19] The determination of the seat or place of arbitration by an institution or by the arbitral tribunal is important, since it will determine the *lex arbitri* and consequently establish a state jurisdiction to supervise the arbitration. It is common practice for arbitral tribunals in these circumstances to establish a seat in a jurisdiction that is a signatory to the New York Convention (for recognition and enforcement purposes) and which has an established reputation as a seat in international disputes.

(iii) Determining the language of the arbitration

Where the language of the arbitration is not established by the arbitration agreement and **5.16** the institutional rules do not provide for determination of this question, the arbitral tribunal must determine the language(s) to be used in the proceedings.[20] Usually, tribunals fix the language of the arbitration as that of the underlying contract, since this is most likely to be the 'common' language of the parties.[21] However, where the parties have used two working languages in negotiations (or have authentic versions of the contract in two languages), the tribunal may order a bilingual arbitration in which two languages may be used interchangeably by the parties, with or without the need for translation or interpretation. Bilingual arbitrations are also commonly ordered in investment arbitrations where a sovereign state insists on presenting its case in its own language whereas the international investor may often prefer English.

(iv) Requiring the production of documents

Where a party has requested production of specific, or a narrow category of, documents by **5.17** the other party and that party has raised objections, the arbitral tribunal will usually receive a request for an order requiring such production. If the arbitral tribunal concludes that the document or category of documents is indeed relevant to the resolution of the dispute, it has the power to order production.[22] In the event that the requested party does not produce

---

[16] Similar rules apply under institutional rules: see the CIETAC Rules, Art. 35.1.

[17] UNCITRAL Rules, Art. 18.1 ('If the parties have not previously agreed on the place of arbitration, the place of arbitration shall be determined by the arbitral tribunal having regard to the circumstances of the case.') LCIA Rules, Art. 16.2 (London, England as the default seat unless the tribunal concludes another seat is more appropriate after hearing the parties).

[18] UNCITRAL Rules, Art. 35.1.

[19] The determination of the applicable law is addressed in detail in Chapter 3.

[20] UNCITRAL Rules, Art. 19.1.

[21] See Chapter 2, paragraphs 2.94–2.95.

[22] The question of the production of documentary evidence is discussed in detail in Chapter 6, paragraphs 6.90*ff.*

the ordered documents, the tribunal has no power (*imperium*) to force production, but may nevertheless 'draw adverse inferences' from such failure or (in French law) impose a financial penalty.[23] A further limitation is that this power may not be exercised by the tribunal against non-parties to the arbitration.[24]

5.18   The law of the place of arbitration may provide supplementary state powers to assist the tribunal. For example, in a tribunal with a seat in the United States, the tribunal may issue a subpoena requiring a person present within the jurisdiction to produce documents. However, the arbitral subpoena can be enforced by a court of the state in which the arbitration is taking place only against a person resident or present within the jurisdiction of that court.[25]

(v) Requiring the presence of witnesses/subpoenas

5.19   The arbitral tribunal has the power to require the presence of witnesses under the control of the parties. However, absent any powers to call upon the forces of public order, if such a witness fails to appear, the arbitral tribunal is again (as with a failure to produce documents) usually limited to drawing adverse inferences from the party's failure to secure the presence of the witness; and once again, the tribunal's powers may be supplemented by the law governing the proceedings (*lex arbitri*) by providing judicial support to the enforceability of orders. For example, in England and Wales, a party may seek a peremptory order from the tribunal requiring the attendance of a witness in the power of a party which, if disobeyed, may be followed by a court order in support. If the court order is disobeyed, it is a contempt of court, which may lead to a criminal prosecution.[26] In the United States, using the same subpoena procedure outlined above for documents, an arbitral subpoena can be issued in respect of a third-party witness present in the jurisdiction of the state in which the arbitration is to take place. In Switzerland, a tribunal may also obtain court assistance for the taking of evidence, such as compelling a witness to appear.[27]

(vi) Examining the subject matter of the dispute

5.20   Where the dispute concerns the state or condition of the subject matter of the contract, such as a cargo of goods or defects in a particular structure in a construction project, it may be useful for the tribunal to see for itself the cargo or the structure in question. A tribunal usually has this power under relevant institutional rules[28] or national laws. The possibility of a 'site visit' is also addressed in the 2020 International Bar Association Rules on the Taking of Evidence in International Arbitration (the IBA Rules).[29] Such visits need to be carefully planned in advance, with appropriate protocols in place. The tribunal will

---

[23] French Code of Civil Procedure, art. 1467: '*Si une partie détient un élément de preuve, le tribunal arbitral peut lui enjoindre de le produire selon les modalités qu'il détermine et au besoin à peine d'astreinte.* [If a party is in possession of evidence, the arbitral tribunal may order it to be produced in a manner that the tribunal decides and if necessary, under penalty for failure to do so.]'

[24] For more detail, see Chapter 6, paragraphs 6.114–6.115.

[25] FAA, § 7, which states that arbitrators 'may summon in writing any person to attend before them […] as a witness and in a proper case to bring with him or them any book, record, document, or paper which may be deemed material as evidence in the case'. For an example of the use of the power and confirmation of its application to non-parties see *Stolt-Nielson SA v Celanese AG*, 430 F.3d 567 (2d Cir. 2005).

[26] See paragraph 5.49.

[27] Swiss PIL, s. 184(2).

[28] For example, LCIA Rules, Art. 22.1.iv; PCA Rules, Art. 27.3.

[29] See IBA Rules, Art. 7 ('Inspection').

usually make the site visit in the presence of the parties and any relevant party or tribunal-appointed experts.

(vii) Appointing experts

Many rules of arbitration permit the tribunal to appoint its own expert.[30] The IBA Rules **5.21** make specific provision for this possibility and establish useful ground rules for such appointment.[31] Where questions of technical expertise are required in an international arbitration, whether arising out of liability or *quantum* issues, it is usual for the parties to present expert reports from independent experts retained for the purpose.[32] It is then for the tribunal to weigh and compare the value of that expert testimony, in order to reach a conclusion. Sometimes, the evidence of the experts is of such technical complexity that the tribunal has difficulty in reaching a decision. At other times the instructions given to the party-appointed experts may differ and the experts fail properly to engage with the adverse party's case. The tribunal may then (after consultation with the parties) decide to seek assistance itself from a neutral expert, either at the outset of a technically complex case or at a later stage, to assist in evaluating the technical evidence.

If the tribunal decides to exercise this power, it is better done sooner rather than later. **5.22** However, typically the need for an independent expert only becomes clear after the tribunal has received the reports of party-appointed experts and (in some cases) after those experts have been heard at a final hearing.[33] Best practice suggests that, wherever possible, the appointment should be made before the final hearing, so that the expert can be present during the oral testimony of the party-appointed experts.

When an arbitral tribunal exercises its power to appoint an expert, it will usually seek the **5.23** views of the parties on the qualifications of the independent expert and the proposed terms of reference which will set out the scope of the exercise, with a list of specific questions and issues to consider (on which the parties should be allowed to comment). The questions should be limited to those that require technical expertise and should not delegate any legal question. The tribunal will then usually establish a shortlist of candidates and ask the parties to confirm the absence of conflicts. Once appointed, the expert will review the evidence in the case and respond to the questions raised by the tribunal in a draft report which should include the methodology and evidence used to arrive at the conclusions. This should then be circulated to the parties for comment. Once comments are received, the expert should prepare a final report and be made available for oral examination by the parties and the tribunal on that report.[34]

A possible variation from this practice would be for the tribunal to appoint two experts, one **5.24** chosen from each of two lists provided by the parties. This 'expert team' would then provide

---

[30] For example, UNCITRAL Rules, Art. 29.1; CIETAC Rules, Art. 44.1.

[31] See IBA Rules, Art. 6 ('Tribunal-Appointed Experts').

[32] See Chapter 6, paragraphs 6.138*ff*.

[33] This was the case of the independent expert appointed in *Suez, Sociedad General de Aguas de Barcelona SA and Vivendi Universal SA v Argentine Republic*, ICSID Case No. ARB/03/19. See Award (9 April 2015), at [7]–[18].

[34] One comprehensive procedure, which may be incorporated or used as a checklist, is established at IBA Rules, Art. 6. For examples of the use of independent experts in investment arbitration, see *Perenco Ecuador Limited v Republic of Ecuador*, ICSID Case No. ARB/08/6, Interim Decision on the Environmental Counterclaim, 11 August 2015, at [585]*ff*; *Abaclat and Others v Argentine Republic*, ICSID Case No. ARB/07/5, Procedural Order No. 15, 20 November 2012, at [11]*ff*.

the tribunal with a single report on the relevant technical issues, based on a single set of questions established in consultation between the arbitrators and the parties.[35] 'Expert teaming' helps to correct the danger of a lone tribunal-appointed expert by requiring two tribunal-appointed experts to work in tandem. By having some input on the choice of one of the experts, parties should feel that they have not lost all control in the selection process. At the same time, the short-list system imposes an incentive on parties to put forward truly independent experts whom a tribunal would be more likely to select.

5.25   It is important to note that the final report of the tribunal's expert(s) is simply another evidentiary element for the arbitral tribunal to consider in its deliberations. It is not binding on the tribunal. The tribunal should not delegate its obligation to reach its own decision on expert issues in dispute through the appointment of an independent expert.[36]

(viii) Interim measures

5.26   During the course of an arbitration, it may become necessary for the arbitral tribunal or a national court to issue orders intended to preserve evidence, to protect assets, to respect procedural rights, and otherwise to maintain the *status quo* pending the outcome of the arbitration proceedings.[37] Such orders take different forms and are known by different names. In the Model Law and in the UNCITRAL Rules, they are known as 'interim measures';[38] in the English version of the ICC Rules, they are known as 'conservatory and interim measures'.[39] Whatever their designation, they are intended to operate as holding orders to protect the *status quo* and the integrity of the proceedings, pending the outcome of the arbitral process. Most major institutional rules now empower arbitral institutions to appoint 'Emergency Arbitrators' for the purpose of providing rapid interim relief before the constitution of a tribunal.[40] An emergency arbitrator usually enjoys the same powers as the definitive tribunal to order interim relief—but once constituted, the arbitral tribunal may review that relief.[41]

5.27   Where interim measures of protection are required, the arbitral tribunal itself generally has the power to order them. For example, Article 28.1 of the ICC Rules provides that 'the Arbitral Tribunal may, at the request of a party, order any interim or conservatory measure it deems appropriate'. There are similar provisions in many arbitration rules.[42] The same powers are usually provided for in arbitration laws. For example, Article 17 of the Model Law (as amended in 2006) states, '[u]nless otherwise agreed by the parties, the arbitral tribunal may, at the request of a party, grant interim measures'.

---

[35] The details of this proposal are set out in Sachs, 'Protocol on expert teaming: A new approach to expert evidence', in ICCA (ed.) *Arbitration Advocacy in Changing Times* (Kluwer, 2011), pp. 135*ff.*

[36] Similar 'ground rules' are established in IBA Rules, Art. 6.

[37] As the tribunal noted in *Burlington Resources v Republic of Ecuador*, ICSID Case No. ARB/08/5, Procedural Order No. 1, 29 June 2009, at [60]: 'In the Tribunal's view, the rights to be preserved by provisional measures are not limited to those which form the subject-matter of the dispute or substantive rights as referred to by the Respondents, but may extend to procedural rights, including the general right to the *status quo* and to the non-aggravation of the dispute.'

[38] Model Law, Chapter IV.A; UNCITRAL Rules, Art. 26.

[39] ICC Rules, Art. 28.

[40] LCIA Rules, Art. 9B; SCC Rules, Art. 37.4 and Appendix II; ICC Rules, Art. 29.1 and Appendix V; ICDR Rules, Art. 7; SIAC Rules, r. 30.2, with proceedings governed by Sch. 1.

[41] See Chapter 4, paragraphs 4.11*ff* for a review of the role of Emergency Arbitrators.

[42] For example, UNCITRAL Rules, Art. 26; LCIA Rules, Art. 25; ICDR Rules, Art. 27.

The ICSID Rules are different, in that they appear to limit the power of the arbitral tribunal   **5.28**
to that of 'recommending' interim measures:

> A party may at any time request that the Tribunal recommend provisional measures to
> preserve that party's rights, including measures to: (a) prevent action that is likely to cause
> current or imminent harm to that party or prejudice to the arbitral process; (b) maintain or
> restore the status quo pending determination of the dispute; or (c) preserve evidence that
> may be relevant to the resolution of the dispute.[43]

The use of the word 'recommended' in this context stems from the concern of the drafters   **5.29**
of the ICSID Convention to be respectful of national sovereignty by not granting powers
to private tribunals to order a state to do, or not do, something on a purely provisional
basis. Arbitral jurisprudence, however, indicates that these measures do constitute binding
obligations.[44] As confirmed by the tribunal in *Valle Verde v Venezuela*,[45] it is now 'well
settled' that ICSID tribunal decisions recommending provisional measures are binding on
the party to whom they are directed.

Whilst most rules and laws of arbitration permit interim measures to be granted at the   **5.30**
tribunal's discretion, they provide little guidance as to how that discretion should be exercised. Traditionally, arbitrators have looked to concepts common to most legal systems in
the granting of such measures—such as the need to establish a *prima facie* case on the merits
and the risk of serious and irreparable harm if the measure is not granted. Recent ICSID
jurisprudence suggests that provisional measures are 'extraordinary measures', which are
recommended in only limited circumstances, such as when such measures are urgent and
necessary to avoid imminent and irreparable harm.[46]

The lack of guidance in many jurisdictions on the applicable test for interim measures was   **5.31**
addressed in the revised Model Law of 2006. Article 17A ('Conditions for granting interim
measures') sets out the applicable test as follows:

> (1) The party requesting an interim measure under article 17(2)*(a)*, *(b)* and *(c)* shall satisfy
>   the arbitral tribunal that:
>   (a) Harm not adequately reparable by an award of damages is likely to result if the
>   measure is not ordered, and such harm substantially outweighs the harm that is
>   likely to result to the party against whom the measure is directed if the measure is
>   granted; and

---

[43] ICSID Rules, r. 47(1); see also ICSID Convention, Art. 47.

[44] In this regard, in *Emilio Agustín Maffezini v Kingdom of Spain*, ICSID Case No. ARB/97/7, Procedural Order No. 2, 28 October 1999, at [9], the ICSID tribunal came to the following conclusion: 'The Tribunal's authority to rule on provisional measures is no less binding than that of a final award. Accordingly, for the purposes of this order, the tribunal deems the word 'recommend' to be of equivalent value as the word "order"'. See also *Quiborax SA v Plurinational State of Bolivia*, ICSID Case No. ARB/06/2, Award, 16 September 2015, at [578]–[582]. The case law is addressed in Kaufmann-Kohler, Antonietti, and Potestà, 'Interim relief in investment arbitration', in Yannaka-Small (ed.) *Arbitration under International Investment Agreements* (Oxford University Press, 2018), pp. 633–678, at [24.149]. See also Sinclair and Repousis, 'An overview of provisional measures in ICSID proceedings' (2017) 32 ICSID Rev—Foreign Investment LJ 431.

[45] *Valle Verde v Bolivarian Republic of Venezuela*, ICSID Case No. ARB/12/18, Decision on Provisional Measures, 25 January 2016, at [75].

[46] *Rizzani de Eccher S.p.A. v State of Kuwait*, ICSID Case No. ARB/17/8, Decision on Provisional Measures, 23 November 2017, at [99], [101] (citing *Occidental Petroleum Corporation and Occidental Exploration and Production Co. v Republic of Ecuador*, ICSID Case No. ARB/06/11, Decision on Provisional Measures, 17 August 2007, at [59]).

(b) There is a reasonable possibility that the requesting party will succeed on the merits of the claim. The determination on this possibility shall not affect the discretion of the arbitral tribunal in making any subsequent determination.

[...]

This test follows earlier arbitral practice. It confirms that the key elements to take into account are: (a) the risk of irreparable harm, if the order is not granted; (b) that the harm to the requesting party, if the order is not granted, will be greater than the harm to the other party if it *is* granted (the 'balance of convenience' test); and (c) that the requesting party has a reasonable chance of success on the merits (that is, a *prima facie* case).

5.32   In most jurisdictions, an arbitral tribunal has the power to issue interim measures provided that both parties are heard (thereby preserving one of the cornerstones of due process). Problems arise, however, when one party seeks to obtain interim measures *ex parte*—that is, in the absence of the opposing party or parties. Institutional rules sometimes authorise the tribunal to grant *ex parte* interim measures under 'exceptional circumstances', subject to the opposing party's right to be heard promptly following the grant of any order.[47] However, some commentators have suggested that such a power is incompatible with the consensual nature of arbitration and with proper respect for due process.[48]

5.33   Article 17B of the revised Model Law sets out a compromise, which provides for emergency relief in the form of a 'preliminary order'. This can be requested on an *ex parte* basis simultaneously with the request for interim relief. A preliminary order is subject to a twenty-day time limit, pursuant to Article 17C(4), and the same conditions apply as for interim measures. Within that twenty-day period, an application may be made to the arbitral tribunal, on notice to the other party, to adopt or vary the preliminary order. In addition, a preliminary order may be granted on an *ex parte* basis if the arbitrator decides that disclosure of the request for interim relief would frustrate the purpose of the measure (for example because the opposing party might seek to hide or remove relevant assets). Article 17C(5) provides that a preliminary order of emergency relief, whilst binding on the parties, is not enforceable by a court.[49]

(ix) Security for costs

5.34   Security for costs is a special form of interim relief, to which the criteria outlined above do not apply. It is an order which seeks to protect the enforceability of an eventual adverse costs order made against an unsuccessful claimant. It is therefore based on the premise that international arbitral tribunals will order the losing party to pay the costs of the winning party. Such costs orders are increasingly frequent in international arbitration but are by no

---

[47] See, e.g., Swiss Rules, Art. 29.3 (emphasis added):

> In *exceptional circumstances*, the arbitral tribunal may rule on a request for interim measures by way of a preliminary order before the request has been communicated to any other party, provided that such communication is made at the latest together with the preliminary order and that the other parties are immediately *granted an opportunity to be heard*.

[48] See van Houtte, 'Ten reasons against a proposal for *ex parte* interim measures of protection in arbitration' (2004) 20 Arb Intl 85, at 89.

[49] Indeed, it is questionable whether any provisional or interim relief ordered by an arbitral tribunal is enforceable by state courts under the New York Convention absent specific authority, since, by definition, such decisions will not be final: see Chapter 7, paragraph 7.26*ff.*

means universal, particularly in the field of investment arbitration where tribunals recognise that some areas of the law are sufficiently in flux that it is reasonable that a successful party should be required to bear its own costs.

The point has already been made that the costs of presenting or defending a claim in an **5.35** international arbitration may run into millions of dollars.[50] Where a claimant considers launching arbitral proceedings, this is—or should be—one of the factors to be taken into account. But what about the respondent, who has no such luxury of choice? If there is a valid arbitration agreement to which the respondent is a party, that respondent may decide not to take part in the proceedings; but if it does so, it runs a very real risk of having a default award made against it that is likely to be enforceable against its worldwide assets.[51]

Whilst a decision to defend the proceedings is usually the safer option, it comes at a consid- **5.36** erable cost. Not only will the respondent have to pay its own legal costs, but it will generally be required to make a substantial advance payment towards the fees and expenses of the arbitral tribunal and, in an institutional arbitration, of the institution under whose rules the proceedings are being conducted. If the respondent is ultimately successful, an award of costs will generally be made in its favour, which will go some way towards repaying the costs actually incurred. However, this will be of no consolation to the respondent if it transpires that the claimant does not have sufficient funds to meet an award of costs against it. The classic example is where a contract is signed with a 'special purpose' vehicle (or shell company) with few assets. If the special purpose vehicle brings a claim, it is likely to be funded by its shareholder. That shareholder will benefit from the claim of its subsidiary if successful. However, if the subsidiary loses, it will have insufficient assets to pay a costs award in favour of the respondent and the shareholder (who would have benefited from a victory) will not be liable.

In this circumstance, an application for security for costs may be made by a respondent to **5.37** protect against the risk that the tribunal may make an order for costs in its favour against an impecunious claimant. In such cases, the tribunal must weigh the risk to a successful respondent of being unable to recover its costs against an unsuccessful claimant versus the risk of stifling a genuine claim by a claimant who is short of funds, possibly because of the very conduct of the respondent that has given rise to the arbitration.

If the application is successful, the consequences are important. First, the respondent will **5.38** know that if it defends the claim successfully and is awarded costs, there will be a mechanism in place (often a bank guarantee or an escrow account) to ensure payment; secondly, if the claimant is unable to provide the requisite security, the proceedings will come to an end.[52]

Historically, applications for costs in international arbitrations were rarely granted, no **5.39** doubt because in many civil law jurisdictions (and the United States) adverse costs orders in the courts for material amounts in favour of the winning respondent are rare.[53] In an early

---

[50] See Chapter 1, paragraphs 1.144–1.146.
[51] Recognition and enforcement of arbitral awards is discussed in Chapter 11.
[52] The LCIA Rules, e.g., provide in Art. 25.2 that if the claimant is unable to provide security as ordered, the tribunal may 'stay that party's claims, counterclaims or cross-claims or dismiss them by an award'.
[53] See the discussion in Redfern and O'Leary, 'Why it is time for international arbitration to embrace security for costs' (2016) 32 Arb Intl 397, at 399.

commentary on the ICC Rules, the authors agreed that an application for security for costs as an interim measure was possible, despite there being no *specific* provision in the rules for such an application. The authors said that:[54]

> Many considered it undesirable to call attention to its availability or to suggest that it was a normal interim measure. The remedy is considered by many to be inappropriate in most circumstances for ICC arbitrations.

5.40   As the burden of costs increases, this historical antipathy to applications for security for costs is changing, particularly in common law jurisdictions. For example, the laws of arbitration of England, Hong Kong, and Singapore explicitly provide for orders for security for costs. Further, as adverse costs orders become more commonplace, institutional rules of leading arbitral institutions have embraced the concept, including those of the LCIA, SIAC, HKIAC, and the Belgian Centre for Arbitration and Mediation (CEPANI).[55] Article 25.2 of the LCIA Rules, for example, confers upon an arbitral tribunal the power to order a claimant or counter-claimant 'to provide or procure security for Legal Costs and Arbitration Costs by way of deposit or bank guarantee or in any other manner and upon such terms as the Arbitral Tribunal considers appropriate in the circumstances'. Under other rules of arbitration, including those of UNCITRAL, ICC, and ICSID, security for costs is not addressed separately but may be ordered under the general provision that authorises an arbitral tribunal to issue interim measures of protection.[56]

5.41   The issue of whether or not to order security for costs is more delicate in investment arbitration than it is before commercial arbitrators because it may have been the very action of the respondent state that has caused the impecuniosity of the claimant. For example, where a claimant's principal producing asset (e.g. a mine) has been seized by a host state without compensation, the claimant may wish to bring a claim under an applicable investment treaty. However, the very action of the host state has stifled the ability of the affected claimant to fund the arbitration. In such cases, affected investors often look to third-party funding to provide access to justice (that is, where its legal costs are paid in whole or in part by a professional funder, who will usually be repaid only in the event of success). The respondent state is usually aware that the claim is funded since some rules (and most tribunals) require the revelation of the existence of funding (and the identity of the funder) for conflicts purposes.[57] The respondent state may use this information to claim that the use of funding is evidence of impecuniosity and thus seek security for costs in respect of the claim.

---

[54] Craig, Park, and Paulson, *International Chamber of Commerce Arbitration* (ICC Publishing, 2000), pp. 467–468.

[55] See Redfern and O'Leary, fn. 53, pp. 401–403.

[56] For ICSID, see *Libananco Holdings v Republic of Turkey*, ICSID Case No. ARB 06/8, Decision on Preliminary Issues, 23 June 2008, at [31], [56]–[60]. For UNCITRAL, see *Guaracachi America, Inc. and Rurelec plc v Plurinational State of Bolivia*, PCA Case No. 2011-17, Procedural Order No. 14, 11 March 2013, at [5]–[6] and *Manuel Garcia Armas et al. v Bolivarian Republic of Venezuela*, PCA Case No. 2016-08, Procedural Order No. 9, 20 June 2018.

[57] Notably, the current ICC Rules require the disclosure of third-party funding. ICC Rules, Art. 11.7. Rule 14(1) of the ICSID Rules also requires such disclosure ('A party shall file a written notice disclosing the name and address of any non-party from which the party, directly or indirectly, has received funds for the pursuit or defense of the proceeding through a donation or grant, or in return for remuneration dependent on the outcome of the proceeding').

In *Guaracachi and Rurelec v Bolivia*,[58] the tribunal was circumspect about this argument, noting: **5.42**

> As a factual matter, the Respondent has not shown a sufficient causal link such that the Tribunal can infer from the mere existence of third-party funding that the Claimants will not be able to pay an eventual award of costs rendered against them, regardless of whether the funder is liable for costs or not.

Investment arbitration tribunals have so far rarely granted security for costs. Indeed, out of nearly seventy known applications filed since 1984, only four requests for security for costs have been granted in investment arbitrations brought under the ICSID, ICSID Additional Facility, and UNCITRAL Rules.[59] This restrained approach is reflected by the comments of the annulment committee noted in *Commerce Group v El Salvador*, who observed that 'the power to order security for costs should be exercised only in extreme circumstances, for example, where abuse or serious misconduct has been evidenced'.[60] The handful of cases in which respondents have successfully obtained security for costs tend to reflect unique circumstances such as repeated failure to pay advances on costs in similar cases[61] or an inability to demonstrate solvency to the satisfaction of the tribunal.[62]   **5.43**

One means for a funded claimant to protect itself in such circumstances from a security for costs order is through the subscription by the claimant (or its funder) of adverse costs insurance (known as ATE or 'after the event' insurance) which will pay any such order. Since the existence of this insurance provides the very guarantee that a respondent will be seeking in a security for costs order, it renders the granting of such an order unlikely.   **5.44**

(x) Power to sanction counsel

Following concerns about the increased abuse by counsel of certain procedural tools with which to delay arbitrations, cause hearings to be annulled, or otherwise frustrate an efficient process, one arbitral institution (the LCIA) has introduced the power to sanction counsel.[63] This permits the tribunal to exercise its discretion to issue a written reprimand or caution as to future conduct in the arbitration, or to take any other measure necessary to fulfil its general duties if counsel: **5.45**

- engages in activities intended unfairly to obstruct the arbitration or to jeopardise the finality of any award, including repeated challenges to an arbitrator's appointment or to the jurisdiction or authority of the tribunal known to be unfounded by counsel;

---

[58] See *Guaracachi*, fn. 56, at [7].

[59] Previti, 'Recently published decision confirms exceptional nature of security for costs' Burford Blog, 7 December 2020. See also Goldberg, Kryvoi, and Philippov, 'Empirical study: Provisional measures in investor-state arbitration' (2019) BIICL/White & Case 14.

[60] *Commerce Group Corp. and San Sebastian Gold Mines, Inc. v Republic of El Salvador*, ICSID Case No. ARB/09/17, Decision on El Salvador's Application for Security for Costs (Annulment Proceeding), 20 September 2012, at [45].

[61] See *RSM Production, Inc. v Saint Lucia*, ICSID Case No. ARB 12/10, Decision on Saint Lucia's Request for Security for Costs, 13 August 2014.

[62] See *Manuel Garcia Armas and ors v Bolivarian Republic of Venezuela*, PCA Case No. 2016-08, Procedural Order No. 9, 20 June 2018. Other successful applications for security for costs were made in *Eugene Kazmin v Republic of Latvia*, ICSID Case No. ARB/17/5, Procedural Order No. 6, 13 April 2020; *Adamakopoulos and ors v Cyprus*, ICSID Case No. ARB/15/49, Procedural Order No. 8, 8 June 2020 (decision not publicly available).

[63] See LCIA Rules, Art. 18.5 and 18.6, and Annex.

- knowingly makes any false statement to the tribunal or the LCIA Court;
- knowingly procures or assists in the preparation of, or relies upon, any false evidence presented to the tribunal or the LCIA Court; or
- knowingly conceals or assists in the concealment of any document ordered to be produced by the tribunal.

(xi) Ordering remote hearings

5.46   One of the consequences of the COVID-19 pandemic for the world of international arbitration was a sudden rise in the number of hearings conducted remotely.[64] This increase in remote proceedings has led to the question of whether tribunals have the power to order remote hearings even over a party's objections, or whether they risk 'due process' and set-aside challenges for doing so. The predominant view is that arbitration-friendly jurisdictions will respect a tribunal's discretion to order remote hearings, subject to certain fundamental procedural safeguards. This is evidenced by national reports commissioned by the International Council for Commercial Arbitration (ICCA). According to these ICCA reports, no jurisdiction's *lex arbitri* contains an express provision setting out a right to a physical hearing, which implies that arbitrators can indeed order a remote hearing if the circumstances so require.[65] In the Netherlands, for example, the *lex arbitri* expressly provides for the possibility of conducting remote hearings, subject to procedural safeguards;[66] similarly, the Austrian Supreme Court confirmed a tribunal's power to hold remote hearings over one party's objections and rejected due process concerns.[67] Arbitral institutions have taken steps to update their rules to provide expressly for the use of remote hearings. Notably, the LCIA and ICC have refined and expanded their provisions on virtual or hybrid (semi-virtual) hearings, removing any ambiguities as to their feasibility and empowering tribunals to order them over a party's opposition.[68]

5.47   The move towards remote proceedings not only affords participants greater flexibility and convenience but also, by eliminating the need for long-distance flights and voluminous hard copies, can also help to reduce international arbitration's significant carbon footprint. According to the Campaign for Greener Arbitrations, nearly 20,000 trees could be required to offset the total carbon emissions resulting from a single arbitration.[69]

---

[64] For instance, from mid-March until mid-December 2020, ICSID administered nearly 150 remote hearings or sessions, up from ninety-five remote hearings or sessions during the same period in 2019. See 'Hearings and Sessions held in ICSID Cases from March to December (2019 vs. 2020)', ICSID, 20 December 2020.

[65] See 'Right to a Physical Hearing Project: The Release of 20 New Reports Reinforces Core Trends and Important Divergences', ICCA, 18 March 2021.

[66] van Zelst, 'The Netherlands', ICCA Projects: Does a Right to a Physical Hearing Exist in International Arbitration?, 2021, at 2–3.

[67] Scherer et al., 'In a "First" Worldwide, Austrian Supreme Court Confirms Arbitral Tribunal's Power to Hold Remote Hearings Over One Party's Objection and Rejects Due Process Concerns', Kluwer Arbitration Blog, 24 October 2020. The Court noted that in situations in which insistence on an in-person hearing could lead to a procedural standstill, videoconferencing can be compatible with a party's right to get effective access to justice and to be heard, which is enshrined in Art. 6 of the European Convention on Human Rights (ECHR).

[68] LCIA Rules, Art. 19.2 ('The Arbitral Tribunal shall have the fullest authority under the Arbitration Agreement to establish the conduct of a hearing, including its date, duration, form, content, procedure, time-limits and geographical place (if applicable). As to form, a hearing may take place in person, or virtually by conference call, videoconference or using other communications technology with participants in one or more geographical places (or in a combined form)'); ICC Rules, Art. 26.1 ('The arbitral tribunal may decide, after consulting the parties, and on the basis of the relevant facts and circumstances of the case, that any hearing will be conducted by physical attendance or remotely by videoconference, telephone or other appropriate means of communication.')

[69] 'A significant impact', Campaign for Greener Arbitrations (2021), available at https://www.greenerarbitrations.com/impact.

(d) Supporting powers of the courts

National courts with an 'arbitration-friendly' law can usually lend support to arbitral tri- **5.48**
bunals, where needed. The United States, for example, provides a formidable array of tools
to enable courts to assist international arbitral tribunals, including, in some cases, arbitral
tribunals with seats outside of the United States, where relevant evidence is in the United
States. These include the power to order depositions, the power to subpoena witnesses present in the jurisdiction to give evidence or to produce documents, and the power to order
production of documents sought by a party to an arbitration with a foreign seat.[70]

Another example is provided by the English system, in which the court can act as a 'backup' **5.49**
to the arbitration by ordering a party to comply with any peremptory order made by the tribunal.[71] This effectively converts the breach of the tribunal's order into a contempt of court.
A court can also assist a tribunal by making its own orders in relation to the proceedings.[72]
These include orders freezing a party's assets,[73] orders permitting the seizure of relevant evidence,[74] and orders securing the attendance of witnesses.[75] This range of powers, whether
exercised directly by the arbitral tribunal itself or indirectly by application to the courts,
provides the support from *national* legal systems that *international* arbitration requires to
achieve its purpose.[76]

C. Duties of Arbitrators

(a) Introduction

The duties of an arbitrator may be divided into three categories: duties imposed by the par- **5.50**
ties; duties imposed by law; and ethical duties. It is a useful discipline for an arbitral tribunal
to draw up for itself a checklist of its specific duties, whatever their origin. Such a list will
differ from case to case, since it must allow for the impact of different rules of arbitration
and for the differing applicable laws.

(b) Duties imposed by the parties

Specific duties may be imposed upon an arbitral tribunal by the parties. This may be done **5.51**
before the arbitrators are appointed, or during the course of the arbitration, or both. If it is
done before the appointment of arbitrators (e.g. in an ad hoc submission agreement), each
arbitrator should check the agreement before accepting the appointment, in case it imposes
unreasonable duties or duties that are incapable of fulfilment. For example, there might be

---

[70] See Chapter 7 for more details on these powers.
[71] English Arbitration Act 1996, s. 42. A court can make such orders only if it is satisfied that the person to whom the tribunal's order was directed has had sufficient time to comply.
[72] Ibid., ss. 43 and 44.
[73] Ibid., s. 44(3).
[74] Ibid., s. 44(2)(c).
[75] Ibid., s. 43(1).
[76] This will be examined in more detail in Chapter 7.

a provision that the award should be made within a limited time after the appointment of the arbitral tribunal. If the agreed time-scale is unacceptable to the arbitrator and cannot be changed, the appointment should be declined.

5.52   Duties may also be imposed on the arbitral tribunal during the course of the proceedings by the parties (but usually only after consultation with the arbitral tribunal). In a dispute arising out of a construction project in a war zone, for example, the parties may decide in the course of the arbitration that they wish the arbitral tribunal to inspect the construction site. The proposal for such a site inspection would usually be discussed with, and agreed by, the arbitral tribunal—but if a particular arbitrator was unwilling to accept the proposal and the parties were to insist upon it, that arbitrator would have to resign.

5.53   Where the arbitration is conducted under specific rules, those rules usually impose particular duties on the arbitral tribunal in addition to any imposed by the parties. A review of the rules of two arbitral institutions indicates the nature of these duties. Under the ICSID Rules, arbitrators must, before or at the first session, sign a declaration of independence and readiness to judge fairly as between the parties.[77] Under the same Rules, the arbitral tribunal must meet for its first session within sixty days of its constitution, or such other period as the parties to the arbitration may agree;[78] it must keep its deliberations private and confidential;[79] it must take decisions by a majority vote;[80] and it must give reasons for its award.[81] The ICC Rules also impose their own obligations upon arbitral tribunals—such as to confirm their availability,[82] to draw up terms of reference,[83] to make an award within a defined period of time,[84] and to submit the award in draft form to the ICC's Court for scrutiny.[85]

(c) Duties imposed by law

5.54   Other duties are imposed by law. For instance, the law may require an arbitral tribunal to decide all procedural and evidential matters,[86] to treat the parties fairly and impartially,[87] or to make the award in a particular form.[88]

(i) Duty to act with due care

5.55   It is generally recognised that members of a profession, such as lawyers, doctors, accountants, architects, and engineers, are under a duty to carry out their professional work with proper skill and care—and that they may be held liable in damages at the suit of an injured

---

[77] ICSID Rules, r. 19(3)(b).
[78] Ibid., r. 29(3).
[79] Ibid., r. 34.
[80] Ibid., r. 35.
[81] Ibid., r. 59.
[82] ICC Rules, Art. 11.2.
[83] Ibid., Art. 23.1.
[84] Ibid., Art. 31.1. Unless extended by the ICC Court under Art. 31.2, this time limit is six months.
[85] Ibid., Art. 34.
[86] English Arbitration Act 1996, s. 34.
[87] Ibid., s. 33(1)(a).
[88] Such as in writing or with reasons: see, e.g., the Mexican Commercial Code, art. 1448 and the ZPO, art. 1054(1) and (2).

party if they fail to do so. In the course of their professional work, such professionals may well be required to formulate a decision that is binding upon two or more parties. For example, an architect may be required, under a standard form of building contract, to certify the value of work as it is performed, by issuing interim certificates. If due care is not taken so that (for instance) the amount certified is too large and the employer loses money as a consequence, the architect may be compelled by legal action to make good the loss caused by his or her negligence.[89] Equally, an accountant may be asked to determine the value of shares in a private company in a way that will be binding upon the parties to an agreement. In this case also, if the accountant acts without due care and a party suffers loss, the accountant may be sued in respect of negligence.[90]

The distinction between a professional adviser, who formulates a decision binding upon two or more parties in the course of a professional activity, and an arbitrator, who formulates a decision binding upon two or more parties in the course of an arbitration, is not easy to identify. It seems appropriate to expect the same standard of professional care from a lawyer (or an accountant, or an architect, or an engineer) who is serving as an arbitrator as would be expected in the course of his or her other professional work. The parties to an arbitration entrust an arbitral tribunal with an important task, for which they are prepared to pay—often generously. They therefore expect the arbitrator to perform the task with due care; and there exists an obvious moral duty for that arbitrator to do so. The question is whether there is also a legal duty. **5.56**

This question goes to the heart of the relationship between the arbitrator and the parties. As the practice of international arbitration becomes increasingly sophisticated and as the sums at stake grow in size, a party that has suffered loss as a result of an arbitrator's manifest lack of care may wish to seek to recover that loss from the arbitrator personally. **5.57**

This raises a preliminary question: under which legal system should the potential liability of an arbitrator be judged? This is relevant since many arbitrators perform arbitral functions outside of their home jurisdiction. For example, should a United States-based arbitrator who performs 90 per cent of her work on a London-seated arbitration be held to the rules applicable to arbitrators in the United States or to those applicable in the United Kingdom? This issue was addressed in France by the Paris Court of Appeal which confirmed that the services performed by an arbitrator are to decide the dispute and to render an award at the seat of arbitration. The Court consequently held that the place of performance of the arbitrator's services must be deemed to be the seat of the arbitration, even if the proceedings and deliberations took place elsewhere.[91] **5.58**

The applicable law will determine the standard by which to judge the potential liability of the arbitrator. This will depend on the characterisation made by that legal system of the relationship between the arbitrators and the parties. There are two schools of thought:[92] the first considers that the relationship between the arbitrator and the parties is established by contract; the second may be identified as the 'status school', which considers that the judicial **5.59**

---

[89] As in the English case *Sutcliffe v Thackrah* [1974] AC 727; [1974] 1 Lloyd's Rep 312 (HL).
[90] *Arenson v Casson Beckman Rutley & Co.* [1977] AC 405; [1976] 1 Lloyd's Rep 179 (HL).
[91] Cour d'appel de Paris, 22 June 2021, Case No. 21/07623.
[92] The two schools are analysed in Mullerat and Blanch, 'The liability of arbitrators: A survey of current practice' (2007) 1 Disp Resol Int'l 99.

nature of an arbitrator's function should result in treatment comparable to that of a judge.[93] In some jurisdictions, equating the role of the arbitrator to that of a judge may give rise to immunity from legal proceedings; in others, it simply results in the application of rules on judicial liability.[94]

5.60   The 'contractual school' considers that an arbitrator is appointed by or on behalf of the parties to an arbitration to perform a service (that of resolving a dispute between them) for a fee. In these circumstances, a contractual relationship arises between the parties and the arbitrator. The terms of this contract may be set out in the submission to arbitration, the relevant rules of arbitration, the terms of reference, and/or the terms of appointment. Other terms may be imposed by operation of law and include the duties to act with due diligence and to act judicially.

5.61   The contractual approach finds favour in most continental European jurisdictions.[95] Austrian law, for instance, takes the position that there is a contract between the arbitrator and the parties. Although this contract resembles a contract for services, it is considered to be *sui generis* by some authors.[96] Certain duties, as well as rights, are imposed upon an arbitrator under the contract. One of the rights is a right to remuneration. The duties include conducting the proceedings in an appropriate way and making an award. The Austrian Arbitration Act provides that an arbitrator who does not fulfil the duties assumed by accepting an appointment, or who does not fulfil them in due time, may be liable to the parties for loss caused by wrongful behaviour.[97]

5.62   A similar position is adopted by Dutch law. An arbitrator is held to be in a contractual relationship with the parties and may be liable for damages in the event of committing gross negligence.[98] Other jurisdictions, such as Argentina, consider that the arbitral contract renders arbitrators liable for losses caused by any failure to perform duties: '[A]cceptance by

---

[93]   The English Supreme Court now seems to have firmly embraced the contractual approach in the case of *Jivraj v Hashwani* [2011] UKSC 40, at [23]: 'It is common ground, at any rate in this class of case, that there is a contract between the parties and the arbitrator or arbitrators appointed under a contract and that his or their services are rendered pursuant to that contract.'

[94]   For a detailed study on the sources of arbitral liability and the implications in connection with immunity, see Franck, 'The liability of international arbitrators: A comparative analysis and proposal for qualified immunity' (2000) 20 NYL Sch J Intl Comp L 1. For a discussion of the status of the arbitrator, see Fouchard, 'Final report on the status of the arbitrator' (1996) 7 ICC International Court of Arbitration Bulletin 1.

[95]   Whilst there is a degree of unity in European civil law jurisdictions on this issue, several jurisdictions in Latin America (such as Colombia and Ecuador) have taken a firm view in favour of the status approach in domestic arbitrations by considering the arbitrator a 'temporary judge', with the same powers and duties as a state-appointed judge during the pendency of his or her appointment (there are no such rules for international arbitrations that take place in those countries).

[96]   See Melis, 'Austria', in Bosman (ed.) *International Handbook on Commercial Arbitration* (ICCA & Kluwer Law International, 2020), p. 17. Swiss law adopts a similar position: see Voser and Fischer, 'The arbitral tribunal', in Geisinger and Voser (eds) *International Arbitration in Switzerland: A Handbook for Practitioners* (Kluwer Law International, 2013), p. 53.

[97]   Austrian Arbitration Act 2013, art. 594(4) states: 'An arbitrator who does not fulfil his obligation resulting from the acceptance of his appointment at all or in a timely manner, shall be liable to the parties for all damages caused by his wrongful refusal or delay.' However, well-established jurisprudence from the Austrian Supreme Court has limited the scope of this provision by ruling that an arbitrator's liability can be triggered only in situations in which the award has successfully been set aside, unless the arbitrator plainly refused to issue an award or failed to comply with the duties resulting from the acceptance of the appointment altogether. For a discussion on such jurisprudence, see Lukic, 'Arbitrators' Liability: Austrian Supreme Court Reconfirms Strict Standards', Kluwer Arbitration Blog, 1 September 2016.

[98]   See van den Berg, 'The Netherlands', in Bosman (ed.) *International Handbook on Commercial Arbitration* (ICCA & Kluwer Law International, 2020), p. 37.

arbitrators of their appointment as such shall entitle the parties to compel them to carry out their functions and to hold them liable for costs and damages derived from the non-performance of arbitral functions.'[99] Chinese law provides for liability for certain arbitral conduct, in addition to sanctions such as removal from the relevant list of arbitrators.[100]

The 'status school' is based on the performance by arbitrators of a judicial or quasi-judicial **5.63** function, which grants an element of 'status' entitling them to treatment similar to that of a judge. Certain rights and duties are conferred on the arbitrator by the very fact of having assumed that office. The arbitrator exercises a compulsory jurisdictional function and enjoys statutory powers. In most common law jurisdictions, this leads to certain immunities,[101] although the immunity may be qualified where the arbitrator has acted in bad faith.[102]

Specifically, arbitrators and arbitral institutions in the United States enjoy a broad degree of **5.64** immunity from suit for actions taken within their mandate.[103] Arbitrators acting in England cannot be held liable for the performance of their arbitral functions, unless bad faith can be proved.[104] Similarly, arbitrators in New Zealand, Australia, Kenya, and Ireland cannot be held liable for negligence.[105] This common law approach has now been followed by institutions such as the ICC and the LCIA, which have adopted rules seeking to exclude liability for arbitrators.[106] Nevertheless, some commentators from common law systems have questioned the appropriateness of almost absolute immunity for arbitrators, and several have argued that arbitrators have professional duties of care, skill, and diligence, and that they should be liable for breach of such duties.[107]

A rigid categorisation of the source of an arbitrator's obligation to act with due care risks **5.65** obscuring the real debate, which is whether it is appropriate, as a matter of policy, to accord immunity, or partial immunity, to arbitrators. Public policy in this context is mainly

---

[99] Argentine National Code of Civil and Commercial Procedure, art. 745.

[100] Arbitration Law of the People's Republic of China, art. 38.

[101] See, e.g., *Austern v Chicago Bd. Options Exchange, Inc.*, 898 F.2d 882, 886 (2d Cir. 1990) ('arbitrators in contractually agreed upon arbitration proceedings are absolutely immune from liability in damages for all acts within the scope of the arbitral process'); *Sutcliffe v Thackrah* [1974] AC 727, at 735; *Pickens v Templeton* [1994] 2 NZLR 718, at 727–728 (although a valuer was technically classified as an arbitrator by the Arbitration Act 1908, his actions were not sufficiently judicial to justify immunity, because they were based on his expertise and he did not make a final determination of the dispute). See also *Sport Maska Inc. v Zittrer* [1988] 1 SCR 564.

[102] The laws of Australia, Canada, England, and New Zealand all provide that arbitrators may be liable for fraud, bad faith, or intentional actions. In the United States, however, arbitrator immunity is subject only to rare exceptions: see, e.g., *Lundgren v Freeman*, 307 F.2d 104, 118 (9th Cir. 1962).

[103] Amirfar, Reid, and Popova, 'United States of America', in Bosman (ed.) *International Handbook on Commercial Arbitration* (ICCA & Kluwer Law International, 2020), p. 41. See also *Corey v New York Stock Exchange*, 691 F.2d 1205 (6th Cir. 1982). Immunity of arbitrators in the United States derives from the view that they are functioning as judges, and is to be contrasted with qualified immunity in Austria, Germany, and Norway, and no immunity in France, Spain, and Sweden: see Lew, 'Introduction', in Lew (ed.) *The Immunity of Arbitrators* (Lloyd's of London Press, 1990), p. 4.

[104] English Arbitration Act 1996, s. 29. See also s. 74, which grants the same immunity to arbitral institutions, appointing authorities, and their respective employees.

[105] New Zealand Arbitration Act 1996, s. 13; Australian International Arbitration Act 1974, s. 28 (which Act was amended to incorporate the 2006 Model Law); Kenyan Arbitration (Amendment) Act No. 11 of 2009, s. 16B(1); Irish Arbitration Act 2010, s. 22(1) ('An arbitrator shall not be liable in any proceedings for anything done or omitted in the discharge or purported discharge of his or her functions').

[106] See LCIA Rules, Art. 31.1, excluding 'conscious and deliberate wrongdoing'; ICC Rules, Art. 41, which excludes only conduct prohibited by applicable law.

[107] See, e.g., Brown, 'The expansion of arbitral immunity: Is absolute immunity a foregone conclusion' [2009] J Disp Res 225, at [237–238], which contends that qualified immunity is the appropriate type of immunity that would 'protect[] arbitral decision making while not shielding non-decisional acts'.

concerned with the independence and integrity of the decision-making process, which could be jeopardised if arbitrators were to be subject to reprisals by disappointed parties.[108]

5.66   Other arguments in favour of immunity are that:

- it helps to ensure the finality of arbitral awards, by preventing an unsuccessful party from suing the arbitrator;[109]
- fewer skilled persons would be prepared to act as arbitrators if they were to run the risk of incurring substantial liability;[110]
- arbitrators have no interest in the outcome of the dispute and should not be compelled to become parties to it.

Some commentators go so far as to base arbitral immunity entirely on public policy grounds, arguing that immunity can be explained satisfactorily only as a concession from the state, which weighs the benefits of arbitration against the risk that granting arbitrators immunity may encourage them to be careless (or even dishonest) in the performance of their duties.[111]

5.67   Indeed, there are a number of policy arguments against immunity. Immunity may encourage carelessness; the finality of the decision is given priority over individual justice; disciplinary remedies are generally unavailable against arbitrators; and alternative remedies, such as *vacatur* of the award and the withholding of fees, may be inadequate.

5.68   One substantial concern is the lack of uniformity in the approach adopted in different states. As a consequence, the source of the arbitrator's duties, and the public policy of the state in which the arbitrator is acting, need to be examined on a case-by-case basis. It would be helpful if some overriding principles could be established at an international level to provide guidance to arbitrators in the exercise of their functions, irrespective of the seat of arbitration.

5.69   In its 1987 Rules of Ethics for International Arbitrators,[112] the IBA stated that 'international arbitrators should in principle be granted immunity from suit under national laws, except in extreme cases of wilful or reckless disregard of their legal obligations'. This appears to be a suitable middle ground, but it remains a wish rather than a reality in many jurisdictions. Pending the establishment of uniform or harmonised rules, arbitrators should ascertain the potential scope of their liability, principally in accordance with the law of the seat.

5.70   Where arbitrators are exposed to a risk of personal liability by the law of the seat, they may consider making their acceptance of an appointment conditional on an indemnity from the parties. In this way, they would obtain immunity from liability by contract, even if they were

---

[108] See, e.g., *Cort v AAA*, 795 F.Supp. 970, 972 (NDCa 1992), determining that, in order to encourage independent judgments, the arbitration process is granted immunity.

[109] See Yat-Sen Li, 'Arbitral immunity: A profession comes of age' (1998) 64 Arbitration 51, at 53.

[110] See, e.g., *Cort*, fn. 108, at [973]. However, some comment that arbitration is now a fully developed profession, the members of which should accept personal responsibility, including full legal liability for loss caused by any failure: see Yat-Sen Li, fn. 109, p. 55.

[111] See Lin Yu and Sauzier, 'From arbitrator's immunity to the fifth theory of international commercial arbitration' (2000) 3 Intl Arb L Rev 114, at [120].

[112] The IBA Rules of Ethics were superseded by the IBA Guidelines, for the matters addressed therein. However, the question of arbitrator immunity was not addressed in the IBA Guidelines, for which the Rules of Ethics continue to apply.

not entitled to it by operation of law. Whether such an indemnity would be enforceable as a matter of public policy is uncertain. Professional liability insurance is also generally available to cover the risks—at a price.

A separate issue is the potential liability of the arbitral institution. Aggrieved parties who have lost an arbitration may look indiscriminately for someone to blame, and arbitral institutions have not escaped this trend.[113] Like the relationship between arbitrators and parties, the relationship between parties and the institution administering the arbitration is generally considered to be contractual. Whereas in common law jurisdictions arbitral institutions have more or less absolute immunity from liability,[114] in civil law jurisdictions they may be held liable for wrongful acts, and such liability will usually be based on general principles of contractual liability. For example, in January 2009, in a case against the ICC, the Paris Court of Appeal held that the waiver of liability contained in the ICC Rules[115] ran contrary to the duty of the ICC as an arbitral institution and should be treated as null and void.[116] As a consequence, the ICC could be held liable for breaches of its obligations to the parties under its contractual relationship. However, the impact of that decision was softened in March 2021 when the Court of Appeal recognised that the ICC's clause excluding liability would operate except in cases of deliberate wrongdoing (*dol*) or gross negligence (*faute lourde*).[117]

5.71

The basis for immunity of arbitral institutions in common law jurisdictions is different from that relating to arbitrators. It is based on their operation as quasi-judicial organisations[118] to protect functions that are (i) closely related to the arbitral process and (ii) sufficiently related to the adjudicative phase of the arbitration. In doing so, they fulfil the necessary requirements for immunity. It is argued (mainly in the United States) that if this immunity was not accorded to the arbitral institutions, the immunity of arbitrators themselves

5.72

---

[113] For example, in 2013, RSM, a US oil company, filed a lawsuit in the United States against ICSID and its secretary-general over the alleged mishandling of an annulment proceeding: see 'Oil investor sues ICSID over annulment case', Global Arb Rev, 3 June 2013. For a more detailed analysis of arbitral institution liability, see van Houtte and McAsey, 'The liability of arbitrators and arbitral institutions', in Habegger, Hochstrasser, Nater-Bass, and Weber-Stecher (eds) *Arbitral Institutions under Scrutiny* (Juris, 2013), p. 133; Rasmussen, 'Overextending immunity: Arbitral institutional liability in the United States, England, and France' (2002) 26 Fordham Intl LJ 1824.

[114] In the United States, institutions, like arbitrators, have absolute immunity. In *Austern v Chicago Board Options Exchange* 716 F.Supp. 121 (SDNY 1989), the plaintiffs sued an arbitral institution for damages for mental anguish, but were barred by the doctrine of immunity. In England, the Arbitration Act 1996, s. 74, provides for immunity in relation to the discharge by the institution of its duties, unless it acts in bad faith.

[115] The provision under analysis was the 1998 ICC Rules, Art. 34 which read: 'Neither the arbitrators, nor the Court and its members, nor the ICC and its employees, nor the ICC National Committees shall be liable to any person for any act or omission in connection with the arbitration.' The current provision in the ICC Rules, Art. 41 builds in an exception for public policy rules: 'The arbitrators, any person appointed by the arbitral tribunal, the emergency arbitrator, the Court and its members, ICC and its employees, and the ICC National Committees and Groups and their employees and representatives shall not be liable to any person for any act or omission in connection with the arbitration, except to the extent such limitation of liability is prohibited by applicable law.'

[116] See *SNF v Chambre de Commerce Internationale*, Paris cour d'appel, 22 January 2009.

[117] See Paris cour d'appel, 23 March 2021, Case No. 18/14817. French courts make a distinction between the institution's jurisdictional role (decisions intimately linked with the process, such as the challenge of arbitrators) and non-jurisdictional conduct, such as when the institution fails to run the arbitration properly: see Dupeyré, 'Les arbitres et centres d'arbitrage face à leurs responsabilités: Le droit français à son point d'équilibre' (2014) 32 ASA Bulletin 265.

[118] See *Rubenstein v Otterbourg*, 357 NYS.2d 62, 64 (NY Misc. 1973); *Boraks v AAA*, 517 NW.2d 771, 772 (Mich. App. 1994).

would be meaningless, since liability would merely shift from the arbitrator to the arbitral organisation.[119]

5.73 Institutional rules usually provide for the institution's immunity in relation to any act or omission in connection with the arbitration, subject to applicable law[120] with the exception of the LCIA which excludes such immunity for conscious or deliberate wrongdoing.[121] The rules of the arbitral institution are usually incorporated in the contract between the parties and the institution, and as such may operate as an exclusion of liability. However, any mandatory rules of the forum providing for liability would be likely to trump such exclusion.[122]

(ii) Duty to act promptly

5.74 An arbitral tribunal has an obvious moral obligation to carry out its task with due diligence. Justice delayed is justice denied. Some systems of law endeavour to ensure that an arbitration is carried out with reasonable speed by setting a time limit within which the arbitral tribunal must make its award.[123] The time limit fixed is sometimes as short as six months (as in the ICC Rules[124]), although generally it may be extended by consent of the parties, or at the initiative of the institution[125] or the tribunal.[126] If an award is not made within the time allowed, the authority of the arbitral tribunal may be regarded as having terminated, with the risk that any award will be null and void.[127] Some systems of law provide that an arbitrator who fails to proceed with reasonable speed in conducting the arbitration and making his or her award may be removed by a competent court,[128] and deprived of any entitlement to remuneration. The Model Law provides that the mandate of an arbitrator terminates if he or she 'fails to act without undue delay'.[129]

5.75 Whilst these sanctions may act as a spur to the indolent arbitrator, they do nothing to compensate a party who has suffered financial loss as a result of delay in the conduct of the arbitration. Delay in the conduct of an arbitration may have serious financial consequences; awards of interest rarely compensate the successful party for the financial loss suffered in the interim. The question accordingly arises as to whether an arbitrator may be made liable in damages for undue delay. No liability is imposed under the established international or

---

[119] See *Corey v New York Stock Exchange*, 691 F.2d 1205, 1211 (6th Cir. 1982).

[120] See ICC Rules, Art. 41; ICSID Convention, Art. 20; NAI Rules, Art. 61; SIAC Rules, Art. 38.1; ICDR Rules, Art. 41.

[121] LCIA Rules, Art. 31.

[122] As occurred in *Société Cubic Défense Système v Chambre de Commerce Internationale* [1997] Rev Arb 417 and *SNF v Chambre de Commerce Internationale*, Paris cour d'appel, 22 January 2009.

[123] For example, the Italian Code of Civil Procedure, as amended in 2006, Arts 813 and 820 (240 days from date of acceptance of appointment by the tribunal); the 2006 Ecuadorean Law of Arbitration and Mediation, art. 25 (150 days from the final hearing).

[124] ICC Rules, Art. 31.1.

[125] Ibid., Art. 31.2. See also the French Code of Civil Procedure, art. 1463(2): 'The statutory or contractual time limit may be extended by agreement between the parties or, where there is no such agreement, by the judge acting in support of the arbitration.'

[126] Article 25 of the 2006 Ecuadorean Law of Arbitration and Mediation permits the tribunal 'where strictly necessary' to grant itself *ex officio* an extension of the 150-day time limit by a further 150 days.

[127] See, e.g., the National Code of Civil Procedure of Argentina, Arts 760 and 771.

[128] As in England: An arbitrator has a duty to act fairly and without unnecessary delay. Arbitration Act 1996, s. 33(1)(b). Breach of this duty may result in the removal of the arbitrator by the court (s. 24(2)) and/or a challenge to the award (s. 68).

[129] Model Law, Art. 14.

institutional rules, and it would be most unusual to find a term imposing liability for delay in an ad hoc submission agreement. Liability might, however, be established on the basis of the contractual duty of care,[130] in those jurisdictions in which the arbitrator does not benefit from immunity.

Faced with increasing delays in the conduct of arbitrations, the major institutions have re- **5.76** vised their rules to improve the speed and efficiency of arbitrations. For example, the ICC Rules now require the tribunal and the parties to 'make every effort' to 'conduct the arbitration in an expeditious and cost-effective manner'.[131] This includes a compulsory case management conference,[132] in which the use of specific case management techniques is encouraged.[133] The tribunal is also required to set an expected date for issue of the award, following the close of the proceedings.[134] Appendix IV sets out case management techniques, and is supplemented by the ICC Commission's updated report on controlling time and costs in arbitration.[135] The ICC Rules also provide a separate set of rules for expedited procedures, which automatically apply to arbitrations where the amount in dispute does not exceed US$ 2 million if the arbitration agreement was concluded between 2017 and 2021 or US$ 3 million if it was concluded on or after 2021.[136]

(iii) Duty to act judicially

It is important that an arbitral tribunal should act, and should be seen to act, judicially (that **5.77** is, respecting the rules of due process). This is more than a mere moral obligation; it is also one that may be enforced under the relevant rules of arbitration or the applicable law. The duty to act judicially is a duty that extends to all aspects of the proceedings.[137]

What does this mean in practice? Neither the arbitral tribunal as a whole nor any of its **5.78** individual members should, for instance, discuss the case with one party in the absence of the other, unless in connection with the nomination of the president of the arbitral tribunal (where this has been agreed), or if the absent party has failed to attend a meeting or a hearing, having been given proper notice to do so. At the hearing, the duty to act judicially means that each party must be accorded equality of treatment and given a fair opportunity to present its case. It would be wrong, for instance, to allow one party to call witnesses and to deny the other party a similar opportunity. Similarly, it would be improper to allow one party to address the arbitral tribunal orally and to deny the same opportunity to the other party. Rules of arbitration, which are usually silent as to the duties of the arbitral tribunal, find common ground on this point. Article 17 of the UNCITRAL Rules provides that the arbitral tribunal may conduct the arbitration in such a manner as it considers appropriate

---

[130] See paragraphs 5.55*ff.*
[131] ICC Rules, Art. 22.1.
[132] Ibid., Art. 24.1.
[133] Ibid., Appendix IV.
[134] Ibid., Art. 27.
[135] ICC Commission on Arbitration and ADR, *ICC Commission Report: Controlling Time and Costs in Arbitration* (2nd edn, ICC, 2018).
[136] ICC Rules, Art. 30 and Appendix VI. See also AAA Rules, Expedited Procedures, Rules E-1 through E-10.
[137] For instance, the cour de cassation upheld the cour d'appel de Paris's decision to partially annul an award for lack of due process because the tribunal had relied on exhibit translations prepared by one of the arbitrators that were not shared with the parties prior to the issuance of the award. See Cass. Civ. 1, 18 March 2015, Case No. 13-22391.

'provided that the parties are treated with equality and that at an appropriate stage of the proceedings each party is given a reasonable opportunity of presenting its case'.[138] The ICSID Rules do not contain such a general statement, but its detailed provisions ensure equality of treatment: and if any party fails to appear or present its case, a special default procedure must be followed.[139] Article 14.4.i. of the LCIA Rules requires arbitrators at all times 'to act fairly and impartially as between all parties, giving each a reasonable opportunity of putting its case and dealing with that of its opponent'.

5.79   The law applicable to the arbitration proceedings often states explicitly that due process must be observed by the arbitral tribunal. For example, article 21(2) of the Brazilian Arbitration Act 1996 states that 'the principles of adversary proceeding, equal treatment of the parties, impartiality of the arbitrator and freedom of decision, shall always be respected'.[140] English law has gone even further. Section 33(1) of the Arbitration Act 1996 provides that an arbitral tribunal shall:

> [...]
> (a) act fairly and impartially as between the parties giving each party a reasonable opportunity of putting his case and dealing with that of his opponent, and
> (b) adopt procedures suitable to the circumstances of the particular case, avoiding unnecessary delay or expense, so as to provide a fair means for the resolution of the matters falling to be determined.

This is a mandatory provision, from which neither the parties nor the tribunal may derogate.[141] An arbitrator acting in breach of this duty can be removed.[142] Perhaps more significantly, awards made in breach of it are open to challenge[143] and would face difficulties of enforcement.[144]

5.80   The duty to act judicially is not simply a matter of ensuring equality between the parties and giving each the right to respond to the other party's position; it also arises where the arbitral tribunal decides to base its decision on an issue not specifically raised by the parties. It is an accepted principle that the tribunal is free to apply any element of applicable law (even where not commented or argued by the parties) under the maxim *juris novit curia* ('the court knows the law' sometimes referred to as *juris novit arbiter* in the arbitration context). However, where the tribunal intends to rely on authorities not cited by the parties, best practice is always to permit the parties to comment before rendering a decision. But what is the consequence under the applicable law when the arbitral tribunal relies on a legal argument not relied upon or addressed by the parties?

5.81   English law is clear in this respect: a tribunal must give the parties an opportunity to be heard. If it fails to do so, then the duty to act judicially will have been infringed. In one case, the English courts noted that an arbitral tribunal must provide each party with a fair

---

[138] The ICC Rules contain provisions to a similar effect: see Art. 22.4.
[139] See ICSID Rules, r. 49.
[140] See also the Mexican Commercial Code, art. 1434: 'The parties shall be treated with equality and each party shall be given a full opportunity to assert their rights.'
[141] English Arbitration Act 1996, s. 4(1) and Sch. 1.
[142] Ibid., s. 24.
[143] Ibid., s. 68(2)(a).
[144] New York Convention, Art. V(1)(d) and possibly also Art. V(2)(b).

opportunity to address all of the essential building blocks in its conclusion.[145] On the facts of the case, the claimant had been deprived of the opportunity to advance submissions on an issue that had formed part of the tribunal's reasoning in the award, but had not been debated by the parties. The court held that such action amounted to a serious irregularity capable of causing substantial injustice, thus meeting the criteria for the setting aside of an award under section 68 of the 1996 Arbitration Act. The court set aside the award and remitted the issue to the arbitral tribunal for further consideration.

The position is less clear in continental Europe. Switzerland, for example, allows arbitrators to reach their conclusions on legal theories not advanced by the parties, without inviting them to comment.[146] By contrast, French courts have ruled that an arbitral tribunal cannot decide a case based on legal grounds not invoked or debated by the parties.[147] In a Dutch case decided in 2021 the District Court of the Hague concluded that 'the adversarial principle does not require the arbitral tribunal to give the parties an opportunity to express themselves in advance on proposed legal considerations'.[148] This lack of uniformity is not helpful to tribunals composed of arbitrators from different legal backgrounds and has prompted calls for harmonisation.[149] **5.82**

Where a tribunal fails in its duty to act judicially, the immediate sanction is for the tribunal to be removed. In some circumstances, this can be done without waiting for the award, either under the rules of the relevant arbitral institution[150] or by a national court, where the applicable law permits the courts at the place of arbitration to intervene.[151] However, in some jurisdictions, such as the United States, there is no opportunity for concurrent court control and the aggrieved party must wait until the end of the proceedings before challenging the award.[152] **5.83**

---

[145] *OAO Northern Shipping Co. v Remolcadores De Marin SL (Remmar)* [2007] EWHC 1821. In *Vee Networks Ltd v Econet Wireless International Ltd* [2005] 1 Lloyd's Rep 192, at 79–91, the Court of Appeal remanded a partial award to the arbitrator for not giving the parties the opportunity to comment on a new legal theory. However, the test is not easily met and if the award would have reached the same conclusion absent the issue not placed before the parties, the challenge is unlikely to succeed: see *ABB AG v Hochtief Airport GmbH* [2006] EWHC 388 (Comm).

[146] *X. v 1. Union Cycliste Internationale (UCI), 2. Fédération Z.*, Decision 4A_110/2012, Federal Supreme Court of Switzerland, 1st Civil Law Chamber, 9 October 2012, at [3.1.1]:

> In Switzerland, the right to be heard mainly relates to the finding of facts. The right of the parties to be asked for their views on legal questions is recognised only restrictively. As a rule, according to the adage *iura novit curia*, state courts or arbitral tribunals freely assess the legal consequences of the facts and they may also base their decisions on rules of law other than those invoked by the parties but in such a case the parties should usually be afforded an opportunity to comment on the arbitrators' conclusions prior to the issue of an award in order to preserve due process.

[147] In a recent decision, the cour d'appel de Paris explained that an arbitral tribunal could not 'rearrange the distribution of contractual rights and obligations' without inviting the parties to express themselves on arrangements which were not part of the parties' claims before the tribunal, and that doing so violated due process. Paris cour d'appel, 13 February 2018, Case No. 15/17137 (*Strube* case).

[148] *Manuel Garcia and ors v Bolivarian Republic of Venezuela*, Judgment of the District Court of the Hague, 19 January 2021 (Case No. 200.280.055/01), at [18].

[149] See Giovannini, 'International arbitration and *jura novit curia*: Towards harmonization' 9 TRANSNAT'L DISP. MGMT. 1, 5 (2012).

[150] For example, ICC Rules, Art. 15.2.

[151] For example, English Arbitration Act 1996, s. 24.

[152] In *PK Time Group, LLC v Robert*, No. 12 Civ 8200 (PAC), 2013 WL 3833084 (SDNY 13 July 2013), a federal district court denied a petition to remove a panel of arbitrators before a final award on damages had been issued, based on alleged misconduct and bias. The court dismissed the application and confirmed its view that the FAA prohibits pre-award challenges to arbitrators.

5.84   The duty to act judicially is to be clearly distinguished from the duty to be independent and impartial. By way of illustration, in a decision of the LCIA Court, a sole arbitrator was challenged for conducting a meeting with representatives of the respondent during two consecutive days in the absence of the claimant or any of its representatives. A verbatim transcript of the meeting was produced for the parties, in which the arbitrator had made clear that the meeting was not a formal hearing. The claimant challenged the arbitrator. The LCIA Court, considering the manner in which the arbitration had been conducted, stated that it had no reason to doubt the arbitrator's independence or impartiality, but, in considering whether the arbitrator had acted fairly between the parties, found that '[f]or the Arbitrator to meet with the representatives of one party in the absence of the other, and to permit any discussion of the merits of the dispute at such a meeting is, to put it no higher, an error of judgment', which in the Court's view, constituted a failure to act fairly between the parties.[153]

5.85   With some rare exceptions,[154] the sanctions for a failure to act judicially normally do not include financial compensation to the aggrieved party. Nevertheless, a party who has suffered financial loss as a result of such a failure may wish to claim personally against the arbitrator. The term 'failure to act judicially' may cover a variety of conduct. Where the behaviour is wilful misconduct or bad faith (for example, the acceptance of a bribe), the party who has suffered loss would be entitled to claim against the offending arbitrator, even in countries that traditionally confer immunity, such as Australia, England, and New Zealand.[155]

(d) Ethical duties

5.86   In addition to specific duties imposed on arbitrators, either by the parties or by law, it is generally considered that an arbitrator has certain moral or ethical obligations. One obvious example, discussed earlier, is the obligation to decline to accept an appointment if sufficient time and attention cannot be given to the case.[156] There has been much discussion as to how these ethical standards—sometimes described as the 'deontology' of arbitrators—might be defined or established in some form of internationally accepted 'code of conduct'.

5.87   The IBA Guidelines[157] recognised the problems posed by possible conflicts of interest in international arbitration, and the increasing recourse to challenges of arbitrators,

---

[153] See Nicholas and Partasides, 'LCIA Court decisions on challenges to arbitrators: A proposal to publish' (2007) 23 Arb Intl 16, referring to Decision No. 10 of the LCIA Court, 13 February 2002.

[154] Following a series of arbitrations involving sportswear brand Puma, the Spanish Supreme Court found that two arbitrators had 'palpably violated the arbitration rules' by excluding a third arbitrator from deliberations, which had led to the setting aside of an initial award and the need for a second arbitration. The pair were found liable pursuant to the Spanish Arbitration Act, art. 21.1 which says that arbitrators must 'faithfully discharge their functions' or they will be 'liable for damages caused in bad faith, willful disregard or fraud', and they were each ordered to reimburse Puma €750,000 in fees plus interest and costs. Ross, 'Spanish Supreme Court declares arbitrators liable for excluding colleague', Global Arb Rev, 21 February 2017, referring to Spanish Supreme Court Judgment of 15 February 2017.

[155] See Arbitration Act 1996, s. 29, for England; Arbitration Act 1996, s. 13, for New Zealand; International Arbitration Act 1974, s. 28(1), for Australia.

[156] See paragraph 5.51.

[157] As discussed earlier in this volume. See Chapter 4, paragraph 4.73.

sometimes brought as a means of delaying arbitrations or of depriving a party of the arbitrator of its choice. We have discussed these Guidelines, and issues relating to the challenge and replacement of international arbitrators, in Chapter 4. It is clear from that discussion that there is no easy solution to the question of what may or may not constitute a conflict of interest.[158] The search for guidance continues. At the time of writing, UNCITRAL Working Group III and ICSID have been collaborating on a draft Code of Conduct for Adjudicators in Investor–State Dispute Settlement.[159]

(i) Use of arbitration to further criminal purposes

Other ethical duties may arise where an arbitrator suspects or has reason to suspect that the **5.88** arbitral process is being hijacked for a criminal purpose.[160] One important concern is the laundering of the proceeds of crime through a fraudulent dispute, which is rapidly settled. The parties ask the tribunal to embody a settlement of their 'dispute' in a consent award, through which an unlawful payment is made and successfully hidden as the proper transfer of funds pursuant to an arbitral award. A tribunal should therefore be particularly cautious in agreeing to an early consent award that simply involves the transfer of money. A consent award is only needed for the payment of money where there is an element of future performance—for instance, an agreement by the winning party to accept payment of the award in instalments, rather than insisting on immediate payment. Otherwise, an agreement by the parties to pay money is usually sufficiently protected by mutual releases in a settlement agreement conditional upon the receipt of funds. Other parties who wish to abuse the arbitral process may be more sophisticated and simply put up a weak defence. There are often 'tell-tale' signs: the entities involved are often recently incorporated; their activities are usually of a nature that does not require any real investment; and the contract in question is rarely detailed or well drafted.

What is an arbitrator to do when confronted with possible criminal activity linked to an **5.89** arbitration? There is a balance to be struck. It is not the job of the arbitrator to seek to uncover criminal activity but rather to resolve the dispute within the scope of the arbitration agreement. Nevertheless, an arbitrator cannot ignore clear signs of criminal activity, especially when the applicable law may impose certain reporting obligations. For example, an arbitrator who is suspicious of criminal activity and is sitting in the European Union (EU) should check on the way in which relevant EU directives[161] have been implemented by local legislation.

---

[158] See Chapter 4, paragraphs 4.69*ff*, for further discussion of the IBA Guidelines.

[159] The third draft was published in September 2021. Apart from more traditional provisions on duties and responsibilities of adjudicators (including arbitrators) as well as disclosure obligations, the Draft Code also addresses 'double-hatting', or the practice of acting in different roles (counsel, arbitrator, or expert) in several investment arbitration proceedings at the same time (by either enjoining adjudicators from double-hatting or, at least, requiring them to disclose it).

[160] For a careful analysis of the interplay between arbitration and criminal law, see Mourre, 'Arbitration and criminal law: Reflections on the duties of the arbitrator' (2006) 22 Arb Intl 95.

[161] See, e.g., Directive 2001/97/EC of the European Parliament and of the Council of 4 December 2001 amending Council Directive 91/308/EEC on prevention of the use of the financial system for the purpose of money laundering, OJ L 344/76, 28 December 2001 (which requires 'auditors, external accountants and tax advisors', as well as 'notaries and other independent legal professionals', to report on their own initiative 'any fact which might indicate money laundering' and to provide the authorities with any information requested); Directive 2005/60/EC of the European Parliament and of the Council of 26 October 2005 on the prevention of the use of the financial system for the purpose of money laundering and terrorist financing, OJ L 309/15, 25 November 2005. It is questionable whether the definition of 'independent legal professionals' would

5.90   If an arbitrator has grounds for suspecting a criminal offence, each party should be given an opportunity to provide an explanation. Once the tribunal believes it has sufficient justification, it can then evaluate the facts. In cases of fraud or corruption, this is likely to have an impact on the outcome of the dispute. In cases of money laundering or other manipulation of the process by the parties, the tribunal should terminate the proceedings on the basis that there is no genuine dispute. In cases of a consent award, the tribunal may issue a ruling refusing to approve the settlement.

5.91   While it may appear contrary to the trust that the parties place in an arbitral tribunal for the tribunal to report to the authorities possible offences, if the parties' trust is simply that the arbitral tribunal act as a mute observer of a criminal offence, then it should not be respected. It seems wrong that the confidential nature of arbitral proceedings and the ultimate enforceability of an award should be open to abuse by international crime. The arbitration community should be vigilant to ensure that it does not unwittingly assist in such ends.

5.92   One issue of increasing concern in international commerce is bribery and corruption.[162] These issues may arise in at least three distinct circumstances. First, there is the possibility of the corruption of an arbitrator; secondly, there is a dispute that arises out of a contract whose purpose is the bribery of state officials (usually disguised as a 'consultancy agreement'); and thirdly, there is the case in which the contract in question was procured by a bribe.

5.93   One of the ethical duties of an arbitrator is to decide fairly in the absence of any corruption or bribe. Unfortunately, arbitration has not escaped the tentacles of corruption that taint many judicial systems and there have been various initiatives to combat corruption in international arbitration. One such initiative is the Additional Protocol to the Criminal Law Convention on Corruption,[163] which requires state parties to create a criminal offence of bribery of a domestic or foreign arbitrator, whether bribery is instigated by an individual ('active bribery') or an arbitrator ('passive bribery').

5.94   The question of the contract whose object is the exercise of influence over state officials was addressed in the well-known decision of Judge Gunnar Lagergren, acting as arbitrator.[164] Although neither party had alleged the nullity of the contract based on its purpose, the arbitrator raised the issue of his own motion. He concluded, on the evidence before him, that he was being asked to enforce a contract for the payment of bribes and consequently declined

---

include arbitrators, or whether resolving a dispute could be said to be assisting a 'client' in the implementation of a transaction. Indeed, the 2005 Directive envisages reporting obligations for legal professionals when assisting in financial or corporate transactions, but excludes such obligations when information is obtained before, during, or after legal proceedings.

[162] For a deep analysis of this complex topic, see Sayed, *Corruption in International Trade and Commercial Arbitration* (Kluwer Law International, 2004). See also (2013) 24 ICC Bulletin, Supplement entitled 'Tackling Corruption in Arbitration', and Lamm, Moloo, and Pham, 'Fraud and corruption in international arbitration', in *Liber Amicorum Bernardo Cremades* (Wolters Kluwer España; La Ley, 2010), p. 699.

[163] As of April 2021, the Protocol had been ratified by forty-five member states. The Protocol was developed by the Council of Europe to supplement the 2002 Criminal Law Convention on Corruption, widening its scope to cover arbitrators.

[164] Award by Gunnar Lagergren, ICC Case No. 1110, (1963) XXI YBCA 47, (1994) 10 Arb Intl 282.

jurisdiction. At the time, this seemed to be the correct approach.[165] An arbitrator should not be asked to enforce an illegal contract. Later, however, a different approach was adopted by arbitral tribunals. It was thought that an arbitrator should *not* decline jurisdiction when confronted with a possibly illegal contract but should go on to investigate the alleged illegality and make the appropriate award.

The issue of a contract obtained through a bribe was considered by the arbitral tribunal **5.95** in the ICSID case *World Duty Free v Kenya*.[166] In this case, the arbitral tribunal was shown evidence that the contract upon which the arbitration was based was procured by the payment of a bribe. The tribunal considered the claim, but had no hesitation in dismissing it as being in clear breach of international public policy. The arbitral tribunal concluded that:

> In light of domestic laws and international conventions relating to corruption, and in light of the decisions taken in this matter by courts and arbitral tribunals, this Tribunal is convinced that bribery is contrary to the international public policy of most, if not all, States or, to use another formula, to transnational public policy. Thus, claims based on contracts of corruption or on contracts obtained by corruption cannot be upheld by this Arbitral Tribunal.[167]

More recently, the Paris Court of Appeal has set aside or refused to enforce awards where **5.96** there was evidence of illegality on the basis of international public policy. In the *Belokon* case, the Court set aside an investment treaty award that ordered the Kyrgyz Republic to pay US$15 million to a bank whose main activity was to devise money laundering schemes.[168] In the 2019 case of *Alstom*, the Court refused to enforce an award that would have obliged the losing party to pay outstanding invoices to an entity engaged in corruption of foreign public officials.[169] In *Sorelec*, which arose out of a dispute regarding the performance of a settlement agreement, the Court set aside a pair of investment treaty awards after it determined that the settlement agreement at issue had been procured through corruption.[170] These and other decisions have sent an important message that international arbitration may not be used as a device to support unlawful contracts. A party that resorts to bribery to obtain a contract is likely to find that the mechanism of international arbitral justice is no longer there to enforce it.

---

[165] It was certainly viewed as such, in the first edition of this book, at p. 108, where it was said to be inappropriate for an arbitral tribunal to assist in the settlement of accounts between parties to an illegal contract.

[166] *World Duty Free Co. Ltd v Republic of Kenya*, ICSID Case No. ARB/00/7, Award, 4 October 2006. Similarly, in the case of *Inceysa Vallisoletana SL v Republic of El Salvador*, ICSID Case No. ARB/03/26, Award, 2 August 2006, a systematic fraud in securing a contract with the Republic of El Salvador, for the operation of vehicle inspection stations, caused the tribunal to deny jurisdiction on a number of grounds, including that the investment was not made in accordance with the laws of El Salvador.

[167] *World Duty Free*, fn. 166, at [157]. See also *Metal-Tech Ltd. v Republic of Uzbekistan*, ICSID Case No. ARB/10/3, Award, 4 October 2013, at [372]–[374] (finding that suspicious payments made by the claimant violated the Uzbek Criminal Code and thereby the legality requirement of the Israel-Uzbekistan BIT, thus depriving the tribunal of jurisdiction).

[168] Paris cour d'appel, 21 February 2017, Case No. 15/01650.

[169] Paris cour d'appel, 28 May 2019, Case No. 16/11182.

[170] Paris cour d'appel, 17 November 2020, Case Nos 18/0737, 18/02568.

D. Jurisdiction

(a) Introduction

5.97 An arbitral tribunal may only validly resolve those disputes that the parties have agreed that it should resolve. This rule is an inevitable and proper consequence of the voluntary nature of arbitration. It is the parties who give to a private tribunal the authority to decide disputes between them, and the arbitral tribunal must take care to stay within the terms of this authority. The rule to this effect is expressed in several different ways. Sometimes, it is said that an arbitral tribunal must conform to the mission entrusted to it,[171] or that it must not exceed its mandate, or that it must stay within its terms of reference,[172] competence, or authority. Another way of expressing the rule (which is followed in this volume) is to state that an arbitral tribunal must not exceed its jurisdiction (this term being used in the sense of mandate, competence, or authority).

5.98 National laws and the international conventions on arbitration emphasise how important it is that an arbitral tribunal should not exceed its jurisdiction. In French law, for example, an award may be challenged where 'the arbitral tribunal wrongly upheld or declined jurisdiction'.[173] Internationally, the New York Convention provides that recognition and enforcement of an award may be refused on proof that '[t]he award deals with a difference not contemplated by or not falling within the terms of the submission to arbitration, or it contains decisions on matters beyond the scope of the submission to arbitration [...]'.[174]

(b) Challenges to jurisdiction

5.99 A challenge to the jurisdiction of an arbitral tribunal may be partial or total. A *partial* challenge raises the question of whether certain (but not all) of the claims or counterclaims that have been submitted to the arbitral tribunal are within its jurisdiction. A challenge of this kind does not amount to a fundamental attack on the jurisdiction of the arbitral tribunal. It is usually dependent on whether a particular matter referred to arbitration falls within the scope of the arbitration agreement. A *total* challenge, by contrast, questions the whole basis upon which the arbitral tribunal is acting.

(i) Partial challenge

5.100 A partial challenge, as we have just indicated, exists where it is asserted that *some* of the claims (or counterclaims) that have been brought before the arbitral tribunal do not

---

[171] See, e.g., French Code of Civil Procedure, art. 1457: 'Arbitrators shall carry out their mission until it is completed.'

[172] Under the ICC Rules, Art. 23, an arbitral tribunal must draw up its own 'terms of reference' for signature by the parties and the tribunal, and for approval by the ICC Court, before proceeding with the arbitration.

[173] French Code of Civil Procedure, art. 1520.1.

[174] New York Convention, Art. V(1)(c). It should be pointed out, however, that the possibility of the 'good' parts of an award being separated from the 'bad' is explicitly recognised, since this paragraph of the New York Convention goes on to state that if the decision on matters submitted to arbitration can be separated from those that were not submitted, 'that part of the award which contains decisions on matters submitted to arbitration may be recognised and enforced'.

properly come within its jurisdiction. For instance, a construction contract may require all claims for varied or additional work to be decided by an engineer *before* being referred to arbitration. If a claimant brings certain claims without asking or waiting for the engineer's decision, the respondent may argue that the failure to do so means that the claims concerned were not properly submitted to arbitration and so were not within the jurisdiction of the arbitral tribunal. Similar issues have been tested in ICSID arbitrations, in which there is usually a requirement to notify disputes for the purpose of seeking an amicable settlement for a period before commencing an arbitration. Respondent states have often argued that certain claims fall outside the parameters of the originally notified dispute.[175]

It is possible to cure such a lack of jurisdiction by agreement of the parties. Even if certain claims or counterclaims are outside the scope of the initial reference to arbitration, the parties may agree that new matters should be brought within the arbitration. By signing an agreement to this effect, they may effectively bring new claims within the jurisdiction of the arbitral tribunal. This is not always as straightforward as might appear: under some arbitration rules, where the arbitral process has already begun, new claims may be added only with the permission of the arbitral tribunal.[176]   **5.101**

Nevertheless, there are many cases in which the other party objects to new claims being brought into the arbitration and has good legal grounds for its objection. In these cases (and indeed in any case in which it seems that it may be exceeding its jurisdiction), the arbitral tribunal should proceed with caution. This issue is of particular concern where there are two or more contracts. In one case, a claim was brought before an arbitral tribunal constituted under the ICC Rules pursuant to a loan agreement. The loan agreement did not specify the seat of the arbitration and Paris was agreed by the parties. In its counterclaim, the respondent raised claims under a second loan agreement between the same parties, which provided for an ICC arbitration with a seat in Madrid. The claimant objected to the inclusion of the counterclaim brought under the second loan agreement and noted that the counterclaim was incompatible with the arbitration in light of the different seat. The arbitral tribunal nevertheless proceeded to review the claim under the second loan within the original arbitration, on the basis that the two loans were commercially connected. The claimant successfully set aside the award on the basis that the tribunal lacked jurisdiction over the second loan agreement due to the incompatible seats.[177] It is apparent that if a tribunal does exceed its jurisdiction, its award will be imperilled, and may be set aside or refused recognition and enforcement in whole or in part by a competent court.[178]   **5.102**

---

[175] These questions have also been referred to as questions of admissibility, that is, have the necessary steps prior to arbitration been completed. See, e.g., *CMS Gas Transmission Co. v Argentine Republic*, ICSID Case No. ARB/01/8, Decision on Objections to Jurisdiction, 17 July 2003, in which the later claims were considered to have been an evolution of a dispute already notified. In contrast, in the case of *Burlington Resources, Inc. v Ecuador*, ICSID Case No. ARB 08/5, Jurisdictional Decision, 2 June 2010, the tribunal rejected jurisdiction over an unrelated claim that had not been the subject of prior notification.

[176] See, e.g., ICC Rules, Art. 23.4, which allows claims made after the drafting of the terms of reference only in the discretion of the arbitral tribunal, which shall consider the nature of such new claims, the stage of the arbitration, and other relevant circumstances.

[177] *Empresa de Telecomunicaciones de Cuba SA (ETECSA) v Telefonica Antillana SA and SNC Banco Nacional de Comercio Exterior*, Paris cour d'appel, 16 November 2006.

[178] In the *ETECSA* case, although the issue of complaint was the exercise of jurisdiction in relation to the second loan agreement, the Paris Court of Appeal was unable to sever the part related to the original loan agreement and the entire award was consequently set aside.

(ii) Total challenge

5.103 A total challenge to the jurisdiction of the arbitral tribunal raises the fundamental question of whether there is a valid arbitration agreement at all. Total challenges to jurisdiction are likely to arise in practice only where the authority (or purported authority) of the arbitral tribunal is derived from a pre-dispute arbitration clause, since an arbitral tribunal that derives its authority from a post-dispute submission agreement will, by definition, have agreed to give the arbitral tribunal jurisdiction to determine specific disputes.

5.104 The grounds for a challenge to jurisdiction are often related to the basic elements of arbitration clauses, as discussed in Chapter 2. One of the alleged parties to an arbitration agreement may argue that it is not bound by the agreement, because the arbitration clause was contained in a document to which it had not consented, or it may claim that the legal entity signing the agreement was a different legal person. Alternatively, it may argue that the arbitration agreement is not an agreement in writing,[179] or that the whole dispute in issue is outside the scope of the arbitration agreement, or not arbitrable under the applicable law. The respondent may assert that the claim is time-barred, or that preconditions to arbitration have not been performed, or that the arbitration clause is otherwise inoperative or incapable of being performed. Challenges to the jurisdiction of the arbitral tribunal of this type raise questions as to who should decide the challenge—the arbitral tribunal or a national court—and whether a ruling on jurisdiction by the arbitral tribunal may be reviewed by a national court and at what stage.

(c) Autonomy (or separability) of the arbitration clause

5.105 The question of whether a total challenge to jurisdiction should be decided by the arbitral tribunal itself, or by the relevant court, is an important one. The answer depends on whether an arbitration clause should be regarded as having a separate and independent existence from the agreement in which it is included. If such a clause did not have an independent existence, an unwilling party could seek to avoid arbitration by simply alleging that the arbitration clause in the contract was invalid because the contract containing the arbitration agreement was itself invalid.

5.106 This concern has been addressed by most jurisdictions by means of the adoption of what is known as the 'doctrine of separability'.[180] In other words, an arbitration clause is considered to be a separate and autonomous agreement from the contract in which it is contained. Consequently, its validity does not depend on the validity of the contract as a whole.[181] By surviving termination of the main contract, the clause also constitutes the necessary agreement of the parties that any disputes between them (even concerning the validity or termination of the contract in which it is contained) should be referred to arbitration. In this way, it provides a legal basis for the appointment of an arbitral tribunal.

---

[179] See Chapter 2, paragraphs 2.15*ff.*
[180] See Chapter 2 on the doctrine of separability.
[181] See, e.g., the UNCITRAL Rules, Art. 23; ICC Rules, Art. 6.9; LCIA Rules, Art. 23; ICDR Rules, Art. 21; Model Law, Art. 16; English Arbitration Act 1996, s. 7. This is the reason why most authors refer to the 'law governing the arbitration agreement', rather than to the 'law governing the contract'. An arbitration clause may be valid even if the contract of which it forms a part is found, under the same law, to be invalid.

In short, if the tribunal is to decide on its own jurisdiction, it must first assume that jurisdiction. **5.107** This is what the doctrine of separability allows it to do. It is apparent that the doctrine is, in many ways, a convenient and pragmatic fiction. If the arbitral tribunal decides that the clause is not a valid agreement to arbitrate, then the basis for its authority disappears. If the clause is not an enforceable agreement to arbitrate, that authority was never there. Nevertheless, because of its obvious practical advantages, this doctrine is widely accepted both by arbitration rules and in national laws.[182] The question of separability was reviewed by the English courts in *Fiona Trust & Holding Corporation and ors v Privalov and ors*. The case concerned charterparties made between, inter alia, the claimants and the defendant charterers. The claimants sought to rescind the charterparties and the arbitration agreements contained within them on the basis they had been procured by bribery. The Court of Appeal, confirming the doctrine of separability of the arbitration agreement from the underlying contract, held that the arbitration agreement would continue to apply unless it was directly impeached for some specific reason.[183] On the facts of the case, there was no evidence to indicate that the bribery impeached the arbitration clause in particular. The House of Lords (now the UK Supreme Court) upheld the decision of the Court of Appeal, concluding that the principle of separability means that the invalidity or rescission of the main contract does not necessarily entail the invalidity or rescission of the arbitration agreement: the arbitration agreement must be treated as a distinct agreement and can be void or voidable only on grounds that relate directly to the arbitration agreement.[184] The validity, existence, or effectiveness of the arbitration agreement is not dependent upon the effectiveness, existence, or validity of the underlying substantive contract unless the parties have agreed to this.[185] The doctrine of separability requires direct impeachment of the arbitration agreement before it can be set aside. This is an exacting test.[186]

But a decision that the arbitration clause is legally separate from the main contract does not **5.108** answer the procedural question: if a challenge to the jurisdiction of the arbitral tribunal is made, by whom is the challenge to be determined? Is it to be determined by the arbitral tribunal itself, by an arbitral institution, by an appointing authority, or by a court of competent jurisdiction?

(i) Who judges?
It is generally accepted that an arbitral tribunal has power to investigate its own jurisdiction. **5.109** This is a power inherent in the appointment of an arbitral tribunal. Indeed, it is an essential power if the arbitral tribunal is to carry out its task properly. An arbitral tribunal must be able to look at the arbitration agreement, the terms of its appointment, and any relevant evidence in order to decide whether or not a particular claim, or series of claims, comes within its jurisdiction. The arbitral tribunal's decision on the issue may be reviewed subsequently by a competent national court—but it is commonly accepted that this does not prevent the tribunal from making the decision in the first place.[187]

---

[182] See Chapter 2, paragraphs 2.107*ff.*
[183] [2007] EWCA Civ 20.
[184] [2007] UKHL 40, at [17].
[185] Ibid., at [32].
[186] Ibid., at [35].
[187] See, e.g., *Insalcor v Prolesa*, Uruguay Court of Appeals, Decision No. 65/2018, 24 May 2018, at [II], where the Court confirmed the principle of competence-competence and referred a dispute to arbitration given the existence of an arbitration clause in one of the contracts underlying the dispute. While one of the parties was claiming

(ii) Competence-competence

5.110 The usual practice under modern international and institutional rules of arbitration is to spell out in express terms the power of an arbitral tribunal to decide upon its own jurisdiction, or (as it is often put) its competence to decide upon its own competence.[188] For example, Article 23.1 of the UNCITRAL Rules provides:

> The arbitral tribunal shall have the power to rule on its own jurisdiction, including any objections with respect to the existence or validity of the arbitration agreement. For that purpose, an arbitration clause that forms part of a contract shall be treated as an agreement independent of the other terms of the contract. A decision by the arbitral tribunal that the contract is null shall not entail automatically the invalidity of the arbitration clause.

5.111 Similarly, under Article 6.9 of the ICC Rules:

> Unless otherwise agreed, the arbitral tribunal shall not cease to have jurisdiction by reason of any allegation that the contract is non-existent or null and void, provided that the arbitral tribunal upholds the validity of the arbitration agreement. The arbitral tribunal shall continue to have jurisdiction to determine the parties' respective rights and to decide their claims and pleas even though the contract itself may be non-existent or null and void.

5.112 The ICC process provides for the possibility of a provisional check on the *prima facie* existence of the arbitration agreement by the ICC Court, at the discretion of the Secretary-General, who may refer the case to the Court for decision.[189] If the Court is satisfied that such an agreement may exist, 'the arbitration shall proceed' and 'any decision as to the jurisdiction of the arbitral tribunal [...] shall then be taken by the arbitral tribunal itself'. If the Court is not so satisfied, then the arbitration cannot proceed under the ICC Rules in respect of the parties or claims in question.

5.113 Most modern national laws governing international arbitration also spell out the power of an arbitral tribunal to rule on its own jurisdiction.[190] For example, Article 16(1) of the Model Law provides that:

> The arbitral tribunal may rule on its own jurisdiction, including any objections with respect to the existence or validity of the arbitration agreement. For that purpose, an arbitration clause which forms part of a contract shall be treated as an agreement independent of the other terms of the contract. A decision by the arbitral tribunal that the contract is null and void shall not entail *ipso jure* the invalidity of the arbitration clause.[191]

---

it had not consented to arbitrate, the Court of Appeals found that, through emails exchanged between the parties pursuant to the negotiation of the agreement, they had ultimately consented to the terms of the contract including an arbitration clause. The Court held that it would be 'useless' to hear the arguments of the alleged non-signatory party because the arbitral tribunal and not the court was the proper forum to first decide on jurisdiction.

[188] This is sometimes described in a form of shorthand as 'competence-competence'. It is expressed in German as *Kompetenz/Kompetenz* and in French as *compétence de la compétence*.

[189] ICC Rules, Art. 6.3. No guidance is given as to how the Secretary-General is expected to exercise the discretion.

[190] See, e.g., *Henry Schein, Inc. v Archer & White Sales, Inc.*, 139 S.Ct. 524, 528 (2019), where the US Supreme Court held unanimously that the FAA does not contain a 'wholly groundless' exception, and that '[w]hen the parties' contract delegates the arbitrability question to an arbitrator, the courts must respect the parties' decision as embodied in the contract'.

[191] For a discussion of the competence-competence principle in the United States, see, e.g., Graves and Davydan, 'Competence-competence and separability—American style', in Kröll, Mistelis, Perales Viscasillas, and Rogers

Support of the principle has not, however, been universal. In India, a series of cases appeared to reject the concept, but more recent case law from the Indian Supreme Court suggests that the approach is changing.[192] Rulings by French and Brazilian courts have also nuanced the competence-competence principle. While observing that an arbitral tribunal has priority to decide on its own jurisdiction and to analyse the validity of the arbitration clause, Brazil's highest court also noted that every rule has its exceptions.[193] In that case, the Court held that a national court 'may in cases where a "pathological", i.e., manifestly illegal, arbitration agreement is *prima facie* identified, declare the nullity of this agreement, regardless of the state of the arbitration proceedings'.[194] A recent decision from the Court of Cassation departed from French case law that had long concluded that the competence-competence principle applies to international consumer contracts.[195] Instead, the Court held that the application of the competence-competence principle in an international contract to which a consumer is a party cannot result in the consumer being effectively deprived of the consumer-protection provisions of European law.[196]

As identified earlier, there are essentially two elements to the separability rule: first, that an arbitral tribunal can rule upon its own jurisdiction; and secondly, that, for this purpose, the arbitration clause is separate and independent from the terms of the contract containing the transaction between the parties. Most countries, including those that have not adopted the Model Law, embrace both propositions.[197] However, the two are inter-related, not identical. To understand the real scope of an arbitrator's power in any given country, it is always important to check whether both propositions appear in its national law. In the English Arbitration Act 1996, for example, the competence of an arbitral tribunal to rule on its own jurisdiction is established in section 30; the separability of the arbitration clause

5.114

(eds) *International Arbitration and International Commercial Law: Synergy, Convergence and Evolution* (Kluwer Law International, 2011), pp. 157–178.

[192] Concern about the application of the concept in India was voiced by Ray and Sabharwal, 'Competence-competence: An Indian trilogy' (2007) 22 Mealey's Intl Arb Rep 15, but this position appears to have softened: see, e.g., *Kvaerner Cementation India Ltd v Bajranglal Aggaral* (2012) 5 SCC 214, in which the Supreme Court found that once an arbitration is initiated, it has no power to rule on the existence or validity of the arbitration clause, and referred the parties to the arbitrator under the Arbitration and Conciliation Act 1996, s. 16. Similarly, in *In World Sport Group (Mauritius) Ltd v MSM Satellite (Singapore) Ltd* (Decision of the Supreme Court dated 24 January 2014 in Civil Appeal No. 895 of 2014), the claimant sought to rescind a contract (and the arbitration agreement it contained) on the basis of fraud and sought relief before the courts. The Indian Supreme Court held that the claim for fraud should be properly heard in the first instance by the arbitral tribunal unless the arbitration agreement itself (not the underlying contract) is 'null and void, inoperative or incapable of being performed' and an arbitration agreement does not become 'inoperative or incapable of being performed' simply because the dispute concerning the underlying contract may involve allegations of fraud. However, the issue is not fully resolved as a recent single judge decision in favour of competence-competence was overruled by the Division Bench of the Delhi High Court, holding that the court has an inherent jurisdiction to determine if a dispute is arbitrable—see *Dr. Bina Modi v Lalit Kumar and ors*, 2020 SCC OnLine Del 1678. For a discussion of the turbulent story of competence-competence in the Indian courts see Tyagi, 'The Muddy Waters of Anti-Arbitration Injunctions in India', American Review of International Arbitration Blog, 17 November 2021.
[193] STJ, *Recurso Especial* No. 1,602,076/SP, 15 September 2016, Reporting Justice Nancy Andrighi.
[194] STJ, *Recurso Especial* No. 1,602,076/SP, 15 September 2016, Reporting Justice Nancy Andrighi, p. 19. See also STJ, *Recurso Especial* No. 1,550,260/RS, 12 December 2017, Reporting Justice Paulo Tarso Sanseverino (the competence-competence principle shall prevail in cases of alleged forgery of signatures in arbitration agreements).
[195] Cass. Civ. 1, 21 May 1997, Case Nos 95-11429, 95-11427 and Cass. Civ. 1, 30 March 2004, Case No. 02-12259.
[196] Cass. Civ. 1, 30 September 2020, Case No. 18-19241.
[197] See, e.g., the Swiss PIL, Ch. 12, ss. 178(3) and 186; Brazilian Arbitration Act 1996, s. 8; English Arbitration Act 1996, ss. 7 and 30.

is established in section 7. The relationship between the two provisions was addressed in *Vee Networks Ltd v Econet Wireless International Ltd*.[198] The case held that separability, as provided in section 7, insulates the arbitration agreement from the underlying contract, and that 'competence-competence', as provided in section 30, reflects the doctrine of separability, but leaves intact the requirement that the arbitration agreement itself should be valid and binding.[199]

(iii) Limitations on jurisdiction

5.115   In addition to checking the applicable rules of procedure that set out the power of an arbitral tribunal to decide on its own jurisdiction, parties should examine carefully the law of the arbitral seat to establish to what extent those powers may be limited by the public policy of the seat. Further, whilst the conventions and rules referred to may define 'the jurisdiction of the arbitrators', that jurisdiction is derived not from any international source, but from the arbitration agreement—and the arbitration agreement, as we have previously stated, can confer only powers that are permissible under the law applicable to the arbitration agreement and under the *lex arbitri*.[200]

(iv) Award made without jurisdiction

5.116   The nullity of an award in the absence of a valid arbitration agreement is recognised both in national laws and in the international conventions governing arbitration. In the Model Law, for example, one of the limited cases in which it is possible to challenge an award is that in which 'the [arbitration] agreement is not valid under the law to which the parties have subjected it [...]'.[201] Likewise, under the New York Convention, recognition and enforcement of an award may be refused if the arbitration agreement 'is not valid under the law to which the parties have subjected it or, failing any indication thereon, under the law of the country where the award was made'.[202] This apparent consistency between the applicable tests at the setting aside and enforcement stages has not avoided conflict. For example, in *Dallah v Pakistan*,[203] the UK Supreme Court and the Paris Court of Appeal reached opposite conclusions under French law regarding the validity of an ICC award that had been rendered by an arbitral tribunal in Paris. The Supreme Court refused to enforce the award, finding that under French law (based on expert evidence) the arbitral tribunal had incorrectly assumed jurisdiction over the government of Pakistan. But, shortly thereafter, the Paris Court of Appeal upheld the tribunal's decision that it had jurisdiction, which was based on its determination that the contract was properly extended to the government as a non-signatory given the heavy involvement of the government during the negotiation

---

[198] [2004] EWHC 2909 (QB), [2004] Arb LR 729.

[199] Ibid., at [20]. For commentary on this decision, see Dundas, 'Separability and jurisdiction: Court assistance to arbitration and a costs horror story—Three recent cases in the English courts' (2005) 71 Arbitration 3.

[200] See e.g., STJ, *Conflito de Competência* No. 139,519/RJ, 11 October 2017, Reporting Justice Napoleão Nunes Maia Filho. Brazil's Superior Court of Justice held that the competence-competence principle applies in disputes involving state entities. In that case, the Court stated '[t]he arbitral jurisdiction precedes state court's jurisdiction, which means the arbitrators have the power to decide on the limits of their jurisdiction before anyone else (the competence-competence principle), as well as on any issues concerning the existence, validity and effectiveness of the arbitration agreement'. The Court, therefore, declared that the ICC tribunal—and not Brazilian federal courts—had competence over the dispute.

[201] Model Law, Art. 34(2)(a)(i).

[202] New York Convention, Art. V(1)(a).

[203] [2010] UKSC 46, [2011] 1 All ER 485.

of the contract.[204] In so finding, the Paris Court of Appeal rejected the government's application to annul the award.[205]

(d) Court control

A decision given by an arbitral tribunal as to its jurisdiction is subject to control by the courts of law, which in this respect have the final word. The relevant procedure and burden of proof vary from country to country, and sometimes even within countries. In practice, recourse to the courts on issues of jurisdiction is likely to take place at one of three stages: at the beginning of the arbitral process; during the course of the process; or following the issuance of the award. These different stages, and the options open both to the arbitral tribunal and to the challenging party, are considered later in this chapter. First, however, it is necessary to review the question of concurrent court control.

5.117

(i) Concurrent control
Any challenge to jurisdiction during the course of the arbitral proceedings is usually made to the arbitral tribunal itself. The arbitral tribunal will decide whether to 'bifurcate' the jurisdictional objection, asking for separate pleadings and holding a hearing before issuing an interim award on jurisdiction, or to hear the jurisdictional objection as part of the case as a whole, which will then be addressed as part of the final award. In many jurisdictions, an interim award on jurisdiction may be challenged immediately in the local courts,[206] which permits a challenge to the arbitral tribunal's jurisdiction *before* any award on the merits has been issued.[207] By this means, a final decision on the issue of jurisdiction may be obtained at an early stage in the arbitral proceedings. One notable exception is the ICSID regime, under which no application to local courts to review a jurisdictional decision is possible and the internal annulment process applies only in respect of final awards, which must 'deal with every question submitted to the Tribunal'.[208] The annulment process is consequently open only in respect of negative jurisdictional decisions that finally dispose of the dispute.[209]

5.118

The system under which a national court may review the issue of jurisdiction before the arbitral tribunal has issued a final award on the merits is known as 'concurrent control'. The advantage of this system is that it will save the cost and time of preparing a case on the merits if the court denies arbitral jurisdiction. There are broadly two arguments against concurrent

5.119

---

[204] *Gouvernement du Pakistan, Ministere des Affaires Religieuses v Société Dallah Real Estate & Tourism Holding Company*, Paris cour d'appel, 17 February 2011, Case No. 09-28533.

[205] For commentary on this decision, see, e.g., Grierson and Taok, '*Dallah*: Conflicting judgments from the UK Supreme Court and the Paris Cour d'Appel' (2011) 28 J Intl Arb 407.

[206] For example, in England, under the Arbitration Act 1996, ss 32 and 67 and in France under the French Code of Civil Procedure, arts 1519 and 1520(1).

[207] For example, English Arbitration Act 1996, s. 32. This particular option for challenging jurisdiction is narrowly drawn and may be pursued only with the permission of the other party (or parties) or the tribunal. It was intended for cases in which a challenge to the courts on jurisdiction would almost inevitably follow an arbitral award on this matter.

[208] ICSID Convention, Art. 48(3).

[209] The ICSID Secretariat will refuse attempts to register applications for annulment of positive jurisdictional decisions. Indeed, where the jurisdictional decision is positive, they are called 'decisions on jurisdiction', and where they are negative and the case is effectively dismissed, they are called 'awards on jurisdiction'. Only awards are subject to a possible annulment process.

control. First, it is argued that recourse to the courts during the course of arbitral proceedings should not be encouraged, since arbitral proceedings should, as far as possible, be conducted without outside 'interference'. Secondly, and more pragmatically, it is argued that to allow recourse to the courts during the course of an arbitration is likely to encourage delaying tactics on the part of a reluctant respondent. This question was much debated during the preparation of the Model Law—but the solution of concurrent control *was* adopted.[210]

(ii) Choices open to the arbitral tribunal

5.120   As the practice of international arbitration has become more sophisticated, challenges to the jurisdiction of arbitral tribunals have become more frequent. An arbitral tribunal faced with a challenge to its jurisdiction will need to decide whether to examine the jurisdictional issue separately and preliminarily or to deal with it as part of the case as a whole (referred to as 'joining the issue to the merits').

5.121   Typically, once a claimant has made its case by way of a full statement of the claim with accompanying documents, witness statements, and expert reports, a tribunal will establish a brief deadline within which the respondent is allowed to indicate whether it wishes to seek the preliminary hearing of any jurisdictional objections it may have through bifurcation of the proceedings. If the respondent uses that opportunity, the claimant will be given the opportunity to respond on the bifurcation request and the tribunal will decide whether the case on the merits should be suspended in order to address the jurisdictional question separately. In the case of bifurcation, the respondent will submit its objections to jurisdiction (to which the claimant will be permitted to respond). A further round of pleadings may then follow and a hearing on jurisdiction will be held and a jurisdictional decision or award issued. On the other hand, if the tribunal denies the request to bifurcate, the respondent will make its objection to jurisdiction as part of its overall defence on the merits of the case and the issue will be argued with the merits and decided in a final award.

5.122   The overarching question for the tribunal is whether bifurcation of the jurisdictional objection(s) will lead to procedural efficiency. For example, the tribunal in *Eco Oro v Colombia* explained that, in deciding whether to bifurcate, the tribunal 'should seek to determine what will best serve the Parties and the sound administration of justice, in particular with respect to procedural efficiency'.[211] In the same vein, the proposed amendments to the ICSID Rules explicitly require the tribunal to consider whether bifurcation 'would materially reduce the time and cost of the proceeding; determination of the questions to be bifurcated would dispose of all or a substantial portion of the dispute; and whether the questions to be addressed in separate phases of the proceeding are so intertwined as to make bifurcation impractical'.[212] Similarly, case law has identified certain factors to be considered by a tribunal when exercising its discretion to decide whether a request for bifurcation is justified or not, namely:

- whether the objection is *prima facie* serious and substantial;
- whether the objection is closely intertwined with the merits of the claim;

---

[210] Model Law, Art. 16(3). The jurisdictional award must be challenged within thirty days of its notification to the competent courts of the seat.

[211] *Eco Oro Minerals Corp v Republic of Colombia*, ICSID Case No. ARB/16/41, Procedural Order 2, 28 June 2018, at [50].

[212] Proposed Amendments of the ICSID Rules—Arbitration Rule 42.4 (November 2021).

- whether the objection is capable of disposing of the entire case; and
- whether procedural economy is served by dealing with the objection prior to the merits.[213]

Any award on jurisdiction made by an arbitral tribunal, whether as an interim or final **5.123** award, is binding on the parties to the arbitration. However, it may be set aside by a competent court, and it may be refused recognition or enforcement. This is the principle adopted in the Model Law with regard to both setting aside and refusal of recognition or enforcement.[214] It is also the principle adopted in the New York Convention with regard to the recognition and enforcement of awards.[215]

(e) Procedural aspects of resolving issues of jurisdiction

Objections to the jurisdiction of the arbitral tribunal are usually raised by a respondent **5.124** in the early stages of the arbitration (or by a claimant in relation to any counterclaims).[216] Indeed, most institutional rules require that an objection be raised no later than the statement of defence, or (for counterclaims) in the reply to the counterclaim.[217] This is a sensible and practical provision. It is undesirable that a party who feels that the case is beginning to go against it should be able to raise objections to jurisdiction at a late stage of the proceedings. National laws often support this position. Under section 31(1) of the English Arbitration Act 1996, an objection to jurisdiction cannot be raised later than 'the time [the party raising the objection] takes the first step in the proceedings to contest the merits'.[218] In Venezuela, any objection to jurisdiction has to be raised within five business days of the procedural hearing.[219]

(f) Options open to the respondent

A respondent has four methods of challenging the jurisdiction of an arbitral tribunal estab- **5.125** lished contrary to its assertion that the tribunal has no jurisdiction. It may:

- boycott the arbitration;
- raise its objections with the tribunal;

---

[213] See, e.g., *Philip Morris Asia Limited v Commonwealth of Australia*, PCA Case No. 2012-12, Procedural Order No. 8, 14 April 2014, at [13]; ICSID 'Proposals for Amendment of the ICSID Rules', Working Paper #1, 2 August 2018, para 393 (citing, e.g., *Tulip Real Estate and Development Netherlands BV v Republic of Turkey*, ICSID Case No. ARB/11/28, Decision on the Respondent's Request for Bifurcation under Article 41(2) of the ICSID Convention, 2 November 2012, at [30]).

[214] Model Law, Art. 16(3). See Chapter 9.

[215] See Chapter 11.

[216] Certain laws require pleas as to the lack of jurisdiction of the tribunal to be raised before the submission of the defence on the merits: see, e.g., Model Law, Art. 16(2). See also the English Arbitration Act 1996, s. 31(1), which requires this plea to be made not later than 'the time [when the objecting party] takes the first step in the proceedings to contest the merits of any matter in relation to which he challenges the tribunal's jurisdiction'.

[217] For example, UNCITRAL Rules, Art. 23.2; LCIA Rules, Art. 23.3.

[218] For the purposes of this section, the 'first step' does not include any participation in the appointment of an arbitrator. See also the Swiss PIL, s. 186(2).

[219] Venezuelan Law on Commercial Arbitration 1998, s. 25.

- apply to the national court to resolve the issue; or
- challenge the award, once it has been made.

(i) Boycott the arbitration

5.126   The first, and most extreme course of action, is to boycott the arbitration altogether. In this event, the arbitration will proceed on an *ex parte* basis and the respondent will seek to set aside the award, or to resist enforcement on the grounds of lack of jurisdiction, after the final award has been issued. The Libyan government took this course in the oil nationalisation cases[220] after writing to the arbitrator in each case to contend that the arbitral proceedings were invalid. Liberia behaved in the same way in *Letco v Liberia* before an ICSID tribunal.[221] It is ill-advised, since, provided that the party has been properly notified of the constitution of the tribunal and of relevant procedural deadlines and hearings, an award will be enforceable against it notwithstanding its non-participation. Further, a costs award against the recalcitrant party is likely.[222] This situation is increasingly rare, because most parties (both states and private parties) are advised about the adverse consequences of such conduct.

(ii) Raise objections with the arbitral tribunal

5.127   The second course of action (which is the most conventional) is to raise objections with the arbitral tribunal itself and to request bifurcation of the jurisdictional question. This possibility, and the ways of dealing with it, has already been discussed, above.

(iii) Apply to a national court

5.128   The third course of action is for the respondent to apply to the relevant court to resolve the issue. There are various ways in which this may be done. The respondent may, for example, seek an injunction or similar remedy to restrain the arbitral tribunal from proceeding (an 'anti-arbitration injunction'), or the respondent may seek a declaration to the effect that the arbitral tribunal does not have jurisdiction in respect of the particular claim(s) put forward by the claimant (for example, on the basis that there was no valid arbitration agreement). Alternatively, the respondent may take the offensive and commence court litigation in respect of the matters in dispute. The claimant in the arbitration would presumably defend such a challenge to the jurisdiction of the arbitral tribunal by seeking to have the arbitration agreement enforced, relying on Article II of the New York Convention, or the relevant provision of domestic law implementing the New York Convention.[223]

5.129   Such challenges to the jurisdiction of an arbitral tribunal are usually addressed to the courts at the seat of arbitration, if these courts have power to intervene concurrently in an

---

[220] See Chapter 6, paragraph 6.206.
[221] See ICSID Case No. ARB/83/2, Award, 31 March 1986, at [378].
[222] In *Letco v Liberia*, the tribunal awarded full costs against Liberia on the basis of 'Liberia's procedural bad faith': ibid., at [378].
[223] Article II requires courts of signatory states to decline jurisdiction and refer the parties to arbitration where an arbitration agreement exists. The relevant national court must simply decide whether the arbitration agreement is null and void, inoperative, or incapable of being performed. If it is not, the parties will be referred to arbitration.

international arbitration during the course of the proceedings.[224] The main disadvantage for a respondent who adopts this course is the risk of an adverse court decision upholding arbitral jurisdiction. This will enhance the standing of the arbitration and make it more difficult to challenge the award subsequently, or to resist enforcement of any subsequent award against the respondent on the grounds of lack of jurisdiction.

(iv) Attack the award

The fourth course of action is for the respondent to participate in the arbitration and to re-   **5.130**
main passive until after the final award has been issued by the arbitral tribunal. It may then either challenge the award in the courts of the country in which the arbitration took place or refuse to implement the award and wait for the successful claimant to attempt to enforce it. When an action for enforcement is taken, the losing party might then argue the objections to jurisdiction as a ground for refusal of enforcement. The disadvantage of this tactic is that most systems of law will consider a failure to raise an objection to jurisdiction promptly as a waiver of the objection, particularly where the applicable institutional rules require that it be made at a particular phase of the arbitration.[225]

(v) A combined approach

What, then, is the reluctant party to do when requested to take part in an arbitration under an   **5.131**
agreement that it considers to be non-existent or invalid? It should take part in the proceedings as respondent and raise the matter with the arbitral tribunal itself at the earliest possible stage; it should insist that all objections be fully argued before the arbitral tribunal and contend that the determination of these objections should be the subject of an interim award. If the arbitral tribunal bifurcates the jurisdictional issue but upholds its own jurisdiction, the respondent should continue to participate in the arbitration, having expressly reserved its position in relation to the issue of jurisdiction, so that this issue may be considered again after the final award is issued. If the tribunal does not bifurcate the issue, the respondent should argue the objection fully in its pleadings in the case and at the final hearing. If the final award confirms the jurisdiction of the tribunal, the respondent may either challenge the award in the courts of the place of arbitration on the basis of the absence of a valid arbitration agreement (or other relevant local ground), or by resisting attempts to obtain recognition or enforcement of the award by asserting Article V of the New York Convention that the arbitration agreement is not valid or addresses a difference beyond the scope of the submission to arbitration.[226]

(vi) Form of court intervention

Although a national court's role in reviewing a tribunal's award on jurisdiction is well es-   **5.132**
tablished, the type of intervention that the court is meant to undertake is not so clear. Is the

---

[224] For example, it would be possible in such countries as England and Switzerland, where the policy is that issues of jurisdiction should be finally resolved at the earliest possible stage by means of concurrent court control. Such control is not possible in the United States.

[225] This would be the position under Model Law, Art. 4. If a party has appeared and participated in the arbitration without raising any objections to the jurisdiction of the tribunal, it may be deemed to have impliedly submitted to the arbitration and any challenge to jurisdiction thereafter might be viewed as a mere device. It is significant, though, that Art. 4 refers to provisions from which the parties 'may derogate', and thus a party is not capable of waiving a mandatory provision of the applicable law.

[226] See New York Convention, Art. V(1)(a) and (c).

court to have a *de novo* hearing, considering the jurisdictional question afresh, or is it merely to review the tribunal's decision, applying the same deferential standard as it would apply to an award on the merits? The United States has adopted a distinction depending on the nature of the jurisdictional decision. If jurisdiction is denied by the arbitral tribunal based upon a failure to comply with a procedural precondition (what the US courts call 'procedural arbitrability' and other jurisdictions would call 'admissibility'), the US Supreme Court has held that the arbitrators must be given deference. This refers to the question 'when' there is a duty to arbitrate. If, on the other hand, jurisdiction has been denied based on an alleged absence of an arbitration agreement, failure of the dispute to fall within the scope of the arbitration agreement, or lack of arbitrability of the dispute given its nature (what the US courts call 'substantive arbitrability'), then the court may exercise a *de novo* review.[227] The court in that case will have the ultimate right to answer the question of 'whether' there is a duty to arbitrate.

5.133   This issue was reviewed in *BG Group v Argentina*,[228] in which an arbitration under the United Kingdom–Argentina BIT had taken place under the UNCITRAL Rules with Washington, DC as the seat of the arbitration. Following BG's victory in the arbitration, Argentina challenged the award before the competent District Court of the District of Columbia, alleging that the arbitrators had no jurisdiction because the claimant had not complied with the BIT's requirement of first submitting the dispute to the courts of Argentina for eighteen months (a requirement that did not require any decision from the courts and under which, even if a decision were issued, the right to arbitrate remained).[229] The arbitral tribunal had analysed and rejected this argument, based on the futility of the requirement in light of restrictions on accessing the Argentine courts and certain provisions of the 1969 Vienna Convention on the Law of Treaties. The District Court rejected the challenge to the award. However, the District of Columbia Court of Appeals upheld the challenge, by reviewing the treaty directly and deciding that the Court need not show deference to the arbitrators' views, but could review the question *de novo*. BG successfully appealed to the US Supreme Court, which confirmed that the eighteen-month requirement was simply a procedural precondition or threshold provision, since the dispute could be definitively resolved only by arbitration. As a consequence, it was no different from any other procedural precondition, since it did not affect 'whether' the dispute could be arbitrated, but only 'when' it could be arbitrated. In accordance with existing case law on procedural preconditions, arbitrators should be given deference and a *de novo* analysis of the question was not permissible.

(g) International agreements on the jurisdiction of national courts

5.134   Whilst any challenge to an arbitral award should be brought before the courts of the seat of the arbitration, the proper judicial forum for other applications may be less clear, particularly where jurisdictional treaties apply. Within the EU, for example, a measure of

---

[227] *Howsam v Dean Witter Reynolds, Inc.*, 537 US 79, 84 (2002).

[228] *BG Group plc v Republic of Argentina*, 572 US 25, 134 S.Ct. 1198 (2014).

[229] The obligation did not require any decision to be made, nor did it prevent any party from subsequently submitting the dispute to arbitration after eighteen months or a decision with which it was not satisfied.

uniformity as to which state courts may accept jurisdiction was originally established by the 2001 Brussels Regulation.[230] Article 1(2)(d) of the Regulation specifically excluded arbitrations from the application of the Regulation. Article 2 established a basic rule (subject to limited exceptions) that persons shall be sued in the courts of the state in which they are domiciled. A potential conflict consequently arose when a legal action was brought in one of the member states, but there was a claim that the dispute was covered by an arbitration clause providing for arbitration in a different member state. The party seeking to avoid arbitration might have claimed that there was no binding arbitration agreement, and that therefore the court of the defendant's domicile had jurisdiction and not the courts at the seat of the arbitration. The other party might have replied that a question as to the validity of an arbitration agreement was itself excluded from the application of the Regulation, under Article 1(2), as being connected with an arbitration.

This situation occurred in the *Marc Rich* case,[231] in which an English court was asked to rule   **5.135**
on the validity of an arbitration agreement as part of the process of considering an application for support of the arbitral process (in the appointment of an arbitrator), while simultaneously an Italian court (which would have had jurisdiction under the Regulation were it not for the arbitration agreement) was asked to act as if no valid arbitration agreement existed. The European Court of Justice (ECJ) held that the arbitration exclusion of the (then) Brussels Convention (later Art. 1(2)(d) of the Brussels Regulation) extended to litigation before a national court in respect of the arbitrator. As a consequence, it was admissible for the English courts to intervene in the appointment of an arbitrator, notwithstanding the domicile of the defendant in Italy. This appears to be sound. The exclusion exception of Article 1(2)(d) would be deprived of any real meaning if the Regulation were to apply to applications in support of arbitration.

Another area of tension between the EU jurisdiction regime and the arbitration excep-   **5.136**
tion was exposed in *Van Uden Maritime v Deco-Line*.[232] The claimant was a Dutch corporation, which had started an arbitration against a German respondent in the Netherlands for monies due under a charterparty. The claimant also sought an interim payment from the national courts in the Netherlands pursuant to the Netherlands Arbitration Act 1986. The Hoge Raad of the Netherlands referred the question to the ECJ as to whether it had jurisdiction to make a provisional order pending determination of a dispute by an arbitral tribunal on the basis of Article 24 of the Brussels Convention (later Art. 31 of the Brussels Regulation), which states:

> Application may be made to the courts of a Contracting State for such provisional, including protective, measures as may be available under the law of that State, even if, under this Convention, the courts of another Contracting State have jurisdiction as to the substance of the matter.

---

[230] Regulation (EU) No. 1215/2012 of 12 December 2012 on jurisdiction and the recognition and enforcement of judgments in civil and commercial matters.

[231] *Marc Rich Co. AG v Societa Italiana Impianti PA (The Atlantic Emperor)* [1989] 1 Lloyd's Rep 548 (CA); appealed to the ECJ and heard on 17 October 1990, [1992] 1 Lloyd's Rep 342 (ECJ). See also the discussion in Hascher, 'Arbitration under the Brussels Convention' (1997) 13 Arb Intl 33.

[232] Case C-391/95 *Van Uden Maritime BV v Kommanditgesellschaft in Firma Deco Line and anor* [1998] 2 WLR 1181.

5.137   The respondent argued that there was no such jurisdiction, since the arbitration exception applied. The ECJ disagreed, holding that:

> [P]rovisional measures are not in principle ancillary to arbitration proceedings but are ordered in parallel to such proceedings and are intended as measures of support. They concern not arbitration as such *but the protection of a wide variety of rights.*[233]

As a consequence, such applications benefited from the protection of the Brussels Regulation such that there could be no concurrent proceedings (Arts 21–23). Further, an application for interim measures from an EU national court in support of an arbitration could be enforced under the Brussels Regulation in any other court in the EU. This was a strong incentive to seek such measures, since interim measures from a national court might not be enforced automatically elsewhere pursuant to the New York Convention.

5.138   The same area of conflict was addressed in the case of *Allianz SpA and anor v West Tankers Inc.* West Tankers Inc. had chartered a vessel to Erg SpA pursuant to a charterparty that provided for disputes to be resolved by arbitration in England. The vessel had collided with a jetty in an Italian port. Erg claimed compensation from its insurer up to the limit of its insurance cover and commenced arbitration proceedings in London against West Tankers for the excess. West Tankers denied liability for the damage caused by the collision. Having paid Erg compensation under the insurance policies for the loss that it had suffered, the insurer brought proceedings against West Tankers before the Italian courts in order to recover the sums that it had paid to Erg, based on its statutory right of subrogation. West Tankers raised an objection of lack of jurisdiction on the basis of the existence of the arbitration agreement.

5.139   In parallel, West Tankers brought proceedings before the English courts, seeking a declaration that the dispute with the insurer was to be settled by arbitration pursuant to the arbitration agreement and an 'anti-suit' injunction restraining the insurer from pursuing the proceedings commenced before the Italian courts. The English High Court upheld West Tankers' claims and granted the anti-suit injunction sought against the insurer.[234] The latter appealed against that judgment to the House of Lords (now the UK Supreme Court), arguing that the grant of such an injunction was contrary to the Brussels Regulation, since it had a right to bring a claim in the Italian courts, and if the Italian courts took jurisdiction, that should be the end of the matter.

5.140   The House of Lords first referred to judgments in which it was held that an anti-suit injunction restraining a party from commencing or continuing proceedings in a court of another member state cannot be compatible with the system established by the Brussels Regulation, even where it is granted by the court having jurisdiction under that regulation.[235] That is because the Brussels Regulation provided a complete set of uniform rules on the allocation of jurisdiction between the courts of the member states, which must trust each other to apply those rules correctly. However, that principle could not, in the view of the House of Lords, be extended to arbitration, which was excluded from the scope of the Brussels Regulation by virtue of Article 1(2)(d). Since there was no set of uniform rules in relation to arbitration, it was clear from the *Marc Rich* case that the exclusion in Article 1(2)(d) applied both to

---

[233] Ibid., at [33] (emphasis added).
[234] *West Tankers Inc. v Allianz SpA and anor* [2005] EWHC 454 (Comm).
[235] *West Tankers Inc. v Allianz SpA and anor* [2007] UKHL 4.

arbitration proceedings and legal proceedings in relation to arbitration. As a consequence, the House of Lords concluded that an anti-suit injunction addressed to the Italian court would not infringe the regulation. However, it stayed its proceedings, pending a preliminary ruling to address the question: 'Is it consistent with Regulation No. 44/2001 for a court of a Member State to make an order to restrain a person from commencing or continuing proceedings in another Member State on the ground that such proceedings are in breach of an arbitration agreement?'

The ECJ concluded that, although the subject matter of the proceedings was arbitration **5.141** (and thus outside of the scope of the Brussels Regulation), an anti-suit injunction against a court of another member state that considered it had validly taken jurisdiction under the Brussels Regulation would have consequences that could undermine its effectiveness.[236] This was particularly so where proceedings were seeking to prevent the exercise by the courts of a member state of their jurisdictional privileges under the Brussels Regulation. In these circumstances, it was exclusively a matter for the courts first seized of the dispute (in this case, the Italian courts) to determine the validity of an arbitration agreement relied upon by a respondent in order to contest its jurisdiction. Otherwise, it would amount to stripping that court of the power to determine its own jurisdiction under the Brussels Regulation. Such anti-suit injunctions were consequently held to be incompatible with the Brussels Regulation. The ECJ noted too that this solution was consistent with Article II(3) of the New York Convention, which vests the courts of a state seized of a matter in respect of which an arbitration agreement exists with the power to refer the matter to arbitration.

The European Court's decision in the *West Tankers* case has been widely criticised by com- **5.142** mentators for not taking into account the fundamental principles of arbitration law and the reality of arbitral practice—namely, that parties select specific jurisdictions as seats for their arbitrations because of their arbitration-friendly judicial systems.[237] It is argued that parties expect the national courts at the seat of the arbitration to enforce agreements to arbitrate and to protect their supervisory jurisdiction. Nevertheless, some commentators have suggested that courts at the seat of the arbitration may continue to enforce arbitration agreements by alternative means, such as declaring the validity of the arbitration agreement, ordering its specific performance, or awarding damages for the breach of agreements to arbitrate.[238]

The scope of the Brussels Regulation was clarified by the superseding Regulation 1215/2012 **5.143** (the Recast Regulation),[239] which came into force on 10 January 2015.[240] Article 1(2)(d) of

[236] Case C-185/07 *Allianz SpA and anor v West Tankers Inc.* [2009] ECR I–663.
[237] See, e.g., Merkin, 'Anti-suit injunctions: The future of anti-suit injunctions in Europe' (2009) 9 Arb LM 1; Clifford and Browne, 'Lost at sea or a storm in a teacup? Anti-suit injunctions after *Allianz SPA (formerly Riunione Adriatica di Sucurta SPA) v West Tankers Inc*' (2009) 12 Intl Arb L Rev 19; Noussia, 'Antisuit injunctions and arbitration proceedings: What does the future hold?' (2009) 26 J Intl Arb 311.
[238] See Byford and Sarwar, 'Arbitration clauses after *West Tankers*: The unanswerable conundrum? Practical solutions for enforcing arbitration clauses' (2009) 12 Intl Arb L Rev 29; Merkin, 'Anti-suit injunctions: The future of anti-suit injunctions in Europe' (2009) 9 Arb LM 1; Michaelson and Blanke, 'Anti-suit injunctions and the recoverability of legal costs as damages for breach of an arbitration agreement' (2008) 74 Arbitration 12; Veeder, 'The Brussels Regulation, the Lugano Convention, the Arbitration Exception and the New Schlosser Report', Paper presented at the ICC UK Annual Arbitration Conference, London, 6 November 2008.
[239] Regulation (EU) No. 1215/2012 of the European Parliament and of the Council of 12 December 2012 on jurisdiction and the recognition and enforcement of judgments in civil and commercial matters (recast), OJ L 351/1, 20 December 2012.
[240] Articles 75 and 76 of Regulation 1215/2012 came into force on 10 January 2014.

the Recast Regulation continues to exclude arbitrations from its application, but provides guidance to courts seized of arbitration matters. Recital 12 states that when a member state court is seized of an action that is subject to an arbitration agreement, the Recast Regulation does not prevent the court from (a) referring those parties to arbitration, (b) staying or dismissing the proceedings, or (c) examining the validity of the arbitration agreement. Recital 12 also excludes rulings from member state courts on the validity of arbitration agreements from the recognition and enforcement regime of the Recast Regulation, regardless of whether the court decided the matter as a principal or incidental issue. However, if a member state court has determined that an arbitration agreement is invalid, then that court's judgment on the substance of the dispute may be recognised or enforced under the Regulation. Recital 12 states that this is without prejudice to member state courts' competence to recognise and enforce arbitral awards in accordance with the New York Convention, 'which takes precedence over' the Recast Regulation.[241] Finally, Recital 12 provides that the Regulation is not applicable to any action or ancillary proceedings relating to the establishment of an arbitral tribunal, the powers of the arbitrators, or the conduct or any other aspect of arbitral procedure, nor to any action or judgment regarding the annulment, review, appeal, recognition, or enforcement of an arbitral award.

[241] Article 73(2) of Regulation 1215/2012 also provides that '[t]his Regulation shall not affect the application of the 1958 New York Convention'.

6

CONDUCT OF THE PROCEEDINGS

A. Overview

(a) Introduction

An international arbitration may be conducted in many different ways. There are few fixed **6.01** rules. Institutional and ad hoc rules of arbitration often provide an outline of the various steps to be taken, but detailed regulation of the procedure to be followed is established either by agreement of the parties, or by directions from the arbitral tribunal, or by a combination of the two. The flexibility that this confers on the arbitral process is a reason why parties choose international arbitration over other forms of dispute resolution in international business and trade. The only certainty is that the parties' counsel should not bring with them the rulebooks from their home courts. The rules of civil procedure that govern proceedings in national courts have no place in arbitrations, unless the parties expressly agree to adopt them.

In general, an arbitral tribunal must conduct the arbitration in accordance with the pro- **6.02** cedure agreed by the parties. If it fails to do so, the award may be set aside, or refused recognition and enforcement.[1] However, the freedom of the parties to dictate the procedure to be followed in an international arbitration is not unrestricted. The procedure that they establish must comply with any mandatory rules[2] and public policy requirements of the law of the juridical seat of the arbitration.[3] It must also take into account the provisions of the international conventions on arbitration, which aim to ensure that arbitral proceedings are conducted fairly, and the tribunal's own view of how the procedure can be conducted most efficiently.[4] Accordingly, a balance must be struck between the parties' wishes concerning

---

[1] An award may be set aside under the Model Law if 'the arbitral procedure was not in accordance with the agreement of the parties', and this is also a ground for refusal of recognition or enforcement: Arts 34(2)(a)(iv) and 36(1)(a)(iv). See also New York Convention, Art. V(1)(d).

[2] See the above provisions of the Model Law and the New York Convention, and see Chapter 2.

[3] For a discussion of the seat of the arbitration, see Chapter 3, paragraphs 3.27*ff.*

[4] See, by way of example, the English Arbitration Act, at s. 33, which imposes a duty on the arbitral tribunal to 'act fairly and impartially as between the parties', and to 'adopt procedures suitable to the circumstances of the particular case, avoiding unnecessary delay or expense'.

the procedure to be followed, the tribunal's views, and any overriding requirements of the legal regime governing the arbitration.

6.03   In some respects, an international arbitration is like a ship. An arbitration may be said to be 'owned' by the parties, just as a ship is owned by shipowners. But the ship is under the day-to-day command of the captain, to whom the owners hand control. The owners may dismiss the captain if they wish (and can agree) and hire a replacement, but there will always be someone on board who is in command.[5]

6.04   At the beginning of an international arbitration, the parties are firmly in control of the process. In arbitration, in which there is no institution involved, they may—and sometimes do—write a complete set of procedural rules to govern the way in which the proceedings are to be handled. When they subsequently appoint an arbitral tribunal, by whatever method they have agreed, that tribunal is constrained by that agreed procedural framework. In institutional arbitration, the procedural framework is provided by the institution's rules, to which the parties agreed when they signed the arbitration agreement and which they put into effect when they referred the resolution of disputes between them to the rules of the institution concerned.

6.05   When an arbitral tribunal is constituted, day-to-day control of the proceedings begins to pass to that tribunal. However, the transfer of control is neither total nor immediate. The tribunal usually engages in a dialogue with the parties on procedural matters, and often a first 'procedural order' is issued to design the essential elements of the process and the time limits within which each stage is to take place.

6.06   Many tribunals make considerable efforts, often adopting compromises in the process, to enable 'Procedural Order No. 1' to carry the subheading 'By Consent'. However, whether or not the procedural order is made by consent, once it is made the procedure will acquire a desirable degree of predictability. The tribunal will be more firmly in control to ensure that the procedural steps are completed on time, and will have a firm basis for determining the almost inevitable procedural issues that will arise between the parties as the arbitration moves forward.[6] By the time of the witness hearings, the tribunal is fully in command (in the sense of being 'captain of the ship'). In any event, by that stage the parties usually find it easier to ask the tribunal for directions on disputed procedural issues than to attempt to reach agreement between themselves.

(b) Party autonomy

6.07   Party autonomy is the guiding principle in determining the procedure to be followed in an international arbitration. It is a principle that is endorsed not only in national laws,

---

[5] See Veeder, 'Whose arbitration is it anyway: The parties' or the arbitration tribunal's? An interesting question', in Hill and Newman (eds) *The Leading Arbitrators' Guide to International Arbitration* (2nd edn, Juris, 2008), p. 337, at pp. 340–341.

[6] Rowley and Wisner, 'Party autonomy and its discontents: The limits imposed by arbitrators and mandatory laws' (2011) 5 World Arb & Med Rev 321, at 321, conceive of this as an expression of party autonomy in which the arbitrator 'giv[es] effect to the parties' choices in running the arbitration'. Pryles, 'Limits to party autonomy in arbitral procedure' (2007) 24 J Intl Arb 327 explains the procedural autonomy of the tribunal as a product of a tripartite contract between parties and tribunal, mandatory law, and institutional rules. Fernandez Arroyo, 'Arbitrator's procedural powers: The last frontier of party autonomy?', in Ferrari (ed.) *Limits to Party Autonomy in International Commercial Arbitration* (JurisNet, 2016), p. 202.

but by international arbitral institutions worldwide and by international instruments such as the New York Convention and the Model Law. The legislative history of the Model Law shows that this guiding principle was adopted without opposition:[7] Article 19(1) of the Model Law itself provides that: 'Subject to the provisions of this Law, the parties are free to agree on the procedure to be followed by the arbitral tribunal in conducting the proceedings.' This principle follows both Article 2 of the 1923 Geneva Protocol, which provided that '[t]he arbitral procedure, including the constitution of the arbitral tribunal, shall be governed by the will of the parties [...]', and Article V(1)(d) of the New York Convention, under which recognition and enforcement of a foreign arbitral award may be refused if 'the arbitral procedure was not in accordance with the agreement of the parties'.

Article 19 of the ICC Rules provides: **6.08**

> The proceedings before the arbitral tribunal shall be governed by the Rules and, where the Rules are silent, by any rules which the parties or, failing them, the arbitral tribunal may settle on, whether or not reference is thereby made to the rules of procedure of a national law to be applied to the arbitration.

Adopting a similar approach, Article 14.4 of the LCIA Rules states that: 'The parties may agree on joint proposals for the conduct of their arbitration for consideration by the Arbitral Tribunal.' In investor–state arbitrations, ICSID adopts a similar approach, its Rule 29.4 requiring that, '[b]efore the first session, the Tribunal shall invite the parties' views on procedural matters' relating to the conduct of the proceedings.

(c) Limitations on party autonomy

In the exercise of their autonomous authority, the parties may confer upon the arbitral tri-   **6.09**
bunal such powers and duties as they consider appropriate to the specific case. They may choose formal or informal methods of conducting the arbitration, adversarial or inquisitorial procedures, documentary or oral methods of presenting evidence, and so forth. They may even dispense with a hearing if they wish to do so. The exercise of this autonomy is, however, limited by certain requirements that may be categorised under the following headings.

(i) Equal treatment
If party autonomy is the first principle to be applied in relation to procedure in international   **6.10**
arbitration, equality of treatment is the second—and it is of equal importance. This principle is given express recognition both in the New York Convention[8] and in the Model Law,

---

Article 18 of which states: 'The parties shall be treated with equality and each party shall be given a full opportunity of presenting his case.'

6.11 The concept of treating the parties with equality is fundamental in all civilised systems of civil justice.[9] The provision in the UNCITRAL Rules to the effect that the arbitral tribunal may conduct the arbitration in such manner as it considers appropriate[10] is qualified by the proviso that it must treat the parties with equality. The same concept underlies other sets of arbitration rules.[11]

6.12 The requirement to treat the parties with equality thus operates as a limitation on party autonomy. For instance, a provision in a submission agreement that only one party should be heard by the arbitral tribunal might well be treated as invalid (for example by an enforcement court) even if both parties originally agreed to it. The UNCITRAL Secretariat recognised the dilemma in the report that led to the Model Law:

> [I]t will be one of the more delicate and complex problems of the preparation of a model law to strike a balance between the interest of the parties to freely determine the procedure to be followed and the interests of the legal system expected to give recognition and effect thereto.[12]

(ii) Public policy

6.13 The parties must not purport to confer powers upon an arbitral tribunal that would cause the arbitration to be conducted in a manner contrary to the mandatory rules or public policy of the state in which the arbitration is held. One important mandatory rule that has already been considered requires that each party should be given a fair hearing or, as the Model Law expresses it, 'a full opportunity of presenting his case'.

6.14 At first sight, the word 'full' can be misleading. It conjures visions of a party being entitled to present as much argument and evidence as it sees fit. But, in this context, the word 'full' must be given a sensible meaning, and in practice it seems unlikely that a national court would set aside an award where the tribunal took a clearly reasonable and proportionate approach to limiting the scope of the evidence that a party wished to present. Indeed, most sets of modern arbitration rules now expressly provide that a party need be given only a '*reasonable* opportunity to present its case', which should encourage arbitral tribunals to balance opportunity with efficiency in determining appropriate arbitral procedures.[13]

---

[9] Kotuby Jr and Sobota, *General Principles of Law and International Due Process: Principles and Norms Applicable in Transnational Disputes* (Oxford University Press, 2017).

[10] UNCITRAL Rules (as revised in 2010), Art. 17.1.

[11] See, e.g., WIPO Rules, Art. 38.b; ICDR Rules, Art. 22.1; AAA Rules, Art. 32.a. See also the Swiss Rules, Art. 19.1, and HKIAC, Art. 13.1, which both refer to 'equal treatment'. The corresponding provisions of the ICC Rules, Art. 22.4, the LCIA Rules, Art. 14.1.i, and the DIAC Rules, Art. 17.2 do not expressly mention 'equality', but the phrase 'fairly and impartially' must encompass it.

[12] UNCITRAL, fn. 7, para. 21.

[13] See, e.g., UNCITRAL Rules, Art. 17.1; ICC Rules, Art. 22.4; LCIA Rules, Art. 14.1.i; SCC Rules, Art. 23.2; CIETAC Rules, Art. 35.1; HKIAC Rules, Art. 13.1. Compare DIAC Rules, Art. 17.2; VIAC Rules, Art. 28.1; Swiss Rules, Art. 19.1.

Any agreement between the parties purporting to confer power on the arbitral tribunal to **6.15** perform an act that would be contrary to a mandatory rule (or to the public policy) of the country in which the arbitration is taking place would be unenforceable in that country, at least to the extent of the offending provision. So would any provision that purports to give the arbitral tribunal power to perform an act that is not capable of being performed by arbitrators under the law applicable to the arbitration agreement, or under the law of the seat of arbitration.[14]

(iii) Arbitration rules

Limitations may also be introduced by the operation of the arbitration rules chosen by the **6.16** parties. Such rules usually contain few mandatory provisions in relation to the conduct of the proceedings. For example, the UNCITRAL Rules specify only the following:

- under Article 17.1, the parties must be treated with equality and, at an appropriate stage of the proceedings, each party must be given a reasonable opportunity of presenting its case;
- under Article 17.3, the tribunal must hold a hearing if either party requests one at an appropriate stage of the proceedings;
- under Articles 20 and 21, there must be one consecutive exchange of written submissions (a 'statement of claim' and a 'statement of defence'); and
- under Article 29.5, if the tribunal appoints an expert, it may give the parties the opportunity to question that expert at a hearing and the parties must be given an opportunity to present their own expert witnesses on the points at issue.

(iv) Third parties

The parties to an arbitration may not validly agree to confer powers on the arbitral tribunal **6.17** that directly affect persons who are *not* parties to the arbitration agreement, unless a special provision of the applicable law enables them to do so. This is rare.[15] This principle applies to matters of substance, as well as procedure. For example, an arbitral tribunal cannot direct a person who is not found to be a party to the arbitration agreement to pay a sum of money or to perform a particular act.

Concerning procedural matters, an arbitral tribunal may direct the parties to produce **6.18** documents, to attend hearings, or to submit to examination—but it usually has no power to compel third parties to do so, even if the parties to the arbitration have purported to confer such a power on the tribunal. The participation of third parties in arbitration proceedings, whether by giving evidence or producing documents, may usually be compelled only by invoking the assistance of a national court of competent jurisdiction.[16] This is not to say that arbitral tribunals cannot give directions that affect the rights of third parties. For example,

---

[14] For example, the administration of oaths by arbitrators in a country in which the law allows oaths to be administered only by judicial officers.

[15] For example, in the United States, the Federal Arbitration Act of 1925 (FAA), § 7, allows an arbitrator to issue a summons to order the attendance of a third party as a witness at the arbitral proceedings; but court assistance is necessary to enforce the summons if the third party refuses to obey it.

[16] This is considered in more detail in Chapter 7, paragraphs 7.46*ff.*

an arbitral tribunal may direct the parties to disclose whether they are receiving third-party funding, and the terms of that funding.[17] Arbitral tribunals may also allow third parties to participate (in some capacity) as *amicus curiae*.[18]

(d) International practice

6.19   There is no universally recognised comprehensive set of detailed procedural rules governing international arbitrations. As described in Chapter 1, each arbitral tribunal is different, each dispute is different, and each case deserves to be treated differently. But there are basic underlying structures, built on three elements: first, the international conventions[19] (and the Model Law), to which reference has been made; secondly, the various established sets of international arbitration rules; and thirdly, the practice of experienced arbitrators and counsel.

6.20   The international conventions and the Model Law do not prescribe the way in which an international arbitration should be conducted, but merely establish general principles intended to ensure a fair procedure and an award that is enforceable both domestically and internationally.

6.21   Even the established sets of international rules—such as those of the ICC, the ICDR, and the LCIA (and, for *ad hoc* arbitrations, those of UNCITRAL)—do not describe in detail the way in which an international arbitration should be conducted. This means that, in practice, it is for the arbitral tribunal and the parties to work together to establish procedures suitable to the circumstances of the particular case. Indeed, many sets of arbitration rules now expressly provide that the tribunal and the parties have a positive duty to design the procedure so that it provides a fair, expeditious, and cost-effective means for the resolution of the matters in dispute.[20] In doing so, the arbitral tribunal and the parties should consider, and find answers to, a series of practical questions, such as the following.

- Is a confidentiality agreement required?[21]
- Is this a case in which it would be helpful for the tribunal to determine preliminary issues, and if so, what type of issue(s)?
- If, as is usual, there are to be written submissions, should they be exchanged sequentially or simultaneously?

---

[17] See, e.g., *Westmoreland Mining Holdings, LLC v Government of Canada*, ICSID Case No. UNCT/20/3, Procedural Order No. 1, [22.1], [22.2].

[18] See, e.g., *Biwater Gauff (Tanzania) Ltd. v United Republic of Tanzania*, ICSID Case No. ARB/05/22, Procedural Order No. 5, 2 February 2007.

[19] This is considered in more detail in Chapter 1, paragraphs 1.98 *ff*.

[20] See, e.g., ICC Rules, Art. 22; UNCITRAL Rules, Art. 17.1; LCIA Rules, Art. 14.1 and 14.5; Swiss Rules, Arts 16 and 19.1; SCC Rules, Art. 23.2; ICDR Rules, Art. 22.1 and 22.2; SIAC Rules, Rule 19.1; HKIAC Rules, Art. 13.1.

[21] Some jurisdictions impose confidentiality obligations upon the arbitrators and parties, as a matter of statute. For example, the Indian Arbitration and Conciliation Act, 1996, at s. 42A (as amended by the Indian Arbitration and Conciliation Act, 2019), provides that 'Notwithstanding anything contained in any other law for the time being in force, the arbitrator, the arbitral institution and the parties to the arbitration agreement shall maintain confidentiality of all arbitral proceedings except award where its disclosure is necessary for the purpose of implementation and enforcement of award'.

- How is the production of documentary evidence to be handled?
- How is the evidence of witnesses to be presented? Are there to be written witness statements and reply statements, and if so, are there are any special considerations to take into account, other than the timing of such statements?
- Is an oral hearing necessary, and if so, how long does it need to be in light of the parties' written submissions and evidence?
- Should there be a pre-hearing conference (if one is not prescribed by the rules adopted by the parties), and if so, at what stage of the proceedings?
- How much time should be reserved for the witness hearing, and when is it likely to be possible to fix dates and make the necessary bookings of hearing rooms, breakout rooms, court reporters, and so forth?

These are all important practical questions that are discussed in this chapter. First, however, it is useful to consider the way in which the procedural 'shape' of an international arbitration differs from that of civil dispute resolution in national courts.

(e) Procedural shape of a typical international arbitration

Two elements in particular distinguish the procedural shape of an international arbitration from civil dispute resolution procedures in national courts. The first is that, unlike judges, it would be unusual for every arbitrator on the tribunal to be resident at the seat of the arbitration. This means that it is difficult to convene a physical hearing or procedural meeting at short notice and at relatively low cost. **6.22**

The second element is that time spent at hearings is 'premium time' in terms of cost to the parties. Not only is each day for which the tribunal is in session likely to be very costly, but the more time that arbitrators and the parties' counsel are expected to spend together, the more difficult it will be to find a date (or dates) on which all concerned can be assembled. **6.23**

There are many different ways of conducting an arbitration, and in drafting the first procedural order, a 'standard form' should not replace an order that is specifically tailored to fit the essential features of the dispute between the parties. But in what follows we try to trace the path along which a typical modern international arbitration will usually proceed. In doing this, we are concerned with what takes place once the arbitral tribunal has been constituted and up to the point at which the proceedings are closed by that tribunal, following delivery of the parties' final oral or written submissions. The work of commencing the arbitration and establishing the arbitral tribunal has been covered earlier in this volume.[22] The award and any proceedings that may follow that award (for instance, in enforcing it if it becomes necessary to do so) are discussed later.[23] **6.24**

---

[22] See Chapter 4.
[23] See Chapter 9.

B. Expedited Procedures

(a) Introduction

6.25   However, before turning to the various procedural steps that are normally followed in an international arbitration, we give brief consideration to the procedural options available for expedited determinations.[24]

6.26   Expedited dispute resolution processes are not a recent development. Nevertheless, in recent years, there has been a growing sense of frustration amongst businessmen involved in international commerce, because of the expense and delays involved in reaching the promised land of the arbitral tribunal's award. Some of the many solutions that are often put forward deserve mention.[25]

(b) Expedited formation

(i) Emergency arbitrator procedures

6.27   As described in more detail in Chapter 4, 'emergency arbitrator' procedures have become a common feature of the main institutional arbitration rules.[26] These procedures provide parties with a means of obtaining interim relief from an emergency arbitrator appointed on an expedited basis (usually within one or two business days) prior to the constitution of the arbitral tribunal, providing an alternative to seeking relief before the national courts. Under some rules, an emergency arbitrator can be appointed before the notice of arbitration is filed[27] and can hear applications *ex parte*.[28]

(ii) Expedited formation of the arbitral tribunal

6.28   The LCIA Rules provide that, in cases of exceptional urgency, a party may apply to the LCIA Court for the expedited formation of an arbitral tribunal.[29] The application must be made in

---

[24] Brief procedures were, for instance, known in Venice between the twelfth and sixteenth centuries, in which decisions were rendered within very short time frames. Marrella and Mozzato, *Alle origini dell'arbitrato commerciale internazionale: L'arbitrato a Venezia tra Medioevo ed età moderna* (CEDAM, 2001).

[25] The debate that followed also gave birth to the notion of 'fast-track' arbitration. The aim of such processes is to accelerate all of the steps, thereby achieving a binding result as quickly as possible, reducing overall costs, and encouraging settlements.

[26] ICC Rules, Art. 29 and Appendix V; ICDR Rules, Art. 7; Swiss Rules, Art. 43; SCC Rules, Appendix II; HKIAC Rules, Sch. 4; SIAC Rules, Sch. 1; LCIA Rules, Art. 9B. Since 1990, the ICC has offered the option to parties to expressly adopt the Pre-Arbitral Referee Rules, which provide for the immediate appointment of a pre-arbitral referee empowered to make certain interim orders prior to the constitution of the arbitral tribunal. However, the Rules have rarely been used, primarily because they require parties to opt in, and are now rendered practically obsolete by the introduction of the emergency arbitrator provisions in Art. 29 and Appendix V of the ICC Rules, which apply unless the parties expressly opt out.

[27] See, e.g., the ICC, SCC, SIAC, and Swiss Rules.

[28] Swiss Rules, Art. 29.3.

[29] LCIA Rules, Art. 9A ('Expedited Formation of Arbitral Tribunal') provides:

> 9.1 In exceptional urgency, any party may apply for the emergency formation of the Arbitral Tribunal by the LCIA Court under Article 5.
> 9.2 Such an application shall be made to the Registrar in writing by electronic means, together with a copy of the Request (if made by a Claimant) or a copy of the Response (if made by a Respondent), and shall be delivered or notified forthwith to all other parties to the arbitration. The application shall set out the specific grounds for exceptional urgency in the formation of the Arbitral Tribunal.

writing to the LCIA Court, with copies sent to all other parties to the arbitration, and must set out the specific grounds for the exceptional urgency in the formation of the arbitral tribunal. For obvious reasons, it is usually the claimant who requests expedited formation.[30]

The LCIA Court has discretion to shorten the time limits for the formation of the arbitral tribunal.[31] There have been a few cases in which the time limit has been 'significantly abridged' and at least one case in which a sole arbitrator was appointed within forty-eight hours of receipt of the request for arbitration.[32]   **6.29**

(c) Fast-track procedures

Following the constitution of the arbitral tribunal, expedition can be achieved by the adoption of 'fast-track' procedures, either by means of simplified procedures available under certain arbitral rules, or by the tribunal exercising its discretion to abridge time limits. Several arbitral institutions have developed rules for the faster resolution of disputes by means of a simplified procedure.[33] As might be expected, the rules differ from one institution to another, but the Swiss Rules serve as a good example of how the procedure can work significantly to reduce the duration of an average arbitration. Under these Rules: **6.30**

- a sole arbitrator is appointed, unless the arbitration agreement otherwise provides and the parties are unable to agree to the appointment of a sole arbitrator;
- written pleadings are limited to a statement of case, a defence, and (if applicable) a counterclaim and reply;
- unless the parties agree to a documents-only arbitration, a single hearing is held for the examination of witnesses and experts, and for oral argument; and
- the award is made within six months of the date of the transmittal of the file to the arbitral tribunal, which may state the arbitrator's reasons in summary form.[34]

It is noteworthy that, while this procedure is mandatory for cases in which the total amount in dispute does not exceed CHF1 million,[35] it is available for disputes of a greater amount if the parties so agree. Such processes offer hope for parties who wish to avoid the delay and cost involved in a traditional international arbitration process.[36]

> 9.3 The LCIA Court shall determine the application as expeditiously as possible in the circumstances. If the application is granted, for the purpose of forming the Arbitral Tribunal the LCIA Court may set or abridge any period of time under the Arbitration Agreement or other agreement of the parties (pursuant to Article 22.5).

---

[30] Turner and Mohtashami, *Guide to the LCIA Arbitration Rules* (Oxford University Press, 2009), paras 4.86*ff*. See Chapter 4 for fuller discussion of the establishment of the arbitral tribunal.
[31] LCIA Rules, Art. 22.5.
[32] Information provided by the LCIA's Registrar.
[33] These include the ICC, AAA, SIAC, CIETAC, HKIAC, WIPO, SCC, and the Swiss Arbitration Centre. See, e.g., ICC Rules, Art. 30 and Appendix VI, AAA Rules, Expedited Procedures, Sections E-1–E-10; see also the ICDR Arbitration Model Clause for Expedited Cases; SIAC Rules, r. 5; CIETAC Rules, Ch. IV (titled 'Summary Procedure'); HKIAC Rules, Art. 42; WIPO Expedited Arbitration Rules; SCC Rules for Expedited Arbitrations; Swiss Rules, Art. 42.
[34] Swiss Rules, Art. 42.
[35] Swiss Rules, Art. 9.4.
[36] The Swiss Federal Supreme Court ruled on a challenge to an award rendered in accordance with the Swiss Arbitration Centre's expedited procedure and held, in the circumstances, that the respondent had not been denied

6.31   A notable example of a fast-track arbitration under standard arbitral rules involved the fast world of Formula One (F1) motor racing.[37] At the time that the dispute arose, the first grand prix of the season was traditionally held in Melbourne in March. In preparation for the race, teams shipped their cars from Europe in mid-February. At the end of one season, in the mid-1990s, one team fell into dispute with the Federation Internationale de l'Automobile (FIA), headquartered in Paris, which regulates the F1 championship in accordance with a comprehensive set of rules. The team in question, which was sponsored by a tobacco company, wished to paint one of its cars in the colours of one of its brands of cigarettes and the other, in the livery of another of its brands. The FIA objected, on the grounds that the championship is a team event, and insisted that all cars from the same team must be painted in identical livery. The constitution of the FIA, to which every team must sign up when entering the championship, contained an ICC arbitration clause.

6.32   By Christmas Eve in the year in question, it became apparent that a resolution of the dispute would not be achieved by negotiation. The team and the FIA agreed that they would submit to a 'fast-track' ICC arbitration with a view to obtaining a final decision by the end of January, so that the cars could be painted and shipped in time to reach Australia by the end of February.

6.33   The F1 team filed a request for arbitration with the ICC between Christmas Day and New Year's Eve. A three-member arbitral tribunal was appointed on New Year's Day. This tribunal circulated draft terms of reference on the same day, which all concerned signed within two more days. A sequential exchange of 'memoranda', to which the parties attached the documents on which they relied, then took place at seven-day intervals, followed by a simultaneous exchange of written witness statements within a few more days. A handful of disputed document requests were resolved by prompt procedural orders from the tribunal and an eight-hour witness hearing took place on the last Saturday of January. The tribunal deliberated on the Sunday, and sent its final award to the ICC Court for scrutiny by fax and courier at lunchtime the next day (Monday), together with separate signed, but undated, signature pages.

6.34   The award was approved at an emergency session of the ICC Court the same afternoon, and the decision was notified to the parties by fax and overnight courier on the same day. The parties received the fully reasoned award on the last day of January, one month precisely from the day on which the tribunal was appointed, and the cars were painted and shipped to Australia in good time for the first grand prix race of the season.[38]

---

its right to be heard nor had it been treated unequally: Decision No. 4A_294/2008, Swiss Federal Supreme Court, 28 October 2008.

[37]   ICC Case No. 10211. None of the material published in this book is confidential, because the proceedings and the procedure were fully reported in various motor racing journals. See also Kaufmann-Kohler and Peter, 'Formula 1 racing and arbitration: The FIA tailor-made system for fast track dispute resolution' (2001) 17 Arb Intl 173.

[38]   As a postscript, one of authors, who was a member of the tribunal (which unanimously upheld the FIA's position), recalls one of the other arbitrators during the deliberation making the observation: 'Of course, you know what they [the F1 team] will do [...] they'll paint each car the same, one side of the car in the livery of one

A Court of Arbitration for Sport (CAS) case provides an even faster example of fast-track arbitration.[39] In 2018, Mr Jeffrey Zina (a Lebanese alpine skier) sued the Lebanon Olympic Committee for failing to select him to represent Lebanon at the 2018 Winter Olympics in Pyeongchang. Mr Zina filed his claim at 10.20 hours on 13 February 2018. The respondent and other interested parties were notified of the claim at 12.35 on the same day. At 13.24 the CAS Ad Hoc Division notified the parties of the composition of the arbitral tribunal, and at 14.30, a hearing was scheduled for 08.00 on the following day. The respondent filed its response to the claim at 20.45 on 13 February 2018, and filed translations of the exhibits on which it sought to rely at 02.45 on 14 February 2018. The hearing commenced at 08.00 on 14 February, with the applicant and two witnesses attending through video-conference. On 14 February 2018 at 14.31 (twenty-eight hours after the institution of the proceedings), the tribunal issued the operative part of its award. These cases demonstrate what can be achieved when all concerned agree that there is a need for speed.[40]

6.35

(d) Early, or summary, determinations

An alternative to 'fast-track' procedures is early, or summary, determination. This involves the early determination of one or more claims or defences, upon application by a party or on the tribunal's own initiative, on the basis that the claim or defence in question has no prospect of success.[41]

6.36

Although arbitration rules have always endowed arbitral tribunals with the broad procedural discretion that would accommodate summary determination, the use of such procedures has been limited.[42] The reasons for such limited use range from reluctance to determine a dispute too swiftly, given the absence of any right of appeal in international arbitration to a far less justified fear of failing to ensure due process. Whether this reluctance is understandable or not, the net result is that the time it takes to dispose of a meritless claim or defence in international arbitration is one way in which the process compares badly to litigation in the courts, where early disposition is often readily

6.37

---

brand and the other side in the livery of the other brand.' His instinct served him well: this is precisely what the team did.

[39] CAS, Ad Hoc Division, XXIII Olympic Winter Games in Pyeongchang, CAS OG 18/06 *Jeffrey Zina v Lebanese Olympic Committee*, Award, 15 February 2018.

[40] See also Rawding, Fullelove, and Martin, 'International arbitration in England: A procedural overview', in Greenaway, Fullelove, Lew, and Bor (eds) *Arbitration in England, with Chapters on Scotland and Ireland* (Kluwer Law International, 2013), p. 361, at paras 18-34–18-38.

[41] Gill, 'Applications for the early disposition of claims in arbitration proceedings' (2009) 14 ICCA Congress Series 513. National court procedures often permit a court to make a summary judgment where a plaintiff or a defendant has no reasonable prospects of succeeding on its claim or defence. However, as Gill points out, 'it is uncontroversial to suggest that tribunals generally do not possess the powers of summary disposition conferred on national courts': ibid., at 515. See also the Centre for Public Resources (CPR) International Committee on Arbitration, Guidelines on Early Disposition of Issues in Arbitration, available online at http://www.cpradr.org/ RulesCaseServices/CPRRules/GuidelinesonEarlyDispositionofIssuesinArbitration.aspx.

[42] Gill, 'Applications for the early disposition of claims in arbitration proceedings' (2009) 14 ICCA Congress Series 513, at 523.

available. As one experienced arbitrator asked a few years ago: 'Why should a party be allowed to pursue an utterly hopeless claim simply because they inserted an arbitration agreement in their contract rather than providing for the jurisdiction of the national courts?'[43] In the authors' view, it should not. And reflecting this growing recognition, an increasing number of arbitration rules now feature express procedures for summary determination.

6.38 The ICSID Rules was the first set of arbitration rules to permit a party to raise a preliminary objection that a claim was 'manifestly without legal merit'.[44] Other institutions have followed suit, and have expressly provided for summary determination of claims and defences. These institutions include the ICC,[45] LCIA,[46] SIAC,[47] and SCC. For example, Rule 29 of the SIAC Rules provides:

> 29.1 A party may apply to the Tribunal for the early dismissal of a claim or defence on the basis that:
> a. a claim or defence is manifestly without legal merit; or
> b. a claim or defence is manifestly outside the jurisdiction of the Tribunal.
> 29.2 An application for the early dismissal of a claim or defence under Rule 29.1 shall state in detail the facts and legal basis supporting the application. The party applying for early dismissal shall, at the same time as it files the application with the Tribunal, send a copy of the application to the other party, and shall notify the Tribunal that it has done so, specifying the mode of service employed and the date of service.

6.39 In the absence of specific provisions authorising summary disposition (or an express agreement by the parties), the use of summary procedures is sometimes thought to run the risk of a claim at the enforcement stage of proceedings that there was a lack of due process.[48] It might be argued that such procedures are inconsistent with the requirement to provide a party with a 'reasonable' opportunity to be heard? While such an argument is perhaps understandable, a summary procedure should not prejudice the 'reasonable' opportunity to be heard. Due process is not a 'one-way street': and summary procedures may, in the right circumstances, be entirely consistent with an arbitral tribunal's duty to adopt procedures that avoid unnecessary delay or expense.

---

[43] Ibid., at 520.
[44] See 2006 ICSID Rules, r. 41.5. ICSID Rule 41.3 provides that: 'If the Tribunal decides that all claims are manifestly without legal merit, it shall render an Award to that effect.' See also AAA Rules, Art. 33. More generally, IBA Rules, Art. 2.3, encourages the arbitral tribunal 'to identify to the Parties, as soon as it considers it to be appropriate, any issues: […] (b) for which a preliminary determination may be appropriate'. See also 1999 IBA Working Party and 2010 IBA Rules of Evidence Review Subcommittee, 'Commentary on the Revised Text of the 2010 IBA Rules on the Taking of Evidence in International Arbitration' (2011) 5(1) DRI 45, at 51: 'While the 1999 Working Party did not want to encourage litigation-style motion practice, the Working Party recognised that in some cases certain issues may resolve all or part of a case.'
[45] The ICC's Note to Parties and Arbitral Tribunals on the Conduct of the Arbitration under the ICC Rules of Arbitration (ICC Practice Note) makes clear that 'an application for the expeditious determination of manifestly unmeritorious claims or defences may be addressed within the broad scope of Article 22.'
[46] LCIA Rules, Art. 22.1.viii.
[47] SIAC Rules, r. 29 (Early dismissal of Claims and Defenses).
[48] Born and Beale, 'Party autonomy and default rules: Reframing the debate over summary disposition in international arbitration' (2010) 21 ICC International Court of Arbitration Bulletin 19.

C. Preliminary Steps

(a) Introduction

(i) Case management conferences

Preliminary procedural hearings at a very early stage of a dispute resolution process may **6.40** not be customary in some countries. Nevertheless, particularly where the parties and their representatives come from different legal systems or different cultural backgrounds, it is sensible for the tribunal to arrange for a conference with the parties, remotely if necessary, as early as possible in the proceedings. This ensures that the arbitral tribunal and the parties have a common understanding of how the arbitration is to be conducted, and enables a carefully designed framework for the conduct of the arbitration to be established.[49] Nowadays, it is common practice for such a case management conference to be conducted by teleconference or video-conference.[50] This saves the costs inevitably incurred when one (or more) of the arbitrators or counsel has to travel across national boundaries, and it also makes it easier for all participants to find common periods of availability that can reduce scheduling delays.

Some institutional rules make it mandatory to hold a 'preliminary meeting',[51] or 'case man- **6.41** agement conference'[52] whilst others provide for such a meeting to be convened at the discretion of the tribunal.[53]

In practice, a first case management conference often proceeds through various stages. The **6.42** members of the arbitral tribunal usually arrange to convene privately, before meeting the parties. This is partly to effect introductions and partly to discuss provisional views as to the organisation of the arbitration.

Similarly, substantial benefits may be gained if the representatives of the parties have an op- **6.43** portunity to discuss procedural and administrative matters before attending the conference with the arbitral tribunal. This is particularly important in ad hoc arbitrations since issues such as the fees and expenses of the arbitrators are generally dealt with at this stage.[54]

(ii) Representation at case management conferences

In order to obtain the maximum benefit from a case management conference with the ar- **6.44** bitral tribunal, each party should be represented by persons with sufficient authority and

---

[49] It is necessary to distinguish between a preliminary meeting (or preliminary hearing) and a pre-hearing conference. A preliminary meeting takes place as early as possible in the proceedings, and certainly before the written stage. A pre-hearing conference takes place after the written stage, and has as its primary objective the organisation and order of proceedings at the evidentiary hearing.

[50] ICSID reported that, in 2019, the year before the COVID-19 pandemic, 'about 60 per cent of the 200 hearings and sessions organized by ICSID were held by video-conference'. ICSID News Releases, *A Brief Guide to Online Hearings at ICSID*, 24 March 2020.

[51] SIAC Rules, r. 19.3; DIAC Rules, Art. 22.

[52] ICC Rules, Art. 24. See also ICC Rules, Appendix IV ('Case Management Techniques').

[53] AAA Rules, Art. 21 (and Sections P-1 and P-2); ICDR Rules, Art. 22.2. Most rules require the tribunal to consult with the parties before it prepares the procedural timetable for the arbitration: see, e.g., ICSID Rules, r. 29; HKIAC Rules, Art. 13.2; SCC Rules, Art. 28. See also UNCITRAL Rules, Art. 17.2.

[54] To avoid awkwardness, it is important that the representatives of the parties should be able to present an agreed position to the arbitral tribunal on the question of the arbitrators' fees and expenses.

knowledge of the case to take 'on the spot' decisions, both in any discussion with the other party's representatives and during the course of the meeting with the arbitral tribunal itself. This means that it is usually necessary for the leader of each party's team of lawyers, as well as a person with appropriate executive authority from the client itself, to attend.

(iii) Items to be covered at case management conferences

6.45   It would be unusual for a preliminary meeting to extend beyond one day, as a maximum, and it may well be disposed of within half a day or less. The items to be addressed at a case management conference will focus on the need to establish terms of appointment of the arbitral tribunal (or Terms of Reference in ICC Proceedings), and a Procedural Order No. 1, including most notably a procedural schedule.

6.46   In particular, the procedure and schedule for the following items will usually be addressed during a preliminary meeting:[55]

- preliminary issues—such as jurisdictional objections, any applications for interim relief, and bifurcation;
- written submissions—including their structure and length, how many there are to be, their timing, and whether they are to be accompanied by documentary and witness evidence;
- document production, including use of the Redfern Schedule;
- witnesses—including their number, the timing of submission of witness statements or expert reports, and any use of tribunal-appointed experts;
- the pre-hearing conference—including the venue and timing;
- the evidentiary hearing—whether actual or remote, and a target date for it;
- other procedural and administrative matters—such as the use as guidelines of the IBA Rules on the Taking of Evidence in International Arbitration, the chairman's power to make procedural orders alone, the appointment of an arbitral secretary, the means of communication with the tribunal, and cybersecurity and data protection measures to be adopted during the arbitration.

(iv) Preparation for the case management conference

6.47   As mentioned in the last section, discussions will have taken place between the members of the arbitral tribunal as they prepare for the case management conference; and between the parties' counsel, in the hope of reaching agreement on as many procedural questions as possible. This is sensible. The members of the tribunal will need to establish a common approach between themselves; and, whatever grievances the parties may have against each other, it is in their common interest that the arbitral proceedings should proceed smoothly and efficiently and indeed, upon an agreed basis, to the extent that this is possible.

6.48   Arbitral tribunals usually prefer to avoid making rulings on disputed procedural matters in the early stages of the arbitration. Where there is disagreement between the parties, arbitrators often suggest compromise solutions. This is probably a matter of tribunal psychology,[56] in consequence of which individual members of the tribunal (and particularly the presiding

---

[55] See also Böckstiegel, 'Party autonomy and case management: Experiences and suggestions of an arbitrator' [2013] SchiedsVZ 1.
[56] See Chapter 9.

arbitrator) are reluctant to make decisions at the very start of the arbitration that one of the parties may regard (however unjustifiably) as unfair or partial.

Nevertheless, if at the end of the case management conference, there are matters out- **6.49** standing upon which the parties are unable to agree, the arbitral tribunal must make a decision. Sometimes, this is done immediately; sometimes, it is reserved and notified to the parties later.

(v) UNCITRAL Notes on Organizing Arbitral Proceedings

It may be useful, at the beginning of an arbitration, for arbitrators, or indeed for parties or **6.50** counsel who are not used to international arbitration, to consult the UNCITRAL Notes on Organizing Arbitral Proceedings. They provide a list of matters that the parties and the tribunal may wish to consider in establishing the procedural rules for their arbitration. Some of these—such as establishing the language of the arbitration—are fairly obvious. Others are more helpful, including arrangements to protect the confidentiality of proprietary information, arrangements for the exchange of memorials and other written submissions, means of communication between the parties (including the extent to which email, or other electronic forms of communication should be used), and so forth.

(vi) 'Procedural Order No. 1'

Many experienced international arbitrators have their own model forms of procedural **6.51** orders. Often, these are sent to the parties' counsel as a first step towards discussing and agreeing the terms of the first procedural order, which will establish an overall procedural scheme for the arbitration. Such a procedural order will usually include dates (or time limits) for the delivery of submissions, for the production of documents and witness statements, and for the production and exchange of expert reports. It may also contain provisional dates for a witness hearing. A procedural order of this type serves as a useful guideline to the parties and to the tribunal in discussing what is required for the actual arbitration with which they are concerned. However, there is a very real risk that the use of such 'model forms', which often go into a considerable degree of detail and which have been drawn up as a template for a 'model arbitration', may lead to the adoption of rigid procedures that are not appropriately tailored to the particular dispute in question. Indeed, the automatic (one might almost say 'lazy') reliance by a tribunal on procedures devised for other arbitrations may lead to a failure on the part of that tribunal to acquire a proper understanding of the case and a consequent failure to deliver one of the key procedural 'promises' of arbitration— namely, 'tailor-made efficiency'.

(b) Preliminary issues

One of the elements that may emerge from the process of formulating Procedural Order **6.52** No. 1 is whether or not there are some issues that should be decided as 'preliminary issues' or 'separate issues'. Apart from jurisdictional issues,[57] other questions may arise that either should be determined as preliminary issues before the arbitral tribunal considers the

---

[57] See Chapter 5.

substance of the claims or, alternatively, may be dealt with more conveniently at an early stage as separate issues, in order to facilitate the efficient and economical conduct of the proceedings.

(i) 'Bifurcation' of liability and quantum

6.53   A question that often arises is whether or not issues of liability and *quantum* should be dealt with separately. In many modern disputes arising out of international trade and commerce, particularly in relation to construction projects or intellectual property disputes, the quantification of claims is a major exercise. It is likely to involve both the parties and the arbitral tribunal in considering large numbers of documents, as well as complex technical matters involving experts appointed by the parties, or by the arbitral tribunal, or sometimes both. In such cases, there may well be savings in costs and overall efficiency if the arbitral tribunal determines questions of liability first. In this way, the parties will avoid the expense and time involved in submitting evidence and argument on detailed aspects of quantification that may turn out to be irrelevant following the arbitral tribunal's decision on liability.[58]

6.54   There are sometimes clear arguments in favour of separating issues of liability from issues of *quantum* in a large and complex case. For example, a claimant may have suffered a substantial loss (including loss of profit) as a result of the breakdown or failure of an important piece of plant or equipment. The claimant may seek to recover this loss by way of arbitration proceedings against a respondent responsible for the manufacture and/or installation of the equipment. In its defence, the respondent may allege, first, that it is the supplier (and not the respondent) who is liable for any breakdown or failure in the plant or equipment supplied: secondly, that liability is limited under the terms of the contract to a sum much smaller than the amount claimed; and, thirdly, and in any event, some of the losses claimed (such as loss of profit) are irrecoverable (because of the conditions of contract or the governing law) and others are not fully recoverable, because they have been quantified on the wrong basis.

6.55   This is a common situation in international disputes, with the respondent putting forward a succession of defences, any one of which, if successful, may limit—or even defeat—the claim. How should an arbitral tribunal deal with such a situation?

6.56   There are various possibilities. For example, the tribunal might decide to hear legal argument as to the effect of the clause limiting liability on the basis that if the clause is found to be effective the respondent may be prepared to pay the limited amount stated in the clause and the case will then be concluded.

6.57   At first sight, this seems to be an attractive option for both parties. There is no point in spending time and money on a complicated factual investigation if the dispute may be resolved by the determination of a legal point as a preliminary issue. It may emerge, however, that the correct legal interpretation to be put upon the clause that limits, or purports to limit, liability depends on the facts—and that, in order to ascertain and understand the factual situation, it is necessary to enquire fully into all of the circumstances of the case, with

---

[58] See also the discussion of partial and interim awards in relation to the separation of liability and *quantum* in Chapter 9. See also ICC Rules, Appendix IV, para. (a); ICDR Rules, Art. 22.4; AAA Rules, Art. 32.b; SIAC Rules, r. 19.4.

the assistance of both fact and expert witnesses on each side. Thus, the findings of the arbitral tribunal on the legal issue might be so dependent on its finding on the fact issues as to make it difficult (and indeed undesirable) to disentangle them. In this event, it would be appropriate for the arbitral tribunal to investigate the relevant facts rather than to attempt to deal with the legal issue in isolation.

Although, in practice, issues of liability and *quantum* may, from time to time, prove to be   **6.58** inextricably interwoven, it is sometimes possible to see a broad division between them. It is also sometimes possible for the arbitral tribunal to determine the principles on which damages should be awarded, while leaving the appropriate calculations to be agreed between the parties or to be determined by the tribunal at a later stage.

(ii) Separation of other issues

It is rarer for an arbitral tribunal to separate issues where there is no clear dividing line—   **6.59** to say, in effect, 'there are only a limited number of issues on which we wish to hear evidence and argument from the parties, and these are as follows'. This course should not be attempted lightly. Before an arbitral tribunal can safely isolate some of the issues for its attention, it must be satisfied that it has been adequately informed of all of the issues that are relevant or likely to be relevant to its decision. This stage is not likely to be reached until the written phase of the proceedings is under way. Where, however, an arbitral tribunal is satisfied that it has been adequately briefed on all of the issues and that the time has come for it to take the initiative in this way, the effect can be dramatic in terms of saving both time and money.

The *Aminoil* arbitration provides a classic example.[59] Many hundreds of millions of dol-   **6.60** lars were at stake, depending upon whether the Kuwait government's act of nationalisation was unlawful (as claimed by Aminoil), thereby giving rise to the possibility of an award of damages on a full indemnity basis, which would have a punitive effect, or lawful (as the government claimed), and thus susceptible to resolution by the payment of fair compensation.

At the close of the written stage of the proceedings, the arbitral tribunal convened a meeting   **6.61** with the parties and their counsel to consider various procedural matters relating to the forthcoming oral hearings. Following this meeting, the arbitral tribunal made an order fixing the hearing date in Paris and specifying, amongst other things, seven specific issues that the parties should address, the order in which they would be taken, and which side should speak first on each issue. This is how the hearing was conducted—and there is no doubt that this intervention by the arbitral tribunal led to a significant saving in time and money for both parties, and, in the end, to an outcome that both parties regarded as fair.[60]

At that time, in the early 1980s, it was relatively rare for an arbitral tribunal to take control of   **6.62** the proceedings in this way.[61] However, since then, international arbitrations have become

---

[59] See Redfern, 'The arbitration between the Government of Kuwait and Aminoil' (1984) 55 BYIL 65.

[60] See Hunter and Sinclair, '*Aminoil* revisited: Reflections on a story of changing circumstances', in Weiler (ed.) *International Investment Law and Arbitration: Leading Cases from the ICSID, NAFTA, Bilateral Treaties and Customary International Law* (Cameron May, 2005), pp. 347–381.

[61] Note that a number of sets of institutional rules permit the tribunal to 'direct the parties to focus their presentations on issues the decision of which could dispose of all or part of the case': ICDR Rules, Art. 22.3; SIAC Rules, r. 19.4. See also ICC Rules, Appendix IV, para. (a); LCIA Rules, Art. 19.2.

more complex and costly. As both arbitral tribunals and practitioners search for quicker and more cost-effective ways of handling disputes, it seems essential that arbitrators should seek to direct the conduct of arbitrations from an early stage—and, in particular, that they should seek to cut through the foliage in order to reach the root issues as quickly as possible.

6.63 Although, like the shipowner mentioned earlier,[62] the parties can agree to dismiss the arbitrators if they jointly lose confidence in them, it is no longer appropriate for arbitrators to sit passively behind their tables and say to themselves, 'this is clearly the wrong way of conducting this case, but the parties have agreed to do it like this so we'll go along with it'.[63]

6.64 To this end, some commentators have advocated the introduction of an early opportunity for the tribunal to discuss the merits of the case, offering preliminary observations, prior to the main evidentiary hearing so as to help focus the parties' ongoing efforts and the evidentiary debate. This can take the form of either an early hearing for opening arguments before the main evidential hearing, or a substantive 'case review conference' following the first full exchange of a first round of statements of claim and defence.[64] Such a way of proceeding would permit an arbitral tribunal to be actively involved in the streamlining of procedures to focus on those issues and evidence that, once they are informed in detail of the parties' cases, are likely to be material to the outcome of the case. The timing of such 'Kaplan Opening' or 'case review conference' would be key. They cannot happen too early, for example at the first case management conference, because at that stage arbitrators and counsel often do not have sufficient information about the case to reach informed decisions about the most efficient procedure to be followed. In the same way, such a 'case review conference' should not happen too late in the process, because that will defeat the purpose. Timed well, such early engagement by the tribunal in the substantive issues can be effective in fulfilling arbitration's promise as a tailored and efficient process.

D. Written Submissions

(a) Introduction

6.65 Following the fixing of a procedural schedule, the first step in addressing the merits of a claim will involve the exchange of detailed written submissions.

6.66 The LCIA Rules, for example, provide that, after the parties have delivered the Request for Arbitration and the Response, written pleadings consisting of a 'Statement of Case', 'Statement of Defence', and 'Statement of Reply' (and any further equivalent written pleadings in the event of a counterclaim, referred to in the Rules as a 'cross-claim') follow each other within certain time limits. It is clear from these Rules that these written statements are

---

[62] See paragraph 6.03.

[63] In this vein, one arbitrator has remarked, 'I am sometimes shocked when I write the award that although we heard 25 witnesses, I am only referring to two, and I think, "why did we spend time hearing them, why did the parties bear the costs of preparing them [...]"': 'Due process must trump efficiency, says Derains', Global Arb Rev, 23 September 2014.

[64] Kaplan, 'If it ain't broke, don't change it' (2014) 80 Arbitration 172. See also Partasides and Vesel, 'A case review conference, or arbitration in two acts' (2015) 81 Arbitration 167.

to be the only pre-hearing written submissions in the arbitration, unless otherwise ordered by the arbitral tribunal.[65]

The Swiss Rules also provide for the exchange of statements of claim and defence, which are to be accompanied by 'all documents and other evidence on which [a party] relies', and states that 'the arbitral tribunal shall decide, after consulting with the parties, which further written statements [...] shall be required from the parties or may be presented by them'.[66] **6.67**

The ICSID Rules refer to the documents that are to be filed by the parties as a 'memorial' and a 'counter-memorial', followed, unless otherwise agreed by the parties, by a reply and a rejoinder.[67] The Rules provide that a memorial should contain a statement of the relevant facts, a statement of law, and submissions, and that the counter-memorial, reply, or rejoinder should respond to these statements and submissions, and add any additional facts, statements of law, or submissions of its own.[68] The Explanatory Note states that the scope of these pleadings represents: **6.68**

> an adaptation of common law practice to the procedure of the civil law. These provisions, tested by international arbitration practice, are designed to prevent procedural arguments concerning the scope of pleadings, even if the parties have differing legal backgrounds. Where, however, the parties share a common experience with an identical or similar system of procedure, they may agree on different contents and functions for the pleadings.[69]

Written pleadings are usually exchanged sequentially, so that the claimant fires the first shot, the statement of claim, and the respondent answers with the statement of defence (and counterclaim, if any). Exceptionally, however, the arbitral tribunal may direct that the parties should submit their written pleadings simultaneously, so that each party delivers a written submission of its claims against the other on a set date, and then, on a subsequent date, the parties exchange their written answers and so forth. Whilst simultaneous exchanges can reduce the overall duration of the written phase, they are more likely to lead to the arbitral equivalent of 'ships passing in the night'. For this reason, simultaneous exchange remains less common than sequential exchange for pre-hearing submissions.[70] **6.69**

With respect to the mode of filing written submissions, there is an increasing trend towards 'electronic-only' filings, which avoids the need for counsel to print and courier (sometimes overseas) large volumes of written submissions to each member of the tribunal, the tribunal secretary, the arbitral institution, and opposing counsel(s). For example, in April 2020, the ICC issued a 'guidance note' recommending that 'tribunals should encourage the parties to use electronic means of communication for the submissions and exhibits to the full extent **6.70**

---

[65] LCIA Rules, Art. 15.6.

[66] Swiss Rules, Arts 20, 21, 24.

[67] ICSID Rules, r. 30.1.

[68] ICSID Rules, r. 30.2.

[69] The Note was included in the Rules of Procedure for Arbitration Proceedings (Arbitration Rules) of January 1968, referring to r. 30.3, which is r. 31.3 in the current 2006 edition of the Rules: see Rayfuse, *ISCID Reports, Vol. 1: Reports of Cases Decided under the Convention on the Settlement of Investment Disputes between States and Nationals of Other States, 1965* (Grotius, 1993), p. 93.

[70] White & Case and Queen Mary University of London, *Current and Preferred Practices in the Arbitral Process* (2012), available online at http://www.arbitration.qmul.ac.uk/research/2012/index.html, found that 82 per cent of respondents said that sequential exchange was the most common approach, with 79 per cent expressing a preference for it.

possible.[71] ICSID has issued similar guidance; and the ICC and ICSID have joined other major institutions like the LCIA, AAA, and SCC in allowing parties to submit new requests for arbitration only in electronic form.[72]

(b) Terminology

6.71   Many different expressions are used to describe written submissions. Examples are 'statement of claim', 'statement of case', 'memorial', and 'points of claim'. These lead to corresponding expressions such as 'statement of defence', 'statement of reply', 'counter-memorial', and so forth, with 'reply', 'rejoinder', 'replique', 'duplique', and similar phrases being used for additional rounds of written submissions.

6.72   The different expressions used to describe written submissions are not wholly interchangeable and none are capable of precise definition. In general, it may be said that the term 'points of claim' indicates a relatively short document, the primary purpose of which is to define the issues and state the facts upon which the claimant's claims are founded. By contrast, the expressions 'statement of claim' and 'memorial' imply a more comprehensive documentary submission, intended to include argument relating to the legal issues, as well as incorporating (in annexes or appendices) the documentary evidence relied upon and the written testimony of witnesses, together with any experts' reports on matters of opinion.

(c) Time and length limits

6.73   There is no such thing as a standard time limit in international arbitration, although periods of up to three months between submissions are not uncommon. Arbitrators should recognise, however, that the longer the time limits, the lengthier the written submissions are likely to be. Whilst this might be considered a matter for the parties (who pay their lawyers' fees), a trend appears to be developing in international arbitration for the submission of exhaustive written submissions, which are heavy with hyperbole and repetition. Not only does this add considerably to the time and cost of proceedings, but it can hinder a tribunal's understanding of a case. Increasingly, therefore, arbitral tribunals (empowered by certain institutional rules) are now considering the imposition of page limits on the parties' written submissions.[73]

---

[71] ICC Guidance Note on Possible Measures Aimed at Mitigating the Effects of the COVID-19 Pandemic, 9 April 2020, para. 13.

[72] Ibid., at para. 11; *ICSID Makes Electronic Filing its Default Procedure*, 13 March 2020, available online at https://icsid.worldbank.org/news-and-events/news-releases/icsid-makes-electronic-filing-its-default-proced ure?CID=359; LCIA Rules, Art. 4; AAA Rules, R-4.f.

[73] Partasides, 'A few words on prolixity in international arbitration', in Carlevaris, Lévy, Mourre, Schwartz (eds.) *International Arbitration Under Review: Essays in Honour of John Beechey* (International Chamber of Commerce, 2015), p. 301; the Iran–United States Claims Tribunal considered 'the reasons for the delay, the prejudice to the other party, and the effect of admitting the late-filed counterclaim on the orderly progress of the case': Holtzmann, 'Some lessons of the Iran–United States Claims Tribunal', in Landwehr (ed.) *Private Investors Abroad: Problems and Solutions in International Business* (Bender, 1988), p. 5. See also UNCITRAL Rules, Art. 22; LCIA Rules, Art. 14.6.i; ICC Rules, Appendix VI, Art. 3.4.

E. Collecting Evidence

(a) Introduction

It is impossible to collect comprehensive and reliable statistics in relation to international **6.74** commercial arbitrations, which are often confidential, but it is probably reasonable to assume that in most cases the tribunal's decision depends on the particular facts and provisions of the contract, rather than on the application of relevant principles of law.

It follows that fact-finding is one of the most significant functions of an arbitral tribunal. **6.75** The relevant facts are determined either by evaluating the presentation by the parties of documentary and/or oral evidence, or by arbitral tribunals making their own efforts, with the assistance of the parties to ascertain the evidence that they consider necessary to establish the relevant facts.

(i) Civil law and common law procedures

In court procedures in most common law countries, the initiative for the collection and **6.76** presentation of evidence is almost wholly in the hands of the parties. The judge acts as a kind of referee, to administer the applicable rules of evidence and to give a decision at the end on who has 'won' the argument in a combative sense. The judge listens to the evidence and may question the witnesses; in general, however, common law judges leave it to the parties to present their respective cases and then form a judgment on the basis of what the parties elect to present to the court. By contrast, in the courts of many civil law countries, the judge takes a far more active role in the conduct of the proceedings and in the collection of evidence, including the examination of witnesses.[74]

The impression we may have given by these brief summaries of the two systems is that **6.77** the differences are fundamental. Yet there is a considerable risk of over-generalisation in drawing distinctions, as we have just done, between the so-called common law and civil law systems. Each system has many variations. The rules of procedure in the United States are different from those in England, just as the German and French rules of procedure are different.

Emphasising this point, a Swiss international arbitration specialist stated: **6.78**

> My first remark is that there is no such thing as 'Civil Law procedure' in civil and commercial litigation. In Common Law countries, there are undoubtedly certain common basic principles of procedure, which go back to the procedure practised in the English courts. In continental Europe, there is no such common origin. In each country, one finds a different blend of civil procedure, largely influenced by local custom, the legal education received by judges and by counsel, and, to a varied extent, by the influence of the procedure practised in the old ecclesiastical courts, although such courts were abolished, in Protestant countries, at the time of the Reformation. [...]

---

[74] See the discussion of comparative arbitration practices in (1987) 3 ICCA Congress Series 98. The extent to which the Iran–United States Claims Tribunal took an active role in obtaining evidence is described by Holtzmann, 'Fact-finding by the Iran–United States Claims Tribunal', in Lillich (ed.) *Fact-Finding before International Tribunals: Eleventh Sokol Colloquium* (Transnational, 1991), pp. 106–110.

The result of this is that there is possibly as much difference between the outlook and practice of a French avocat and of a German Rechtsanwalt as between those of an English and of an Italian lawyer. The same applies within my own country, Switzerland, where civil and criminal procedure remain in the realm of the 26 sovereign States of the Confederation, thus leading to the existence of 26 different codes of civil or criminal procedure, plus a Civil Procedure Act for the Federal Supreme Court. There is as much difference between the type of civil procedure practised in Geneva and that practised in Zurich as between those featured in Madrid and Stockholm.

These differences are experienced daily in international arbitration, where they are sometimes the source of great difficulties. Certainly these difficulties are due, to a large extent, to the different patterns of civil procedure law, but, in my experience, to a far greater extent to the undisclosed assumptions and prejudices of municipal lawyers faced for the first time in their lives with a system of which they are not aware. Just to take a simple example, a common lawyer expects the claimant as a matter of course to have the last word at the end of the day, whereas a continental lawyer considers it a requirement of natural justice that the defendant should be the last to address the Court.[75]

6.79   Nevertheless, there is probably just enough uniformity in the usual approach to such matters as the presentation of evidence to justify using the expression 'civil law countries' by way of contrast to the 'common law countries' in the discussion that follows. Where there are differences between the two systems, they are most noticeable in the procedures that lead to fact-finding. The most important elements include the following.

(ii) Admissibility

6.80   In practice, tribunals composed of three experienced international arbitrators from different legal systems approach the question of the reception of evidence in a pragmatic way. Whether they are from common law or civil law countries, they tend to focus on establishing the facts necessary for the determination of the issues between the parties and are reluctant to be limited by technical rules of evidence that might prevent them from achieving this goal. This is especially so where the rules in question were originally designed for use in jury trials, centuries ago, at a time when many jurors were not able to read or write, so that it was necessary for documents to be read aloud at hearings.

6.81   It is essential for practitioners who have been raised in the common law tradition to appreciate this and to learn not to rely overly on technical rules from their own jurisdictions concerning the admissibility of evidence during the course of the proceedings, particularly at witness hearings. Conversely, where all three arbitrators come from the same legal tradition, whether common law or civil law, it is nevertheless sensible for the team of lawyers retained to represent each party to include at least one member who is familiar with the approach to the presentation and reception of evidence that that particular arbitral tribunal is likely to apply.[76]

---

[75] Reymond, 'Part 2: Common law and civil law procedures—Which is the more inquisitorial?' (1989) 55 Arbitration 155, at 159.

[76] Holtzmann, 'Fact-finding by the Iran–United States Claims Tribunal', in Lillich (ed.) *Fact-Finding before International Tribunals: Eleventh Sokol Colloquium* (Transnational, 1991), pp. 118–119. See also Holtzmann, 'Streamlining arbitral proceedings: Some techniques of the Iran–United States Claims Tribunal' (1995) 11 Arb Intl 39; Straus, 'The practice of the Iran–US Claims Tribunal in receiving evidence from parties and from experts' (1986) 3 J Intl Arb 57. See also IBA Rules, Art. 9.1.

(iii) Burden of proof

A question that often arises in an international arbitration is that of knowing which party   **6.82** has the responsibility for proving a particular allegation or set of allegations. The gener- ally accepted answer is that the 'burden of proof' of any particular factual allegation is upon that party which makes the allegation. This is recognised explicitly in Article 27.1 of the UNCITRAL Rules: 'Each party will have the burden of proving the facts relied on to support its claim or defence.' The UNCITRAL Rules then go on to make it clear that this burden of proof may be discharged by the evidence of witnesses, including expert witnesses, or by the production of documents, exhibits, or other evidence, or (of course) by a combination of the two. Further, there are some propositions that are so obvious that proof is not required.[77]

(iv) Standard of proof

The degree of proof that must be achieved in practice before an international arbitral tri-   **6.83** bunal is not capable of precise definition, but it is generally based on the 'balance of prob- ability' standard (that is, 'more likely than not'). This standard is to be distinguished from the concept of 'beyond all reasonable doubt' required, for example, in countries such as the United States and England to prove guilt in a criminal trial before a jury.[78]

The practice of arbitral tribunals in international arbitrations is to assess the weight to be   **6.84** given to the evidence presented in favour of any particular proposition by reference to the nature of the proposition to be proved. For example, if the weather at a particular airport on a particular day is an important element in the factual matrix, it is probably sufficient to produce a copy of a contemporary report from a reputable newspaper, rather than to engage a meteorological expert to advise the tribunal.

In general, the more startling the proposition that a party seeks to prove, the more rigorous   **6.85** the arbitral tribunal will be in requiring that proposition to be fully established. A classic ex- ample of this general rule involves allegations of fraud or illegality. Whilst the standard will remain the 'balance of probabilities', an arbitral tribunal is likely to look even more closely at the evidence to determine whether such a standard has been adequately met. In the words of an English case heard in the (then) House of Lords:

> The civil standard of proof always means more likely than not. The only higher degree
> of probability required by the law is the criminal standard. But, as Lord Nicholls of
> Birkenhead explained in *In re H (Sexual Abuse, Standard of Proof) (Minors)* [1996]
> AC 563 at 586, some things are inherently more likely than others. It would need more
> cogent evidence to satisfy one that the creature seen walking in Regent's Park was
> more likely than not to have been a lioness than to be satisfied to the same standard of

---

[77] One such proposition might be that the earth is an oblate spheroid, although members of the Flat Earth Society would not agree.

[78] In *Parker* (1926) 4 Rep Intl Arb Awards 25, at 39, the Mexican–US General Claims Commission held that, 'when the claimant has established a *prima facie* case and the respondent has offered no evidence in rebuttal the latter may not insist that the former pile up evidence to establish its allegations beyond a reasonable doubt without pointing out some reason for doubting'. See also Eveleigh, Hanotiau, Menzies, Philip, Redfern, Reiner, and Reymond, 'The standards and burden of proof in international arbitration' (1994) 10 Arb Intl 317, at 320–321; Pietrowski, 'Evidence in international arbitration' (2006) 22 Arb Intl 373.

probability that it was an Alsatian. In this basis, cogent evidence is generally required to satisfy a civil tribunal that a person has been fraudulent or behaved in some other reprehensible manner. But the question is always whether the tribunal thinks it more probable than not.[79]

6.86 In deciding what evidence to produce and the means by which it should be presented, the practitioner should therefore make an evaluation of the degree of proof that the tribunal is likely to require before being sufficiently satisfied to make the finding of fact that his or her client is seeking.

(b) Categories of evidence

6.87 The evidence presented to arbitral tribunals on disputed issues of fact may be divided into four categories:

(1) production of contemporaneous documents;
(2) testimony of witnesses of fact (written and/or oral);
(3) opinions of expert witnesses (written and/or oral); and
(4) inspection of the subject matter of the dispute.

These methods may be used, or combined, in many different ways for the purpose of discharging the burden of proof to the standard required by an arbitral tribunal. It is important to recognise that each different arbitral tribunal may adopt a different approach not only to the manner in which it wishes the evidence to be presented, but also to the weight that it is willing to give to any particular type of evidence.

6.88 Modern international arbitral tribunals accord greater weight to the contents of contemporary documents than to written and oral testimony given, possibly years after the event, by witnesses who have obviously been 'prepared' by lawyers representing the parties. In international arbitrations, the best evidence that can be presented in relation to any issue of fact is almost invariably contained in the documents that came into existence at the time of the events giving rise to the dispute.[80]

6.89 Unsurprisingly, the evidence-gathering activity in international arbitrations usually takes place in the period after the facts in dispute have been identified, through the written submissions delivered by the parties, and before the witness hearings begin.

---

[79] *Secretary of State for the Home Department v Rehman* [2001] UKHL 47, at [140]–[141] *per* Lord Hoffmann. (There was a time when there were lions and lionesses in the zoo at Regent's Park, so the creature might then have been a lioness.) See also Partasides, 'Proving corruption in international arbitration: A balanced standard for the real world' (2010) 25 ICSID Rev—Foreign Investment LJ 472.

[80] In two cases before the Iran–United States Claims Tribunal, fact-finding on jurisdictional issues was based entirely on documentary evidence consisting of official documents, corporate documents prepared in the ordinary course of business, publications of which the Tribunal took judicial notice, certificates by independent certified public accountants, and affidavits of corporate officers: see Holtzmann, 'Fact-finding by the Iran–United States Claims Tribunal', in Lillich (ed.) *Fact-Finding before International Tribunals: Eleventh Sokol Colloquium* (Transnational, 1991), pp. 110–114.

(c) Documentary evidence

The parties produce the documents on which they intend to rely at an early stage in an inter- **6.90** national arbitration. This will usually be with their written submissions, which has the merit of placing the principal documents 'on the table' at the earliest practicable moment.

The story becomes more complicated in the context of documents that the parties have **6.91** not chosen to produce voluntarily. The phrase 'culture clash' is overused in the lexicon of modern arbitration, but it often seems appropriate in the context of document production.

It is thus not unusual for US lawyers to come to hearings in European (and other) prom- **6.92** inent arbitration venues carrying with them a belief in the entitlement to 'discovery'[81] of a certain document, or groups of documents. By contrast, in some civil law countries, it may be professional malpractice for a lawyer to disclose such documents to the arbitral tribunal or to the opposing party.[82] The result can be that a huge amount of time and expense is incurred in dealing with disputes concerning document production.

(i) IBA Rules on the Taking of Evidence in International Arbitration
In the late 1990s, building on experience gained from the (not particularly suc- **6.93** cessful) Supplementary Rules Governing the Presentation and Reception of Evidence in International Commercial Arbitration that it had adopted in 1983, the International Bar Association (IBA) embarked on a project to produce a new more 'internationalised' version. This project led to the 1999 edition, entitled the IBA Rules on the Taking of Evidence in International Commercial Arbitration, which became almost universally recognised as the international standard for an effective, pragmatic, and relatively economical document production regime. Following a two-year review process that included a public consultation, a substantially revised version of the Rules (now titled the IBA Rules on the Taking of Evidence in International Arbitration[83] and herein simply 'the IBA Rules') was adopted by the IBA Council on 29 May 2010. The 2010 edition enjoyed wide acceptance such that, in 2019, the IBA created a task force charged with revising the 2010 edition. Given the general satisfaction with the 2010 edition, the task force proposed only modest revisions to the 2010 edition and, on 15 February 2021, the 2020 edition was formally issued. The remainder of this section of the current chapter is therefore presented by reference to the principles and provisions contained in the 2020 edition.[84]

---

[81] The word 'discovery' is a term of art used in the United States and some other common law countries (no longer in England, where the term was abolished under the Civil Procedure Rules 1996) to describe a process whereby the parties (and their lawyers) are legally obliged to produce documents that are 'relevant to the pleaded issues', even if they are prejudicial to that party's case. Subject to any mandatory rules of the *lex arbitri*, or agreement of the parties, the process known as 'discovery' has no place in international arbitration.

[82] Other than where the applicable arbitration rules expressly permit such an order.

[83] The deletion of the word 'Commercial' from their title was intended to reflect the fact that the Rules may be, and indeed already are, applied in both commercial and investment treaty arbitration.

[84] The Preamble to the Rules provides that:

> They are designed to supplement the legal provisions and the institutional, ad hoc or other rules that apply to the conduct of the arbitration [...] Parties and Arbitral Tribunals may adopt the IBA Rules of Evidence, in whole or in part, to govern arbitration proceedings, or they may vary them or use them as guidelines in developing their own procedures. The Rules are not intended to limit the flexibility that is inherent in, and an advantage of, international arbitration, and Parties and Arbitral Tribunals are free to adapt them to the particular circumstances of each arbitration.

6.94 Article 3 of the IBA Rules deals with document production. Its main provisions are as follows:

1. Within the time ordered by the Arbitral Tribunal, each Party shall submit to the Arbitral Tribunal and to the other Parties all Documents available to it on which it relies, including public Documents and those in the public domain, except for any Documents that have already been submitted by another Party.

2. Within the time ordered by the Arbitral Tribunal, any Party may submit to the Arbitral Tribunal and to the other Parties a Request to Produce.

3. A Request to Produce shall contain:
   (a) (i) a description of each requested Document sufficient to identify it, or
       (ii) a description in sufficient detail (including subject matter) of a narrow and specific requested category of Documents that are reasonably believed to exist; in the case of Documents maintained in electronic form, the requesting Party may, or the Arbitral Tribunal may order that it shall be required to, identify specific files, search terms, individuals or other means of searching for such Documents in an efficient and economical manner;
   (b) a statement as to how the Documents requested are relevant to the case and material to its outcome; and
   (c) (i) a statement that the Documents requested are not in the possession, custody or control of the requesting Party or a statement of the reasons why it would be unreasonably burdensome for the requesting Party to produce such Documents, and
       (ii) a statement of the reasons why the requesting Party assumes the Documents requested are in the possession, custody or control of another Party.

4. Within the time ordered by the Arbitral Tribunal, the Party to whom the Request to Produce is addressed shall produce to the other Parties and, if the Arbitral Tribunal so orders, to it, all the Documents requested in its possession, custody or control as to which it makes no objection.

   [...]

6.95 These provisions are admirably clear and self-explanatory. They establish the principle, referred to earlier, that the parties should produce the evidentiary documents on which they rely as the first stage. They make provision for requests by each party to the other(s) for further documents, with appropriate limitations. The most significant limitation is in the expression 'relevant to the case and material to its outcome' in Article 3.3.b, which is considered further later in this chapter.[85]

Article 1 of the Rules further includes various provisions aimed at resolving conflicts between the Rules, mandatory provisions of law, and the institutional, ad hoc, or other rules that apply to the conduct of the arbitration.

[85] See paragraph 6.103. This formulation (introduced in the 2010 edition) was intended to be a clarification, rather than a modification, of the criteria under the 1999 Rules, which required a document to be 'relevant and material to the outcome of the case'. The change of wording is not mentioned in the IBA Commentary on the 2010 Rules: Ashford, *The IBA Rules on the Taking of Evidence in International Arbitration: A Guide* (Cambridge

Most legal practitioners are accustomed to the obligation to satisfy a court, or arbitral tri-   **6.96**
bunal, as to the question of relevance of documents or other information that they are
seeking from the opposing party. But the requirement of showing 'materiality' to the outcome of the case is an increased burden. It also enables arbitral tribunals to deny document
requests where, although the requested documents would generally be relevant, they consider that their production will not affect the outcome of the proceedings.

Dealing with disputed document production requests can be a laborious and time-   **6.97**
consuming process for all concerned, and different arbitral tribunals adopt various techniques to cut through the detail involved in resolving such disputed requests. Article 3 of the
IBA Rules (to continue the extract set out above), contains the following relevant provisions:

> […]
> 5. If the Party to whom the Request to Produce is addressed has an objection to some or
>   all of the Documents requested, it shall state the objection in writing to the Arbitral
>   Tribunal and the other Parties within the time ordered by the Arbitral Tribunal. The
>   reasons for such objection shall be any of those set forth in Article 9.2[86] or a failure to
>   satisfy any of the requirements of Article 3.3.
> 6. Upon receipt of any such objection, the Arbitral Tribunal may invite the relevant Parties
>   to consult with each other with a view to resolving the objection.
> 7. Either Party may, within the time ordered by the Arbitral Tribunal, request the Arbitral
>   Tribunal to rule on the objection. The Arbitral Tribunal shall then, in consultation
>   with the Parties and in timely fashion, consider the Request to Produce and the ob-
>   jection. The Arbitral Tribunal may order the Party to whom such Request is addressed
>   to produce any requested Document in its possession, custody or control as to which
>   the Arbitral Tribunal determines that *(i)* the issues that the requesting Party wishes to
>   prove are relevant to the case and material to its outcome; *(ii)* none of the reasons for
>   objection set forth in Article 9.2 applies; and *(iii)* the requirements of Article 3.3 have
>   been satisfied. Any such Document shall be produced to the other Parties and, if the
>   Arbitral Tribunal so orders, to it.
> […]

University Press, 2013), paras P-5–P-38. See also Kläsener, 'The duty of good faith in the 2010 IBA Rules on the
Taking of Evidence in International Arbitration' (2010) 13 Intl Arb LR 160.

[86] Article 9.2 states:
> 2. The Arbitral Tribunal shall, at the request of a Party or on its own motion, exclude from evidence or
>   production any Document, statement, oral testimony or inspection for any of the following reasons:
>   (a) lack of sufficient relevance to the case or materiality to its outcome;
>   (b) legal impediment or privilege under the legal or ethical rules determined by the Arbitral Tribunal
>   to be applicable;
>   (c) unreasonable burden to produce the requested evidence;
>   (d) loss or destruction of the Document that has been shown with reasonable likelihood to have
>   occurred;
>   (e) grounds of commercial or technical confidentiality that the Arbitral Tribunal determines to be
>   compelling;
>   (f) grounds of special political or institutional sensitivity (including evidence that has been classified
>   as secret by a government or a public international institution) that the Arbitral Tribunal deter-
>   mines to be compelling; or
>   (g) considerations of procedural economy, proportionality, fairness or equality of the Parties that the
>   Arbitral Tribunal determines to be compelling.

(ii) The Redfern Schedule

6.98   The IBA Rules, as we have seen, suggest (at Article 3.6) that faced with an objection to a request for production of documents, the arbitral tribunal should ask the parties to try to settle their differences before asking the tribunal itself to intervene. In practice, the parties' counsel will almost certainly have been engaged, often for weeks or months, in discussions and correspondence about their respective Requests for Production of Documents, before any reference is made to the tribunal. Requests for production have become a prominent part of the evidentiary process in international arbitration, with each party hoping to find documents in the control or possession of the opposing party that will either help the requesting party's case or damage that of its opponent. There may be no 'smoking gun', but there may still be documents (internal memoranda, for example) that throw a different light on the case from that shown by the documents or witness statements previously put forward by the party that is now trying to resist disclosure.

6.99   In consequence, the search for such documents is often a protracted process, with lengthy exchanges between counsel in their respective requests for production of documents by their opponents. During the course of these exchanges, some requests may have been agreed in whole or in part, others may have been modified or withdrawn, others still may have been added to the list, as fresh information emerged as to the type of documentary information potentially available. Only when a final impasse has been reached, with each party feeling that it has gone as far as it reasonably can in complying with the requests for production, will a reference to the tribunal become necessary.

6.100   It is at this stage that the Redfern Schedule is likely to come into play. The schedule was designed in the year 2000,[87] as a convenient tool for addressing disputed requests for the production of documents in an ongoing international arbitration. Counsel for the parties, three major oil companies, had spent several months in correspondence and discussions about their respective requests for production of documents, with the picture changing constantly as some requests were met, others were withdrawn, and others still were added to each party's lists. Finally, when the parties' counsel had done all they could to reach agreement, the arbitral tribunal was given an agreed bundle of emails and memoranda, and asked to rule on the remaining disputed requests.

6.101   The first problem for the arbitral tribunal was to find out from the ebb and flow of the communications between the parties, what precisely were the requests on which it was expected to make a ruling? It would take considerable time for the tribunal itself to do this. Accordingly, it was proposed that each requesting party should draw up a schedule showing in the first column what documents it wanted to see, which it believed were in the possession or control of the other party; and in the second column, why it thought that these documents were relevant to the case and material to its outcome. This schedule would then be passed to the opposing party's counsel who would complete a third column, stating why there was an objection to production of the documents

---

[87]   It was given its title, somewhat jocularly, by the presiding arbitrator in the international arbitration for which it was devised. See 'The Redfern Schedule' in the ICCA Review of April 2013, 'Efficiency in Arbitration', pp. 9 and 12.

requested—for instance, because they were not considered to be relevant, or because they could not be found, or because they were protected by legal professional privilege—and so forth. Then and only then would the schedule be forwarded to the tribunal for its decision on the disputed requests.

The purpose of the Redfern Schedule, then, is to crystallise the precise issues in dispute in relation to the production of documents so that the arbitral tribunal knows the position that the parties have reached following the various exchanges between them.[88] This makes it possible for the arbitral tribunal to make an informed decision as to whether or not a particular document, or class of documents, should be produced, without becoming involved in the details of the exchanges between the parties' lawyers.   **6.102**

To achieve this purpose, a schedule with at least four columns is drawn up. Each column of the schedule is intended to be completed as briefly as possible by the parties' lawyers.   **6.103**

- In the first column, the 'requesting party' sets out (a) a brief description of the requested document in sufficient detail to identify it, or (b) a description in sufficient detail to identify a narrow and specific category of documents that are reasonably believed to exist.
- In the second column, the requesting party states why the requested document(s) are both relevant to the case and material to its outcome, as well as the statements required by Article 3.3.c.i and ii of the IBA Rules.
- In the third column, the requested party states the extent to which, if at all, it is prepared to accede to the request, and if it objects, the grounds on which it does so.[89]
- The fourth column is left blank for the arbitral tribunal's decision.

Although this organisation of the Redfern Schedule remains common, it is not set in stone, and some tribunals request the parties to organise the schedule so that the columns referenced above are presented instead as rows.[90]

In most cases, the arbitral tribunal should be able to make a decision on the disputed requests on the basis of the information set out in the schedule. However, if the tribunal considers   **6.104**

---

[88] The requirement to present document requests in the form of a Redfern Schedule is usually set out in the first procedural order, as part of the 'ground rules' for the arbitration: see the ICC Report on the 'Effective Management of Arbitration' mentioned below. The first report by the ICC Commission on the Redfern Schedule was published in November 2007 and entitled 'Techniques for Controlling Time and Costs in Arbitration'; it suggested that one way of managing requests for production of documents efficiently was by 'using the Schedule of Document Production devised by Alan Redfern and often referred to as the Redfern Schedule, in the form of a chart containing the following four columns' (which were then listed): see ICC Publication No. 843 at p. 32. In the later ICC Commission's Report on 'Effective Management of Arbitration', published in 2014, the advice was shortened to read: 'Consider the ground rules to be adopted for implementing document production, including the use of a Redfern Schedule and the setting of the shortest reasonable time frames for production': see ICC Publication No. 866 at p. 36.

[89] As a further efficiency in the use of Redfern schedules, VV Veeder KC (who seems to have been the first arbitrator to bring the Schedule into the public domain) proposed a set of 'Veeder codes', in the form of abbreviations of the reasons for objection set out in IBA Rules, Art. 3.5, for use in the drafting of objections to documents requests made in Redfern Schedules. For example, where the requested party objects on the grounds that the requested document is not material to the outcome of the case (pursuant to Arts 3.3.b and 9.2.a), it would enter the code 'M' in the third column of the Redfern Schedule; where the requested party objects on the basis that the request is excessively broad (pursuant to Art. 3.3.a.ii), it would enter the code 'B'.

[90] See, e.g., *Global Telecom Holding S.A.E. v Canada*, ICSID Case No. ARB/16/16, Procedural Order No. 1, 13 July 2017, at [15.2], Annex B. This organisation of the Redfern Schedule is referred to as the 'Stern format'.

that the schedule as it stands does not contain sufficient information for it to make a properly informed decision, it will either (a) call for additional information, or (b) hold a procedural hearing with the parties' counsel (perhaps a 'case review conference') to explore, for instance, the validity of an objection on the grounds of legal professional privilege or to discuss some of the disputed claims in more detail. Once the tribunal has made its decisions on all of the disputed requests, the documentary disclosure phase of the arbitration should be over.

6.105   It is apparent from what has been said above that, as with much else in an international arbitration, the process depends for its proper and fair operation on the integrity of counsel for the parties. But if, for instance, a witness at a hearing referred to documents that had previously been said to have been destroyed, the tribunal would need a very good explanation from counsel before drawing an inference adverse both to that counsel and to the party they represented.[91]

(iii) The Prague Rules

6.106   Before turning to other issues concerning documentary evidence, it is worth noting the 'Rules on the Efficient Conduct of Proceedings in International Arbitration' (or the 'Prague Rules'), which were developed because of a concern that international arbitration was being 'Americanised' and that there was a common law bias in the IBA Rules.[92] The Prague Rules are put forward as an attempt to give a more 'civil law' flavour to international arbitral procedure. They attempt to do so, amongst other things, by encouraging arbitral tribunals to play a more proactive role in establishing the facts of the case, and by encouraging the parties to 'avoid any form of document production [requests], including e-discovery'.[93] However, the Prague Rules do allow for document production requests if the requesting party satisfies the arbitral tribunal at the outset of the proceedings that 'document production may be needed',[94] and it is not yet apparent at the time of writing whether the Prague Rules are having a significant effect in reducing document production requests in many international arbitrations.

(iv) Production of electronic documents

6.107   International arbitral tribunals generally place more reliance on contemporary documentary evidence than on witness statements written years later for the purpose of the arbitration, which often betray a distinct harmony of views. It is therefore not surprising that there has been much discussion concerning the ways in which electronically stored documents may, or should, be used in international arbitration.

6.108   If we take as the starting point what happens in civil law countries, it is probably broadly correct to say that there is generally no obligation on the parties to produce documents other than those on which they rely (unless, exceptionally, the judge orders a party to produce documents as part of his or her investigation of the facts). It follows that, in many civil

---

[91] See paragraph 6.116 below. See also Chapter 5.

[92] *Is it time for a change?*, Prague Rules Website, 20 April 2017, available online at https://praguerules.com/news/is-it-time-for-a-change-/; *Prague Rules* (Draft of 1 September 2018), Note from the Working Group.

[93] Prague Rules, Arts 3 and 4.

[94] Prague Rules, Art. 4.3. In such circumstances, 'a party may request the arbitral tribunal to order another party to produce a specific document which: a. is relevant and material to the outcome of the case; b. is not in the public domain; and c. is in the possession of another party or within its power or control'. Prague Rules, Art. 4.5.

law systems, the existence of many hundreds of thousands of pages of electronically stored documents relating to a transaction does not give rise to practical problems.

However, in many common law countries, the rules of procedure in the law courts place **6.109** an obligation on the parties to disclose all documents 'relevant' to the issues in dispute. The sheer scale of complying with this obligation may place an intolerable burden in terms of cost and effort not only on the producing party, but also on the opposing party, and on the judges who have to make the findings of fact on which their judgments are based. For proceedings in the common law courts, a partial solution to this problem was developed in the form of the so-called Sedona Principles,[95] which are aimed primarily at limiting to a reasonable level the extent of the resources that parties may be obliged to expend in identifying documents that might be required to be disclosed in litigation.

Techniques to limit the burden of searching for relevant documents making use of artificial **6.110** intelligence are now frequently relied upon by lawyers. For example, several electronic discovery software products offer technology that can be used to segregate for lawyers' review information that is likely to be relevant from that which is likely to be irrelevant.[96] Similarly, 'Technology-Assisted Review' or predictive coding, in which 'a computer learns to distinguish relevant from non-relevant documents based on the coding [that is, relevancy decisions] of human reviewers and can then classify unlabeled documents on its own'[97] is widely available. It is likely that the use of such techniques will become commonplace in international arbitrations.

As stated earlier in this chapter,[98] rules of court do not apply in international arbitrations **6.111** unless either the parties agree to adopt them or, exceptionally, the arbitral tribunal should for some reason seek to impose them by a procedural direction.[99] It follows that, absent agreement of the parties, the basis for production of documents is in the discretion of the arbitral tribunal.

It is therefore appropriate to assess the question of electronic production against the back- **6.112** ground of the current version of the IBA Rules, by which many tribunals will today be guided in the exercise of their discretion. First, the IBA Rules define the term 'document' as 'a writing, communication, picture, drawing, program or data of any kind, whether recorded or maintained on paper or by electronic, audio, visual or any other means'.[100]

---

[95] *Best Practices, Recommendations and Principles for Addressing Electronic Document Production* (3rd edn, 2018), named after The Sedona Conference (held at the Sedona Hilton in the United States). The first edition of the Principles published in 2004 clearly inspired the conclusions reached by the Cresswell Committee in England, whose report in turn led to a Practice Direction under the English Civil Procedure Rules, Pt. 31, and, later, to an amendment of the FRCP. See also Hedges, 'Litigation lessons? US Federal Rules of Civil Procedure, The Sedona Principles, and Part 31 of the English Civil Procedure Rules', in Howell (ed.) *Electronic Disclosure in International Arbitration* (JurisNet, 2008), pp. 107–117.

[96] EDRM, *The Use of Artificial Intelligence in eDiscovery*, February 2021, p. 5.

[97] Ibid. at p. 4.

[98] See paragraph 6.01.

[99] Which would generally be inappropriate unless both parties come from the seat of the arbitration, in which case the arbitration would not, in fact, be an *international* arbitration.

[100] IBA Rules, Definitions. The Introduction to the Sedona Principles defines ESI as including:

> email, web pages, word processing files, audio and video files, images, computer databases [...] including but not limited to servers, desktops, laptops, cell phones, hard drives, flash drives, PDAs and MP3 players. Technically, information is 'electronic' if it exists in a medium that can only be read through the use of computers. Such media include cache memory, magnetic disks (such as computer hard drives or floppy disks), optical disks (such as DVDs or CDs), and magnetic tapes.

6.113 In the context of production of documents pursuant to Article 3 of the IBA Rules, it seems clear that there is no difference in principle between 'hard copy' documents and 'soft copy' documents. It follows that the same general criteria should apply to the approach by arbitral tribunals to resolving disputes between the parties as to whether or not they should order the production of requested documents. The most important of these are 'unreasonable burden', 'proportionality', and 'considerations of procedural economy, fairness or equality'. To a certain extent, these elements are intertwined. It is for the arbitral tribunal to weigh the 'materiality to the outcome' against 'proportionality' (including the cost and burden involved in complying with the contemplated procedural order).[101]

(v) Documents in the possession of third parties

6.114 An arbitral tribunal lacks power to order production of documents in the possession of a third party even where such documents may be relevant to the matters in issue. However, in some countries, a third party may be compelled by subpoena to attend at the hearings to give evidence and the courts can assist the arbitral tribunal in enforcing the attendance of such witnesses. In England, a party may apply to a court to compel the attendance of a witness who is within the jurisdiction of the court and to bring with him or her any material documents in his or her possession.[102] Similarly in the United States, the Federal Arbitration Act of 1925 (FAA) provides that the arbitrators may summon a person to attend before them and to produce any material documents.[103] However, following the US Supreme Court's decision in *ZF Automotive US, Inc. v Luxshare, Ltd. and AlixPartners LLP v Fund for Protection Investors' Rights in Foreign States*, it will—in most circumstances—no longer be possible to obtain discovery from third parties in the United States in support of foreign arbitration proceedings pursuant to section 1782 of Title 28 of the US Code.

6.115 It sometimes happens in arbitration proceedings that a third party appears voluntarily at the request of one of the parties to provide testimony helpful to that party. On questioning by the other party's counsel, the witness may then object to the production of requested documents. While the arbitral tribunal may not have the power to order such a third party to produce documents, it may draw an adverse inference in respect of the evidence of the witness in question if it appears to the tribunal that the witness is withholding documents without good reason.

As the definition of 'Documents' contained in the 1999 edition of the IBA Rules was sufficiently broad to encompass most forms of ESI, it was decided that minor changes would be made in the 2010 edition to ensure that all known forms of ESI evidence would be subject to the IBA Rules: 1999 IBA Working Party and 2010 IBA Rules of Evidence Review Subcommittee, 'Commentary on the Revised Text of the 2010 IBA Rules on the Taking of Evidence in International Arbitration' (2011) 5(1) DRI 45, at 49.

[101] In respect of the production of electronic documents, the power of the tribunal under IBA Rules, Art. 3.3.a.ii, to require a requesting party to 'identify specific files, search terms, individuals or other means of searching for such Documents in an efficient and economical manner' provides a way in which to reduce the burden imposed on a requested party. See also Art. 3.12.b (a party need produce electronic documents only 'in the form most convenient or economical to it that is reasonably usable by the recipients') and c. (a party is not required to produce 'multiple copies of Documents which are essentially identical'). See also Smit, 'E-disclosure under the Revised IBA Rules on the Taking of Evidence in International Arbitration' (2010) 13 Intl Arb L Rev 201.

[102] English Arbitration Act 1996, s. 43.

[103] US FAA, § 7.

(vi) Adverse inferences

A technique followed by arbitral tribunals coming from different systems and cultures is to draw an 'adverse inference' from the silence of a party, or failure to comply with an order of the arbitral tribunal for the production of documentary or witness evidence.[104] This is covered in Article 9.6 and 9.7 of the IBA Rules, which state: **6.116**

> 6. If a Party fails without satisfactory explanation to produce any Document requested in a Request to Produce to which it has not objected in due time or fails to produce any Document ordered to be produced by the Arbitral Tribunal, the Arbitral Tribunal may infer that such document would be adverse to the interests of that Party.
> 7. If a Party fails without satisfactory explanation to make available any other relevant evidence, including testimony, sought by one Party to which the Party to whom the request was addressed has not objected in due time or fails to make available any evidence, including testimony, ordered by the Arbitral Tribunal to be produced, the Arbitral Tribunal may infer that such evidence would be adverse to the interests of that Party.

In this way, two important limitations apply where the IBA Rules are applicable. The first is that there must have been an order of the arbitral tribunal for production of the documents or other testimony concerned; the second is that the requested party must have failed to provide a 'satisfactory explanation' for not having produced the material in question.[105] Whether or not an explanation to the effect that the material 'does not exist' or 'no longer exists' is satisfactory is a matter for the arbitral tribunal to decide after taking all of the relevant circumstances into consideration. **6.117**

For example, if a document had been destroyed before the dispute arose, pursuant to a well-established (and reasonable) corporate document retention policy, many arbitral tribunals would consider such an explanation to be reasonable. However, if a document had been destroyed soon after a new document retention policy had been implemented, particularly if the policy was devised after the dispute arose, it would not be surprising if the tribunal were to take a sceptical view of the explanation. **6.118**

(vii) Presentation of documents

It is of considerable assistance to the arbitral tribunal if the parties are able to present the documentary evidence in the form of a volume (or volumes) of documents, in chronological order, with each page numbered like those of a book, for use at the hearing. In this way, each member of the arbitral tribunal, and each party, has a complete set of documents with identical numbering. If there is a huge number of documents, it may be sensible to identify the most important documents and to include them in a separate volume or volumes (sometimes known as a 'core bundle'). **6.119**

---

[104] The Iran–United States Claims Tribunal drew adverse inferences from the silence of a party in the face of alleged breach or non-performance of the contract when some complaint would have been expected, and from failure of a party to mention a point in a contract or in contemporaneous correspondence consistent with that party's position in the arbitration: Holtzmann, 'Fact-finding by the Iran–United States Claims Tribunal', in Lillich (ed.) *Fact-Finding before International Tribunals: Eleventh Sokol Colloquium* (Transnational, 1991), pp. 126–127.

[105] The Prague Rules, too, address the issue of adverse inferences. Article 10 of the Prague Rules provides that '[i]f a party does not comply with the arbitral tribunal's order(s) or instruction(s), without justifiable grounds, the arbitral tribunal may draw, where it considers appropriate, an adverse inference with regard to such party's respective case or issue'. Thus the same limitations to an arbitral tribunal's power to draw an adverse inference that exist under the IBA Rules, also apply when the Prague Rules are applicable.

6.120   It is increasingly common for arbitral tribunals to request the parties to prepare hyper-linked versions of their written submissions, and hyperlinked indices of the fact evidence and legal authorities placed in the record by the parties. Such hyperlinked documents allow the tribunal members to navigate easily between documents at the hearing, and often prove useful to the arbitral tribunal while it is writing its award.[106] Arbitral tribunals and parties may also find utility in arranging for an 'electronic hearing bundle' which is an organised collection of the electronic documents sought to be relied upon at the hearing. There now exist several document-sharing platforms that support electronic bundles.[107]

6.121   The use of the word 'agreed' in the context of volumes of documents occasionally gives rise to misunderstanding. The word is not intended to indicate that the parties are agreed on the meaning of the contents of the document, or its evidentiary weight, or even its admissibility. It simply indicates that the authenticity of the document is 'agreed' in the sense that each party agrees that it is an accurate copy of an existing document.

6.122   When the authenticity of documents is disputed, the arbitral tribunal usually orders that the originals (or certified copies, when appropriate) must be produced for inspection.[108] This may be carried out by forensic experts, if necessary. If the originals are not produced, the arbitral tribunal may disregard the documents in question as unreliable.

(viii)   Translations
6.123   It is usually necessary to provide translations of any documents that are not already in the language of the arbitration. Such translations should, if possible, be submitted to the arbitral tribunal jointly by the parties as 'agreed translations'. The most convenient practice is to include the document in its original language first, immediately following it in the volume with the translation (of the relevant extract if the document is lengthy) into the language of the arbitration.[109] If the correctness of the translation is disputed, each party's version may be inserted following the original and the tribunal may involve an expert translator of its own to resolve such a dispute.

(d)   Fact witness evidence

6.124   The role of fact witnesses is to explain or supplement the evidentiary documents, so as to help the arbitral tribunal to perform its fact-finding function. In commercial transactions, as compared with accident cases, for example, most of the witnesses are likely to have had some connection with the transaction on one side or the other. They therefore tend to have a direct or indirect interest in the outcome of the case.[110] It is perhaps not surprising that

---

[106] Such documents should ordinarily be 'readable' (that is, be the subject of optical character recognition) so that users can search for particular words or phrases in the document.

[107] See ICC Note to Parties and Arbitral Tribunals on the Conduct of the Arbitration under the ICC Rules of Arbitration, para. 107.

[108] IBA Rules, Art. 3.12.a.

[109] IBA Rules, Art. 3.12.d.

[110] Although this does not mean that fact witnesses are inclined deliberately to misrepresent facts to an arbitral tribunal, it is worth noting that studies have shown that 'taking a particular perspective *after* an event is encoded

most arbitral tribunals regard the testimony of fact witnesses as generally less reliable than the contemporaneous documents, brought into existence at the time of the events that gave rise to the dispute, particularly when their written witness statements bear a striking resemblance to each other.

Article 4 of the IBA Rules deals with the presentation of fact witness evidence. It provides, **6.125** in part, as follows:

1. Within the time ordered by the Arbitral Tribunal, each Party shall identify the witnesses on whose testimony it intends to rely and the subject matter of that testimony.
2. Any person may present evidence as a witness, including a Party or a Party's officer, employee or other representative.
3. It shall not be improper for a Party, its officers, employees, legal advisors or other representatives to interview its witnesses or potential witnesses and to discuss their prospective testimony with them.
4. The Arbitral Tribunal may order each Party to submit within a specified time to the Arbitral Tribunal and to the other Parties Witness Statements by each witness on whose testimony it intends to rely, except for those witnesses whose testimony is sought pursuant to Articles 4.9 or 4.10. If Evidentiary Hearings are organised into separate issues or phases (such as jursidiction, preliminary determinations, liability or damages), the Arbitral Tribunal or the Parties by agreement may schedule the submission of Witness Statements separately for each issue or phase.
5. Each Witness Statement shall contain:
   (a) the full name and address of the witness, a statement regarding his or her present and past relationship (if any) with any of the Parties, and a description of his or her background, qualifications, training and experience, if such a description may be relevant to the dispute or to the contents of the statement;
   (b) a full and detailed description of the facts, and the source of the witness's information as to those facts, sufficient to serve as that witness's evidence in the matter in dispute. Documents on which the witness relies that have not already been submitted shall be provided;
   (c) a statement as to the language in which the Witness Statement was originally prepared and the language in which the witness anticipates giving testimony at the Evidentiary Hearing;
   (d) an affirmation of the truth of the Witness Statement; and
   (e) the signature of the witness and its date and place.
   […]
7. If a witness whose appearance has been requested pursuant to Article 8.1 fails without a valid reason to appear for testimony at an Evidentiary Hearing, the Arbitral Tribunal shall disregard any Witness Statement related to that Evidentiary Hearing by that witness unless, in exceptional circumstances, the Arbitral Tribunal decides otherwise.

into memory can bias later recall of that event towards the biased perspective.' ICC Commission Report: The Accuracy of Fact Witness Memory in International Arbitration, p. 38.

8. If the appearance of a witness has not been requested pursuant to Article 8.1, none of the other Parties shall be deemed to have agreed to the correctness of the content of the Witness Statement.[111]

[...]

In effect, this scheme codifies the procedures that have been developed by international arbitrators and arbitral institutions over the years,[112] during which it has gradually become common practice to present the direct testimony of fact witnesses in writing in advance of the witness hearing.

(i) Presentation of witness evidence

6.126   The IBA Rules requires each party to indicate to the arbitral tribunal which of the other party's witnesses should be required to attend the hearing for oral examination, and the arbitral tribunal may itself indicates to the parties which, if any, of the other witnesses it wishes to hear in person.[113] The 2020 IBA Rules have introduced a new provision which makes clear that even if the parties agree that a witness statement shall serve as that witness's direct testimony, the arbitral tribunal 'may nevertheless permit further oral direct testimony'.[114] This new provision allows a witness to give oral evidence even when not called for cross-examination by the other party. Although it is relatively rare for the arbitral tribunal to require a witness to be present if neither party requires that witness to attend, the arbitral tribunal has the power to do so.[115]

6.127   The Prague Rules adopt a slightly different approach to the presentation of witnesses, and by default allow for the arbitral tribunal to determine which of the witnesses it wishes to hear in person. Specifically, Article 5.2 of the Prague Rules provides: 'The arbitral tribunal, after having heard the parties, will decide which witnesses are to be called for examination during the hearing [...]'.[116]

(ii) Preparation of witnesses

6.128   An important aspect of the presentation of witness evidence is the question of whether, and if so, to what extent, it is permissible for a party, its employees, or counsel to interview and prepare those witnesses whose testimony they intend to present to the arbitral tribunal. This is largely a cultural matter, although the rules of some national courts (and/or bar associations) forbid, or make it unethical for, parties or their counsel to contact witnesses before they give their testimony in person.[117]

---

[111]   This provision and Art. 8.1 are intended to save on time and expense by requiring witnesses to attend only where they are requested to do so, and by providing that a witness statement is not deemed to be accepted by the other parties in the absence of any such request (whether by agreement or otherwise): 1999 IBA Working Party and 2010 IBA Rules of Evidence Review Subcommittee, 'Commentary on the Revised Text of the 2010 IBA Rules on the Taking of Evidence in International Arbitration' (2011) 5(1) DRI 45, at 64–66; Ashford, *The IBA Rules on the Taking of Evidence in International Arbitration: A Guide* (Cambridge University Press, 2013), paras 4-13–4-14.

[112]   See, e.g., LCIA Rules, Art. 20; SIAC Rules, r. 25.

[113]   Article 8.3 provides that the right to call witnesses is subject to the tribunal's power to exclude any appearance that it considers to be 'irrelevant, immaterial, unreasonably burdensome, duplicative or otherwise covered by a reason for objection set forth in Articles 9.2 or 9.3'.

[114]   IBA Rules, Art. 8.5.

[115]   See also IBA Rules, Arts 3.10 and 8.5.

[116]   Prague Rules, Art. 5.2.

[117]   See the paper presented by Doak Bishop at the 2012 ICCA Congress held in Singapore in the context of a panel discussion on the merits of uniform ethical regulation of international arbitration. See also Bishop and

In international arbitration, it is well recognised that witnesses may be interviewed and **6.129** prepared prior to giving their oral testimony.[118] This is confirmed by at least three of the sets of institutional rules in common use. The LCIA Rules expressly permit it, subject to any mandatory provisions of any law governing the arbitration, other rules of law, or an order of the tribunal to the contrary,[119] and the Swiss Rules and the SIAC Rules also permit such contact.[120] Article 4.3 of the IBA Rules also provides: 'It shall not be improper for a Party, its officers, employees, legal advisors or other representatives to interview its witnesses or potential witnesses and to discuss their prospective testimony with them.'[121] However, it is generally accepted that there are certain limits. It would be professional misconduct if a lawyer were to try to persuade a fact witness to tell a story that both the lawyer and the witness know to be untrue, and to prepare the witness to make such a story sound as credible as possible.[122] It would also almost always be counterproductive. Experienced arbitral tribunals tend to have good 'noses' for sniffing out inaccuracies in stories told by witnesses, and invariably cross-check oral testimony against the available corroborative documentary and other evidence.

(iii) Parties as witnesses

Another cultural division arises between lawyers from jurisdictions in which a party is not **6.130** allowed to be called as a 'witness'. This stems from the rules of court in some civil law countries under which a person (or officer, or employee, in the case of corporate entities) cannot be treated as a witness in his or her own cause.[123] However, even in the courts of these countries, a party can be heard; the rule merely forbids him or her from being categorised as a 'witness'.

As in the case of other rules of national court procedure, this rule does not apply in inter- **6.131** national arbitrations,[124] unless the parties have expressly agreed that such rules should be applied. It may be that an arbitral tribunal will tend to give greater weight to the testimony

---

Stevens, 'The compelling need for a code of ethics in international arbitration: Transparency, integrity and legitimacy' (2011) 15 ICCA Congress Series 391, at 394.

[118] Blackaby, 'Witness preparation: A key to effective advocacy in international arbitration' (2010) 15 ICCA Congress Series 118.

[119] LCIA Rules, Art. 20.6.

[120] Swiss Rules, Art. 27.3; SIAC Rules, r. 25.5.

[121] The final phrase, 'and to discuss their prospective testimony with them', was introduced in the 2010 edition to clarify 'that such an interview need not remain general, but may indeed relate to the subject-matter of the prospective testimony': 1999 IBA Working Party and 2010 IBA Rules of Evidence Review Subcommittee, 'Commentary on the Revised Text of the 2010 IBA Rules on the Taking of Evidence in International Arbitration' (2011) 5(1) DRI 45, at 63–64; Ashford, *The IBA Rules on the Taking of Evidence in International Arbitration: A Guide* (Cambridge University Press, 2013), paras 4-7–4-8. See also the IBA Guidelines on Party Representation, Guideline 24, which similarly provides that: 'A Party Representative […] may meet or interact with Witnesses and Experts in order to discuss and prepare their prospective testimony.' See also the UNCITRAL Notes, para. 90. However, in exercise of its discretion under IBA Rules, Art. 9.1, a tribunal may take into account extensive interviewing and preparation in determining the weight that it will accord to a witness's evidence.

[122] See the IBA Guidelines on Party Representation, Guidelines 26 and 27. See also LCIA Rules, Annex.

[123] Germany is a significant example, followed by countries in which the code of civil procedure broadly follows the German tradition, such as Austria and the Czech Republic. See also 1999 IBA Working Party, fn. 121, at 63.

[124] IBA Rules, Art. 4.2.

of a witness who has no financial or other interest in the outcome of the arbitration, but that is a different question.[125]

(iv) Admissibility and weight of witness evidence

6.132   The rules concerning admissibility of witness testimony are, in principle, the same for written testimony as those that are applied to witnesses when they are giving oral testimony at a hearing before the arbitral tribunal.[126] In practice, it is rare for an arbitral tribunal to order written witness testimony to be withdrawn as inadmissible; rather, an arbitral tribunal is far more likely to address such issues as a matter of the evidentiary weight to be accorded the contents of the witness evidence concerned.

6.133   An arbitral tribunal has discretion to determine the evidentiary weight to be given to witness evidence.[127] This arises from the general principles applicable to arbitration proceedings and is expressly affirmed, for example, in Article 27.4 of the UNCITRAL Rules.[128]

6.134   In general, arbitral tribunals tend to give less weight to uncorroborated witness testimony than to evidence contained in contemporaneous documents. This is not altogether surprising given recent scientific studies on the fallibility of human memory. For example, a recent ICC Report on the 'Accuracy of Fact Witness Memory in International Arbitration' notes that '[s]cientific studies and human experience show that witness memory is imperfect and is subject to possible distorting influences as soon as it is formed'.[129] Mr Justice Legatt has similarly observed that '[a]n obvious difficulty which affects allegations and oral evidence based on recollection of events which occurred several years ago is the unreliability of human memory', and that 'the best approach for a judge to adopt in the trial of a commercial case is, in my view, to place little if any reliance at all on a witness's recollections of what was said in meetings and conversations'.[130] He has added that '[t]his does not mean that oral testimony serves no useful purpose […] its value lies, as I see it, in the opportunity which cross-examination affords to subject the documentary record to critical scrutiny and to gauge the personality, motivations and working practices of a witness, rather than in testimony of what the witness recalls of particular conversations and events'.[131] Legatt's observations are likely to be shared by many international arbitrators, and that is no doubt why arbitral tribunals give greater weight to the evidence of a witness that has been tested by cross-examination, or by an examination by the arbitral tribunal itself. Arbitral tribunals usually reject any submission that they should not hear the evidence of any particular witness, even if it is secondary or 'hearsay' evidence. However, an arbitral tribunal will give less weight to secondary evidence if, in its opinion, the party calling that evidence could have produced a witness who would have been able to give direct first-hand evidence on the factual issue in question.

---

[125] 1999 IBA Working Party, fn. 121, at 63.

[126] See paragraphs 6.80–6.81.

[127] IBA Rules, Art. 9.1. The practice of the Iran–United States Claims Tribunal concerning the weight to be given to affidavits is discussed by Holtzmann, 'Fact-finding by the Iran–United States Claims Tribunal', in Lillich (ed.) *Fact-Finding before International Tribunals: Eleventh Sokol Colloquium* (Transnational, 1991), pp. 113–114.

[128] See also, e.g., LCIA Rules, Art. 22.1.vi; Swiss Rules, Art. 26.1; SCC Rules, Art. 31.1; HKIAC Rules, Art. 22.1.

[129] ICC Commission Report, *The Accuracy of Fact Witness Memory in International Arbitration: Current Issues and Possible Solutions* (2020), p. 7.

[130] *Gestmin v Credit Suisse* [2013] EWHC 3560 (Comm).

[131] Ibid.

(v) Taking evidence outside the seat

Problems arise when an arbitral tribunal wishes to obtain evidence from outside of the jur- **6.135**
isdiction in which the arbitration takes place. In most countries, arbitrators do not have
subpoena powers and thus have to request the assistance of courts if they want to compel
the attendance of third-party witnesses, or to compel the production of documents in the
possession of third parties, whether they are located within the seat of the arbitration or
beyond.

The 1970 Hague Convention streamlines procedures for obtaining evidence in response **6.136**
to a request for assistance from 'judicial authorities'—but an arbitral tribunal is not a judicial authority. Accordingly, a request made from an arbitral tribunal does not fall within
the scope of the 1970 Hague Convention. Nonetheless, many of the signatory states to
the Hague Convention lend their judicial assistance to an arbitral tribunal with its juridical seat in another contracting state, or have otherwise enacted legislation that permits
courts to provide assistance to foreign tribunals.[132] In the United States, courts have the
power under section 1782 of Title 28 of the US Code to order non-parties within their
jurisdiction to give testimony or to produce documents for use in proceedings 'in a foreign or international tribunal' at the request of the tribunal or 'any interested person'.[133]
From the mid-2000s onwards, parties increasingly sought to rely on this power to secure
expansive forms of discovery in aid of foreign arbitrations.[134] However, in June 2022, the
US Supreme Court put an end to this—at least for international commercial arbitration—
holding that section 1782 applies only to foreign or international tribunals that are governmental or intergovernmental, rather than also encompassing '[p]rivate adjudicatory
bodies'.[135]

The Model Law also deals with court assistance in the production of evidence.[136] **6.137**
However, it was determined that questions of international cooperation in the taking
of evidence should not be governed by a model law, but through bilateral or multilateral
conventions. Thus, it is restricted to obtaining evidence where both the state in which
the arbitration takes place and the state in which the evidence is located are signatories
of the Model Law. In the light of inherent limitations, the most common way of compelling the production of evidence in arbitration is indirectly, by means of the ability of
arbitrators to draw adverse inferences from unexcused failure to produce the requested
evidence.[137]

---

[132] For example, the English Arbitration Act 1996, at s. 44, permits English courts to provide assistance to foreign arbitral tribunals, but s. 2(3) provides that the courts can refuse to do so if 'the fact that the seat of the arbitration is outside England and Wales or Northern Ireland, or that when designated or determined the seat is likely to
be outside England and Wales or Northern Ireland, makes it inappropriate to do so'.

[133] 28 USC § 1782.

[134] This was particularly so after the US Supreme Court's decision in *Intel Corporation v Advanced Micro Devices,
Inc.* 542 US 241 (2004), in which it adopted an expansive view of the scope of § 1782, holding that the Court's
power extends to 'administrative and quasi judicial proceedings abroad'.

[135] *ZF Automotive US, Inc. v Luxshare, Ltd. and AlixPartners LLP v Fund for Protection Investors' Rights in Foreign
States* 596 US ____ (2022), p. 11. See paragraphs 7.45ff for a fuller discussion of this issue.

[136] Model Law, Art. 27.

[137] IBA Rules, Art. 9.6 and 9.7.

(e) Experts

(i) Role of experts in international arbitration

6.138   We have already discussed the presentation of evidence to a tribunal, first by means of the production of contemporaneous documents, and secondly, by means of the testimony of witnesses of fact. The third method of presenting evidence to an arbitral tribunal is by the use of expert witnesses. Some issues can be determined only by the arbitral tribunal deciding on differences that are essentially matters of opinion. Thus in a construction dispute, the contemporary documents (comprising correspondence, progress reports, site diaries, and other memoranda), together with the evidence of witnesses who were actually present on the site, should enable the arbitral tribunal to determine what *actually* happened. There may then be a further question to be determined—namely, whether what actually happened was the result of, for example, a design error or defective construction practices. The determination of such an issue can probably be made by the arbitral tribunal only with the assistance of experts, unless the tribunal itself possesses the relevant expertise. Equally, in shipping arbitrations, the performance of a vessel or its equipment may need to be evaluated by experts, so that the arbitral tribunal may make the relevant findings of fact.

6.139   There are two basic methods of proceeding where the arbitral tribunal itself does not have the relevant expertise. The first is for the arbitral tribunal to appoint its own expert or experts. The second is for the parties to engage its own 'independent' experts to work on the case and to give expert evidence to the tribunal. Since this evidence is extremely likely to differ from the evidence of the other side's experts, it will be for the arbitral tribunal to evaluate it. This evaluation is usually carried out after the evidence of each expert has been tested by cross-examination, leaving the tribunal to decide which expert or experts it finds the most credible.

(ii) Experts appointed by the arbitral tribunal

6.140   In international arbitration, the arbitral tribunal is usually composed of lawyers.[138] Where matters of a specialist or technical nature arise, such an arbitral tribunal often needs expert assistance in reaching its conclusions, in order 'to obtain any technical information that might guide it in the search for the truth'.[139]

6.141   International arbitral tribunals have the power to appoint experts under most arbitration rules.[140] Although it is a well-established principle of most national systems of law that someone to whom a duty has been delegated must not delegate that duty to someone else, it is difficult to see any objection in principle to the appointment of an expert by an arbitral tribunal.[141] If an arbitral tribunal needs expert technical assistance in order to understand

---

[138] See Chapter 4, paragraphs 4.48*ff.*

[139] See *Starrett Housing Corporation v Government of the Islamic Republic of Iran* (1987) 16 Iran–US CTR 112, Award No. 314-21-1, 14 August 1987, at [264], quoting the International Court of Justice (ICJ) in *United Kingdom of Great Britain and Northern Ireland v Albania (Corfu Channel)* [1949] ICJ Rep 4, at 20.

[140] See, e.g., UNCITRAL Rules, Art. 29; ICC Rules, Art. 25.4; Swiss Rules, Art. 28; SCC Rules, Art. 34; ICDR Rules, Art. 28; SIAC Rules, r. 26; HKIAC Rules, Art. 25; LCIA Rules, Art. 21.

[141] This principle was expressed by the Iran–United States Claims Tribunal in *Starrett Housing*, at [266]: 'No matter how well qualified an expert may be, however, it is fundamental that an arbitral tribunal cannot delegate to him the duty of deciding the case.' In applying this principle, the Tribunal cited earlier international tribunals

complex technical matters and it decides that it is in need of expert assistance to understand these matters in order to arrive at a proper decision, there is no good reason to prevent it from obtaining such assistance.

If the tribunal decides to appoint its own expert, it will probably first ask the parties to try to agree upon a suitable candidate, since they are more likely to know who are the best people for the job. If this doesn't work, the tribunal may present the parties with a list of individuals and institutions from which to choose, stating that if the parties are still unable to agree, the tribunal will choose the expert itself.   **6.142**

Similarly, the tribunal may seek input from the parties as to the expert's terms of reference. Once the expert has prepared a preliminary report, the parties will be given an opportunity to comment; and the expert is expected to take these comments into account when finalising his or her report. In this way, the parties can assist the expert in making the report complete, while being reassured that important aspects of the case are not being decided without their involvement.[142]   **6.143**

(iii) Expert witnesses presented by the parties

One of the least satisfactory features of modern international arbitrations is the prevailing practice of presenting conflicting expert evidence of opinion on matters of great technical complexity. However well the advocates for the parties are able to test evidence of expert opinion presented by the other side through cross-examination, 'how can the jury judge between two statements each founded upon an experience confessedly foreign in kind to their own?'[143]   **6.144**

Although professional triers of fact should fare better than a jury, it is sometimes difficult for an arbitral tribunal to make a reasoned judgment as between two conflicting professional opinions on complex technical matters. Nevertheless, this remains by far the most common method of presenting expert evidence, regardless of where the arbitration takes place.[144]   **6.145**

The parties' expert evidence is normally delivered initially in the form of written expert reports, usually at the same time as any written statements of witnesses of fact, or shortly thereafter, but in any event well in advance of the hearing.[145]   **6.146**

---

and stated, at [273]: '[T]he Tribunal adopts as its own the conclusions of the Expert on matters within his area of expertise when it is satisfied that sufficient reasons have not been shown that the Expert's view is contrary to the evidence, the governing law, or common sense.' See also the comment and cases cited at [271]–[272]. See also IBA Rules, Art. 6.7.

[142] The IBA Rules provide for the involvement of the parties in the appointment of the expert, and also recommend that the parties (or their experts) have an opportunity to comment on and question the expert's report: see IBA Rules, Art. 6.1, 6.2, 6.5, and 6.6.

[143] Learned Hand, 'Historical and practical considerations regarding expert testimony' (1901) 15 Harv L Rev 40, at 54–55.

[144] A number of international arbitration rules provide for the use of party-appointed experts: see, e.g., UNCITRAL Rules, Art. 27.2; LCIA Rules, Art. 20; Swiss Rules, Art. 25.1, 25.4, and 25.5; SCC Rules, Art. 33; SIAC Rules, r. 25; HKIAC Rules, Art. 22.5.

[145] IBA Rules, Art. 5.1. See also Ashford, *The IBA Rules on the Taking of Evidence in International Arbitration: A Guide* (Cambridge University Press, 2013), para. 2-10.

6.147   Article 5.2 of the IBA Rules provides a useful summary of the expected contents of a party-appointed expert report:[146]

> 2. The Expert Report shall contain:
>
> (a) the full name and address of the Party-Appointed Expert, a statement regarding his or her present and past relationship (if any) with any of the Parties, their legal advisors and the Arbitral Tribunal, and a description of his or her background, qualifications, training and experience;
>
> (b) a description of the instructions pursuant to which he or she is providing his or her opinions and conclusions;
>
> (c) a statement of his or her independence from the Parties, their legal advisors and the Arbitral Tribunal;
>
> (d) a statement of the facts on which he or she is basing his or her expert opinions and conclusions;
>
> (e) his or her expert opinions and conclusions, including a description of the methods, evidence and information used in arriving at the conclusions. Documents on which the Party-Appointed Expert relies that have not already been submitted shall be provided;
>
> (f) if the Expert Report has been translated, a statement as to the language in which it was originally prepared, and the language in which the Party-Appointed Expert anticipates giving testimony at the Evidentiary Hearing;
>
> (g) an affirmation of his or her genuine belief in the opinions expressed in the Expert Report;
>
> (h) the signature of the Party-Appointed Expert and its date and place; and
>
> (i) if the Expert Report has been signed by more than one person, an attribution of the entirety or specific parts of the Expert Report to each author.

6.148   The tribunal may also direct that experts be bound by the Chartered Institute of Arbitrators' Protocol for the Use of Party-Appointed Expert Witnesses in International Arbitration in preparing their opinions. The Chartered Institute's protocol 'expands upon the IBA Rules' in that it gives 'more detailed guidance as to what should (and should not) be in an expert's written opinion and it deals with independence and privilege'.[147]

(iv) Admissibility of expert evidence

6.149   Where expert evidence is introduced by the parties, the rules regarding the admissibility of expert evidence applied by arbitral tribunals will be, in general, the same as those applied to other forms of evidence in the same arbitration. If the evidence of technical opinion is conflicting (which is usually the case), the expert witnesses must be prepared to appear in person before the arbitral tribunal for examination. Consistent with the approach to fact witnesses, the IBA Rules provide that party-appointed experts need not appear for

---

[146] The key amendments introduced in the 2010 edition of the Rules were the requirements to (a) include a description of expert's instructions, (b) provide a statement of independence, and (c) append copies of the documents on which the experts relies, unless they are already on the record of the arbitration. The report must also now include statements regarding translation and be signed with an affirmation of genuine belief in the opinions expressed (rather than an affirmation of the truth of the report, as was required under the 1999 edition of the Rules). See also ibid., at paras 5-4–5-27, and the Chartered Institute of Arbitrators (CIArb) Protocol for the Use of Party-Appointed Expert Witnesses in International Arbitration.

[147] CIArb, Protocol for the Use of Party-Appointment Expert Witnesses in International Arbitration (2007), Foreword.

testimony at an evidentiary hearing unless they are requested to do so and that, in the absence of any such request, the other parties shall not be deemed to have accepted the correctness of the expert's report.[148]

(v) Categories of expert evidence

The evidence of experts is presented in relation to all kinds of matters of opinion. Engineers **6.150** and scientists are frequently called upon to present reports, and to give evidence, in relation to disputes in which the quality of building work or the performance of plant and equipment is in issue. Accountants are called upon to give evidence as to the *quantum* of claims; lawyers may sometimes be required to give evidence where provisions of a 'foreign' system of law have to be explained to the arbitral tribunal. In addition, it is not unknown for handwriting experts, or other persons expert in the forensic examination of documents, to be called upon where the authenticity of a document is in question.

(vi) Experts on 'foreign' law

In the common law system, judges sitting in their national courts expect the substantive **6.151** law of a foreign country to be 'proved as fact' by expert evidence. This convenient fiction has worked satisfactorily for hundreds of years in the court system. However, it takes only a brief moment of reflection to appreciate that the convenient fiction that 'foreign law is fact' does not work in the context of an international arbitration. Imagine three French lawyer arbitrators, sitting in England, with French avocats presenting arguments on the applicable French substantive law: any suggestion that English procedural law would require the relevant 'foreign' French substantive law to be proved as 'fact' would surely be greeted with some hilarity.

In practice, the international arbitration community has solved this dilemma in a prag- **6.152** matic and efficient way. Nowadays, in almost all international arbitrations, 'law' is treated as 'law'. The relevant provisions of that law are then identified and substantiated either in written submissions by counsel (or by a lawyer experienced in that law acting as co-counsel), or by way of expert testimony in the form of an expert opinion by legal experts on the law in issue, with the possibility that those experts may be called as witnesses to explain their reasoning and conclusions.

(f) Inspection of the subject matter of the dispute

The fourth method of presenting evidence to an arbitral tribunal is for the arbitral tri- **6.153** bunal itself to inspect the subject matter of the dispute. This is usually a site inspection, and mainly arises in connection with construction contracts and disputes arising out of the performance of process plant and so forth. However, it may also apply in other types of case, for example it is common in commodity arbitrations for the arbitrator to inspect the cargo or consignment if the dispute concerns the quality of the goods supplied.[149]

---

[148] IBA Rules, Art. 5.6.
[149] Ashford, *The IBA Rules on the Taking of Evidence in International Arbitration: A Guide* (Cambridge University Press, 2013), para. 7-02.

6.154 Article 7 of the IBA Rules provides that:

> Subject to the provisions of Articles 9.2 and 9.3, the Arbitral Tribunal may, at the request of a Party or on its own motion, inspect or require the inspection by a Tribunal-Appointed Expert or a Party-Appointed Expert of any site, property, machinery or any other goods, samples, systems, processes or Documents, as it deems appropriate. The Arbitral Tribunal shall, in consultation with the Parties, determine the timing and arrangements for the inspection. The Parties and their representatives shall have the right to attend any such inspection.[150]

6.155 Although this power exists, arbitral tribunals do not often use this opportunity to supplement the information and evidence available to them, probably because the additional expense involved is likely to be substantial in relation to the benefit gained. It is more common, in current practice, for models, photographs, drawings, or even films to be used to fulfil the purpose that would have been served by a site inspection. For example, in an ICC arbitration, it was proposed to charter a helicopter to make a video showing the terrain in which a road was constructed over a length of some 60 km.[151] And in public international law cases between states, for example involving a boundary dispute, film and photographic evidence is often presented at hearings.[152]

(i) Procedure for inspection

6.156 An arbitral tribunal has broad discretion as to the manner in which it undertakes an inspection of the subject matter of the dispute. Unless the parties specifically agree otherwise, the arbitral tribunal will normally be careful to ensure that the principle of equality of treatment is strictly observed. In particular, the arbitral tribunal will not normally make a site inspection except in the presence of representatives of both parties, and the arbitrators will not normally put questions directly concerning the case to persons working on the site unless counsel for each of the parties also has the right to ask additional questions of those persons.

6.157 Occasionally, parties may agree that the arbitral tribunal should inspect a site, or the subject matter of the dispute, without being accompanied at all. However, it would be inappropriate, and potentially dangerous when the award comes to be enforced, if the arbitral tribunal were to make an inspection in the presence of one party alone.[153]

6.158 If a site inspection is to be made, it is good practice for the arbitral tribunal to issue a procedural direction in advance. Who is to be present? Who will make the arrangements? Will questions and answers or any discussion be transcribed and form part of the record? In general, it is suggested that best practice is to direct that there will be no transcript and that

---

[150] See IBA Rules, Art. 6.3 and 6.5, subject to Art. 9.2 and 9.3. See also the ICDR Guidelines for Arbitrators Concerning Exchanges of Information, para. 5.

[151] In fact, the dispute was settled before this was done.

[152] Regarding inspections, see Art. 66 of the 1978 ICJ Rules of Court (adopted on 14 April 1978 and entered into force on 1 July 1978).

[153] UNICTRAL Notes on Organizing Arbitral Proceedings, para. 57.

what is said should not form part of the record.[154] Otherwise, much of the usefulness of the inspection may be lost as a result of the inevitable delay and formality that accompanies the presence of a reporter.

(ii) Inspection under ad hoc and institutional rules of arbitration

The UNCITRAL Rules and the ICC Rules are silent on the question of inspection of the **6.159** subject matter of the dispute, although the UNCITRAL Rules refer to the obligation of the parties to make available to any experts appointed by the arbitral tribunal any relevant information for inspection.[155] The LCIA Rules,[156] the SIAC Rules,[157] CIETAC Rules,[158] the DIAC Rules,[159] the AAA Rules,[160] and the WIPO Rules[161] make specific provision for any inspection or investigation that the arbitral tribunal may require.

The ICSID Rules contemplate that a site inspection may be necessary. They contain power **6.160** for the arbitral tribunal to 'order a visit to any place connected with the dispute if the arbitral tribunal deems it necessary.[162]

The WIPO Rules also provide for experiments to be conducted,[163] and for the provision by **6.161** the parties of 'primers' and 'models'.[164]

F. Hearings

(a) Introduction

It has been said that the only thing wrong with 'documents only' arbitrations is that **6.162** there are not enough of them. Such arbitrations are commonplace in certain categories of domestic arbitrations—notably, in relation to small claims cases. In the international context, the main examples of 'documents only' arbitrations are those conducted under the LMAA Rules in connection with disputes arising out of charterparties and related documents.

However, in mainstream international arbitration, it is unusual for the arbitral proceedings **6.163** to be concluded without at least a brief hearing at which the representatives of the parties have an opportunity to make oral submissions to the arbitral tribunal, and at which the arbitral tribunal itself is able to ask for clarification of matters contained in the written submissions and in the written evidence of witnesses.

---

[154] Ibid., para. 58.
[155] UNCITRAL Rules, Art. 29.3. See also the LCIA Rules, Art. 21.3; Swiss Rules, Art. 28.2; ICDR Rules, Art. 28.2; SIAC Rules, r. 26.1.b; HKIAC Rules, Art. 25.2; CIETAC Rules, Art. 44.2.
[156] LCIA Rules, Art. 22.1.iv.
[157] SIAC Rules, Rule 27.d.
[158] CIETAC Rules, Art. 44.2.
[159] DIAC Rules, Art. 27.4.
[160] AAA Rules, Art. 36.
[161] WIPO Rules, Art. 50.
[162] ICSID Rules, r. 40.1.
[163] WIPO Rules, Art. 49 (on motion of a party).
[164] WIPO Rules, Art. 51 (with the agreement of the parties).

6.164   All of the rules of the major international arbitration institutions provide for a hearing to take place at the request of either party, or at the instigation of the arbitral tribunal itself. Whilst an arbitral tribunal must proceed to make its award without a hearing if the parties have expressly so agreed,[165] such an agreement is rare in modern international arbitration.

(b) Organisation of hearings

6.165   Hearings are normally held on a date fixed by the arbitral tribunal, either at the request of one or both of the parties, or on its own initiative. The administrative arrangements may be made by one of the parties, often the claimant, with the agreement of the other. Alternatively, they may be made by the sole or presiding arbitrator, or by the tribunal secretary (if there is one).

6.166   In fully administered arbitrations, the institution itself (for example, the AAA or the LCIA) sometimes makes the arrangements; in others, these matters are left to the arbitral tribunal and the parties.[166]

6.167   The task of organising hearings in a major international arbitration should not be underestimated nor should the cost. In the case of a physical hearing, a suitable hearing room must be provided, with ancillary breakout rooms and facilities for the parties and the arbitral tribunal. Access to printing facilities, and a Wi-Fi connection, are invariably essential. A live transcript and verbatim record of the proceedings are often considered essential. Accommodation is also required for witnesses, experts, and the parties' legal teams.[167] Hearings conducted remotely over video-conference avoid some of these costs. However, the largest single element of costs associated with an oral hearing—those relating to the time spent by the arbitral tribunal and counsel on both sides—will still be incurred.

6.168   In short, oral hearings are the most cost-intensive periods of any arbitration and their scheduling often leads to the greatest delays, because availability of all essential participants must be coordinated. Efforts should therefore be made by arbitrators and counsel to limit their duration. To this end, the following matters should be considered.

- Should there be one hearing or several?
- Should there be time limits for the presentation of oral arguments?
- Should there be a limit on the time allowed for the examination and re-examination of witnesses?
- Should there be post-hearing briefs, rather than oral closing submissions?[168]

(i) Location

6.169   In most cases, physical hearings may be held at any location that is convenient for all concerned. Subject to any mandatory provisions of law in the seat of the arbitration, there is generally no requirement that all hearings be physically conducted in the territory of the

---

[165] See, e.g., LCIA Rules, Art. 19.1.

[166] See UNCITRAL Notes, para. 34. The ICC Secretariat is usually willing to make the necessary arrangements if requested to do so by the arbitral tribunal.

[167] For further discussion of administrative arrangements of an arbitral tribunal, see Chapter 4, paragraphs 4.183*ff.*

[168] See UNCITRAL Notes, Note 17.

seat of the arbitration.[169] As a result, most current rules of arbitration permit oral hearings to be conducted at any location (different from the legal place of arbitration) that the tribunal considers appropriate.[170] While it remains usual to hold the main physical evidential hearing in the place of arbitration, the option not to do so can, on occasion, bring real benefits and savings in convenience and cost (for example, when many of the participants in a hearing are all based in another city), and should be considered in appropriate cases.

(ii) Remote hearings

Although remote hearings in international arbitration were not unheard of prior to 2020, they were typically restricted to hearings on procedural or urgent matters (for example, interim measures). In 2020, the COVID-19 pandemic and associated lockdowns and travel restrictions across the world, led to an increasing number of oral hearings being held remotely over video-conferencing platforms. **6.170**

The shift towards remote hearings during the COVID-19 pandemic was partly facilitated by leading arbitral institutions, some of which explicitly stated that remote hearings were permissible under their institutional rules. For example, the LCIA Rules provide that 'a hearing may take place in person, or virtually by conference call, videoconference or using other communications technology with participants in one or more geographic places (or in a combined form)'.[171] The ICC has made it clear that arbitral tribunals possess 'broad procedural authority under Article 22(2)', and that this authority extends to conducting 'any hearing either by physical attendance or by remote means of communication, such as videoconference ("virtual hearing"), or both'.[172] Even with the institutions that do not expressly address remote hearings in their rules, there is consensus that remote hearings are allowed under the broad procedural discretion allocated to arbitral tribunals under most institutional rules.[173] **6.171**

Although remote hearings offer certain advantages, arbitration counsel should assess carefully whether the particular international arbitration with which they are dealing is best suited to a remote hearing. This is because remote hearings are not without their drawbacks. Oral advocacy on a video-conference to a generally static, and muted, image may make it more difficult for the arbitral tribunal and counsel to engage in the substance of complicated arguments. Indeed, a study of US appellate judges found that judges were less likely **6.172**

---

[169] In a decision that was widely criticised, the Swedish Svea Court of Appeal held, in *Titan Corporation v Alcatel CIT SA*, Case No. RH 2005:1 (T 1038-05) YCA XXX (2005), 139, that Titan Corporation could not request the Swedish courts to set aside an ICC award in an arbitration in which the seat was Stockholm because the parties had not conducted any of the hearings in Stockholm (consistent with the discretion to hold hearings other than in the place of arbitration that exists under the ICC Rules). In 2010, the Supreme Court reversed the decision. See 'Decision by the Svea Court of Appeal in Sweden rendered in 2005 Case No. T 1038–05' (2005) 2 Stockholm Intl Arb Rev 259; Ewerlöf, 'Chapter 10 application of the New York Convention by Swedish courts', in Wallin, Regnwaldh, Magnusson, and Franke (eds) *International Arbitration in Sweden: A Practitioner's Guide* (Kluwer Law International, 2013), p. 267, at pp. 270–271.

[170] LCIA Rules, Art. 16.3.

[171] LCIA Rules, Art. 19.2.

[172] ICC, Note to Parties and Arbitral Tribunals on the Conduct of the Arbitration under the ICC Rules of Arbitration, 1 January 2021. See also ICC Rules, Art. 26.1. The 2020 IBA Rules also expressly address remote hearings. IBA Rules, Art. 8.2.

[173] See, e.g., Maxi Scherer, 'Remote hearings in international arbitration: An analytical framework' (2020) 37(4) J Intl Arb 407. See also SIAC Rules, r. 21.2; SCC Rules, Art. 23.1. Although they are not institutional rules, it is worth noting that the IBA Rules and the UNCITRAL Notes both expressly recognise that hearings may be held virtually. See IBA Rules, Art. 8.2; UNCITRAL Notes, para. 122.

to interrupt oral arguments with questions during a remote hearing.[174] The lack of a court-room dynamic may also make effective cross-examination more difficult, where it is being conducted remotely and through language interpretation. There are other disadvantages too. Accommodating every participant in a wide variety of home bases may involve some difficult time-zone jockeying. It is equally easy to imagine circumstances where different participants in an international arbitration have differing access to technology to allow their participation in a remote hearing.

6.173   The ICC has identified certain considerations that should be taken into account before an arbitral tribunal decides to hold a remote hearing, which may be helpful.

> The arbitral tribunal must take any decision to hold an evidentiary hearing by remote means of communication rather than by physical attendance after careful consideration of all relevant circumstances, including the nature of the hearing, the possible existence of travel constraints, the planned duration of the hearing, the number of participants and of witnesses and experts to be examined, the size and complexity of the case, the need for the parties to properly prepare for the hearing, the costs and the gains of efficiency that may be expected by resorting to virtual means of communication, and whether rescheduling the hearing would entail unwarranted or excessive delays.
>
> If an arbitral tribunal determines to proceed with a virtual hearing without party agreement, or over party objection, it should carefully consider the relevant circumstances, including those mentioned in [the prior paragraph], assess whether the award will be enforceable at law, as provided by Article 42, and provide reasons for that determination. In making such a determination, arbitral tribunals may take into account their broad procedural authority under Article 22(2), to, after consulting the parties, adopt such procedural measures as they consider appropriate, provided that they are not contrary to any agreement of the parties.[175]

6.174   As a result, an arbitral tribunal must consider carefully its decision to hold a remote hearing. Such a decision may be straightforward in circumstances where both the tribunal and the parties agree on a remote hearing but it is more delicate where one party insists on having a physical hearing or where, for example, the arbitral tribunal wants a remote hearing but the parties have agreed on a physical hearing. Ultimately, it is important for the arbitral tribunal to ensure that neither party has a legitimate 'due process' objection to having a remote hearing.

6.175   Once an arbitral tribunal has determined that it will hold a remote hearing instead of a physical hearing, it must take steps to ensure equality of arms between the parties. An important consideration to be borne in mind is whether both parties are going to appear remotely, or if only one party will do so. In the latter case, the CIArb's Guidance Note on Remote Dispute Resolution Proceedings advises that 'in the interests of equality, it is preferable that if one

---

[174] Dunn and Norwick, 'Report of a survey of videoconferencing in the courts of appeals', Federal Judicial Center, 2006, p. 13, available online at https://www.fjc.gov/sites/default/files/2012/VidConCA.pdf.
[175] ICC, Note to Parties and Arbitral Tribunals on the Conduct of the Arbitration under the ICC Rules of Arbitration, 1 January 2021, paras 99–100.

party must appear to the tribunal remotely, both parties should do so. However, the parties may agree otherwise.'[176]

(iii) Pre-hearing conference

In large and complex cases, a properly planned pre-hearing meeting or conference can pay substantial dividends in terms of saving time and money at the hearing itself. Such conferences should be organised efficiently, both as to timing and content. The timing is extremely important. If a pre-hearing conference takes place too near to the hearing itself, it will be too late for the 'shape' of the hearing to be influenced. However, if it takes place too early, the arbitral tribunal will almost certainly not be sufficiently well informed about both the issues, and the evidence needed to supplement the parties' written submissions, to enable useful decisions to be taken with regard to the structure of the hearing. **6.176**

Items to be covered at a pre-hearing conference are likely to include the allocation of time as between the parties, the running order, length, and format of opening statements, whether there is to be sequestration of witnesses, the scope and length of direct cross- and re-direct examination, whether there are to be oral closing statements and/or post-hearing briefs, arrangement for transcripts and possibly interpreters, and the preparation of hearing bundles. These matters may be agreed by the parties or if they cannot agree, be decided by the tribunal, but in any event, they should be recorded in a procedural order. **6.177**

For remote hearings, the pre-hearing conference is also an appropriate time for the tribunal and the parties to decide and agree on the issues unique to such hearings. To that end, in addition to the agenda items discussed above, the following issues might also be raised for discussion during the pre-hearing conference: **6.178**

(1) The hearing platform to be used (Zoom, Microsoft Teams, WebEx, etc.).

(2) Service providers who may be retained to provide remote hearing support.

(3) Minimum technical requirements for participating in the remote hearing (for example, a private and stable internet connection with sufficient bandwidth, camera, microphone, speaker of adequate quality, access to a telephone connection in case difficulties are encountered using a computer).

(4) Online etiquette, including the identification of lead speakers for each day of the hearing, and the permissibility of using virtual backgrounds (or other screen filters!) during the hearing.[177]

(5) The cyber-security measures to be adopted.

(6) Determining whether the hearing shall be recorded, and if so, whether it should be video-recorded or only audio-recorded.

(7) The dress code for the remote hearing. Although tribunals and courts have made formal attire optional during remote hearings, some have been careful to specify that counsel must nonetheless be clothed![178]

---

[176] CIArb, *Guidance Note on Remote Dispute Resolution Proceedings*, Section 1.6.

[177] Although some tribunals may allow counsel to use a plain virtual background during the hearing, they are unlikely to allow any participant to use virtual face filters. See Daniel Victor, 'I'm not a cat,' says lawyer having Zoom difficulties, New York Times, 9 February 2021.

[178] See Dorothy Atkins, 'Judge says Zoom formal attire optional, but clothing a must', Law360, 29 July 2021; 'Florida judge: Get out of bed, get dressed for Zoom hearings', AP News, 14 April 2020.

(8) The protocol for the examination of witnesses/experts, which might include measures to ensure that the witness/expert is not communicating with any other person during the examination, whether the witness/expert may be joined in the room by an IT assistance, and determining whether a 360° view of the room in which the witness/expert is appearing is necessary.

(9) The manner in which documents and demonstratives will be displayed.

(10) The need for scheduling test sessions prior to the hearing to ensure that the remote hearing proceeds as smoothly as possible.

6.179 Pre-hearing conferences are a very effective way of ensuring that the hearing itself runs as smoothly as possible, with as few interruptions for discussion of procedural or administrative issues as can reasonably be expected. The value of such conferences has been acknowledged by the report of the ICC Commission on Arbitration and ADR Task Force on Reducing Time and Costs, which has recommended that parties consider 'organizing a conference with the arbitral tribunal, which may be by telephone, to discuss the arrangements for any hearing. At such a prehearing conference, held a suitable time before the hearing itself, the parties and the arbitral tribunal can discuss matters such as time allocation, use of transcripts, translation issues, order of witnesses and other practical arrangements that will facilitate the smooth conduct of the hearing.' [179]

6.180 Whether rules provide for oral pre-hearing conferences explicitly or not,[180] they have become common practice in the exercise of an arbitral tribunal's general procedural discretion. Indeed, the most proactive tribunals will use them to go beyond a purely organisational agenda and indicate to the parties issues on which it would like them to focus at the hearing.[181]

(c) Procedure at hearings

6.181 Individual arbitral tribunals approach the determination of the procedure to be followed at the hearing in different ways. Most have the common aim of keeping the duration of the hearing to a minimum so far as practicable, in order to assist the busy schedules of the arbitrators and parties and to reduce expense.

6.182 Ideas as to what is a reasonable length of time for a hearing differ. Formerly,[182] in English court practice, hearings could last for many weeks, causing great inconvenience, expense, and exhaustion to all concerned.[183] By contrast, arbitrators from the civil law countries tend to regard any hearing that takes more than three days as a long one. Although we hear of exceptions, the general tendency in international arbitration is towards shorter hearings, with greater reliance upon documentary evidence for the reasons already discussed. This is a necessary step in the

---

[179] ICC Commission Report, *Techniques for Controlling Time and Costs in Arbitration* (2nd edn, 2018), paragraph 37.

[180] Only a few do: see WIPO Rules, Art. 47; CIETAC Rules, Art. 33.5.

[181] In this regard, see ICC Rules, Appendix IV, para. (g) ('Case Management Techniques').

[182] Under the English Civil Procedure Rules 1998, however, the length of the hearing is restricted according to the value or complexity of the case.

[183] The oral tradition in England owes its origin to the 'man who is no longer there'—that is, the juror. Jury trials led to two inescapable procedural features. First, once started, the oral proceedings had to be completed, because, once assembled, there was no real practical possibility of reconvening the same jury many weeks, or even months, later. Secondly, although jurors had to be property owners, there was no guarantee that they were literate; hence the need for all of the documents to be read aloud at the hearing.

interests of economy of time and costs in cases that often involve arbitrators, lawyers, experts, company executives, and other participants operating away from their home bases.

The procedure at a hearing is not fixed in stone. As the UNCITRAL Notes on Organizing   **6.183**
Arbitral Proceedings describe:

> Arbitration rules typically give broad latitude to the arbitral tribunal to determine the
> order of presentations at the hearings. Within that latitude, practices differ, for example, as
> to whether opening or closing statements are heard and if they are, their sequence and dur-
> ation, and which of the parties has the last word. The broad latitude of the arbitral tribunal
> also applies to the manner and sequence in which witnesses are heard and to other issues
> addressed at any hearing. When several witnesses are to be heard and longer testimony is
> expected, it is useful to determine in advance the order in which they will be called. In cer-
> tain circumstances, it may be desirable to hear collectively several witnesses on the same
> subject matter. This is likely to reduce costs and facilitate scheduling. Each party might be
> invited to suggest the order in which it proposes to have its own witnesses testify.[184]

Against the backdrop of procedural freedom, a usual practice (or practices) has emerged in   **6.184**
international arbitration that is described next.

(i) Opening statements

The usual practice in international arbitration, given the necessary time limits, is to allocate   **6.185**
to each side only a limited opening statement, in which the advocates assume that the arbitrators have a full knowledge of the written submissions and evidence that is already on the
record. This is followed by the main event: the oral testimony of the witnesses for each party.
An English international arbitrator put it thus:

> Finally, since the arbitrators are likely to be busy professional people and often from dif-
> ferent countries, the oral hearings will usually be remarkably short by English standards.
> Their main purpose is to hear the cross-examination of the witnesses, bracketed by short
> opening and closing remarks from both sides, which are often supplemented by written
> post-hearing submissions.[185]

(ii) Examination of witnesses

Although the examination of witnesses owes much to the common law tradition, it has   **6.186**
become a standard feature of evidential hearings in international arbitration. For this
reason, witness preparation has become a significant part of hearing preparation for parties involved in international arbitration and cross-examination has become a key skill for
counsel in the conduct of a hearing.

Of course, there are important limits in the preparation of witnesses. The role of counsel   **6.187**
should be to assist witnesses 'in developing the confidence and clarity of thought required to testify truthfully and effectively based upon their own knowledge or recollection
of the facts'.[186] Counsel should not be instructing witnesses to change their evidence. In

---

[184] UNCITRAL Notes, paras 127–128.
[185] Kerr, 'Concord and conflict in international arbitration' (1997) 13 Arb Intl 121, at 126–127.
[186] Roney, 'Effective witness preparation for international commercial arbitration: A practical guide for counsel' (2003) 20 J Intl Arb 429, at 430. This article provides a useful practical six-step guide for the preparation of witnesses.

this regard, the IBA Guidelines on Party Representation contain advice as to the appropriate limits of such preparation, providing that contact between counsel and witnesses should not 'alter the genuineness of the Witness or Expert evidence, which should always reflect the Witness's own account of relevant facts, events or circumstances'.[187] It should be borne in mind that being examined in the 'witness box' is, for most witnesses, an unfamiliar and sometimes even intimidating experience.[188] Once the hearing begins, styles of witness examination vary and tribunals will typically allow counsel some leeway to test the evidence in the way that they prefer. As a general matter, however, tribunals do not appreciate overly aggressive or discourteous attacks by counsel. Since being examined in the 'witness box' is, for most witnesses, an intimidating experience, an aggressive comportment by counsel can easily backfire. Experienced arbitrators often discount severe or bullying cross-examinations on the basis that they are evidence of the self-importance of the cross-examiner rather than the lack of credibility of the witness.[189]

6.188   Article 8 of the IBA Rules confirms the current international standard generally adopted by international arbitral tribunals:

> [...]
>
> 3. The Arbitral Tribunal shall at all times have complete control over the Evidentiary Hearing. The Arbitral Tribunal may limit or exclude any question to, answer by or appearance of a witness, if it considers such question, answer or appearance to be irrelevant, immaterial, unreasonably burdensome, duplicative or otherwise covered by a reason for objection set forth in Articles 9.2 or 9.3. Questions to a witness during direct and re-direct testimony may not be unreasonably leading.
>
> 4. With respect to oral testimony at an Evidentiary Hearing:
>
>   (a) the Claimant shall ordinarily first present the testimony of its witnesses, followed by the Respondent presenting testimony of its witnesses;
>
>   (b) following direct testimony, any other Party may question such witness, in an order to be determined by the Arbitral Tribunal. The Party who initially presented the witness shall subsequently have the opportunity to ask additional questions on the matters raised in the other Parties' questioning;
>
>   (c) thereafter, the Claimant shall ordinarily first present the testimony of its Party-Appointed Experts, followed by the Respondent presenting the testimony of its Party-Appointed Experts. The Party who initially presented the Party-Appointed Expert shall subsequently have the opportunity to ask additional questions on the matters raised in the other Parties' questioning;
>
>   (d) the Arbitral Tribunal may question a Tribunal-Appointed Expert, and he or she may be questioned by the Parties or by any Party-Appointed Expert, on issues raised in the Tribunal-Appointed Expert Report, in the Parties' submissions or in the Expert Reports made by the Party-Appointed Experts;
>
>   (e) if the arbitration is organised into separate issues or phases (such as jurisdiction, preliminary determinations, liability and damages), the Parties may agree or the

---

[187] See IBA Guidelines on Party Representation, Guidelines 20–24, and the accompanying commentary.
[188] Ibid.
[189] Veeder, 'The 2001 Goff Lecture: The lawyer's duty to arbitrate in good faith' (2002) 18 Arb Intl 431, at 445. See also ICCA Guidelines on Standards of Practice in International Arbitration (2021).

Arbitral Tribunal may order the scheduling of testimony separately on each issue or phase;

(f) the Arbitral Tribunal, upon request of a Party or on its own motion, may vary this order of proceeding, including the arrangement of testimony by particular issues or in such a manner that witnesses be questioned at the same time and in confrontation with each other (witness conferencing);

(g) the Arbitral Tribunal may ask questions to a witness at any time.

5. A witness of fact providing testimony shall first affirm, in a manner determined appropriate by the Arbitral Tribunal, that he or she commits to tell the truth or, in the case of an expert witness, his or her genuine belief in the opinions to be expressed at the Evidentiary Hearing. If the witness has submitted a Witness Statement or an Expert Report, the witness shall confirm it. The Parties may agree or the Arbitral Tribunal may order that the Witness Statement or Expert Report shall serve as that witness's direct testimony.

6. Subject to the provisions of Articles 9.2 and 9.3, the Arbitral Tribunal may request any person to give oral or written evidence on any issue that the Arbitral Tribunal considers to be relevant to the case and material to its outcome. Any witness called and questioned by the Arbitral Tribunal may also be questioned by the Parties.

In the courts of common law countries, elaborate rules of evidence are still deployed even **6.189** though they were designed for use in jury trials, which (other than in the United States) are largely used only in criminal cases. Such rules of evidence are not necessary in the courts of civil law countries because, in general, fact-finding is the responsibility of the judge based on his or her own enquiries and collection of the evidence. In any event, the civil procedure rules applicable in national courts do not apply to international arbitrations unless the parties agree otherwise, or the local law at the seat of arbitration provides that they do apply to international arbitrations held in that country as the juridical seat.

Fact witnesses are usually first 'examined' by counsel for the party presenting that wit- **6.190** ness, then 'cross-examined' by counsel for the other party, then 're-examined' by the first counsel, if necessary. Additional cross-examination may be introduced, with permission of the arbitral tribunal, where the witness has given new 'direct' testimony during the re-examination.[190]

Arbitral tribunals may sustain objections to direct or redirect examination questions based **6.191** on characterising them as 'leading', or 'closed' (that is, questions that prompt the answer that the examining counsel wishes to obtain).[191] This is not because there is a binding evidential rule against putting such questions in international arbitration, but because the value of a witness's testimony is reduced if it is given pursuant to a question that has suggested the answer. This constraint does not apply to cross-examining counsel, who may ask any type of question as long as it is fair and relevant to the issues in dispute.

---

[190] Although witnesses 'shall' appear 'for testimony at the Evidentiary Hearing', the IBA Rules make clear that an 'Evidentiary Hearing' includes 'any hearing […] whether in person, by teleconference, videoconference or other method'. IBA Rules, Art. 8.1 and Definitions. See also UNCITRAL Rules, Art. 28.4 ('The arbitral tribunal may direct that witnesses, including expert witnesses, be examined through means of telecommunication that do not require their physical presence at the hearing (such as videoconference)').

[191] See IBA Rules, Art. 8.3.

6.192   Witnesses are sometimes excluded, or 'sequestered', until they have given their testimony, although this practice is often dispensed with, particularly if a witness also happens to be a party representative. Much depends on whether or not a party is likely to gain an unfair advantage by having a particular witness present while the corresponding witness presented by the opposing party gives evidence. Fact witnesses are not allowed to discuss the case with any member of the 'team', whether lawyers or other witnesses presented by the same party, during overnight or refreshment breaks whilst they are under examination. This is an obvious way of ensuring that the witness is not 'coached' on how to answer questions during an examination or re-examination ('re-direct'). Sometimes, they are permitted to eat meals together, or drink coffee, on the understanding that the case will not be discussed in his presence. In the case of remote hearings, the arbitral tribunal and the parties may agree on a set of procedures to ensure that a fact witness is not improperly assisted during a cross-examination.[192]

(iii) 'Witness conferencing'

6.193   An alternative to traditional cross-examination is to put two or more witnesses from each side together to answer questions from the tribunal. This technique, which was described in the 1999 edition of the IBA Rules as 'witness confrontation', is now better known as 'witness conferencing'.[193] Where fact witnesses are concerned, it is a somewhat adventurous path for an arbitral tribunal to take. But, used together with traditional cross-examination, it may provide an effective way of identifying areas of agreement and disagreement between witnesses. It also offers an opportunity for an immediate and direct comparison between the witness's earlier testimony, both in writing and at the hearing.

6.194   In the context of expert witnesses, the practice of 'witness conferencing' is much better established. It can be a very effective way of highlighting the points of agreement and disagreement between the experts, and it often leads, if not to agreement, then at least to a narrowing of the points of difference—that is, the conflicting expert testimony between which the arbitral tribunal may have difficulty deciding.[194]

6.195   Where a bridge has collapsed into a river, for example, a fact witness will testify as to what he or she saw and the way in which the bridge fell, while the expert witness will testify as to what, in his or her opinion, caused the bridge to collapse. Was it defective design, or defective workmanship or materials? Where the parties' respective experts disagree, after submitting lengthy and persuasive expert reports, how is the arbitral tribunal to decide which explanation is more persuasive?

6.196   The role of experts in this context is to assist, educate, and advise the arbitral tribunal, in a fair and impartial manner, in specialist fields (such as technical, forensic accountancy, or legal) relevant to specific issues in dispute between the parties in which (some of) the arbitrators do not themselves have relevant expertise. The result is that arbitral tribunals find themselves faced with deciding between the opinions of opposing experts who have

---

[192]   See e.g., Seoul Protocol on Video Conferencing in International Arbitration. See also IBA Rules, Art. 8.2 (discussing the importance of 'measures to ensure that witnesses giving oral testimony [during a remote hearing] are not properly influenced or distracted').

[193]   See IBA Rules, Art. 8.4.f. It is also more colloquially referred to as 'hot tubbing'.

[194]   See Peter, 'Witness conferencing' (2002) 18 Arb Intl 47.

provided diametrically opposite opinions to questions such as, 'why did the bridge fall down?',[195] with little or no unbiased expert advice to guide them.

In an effort to find a practical solution, a number of experienced international arbitrators[196] developed 'expert conferencing' techniques instead of, or (more typically) in addition to, traditional cross-examination. In this kind of procedure, either before or (more commonly) after the experts have drafted their written expert reports, the experts are required to meet and draw up lists of (a) matters on which they agree, and (b) matters on which they do not agree, and the reasons for their disagreement.[197]   **6.197**

Based on list (b), the arbitral tribunal prepares an agenda designed to encompass the matters on which the experts are not agreed, and presents it to the parties and their advocates in advance of the hearing. Then, after all of the fact witnesses from both sides have been heard and often after the experts have been subject to individual cross-examination, the independent experts retained by the opposing parties come before the arbitral tribunal, seated alongside each other at the witness table.[198]   **6.198**

The chairman of the arbitral tribunal then takes the experts through the agenda, item by item. The experts are requested to explain in their own words the basis for reaching the opinions set out in their written reports and to answer each other's main points. They may also be encouraged to debate these points directly with each other if the arbitral tribunal considers that this would be useful.   **6.199**

(iv) Closing submissions

As with opening statements, it is relatively rare in modern international arbitration for lengthy oral submissions to be made after the witness testimony has been heard. There are two reasons for this. The first relates to time and cost. It has been noted already that the most expensive phase of an international arbitration is the time during which all of the players must be gathered in a city that will be foreign to most of them. The accommodation costs are high, but these are dwarfed by the 'time costs' of the parties: the tribunal, the parties' representatives, their counsel, and the witnesses. The second reason is that it can be challenging, alongside intensive witness examination, for counsel to review quickly and evaluate the transcripts obtained throughout the hearing, and to craft a closing statement that will deal adequately with the tribunal's concerns.   **6.200**

It is more usual, in modern international arbitrations, for the closing submissions to be in writing, in the form of post-hearing briefs, delivered after the parties have had the opportunity to review (and, where necessary, correct) the transcripts, within a time for delivery to be agreed between the parties or fixed by the arbitral tribunal. These documents will contain footnote references to the transcripts of the evidence and are designed to facilitate the drafting of the award.   **6.201**

---

[195] One side's expert says, with great conviction, 'faulty design of the bridge'; equally convincingly, the other side's expert says, 'defective materials used in construction of the bridge'. Cross-examination of experts by counsel is considered by many international arbitrators to be an inadequate tool to help them to make a determination between the opposing views of such experts.

[196] Notably Peter, 'Witness conferencing' (2002) 18 Arb Intl 47.

[197] IBA Rules, Art. 5.4. See also the CIArb Protocol for the Use of Party-Appointed Expert Witnesses in International Arbitration, Arts 6 and 7(2).

[198] IBA Rules, Art. 8.4.f.

6.202 However, this does not exclude the possibility of counsel being permitted to present some form of oral closing statement after the witness testimony has been heard, if they prefer, or to answer questions from the arbitral tribunal.

(v) Who has the last word?

6.203 In common law practice, it is the claimant (or 'plaintiff', in some jurisdictions) in a national court that is given the 'last word', on the basis that the claimant bears the burden of proof. In international arbitrations, however, this practice is rarely followed, since arbitrators tend to feel, instinctively, that due process is generally served only if the respondent has the privilege of having the last word to balance the claimant's privilege of going first. Furthermore, the 'burden of proof' point is not wholly valid, because, in most international arbitrations, the burden falls on each party to prove the facts on which it relies.

(d) Default hearings

6.204 An arbitral tribunal may, and indeed should, proceed *ex parte* if one of the parties (almost invariably the respondent) refuses or fails to appear. In such cases, the arbitral tribunal should proceed with the hearing and issue its award, making sure that the precise circumstances in which the proceedings have taken place are specified in the award itself.[199]

6.205 This is necessary because it is likely that a party who boycotts an international arbitration intends to resist enforcement of any award ultimately rendered. Since it is a legitimate ground for refusal of recognition or enforcement of an award, whether under the New York Convention or otherwise, that a party has not had a reasonable opportunity to present its case, it is desirable that the award should itself show, on its face, the circumstances in which the respondent did not participate. Two main problems commonly arise in relation to such *ex parte* hearings: the first is what constitutes a 'refusal' to participate; the second is how the arbitral tribunal should proceed in such circumstances.

(i) Refusal to participate

6.206 In some circumstances, the situation is clear. This was so in the three Libyan oil nationalisation cases[200] in which the Libyan government stated at the outset that it refused to take any part in the proceedings, on the grounds that the arbitral tribunals, in each case, had no jurisdiction. It will also be clear if a respondent expressly refuses to reply to correspondence from the arbitral tribunal, or to comply with any procedural directions as to the submission of written pleadings, and so forth.

6.207 There are two other circumstances in which an arbitral tribunal should proceed *ex parte*, but these are more difficult to identify. The first is where a party does not notify its unwillingness to participate, but creates a delay so unreasonable that the arbitral tribunal (on the application of the other party) would be justified if it were to treat the party in default as

---

[199] For a discussion of practice under various arbitration rules and national laws, see van den Berg, 'Preventing delay and disruption of arbitration' (1990) 5 ICCA Congress Series 17. See also ICSID Rules, r. 49; UNICTRAL Rules, Art. 30; Swiss Rules, Art. 30; SCC Rules, Art. 35; ICDR Rules, Art. 29; AAA Rules, Art. 31; HKIAC Rules, Art. 26.

[200] The *Texaco*, *BP*, and *Liamco* arbitrations; see Chapter 3, paragraphs 3.163*ff*.

having abandoned its right to present its case. It is impossible to specify precisely when this point arises in any given proceedings and an arbitral tribunal must use its best judgement, balancing the various factors involved. However, the arbitral tribunal should bear in mind that it may not be doing the claimant any favours if it accedes too early to an application to proceed *ex parte*, because the award may become the subject of a successful challenge when the claimant seeks to enforce it.[201]

The second situation is where a party so disrupts the hearing that it becomes impossible to conduct it in an orderly manner. Experience of such a situation is hard to find, but theoretically it could happen; the arbitral tribunal would then need to treat the defaulting party's conduct as being equivalent to a refusal to participate. **6.208**

(ii) Procedure in default hearings

Unlike a court, an arbitral tribunal has no authority to issue an award akin to a default judgment. Its task is to make a determination of the disputes submitted to it. Accordingly, even if a party fails to present its case, the arbitral tribunal must consider the merits and make a determination of the substance of the dispute. Where it is clear from the beginning that a party (usually the respondent) does not propose to take part, the arbitral tribunal usually ensures that all notifications of hearings and correspondence continue to be sent to the defaulting party, and that all of the participating party's submissions and evidence are placed before the defaulting party in written form. The tribunal will then be justified in holding only a brief hearing, on an *ex parte* basis, to review the claims and raise any questions. **6.209**

A reliable guideline as to how such a proceeding should take place is that the party who is taking part must prove its case to the satisfaction of the arbitral tribunal. The arbitral tribunal has no duty to act as advocate for a party who has elected not to appear, but it must examine the merits of the arguments of law and fact put to it by the participating party, so as to satisfy itself that these are well founded. It must then make a reasoned determination of the issues. **6.210**

The practice of arbitral tribunals varies as regards hearings in such situations. Much will depend on the form in which the written stages of the arbitration have taken place. If the written stages have been comprehensive, the arbitral tribunal may feel justified in holding a brief and purely formal hearing prior to issuing its award. If, on the other hand, the written pleadings have been skeletal, formal documents in which only the issues have been defined and no documentary or witness evidence has been submitted in writing, the arbitral tribunal would probably consider it necessary to hear oral evidence before being satisfied that the participating party has discharged the burden of proof in relation to its claims (or defences). **6.211**

The Model Law contains a provision empowering the arbitral tribunal to continue the proceedings and to make an award where a party fails to comply with the requirements of the procedure agreed by the parties or established by the arbitral tribunal.[202] Similar provisions **6.212**

---

[201] It is rare, but not unknown, for the respondent to want the proceedings to go ahead, when the claimant has failed to take them forward, in order to obtain an award that will put an end to the claim. In such a case, similar considerations will apply: the respondent will require a solid award, capable of being *recognised* by the courts, if this becomes necessary.

[202] Model Law, Art. 25.

are to be found in modern laws of arbitration, even if they are not directly based on the Model Law.

G. Proceedings After the Hearing

(a) Introduction

6.213   In theory, the hearing should conclude the participation of the parties in the arbitration. Indeed, it is good practice for the arbitral tribunal to declare the evidentiary record closed.[203] This will not prevent the parties, if so agreed by the tribunal, from submitting post-hearing briefs, but it will prevent them from submitting new unsolicited material after the hearing, which will require further procedural orders to enable the other party to reply.

(b) Post-hearing briefs

6.214   It is increasingly common for the parties to submit post-hearing briefs, often of limited length, summarising the main points that have emerged in evidence and argument. The emergence of such a practice may be seen as a direct corollary of the practice of limiting the length of the hearing—and, indeed, of imposing time constraints on the parties at the hearing.[204]

6.215   Thus the most frequently adopted form of proceedings after the closure of the hearings is an exchange of post-hearing briefs. Such a final written opportunity to make submissions is particularly useful where the arbitral tribunal has raised questions during the closing arguments and the parties' counsel wish to have time to undertake research before giving their answers.[205]

(c) Introduction of new evidence

6.216   The post-hearing briefs may not always be the end of the proceedings. First, fresh evidence may come to light after the hearing, but before the arbitral tribunal has issued its award. In these circumstances, the arbitral tribunal has discretion to reopen the proceedings at the request of the party wishing to present the new evidence.[206] Clearly, it should refuse to do so where the fresh evidence is not needed for its deliberations, or if the new material appears to be a spurious attempt to delay the proceedings. But, in general, arbitral tribunals prefer to determine a dispute with the benefit of all of the relevant evidence in their possession. If the fresh evidence turns out to be valueless, or without merit, the opposing party may be

---

[203] Some sets of institutional rules require it: e.g., ICC Rules, Art. 27; DIAC Rules, Art. 34; SIAC Rules, r. 32.1.
[204] See section on 'Hearings' above.
[205] AAA Case No. 13T1810031097.
[206] See, e.g., UNCITRAL Rules, Art. 31.2; Swiss Rules, Art. 31; VIAC Rules, Art. 32; SIAC Rules, r. 32.1.

compensated by the arbitral tribunal in relation to the additional costs incurred, and by an award of interest where this is appropriate.

The course that should be adopted by the arbitral tribunal depends on the circumstances of each case and the nature of the material to which a response must be made. However, arbitral tribunals normally (and rightly) try to ensure that additional hearings do not take place unless they are really necessary; they generally permit one party to put in further written evidence and submissions only if the other has presented fresh material at, or subsequent to, the hearing.   **6.217**

7

ROLE OF NATIONAL COURTS DURING THE PROCEEDINGS

A. Introduction

The relationship between national courts and arbitral tribunals presents a paradox. **7.01**
Arbitration, founded on the agreement of the parties, is an alternative to litigation before a national court. Nevertheless, at various stages of the process, arbitration is dependent on the underlying support of national courts. As Lord Mustill, a former senior English judge and arbitrator, has stated:

> [T]here is plainly a tension here. On the one hand the concept of arbitration as a consensual process reinforced by the ideas of transnationalism leans against the involvement of the mechanisms of state through the medium of a municipal court. On the other side there is the plain fact, palatable or not, that it is only a Court possessing coercive powers which could rescue the arbitration if it is in danger of foundering.[1]

A party who chooses to refer disputes to arbitration chooses a private system of justice. But **7.02**
considerations of public policy impose restrictions upon this freedom of choice. Most states limit the scope of arbitration to disputes that the state itself considers suitable for determination by this private system of justice —that is to say, disputes that are, because of their subject matter, 'arbitrable' in the sense discussed elsewhere in this volume.[2] But, as we have seen, the concept of what is and what is not 'arbitrable' differs from one country to another, and even over time.[3] The state prescribes the boundaries of arbitration and enforces these boundaries through its courts. The state also determines other limitations upon the arbitral process: for instance, whether arbitrators have the power to compel the attendance of witnesses or the disclosure of documents and more importantly, whether or not any appeal to the state's national court is possible, and if so, how, when, and upon what terms.[4]

The paradoxical relationship between arbitral tribunals and the courts oscillates between **7.03**
partnership and forced cohabitation. To the extent that the relationship between national

---

[1] *Coppée Levalin NV v Ken-Ren Fertilisers and Chemicals* [1994] 2 Lloyd's Rep 109 (HL), at 116 *per* Lord Mustill.
[2] See Chapter 2.E.
[3] See, e.g., the changed attitude of the US courts towards the arbitration of antitrust, securities, or patent issues.
[4] See Chapter 10.

courts and arbitral tribunals is said to be one of 'partnership',[5] it is not a partnership of equals. Arbitration depends upon the agreement of the parties, but it is also a system built on law, which relies upon that law to make it effective both nationally and internationally. National courts could exist without arbitration, but arbitration could not exist without national courts. The real issue is to define the point at which this reliance of arbitration on the courts begins and that at which it ends. That point is constantly changing over time and across jurisdictions.[6]

(a) The increasing independence of arbitration

7.04   As noted in Chapter 1, arbitration is now the principal method of resolving international disputes involving states, individuals, and corporations. This reality has led the arbitral process to distance itself, where possible, from the risk of domestic judicial parochialism. Modern international arbitration has consequently achieved a considerable degree of independence from national courts. For example, the arbitration clause in an international contract is generally recognised as being an independent agreement, which survives any termination of the contract in which it is contained.[7] The parties themselves are generally free to determine how their disputes are to be resolved, subject only to such safeguards as may be considered necessary as a matter of public policy; and arbitrators are free to decide on their own jurisdiction, subject only to differing degrees of review by the national courts of the seat of the arbitration and of the place of recognition or enforcement. The parties are free to choose which system or rules of law will govern the dispute between them[8]— and, indeed, they may even select general principles, such as the UNIDROIT Principles of International Commercial Contracts.[9] Finally, judicial control of errors of law in international arbitration has been virtually abandoned, leaving courts the limited role of policing only public policy and procedural due process, such as the obligation of the tribunal to give each party a fair hearing.

7.05   Nonetheless, the arbitral process remains (primarily) subject to the arbitration law of the country in which it has its juridical seat, which, as observed by Rawding and Snodgrass, 'should be the first port of call for any necessary judicial assistance to allow the arbitration to

---

[5] See, e.g., Goldman, *The Complementary Role of Judges and Arbitrators*, ICC Publication No. 412 (ICC, 1984), p. 259.

[6] The relationship between arbitration and national courts is one of continuous evolution. The Rt. Hon. Dame Elizabeth Gloster DBE, PC observed that this ongoing change is the product inter alia of 'a broader, international conversation' taking place at fora such as the Standing International Forum of Commercial Courts, which discussed at its inauguration in May 2017 'how international commercial courts and arbitration could best work together': Gloster, 'Symbiosis or sadomasochism?' (2018) 34 Arb Intl 321, at 322; Courts and Tribunals Judiciary, 'A Unique Gathering of Commercial Courts', 15 May 2017, available online at https://www.judiciary.uk/announcements/a-unique-gathering-of-commercial-courts/.

[7] See the discussion of separability in Chapter 2, paragraphs 2.107*ff*.

[8] Model Law, Art. 28(1): 'The arbitral tribunal shall decide the dispute in accordance with such rules of law as are chosen by the parties as applicable to the substance of the dispute.'

[9] The UNIDROIT Principles represent a private codification or 'restatement' of international contract law. What was at the time one of the largest disputes referred to international arbitration was decided under these Principles: see Bonell, 'A "global" arbitration decided on the basis of the UNIDROIT Principles' (2001) 17 Arb Intl 249. See also Bonell, *An International Restatement of Contract Law: The UNIDROIT Principles of International Commercial Contracts* (Brill, 2005), pp. 273–274. For a detailed analysis, see Vogenauer and Kleinheisterkamp (eds) *Commentary on the UNIDROIT Principles of International Commercial Contracts (PICC)* (Oxford University Press, 2009).

proceed or to secure the parties' rights while the arbitration is pending'.[10] It is (secondarily) also subject to the arbitration law of the country, or countries, in which a winning party may seek to recognise or enforce the eventual award.[11] In other words, the involvement of national courts in the international arbitration process remains essential to its effectiveness. For instance, the ever-increasing trend to seek interim measures, or interlocutory support for the arbitral process, has placed a renewed focus on the respective roles of the arbitral tribunal and the courts.

(b) Limitations on independence

Article 5 of the Model Law declares that no court shall intervene in matters governed by the Model Law, except where permitted by that law. At first sight, this is a powerful declaration of independence. Yet the Model Law does not seek to exclude the participation of what it calls the 'competent court'[12] in carrying out 'certain functions of arbitration assistance and supervision'. On closer examination of the Model Law itself, it becomes apparent that of its thirty-six Articles, no fewer than ten recognise a possible role for the 'competent court'. For example, Article 11 acknowledges that the help of the competent court may be necessary to constitute the arbitral tribunal; Article 13 acknowledges that the competent court may have to decide upon a challenge to an arbitrator if there are justifiable doubts as to that arbitrator's impartiality or independence; Article 16 acknowledges that a party to an international arbitration may apply to the competent court to review the decision of the arbitral tribunal on jurisdiction—in which case, it is the decision of that court (and not the decision of the arbitral tribunal) that is final and binding. The Model Law also acknowledges that the assistance of the competent court may be necessary in the taking of evidence,[13] and that, in any challenge to the arbitral award, or to its recognition and enforcement, the judgment of the competent court will be decisive.[14]

7.06

(c) 'A relay race'

If there is a resulting partnership between arbitrators and the national courts, it is one in which each has a different role to play at different times. This relationship between courts and arbitrators has been imaginatively compared to a relay race:

7.07

> Ideally, the handling of arbitral disputes should resemble a relay race. In the initial stages, before the arbitrators are seized of the dispute, the baton is in the grasp of the court; for

---

[10] Rawding and Snodgrass, 'Global Overview', in Nairn KC and Heneghan (eds) *Arbitration World* (5th edn, Sweet & Maxwell, 2015), para. 2.3.3.

[11] Lew, 'Does national court involvement undermine the international arbitration processes?' (2009) 24(3) Am Uni Intl Law Rev 489, at 494, citing *Karaha Bodas Co. v Perusahaan Pertambangan Minyak Dan Gas Bumi Negara*, 335 F.3d 357, 364 (5th Cir. 2003): 'Under the [New York] Convention, "the country in which, or under the [arbitration] law of which, [an] award was made" is said to have primary jurisdiction over the arbitration award. All other signatory States are secondary jurisdictions, in which parties can only contest whether that State should enforce the arbitral award.'

[12] The competent court is defined in Model Law, Art. 6, as the court or other authority specified by each state as being competent to perform the functions entrusted to it by the Model Law.

[13] Model Law, Art. 27.

[14] Ibid., Arts 34–36.

at that stage there is no other organisation which could take steps to prevent the arbitration agreement from being ineffectual. When the arbitrators take charge they take over the baton and retain it until they have made an award. At this point, having no longer a function to fulfil, the arbitrators hand back the baton so that the court can in case of need lend its coercive powers to the enforcement of the award.[15]

In principle, there should be no disputes as to where the frontier between the public world of the courts and the private world of arbitration lies. At the beginning of an arbitration, national courts (not the arbitrators) have the task of enforcing the agreement to arbitrate if one of the parties should seek to avoid it. At the end of the arbitral process, national courts (not the arbitrators) must also enforce the arbitral award if the losing party is not prepared to comply with it voluntarily. During the arbitral process, the arbitrators (not the courts) must take charge of the proceedings, set time limits, organise meetings and hearings, issue procedural directions, consider the arguments of fact and law put forward by, or on behalf of, the parties, and make their award.

7.08   Unfortunately, the respective dominions of arbitral tribunals and national courts are not as clearly distinguished as this metaphor suggests. As Lord Mustill went on to observe:

> In real life the position is not so clear-cut. Very few commentators would now assert that the legitimate functions of the Court entirely cease when the arbitrators receive the file, and conversely very few would doubt that there is a point at which the Court takes on a purely subordinate role. But when does this happen? And what is the position at the further end of the process? Does the Court retake the baton only if and when invited to enforce the award, or does it have functions to be exercised at an earlier stage, if something has gone wrong with the arbitration, by setting aside the award or intervening in some other way?[16]

B. At the Beginning of the Arbitration

7.09   There are at least three situations in which the intervention of the court may be necessary at the beginning of the arbitral process:

- the enforcement of the arbitration agreement;
- the establishment of the tribunal; and
- challenges to jurisdiction.

(a) The enforcement of the arbitration agreement

7.10   An agreement to arbitrate confers two types of obligations: *first*, a positive obligation to arbitrate disputes that arise between the parties cooperatively and in good faith; and *second*, a

---

[15] Mustill, 'Comments and conclusions', in International Chamber of Commerce (ICC) (ed.) *Conservatory Provisional Measures in International Arbitration: 9th Joint Colloquium* (ICC, 1993), p. 118.
[16] Ibid.

negative obligation to refrain from litigating arbitrable disputes. In respect of the former, US courts order recalcitrant parties to arbitration agreements to participate in arbitration proceedings.[17] As one senior arbitrator has observed, the value of such orders lies in foreclosing the ability of the would-be non-participating party to 'decide for tactical reasons, which may assist in resisting enforcement, to refuse to participate in the arbitration despite the arbitration agreement'.[18]

It would no doubt have been possible to provide in the New York Convention for such posi-   **7.11** tive enforcement of an agreement to arbitrate. Instead, the Convention relies on the negative obligation. If a national court is seized of an action in respect of a claim that the parties have agreed to refer to arbitration, the court should order the matter to go to arbitration, unless it finds that the agreement to arbitrate was null and void, inoperative, or incapable of being performed.[19] If a party to an arbitration agreement decides to issue proceedings in a court of law, rather than to take the dispute to arbitration, and the respondent acquiesces, then the arbitration agreement will be deemed to have been waived and the court action will proceed. However, a respondent that has entered into an arbitration agreement will usually wish to have the dispute decided by arbitrators rather than by a national court.

The principal remedy for breach of the negative obligation is almost universally either a   **7.12** mandatory stay or the dismissal for lack of jurisdiction of the litigation brought before the national court in breach of the arbitration agreement.

In addition, where litigation has been brought or is threatened before the courts of another   **7.13** jurisdiction, in breach of an arbitration agreement, that litigation may be suspended or prevented by enforcing the negative obligation through an anti-suit injunction, viewed as 'one of the most controversial and contested remedies in the court's armoury'.[20] Raphael defines an anti-suit injunction as:

> an order of the court requiring the injunction defendant not to commence, or to cease to pursue, or not to advance particular claims within, or to take steps to terminate or suspend, court or arbitration proceedings in a foreign country [...] The order is addressed to, and binds, the actual or potential litigant in the other proceedings, and is not addressed to, and has no effect on, the other court.[21]

Anti-suit injunctions are generally available in common law jurisdictions but not in civil   **7.14** law systems, and under certain laws may be granted by a tribunal as well as by the courts.[22] But as noted in Chapter 5, following *Allianz SpA and anor v West Tankers Inc.*, courts in European Union (EU) member states are not permitted to issue anti-suit injunctions against proceedings in other member states, even if those proceedings were brought in violation of a valid arbitration agreement.

---

[17] Pursuant to the Federal Arbitration Act, ss. 4, 206, and 303.
[18] Lew, 'Does national court involvement undermine the international arbitration processes?' (2009) 24(3) Am Uni Intl Law Rev 489, at 527.
[19] New York Convention, Art. II(3).
[20] Raphael, *The Anti-Suit Injunction* (Oxford University Press, 2008), para. 1.01.
[21] Ibid., at para. 1.05.
[22] See *Steamship Mutual Underwriting Association (Bermuda) Ltd v Sulpicio Lines Inc* [2008] EWHC 914 (Comm), at [33], confirming arbitral tribunals' competence to issue anti-suit injunctions under English law.

(b) Establishing the arbitral tribunal

7.15   If (i) the parties have failed to make adequate provision for the constitution of an arbitral tribunal, or (ii) the agreed appointment procedure is not successfully carried out, and there is no fallback mechanism in the applicable institutional or other rules (such as the UNCITRAL Rules), then the assistance of a national court may be required to complete the constitution of the arbitral tribunal—for instance, by appointing the presiding arbitrator, if there is no agreement between the parties as to a suitable appointment.

7.16   As discussed in Chapter 4, the national court may also be asked to decide on a challenge to the independence or impartiality of an arbitrator, and to remove that arbitrator if the challenge is successful.[23] However, the power of removal is generally exercised sparingly by national courts.[24]

(c) Challenges to jurisdiction

7.17   If any issue is raised as to the jurisdiction of the arbitral tribunal, it will generally (although not always) be made at the beginning of the arbitration. If the objection is successful, the arbitration will be terminated. The issue of challenges to jurisdiction is one of growing importance and is dealt with in Chapter 5. The only point that should be made here, in the context of the relationship between national courts and arbitral tribunals, is that it is recognised in the Model Law (and in many national systems of law) that whilst any challenge to the jurisdiction of an arbitral tribunal may be dealt with *initially* by the tribunal itself, the final decision on jurisdiction rests with the relevant national court.[25] This is either the court at the seat of the arbitration, or the court of the state(s) in which recognition and enforcement of the arbitral award is sought.

C. During the Arbitral Proceedings

7.18   What happens in the most important phase of an arbitration, when the arbitrators begin their task? The baton has been passed to them. Is there any need for national courts to be involved in the arbitral process? The answer in almost every case is 'no', and the recent changes to major arbitration rules which provide for Emergency Arbitrators or the expedited formation of arbitral tribunals have made that 'no' more emphatic.[26] Once an arbitral tribunal has been constituted, most arbitrations are conducted without any need to refer to a national court, even if one of the parties fails or refuses to take part in the proceedings. There may be

---

[23] Paragraphs 4.115*ff.*

[24] Lew, Mistelis, and Kroll, *Comparative International Commercial Arbitration* (Kluwer Law International, 2003), para. 15-37.

[25] Model Law, Art. 16(3). Unusually, English (Arbitration Act 1996, s. 32) and German law (ZPO, s. 1032(2)) both provide for an action to be brought before the courts to determine preliminary points of jurisdiction prior to the tribunal's jurisdictional award, subject to narrow limits.

[26] For data on the relative (in)frequency of different types of national court involvement in arbitration cases, see Korzun and Lee, 'An empirical survey of international commercial arbitration cases in the US District Court for the Southern District of New York, 1970–2014' (2016) 39(2) Fordham Intl Law J 307.

times, however, when the involvement of a national court *is* necessary in order to ensure the proper conduct of the arbitration. It may become necessary, for instance, to ask the competent court to assist in taking evidence or to make an order for the preservation of property that is the subject of the dispute or to enforce tribunal-ordered interim measures. The question that then arises is whether a national court may (or indeed should) become involved in a dispute that is subject to arbitration, and if so, how far this involvement should extend.

(a) Interim measures—powers of the arbitral tribunal

As discussed in Chapter 5, it may become necessary during the course of an arbitration for the arbitral tribunal or a national court to issue orders intended to preserve evidence, to protect assets, or in some other way to maintain the *status quo* pending the outcome of the arbitration. The purpose of interim measures has been described by the EU's former Advocate General Tesauro as being 'to achieve that fundamental objective of every legal system, the effectiveness of judicial protection', by ensuring 'that the time needed to establish the existence of the right does not in the end have the effect of irremediably depriving the right of substance'.[27]   **7.19**

Such measures of protection take different forms and go under different names. In the Model Law[28] and in the UNCITRAL Rules,[29] they are known as 'interim measures'. In the English version of the ICC Rules, they are known as 'interim or conservatory measures and in the French version, as '*mesures conservatoires ou provisoires*'.[30] In the Swiss law governing international arbitration, they are referred to as 'provisional or conservatory measures'.[31] Whatever their designation, however, they are intended in principle to operate as holding orders and to apply only pending the issue of the final arbitral award.   **7.20**

In many cases in which interim measures of protection are required, the arbitral tribunal itself has the power to issue them, as considered in Chapter 5. There are, however, five situations in which a party seeking interim relief will need to refer to a national court.   **7.21**

(i) No powers

First, the arbitral tribunal *may not have* the necessary powers. This is usually a result of antique domestic legislation, going back to a time when, for reasons of public policy, the power to grant such measures was considered to be a prerogative of the national courts. Such limitations are today very rarely encountered in practice.[32]   **7.22**

---

[27] Opinion of Advocate General Tesauro, *R. v Secretary of State for Transport, ex parte Factortame Ltd*, Case No. 2-13/89, [1990] ECR I-02433, at [18] (ECJ).

[28] Model Law, Art. 17.

[29] UNCITRAL Rules, Art. 26.

[30] ICC Rules, Art. 28.

[31] Swiss PIL, art. 183.

[32] Argentina was one of the last jurisdictions to remove this restriction, codified in Art. 753 of the Argentine Code of Civil Procedure, which states: 'Arbitrators may not issue binding measures, but shall request them from the judge, who shall provide its jurisdictional assistance for the fastest and most effective conduct of the arbitration proceedings.' This provision, though still technically in force, is overridden in respect of international arbitration by Law No. 27,449 on International Commercial Arbitration (2018), which incorporates the Model Law's interim measures regime, and in respect of domestic arbitration by Art. 1655 of the National Joint Civil and Commercial Code (2015).

(ii) Inability to act prior to the formation of the tribunal

7.23   Second, it is evident that an arbitral tribunal cannot issue interim measures until it has been established.[33] The point may seem obvious, yet it is frequently overlooked until a crisis arises. The problem is that it takes time to establish an arbitral tribunal and, during that time, vital evidence or assets may disappear.

7.24   Most international institutional rules have sought to address this problem through rules allowing for the appointment of so-called Emergency Arbitrators.[34] The idea is that so-called 'Emergency Arbitrators' may be appointed at short notice by the institution to re-solve problems (such as the threatened transfer of assets by the respondent) that may arise prior to the constitution of the formal tribunal. Once appointed, the Emergency Arbitrators will do their job and then take no further part in the proceedings. However, in circum-stances of great urgency, it may happen that, even if there is provision for the appointment of Emergency Arbitrators, they would not be appointed quickly enough, so that the appli-cant would be obliged to resort to the national courts to obtain interim measures within the required timeframe.[35] For example, the LCIA Rules permit the Emergency Arbitrator a maximum of fourteen days from the date of appointment to determine the application,[36] while the ICC Rules permit a maximum of fifteen days from the date on which the file was transmitted to the Emergency Arbitrator.[37] Certain courts may determine applications for interim measures even more quickly than the 'Emergency Arbitrator' mechanism allows. This is often because courts are ready to hear applications on an *ex parte* basis, which (as ad-dressed below) Emergency Arbitrators are generally prohibited from doing.

(iii) An order can affect only the parties to the arbitration

7.25   The third factor that may make the assistance of a national court necessary is that the powers of an arbitral tribunal are generally limited to the parties to the arbitration. The Model Law makes it plain that an arbitral tribunal may order interim measures only against 'a party'.[38] A third-party order, for example, addressed to a bank holding deposits of a party would not be enforceable against the bank, and multiparty or multi-contract disputes may also pose similar problems, requiring national court assistance.

(iv) Enforcement difficulties

7.26   Fourth, as discussed below,[39] enforcement of interim measures ordered by an arbitral tri-bunal is not always straightforward, because it is uncertain where such orders may rank under the enforcement regime of the New York Convention. That regime applies only to 'awards',[40] for which finality is considered an essential characteristic in many jurisdictions,

---

[33] Indeed, in the case of ICC arbitrations, interim measures cannot be issued by the tribunal until the file has been transmitted to it: see ICC Rules, Art. 28.

[34] SCC Rules, Art. 37.4 and Appendix II; ICC Rules, Art. 29.1 and Appendix V; SIAC Rules, Art. 30.2 and Sch. 1; HKIAC Rules, Art. 23.1 and Sch. 4, Art. 1; ICDR Rules, Art. 6; LCIA Rules, Art. 9B; JAMS Rules, r. 2(c); AAA Rules, R-38; NAI Rules, Art. 36.4.

[35] See, e.g., *Gerald Metals S.A v Timis & Ors* [2016] EWHC 2327 (CH), at [53]: 'It is common ground that there can be situations where the need for relief, for example in the form of a freezing injunction, is so urgent that the power to appoint an emergency arbitrator is insufficient and the court may properly act under section 44 of the Arbitration Act—for example if the application is one that needs to be made without notice.'

[36] LCIA Rules, Art. 9.8.

[37] ICC Rules, Appendix V, Art. 6.4.

[38] Model Law, Art. 17(2).

[39] Paragraphs 7.63*ff.*

[40] Pursuant to Art. III of the New York Convention.

and the New York Convention is silent as to whether it applies to interim awards by an arbitral tribunal. Consequently, in circumstances where there may be a need for international enforcement of an interim measure in a jurisdiction that lacks an available mechanism for such enforcement,[41] parties should consider the possibility of applying for such measures before the courts of the place of execution.

(v) No *ex parte* application

Fifth, a party may need to make an application *ex parte* (that is, without notice to the party against whom the measure is directed) for example, to freeze the opposing party's bank account in order to prevent the transfer of funds abroad. As discussed in Chapter 5, the revised Model Law offers the possibility of limited *ex parte* applications to the arbitral tribunal.[42] However, 'preliminary orders' for interim measures obtained from tribunals through *ex parte* applications are not enforceable,[43] which considerably reduces their effectiveness, and the rules of the leading institutions do not currently expressly envisage giving such powers to arbitrators. As a consequence, in most cases in which *ex parte* relief is important, such as where there is a risk of dissipation of assets or of important evidence being destroyed, the only option is to apply to the competent court.

7.27

(b) Interim measures—powers of the competent court

For these reasons, it is important that the competent court should have the power to issue interim measures in support of the arbitral process. In situations of extreme urgency, in which third parties need to be involved or in which there is a strong possibility that a party will not voluntarily execute the tribunal's order, there may be little option but to identify the appropriate state court and to make the application to that court. The measures requested may include the granting of an injunction to preserve the *status quo* or to prevent the disappearance of assets; or the issue of an order to assist in the taking of evidence from witnesses or to ensure the preservation of property or evidence.

7.28

An application to a court for interim measures may give rise to at least two problems. First, if a party to an arbitration agreement makes an application for interim measures to the court rather than to the arbitral tribunal, will this be regarded as a breach of the agreement to arbitrate? Second, if the choice between seeking interim measures from the courts or from the

7.29

---

[41] As examples of such jurisdictions, Castello and Chahine list the following: 'although the Korean Arbitration Act was revised in 2016 and largely incorporated provisions on interim measures from the 2006 Model Law, it nevertheless limits enforcement of interim measures to those issued by tribunals seated in Korea. In 2010, the Chilean Supreme Court rejected the exequatur of arbitral interim measures granted abroad regarding assets located in Chile. Similarly, in Russia, the Presidium of the Highest Arbitrazh Court reaffirmed in 2010 its position that only awards finally deciding (part of) the merits of a dispute can be enforced in the Russian Federation': Castello and Chahine, 'Enforcement of interim measures', in Rowley KC, Gaillard, and Kaiser (eds) *The Guide to Challenging and Enforcing Arbitration Awards* (Global Arbitration Review, 2019), p. 111.

[42] Model Law, Art. 17B(1): 'Unless otherwise agreed by the parties, a party may, without notice to any other party, make a request for an interim measure together with an application for a preliminary order directing a party not to frustrate the purpose of the interim measure requested.' Jurisdictions that have adopted legislation based on the revised Model Law allowing for *ex parte* preliminary orders include Australia, Colombia, Costa Rica, Hong Kong, Ireland, Lithuania, Panama, Peru, and Rwanda.

[43] Model Law, Art. 17 C(5).

arbitral tribunal is truly an open choice, should the application be made to the courts or to the arbitral tribunal?

(i) Incompatibility with the arbitration agreement?

7.30   The risk that resort to interim measures before a court might operate as a waiver of the arbitration agreement, or that any order so obtained might be dissolved in the face of a valid arbitration clause, appears now to be negligible. Most arbitration rules are explicit in confirming that an application for interim relief from a court is not incompatible with an arbitration agreement.[44] For example, Article 9 of the Model Law states categorically that: 'It is not incompatible with an arbitration agreement for a party to request, before or during arbitral proceedings, from a court an interim measure of protection and for a court to grant such measure.'

(ii) Should an application be made to a national court or to the arbitrators?

7.31   On the question of whether to seek interim relief from the relevant court or the arbitral tribunal, much depends on the relevant law, the applicable institutional rules, and the nature of the relief sought. The relevant law may make it clear, for instance, that any application should be made first to the arbitral tribunal, and only then to the court of the seat of arbitration. This is the position taken by Swiss law, which empowers the arbitral tribunal to take 'provisional', or conservatory, measures (unless the parties otherwise agree), then states that if the party against whom the order is made fails to comply, the arbitral tribunal may request assistance from the competent court.[45]

7.32   English law is equally careful to spell out the position. It does so in three provisos to the court's 'powers exercisable in support of arbitral proceedings', including the preservation of evidence, the inspection of property, the granting of an interim injunction, and the appointment of a receiver. These three provisos are set out at section 44(3)–(5) of the English Arbitration Act 1996:

> (3) If the case is one of urgency, the court may, on the application of a party or proposed party to the arbitral proceedings, make such order as it thinks necessary for the purpose of preserving evidence or assets.
>
> (4) If the case is not one of urgency, the court shall act only on the application of a party to the arbitral proceedings [...] made with the permission of the tribunal or with the agreement in writing of the other parties.
>
> (5) In any case the court shall act only if or to the extent that the arbitral tribunal [...] has no power or is unable for the time being to act effectively.

7.33   Similarly, various institutional rules set additional hurdles which must be cleared before an application to court for interim measures is permissible. For example, such

---

[44] For example, ICC Rules, Art. 28.2; UNCITRAL Rules, Art. 26.9; ICDR Rules, Art. 24.3; SCC Rules, Art. 37.5; ICC Rules, Art. 28.2; SIAC Rules, Art. 30.3; HKIAC Rules, Art. 23.9; LCIA Rules, Art. 25.3; Swiss Rules, Art. 26.5; JAMS Rules, r. 24(e); AAA Rules, R-37.c.

[45] Swiss PIL, Ch. 12, s. 183(1) and (2). In France, in a 2012 decision, the Reims cour d'appel held that, after the tribunal has been constituted, applications for provisional or conservatory measures or measures relating to the taking of evidence can no longer be made to domestic courts: see *SA Clinique de Champagne v Enrico Ambrosini*, Reims cour d'appel, 1ere Ch. Civ., 3 July 2012, [2012] Rev Arb 681.

applications may only be made pursuant to Article 25.3 of the LCIA Rules, 'after the formation of the Arbitral Tribunal, in exceptional cases and with the tribunal's authorisation'. Similarly, pursuant to Rule 30.3 of the SIAC Rules, a court application for interim relief can only be made 'in exceptional circumstances' after the tribunal's constitution. The ICC Rules are somewhat more permissive, providing at Article 28.1 that court applications may be made 'in appropriate circumstances' after the case file has been transmitted to the arbitral tribunal.

Where the position is not spelled out clearly by the national law or by institutional rules, the answer to the question of whether to seek interim relief from the court or from the arbitral tribunal is likely to depend upon the particular circumstances of each case. If, for example, the tribunal has not been constituted, the matter is one of urgency, and there is a concern that an order by an emergency arbitrator may not be voluntarily executed, the only possibility is to apply to the relevant national court for interim measures. At the same time, the party seeking such an order should take steps to advance the arbitration, so as to show that there is every intention of respecting the agreement to arbitrate.[46] Where the arbitral tribunal *is* in existence, or where the appointment of an emergency arbitrator is possible and likely to be effective, it would be appropriate to apply first to that tribunal or emergency arbitrator unless international enforcement may be required. **7.34**

This is not simply a question of division of labour. Although an arbitral tribunal or an emergency arbitrator lacks the coercive powers of a court of law, and although there are questions concerning the international enforceability of an order for interim measures, parties should not forget that any order is binding as between the parties themselves. It is a brave (or foolish) party who deliberately chooses to ignore interim measures ordered by the tribunal that is charged with deciding the merits of its dispute. As one experienced commentator has asserted: **7.35**

> Ultimately, of course, the arbitrators' greatest source of coercive power lies in their position as arbiters of the merits of the dispute between the parties. Parties seeking to appear before arbitrators as good citizens who have been wronged by their adversary would generally not wish to defy instructions given to them by those whom they wished to convince of the justice of their claims.[47]

---

[46] In circumstances where national courts effectively 'step into the shoes' of the as yet un-constituted arbitral tribunal by granting interim measures, English law requires that the applicant undertake to have the tribunal formed as soon as possible thereafter: *Econet Wireless Ltd v Vee Networks and Ors* [2006] EWHC 1568 (Comm), at [14]. Similarly, Brazilian law requires a party seeking interim measures prior to the commencement of arbitration to undertake to initiate proceedings within 30 days: São Paulo Court of Appeals, Interlocutory Appeal 614.006-4/4/00.

[47] Schwartz, 'The practices and experience of the ICC Court', in ICC (ed.) *Conservatory and Provisional Measures in International Arbitration*, ICC Publication No. 519 (ICC, 1993), p. 59. The Analytical Commentary to the Model Law expressly stipulates that 'if a party does not take the interim measure of protection as ordered by the arbitral tribunal, such failure may be taken into account in the final decision, in particular in any assessment of damages': UNCITRAL, *Analytical Commentary on Draft Text of a Model Law on International Commercial Arbitration, Report of the Secretary-General*, 25 March 1985, Art. 18, para. 5, p. 43. However, Binder criticises this guidance on the basis that 'it implies that the tribunal could act in a prejudiced way towards the party which did not obey the tribunal's orders', suggesting that such an approach 'could cause a tribunal to be challenged due to misconduct': Binder, *International Commercial Arbitration and Mediation in UNCITRAL Model Law Jurisdictions* (4th edn, Kluwer Law International, 2019), p. 281.

7.36   There are other logistical problems inherent in applying to a court for interim measures.[48] Often, the merits of the dispute will fall to be determined under a foreign law, which the local court would be ill-prepared to consider at an interim stage. In addition, the language of the dispute and the contract may be different from that of the foreign court. Finally, the chosen court is likely to be at the place of execution of the order to avoid concerns as to enforceability. This may give rise to a difficulty in persuading the court that the measures are necessary, if they are being sought against a state or local entity, in favour of a foreign corporation.[49]

7.37   The nature of the relief sought is also likely to have an important bearing on the question of whether to go to a national court or to the arbitral tribunal. Interim measures of relief take many forms and differ from state to state. In addition, new and important forms of relief may be crafted by the courts or set out in legislation, so that it would be unwise to regard the categories of interim measures as being in any sense closed.[50] The following classification may, however, be helpful:

- measures relating to the attendance of witnesses;
- measures related to preservation of evidence;
- measures related to documentary disclosure;
- measures aimed at preserving the *status quo*; and
- measures aimed at relief in respect of parallel proceedings.

(c) Measures relating to the attendance of witnesses

7.38   The first category of interim measures, directed towards the taking of witness evidence, is one of obvious concern. Since an arbitral tribunal does not generally possess the power to compel the attendance of relevant witnesses, it may be necessary to resort to the courts, particularly if the witness whose presence is required is not in any employment or other dependent relationship to the parties to the arbitration and so cannot be persuaded to attend voluntarily. This need for the assistance of the court is recognised by Article 27 of the Model Law:

> The arbitral tribunal or a party with the approval of the arbitral tribunal may request from a competent court of this State assistance in taking evidence. The court may execute the request within its competence and according to its rules on taking evidence.

7.39   Some national arbitration laws, including those of countries such as Switzerland, which have not adopted the Model Law as it stands, nevertheless follow this form of wording very

---

[48] See Voser, 'Interim relief in international arbitration: the tendency towards a more business-oriented approach' (2007) 1(2) Disp Res Intl 171, at 173.

[49] In an ICC arbitration in which one of the authors was involved (ICC Case No. 11681), the parties had to consider whether to apply to the tribunal or to the local courts of the respondent for an interim measure. Given that the applicable law and language were foreign to the local court, and that the measure sought to stop an important commercial transaction of an entity local to the court, a decision was taken to apply to the arbitral tribunal. The measure was awarded and the respondent complied voluntarily.

[50] This is confirmed by Art. 17J of the Model Law, pursuant to which the nature of interim measures that can be granted by national courts in support of arbitration mirrors the types of interim measures each court may grant in relation to court proceedings. English law also follows this approach: Arbitration Act 1996, s. 44(1).

closely.[51] In other arbitration laws, the position may be set out more fully. For example, section 43 of the English Arbitration Act 1996 provides that:

(1) A party to arbitral proceedings may use the same court procedures as are available in relation to legal proceedings to secure the attendance before the tribunal of a witness in order to give oral testimony or to produce documents or other material evidence.

(2) This may only be done with the permission of the tribunal or the agreement of the other parties.

(3) The court procedures may only be used if—
   (a) the witness is in the United Kingdom, and
   (b) the arbitral proceedings are being conducted in England and Wales or, as the case may be, Northern Ireland.

(4) A person shall not be compelled by virtue of this section to produce any document or other material evidence which he could not be compelled to produce in legal proceedings.[52]

In an arbitration seated in the United States, section 7 FAA grants arbitrators the power to subpoena witnesses within the jurisdiction either to appear to give oral evidence or to disclose relevant documentary evidence in their possession.[53]   **7.40**

Practically, a subpoena can be issued by tribunals only in respect of witnesses present in the jurisdiction, and there appear to be few instances of the power having been exercised in the context of international arbitrations.[54] In one unreported ICC case, a tribunal refused to exercise its power to issue a subpoena to produce documents against a foreign national present in New York only for the arbitration hearing. The tribunal considered that the parties would not have contemplated the exercise of such power when selecting New York as a seat for a dispute that otherwise had no connection with the United States.   **7.41**

---

[51] Swiss PIL, s. 184(2).

[52] Under English Arbitration Act 1996, s. 2(3), this section of the Act (and that concerning court powers exercisable in support of arbitral proceedings) applies even if (a) the seat of the arbitration is outside England, Wales, or Northern Ireland, or (b) no seat has been designated or determined.

[53] The section reads: 'The arbitrators selected either as prescribed in this title or otherwise, or a majority of them, may summon in writing any person to attend before them or any of them as a witness and in a proper case to bring with him or them any book, record, document, or paper which may be deemed material as evidence in the case. [...] Said summons shall issue in the name of the arbitrator or arbitrators, or a majority of them, and shall be signed by the arbitrators, or a majority of them, and shall be directed to the said person and shall be served in the same manner as subpoenas to appear and testify before the court; if any person or persons so summoned to testify shall refuse or neglect to obey said summons, upon petition the United States district court for the district in which such arbitrators, or a majority of them are sitting may compel the attendance of such person or persons before said arbitrator or arbitrators, or punish said person or persons for contempt in the same manner provided by law for securing the attendance of witnesses or their punishment for neglect or refusal to attend in the courts of the United States.'

[54] In the United States, r. 45(b)(2) of the Federal Rules of Civil Procedure (FRCP) originally provided that a subpoena 'may be served at any place within the district of the court by which it is issued, or at any place without the district that is within 100 miles of the place of the deposition, hearing, trial, production, or inspection specified in the subpoena'. Finding that the FRCP was incorporated by FAA, s. 7, the Second Circuit concluded that arbitrators could not issue subpoenas beyond the territorial limit in r. 45(b)(2). *Dynegy Midstream Services v Trammochem*, 451 F.3d 89, 96 (2d Cir. 2006). On the other hand, the Eighth Circuit chose not to apply the territorial limit in r. 45(b)(2) to arbitral subpoenas to produce documents, since 'the burden of producing documents need not increase appreciably with an increase in the distance those documents must travel'. In 2013, r. 45(b)(2) FRCP was amended to eliminate the territorial limit on the service of subpoenas, permitting service 'at any place within the United States'. Relying on this amendment, the Eleventh Circuit held that nationwide service of arbitral summonses was appropriate. *Managed Care Advisory Grp., LLC v CIGNA Healthcare, Inc.*, 939 F.3d 1145, 1157 (11th Cir. 2019).

7.42   The 'any person' wording of section 7 of the FAA expressly authorises tribunals to subpoena parties and non-parties to the arbitration agreement to attend hearings. However, there is conflicting authority at the Circuit level regarding whether this power extends to ordering pre-hearing discovery from non-parties (for example, in the form of interrogatories and depositions). The Sixth and Eighth Circuits have held that section 7 applies to pre-hearing discovery of documents in the possession of third parties,[55] while the Fourth Circuit permits pre-hearing discovery of non-parties where a party demonstrates a 'special need or hardship', such as where the information sought is otherwise unavailable.[56] Conversely, the Second, Third, Ninth, and Eleventh Circuits have all taken the opposite stance.[57] The Second Circuit has distinguished between depositions of non-parties and testimony of non-parties at preliminary hearings, finding only the latter permissible under section 7.[58] The key difference is that preliminary hearings are conducted before the arbitrators, unlike depositions.

(d) Measures related to the preservation of evidence

7.43   As far as the preservation of evidence is concerned, it is obviously important that evidence should *not* be destroyed before a proper record can be made of it.[59] If, for example, the dispute is over the quality of a consignment of coffee or cocoa beans, then some assessment of that quality must be made before the consignment is either sold or perishes. Or again for example, if the dispute is over the number or quality of reinforcing bars used in the concrete foundations of a road, bridge, or dam, some record must be preserved, preferably by independent experts, before those foundations are covered over. Moreover, given that the preservation of evidence is a matter of particular concern right at the beginning of the case, and probably well before the formation of the arbitral tribunal, this is an area in which parties are likely to rely heavily either on assistance from the competent national court or from an Emergency Arbitrator.

7.44   Arbitration laws may grant specific powers to national courts to support arbitration by means of the granting of interim injunctions to preserve evidence. For example, section 44 of the English Arbitration Act 1996 grants to the courts in cases of urgency the same powers

---

[55] *Am. Fed. Of Television & Radio Artists*, 164 F.3d 1004, 1009 (6th Cir. 1999); *In re Sec. Life Ins. Co. of Am.*, 228 F.3d 865, 870–871 (8th Cir. 2000). Later decisions by district courts in the Eighth Circuit have limited the application of this holding to document production, reasoning that 'the production of documents is less onerous and imposes a lesser burden than does a witness deposition'. *SchlumbergerSema, Inc. v Xcel Energy, Inc.*, No. CIV. 02-4304PAMJSM, 2004 WL 67647, at *2 (D. Minn. 2004).

[56] See *COMSAT Corporation v NSF*, 190 F.3d 269, 276 (4th Cir. 1999); *Application of Deiulemar Compagnia Di Navigazione S.p.A. v M/V Allegra*, 198 F.3d 473, 479–481 (4th Cir. 1999). The same test has also been applied by New York State courts. *Imclone Systems, Inc. v Waksal*, 22 A.D.3d 387, 388 (NY App Div 2005); *Matter of Roche Molecular Sys. Inc. (Gutry)*, 76 NYS.3d 752, 758 (NY Sup Ct 2018).

[57] *Life Receivables Tr. v Syndicate 102 at Lloyd's of London*, 549 F.3d 210, 216 (2d Cir. 2008); *Hay Group, Inc. v E.B.S. Acquisition Corp.*, 360 F.3d 404 (3d Cir. 2008); *CVS Health Corporation v Vividus, LLC*, 878 F.3d 703, 706 (9th Cir. 2017); *Managed Care Advisory Grp. v CIGNA Healthcare*, 939 F.3d 1145, 1161 (11th Cir. 2019).

[58] *Stolt-Nielsen Transp. Grp., Inc. v Celanese AG*, 430 F.3d 567, 578 (2d Cir. 2005); *Life Receivables Tr. v Syndicate 102 at Lloyd's of London*, 549 F.3d 210, 217–218 (2d Cir. 2008); *Washington Nat'l Ins. Co. v OBEX Grp. LLC*, 958 F.3d 126, 136 (2d Cir. 2020).

[59] This is not least because counsel is likely to be bound under national rules of professional conduct to ensure document retention or at least to prevent the destruction of evidence, whilst Guideline 12 of the IBA Guidelines on Party Representation imposes a duty on counsel to inform clients about the necessity of document preservation.

in arbitration to order the preservation of evidence, or the inspection, photographing, or preservation of property, as in court proceedings.[60] In one case, pending initiation of an arbitration, the Court of Appeal granted a freezing order preventing a respondent from disposing or otherwise dealing with shares in order to protect a disputed right to purchase under a share purchase agreement.[61] The Court considered that property could include contractual rights and that there was no bar to the issuing of a mandatory injunction. The key issue was the need to protect the rights that would be the subject of the arbitration.

(e) Measures related to documentary disclosure

As observed in Chapter 6, the arbitral tribunal's power to order disclosure of documents is generally limited to the parties to the arbitration. Yet, in certain circumstances, relevant documents may be in the hands of a third party. Whilst the courts of the seat of the arbitration may offer some assistance,[62] that seat has usually been chosen for its neutrality, and so the relevant third party is unlikely to be within its jurisdiction. The usual result is that third-party documents remain outside the scope of the arbitral process. Prior to the US Supreme Court's June 2022 judgment in the joined cases of *ZF Automotive US, Inc. v Luxshare, Ltd. and AlixPartners LLP v Fund for Protection Investors' Rights in Foreign States*, there were states in the United States where an application to obtain disclosure of documents in support of a foreign arbitration was possible. The importance of this tool was magnified by, the expansiveness of US discovery processes, which could yield access to forms of disclosure (such as depositions) from third parties that would not be normally available in an international arbitration from the parties themselves.   **7.45**

It was argued that this contested power arose from section 1782(a) of Title 28 of the US Code, which permits a district court to order a person who 'resides or is found' in the district to give testimony or produce documents 'for use in a foreign or international tribunal […] upon the application of any interested person'. In 2004, contrary to the prevailing view until then that this power was limited to judicial courts and thus did not extend to arbitration proceedings,[63] the US Supreme Court remarked *obiter* in *Intel Corporation v Advanced Micro Devices, Inc* that this power does in fact extend to foreign arbitral tribunals, subject to the following four discretionary factors: **7.46**

a) whether the material sought is accessible to the foreign tribunal absent section 1782;
b) the nature of the tribunal, the character of the proceedings, and the receptivity of the tribunal to US assistance;
c) whether the request conceals an attempt to circumvent foreign proof-gathering restrictions or other policies; and
d) whether the request is unduly intrusive or burdensome.[64]

---

[60] English Arbitration Act 1996, s. 44(3).
[61] *Cetelem SA v Roust Holdings Ltd* [2005] EWCA Civ 618.
[62] See Dupeyon, 'Shall national courts assist arbitral tribunals in gathering evidence?' (2016) ICCA Mauritius, Section III.2.a.
[63] *National Broadcasting Co., Inc. v Bear Stearns & Co., Inc.*, 165 F.3d 184 (2d Cir. 1999); *Republic of Kazakhstan v Biedermann International* 168 F.3d 880 (5th Cir. 1999).
[64] *Intel Corporation v Advanced Micro Devices, Inc.*, 542 US 241, 124 S.Ct. 2466, 159 L.Ed.2d 355 (2004).

7.47   Following *Intel* and prior to *ZF Automotive*, a consistent line of case law supported the view that section 1782 was applicable in relation to investor–state arbitration.[65] Much of this jurisprudence flowed from the Chevron-Ecuador dispute, in which section 1782 was deployed repeatedly by both parties to the dispute.[66]

7.48   By contrast, no unanimous approach emerged in respect of the provision's applicability to international commercial arbitration. Instead, the ensuing inter-Circuit (and even intra-Circuit) splits caused this jurisprudence to take on what one author has described as a 'wheel-of-fortune like nature'.[67] The Fourth and Sixth Circuits, for instance, took the position that it was applicable,[68] whilst other circuits, including the Second, Fifth, and Seventh, adopted either contrary or inconsistent views.[69]

7.49   This legal uncertainty was clearly unsatisfactory, particularly in light of the increasing use of section 1782 applications by parties to foreign-seated international arbitrations. The US Supreme Court's intervention now resolves (at least much of) that uncertainty. In its unanimous judgment, the Court held that section 1782 required a 'foreign or international tribunal' to be 'governmental or intergovernmental' to fall within its scope, rather than also encompassing '[p]rivate adjudicatory bodies'.[70] It based this determination on a contextual and purposive interpretation of the statute.[71] The Court found it to be a 'straightforward' matter that the commercial arbitral tribunal in question in the former of the joined appeals could not qualify as governmental.[72] And although the Court considered that the investment tribunal at issue in the latter of the appeals (an ad hoc UNCITRAL tribunal constituted pursuant to a bilateral investment treaty) posed 'a harder question', it nevertheless again rejected the argument that this tribunal qualified as governmental.[73] In both determinations, the Court dispensed with any recourse to the discretionary factors previously considered in Intel. It did, however, reserve judgment on 'the possibility that sovereigns might imbue an ad hoc arbitration panel with official authority'.[74] The Court thereby preserved some room for continued jurisprudential and scholarly debate as to whether other *investment* tribunals—notably, those constituted pursuant to the ICSID Convention, or under the auspices of an often mooted multilateral investment court—might be deemed to qualify as governmental, and therefore fall within section 1782's scope. However, that room appears to be limited.

---

[65] See, e.g., *In re Petition of the Republic of Turkey for an Order Directing Discovery From Hamit Çiçek Pursuant to 28 U.S.C. § 1782*, 2020 WL 4035499, at *3 (DNJ 17 July 2020); *Pakistan v Arnold & Porter Kaye Scholer LLP*, 2019 WL 1559433, at *7 (DDC); Stute, '28 USC § 1782—looking for consensus' (2019) 35 Arb Intl 331, at 336.

[66] Strong, 'Discovery under 28 U.S.C. §1782: Distinguishing international commercial arbitration and international investment arbitration' (2013) University of Missouri School of Law Scholarship Repository, p. 20 *et seq.*

[67] Stute, '28 USC § 1782—looking for consensus' (2019) 35 Arb Intl 331, at 342.

[68] *Servotronics, Inc. v Boeing Co.*, 2020 WL 1501954 (4th Cir. 2020); *Abdul Latif Jameel Trans. Co. Ltd. v FedEx Corp.*, 2019 WL 4509287 (6th Cir. Case No. 19-5315).

[69] See, e.g., *Servotronics Inc. v Rolls-Royce PLC*, 975 F.3d 689 (7th Cir. 2020); *In re Application and Petition of Hanwei Guo for an Order to take Discovery for Use in a Foreign Proceeding Pursuant to 28 U.S.C., 1782*, 965 F.3d 96 (2d Cir. 2020); *El Paso Corporation v La Comision Ejecutiva Hidroelectrica Del Rio Lempa*, 341 Fed.Appx 31 (5th Cir. 2009); *Kleimar N.V.*, US Dist Court, SD New York, Nov 16, 2016, 220 F.Supp. 3d 517 (SDNY 2016); *In re Children's Investment Fund Foundation (UK)*, 363 F.Supp.3d 361 (SDNY, 30 January 2019); *In re Hanwei Guo*, 2019 WL 917076 (SDNY, 25 February 2019).

[70] *ZF Automotive US, Inc. v Luxshare, Ltd. and AlixPartners LLP v Fund for Protection Investors' Rights in Foreign States* 596 US (2022), p. 11.

[71] Ibid., pp. 6–11.

[72] Ibid., p. 12.

[73] Ibid., pp. 12–16.

[74] Ibid., p. 15.

Therefore, section 1782's application to international arbitration appears now in large part   **7.50**
to have run its course.

(f) Measures aimed at preserving the *status quo*

There are many cases in which an award of damages, however substantial, does not ad-   **7.51**
equately compensate the injured party for the loss that it has suffered. This may include
damage to reputation, loss of business opportunities, and similar heads of claim, which are
real enough, but difficult to prove and to quantify, even if they are considered to be legally
admissible. For example, a manufacturer may refuse to continue supplies under a distribution agreement, alleging breach of contract. If the distributor does not receive the supplies
for which it has contracted, it may not be able to fulfil the contracts that it, in turn, has made.
This may damage the distributor's reputation. In such a case, the distributor would no doubt
wish to argue that the *status quo* should be maintained and that the manufacturer should
continue to supply, pending resolution of the dispute by arbitration. Similarly, a pharma-
ceutical company may produce a particular drug under licence, then decide to manufacture and market a competing product under its own name, claiming that there is nothing
in the licence agreement to prevent it doing so. In such a case, the licensor probably wishes
to argue that, until the dispute is resolved by arbitration, the licensee should be restrained
from manufacturing and marketing the competing product.

A key consideration which governs applications for this category of interim measures is   **7.52**
not only whether they should be made to a national court or to an arbitral tribunal, but also
whether ordering such interim relief 'would be equivalent to pre-judging the merits of the
case'.[75] An application is likely to fail if it is found that granting the interim measures sought
would have this effect. This consideration confronted the English courts in the *Channel
Tunnel* case. This was a case that went on appeal from the court of first instance to the Court
of Appeal and then to the (then) highest English court, the House of Lords. Each court gave
a different answer to the two questions posed.

The contract for the construction of the Channel Tunnel was between Eurotunnel (the   **7.53**
owner and intended operator of the tunnel) and Trans-Manche Link (TML), a consortium
of five French and five British construction companies that had agreed to construct the
land terminals, bore and equip the tunnels, and provide the necessary rolling stock. One
serious dispute that arose between the parties was about payment for the Tunnel's cooling
system. This was not part of the original specification, but was added by a variation order.
TML claimed that the monthly payments it received for the cooling system were insufficient. By the end of September 1991, the gap between what Eurotunnel had paid and what
TML claimed had grown to approximately £17 million. In October 1991, TML wrote to
Eurotunnel, threatening to suspend work on the cooling system unless its claim was met in
full and pointing out the 'very serious' consequences that this would have for completion of
the project, with subcontractors and other workers having to be laid off, equipment orders
being delayed or cancelled, and so forth. In reply, Eurotunnel applied to the English court

---

[75] Yesilirmak, 'Interim and conservatory measures in ICC arbitral practice, 1999–2008' (2011) Special
Supplements of the ICC Bulletin: Interim, Conservatory and Emergency Measures in ICC Arbitration 6.

for an interim injunction to restrain TML from carrying out its threat. TML argued that the English courts had no power to intervene by granting the injunction that was sought; instead, it said, the court should stay the litigation and refer the parties to arbitration, in accordance with the then governing statute.[76]

7.54 The judge who heard the case at first instance decided that he *did* have the power to grant an injunction and would have done so, but for an undertaking by TML to continue working pending further court proceedings.[77] The Court of Appeal considered that it was an appropriate case for an injunction, but that it had no power to grant one, because of the arbitration agreement.[78] The House of Lords considered that it *did* have power to grant an injunction, but thought it inappropriate to do so. In giving the House of Lords' judgment, Lord Mustill highlighted the problem to which this kind of application for interim relief may give rise:

> It is true that mandatory interlocutory relief may be granted even where it substantially overlaps the final relief claimed in the action; and I also accept that it is possible for the court at the pre-trial stage of the dispute arising under a construction contract to order the defendant to continue with a performance of the works. But the court should approach the making of such an order with the utmost caution and should be prepared to act only when the balance of advantage plainly favours the grant of relief. In the combination of circumstances which we find in the present case, I would have hesitated long before proposing that such an order should be made, even if the action had been destined to remain in the High Court.[79]

7.55 That in the *Channel Tunnel* case, three different courts gave different answers to the questions of whether or not there was power to issue an injunction, and if so, whether it would be appropriate to do so, underlines the difficulties posed by such questions.[80] It is no comfort to the practitioner to say so, but there is no clear rule as to whether or not an injunction will be issued in particular circumstances.[81] Each case has to be assessed individually.

(g) Interim relief in respect of parallel proceedings

7.56 Whilst an uneasy truce may have been signed between the courts and arbitral tribunals in developed arbitral jurisdictions,[82] a 'turf war' continues in other parts of the world, where

---

[76] English Arbitration Act 1975.

[77] *Channel Tunnel Group v Balfour Beatty Ltd*, Commercial Court, 27 November 1991, at [367].

[78] *Channel Tunnel Group v Balfour Beatty Ltd*, Court of Appeal, 22 January 1992.

[79] *Channel Tunnel Group v Balfour Beatty Ltd* [1993] AC 334, at 367.

[80] The former English arbitration legislation was amended to take account, inter alia, of some of the difficulties that the courts faced in the *Channel Tunnel* case. The Court of Appeal, which would have been prepared to grant an injunction, considered that it had no power to do so, because the arbitration agreement provided for arbitration in Brussels. The English Arbitration Act 1996, s. 44(2)(e), provides that the powers of the court that are 'exercisable in support of arbitral proceedings' include the granting of an interim injunction, and this section of the Act applies even if the seat of the arbitration is outside England (s. 2(3)). There may be resort to the courts if, or to the extent that, the arbitral tribunal or any other person empowered by the parties to decide the case 'has no power or is unable for the time being to act effectively' (s. 44(5)).

[81] For different approaches to the granting of court injunctions pending arbitration, see Judgment of 14 October 2016, *Civil Procedure Preservation Ruling Regarding Ocean Eleven Shipping Corp. v Lao Kaiyuan Mining Sole Co. Ltd*, E72 Cai Bao No. 427 (Wuhan Maritime Ct.); *Chen Hongqing v Mi Jingtian and another* [2017] HKCFI 1148 (Hong Kong High Court); *Petrobras v Tractebel Energia & MSGAS*, Case No. AgRg MC 19.226-MS (2012/0080171-0), Superior Court of Justice of Brazil, 29 June 2012; *Discovery Geo Corporation v STP Energy Pte Ltd*, High Court of New Zealand, 19 December 2013.

[82] For example, in a 2010 decision, a Paris court held that French courts cannot interfere with arbitral proceedings: *SA Elf Aquitaine and Total v Mattei, Lai. Kamara and Reiner*, Paris Court of First Instance, 6 January 2010.

there is an uncomfortable trend towards the issue of 'anti-arbitration' injunctions, either by the courts of the seat or by the courts of the place of eventual enforcement. The fact pattern is often similar: a dispute arises between a foreign party and a state, or state-owned entity, which has signed an arbitration agreement. The state entity wishes to sabotage the arbitral proceedings and to have the case remitted for judicial determination in its own courts. It therefore seeks an injunction before those courts, seeking to challenge the jurisdiction of the tribunal, and an order requiring the arbitrators and adverse party to suspend or abandon the arbitral proceedings on pain of daily fines (or worse). This problem has raised serious challenges for the modern arbitrator: should such orders be obeyed, even where they are the product of improper intervention at the local or state level, or should the arbitrator seek to ensure justice in the individual case, often at risk of monetary penalties (or worse)?

In one such case, a subsidiary of a US corporation, Himpurna, had entered into a contract **7.57**
with the Indonesian state electricity corporation, PLN, to explore and develop geothermal resources in Indonesia and subsequently to sell the power to PLN. In the wake of the Asian economic crisis, PLN failed to purchase the electricity supplied. Himpurna relied on the arbitration clause in the contract to commence an arbitration under the UNCITRAL Rules against PLN. A final award was made in favour of Himpurna, which PLN refused to pay. Himpurna subsequently commenced a second arbitration proceeding against Indonesia, based on Indonesia's pledge to secure PLN's performance. Shortly after serving the statement of claim, proceedings were commenced by both PLN and Indonesia in the Indonesian courts, which resulted in interim injunctions ordering the suspension of the arbitral proceedings pending a court decision on the merits, with an attached fine of US$1 million per day for breach of the order.

The tribunal considered that the injunction was a transparent attempt to avoid the conse- **7.58**
quences of a freely signed arbitration agreement and refused to abandon the arbitration. To avoid the risk of breaching the Indonesian court order, the tribunal moved the place of the hearing to The Hague and convened witnesses. Indonesia tried to stop such hearings from proceeding by seeking an injunction from the Dutch courts. This attempt failed, and the hearings were held (albeit in truncated form without the presence of the Indonesian arbitrator) and a final award issued.

The colourful facts of this case raise important questions as to how an arbitral tribunal can **7.59**
seek to avoid injunctions of national courts in extreme circumstances. First, hearings in an UNCITRAL case can be held 'at any place [the tribunal] deems appropriate', and so the physical transfer of the hearings to The Hague was permitted by the Rules. In connection with the injunction itself, Article 28 of the UNCITRAL Rules allows a tribunal to proceed with the arbitration notwithstanding one party's default whenever the defaulting party has failed to show 'sufficient cause' for its default. In this regard, the arbitral tribunal found that the Indonesian injunction did not constitute 'sufficient cause', because (a) it was sought and obtained by a state agency that was under the *de jure* control of the government of Indonesia, and (b) the government of Indonesia had *de facto* made no attempt to rein in those actions that were inconsistent with its obligations under the parties' arbitration agreement.

While in less categorical terms, US and English courts have expressed great reluctance to issue anti-arbitration injunctions: see Reisman and Iravani, 'The changing relation of national courts and international commercial arbitration' (2010) 21 Am Rev Intl Arb 33; see also *Sabbagh v Khoury* [2019] EWCA Civ. 1219, at [110]*ff* emphasising the exceptional nature of the grant of an anti-arbitration injunction.

7.60   As a second ground, the arbitral tribunal held that the very existence of an arbitration agreement, and the involvement of a state party, entitled the tribunal to apply international law. As a matter of international law, the actions of the Indonesian courts were attributable to the Republic of Indonesia. In *Benteler v Belgium*,[83] an international tribunal had held that 'a state which has signed an arbitration clause or agreement would be acting contrary to international public policy if it subsequently relied on the incompatibility of such an obligation with its internal legal system'.[84] The arbitral tribunal held that it would constitute 'a denial of justice for the courts of a State to prevent a foreign party from pursuing its remedies before a forum to the authority of which the State consented'.[85] Thirdly, the tribunal held that an international arbitral tribunal is not 'unconditionally subject' to the jurisdiction of the courts at the seat of the arbitration. Specifically, the 'adjudicatory authority' of an international tribunal 'does not emanate from a discrete sovereign but rather from an international order'.[86]

7.61   There are also examples of national courts with no supervisory jurisdiction that have sought to stay foreign arbitral proceedings. In *National Grid v Argentina*,[87] the claimant had instituted proceedings under the UNCITRAL Rules against Argentina, pursuant to the United Kingdom–Argentina BIT. The parties agreed to a juridical seat of Washington, DC, and the ICC was designated as appointing authority. In the course of proceedings, Argentina unsuccessfully challenged the president of the tribunal before the ICC and then brought a claim against the ICC before its own courts in Buenos Aires. Less than a week before the final hearing, Argentina obtained an interim injunction in its domestic proceedings against the ICC to stay the arbitration in Washington, DC. The tribunal refused to suspend the proceedings, noting that the procedure for the challenge of arbitrators was a self-contained procedure under the UNCITRAL Rules, agreed by the parties, and further that the supervisory courts were those of the agreed seat, being Washington, DC, and not Argentina. Similarly, in *SGS v Pakistan*,[88] the Pakistan Supreme Court issued an order against SGS restraining it from taking any action to pursue arbitration proceedings that it had commenced under the Arbitration Rules of the International Centre for the Settlement of Investment Disputes (ICSID) on the basis of a BIT. SGS nevertheless pursued its case, considering that the Pakistani courts had no supervisory jurisdiction over an ICSID claim.

7.62   Such cases nevertheless remain rare. The vast majority of arbitrations are pursued without interference from domestic courts. Nevertheless, the evolution of an international law principle by which tribunals must abide, even if in conflict with the dictates of the courts of the seat, may cause such courts to curtail their partisan zeal and conform to accepted international norms.

---

[83]   *Benteler v Belgium* (1985) 8 European Commercial Cases 101.
[84]   Quoted in *Himpurna California Energy Ltd (Bermuda) v Republic of Indonesia* (2000) XXV YBCA 11, at [169].
[85]   Ibid., at [184].
[86]   Ibid., at [181].
[87]   *National Grid v Argentina*, Decision of the Fourth Chamber of the Camera Contencioso-Administrativa Federal, 2 July 2007.
[88]   *Société Générale de Surveillance SA (SGS) v Islamic Republic of Pakistan*, Pakistan Supreme Court, 3 July 2002. For a detailed analysis of the case, see Lau, 'Note on *Société Générale de Surveillance v Pakistan*' (2003) 19 Arb Intl 179.

(h) Court enforcement of tribunal-ordered interim measures

As discussed above,[89] when a party is subject to interim measures ordered by an arbitral tri-   **7.63**
bunal, it has a powerful incentive to comply with the order voluntarily to avoid prejudicing
its standing in the eyes of the tribunal that will adjudicate upon the merits of its dispute.
However, in the absence of such voluntary compliance, an arbitral tribunal lacks the authority directly to enforce its orders of interim measures (just as tribunals also lack the authority to directly enforce their own final awards). In such circumstances, it is therefore
necessary for the applicant party to apply to the national courts to compel compliance.

As already mentioned, there have been difficulties in enforcing arbitral interim measures   **7.64**
internationally as a consequence of the uncertainty that remains as to whether they come
within the enforcement regime of the New York Convention.[90] The Convention is silent
on this point,[91] a by-product of its adoption in 1958, a time when arbitral interim measures were far rarer than they are today. The ongoing debate has centred upon whether such
interim measures possess the necessary characteristic of finality to qualify as 'awards' enforceable under the Convention, a question on which commentators have expressed varied
positions.[92]

To address this uncertainty, the Model Law and numerous other national arbitration statutes   **7.65**
provide for a *sui generis* enforcement mechanism for arbitral interim measures. Pursuant to
Article 17 H(1), the Model Law's regime applies irrespective of the seat of the tribunal that
ordered the interim measures in question, and regardless of whether the interim measure
is styled as an award, an order, or a decision. Interim measures are required to be enforced
subject to certain limited grounds for non-enforcement set forth in Article 17 I, which includes the standard grounds for non-enforcement of awards on the merits under Article 36
and further grounds relevant specifically to interim measures, for example a party having
not fulfilled a tribunal's order to post security for the interim measure.

An enforcement mechanism for arbitral interim measures is also enshrined, for instance,   **7.66**
in English law, although it does not apply to interim measures ordered by foreign-seated

---

[89] Paragraph 7.35.

[90] These complications appear to be decreasing over time, due to the 'trend toward broader recognition
and enforcement of arbitral interim measures, even in the absence of an express statutory provision to that effect': Castello and Chahine, 'Enforcement of interim measures', in Rowley KC, Gaillard, and Kaiser (eds) *The Guide
to Challenging and Enforcing Arbitration Awards* (Global Arbitration Review, 2019), p. 108.

[91] New York Convention, Art. III: 'Each Contracting State shall recognize arbitral awards as binding and enforce
them in accordance with the rules of procedure of the territory where the award is relied upon, under the conditions laid down in the following articles.' Crucially, this provision does not define an 'award'.

[92] Against this proposition, see V. V. Veeder: 'the better view of [the New York Convention's] application excludes any provisional order for interim measures from enforcement abroad as a Convention award'. Castello and
Chahine, 'Enforcement of interim measures', in Rowley KC, Gaillard, and Kaiser (eds) *The Guide to Challenging
and Enforcing Arbitration Awards* (Global Arbitration Review, 2019), p. 101, fn. 2. In favour, see Born: 'The better
view is that provisional measures should be and are enforceable as arbitral awards under generally-applicable provisions for the recognition and enforcement of awards in the Convention and most national arbitration regimes.
Provisional measures are "final" in the sense that they dispose of a request for relief pending the conclusion of
the arbitration [...] T]here is no reason that the term "award" should not include reasoned, signed decisions by
arbitrators on requests for provisional measures when Contracting States have (almost universally) recognized
the authority of arbitrators to grant such relief'. Born, *International Commercial Arbitration* (3rd edn, Kluwer
Law International, 2021), pp. 2703–2704. Agnostic, see van den Berg: 'there does not seem to be a "prevailing
view" on this question'. Cited in Castello and Chahine, 'Enforcement of interim measures', in Rowley KC, Gaillard,
and Kaiser (eds) *The Guide to Challenging and Enforcing Arbitration Awards* (Global Arbitration Review, 2019),
pp. 101, 104.

arbitral tribunals.[93] English law provides a two-stage process. First, under section 41(5) of the English Arbitration Act 1996, a tribunal may grant a peremptory order against a party that is in default of any order or directions (including interim measures); secondly, the peremptory order may be enforced by the courts pursuant to section 42(1) of the 1996 Act. *Pearl Petroleum & Others v The Kurdistan Regional Government* provides a high-profile example of this process in action, in which the English High Court enforced a US$100 million peremptory order issued in an LCIA arbitration against the respondent state, after confirming that the court has discretion to review the order and was not obliged to 'act as a rubber stamp on orders made by the tribunal'.[94]

7.67   A further approach to enforcement that some states have taken is to label certain interim measures ordered by tribunals as 'awards', at least as far as their own legislation is concerned. This is the case in Israel and Malaysia, which define 'award' to include an interim award,[95] and New Zealand,[96] which makes the provisions on enforcement of awards applicable to an interim measures order (unless the tribunal provides otherwise). Institutional rules typically leave the form in which arbitral interim measures are granted at the discretion of the tribunal.[97] In the context of an ICC arbitration, granting such measures in the form of an order rather than an award may add considerably to the speed of the process, because an order, unlike an award, will not need to be scrutinised by the ICC Court before issuance.[98]

D. At the End of the Arbitration

7.68   One final aspect of the relationship between national courts and arbitral tribunals remains to be considered: the extent to which, if at all, national courts should exercise judicial control over the conduct of international arbitrations and the resulting award. There are two extreme positions. As one English judge recognised:

> It can be said on the one side that if parties agree to resolve their disputes through the use of a private rather than a public tribunal, then the court system should play no part at all, save perhaps to enforce awards in the same way as they enforce any other rights and obligations to which the parties have agreed. To do otherwise is unwarrantably to interfere with the parties' right to conduct their affairs as they choose.
>
> The other extreme position reaches a very different conclusion. Arbitration has this in common with the court system; both are a form of dispute resolution which depends on the decision of a third party. Justice dictates that certain rules should apply to dispute resolution of this kind. Since the state is in overall charge of justice, and since justice is an integral part of any civilised democratic society, the courts should not hesitate to

---

[93]   English Arbitration Act, s. 42(1); see also Sutton et al., *Russell on Arbitration* (24th edn, Sweet & Maxwell, 2015), para. 7-208.

[94]   *(1) Pearl Petroleum Company Limited (2) Dana Gas PJSC (3) Crescent Petroleum Company Limited v The Kurdistan Regional Government of Iraq* [2015] EWHC 3361 (Comm), at [16].

[95]   Israel Arbitration Law of 1968, s. 1; Malaysia Arbitration Act 2005, s. 2.

[96]   New Zealand Arbitration Act 1996, Sch. 1, Art. 17L.

[97]   Swiss Rules, Art. 26.2; SIAC, Art. 30.1; SCC, Art. 37.3; NAI, Art. 35.4; JAMS, r. 24(e); ICDR, Art. 24.2; ICC, Art. 28.1; HKIAC Administered Rules, Art. 23.3; AAA, R-37.b; LCIA Rules, Art. 25 (silent as to the form of interim measures).

[98]   ICC Rules, Art. 33.

intervene as and when necessary, so as to ensure that justice is done in private as well as public tribunals.[99]

The extent to which there should be judicial control at the seat of the arbitration and at the place of enforcement over both the conduct of the arbitration and the resulting award is a matter on which different commentators and, more importantly, different states have taken different views. It is an important matter and is considered in more detail in Chapters 10 and 11.

E. Conclusion

Powers which have been conferred on national courts by legislation, or which have **7.69** been developed by the courts themselves (such as the powers to attach bank accounts, to appoint liquidators, or to issue injunctions) are there to serve the interests of justice. They are there to ensure that the ultimate purpose of legal proceedings is not frustrated by evidence or assets disappearing, or by parties taking the law into their own hands. As international commercial transactions and foreign direct investment increase, recourse to the courts, even where there is an arbitration agreement, may be essential if the aims of justice are to be properly served. As one experienced Swiss arbitrator expressed it:

> [T]he development of law and international arbitration has been marked by an obvious tendency to limit the possibilities of court intervention in the course of an arbitration.
> [...] It may be that the tide is now turning: it is increasingly realised in international arbitration circles that the intervention of the courts is not *necessarily* disruptive of the arbitration. It may equally be definitely *supportive* [...][100]

As in all relationships, the appropriate balance must be found between the rights of the **7.70** courts to supervise arbitrations and the rights of parties to solicit the courts' assistance in times of need. As succinctly put by Hwang, 'courts should supervise with a light touch but assist with a strong hand'.[101]

---

[99] Saville, 'The Denning Lecture 1995: Arbitration and the courts' (1995) 61 Arbitration 157, at 157.

[100] Reymond, 'The *Channel Tunnel* case and the law of international arbitration' (1993) 109 LQR 337, at [341] (emphasis added).

[101] Hwang, 'Commercial courts and international arbitration—competitors or partners?' (2015) 31 Arb Intl 193, at 194.

8

ARBITRATION UNDER INVESTMENT TREATIES

A. Introduction

Historically, an individual or a corporation who wished to assert a claim against a foreign **8.01** state for breach of customary international law could not do so directly. Instead, the individual or corporation who believed its rights had been violated by another state had to petition its government to take up, or 'espouse', a claim on its behalf by way of diplomatic protection. In the course of the nineteenth century, influential individuals or corporations would seek to convince their government to send a small contingent of warships to moor off the coast of the offending state until reparation was forthcoming. This form of 'gunboat diplomacy' was exercised frequently by European powers on behalf of their subjects in the not-so-distant past. For example, the British government successfully obtained compensation from Greece for the destruction in a riot of the home of a British subject in the well-documented Don Pacifico affair.[1] When faced with Venezuela's default on its sovereign debt in 1902, the governments of Great Britain, Germany, and Italy sent warships to the Venezuelan coast to demand reparation for the losses incurred by their nationals.

Argentine jurist and diplomat Carlos Calvo fought for the right of newly independent **8.02** states to be free of such intervention by foreign powers and promoted the so-called Calvo doctrine, whereby foreign investors should be in no better position than local investors, with their rights and obligations to be determined through the exclusive jurisdiction of the courts of that state.[2] His position was adopted by the First International Conference of American States in 1889, which concluded (without the support of the United States):

---

[1] David Pacifico (known as Don Pacifico) was a Greek resident who was a British subject by virtue of his birth in Gibraltar. In 1847 his house was burned down in an anti-Semitic riot without intervention by the Greek authorities. Pacifico demanded compensation from the Greek government and when that was not forthcoming sought diplomatic protection from Britain. Then Foreign Secretary Lord Palmerston sent a naval squadron to blockade the Greek coast and compensation was obtained. After grave concerns were voiced in Parliament, Palmerston gave a historic five-hour speech which changed public opinion noting 'a British subject, in whatever land he may be, shall feel confident that the watchful eye and the strong arm of England will protect him against injustice and wrong'.

[2] This thesis was developed by Calvo in his 1868 treatise, *Derecho internacional teórico y práctico de Europa y América* (D'Amyot, 1868).

Foreigners are entitled to enjoy all the civil rights enjoyed by natives and they shall be accorded all the benefits of said rights in all that is essential as well as in the form or procedure, and the legal remedies incident thereto, absolutely in like manner as said natives. A nation has not, nor recognizes in favour to foreigners, any other obligations or responsibilities than those which in favour of the natives are established in like cases by the constitution and the laws.[3]

8.03   This doctrine of non-intervention was adopted in many treaties of friendship, commerce, and navigation (FCN treaties) with important exceptions limited to denial of justice or extraordinary delay in justice. For example, Article 21 of the FCN treaty between Italy and Colombia of 1894 stated:

The Contracting Parties express their desire to avoid all types of disputes which might affect their cordial relations and agree that, in connection with disputes which involve individuals arising out of criminal, civil or administrative matters, their diplomatic agents will abstain from intervening except in cases of denial of justice or extraordinary or unlawful delay in the administration of justice.[4]

8.04   Gunboat diplomacy as a means of asserting rights of nationals was finally laid to rest at the Second International Peace Conference of The Hague in 1907, when the Convention on the Peaceful Resolution of International Disputes was signed. The Convention provided the framework for the conclusion of bilateral arbitration treaties. In accordance with these treaties, in the event of a dispute between two states arising out of the interests of a national of one of those states, an independent arbitral tribunal would be formed. In effect, a state could espouse the claim of its national by means of a horizontal inter-state procedure. There was no direct cause of action by the foreign national whose interests had been harmed against the offending state.

8.05   In the words of the Permanent Court of International Justice (PCIJ) in the *Panevezys-Saldutiskis Railway* case, in asserting diplomatic protection, a state was in fact asserting its own right that international law be respected:

[I]n taking up the case of one of its nationals, by resorting to diplomatic action or international judicial proceedings on his behalf, a state is in reality asserting its own right, the right to ensure in the person of its nationals respect for the rules of international law. This right is necessarily limited to the intervention on behalf of its own nationals because, in the absence of a special agreement, it is the bond of nationality between the state and the individual which alone confers upon the state the right of diplomatic protection, and it is as a part of the function of diplomatic protection that the right to take up a claim and to ensure respect for the rules of international law must be envisaged.[5]

8.06   As Sir Humphrey Waldock stated in 1963, the procedure was unsatisfactory from the individual claimant's point of view:

He has no remedy of his own, and the state to which he belongs may be unwilling to take up his case for reasons which have nothing to do with its merits; and even if it is

---

[3] Scott, *The International Conferences of American States (1889–1928)* (Oxford University Press, 1931), p. 45.
[4] Free translation from the Italian.
[5] *Panevezys-Saldutiskis Railway (Estonia v Lithuania)* [1939] PCIJ Series A/B 76, ICGJ 328 (1939), at [16].

willing to do so, there may be interminable delays before, if ever, the defendant state can be induced to let the matter go to arbitration. [...] It has been suggested that a solution might be found by allowing individuals access in their own right to some form of international tribunal for the purpose, and if proper safeguards against merely frivolous or vexatious claims could be devised, that is a possible reform which deserves to be considered. For the time being, however, the prospect of states accepting such a change is not very great.[6]

Since that text was written, the situation has changed dramatically and what Humphrey Waldock thought unlikely has become a commonplace reality. The validity of his concerns, and the inevitable 'politicisation' of disputes 'leaving investors, particularly small and medium-sized enterprises, with little recourse save what their government cares to give them after weighing the diplomatic pros and cons of bringing any particular claim',[7] led to what we now know as investor–state arbitration provisions in bilateral and multilateral investment treaties.   **8.07**

The radical solution of allowing individuals to assert rights directly against states through arbitration provisions in investment treaties was facilitated by the conclusion of the ICSID Convention.[8] The Convention was aimed primarily at creating a new arbitral forum for the resolution of disputes between investors and states by means of the inclusion of arbitration clauses in state contracts or (as the *travaux préparatoires* of the Convention made clear) through the consent of the state to arbitration under the provisions of an investment law.[9] Following the 1959 Abs-Shawcross Draft Convention on Investments Abroad and the 1967 Organisation for Economic Co-operation and Development (OECD) Draft Convention on the Protection of Foreign Property,[10] many states had begun a programme of bilateral treaties for the promotion and protection of investments (the so-called BITs) that set out explicit substantive protections in favour of foreign investment.[11] They were a natural successor to the FCN treaties of the early part of the twentieth century, but still suffered from the limitations imposed by diplomatic protection. However, once the ICSID Convention was in place, treaty drafters from signatory states recognised the possibility   **8.08**

---

[6] Brierley, *The Law of Nations* (6th edn by Sir Humphrey Waldock, Oxford University Press, 1963), p. 277. Humphrey Waldock served as the British judge in the ECtHR from 1966 until 1974 and in the ICJ from 1973 until 1981. He was also the President of the ICJ between 1979 and 1981.

[7] Testimony of Dan Price, one of the negotiators of the NAFTA, addressing investment protection issues before a US Senate Ways and Means Committee Hearing on the Free Trade Area of the Americas.

[8] The Convention (also known as the Washington Convention) has been ratified by 156 states. The history of the Convention is detailed in Parra, *The History of ICSID* (Oxford University Press, 2012). For a detailed analysis of the provisions of the ICSID Convention, see Schreuer, Malintoppi, Reinisch, and Sinclair, *The ICSID Convention: A Commentary* (2nd edn, Cambridge University Press, 2009). A simple guide to the ICSID arbitration process is contained in Reed, Paulsson and Blackaby, *Guide to ICSID Arbitration* (2nd edn, Kluwer Law International, 2011).

[9] See ICSID, 'Report of the Executive Directors of the International Bank for Reconstruction and Development on the [ICSID Convention]', in *ICSID Convention, Regulations and Rules* (ICSID, 2006), p. 43, para. 24: 'Nor does the Convention require that the consent of both parties be expressed in a single instrument. Thus, a Host State might in its investment protection legislation offer to submit disputes arising out of certain classes of investments to the jurisdiction of the Centre, and the investor might give his consent by accepting the offer in writing.'

[10] See 1967 OECD Draft Convention on the Protection of Foreign Property (1968) 7 ILM 117; see also earlier draft at (1963) 2 ILM 241.

[11] The history of BITs is described in greater detail in Vandevelde, *Bilateral Investment Treaties: History, Policy, and Interpretation* (Oxford University Press, 2010).

of using this new specialist forum designed for the resolution of disputes directly between states and investors within the new investment treaties. They did so by incorporating a provision establishing the consent of the state to arbitrate with qualifying investors who had made protected investments. Humphrey Waldock's vision of a diagonal clause, permitting investors to claim directly under a treaty against the state in which the investment was made (the 'host state'), thus became a reality. Switzerland, for example, inserted a diagonal clause for the first time in its 1981 BIT with Sri Lanka,[12] and has done so systematically ever since.[13]

8.09   This right of direct recourse ensures that the investor's claim is not subject to the political considerations inherent in diplomatic protection. Even if there is no contract between the investor and the host state, a qualifying investor with a qualifying investment may commence arbitration directly against the host state if it believes that the host state has breached the substantive protections in the applicable treaty.[14] Foreign investors were nevertheless slow to take up their newfound rights: the first case brought by an investor under the investment protections of a BIT was not decided until 1990.[15]

8.10   In light of the dramatic increase in the number of BITs and other treaties with investment chapters[16] and the emergence of clearer legal principles through case law, the number of investment arbitrations has mushroomed. In 2021, ICSID registered sixty-one new cases— some ten times the number of cases registered during the whole of ICSID's first ten years of existence.[17] By the end of 2020, the number of known investment arbitrations cases had reached 1104, almost twenty times the figure as it stood in 2000.[18]

8.11   The dramatic growth of BITs since the mid-1980s has led to the adoption of similar provisions in the 'investment chapters', or collateral agreements, to multilateral economic cooperation treaties. These include the Association of Southeast Asian Nations (ASEAN) Comprehensive Investment Agreement,[19] the US–Mexico–Canada Agreement (USMCA),[20]

---

[12] Agreement between the Government of the Swiss Confederation and the Government of the Democratic Socialist Republic of Sri Lanka for the Reciprocal Promotion and Protection of Investments, signed on 23 September 1981, entered into force on 12 February 1982.

[13] See Liebeskind, 'State–investor dispute settlement clauses in Swiss bilateral investment treaties' (2002) 20 ASA Bulletin 1, at 27.

[14] Obviously, the investor could have access to litigation before the courts of the host state. However, this would likely be a last resort since it raises serious questions of neutrality of forum and ultimate enforceability of the judgment elsewhere.

[15] *Asian Agricultural Products Ltd (AAPL) v Democratic Socialist Republic of Sri Lanka*, ICSID Case No. ARB/87/3, Final Award, 27 June 1990.

[16] According to the UNCTAD, there were a total of 3,218 treaties with investment provisions as of 31 January 2022 (2794 BITs and 424 other treaties (multilateral and free trade agreements)): see https://investmentpolicy.unctad.org/international-investment-agreements. It should be noted that *most* intra-EU BITs have been terminated following the Agreement for the Termination of all Intra-EU BITs signed by twenty-three member states of the European Union (EU) on 5 May 2020, following the decision in *Achmea v Slovak Republic*. The Agreement entered into force on 29 August 2020.

[17] See ICSID, 2021—The Year in Review available online at https://icsid.worldbank.org.

[18] See UNCTAD, Investor–State Dispute Settlement Cases: Facts and Figures 2020, International Investment Agreements (IIA) Issues Notes 4 (UN, 2021), available online at http://unctad.org/.

[19] Signed on 26 February 2009, entered into force on 29 March 2012. This agreement covers investments from investors of Brunei, Cambodia, Indonesia, Laos, Malaysia, Myanmar, Philippines, Singapore, Thailand, and Vietnam in the territory of these states.

[20] USMCA, Ch. 14 ('Investment'). This agreement replaced the NAFTA, which covered investments from investors of Canada, Mexico, and the United States in the territory of these states. The investor–state arbitration

the Energy Charter Treaty (ECT),[21] the Dominican Republic and Central America–United States Free Trade Agreement (DR-CAFTA),[22] and the Comprehensive and Progressive Agreement for Trans-Pacific Partnership (CPTPP).[23] Similar provisions have found their way into many bilateral free trade agreements (FTAs) such as the United States–Korea FTA[24] and the 2019 EU–Vietnam Investment Protection Agreement.[25]

As the number of investment treaty arbitrations has grown, concerns over the investment **8.12** treaty system have arisen. These concerns include a perceived deficit of legitimacy given that states are being judged on their conduct by private non-elected individuals often in the context of hearings that are not open to the public. Concerns have also arisen in respect of inconsistent arbitral awards, the independence and impartiality of arbitrators, and the delays and costs of arbitral procedures.[26] These complaints have resonated in some scholarly publications[27] and popular media outlets.[28] At the same time, between 2007 and 2012, a small group of Latin American countries defending multiple claims—Bolivia, Ecuador, and Venezuela—denounced the ICSID Convention and certain BITs.[29] These concerns and isolated denunciations are not symptomatic of an exodus from the investment treaty system. Indeed, Ecuador's departure was short-lived as it signed the ICSID Convention again on 21 June 2021, becoming the first state to leave and return to the system.[30]

---

under the USMCA is significantly more limited than that under NAFTA, including by covering only investments from investors of the United States and Mexico, restricting full protection to investments in limited 'covered sectors' and substantially restricting substantive protections for all other investments.

[21] Signed on 17 December 1994, entered into force on 16 April 1998. The ECT covers investments in the energy sector for investors of its state parties (which number more than fifty) within the territory of those states.

[22] DR-CAFTA, Ch. 10 ('Investment'), signed on 5 August 2004, entered into force between 2006 and 2009 in seven signatory countries. This agreement covers investments from investors from the United States, Costa Rica, El Salvador, Guatemala, Honduras, Nicaragua, and the Dominican Republic in the territory of these states.

[23] Signed on 8 March 2018, entered into force 30 December 2018. This agreement covers investments of investors from Australia, Brunei Darussalam, Canada, Chile, Japan, Malaysia, Mexico, New Zealand, Peru, Singapore, and Vietnam in the territory of those states.

[24] Signed on 30 June 2007, entered into force on 15 March 2012.

[25] European Union–Vietnam Agreement and Investment Protection Agreement, signed on 30 June 2019, entered into force on 1 August 2020.

[26] See UNCTAD, *World Investment Report 2015* (UN, 2015). See also UNCTAD, *Investment Policy Monitor 2020* (UN, 2021), available online at http://unctad.org.

[27] See generally, e.g., Waibel, Kaushal, Chung, and Balchin, *The Backlash against Investment Arbitration* (Kluwer Law International, 2010); Marceddu and Ortolani, 'What is wrong with investment arbitration? Evidence from a set of behavioural experiments' (2020) 31(2) The European Journal of International Law; Nolan, 'Challenges to the credibility of the investor state arbitration system' (2015) American University Business Law Review.

[28] See, e.g., Ranald, 'A clause in the UK-Australia trade deal could let companies sue governments. We have been here before', *The Guardian*, 1 June 2021; Farrell, 'People are freaking out about the Trans Pacific Partnership's investor dispute settlement mechanism. Why should you care?', *The Washington Post*, 26 March 2015.

[29] See UNCTAD, *Denunciation of the ICSID Convention and BITs: Impact on Investor–State Claims*, IIA Issue Notes No. 2 (UN, 2010), available online at http://unctad.org/en/Docs/webdiaeia20106_en.pdf; State Department and the Trade Representative, Office of the United States, *Notice of Termination of United States–Bolivia Bilateral Investment Treaty*, Federal Register, 23 May 2012; Blackaby, 'ICSID withdrawal: A storm in a teacup?' (2010) 1 Les Cahiers de l'Arbitrage 45; ICSID, 'Venezuela submits a notice under Article 71 of the ICSID Convention', ICSID News Release, 26 January 2012, available online at https://icsid.worldbank.org.

[30] See ICSID, 'Ecuador Signs the ICSID Convention', available online at https://icsid.worldbank.org/news-and-events/news-releases/ecuador-signs-icsid-convention.

According to the United Nations Conference on Trade and Development (UNCTAD), 478 new investment treaties were concluded between 2010 and 2019.[31] During that same period, ICSID gained ten new signatory states.[32] Between 2019 and 2020 the number of investment treaties terminated (seventy-six) outstripped the number of treaties signed (forty-three) mainly linked to the termination of intra-EU BITs following the *Achmea v Slovak Republic* decision.[33]

8.13   Systemic reforms are being considered.[34] A critical advance has been the adoption of the UNCITRAL Transparency Rules. Where the parties to an arbitration agree to their application, they provide for public access to transcripts of hearings, a list of documents, expert reports, witness statements presented in the proceedings, and awards.[35] In parallel to this initiative (and since the Transparency Rules only apply to arbitrations commenced under treaties concluded after 1 April 2014) the United Nations Convention on Transparency in Treaty-based Investor–State Arbitration (known as the 'Mauritius Convention') was adopted on 10 December 2014 and entered into force on 18 October 2017.[36] The Convention is an instrument by which the Contracting Parties broaden the scope of the Transparency Rules by expressing their consent to apply them to arbitrations commenced under investment treaties concluded *prior to* 1 April 2014.

8.14   ICSID has been actively promoting greater transparency in its 2022 Rules. For example, in proceedings filed under the 2006 Rules, the publication of awards without the consent of the parties was prohibited.[37] Under the current rules, however, ICSID may publish orders and awards subject only to any redactions agreed by the parties and jointly notified to the Secretary-General within sixty days after the order or decision is issued.[38] The current rules also require parties to disclose the name and address of any non-party from which they received funding, directly or indirectly on an ongoing basis.[39]

8.15   As a result of the growth in investment treaties, many foreign investments are now protected. The question is whether an investor can rely on one or more of these investment treaties to vindicate its legal rights in a particular case. This raises fundamental issues relating to the scope and application of those treaties, which we shall now address.

---

[31] See UNCTAD, *World Investment Reports* (UN, 2011–15) and UNCTAD, World Investment Reports (UN, 2016–20), available online at http://unctad.org.

[32] See the list of ICSID contracting states online at https://icsid.worldbank.org/. Among the state signatories during this period was Ecuador, which, together with Bolivia and Venezuela, earlier withdrew from the ICSID Convention.

[33] UNCTAD, *The Changing IIA Landscape: New Treaties and Recent Policy Developments*, International Investment Agreements (IIA) Issues Notes 1 (UN, 2020); UNCTAD, World Investment Report 2020, p. xii; and UNCTAD, World Investment Report 2021, p. 121, both available online at https://unctad.org/.

[34] See UNCITRAL Working Group III (Investor–State Dispute Settlement Reform) Workplan to implement investor–State dispute settlement (ISDS) reform and resource requirements, Doc. No. A/CN.9/WG.III/WP.206, 4–5 May 2021. More information on the progress of Working Group III (Investor–State Dispute Settlement Reform) is available online at https://uncitral.un.org/en/working_groups/3/investor-state.

[35] See UNCITRAL Transparency Rules.

[36] See Mauritius Convention.

[37] 2006 ICSID Rules, r. 48.

[38] ICSID, r. 63.

[39] ICSID, r. 14.

B. Jurisdictional Issues

(a) Existence of an applicable treaty

To determine whether an investor enjoys investment treaty protection, an applicable treaty **8.16** between the state in which the investment was made and the home state of the investor must be identified.[40] It is easy to identify multilateral investment treaties, because they are sufficiently notorious. It is, however, more difficult to detect applicable BITs, considering their number and the absence of a comprehensive list.[41] Although the list prepared by UNCTAD is helpful, the only definitive means of verifying the existence of a BIT, and whether it is in force,[42] is by contacting the treaty section of the relevant government or embassy.

Most treaties contain provisions with respect to their effective date and duration. An issue may **8.17** arise as to whether investments made prior to the date on which the treaty came into effect are eligible for protection under it. Tribunals have generally taken the position that prior investments are afforded protection and some treaties are explicit in this regard. The United States–Argentina BIT, for example, provides that it shall apply to investments existing at the time of entry into force, as well as to investments made or acquired thereafter.[43] A distinction should be drawn between application of a treaty to investments made prior to its entry in force and its application to alleged breaches that occurred prior to that date. In *Técnicas Medioambientales Tecmed SA v Mexico*, for example,[44] the tribunal held that while the concerned investment was eligible for protection under the treaty, the treaty could not have retrospective application to actions by the host state prior to its entry into force.

Investment treaties also commonly include provisions regarding the legal status of invest- **8.18** ments after the termination or expiry of the particular BIT. Generally, such provisions indicate that investments that were otherwise covered by the treaty whilst in force will continue to benefit from the same protection for a specified 'sunset' period, usually of between ten and fifteen years after termination or expiry.[45]

---

[40] An investor may derive protections for the same investment from more than one treaty or from other non-treaty sources, such as foreign investment laws or contracts. It may be possible for claims based on different instruments to be dealt with in the same arbitral proceedings: see *Pac Rim Cayman LLC v Republic of El Salvador*, ICSID Case No. ARB/09/12, Decision on the Respondent's Jurisdictional Objections, 1 June 2012, at [4.45]: '[T]he Tribunal finds no juridical difficulty in having an ICSID arbitration based on different claims arising from separate investment protections and separate but identical arbitration provisions, here CAFTA and the Investment Law.'

[41] The UNCTAD website provides a database of international investment agreements at http://investmentpolicyhub.unctad.org/IIA.

[42] Treaties that have been signed may not necessarily be in force. A treaty enters into force in accordance with the procedure provided for within the treaty itself. This usually involves the exchange of instruments of ratification between the contracting states.

[43] Treaty between the United States and the Argentine Republic Concerning the Reciprocal Encouragement and Protection of Investment, signed on 14 November 1991, entered into force on 20 October 1994, Art. XIV(1).

[44] ICSID Case No. ARB(AF)/00/02, Award, 29 May 2003. The tribunal noted, however, that the pre-BIT acts of the host state would be relevant to consider a continuing or aggravating breach of the BIT. See also *Mesa Power Group LLC v Government of Canada*, PCA Case No. 2012-17, Award, 24 March 2016, at [326].

[45] For instance, in May 2008, the Bolivarian Republic of Venezuela denounced its BIT with the Netherlands. In accordance with its terms, the termination of the BIT took effect on 1 November 2008. However, in view of its fifteen-year survival clause, investments made prior to 1 November 2008 remain protected by the BIT until 2023: see Agreement on Encouragement and Reciprocal Protection of Investments between the Kingdom of the

(b) Protected investors

8.19   Once a potentially applicable treaty has been identified, the relevant treaty provisions de-fining the eligible 'investors', or 'nationals', should be reviewed. Although treaties may vary substantially in this respect, the following provision of the Lithuania–Poland BIT is representative:

> For the purposes of this Agreement:
>
> (1) The term 'investor' refers with regard to either Contracting Party to:
>   (a) natural persons having the nationality of the Contracting Party;
>   (b) legal entities, including companies, corporations, business associations and other organizations, which are constituted or otherwise duly organized under the law of that Party and have their seat, together with real economic activities, in the territory of that same Contracting Party;
>   (c) legal entities established under the law of any country which are, directly or indir-ectly, controlled by nationals of that Contracting Party or by legal entities having their seat, together with real economic activities, in the territory of that same Contracting Party; it being understood that control requires a substantial part in the ownership.[46]

Investors covered by protection of investment treaties can thus be divided into natural per-sons and legal entities.

(i) Natural persons

8.20   Most BIT provisions establish the nationality of a natural person by reference to the do-mestic laws of the respective contracting states. This is consistent with the concept of state sovereignty in deciding the criteria for identifying its nationals. Certain BITs may contain an additional requirement of residence,[47] or domicile.[48]

8.21   Difficulties may arise where the purported investor is a dual national who is a national of both state parties to the BIT. The ICSID Convention precludes individuals from suing any state of which they are nationals.[49] While most tribunals have not found dual nationality to be an obstacle to a claim under a treaty absent any specific exclusionary language,[50] a

---

Netherlands and the Bolivarian Republic of Venezuela, signed on 22 October 1991, entered into force 1 November 1993, Art. 14.

[46] Agreement between the Republic of Lithuania and the Republic of Poland on the Reciprocal Promotion and Protection of Investments, signed on 28 September 1992, entered into force on 6 August 1993, Art. 1.

[47] See, e.g., Treaty between the Federal Republic of Germany and the State of Israel concerning the Encouragement and the Reciprocal Protection of Investments, signed on 24 June 1976, entered into force on 14 April 1980, Art. 1(3)(b).

[48] See, e.g., Agreement between the Government of Denmark and the Government of the Republic of Indonesia Concerning the Encouragement and the Reciprocal Protection of Investments, signed on 30 January 1968, entered into force on 10 March 1970, Art. 1.

[49] ICSID Convention, Art. 25(2)(a).

[50] See *Victor Pey Casado and Fundación Presidente Allende v Republic of Chile*, ICSID Case No. ARB/98/2, Award, 8 May 2008; *Serafín García Armas y Karina García Gruber v Bolivarian Republic of Venezuela*, PCA Case No. 2013-3, Decision on Jurisdiction, 15 December 2014; *Mohamed Abdel Raouf Bahgat v Arab Republic of Egypt*, PCA Case No. 2012-07, Decision on Jurisdiction, 30 November 2017; *Dawood Rawat v Republic of Mauritius*,

minority has applied a test of effective (or dominant) nationality that had been used in inter-state cases of diplomatic protection.[51]

(ii) Legal entities

All investment treaties extend the benefit of their protection to legal entities such as com-   **8.22**
panies. Many treaties simply require that the entity be incorporated or constituted under the laws of one of the Contracting Parties. Some treaties add other requirements of substantive activity in the home state, such as the need to carry out business or have a place of effective management there.[52]

Where no such additional requirements have been stipulated, tribunals generally conduct   **8.23**
a review limited to determining whether the legal entity satisfies the formal definition of investor under the treaty and refuse to incorporate additional requirements that the treaty drafters did not include. For instance, in *Yukos Universal Ltd (Isle of Man) v Russia*,[53] Russia argued that the claimant should not qualify as an investor under the ECT (which defines 'investors' based on the law under which an entity is organised), because it was a shell company that was owned and controlled by Russian nationals. In rejecting this argument, the tribunal held that it knew of 'no general principles of international law that would require investigating how a company or another organization operates when the applicable treaty simply requires it to be organized in accordance with the laws of a Contracting Party' and refused to 'write new, additional requirements—which the drafters did not include—into a treaty, no matter how auspicious or appropriate they may appear'.[54]

Similarly, in *Tokios Tokelės v Ukraine*,[55] a majority of the arbitrators held that an in-   **8.24**
vestor incorporated in Lithuania qualified as an investor under the Lithuania–Ukraine BIT,[56] even though 99 per cent of its shares were owned by Ukrainian nationals. By

---

PCA Case No. 2016-20, Award on Jurisdiction, 6 April 2018; *Sergei Viktorovich Pugachev v Russian Federation*, UNCITRAL, Award on Jurisdiction, 18 June 2020.

[51] See *Manuel Garcia Armas and ors v Bolivarian Republic of Venezuela*, UNCITRAL, Award on Jurisdiction, 13 December 2019; *Enrique Heemsen and ors v Bolivarian Republic of Venezuela*, UNCITRAL, Award on Jurisdiction, 29 October 2019.

[52] See, e.g., Agreement on Encouragement and Reciprocal Protection of Investments between the Kingdom of the Netherlands and the Argentine Republic, signed on 20 October 1992, entered into force on 1 October 1994, Art. 1(b): '[T]he term "investor" shall comprise with regard to either Contracting Party: […] (ii) […] legal persons constituted under the law of that Contracting Party and actually doing business under the laws in force in any part of the territory of that Contracting Party in which a place of effective management is situated; and (iii) legal persons, wherever located, controlled, directly or indirectly, by nationals of that Contracting Party.'

[53] UNCITRAL, PCA Case No. AA 228, Interim Award on Jurisdiction and Admissibility, 30 November 2009.

[54] Ibid., at [415]. Similarly, in *KT Asia Investment Group BV v Republic of Kazakhstan*, ICSID Case No. ARB/09/8, Award, 17 October 2013, the host state, Kazakhstan, argued, among other things, that the claimant entity was not protected by the Netherlands–Kazakhstan BIT because the company was wholly owned and controlled by a Kazakh national. The tribunal upheld jurisdiction, finding that the claimant satisfied the formal requirements of the BIT, which required only incorporation in the Netherlands and declining to import additional obligations into the BIT.

[55] ICSID Case No. ARB/02/18, Decision on Jurisdiction, 29 April 2004. The tribunal refused to pierce the corporate veil because there was no evidence that the claimant had used its status as a Lithuanian entity for an improper purpose, noting, at [56], that 'the Claimant manifestly did not create Tokios Tokelės for the purpose of gaining access to ICSID arbitration under the BIT against Ukraine, as the enterprise was founded six years before the BIT between Ukraine and Lithuania entered into force'. See also *Mabco Constructions SA v Republic of Kosovo*, ICSID Case No. ARB/17/25, Decision on Jurisdiction, 30 October 2020, at [490].

[56] Agreement between the Government of Lithuania and the Government of Ukraine Concerning the Protection and Promotion of Investment, signed on 8 February 1994, entered into force on 6 March 1995.

contrast, in *TSA Spectrum de Argentina SA v Argentina*,[57] a majority denied jurisdiction under the Netherlands–Argentina BIT[58] over a claim against Argentina brought by an Argentine company claiming to be 'controlled' by its Dutch parent (which owned 100 per cent of its shares). The tribunal looked beyond the claimant's immediate (Dutch) parent company and found that its 'ultimate owner' was an Argentine national. The tribunal then held that Article 25(2)(b) of the ICSID Convention's 'foreign control' requirement for juridical entities having the nationality of the state party to the arbitration had not been met.

8.25   The natural consequence of the formalistic language of many treaties is that adopting a particular corporate structure for the purposes of attracting the protection of an investment treaty is wholly legitimate (as it is in the case of tax structuring). In *Aguas del Tunari SA v Bolivia*,[59] the tribunal rejected Bolivia's objection that the 'availability of the BIT was the result of strategic changes in the corporate structure', noting that:

> [I]t is not uncommon in practice, and—absent a particular limitation—not illegal to locate one's operations in a jurisdiction perceived to provide a beneficial regulatory and legal environment in terms, for examples, of taxation or the substantive law of the jurisdiction, including the availability of a BIT.[60]

8.26   Some tribunals have nevertheless drawn the line where the restructuring of an investment has been undertaken solely to gain treaty protections in relation to an earlier dispute, holding that this would amount to a lack of good faith and an 'abusive manipulation of the system'.[61] Thus, in *Mobil Corporation Venezuela Holdings BV v Venezuela*,[62] the tribunal held that it had jurisdiction over claims relating to nationalisation measures taken by Venezuela after the corporate restructuring in question had taken place, but not claims relating to disputes over royalty and tax rates that had arisen prior to the restructuring. Similarly, in *Philip Morris v Australia*, the tribunal concluded that the commencement of an arbitration was an abuse of rights because the claimant had changed its corporate structure to gain the protection of the BIT when the specific dispute object of the claim was reasonably foreseeable.[63]

8.27   Some treaties seek to limit the scope of protection to protected investors by means of treaty clauses allowing the state parties to deny treaty benefits to investors that do not have substantial business activities in their home state and which are controlled by entities or

---

[57]   ICSID Case No. ARB/05/5, IIC 358, Award, 19 December 2008, at [160]–[162].

[58]   Agreement on Encouragement and Reciprocal Protection of Investments between the Kingdom of the Netherlands and the Argentine Republic, signed on 20 October 1992, entered into force on 1 October 1994.

[59]   ICSID Case No. ARB/02/3, Decision on Respondent's Objections to Jurisdiction (2005).

[60]   Ibid., at [330]. See also *MNSS BV and Recupero Credito Acciaio NV v Montenegro*, ICSID Case No. ARB(AF)/12/8, Award, 4 May 2016, at [182].

[61]   *Mobil Corporation, Venezuela Holdings BV and ors v Bolivarian Republic of Venezuela*, ICSID Case No. ARB/07/27, Decision on Jurisdiction, 10 June 2010, at [205], citing *Phoenix Action Ltd v Czech Republic*, Award, fn. 36, at [93] and [144]. See also *Tidewater Inc. and ors v The Bolivarian Republic of Venezuela*, ICSID Case No. ARB/10/5, Decision on Jurisdiction, 8 February 2013, at [146]; and *Philip Morris Asia Limited v Commonwealth of Australia*, PCA Case No. 2012-12, Award on Jurisdiction and Admissibility, 17 December 2015, at [554], [585]–[586].

[62]   See fn. 61, at [205]–[206].

[63]   *Philip Morris Asia*, fn. 61.

persons of a third state (known as 'denial of benefits' clauses).[64] While it remains a matter of debate whether these clauses can be applied retroactively (that is, after an investment is made),[65] tribunals have held that respondent states bear the burden of proving that the requisite elements have been satisfied.[66]

Legal entities established in the host state (and therefore having the nationality of the re-   **8.28** spondent state) may receive treaty protection if (a) they are controlled by entities incorporated in the other contracting state, and (b) both states have agreed in the applicable treaty to extend the protection of the treaty to such controlled entities. This extension is expressly permitted by Article 25(2)(b) of the ICSID Convention.[67] For example, Article 1(2)(c) of the Switzerland–Guyana BIT extends protection, with regard to either contracting party, to:

> legal entities, including companies, corporations, business associations and other organisations, which are constituted or otherwise duly organised under the law of that Contracting Party and have their seat, together with real economic activities, in the territory of the same Contracting Party; [and] legal entities not established under the law of that Contracting Party but effectively controlled by natural persons as defined in (a) above or by legal entities as defined in (b) above.[68]

Thus a locally incorporated entity may claim against its state of incorporation if controlled   **8.29** by a national or company of the other contracting state. This is significant because it is often expedient, or even necessary, to incorporate a local entity to hold an investment, and this extension of protection allows the local entity to bring a claim for its direct losses. It also enables minority shareholders in the local entity (many of whom may be local investors) to obtain indirect relief through treaty arbitration.

---

[64] See, e.g., Agreement between the Republic of Austria and the Great Socialist People's Libyan Arab Jamahiriya for the Promotion and Protection of Investments, signed on 18 June 2002, entered into force on 1 January 2004, Art. 9: 'A Contracting Party may deny the benefits of this Agreement to an investor of the other Contracting Party and to its investments, if investors of a Non-Contracting Party own or control the first mentioned investor and that investor has no substantial business activity in the territory of the Contracting Party under whose law it is constituted or organized.'

[65] See *Plama Consortium Ltd v Republic of Bulgaria*, ICSID Case No. ARB/03/24, Decision on Jurisdiction, 8 February 2005, at [162]–[165] (holding that denial-of-benefits clause cannot be invoked retroactively, after an investment has been made); but see *Gran Colombia Gold Corp. v Republic of Colombia*, ICSID Case No. ARB/18/23, Decision on the Bifurcated Jurisdictional Issue, 23 November 2020, at [130] (rejecting the view that denial-of-benefits clause could be invoked only up until the date the investor files its request for arbitration).

[66] See, e.g., *Ulysseas Inc. v Republic of Ecuador*, UNCITRAL, Interim Award, 28 September 2010, at [166]; *Liman Caspian Oil BV and NCL Dutch Investment BV v Republic of Kazakhstan*, ICSID Case No. ARB/07/14, Award, 22 June 2010, at [164].

[67] Article 25(2)(b) states: National of another Contracting state means: '[…] any juridical person which had the nationality of the Contracting state party to the dispute […] and which, because of foreign control, the parties have agreed should be treated as a national of another Contracting state for the purposes of this Convention.' This 'agreement' is usually explicit (e.g. in the definition of 'investor' in a BIT). It may also be implicit: see *Millicom International Operations BV and Sentel GSM SA v Republic of Senegal*, ICSID Case No. ARB/08/20, Decision on Jurisdiction, 16 July 2010, at [109]–[115] (holding that consent can be implied where the host state entered into an agreement with a local entity containing an ICSID arbitration clause); and *AHS Niger and Menzies Middle East and Africa SA v Republic of Niger*, ICSID Case No. ARB/11/11, Decision on Jurisdiction, 15 July 2013, at [147]–[148] (holding that consent was implied where the host state objected to proceedings before local courts on the basis that ICSID was the appropriate forum for the dispute to be heard).

[68] Agreement between the Swiss Confederation and the Republic of Guyana on the Promotion and Reciprocal Protection of Investments, signed on 13 December 2005, entered into force on 2 May 2018, Art. 1(2).

(c) Protected investments

8.30   In order to rely on an investment treaty, a qualifying 'investor' must establish that it has made a protected 'investment'. Most investment treaties contain a definition of what constitutes an 'investment'.[69] They tend to provide a definition that commences with a broad statement, often referring to 'every kind of asset',[70] or 'every kind of investment in the territory',[71] and then add a non-exhaustive list of examples. The United Kingdom–Chile treaty[72] is typical in this respect and provides, at Article 1(a), that:

> 'investment' means every kind of asset and in particular, though not exclusively, includes:
>   (i)   movable and immovable property and any other property rights such as mortgages, liens and pledges;
>   (ii) shares in, and stock and debentures of a company, and any other form of participation in a company;
>   (iii) claims to money or to any performance under contract having a financial value;
>   (iv) intellectual property rights, goodwill, technical processes and know-how;
>   (v)   business concessions conferred by law or under contract, including concessions to search for, cultivate or extract or exploitation of natural resources.

8.31   The open-ended definition acknowledges that the concept of 'investment' is dynamic and may evolve over time. A tribunal considering an investment treaty claim must therefore analyse whether the claimant's investment satisfies the definition in the treaty that has been invoked.

8.32   Most treaties provide that a shareholding in a company established in the host country constitutes an investment. In *AMT v Zaire*,[73] the ICSID tribunal rejected Zaire's argument that AMT, an American company, had not made any direct investment in Zaire, because it had merely participated in the share capital of a Zairian company. The arbitral tribunal held that investments via the share capital of a local entity were eligible for protection under the United States–Zaire BIT.[74] And, in *CMS v Argentina*,[75] the tribunal held that the American claimant's minority shareholding in an Argentine company qualified as a protected

---

[69]   See UNCTAD, *Scope and Definitions (A Sequel)*, Series on Issues in International Investment Agreements II (UN, 2011), available online at http://unctad.org/.

[70]   See ECT, Art. 1(6).

[71]   See Treaty between the United States of America and the Argentine Republic Concerning the Reciprocal Encouragement and Protection of Investments, signed on 14 November 1991, entered into force on 20 October 1994, Art. I(1)(a).

[72]   Agreement between the Government of the United Kingdom of Great Britain and Northern Ireland and the Government of Chile for the Promotion and Protection of Investments, signed on 8 January 1996, entered into force on 21 April 1997.

[73]   *American Manufacturing and Trading Inc. v Republic of Zaire*, ICSID Case No. ARB/93/1, Award, 27 February 1997, at [5.08]–[5.15].

[74]   Treaty between the United States of America and the Republic of Zaire concerning the Reciprocal Encouragement and Protection of Investment, signed on 3 August 1994, entered into force on 28 July 1989, defining 'investments' as including 'a company or shares of stock or other interests in a company or interests in the assets thereof'.

[75]   *CMS Gas Transmission Co. v Argentine Republic*, ICSID Case No. ARB/01/8, Decision on Jurisdiction, 17 July 2003, at [36]–[65]. See also *Fouad Alghanim & Sons Co. for General Trading & Contracting and ors v Hashemite Kingdom of Jordan*, ICSID Case No. ARB/13/38, Award, 14 December 2017, at [120].

investment. Such decisions are important because host states often impose an obligation that the ultimate investment vehicle be a locally incorporated entity.

The definition of 'investment' has been interpreted to cover direct and indirect investments, **8.33** and modern contractual and other transactions having economic value.[76]

An indirect shareholding in a local company via one or several intermediary companies **8.34** has been held to constitute a protected investment, even where the treaty's definition of 'investment' does not expressly include 'indirect' investments. In *Tza Yap Shum v Peru*,[77] the tribunal held that a Chinese national's indirect shareholding in a local Peruvian company, which was held via an intermediary company established in the British Virgin Islands, could be considered a protected investment for the purposes of the Peru–China BIT.

Indirect investments in assets, rather than shareholdings, have also been held to be pro- **8.35** tected. In *Mobil Corporation v Venezuela*[78] the tribunal held that a Dutch company had a qualifying investment in a Venezuelan joint venture, even though the party to that agreement was its Bahamian subsidiary, and the Netherlands–Argentina BIT[79] did not expressly specify that both direct and indirect investments were covered.[80]

Tribunals have also recognised that financial investments qualify for protection under BITs, **8.36** even though they do not correspond to the conventional notion of 'foreign investment' in that they do not necessarily involve an inflow of funds into the host state or the active management of an investment. For example, in *Fedax NV v Venezuela*,[81] the arbitral tribunal held that promissory notes issued by Venezuela, acquired by the claimant from the original holder in the secondary market by way of endorsement, constituted an investment under the Netherlands–Venezuela BIT. The relevant BIT included 'titles to money' as a category of investment, and the tribunal rejected the contention of Venezuela that this item was restricted to classic forms of direct foreign investment—that is, 'the laying out of money or property in business ventures, so that it may produce a revenue or income'.[82] The tribunal also held that 'it is a standard feature of many international finance transactions that the funds involved are not physically transferred to the territory of the host country but are put at its disposal elsewhere'.[83]

---

[76] See, e.g., Parra, 'The scope of new investment laws and international instruments', in Pritchard (ed.) *Economic Development, Foreign Investment and the Law* (Kluwer Law International, 1996), p. 35.
[77] *Tza Yap Shum v Republic of Peru*, ICSID Case No. ARB/07/6, Decision on Jurisdiction and Competence, 19 June 2009; Agreement between the Government of the Republic of Peru and the Government of the People's Republic of China Concerning the Encouragement and Reciprocal Protection of Investments, signed on 9 June 1994, entered into force on 1 February 1995. See also *Lee-Chin v Dominican Republic*, ICSID Case No. UNCT/13/3, Partial Award on Jurisdiction, at [208]–[219].
[78] See fn. 56. See also *Indian Metals & Ferro Alloys Ltd v Republic of Indonesia*, PCA Case No. 2015-40, Award, 29 March 2019, at [179].
[79] See fn. 52.
[80] But see *Standard Chartered Bank v United Republic of Tanzania*, ICSID Case No. ARB/10/12, Award, 2 November 2012. In this case, the tribunal held that a loan made in Tanzania was not a protected investment. The passive indirect ownership of the loan by the claimant, a British company, did not suffice for the purposes of the United Kingdom–Tanzania BIT, which it interpreted as requiring an investor to contribute actively to an investment.
[81] ICSID Case No ARB/96/3, Decision on Objections to Jurisdiction, 11 July 1997. The definition contained in the applicable BIT was substantially the same as that one quoted at paragraph 8.28.
[82] Ibid., at [41].
[83] Ibid. See also *Tokios Tokelės*, fn. 55, at [77]–[80], in which the tribunal noted that the requirement that there be a transfer of capital was absent from the text, and contrary to the object and purpose of the BIT.

8.37   Subsequent tribunals have opined that loans,[84] hedging agreements,[85] government bonds, and related security entitlements[86] can constitute protected 'investments' under the broad headings of the relevant BIT's definition of investment, such as 'assets', 'claims to money', or 'obligations'. Some tribunals have held that whilst certain financial transactions taken in isolation might not qualify as investments, they may nevertheless be so considered if the overall operation of which they are part, or to which they are connected, constitutes an investment.[87]

8.38   In order to determine whether a purported 'investment' qualifies for protection under the treaty, it may be necessary to consider the conditions under which the investment was admitted into the host state.[88] Investments procured by fraud or corruption or made in violation of the host state's public policy laws or international principles of good faith, will generally not be protected. For instance, the tribunal in *Inceysa Vallisoletana SL v El Salvador*[89] declined jurisdiction on the basis that the investment, a concession contract, was obtained through fraud. And in *Phoenix Action Ltd v Czech Republic*,[90] the tribunal declined jurisdiction on the basis that the claimant's acquisition of an interest in two Czech companies for the sole purpose of bringing a claim against the Czech Republic was not an 'investment' under the BIT, because it was not made in good faith.

8.39   Moreover, some treaties contain conditions requiring that the investment be specifically approved, or 'classified', by the host state. In *Philippe Gruslin v Malaysia*,[91] the tribunal declined jurisdiction on the ground that the concerned investment was not made in a project *approved* by Malaysia, which was a precondition to accessing the protection of the agreement. However, some tribunals have prevented states from relying on formal requirements where the investment has otherwise been clearly approved by the state. In *Desert Line Projects LLC v Yemen*,[92] the tribunal upheld its jurisdiction despite the claimant's failure to produce an 'investment certificate'—a requirement under the BIT. The tribunal did not consider that the granting of a specific certificate was an indispensable formality for

---

[84]   *Ceskoslovenska Obchodni Banka AS v Slovak Republic*, ICSID Case No. ARB/97/4, Decision on Objections to Jurisdiction, 24 May 1999. In this case, no funds were actually transferred to the Slovak Republic pursuant to the loan. However, owing to the close connection of the loan facility to the development of banking facilities in the Slovak Republic, the same was held to be an investment. See also Apostolova, 'Portigon v Spain: new frontiers for financial institutions in investor–state arbitration?' (2020) 36 Arb Intl 4 (discussing case finding claimant's financing of energy project, in the form of long-term loans and swaps, to constitute a protected investment).

[85]   *Deutsche Bank AG v Democratic Socialist Republic of Sri Lanka*, ICSID Case No. ARB/09/02, Award, 31 October 2012, at [291]–[292].

[86]   *Abaclat and ors v Argentine Republic*, ICSID Case No. ARB/07/5, Decision on Jurisdiction and Admissibility, 4 August 2011; see also *Ambiente Ufficio SPA and ors v Argentine Republic*, ICSID Case No. ARB/08/9, Decision on Jurisdiction and Admissibility, 8 February 2013.

[87]   *Ceskoslovenska Obchodni Banka*, fn. 84.

[88]   See, e.g., Agreement between the Government of Canada and the Government of the Argentine Republic for the Protection and Promotion of Investments, signed on 5 November 1991, entered into force on 29 April 1993, Art. 1(a), requiring that the investment be 'made in accordance with the laws' of the host state.

[89]   ICSID Case No. ARB/03/26, Decision on Jurisdiction, 2 August 2006. See also *Gustav F W Hamester GmbH & Co. KG v Republic of Ghana*, ICSID Case No. ARB/07/24, Award, 18 June 2010, at [122]–[124]; *Metal-Tech Ltd. v Republic of Uzbekistan*, ICSID Case No. ARB/10/3, Award, 4 October 2013, at [372].

[90]   *Phoenix Action*, fn. 61, at [144]–[145]. See also *Cementownia 'Nowa Huta' SA v Republic of Turkey*, ICSID Case No. ARB(AF)/06/2, Award, 17 September 2009, at [146]–[149].

[91]   ICSID Case No. ARB/99/3, Award, 27 November 2000.

[92]   ICSID Case No. ARB/05/17, Award, 6 February 2008, at [116]–[118].

jurisdictional purposes and it emphasised that the investment had been endorsed at the highest level of the state.

In addition to satisfying the definition of 'investment' in the BIT, several tribunals have re- **8.40**
quired that an investment also possess certain objective characteristics in order to qualify for protection. This case law was developed in the context of Article 25 of the ICSID Convention, which requires that legal disputes arise directly out of an 'investment'.[93] The Convention, however, does not define the term 'investment',[94] leaving it to contracting states to do so, such as by means of BIT clauses. However, certain tribunals and commentators have opined that the term 'investment' in the ICSID Convention must be understood as setting 'outer limits' to, or mandatory requirements for, ICSID's jurisdiction that cannot be left to the discretion of the parties.[95] In this regard, it is often noted that a simple contract for the sale of goods, without more, could not qualify as an investment under Article 25 of the Convention, even if this were the subject of an agreement by the parties.[96]

The tribunals that adhere to this view typically apply some version of the so-called *Salini* **8.41**
test, which was laid out in *Salini v Morocco*—although it originally derives from *Fedax v Venezuela*.[97] The tribunal in that latter case opined that '[t]he basic features of an investment have been described as involving a certain duration, a certain regularity of profit and return, assumption of risk, a substantial commitment and a significance for the host State's development'.[98]

Among the tribunals that have applied the *Salini* test, there is disagreement as to how it **8.42**
should be applied and which factors should be considered. Perhaps the most controversial aspect is whether (and to what extent) investments must contribute to the economic development of a state (a factor drawn from the Preamble of the ICSID Convention[99]). The tribunal in *LESI SpA and ASTALDI SpA v Algeria*[100] considered this requirement to be irrelevant. By contrast, the ad hoc committee in *Patrick Mitchell v Democratic Republic of the Congo*[101] held that 'the existence of a contribution to the economic development of the host State as an essential—although not sufficient—characteristic or unquestionable criterion of the investment, does not mean that this contribution must always be sizable or successful'.[102]

---

[93] See paragraph 8.44.
[94] ICSID, 'Report of the Executive Directors of the International Bank for Reconstruction and Development on the ICSID Convention', fn. 9, p. 44, para. 27 explains that: '[N]o attempt was made to define the term "investment" given the essential requirement of consent by the parties, and the mechanism through which Contracting States can make known in advance, if they so desire, the classes of disputes which they would or would not consider submitting to the Centre' (Art. 25(4)).
[95] Schreuer, Malintoppi, Reinisch, and Sinclair, fn. 8, p. 83.
[96] See, e.g., *SGS Société Générale de Surveillance SA v Republic of Paraguay*, ICSID Case No. ARB/07/29, Decision on Jurisdiction, 12 February 2010 at [93].
[97] *Salini Costruttori SpA and Italstrade SpA v Morocco*, ICSID Case No. ARB/00/4, Decision on Jurisdiction, 29 November 2004; *Fedax NV v Bolivarian Republic of Venezuela*, fn. 81.
[98] *Fedax NV v Bolivarian Republic of Venezuela*, fn. 81, at [43].
[99] The first paragraph of the Preamble to the ICSID Convention reads: 'Considering the need for international cooperation for economic development, and the role of private international investment therein [...]'.
[100] ICSID Case No. ARB/05/3, Award, 12 November 2008. See also *KT Asia Investment Group BV v Republic of Kazakhstan*, ICSID Case No. ARB/09/8, Award, 17 October 2013, at [170]–[173].
[101] ICSID Case No. ARB/99/7, Decision on the Application for Annulment of the Award, 1 November 2006.
[102] Ibid., at [33].

8.43   Other tribunals, however, reject the *Salini* test as inappropriately narrowing the definition of 'investment' in the investment treaty. The annulment committee in *Malaysian Historical Salvors, SDN, BHD v Malaysia*[103] decided, by majority, to annul the original sole arbitrator's decision that a salvage contract was not an 'investment' under Article 25 of the ICSID Convention because it did not sufficiently contribute to Malaysia's economic development. The decision rejected the elevation of the *Salini* criteria to jurisdictional conditions and criticised the arbitrator's failure to apply the broad definition of investment in the applicable BIT.

8.44   This doctrine of the objective notion of investment has been applied outside the ICSID context, in an UNCITRAL case: *Romak SA (Switzerland) v Uzbekistan*.[104] In that case, the tribunal was asked to determine whether a transfer of title to wheat amounted to an investment. Referring to the 'inherent meaning' of the term 'investments' under the BIT—which the tribunal held included a contribution over a certain period of time involving some risk—the tribunal concluded that this one-off transaction did not constitute an investment. This approach in a non-ICSID context was criticised in *Guaracachi America Inc. and Rurelec Plc v Bolivia*,[105] in which it was held that:

> [I]t is not appropriate to import 'objective' definitions of investment […] when in the context of a non-ICSID arbitration such as the present case. On the contrary, the definition of protected investment, at least in non-ICSID arbitrations, is to be obtained only from the (very broad) definition contained in the BIT […]

8.45   Whilst the notion of investment has been expanding, it has its limitations. As noted already, ordinary commercial transactions are generally not protected by investment treaties or the ICSID Convention.[106] In other cases, tribunals have found that bank guarantees contingent on a sales contract[107] and expenses incurred in bidding for a public contract were not investments under the applicable treaty.[108]

8.46   Moreover, in some investment treaties, states have narrowed the scope of protection by expressly excluding portfolio investments[109] and commercial contracts for the sale of a good or service,[110] or by requiring that investments have certain inherent characteristics by

---

[103] ICSID Case No. ARB/05/10, Award on Jurisdiction, 17 May 2007. See also *Gavrilovic and Gavrilovic d.o.o. v Republic of Croatia*, ICSID Case No. ARB/12/39, Award, 26 July 2018, at [193].

[104] PCA Case No. AA280, Award, 26 November 2009. See also *A.M.F. Aircraftleasing Meier & Fischer GmbH & Co. KG v Czech Republic*, PCA Case No. 2017-15, Final Award, 11 May 2020, at [472].

[105] See *Guaracachi America Inc. and Rurelec Plc v Plurinational State of Bolivia*, PCA Case No. 2011-17, Award, 31 January 2014, at [364].

[106] See paragraph 8.40. However, in *GEA Group Aktiengesellschaft v Ukraine*, ICSID Case No. ARB/05/18, Award, 31 May 2011, the tribunal found that a conversion contract involving the delivery of diesel, catalysts, and other materials, as well as know-how on logistics and market and other services, was a 'complex relationship going far beyond the simple sale of raw materials', and therefore constituted a protected investment.

[107] *Joy Mining Machinery Ltd v Arab Republic of Egypt*, ICSID Case No. ARB/03/11, Award on Jurisdiction, 6 August 2004, at [44]–[47]. The tribunal reached this conclusion notwithstanding the fact that the BIT defined 'investment' as every kind of asset, including mortgage, lien or pledge, and claims to money or to any other performance under contract having a financial value: see ibid., at [38].

[108] *Mihaly International Corporation v Democratic Socialist Republic of Sri Lanka*, ICSID Case No. ARB/00/2, Award, 15 March 2002.

[109] See, e.g., EFTA–Mexico FTA, signed 27 November 2000, entered into force on 1 July 2001, Art. 45.

[110] See, e.g., Canada Model BIT (2021), Art. 1. Definition of 'investment'.

reference to criteria associated with the *Salini* test.[111] Other states have limited the scope of their treaties by excluding certain classes of dispute arising out of investments in certain sectors, which they are permitted to do under Article 25(4) of the ICSID Convention, although such exclusions are unlikely to affect treaties already in place.[112]

(d) Consent and conditions to access investment treaty arbitration

It is important at the outset to distinguish consent from procedural preconditions. **8.47** Whether or not a state has consented to arbitration will go to the question of jurisdiction, that is, 'if' there has been an agreement to arbitrate. Procedural preconditions on the other hand go to the question of admissibility, that is, 'when' the dispute can be arbitrated. Typical procedural preconditions include the written notification of a dispute and the expiry of a specified period within which the investor seeks to engage the host state in amicable consultations (also known as a 'cooling-off period'). Other treaties require the investor to pursue remedies before the courts of the host state for a minimum period prior to commencing arbitration. The question arises: what happens if an investor fails to comply with such conditions?

The level of detail required for notifications of disputes sent under investment treaties **8.48** depends upon the requirements set out in the text of the treaty and their interpretation. Several tribunals have held it to be unnecessary for the investor to 'spell out its legal case in detail'[113] or even to allege a breach of the BIT itself,[114] during the initial negotiation process and that it is sufficient for it to inform the state of the allegations that may later be invoked to engage the host state's international responsibility before an international tribunal.[115] Other tribunals, including the tribunal in *Burlington Resources Inc. v Ecuador*,[116] declined jurisdiction over one of several claims on the basis that it had not been specifically notified.

Consultation periods are generally considered to be procedural in nature. As a conse- **8.49** quence, failure to comply where the purpose of the clause is frustrated (e.g. when the host state has failed to engage in discussions) does not impact the state's consent to arbitrate.[117]

---

[111] See, e.g., United States Model BIT (2012), Art. 1, which defines 'investment' as 'every asset that an investor owns or controls, directly or indirectly, that has the characteristics of an investment, including such characteristics as the commitment of capital or other resources, the expectation of gain or profit, or the assumption of risk'.

[112] For instance, in 1974, Jamaica excluded legal disputes arising directly out of an investment relating to minerals or other natural resources. In 2007, Ecuador provided a similar notice under Art. 25(4) of the ICSID Convention in respect of disputes arising out of investments in the natural resources sector.

[113] *Tulip Real Estate Investment and Development Netherlands BV v Republic of Turkey*, ICSID Case No. ARB/11/28, Decision on Bifurcated Jurisdictional Issue, 5 March 2013, at [83]. See also *Hydro Srl and ors v Republic of Albania*, ICSID Case No. ARB/15/28, Award, 4 June 2019, at [506]–[507].

[114] *Compañía de Aguas del Aconquija SA and Vivendi Universal SA v Argentine Republic*, ICSID Case No. ARB/97/3, Decision on Annulment, 3 July 2002.

[115] *Tulip Real Estate*, fn. 113, at [83].

[116] ICSID Case No. ARB/08/5, Decision on Jurisdiction, 2 June 2010, at [334]–[337]. See also *Murphy Exploration and Production Co. International v Republic of Ecuador*, ICSID Case No. ARB/08/4, Award on Jurisdiction, 15 December 2010, at [102]–[105].

[117] See, e.g., *Abaclat and ors v Argentine Republic*, fn. 86; *Alps Finance and Trade AG v Slovak Republic*, UNCITRAL, Award, 5 March 2011, at [200]–[212]; *Teinver SA, Transportes de Cercanías SA, Autobuses Urbanos del Sur SA v Argentine Republic*, ICSID Case No. ARB/09/1, Decision on Jurisdiction, 21 December 2012, at [107].

For example, in *Ronald S Lauder v Czech Republic*,[118] the tribunal waived the waiting period in the following terms:

> However, the Arbitral Tribunal considers that this requirement of a six-month waiting pe-
> riod of Art VI(3)(a) of the Treaty is not a jurisdictional provision, ie a limit set to the au-
> thority of the Arbitral Tribunal to decide on the merits of the dispute, but a procedural rule
> that must be satisfied by the Claimant (*Ethyl Corp v Canada*, UNCITRAL June 24, 1998, 38
> ILM 708 (1999), paras 74–88). As stated above, the purpose of this rule is to allow the par-
> ties to engage in good-faith negotiations before initiating arbitration.[119]

8.50   Similarly, the tribunal in *Biwater Gauff (Tanzania) Ltd v Tanzania*[120] held that the six-month amicable settlement period under the BIT was 'procedural and directory in nature', the purpose of which was 'to facilitate opportunities for amicable settlement [...] not to impede or obstruct arbitration proceedings'.

8.51   The same conclusion has been reached with other preconditions to arbitration, such as the obligation to pursue local court remedies for a set period of time before accessing arbitration irrespective of whether or not the local court had issued a decision. In the case of *BG Group v Argentina*,[121] a treaty requirement to submit the dispute to the Argentine courts for eighteen months (without any obligation to be bound by the result, or even to reach a decision) before accessing arbitration was not held to be 'an absolute impediment to arbitration' where the host state had severely restricted access to those local courts.[122]

8.52   The position is not, however unanimous. Other tribunals have held that conditions to access arbitration under a BIT, such as consultation periods, are jurisdictional prerequisites. For instance, in *Guaracachi America Inc. and Rurelec PLC v of Bolivia*,[123] the tribunal concluded that it lacked jurisdiction over certain claims because the claimants failed to observe a six-month 'cooling-off period', even though it considered that to have done so would have been likely to prove futile.

8.53   A separate issue is whether preconditions to arbitration can be avoided (or replaced) by relying on the 'most favoured nation' (MFN) clause of the applicable treaty in order to access more favourable preconditions in other treaties concluded by the host state of the investment.

---

[118] UNCITRAL, Final Award, 3 September 2001.

[119] Ibid., at [187]. Moreover, in the tribunal's view (at [190]), '[t]o insist that the arbitration proceedings cannot be commenced until six months after the 19 August 1999 Notice of Arbitration would, in the circumstances of this case, amount to an unnecessary, overly formalistic approach which would not serve to protect any legitimate interests of the Parties'. See also *Evrobalt LLC v Republic of Moldova*, SCC Emergency Arbitration No. EA (2016/082), Award on Emergency Measures, 30 May 2016, at [22].

[120] ICSID Case No. ARB/05/22, Award, 24 July 2008, at [343].

[121] UNCITRAL, Final Award, 24 December 2007.

[122] Ibid., at [147]. The conclusion of the tribunal on this point led Argentina to challenge the award before the courts of the seat, which was Washington, DC. Under the terms of the *lex arbitri*, the FAA, the District Court confirmed the award. However, the award was subsequently set aside by the DC Circuit Court of Appeals. An application for certiorari to the US Supreme Court was made and granted. The justices overruled the appellate court and held that the obligation to pursue remedies before local courts for a set period without any obligation to await a final decision (or to agree to the final decision) was effectively a procedural precondition, which, in light of Supreme Court precedent, meant that deference should be given to the arbitral tribunal's decision (572 US 25, 134 S.Ct. 1198 (2014)).

[123] See fn. 105 at [386] and [388]. See also *Burlington Resources Inc.*, fn. 116; *Tulip Real Estate*, fn. 113; *Mabco Constructions SA v Republic of Kosovo*, ICSID Case No. ARB/17/25, Decision on Jurisdiction, 30 October 2020, at [445].

There is much debate as to whether MFN clauses can be applied to dispute settlement   **8.54**
clauses in investment treaties. This possibility was upheld by an ICSID tribunal in the
Maffezini case.[124] Mr Maffezini was an Argentine investor, who had a dispute with the government of Spain arising out of an investment that he had made in Spain. He submitted his
dispute directly to ICSID arbitration under the Spain–Argentina BIT,[125] despite the fact
that the treaty had a dispute settlement clause requiring prior recourse to local courts for a
period of eighteen months. Mr Maffezini pointed out that the MFN clause of the Spanish
treaty obliged Spain to treat investors of Argentina no less favourably than third-party investors. Consequently, rather than taking his dispute to local courts, he invoked the MFN
clause of the Spanish treaty in order to rely on the more favourable dispute settlement clause
of another BIT concluded between Spain and Chile.[126] This treaty provided for access to
international arbitration after only a six-month negotiation period.

The ICSID tribunal held that the text of the MFN clause of the Spanish treaty was broad   **8.55**
enough to include the dispute settlement provisions of that treaty. Therefore, relying on
the more favourable arrangements contained in the Chile–Spain BIT, Mr Maffezini had the
right to submit the dispute to international arbitration without first accessing the Spanish
courts. This position was upheld by a number of later tribunals,[127] but is closely linked to the
drafting of the particular MFN clause. In *Wintershall Aktiengesellschaft v Argentina*,[128] for
example, the tribunal declined jurisdiction on the basis that the MFN clause was not broad
enough to embrace the dispute resolution provision.

(e) Bilateral investment treaties and contractual dispute resolution clauses

Another issue is whether a state's consent to arbitration in a BIT is overridden by an exclu-   **8.56**
sive choice-of-forum clause in a related investment contract. Tribunals have generally held
that, as long as the claims allege a breach of the relevant treaty, they are not subject to the
contractually elected jurisdiction. In *Lanco v Argentina*,[129] for example, the contract contained an exclusive jurisdiction clause in favour of the Argentine courts. Argentina argued
that this clause applied and that the dispute was not within the jurisdiction of the ICSID tribunal. The tribunal rejected this argument, holding that the exclusive jurisdiction clause in
the contract could not exclude the jurisdiction of the ICSID tribunal in relation to the treaty

---

[124] *Emilio Agustín Maffezini v The Kingdom of Spain*, ICSID Case No. ARB/97/7, Award on Jurisdiction, 25 January 2000.

[125] Agreement between the Government of the Argentine Republic and the Kingdom of Spain for the Promotion and Reciprocal Protection of Investments, signed on 3 October 1991, entered into force on 28 September 1992.

[126] Agreement between the Republic of Chile and the Kingdom of Spain concerning the Reciprocal Encouragement and Protection of Investments, signed on 2 October 1991, entered into force on 29 March 1994.

[127] Since *Maffezini*, several tribunals have applied MFN clauses in order to bypass conditions for access to arbi-tration: see, e.g., *Gas Natural SDG, SA v Argentine Republic*, ICSID Case No. ARB/03/10, Decision on Jurisdiction, 17 June 2005, at [30]–[31]; *Suez, Sociedad General de Aguas de Barcelona SA and InterAguas Servicios Integrales del Agua SA v Argentine Republic*, ICSID Case No. ARB/03/17, Decision on Jurisdiction, 3 August 2006.

[128] ICSID Case No. ARB/04/14, Award, 8 December 2008. Similarly, in *Daimler Financial Services v Argentine Republic*, ICSID Case No. ARB/05/1, Award, 22 August 2012, the tribunal held, by majority, that the clause re-quiring the pursuit of remedies before local courts for eighteen months was a condition precedent to arbitration that could not be altered through the application of the MFN clause.

[129] *Lanco International Inc. v Argentine Republic*, Award, ICSID Case No. ARB/97/6, Award, 8 December 1998.

claim. Each claim had a separate legal source (one was based on the contract and the other on the treaty) and each source had a separate dispute resolution provision.

8.57   In the *Vivendi* case,[130] the relevant investment was a concession contract concluded by the claimant with Tucumán, a province of Argentina. The claims concerned acts by Tucumán authorities interfering with the claimant's rights under the concession contract. Argentina argued that the dispute resolution clause of the contract, establishing the jurisdiction of the local courts for the purpose of interpretation and application of the contract, precluded jurisdiction under the French treaty. Rejecting this argument, an ICSID annulment committee held that:

> [W]here 'the fundamental basis of a claim' is a treaty laying down an *independent standard* by which the conduct of the parties is to be judged, the existence of an exclusive jurisdiction clause in the contract between the Claimant and the respondent state or one of its subdivisions cannot operate as a bar to the application of the treaty standard.[131]

The committee went on to state that treaty claims often involve taking into account the terms of a contract in determining whether there has been a breach of the treaty. This does not prevent the claims being treaty claims for which arbitration is available.

8.58   The case law also suggests, however, that there may be cases in which the claims are so linked to the underlying contract that the contract is the 'fundamental basis' of the claims, rather than the BIT. In this case, the contract clause may apply even if the claims are formally 'dressed up' as BIT claims.[132] This issue is further complicated by the issue of 'observance of undertakings', or 'umbrella', clauses in which the treaty elevates contractual rights to the level of treaty rights. In such cases, purely contractual claims may also be categorised as treaty claims. In such cases, there may be issues of admissibility where the relevant contract also includes an exclusive jurisdiction clause.[133]

(f)   Parallel claims before local courts

8.59   Many dispute settlement clauses of BITs provide that investors may choose to submit an investment dispute *either* to the local courts of the host state *or* to arbitration, and once made, the choice is final.[134] Thus if the investor has already submitted the investment dispute to the local courts, it may no longer resort to arbitration. This is known as the 'fork in the road' provision.

---

[130] *Compañía de Aguas del Aconquija*, fn. 114.
[131] Ibid., at [101] (emphasis added). See also *Tenaris SA and Talta—Trading e Marketing Sociedade Unipessoal Lda. v Bolivarian Republic of Venezuela*, ICSID Case No. ARB/11/26, Award, 8 December 1998, at [307]; *Silver Ridge Power BV v Italian Republic*, ICSID Case No. ARB/15/37, Award, 26 February 2021, at [263].
[132] See, e.g., *Camuzzi International SA v Argentine Republic*, ICSID Case No. ARB/03/2, Decision on Objections to Jurisdiction, 10 June 2005, at [89].
[133] See paragraphs 8.138–8.142 for a more detailed discussion of the scope of the 'umbrella clause' provisions.
[134] See, e.g., Agreement Between the Government of the Republic of South Africa and the Government of the Republic of Zimbabwe for the Promotion and Reciprocal Protection of Investments, signed on 27 November 2009, entered into force on 15 September 2010, Art. 7(3): 'If the investor submits the dispute to the competent court of the host Party or to international arbitration [...], the choice shall be final.'

Most tribunals have generally held that 'fork in the road' clauses bar arbitration claims   **8.60**
under a treaty only where there is a 'triple identity', that is to say the arbitration claim
has the same object, the same parties, and the same cause of action being pursued simultaneously before local courts. As the tribunal in *Toto Construzioni Generali Spa v
Lebanon* held:

> In order for a fork-in-the-road clause to preclude claims from being considered by the
> Tribunal, the Tribunal has to consider whether the same claim is 'on a different road', ie
> that a claim with the same object, parties and cause of action, is already brought before a
> different judicial forum.[135]

Since disputes submitted to local courts tend to relate to local contractual or regulatory   **8.61**
issues that are distinct from the treaty breach issues submitted to arbitration, they do not
usually trigger the fork-in-the-road provision.[136] As stated by the *CMS* tribunal in its decision on jurisdiction: 'As contractual claims are different from treaty claims, even if there had
been or there currently was a recourse to local courts for breach of contract, this would not
have prevented submission of the treaty claims to arbitration.'[137]

The case law, however, is not unanimous on this subject. In the *Pantechniki* award,[138] the   **8.62**
tribunal dismissed a claim by the same claimant based on a fork-in-the-road clause because the 'fundamental basis of the claim' in the arbitration matched that of the local court
proceeding. In this regard, the tribunal noted that the prayer for relief in the local court
proceedings—namely, of payment amounts due under a contract—matched the relief
sought before the tribunal:

> To the extent that this prayer was accepted it would grant the Claimant exactly what it is
> seeking before ICSID—and on the same 'fundamental basis'. The Claimant's grievance
> thus arises out of the same purported entitlement that it invoked in the contractual de-
> bate it began with the General Roads Directorate. The Claimant chose to take this matter
> to the Albanian courts. It cannot now adopt the same fundamental basis as the founda-
> tion of a Treaty claim. Having made the election to seize the national jurisdiction the
> Claimant is no longer permitted to raise the same contention before ICSID.[139]

Moreover, much may depend on the language of the treaty. Where a claimant is simultan-   **8.63**
eously pursuing a local remedy in respect of the same measures,[140] a tribunal constituted
under an investment treaty should look carefully at whether the fork-in-the-road provision
is limited to claims under the treaty, or merely to the resolution of a dispute arising out of
the investment.

---

[135] *Toto Costruzioni Generali SpA v Republic of Lebanon*, ICSID Case No. ARB/07/12, Decision on Jurisdiction, 11 September 2009, at [211].

[136] Ibid., at [211]–[212]; *Total SA v The Argentine Republic*, ICSID Case No. ARB/04/01, Decision on Liability, 27 December 2010, at [443].

[137] *CMS Gas*, fn. 75. See Schreuer, 'Travelling the BIT route: Of waiting periods, umbrella clauses and forks in the road' (2004) 5 JWIT 231, at [247].

[138] *Pantechniki SA Contractors & Engineers (Greece) v Republic of Albania*, ICSID Case No. ARB/07/21, Award, 30 July 2009, at [61] and [67].

[139] Ibid., at [67].

[140] Defensive local actions that challenge measures impairing investments have been found not to trigger fork-in-the-road clauses: see, e.g., *Genin and ors v Republic of Estonia*, ICSID Case No. ARB/99/2, Award, 25 June 2001.

C. Law Applicable to the Substance of the Dispute

8.64 Investment treaties do not always contain specific provisions on the law to be applied by arbitral tribunals appointed under their provisions. Those treaties that do contain applicable law provisions often list both international law and domestic law, without indicating which is pre-eminent or how they are to be combined. By way of example, Article 10.6 of the Ukraine–Turkey BIT[141] provides that:

> The arbitral tribunal shall take its decisions in accordance with the provisions of this Agreement, the laws and regulations of the Contracting Party involved in the dispute on which territory the investment is made (including its rules on the conflict of laws) and the relevant principles of international law as accepted by both Contracting Parties.

8.65 Where the investment treaty is silent as to the applicable law, other instruments may provide guidance. Article 35.1 of the UNCITRAL Rules provides that, failing a designation of the applicable law by the parties, 'the arbitral tribunal shall apply the law which it determines to be appropriate'.[142] Article 42 of the ICSID Convention provides that, in the absence of an agreement on the applicable law, 'the Tribunal shall apply the law of the Contracting State party to the dispute (including its rules on the conflict of laws) and such rules of international law as may be applicable'.

8.66 Ultimately, however, whether or not a treaty specifies the applicable law, the tribunal will apply and accord a controlling role to international law.[143] Because treaties are international law instruments, international law is applicable by virtue of the 1969 Vienna Convention on the Law of Treaties, which provides that treaties are 'governed by international law' and must be interpreted in the light of 'any relevant rules of international law applicable'.[144]

8.67 In this regard, in the *AAPL v Sri Lanka* case,[145] which was brought under the Sri Lanka–United Kingdom BIT,[146] the tribunal held the BIT to be the 'primary source of the applicable legal rules' and added that the BIT was not a 'closed legal system' but had to be seen in the 'wider juridical context' of international law. This led the tribunal to apply general international law to complement the provisions of the BIT. Similarly, the annulment committee in the *Vivendi* case held that:

---

[141] Agreement between the Government of the United Kingdom of Great Britain and Northern Ireland and the Government of the Argentine Republic for the Promotion and Protection of Investments, signed on 11 December 1990, entered into force on 19 February 1993.

[142] This stands in contrast to the less flexible approach set out in the 1976 UNCITRAL Rules, Art. 33.1 which provided that 'failing such designation by the parties, the arbitral tribunal shall apply the law determined by the conflict of laws rules which it considers applicable'. See Caron and Caplan, *The UNCITRAL Arbitration Rules* (2nd edn, Oxford University Press, 2013), p. 112.

[143] *Lidercón, SL v Republic of Peru*, ICSID Case No. ARB/17/9, Award, 6 March 2020, at [177]; *Middle East Cement Shipping and Handling Co. SA v Arab Republic of Egypt*, ICSID Case No. ARB/99/6, Award, 12 April 2002, at [86]. See also Kjos, *Applicable Law in Investor–State Arbitration: The Interplay Between National and International Law* (Oxford University Press, 2013).

[144] Vienna Convention on the Law of Treaties, opened for signature 23 May 1969, Arts 2(1)(a) and 31(3)(c), 1155 United Nations Treaty Series 331, reprinted in 8 ILM 679 (1969).

[145] *Asian Agricultural Products Ltd (AAPL)*, fn. 15, at [20]–[21].

[146] Agreement between the Government of the United Kingdom of Great Britain and Northern Ireland and the Government of Sri Lanka for the Promotion and Protection of Investments, signed on 13 February 1980, entered into force on 18 December 1980.

[I]n respect of a claim based upon a substantive provision of that BIT [...] the inquiry which the ICSID tribunal is required to undertake is one governed by the ICSID Convention, by the BIT and by applicable international law. Such an inquiry is neither in principle determined, nor precluded, by any issue of municipal law [...][147]

International law provides the standard by reference to which the legality of the conduct of the host state is to be assessed.[148] This is made clear by Article 3 of the International Law Commission's Articles on State Responsibility,[149] which provides that the 'characterisation of an act of a State as internationally wrongful is governed by international law'.   **8.68**

In this sense, it may be necessary to refer to international law in order to interpret the terms of an investment treaty. For instance, while investment treaties generally include provisions regarding the expropriation of investments, they typically do not define the term 'expropriation'. Tribunals can therefore refer to the concept of expropriation under customary international law in order to interpret the scope and content of the investment treaty.[150] The application of international law, however, does not allow claimants to assert claims under customary international law as an independent cause of action.[151]   **8.69**

The applicable law provisions in investment contracts or other agreements forming part of the background of the dispute do not preclude the application of international law. In *Wena Hotels Ltd v Egypt*,[152] the annulment committee rejected the argument that the applicable law clauses of the lease agreements between Wena Hotels and an Egyptian state authority, which selected Egyptian law, applied to the BIT dispute: **8.70**

> The leases deal with questions that are by definition of a commercial nature. The [BIT] deals with questions that are essentially of a governmental nature, namely the standards of treatment accorded by the State to foreign investors. It is therefore apparent that Wena and EHC agreed to a particular contract, the applicable law and the dispute settlement arrangement in respect of one kind of subject, that relating to commercial problems under the leases. It is also apparent that Wena as a national of a contracting state could invoke the [BIT] for the purpose of a different kind of dispute, that concerning the treatment of foreign investors by

---

[147] *Compañía de Aguas del Aconquija*, fn. 114, at [102]. See also *Crystallex International Corporation v Bolivarian Republic of Venezuela*, Award, ICSID Case No. ARB(AF)/11/2, Award, 4 April 2016, at [474].

[148] See Parra, 'Applicable law in investor–state arbitration', in Rovine (ed.) *Contemporary Issues in International Arbitration and Mediation: The Fordham Papers* (Brill, 2008), p. 11. See also *Electrabel SA v Republic of Hungary*, ICSID Case No. ARB/07/19, Decision on Jurisdiction, Applicable Law and Liability, 25 November 2015, at [4.128]–[4.129]; *CMC Africa Austral et al., Republic of Mozambique*, ICSID Case No. ARB/17/23, Award, 24 October 2019, at [220].

[149] See the ICSID Annulment Committee's reliance on this provision in *Compañía de Aguas del Aconquija*, fn. 114, at [95]–[96].

[150] *Accession Mezzanine Capital LP v Republic of Hungary*, ICSID Case No. ARB/12/3, Decision on Respondent's Objection under Arbitration Rule 41(5), 16 January 2013, at [68]–[70]. See also 2012 United States Model BIT, Annex B, which states the 'shared understanding' of the parties that expropriation (Art. 6(1)) 'is intended to reflect customary international law concerning the obligation of States with respect to expropriation'.

[151] *Generation Ukraine Inc. v Ukraine*, ICSID Case No. ARB/00/9, Award, 16 September 2003, at [11.3]; *Emmis International Holding, BV et al.*, ICSID Case No. ARB/12/2, Decision on Respondent's Objection Under ICSID Arbitration Rule 41(5), 11 March 2013, at [84]; *Accession Mezzanine Capital LP*, fn. 150, at [72].

[152] *Wena Hotels Ltd v Arab Republic of Egypt*, ICSID Case No. ARB/98/4, Decision on Annulment Application, 5 February 2002.

Egypt. This other mechanism has a different and separate dispute settlement arrangement and might include a different choice of law provision or make no choice at all.

[...]

This Committee accordingly concludes that the subject matter of the lease agreements submitted to Egyptian law was different from the subject matter brought before ICSID arbitration under the [BIT].[153]

8.71   This approach does not ignore domestic law or the text of Article 42(1) of the ICSID Convention set out earlier.[154] However, it should be remembered that the Convention was itself drafted principally with investor–state contracts in mind, in which domestic law would play the critical, if not exclusive, role.[155] Treaty interpretation, however, calls for a different approach. If a domestic legal system were to provide rules of decision, then a state could simply legislate itself out of a breach of treaty, contrary to Article 27 of the Vienna Convention ('[a state] may not invoke the provisions of its internal law as justification for its failure to perform a treaty'). As the tribunal held in the *Santa Elena* case:

> To the extent that there may be any inconsistency between the two bodies of law, the rules of public international law must prevail. Were this not so in relation to takings of property, the protection of international law would be denied to the foreign investor and the purpose of the ICSID Convention would, in this respect, be frustrated.[156]

8.72   This does not mean that the domestic law of the host state does not have a role to play. The domestic law of the host state will be taken into consideration to establish the facts to be analysed in determining whether the state is liable under the investment treaty. For instance, a tribunal will consider domestic law in determining whether particular assets or rights constituting an alleged investment exist and in whom they vest; the question of whether these assets or rights constitute an investment under the treaty will, however, be a question governed by the treaty and international law.

8.73   Similarly, the domestic law of the host state will typically constitute evidence of the measures taken by the state that are alleged to be in breach of the treaty, since the misconduct of the state will usually manifest itself through internal legal acts. The analysis of whether these acts or measures engage the host state's liability under the treaty will, however, be governed by the terms of the treaty and international law.

8.74   The practice of BIT tribunals has been summarised by one commentator as follows:

> The principle that treaties are on the plane of international law is too well established to warrant much argument. Therefore, alleged breaches of a BIT by a state are prima facie

---

[153] Ibid., at [31]–[36].

[154] See paragraph 8.65.

[155] See *Autopista Concessionada de Venezuela CA v Bolivarian Republic of Venezuela*, ICSID Case No. ARB/00/5, Award, 23 September 2003, at [102]: '[T]his Tribunal believes that there is no reason in this case, especially considering that it is a contract and not a treaty arbitration, to go beyond the corrective and supplemental functions of international law.'

[156] *Compañía del Desarrollo de Santa Elena SA v Republic of Costa Rica*, ICSID Case No. ARB/96/1, Award, 17 February 2000, at [64]. See also *Pac Rim Cayman LLC v Republic of El Salvador*, ICSID Case No. ARB/09/12, Award, 14 October 2016, at [5.62]; *LG&E Energy Corporation and ors v Argentine Republic*, ICSID Case No. ARB/02/1, Decision on Liability, 3 October 2006, at [98].

governed by international law. Be that as it may, the complex questions that arise in for-eign investment disputes cannot simply be answered by a prior assumption of the sole ap-plicability of international law. As is always the case, foreign investments are intrinsically connected to the national law of the host state. Suffice to say that questions as to whether an investment is properly made or whether a measure or regulation taken by a state meets the threshold of treaty violation may not be disposed of without a thorough examination of that state's national law. Even if the relevant treaty does not provide for a choice of sub-stantive law, arbitrators still have the obligation to consider the relevant national laws of the host state, with the caveat that such law may not be applicable if it is contrary to the obli-gations assumed by the state under the treaty—the principle that a state cannot rely on its internal laws to derogate from or modify its treaty obligations. To that extent, it is conceded that the arbitrators may have a certain margin and power of interpretation.[157]

Potential conflicts between international and domestic law often fall away when tribunals take note that international legal principles and treaties are in any event frequently incorp-orated into domestic law, as the tribunal noted in *BG Group PLC v Argentina*:   **8.75**

> [T]he challenge of discerning the role that international law ought to play in the settlement of this dispute, vis-à-vis domestic law, disappears if one were to take into account that the BIT and underlying principles of international law, as 'the supreme law of the land', are in-corporated into Argentine domestic law, superseding conflicting domestic statutes.[158]

As for conflicts between two international law instruments, these may fall away if it is possible to interpret both instruments harmoniously. Such issues have arisen in the context of BITs entered into by a non-EU member state with an EU member state when the former accedes to the European Union. The newly acceded states have argued that their BIT obligations were terminated, or modified, as a result of their accession. For instance, in *Achmea BV v Slovak Republic*,[159] the Slovak Republic argued that the dispute settlement clause in the Netherlands–Slovakia BIT was inapplicable as a consequence of Slovakia's accession to the European Union, because the BIT was incompatible with Slovakia's obligations under EU law. The tribunal dis-agreed, holding that the BIT established rights that were neither duplicated by nor incompat-ible with EU law. The tribunal also held that the fact that it was bound to apply EU law to the extent that it formed part of the applicable laws did not deprive it of jurisdiction.   **8.76**

However, the tribunal's view of the compatibility between the two instruments was ques-tioned by the Slovak Republic before the German courts (the courts of the seat of the arbi-tration). Upon referral from the German courts, the Court of Justice of the European Union (CJEU) considered that the dispute resolution clause in the BIT was inconsistent with the Treaty on the Functioning of the European Union (TFEU) and therefore invalid.[160] This   **8.77**

---

[157] Igbokwe, 'Determination, interpretation and application of substantive law in foreign investment treaty arbi-trations' (2006) 23 J Intl Arb 267, at 297–298. See also *Vestey Group Ltd v Bolivarian Republic of Venezuela*, ICSID Case No. ARB/06/4, Award, 15 April 2016, at [116]–[117]; *El Paso Energy International Co. v Argentine Republic*, ICSID Case No. ARB/03/15, Award, 30 October 2011, at [129].

[158] *BG Group PLC*, fn. 121, at [97]. See also *Siemens AG v Argentine Republic*, ICSID Case No. ARB/02/8, Award, 6 February 2007, at [78]–[79].

[159] *Achmea BV (formerly known as Eureko BV) v Slovak Republic*, UNCITRAL, PCA Case No. 2008-13 (2010), Award on Jurisdiction, Arbitrability and Suspension, 26 October 2010, at [244]–[246].

[160] Case C-284/16 *Slovak Republic v Achmea BV*, 6 March 2018.

ultimately led (at the call of the European Commission) to an Agreement for the Termination of all Intra-EU BITs signed by 23 Member States of the European Union on 5 May 2020. Arbitral tribunals have, however, not considered themselves bound by the *Achmea* decision and have predominantly held that the BIT obligations are not inconsistent with the obligations of the host state under the TFEU. For example, in *GPF GP S.à.r.l v Poland*, the tribunal found that, despite the termination of the Belgium–Luxembourg Economic Union–Poland BIT, resulting from Poland's accession to the European Union, the substantive protections afforded under the BIT were not incompatible with EU law, nor did EU law deprive the tribunal of jurisdiction.[161] Some fifty tribunals have refused to follow the logic of the *Achmea* decision and have upheld the right to arbitrate under intra-EU BITs.

8.78   Finally, it should be noted that although there is 'a progressive emergence of rules through lines of consistent cases on certain issues',[162] there is no doctrine of precedent in investment treaty arbitration.[163] Therefore while investment treaty case law may be a subsidiary means for the determination of rules of international law,[164] tribunals are not bound by the decisions of other tribunals. Commenting on this issue, the tribunal in the *SGS Société Générale de Surveillance SA v Philippines* case noted:

> Moreover there is no doctrine of precedent in international law, if by precedent is meant a rule of the binding effect of a single decision. There is no hierarchy of international tribunals, and even if there were, there is no good reason for allowing the first tribunal in time to resolve issues for all later tribunals. It must be initially for the control mechanisms provided for under the BIT and the ICSID Convention, and in the longer term for the development of a common legal opinion or *jurisprudence constante*, to resolve the difficult legal questions […][165]

8.79   The consequences of failing to identify and apply the applicable law may be grave. It can expose the tribunal's award to a challenge, or even annulment. Indeed, in the ICSID context, ad hoc committees annulled the awards rendered in *Helnan v Egypt*, *Enron v Argentina*, and *Sempra v Argentina* on the basis that the arbitral tribunals exceeded their powers by failing to apply the applicable law.[166]

---

[161]   SCC Case No. 2014/168, Final Award, 29 April 2020, at [363]–[380].
[162]   Kaufmann-Kohler, 'Arbitral precedent: Dream, necessity or excuse? The 2006 Freshfields Lecture' (2007) 23 Arb Intl 357. See also *Daimler Financial Services*, fn. 128, at [52].
[163]   Indeed, tribunals have reached different conclusions based on the same facts and law. See, e.g., the decisions in *CME Czech Republic BV (The Netherlands) v Czech Republic*, UNCITRAL, Partial Award, 13 September 2001, IIC 61 (2001); *Ronald S Lauder*, fn. 118, in which claims were brought under two different treaties based on identical facts. In *Lauder*, the case was dismissed. In *CME*, the Czech state was ordered to pay over US$300 million. On legal issues, there has been a clear split on the scope of the so-called umbrella clause in the cases of *Bureau Veritas, Inspection, Valuation, Assessment and Control, BIVAC BV v Republic of Paraguay*, ICSID Case No. ARB/07/9, Decision on Jurisdiction, 9 October 2012, and *SGS Société Générale de Surveillance SA v Republic of Paraguay*, fn. 96. Both cases were based on nearly identical facts.
[164]   ICJ Statute, Art. 38(d).
[165]   *SGS Société Générale de Surveillance SA v Republic of the Philippines*, ICSID Case No. ARB/02/6, Decision on Jurisdiction, 29 January 2004, at [97]. See also *Suez, Sociedad General de Aguas de Barcelona SA and InterAguas Servicios Integrales del Agua SA v Argentine Republic*, fn. 127, at [189].
[166]   *Helnan International Hotels AS v Arab Republic of Egypt*, ICSID Case No. ARB/05/19, Decision of the ad hoc Committee, 14 June 2010; *Enron Creditors Recovery Corporation (formerly Enron Corporation) and Ponderosa Assets LP v Argentine Republic*, ICSID Case No. ARB/01/3, Decision on Application for Annulment, 30 July 2010; *Sempra Energy International v Argentine Republic*, ICSID Case No. ARB/02/16, Decision on Annulment, 29 June 2010.

D. Merits of the Dispute

If jurisdictional hurdles are overcome, the question arises whether the host state has **8.80** breached its substantive treaty obligations. There is a surprising degree of uniformity between substantive protections in the treaties, aided by model treaties established as negotiating guidelines by both capital-exporting and capital-importing nations. The essential protections are:

- the protection against expropriation or measures equivalent to expropriation without compensation;
- the right to be treated fairly and equitably;
- the right to full protection and security;
- the protection against arbitrary or discriminatory treatment;
- the right to national and MFN treatment;
- the right to the free transfer of funds and assets; and
- the protection against a state's breaches of its investment obligations and undertakings.[167]

(a) No expropriation without prompt, adequate, and effective compensation

The obligation to compensate for expropriation is among the most crucial protections pro- **8.81** vided by investment treaties. This provision is frequently relied upon by foreign investors in treaty arbitration. The expropriation provisions in investment treaties are quite similar. A typical provision is, for example, Article 3(1) of the United States–Argentina BIT,[168] which states:

> Investments shall not be expropriated or nationalized either directly or indirectly through measures tantamount to expropriation or nationalization ('expropriation') except for a public purpose; in a non-discriminatory manner; upon payment of prompt, adequate and effective compensation; and in accordance with due process of law and the general principles of treatment provided for in Article II(2). Compensation shall be equivalent to the fair market value of the expropriated investment immediately before the expropriatory action was taken or became known, whichever is earlier; be paid without delay; include interest at a commercially reasonable rate from the date of expropriation; be fully realizable; and be freely transferable at the prevailing market rate of exchange on the date of expropriation.

Thus, in order to be lawful, BITs generally require that the expropriation fulfil the fol- **8.82** lowing cumulative requirements: (a) it must be for a public purpose, (b) it must be

---

[167] For a detailed analysis of these substantive treaty obligations, see Salacuse, *The Law of Investment Treaties* (3rd edn, Oxford University Press, 2021); McLachlan, Shore, and Weiniger, *International Investment Arbitration: Substantive Principles* (2nd edn, Oxford University Press, 2017); Yannaca-Small, *Arbitration under International Investment Agreements* (2nd edn, Oxford University Press, 2018); Schreuer and Dolzer, *Principles of International Investment Law* (Oxford University Press, 2012).
[168] See fn. 43.

non-discriminatory, (c) it must be in accordance with due process, and (d) only effected upon payment of prompt, adequate, and effective compensation.

(i) Direct expropriation

8.83 A direct expropriation involves the outright physical seizure of a foreign investor's property, or the title to such property, by the host state. In such cases, 'there is an open, deliberate and unequivocal intent, as reflected in a formal law or decree or physical act, to deprive the owner of his or her property through the transfer of title or outright seizure'.[169] For instance, in *Saint-Gobain v Venezuela*,[170] the tribunal held that Venezuela had expropriated the claimant's investments in a plant that produced ceramic proppants (used in hydrocarbon production) by means of an actual physical takeover, followed by a legislative decree.

(ii) Indirect expropriation

8.84 It is now a well-accepted principle of international law that expropriation may occur indirectly, by measures resulting in a substantial deprivation of the use and value of the investment, even though the actual title of the asset remains with the investor.[171] As explained in *Ronald S Lauder v Czech Republic*: 'The concept of indirect (or "de facto", or "creeping") expropriation is not clearly defined. Indirect expropriation or nationalization is a measure that does not involve an overt taking, but that effectively neutralizes the enjoyment of the property.'[172]

8.85 International arbitral tribunals have recognised this principle and upheld claims for indirect expropriation when the state has not seized the investment but has taken measures that have destroyed its value. For example, in *Total v Argentina*, the tribunal explained:

> [U]nder international law a measure which does not have all the features of a formal expropriation could be equivalent to an expropriation if an effective deprivation of the investment is thereby caused. An effective deprivation requires, however, a total loss of value of the property such as when the property affected is rendered worthless by the measure, as in case of direct expropriation, even if formal title continues to be held.[173]

8.86 Indirect expropriation can also arise from a deprivation of control or interference in management by the state, thus preventing the investor from controlling the day-to-day operation of the investment. Such measures would include:

> depriving the investor of control over the investment, managing the day-to-day operations of the company, arresting and detaining company officials or employees, supervising the

---

[169] UNCTAD, *Expropriation: A Sequel*, Series on Issues in International Investment Agreements II (UN, 2012), available online at http://unctad.org/

[170] *Saint-Gobain Performance Plastics Europe v Bolivarian Republic of Venezuela*, ICSID Case No. ARB/12/13, Decision on Liability and the Principles of Quantum, 30 December 2016.

[171] OECD, '"Indirect expropriation" and the "right to regulate" in international investment law', Working Paper on International Investment No. 2004/4 (September 2004), available online at http://www.oecd.org/daf/inv/investment-policy/WP-2004_4.pdf.

[172] *Ronald S Lauder v Czech Republic*, fn. 118, at [200].

[173] *Total SA v Argentine Republic*, fn. 136, at [195]–[196].

work of officials, interfering in administration, impeding the distribution of dividends, interfering in the appointment of officials or managers, or depriving the company of its property or control in whole or in part.[174]

In evaluating the degree to which the host state's measures have interfered with the investor's rights, tribunals typically consider the economic impact of the measures on the investment, their interference with the investor's reasonable expectations, and their duration.[175]

Under exceptional or 'extreme' circumstances, the imposition of taxes, which are con-   **8.87**
sidered part of a state's regulatory powers, can be expropriatory. In the *Burlington* case,[176] the tribunal explained that 'a tax measure may be tantamount to expropriation if (i) it produces the effects required for any indirect expropriation and (ii) in addition, it is discriminatory, arbitrary, involves a denial of due process or an abuse of rights'.

(iii) Acts contrary to undertakings and assurances granted to investors may constitute indirect expropriation

States may also expropriate foreign investments by means of measures that interfere   **8.88**
with assurances that they offered to investors to induce them to invest. The assurances that states offer to create a favourable investment environment may amount to essential conditions for those investments and, as such, may form part of the legal framework underlying, and protecting, those investments. A failure by the state to honour those undertakings may give investors who reasonably relied on them a right to compensation.

International arbitral tribunals have held that government assurances and undertakings   **8.89**
create 'acquired rights' for investors.[177] The rationale is simple. Investors looking to invest in developing countries cannot predict with confidence that conditions of stability and security will exist throughout the period of their investment; thus the state may provide certain core promises to foreign investors (in contracts, concessions or licences), which motivate the decision to invest. If those promises are unilaterally withdrawn by the state

---

[174] *Sempra Energy International v Argentine Republic*, ICSID Case No. ARB/02/16, Award, 28 September 2007, at [284], endorsing the criteria set out in *Pope & Talbot Inc. v Government of Canada*, UNCITRAL, Award on Damages, 31 May 2002, IIC 195 (2002). See also *PSEG Global, Inc., The North American Coal Corporation, and Konya Ingin Electrik Üretim ve Ticaret Ltd Şirketi v Republic of Turkey*, ICSID Case No. ARB/02/5, Award, 19 January 2007, at [278]: 'The Tribunal has no doubt that indirect expropriation can take many forms. Yet, as the tribunal in *Pope & Talbot* found, there must be some form of deprivation of the investor in the control of the investment, the management of day-to-day operations of the company, interfering in the administration, impeding the distribution of dividends, interfering in the appoint of officials and managers, or depriving the company of its property or control in total or in part.'

[175] *LG&E Energy Corporation*, fn. 156, at [190].

[176] *Burlington Resources Inc.*, fn. 116 at [375]. See also *Ampal-American Israel Corporation and ors v Arab Republic of Egypt*, ICSID Case No. ARB/12/11, Decision on Liability and Heads of Loss, 21 February 2017, at [183] (finding that the host state's removal of the investor's tax-free status constituted an expropriation of a 'defined and valuable interest that had been validly conferred' under local law and 'guaranteed by the State for a defined period').

[177] Acquired rights have been defined as follows: 'Acquired rights are any rights, corporeal or incorporeal, properly vested under municipal law in a natural or juristic person and of an assessable monetary value. Within the scope of such rights fall interests which have their basis in contract as well as in property, provided they concern an undertaking or investment of a more or less permanent character.' See O'Connell, *International Law, Vol. II* (2nd edn, Stevens & Sons, 1970), pp. 763–764.

within the agreed lifespan of the investment (for example a thirty-year concession) in a manner that destroys the value of the investment, then an indirect expropriation may have occurred.[178]

8.90   The tribunal in *CME v Czech Republic*[179] reached such a conclusion when it was asked to consider the expropriation claim of an investor in a joint venture in the Czech Republic. The investor alleged that the joint venture collapsed after the Czech broadcasting authority forced the investor to give up its exclusive licensing rights and changed other key terms of the joint venture agreement. The tribunal held that the acts of the Czech regulatory authority interfered with the 'economic and legal basis of CME's investment' and 'destroy[ed] the legal basis ("the safety net") of the Claimant's investment', which ruined the 'commercial value of the investment' and thus amounted to expropriation.

8.91   However, in the absence of such government assurances or undertakings, the effects alone (as grave as they may be) may be insufficient to constitute expropriation. In the *Methanex* case,[180] the tribunal held that a non-discriminatory, bona fide regulation within the police powers of the state, which banned a harmful gasoline additive containing methanol, had not expropriated Methanex, a Canadian producer of methanol, in the absence of a breach of specific commitments by the state.

8.92   Similarly, a simple breach of contract by a state does not amount to an expropriation in the absence of an act of the state in its sovereign (as opposed to contractual) capacity.[181] The *Waste Management*[182] tribunal explained: '[I]t is one thing to expropriate a right under a contract and another to fail to comply with the contract. Non-compliance by a government with contractual obligations is not the same thing as, or equivalent or tantamount to, an expropriation.' Tribunals have nevertheless found that contractual rights were expropriated where a state acted in a sovereign manner by terminating a contract by decree,[183] and following a series of 'sovereign acts designed illegitimately to end the concession or to force its renegotiation'.[184]

8.93   In sum, the paramount concern of tribunals in indirect expropriation cases is whether a state's interference with prior assurances that it gave to an investor, be it direct or indirect, express or covert, creeping or not, deprives the investor, in whole or in significant part, of the use or reasonably expected benefit of its investment.[185]

---

[178] Fatouros, *Government Guarantees to Foreign Investors* (Columbia University Press, 1962).

[179] *CME Czech Republic BV*, fn. 163, at [551], [554]–[555], and [591].

[180] *Methanex Corporation v United States of America*, UNCITRAL, Final Award on Jurisdiction and Merits, 19 August 2005, at [7].

[181] See *Parkerings-Compagniet AS v Republic of Lithuania*, ICSID Case No. ARB/05/8, Award, 11 September 2007, at [443]–[445]; *Azurix Corporation v Argentine Republic*, ICSID Case No. ARB/01/12, Award, 14 July 2006, at [315]; *Suez, Sociedad General de Aguas de Barcelona SA and InterAguas Servicios Integrales del Agua SA v Argentine Republic*, ICSID Case No. ARB/03/17, Decision on Liability, 30 July 2010, at [140]–[145]. See also *Cairn Energy PLC and Cairn UK Holdings Limited v Republic of India*, A Case No. 2016-07, Final Award, 21 December 2020, at [871].

[182] *Waste Management Inc. v United Mexican States*, ICSID Case No. ARB(AF)/00/3, Award, 30 April 2004, at [175]. See also *Biwater Gauff*, fn. 120, at [458].

[183] *Siemens AG*, Award, fn. 158, at [271].

[184] *Compañia de Aguas del Aconquija*, fn. 144, at [7.5.22].

[185] *Eureko BV v Republic of Poland*, UNCITRAL, Partial Award of the Ad Hoc Committee, 19 August 2005, at [242]; *ADC Affiliate Ltd and ADC & ADMC Management Ltd v Republic of Hungary*, ICSID Case No. ARB/03/16,

(iv) Purpose of the host state's measures does not affect their characterisation

The form of measures or their motive is irrelevant if the *effect* is to deprive the owner of **8.94** the economic benefit of the asset.[186] Arbitral tribunals have held that it is immaterial that the property was expropriated for laudable environmental reasons,[187] or as part of the political reorientation of the country.[188]

Although the purpose of an expropriatory measure may affect its legality, it does not af- **8.95** fect the host state's obligation to provide the expropriated investor with prompt and adequate compensation. This point was affirmed by the ICSID tribunal in *Compañía del Desarrollo de Santa Elena SA v Costa Rica*:

> Expropriatory environmental measures—no matter how laudable and beneficial to society as a whole—are, in this respect, similar to any other expropriatory measures that a state may take in order to implement its policies: where property is expropriated, even for environmental purposes, whether domestic or international, the state's obligation to pay compensation remains.[189]

Whilst considering whether there has been expropriation in a particular case, a tribunal **8.96** need not examine each state measure in isolation. If the cumulative effect of multiple state measures is substantially to deprive the investor of the use, value, and enjoyment of its investment, expropriation may still be construed.[190] This is known as 'creeping expropriation'. As the tribunal noted in *Siemens AG v Argentina*:

> By definition, creeping expropriation refers to a process, to steps that eventually have the effect of an expropriation. Obviously, each step must have an adverse effect but by itself may not be significant or considered an illegal act. The last step in a creeping expropriation that tilts the balance is similar to the straw that breaks the camel's back. The preceding straws may not have a perceptible effect but are part of the process that led to the break.[191]

Award, 2 October 2006, at [424]; *LG&E Energy Corporation*, fn. 156, at [190]; *Mohamed Abdel Raouf Bahgat v Arab Republic of Egypt*, Final Award, PCA Case No. 2012-07, Final Award, 23 December 2019, at [221].

[186] *Compañia de Aguas del Aconquija*, fn. 114 at [7.5.20]: 'There is extensive authority for the proposition that the state's intent, or its subjective motives are at most a secondary consideration. While intent will weigh in favour of showing a measure to be expropriatory, it is not a requirement, because the effect of the measure on the investor, not the state's intent, is the critical factor'. But see *UAB E Energija (Lithuania) v Republic of Latvia*, ICSID Case No. ARB/12/33, Award, 22 December 2017, at [1079] (finding that, while the effect of the measure is the 'crucial test', some relevance must be attached to intention, and any evidence of expropriatory intention should be carefully weighed).

[187] *Compañía del Desarrollo de Santa Elena*, fn. 156, at [71]–[72].
[188] *Phillips Petroleum Co. Iran v Islamic Republic of Iran* (1989) 21 Iran–US CTR 79, at [115]–[116].
[189] *Compañía del Desarrollo de Santa Elena*, fn. 156, at [71]–[72].
[190] *Teinver SA, Transportes de Cercanías SA and Autobuses Urbanos del Sur SA v Argentine Republic*, ICSID Case No. ARB/09/01, Award, 21 July 2017, at [948]–[951]; *Biwater Gauff*, fn. 120, at [455]. See also Weston, 'Constructive takings under international law: A modest foray into the problem of creeping expropriation' (1976) 16 VJIL 103; UNCTAD, *Taking of Property*, Series on Issues in International Investment Agreements (UN, 2000), available online at http://unctad.org/en/docs/psiteiitd15.en.pdf, p. 11; Restatement (Third) of Foreign Relations Law of the United States, § 712.
[191] *Siemens AG*, fn. 158, at [263]. See also *UP (formerly Le Chèque Déjeuner) and C.D Holding Internationale v Republic of Hungary*, ICSID Case No. ARB/13/35, Award, 9 October 2018, at [331].

(b) 'Fair and equitable treatment' and the international minimum standard

8.97   Almost all investment treaties require host states to accord 'fair and equitable treatment' to investors of the other contracting state.[192] It is the treaty standard most frequently invoked before investment tribunals and the one most frequently found to be breached. To highlight the significance of this standard of protection, it is frequently addressed at the beginning of the general treatment clauses. For example, Article II(2)(a) of the United States–Argentina BIT[193] provides: 'Investment shall at all times be accorded fair and equitable treatment, shall enjoy full protection and security and shall in no case be accorded treatment less than that required by international law.'

8.98   It is difficult to reduce the words 'fair and equitable treatment' to a precise statement of a legal obligation. They grant considerable discretion to tribunals to review the 'fairness' and 'equity' of government actions in light of all of the facts and circumstances of the case.[194]

8.99   International arbitral tribunals called upon to decide cases on the basis of the 'fair and equitable treatment' standard have developed the elements of the obligation that it imposes upon states.[195] In accordance with the 'plain meaning' approach required by the Vienna Convention, tribunals have concluded, based on the object and purpose of the treaties, that the standard is intended to accord to foreign investors broad objective protections. These include a stable and predictable investment environment, in order to maximise investments.[196] As the tribunal noted in *LG&E Energy Corporation and ors v Argentina*:

> [T]he stability of the legal and business framework in the State party is an essential element in the standard of what is fair and equitable treatment. As such, the Tribunal considers this interpretation to be an emerging standard of fair and equitable treatment in international law.[197]

8.100   However, other tribunals have stressed that the fair and equitable treatment standard does not provide investors with blanket protection against changes in the host state's law. The inquiry is properly focused on reasonableness and proportionality, and 'a foreign investor can expect that the rules will not be changed without justification of an economic, social or

---

[192] UNCTAD, *Fair and Equitable Treatment: A Sequel*, Series on Issues in International Investment Agreements II (UN, 2012), available online at http://unctad.org/ pp. 17–35 (identifying the five 'most important and widespread approaches to the FET standard in treaty practice').

[193] See fn. 43.

[194] See, e.g., Schreuer, 'Fair and equitable treatment in arbitral practice' (2005) 6 JWIT 357; Kalicki and Medeiros, 'Fair, equitable and ambiguous: What is fair and equitable treatment in international investment law?' (2007) 22 ICSID Rev—Foreign Investment LJ 24; Kinnear, 'The continuing development of the fair and equitable treatment standard', in Bjorklund, Laird, and Ripinsky (eds) *Investment Treaty Law: Current Issues III* (British Institute of International and Comparative Law, 2009), p. 214; Yannaca-Small, 'Fair and equitable treatment', in Yannaca-Small (ed.) *Arbitration under International Investment Agreements* (2nd edn, Oxford University Press, 2018), pp. 510–511; UNCTAD, *Fair and Equitable Treatment: A Sequel*, Series on Issues in International Investment Agreements II (UN, 2012), available online at http://unctad.org.

[195] *Enron Corporation and Ponderosa Assets LP v Argentine Republic*, ICSID Case No. ARB/01/3, IIC 292 Award, 12 May 2007, at [256]–[257].

[196] See decisions in which tribunals have referred to the object and purpose of the BIT to interpret the fair and equitable treatment standard: *Azurix Corporation*, Award, fn. 181, at [360]; *MTD Equity Sdn Bhd, MTD Chile SA v Republic of Chile*, ICSID Case No. ARB/01/17, Award, 24 May 2004, at [109]–[113]; *Saluka Investments BV v Czech Republic*, UNCITRAL, Partial Award, 17 March 2006, at [300].

[197] fn. 156, at [12].

other nature'.[198] However, in the absence of a specific commitment from the state, a change in the legal framework will not typically breach the fair and equitable treatment standard unless such alteration is 'total',[199] or amounts to a 'radical unpredictable transformation in the conditions of the investment'.[200]

International arbitral tribunals have identified the protection of investors' legitimate expectations as the 'dominant element'[201] of the fair and equitable treatment standard. In order to determine if a state's measures violate the standard, tribunals frequently examine 'the impact of the measure on the reasonable investment-backed expectations of the investor; and whether the state is attempting to avoid investment-backed expectations that the state created or reinforced through its own acts'.[202] It is on this basis that the UNCITRAL ad hoc tribunal in *CME v Czech Republic*[203] found that the Czech Republic's legislative and regulatory changes had unlawfully harmed CME's investment by altering the country's investment framework, and held that the government had 'breached its obligation of fair and equitable treatment by evisceration of the arrangements in reliance upon [which] the foreign investor was induced to invest'.   **8.101**

In *Técnicas Medioambientales Tecmed SA v Mexico*,[204] the basic expectation of the claimant was that the laws applicable to its investment in a landfill for hazardous waste would be used by the government for the purpose of assuring compliance with the environmental and health goals underlying such laws. In particular, upon making its investment, the claimant 'reasonably trusted, on the basis of existing agreements and of the good faith principle' that the permit it acquired in order to make its investment would continue in full force and effect.[205] As held by the tribunal, however, the relevant Mexican federal agency later refused to renew the claimant's permit for political reasons arising from local community opposition unrelated to the underlying environmental and health goals.[206] This conduct constituted a breach of the fair and equitable treatment standard.   **8.102**

In order to qualify for protection, the investor's expectations must be reasonable, based on the conduct of the state and reasonable reliance by the investor in making the investment, as explained by the tribunal in *LG&E*:   **8.103**

> [T]he investor's fair expectations have the following characteristics: they are based on the conditions offered by the host State at the time of the investment; they may not be established unilaterally by one of the parties; they must exist and be enforceable by law;

---

[198] *El Paso Energy International Co.*, fn. 157, at [372]–[374].

[199] Ibid., at [374].

[200] *RREEF Infrastructure (GP) Limited and RREEF Pan-European Infrastructure Two Lux Sàrl v Kingdom of Spain*, ICSID Case No. ARB/13/30, Decision on Responsibility and on the Principles of Quantum, 30 November 2018 at [315]; *Silver Ridge Power*, fn. 131, at [414]–[415].

[201] *Saluka*, fn. 196, at [302]. But see *Cairn Energy PLC*, fn. 181, at [1723], finding that '[l]egitimate expectations might be the relevant analytical tool in some cases, but it is not to be considered the primary tool. [...] the Tribunal cannot accept that the doctrine of legitimate expectations is to be treated as essentially co-extensive with the ambit of FET'.

[202] Paulsson, 'Investment protection provisions in treaties', in ICC (ed.) *Investment Protection* (ICC, 2000), p. 22, para. 19.

[203] *CME Czech Republic BV*, fn. 163, at [611].

[204] ICSID Case No ARB(AF)/00/02, Award, 29 May 2003, at [157].

[205] Ibid., at [160].

[206] Ibid., at [164].

in the event of infringement by the host State, a duty to compensate the investor for damages arises except for those caused in the event of state of necessity; however, the investor's fair expectations cannot fail to consider parameters such as business risk or industry's regular patterns.[207]

8.104   It has been held that failure to ensure due process, consistency, and transparency in the functioning of public authorities,[208] and the lack of a predictable and stable framework for investment contrary to the legitimate expectations of the investor and commitments made by the host state,[209] are breaches of fair and equitable treatment standards.[210] The legal stability requirement does not require that a state's legal system remain frozen in time. However, legislative changes that are unfair and inequitable in the face of specific commitments to the contrary may constitute a compensable treaty breach:

> Save for the existence of an agreement, in the form of a stabilisation clause or otherwise, there is nothing objectionable about the amendment brought to the regulatory framework existing at the time an investor made its investment [...] What is prohibited however is for a State to act unfairly, unreasonably or inequitably in the exercise of its legislative power.[211]

8.105   The fair and equitable standard has also been held to be breached by the effective discrimination of host states in favour of domestic entities. In *Eastern Sugar BV v Czech Republic*,[212] the claimant invested in sugar factories in the Czech Republic. Those subsidiaries were then targeted by a decree passed by the Czech authorities in a very different manner from its application to domestic entities.[213] As explained by the tribunal, 'the Czech Republic penalized a foreign company that had done nothing illegal in the previous years, while Czech newcomers who had exceeded their quota within the previous years were now rewarded for having done so'.[214] As a result, the tribunal held that the effect of one of the decrees was

---

[207] *LG&E Energy Corporation*, fn. 156, at [130]; *Saluka*, fn. 196, at [304]. Tribunals have enquired on the level of investors' due diligence in considering the extent to which the investor actually relied on the state's representations when investing: see *FREIF Eurowind v Kingdom of Spain*, SCC Case No. 2017/060, Final Award, 8 March 2021, at [545]–[553]; *RWE Innogy GmbH and RWE Innogy Aersa SAU v Kingdom of Spain*, ICSID Case No. ARB/14/34, Decision on Jurisdiction, Liability and Certain Issues of Quantum, 30 December 2019, at [507], [513]; *Parkerings-Compagniet AS*, fn. 181, at [335]–[336].

[208] *Crystallex International Corporation v Bolivarian Republic of Venezuela*, fn. 147, at [623]; *Emilio Agustín Maffezini v Kingdom of Spain*, ICSID Case No. ARB/97/7, Award, 13 November 2000, at [83].

[209] *Murphy Exploration & Production Company–International v Republic of Ecuador (II)*, PCA Case No. 2012-16, Partial Final Award, 6 May 2016, at [292]–[293]; *CME Czech Republic BV*, fn. 163, at [611]; *Saluka*, fn. 196, at [279] and [309].

[210] *CMS Gas Transmission Co. v Argentine Republic*, ICSID Case No. ARB/01/8, Award, 12 May 2005, at [276] ('fair and equitable treatment is inseparable from stability and predictability'); see also *Occidental Petroleum Corporation and ors v Republic of Ecuador*, LCIA Case No. UN 3467, Final Award, 5 October 2012, at [183].

[211] *Parkerings-Compagniet AS*, fn. 181, at [332]; *CMS Gas Transmission Co. v Argentine Republic*, fn. 210, at [277] ('It is not a question of whether the legal framework might need to be frozen as it can always evolve and be adapted to changing circumstances, but neither is it a question of whether the framework can be dispensed with altogether when specific commitments to the contrary have been made').

[212] SCC Case No. 088/2004, Partial Award, 27 March 2007.

[213] Ibid., at [335].

[214] Ibid., at [337].

discriminatory, and therefore in violation of the Netherlands–Czech and Slovak Federal Republic BIT.[215]

The standard also requires host states to offer basic protections in their internal judicial **8.106** systems. Failure to provide such protection is categorised as 'denial of justice'.[216] Such a finding can be made 'whenever an uncorrected national judgment is vitiated by fundamental unfairness'.[217] Specifically, the tribunal in *Azinian v Mexico*[218] explained how such a claim could be advanced in the following terms:

> [A] denial of justice could be pleaded if the relevant courts refuse to entertain a suit, if they subject it to undue delay, of if they administer justice in a seriously inadequate way [...] There is a fourth type of denial if justice, namely the clear and malicious misapplication of the law.[219]

In summary, it is therefore now possible to identify certain kinds of conduct and **8.107** treatment that would be likely to constitute a violation of the fair and equitable treatment standard. As explained by the tribunal in *Joseph Charles Lemire v Ukraine*,[220] the standard requires 'an action or omission by the State which violates a certain threshold of propriety, causing harm to the investor, and with a causal link between action or omission and harm'. In assessing that threshold of propriety, a tribunal will consider whether:

- the state has failed to offer a stable and predictable legal framework;
- the state made specific representations to the investor;
- due process has been denied to the investor;
- there is an absence of transparency in the legal procedure or in the actions of the state;
- there has been harassment, coercion, abuse of power, or other bad faith conduct by the host state; and
- any of the actions of the state can be labelled as arbitrary, discriminatory, or inconsistent.[221]

There is disagreement over whether the concept of 'fair and equitable treatment' is syn- **8.108** onymous with the minimum standard of protection required by customary international law, or whether it represents an independent concept requiring greater protection.[222] Under customary international law, the minimum standard has traditionally been understood to

---

[215] Ibid., at [338].
[216] NAFTA tribunals have held that a denial of justice would constitute a breach of the standard: see *The Loewen Group Inc. and Raymond L Loewen v United States of America*, ICSID Case No. ARB(AF)/98/3, Award, 26 June 2003, at [132]; *Waste Management*, fn. 182, at [98]; *International Thunderbird Gaming Corporation v United Mexican States*, UNCITRAL, Award, 26 January 2006, at [194], rejecting the investors' denial of justice claims. For a comprehensive analysis, see Paulsson, *Denial of Justice in International Law* (Cambridge University Press, 2005).
[217] Ibid., at 5.
[218] *Azinian and ors v United Mexican States*, ICSID Case No. ARB(AF)/97/2, Award on Jurisdiction and Merits, 1 November 1999.
[219] Ibid., at [102]–[103]. See also *Krederi Ltd. v Ukraine*, ICSID Case No. ARB/14/17, IIC 1636, Award (2018), at [455].
[220] ICSID Case No ARB/06/18, Decision on Jurisdiction and Liability, 14 January 2010, at [284].
[221] Ibid.
[222] See Dolzer and Stevens, *Bilateral Investment Treaties* (Martinus Nijhoff, 1995), p. 59; *BG Group PLC*, fn. 121 at [275]–[310].

be based on a standard of review that was set out in the 1926 *Neer* decision of the United States–Mexico General Claims Commission:

> [T]he treatment of an alien, in order to constitute an international delinquency, should amount to an outrage, to bad faith, to wilful neglect of duty, or to an insufficiency of governmental action so far short of international standards that every reasonable and impartial man would readily recognize its insufficiency.[223]

8.109   The *Neer* standard, however, has been subject to considerable criticism on the grounds that 'it did not lay down a general rule' and is of only 'limited import' in the interpretation of investment treaties.[224]

8.110   In an oft-cited article on British investment treaty practice, one commentator concluded that:

> [T]he terms 'fair and equitable treatment' envisage conduct which goes far beyond the minimum standard and afford protection to a greater extent and according to a much more objective standard than any previously employed form of words [...] The terms are likely to be understood and applied independently and autonomously.[225]

8.111   Unless there is a clear and express link with the international minimum standard, tribunals have overwhelmingly interpreted fair and equitable treatment provisions in BITs as an independent and self-contained treaty standard with an autonomous meaning, which provides protections beyond the customary international law standard.[226]

8.112   A difficulty occurs when treaties link the fair and equitable standard to 'international law'. Typical language is 'fair and equitable treatment in accordance with international law'. The argument has frequently been made that this type of reference restricts the protection to the customary international law minimum standard of treatment.[227] However, several tribunals have concluded that this cannot be the case, since 'international law', as a general reference, must also take into account treaty practice. As the tribunal in the *Vivendi* case held:

> The Tribunal sees no basis for equating principles of international law with the minimum standard of treatment. First, the reference to principles of international law supports a broader reading that invites consideration of a wider range of international law principles than the minimum standard alone. [... T]he language of the provision suggests that one should also look to contemporary principles of international law, not only to principles from almost a century ago.[228]

8.113   But what happens where there is a clear reference to the customary international law standard, and is it different from a stand-alone fair and equitable treatment standard? Some

---

[223] *Neer v Mexico*, Opinion, United States–Mexico General Claims Commission, (1926) 4 RIAA 60, at 61–62.
[224] Paulsson and Petrochilos, 'Neer-ly misled?' (2007) 22 ICSID Rev—Foreign Investment LJ 242, at 257.
[225] Mann, 'British treaties for the promotion and protection of investments' (1981) 52 BYIL 241, at 244.
[226] See, e.g., *Cairn Energy*, fn. 201, at [1702]–[1704]; *Global Telecom Holding SAE v Government of Canada*, ICSID Case No. ARB/16/16, Award, 27 March 2020, at [484]. See generally Schreuer and Dolzer, fn. 167, pp. 137–138.
[227] The content of the international minimum standard is itself open to debate: see UNCTAD, *Fair and Equitable Treatment*, Series on Issues in International Investment Agreements (UN, 1999), available online at http://unctad.org, pp. 39–40. See also *CC/Devas (Mauritius) Ltd, Devas Employees Mauritius Private Limited and Telcom Devas Mauritius Limited v Republic of India*, PCA Case No. 2013-09, Award on Jurisdiction and Merits, 25 July 2016, at [456]; Paulsson and Petrochilos, 'Neer-ly misled?' (2007) 22 ICSID Rev—FILJ 242.
[228] *Compañía de Aguas del Aconquija*, fn. 114 at [7.4.7].

tribunals have concluded that the evolution of the customary standard makes the analysis a distinction without a difference.[229] For example, the NAFTA tribunal in *Mondev v United States*,[230] applying the customary international law standard, made a clear distinction with the Neer standard and held that: 'To the modern eye, what is unfair or inequitable need not equate with the outrageous or the egregious. In particular, a State may treat foreign investment unfairly and inequitably without necessarily acting in bad faith.'[231]

It is clear that there is significant overlap between the customary and the treaty standards, and **8.114** that the distinctions between the two 'may well be more apparent than real'.[232] Whilst the argument about the distinction between the FET and the minimum standard of treatment continues to be made, tribunals have 'seemed to be less interested in the theoretical discussion on the relationship between the FET and the MST [minimum standard of treatment] and turned their attention primarily to the content of the FET [fair and equitable treatment] obligation, whether or not it is qualified by the MST'.[233]

(c) Full protection and security

As in the case of 'fair and equitable treatment', it is difficult to give a precise meaning to the **8.115** notion of 'full protection and security'. However, its scope may be illustrated by reference to its practical application. In contrast with most of the other investor protections, which impose restrictions or prohibitions on certain types of host state activity, the 'full protection and security' clause seeks to impose certain positive obligations on the host state to protect investments.

Arbitral tribunals have traditionally found breaches of the 'full protection and security' ob- **8.116** ligation in situations in which the host state failed to prevent physical damage to qualifying investments by not taking measures that fell within the normal exercise of governmental functions of policing and maintenance of law and order.[234] For example, in *AAPL v Sri Lanka*,[235] the tribunal held that Sri Lanka violated its obligation of full protection and

---

[229] *Pope & Talbot Inc. v Government of Canada*, UNCITRAL, Award on Damages, 31 May 2002, at [52] and [55]; *International Thunderbird Gaming Corporation*, fn. 216, at [194].

[230] *Mondev International Ltd v United States of America*, ICSID Case No. ARB(AF)/99/2, Final Award, IIC 173 (2002).

[231] Ibid., at [116]. See also *CC/Devas (Mauritius) Ltd*, fn. 227 at [457]: 'The Tribunal does not subscribe to the view that, today, a violation of the customary international minimum standard was frozen as defined in *Neer* [...] It is now generally recognized that customary international law has evolved since 1926, some awards giving the required minimum treatment a wider interpretation than others.'

[232] *Saluka*, fn. 196, at [292]–[295]. See also *CMS Gas Transmission Co.*, fn. 210, at [284]: 'While the choice between requiring a higher treaty standard and that of equating it with the international minimum standard might have relevance in the context of some disputes, the Tribunal is not persuaded that it is relevant in this case. In fact, the Treaty standard of fair and equitable treatment and its connection with the required stability and predictability of the business environment, founded on solemn legal and contractual commitments, is not different from the international law minimum standard and its evolution under customary law.'

[233] UNCTAD, *Fair and Equitable Treatment: A Sequel*, Series on Issues in International Investment Agreements II (UN, 2012), available online at http://unctad.org/en/Docs/unctaddiaeia2011d5_en.pdf, p. 59.

[234] *Cengiz Insaat Sanayi ve Ticaret AS v Libya*, ICC Case No. 21537/ZF/AYZ, Award, 7 November 2018; *Asian Agricultural Products Ltd (AAPL)*, fn. 15; *American Manufacturing and Trading*, fn. 73; *Rumeli Telekom AS and Telsim Mobil Telekomunikasyon Hizmetleri AS v Republic of Kazakhstan*, ICSID Case No. ARB/05/16, Award, 29 July 2008. See generally Schreuer, 'Full protection and security' (2010) 1 J Intl Disp Settlement 353.

[235] *Asian Agricultural Products Ltd (AAPL)*, fn. 15.

security by not taking appropriate measures to prevent the destruction of an investor's shrimp farm and the killing of more than twenty of its employees during a counterinsurgency operation.

8.117   The standard applied is one of 'due diligence', or an *obligation de moyens*, requiring the host state to exercise reasonable care, within its means,[236] to protect investments, rather than a 'strict liability' standard. However, there is no need for the claimant to establish negligence or bad faith.

8.118   The obligation of the host state to provide full protection and security to investors is independent, and not relative to the level of protection provided by the state to its own nationals or to nationals of other states. Therefore the fact that the state did not protect the property of its own nationals is no defence to a claim by an investor of breach of this obligation.[237] However, the resources available to a state and the reasonable deployment of those resources will be elements that are taken into account. For example, if, in the context of civil disturbances, a factory belonging to a foreign investor were destroyed because the police were all protecting a neighbouring domestically owned installation, liability might well be established. If, however, the police were fully engaged in protecting the population, and many local businesses, whether locally or foreign-owned, were damaged, it will be difficult to establish liability.

8.119   Whilst this standard has normally been applied in situations of physical protection of real and tangible property, its scope has been extended to other circumstances.[238] For instance, it has been held that withdrawal of an authorisation vital to the operation of the investment amounts to a breach of 'full protection and security'.[239] Similarly, a change in the legal framework, making it impossible to preserve and continue contractual arrangements underpinning the investment, has also been found to be incompatible with a BIT's 'full protection and security' provision.[240]

(d) No arbitrary or discriminatory measures impairing the investment

8.120   Most investment treaties impose an obligation upon the host state not to impair the management or operation of the investment by arbitrary or discriminatory measures.[241]

[236] *Pantechniki SA*, fn. 138, at [81]–[84]; *Peter A Allard v Government of Barbados*, PCA, Award, 13 June 2014, at [243]–[244].
[237] *American Manufacturing and Trading Inc.*, fn. 73.
[238] *Waguih Elie George Siag and Clorinda Vecchi v Arab Republic of Egypt*, ICSID Case No. ARB/05/15, Award, 1 June 2009, at [445]–[448]; *AES Summit Generation Ltd and AES-Tisza Erömü Kft v Republic of Hungary*, ICSID Case No. ARB/07/22, Award, 23 September 2010, at [13.3.2]; *Marion Unglaube and Reinhard Unglaube v Republic of Costa Rica*, ICSID Case Nos ARB/08/1 and ARB/09/20, Award, 16 May 2012, at [281]. Other tribunals, however, have rejected this extension of the standard: see, e.g., *Rumeli Telekom AS*, fn. 234, at [668]–[669]; *Indian Metals & Ferro Alloys Ltd v Republic of Indonesia*, PCA Case No. 2015-40, Award, 29 March 2019, at [267].
[239] *Antoine Goetz and ors v Republic of Burundi*, ICSID Case No. ARB/95/3, Award, 10 February 1999, at [125]–[131].
[240] *CME Czech Republic BV*, fn. 163, at [613]; *National Grid Plc v Argentine Republic*, UNCITRAL, Award, 3 November 2008, at [189]; *Azurix Corporation*, fn. 181, at [408].
[241] Not all investment treaties use the term 'arbitrary'; some instead refer to 'unreasonable or discriminatory' measures. Tribunals differ as to the significance of this variance in the language. According to the tribunal in *National Grid*, fn. 240, at [197], the terms are synonymous: 'It is the view of the Tribunal that the plain meaning of the terms "unreasonable" and "arbitrary" is substantially the same in the sense of something

For instance, Article II(3)(b) of the United States–Ecuador BIT[242] provides: 'Neither Party shall in any way impair by arbitrary or discriminatory measures the management, operation, maintenance, use, enjoyment, acquisition, expansion, or disposal of investments […]'.

The concepts of 'arbitrary', or 'discriminatory', measures are not defined in the treaties. The International Court of Justice (ICJ) formulated the test of 'arbitrariness' in the context of investment protection in the *ELSI* case.[243] The Court observed: **8.121**

> Arbitrariness is not so much something opposed to a rule of law, as something opposed to the rule of law […] It is a wilful disregard of due process of law, an act which shocks, or at least surprises, a sense of juridical propriety.[244]

In the words of the tribunal in *Joseph Charles Lemire v Ukraine*,[245] arbitrariness is defined as: **8.122**

[…]
  a. a measure that inflicts damage on the investor without serving any apparent legitimate purpose;
  b. a measure that is not based on legal standards but on discretion, prejudice or personal preference;
  c. a measure taken for reasons that are different from those put forward by the decision maker;
  d. a measure taken in wilful disregard of due process and proper procedure.[246]

For instance, in the *Azurix* case,[247] involving an investment in a water concession, government measures that included inciting consumers not to pay their bills, requiring the concessionaire not to apply the new tariffs resulting from a review, and denying the concessionaire access to documentation on the basis of which it had been sanctioned, were considered to be arbitrary.   **8.123**

By contrast, in the *El Paso* case,[248] the tribunal concluded that certain measures taken by Argentina to address the economic crisis at the end of 2001 were reasonable, consistent with the aim pursued, had the desired result, and therefore were not tainted by arbitrariness. The tribunal observed that there were several methods that Argentina could have employed to address the crisis, that evidence presented by the experts demonstrated a difference of   **8.124**

---

done capriciously, without reason.' Meanwhile, the tribunal in *Glencore International AG and CI Prodeco SA v Republic of Colombia*, ICSID Case No. ARB/16/6, Award, 27 August 2019, found that '[t]he set of unreasonable measures is wider than that of arbitrary measures' (at [1446]), and that ' "unreasonable" [includes] not only "arbitrary measures" but also measures that are irrational in themselves or result from an irrational decision-making process' (at [1452]).

[242] Treaty between the United States of America and the Republic of Ecuador Concerning the Encouragement and Reciprocal Protection of Investment, signed on 27 August 1993, entered into force on 11 May 1997.

[243] *Case Concerning Elettronica Sicula SpA (ELSI) (United States of America v Italy)*, Judgment, 15 ICJ 76 (1999), ICGJ 95 (1989). See also *LG&E Energy Corporation*, fn. 156, at [158]. For a definition based on the plain meaning of the term 'arbitrary', *see Azurix Corporation*, fn. 181, at [392] ('In its ordinary meaning, "arbitrary" means "derived from mere opinion", "capricious", "unrestrained", "despotic" ').

[244] *ELSI*, fn. 243, at [128].

[245] fn. 220.

[246] Ibid., at [262].

[247] *Azurix Corporation*, fn. 181, at [393].

[248] *El Paso Energy International Co.*, fn. 157 at [319]–[325].

opinion as to which would have been the preferred solution, and that, ultimately, the measures resulted in the positive evolution of Argentina's economy.

8.125   In relation to 'discriminatory' treatment, a measure is considered discriminatory if (a) 'the intent of the measure is to discriminate', or (b) 'if the measure has a discriminatory effect'.[249] As a result, although evidence of discriminatory intent may be relevant, it is 'the fact of unequal treatment which is key'.[250] Thus it is not essential to establish any bad faith on the part of the host state.[251] It has been held that, in general, a measure is discriminatory in effect if it results in a treatment of an investor that is different from that accorded to other investors in a similar or comparable situation, where there appears to be no reasonable basis for such differentiation.[252] The issue of whether investors are in such a comparable situation is a question of fact. Typically, tribunals have been reluctant to find that investors are in sufficiently comparable positions to take advantage of this protection.

(e) National and 'most favoured nation' treatment

8.126   Investment treaties also provide comparative protection standards—that is, standards that do not set an autonomous standard of treatment, but rather require treatment no less favourable than that of nationals and companies of the host state (national treatment), or of any other state (MFN treatment). Article 3(1) of the United Kingdom–Egypt BIT[253] is a representative provision:

> Neither Contracting Party shall in its territory subject investments or returns of investors of the other Contracting Party to treatment less favourable than that which it accords to investment or returns of its own nationals or companies or to investments or returns of nationals or companies of any third State.

8.127   Since these are relative standards of protection, their scope cannot be defined in the abstract, but will vary according to the circumstances of each case. This requires an analysis of facts, including the protections and assurances granted by the host state to other investors.

8.128   In order to succeed in a claim based on the national treatment or MFN provisions of a BIT, a claimant must establish that *more* favourable treatment has been granted to another foreign investor or national in similar circumstances.[254] The requirement for a

---

[249] *LG&E Energy Corporation*, fn. 156, at [146].

[250] *Marion Unglaube*, fn. 238, at [263].

[251] *The Loewen Group Inc.*, fn. 216, at [132]. The tribunal was considering the judgment of a US trial court. The tribunal observed that bad faith or malicious intention is not an essential element of unfair and inequitable treatment, and it is sufficient if there is a lack of due process that offends a sense of judicial propriety. Although the tribunal found the trial court proceedings to be improper and discreditable, it held against the claimant, as a result of its failure to exhaust all remedies under the US legal system.

[252] *Lidercón*, fn. 153, at [169]; *Nykomb Synergetics Technology Holding AB v Republic of Latvia*, Stockholm Rules, Award, 16 December 2003, at [64]; *Saluka*, fn. 196, at [313] ('State conduct is discriminatory, if (i) similar cases are (ii) treated differently (iii) and without reasonable justification').

[253] Treaty between the United States of America and the Arab Republic of Egypt Concerning the Reciprocal Encouragement and Protection of Investments, signed on 29 September 1982, entered into force on 27 June 1992.

[254] *İçkale İnşaat Limited Şirketi v Turkmenistan*, ICSID Case No. ARB/10/24, Award, 8 March 2016, at [328]–[329]; *Parkerings-Compagniet AS*, fn. 181, at [368]; *United Parcel Service of America Inc. v Government of Canada*, UNCITRAL, Award, 24 May 2007, at [173]–[184].

similar basis of comparison is explicit in the USMCA, which provides that national treatment applies only where the foreign and domestic investor are 'in like circumstances'.[255] Tribunals do not require proof of discriminatory or protectionist intent in order to find a treaty breach. However, the pursuit of legitimate policy objectives may justify differential treatment.[256]

Traditionally, the MFN clause is relied on in the context of substantive rights. For example, **8.129** the host state of an investment may provide tax concessions to French investors in the oil industry, but not to British investors in that industry. In those circumstances, the British investor could rely on an MFN clause in the UK treaty with the host state to claim the same treatment or compensation for the loss suffered as a result of the discrimination. However, as seen earlier, tribunals in *Maffezini* and other cases[257] have extended the application of this provision from substantive to procedural matters, such as the dispute resolution mechanism between the host state and investors.[258] This trend has led to a new generation of investment treaties that include more deliberate language to exclude procedural rights from the reach of the MFN clause.[259]

The presence of MFN clauses in investment treaties creates a diffusive effect of investor **8.130** protection, as additional gains obtained by one state flow to other states. This can lead to the creation of a single 'highest' standard for all contracting parties to BITs with a particular state.

(f) Free transfer of funds related to investments

Many investment treaties provide guarantees relating to the free transfer of funds related to **8.131** investments. For example, Article 11 of the Canada–Mongolia BIT[260] provides:

1. Each Party shall permit all transfers relating to covered investments to be made freely, and without delay, into and out of its territory. Such transfers include:
    1. contributions to capital; 2. profits, dividends, interest, capital gains, royalty payments, management fees, technical assistance and other fees, returns in kind and other amounts derived from the covered investment; 3. proceeds from the sale of all or any part of covered investments or from the partial or complete liquidation of covered investments; 4. payments made under a contract entered into by the investor, or covered investments, including payments made pursuant to a loan agreement; 5. payments made pursuant to Articles 7 (Compensation for Losses)

---

[255] USMCA, Arts 14.4 and 14.5.

[256] *Gami Investments Inc. v United Mexican States*, UNCITRAL, Award, 15 November 2004, at [114]; *Parkerings-Compagniet AS*, fn. 181, at [371]. See also *William Ralph Clayton and ors v Government of Canada*, PCA Case No. 2009-04, Award on Jurisdiction and Liability, 17 March 2015, at [720].

[257] See *Suez, Sociedad General de Aguas de Barcelona SA*, fn. 127.

[258] See paragraphs 8.54–8.55.

[259] See, e.g., UNCTAD, *Most-Favored-Nation Treatment: A Sequel*, Series on Issues in International Investment Agreements II (UN, 2010), available online at http://unctad.org/en/Docs/diaeia20101_en.pdf, pp. 85–86 (referring to the Chile–Colombia FTA of 2006, Annex 9.3, the Canada–Peru FTA of 2008, Annex 804.1, and the Japan–Switzerland EPA of 2009, Art. 88).

[260] Agreement between Canada and Mongolia for the Promotion and Protection of Investments, signed on 8 September 2016, entered into force on 24 February 2017.

and 10 (Expropriation); and 6. payments arising under Section C (Settlement of Disputes between an Investor and the Host Party).

2. Each Party shall permit transfers relating to covered investments to be made in the convertible currency in which the capital was originally invested, or in any other convertible currency agreed to by the investor and the Party concerned. Unless otherwise agreed by the investor, transfers shall be made at the market rate of exchange applicable on the date of transfer.

8.132   This obligation entitles foreign investors to compensation if they are affected by currency control regulations or other host state acts that effectively block the investor's money in the host state. The right to free transfer of funds is critical to the value of a foreign investment. As one tribunal noted, such guarantees are 'fundamental to the freedom to make a foreign investment and an essential element of the promotional role of BITs'.[261]

8.133   Free transfer provisions are generally broad in scope and are not limited to the money originally invested but also cover (as in the Canada–Mongolia Treaty) any amounts derived from or associated with the investment, including profits, dividends, interest, capital gains, royalty payments, management, technical assistance or other fees, or returns in kind. However, not every cross-border movement of funds will be 'related to the investment' and protected by the BIT. In *Continental Casualty Co. v Argentina*,[262] the tribunal held that the frustrated transfer at issue—a short-term placement to a bank account outside Argentina for the purpose of protecting the funds from an impending devaluation of the Argentine peso—was not a transfer protected by the BIT.

8.134   The right to transfer funds is not to be confused with assertion of contested rights over funds. For example, in *White Industries v India*,[263] the tribunal held that the retention of bank guarantees by Coal India (a state-owned company) was not a violation of India's obligation to 'permit all funds of an investor related to an investment to be transferred freely without unreasonable delay' because the provision was meant to apply to the movement of capital and exchange of currency, not assertions of contractual rights.[264]

8.135   Treaties often provide for exceptions to the free movement of funds by allowing host states to restrict transfers during unusual periods of low foreign exchange or balance-of-payments problems.[265] Further, it may be permissible for the host state to maintain laws and regulations requiring reports of currency transfer, or to take measures for protection of creditor interests. Such regulations must nevertheless comply with the other investor treaty provisions requiring fair and equitable and non-discriminatory treatment. As the tribunal in *Rusoro v Venezuela* noted:[266] '[The free transfer of funds clause] guarantee[s] investors that they will be able to transfer funds related to their investments and returns without delay, in

---

[261] One tribunal noted that the guarantees provided by free transfer of funds provisions are 'fundamental to the freedom to make a foreign investment and an essential element of the promotional role of BITs': see *Continental Casualty Co. v Argentine Republic*, ICSID Case No. ARB/03/9, Award, 5 September 2008, at [239].

[262] See fn. 261.

[263] *White Industries Australia Ltd v Republic of India*, UNCITRAL, Final Award, 30 November 2011.

[264] Ibid., at [13.2.1]–[13.2.4].

[265] See, e.g., the Protocol attached to the Treaty between the United States of America and the Arab Republic of Egypt Concerning the Reciprocal Encouragement and Protection of Investments, 29 September 1982, para. 10.

[266] *Rusoro Mining Ltd. v Bolivarian Republic of Venezuela*, ICSID Case No. ARB(AF)/12/5, Award, 22 August 2016, at [576]–[578].

a convertible currency and at the exchange rate prevailing at the date of transfer. Provided that this triple guarantee is complied with, the BIT does not impose restrictions on the manner in which Contracting States decide to regulate their exchange control regime.'

In order to access the protection of the free transfer of funds provision, tribunals have held   **8.136** that investors need to comply with reasonable internal formalities to transfer currency abroad. In *Metalpar v Argentina*[267] the tribunal refused to hold a breach of the free transfer provision because the claimants had not complied with the established procedure for transferring funds abroad (that is, seeking the authorisation of the central bank).

The question arises as to what constitutes a transfer 'without delay' when a host state has in   **8.137** place a system of applications for foreign currency. The tribunal in *Air Canada v Venezuela*[268] concluded that 'the time frame should reflect the period of time normally required to complete the necessary formalities related to the requested transfer' by the host state.[269] In that case, Venezuela failed to approve the conversion to hard currency of proceeds from ticket sales Air Canada earned in local currency (the bolivar), contrary to its prior practice and thus locked Air Canada's rapidly devaluing bolivares in Venezuela. Venezuela's conduct was held in breach of the free transfer of funds protection.

(g) Observance of specific investment undertakings

Some treaties contain a clause whereby the host state commits to respect specific undertak-   **8.138** ings towards investors or investments. This clause is known as the 'umbrella clause' due to the wide scope of protection it may potentially offer. Unlike the other protections that we have considered, which are present in nearly all treaties, umbrella clauses are, according to one study, only present in 40 per cent of treaties.[270] There is no standard form of wording and so each 'umbrella clause' needs to be carefully considered on its own language. One example is the final sentence of Article II(2)(c) of the United States–Argentina Treaty[271] which sets out the obligation in the following terms: 'Each Party shall observe any obligation it may have entered into with regard to investments.'

There is disagreement as to the whether the legal effect of umbrella clauses is to elevate any   **8.139** breach of contractual obligations in direct agreements between states and investors to the level of treaty breach.[272] The award in *SGS v Pakistan*[273] was the first to consider the issue of the scope of umbrella clauses. The tribunal concluded, on the terms of the particular clause in question, that it did 'not believe that transmutation of SGS's contract claims into BIT

---

[267] *Metalpar SA and Buen Aire SA v Argentine Republic*, ICSID Case No. ARB/03/5, Award, 6 June 2008, at [179].

[268] ICSID Case No. ARB (AF)17/1, Award, 13 September 2021.

[269] Ibid., at [362].

[270] Yannaca-Small, *Interpretation of the Umbrella Clause in Investment Agreements, OECD Working Papers on International Investment, 2006/03* (OECD Publishing, 2006), p. 5.

[271] See fn. 43.

[272] See OECD, 'Interpretation of the umbrella clause in investment agreements', Working Paper on International Investment No. 2006/3 (October 2006), available online at http://www.oecd.org/; Crawford, 'Treaty and contract in investment arbitration' (2008) 24 Arb Intl 351; Kunoy, 'Singing in the rain: Developments in the interpretation of umbrella clauses' (2006) 7 JWIT 275.

[273] *SGS Société Générale de Surveillance SA v Islamic Republic of Pakistan*, ICSID Case No. ARB/01/13, Decision on Jurisdiction, 6 August 2003, at [156].

claims has occurred' through the operation of such a clause. That tribunal also concluded that the legal consequences of such an interpretation of the BIT were 'so far-reaching in scope, and so automatic and unqualified and sweeping in their apparent operation, so burdensome in their potential impact upon the contracting party',[274] that clear and convincing evidence had to be adduced by the claimant to demonstrate that such was the shared intent of the contracting parties to the BIT. In the absence of such evidence, the arbitral tribunal rejected the claimant's interpretation, which would, according to the tribunal, amount to 'incorporating by reference an unlimited number of state contracts as well as other municipal law instruments setting out state commitments including unilateral commitments to an investor of the other contracting party'.[275]

8.140   This narrow interpretation of umbrella clauses was rejected in another case[276] brought by the same investor against the Philippines under the Switzerland–Philippines BIT.[277] That case concerned Article X(2) of that treaty which stated: 'Each Contracting Party shall observe any obligation it has assumed with regard to specific investments in its territory by investors of the other Contracting Party.' The tribunal concluded that this clause did make it a breach of the BIT for the host state to fail to observe binding contractual commitments. However, the obligations contained in the investment agreement remained governed by the applicable law of the contract and were not elevated to international law. The practical impact of the decision was further limited by the conclusion that compliance with undertakings was a 'two-way street'—in other words the investor was also bound by its obligations under a covered instrument. In the *SGS v Philippines* case that meant that the investor could not bypass the contract's dispute resolution clause and that it first had to comply with its obligation to submit its claim to local jurisdiction in accordance with the dispute resolution clause as a precondition to an international arbitration.[278]

8.141   The diverging approaches adopted by the *SGS v Pakistan* and *SGS v Philippines* tribunals have led to the development of conflicting lines of jurisprudence, which one leading commentator, Professor James Crawford, grouped into four 'camps':

> The first camp adopts an extremely narrow interpretation of umbrella clauses, holding that they are operative only where it is possible to discern a shared intent of the parties that any breach of contract is a breach of the BIT (*SGS v Pakistan*; *Joy Mining v Egypt*).
>
> The second camp seeks to limit umbrella clauses to breaches of contract committed by the host State in the exercise of sovereign authority (*Pan American Energy v Argentina*; *El Paso Energy v Argentina*).
>
> A third view goes to the other extreme: the effect of umbrella clauses is to internationalise investment contracts, thereby transforming contractual claims into treaty claims directly subject to treaty rules (*Fedax v Venezuela*; *Eureko v Poland*; *Noble Ventures v Romania*).

---

[274] Ibid., at [167].
[275] Ibid., at [168].
[276] *SGS Société Générale de Surveillance SA*, fn. 165.
[277] Agreement between the Swiss Confederation and the Republic of the Philippines on the Promotion and Reciprocal Protection of Investments, signed on 23 August 1991, entered into force on 23 April 1999.
[278] *SGS Société Générale de Surveillance SA*, fn. 165, at [155].

Finally there is the view that an umbrella clause is operative and may form the basis for a substantive treaty claim, but that it does not convert a contractual claim into a treaty claim. On the one hand it provides, or at least may provide, a basis for a treaty claim even if the BIT in question contains no generic claims clause (*SGS v Philippines*; *CMS v Argentina* (Annulment)); on the other hand, the umbrella clause does not change the proper law of the contract or its legal incidents, including its provisions for dispute settlement.[279]

Later cases involving umbrella clauses have continued to divide into these camps.[280] For in-   **8.142** stance, in interpreting nearly identical umbrella clauses, the tribunals in *BIVAC v Paraguay* and *SGS v Paraguay* came to opposite conclusions. Both tribunals determined that the umbrella clause imports contractual obligations into the investment treaty. However, the *BIVAC* tribunal (like the *SGS v Philippines* tribunal) determined that the claim was premature because the parties had agreed to the exclusive jurisdiction of national courts,[281] whereas the *SGS* tribunal determined that the forum selection clause was not a bar to the claim's admissibility.[282] In the words of one commentator, 'the situation seems to remain as uncertain today as it was 10 years ago when the first two *SGS* Tribunals were called to interpret and apply the clause for the first time in a legal vacuum'.[283]

E. Measures of Compensation

In the context of investment treaty arbitration, the term 'compensation' is commonly used   **8.143** to describe (a) a prerequisite for a lawful expropriation of private property, (b) one form of reparation for injury caused by a state's unlawful act under international law, and/or (c) the obligation to pay damages as a consequence for a breach of contract.[284] In customary international law, compensation is considered an alternative to restitution in the sense that 'restitution is a primary remedy for international wrongs, while compensation has a supplementary function in achieving the ultimate objective of reparation, viz wiping out all the consequences of the illegal act'.[285]

---

[279] Crawford, 'Treaty and contract in investment arbitration' (2008) 24 Arb Intl 351, at 366–367.

[280] See, e.g., *Strabag SE v Libya*, ICSID Case No. ARB(AF)/15/1, Award, 29 June 2020, at [164] (declining to read into the treaty a requirement that the state act in a sovereign capacity in order to trigger umbrella clause protection); *Supervisión y Control SA v Republic of Costa Rica*, ICSID Case No. ARB/12/4, Award, 18 January 2017, at [287] (finding that the treaty's umbrella clause encompassed obligations entered into by a company controlled by the claimant); *Gustav F W Hamester*, fn. 89, at [348] (declining to interpret the umbrella clause as encompassing obligations undertaken in a contract entered into by an entity separate from the host state); *EDF International and ors v Argentine Republic*, ICSID Case No. ARB/03/23, Award, IIC 556 (2012), at [939] (finding that concession agreements for specific investments fell within the ambit of the umbrella clause); *Bosh International, Inc. and B&P Ltd Foreign Investments Enterprise v Ukraine*, ICSID Case No. ARB/08/11, Award, 25 October 2012, at [246] (finding that the umbrella clause did not cover contractual undertakings made by a third party whose acts were not attributable to the host state).

[281] *Bureau Veritas*, fn. 163, at [141]–[142], and [159].

[282] *SGS Société Générale de Surveillance SA*, fn. 96, at [162]–[171].

[283] Yannaca-Small, '*BIVAC BV v Paraguay* versus *SGS v Paraguay*: The umbrella clause still in search of one identity' (2013) 28 ICSID Rev—FILJ 307, at 313.

[284] Marboe, 'Compensation in investment law and arbitration', in Bjorklund, Laird, and Ripinsky (eds) *Investment Treaty Law: Current Issues III* (British Institute of International and Comparative Law, 2009), pp. 29–32.

[285] Ripinsky and Williams, *Damages in International Investment Law* (British Institute of International and Comparative Law, 2008), p. 55, citing the ruling in *Chorzów Factory* that the state was under 'the obligation to restore the undertaking [that is, restitution] and, if this be not possible, to pay its value at the time of the indemnification [that is, compensation], which value is designed to take the place of restitution which has become

8.144   The quantification of compensation is left to the arbitral tribunal's discretion as the tribunal in *Rumeli v Kazakhstan* noted:

> This is not a matter to be resolved simply on the basis of the burden of proof. To be sure, the tribunal must be satisfied that the claimant has suffered some damage under the relevant head as a result of the respondent's breach. But once it is satisfied of this, *the determination of the precise amount of this damage is a matter for the tribunal's informed estimation* in the light of all the evidence available to it.[286]

8.145   A tribunal will award compensation, however, only if the party seeking it has established causation. As articulated by the majority in *Biwater Gauff (Tanzania) Ltd v Tanzania*:

> Compensation for any violation of the BIT, whether in the context of unlawful expropriation or the breach of any other treaty standard, will only be due if there is a sufficient causal link between the actual breach of the BIT and the loss sustained by [the claimant].[287]

8.146   The elements of causation include, inter alia, '(a) a sufficient link between the wrongful act and the damage in question, and (b) a threshold beyond which damage, albeit linked to the wrongful act, is considered too indirect or remote'.[288] In other words, proof of causation requires cause, effect, and a logical link between the two.[289]

8.147   The issue of compensation can be usefully considered first in terms of remedies for expropriation and remedies for other international law breaches, before turning to certain ancillary issues (moral damages, interest, costs, and attorneys' fees).

(a) Expropriation remedies

8.148   The almost universal standard of compensation in expropriation established by BITs for lawful expropriations is the 'fair market value' of the expropriated investment immediately prior to the expropriatory measure. This standard dates from 1938 and is known as the 'Hull formula' after US Secretary of State Cordell Hull, who declared, in a dispute between

---

impossible': see *Case Concerning the Factory at Chorzów (Claim for Indemnity) (Germany v Poland)* [1928] PCIJ Series A No. 17, at 48.

[286] *Rumeli Telekom AS*, fn. 234, at [147] (emphasis added); see also *Tidewater Investment SRL and Tidewater Caribe CA v Bolivarian Republic of Venezuela*, ICSID Case no ARB/10/5, Decision on Annulment, 27 December 2016, at [192].

[287] *Biwater Gauff (Tanzania) Ltd v United Republic of Tanzania*, fn. 120, at [779].

[288] Ibid., at [785], citing Crawford, *The International Law Commission's Articles on State Responsibility: Introduction, Text and Commentaries* (Cambridge University Press, 2002), pp. 204–205. The majority determined that although Tanzania had violated the BIT, none of the violations caused the loss and damage in question: *Biwater Gauff*, fn. 120, at [797]–[798]. The concurring and dissenting opinion, at [16]–[19], considered the majority's analysis to confuse issues of causation, on the one hand, and quantum of damages, on the other. Tanzania seized the claimant's business, which clearly caused injury to it. However, the claimant had failed to demonstrate damages, so the majority's analytical confusion was not decisive in the outcome.

[289] *Joseph Charles Lemire*, fn. 220, at [157]. That a claimant could potentially recover against a respondent state on the basis of a contract does not preclude the claimant for recovering damages for the state's breach of the relevant BIT: see, e.g., *Deutsche Bank*, fn. 85.

the United States and Mexico concerning the expropriation of US oil fields, that international law required Mexico to pay 'prompt, adequate and effective' compensation.[290] The standard requires the payment of full market value of the expropriated asset speedily in a convertible currency. The World Bank Guidelines on the Treatment of Foreign Direct Investment state:

1. Compensation for a specific investment taken by the State will, according to the details provided below, be deemed 'appropriate' if it is adequate, effective and prompt.
2. Compensation will be deemed 'adequate' if it is based on the fair market value of the taken asset as such value is determined immediately before the time at which the taking occurred or the decision to take the asset became publicly known.[291]

Fair market value is generally accepted to mean the price at which a willing buyer and willing seller would conclude an arm's-length transaction.[292] As the tribunal in *Starrett Housing Corporation v Iran*[293] summarised it: **8.149**

[…] the price [at which] a willing buyer would buy […] and the price at which a willing seller would sell […] on condition that none of the two parties [is] under any kind of duress and that both parties have good information about all relevant circumstances involved in the purchase.[294]

There are various accepted methods of calculating the fair market value of an asset. The fair   **8.150** market value of an income-producing asset, or 'going concern', is often calculated by measuring its future prospects by using the discounted cash flow (DCF) analysis. The World Bank Guidelines define DCF as:

the cash receipts realistically expected from the enterprise in each future year of its economic life as reasonably projected minus that year's expected cash expenditure, after discounting this net cash flow for each year by a factor which reflects the time value of money, expected inflation, and the risk associated with such cash flow under realistic circumstances.[295]

This is exactly what a willing buyer and seller would do in the real world when fixing a price   **8.151** for a business. In order to calculate future cash flows, future revenues, operating expenditure, capital expenditure, and applicable taxes will all need to be estimated.[296] The discount rate will, in turn, be established using a formula that takes into account the particular risk of the industry in question by means of what is known as the 'beta'[297] and the relevant country risk. This exercise is usually undertaken by expert economic witnesses.

---

[290] Hackworth, *Digest of International Law*, vol. 3 (Government Printing Office, 1942), p. 659.
[291] Reprinted in Shihata, *Legal Treatment of Foreign Investment: The World Bank Guidelines* (Martinus Nijhoff, 1993), p. 193.
[292] Ripinsky and Williams, *Damages in International Investment Law* (British Institute of International and Comparative Law, 2008), pp. 183–186, citing *Black's Law Dictionary*.
[293] *Starrett Housing Corporation and ors v Islamic Republic of Iran*, 16 IRAN-U.S. C.T.R., 112.
[294] Ibid., at [18], [27], and [274]. See also *Rusoro Mining Ltd.*, fn. 266 at [647].
[295] *World Bank Guidelines on the Treatment of Foreign Direct Investment*, s. IV(6).
[296] See *Phillips Petroleum Co. Iran*, fn. 188, at [111]; see also *Burlington Resources Inc.*, fn. 116, at [374].
[297] The 'beta' measures the volatility of the particular industry vis-à-vis the stock market as a whole.

8.152   Once a figure is obtained from the DCF analysis, it is often supported by reference to comparative transactions, which show what comparable assets in comparable countries have been sold for at similar moments in time.

8.153   Another common valuation methodology where the affected asset is part of a publicly traded company is to look to the stock market valuation. This is of greater value where the affected asset represents the whole (or the bulk of) the traded corporation and the market in question is liquid.

8.154   Where the affected asset is not publicly traded, is not a going concern, and has no clear prospect of future earning power (e.g., a factory as yet unopened, which was to make a product in respect of which the local market is uncertain), tribunals have looked to book value (using the numbers appearing in the asset's accounting books or balance sheets) or 'sunk costs' (the repayment of investments undertaken that cannot be recovered), with interest appropriate to the country in which the asset is located.[298]

8.155   In other contexts where the business has no inherent store of value such as mineral reserves, tribunals only establish the value based on forward looking methodologies if future profitability can be reasonably established with a sufficient degree of certainty.[299] This approach had been adopted earlier by the Iran–United States Claims Tribunal, where an American investor was unable to obtain damages based on forward-looking methodology for a factory that had been expropriated before it had started operations.[300]

8.156   The question remains as to the circumstances in which an asset with no history of revenue production may properly give rise to a DCF-type calculation. In the *Karaha Bodas* and *Himpurna* arbitrations, which involved a geothermal power project that was terminated, damages were awarded for lost profits notwithstanding the absence of any revenue-generating activity based on expected future demand.[301]

8.157   Similarly, assets linked to natural resources with proven or probable reserves (such as oil fields or mines) are one class of investments for which the market value is intrinsically linked to those reserves, rather than simply the result of a historic analysis of revenue generation. In such circumstances, whether or not the assets are in production will not affect market value materially, because the market values the resources proven in the ground, which will be eventually extracted by a 'willing buyer'.[302] For example, although the claimant in *Crystallex v Venezuela* had no proven track record of revenue generation from the gold mine that it had the right to exploit, it had established proven gold reserves and resources. Since future income from ascertained reserves could be calculated with a significant degree of certainty, even without a record of past production, Crystallex was awarded damages based on forward-looking methodologies.[303]

---

[298] See Marboe, *Calculation of Compensation and Damages in International Investment Law* (2nd edn, Oxford University Press, 2017), pp. 278–288.
[299] *Asian Agricultural Products Ltd (AAPL)*, fn. 15.
[300] *Phelps Dodge Corporation v Islamic Republic of Iran* (1986) 10 Iran–US CTR 121.
[301] *Karaha Bodas Co. LLC v Perusahaan Pertambangan Minyak Dan Gasi Bumi Nehara*, UNCITRAL, Award, 18 December 2000; *Himpurna California Energy Ltd v PT PLN*, UNCITRAL, 4 May 1999, both available at (2000) XXV YBCA 13.
[302] *Occidental Petroleum Corporation and ors v Republic of Ecuador*, Award, ICSID Case No. ARB/06/11, Award, 5 October 2012, at [707]–[708], [722], [733], and [737]–[738].
[303] fn. 147, at [916].

There is a distinction to be drawn between the standard of compensation for lawful expro-   **8.158**
priations[304] and unlawful expropriations.[305] In *ADC v Hungary*,[306] the tribunal stated that:

> [T]he BIT only stipulates the standard of compensation that is payable in the case of a
> lawful expropriation, and these cannot be used to determine the issue of damages payable
> in the case of an unlawful expropriation since this would be to conflate compensation for a
> lawful expropriation with damages for an unlawful expropriation.

In other words, if any of the cumulative conditions set out in the treaty expropriation art-   **8.159**
icle are not met, then (by definition) the expropriation has not complied with the treaty
obligations and the treaty standard need no longer apply. As a consequence, tribunals have
held that unlawful expropriations are to be compensated under the customary international
law standard, rather than under the express terms of the BIT.[307] The customary standard of
compensation is set out in the famous *Chorzów Factory* case as one of full reparation, which
'must, as far as possible, wipe out all the consequences of the illegal act and re-establish the
situation which would, in all probability, have existed if that act had not been committed'.[308]

The application of this standard may lead to higher compensation than for lawful ex-   **8.160**
propriation.[309] For example, in *ADC v Hungary*,[310] the asset expropriated—an airport
concession—increased in value after its expropriation by the state. The tribunal held that,
in order to restore the investor to the position in which it would have been 'but for' the expropriation, the investor should be awarded the higher value of the asset at the time of the
award, rather than the value of the asset at the time of expropriation (the valuation date set
out in the BIT).[311] This approach was also adopted by the majority in the *ConocoPhillips
v Venezuela* arbitration.[312] Other tribunals, however, have found that, in certain circumstances, 'the distinction between compensation for a lawful expropriation and compensation for an unlawful expropriation may not make a significant practical difference'.[313]

(b) Compensation for other treaty breaches

As in the expropriation context, a claimant who has prevailed in establishing other types of   **8.161**
treaty breach—that is, breaches of the 'fair and equitable', and other, treatment protections

---

[304] Namely, the treaty standard described at paragraphs 8.81–8.96.

[305] *ADC Affiliate Ltd.*, fn. 185.

[306] Ibid at [481]. See also *Saipem SpA v People's Republic of Bangladesh*, ICSID Case No. ARB/05/07, Award, 30 June 2009, at [201]; *ConocoPhillips Petrozuata BV and ors v Bolivarian Republic of Venezuela*, ICSID Case No ARB/07/30, Award, 8 March 2019, at [211]–[227].

[307] *ADC Affiliate Ltd*, fn. 185.

[308] *Case Concerning the Factory at Chorzów (Claim for Indemnity) (Germany v Poland)* [1928] PCIJ Series A No. 17, at 47. See Abdala and Spiller, 'Chorzow's standard rejuvenated: Assessing damages in investment treaty arbitrations' (2008) 25 J Intl Arb 103.

[309] *Compañía de Aguas del Aconquija*, fn. 114, at [8.2.5].

[310] *ADC Affiliate Ltd*, fn. 185.

[311] Ibid., at [496].

[312] *ConocoPhillips Petrozuata BV and ors v Bolivarian Republic of Venezuela*, ICSID Case No. ARB/07/30, Decision on Jurisdiction and the Merits, 3 September 2013, at [343].

[313] *Waguih Elie George Siag*, fn. 238, at [539]–[542]; *Bernardus Henricus Funnekotter and ors v Republic of Zimbabwe*, ICSID Case No. ARB/05/6, Award, 22 April 2009, at [124]; *Marion Unglaube*, fn. 238, at [305] and [307].

provided in the treaties—must also establish its entitlement to compensation for those breaches. For instance, the tribunal in *Rompetrol Group NV v Romania*[314] found that the claimant had established Romania's breach of the BIT's fair and equitable treatment provision but had not proven that it suffered economic loss or damage as a result of that breach. Consequently, the tribunal awarded no compensation. By way of contrast, in *Joseph Charles Lemire v Ukraine*,[315] the claimant demonstrated a causal link between the host state's wrongful denial of public tenders and the loss in value of his broadcasting company, showing that it was 'probable—and not simply possible' that his company would have been awarded the tender but for the wrongful acts.

8.162 Investment treaties usually do not specify the damages to which the claimant would be entitled as compensation for the host state's other treaty breaches. However, international tribunals have awarded damages for breach of the fair and equitable treatment standard according to the *Chorzów Factory* case—that is, the 'wiping out' of all consequences of the illegal act.

8.163 International tribunals have applied the *Chorzów Factory* principle, confirming that, under international law, treaty breaches give rise to the obligation to compensate the economic harm that they cause in an amount equivalent to the losses that the claimant can prove were caused by the measures in question.[316] It should be noted that, in case of successful claims for expropriation and other treaty breaches, compensation will not be cumulative.

8.164 In applying the *Chorzów Factory* principle, several tribunals have used the standard of fair market value in determining damages for violations of fair and equitable treatment.[317] Although 'fair market value' is a standard employed in compensating for an expropriation, in *CMS v Argentina*,[318] the tribunal resorted to the fair market value standard in assessing damages arising out of Argentina's breach of the treaty, noting that the standard 'might be appropriate for breaches different from expropriation if their effect results in important long-term losses'. The tribunal established the *quantum* of damages using the DCF method to calculate the net present value (NPV) of expected cash flows. It adopted a (hypothetical) scenario *without* the adverse measures, from which it subtracted the NPV of expected cash flows in the (actual) scenario *with* the adverse measures.[319]

8.165 Restitution also remains available as a remedy for fair and equitable treatment breaches. In *Mr Franck Charles Arif v Moldova*,[320] the respondent requested the option to offer

---

[314] ICSID Case No. ARB/06/3, Award, 6 May 2013, at [283], [286], and [288]. See also *Nordzucker AG v Republic of Poland*, UNCITRAL, Third Partial and Final Award, 28 January 2009.

[315] See fn. 220, at [163]. Ukraine objected that any such analysis would be inherently speculative.

[316] *MTD Equity Sdn Bhd*, fn. 196; *Petrobart Ltd v Kyrgyz Republic*, SCC Arbitration No. 126/2003, Award, 29 March 2005; *Azurix Corporation*, fn. 181; *SD Myers Inc. v Government of Canada*, UNCITRAL, Final Award, 30 December 2002; *Metalclad Corporation v United Mexican States*, ICSID Case No. ARB(AF)/97/1, Award, 30 August 2000.

[317] Reed and Bray, *Fair and Equitable Treatment: Fairly and Equitably Applied In Lieu of Unlawful Indirect Expropriation?* (Brill, 2007); *CMS Gas Transmission Co. v Argentine Republic*, fn. 210; *Enron Corporation*, fn. 195; *Azurix Corporation*, fn. 181; *Saluka*, fn. 196.

[318] *CMS Gas Transmission*, fn. 210, at [410].

[319] One possible measure of the value of a claimant's investment in a company 'but for' the respondent state's measures is the actual price paid for the claimant's shares: see *EDF Internationa*, fn. 280, at [1232].

[320] *Mr Franck Charles Arif v Republic of Moldova*, ICSID Case No. ARB/11/23, Award, 8 April 2013.

restitution instead of damages were it found to have breached its treaty obligations. The tribunal obliged, noting that 'restitution is more consistent with the objective of bilateral investment treaties, as it preserves both the investment and the relationship between the investor and Host State'.[321] The tribunal gave Moldova sixty days in which to make proposals for restitution and allowed the claimant to accept or reject those proposals.[322]

(c) Moral damages

It has become increasingly frequent for claimants to bring claims for 'moral damages', a compensatory remedy for a category of intangible harm.[323] The first example of an award of such damages under an investment treaty was the 2008 decision in *Desert Line v Yemen*.[324] The *Desert Line* tribunal found that it had jurisdiction to award moral damages, which may be requested in 'exceptional circumstances' and by corporate claimants only in 'specific circumstances'. It then awarded US$1 million in damages for physical duress suffered by executives of the claimant company at the hands of government security forces, as well as for the company's loss to its 'credit and reputation'.[325]   **8.166**

In the wake of *Desert Line*, a significant number of claimants have, unsuccessfully, sought moral damages. In denying a claim for moral damages, the *Lemire* majority articulated a test that has been adopted in several subsequent cases, holding that moral damages can be awarded only in exceptional cases in which: **8.167**

- the state's actions imply physical threat, illegal detention, or other analogous situations in which the ill-treatment contravenes the norms according to which civilised nations are expected to act;
- the state's actions cause a deterioration of health, stress, anxiety, other mental suffering such as humiliation, shame and degradation, or loss of reputation, credit and social position; and
- both cause and effect are grave or substantial.[326]

Another approach was taken by an ICSID tribunal that rendered an award rejecting a claim for moral damages in a dispute between a group of Turkish businessmen and the   **8.168**

---

[321] Ibid., at [570].

[322] Ibid., at [633].

[323] The origins and developments of moral damages in international investment arbitration are addressed in Weber, 'Demystifying moral damages in international investment arbitration' (2020) 19 The Law and Practice of International Courts and Tribunals 417–450. See also Dumberry, 'Compensation for moral damages in investor-state arbitration disputes' (2010) 27(3) J Intl Arb 247 and Jagusch and Sebastian, 'Moral damages in investment arbitration: Punitive damages in compensatory clothing?' (2013) 29 Arb Intl 45, at 45–46.

[324] *Desert Line*, fn. 92. The previous case was *SARL Benvenuti & Bonfant v People's Republic of the Congo*, ICSID Case No. ARB/77/2, Award, 8 August 1980, (1982), which was decided *ex aequo et bono* rather than under a BIT.

[325] *Desert Line*, fn. 92, at [289]–[290].

[326] *Joseph Charles Lemire*, fn. 220, at [333]. The majority was sympathetic to the claimant's claim that recurring rejections of his applications had a negative impact on his entrepreneurial image, which would be likely to satisfy the second requirement for moral damages. Nevertheless, the 'gravity' required under the moral damages standard was not present, for Lemire's situations could not be compared to the armed threats or witnessing of deaths for which other tribunals have awarded moral damages: ibid., at [339]. The *Lemire* test has been adopted in other cases: see, e.g., *Mr Franck Charles Arif*, fn. 320, at [584]–[592], and [615].

state of Uzbekistan on basis that the BIT in question did not protect 'investors' but only 'investments'.[327]

(d) Interest

8.169 Investment arbitration tribunals routinely award interest, which forms part of the overall compensation for loss owed to a prevailing party. For example, in the case of an expropriation, the obligation to compensate arises immediately prior to the expropriatory act. Failure to pay compensation causes the affected investor to lose the use of those funds in the period between the taking and payment and is part of the loss. As noted by one leading commentator: 'The most commonly cited reason for awarding interest is to compensate the claimant for the loss of the ability to benefit from the use of the principal sum.'[328]

8.170 Many investment treaties provide for payment of interest in their expropriation clauses, and the International Law Commission's Draft Articles of State Responsibility codify the customary international law view that interest is part of full reparation for other types of breach.[329] In deciding whether to award interest, investment arbitration tribunals consider the applicable interest rate, the starting date for the calculation (e.g. date of expropriation), whether compounding of interest is appropriate, and whether to grant post-award interest.[330] In the terms of the rate of interest, tribunals have adopted a number of different approaches, including the rate in the host country,[331] the cost of capital of the investor,[332] or the borrowing rate that an investor would have been charged,[333] among others.[334] As to the award of simple versus compound interest, the 'overwhelming trend' is to award compound interest,[335] such that there is now a 'jurisprudence *constante* where the presumption has shifted from a decade or so ago with the result that it would now be more appropriate to order compound interest'.[336]

(e) Costs and attorneys' fees

8.171 The traditional position in investment treaty arbitration, in comparison to commercial arbitration, has been for each party to bear its own costs of legal representation and related

---

[327] *Güneş Tekstil Konfeksiyon Sanayi ve Ticaret Limited Şirketi and ors v Republic of Uzbekistan*, ICSID Case No. ARB/13/19, Award, 4 October 2019.

[328] Crawford, *State Responsibility: The General Part* (Oxford University Press, 2013), pp. 532–533.

[329] Ibid., citing the International Law Commission's Draft Articles of State Responsibility, Art. 38.

[330] See Ripinsky and Williams, fn. 285, p. 362; Marboe, fn. 298, pp. 337–403; Sabahi, *Compensation and Restitution in Investor–State Arbitration: Principles and Practice* (Oxford University Press, 2011), pp. 148–153. For a detailed discussion of interest in international commercial arbitrations, see Chapter 9.

[331] *CME Czech Republic BV*, fn. 163, at [636]–[641].

[332] *Compañía de Aguas del Aconquija*, fn. 114, at [9.2.8].

[333] *Alpha Projektholding GmbH v Ukraine*, ICSID Case No. ARB/07/16, Award, 8 November 2010, at [514].

[334] See Marboe, fn. 298, pp. 338–375. See generally Ripinsky and Williams, fn. 285, ch. 9.

[335] *Ioan Micula and ors v Romania*, ICSID Case No. ARB/05/20, Decision on Jurisdiction and Admissibility, 24 September 2008, at [1266].

[336] *Gemplus SA and ors v United Mexican States*, ICSID Case No. ARB(AF)/04/3, Award, 16 June 2010; *Bear Creek Mining Corporation v Republic of Peru*, ICSID Case No. ARB/14/21, Award, 30 November 2017, at [714]–[716].

expenses, and to divide tribunal costs equally.[337] There has, however, been a trend towards requiring the losing party to pay the costs and legal fees of the prevailing party in certain circumstances, based on the parties' degree of success and/or conduct.[338] As summarised by one commentator, those circumstances may include where the unsuccessful party (a) advances patently unmeritorious or legally untenable claims, (b) abuses the investment arbitration process, (c) presents poor and inefficient pleadings, or (d) engages in egregious underlying conduct.[339]

This practice is consistent with the ICSID Rules and the UNCITRAL Rules. Indeed, Article   **8.172** 42 of the UNCITRAL Rules was revised in 2010, and now includes a default principle that costs *and* legal fees shall be borne by the unsuccessful party.[340] Similarly, while the 2006 ICSID Rules did not contain any default principle concerning the allocation of costs and legal fees,[341] the 2022 Rules make it clear that in allocating the costs of the proceeding, the tribunal shall consider all relevant circumstances, including: (a) the outcome of the proceeding or any part of it; (b) the conduct of the parties during the proceeding, including the extent to which they acted in an expeditious and cost-effective manner and complied with these Rules and the orders and decisions of the tribunal; (c) the complexity of the issues; and (d) the reasonableness of the costs claimed. Further, the tribunal shall award the prevailing party its reasonable costs, unless the tribunal determines that there are special circumstances justifying a different allocation of costs.[342]

---

[337] See, e.g., *ICS Inspection and Control Services Ltd (United Kingdom) v Argentine Republic*, UNCITRAL, PCA Case No. 2010-9, Award on Jurisdiction, at [340]; *Chevron Corporation and Texaco Petroleum Co. v Republic of Ecuador*, UNCITRAL, Final Award, 31 August 2011, IIC 505 (2011), at [375]. For a detailed discussion of costs and fees in international commercial arbitrations, see Chapter 9.

[338] See, e.g., *TECO Guatemala Holdings LLC v Republic of Guatemala*, ICSID Case No. ARB/10/17, Award, 19 December 2013, at [769]–[779] (ordering the Republic of Guatemala to reimburse 75 per cent of the claimant's costs, amounting to US$7.5 million); *ConocoPhillips BV*, fn. 306 at [1004].

[339] Reed, 'Allocation of costs in international arbitration' (2011) 26 ICSID Rev—FILJ 76.

[340] See Caron and Caplan, *The UNCITRAL Arbitration Rules* (Oxford University Press, 2013), p. 867 (noting that the 1976 UNCITRAL Rules, Art. 40.1 addressed the costs of legal representation and assistance but did not apply any default principle to those costs).

[341] See 2006 ICSID Rules, r. 28(1).

[342] See ICSID Rules, r. 52.

9

AWARD

A. Introduction

(a) Destination of an international arbitration—the award

Parties to transborder transactions who go to the trouble and expense of taking their **9.01** disputes to international arbitration do so in the expectation that, unless a settlement is reached along the way, the process will lead to an award. They also expect that, subject to any right of recourse, the award will be final and binding upon them. Both international and institutional rules of arbitration reflect this expectation. Article 34.2 of the Arbitration Rules of the United Nations Commission on International Trade Law (UNCITRAL) states simply: 'All awards shall be made in writing and shall be final and binding on the parties. The parties shall carry out all awards without delay.' The Rules of the International Chamber of Commerce (ICC), recognising the possibility of some form of challenge to an award at the place of arbitration under the *lex arbitri*, are more circumspect:

> Every award shall be binding on the parties. By submitting the dispute to arbitration under the Rules, the parties undertake to carry out any award without delay and shall be deemed to have waived their right to any form of recourse insofar as such waiver can validly be made.[1]

As the UNCITRAL Rules suggest, there may be more than one award in any given dis- **9.02** pute. Indeed, a number of institutional rules expressly empower arbitral tribunals to make separate awards on different issues at different times.[2] These powers reflect the practical reality that, during the course of an arbitration, an arbitral tribunal may be called upon to make more than one award at different times on different issues between the parties.[3]

---

[1] ICC Rules, Art. 35.6. See also SIAC Rules, r. 32.11.
[2] SIAC Rules, r. 32.5; and LCIA Rules, Art. 26.1.
[3] The authors recommend use of the term 'partial awards', rather than 'interim', or 'provisional', awards. The latter terms, particularly in the civil law context, can be interpreted to mean that such awards are not final, when they are indeed final.

For example, the tribunal may make an early decision on its jurisdiction, rather than take the risk of proceeding to the merits of the case and then, perhaps, deciding later that it lacks jurisdiction. Alternatively, it may make a partial award of a sum of money that it considers to be indisputably due and payable by one party to the other.[4]

9.03 All 'awards' are 'final' in the sense that they dispose 'finally' of the issues decided in them (subject to any challenge or available procedure for correction or interpretation), and they are 'binding' on the parties.[5] The award that disposes 'finally' of all outstanding issues is known as the 'final award'. A final award, in this sense, is usually the outcome of arbitral proceedings that have been contested throughout. However, it may embody an agreed settlement between the parties, in which case it is generally known as a 'consent award'.[6] Another category is an award in proceedings in which a party has failed or refused to participate, in which case it is usually described as a 'default award'.

9.04 Each of these different types of award are considered in this chapter. Since all awards are dispositive of the issues that they determine, it is important that the arbitral tribunal does its best to ensure not only that the award is correct, but also that it is enforceable across international frontiers. Indeed, several institutional rules impose an express obligation on arbitral tribunals to make every effort to ensure the enforceability of their awards.[7]

(b) Definition of an award

9.05 There is no internationally accepted definition of the term 'award'. Indeed, no definition is to be found in the main international conventions dealing with arbitration, including the Geneva treaties, the New York Convention, and the Model Law. Although the New York Convention is directed to the recognition and enforcement of arbitral awards,[8] the nearest that it comes to a definition is in Article I(2): 'The term "arbitral awards" shall include not only awards made by arbitrators appointed for each case but also those made by permanent arbitral bodies to which the parties have submitted.'

---

[4] Some modern arbitration statutes make a specific distinction between interim, partial, and final awards. The Netherlands Arbitration Act 2015, s. 1049, provides that: 'The arbitral tribunal may render a final award, a partial final award, or an interim award.' Commentary on the materially identical version of this article in the 1986 Netherlands Arbitration Act by Sanders and van den Berg, *The Netherlands Arbitration Act 1986* (Kluwer International Law, 1987) suggests that partial awards are given in respect of substantive issues that are separated, such as liability and quantum; interim awards are given on jurisdictional issues; and simple orders are made in respect of procedural issues. The Swiss Private International Law Act 1987 (Swiss PIL), Ch. 12, provides for 'preliminary awards' in relation to jurisdictional issues in s. 186(3), while 'partial awards' that finally determine the issue are provided for in s. 188: see Geisinger, *International Arbitration in Switzerland: A Handbook for Practitioners* (2nd edn, Wolters Kluwer, 2013), pp. 226–227.

[5] The English Arbitration Act 1996, s. 39, is an exception to this general rule in granting a power to make 'provisional awards' if the parties agree that the arbitral tribunal shall have such power. Interestingly, s. 39 mentions the word 'award' only in the marginal note and the body of the section refers to 'orders'. Whether such provisional orders are enforceable under the New York Convention is questionable and would be a matter for the courts of the country in which enforcement is sought: see Hunter and Landau, *The English Arbitration Act 1996: Text and Notes* (Wolters Kluwer, 1998), p. 35. For an example of the English courts enforcing a provisional order made by a tribunal under s. 39, see *Pearl Petroleum Co Ltd v Kurdistan Regional Govt of Iraq* [2016] 1 Lloyd's Rep 441.

[6] See English Arbitration Act 1996, s. 51(2)–(3).

[7] See, e.g., ICC Rules, Art. 42 ('the arbitral tribunal [...] shall make every effort to make sure that the award is enforceable at law'). See also LCIA Rules, Art. 32.2, and SIAC Rules, r. 41.2.

[8] And of arbitration agreements: see Chapter 2.

At one stage, it was proposed that there should be a definition of the term 'award' in the   **9.06**
Model Law, but ultimately none was adopted. One suggested solution illustrates the difficulty of finding a definition that encompasses not only final awards, but also partial
awards, which dispose of only some issues. The proposed definition was as follows:

> 'Award' means a final award which disposes of all issues submitted to the arbitral tribunal
> and any other decision of the arbitral tribunal which finally determines any question of
> substance or the question of its competence or any other question of procedure but, in the
> latter case, only if the arbitral tribunal terms its decision an award.[9]

As this proposed definition shows, the need to distinguish between awards that are final
and other decisions of a tribunal that are not is a complicating factor. The possible solution
of defining each separately was not adopted. The Model Law also plainly contemplates that
there may be more than one award during the course of an arbitration. For example, a plea
that the arbitral tribunal does not have jurisdiction may be dealt with either in the final
award or as a 'preliminary question'; thus, in a 'Model Law country', if the tribunal takes
the second course, its partial award may be challenged in the competent court within thirty
days of its notification to the parties.[10]

The time limit for challenge of an award generally begins to run from the date on which   **9.07**
the award was issued.[11] Once the final award has been made, it may be impossible for a
party to challenge any element in it that flows from a previously unchallenged partial
award. Moreover, only an 'award' will qualify for recognition and enforcement under the
relevant international conventions, including the New York Convention. Thus important
consequences flow from a ruling or decision of the arbitral tribunal that has the status of
an award.

The term 'award' should generally be reserved for decisions that finally determine the sub-   **9.08**
stantive issues with which they deal.[12] This involves distinguishing between awards, which
are concerned with substantive issues, and procedural orders and directions, which are concerned with the conduct of the arbitration. Procedural orders and directions help to move
the arbitration forward; they deal with such matters as the exchange of written evidence,
the production of documents, protective measures, and the arrangements for the conduct
of the hearing. They do not have the status of awards and they may perhaps be called into

---

[9] Broches, 'Recourse against the award; Enforcement of the award: UNCITRAL's Project for a Model Law on International Commercial Arbitration' (1984) 2 ICCA Congress Series 201, at 208.

[10] Model Law, Art. 16(3). Model Law jurisdictions have taken differing approaches to determining the consequences of a failure to challenge a partial award on jurisdiction within the specified time limit. New Zealand recently passed an amendment to its 1996 Arbitration Act clarifying that failure to make a request to the High Court challenging a jurisdictional decision within thirty days 'operates as a waiver of any right to later object' (NZ Arbitration Amendment Act 2019, 7 May 2019, s. 4). In contrast, in Singapore, a non-participating respondent who fails to challenge a jurisdictional award retains the right to challenge the tribunal's jurisdiction in set-aside proceedings (see *Rakna Arakshaka Lanka Ltd v Avant Garde Maritime Services (Private) Limited* [2019] SGCA 33).

[11] See, e.g., English Arbitration Act, s.70(3). Where there has been any arbitral process of appeal or review, the relevant time limit in England runs from the date when the applicant invoking any such post-award remedy is notified of the result of such process (English Arbitration Act, s. 70(3)).

[12] Some commentators have suggested that a 'preliminary award' may be treated as 'provisional'. However, this concept seems to be fraught with peril; the authors suggest that any decision that is *not* finally determinative of the issues with which it deals should not be described as an 'award'.

question after the final award has been made (for example as evidence of 'bias', or 'lack of due process').[13]

(c) Which decisions have the status of an award?

9.09   Distinguishing between an 'award' and an 'order' may not be as easy as simply reading the title that an arbitral tribunal chooses to give to its ruling; it is a matter of substance not form. The English High Court identified the following factors as being relevant to distinguishing an award from an order:[14]

- real weight is to be given to the substance and not merely the form of the decision;
- a decision is more likely to be an award if it finally disposes of the matters submitted to arbitration so as to render the tribunal *functus officio*, either entirely or in relation to that issue or claim;
- the nature of the issues considered in the decision is significant, as substantive rights and liabilities of parties are likely to be dealt with in the form of an award, whereas a decision dealing purely with procedural issues is less likely to be an award;
- the tribunal's own description of the decision is relevant but not conclusive;
- the perception of a reasonable recipient of the tribunal's decision is relevant;
- the reasonable recipient is likely to take into account the objective attributes of the decision, including the formality of the language, the level of detail in the reasoning, and whether the decision complies with the formal requirements for an award under any applicable rules.

9.10   Both the Paris Court of Appeal and a US Federal Court of Appeals have classified certain arbitral decisions as awards, even though they have been entitled 'orders' by tribunals.

9.11   The Paris Court of Appeal decision in *Brasoil*[15] arose from an ICC arbitration under a contract whereby Brasoil agreed to drill a number of wells in the Libyan desert for the Management and Implementation Authority of the 'Great Man-Made River Project'. Brasoil started an ICC arbitration following termination of the contract by the Authority in 1990. In 1995, the arbitral tribunal issued a partial award in which it held Brasoil liable for the malfunctioning of the wells that it had constructed. In 1997, during the damages phase of the proceedings, the Authority submitted certain documents that Brasoil alleged had been fraudulently withheld during the liability phase. Brasoil requested that the tribunal review its partial award on liability. In May 1998, the tribunal denied Brasoil's request in what it described as an 'order'. In subsequent challenge proceedings, the Paris Court of Appeal granted Brasoil's request to have the 'order' set aside. The Court held that, although

---

[13] If a party is aggrieved by a procedural order or direction, it is sensible for that party to make a formal protest. In this way, it will reserve the position in case it emerges, at a later stage, that the ruling in question has, e.g., denied that party a proper opportunity to present its case or to respond to the case submitted by the opposing party.

[14] *ZCCM Investments Holdings PLC v Kansanshi Holdings PLC & Anor* [2019] EWHC 1285 (Comm), at 40. See also *Uganda v Rift Valley Railways Uganda Ltd* [2021] EWHC 970 (in which the Republic of Uganda's application to set aside a procedural order was dismissed on the ground that the order would not have been understood by a reasonable recipient as an award and did not finally determine any issues between the parties).

[15] *Braspetro Oil Services Co. v The Management and Implementation Authority of the Great Man-Made River Project*, Paris cour d'appel, 1 July 1999, (1999) 14 Mealey's Intl Arb Rep 8, at [G-1]–[G-7].

described as an 'order', the tribunal's decision was, in fact, an 'award', because it purported to make a final determination of a substantive issue between the parties.[16] In so finding, the Court of Appeal noted that:

> The qualification of [a decision as an] award does not depend on the terms used by the arbitrators or by the parties [...] after a five-month deliberation, the arbitral tribunal rendered the 'order' of 14 May 1998, by which, after a lengthy examination of the parties' positions, it declared that the request could not be granted because Brasoil had not proven that there had been fraud as alleged. This reasoned decision—by which the arbitrators considered the contradictory theories of the parties and examined in detail whether they were founded, and solved, in a final manner, the dispute between the parties concerning the admissibility of Brasoil's request for a review, by denying it and thereby ending the dispute submitted to them—appears to be an exercise of its jurisdictional power by the arbitral tribunal [...] Notwithstanding its qualification as an 'order', the decision of 14 May 1998 [...] is thus indeed an award.[17]

Some years later, the French Supreme Court provided a definition of an arbitral award that **9.12** supported this interpretation. Addressing a challenge to an award on the basis of an alleged professional relationship between the chairman of the arbitral tribunal and the parent company of the guarantor of debts owed by the respondent, the Court of Cassation held that 'only proper arbitral awards may be challenged through an action to set aside' and went on to define awards as:

> [...] decisions made by the arbitrators which resolve in a definitive manner all or part of the dispute that is submitted to them on the merits, jurisdiction or a procedural matter which leads them to put an end to the proceedings.[18]

The decision of the Seventh Circuit Federal Court of Appeal in *True North*[19] addressed **9.13** similar issues. True North, a US advertising company, and Publicis Communications, an affiliate of the Publicis global communications group, entered into a joint venture in 1989, which eventually led the parties to arbitration in London. As one of its requests for relief in the arbitration, True North requested that Publicis disclose tax records filed with the US Internal Revenue Service and the Securities and Exchange Commission (SEC). In October 1998, the chairman of the arbitral tribunal, 'for and on behalf of the arbitrators', signed an unreasoned 'order' directing Publicis to disclose the requested tax records to True North. Publicis failed to comply and True North applied to the court to confirm the arbitral decision. Publicis argued that the tribunal's decision constituted no more than a procedural order and that only finally determinative 'awards' are subject to confirmation or enforcement. The issue ultimately came before the Seventh Circuit Federal Court of Appeals, which disagreed, reasoning that the finality of a decision was the key to its recognition or

---

[16] For a commentary on this decision, see Gill, 'The definition of award under the New York Convention' (2008) 2 Disp Res Intl 114, at 119, in which the author writes that 'the court found that the "procedural order" was effectively an award because it settled a substantive issue between the parties. The tribunal was exercising its jurisdictional power and its decision was therefore an award.'

[17] *Braspetro Oil Services Co. v The Management and Implementation Authority of the Great Man-Made River Project*, Paris cour d'appel, 1 July 1999, (1999) XXIVa YBCA 297, at [1]–[4].

[18] *Groupe Antoine Tabet v République du Congo*, Case No. 09-72.439, Cass. Civ. 1ere, 12 October 2011, n.p.

[19] *Publicis Communications and Publicis SA v True North Communications Inc.* (2000) XXV YBCA 1152.

enforcement under the New York Convention. In so doing, it described Publicis's approach as 'extreme and untenable formalism', and observed:

> Although Publicis suggests that our ruling will cause the international arbitration earth to quake and mountains to crumble, resolving this case actually requires determining only whether or not this particular order by this particular arbitration tribunal regarding these particular tax records was final. If the arbitration tribunal's 30 October 1998 decision was final, then [the district court judge] had the authority to confirm it. If the arbitrators' decision was not final, then the district court jumped the gun.[20]

9.14   Referring to an earlier edition of this volume, the Federal Court of Appeals noted that the arbitral tribunal's decision on the tax records was intended to be final and stated that the fact that the 'order' was issued prior to the conclusion of the arbitration was no bar to its enforceability or finality:

> The tribunal's order resolved the dispute, or was supposed to, at any rate. Producing the documents wasn't just some procedural matter—it was the very issue True North wanted arbitrated [...] The tribunal explicitly carved out the tax records issue for immediate action from the bulk of the matter still pending, stating that 'the delivery of the documents should not await final confirmation in the Final Award'. Requiring the unrelated issues to be arbitrated to finality before allowing True North to enforce a decision the tribunal called urgent would defeat the purpose of the tribunal's order. A ruling on a discreet, time-sensitive issue may be final and ripe for confirmation even though other claims remain to be addressed by arbitrators.[21]

(d) Rendering an internationally enforceable award

9.15   No arbitral tribunal can be expected to *guarantee* that its award will be enforceable in whatever country the winner chooses to enforce it. However, as noted above, every arbitral tribunal must do its best. As Article 42 of the ICC Rules provides: 'In all matters not expressly provided for in the Rules, the Court and the arbitral tribunal shall act in the spirit of these Rules and shall make every effort to make sure that the award is enforceable at law.'[22] Phrases such as 'make every effort' imply an 'obligation to perform', rather than an 'obligation to achieve a defined result'. Nonetheless, the message is clear: in principle, the eventual

---

[20]   Ibid., at [4].

[21]   Ibid., at [9]. For a commentary on this decision, see Murphy, 'Enforceability of foreign arbitral decisions' (2001) 67 Arbitration 369, at 371, in which the author concludes that: '[T]his decision has clearly announced that all orders or awards made in the arbitral process are capable of recognition and enforcement abroad by means of the New York Convention, so long as the finality test is satisfied [...] when rendering any decision, it may be prudent to determine whether or not the issue is being dealt with finally, to recite that in the decision and, despite the approach of the Seventh Circuit, to label the decision or order as an award to ensure that no argument of form over substance can take place.' See also, e.g., *Santos v GE Co.*, No. 10 Civ. 6948, 2011 US Dist. LEXIS 131925 (SDNY 2011), at [14]–[15]; *Yonir Techs, Inc. v Duration System (1992) Ltd*, 244 F.Supp.2d 195, 204 (SDNY 2002). '[T]hese authorities suggest that, regardless of whether the form of the arbitral measure (*e.g.*, an award or order) resembles a final award, if the substance of the measure serves a discrete function and effects a final disposition of a particular issue, the interim measure is confirmable and enforceable': Sherwin and Rennie, 'Interim relief under international arbitration rules and guidelines: A comparative analysis' (2009) 20 Am Rev Int'l Arb 318, at 326.

[22]   See also LCIA Rules, Art. 32.2.

outcome of every arbitration is intended to be a final, enforceable award—as opposed to the outcome of a mediation, which is intended to be an agreement between the parties.

For an arbitral tribunal to achieve the standard of performance required to make an inter-   **9.16** nationally enforceable award, it must first ensure that it has jurisdiction to decide all of the issues before it. The arbitral tribunal must also comply with any procedural rules governing the arbitration. Such rules commonly include, for example, allocation of the costs of the ar-bitration,[23] identifying the seat of the arbitration, and having the award formally approved by an arbitral institution (as with an ICC award).[24] The arbitral tribunal must also sign and date the award, and arrange for it to be delivered to the parties in the manner laid down in the relevant law or by the rules that apply to the arbitration. If the arbitral tribunal has carried out its work adequately, its decision should not be susceptible to any post-award re-course that may otherwise be available to the parties.[25]

Moreover, Article V(2)(b) of the New York Convention provides that, even when these con-   **9.17** ditions have been met, an award need not be enforced if it violates the public policy of the place of enforcement:

> Recognition and enforcement of an arbitral award may also be refused if the competent authority in the country where recognition and enforcement is sought finds that […] the recognition or enforcement of the award would be contrary to the public policy of that country.

This provision gives discretion to the judicial authority at the recognition and enforcement stage, highlighting the impossibility of guaranteeing international enforceability at the time of issuing the award (particularly given that the jurisdiction(s) in which a tribunal's award will ultimately be enforced are often difficult to predict at the time when the award is issued).

Given the complexity of the task facing an arbitral tribunal, the arbitrators should be ad-   **9.18** equately trained and experienced.[26] An award may comply meticulously with the agreed rules of procedure and with the law governing the arbitration, but may fail to comply with some special requirement of the law of the place of enforcement, so that the award may be unenforceable in that jurisdiction.

B. Categories of Award

All awards are final and binding, subject to any available challenges.[27] However, the term   **9.19** 'final award' is customarily reserved for an award that completes the mission of the arbitral tribunal. Subject to certain exceptions, the delivery of a final award renders the arbitral tri-bunal *functus officio*: it ceases to have any further jurisdiction in respect of the dispute, and the special relationship that exists between the arbitral tribunal and the parties during the currency of the arbitration ends. This has significant consequences. An arbitral tribunal

---

[23] For example, ICC Rules, Art. 38.6; UNCITRAL Rules, Art. 40.
[24] ICC Rules, Art. 34.
[25] For further discussion of interpretation, correction, and revision of awards, see paragraphs 9.206*ff.*
[26] See Chapter 10, paragraphs 10.02, 10.08, and 10.61.
[27] See, e.g., UNCITRAL Rules, Art. 34.2.

should not issue a final award until it is satisfied that its mission has actually been completed. If there are outstanding matters to be determined, such as questions relating to costs (including the arbitral tribunal's own costs), the arbitral tribunal should issue an award expressly designated as a partial award.

(a) Partial awards

9.20 The power to issue a partial award is a useful weapon in the armoury of an arbitral tribunal. A partial award is an effective way of determining matters that are susceptible to determination during the course of the proceedings, and which, once determined, may save considerable time and money for all involved.[28] One obvious example that has already been given is where an issue of jurisdiction is involved: a partial award on such an issue may shorten, or at least simplify, the proceedings considerably. An arbitral tribunal that spent months hearing a dispute, only to rule in its final award that it had no jurisdiction, would (to put it mildly) appear inefficient (unless the issue of jurisdiction were inseparably bound up with the merits of the case). Another example is a partial award that makes an early determination that a particular claim or defence is manifestly without legal merit (as is now possible under some but not all institutional rules).[29] Such an early partial award avoids the time and expense that would otherwise be incurred in litigating a manifestly unmeritorious claim or defence in full.

9.21 The power of an arbitral tribunal to issue partial awards may derive from the arbitration agreement or from the applicable law. Where the arbitration agreement incorporates international or institutional rules of arbitration, these rules generally contain provisions for the making of such awards.[30]

9.22 The ICC Rules, for instance, define the term 'award' to include 'an interim, partial, or final award'.[31] In practice, partial awards are frequently made in ICC arbitrations, particularly where jurisdiction is challenged or the proper law has to be determined by the arbitral tribunal.[32] The Rules of the LCIA follow the same approach: 'The Arbitral Tribunal may make separate awards on different issues at different times. Such awards shall have the same status

---

[28] See the discussion of enforceability of partial awards in the United States in von Mehren, 'The enforcement of arbitral awards under conventions and United States law' (1985) 9 Yale Journal of World Public Order 343, at 362. The approach of the case that von Mehren cites, *Sperry International Trade, Inc. v Government of Israel*, 532 F.Supp. 901 (SDNY 1982), continues to be followed for its proposition that partial awards disposing of issues separable from those that continue to be disputed are final for the purposes of judicial review and enforcement: 'The New York Convention, the United Nations arbitration rules, and the commentators' consistent use of the label 'award' when discussing final arbitral decisions does not bestow transcendental significance on the term. Their treatment of 'award' as interchangeable with final does not necessarily mean that synonyms such as decision, opinion, order, or ruling could not also be final. The content of a decision—not its nomenclature—determines finality.'

[29] SIAC Rules, r. 29; LCIA Rules, Art. 22.viii; ICSID Rules, r. 41.5.

[30] See, e.g., UNCITRAL Rules, Art. 26 ('Interim measures').

[31] ICC Rules, Art. 2.v.

[32] For further discussion of partial awards in ICC arbitrations, see ICC, *Final Report on Interim and Partial Awards of a Working Party of the ICC's Commission on International Arbitration* (1990) 2 ICC International Court of Arbitration Bulletin 26, at 30, in particular the discussion about terminology. The term 'interlocutory award' should never be used, because it leads to confusion with procedural directions, which are not given in the form of an award.

and effect as any other award made by the Arbitral Tribunal.'[33] The SIAC Rules similarly provide that the 'Tribunal may make separate Awards on different issues at different times'.[34]

In an ad hoc arbitration, it is usual to make express provision in the submission agreement **9.23** for the arbitral tribunal to issue partial awards, if it sees fit to do so. Where the power is not conferred expressly upon the arbitral tribunal by the agreement of the parties, it may nevertheless be conferred by operation of law. For example, section 47 of the English Arbitration Act 1996 provides:

(1) Unless otherwise agreed by the parties, the tribunal may make more than one award at different times on different aspects of the matters to be determined.
(2) The tribunal may, in particular, make an award relating to:
   (a) an issue affecting the whole claim, or
   (b) a part only of the claims or cross-claims submitted to it for decision.
(3) If the tribunal does so, it shall specify in its award the issue, or the claim or part of a claim, that is the subject-matter of the award.

Other modern arbitration laws contain similar provisions. Although the Model Law itself **9.24** does not otherwise expressly refer to partial awards, it is clear from the context in which the expression 'final award' is used, and from the *travaux préparatoires*, that the draftsmen intended that the arbitral tribunal should have such a power.[35] However, if there is no express or implied provision for an arbitral tribunal to make a partial award—either in the arbitration agreement, the applicable arbitration rules, or the applicable law—it is doubtful that the tribunal has power to do so.[36] It is usually apparent from its content that a partial award is not the 'last' award; nevertheless, the award should state clearly that it is a partial award. As mentioned earlier,[37] the issuance of a final award renders the arbitral tribunal *functus officio*, except for the purpose of correcting minor or clerical errors. It is important not to allow either party an opportunity to claim that the arbitral tribunal has no further jurisdiction on the grounds that it has issued a final award, when it intended to issue only a partial award.[38]

The main disadvantage of a partial award is that it opens the way for a challenge, which in **9.25** turn would lead to delay, since the relevant court would then become involved in dealing with an application by one of the parties to annul (or set aside) the partial award, or to confirm it.[39] As noted above, the Model Law limits the potential for delay by specifying that an

---

[33] LCIA Rules, Art. 26.1.

[34] SIAC Rules, r. 32.5.

[35] Model Law, Art. 32(1). See Holtzmann and Neuhaus, *A Guide to the UNCITRAL Model Law on International Commercial Arbitration* (Kluwer Law, 1989), p. 868. The Model Law, Ch. IVA, does, however, expressly refer to interim measures and preliminary orders.

[36] It was perhaps to avoid uncertainty in this respect that some jurisdictions amended the Model Law to provide specifically so that the arbitral tribunal may make a partial award on any matter on which it may make a final award: see, e.g., the British Columbia International Commercial Arbitration Act, s. 31(6).

[37] See paragraph 9.19.

[38] In a 2017 case, the VSC held that an award labelled 'Final Award' was not final, since it did not address all the issues that had been submitted to the arbitrator. Consequently, the arbitrator was not *functus officio* and it was open to either party to apply to continue the arbitration and seek a determination of the outstanding issues (*Blanalko Pty Ltd v Lysaght Building Solutions Pty Ltd* [2017] VSC 97 (10 March 2017)).

[39] In the United States, a partial award for the payment of freight was 'confirmed' by a court while there were still outstanding matters in dispute in the arbitration: *Metallgesellschaft AG v M/V Capitan Constante and Yacimientos Petroliferos Fiscales*, 790 F.2d 280 (2d Cir. 1986). The majority judgment lists cases endorsing the 'proposition that an award which finally and definitely disposes of a separate independent claim may be confirmed although it does

application to review a partial award on jurisdiction must be lodged within thirty days of receipt of notice of the ruling, with no appeal beyond the first level of court in which the decision is made.[40] As also noted above, the relevant decision need not have the title 'award' to be subject to judicial review or confirmation.[41]

(i) Issues concerning the applicable law

9.26   An example of a situation in which a partial award is likely to prove useful is where there is a dispute between the parties as to the law(s) applicable to the merits of the case. If this is not resolved at an early stage, the parties must argue their respective cases by reference to different systems of law. They may even need to introduce evidence from lawyers experienced in each of these different systems. In such circumstances, it may be sensible for the arbitral tribunal to issue a preliminary decision on the question of the applicable law (although in the authors' experience such disputes are rare in practice).

(ii) Separation of issues (jurisdiction, liability, *quantum*)

9.27   A further example of the type of case in which it may be convenient to issue a partial award is where issues of liability may be separated from those of *quantum*, which is often worth doing if it is possible to disentangle these issues. Most obviously, the determination of a particular issue of liability in favour of the respondent may make it unnecessary for the arbitral tribunal to investigate questions of *quantum*.[42] Even if it is not determinative, a decision by an arbitral tribunal on certain issues of principle in a dispute may well encourage the parties to reach a settlement on *quantum*. They are usually well aware of the costs likely to be involved if the arbitral tribunal itself has to go into the detailed quantification of a claim—a process that often involves taking evidence from accountants, technical experts, and others.

9.28   However, there are real dangers in attempting to isolate determinative issues at an early stage of the proceedings. The nature of the dispute and the way in which the parties present their cases may change during the course of the proceedings, and it is not unknown for parties to amend their cases radically in order to take advantage of a preliminary award on liability. Where this happens, savings of time and cost will not be achieved, and the result will be the opposite of that intended. Moreover, the process of rendering a preliminary award can itself be a time-consuming and expensive one. It is suggested that an arbitral tribunal should not normally decide to issue a partial award on its own initiative,[43] but should do so

---

not dispose of all the claims that were submitted to arbitration': ibid., at [3]. However, the dissent of Feinberg CJ noted the dangers of piecemeal review of arbitral awards. Since then, US courts of appeal in several circuits have held that a partial award disposing definitively of fewer than all of the issues lying before the arbitral tribunal may be confirmed: see, e.g., *Zeiler v Deitsch*, 500 F.3d 157, 168 (2d Cir. 2007); *Hart Surgical, Inc. v Ultracision Inc.*, 244 F.3d 231 (1st Cir. 2001); *Publicis Communication v True North Communications Inc.*, 206 F.3d 725, 727 (7th Cir. 2000); *Pacific Reinsurance Management Corp. v Ohio Reinsurance Corp.*, 935 F.2d 1019, 1022–23 (9th Cir. 1991). This approach has not, however, been consistently applied in all circuits (*Quixtar Inc. v Brady*, Nos. 08-14346, 08-14347, 2008 WL 5386774, at *13–14 (E.D. Mich. 17 December 2008), *aff'd sub nom. Quixtar, Inc. v Brady*, 328 F. App'x 317, 322–23 (6th Cir. 2009) (refusing judicial review of a partial award disposing of the issue of arbitrability).

[40] Model Law, Art. 16(3).
[41] See paragraphs 9.09–9.14.
[42] See Chapter 6, paragraphs 6.53 to 6.58.
[43] Except in relation to issues of jurisdiction, where the respondent has not raised them, or has elected not to participate, as in *Liberian Eastern Timber Corporation v Government of the Republic of Liberia* (1987) 26 ILM 647, in which the government nominated one of the authors as an arbitrator, but then refused to take part in the

only following a request by one of the parties. Where both parties agree that a partial award should be made, the arbitral tribunal must follow the agreement of the parties. Where only one party requests a partial award, a tribunal with the power to make such an award should reach its decision as to whether or not to comply with the request only after receiving the submissions of both parties and giving each party a reasonable opportunity to explain its position.

(iii) Limitation and exclusion clauses in a contract

9.29 Major commercial contracts—for example for the supply of a process plant or for a construction project—often contain a clause that limits, or purports to limit, the type or amount of damages payable in the event of breach. A typical example is a clause providing that in no event will loss of profits be payable. There may be occasions on which a partial award on the meaning and effect of such clauses will help to define the amount of the claim, and may make the prospect of settlement more likely.

(b) Foreign and domestic awards

9.30 The distinction between foreign and domestic awards is especially significant in the context of challenging and enforcement of awards in national courts, which is addressed in Chapter 10. In India, the Arbitration and Conciliation Act 1996 defines a 'foreign award', inter alia, as an award that arises out of an arbitration agreement to which the New York Convention applies, and which is issued in a territory (other than India).[44] Conversely, the Indian Supreme Court has held that the term 'domestic award' means an award made in India whether or not this is in a purely domestic context; thus the definition will include a 'domestically rendered' award in a domestic arbitration or in an international arbitration. The distinction is significant in India because, inter alia, domestic awards are generally subject to a higher degree of judicial scrutiny than foreign awards at the enforcement stage.[45]

(c) Default awards

9.31 Occasionally, international arbitrations are commenced in which one party (usually the respondent) fails or refuses to take part. This failure or refusal may be complete—that is, it occurs from the outset of the proceedings—or it may happen during the proceedings as a result of a change of mind or strategy. The arbitral tribunal is compelled to take a more proactive role in these circumstances, making its task more difficult. The task of an arbitral

proceedings, and the arbitral tribunal examined its jurisdiction—as required by the ICSID Rules, r. 42(4)—and issued a partial award.

[44] Indian Arbitration and Conciliation Act 1996, s. 53 provides a similar definition of 'foreign award' in relation to the Geneva Protocol of 1923.

[45] Indian Arbitration and Conciliation Act 1996, s. 34 sets out wider grounds for refusal of enforcement of a domestic award than those available in respect of a foreign award under s. 48. Brazil follows a similar, territorial approach to determining the nationality of an award (see Brazil Arbitration Act, art. 34, pursuant to which an arbitral award is domestic if rendered within the Brazilian territory and foreign if rendered outside the Brazilian territory).

tribunal is not to 'rubber stamp' claims that are presented to it; rather, it must make a *determination* of these claims, so the tribunal must take upon itself the burden of testing the assertions made by the active party, and it must call for such evidence and legal argument as it may require for this purpose.[46]

9.32   If the arbitral tribunal makes an award in favour of the active party in the proceedings, it will wish to ensure that the award is effective. To this end, it should ensure, in particular, that the award recites in considerable detail the procedure followed by the arbitral tribunal and the efforts made by the arbitral tribunal to communicate the active party's case to the defaulting party, so as to give that party every opportunity to present its own arguments and evidence. Further, the motivation, or reasons, given in the award should (without necessarily being lengthy) reflect the fact that the arbitral tribunal has genuinely addressed the merits of the case, in order to show that a reasoned determination has been made.

9.33   The award should also deal with any questions of jurisdiction that appear to the arbitral tribunal to be relevant, whether or not such issues have been raised by one or other of the parties. In this context, the Arbitration Rules of the International Centre for the Settlement of Investment Disputes (ICSID), which contain detailed provisions for default proceedings, expressly stipulate, at Rule 42.4, that '[t]he Tribunal shall examine the jurisdiction of the Centre and its own competence in the dispute and, if it is satisfied, decide whether the submissions made are well-founded in fact and in law'. If the arbitral tribunal follows these guidelines, there is less risk of the money spent by the active party in obtaining the award being wasted as a result of a subsequent decision by national courts that the award is unenforceable.

(d) Additional awards

9.34   When the tribunal renders an award that does not address all of the issues presented, the parties may, within a limited time frame, request an additional award to remedy this gap. Many arbitration rules expressly provide for additional awards,[47] and even where they are not expressly provided for, there is generally a procedural tool by which they can, in essence, be accomplished.[48]

(e) Consent awards and termination of proceedings without an award

9.35   As in litigation in national courts, parties to an international arbitration often arrive at a settlement during the proceedings. Where this occurs, the parties may simply implement the settlement agreement and thus revoke the mandate of the arbitral tribunal. This

---

[46] For a discussion of the procedure to be followed where one party fails or refuses to participate in an arbitration, see Chapter 6, paragraphs 6.204–6.205.

[47] See UNCITRAL Rules, Art. 39; LCIA Rules, Art. 27; International Dispute Resolution Procedures (International Arbitration), Art. 36; SCC Rules, Art. 48; English Arbitration Act 1996, s. 57(3)(b); Model Law, Art. 33(1)(b).

[48] See, e.g., ICSID Rules, r. 49.2.

means that the jurisdiction and powers conferred on the arbitral tribunal by the parties are terminated.[49]

In many cases, however, the parties find it desirable for the terms of settlement to be em-   **9.36** bodied in an award. There are many reasons for this. The most important is that it is usually easier for a party to enforce performance by the other party of a future obligation if that obligation is contained in an award (in respect of which the assistance of the New York Convention may be available), rather than to take further steps to enforce a settlement agreement.[50] Other reasons for obtaining a consent award include the desirability (particularly where a state or state agency is involved) of having a definite and identifiable 'result' of the arbitral proceedings, in the form of an award, which may be passed to the appropriate paying authority for implementation. In this context, the signatures of the arbitrators on the consent award indicate a measure of approval by the arbitral tribunal to the agreement reached by the parties. This may help to meet politically motivated criticism of those responsible for taking the decision to reach a compromise settlement.

There should be little or no problem as far as capacity to compromise is concerned. Many   **9.37** countries adopt as their definition of matters that are capable of resolution by arbitration (that is, matters that are 'arbitrable') the concept that parties may refer to arbitration any disputes in respect of which they are entitled to reach a compromise. The reverse holds good: if parties are entitled to refer a dispute to arbitration, they are entitled to reach a compromise in respect of that dispute.

No restrictions are imposed by national law, or international or institutional rules of ar-   **9.38** bitration, to the effect that, once arbitral proceedings have been commenced, the parties cannot terminate them by agreement. On the contrary, a settlement is invariably welcomed, and it may be possible to have it recorded in a consent award. Article 30 of the Model Law provides for 'an arbitral award on agreed terms.' Article 36.1 of the UNCITRAL Rules provides for a settlement to be recorded by an order or by an award:

> If, before the award is made, the parties agree on a settlement of the dispute, the arbitral tribunal shall either issue an order for the termination of the arbitral proceedings or, if requested by the parties and accepted by the tribunal, record the settlement in the form of an arbitral award on agreed terms. The arbitral tribunal is not obliged to give reasons for such an award.

The ICC Rules contain a similar provision, at Article 33: if the parties reach a settlement, after the file has been transmitted to the arbitral tribunal in accordance with Article 13, then 'the settlement *shall* be recorded in the form of an award made by consent of the parties, if so requested by the parties and if the arbitral tribunal agrees to do so'.[51] The word 'shall' is mandatory and suggests an obligation to record any settlement in a consent award. However, it is qualified by the requirements that the parties must request such an award and the tribunal must agree to it. Similarly, the LCIA Rules provide that, in the event of any final settlement, the tribunal '*may* decide' to make an award recording the settlement if the parties jointly so

---

[49] This follows from the consensual nature of arbitration: see Chapter 5, paragraph 5.32.
[50] See, e.g., English Arbitration Act 1996, s. 51(3) (which provides that an 'agreed award' shall 'have the same status and effect as any other award on the merits of the case').
[51] Emphasis added.

request.[52] This indicates that, under the UNCITRAL, LCIA, and ICC Rules, there is no obligation for either the parties or the tribunal to make a consent award.

9.39   Under whatever rules the parties are proceeding, however, it would be a normal act of courtesy to inform the arbitral tribunal (and the appropriate arbitral institution, if one is involved) of any settlement agreement reached between the parties, particularly if meetings or hearings have already been held. There may also be sound financial reasons for doing what normal courtesy demands. First, notifying the arbitral tribunal of a settlement will ensure that it does not incur further fees and expenses (other than any cancellation fees that may have been agreed). Secondly, such notification might lead to a refund of advance payments made to cover fees and expenses, since the actual costs incurred may well be less than expected if the case has been settled without a hearing. Thirdly, as already indicated, it may be desirable to put the terms of settlement into an enforceable form when there is an element of future performance. Although most settlements involve immediate implementation of the agreed terms, it is nevertheless not unusual for there to be provision for payment by instalments, or for some future transaction between the parties to be carried out.

9.40   A question occasionally arises as to the role of an arbitral tribunal that is requested by the parties to make a consent award ordering the performance of an unlawful act. Examples might be the manufacture of an internationally banned drug, or the smuggling of contraband or—perhaps more realistically—an agreement that manifestly contravenes relevant competition or antitrust laws. At one time, various sets of rules (including the ICC Rules prior to 1998) seemed to leave the tribunal with no discretion, but modern rules and legislation permit the arbitral tribunal to refuse to make a consent award.[53]

C. Remedies

9.41   The arbitral tribunal's power to grant appropriate relief is based on the arbitration agreement and on the relevant applicable law. While in principle an arbitration agreement could specify the remedial measures to be conferred upon the tribunal, the usual position is that the agreement is silent on that point. In such circumstances, the tribunal must look into the relevant arbitration rules or the applicable law. Arbitration awards may cover a range of remedies, including:

- monetary compensation;
- punitive damages and other penalties;
- specific performance and restitution;
- injunctions;
- declaratory relief;
- rectification;
- filling gaps and adaptation of contracts;
- interest; and
- costs.

---

[52]   LCIA Rules, Art. 26.9.
[53]   See, e.g., ICC Rules, Art. 33.

(a) Monetary compensation

The type of award most often made by an international arbitral tribunal is one that dir- **9.42**
ects the payment of a sum of money by one party to the other. This payment may represent money due under a contract (debt), or compensation (damages) for loss suffered, or
both. The sum of money awarded is usually expressed in the currency of the contract or
the currency of the loss. In large transnational projects, however, it is not unusual for reference to be made to several different currencies—so that, for example, plant and equipment
manufactured or purchased overseas may be paid for in US dollars, whilst labour, plant, and
equipment made or purchased locally may be paid for in the local currency. In such cases,
unless the parties agree, the arbitral tribunal must receive submissions and decide on the
currency or currencies in which the award is to be made.

Under many national arbitration laws, arbitral tribunals have discretion to make awards **9.43**
in any currency deemed appropriate. The *Lesotho Highlands* case is illustrative of both
the exercise of such discretion and the potential consequences of doing so. The case concerned the construction of a dam in Lesotho by a consortium of foreign companies. The
consortium claimed amounts that, had they been paid when due, would have been payable
in Lesotho loti, as owed under the relevant contract. However, by the time the award was
made, the value of the loti had diminished against international currency values. The consortium therefore claimed payment of the award in four European currencies contractually
designated as currencies for non-loti payments. In rendering the award in the currencies requested, the arbitral tribunal invoked section 48 of the English Arbitration Act 1996, which
allows a tribunal to order payment of an award in any currency (unless agreed otherwise by
the parties).

The employer challenged the award in the English courts, under section 68(2)(b), for excess **9.44**
of power.[54] In so doing, the employer contended that the provisions in the contract on currencies effectively excluded the tribunal's power to select the currency of the award. On appeal to the House of Lords, the employer's challenge was dismissed by a majority of four to
one.[55] Of the major institutional rules, the LCIA expressly permits an award to be expressed
in any currency (unless the parties have agreed otherwise).[56] The ICDR Rules go further in
granting the tribunal power to issue a monetary award in a currency other than that of the
contract if it considers such alternative currency to be 'more appropriate'.[57]

(b) Punitive damages and other penalties

Punitive damages are not awarded to compensate the wronged party, but instead to punish **9.45**
and deter the wrongdoer. In general, punitive damages are an exceptional and extreme
measure permitted only, for example, in cases of fraud and substantial malice.[58] In the

[54] *Lesotho Highlands Development Authority v Impregilo SpA and ors* [2003] EWCA Civ 1159.
[55] *Lesotho Highlands Development Authority v Impregilo SpA and ors* [2005] UKHL 43.
[56] LCIA Rules, Art. 26.3.
[57] ICDR Rules, Art. 34.4.
[58] Lew, Mistelis, and Kröll, *Comparative International Commercial Arbitration* (Kluwer Law International,
2003), p. 651.

context of awarding punitive damages, it is tempting to think that an arbitral tribunal has precisely parallel powers to those of a national court to award damages in accordance with the law applicable to the substantive merits of the dispute. However, the powers of an arbitral tribunal are not necessarily the same as those of a court.

9.46 An arbitral tribunal may, in certain respects, have *wider* powers than those of a judge, because the tribunal's powers flow from, inter alia, the arbitration agreement. Thus, in England, a court applying US law has no power to order the payment of triple damages—a power provided under US antitrust legislation.[59] But an arbitral tribunal sitting in England *does* have the power to award triple damages provided that the parties' arbitration agreement is sufficiently wide to encompass the determination of US antitrust law claims—although, for public policy reasons, there may be problems of enforcement, as will be discussed later.[60]

9.47 To determine the power of an arbitral tribunal to award a particular remedy, it is necessary to look at the law applicable to the substance of the dispute, or the law of the seat of the arbitration, depending on the applicable conflict of laws rules applicable (often determined by the seat). In civil law countries, for example, the concept of punitive damages is almost unknown, whether in breach-of-contract cases or otherwise, with a limited exception in some countries where there has been a wilful intention to harm the claimant amounting, in effect, to fraud.[61] Under French law, punitive damages are not recoverable, although 'moral damages' (to reflect the tribunal's disapproval) may be recoverable. Under English law, punitive damages may be awarded only in actions in tort—and even then only in three categories of case.[62] Punitive damages may not be awarded for breach of contract.[63] However, such claims are permissible in the United States, where statutes may provide expressly for the payment of multiple damages by one party to the other.[64]

9.48 With regard to enforcement, the key question is whether an award of punitive damages would be enforceable under the New York Convention in a country that does not itself recognise such a remedy. The ground for refusal of enforcement would be Article V(2) of the Convention, which allows refusal of recognition or enforcement of an award if recognition or enforcement would be contrary to public policy. For example, in a leading judgment

---

[59] *British Airways Board v Laker Airways Ltd* [1985] AC 58 (HL).

[60] See paragraph 9.161. It would lead to an absurd result if an arbitral tribunal applying US antitrust law could determine the issue of liability under that law, but not award the mandatory remedy provided for in that law. The point was considered by a US court in *PPG Inc v Pilkington Plc* (1995) XX YBCA 885.

[61] In ICC Case No. 5946 (1991) XVI YBCA 97, at 113, an ICC arbitration held in Geneva, a claim was made for exemplary damages, but this claim was refused on the basis that: 'damages that go beyond compensatory damages to constitute a punishment of the wrongdoer [... punitive or exemplary damages], are considered contrary to Swiss public policy, which must be respected by an arbitral tribunal sitting in Switzerland even if the arbitral tribunal must decide a dispute according to a law that may allow punitive or exemplary damages as such: see Art 135(2) Switzerland's Federal Code on Private International Law of December 1987, which refuses to allow enforcement of a judgment awarding damages that cannot be awarded in Switzerland [...]'.

[62] See *Rookes v Barnard* [1964] AC 1129. The three categories are: (a) abuse of power by servants of the government; (b) conduct that was motivated by the pursuit of profits; and (c) where punitive, or 'exemplary', damages expressly authorised by statute.

[63] For contract cases, see *Addis v Gramophone Co. Ltd* [1909] AC 488, with exceptions to the general rule at 495. For actions in tort, see *Rookes v Barnard* [1964] AC 1129, [1967] 1 Lloyd's Rep 28 (HL).

[64] Examples of statutes that provide for multiple damages in the United States are the Racketeer Influenced and Corrupt Organizations Act of 1970 (RICO) and antitrust laws that provide for triple damages.

rendered in Germany in 1992, the Federal Supreme Court (*Bundesgerichtshof*) refused to enforce part of a US court decision that provided for the recovery of punitive damages, on the grounds that such recovery was contrary to German public policy.[65] The authors are not aware of any German court decisions relating to attempts to enforce a foreign arbitral award providing for the recovery of punitive damages, but the same result is likely.[66]

In summary, it is suggested that arbitral tribunals should treat claims for punitive damages and other penalties with considerable caution. They should address themselves to the threshold question as to whether or not they have the power to make such an award, even if a claim for punitive damages is admissible under the law applicable to the substance of the dispute, by examining both the *lex arbitri* and the scope of the arbitration agreement.[67] If the remedy is permissible, it then becomes a question of enforcement, which is dealt with in Chapter 11.   **9.49**

Problems concerning enforceability should be left for the courts at the place of enforcement. However, it is preferable for arbitral tribunals to treat any award in respect of punitive damages or any other penalties as an entirely separate claim, in order to ensure that the punitive portion of the award is severable in the event of a successful challenge in the courts at the place of enforcement.   **9.50**

(c) Specific performance

An arbitral tribunal may be authorised by the parties or by the applicable law (either the substantive law or the *lex arbitri*,) to order specific performance of a contract. An international arbitral tribunal sitting in the United States will have the power to award specific performance,[68] and English law empowers an arbitral tribunal sitting in England 'to order specific performance of a contract (other than a contract relating to land)' unless a contrary intention is expressed in the arbitration agreement.[69] In civil law jurisdictions, specific performance is a primary remedy for breach of contract. Orders of specific performance are therefore not uncommon in international arbitration.[70]   **9.51**

---

[65] *Bundesgerichtshof* (Neue Juristische Wochenschrift, 1992), at 3096*ff.* The Court has affirmed it in two more recent decisions: BVerfG, Beschluß vom 24.01.2007—2 BvR 1133/04; BVerfG, Beschluß vom 14.06.2007—2 BvR 2247/06.

[66] Similarly, Dutch courts have held that a judgment to pay punitive damages cannot be recognised and enforced in the Netherlands without further enquiry: see the decision of the District Court of Rotterdam, 17 February 1995, [1996] NIPR 205, at 207.

[67] For a comprehensive review of the powers of arbitrators to award punitive damages, see Gotanda, *Supplemental Damages in Private International Law* (Kluwer Law International, 1998), pp. 226–229.

[68] While neither the US Federal Arbitration Act of 1925 (FAA) nor the Uniform Arbitration Act of 1955, as amended (UAA), expressly specifies the remedies available in international arbitrations taking place in the United States (e.g., the UAA, s. 21, empowers arbitrators to 'order such remedies as the arbitrator considers just and appropriate under the circumstances of the arbitration proceeding'), courts have confirmed that arbitrators have the power to award specific performance even if the arbitration agreement does not specify this remedy: see, e.g., *Brandon v MedPartners Inc.*, 203 FRD 677, 686 (SD Fla. 2001).

[69] English Arbitration Act 1996, s. 48(5)(b).

[70] Where enforcement takes place in a New York Convention State, there is nothing in the New York Convention that gives the court power to resist enforcement simply on the basis that the award contains an order for specific performance.

(d) Restitution

9.52   Restitution seeks to put the aggrieved party in the same position as that in which it would have been had the wrongful act not taken place. In common law terminology, it is a form of specific performance. By way of example, in England, unless the parties otherwise agree, an arbitral tribunal has the same powers as an English court 'to order a party to do or refrain from doing anything'.[71]

9.53   An example of the use of this remedy in public international law is provided by the *Temple of Preah-Vihear* case,[72] in which the International Court of Justice (ICJ) ordered the government of Thailand to restore to Cambodia certain sculptures and other objects that it had removed from the temple on the border between the two countries. In 2003, the ICJ in its advisory opinion about *Legal Consequences of the Construction of a Wall in the Occupied Palestinian Territory*,[73] held that Israel had an obligation to return the 'land, orchards, olive groves and other immovable property seized from any natural or legal person for purposes of construction of the wall in the Occupied Palestinian Territory'.[74] A further example in the investment treaty context is *Von Pezold v Zimbabwe*, where the tribunal granted claimants restitution of certain properties expropriated by the state.[75]

9.54   Even in the field of public international law, however, the remedy is less common than monetary compensation:

> The essential principle contained in the actual notion of an illegal act—a principle which seems to be established by international practice and in particular by the decisions of arbitral tribunals—is that reparation must, as far as possible, wipe out all the consequences of the illegal act and re-establish the situation which would, in all probability, have existed if that act had not been committed. Restitution in kind, or, if this is not possible, *payment of a sum corresponding to the value which a restitution in kind would bear*; the award, if need be, of damages for loss sustained which would not be covered by restitution in kind or payment in place of it—such are the principles which should serve to determine the amount of compensation due for an act contrary to international law.[76]

9.55   The relief sought and granted in the growing number of investment arbitrations confirms that, in practice, monetary compensation, rather than restitution, is the principal remedy sought and granted in international arbitration. By way of example, Article 1135 of Chapter 11 of the North American Free Trade Agreement (NAFTA) provides that although a tribunal may award 'restitution of property', such awards 'shall provide that the disputing party may pay monetary damages and any applicable interest in lieu of restitution'. Thus the

---

[71]   English Arbitration Act 1996, s. 48(5)(a).

[72]   *Cambodia v Thailand* [1962] ICJ Rep 6.

[73]   *Legal Consequences of the Construction of a Wall in the Occupied Palestinian Territory, Advisory Opinion* [2004] ICJ Rep 136.

[74]   Ibid., at [153].

[75]   *Bernhard von Pezold and others v Republic of Zimbabwe*, ICSID Case No. ARB/10/15, Award, 28 July 2015, at [744]. In this case, the tribunal considered that, in order to achieve full reparation, it was also necessary to award claimants compensation for losses incurred as a result of the expropriations.

[76]   *Case Concerning the Factory at Chorzów (Claim for Indemnity) (Germany v Poland)* (the *Chorzów Factory* case) [1928] PCIJ Series A No. 17, at 47 (emphasis added).

host state of an investment that is condemned under a Chapter 11 arbitral award will always have the right to pay damages in place of restitution.

In *Occidental Petroleum Corporation and Occidental Exploration and Production Co. v Ecuador*,[77] the tribunal refused to grant an order that Ecuador fully reinstate the claimants' rights under the relevant contracts. In an interim award dated 17 August 2007,[78] the tribunal refused to grant such relief partly on the basis that the claimants could not establish a right to an award of specific performance of the contracts. The tribunal held that an order reinstating the claimants' contract could be made only if (a) it was not legally impossible to revive the contract, (b) such a remedy would not involve a disproportionate interference with state sovereignty, as compared to an award of damages, and (c) damages could not otherwise make the claimants whole for their losses.[79]   **9.56**

(e) Injunctions

There is no objection in principle to an arbitral tribunal granting relief by way of injunction, if requested to do so, either on an interim basis or as final relief. Injunctive relief is addressed in detail in Chapter 7. For present purposes, it is sufficient to state that an arbitral tribunal is not usually empowered to make effective orders against third parties, and if injunctive relief against third parties is required, it is generally quicker and more effective to seek it directly from a national court. Most sets of international and institutional rules make it clear that an arbitration clause is not to be taken as excluding the jurisdiction of the relevant national court to make orders for interim measures of protection.[80] However, Article 26.3 of the UNCITRAL Rules, for example, contains the qualification requiring that an applicant must satisfy the tribunal that: **9.57**

[...]

(i) harm not adequately reparable by an award of damages is likely to result if the measure is not ordered, and such harm substantially outweighs the harm that is likely to result to the party against whom the measure is directed if the measure is granted; and

(ii) there is a reasonable possibility that the requesting party will succeed on the merits of the claim.

In some jurisdictions, there was previously doubt as to whether the power of national courts to grant interim relief in support of arbitration was limited to domestic seated arbitrations. For example, in India, following the Supreme Court's 2012 decision in *Balco*,[81] no application for interim relief under section 9 of the 1996 Indian Arbitration Act was available from Indian courts in support of international arbitrations seated outside India.[82] However,   **9.58**

---

[77] ICSID Case No. ARB/06/11, Decision on Provisional Measures, 17 August 2007, IIC 305 (2007).

[78] IIC 305 (2007).

[79] See also *RREEF v Kingdom of Spain*, ICSID Case No. ARB/13/30, at 473 (in which the tribunal held that restitution would not be an appropriate remedy as it would imply 'repealing laws and regulations' and would accordingly amount to a disproportionate interference with Spain's sovereignty). To the same effect, see also *Antin v Kingdom of Spain*, ICSID Case No. ARB/13/3, at 636 and *Masdar v Kingdom of Spain*, ICSID Case No. ARB/14/1, at 559.

[80] See, e.g., ICC Rules, Art. 28.2; UNCITRAL Rules, Art. 26. See paragraphs 7.28*ff*.

[81] *Bharat Aluminium Co. v Kaiser Aluminium Technical Services Inc.* (2012) 9 SCC 552.

[82] This prior rule was applicable only in respect of proceedings pursuant to arbitration agreements executed after 6 September 2012. In respect of arbitration agreements executed prior to this date, the pre-*Balco* regime as set

following significant amendments to India's Arbitration Act in 2015, it is now clear that interim relief from Indian courts is available in respect of foreign seated 'international commercial arbitrations' (subject to any agreement to the contrary).[83] A recent decision of the Supreme Court has clarified that the phrase 'international commercial arbitration' in this context also captures an arbitration between two Indian parties with a foreign seat (which was previously a somewhat vexed issue as a matter of Indian law).[84]

(f) Declaratory relief

9.59 An arbitral tribunal may be asked to make an award that is simply declaratory of the rights of the parties. Modern arbitration legislation[85] often makes express provision for the granting of declaratory relief. Even when there is no such express provision, however, there is no reason in principle why an arbitral tribunal should not grant such relief. Indeed, declaratory relief has become a common remedy in international arbitration, with requests for contractual damages usually coupled with a request for a declaration that there has been a breach of contract.

9.60 The *Aramco* arbitration provides a classic example of an arbitration in which the parties only claimed declaratory relief.[86] Aramco claimed that its exclusive right to transport oil from its concession area in Saudi Arabia had been infringed by the agreement made between the Saudi Arabian government and the late Aristotle Onassis, the Greek shipping magnate, and his company, the Saudi Arabian Maritime Tankers Company. The dispute was significant—but neither party wished it to jeopardise their trading relationship, which was a continuing relationship dating back many years.[87] Accordingly, it was agreed that the dispute should be referred to an ad hoc tribunal of three arbitrators based in Geneva. It was further agreed that the award should be of declaratory effect only, with neither of the parties claiming damages for any alleged injury. The arbitral tribunal said:

> There is no objection whatsoever to Parties limiting the scope of the arbitration agreement to the question of what exactly is their legal position. When the competence of the arbitrators is limited to such a statement of the law and does not allow them to impose the execution of an obligation on either of the Parties, the Arbitration Tribunal can only give a declaratory award.[88]

9.61 A declaratory award establishes the legal position definitively and has a binding effect as between the parties. It is a useful device, particularly where the parties have a continuing relationship and want to resolve a dispute without the risk of damaging that relationship by a demand for monetary compensation. In England, an award containing a negative

out in *Bhatia International v Bulk Trading S.A.* (2002) 4 SCC 105 applied. Under the rule in *Bhatia*, interim relief from Indian courts was available in respect of foreign seated arbitrations.

[83] Indian Arbitration and Conciliation Act 1996, s. 2(2) (as amended).
[84] *PASL Wind Solutions v GE Power Conversion India*, Civil Appeal No. 1647 of 2021, 20 April 2021.
[85] See, e.g., the English Arbitration Act 1996, s. 48(3).
[86] For further discussion of this arbitration, see Chapter 3.
[87] The original concession was granted by King Saud of Saudi Arabia in 1933, for a period of sixty years.
[88] *Saudi Arabia v Arabian American Oil Co. (Aramco)* (1963) 27 ILR 117, at 145.

declaration is capable both of recognition and enforcement (depending on the terms of the order in question).[89]

(g) Rectification

Rectification essentially is a common law equitable remedy, and is virtually unknown in civil law countries, where it tends to be treated in the same sense as adaptation of contracts and 'filling gaps'. In common law countries, these concepts are considered separately. However, in general, an arbitral tribunal may make an order for rectification of a contract if empowered to do so by the parties.   **9.62**

In England, any doubt about the position was resolved by the Arbitration Act 1996: an arbitral tribunal has the power 'to order the rectification, setting aside or cancellation of a deed or other document', unless the parties agree otherwise.[90]   **9.63**

(h) Filling gaps and adaptation of contracts

An arbitral tribunal does not, in general, have power to create, or write, a contract between the parties. Its role in a contractual dispute is usually to interpret the contract as signed by the parties. However, almost anything is possible by clear consent of the parties.[91] In particular, it is now generally accepted that an arbitral tribunal has implied consent to 'fill gaps' by making a determination as to the presumed intention of the parties in order to make a contract operable. In England, a relatively mature authority for this proposition may be found in the famous 'chickens' case,[92] to which reference is still made from time to time by the English courts.   **9.64**

The principle was clarified and expanded in the later *Mamidoil* line of cases. In *Mamidoil*,[93] the English Court of Appeal stated: **9.65**

> [...]
> (vi) Particularly in the case of contracts for future performance over a period, where the parties may desire or need to leave matters to be adjusted in the working out of their contract, the courts will assist the parties to do so, so as to preserve rather than destroy bargains, on the basis that what can be made certain is itself certain. *Certum est quod certum reddi potest.*

---

[89] See *West Tankers Inc v Allianz Spa and another* [2012] EWCA Civ 27 (in which the English Court of Appeal confirmed that the phrase 'enforced in the same manner as a judgment to the same effect' in the English Arbitration Act, s. 66(1), allows a court to give leave for a declaratory award to be enforced as a judgment). As is clear from the judgment, however, this is not a blanket rule and it will be necessary to satisfy the court that such enforcement is appropriate in each case.

[90] English Arbitration Act 1996, s. 48(5)(c). See also the discussion of the scope of the arbitration clause in Chapter 2, paragraphs 2.70–2.80.

[91] Provided that it is not unlawful or contrary to public policy.

[92] *F & G Sykes (Wessex) Ltd v Fine Fare Ltd* [1967] 1 Lloyd's Rep 53. See also Veeder, 'England', in Paulsson and Bosman (eds) *ICCA International Handbook on Commercial Arbitration* (Kluwer Law International, 1984).

[93] *Mamidoil-Jetoil Greek Petroleum Co. SA v Okta Crude Oil Refinery AD* [2001] 2 All ER (Comm) 193, at 215.

[…]

(viii) For these purposes, an express stipulation for a reasonable fair measure or price will be a sufficient criterion for the courts to act on. But even in the absence of express language, the courts are prepared to imply an obligation in terms of what is reasonable.

[…]

(x) The presence of an arbitration clause may assist the courts to hold a contract to be sufficiently certain or to be capable of being rendered so, as indicating a commercial and contractual mechanism which can be operated with the assistance of experts in the field, by which the parties, in the absence of agreement, may resolve their dispute.

9.66   A similar position exists in civil law countries, where the courts appear to go directly to what they call the 'intention of the parties', rather than use the 'implied term' device that is a feature of English contractual interpretation. In a note on 'L'Interprétation Arbitrale',[94] a distinguished Swiss commentator suggested that, in French law, the arbitrator takes account of the commercial context in which an agreement is made—but if the parties have omitted an important provision from their contract on a particular point, it is perhaps because they prefer to leave it open, rather than not to agree upon a contract at all.

9.67   A more difficult question is whether or not an arbitral tribunal has power to change the unambiguous terms of a contract. This is certainly possible where the relevant contract contains a provision authorising the arbitral tribunal to do so. Such provisions are commonly found in long-term gas contracts. Many such contracts contain clauses that provide for price reviews. Indeed, these have led to a whole wave of price review arbitrations in recent years, which have focused on often complex price review formulae and that are heavy on economic expert evidence.[95]

9.68   A device once used was reliance on the so-called 'hardship clause'. The 1978 ICC Rules for the Adaptation of Contracts, the 1994 Model Exploration and Production Sharing Agreement of Qatar and Principles 6.2.2 and 6.2.3 of the 2004 UNIDROIT Principles of International Commercial Contracts[96] served as a 'blueprint' for such provisions. However, an express provision in the relevant contract was required to bring them into operation and in practice 'hardship clauses' are rarely seen in modern contracts. What happens instead is that commercial parties (or their lawyers) insert tailor-made price-review, 'balancing', or 'economic equilibrium' provisions in long-term supply contracts, so as to enable mediators and/or arbitral tribunals to adapt their contracts when circumstances change in a manner that was unforeseen when the contract was signed.[97]

---

[94] Levy, 'L'interprétation arbitrale' (2013–14) 4 Rev Arb 861.
[95] See Anway and von Mehren, 'The evolution of gas price review arbitrations', in Rowley KC, Bishop, and Kaiser (eds) The Guide to Energy Arbitrations (4th edn, Global Arbitration Review, 2020).
[96] Available online at http://www.unidroit.org/english/principles/contracts/principles2004/blackletter2004.pdf.
[97] Unlike classic 'freezing' clauses, such provisions are not designed to freeze the legal regime applicable to a contract. Rather, they attempt to deal with the consequences of change by providing for the negotiation of contractual amendments to reinstate the initial economic balance of the contract (see Partasides and Martinez, 'Of taxes and stabilization', in Rowley et al. (eds) The GAR Guide to Energy Arbitrations (3rd edn, Global Arbitration Review, 2019)).

Occasionally, arbitral tribunals issue awards that have the effect of changing the express **9.69** terms of a contract in which there is no clear provision authorising them to do so. Where the applicable substantive law is that of a civil law jurisdiction, the justification usually given is the application of the doctrine of *rebus sic stantibus*. In the common law world, the parties' legal representatives and arbitrators tend to place reliance on 'implied terms' to the effect that this is what the parties must have intended to happen in the new circumstances that have arisen.

(i) Interest

The payment of interest on a loan, or in respect of money that is paid later than it should **9.70** have been, is a common feature of modern business relationships, and the award of compensatory interest in international arbitration has likewise become routine. Indeed, it has become rare for interest not to be awarded where an award provides for the payment of monies due. As one international arbitrator has said:

> In all international commercial arbitrations where a claim for the payment of money is advanced, whether debt or damages, it is highly probable that the claimant has also suffered a financial loss resulting from late payment of the principal amount. That loss can amount to a significant proportion of the total claim; and in certain cases, it can exceed the principal amount. In a modern arbitration régime, it is unthinkable that a claimant should not have the right to recover that loss in the form of interest.[98]

However, the situation is different in some Muslim countries—such as Saudi Arabia[99]—in **9.71** which the law against usury (*riba*) prevents the levying of interest:

> The proposition of interest, strictly applied in Hanbali law (Saudi Arabia, Qatar) and Zayydi law (North Yemen) is linked in the minds of Muslim lawyers and economists with the rejection of the idea of the *homo economicus* as devised by the West, and with the integration of religious principles into the commercial life of the Muslim businessman, while the businessman should be solvent he should also conform to Qur'anic teaching, for although the Prophet did not condemn profit arising from sale or from a partnership he did prohibit the charging of interest on a loan [...][100]

---

[98] Veeder, 'Whose arbitration is it anyway: The parties' or the arbitration tribunal's? An interesting question?', in Newman and Hill (eds) *The Leading Arbitrators' Guide to International Arbitration* (2nd edn, Juris, 2008), p. 344. See also Brower and Sharpe, 'Awards of compound interest in international arbitration: The *Aminoil* non-precedent' (2006) 3 TDM 5.

[99] The approach to interest in Saudi Arabia appears to be the most restrictive amongst Islamic jurisdictions (Saudi Arbitration Law, art 55(2)(b); see also Al-Ammari, 'Arbitration in the Kingdom of Saudi Arabia' (2014) 30 Arb Intl 387, at 406). In contrast, arbitral awards dealing with interest under *Shari'ah* law in other Islamic jurisdictions have shown that it is possible to grant interest, or something akin to interest under another name (see *ICC case 7373*, Final Award, (2004) 15(1) ICC International Court of Arbitration Bulletin 72, in which the tribunal noted that 'numerous statute laws of the Islamic world permit the tribunal to award interest to compensate financial damages. It is well known that Islamic banks grant interest to their clients without using the word "interest" '). See also the decision of the English courts in *Sanghi Polyesters Ltd (India) v The International Investor KCFC (Kuwait)* [2000] 1 Lloyd's Rep 480.

[100] Saleh, 'The recognition and enforcement of foreign arbitral awards in the states of the Arab Middle East', in Lew (ed.) *Contemporary Problems in International Arbitration* (CCLS/Kluwer, 1986), pp. 348–349.

(i) Basis upon which interest can be awarded

9.72   While the availability of interest in international arbitration is for the large part uncontroversial, the basis upon which interest is awarded varies. Most institutional rules of arbitration do not contain express provisions for the payment of interest, largely because it was assumed that an arbitral tribunal had the power to make an award in respect of interest, in just the same way as it has the power to make an award in respect of any other claims submitted to it.[101] The right to interest will therefore flow from the parties' underlying contract (that is, from a contractual provision for the levying of interest for late payment), or by virtue of the applicable law.[102] The laws that govern the power of a tribunal to award interest also vary. In some jurisdictions, for example Bermuda, Hong Kong, England, and Scotland, the power to award interest is governed by the law of the place of arbitration.[103] In others, for example under German conflict-of-laws rules, the liability to pay interest is a question of substantive law and thus governed by the law of the contract.[104]

(ii) How much interest to award

9.73   More problematic in practice than the question of whether an arbitral tribunal can award interest in principle are questions concerning the rate of interest to be awarded, from which start date, and in which currency. Most applicable laws leave these questions to the tribunal's discretion. Thus the English Arbitration Act 1996 empowers a tribunal seated in England to award interest 'from such dates, at such rates and with such rests as it considers meets the justice of the case'.[105] Similarly, the law of Australia permits a tribunal to award interest 'at such reasonable rate as the tribunal determines for the whole or any part of the money, for the whole or any part of the period between the date on which the cause of action arose and the date on which the award is made', and thereafter 'from the day of the making of the award or such later day as the tribunal specifies, on so much of the money as is from time to time unpaid'.[106] Other jurisdictions, such as Hong Kong, India, and Singapore, have also enacted laws that give arbitrators similar discretion in the award of interest.[107]

9.74   In exercising this discretion, the tribunal will typically invite submissions and evidence from the parties on these issues in the same way as it would in respect of any other request for relief. Parties will thus usually have an opportunity to set out their respective positions

---

[101] Exceptionally, the LCIA Rules, Art. 26.4, provides that the arbitral tribunal may award simple or compound interest up to the date of compliance with the award, and without being bound by the rates of interest practised by any state court or other legal authority. See also SIAC Rules, r. 32.9. For a discussion of compound interest, see paragraphs 9.75*ff*.

[102] See Gotanda, 'Awarding interest in international arbitration' (1996) 90 Am J Intl L 40, at 50*ff*; Gotanda, 'A study of interest', Villanova University School of Law Working Paper Series No. 83 (August 2007), available online at http://digitalcommons.law.villanova.edu/wps/art83/, pp. 3*ff*.

[103] See, e.g., the English Arbitration Act 1996, s. 49.

[104] Accordingly, under German conflict-of-laws rules, if an arbitral tribunal sitting in Germany were to conclude that the substantive law of the contract was English, it would apply not only those rules of English law governing interest that English law classifies as substantive, but also those rules that English law classifies as procedural, because a court or arbitral tribunal sitting in Germany would classify such *procedural* rules as being of a *substantive* nature for this purpose.

[105] English Arbitration Act 1996, s. 49(3). Almost identical provisions are found in the Irish Arbitration (International) Commercial Act 1998, s. 10(2), and the Singapore International Arbitration Act, s. 20(1).

[106] Australian International Arbitration Acts 1974–1989, ss. 25(1) and 26; equivalent provisions are also found in the Maltese Arbitration Act 1996, ss. 63(1) and 64.

[107] Hong Kong Arbitration Ordinance 1997, Ch. 341, ss. 2GH and 2GI; Indian Arbitration and Conciliation Act 1996, s. 31(7)(a) and (b); Singapore International Arbitration Act (Ch. 143A) 2002, ss. 12(5)(b) and 20.

on the rate of interest to be applied, the period for which it should be applied, and whether a different rate (such as a statutory legal interest rate) should be applied for the period following the rendering of an award until payment. In making such submissions, parties would do well to make it as easy as possible for a tribunal to award interest by providing the calculations upon which such an award would be based (for example, in any damages model prepared by a party's *quantum* expert).[108]

(iii) Compound interest

Most systems of national law expressly permit arbitral tribunals to award some form of interest on the amount awarded in respect of a claim or counterclaim, whether the amount awarded is due under a contract or as compensation or as restitution. However, whether there is a power to award compound (as opposed to simple) interest remains less clear.[109] Although the Model Law does not contain any express provisions concerning interest, arbitration legislation in common law jurisdictions such as England, Ireland, Hong Kong, and Bermuda give arbitral tribunals express power to award compound interest. Thus section 49 of the English Arbitration Act 1996 provides that, unless otherwise agreed by the parties, the tribunal may award simple or compound interest. This is, however, by no means a feature of all common law jurisdictions: in Canada and the United States, the power to award compound interest varies from state to state and province to province; in Australia and New Zealand, the power to award compound interest is strictly limited.   **9.75**

In civil law jurisdictions, arbitral tribunals typically have the power to award a statutory (or legal) rate of interest, which is simple interest at a rate defined by statute. Like the common law, however, there are once again exceptions to the rule: the Dutch and Japanese civil codes provide, for example, that statutory interest is automatically capitalised at the end of each year.[110] An ICC arbitral tribunal in Geneva once awarded compound interest in a dispute between a state and a French entity on the basis of trade usage under Article 13 of the ICC Rules.[111] Sources of international law are no clearer. Article 38 of the International Law Commission's Draft Articles on 'Responsibility of States for Internationally Wrongful Acts'[112] provides simply that 'interest shall be payable on any principal sum when necessary in order to ensure full reparation'.   **9.76**

Although the law on this issue varies from jurisdiction to jurisdiction, awards of compound interest appear to have become more common. In the *Santa Elena* arbitration,[113] an international tribunal found that although simple interest seemed, at that time, to be awarded more frequently than compound interest, 'no uniform rule of law has emerged from the practice in international arbitration as regards the determination of whether   **9.77**

---

[108] As Professor Park observed in his 2002 Freshfields Lecture, there are, in theory, three kinds of arbitrator—namely, those who can count and those who cannot: see Park, 'Arbitration's Protean nature: The value of rules and the risks of discretion' (2003) 19 Arb Intl 279.

[109] For the avoidance of doubt, compounding interest involves capitalising interest and accruing further interest on such capitalised interest. The difference between simple and compound interest can be significant where the amount in dispute is large and the time periods involved are lengthy.

[110] See also French Civil Code, Art. 1343-2 (providing for the capitalisation of judgment debts after one year); and Brazilian Civil Code, Art. 591 (permitting the annual compounding of interest on certain outstanding debts).

[111] Arnaldez, Derains, and Hascher, *Collection of ICC Arbitral Awards 1991–1995* (Kluwer Law International, 1997), p. 459.

[112] Official Records of the General Assembly, F50, 6th Session, Supplement No. 10 (AR/56/10), Ch. IV, E.1.

[113] *Compañía del Desarollo de Santa Elena SA v Republic of Costa Rica* (2000) 39 ILM 1317, at [103].

compound or simple interest is appropriate in any given case'.[114] In *Wena Hotels*,[115] an ICSID tribunal went further and found that an award of compound interest is generally appropriate in modern arbitration. In recent years, the approach in the *Santa Elena* and *Wena Hotels* arbitrations has been followed by a large number of arbitral tribunals, such that the award of compound interest is no longer an exception.[116] In fact, studies have shown that ICSID awards issued subsequent to *Santa Elena* have more often than not awarded compound interest.[117]

9.78   The reason for this change is that, where the applicable law allows, international arbitral tribunals are reaching the same view as that reached nearly 40 years ago by Judge Howard Holtzmann in his dissenting opinion in *Starrett Housing Corporation v Iran*[118]—namely, that simple interest may not always, in the language of Article 38 of the Draft Articles on Responsibility of States, 'ensure *full* reparation of loss suffered'. As a leading academic in this field has observed:

> [A]lmost all financing and investment vehicles involve compound interest [...] if the claimant could have received compound interest merely by placing its money in a readily available and commonly used investment vehicle, it is neither logical nor equitable to award the claimant only simple interest.[119]

(iv) Enforcing awards that carry interest

9.79   It has already been seen that an award of interest (whether simple or compound) may be prohibited by the relevant national law. If this is the law of the arbitration agreement, or of the contract under which the dispute arose, it seems that an arbitral tribunal has no option but to apply it. Where parties to a contract have chosen (or are deemed to have chosen) as the substantive law of their agreement a law that prohibits the payment of interest, they can scarcely complain if interest is not payable.

9.80   If the law of the place of arbitration (the *lex arbitri*) forbids the payment of interest, it may theoretically be possible for the arbitral tribunal to disregard this local law and apply the substantive law of the contract. But if the provisions of the local law are mandatory, there is a

---

[114] The tribunal in *Santa Elena* set out a number of reasons why compound interest may be justified on an expropriation award, including in order to ensure full reparation under international law (see Secomb, *Interest in International Arbitration* (Oxford University Press, 2019), at 4.133–4.141).

[115] *Wena Hotels Ltd v Egypt*, ICSID Case No. ARB/98/4, Award; IIC 273 (2000), (2002) 41 ILM 896.

[116] With respect to NAFTA claims, see *Pope Talbot v Government of Canada*, Award on Damages, Ad hoc UNCITRAL, IIC 195 (2002); *SD Myers Inc. v Government of Canada*, Second Partial Award, Ad hoc UNCITRAL, IIC 250 (2002). Other awards include *Middle East Cement Shipping and Handling G SA v Arab Republic of Egypt*, ICSID Case No. ARB/99/6, Award, IIC 169 (2002); *CME Czech Republic BV v Czech Republic*, Ad hoc UNCITRAL, Final Award and Separate Opinion, IIC 62 (2003); *Azurix Corporation v Argentine Republic*, ICSID Case No. ARB/ 01/12, Award, IIC 24 (2006); *ADC Affiliate Ltd, ADC & ADMC Management Ltd v Republic of Hungary*, ICSID Case No. ARB/03/16, Award, IIC 1 (2006); *UAB E Energija (Lithuania) v Republic of Latvia*, ICSID Case No. ARB/ 12/33, Award, 22 December 2017; *Gavrilovic and Gavrilovic d.o.o. v Republic of Croatia*, ICSID Case No. ARB/12/ 39, Award, 26 July 2018; *RREEF Infrastructure (G.P.) Limited and RREEF Pan-European Infrastructure Two Lux S.à r.l. v Kingdom of Spain*, ICSID Case No. ARB/13/30, Award, 11 December 2019. All of these decisions are in the public domain and can be found online at http://icsid.worldbank.org.

[117] Uchkunova and Temnikov, 'A procrustean bed: Pre- and post- award interest in ICSID arbitration' (2014) 29 ICSID Rev 648, at 659 (finding that only 10 out of 42 awards post *Saint Elena* applied simple interest).

[118] Iran–US CTR 122, 269 (1983).

[119] Gotanda, 'Awarding interest in international arbitration' (1996) 90 Am J Intl L 40, at 61.

risk that the award could be attacked and rendered invalid under the law of the place where it was made. It follows that an arbitral tribunal sitting, for example, in Saudi Arabia but applying French law as the substantive law of the contract, should be cautious when considering an award in respect of interest, even though this is permitted by the substantive law of the contract. Certainly, any award of interest should be clearly separated from the other parts of the award.[120]

What of the law of the place of enforcement? At the time of the arbitration, it is hardly possible for an arbitral tribunal to do more than make an informed guess as to the likely place of enforcement of its eventual award—and even this will be difficult until the arbitral tribunal has formed a view as to which party is likely to win the arbitration. It is suggested that, in deciding whether or not to award interest, an arbitral tribunal cannot be expected to take into account the likely consequences of such an award in a potential place of enforcement unless the point is expressly brought to its attention by one or both of the parties, in which case the point would have to be considered.   **9.81**

(v) Post-award interest

In general, it is also open to arbitrators to set a rate of post-award interest at any reasonable percentage that they deem appropriate.[121] This is often the rate that would apply to a judgment in the country in which the award is made. But, in modern practice, arbitral tribunals often decline to distinguish between pre- and post-award interest; instead, arbitral tribunals often award a single rate of interest to run for the whole period from a certain date (which may include the date of the breach, or the date on which the loss was suffered, or the date of the request for arbitration, depending on the applicable law and on the way in which the arbitral tribunal decides to exercise any discretion available to it) up to the date of payment of the award.[122]   **9.82**

In some instances, once an arbitral award is enforced in a particular country as a judgment of a court, the post-award interest rate may be replaced by the rate applicable to civil judgments.[123] In England, however, section 49(3) of the English Arbitration Act 1996 permits the arbitral tribunal to exercise its discretion to award interest up to the date of payment.   **9.83**

---

[120] Commentators recommend that awards that might potentially be enforced in Saudi Arabia should contain separate dispositions for compensation and interest respectively (see Secomb, *Interest in International Arbitration* (Oxford University Press, 2019), at 2.136).

[121] For a comprehensive review of the power of arbitrators to award post-award interest, see Gotanda, *Supplemental Damages in Private International Law* (Kluwer Law International, 1998), pp. 85–93.

[122] Sometimes tribunals may impose a higher rate for post-award interest than pre-award interest (see, e.g., *Gold Reserve Inc. v Venezuela,* ICSID Case No. ARB(AF)/09/1, Award of 22 September 2014, at [856]). This approach is intended to incentivise the award-debtor to satisfy the award promptly. In the investment treaty context, however, this approach has been criticised as unjustifiably 'imply[ing]' that there are reasons to believe that the State will not fulfil its international obligation to comply promptly' (see, e.g., *Antin Infrastructure Services Luxembourg S.à.r.l. and Antin Energia Termosolar B.V. v Kingdom of Spain,* ICSID Case No. ARB/13/31, Award, 15 June 2018, at [733]).

[123] In respect of the US see, e.g., *Carte Blanche (Singapore) Pte Ltd v Carte Blanche Intl Ltd,* 888 F2d 260 (2d Cir 1989) 268–70 (holding that the relevant statutory rate was mandatory once the award was submitted to court for enforcement).

(j) Costs

9.84   A claim in respect of the costs incurred by a party in connection with an international arbitration is, in principle, no different from any other claim, except that it is not usually quantified until the end of the arbitral proceedings.

9.85   Given the growing scale and costs of many international arbitrations, it is not surprising that the allocation of costs as between the parties is an increasingly important feature of any proceeding.

9.86   The world's major arbitral institutions generally distinguish between the 'costs of the arbitration' and 'costs of the parties'. These are broad summaries of the terminology used in the UNCITRAL Rules,[124] the ICC Rules,[125] the ICDR Rules,[126] SCC Rules,[127] the Rules of the SIAC,[128] and the LCIA Rules.[129] However, as in the previous edition of this book, this section addresses three separate categories for the purpose of discussing claims in respect of costs:

- 'costs of the tribunal' (that is, the fees and expenses of the tribunal);
- 'costs of the arbitration' (including the charges for administration of the arbitration by an arbitral institution, the hiring of hearing rooms, interpreters and transcript preparation, amongst other things); and
- 'costs of the parties' (including the costs of legal representation, expert witnesses, witness and other travel-related expenditure, amongst other things).

Each of these categories is now considered in turn.

(i) Costs of the tribunal

9.87   The costs of the tribunal usually include not only the fees, and travel-related and other expenses, payable to the individual members of the arbitral tribunal itself, but also any directly related expenses, such as the fees and expenses of any experts appointed by the arbitral tribunal. Also included in the tribunal costs are the fees and expenses of any administrative secretary or registrar,[130] and any other incidental expenses incurred by the arbitral tribunal for the account of the case. In institutional arbitration, the costs of the tribunal are usually fixed or approved by the relevant institution pursuant to its rules. Some institutions, as already stated, adopt an *ad valorem* system of remuneration; others adopt a time/cost system, with an hourly rate that will be fixed by the institution, and will usually be subject to an upper limit. The UNCITRAL Rules require the tribunal to inform the parties of the methodology that it proposes to use in determining its costs and expenses. This methodology is then subject to challenge by the parties. Thereafter, in any award rendered, the tribunal must fix its costs and expenses consistently with this methodology, and any party

---

[124] UNCITRAL Rules, Art. 40.1 and 40.2.
[125] ICC Rules, Art. 38.1.
[126] ICDR Rules, r. 34.
[127] SCC Rules, Arts 49 and 50.
[128] SIAC Rules, Art. 35.1 and 35.2.
[129] LCIA Rules, Art. 28.1.
[130] LCIA Rules, Art. 14.13; SIAC Rules, Art. 35.2.c.

may request the appointing authority or the Secretary-General of the Permanent Court of Arbitration (PCA) to review the calculations.[131]

(ii) Costs of the arbitration

The costs of the arbitration include the charges for administration of the arbitration by an **9.88** arbitral institution (if the arbitration is administered), the costs of hiring rooms for hearings, as well as the fees and expenses of court reporters and interpreters and, where appropriate, those who provide remote hearing services. These costs, except those of the arbitral institution, are usually paid directly by the parties in equal shares, pending the tribunal's determination regarding allocation of costs in its final award. Occasionally, where the arrangements are made by the chairman of the tribunal, or by an administering institution, such costs are paid from the deposits held by the arbitral tribunal or the institution.

(iii) Costs of the parties

The costs of the parties include not only the fees and expenses of the legal representatives **9.89** engaged to represent the parties at the arbitration hearing, but also the costs incurred in the preparation of the case. There will also be other professional fees and expenses, such as those of accountants or expert witnesses, as well as the hotel and travelling expenses of the lawyers, witnesses, and others involved in the case as well as copying and printing charges, telephone, email, and other data expenses. All of these costs are likely to be substantial in a major case.

The parties also incur costs that may be considerable in terms of the time spent on the case **9.90** by senior officials, directors, or employees of the parties themselves, to say nothing of the indirect costs of disruption to their ordinary business. In a major arbitration, a small management team may be constituted to take charge of the case, liaising with the lawyers and reporting back to senior management. The cost of such 'executive', or 'management', time may be high. This poses an important question. If it is possible to recover the legal costs and expenses of bringing or defending a claim in arbitration, should it be possible to recover the cost of executive time, particularly if this includes—as it often does—the cost of in-house counsel?

Traditionally, such costs have been regarded as part of the normal cost of running a business **9.91** enterprise or a government department, rather than the recoverable costs of the winning party.[132] The UNCITRAL Rules, for example, do not include such costs in the definition of what constitutes the 'costs of the arbitration'.[133] It may be possible to include them, however, as part of a claim for the damages caused, for example, by the respondent's breach of contract, although this would pose questions as to whether or not such losses were too remote to be recoverable.

Parties to international arbitrations are increasingly making use of third-party funding, **9.92** which in turn is leading to claims for the award of such costs as part of the 'other costs' incurred in connection with the arbitration. There is authority in England that an arbitrator's general power to award costs includes the power to award the costs of third-party funding

---

[131] UNCITRAL Rules, Art. 41.3 and 41.4.
[132] See Gotanda, *Supplemental Damages in Private International Law* (Kluwer Law International, 1998), p. 191.
[133] UNCITRAL Rules, Art. 40.

as 'other costs' of a party,[134] and given the increasing use of such funding in international arbitration it seems certain that such claims will become more common in the future.

(iv) Assessment

9.93   In assessing how costs should be allocated, many institutional rules expressly adopt the principle that 'costs follow the event'[135] (which used to mean 'winner takes all' but now means, more appropriately, that the allocation of costs between the parties should reflect their relative success or failure in the arbitration). Other rules, however, are less explicit. For example, the SIAC Rules, while recognising the tribunal's power to determine the apportionment of costs, provide no guidance on how it should do so.[136] In the authors' experience, it is increasingly common for arbitral tribunals broadly to adopt the principle that 'costs follow the event' as a starting point, thereafter adjusting the allocation of costs as necessary depending on the specific circumstances of the case.[137]

9.94   Many sets of arbitration rules provide further guidance on the circumstances a tribunal may take into account in allocating costs. For example, the ICC Rules indicate that the tribunal may consider such circumstances as it considers relevant (including the extent to which each party has conducted the arbitration in an expeditious and cost-effective manner) before making a decision on the amount of costs to be awarded.[138] A similar provision appears in the 2020 version of the LCIA Rules.[139] The UNCITRAL Rules adopt a more conservative approach: while recognising that the arbitral tribunal may take into account the circumstances of the case when allocating costs between the parties, they do not explicitly mention cooperative or disruptive behaviour of the parties as a factor.

9.95   Claims for recovery of parties' legal costs usually set out the time spent on the case by individual lawyers within the parties' legal team, together with a note of their individual 'charge-out' rates as fixed by their particular firm. It is then a simple matter of multiplication to arrive at a figure for the total costs of the legal fees. However, there is no necessary correlation between the *time* spent by a lawyer on a particular line of enquiry, research, or argument and the *value* of that time, in terms of the end result. Even if it is assumed that every minute spent on the case was of value—a somewhat brave assumption—the hourly 'charge-out rate' of the lawyers concerned will almost certainly vary from one country to another, and from place to place within the same country. In consequence, the tribunal will need to exercise its own judgement and experience in deciding (in retrospect) broadly how much time should reasonably have been spent on the case and what hourly rates should reasonably have been charged.

9.96   A less difficult problem is that of deciding *when* the assessment of costs should be made. Arbitration rules, such as those of UNCITRAL[140] and the SCC,[141] give their answer,

---

[134]   *Essar Oilfields Services Limited v Norscot Rig Management PVT Limited* [2016] EWHC 2361 (dismissing a serious irregularity challenge under the English Arbitration Act, s. 68(2)(b) to an ICC award in which the arbitrator awarded Norscot the £1.94 million costs of third-party funding it had obtained in order to bring the arbitration).

[135]   CIETAC Rules, Art. 52(2); DIS Rules, Art. 35.2; LCIA Rules, Art. 28.4; PCA Rules, Art. 42(1); UNCITRAL Rules, Art. 42(1).

[136]   SIAC Rules, rr. 35.2, 37.

[137]   Decisions on Costs in International Arbitration, 2015(2) ICC Dispute Resolution Bulletin, para. 13.

[138]   ICC Rules, Art. 38.5.

[139]   LCIA Rules, Art. 28.4.

[140]   UNCITRAL Rules, Art. 40.

[141]   SCC Rules, Art. 49.5.

providing for the costs of the arbitration to be fixed in the award. The ICC Rules[142] provide differently, permitting the tribunal to make decisions as to costs at any time during
the arbitration. This means that if there is, for instance, an application to stop the arbitration on the grounds of lack of jurisdiction and this application is refused, the arbitral tribunal, in giving its decision, would be entitled to order the unsuccessful applicant
to pay the costs of the application. In practice, most tribunals prefer not to spend time
dealing with applications for costs during the course of the proceedings, but leave it to
their final award.

In the authors' experience, there is very much more concern by lawyers and their clients   **9.97**
than was once the case, about the money they have spent and are spending on the arbitration and the likelihood of recovering some, if not all, of that money. This is not surprising,
given the very substantial costs that may be incurred, with the total sum in high profile
cases running into many millions of dollars. This emphasis on costs places an additional
burden on the tribunal, in deciding what specific items of costs to award and how to allocate them as between the parties.

In previous editions of this book, the authors suggested that most international arbitral   **9.98**
tribunals that make an award of costs in favour of the winning party tend to adopt a
'broad-brush' approach in assessing the amount to be paid, rather than going through the
bill item by item as a trained and experienced costs assessor would do. Based on our experience both as counsel and as arbitrator, we still think this is the case. However, we then
went on to commend the approach of Judge Holtzmann, an experienced US arbitrator
who, in a case in the Iran–United States Claims Tribunal, proposed criteria that included
the following questions for the tribunal to ask itself:

- Is the amount of the costs claimed reasonable?
- Are the circumstances of the particular case such as to make it reasonable to apportion
  such costs?

On the criteria of reasonableness, Judge Holtzmann said: **9.99**

> The classic test of reasonableness is not, however, an invitation to mere subjectivity.
> Objective tests of reasonableness of lawyers' fees are well known. Such tests typically as-
> sign weight primarily to the time spent and complexity of the case. In modern practice,
> the amount of time required to be spent is often a gauge of the extent of the complex-
> ities involved. Where the Tribunal is presented with copies of bills for services, or other
> appropriate evidence, indicating the time spent, the hourly billing rate, and a general
> description of the professional services rendered, its task need be neither onerous nor
> mysterious. The range of typical hourly billing rates is generally known and, as evidence
> before the Tribunal in various cases including this one indicates, it does not greatly differ
> between the US and countries of Western Europe, where both claimants and respondents
> before the Tribunal typically hire their outside counsel. Just how much time any lawyer
> reasonably needs to accomplish a task can be measured by the number of issues involved
> in a case and the amount of evidence requiring analysis and presentation. While legal
> fees are not to be calculated on the basis of the pounds of paper involved, the Tribunal by

---

[142] ICC Rules, Art. 38.3.

the end of a case is able to have a fair idea, on the basis of the submissions made by both sides, of the approximate extent of the effort that was reasonably required. Nor should the Tribunal neglect to consider the reality that legal bills are usually first submitted to businessmen. The pragmatic fact that a businessman has agreed to pay a bill, not knowing whether or not the Tribunal would reimburse the expenses, is a strong indication that the amount billed was considered reasonable by a reasonable man spending his own money, or the money of the corporation he serves.[143]

9.100   A number of subsequent Iran–United States Claims Tribunal awards have referred to, and adopted, this test as a guide.[144] Furthermore, in the more recent, much publicised, and very substantial *Yukos* cases,[145] a highly distinguished tribunal, also applying the UNCITRAL Rules, adopted a similar approach. Judge Holtzmann's statement, made over thirty years ago, has stood the test of time well. However, there are now two comments which we think we should make. First, whilst the fees charged by US lawyers in international arbitrations are perhaps, as Judge Holtzmann says, still comparable 'to those charged in countries of Western Europe', this may not be correct for all of the rest of the world; secondly, whilst the fact that the client ('a businessman') has agreed to the amount of the fees is certainly a factor to be taken into consideration, it may not be a 'strong indication' that those fees are reasonable, but merely that the businessman concerned is accustomed to a level of fees that may well be very much higher than other businessmen, states, or corporations can afford.

(k) Requirements imposed by national law

9.101   Most national legislation is silent concerning awards of costs in international arbitrations.[146] The Model Law also does not address this question. Some states that have adopted the Model Law have added provisions regarding awards of the costs of arbitration, but not many.[147] As with interest, and indeed all other matters concerning the powers of the tribunal, any specific provisions of the *lex arbitri* concerning costs must be respected. However, the practices of national courts in following their own rules in relation to awarding costs do not appear to be an appropriate guide for the way in which an international tribunal should exercise the discretion granted to it under either the relevant set of rules or the *lex arbitri*.[148] It is suggested that international tribunals, wherever the seat of arbitration, should be guided by the *lex arbitri* and by the applicable substantive law as to the scope of its discretion, and by the applicable arbitration rules (if any) as to the exercise of that discretion.

---

[143] Separate opinion of Judge Holtzmann, reported in [1985] Iranian Assets Litigation Reporter 10860, at 10863; (1985) 8 Iran–US CTR 329, at 332–333.

[144] For a detailed review of the practices of the Iran–United States Claims Tribunal, see van Hof, *Commentary on the UNCITRAL Arbitration Rules* (Kluwer Law International, 1991), pp. 293–311.

[145] For example, see *Yukos Universal Ltd (Isle of Man) v The Russian Federation*, PCA Case No. AA 227, UNCITRAL, 18 July 2014, at [1887].

[146] By way of exception, see the English Arbitration Act, s. 61.

[147] Born, *International Commercial Arbitration* (2nd edn, Kluwer Law International, 2014), p. 3087.

[148] For a comprehensive review of the practices of international tribunals concerning the award of costs, see Gotanda, *Supplemental Damages in Private International Law* (Kluwer Law International, 1998), pp. 173–192.

D. Deliberations and Decisions of the Tribunal

(a) Introduction

The purpose of an arbitration is to arrive at a binding and enforceable decision. For the parties and their lawyers, it is the dispositive section of an award that is most important. Yet there is more to an award, including how a tribunal of arbitrators goes about reaching its decision, which has become an increasing feature of the literature concerning international arbitration.[149] **9.102**

The task that faces arbitral tribunals is not easy. A leading English judge described judicial decision making as follows: **9.103**

> The judge's role in determining what happened at some time in the past is not of course peculiar to him. Historians, auditors, accident investigators of all kinds, loss adjusters and doctors are among those who, to a greater or lesser extent, may be called upon to perform a similar function. But there are three features of the judge's role which will not apply to all these other investigations. First, he is always presented with conflicting versions of the events in question: if there is no effective dispute, there is nothing for him to decide. Secondly, his determination necessarily takes place subject to formality and restraints (evidential or otherwise) attendant upon proceedings in court. Thirdly, his determination has a direct practical effect upon people's lives in terms of their pockets, activities or reputations.[150]

The same task faces an arbitral tribunal, but with a number of important differences. **9.104**

First, such an arbitral tribunal is not a permanent court or tribunal (except in special cases such as the Iran–US Claims Tribunal). Secondly, the tribunal may be composed of arbitrators of different professions: accountants, engineers, or whatever the case may require. Thirdly, even if all of the members of the tribunal are lawyers, they will often be of different nationalities, with different languages and different legal backgrounds—common law, civil law, *Shari'ah*, and so forth. **9.105**

How will this disparate, ad hoc group of people set about trying to reach their decision? They will read the parties' submissions, the witness statements, and the (sometimes copious) number of documents filed in support of each party's case; they will listen to evidence and oral argument. After this, although (as the saying goes) they may not be any wiser, they should certainly be better informed. As a case proceeds, each arbitrator will no doubt begin to form his or her own view as to how the various issues that have arisen ought to be determined, but the tribunal should arrive at a decision together. If the tribunal consists of three arbitrators, there must be some exchange of views, some dialogue between them, if they are to do so. **9.106**

---

[149] See, e.g., Reed, 'Chapter 6: Arbitral decision-making: Art, science or sport? (Sixth Kaplan Lecture, December 3, 2012)', in Hong Kong International Arbitration Centre (ed) *International Arbitration: Issues, Perspectives and Practice: Liber Amicorum Neil Kaplan* (Kluwer Law International, 2018), pp. 161–174.

[150] Bingham, *The Business of Judging* (Oxford University Press, 2000), p. 4.

9.107   There are no set rules as to how a decision should be made. Each arbitration is different and each arbitral tribunal is different. What works well with one tribunal may not work at all with another. However, the advice written by a former president of the LCIA may serve as a useful guideline:

> While it is important for the chairman not to rush his fellow arbitrators into reaching a definitive decision on all outstanding issues—indeed, it is incumbent on the chairman to remind the members of the tribunal that their work is only just beginning and that any opinions expressed will be considered to be provisional—it is, however, crucial to ascertain whether or not a consensus seems likely to emerge on one or more of the issues to be decided. If there is disagreement between the two party-appointed arbitrators, the chairman will begin to earn his extra stipend. In the event a consensus on certain issues is clear, the chairman will generally offer to prepare a first draft of an eventual award, for discussion at a later date.
>
> No member of the tribunal must exert any pressure on his colleagues during this first session. This initial session should provide an opportunity for all arbitrators to engage in a relaxed dialogue with one another.
>
> Each arbitrator must feel that he is allowed to 'think out loud' in this informal setting. Personally, whether I serve as chairman or party-designated arbitrator, I tend to listen at least as much as to speak during such a first encounter. I wish my colleagues to know what my initial views are, but I also want to know how my colleagues believe they can inform the decision-making process which has begun.[151]

9.108   This passage raises an interesting question as to whether there is any difference between, on the one hand, informal discussions among members of the tribunal (for example over a meal or during a coffee break) and, on the other, formal deliberations (in the French sense). One of the reasons why the issue of deliberations is infrequently addressed is undoubtedly the fact that some systems encourage secrecy in the deliberative process. For example, in French law, as in some other civil law countries, the deliberations of the arbitrators are indeed 'secret'.[152] In French law, the interchange of views between arbitrators is formalised as a '*deliberation*'. The Civil Code that governs French internal (or domestic) arbitrations requires the arbitrators to fix the date at which their deliberations will start (*le délibéré sera prononcé*),[153] after which no further submissions by the parties are allowed. One distinguished French academician and author considers the rule that there must be a '*deliberation*' before there is any award by the tribunal to be a rule of international public order.[154] Although it does not necessarily follow that the deliberations should be secret, for another French commentator the rule that such a '*deliberation*' should be, and should remain, so is a 'fundamental principle, which constitutes one of the mainsprings of arbitration, as it does of

---

[151] Fortier, 'The tribunal's deliberations', in Newman and Hill (eds) *The Leading Arbitrators' Guide to International Arbitration* (2nd edn, Juris, 2008), pp. 479–480.

[152] French Civil Code, Art. 1479, states: 'Les délibérations du tribunal arbitral sont secrètes.'

[153] French Civil Code, Art. 1468, states: 'Le tribunal arbitral fixe la date à laquelle le délibéré sera prononcé. Au cours du délibéré, aucune demande ne peut être formée, aucun moyen soulevé et aucune pièce produite, si ce n'est à la demande du tribunal arbitral.'

[154] Bredin, 'Le secret du délibéré arbitral', in *Études Offertes à Pierre Bellet* (Litec, 1991). See also Savage and Gaillard (eds) *Fouchard, Gaillard, Goldman on International Commercial Arbitration* (Kluwer, 1999), para. 1369 (where proper deliberations are considered 'a requirement of international procedural public policy').

all judicial decisions'.[155] However, this is not solely a French position. Rule 15 of the ICSID Rules states:

(1) The deliberations of the Tribunal shall take place in private and remain secret.

(2) Only members of the Tribunal shall take part in its deliberations. No other person shall be admitted unless the Tribunal decides otherwise.

In a well-known case,[156] the Swedish Court of Appeal discussed what is necessary for a proper deliberation when considering a request by the Czech Republic to set aside an arbitral award. One of the grounds put forward was that the arbitrator nominated by the Czech Republic had, as he alleged in his dissenting opinion, been deliberately excluded by his fellow arbitrators from the deliberations of the tribunal. The Court referred to a seemingly conflicting balance of considerations: the equality of the arbitrators, balanced against the need for the tribunal to reach a conclusion without undue delay. The Court said, in summary, that the arbitrators should be treated equally, but that the procedures adopted should also be cost-effective and flexible. There were no formal rules, and so the deliberations might be oral or written, or both; deadlines could be set, but could also be changed as required, and so forth. The Swedish Court of Appeal added that whilst due process must be guaranteed: **9.109**

[W]hen two arbitrators have agreed upon the outcome of the dispute, the third arbitrator cannot prolong the deliberations by demanding continued discussions in an attempt to persuade the others as to the correctness of his opinion. The dissenting arbitrator is thus not afforded any opportunity to delay the writing of the award.[157]

The rule as to the secrecy, or confidentiality, of the tribunal's discussions has significant consequences.[158] It was considered by a former president of the ICJ, in considering a challenge to one of the members of the Iran–United States Claims Tribunal, whose impartiality had been questioned on the basis of a dissenting opinion that he had issued. In the course of the decision on the challenge, it was held that: **9.110**

A rule of the confidentiality of the deliberations must, if it is to be effective, apply generally to the deliberation stage of a tribunal's proceedings and cannot realistically be confined to what is said in a formal meeting of all the members in the deliberation room. The form or forms the deliberation takes varies greatly from one tribunal to another. Anybody who has had experience of courts and tribunals knows perfectly well that much of the deliberation

---

[155] De Boisséson, *Le Droit Français de l'Arbitrage National et International* (Joly, 1990), p. 296. See also the comment in Robert, *L'Arbitrage: Droit Interne, Droit International Privé* (5th edn, Dalloz, 1983), para. 360 (authors' translation): 'Although it is practised according to a certain number of foreign laws, notably Anglo-Saxon, the dissenting opinion is prohibited in French domestic law since it violates the secrecy of the tribunal's deliberation [...]. ' Under German law, unless provided otherwise by the arbitration agreement, deliberations are also secret: see *Münchener Kommentar zur Zivilprozessordnung: ZPO*, § 1052 Rn 1-5. In France, there may be limited exceptions to the general rule (e.g., in the context of allegations of fraud or corruption). For example, in the *Tapie* case the French courts did have regard to communications between a party, its appointee on the tribunal, and the tribunal president, in order to establish whether the deliberative process was free of external influence (see Arrêt No. 842 du 18 mai 2017 (15-2.683, 16-10.339, 16-10.344), Cass Comm, 18 May 2017).

[156] *Czech Republic v CME Czech Republic BV*, Case No. T 8735–01, Svea Court of Appeal, IIC 63 (2003). An English translation of the judgment can be found online at http://italaw.com/sites/default/files/case-documents/ita0182.pdf; a case summary is available at [2003] Stockholm Arb Rep 167.

[157] *Czech Republic v CME Czech Republic BV*, in the English translation, at 87; in the case summary, at 180.

[158] See Gaillard and Savage (eds) *Fouchard, Gaillard, and Goldman on International Commercial Arbitration* (Kluwer Law International, 1999), para. 1374.

work, even in courts like the ICJ which have formal rules governing the deliberation, is done less formally. In particular the task of drafting is better done in small groups rather than by the whole court attempting to draft round the table. Revelations of such informal discussion and of suggestions made could be very damaging and seriously threaten the whole deliberation process.[159]

9.111 As noted, there must obviously be a serious interchange of views between the members of the tribunal as they try to arrive at a decision that can be expressed in their award. This interchange of views may be characterised, as it is in the ICSID Rules and in the French Civil Code, as a '*deliberation*', but this does not mean that the members of the tribunal have to sit together in solemn conclave, like cardinals electing a new pope, until a decision is reached.

9.112 What is likely to happen in practice is that the arbitrators exchange views informally, as the case progresses—particularly in the course of the hearing or immediately upon its conclusion—and then decide how to proceed with the formulation of their award. The chairman of the tribunal often prepares a list of the issues that he or she considers critical, then asks the co-arbitrators to amend, or add to, this list and perhaps express a preliminary view on the issues raised—either orally or, more commonly, in writing— with each arbitrator being given the opportunity to comment upon what the others have written.

9.113 Where the arbitral tribunal consists of a sole arbitrator, the need to consult with other members of the tribunal and to try to reconcile possibly differing opinions does not arise. However, the sole arbitrator will still need to consider the evidence and arguments of the parties, work through a list of the significant issues, and generally come to a conclusion on the matters in dispute as part of the process of drafting an award.

9.114 For a sole arbitrator, it is only his or her decision that counts. But what happens when there is a tribunal of three arbitrators and, despite their best efforts, they find themselves unable to agree? Ideally, decisions are made unanimously; but there must be a 'fall-back' position, and, on this, the international and institutional rules of arbitration differ. Some favour majority voting; others give the presiding arbitrator a decisive role.

(b) Tribunal psychology

9.115 Most international arbitrations are determined by an arbitral tribunal composed of three arbitrators. The aim of their deliberations must be to achieve a unanimous award, since this will be seen as both authoritative and conclusive. If unanimity cannot be achieved, however, the next best thing is to have a majority award, rather than an award by the chairman alone—or no award at all. In one of the Iran–United States arbitrations, a US-appointed arbitrator concurred in a majority award, although he thought that the damages awarded were half what they should have been. 'Why then do I concur in this inadequate award?' he

---

[159] Sir Robert Jennings, Decision of 7 May 2001, at 7. A summary of the decision was published at (2001) 16 Mealey's Int Arb Rep 2. The full text is available for purchase from Mealey's online.

asked rhetorically; 'Because', he answered, 'there are circumstances in which "something is better than nothing".[160]

There may be concern over the way in which arbitrators will conduct themselves in deliberations when they have been directly appointed by one of the parties to a dispute. However, parties rarely abuse the arbitral process to the extent of nominating an arbitrator whose specific function is to vote for the party who nominated him or her, although they do appoint arbitrators whom they believe are likely to be sympathetic to the case that they wish to advance during the proceedings. As has been said: **9.116**

> It should not be surprising if party appointed arbitrators tend to view the facts and law in a light similar to their appointing parties. After all, the parties are careful to select arbitrators with views similar to theirs. But this does not mean that arbitrators will violate their duty of impartiality and independence.[161]

In an international arbitration, each arbitrator, however appointed, is under a duty to act impartially and to reach a determination of the issues in a fair and unbiased manner.[162] It follows that it would be entirely improper if a party-nominated arbitrator were to hold private discussions with the party who nominated that arbitrator about the substance of the dispute. However, it is not improper for a party-nominated arbitrator to ensure that the arbitral tribunal properly understands the case being advanced by that party,[163] and a party-nominated arbitrator who is convinced of the merits of the case being put forward by the appointing party can have a significant impact on the private deliberations of the arbitral tribunal when the award is discussed. Interestingly, the UNCITRAL Rules extend the duty of the arbitrator in relation to disclosing circumstances giving rise to a potential conflict of interest so that it is owed not only to the parties, but also to the other members of the tribunal.[164]   **9.117**

The behaviour of the party-appointed arbitrators affects the dynamics of deliberations for the presiding arbitrator, although the presiding arbitrator will form his or her own view of the case. If it is difficult to achieve a majority award, inevitably the presiding arbitrator leans towards a compromise with a party-nominated arbitrator who follows the proceedings intelligently, asks good questions of each party, and puts forward well-reasoned arguments,   **9.118**

---

[160] *Economy Forms Corporation v Islamic Republic of Iran*, Award, Case No. 55-165-1, 13 June 1983, quoted in Schwebel, 'The majority vote of an arbitral tribunal' (1991) 2 Am Rev Intl Arb 402, at 409.

[161] Mosk and Ginsburg, *Dissenting Opinions in International Arbitration* (Liber Amicorum Bengt Broms, 1999), p. 275.

[162] See Chapter 5, paragraphs 5.77–5.85. In England, a party-appointed arbitrator is expected to come up to the same high standards of fairness and impartiality as the person chairing the tribunal (see *Halliburton v Chubb* [2020] UKSC 48, at 63).

[163] Indeed, this is a material part of the duties of party-nominated arbitrators. A party-nominated arbitrator should do his or her best to ensure that he or she understands the case being put forward by the party that nominated him or her and should seek to make sure that the arbitral tribunal as a whole is in the same position. It is, of course, necessary for party-nominated arbitrators to consider carefully the merits of the arguments on both sides and not to be seen as favouring appointing parties. For concerns about partisanship amongst party-appointed arbitrators, see Paulsson, 'Moral hazard in international dispute resolution' (2010) 25 ICSID Review, Foreign Investment Law Journal 339 and van den Berg, 'Dissenting opinions by party-appointed arbitrators in investment arbitration', in Mahnoush Arsanjani et al. (eds) *Looking to the Future: Essays on International Law in Honor of W Michael Reisman* (Brill Academic, 2010), p. 821. In contrast, for a defence of party-appointed arbitrators, see Brower and Rosenberg, 'The death of the two-headed nightingale: Why the Paulsson-van den Berg presumption that party-appointed arbitrators are untrustworthy is wrongheaded' (2013) Arb Intl 29(1) 7–44.

[164] UNCITRAL Rules, Art. 11.

rather than with someone who shows little interest in the proceedings and gives the impression of being there simply as the advocate nominee or mouthpiece of the appointing party.

(c) Bargaining process

9.119   An award of monetary compensation arrived at by a majority vote is sometimes the result of a bargaining process in the deliberations that might be more common in a marketplace than in a judicial, or quasi-judicial, proceeding. To describe it as a process of eliminating alternatives by 'a proper sequence of votes' is a euphemism. However, particularly when carried out in a structured manner and in relation to pre-defined issues, 'bargaining' may be a sensible way in which to proceed. Indeed, such a procedure is envisaged in the 1966 European Convention providing a Uniform Law on Arbitration (known as the 'Strasbourg Uniform Law'), which provides that:

> Except where otherwise stipulated, if the arbitrators are to award a sum of money, and a majority cannot be obtained for any particular sum, the votes for the highest sum shall be counted as votes for the next highest sum until a majority is obtained.[165]

9.120   Where there are a number of different issues, it is theoretically possible for the members of the arbitral tribunal to be split on some issues and unanimous on others. In such cases, the question arises as to whether all of the issues should be decided by the presiding arbitrator alone (if this is permitted under the relevant rules of arbitration)[166] or whether the award may be divided into various parts. If there is lack of unanimity in relation to one or two issues out of many issues, the dispositive part of the award could reflect this by recording that those issues were decided by a majority of the tribunal, rather than by the tribunal as a whole. If there is no majority in relation to a considerable number of issues, the award as a whole may have to be that of the presiding arbitrator if the relevant rules permit; otherwise, the arbitrators will have to continue, in one way or another, to try to reach a majority decision.

(d) Majority voting

9.121   As an example of majority voting, Article 33.1 of the UNCITRAL Rules provides: 'When there is more than one arbitrator, any award or other decision of the arbitral tribunal shall be made by a majority of the arbitrators.' However, Article 33.2 makes an exception to this rule in relation to questions of procedure and allows the presiding arbitrator to decide such questions on his or her own, subject to revision by the tribunal. This provision gives rise to two potential problems.

9.122   The first is how to identify procedural issues: for example, is a determination of the place of arbitration under Article 18 of the Rules a question of procedure? If it is, then, in the absence of a majority, the presiding arbitrator may decide. However, Professor Pieter Sanders,

---

[165] Strasbourg Uniform Law, Annex I, Art. 22(3).
[166] See, e.g., LCIA Rules, Art. 26.5.

as special consultant to the UNCITRAL Secretariat, played a major role in drafting the original UNCITRAL Rules. He expressed the view that the determination of the place of arbitration should *not* be considered a procedural question; and should therefore not be a function of the presiding arbitrator alone.[167]

The second problem is that, in order to achieve an award, a majority must be reached, because there is no fall-back position under Article 33.1. Professor Sanders stated that 'the arbitrators are [...] forced to continue their deliberations until a majority, and probably a compromise solution, has been reached'.[168] **9.123**

This is a potentially serious defect in the UNCITRAL Rules, since there may be cases in which it is genuinely impossible to achieve a majority.[169] In construction arbitrations, for example, there are often many different issues in relation to separate claims and it is possible for each individual arbitrator to have a different view on these different issues. Furthermore, the arbitrators may have widely differing views on questions of *quantum* in such cases, with no real possibility of a compromise solution being achieved in order to obtain a majority award. The Model Law, Article 29 of which adopts the same position as the UNCITRAL Rules, is open to the same criticism. **9.124**

The approach in the ICC Rules is different. These rules provide that where the arbitral tribunal is composed of more than one arbitrator, the award, if not unanimous, may be made by a majority of the tribunal; and if there is no majority, the chairman of the arbitral tribunal makes the decision alone.[170] The same approach is adopted in the Swiss Private International Law Act 1987 (Swiss PIL), the Swiss Rules, the English Arbitration Act 1996, and the LCIA Rules.[171] **9.125**

In contrast to the UNCITRAL Rules, under the ICC Rules, the Swiss Rules, and the LCIA Rules, the pressure is on each of the co-arbitrators to join the presiding arbitrator in forming a majority. This is because the presiding arbitrator is entitled to make an award alone. However, if this happens, the party-chosen arbitrators will not have participated in the award;[172] instead, the award will have been made by a person who may have been chosen for the parties by an arbitral institution or some other appointing authority. **9.126**

In ICSID arbitrations, majority rule also prevails. The ICSID Convention provides that '[t]he Tribunal shall decide questions by a majority of the votes of all its members',[173] and this provision is carried into effect by the ICSID Rules, Rule 16.1 which states: 'Decisions **9.127**

---

[167] (1977) II YBCA 172, at 194.

[168] Ibid., at 208.

[169] Parties may of course consider modifying Art. 33(1) in order to remove the majority requirement in the event of a deadlock (see UNCITRAL Report of 51st Session, 10 November 2009, UN Doc A/CN.9/684, para. 61 ('the Working Group emphasized that the parties had the ability in such situations to agree to another method of decision-making')).

[170] ICC Rules, Art. 32.1. In such a case, the presiding arbitrator's role is very similar, but not identical, to that of an umpire. The difference is that an umpire is not required to make a decision unless and until the arbitrators appointed by the parties disagree. If they disagree, they take no further part in the proceedings and the umpire proceeds as if he or she were sole arbitrator.

[171] LCIA Rules, Art. 26.5; Swiss PIL, Ch. 12, s. 189; English Arbitration Act 1996, s. 20(3)–(4); Swiss Rules, Art. 31.1. In the authors' experience, president-only awards are a rare occurrence. One reported example is the RAKTA case under the 1955 ICC Rules (see ICC Case No. 1703/1971, summarised in Craig, Park, and Paulsson, *International Chamber of Commerce Arbitration* (3rd edn, Oceana Publications, 2000), p. 370).

[172] LCIA Rules, Art. 26.5.

[173] ICSID Convention, Art. 48(1).

of the Commission shall be taken by a majority of the votes of all its members. Abstention shall count as a negative vote.' In this context, 'majority rule' means that at least two of the three members of the arbitral tribunal must be prepared to agree with each other, whatever element of bargaining or compromise this might involve. An arbitral tribunal is bound to render a decision or to resign. It is not permitted to say that it is undecided and unable to make an award. It may not bring in a finding of *non liquet* (on the ground of silence, or obscurity of the law, or otherwise).[174]

9.128   It may be difficult for individual members of an arbitral tribunal to alter their respective positions so as to achieve the necessary majority. The notes to the ICSID Rules record that, when the Rules were originally formulated, consideration was given to providing for the possibility of the arbitral tribunal being unable to reach a majority decision. It was concluded, however, that no problem would arise with questions that admitted of only a positive or a negative answer. If a positive proposition were to fail to achieve a majority, it would automatically fail since, under the ICSID Rules, an abstention is counted as a negative vote. Where the question could not be answered by a simple 'yes' or 'no', as in the determination of the amount of compensation to be awarded, it was concluded that 'a decision can normally be reached by a proper sequence of votes by which alternatives are successively eliminated'.[175]

9.129   Thus there are various ways in which the awards of three-member arbitral tribunals may be made. They may be made unanimously, or by a majority, or by the presiding arbitrator alone if he or she is empowered to decide alone under the rules governing the proceedings.

(e) Concurring and dissenting opinions

(i) Concurring opinions

9.130   A 'separate', or 'concurring', opinion is one that is given by an arbitrator who agrees with the result of the arbitration, but who either does not agree with the reasoning or does not agree with the way in which the award is formulated. These opinions are rarely given in commercial arbitrations. They are more frequently found in investment treaty arbitrations, in which the practice of the ICJ tends to be followed.[176]

(ii) Dissenting opinions

9.131   Dissenting opinions pose greater problems and are less frequently delivered. There is a broad division of philosophy and practice as to whether the giving of dissenting opinions should be permitted. In arbitrations between states, the right to submit a dissenting opinion was asserted as long ago as the middle of the nineteenth century, in the *Alabama Claims* arbitration[177] between the United Kingdom and the United States. The Statute of the ICJ

---

[174] ICSID Convention, Art. 42(2). If it is not possible to form a majority, the proper course is for the arbitrators to resign and for a replacement tribunal to be appointed. For an example in which this occurred, see *Tokios Tokeles v Ukraine*, ICSID Case No. ARB/02/18, Decision on Jurisdiction, 29 April 2004.

[175] Note D to Arbitration Rule 47 of 1968, (1968) 1 ICSID Reports 108.

[176] The ICJ Statute, Art. 57 is generally interpreted as permitting the practice of giving separate opinions: see Born, *International Commercial Arbitration* (2nd edn, Kluwer Law International, 2014), pp. 3052–3053.

[177] Alabama Claims of the United States of America against Great Britain, Award rendered on 14 September 1872 by the Tribunal of Arbitration established by Article I of the Treaty of Washington of 8 May 1871. For a discussion of the proceedings, see Cushing, *The Treaty of Washington: Its Negotiation, Execution, and the Discussions*

expressly entitles judges in the minority to deliver dissenting opinions,[178] and this right has been exercised frequently not only in judgments, but also in connection with procedural orders, advisory opinions, and interim proceedings.

When arbitrators dissent in international arbitrations, they often simply refuse to sign the award. Where this is done, the dissenting opinion may be annexed to the award if the other arbitrators agree, or it may be delivered to the parties separately. In either case, the dissenting opinion does not form part of the award itself: it is not an 'award', but an *opinion*.[179]   **9.132**

(iii) Position in national laws

While modern arbitration legislation tends not to refer expressly to dissenting opinions, many such laws permit such opinions. For example, although there is no mention of dissenting opinions in the Swiss PIL, a commentator states that an arbitrator has the right to give reasons for his dissent.[180] Similarly, section 52(3) of the English Arbitration Act 1996 provides that the award shall be signed by all the arbitrators or all those assenting to the award, thus envisaging the possibility that an arbitrator might dissent.[181] The Netherlands Arbitration Act 2015 provides that if 'a minority of the arbitrators refuse to sign [the award], the other arbitrators shall make mention thereof in the award signed by them', similarly envisaging both the possibility that an arbitrator may dissent, and confirming that such dissent will not form part of the award.[182] In France, it is sometimes said that the principle of the secrecy of the deliberations is such that even to disclose that the decision was unanimous is a breach of secrecy.[183] On the face of it, such an approach is not favourable to dissenting opinions, yet such opinions are given in international arbitration, even in France. No prohibition against dissenting opinions is known in the common law countries. Indeed, it is not unusual for common law arbitrators to consider themselves under a duty to inform the tribunal and the parties of their reasons for any dissent.   **9.133**

(iv) Position under institutional rules

ICSID is alone amongst the leading arbitral institutions in expressly recognising in its Rules the right of an arbitrator to issue an individual opinion and, in particular, a dissenting opinion: 'Any member of the Tribunal may attach his individual opinion to the award, whether he dissents from the majority or not, or a statement of his dissent.'[184] The LCIA   **9.134**

Relating Thereto (Harper & Bros, 1873). See also Bingham, *Lives of the Law* (Oxford University Press, 2011), 'The *Alabama* Claims and the International Rule of Law'.

[178] ICJ Statute, Art. 57.
[179] See, e.g., Redfern, 'Dissenting opinions in international commercial arbitration: The good, the bad and the ugly' (2004) 20 Arb Intl 223, at 236, arguing that dissenting opinions are unwelcome in international commercial arbitration, because: 'It is the *decision* which matters; and it matters *not* as a guide to the opinions of a particular arbitrator, or as an indication of the future development of the law, but because it resolves the particular dispute that divides the parties; and it resolves that dispute as part of a private, not public, dispute resolution process that the parties themselves have chosen.'
[180] Blessing, 'The new International Arbitration Law in Switzerland' (1988) 5 J Intl Arb 9, at 66.
[181] Other laws are more explicit. For example, the Brazilian Arbitration Act provides that '[A] dissenting arbitrator may, if he so wishes, render a separate decision' (Art. 24(2)).
[182] Netherlands Arbitration Act 2015, Art. 1057(3). See also Sanders and van den Berg, *The Netherlands Arbitration Act 1986* (Kluwer Law and Taxation, 1987), p. 33.
[183] Cass. Soc. 9 November 1945, Gaz. Pal. 1946 1.22. Note, however, Professor Bredin's comment that legal opinion on this point seems to be divided: Bredin, 'Le secret du délibéré arbitral', in *Études Offertes à Pierre Bellet* (Litec, 1991), p. 71.
[184] ICSID Rules, r. 47(3); ICSID Convention, Art. 48(4).

Rules do not mention dissenting opinions, although, as already stated, the right of an arbitrator to issue a dissenting opinion is recognised in England[185] and it may be assumed that the draftsmen considered that no express provision was necessary. Nor do the ICDR or ICC Rules contain any provision relating to dissenting opinions.

9.135   The way in which dissenting opinions are handled in ICC arbitrations is unique because of the provisions of the ICC Rules relating to scrutiny of awards.[186] At one time, the ICC discouraged the submission of dissenting opinions, but in 1985 a working party was set up to consider dissenting opinions, and its final report was adopted in 1988.[187] The report did not rule out dissenting opinions; instead, it suggested that the only circumstances in which a dissenting opinion should *not* be sent to the parties with the award was where it is prohibited by law, or where the validity of the award might be imperilled, either in the place of arbitration or (to the extent that this could be foreseen) in the country of enforcement. The ICC has issued guidelines to its staff that reflect the conclusions of the working group and, in practice, dissenting opinions are sent out by the ICC with the majority award (where applicable). (The ICC regularly issues statistics which, in relation to dissenting opinions, usually reveal that almost all dissenting opinions are given by party-appointed arbitrators in favour of the party that appointed them.)[188]

(v) Practice at the Iran–United States Claims Tribunal

9.136   Separate and dissenting opinions were submitted by both the Iranian and US arbitrators in many reported cases. In one of these, the dissenting arbitrator went too far, when the dissenting judge indicated that the other two arbitrators had agreed with one of his views in deliberations.[189] In another case, problems were caused when the dissenting opinion was issued after the majority decision was published and contained allegations of procedural misconduct on the part of the majority arbitrators.[190] The majority arbitrators felt compelled to file an additional opinion, whereupon the dissenting arbitrator continued the process by issuing yet another opinion. This was, in turn, followed by a second additional opinion by the chairman, who, whilst stating that he would make no further response, indicated that he considered this exceptional procedure to be necessary to vindicate the integrity of the tribunal and its staff, and to answer allegations that were factually incorrect. Acrimonious trading of allegations and insults could go on indefinitely, and it is clearly desirable that the arbitrators should disclose their concerns to each other in an exchange of draft opinions *before* the formal issue of the majority award and the dissenting opinion.

---

[185] See, e.g., *Bank Mellat v GAA Development Construction Co.* [1988] 2 Lloyd's Rep 44, *per* Steyn J, (1990) XV YBCA 521.

[186] Discussed further in paragraph 9.201. The ICC Rules, Art. 34 provides that no award shall be rendered by the arbitral tribunal until it has been approved by the ICC Court.

[187] ICC, *Final Report of the Working Party on Dissenting Opinions* (1991) 2 ICC International Court of Arbitration Bulletin 32.

[188] For arbitrations involving dissenting opinions, an ICC Court member will generally draft a report with recommendations on the draft dissenting opinion during the scrutiny process (see ICC Note to Parties and Arbitral Tribunals, 1 January 2021, at 163). (For a discussion on dissenting opinions and party-appointed arbitrators, see Chapter 1, paragraphs 1.53–1.55 and footnotes.)

[189] Decision of 7 May 2001, at 7.

[190] *Grainger Associates v Islamic Republic of Iran* (1987) 16 Iran–US CTR 317.

(vi) When and how should dissenting opinions be given in international arbitrations?

As already indicated, there is no tradition of dissenting opinions in civil law systems.[191]   **9.137**
Dissenting opinions have come to international arbitration from the common law tradition
and it is a disputed question whether they have added value to the arbitral process.[192] The
traditional justification for dissenting opinions in common law judicial systems is that they
may contribute to the development of the law. Although rare, there are examples of higher
courts adopting dissenting opinions rather than the judgment of the majority. It might well
be said—particularly by common lawyers—that if dissenting opinions can contribute in
this way to a national judicial system of justice, why might they not also contribute to the
system of international arbitration? To this, there are at least three responses.

First, in most cases, there is no appeal from the award of an arbitral tribunal and, more-   **9.138**
over, there exists no system of *stare decisis* in international arbitration. A dissenting opinion
cannot therefore inform an appellate arbitral jurisdiction nor will it guide future arbitral
tribunals searching for the wisdom of precedent. Dissenting opinions therefore have far less
to contribute to the arbitral process than to a common law judicial system. (An exception to
this may arise in investment arbitrations where the dissenting opinion may become public
and influence later decisions, as sometimes happens with dissents in judgments of the law
courts.)[193]

Secondly, rather than contribute to the arbitral process, dissenting opinions may endanger   **9.139**
its efficacy by threatening the validity and enforceability of the award. It might be argued, in
response to this concern, that if an award *is* flawed, then a dissenting arbitrator has a right,
and perhaps even a duty, to provide ammunition that may assist the losing party in challenging the award. However, such an argument ignores the very purpose of an arbitration,
which is to arrive at a decision, not a debate. It is the *decision* that matters, and it matters
not as a guide to the opinions of a particular arbitrator or as an indication of the future development of the law, but because it resolves the particular dispute that divides the parties,
in the manner chosen by the parties, even if one of the arbitrators believes that decision to
be wrong.

The third and final reason follows from the different way in which arbitrators—as opposed   **9.140**
to judges—are appointed. Judges are appointed by the state. They do not depend in any way
on the parties who appear before them. In an international arbitration, by contrast, two of
the three members of the tribunal will usually have been appointed (or nominated) by the
parties. When a dissenting arbitrator disagrees with the majority, and does so in terms that
favour the party that appointed him or her, it may cause some concern. Does the dissent
arise from an honest difference of opinion, or is it influenced by a desire to keep favour with
the party that appointed the dissenting arbitrator? As one commentator has said:

---

[191] Lévy, 'Dissenting opinions in international arbitration in Switzerland' (1989) 5 Arb Intl 35, at 35.

[192] This question was answered in the negative in Alan Redfern's 2003 Freshfields Lecture: see Redfern,
'Dissenting opinions in international commercial arbitration: The good, the bad and the ugly' (2004) 20 Arb Intl
223. It would be right to say that the lecture itself gave rise to much dissent, as indicated in paragraphs 1.53–1.55 of
this book.

[193] The ICSID Rules, r. 46, defines an award to include any individual or dissenting opinions, and so make dissent something that is expressly permitted.

Certain arbitrators, so as not to lose the confidence of the company or the state which appointed them, will be tempted, if they have not put their point of view successfully in the course of the tribunal's deliberation, systematically to draw up a dissenting opinion and to insist that it be communicated to the parties.[194]

Other authors concur:

Although party-appointed arbitrators are supposed to be impartial and independent in international arbitrations, some believe that with the availability of dissent, arbitrators may feel pressure to support the party that appointed them and to disclose that support.[195]

E. Form and Content of Awards

(a) Generally

9.141   The best awards are short, reasoned, and simply written in clear, unambiguous language. An arbitral tribunal should aim at rendering a correct, valid, and enforceable award. Under some systems of law, it may have to do so as a matter of legal obligation;[196] or it may be required to do so under the applicable institutional rules. Whether or not there is a legal obligation, the arbitral tribunal will want to do its best, as a matter of professional pride, to ensure that the award is enforceable: having been entrusted with the duty of determining a dispute for the parties, it will naturally wish to ensure that its duty is properly and effectively discharged.

9.142   A distinguished arbitrator has suggested that:

A valid yardstick for assessing the diligence shown by the arbitrators in drawing up an arbitral award that is enforceable and likely to be recognised, is to apply the criteria established under the New York Convention, since compliance therewith will enable recognition and enforcement of the arbitral award in all the signatory countries. Consequently, no arbitral tribunal could be held responsible in a case where its decision was not recognised in a given country for failing to fulfil some mandatory requirement imposed by that country's domestic law, unless the parties had expressly advised the tribunal of this circumstance, which should rightly have been taken into account when the arbitral award was drawn up.[197]

---

[194] De Boisséson, *Le Droit Français de l'Arbitrage National et International* (Joly, 1990), p. 802 (author's translation).

[195] Mosk and Ginsburg, *Dissenting Opinions in International Arbitration* (Liber Amicorum Bengt Broms, 1999), p. 275. See also De Boisséson, *Le Droit Français de l'Arbitrage National et International* (Joly, 1990), p. 802. For an analysis of the perceived problems with dissenting opinions in the investment treaty context, see Van den Berg, 'Dissenting opinions by party-appointed arbitrators in investment arbitration', in Mahnoush Arsanjani et al. (eds) *Looking to the Future: Essays on International Law in Honor of W Michael Reisman* (Brill Academic, 2010), p. 821.

[196] See Chapter 5.

[197] Cremades, 'The arbitral award', in Newman and Hill (eds) *The Leading Arbitrators' Guide to International Arbitration* (2nd edn, Juris, 2008), p. 500.

The award of an international arbitral tribunal may be challenged in the courts of the seat of ar-   **9.143**
bitration;[198] and recognition and enforcement of the award may be refused by a competent court
in the place(s) in which such recognition or enforcement is sought. This subject is discussed in
detail later.[199] The point to be made here is that an arbitral tribunal should bear the possibilities
of challenge and post-award recourse in mind when drawing up its award. Against this background, the validity of an award must be considered under two headings: form and content.

(b) Form of the award

In general, the requirements of form are dictated by the arbitration agreement (including   **9.144**
the rules of any arbitral institution chosen by the parties) and the law governing the arbitration (the *lex arbitri*).

(i) Arbitration agreement
It is necessary to check whether the arbitration agreement specifies any particular formal-   **9.145**
ities for the award. In practice, this means examining any set of rules that the parties have
adopted. The UNCITRAL Rules, for example, lay down the following requirements:

- the award shall be made in writing;
- the reasons upon which the award is based shall be stated (unless otherwise agreed);
- the award shall be signed by the arbitrators, and shall contain the date on which and
  the place where it was made; and
- where there are three arbitrators and one of them fails to sign, the award shall state the
  reason for the absence of the signature.[200]

The only arbitral institution that sets out the detailed obligations for an arbitrator when   **9.146**
writing an award is ICSID. Rule 47 of the ICSID Rules states:

(1) The award shall be in writing and shall contain:
  (a) a precise designation of each party;
  (b) a statement that the Tribunal was established under the Convention, and a de-
       scription of the method of its constitution;
  (c) the name of each member of the Tribunal, and an identification of the appointing
       authority of each;
  (d) the names of the agents, counsel and advocates of the parties;
  (e) the dates and place of the sittings of the Tribunal;
  (f) a summary of the proceeding;
  (g) a statement of the facts as found by the Tribunal;
  (h) the submissions of the parties;
  (i) the decision of the Tribunal on every question submitted to it, *together with the
       reasons upon which the decision is based*; and
  (j) any decision of the Tribunal regarding the cost of the proceeding.

---

[198] Or, exceptionally, if the parties have agreed to subject the arbitration to the law of a 'foreign' country, in the
courts of that country.
[199] See Chapter 11, paragraphs 11.54 to 11.105.
[200] UNCITRAL Rules, Art. 34. See also Swiss Rules, Art. 32.

(2) The award shall be signed by the members of the Tribunal who voted for it; the date of each signature shall be indicated.

(3) Any member of the Tribunal may attach his individual opinion to the award, whether he dissents from the majority or not, or a statement of his dissent. (Emphasis added)

9.147   These two examples, drawn from institutional rules of arbitration, indicate the importance for the arbitral tribunal of checking the form (and contents) of its award against the relevant rules.

(ii) Law governing the arbitration

9.148   The requirements of form imposed by national systems of law vary from the comprehensive to the virtually non-existent. The Swiss Code of Civil Procedure, under Part III, which govern domestic arbitrations in Switzerland, lays down detailed requirements,[201] but for international cases, these are narrowed to just four—namely, that the award be in writing, reasoned, dated, and signed.[202] Section 52 of the English Arbitration Act 1996 follows the same lines:

(1) The parties are free to agree on the form of an award.

(2) If or to the extent that there is no such agreement, the following provisions apply.

(3) The award shall be in writing signed by all the arbitrators or all those assenting to the award.

(4) The award shall contain the reasons for the award unless it is an agreed award or the parties have agreed to dispense with reasons.

(5) The award shall state the seat of the arbitration and the date when the award is made.

(iii) Introductory section of an award

9.149   Awards will usually begin by setting out the names and addresses of the parties, and the names and contact details of their representatives and of the tribunal, and any tribunal secretary. The award will then usually contain a brief, preliminary narrative setting out the background to the dispute between the parties. This preliminary narrative should include an identification of the arbitration agreement or document containing the arbitration clause, which it is usual to set out in detail, since it is the foundation on which the arbitration is built. It will then usually be followed by a brief outline of the dispute or disputes that have arisen between the parties, the relief claimed (including interest and costs, if claimed, as they normally would be), the dates on which the arbitrator or arbitrators were appointed, and by whom this was done.

9.150   This will then generally be followed by the procedural history of the arbitral proceedings, which ideally will serve to show that the parties were treated equally and had a reasonable opportunity to present their cases to the tribunal. There will then usually follow a discussion of the merits of the issues in dispute, where the tribunal will do its best to summarise the evidence and arguments of the parties as briefly but as accurately as possible. This summary will generally be followed by the tribunal's detailed analysis of the parties' evidence and argument, and a 'discussion' of its conclusions and of its reasons for reaching those

---

[201] Swiss Code of Civil Procedure, Pt. III, Art. 384.
[202] Swiss PIL, Ch. 12, s. 189(2).

conclusions. Finally, the tribunal will then record its decisions on the issues before it, including any claims for interest and costs, in the final, dispositive section of its award.

We started this discussion of the form and content of an award by stating that the best **9.151** awards are short, reasoned, and simply written, in clear and unambiguous language. This remains true. It must be admitted, however, that in all but the very simplest of cases, it is difficult now to produce an award that is short. In part, this is due to the increasing number of challenges to awards, so that tribunals feel obliged to enter into more detail than they would have done in the past about the procedure that has been followed, the arguments that have been raised, and the way in which those arguments have been dealt with. In part too, it is due to the requirements of the arbitral institutions. They are naturally concerned about the quality of awards issued under their rules, by arbitrators coming from all kinds of professional and cultural backgrounds, and they want to ensure that essential points are not overlooked.

The ICC, for example, issues arbitrators with an 'ICC Award Checklist' which provides guid- **9.152** ance on the drafting of an ICC award. This checklist itself is a detailed document, with guidance on such matters as page and paragraph numbering and, more importantly, with seven major headings. These include identifying the parties and their representatives, with their correct names and addresses; quotation of the entire arbitration agreement and any relevant choice of law clause; a history of the arbitral proceedings, including details of the appointment of the tribunal, again with correct names and addresses; a note on the jurisdiction of the tribunal, if it was at issue; costs; and a dispositive section, dealing with all the parties' issues and claims, including the most recent claims for relief, and noting the place of arbitration, the date on which the award is made, and the signatures of the members of the tribunal. In a world in which awards are increasingly subject to challenge, it is right for a tribunal to check carefully that it has done all that is required in drafting its award, in terms both of form and of substance. But it is difficult to do this briefly.

(iv) Signatures

Some national systems of law require all arbitrators to sign the award in order for it to be **9.153** valid. Formalities with regards to signature still exist in the United Arab Emirates (UAE), for example, and are important to follow. A decision by the Dubai Court of Cassation in 2009[203] distinguished between awards in which the grounds were included in the same document as the award itself and awards in which the grounds and the award were in separate documents. It was held that arbitrators could sign the final page on which the award appears, if it is attached to the grounds; if they are in separate documents, then the Court held that the page with the grounds must be signed, as well as *each* page of the award by all of the arbitrators.[204] In practice, arbitrators sitting in arbitration proceedings in the UAE normally sign every page of the award.

---

[203] Dubai Court of Cassation, Petition No. 156/2009 (considering the signature requirement under Art. 212(5) of the former UAE Arbitration Chapter).

[204] In a recent ruling (14 June 2020), the Dubai Court of Cassation confirmed that the position remains the same under UAE's new federal arbitration law, which entered into force in June 2018 (see *Ali & Sons Marine Engineering Factory LLC v E-Marine FZC*, Civil Cassation Appeal No. 1083/2019). In this case, rather than accede to the applicant's request to annul the award on the ground that the arbitrators had not signed the pages of the award

9.154 The major institutional rules all deal expressly or impliedly with signature of the award. The ICC Rules, as already noted, make it clear that the award must be signed, but the award of a majority of the arbitrators or, if there is no majority, the award of the presiding arbitrator alone is effective.[205] As noted above, a similar provision is found in the LCIA Rules.[206]

(v) Language of the award

9.155 The award will normally be rendered in the language of the arbitration. Nevertheless, it is a condition of recognition and enforcement under the New York Convention that a foreign arbitral award must be accompanied by an officially certified translation into the language of the place in which recognition or enforcement of the award is sought, when this is not the language of the award.[207]

(c) Contents of the award

9.156 The contents of an award, like its form, are dictated primarily by the arbitration agreement and the law governing the arbitration (the *lex arbitri*).

(i) Arbitration agreement

9.157 Arbitration agreements usually provide that the award is to be final and binding upon the parties. It follows that the award should deal with all matters referred to arbitration, insofar as they have not been dealt with by any interim or partial awards. However, arbitration agreements rarely go on to describe the content of the award; the nearest they get is to incorporate a set of arbitration rules. Such rules invariably also provide that the award should deal with such matters as the costs of the arbitration[208] and the payment of interest. The rules may also provide that the award shall state the reasons upon which it is based.[209] Even if not specifically required, the giving of reasons is a practice that should be followed unless there is some very good reason why it should not be (for example, because the parties have agreed to dispense with reasons).[210]

(ii) Unambiguous

9.158 Most national systems of law require an award to be unambiguous and dispositive. Ambiguity is often capable of being cured, either by the arbitral tribunal interpreting the award at the request of the parties (or occasionally at the request of only one of them),[211] or by an application to the relevant national court for an order that the award should be

---

containing the grounds or the operative part of the award, the Court of Cassation instead directed the matter to be remitted to the tribunal so that this clerical error could be rectified.

[205] ICC Rules, Art. 32.1.
[206] LCIA Rules, Art. 26.5.
[207] New York Convention, Art. IV(2).
[208] See, e.g., UNCITRAL Rules, Art. 40; ICC Rules, Art. 38; LCIA Rules, Art. 28.
[209] See, e.g., UNCITRAL Rules, Art. 34.3; ICSID Rules, r. 47.1.i.
[210] For further discussion on this topic, see paragraphs 9.162–9.165.
[211] See paragraphs 9.193 and 9.196–9.200.

remitted to the arbitral tribunal for clarification.[212] The position is similar where the award contains provisions that are inconsistent.

(iii) Determination of the issues

An award must also be dispositive, in that it must constitute an effective determination of the issues in dispute. It is not sufficient for the arbitral tribunal to issue a vague expression of opinion. The award must be formulated in an imperative tone: 'we award', 'we direct', 'we order', or the equivalent.   **9.159**

Equally, if there is more than one respondent and a monetary award is made in favour of the claimant, it is essential for the arbitral tribunal to make it clear whether one of the respondents, and if so, which one, has the obligation to make the payment, or whether the obligation is joint and several.   **9.160**

An award should not direct the parties to perform an illegal act or require the parties to do anything that may be considered contrary to public policy,[213] nor should the award contain any directions that are outside the scope of authority of the arbitral tribunal.   **9.161**

(iv) Reasons

The way in which reasons are given in arbitral awards varies considerably. Sometimes, the reasoning, or 'motivation', is set out with extreme brevity. However, a mere statement that the arbitral tribunal accepted the evidence of one party and rejected the evidence of the other, which was common practice for some arbitrators, has fallen into disrepute.   **9.162**

Even today, there are arbitrations in which providing reasons is likely to seem unnecessary. An arbitrator in a quality arbitration, for example, who is asked to decide whether goods supplied do or do not correspond to sample, can hardly do much more than answer 'yes' or 'no'. That said, for the vast majority of international arbitrations, a reasoned award is not only appropriate, but will probably be obligatory under the applicable arbitration rules or the *lex arbitri*.   **9.163**

The ICSID Convention, as already stated, calls for a reasoned award, without any exceptions;[214] and in practice, the ICC Court considers awards that are insufficiently reasoned to be defective as to form. They are therefore sent back to the arbitral tribunal for amendment, before they can be approved. The UNCITRAL Rules take the same approach as the Model Law: reasons should be given, unless the parties agree otherwise.[215] The requirement that an award be reasoned is also commonly found in national laws governing arbitrations.[216]   **9.164**

The New Zealand Court of Appeal, in setting aside an award in which the reasoning comprised only five paragraphs, explained that reasons 'must be coherent and comply with an   **9.165**

---

[212] See, e.g., English Arbitration Act, s. 57(3) (permitting a party to apply for correction of an award to 'clarify or remove any ambiguity').

[213] However, since public policy considerations vary from country to country, it may be difficult to avoid this in all cases, e.g. an award of interest may be acceptable in the country in which the award is made, but not in the country of eventual enforcement (which will often be difficult for the tribunal to predict at the time of issuing its award).

[214] ICSID Convention, Art. 48(3).

[215] UNCITRAL Rules, Art. 34.3. See also LCIA Rules, Art. 26.2.

[216] See, e.g., English Arbitration Act, s. 52(4) and New Zealand Arbitration Act 1996, s. 31(2).

elementary level of logic of adequate substance to enable the parties to understand how and why [the tribunal reached its decision]'. It went on to hold that the extent of the reasons to be given will be dictated by context and 'must reflect the importance of the arbitral reference and the panel's conclusion'.[217] In contrast, the English Commercial Court recently held that a failure to provide adequate reasons cannot amount to a serious irregularity under section 68(2)(c) or 68(2)(h) of the English Arbitration Act.[218]

(d) Time limits

9.166 A limit may be imposed as to the time within which the arbitral tribunal must make its award. When this limit is reached, the authority or mandate of the arbitral tribunal is at an end and it no longer has jurisdiction to make a valid award. This means that, where a time limit exists, care must be taken to see that either the time limit is observed, or that the time limit is extended before it expires. The purpose of time limits is to ensure that the case is dealt with speedily. Such limits may be imposed on the arbitral tribunal by the rules of an arbitral institution, by the *lex arbitri*, or by agreement of the parties.

9.167 The laws of a number of countries provide for the time limits within which an award must be made, sometimes starting from the date upon which the arbitration itself commenced. In India, 2015 amendments to the Arbitration and Conciliation Act 1996 imposed an obligation on arbitral tribunals to render an award within twelve months from the date of the tribunal's constitution (which time limit could be extended by a further six months only).[219] This reform was subject to widespread criticism, particularly given its one-size-fits-all approach. Accordingly, the Indian Act was further amended in 2019 to clarify that international commercial arbitrations seated in India are not subject to strict application of the twelve-month time limit.[220] In the United States, the position varies from state to state. In some states, the limit is thirty days from the date on which the hearings are closed. However, time limits in the United States may also be extended by mutual agreement of the parties or by court order.

9.168 In the institutional context, the ICC 'expects arbitral tribunals to render awards within six months from the establishment of the Terms of Reference, or within the time limit fixed by the Court'.[221] In the authors' experience, however, this time limit is routinely extended by the Court. The ICC does, however, employ a 'stick and carrot' approach to incentivise efficiency. For example, if a tribunal exceeds the agreed time limit for rendering an award, the ICC may lower the tribunal's fees.[222] Conversely, if the tribunal conducts the arbitration expeditiously, the ICC may increase its fees.[223]

---

[217] *Ngāti Hurungaterangi & Ors v Ngāti Wahiao* [2017] NZCA 429, New Zealand Court of Appeal.

[218] *Islamic Republic of Pakistan v Broadsheet LLC* [2019] EWHC 1832 (Comm).

[219] If the arbitral tribunal failed to issue an award within the maximum available period of 18 months, its mandate was to stand terminated unless the court, either prior to or after expiry of the specified period, extended the period on a showing by a party of 'sufficient cause' (Indian Arbitration and Conciliation (Amendment) Act 2015, s. 15).

[220] Indian Arbitration and Conciliation (Amendment) Act 2019, s. 6 (revising s. 29A of the Act). These reforms also provided that the twelve-month time limit now commences from the date of completion of pleadings and not from the Tribunal's constitution.

[221] ICC Note to Parties and Arbitral Tribunals, 1 January 2021, at 152.

[222] Ibid., at 155.

[223] Ibid., at 154.

It is important that a fixed time limit for rendering the award should not enable one of the   **9.169**
parties to frustrate the arbitration. This might happen if a fixed limit were to run from the
date of the appointment of the arbitral tribunal, rather than, for example, that of the end of
the hearings. If a court has no power to intervene on the application of one party alone and
the time limit can be extended only by agreement of the parties, a party might frustrate the
proceedings simply by refusing to agree to any extension of time. However, the courts of
many countries would be reluctant to invalidate a late award in such a case. For example,
in New York, it was held that an untimely award was not a nullity, even though the issue of
timeliness was properly raised: the court stated that, without a finding of prejudice, there
was no justification for denying confirmation of the award.[224]

(i) Disadvantages of mandatory time limits

It is rare to find time limits for delivery of the award in non-institutional rules. Where such   **9.170**
limits are imposed, it may be by the national law although it is usually by an express agreement between the parties, contained in the arbitration clause or the submission agreement.
Undoubtedly, such a provision is inserted with the intention of putting pressure on the arbitral tribunal to complete its work with due despatch and in order to minimise the opportunities for delaying the resolution of disputes by the parties themselves. However, it is
a strategy that may well prove to be counterproductive. In most substantial international
cases before an arbitral tribunal consisting of three arbitrators, it is usually impracticable
to complete the arbitration within such a short period of time as six months. The result is
that the arbitral tribunal may be forced into a situation in which, in order to comply with
the time limit, it must issue its award without giving the respondent a proper opportunity
to present its case. Such an award is vulnerable to an action for nullity or to a successful defence to enforcement proceedings. Thus the successful party finds that, far from the time
limit having assisted in a speedy resolution of the dispute, it contributes to overall delay and
ineffectiveness in the arbitral process.[225] In addition, a number of arbitral institutions have
now introduced expedited procedures for the conduct of an international arbitration, and
a standard feature of these procedures is a provision for the award to be made within a relatively short time.[226]

In general, it is preferable that no time limit should be prescribed for the making of the   **9.171**
award in an arbitration clause or submission agreement. However, if the parties consider it
desirable to set a limit, or if it is necessary to do so under the applicable law, the time limit
should, if possible, be related to the closure of the hearings and not to the appointment of
the arbitral tribunal, or to some other stage in the arbitration at which the respondent will
have opportunities to create delay. A provision that the award must be issued within a certain time after the closure of the hearings helps to ensure that the arbitral tribunal proceeds
diligently with its task. It is frustrating for the parties if the arbitral tribunal takes many

---

[224] *State of New York Department of Taxation and Finance v Valenti* 57 AD 2d 174, 393 NYS 2d 797 (1977). In
contrast, the Belgian Supreme Court annulled an award issued only eight days after the deadline fixed by the parties on the basis that the late issuance amounted to an excess of powers (*X. v Y.*, Court of Cassation of Belgium,
Third Civil Law Chamber, Case No. C.13.0264.N., 26 October 2015).

[225] For a potential horror story, see *Staatsrechtliche v ICC Schiedsgerichtsentschied*, Bundesgericht,
I. Zivilabteilung (Federal Court, First Civil Division), 24 March 1997, (1997) 2 ASA Bulletin 316. For commentary,
see Kreindler and Kautz, 'Agreed deadlines and the setting aside of arbitral awards' (1997) 4 ASA Bulletin 576.

[226] See Chapters 1 and 6.

months to deliberate and to issue its award. However, any time limit should be realistic and not merely one that incites the arbitral tribunal to make the award in too great a hurry, thus potentially exposing the award to a successful challenge.

(ii) Non-mandatory provisions

9.172 Perhaps the best way in which the parties can put time pressure on an arbitral tribunal, without placing the effectiveness of the proceedings at risk, is to insert some form of non-mandatory provision. In one ICC case,[227] the arbitration clause contained a provision to the effect that 'the parties wish that the award shall be issued within five months of the date of the appointment of the third arbitrator'.

9.173 The arbitral tribunal considered it necessary to clarify the position and, at its request, the parties confirmed that this provision:

- superseded the provision of Article 18.1 of the then applicable 1998 ICC Rules, which provided that the award was to be made within six months of the signing of the terms of reference; and
- did not affect the power of the ICC Court to extend the time limit provided for by the parties, in accordance with Article 18.2 of the then applicable 1998 ICC Rules.

9.174 In effect, therefore, the parties set a *target* for the arbitral tribunal in their arbitration agreement, without imposing any mandatory provision that might have placed at risk the effectiveness of that agreement.

(e) Notification of awards

9.175 International and institutional rules of arbitration generally make provision for the notification of the award to the parties. The UNCITRAL Rules provide, at Article 34.6, that '[c]opies of the award signed by the arbitrators shall be communicated to the parties by the arbitral tribunal'. However, no time limit is imposed within which this must be done. The position is similar under the ICSID Rules, Rule 48.1 of which merely states that a certified copy of the award (including individual opinions and statements of dissent) will be sent to the parties 'promptly' when the last arbitrator has signed it. Article 35.1 of the ICC Rules provides that the Secretariat will notify the parties once an award has been made, provided that the costs have been fully paid.[228]

9.176 That party which expects to have won the case will invariably make it its business to obtain a copy of the award as soon as practicable, either directly from the arbitral tribunal or from the relevant arbitral institution. If that party has won, it will immediately communicate the

---

[227] ICC Case No. 5051.

[228] The potential problems with delayed notification have been obviated in recent years by the increasing facilitation in institutional rules of electronic notification of awards (with original copies to follow by courier). For example, the LCIA Rules make clear that the transmission of an award to parties by the LCIA Court 'may be made by any electronic means' (Art. 26.7). Similarly, ICC guidance notes that, 'subject to any applicable mandatory law requirements', any award may be 'notified to the parties by the Secretariat by email or any other means of telecommunication that provides a record of the sending' (ICC Note to Parties and Arbitral Tribunals, 1 January 2021, at 199).

award to the unsuccessful party. The time limit within which a party may apply to the appropriate court for recourse against the award may run from the date of communication of the award and not from the making of the award itself. However, the position should be checked under the law of the place in which recourse may be sought, which is normally the place of arbitration.

(f) Registration or deposit of awards

In some countries, registration for the purposes of recognition by the courts is unnecessary   **9.177**
or optional. In others, it may be a necessary prelude to enforcement of a foreign award. In such cases, there may be an element of 'double *exequatur*', which has been strongly criticised by the draftsmen of the New York Convention, amongst others.[229] The principle on which the New York Convention is based is that the award needs only to be binding on the parties in order for it to be enforceable. Nonetheless, registration is a matter that may affect the validity of the award if the mandatory provisions of the place in which the arbitration is held require it.[230] Where the requirement is mandatory, it *must* be deposited in order to protect the validity of the award.

Even when it is not mandatory, registration or deposit of an award may be desirable in order   **9.178**
to put pressure on the unsuccessful party. In some cases, registration of the award is relevant for the purposes of the time limit within which any application for annulment of the award must be made. Although registration will not necessarily assist the successful party in relation to enforcement actions in other countries, it may protect the award from any further challenge in the country in which the arbitration took place.

F. Effect of Awards

(a) *Res judicata*

The basic principle of *res judicata* is that a legal right or obligation, or any facts, specifically   **9.179**
put in issue and determined by a court or tribunal of competent jurisdiction, cannot later be put back into question as between the same parties.[231]

Despite general recognition, the application of the principle of *res judicata* varies as be-   **9.180**
tween jurisdictions. In common law jurisdictions, *res judicata* falls broadly into two categories: claim estoppel, which prevents either party from re-litigating the same claim against the other; and issue estoppel, which prevents a party from questioning or denying an issue already decided in previous proceedings between the parties. Many civil law

---

[229] See Chapter 11, paragraph 11.90.
[230] This must be considered separately from any requirement for the deposit of the award with an arbitral institution.
[231] See the award in *Amco Asia Corporation v Indonesia (Resubmission: Jurisdiction)*, ICSID Case No. ARB/81/1, (1992) 89 ILR 552, at 560.

jurisdictions apply *res judicata* only as a claim estoppel, and the estoppel is said to attach only to the dispositive part of the judgment/award, not to the reasons.[232]

9.181 Given the difficulties that can arise as a result of the varying interpretations of the principle of *res judicata*, the International Commercial Arbitration Committee of the International Law Association (ILA) set about creating a transnational body of rules that could be referred to as guidance, or adopted by the parties if they so choose, in international arbitrations. Since 2004, the Committee has published interim and final reports on *res judicata* and *lis pendens*, and, at the same time as its final report, the Committee adopted its Recommendations on *Lis Pendens* and *Res Judicata* and Arbitration.[233] In setting forth a transnational approach, the Committee commented in its final report that:

> *Res judicata* regarding international arbitral awards should not necessarily be equated to *res judicata* effects of judgments of state courts and, thus, may be treated differently than *res judicata* under domestic law. International arbitral awards in accordance with the Recommendations are to be treated differently than judgments. This is due to the differences between international arbitration and domestic court dispute settlement, as well as to the international character of arbitration, which should not be reduced to domestic notions regarding *res judicata* that are valid in a domestic setting but are hardly appropriate in an international context.[234]

9.182 The doctrine of *res judicata* can be applicable in international arbitration in a variety of ways. Broadly, there are three different aspects of *res judicata*: first, the effect of an award on existing disputes between the parties; secondly, its effect on subsequent disputes between the parties; and thirdly, its effect on third parties.

(b) Existing disputes

9.183 As far as the parties themselves are concerned, it is clear that (subject to challenge before a competent court) the award disposes of those disputes between the parties that were submitted to arbitration.[235] This even extends to cases in which the arbitrators acted as *amiables compositeurs*.[236] If one party were to bring a court or arbitral action against the other in relation to the subject matter of the arbitration, based on the same cause of action between the same parties, the court or tribunal would dismiss the action on the ground that the issues had been disposed of and were *res judicata*.[237] In the United States, courts have often applied *res judicata* (also referred to as 'claim preclusion') to bar claims that could have been, but

---

[232] In France, Belgium, and the Netherlands, some recourse can be had to the reasons in order to explain the meaning and scope of the *dispositif*. In Italy, certain cases suggest that *res judicata* may include the entire reasoning. See, in this regard, ILA, 'Interim Report on *Res Judicata* and Arbitration' (2009) 25 Intl Arb 1, at 51, 52, and 65.

[233] The ILA interim report, the final report, and the ILA Recommendations can all be found at (2009) 25 Arb Intl or online at http://www.ila-hq.org.

[234] ILA, 'Final Report on *Res Judicata* and Arbitration' (2009) 25 Intl Arb 72, at para. 25.

[235] See the commentary on the award in ICC Case No. 3383, Jarvin and Derains, *Collection of ICC Arbitral Awards 1974–1985* (Kluwer Law International, 1994), pp. 394 and 397.

[236] Söderlund, '*Lis pendens, res judicata* and the issue of parallel judicial proceedings' (2005) 22 J Intl Arb 4.

[237] In France, Arts 1476 and 1500 of the *Nouveau Code de Procédure Civile* provide that an arbitral award has a *res judicata* effect with respect to the dispute that it determines. Similar provisions also exist in Belgium, Spain, Germany, Austria, and Switzerland. See Hanotiau, 'The *res judicata* effect of arbitral awards' (2003) *Supplement* ICC International Court of Arbitration Bulletin 43.

were not, asserted in a prior arbitral proceeding. However, if the award is deemed invalid and is set aside by a court of competent jurisdiction, the nullified award does not operate as *res judicata* in any subsequent proceedings. An example of this is the classic *Pyramids* arbitration, in which the claimant started an ICSID arbitration after the award in the ICC arbitration was nullified in the French courts.[238]

The ILA's Committee has endorsed this basic application of *res judicata*, which depends on **9.184** the 'triple identity test' (the same parties, the same subject matter, and the same claim for relief). In particular, Recommendation 3 of Part II of the ILA Recommendations provides as follows:

3. An arbitral award has conclusive and preclusive effects in further arbitral proceedings if:
    - it has become final and binding in the country of origin and there is no impediment to recognition in the country of the place of subsequent arbitration;
    - it has decided on or disposed of a claim for relief which is sought or is being reargued in the further arbitration proceedings;
    - it is based upon a cause of action which is invoked in the further arbitration proceedings or which forms the basis for the subsequent arbitration proceedings; and
    - it has been rendered between the same parties.

(c) Subsequent disputes

Where there are subsequent disputes between the same parties, more difficult questions **9.185** arise. Because there is no doctrine of *stare decisis* in arbitration, the previous decision of an arbitral tribunal will not be binding on any subsequent disputes that arise between the same parties over different subject matter or a different cause of action (even if related). But it does not follow that a previous decision will necessarily be irrelevant to the resolution of a subsequent dispute between the same parties. In this context, it is necessary to consider the principle of issue estoppel. This precludes a party in subsequent proceedings from contradicting an issue of fact or the legal consequences of a fact that has already been raised and decided in earlier proceedings between the same parties, even if the causes of action in both proceedings are not identical.[239]

By way of example, the English Privy Council decided that, notwithstanding a confidenti- **9.186** ality agreement concluded by the parties to an arbitration not to disclose material generated therein to third parties, an award rendered in that arbitration could be relied upon by one of the parties in a subsequent arbitration to found a plea of issue estoppel. The second arbitration took place between the same parties and concerned the same clause under the same reinsurance agreement as the first arbitration. In so finding, the Privy Council reasoned that relying on an issue estoppel in a subsequent arbitration was 'a species of the enforcement of

---

[238] For further discussion of the *Pyramids* arbitration, see Chapter 11, fn 102.

[239] Cremades and Madalena, 'Parallel proceedings in international arbitration' (2008) 24 Arb Intl 4, at 507; Sheppard, 'Res judicata and estoppel', in ICC (ed.) *Parallel State and Arbitral Procedures in International Arbitration*, ICC Publications No. 692 (ICC, 2005), p. 225; Barnett, *Res Judicata, Estoppel, and Foreign Judgments: The Preclusive Effects of Foreign Judgments in Private International Law* (Oxford University Press, 2001), p. 135.

the rights given by the [previous] award' and that this legitimate use of the earlier award was not a breach of the confidentiality agreement.[240] In the same way, US courts have also invoked principles of collateral estoppel, or 'issue preclusion', to exclude issues raised in litigation that were previously adjudicated fully and fairly during an arbitration, and vice versa.[241]

9.187 Although issue estoppel is less common outside the common law world, the ILA Committee has endorsed the application of 'issue estoppel' in international arbitration,[242] including Recommendations 4 and 5 (of Part II of the ILA Recommendations) which read as follows:

> 4. An arbitral award has conclusive and preclusive effects in the further arbitral proceedings as to:
>   - Determinations and relief contained in its dispositive part as well as in all reasoning necessary thereto;
>   - Issues of fact or law which have actually been arbitrated and determined by it, provided any such determination was essential or fundamental to the dispositive part of the arbitral award.
> 5. An arbitral award has preclusive effects in the further arbitral proceedings as to a claim, cause of action or issue of fact or law, which could have been raised, but was not, in the proceedings resulting in that award, provided that the raising of any such new claim, cause of action or new issue of fact or law amounts to procedural unfairness or abuse.

(d) Effect of award on third parties

9.188 An arbitral tribunal has no power to make orders or to give directions against someone who is not a party to the arbitration agreement, unless that party has in some way acquiesced in a manner that, without actually making it a party to the arbitration agreement, indicates an intention on its part to be bound by the award.

9.189 It follows that an award can neither directly confer rights nor impose obligations upon a non-party to the arbitration agreement.[243] For example, the award of an arbitral tribunal in the main arbitration between an employer and a contractor under a building contract does not have the effect of *res judicata* in respect of a claim for an indemnity by the contractor against its subcontractor in a subsequent arbitration. Although the facts in both arbitrations

---

[240] *Associated Electric and Gas Insurance Services Ltd v European Reinsurance Co. of Zurich* [2003] 1 WLR 1041. See also *Daewoo Shipbuilding & Marine Engineering v Songa Offshore Equinox Ltd* [2020] EWHC 2353.

[241] *In the matter of petition of Gemstar TV Guide International Inc. v Henry C Yuen*, Index No. 602094/07, NY Sup., New York Co., NY Misc. LEXIS 7845 (2007).

[242] ILA, 'Final Report on *Res Judicata* and Arbitration' (2009) 25 Intl Arb 72, at 77; 'ILA Recommendations on *Lis Pendens* and *Res Judicata* and Arbitration, Pt. II, paras 4 and 5' (2009) 25 Intl Arb 1, at 85.

[243] By way of rare exception, the Belgian Constitutional Court recently extended to arbitration the rule under the Belgian Code of Civil Procedure, Art. 1122, permitting third parties to challenge court decisions that prejudice their rights (Judgment no. 21/2017 of the Belgian Constitutional Court dated 16 February 2017). Following this decision, the Brussels Court of First Instance annulled a 2012 ICC award on the basis of a third party's challenge ('La société de droit grec X. v. la SPRL Y. et A.K., Court of First Instance of Brussels, Case Nos 2014/480/A and 2015/6305/A, 29 January 2016 and 12 April 2018', in Annet van Hooft and Jean-François Tossens (eds) *b-Arbitra, Belgian Review of Arbitration* (Wolters Kluwer, 2018, Vol. 2018 Issue 1), pp. 195–218).

may be substantially the same, the second arbitral tribunal may come to a different conclusion from the first—and there is very little that the subcontractor can do apart from agreeing (with the consent of both parties to the main arbitration) to be joined as an additional party in the main arbitration. This gives the subcontractor the right to present evidence and argument in relation to any claims that affected it.[244]

Nonetheless, an award may often have a significant *indirect* effect on persons who were not parties to the arbitration. For example, a third party may be affected by an award where one person is jointly liable with another who is a party to the arbitration. The award would not be *res judicata* in any subsequent claim against that third party, but it should be of persuasive significance in that a tribunal is likely to consider the findings of the earlier award to inform its own findings. Conversely, it is possible that an award (even if unsatisfied) against one of the persons who was jointly liable would have the effect of discharging the third party's liability. Finally, where an award orders performance (for example in relation to the delivery of property by one of the parties), it is doubtful whether it is effective if the property concerned is temporarily in the hands of a third party under a licence. **9.190**

In the United States, issue estoppel can, in certain circumstances, be relied upon in subsequent litigation involving a different party.[245] Further, in both the United States and England, certain parties that are closely linked to the original parties might be bound by an earlier award where the connection is close enough to establish privity between such parties. In an English case, the court held that a director of the claimant company was a privy of the company and therefore had an interest in the arbitration.[246] It has been argued in the international sphere that 'sister companies' constituting a single 'economic entity' should all be bound by the *res judicata* effect of an award involving one of those companies.[247] The ILA Committee noted, in its interim report, that ICSID tribunals have followed this 'single economic entity' analysis in relation to questions of jurisdiction, and asked whether it might also usefully be relied upon in relation to *res judicata* in order to prevent companies from a corporate group 'endlessly re-litigat[ing] the same dispute under the disguise of formally separate legal identities'.[248] However, for the time being, this approach has not been adopted and the ILA has made no recommendation in this regard. **9.191**

G. Proceedings After the Award

Exceptions to the general rule that an arbitral tribunal becomes *functus officio* on the issue of a final award arise from specific provisions of the national system of law governing the arbitration, from the parties' arbitration agreement, or from any rules of arbitration adopted by them.[249] **9.192**

---

[244] For further discussion of consolidation of arbitrations, see Chapter 2, paragraphs 2.246 to 2.254.

[245] See, e.g., *Parklane Hosiery Co. v Shore* 439 US 322 (1979); ILA, 'Interim Report on *Res Judicata* and Arbitration' (2009) 25 Intl Arb 1, at 48.

[246] *Dadourian Group International Inc. v Simms and ors* [2004] EWHC 450 (Ch), [2004] Arb LR 17, with commentary in 'The effect of an arbitration award' (2005) 5 Arb LM 4.

[247] ILA, 'Interim Report on *Res Judicata* and Arbitration' (2009) 25 Intl Arb 1, at 21.

[248] Ibid., at 58 and 59.

[249] See Chapter 10.

9.193 These exceptions typically include applications to interpret an award or correct typographical or calculating errors. Corrections are self-evidently limited in scope. The problem with
'interpretation', as opposed to 'correction', of an award is that it is sometimes used to re-open
decisions reached by the tribunal in the guise of an 'interpretation'.

(a) Under national law

9.194 Many systems of national law with developed arbitral rules permit the correction of minor
clerical or typographical errors in awards, a so-called 'slip rule', either at the request of
one or both of the parties, or by the arbitral tribunal on its own initiative. For example,
in England, this power is conferred expressly by statute. Section 57 of the Arbitration Act
1996 provides:

> (1) The parties are free to agree on the powers of the tribunal to correct an award or make
>   an additional award.
> (2) If or to the extent there is no such agreement, the following provisions apply.
> (3) The tribunal may on its own initiative or on the application of a party:
>   (a) correct an award so as to remove any clerical mistake or error arising from an ac-
>   cidental slip or omission or clarify or remove any ambiguity in the award, or
>   (b) make an additional award in respect of any claim (including a claim for interest or
>   costs) which was presented to the tribunal but was not dealt with in the award.
>
> These powers shall not be exercised without first affording the other parties a
> reasonable opportunity to make representations to the tribunal.[250]
>
> [...]

9.195 The US Federal Arbitration Act of 1925 (FAA) provides that the relevant district court
may make an order modifying or correcting errors.[251] The grounds for modifying or
correcting an award include 'evident material miscalculation', 'evident material mistake', and 'imperfect[ions] in a manner of form not affecting the merits'.[252] Similar provisions are contained in the arbitration statutes of many individual states in the United
States, some of which also permit corrections and modifications on the initiative of the
arbitral tribunal. Additionally, in some countries, the arbitral tribunal may complete
the award where a determination of a claim, or ruling as to costs, has been omitted.[253]
The Model Law imposes a thirty-day time limit within which requests to correct 'any
errors in computation, any clerical or typographical errors or any errors of similar nature'
may be made.[254]

---

[250] For an example of how and when awards can be considered under s. 57, see *Gold Coast Ltd v Naval Gijon SA* [2006] EWHC 1044 (Comm), [2006] Arb LR 381.

[251] FAA, s. 11.

[252] FAA, s. 11(c). See *Hall Street Associates LLC v Mattel Inc.* 552 US 576 (2008).

[253] For the powers of an arbitral tribunal to correct or complete an award in various national states, see the national reports in Paulsson and Bosman (eds) *ICCA International Handbook on Commercial Arbitration* (Kluwer
Law International, 1984).

[254] Model Law, Art. 33(1). Such time limit does not apply where an arbitrator makes a 'conscious choice not to
deal with an issue', in which case the tribunal is left with an 'undischarged mandate to complete' (see *Blanalko Pty
Ltd v Lysaght Building Solutions Pty Ltd* [2017] VSC 97).

(b) Under rules of arbitration

Exceptions to the general rule of *functus officio* vary under different sets of arbitration rules. **9.196** The LCIA Rules contain an express power for the arbitral tribunal to correct 'any error in computation, any clerical or typographical error, any ambiguity or any mistake of a similar nature', but not to make interpretations of awards.[255] Prior to 1998, the ICC Rules did not mention either correction or interpretation. This was presumably on the basis that the process of scrutiny under Article 21 of the previous version of the Rules should be sufficient to ensure that all mistakes would be identified. However, this absence was addressed some time ago, and the 2021 Rules contain the following provision:

> On its own initiative, the arbitral tribunal may correct a clerical, computational or typographical error, or any errors of similar nature contained in an award, provided such correction is submitted for approval to the Court within 30 days from notification of the award by the Secretariat pursuant to Article 35(1).
>
> Any application of a party for the correction of an error of the kind referred to in Article 36(1), or for the interpretation of an award, must be made to the Secretariat within 30 days from receipt of the award by such party.[256]

Similarly, the SCC Rules contain an explicit provision granting the arbitral tribunal power **9.197** to give a written interpretation of its award at the request of a party, in addition to the power to correct clerical errors:

> Within 30 days of receiving an award, a party may, upon notice to the other party, request that the Arbitral Tribunal correct any clerical, typographical or computational errors in the award, or provide an interpretation of a specific point or part of the award. After giving the other party an opportunity to comment on the request, and if the Arbitral Tribunal considers the request justified, it shall make the correction or provide the interpretation within 30 days of receiving the request.[257]

The UNCITRAL Rules contain powers for the arbitral tribunal to correct its award, issue **9.198** additional awards, and interpret its award (if so requested) within narrow time limits. The *correction* of an award (in relation to clerical or typographical errors) may take place either at the request of the party or on the initiative of the arbitral tribunal itself.[258] Yet the arbitral tribunal may issue an interpretation only at the request of a party, not on its own initiative.[259] Similarly, the arbitral tribunal may issue an additional award only at the request of a party.[260] The purpose of the provision relating to additional awards is to ensure that the arbitrators may complete their mission if they have omitted from their award decisions in

---

[255] LCIA Rules, Art. 27.

[256] ICC Rules, Art. 36.1 and 36.2. For a comprehensive survey of applications for correction and/or interpretation of awards under the ICC Rules that have been made since the original introduction of this provision, see Daly, 'Correction and interpretation of arbitral awards under the ICC Rules of Arbitration' (2002) 13 ICC International Court of Arbitration Bulletin 1.

[257] SCC Rules, Art. 47.

[258] UNCITRAL Rules, Art. 38.2.

[259] UNCITRAL Rules, Art. 37.1. Curiously, Art. 37.2 does not contain the express safeguard for the arbitral tribunal that appears in Art. 39.2, '[i]f the arbitral tribunal considers the request for an award or additional award to be justified'. But common sense dictates that the literal language meaning of Art. 37.2 could not be used to force the arbitral tribunal to give an interpretation, at least when it considers the request to be spurious.

[260] UNCITRAL Rules, Art. 39.1.

relation to any of the claims presented in the proceedings. Time limits for complying with each of these provisions are set out in the relevant Articles. In each case, the provisions of Article 34, relating to the formalities required in making an award, must be observed.

9.199 Where the arbitral tribunal is asked to issue an interpretation of its award,[261] whether under the UNCITRAL Rules or otherwise,[262] this may pose difficulties for the tribunal. Its members will have to recapitulate their thinking as best they can and clarify what is unclear—unless they take the view that the request is without substance and may be dealt with in a summary manner.

9.200 The ICSID Rules go further than those of other arbitral institutions. They permit applications for the award to be interpreted and revised not only by the original arbitral tribunal,[263] but also, if that arbitral tribunal cannot be reconstituted, by a new one specially appointed for the purpose.[264] This is a cumbersome procedure, but it appears to be part of the price to be paid for the self-contained and autonomous nature of ICSID arbitrations, which means that even obvious errors may be corrected only within the system and not by an outside authority such as a national court.[265]

(c) Review procedures other than by national courts

9.201 Challenging awards in national courts is considered in Chapter 10. However, in a limited number of cases, there may be a prior review of awards by some other authority. The main instances in which this arises are as follows. First, in certain specialised types of arbitration, particularly in the commodity trades, there is sometimes provision for either party to appeal to a specially constituted arbitral appeals tribunal.[266] Secondly, in a small number of countries, parties may raise an objection to an award before a body other than a national court. Thirdly, in the ICC system, the award must not be signed by the arbitral tribunal until it has been scrutinised by the ICC Court. This provision states:

> Before signing any award, the arbitral tribunal shall submit it in draft form to the Court. The Court may lay down modifications as to the form of the award and, without affecting the arbitral tribunal's liberty of decision, may also draw its attention to points of substance. No award shall be rendered by the arbitral tribunal until it has been approved by the Court as to its form.[267]

9.202 It calls for two different standards of review: the first is as to *form*, with respect to which the ICC Court may 'lay down' modifications; the second is as to points of *substance*, which the ICC Court may only 'draw to the attention' of the arbitrator.

---

[261] In a case in which one of the authors was an arbitrator, the losing respondent requested an interpretation, but the arbitral tribunal determined that this was a manifest attempt by that party to cause the arbitral tribunal to review its decision on the merits of the case.

[262] The ICDR Rules, Art. 36, contains similar provisions to those of the UNCITRAL Rules.

[263] ICSID Rules, rr. 50–52.

[264] ICSID Rules, r. 51(3).

[265] For an example of the relevant ICSID Rules in practice, see *Marvin Feldman v Mexico*, Correction and Interpretation of the Award, ICSID Case No. ARB(AF)/99/1, IIC 158 (2003).

[266] See Chapter 10, paragraph 10.11.

[267] ICC Rules, Art. 34.

The review of awards by the ICC Court sometimes causes concern to arbitrators, who con-   **9.203**
sider it unnecessary and time-consuming. It may also arouse concerns on the part of some
parties, who fear that the case will be reviewed by a 'court' before which they have had no
opportunity of presenting their cases. However, by adopting the Rules, the parties agreed
that the ICC Court should act as the auxiliary of the arbitral tribunal in relation to the form
of the award and as adviser to the tribunal in relation to the substance of the award and they
can hardly complain if the ICC Court carries out the functions that they have empowered it
to carry out.

(d) Review of the award by way of settlement

After the award has been rendered, parties can also settle a dispute by voluntarily agreeing   **9.204**
to vary the terms of the award. In one study of the record of compliance with, and variation
of, awards once rendered, it was found that more than 18 per cent had been renegotiated
post-award to establish final settlement claims.[268] Citing even higher figures, another study
found that 40 per cent of corporations negotiated a settlement after the arbitral award was
rendered.[269] While more recent statistics are not available, it seems that parties commonly
conclude the matter by entering into a negotiation either to establish terms of payment or to
establish a new settlement, using the award as a bargaining tool.

(e) Publication of awards

A conflict emerged some years ago between the 'inherent confidentiality' of the arbitral   **9.205**
process and the desire for publication of awards in the interests of establishing a body of
learning that might guide—if not bind—other arbitrators. The prevailing trend appears to
favour publication. Awards of the Iran–United States Claims Tribunal have been comprehensively reported and have been used as guidance in other arbitrations. The ICDR Rules
provide that, unless otherwise agreed by the parties, selected awards may be made publicly
available, with the names of the parties and other identifying features removed. Similarly,
as of 1 January 2019, the ICC may publish awards and/or orders, subject to any party's
objection and/or to applicable confidentiality constraints.[270] In the ICC's own words,
'[p]ublicising and disseminating information about arbitration has been one of ICC's commitments since its creation and an instrumental factor in facilitating the development of
trade worldwide'.[271] Under the ICSID Rules, excerpts of an award may be published even
without the consent of the parties.[272] There are other circumstances in which, even without
the consent of the parties, an award may find its way into the public domain. This may
occur, for example, during court proceedings to challenge or enforce an award,[273] or when

---

[268] Of 118 cases, 22 had been renegotiated: Naimark and Keer, 'Post-award experience in international commercial arbitration' (2005) 60 Disp Res J 94.
[269] Mistelis and Baltag, 'Recognition and enforcement of arbitral awards and settlement in international arbitration: Corporate attitudes and practices' (2008) 19 Am Rev Intl Arb 319, at 324.
[270] ICC Note to Parties and Arbitral Tribunals, 1 January 2021, Pt. IV(C).
[271] Ibid., at 56.
[272] ICSID Rules, r. 48(4).
[273] See, e.g., *Emmott v Michael Wilson & Partners Ltd* [2008] EWCA Civ 184.

a publicly quoted corporation is obliged to disclose in its published accounts material information relating to its liabilities.[274]

9.206 In a less official context, in a form of post-Soviet legal *samizdat*,[275] it is becoming increasingly common for awards rendered in investment treaty arbitrations to be circulated via email and the Internet between practitioners and academics active in the field. During the second decade of the twenty-first century, online communities sprang up to exchange information and views on matters related to arbitration and international law. One of the most prominent among these is the Oil Gas Energy Mining Infrastructure Dispute Management (OGEMID) email list.[276]

9.207 Together with other similar forums and websites,[277] OGEMID informally introduced an era of greater (although haphazard) transparency within the world of international arbitration. The advantages and disadvantages of transparency versus confidentiality continue to be debated within the international arbitration community, with many drawing a distinction between investment treaty arbitration and commercial arbitration arising between parties to private contracts.[278]

9.208 Further, after several years of debate, in 2014 the UNCITRAL Rules on Transparency in Treaty-based Investor–State Arbitration were promulgated (the UNCITRAL Transparency Rules) in relation to treaties concluded after 1 April 2014, providing for automatic publication of all submissions, orders, hearing transcripts, and awards in treaty-based UNCITRAL cases (unless the parties opt-out).[279] In 2017, the Mauritius Convention on Transparency in Treaty-based Investor–State Arbitration entered into force, applying the UNCITRAL Transparency Rules to all treaty-based arbitrations where both the host state and investor's home state are parties to the Convention.

9.209 At the time of writing, it is still too early to predict the extent to which these recent changes will result in an increased level of transparency in treaty-based investor–state arbitrations; and whether, in the medium or long term, the trend towards greater transparency will be extended to international arbitrations between private commercial parties.

---

[274] See Chapter 2. See also Paulsson and Rawding, 'The trouble with confidentiality' (1995) 11 Arb Intl 303.

[275] *Samizdat*, meaning literally 'self-publishing', was the clandestine copying and onward distribution of government-suppressed literature in Soviet states. Individuals who received a copy of a censored text would be expected to make copies, often by hand, and then to hand those out for further consumption, copying, and distribution.

[276] The list, set up by the late Professor Thomas Wälde, has been described as a 'vehicle where the blue-eyed theorists meet the rock of reality [… where] theoreticians [can no longer] graze on the prairies of theory in groups of like-minded people rather than slog it out at the coalface of legal practice': 'OGEMID: An exchange practice–theory vehicle', posted online at OGEMID, 23 May 2008.

[277] See, e.g., https://www.italaw.com .

[278] For a discussion of whether such a distinction remains viable in the face of increased public scrutiny of arbitration as a mainstream dispute resolution process, see Partasides, 'What has been the "spillover" effect of the transparency debate on commercial arbitrations?', in Kalicki and Raouf (eds) *Evolution and Adaptation: The Future of International Arbitration*, ICCA Congress Series, Vol. 20 (Kluwer Law, 2019) pp. 699–705.

[279] UNCITRAL Transparency Rules, Art. 1.1, 1.2.

10

CHALLENGE OF ARBITRAL AWARDS

A. Introduction

No one likes losing. So it is not surprising that, when a client is disappointed with an arbitral **10.01** award, the first question the lawyer is asked is: 'How can I appeal?' As is so often the case when a lawyer is asked a question, the answer is: 'It depends.'

First, it depends on whether the relevant rules of arbitration establish any internal ap- **10.02** peal procedure, as is the case in certain maritime and commodity arbitration systems,[1] and in certain investment arbitration systems such as in the EU-Canada Comprehensive Economic and Trade Agreement (known as 'CETA').[2] However, a right of appeal is the exception and most arbitration rules provide unequivocally that an arbitral award is final and binding.[3] These are not intended to be empty words. One of the advantages of arbitration is that it is intended to result in the final determination of the dispute between the parties. If the parties want a compromise solution to be proposed, they should opt for mediation. If they are prepared to fight the case to the highest court in the land, they should opt for litigation. By choosing arbitration, the parties choose, in principle, finality. An arbitral award is not intended to be a mere proposal as to how the dispute might be resolved, nor is it intended to be the first step on a ladder of appeals.

To the losing party, this 'advantage' of arbitration may seem, in retrospect, to be the very **10.03** opposite. However, the laws of many countries, reflecting the policy of the New York Convention and of the Model Law, have traditionally manifested what has been described by the US federal courts as 'a pro-enforcement bias'.[4] This means that whilst it may be possible to challenge an arbitral award, the available options are likely to be limited—and intentionally so.

---

[1] See paragraph 10.11.

[2] CETA provides for a CETA Appellate Tribunal, with the power to review first instance arbitral decisions on wide grounds, including 'errors in the application or interpretation of applicable law' (Art. 8.28(2)(a)) and 'manifest errors in the appreciation of the facts' (Art. 8.28(2)(b)).

[3] See, e.g., LCIA Rules, Art. 26.8; ICC Rules, Art. 35.6; ICDR Rules, Art. 30.1.

[4] *Parsons Whittemore Overseas Co. Inc. v Société Générale de l'Industrie du Papier*, 508 F.2d 969, 973 (2d Cir. 1974).

10.04 It is usually the law of the seat of the arbitration[5] that contains these limited provisions for challenging an arbitral award.[6] Such laws are principally focused on ensuring that the arbitration has been conducted in accordance with basic rules of due process, respecting the parties' equal right to be heard before an independent and impartial arbitral tribunal within the boundaries of their arbitration agreement. Grounds of challenge are rarely concerned with a review of the merits of the tribunal's decision on the law or facts, thus distinguishing challenge from an appeal.

10.05 It is important at the outset to make a clear distinction between actions to challenge an award[7] and opposition to actions seeking to recognise and enforce an award. A challenge to an award (usually) takes place in the courts of the seat of the arbitration. It is an attempt by the losing party to invalidate the award on the basis of the statutory grounds available under the law of the seat. In contrast, actions seeking to recognise and enforce an award, which are fully discussed in the next chapter, may take place in any jurisdiction signatory to the New York Convention, or one that has adopted the relevant provisions of the Model Law. In such actions, the party against whom recognition and enforcement is sought may rely on the limited exceptions contained in Article V of the New York Convention or the corresponding provisions of the Model Law to seek to block enforcement.

(a) Purpose of challenge

10.06 The purpose of challenging an award before a national court at the seat of arbitration is to have that court declare all, or part, of the award null and void. If an award is set aside or annulled by the relevant court, it will usually be treated as invalid, and accordingly unenforceable, not only by the courts of the seat of arbitration, but also by national courts elsewhere.[8] This is because, under both the New York Convention and the Model Law, a competent court may refuse to grant recognition and enforcement of an award that has been set aside by a court of the seat of arbitration.[9] It is important to note that, following

[5] Or, if the parties have chosen a different procedural law to govern the arbitration, under that law: New York Convention, Art. V.1(e); Model Law, Art. 36(1)(a)(v).

[6] Including a partial, or interim, award that is final as to the issue(s) it addresses.

[7] Also referred to as 'actions to set aside an award', 'actions seeking annulment of the award' or (in the United States) 'actions seeking to vacate the award'.

[8] New York Convention, Art. V, provides only that a competent national authority *may* refuse to enforce an award that has been annulled at the seat. It is not obliged to do so; accordingly, an award that has been set aside by the court of the seat of arbitration may be granted recognition and enforcement if the enforcing court so concludes. France is one of the more liberal jurisdictions in this regard, famously granting recognition to a Swiss-seated award that had been set aside by Swiss courts: *Hilmarton I*, Cass. Civ., 1ère Civ., 23 Mar. 1994, [1994] Rev Arb 437. See also *PT Putrabali Adyamulia v Rena Holdings*, Cass. Civ., Ch. Civ. 1ere, 29 June 2007, in which a French court enforced an award that had been set aside at the seat in England. Similarly, the District Court for the District of Columbia in *Chromalloy Aeroservices v Arab Republic of Egypt*, 939 F.Supp. 907, 909 (DDC 1996) enforced an award that had been annulled at its seat in Egypt. In *Corporacion Mexicana de Mantenimiento Integral, S. de RL de CV v PEMEX-Exploracion y Produccion*, Docket No. 13-4022 (2d Cir. 2016), the US courts enforced an ICC award set aside in Mexico where denying enforcement would be fundamentally unfair and violate basic notions of justice. However, much will depend on the particular award and the enforcing court will still give great weight to the courts of the seat: see, e.g., *TermoRio SA ESP v Electranta SP*, 487 F.3d 928 (DCC 2007) (refusing to enforce an award annulled by the courts of the seat in Colombia) and *Getma International v Republic of Guinea*, 862 F.3d 45 (DDC 2017) (refusing to enforce an award annulled in Guinea). For further discussion of this concept, see Chapter 11.

[9] New York Convention, Art. V.1(e); Model Law, Art. 36(1)(a)(v).

complete annulment, the claimant can recommence proceedings because the award simply does not exist—that is, the *status quo ante* is restored. The reviewing court cannot alter the terms of an award nor can it decide the dispute based on its own view of the merits. Unless the reviewing court has a power to remit the fault to the original tribunal,[10] any new submission of the dispute to arbitration after annulment has to be undertaken by commencement of a new arbitration with a new arbitral tribunal.

(b) Preconditions to challenge

Before challenging an award before the relevant court, it will usually be necessary to 'exhaust' any other remedies: these may include any available process of appeal or review under the applicable rules or law, and any available provision for the correction of the award or for an additional award.[11]   **10.07**

With regard to appeal or review, certain rules of arbitration and certain arbitration agreements provide for appeals to 'second-tier' tribunals.[12] Subject to the applicable rules, it is usually the award of that second tribunal, and not any earlier award, that is final and binding upon the parties and which may be subject to challenge before the competent courts. With regard to correction of the award or supplemental decision, it is usual for rules of arbitration, as well as national legislation, to provide a mechanism for the correction of awards by the arbitral tribunal itself and it is the corrected or supplemented award which will be subject to judicial review.[13]   **10.08**

(c) Time limits for challenge

Time limits for applying to correct or amend an arbitral award, or to challenge an award by an application to the relevant national court, are likely to be short and strictly enforced.[14] The position in each case will depend upon the relevant rules or legislation, but by way of example: **10.09**

- under the UNCITRAL Rules, requests for interpretation or correction of an award, or for an additional award, must be made within thirty days after receipt of the award;[15]

---

[10] See paragraphs 10.18–10.20

[11] See, e.g., the English Arbitration Act 1996, s. 70(2), which states that an application or appeal may not be brought if the applicant or appellant has not first exhausted (a) any available arbitral process of appeal or review, and (b) any available recourse under s. 57 (correction of award or additional award).

[12] See paragraph 10.11.

[13] See paragraphs 10.14 and 10.16–10.17.

[14] See, e.g., *Terna Bahrain v Bin Kamil* [2012] EWHC 3283, in which the applicant tried to challenge an award under the English Arbitration Act 1996 for procedural irregularity, but the English court refused to hear the challenge because the application was made after the twenty-eight-day period for doing so had expired. The same strict approach is taken in the United States—see *Glaser v Legg*, Case No. 12-cv-00805, 2013 WL 870382 (DDC, 11 March 2013), in which a petition to vacate award was untimely, because it was filed more than three months after the award was issued. In Brazil, the Court of Appeals of São Paulo in *Companhia do Metropolitano de São Paulo—Metrô v Consórcio Via Amarela*, Appeal No. 0177130-22.2010.8.26.0100, 3 December 2012, held that the Brazilian statutory period of ninety days for challenging an award does not run while a valid request for the correction and interpretation of award is pending, but found the request for annulment to be nonetheless untimely because the party had not first filed a valid request for clarification of the award under the ICC Rules.

[15] UNCITRAL Rules, Arts 37–39.

- under the Model Law, an application for setting aside an award must be made within three months of receiving the award or, if a request for an interpretation, correction, or additional award has been made, within three months of that request being disposed of by the arbitral tribunal.[16]

B. Methods of Challenge

10.10   The relevant arbitration rules sometimes provide for 'internal' challenges to an award. This form of challenge is considered first. The correction and interpretation of awards is then considered before the challenge of awards by application to national courts.

(a) Internal challenge

10.11   The rules under which an arbitration was conducted may provide for review of the award. This is frequently the case with maritime and commodity arbitrations, and other forms of arbitration established by trade associations. For example, the Grain and Feed Trade Association (GAFTA) arbitration rules incorporated into all GAFTA standard form contracts provide for a right of appeal within a two-stage arbitration system.[17]

10.12   One frequently used provision for the challenge of arbitral awards by means of an internal review procedure is that of the ICSID Convention and ICSID Rules. A party who is dissatisfied with the award of an ICSID arbitral tribunal may apply for the annulment of the award before an ad hoc committee of three adjudicators who will all be appointed by ICSID from its list of arbitrators.[18] The committee will apply the grounds set out at Article 52 of the ICSID Convention which are far narrower than a general appeal and include that the tribunal 'was not properly constituted', that the tribunal has 'manifestly exceeded its powers', that there 'was corruption on the part of a member of the tribunal', that there has been 'a serious departure from a fundamental rule of procedure', or that the award has 'failed to state the reasons on which it is based'. These grounds are very similar to the grounds contained in national arbitral systems for the judicial challenge of arbitral awards. This is not surprising. As discussed in Chapter 8, the ICSID system is a self-contained system governed by the ICSID Convention, which does not permit judicial challenge of awards. The internal review mechanism therefore effectively replaces the system of judicial challenge.

---

[16]   Model Law, Art. 34(3).

[17]   The latest version of the No. 125 Arbitration Rules is effective from 1 March 2022. A similar approach is taken by the arbitration rules of the Chambre Arbitrale Maritime de Paris, effective 21 September 2020. The CAS Arbitration Rules (r. 47) provide for an internal appeal procedure within CAS, so long as the relevant sports federation or body has expressly provided for such an appeal in its rules. See also arbitration rules of the European Court of Arbitration, Arts 2.12 and 2.28, under which the parties are deemed to have waived any right to challenge, except by appeal to an appellate tribunal consisting of three arbitrators. To appeal, the losing party must deposit the amount of original award with the court, and if it loses the appeal, the award is automatically paid to the prevailing party.

[18]   ICSID Convention Art. 52(3) and ICSID Rules, r. 71(1). Unlike the constitution of the original arbitral tribunal, there are no party appointments of annulment panel members.

If the award is annulled, in whole or in part, either party may ask for the dispute to be **10.13** submitted to a new tribunal, which hears the dispute again and then delivers a new award.[19]

(b) Correction and interpretation of awards; additional awards; remission of awards

(i) Correction

There is usually a provision in the relevant arbitration rules, or in the law governing the **10.14** arbitration, for the correction of computational, clerical, or similar errors.[20] These are primarily intended to allow correction of 'slips' that are obvious on the face of the award. For example, the ICC Rules provide that the arbitral tribunal, on its own initiative or at the request of a party, may correct 'a clerical, computational or typographical error, or any errors of similar nature contained in an Award'.[21]

(ii) Interpretation

Some arbitral rules permit an arbitral tribunal to issue an 'interpretation' of its award.[22] **10.15** For example, the ICC Rules provide that, at the request of a party, the arbitral tribunal may issue an 'interpretation' of the award.[23] The UNCITRAL Rules provide a similar interpretation rule.[24] Whilst dissatisfied parties are sometimes tempted to use this facility to invite an arbitral tribunal to revisit the merits of its decision, it is intended only to resolve any uncertainty as to the precise meaning of an award and therefore the manner in which it is to be performed.

(iii) Additional award

A further power is given to an arbitral tribunal under some rules and national laws to deal **10.16** with any claims that were presented in the arbitral proceedings, but which the tribunal omitted to address in its award.[25] Since an arbitral award may be challenged under many legal systems if the arbitral tribunal fails to decide all of the issues that were put to it,[26] this is a sensible solution.

---

[19] ICSID Rules, r. 74. If the original award has been annulled only in part, the new tribunal will not reconsider any portion of the award that has *not* been annulled: ibid., r. 55(3).

[20] See, e.g., UNCITRAL Rules, Art. 38; ICSID Additional Facility Rules, r. 72.1; LCIA Rules, Art. 27.1 and 27.2; SIAC Rules, r. 33. The UNCITRAL Rules allow a party to request the tribunal to correct not only 'any error in computation, any clerical or typographical error', but also any erroneous 'omission'. Furthermore, under UNCITRAL Rules, Art. 38, any such corrections shall be deemed to 'form part of the award'.

[21] ICC Rules, Art. 36.

[22] Daly, 'Correction and interpretation of arbitral awards under the ICC Rules of Arbitration' (2002) 13 ICC International Court of Arbitration Bulletin 62. For example, in ICC Case No. 10189, the tribunal amended the text of an award in order to avoid any uncertainty as to the time period of the royalty payments owed by the claimant.

[23] The ICC Rules, Art. 36 is based on the 1998 ICC Rules, Art. 29. The interpretation of an award should not be an indirect means of appealing or altering the award. See Verbist and others, *ICC Arbitration in Practice* (2nd edn, Kluwer International Law, 2015), p. 194.

[24] UNCITRAL Rules, Art. 35.

[25] See, e.g., the English Arbitration Act 1996, s. 57; UNCITRAL Rules, Art. 39.1.

[26] An award that is *infra petita*. See, e.g., English Arbitration Act 1996, s. 68(2)(d).

10.17   In addition, certain national laws provide for tribunals to revisit their awards where evidence is later produced of fraud, forgery, or concealment of evidence. By way of example, subsequently revealed fraud is considered to be a ground for revising an award both under French and Swiss law.[27]

(iv) Remission of award

10.18   Certain national laws further provide the domestic courts with the power to remit or send back disputes, requiring the tribunal to revisit some or all of its findings. In contrast to requests for correction, interpretation, or additional awards where a party makes a request of the arbitral tribunal, a request for remission will be made to the courts of the seat of the arbitration.

10.19   Powers of remission are derived from national arbitration statutes. For example, section 68(3) of the English Arbitration Act 1996 provides that '[t]he court shall not exercise its power to set aside or to declare an award to be of no effect, in whole or in part, unless it is satisfied that it would be inappropriate to remit the matters to the tribunal for reconsideration'. In the United States, the power has been established by means of case law.[28] The ICC Rules acknowledge the possibility of remission and establish the mechanism applicable to the administration of the arbitration in that eventuality.[29]

10.20   It should be noted that national arbitration laws vary widely regarding the scope of the courts' power of remission. Many take their cue from the Model Law by linking remission to setting-aside proceedings and thereby limiting the scope of grounds for remission to the narrow grounds available for setting aside.[30] In these countries, the power to remit is essentially a means to 'cure' awards that might otherwise need to be set aside. By contrast, some national laws adopt a more flexible approach—such as the United States, where the courts do not necessarily limit remission to situations in which the only alternative is to vacate (that is, set aside) the award.[31]

(c) Recourse to the courts

10.21   What is a losing party to do if its grievance is not something that can be put right by correction or interpretation of the award and there is no provision for internal review

---

[27]   See, e.g., French law (cour de cassation in *Fougerolle v Procofrance* [1992] J du Droit Intl 974; cour d'appel de Paris in *European Gas Turbines SA v Westman International Ltd*, Rev Arb 1994, 359 (Fr.) and Swiss law (Swiss Federal Supreme Court in *Sovereign Participations International SA v Chadmore Developments Ltd* (2001) XXVI YBCA 299, at 301*ff*). This principle was confirmed in the 2011 French Arbitration Law, art. 1502.

[28]   See ALI, Draft Restatement of the US Law of International Commercial and Investor–State Arbitration (2019), §4.34, restating the US case-generated rule as positing that '[a] court may in exceptional circumstances remand a U.S. Convention award to the arbitral tribunal with instructions to complete the award or to clarify its meanings'. The Draft represents the official position of the ALI until the official text of the restatement expected to be published in 2022.

[29]   ICC Rules, Art. 36.5.

[30]   Model Law, Art. 34(4).

[31]   See *Weinburg v Silber*, 140 F.Supp.2d 712 (Tex. 2001), remanding the award to the tribunal to explain how it should be discharged in view of the emergence of certain apparently unforeseen circumstances; *Fisher v General Steel Domestic Sales, LLC*, Slip Copy No. 10-cv-0109-WYD-BNB, 2011 WL 524362 (D. Colo., 31 October 2011), remitting to the tribunal to address a jurisdictional issue left undecided. See also Coe, 'Making remission and other "curative" mechanisms part of the forum shopping conversation: A view from the US with comparative notes', in Ferrari (ed.) *Forum Shopping in the International Commercial Arbitration Context* (Sellier European Law, 2013), pp. 382–383.

of the award? It should consider whether there are grounds on which the arbitral award may be challenged before a national court at the place of arbitration (the 'competent court', as it is described in the Model Law).[32] However, there are two preliminary issues that need to be addressed before considering the typical grounds for challenging an award:

(i) Place of challenge

Any challenge to the validity or effect of an award must be addressed to the designated competent court of the seat of the arbitration.[33] If the arbitration had its seat in Switzerland, for example, the competent court is the Swiss Federal Supreme Court (although the parties may agree to the court of the canton in which the arbitration took place).[34] In France, it is the Paris Court of Appeal.[35] In England, it is the Commercial Court of the Queen's Bench Division in the High Court of Justice. In the United States, it is the District Court (the federal first-instance court) of the seat of the arbitration.[36]   **10.22**

There is one notable exception to this general rule, although it is probably more theoretical than real: the freedom of the parties to decide how an international arbitration should be conducted includes the freedom to subject the arbitration to the procedural law of a country *other than* that in which the arbitration is held. It seems to be both unnecessary and unhelpful for parties to use their freedom in this way.[37] However, the New York Convention itself acknowledges that recognition and enforcement of an award may be refused on the basis that the award has been 'set aside or suspended by a competent authority of the country in which, *or under the law of which*, that award was made'.[38] Some courts have read the reference to 'the country under whose law the award was made' as a licence to set aside an award that was not made in their own country, but which was governed by their country's substantive law.   **10.23**

For example, in 2008 the Indian courts exercised supervisory jurisdiction in cases in which the seat was not India but where the substance of the dispute was governed by Indian   **10.24**

---

[32] Model Law, Art. 6, provides for each state to designate the court, courts, or other authority competent to perform the functions laid down by the Model Law, which include the setting aside of awards under Art. 34.

[33] For example, the Model Law provides that each State is free to determine which specific courts or authorities are competent to hear the requests for setting aside an award. See Model Law, Arts 6, 34, and Explanatory Note, para. 45.

[34] Swiss PIL, Ch. 12, s. 191, as amended.

[35] In 2018, the cour d'appel de Paris established an 'International Chamber' to hear challenges against international awards as of 1 March 2018. This chamber allows limited use of English in the proceedings to make French courts more accessible to non-French speakers (e.g. by allowing the submission of exhibits in English and allowing foreign advocates to plead in English).

[36] FAA, § 10(a).

[37] 'Unnecessary', because if the law of a particular country contains procedures that the parties prefer, the parties would do better to adopt those specific procedures rather than to try to adopt a law of procedure that is alien to the *lex arbitri* with which it might be in conflict. 'Unhelpful', because it means adding another set of legal rules to which the arbitration will be subject, in addition to those agreed by the parties or imposed by the *lex arbitri*. This topic is discussed more fully in Chapter 3.

[38] New York Convention, Art. V(1)(e) (emphasis added). Art. 5(1)(e) of the Inter-American Convention on International Commercial Arbitration contains a similar provision. See also *International Electric Corporation v Bridas Sociedad Anonima Petrolera, Industrial y Comercial*, 745 F.Supp. 172, 178 (SDNY 1990), in which the court held that the italicised words ('since the *situs* of the arbitration is Mexico, and the governing procedural law that of Mexico, only Mexican courts have jurisdiction under the Convention to vacate the award') referred to the procedural law governing the arbitration and not to the substantive law governing the agreement between the parties. See also the decision of the Mexican Supreme Court in *Amparo Directo en Revisión* No. 8/2011, which deemed that only judges at the seat of the arbitration are competent to annul an award.

law.[39] Four years later, in 2012, the Indian Supreme Court reversed course with its decision in *Bharat Aluminium Co. (Balco) v Kaiser Aluminium Technical Services,*[40] confirming the international practice that the power to set aside is limited to the courts of the seat of the arbitration. In 2015, India issued an ordinance amending its arbitration law and clarifying the scope of the *Balco* decision, stating that Indian courts are still empowered to issue orders in aid of international arbitration seated outside India, such as interim measures and those related to the taking of evidence.[41]

(ii) Exclusion and waiver of challenge

10.25   In some jurisdictions, parties to arbitrations may be able to exclude their right to challenge an award.[42] Thus, under the arbitration laws of both Switzerland[43] and Belgium,[44] if all parties to an arbitration are foreign, they may agree to exclude the right to challenge the arbitral award. Under the French law governing international arbitrations, any party may waive the right to challenge.[45]

10.26   In general, a waiver of a right to challenge must be express; general waivers by incorporation, such as that contained in the ICC Rules,[46] will not usually suffice.[47] In 2012, the ICC Secretariat confirmed that this type of provision was '*unlikely to be deemed sufficient* to constitute a waiver of the right to bring proceedings to set aside an award even in those jurisdictions where such a waiver is possible.'[48]

10.27   Parties are unlikely to succeed in any challenge to an award based on an objection that they could have raised but failed to raise during the arbitral proceedings.[49] In these

---

[39]   See *Venture Global Engineering v Satyam Computer Services Ltd and anor*, Civil Appeal No. 309 of 2008, Supreme Court of India (arising out of SLP (C) No. 8491 of 2007); *Bhatia International v Bulk Trading SA* (2002) 4 SCC 105.

[40]   Civil Appeal No. 7019 of 2005, 6 September 2012 (holding that Indian courts will no longer be able to vacate international arbitral awards not seated in India or issue interim measures concerning ongoing international arbitrations seated abroad). The problem was also addressed in Uruguay in *YPF v AESU, Sulgás, TGM,* Decision No. SEF 0005-000152/2014, in which (in 2014) the Uruguayan Court of Appeals held invalid the provision of an arbitration clause in which the parties agreed that challenges against awards rendered in an arbitration seated in Uruguay would be heard by Argentinian courts. The Uruguayan court reasoned that parties to an arbitration agreement are not allowed to remove the authority of the Uruguayan courts over arbitrations seated in Uruguay.

[41]   See 2015 Arbitration and Conciliation (Amendment) Ordinance, § 2(2).

[42]   See *Sociedad de Inversiones Inmobiliarias Del Puerto SA v Constructora Iberoamericana SA*, Court of Appeals on Commercial Matters, Division D, 7 February 2011, in which the Argentina Court of Appeals on Commercial Matters held that parties may validly waive the right to challenge an arbitral award. However, for a contrary view, see the Swiss Supreme Court's annulment of an award rendered by CAS, in which waivers to challenge awards were held to be invalid: Case No. 4P–172/2006, 22 March 2007.

[43]   Swiss PIL, Ch. 12, s. 192.

[44]   See Belgian Judicial Code, art. 1718, as amended in 2013.

[45]   French Arbitration Law, Arts 1520, 1522 CCP.

[46]   ICC Rules, Art. 35.6.

[47]   General waivers may suffice to waive some rights, such as the right to appeal an arbitral award on points of English law contemplated in the English Arbitration Act 1996, s. 69. See *Lesotho Highlands Development Authority v Impreglio SpA and ors* [2005] UKHL 43, [2005] Arb LR 557, at [3] *per* Lord Steyn, finding that, by submitting to ICC arbitration, current Art. 35.6 (then Art. 28.6) of the ICC Rules sufficed to waive the parties' right to appeal.

[48]   Fry, Greenberg, and Mazza, *The Secretariat's Guide to ICC Arbitration* (ICC, 2012), paras 3.1254–3.1255 (emphasis added). This statement was issued in context of discussing the 2012 ICC Rules, Article 34.6—identical to the ICC Rules, Art. 35.6 now in force.

[49]   See, e.g., *Thyssen Canada Ltd v Mariana Maritime SA and ors* [2005] EWHC 219, in which it was held that a party who takes part in arbitral proceedings and fails to raise an objection as to a serious irregularity affecting the proceedings will lose the right to object, unless it can show that, at the time that it took part or continued to take

circumstances, they will usually be taken to have waived any objection. The possibility of waiver is often set out in national arbitration legislation[50] and in the major arbitration rules.[51] Take, for example, an international arbitration in London, in which the respondent is in doubt as to the validity of the arbitration agreement, but nevertheless participates in the arbitration. The tribunal makes an award against the respondent, who then seeks to challenge it on the ground that the tribunal lacked jurisdiction. The respondent will find that it is too late to rely on such a ground, since English law requires an objection to jurisdiction to be raised at the earliest possible opportunity[52] and provides that if this is not done, the right to object is lost.[53] The Paris Court of Appeal has also rejected challenges based on objections that the challenging party failed to raise—and was therefore deemed to have waived—during the arbitration itself.[54] The UNCITRAL Rules and the Model Law contain provisions requiring a plea as to lack of jurisdiction to be raised at an early stage (failing which, it is waived).[55]

Case law in the United States also supports the proposition that a party will have waived its right to seek judicial relief of the arbitrator's award, having participated in the arbitration process and failed to object that the claim was not arbitrable.[56]   **10.28**

Indeed, most developed arbitral jurisdictions uphold awards where an objection is raised too late; and most states that are parties to the New York Convention are ready to enforce such awards. Less commonly, courts may refuse to set aside an award where the party challenging the award fails to raise its complaint with sufficient force and clarity during the arbitral proceedings.[57] Put simply, and as a matter of practice, if an objection is to be taken, it should be taken without delay and in the clearest terms possible.   **10.29**

---

part in the proceedings, it did not know and could not with reasonable diligence have discovered the grounds for the objection.

[50] See, e.g., English Arbitration Act 1996, s. 73; Belgian Judicial Code, art. 1679; Dutch Code of Civil Procedure, art. 1048a.

[51] See, e.g., ICC Rules, Art. 40; UNCITRAL Rules, Art. 32; ICDR Rules, Art. 28; ICSID Rules, r. 27; LCIA, Art. 32.1; SIAC Rules, r. 41.1.

[52] English Arbitration Act 1996, s. 31.

[53] English Arbitration Act 1996, s. 73. See also *Emirates Trading Agency LLC v Sociedade de Fomento Industrial Private Ltd* [2015] EWHC 1452 (Comm), in which the English court refused to consider a party's challenge to an arbitral award because the party had failed to timely object to the tribunal's preliminary ruling on jurisdiction.

[54] See, e.g., the cour d'appel de Paris decision in *SA Caisse Fédérale de Crédit Mutuel du Nord de la France v Banque Delubac et Compagnie* [2001] Rev Arb 918. See also the cour d'appel de Paris decision in *Exodis c/Ricoh France* [2004] 683. It is noteworthy that, in *A Rahman Golshani v Iran* [2005] Rev Arb 993, the French cour de cassation referred to and applied the notion of estoppel in an international arbitration case. In this case, the cour de cassation held that a party which had itself commenced the arbitration and participated without any reservation for more than nine years was estopped from arguing that that tribunal had rendered its decision in the absence of an arbitration agreement, or on the basis of an arbitration agreement that was null and void.

[55] UNCITRAL Rules, Art. 23.2 ('no later than in the statement of defence or, with respect to a counterclaim or a claim for the purpose of a set-off, in the reply to the counterclaim or to the claim for the purpose of set-off'); Model Law, Art. 16(2) ('not later than the submission of the statement of defence').

[56] See *Howard University v Metropolitan Campus Police Officer's Union* 519 F.Supp.2d 27, 35 (DDC 2007). See also *United Industrial Workers v Government of the Virgin Islands*, 987 F.2d 162, 168 (3d Cir. 1993), in which it was held: 'Because arbitrators derive their authority from the contractual agreement of the parties, a party may waive its right to challenge an arbitrator's authority to decide a matter by voluntarily participating in an arbitration and failing to object on the grounds that there was no agreement to arbitrate.'

[57] For example, in rejecting a challenge to an ICC arbitration, a Swiss court held that the challenging party had not made 'a sufficiently clear complaint' during the original arbitration, thus waiving its right to challenge. *X. SE & Y. GmbH v Z. BV*, Case No. 4A_407/2012, First Civil Law Court (Switzerland), 20 February 2013.

C. Grounds for Challenge

10.30   Each state has its own concept of what measure of control it wishes to exercise over an arbitral process that takes place in its territory and, in particular, whether it wishes in this respect to distinguish between 'domestic' and 'international' arbitration. It is thus necessary to consult the law of the arbitral seat in order to determine the grounds on which a particular award may be challenged.

10.31   It is beyond the scope of this book to review all these different legal systems. It may nevertheless be helpful to discern the areas in which judicial control, or review, is likely to occur.

10.32   There are essentially three broad areas in which an arbitral award is likely to be challenged before a national court at the seat of the arbitration. First, an award may be challenged on jurisdictional grounds—for example, the non-existence of a valid and binding arbitration agreement—or on grounds that go to the admissibility of the claim determined by the tribunal. Secondly, an award may be challenged on what may broadly be described as 'procedural' grounds, such as failure to give a party an equal opportunity to be heard. Thirdly, and most rarely, an award may be challenged on substantive grounds, on the basis that the arbitral tribunal made a mistake of law. We will illustrate these broad categories by reference to the grounds for challenge set out in the Model Law[58] which has now been adapted or adopted by eighty-five states[59] and has been a strong influence on other states, such as the United Kingdom, when drafting their laws governing arbitration.

(a) Grounds under the Model Law

10.33   The Model Law provides that an action for setting aside an award may be brought before the designated courts of the state in which an award was made[60] pursuant only to the grounds exhaustively set out in the Law. These grounds are taken from Article V of the New York Convention. There is a pleasing symmetry here: Article V of the New York Convention sets out the grounds on which recognition and enforcement of an international award may be refused, while Article 34 of the Model Law sets out the same grounds (with only slight differences of language) on which an award may be set aside. These grounds are:

- lack of capacity to conclude an arbitration agreement, or lack of a valid arbitration agreement;
- the aggrieved party was not given proper notice of the appointment of the arbitral tribunal, or the arbitral proceedings, or was otherwise unable to present its case;

---

[58] The full title of the Model Law is the 'Model Law on *International* Commercial Arbitration' (emphasis added). Some states, such as Australia, Canada, Germany, or Singapore have either adopted or adapted the Model Law for both 'international' and 'domestic' arbitration.

[59] See UNCITRAL website https://uncitral.un.org/en/texts/arbitration/modellaw/commercial_arbitration/status.

[60] Model Law, Art. 1(2). Under Art. 6, a state that enacts the Model Law must designate the court(s) within its territory that will fulfil the various functions entrusted to the courts.

- the award deals with matters not contemplated by, or falling within, the arbitration clause or submission agreement, or goes beyond the scope of what was submitted;
- the composition of the arbitral tribunal or the arbitral procedure was not in accordance with the agreement of the parties, or with the mandatory provisions of the Model Law itself;
- the subject matter of the dispute is not capable of settlement by arbitration under the law of the state in which the arbitration takes place; and/or
- the award (or any decision within it) is in conflict with the public policy of the state in which the arbitration takes place.[61]

One provision of the Model Law mitigates, to some extent, the 'all or nothing' approach of the Model Law, under which an award is either set aside or left to stand. Where appropriate, upon application by a party, the court may suspend the setting-aside proceedings in order to give the arbitral tribunal an opportunity to resume the arbitral proceedings, or to take such other action as, in the arbitral tribunal's opinion, will eliminate the grounds for setting aside.[62] In effect, this is an equivalent provision to that of remitting the award to the tribunal for reconsideration.   **10.34**

The grounds for challenge may be broadly categorised as: **10.35**

- grounds that concern whether the claim in question is capable of adjudication (including issues of incapacity, invalid agreements to arbitrate, a tribunal's excess of powers, or the arbitrability of the subject matter of the dispute);
- procedural grounds (including issues relating to the composition of the arbitral tribunal); and
- substantive grounds (including mistakes of law, mistakes of fact, and public policy).

(b) Adjudicability

As discussed in Chapter 5, an arbitral tribunal is empowered to decide for itself whether or not it has jurisdiction over a particular dispute under the doctrine of 'competence-competence'. If its jurisdiction is challenged, the arbitral tribunal may decide the point as a preliminary issue in an interim award or as part of its award on the merits. In either case, however, the decision of the arbitral tribunal is not necessarily the last word on the subject: that rests with the national court which, depending on the jurisdiction, may have the power to review the question *de novo* or review the decision deferentially. The Model Law provides for a *de novo* review by stating that if the arbitral tribunal rules as a preliminary question that it has jurisdiction, this ruling may be referred to the competent court (within thirty days) for the court's decision, which is final.[63] In England, the courts have power to review the jurisdictional decision *de novo*.[64] The same is true   **10.36**

---

[61] Model Law, Art. 34(2).
[62] Model Law, Art. 34(4). For a detailed commentary on this Article, see Holtzmann and Neuhaus, *A Guide to the UNCITRAL Model Law on International Commercial Arbitration* (Kluwer Law International, 1995), p. 967.
[63] Model Law, Art. 16(3).
[64] See English Arbitration Act 1996, s. 67.

in France.[65] Curiously, in the Netherlands, only a decision accepting jurisdiction is reviewable *de novo* and a decision denying jurisdiction is given the same deference as a decision on the merits.[66] In the United States, the standard depends on whether the jurisdictional decision was based on compliance with procedural preconditions (that is, *when* the obligation to arbitrate arises), in which case deferential review applies, or consent to arbitrate at all (that is, *if* the obligation to arbitrate arises). Only in the second case a *de novo* test will be applied.[67]

(i) Incapacity to consent to arbitration or invalid arbitration agreement

10.37   The first ground for challenging an award under Article 34(2)(a)(i) of the Model Law provides that:

> (i) a party to the arbitration agreement [...] was under some incapacity; or the said agreement is not valid under the law to which the parties have subjected it or, failing any indication thereon, under the law of this State; [...]

10.38   This conflates two separate grounds. Both the issue of 'capacity' and the requirements for an enforceable arbitration agreement are discussed in detail in Chapter 2. Challenges based on the absence of a valid and binding arbitration agreement are not an uncommon ground for challenge. They are often made by non-signatories who have been brought into arbitral proceedings contrary to their wishes.[68]

10.39   Another challenge as to the validity of the arbitration agreement arose out of great tension between European Union (EU) law and international investment arbitration. In *Achmea*, an arbitral tribunal seated in Germany constituted under the UNCITRAL Rules pursuant to the BIT between the Netherlands and Slovakia awarded the claimant investor damages of €22.1 million against Slovakia. Slovakia then applied to set aside the award before the German courts on the basis, inter alia, that there was no valid arbitration agreement since it was inconsistent with EU law. The application was dismissed, and subsequently reached the German Federal Court of Justice. The Federal Court confirmed that the case raised untested questions about the interpretation of EU law and referred the question to the Court of Justice of the European Union (the CJEU) under the preliminary reference procedure

---

[65] French Code of Civil Procedure, art. 1520(1).

[66] Civil Procedure Code, Art. 1065(1). Case law has concluded that only a positive conclusion in favour of jurisdiction is subject to a full review. A negative conclusion is subject to the ordinary deferential level of review. See, e.g. *Manuel Garcia et al v Bolivarian Republic of Venezuela*, District Court of the Hague, 26 January 2021, at [14].

[67] See *BG Group plc v Argentine Republic*, 572 US 25, 134 S.Ct. 1198 (2014).

[68] See, e.g., *Arab National Bank v El Sharif Saoud Bin Masoud Bin Haza'a El-Abdali* [2004] EWHC 2381; *Republic of Kazakhstan v Istil Group Inc.* [2004] Eng Comm QBD 579, in which an award was set aside based on the Republic of Kazakhstan not having been a party to the relevant arbitration agreement. See also *Kabab-Ji v Kout Food Group* (cour d'appel de Paris, 23 June 2020, Case No. 17/22942), in which, in an ICC arbitration with its seat in Paris, the tribunal determined that it had jurisdiction over a non-signatory to the arbitration agreement. The non-signatory losing party challenged the award, alleging that the underlying contract was governed by English law, which should have led to the tribunal to decline jurisdiction. The cour d'appel de Paris rejected the challenge finding that, regardless of the law governing the contract, the law of the seat is applicable to the arbitration clause in the absence of an agreement on the contrary, and thus a non-signatory of an arbitration agreement governed by French law may be compelled to arbitrate. In another case, the cour d'appel de Paris partially annulled an arbitral award that had declined jurisdiction to hear a dispute involving four non-signatory parties. The Court held that two of the four non-signatory parties had knowledge of the arbitration agreement and were directly involved in the performance of the contract and were therefore bound to arbitrate any dispute arising from that contract. cour d'appel de Paris, 18 December 2018, Case No. 16/24924.

to opine on the compatibility of investor–state arbitration under an intra-EU BIT with the Treaty on the Functioning of the European Union (TFEU).[69] The CJEU concluded[70] that the investor–state arbitration provision of an investment treaty between two EU states was incompatible with EU law as investment arbitration tribunals may be called upon to decide questions of EU law (since EU law is part of a member state's domestic and international law obligations). However, since an investment arbitration tribunal is not part of the EU judicial system, the tribunal would not have the power to refer any question concerning EU law to the CJEU (as would a national court). Consequently, the arbitration provision of intra-EU BITs would be contrary to EU law (as it would effectively bypass the protection of the CJEU as a guarantee of uniformity of interpretation of EU law).

In applying this decision, the German Federal Supreme Court set aside the award in favour of Achmea on the basis that there was no valid arbitration agreement[71] since Slovakia's offer to arbitrate in the Treaty was inapplicable and could not give rise to an arbitration agreement.[72]   **10.40**

The risks of an arbitral award made pursuant to an intra EU BIT being set aside are therefore high (particularly in cases seated in an EU jurisdiction).[73] Those risks may be mitigated if a London seat is chosen since the UK courts have proven to be less deferential to the idea that EU law trumps other international obligations that arise from investment treaties or the ICSID Convention.[74]   **10.41**

(ii) An arbitral tribunal's excess of powers

A further ground for challenge under the Model Law is that the arbitral tribunal has exceeded its powers in the decision that it has rendered. In the words of Article 34(2)(a)(iii):   **10.42**

> (iii) the award deals with a dispute not contemplated by or not falling within the terms of the submission to arbitration, or contains decisions on matters beyond the scope of the submission to arbitration, provided that, if the decisions on matters submitted to arbitration can be separated from those not so submitted, only that part of the award which contains decisions on matters not submitted to arbitration may be set aside; […]

This ground of challenge contemplates a situation in which an award has been made by a tribunal that did have jurisdiction to deal with the dispute, but which exceeded its powers by dealing with claims that had not been submitted to it.[75] By way of example, the Paris Court of Appeal found that a tribunal exceeded its powers by awarding a party damages in an amount that significantly exceeded the damages claimed.[76]   **10.43**

---

[69] Judgment of the Higher Regional Court of Frankfurt, 18 December 2014.

[70] Case C-284/16 *Slovak Republic v Achmea BV*, 6 March 2018.

[71] See the ZPO, s. 1059(2)(1)(a).

[72] German Federal Supreme Court (BGH) Decision of 31 October 2018.

[73] The number of new awards under intra-EU BITs will be restricted by the Agreement for the Termination of all Intra-EU BITs signed by 23 Member States of the European Union on 5 May 2020, following the decision in *Achmea*. The Agreement entered into force on 29 August 2020.

[74] See, e.g. the decision of the UK Supreme Court in *Micula and ors v Romania* [2020] UKSC 5, at [84]–[86] where it held that the UK's obligations under the ICSID Convention were not impacted by its obligations under the TFEU.

[75] See Liebscher, *The Healthy Award: Challenge in International Commercial Arbitration* (Kluwer Law International, 2003), ch. V(6).

[76] *Paris Lapeyre v Sauvage* [2001] Rev Arb 806, n. Derains.

10.44   Where an arbitral tribunal fails to deal with *all* of the issues referred to it for determination, it is usually said that the award should at least be upheld in respect of the issues with which it *does* deal. However, this is perhaps too simplistic. The significance of the issues that were not addressed must be considered in relation to the award as a whole. A situation might be envisaged in which the issues that were overlooked were of such importance that, if they had been dealt with, the whole balance of the award would have been altered and its effect would have been different.[77]

10.45   In such circumstances, it seems fair that the aggrieved party should have a right of recourse against the entire award. However, national laws are divided on the subject and no right of recourse against the entire award is available under the Model Law.[78]

(iii) Arbitrability

10.46   The concept of 'arbitrability', which provides another ground on which to challenge an award, has already been discussed in detail.[79] Under the Model Law, an award can be challenged if 'the subject matter of the dispute is not capable of settlement by arbitration'.[80] As discussed in Chapter 2, the arbitrability of a dispute is usually linked to the underlying public policy of the state in which the arbitration takes place.[81] The law applicable to the dispute, however, may also curtail the parties' freedom to submit certain disputes to arbitration. In Belgium, for example, a Brussels court annulled an award after concluding that the subject matter was not arbitrable under the law governing the dispute, namely, Greek law.[82] Many states prohibit the arbitration of disputes that are not suited to the confidential nature

---

[77] For example, in *BLB and anor v BLC and ors*, the Singapore High Court set aside an award on *infra petita* grounds. In that case, the respondent BLC had originally advanced a counterclaim, but the tribunal omitted to decide the counterclaim after wrongly characterising it as a substantive defence to liability. The High Court annulled the award finding that the tribunal had failed to exercise its powers and that the *infra petita* doctrine applied. See Tan and Ahmad, 'The UNCITRAL Model Law and awards infra petita' (2014) 31(3) J Intl Arb 413, at 414–415.

[78] See the Netherlands Arbitration Act 2015, s. 1065, for an example of a national system permitting a challenge to the entire award for an *infra petita* decision. But note that where the parties have discovered that the arbitral tribunal omitted to decide an issue before it, an additional award must first have been applied for and rejected before there is an admissible ground for setting aside: s. 1065(6). However, certain countries, such as Belgium and France, do not allow a challenge to an award on the basis that a tribunal has not ruled on certain issues. See Belgian Arbitration Law 2013, s. 1717(3); French Code of Civil Procedure, art. 1502(3). See also Meijer, 'Concluding Remarks', in Cooper, Gerbay, Kühner, Goldman, and Van Rompaey (eds) *Annulment and Enforcement of Arbitral Awards from a Comparative Law Perspective*, (Wolters Kluwer, 2018) pp. 107–131, at 129. The Model Law, Art. 33(3), may provide the answer to this problem, in that, at the request of a party, the arbitral tribunal may make an additional award where claims have not been dealt with in the award.

[79] See Chapter 2.

[80] Model Law, Art. 34(2)(b)(i). See, e.g., Belgian Arbitration Law 2013, s. 1676(5), providing that certain categories of labour disputes are not arbitrable, and that any arbitration agreement relating to such disputes shall be null and void.

[81] For example, in France, limits to arbitrability are set by French concepts of international public policy. In other countries such as the United States, Germany, and China, those limits are set by mandatory rules (*lois de police*). See, e.g., Kleiman and Pauly, 'Arbitrability and public policy challenges', in Rowley (ed.) *The Guide to Challenging and Enforcing Arbitration Awards* (Global Arbitration Review, 2019), pp. 33–42.

[82] *La société de droit grec X. v la SPRL Y. et A.K.*, Court of First Instance of Brussels, Case Nos 2014/480/A and 2015/6305/A, 29 January 2016 and 12 April 2018. In *Reliance Industries Ltd & Anor v The Union of India* [2018] EWHC 822 (Comm), the English High Court considered nine challenges to a final partial award, in which the majority of an arbitral tribunal, inter alia, had declined jurisdiction to hear a claim relating to the decision of the Indian government to withhold certain payments to its private counterparty. Challenge 6 concerned the arbitrability of the claim based on this government act. The Court found that '[t]he jurisdiction being conferred on the tribunal is to decide disputes in accordance with the relevant principles of law which are applicable, and if the relevant applicable principles of private international law make some issues non-justiciable, they form just as much a part of the body of legal rules which the state is asking the tribunal to apply'.

of the arbitral process and which have effects on third parties. Typically, these include questions of insolvency, personal status, and certain types of intellectual property dispute (such as the validity of patents).

(c) Procedural grounds

The second broad category of grounds for challenging arbitral awards relates to deficiencies in the way in which the arbitral tribunal was appointed or the arbitral procedure was conducted. As set out in Article 34(2)(c)(ii) of the Model Law, an award can be challenged when 'the party making the application was not given proper notice of the appointment of an arbitrator or of the arbitral proceedings or was otherwise unable to present his case'.   **10.47**

(i) Lack of due process—procedural irregularity

Certain minimum procedural standards must be observed in the fair and proper conduct of an international arbitration. These procedural standards are designed to ensure that the arbitral tribunal is properly constituted, that the arbitral procedure is in accordance with the agreement of the parties (subject to any mandatory provisions of the applicable law), and that the parties are given proper notice of the proceedings, hearings, and awards. In short, the aim is to ensure that the parties are treated with equality and are given a fair hearing, with a proper opportunity to present their respective cases.[83]   **10.48**

Most lawyers with experience of litigation or arbitration should find it relatively easy to agree upon these basic principles. The same body of lawyers, however, might find it more difficult to agree upon a set of rules to implement them. Some national systems of law, whilst rightly insisting upon the need for each of the parties to an arbitration to be given a fair hearing, have little or no legislation to guide the parties or the arbitral tribunal. In practice, it is left to national courts to determine, from case to case, exactly what is required to constitute a 'fair hearing'. This may require that the parties be heard, be allowed to attend any oral hearings, and be represented or assisted by a representative of their choice. Failure to observe these rules of procedure may be a ground for the challenge of an award,[84] although procedural grounds for challenge are often rightly viewed by many national courts with circumspection, because they are often employed by unsuccessful parties in an opportunistic attempt to avoid compliance with the award.[85]   **10.49**

---

[83] The requirement of equality is a specific requirement of some laws: see, e.g., Swiss PIL, Ch. 12, s. 190. The Swiss courts, however, have adopted an increasingly restrictive approach to equality and, in particular, the right to be heard, to the extent that, in 2019, the Swiss Federal Supreme Court determined that a violation of the right to be heard warranted annulment only if its violation was determinative to the outcome of the procedure. See Gabriel and Schregenberger, 'The new Swiss approach to the right to be heard—Balancing challenging fairness and efficiency concerns' (2019) III(2) Indian Journal of Arbitration Law 48. See also *Sara Errani v International Tennis Federation and CAS*, Case BGE 4A_424/2018, Decision of the Swiss Supreme Court, 29 January 2019. Other courts have been less strict. For example, in two parallel cases *Hui v Esposito Holdings* [2017] FCA 648 and [2017] FCA 728, an Australian court observed that a party must prove that the procedural breach resulted in real unfairness or real practical injustice, leading to a possibility that the arbitration may have had a different outcome.

[84] See, e.g., the kinds of 'serious irregularity' referred to in the English Arbitration Act 1996, s. 68(1)–(3). The English view is that there must be an irregularity of a specified kind and that the court must consider that the irregularity has caused or will cause substantial injustice: Shore and Carey, 'Procedural irregularity: Setting aside or remitting awards under English and Irish law—A comparative assessment' (2005) Intl ALR 58.

[85] See, e.g., Decision of 7 January 2004, Case No. 4P_196/2003 (2004) 3 ASA Bulletin 592, in which the Swiss Federal Supreme Court held that there was no absolute right for a party to hear a witness orally or to ask questions

10.50   By way of example, US federal courts have regarded the failure to give the parties an oral hearing where one is requested to be a violation of due process, and they recognise this as a ground for setting aside an award or for refusing recognition and enforcement under the New York Convention.[86] In civil law systems, the right of the parties to have a full opportunity to present their case—the classic *droit de la défense*—often incorporates the *principe du contradictoire*, which requires that no evidence or argument should serve as a basis for a decision unless it has been subject to the possibility of comment and contradiction by the other parties.[87]

10.51   Thus, when a question arises as to whether or not an arbitration was conducted properly, each national court approaches the question from its own particular national standpoint. This is understandable, but it may lead to difficulties. The arbitration proceedings may have been conducted by lawyers from different legal backgrounds, accustomed to different procedures and professional ethics.[88] The rules of the leading arbitral institutions are themselves vague on the question of what procedure should be followed. This is a deliberate policy, since the rules are intended to be suitable for use in many different countries of the world, with many different systems of trial.[89] However, international arbitration has become sufficiently established and widespread for the development of some common procedures, as discussed in Chapter 6.[90]

---

to witnesses who the arbitrators had refused to hear. See also, e.g., Decision of 1 July 2004, Case No. 4P_93/2004 (2005) 1 ASA Bulletin 139, in which the Swiss Federal Tribunal Supreme Court held that the mere violation of a procedural rule was not sufficient to have an award set aside. In England, see, e.g., *Lesotho Highlands Development Authority v Impregilo SpA and ors* [2005] 3 WLR 129, in which the House of Lords (now the UK Supreme Court) confirmed the exceptional nature of the remedy available for serious irregularity under the English Arbitration Act 1996, s. 68. With respect to Hong Kong, see, e.g., *Grand Pacific Holdings Ltd v Pacific China Holdings Ltd*, CACV 136/2011, 19 February 2013, in which the Court of Final Appeal affirmed the Court of Appeal's decision that the procedural irregularities alleged by the losing party were not 'egregious' enough to warrant annulment.

[86]   See *Parsons Whittemore Overseas Co. Inc. v Société Générale de l'Industrie du Papier (RAKTA)*, 508 F.2d 969 (2d Cir. 1974).

[87]   See, e.g., the decision of the cour d'appel de Paris in *Burkinabe des Ciments et Matérieux (CIMAT) v Société des Ciments d'Abidjan (SCA)* [2001] Rev Arb 165, n. Cohen. See also *Gouvernement de la République arabe d'Egypte v Société Malicorp Ltd*, Cass. Civ., Ch. Civ. 1ere, 23 June 2010, [2011] Rev Arb 446; *France Telecom-Orange FCR v Equatorial Guinea*, cour d'appel de Paris, 22 September 2015, Case No. 14/17200 and *Société Strube GmbH & Co. KG v Société SESVanderHave*, Case No. 15/17/137, in which the French court set aside the award because it was based on legal grounds or documents not raised with the parties. See also *Fleetwood Wanderers Ltd. (t/a Fleetwood Town Football Club) v AFC Fylde Ltd.* [2018] EWHC 3318 (Comm), in which the English High Court set aside the award on the basis that the tribunal had rendered its award on grounds not raised by parties. See also *RJ and ors v HB* [2018] EWHC 2833 (Comm). In turn, see *Terna Bahrain Holding Co. v Ali Marzook Ali Bin Kamil Al Shamsi ors* [2012] EWHC 3283 (Comm), in which the London High Court dismissed the challengers' contention that the arbitrator had engaged in a serious irregularity of procedure under the English Arbitration Act 1996, s. 68 by deciding the case on a basis allegedly not advanced by a party. According to Popplewell J, at [85]: 'Relief under section 68 will only be appropriate where the tribunal has gone so wrong in its conduct of the arbitration, and where its conduct is so far removed from what could reasonably be expected from the arbitral process, that justice calls out for it to be corrected.' The court found that no such situation existed in that case.

[88]   For example, in some common law systems, it is usual for lawyers to interview witnesses and take statements from them before the hearing—a practice that may be frowned upon (and, indeed, regarded as a breach of professional ethics) in other countries. A recent industry survey identified what was labelled as 'due process paranoia' in reference to the reluctance of tribunals to act decisively on certain issues for fear of an award being challenged for violations of due process. See Sharma, 'Due process "paranoia": Turning away from judicial attitudes and looking for answers within' (2018) 84(4) Arbitration: The International Journal of Arbitration, Mediation and Dispute Management 314.

[89]   Berger, 'Art. 15 UNCITRAL Arbitration Rules: The eternal conflict between arbitral discretion and the parties' due process rights' (2006) 21 Mealey's Intl Arb Rep 29: 'It will ultimately rest on the arbitrators to reconcile the procedural rules with the mandatory rules of due process in order to ensure the integrity of the award.'

[90]   Of particular note, the 2016 UNCITRAL Notes, discussed in Chapter 6, should assist in establishing common and acceptable procedures.

In 2020, the degree of consensus on due process in international arbitration was put to test **10.52** by the COVID-19 pandemic, which unexpectedly forced parties and tribunals to adapt to remote proceedings and hearings. As discussed in Chapter 4, several arbitral institutions such as the LCIA and the ICC issued protocols and now expressly provide for remote hearings in their rules. They have also embraced electronic communications and filings. The question has arisen as to whether the imposition of remote proceedings over a party's objection could constitute a procedural irregularity sufficient to set aside of the award. As noted in Chapter 5, a report commissioned by the International Council for Commercial Arbitration (ICCA) concluded that no jurisdiction's *lex arbitri* contained an express provision setting out a right to a physical hearing, which implies that arbitrators can indeed order a remote hearing if the circumstances so require, provided the parties are equally heard within that procedure.[91]

In Europe, the concept of 'due process' is reflected in the European Convention on Human **10.53** Rights (ECHR),[92] Article 6(1) of which provides that: 'In the determination of his civil rights and obligations or of any criminal charge against him, everyone is entitled to a fair and public hearing within a reasonable time by an independent and impartial tribunal established by law.'

An agreement to arbitrate under rules which establish that hearings are private operates as **10.54** a waiver of the entitlement under Article 6 ECHR to a public hearing. However, in *BEG SpA v Italy*,[93] the ECtHR confirmed that a voluntary arbitration agreement did not represent a waiver of other rights enshrined in Article 6 (such as the independence and impartiality of arbitrators). It consequently held that it had jurisdiction to review an arbitral award issued by a tribunal constituted under the arbitration rules of the Rome Chamber of Commerce and the related challenged decisions of the Italian courts for their compatibility with Article 6 ECHR. It concluded on the facts of the case that Italy had breached its obligations under Article 6 ECHR for failing to annul an award issued by an arbitrator who was not independent or impartial.

In summary, an arbitration agreement may constitute a waiver of the right to a public **10.55** hearing but is not intended to be a blanket waiver of the guarantees to a 'fair hearing' contained in Article 6 ECHR.[94] When considering a challenge to an award on grounds of a violation of 'due process', courts in Europe should therefore have regard to the safeguards of Article 6 and their failure to do so could result in their condemnation before the ECtHR.[95]

---

[91] See 'Right to a Physical Hearing Project: The Release of 20 New Reports Reinforces Core Trends and Important Divergences,' ICCA, 18 March 2021.

[92] Convention for the Protection of Human Rights and Fundamental Freedoms (Rome, 4 November 1950) (as amended).

[93] *BEG SpA v Italy* (Case 5212/11), Judgment of 20 May 2021.

[94] For other examples, in two decisions from 2018 and 2019, the ECtHR held that a party did not waive the protections of Art. 6 ECHR in cases of compulsory arbitration, such as in the CAS Arbitration Rules. See *Mutu and Pechstein v Switzerland*, Cases Nos 40575/10 and 67474/10, 2 October 2018, para. 115; *Ali Riza and others v Turkey*, Cases Nos. 30226/10, 17880/11, 17887/11, 17891/11 and 5506/16, 175–177, 181, 28 January 2020.

[95] For a thorough analysis of the interaction between human rights (including Art. 6 ECHR) and international arbitration, see Benedettelli, 'Human rights as a litigation tool in international arbitration: reflecting on the ECHR experience' (2015) 31 Arb Intl 631.

(ii) Further procedural issues

10.56   An award is also at risk of challenge where the composition of the arbitral tribunal and the procedure adopted in the arbitration are not in conformity with the agreement of the parties or, failing such agreement, with the law.[96] By way of example, a failure to comply with the agreement of the parties as to the appointment of the tribunal could include cases in which an arbitrator does not meet the particular qualifications specified in the arbitration agreement; failure to comply with the required procedure could include the rendering of an award without reasons where such a requirement is imposed by law.

10.57   If there is no specific agreement between the parties as to the composition of the tribunal, there can be no complaint if the arbitrators are selected according to the method prescribed by the applicable rules or law. But it is noteworthy that the constitution of the arbitral tribunal in accordance with the agreement of the parties will incorporate the relevant institutional rules as to independence and impartiality. So even if a challenge to an arbitrator for lack of independence and impartiality fails during the arbitral process itself, it can be argued again as a ground to set aside an adverse award.

10.58   For example, in 2019, the French Court of Cassation confirmed the decision of the Paris Court of Appeal to set aside an award based on the failure by the respondent's arbitrator to disclose that his law firm represented an entity that was part of the respondent's corporate group in unrelated proceedings.[97]

10.59   Similarly, in June 2020, the ICSID ad hoc committee in *Eiser v Spain* annulled a €128 million award on the basis that the arbitrator appointed by the claimant had failed to disclose numerous past and present connections with the claimant's damages expert in cases where the arbitrator acted as counsel.[98] The ad hoc committee found that those connections created an 'obvious appearance of lack of impartiality' and that the failure to disclose them to the co-arbitrators during the deliberations may have had a material effect on the award, thus amounting to a serious departure from the fundamental rule of procedure guaranteeing an independent and impartial tribunal.

10.60   Not all procedural irregularities are sufficient to set aside an award. The materiality to the outcome of the proceedings may be relevant. In *Chantiers de l'Atlantique SA v Gaztransport & Technigaz SAS*,[99] the Commercial Court in London held that even fraud in the arbitral proceedings would not necessarily justify setting the award aside. The court held that a witness for Gaztransport had deliberately misled the arbitral tribunal. However, despite agreeing with the claimant on the existence of fraud in the proceedings, the court held that the fraudulent testimony did not justify setting the award aside,

---

[96] See Model Law, Art. 34(2)(a)(iv). But note that the Belgian Arbitration Law of 2013 limits the Model Law's grounds for challenge. Under the Model Law, an award may be set aside if the procedure deviates from that agreed upon by the parties; under Belgian law, the award may be set aside only if that deviation was so significant that it actually affected the outcome.

[97] *Société Saad Buzwair Automotive Co. v Société Audi Volkswagen Middle East Fze LLC*, Case No. 18-15755, Decision of the cour de cassation of 3 October 2019.

[98] *Eiser Infrastructure Limited and Energía Solar Luxembourg Sarl v Kingdom of Spain*, ICSID Case No. ARB/13/36, Decision of Ad Hoc Committee, 11 June 2020.

[99] [2011] EWHC 3383.

because 'even if the true position had been disclosed to the tribunal, that would, in all probability, not have affected the result of the arbitration'.[100]

(d) Substantive grounds

Few jurisdictions permit any form of appeal on the law or facts from an international arbitral award. If the tribunal has jurisdiction, the correct procedures are followed and the correct formalities are observed, the award—good, bad, or indifferent—is final and binding on the parties. It matters not that the tribunal erred in its review of the evidence or misapplied the applicable law.

10.61

The question, however, arises as to whether this approach is the right one or whether there should be a greater degree of judicial review of the merits: is it enough to ensure that the correct procedures have been observed, as the Model Law requires, or is something more needed—ranging from correction of any mistakes of law to a complete review of the dispute—so as to ensure that the arbitral tribunal has reached the correct decision?

10.62

(i) Mistake of law

The argument in favour of reviewing arbitral decisions in order to guard against mistakes of law is not difficult to make. There are obvious risks in having a legal system that leaves arbitral awards entirely free from appeal or judicial review. First, there is the risk of inconsistent decisions as the same or similar points come before different tribunals, each one of which is independent of the other. Such tribunals are generally unaware that the same point of law may already have been decided in a different way by another tribunal (although this is not so in ICSID cases, in which later tribunals have decided the same point of law differently in full knowledge of the earlier decision[101]). This is likely to be of particular importance where the decision turns upon the correct interpretation of a standard form clause in a widely used contract—such as the standard form contracts used throughout the worldwide commodity, construction, shipping, insurance, or reinsurance markets, or the basic concepts underpinning the substantive protections of investment treaties. Secondly, there is the risk that the arbitral tribunal may not do its work as competently or as professionally as it should if its awards are not subject to substantive scrutiny, either by an arbitral institution[102] or by a competent court.

10.63

There are nevertheless serious disadvantages in having a system of arbitration that gives an unrestricted right of appeal from arbitral awards. First, the decisions of national judges would effectively replace the decisions of an arbitral tribunal specifically selected by, or on behalf of, the parties. Secondly, a party that agreed to arbitration as a private method of resolving disputes may find itself brought unwillingly before national courts that hold their

10.64

---

[100] Ibid., at [369]. (The English Arbitration Act 1996, s. 68 allows, but does not require, a court to set aside an award on the grounds of 'serious irregularity', including where an award is 'obtained by fraud'.) A different position was endorsed by a Hong Kong court in *Z v Y* [2018] HKCFI 2342, in which the court annulled an arbitral award on the basis that the arbitral tribunal failed to properly address the party's allegation that the arbitration had arisen from fraudulent contracts.

[101] This is because ICSID awards (unlike other awards) are nearly always published.

[102] Whilst the ICC Rules, Art. 34, provide for the scrutiny of an award by the ICC Court before the award is finalised and issued to the parties, it is principally as to form and not substance.

hearings in public. Thirdly, the appeal process may be invoked simply to postpone the day on which payment is due. It is not easy to strike a balance between the need for finality in the arbitral process and the wider public interest in some measure of judicial control, if only to ensure consistency of decisions and predictability of the operation of the law. Internationally, however, the balance has come down overwhelmingly in favour of finality and against judicial review of substance, except in very limited circumstances. The Model Law sets the tone, as has been seen, when Article 5 proclaims that, '[i]n matters governed by this Law, no court shall intervene except where so provided in this Law'.

10.65   The extent of intervention by the courts on questions of law permitted by different states may be viewed as a spectrum. At one end of the spectrum are states such as Belgium, France, and Switzerland, which exercise a very limited control over international arbitral awards and permit parties to 'contract out' of control by the courts of the seat altogether. In the middle of the scale, a large number of states have adopted (either in full or with some modifications) the limited grounds of recourse laid down in the Model Law, which mirror the grounds for refusal of enforcement under the New York Convention. At the other end of the spectrum are countries such as England, which operate a range of controls, including a limited right of appeal on questions of law, which the parties may agree to waive. The examples that follow illustrate the different approaches, including the systems adopted by some of the major countries selected as seats for international arbitration.

10.66   The admonition in the Model Law *against* intervention by national courts in the process of international arbitration was taken to extremes by Belgium, which, at one time, 'delocalised' international arbitration by eliminating the possibility of setting aside an award made in Belgium when none of the parties had Belgian nationality or domicile. However, rather than encouraging parties to select Belgium as a seat, it had the opposite effect. The experiment was abandoned and, since 1998, recourse to the Belgian courts to set aside an award made in Belgium is once again available even for foreign nationals or corporations, unless they expressly exclude any such application.[103]

10.67   France distinguishes between 'domestic' and 'international' arbitrations and does not permit appeals on points of law to its courts from an international award. The grounds for recourse against an international award made in France are also more limited than those set out in the Model Law,[104] being:

- if the arbitral tribunal wrongly upheld or declined jurisdiction;
- if the arbitral tribunal was not properly constituted;
- if the arbitral tribunal ruled without complying with the mandate conferred upon it;
- if due process has been violated; and/or
- if the recognition or enforcement is contrary to international public policy (*ordre public international*).[105]

---

[103] Belgian Judicial Code, art. 1718, as amended in 2013. Belgium internationalised its legislation on arbitration when it adopted the Model Law in 2013. In addition to the grounds provided for in the Model Law, the 2013 Belgian Arbitration Law includes three additional grounds to set aside an award: failure to state reasons (art. 1717.3(a)(iv)), excess of powers (art. 1717.3(a)(vi)), and obtaining an award by fraud (art. 1717.3(b)(iii)).

[104] Compare arts 1518*ff* of the French Code of Civil Procedure (incorporating the French 2011 Arbitration Law) with the Model Law, Art. 34.

[105] See French Code of Civil Procedure, art. 1520. Recently, the French courts have clarified further the grounds for annulment by distinguishing between mistakes of law in decisions on jurisdiction—which are challengeable—from

Since 2011, French law has adopted the Belgian approach and permits parties to contract **10.68** out of court control.[106] Indeed, it has gone further, since it does not limit that power to parties who have no connection with France. Similarly, in Switzerland, if none of the parties has its domicile, habitual residence, or business establishment in Switzerland, parties may agree to exclude all setting-aside proceedings or to limit such proceedings to one or more of the grounds listed in the Act.[107]

The next group of states do not permit parties to contract out of judicial review when arbitrations have their seat in their territory. These are the Model Law states and the United **10.69** States. The judicial review of awards issued in the United States is set out at section 10(a) of the US Federal Arbitration Act of 1925 (FAA). A court may set aside (or, in the language of the statute, 'vacate') an award in the following circumstances:

(1) where the award was procured by corruption, fraud, or undue means;
(2) where there was evident partiality or corruption in the arbitrators, or [any] of them;
(3) where the arbitrators were guilty of misconduct in refusing to postpone the hearing, upon sufficient cause shown, or in refusing to hear evidence pertinent and material to the controversy; or any other misbehaviour by which the rights of any party have been prejudiced; or
(4) where the arbitrators exceeded their powers, or so imperfectly executed them that a mutual, final, and definite award upon the subject matter submitted was not made.[108]

The statute does not provide expressly for any judicial review of an arbitral award on the **10.70** basis of a mistake of law. Some circuits have followed the dictum in *Wilko v Swan*,[109] which concluded that awards could be set aside for 'manifest disregard of the law'. However, US courts have now mostly taken a very restrictive view on challenging awards based on this jurisprudential standard[110] and some circuits have rejected the doctrine in its entirety.[111] This approach can be contrasted with the Model Law, where there is no possibility for challenging an award on the basis of mistake of law, however egregious.

In England, a limited right to seek appeal on a point of law is preserved by section 69 of **10.71** the Arbitration Act 1996, but it is not unrestricted. First, the parties may 'contract out' of

---

mistakes of law on questions of admissibility—which are not. See *Jnah Development SAL v Marriott International Hotels Inc.*, Case No. 16-21.391, Decision of the French cour de cassation, January 2018, p. 3.

[106] See French Code of Civil Procedure, art. 1522 ('By way of a specific agreement the parties may, at any time, expressly waive their right to bring an action to set aside').

[107] Swiss PIL, Ch. 12, s. 192(1).

[108] There is a possibility of the award being remitted to the arbitrators, where the time within which the award was to be made has not expired: FAA, § 10(b).

[109] 346 US 427, 74 S.Ct. 182 (1953). In *Shanghai Foodstuffs Import & Export Corporation v International Chemical, Inc.*, Case No. 99 CV 3320, 2004 US Dist. LEXIS 1423 (SDNY, 2004), it was acknowledged that US courts had the authority to set aside non-domestic awards that were rendered in the United States on the basis of 'manifest disregard of the law'.

[110] See, e.g., *Hall Street Associates, LLC v Mattel, Inc.*, 552 US 576 (2008) and Beraudo, 'Egregious error of law as grounds for setting aside an arbitral award' (2006) 23 J Intl Arb 351.

[111] However, the Second Circuit has held that the doctrine survives as valid (though narrow) ground for challenge. See *Citigroup Global Markets v Bacon*, 562 F.3d 349, 350 (5th Cir. 2009): '*Hall Street* restricts the grounds for vacatur to those set forth in § 10 of the FAA, and consequently manifest disregard of the law is no longer an independent ground for vacating arbitral awards'; *Goldman Sachs Execution & Clearing v Official Unsecured Creditors Committee of Bayou Group*, 491 Fed. Appx 201, 2012 US App. LEXIS 13531, 3–4 (2012). See also *Zurich Am. Ins. Co. v Team Tankers AS*, 811 F.3d 584, 589 (2d Cir. 2016) finding that a challenge on the basis of manifest disregard of law imposes a 'heavy burden' on the applicant.

any right of appeal to the national court before or after the start of arbitration proceedings. Although their agreement to do so must be in writing, the provision contained in standard form rules of arbitration to the effect that the award shall be final and binding has been held to constitute a valid agreement to waive the right of appeal.[112] Secondly, even if the right of appeal has been retained, it is in effect a right of appeal only on questions of *English* law.[113] This is important because, given London's position as a neutral international seat, the law governing the substance of the dispute may well be that of another state.[114] Thirdly, the right of appeal is available only with leave of the court, and then only if the decision of the tribunal on the question of law is 'obviously wrong', the question is one of 'general public importance', or the decision 'is at least open to serious doubt', so that it would be 'just and proper in all the circumstances for the court to determine the question'.[115] As a matter of practice, English courts have taken a restrictive view on allowing challenges on grounds of a mistake of law.[116]

10.72   On an appeal on a point of English law, the English court has power to confirm the award, to vary it, to remit it to the arbitral tribunal, or to set it aside, but the court should not set aside the award, in whole or in part, unless satisfied that it would be inappropriate to submit the matters in question to the tribunal for reconsideration.[117] No further appeal is possible, unless the court considers the question to be one of general importance or one that, for some special reason, should be considered by the Court of Appeal.

(ii) Mistake of fact

10.73   The principal justification for allowing an appeal from the award of an arbitral tribunal on questions of law is that it is in the public interest that the law should be certain, and that, in particular, there should be consistent findings by different tribunals as to the meaning and effect of the same legal principles or the same standard form contracts.[118] There can be no such general interest in the findings of fact of a particular tribunal in a particular case. Accordingly, almost all states with developed laws of arbitration refuse to allow appeals from arbitral tribunals on issues of fact.[119]

10.74   The question may then be posed: what if the parties wish to expand, by contract, the scope of the reviewing court's powers? This issue was addressed in the US case *LaPine Technology*

---

[112] See, e.g., *Sanghi Polyesters Ltd v The International Investor (KCFC)* [2001] 1 Lloyd's Rep 480. See also *Lesotho Highlands Development Authority v Impreglio SpA and ors* [2005] UKHL 43, at [3] *per* Lord Steyn, in which it was held that the ICC Rules, Art. 28.6 (now the ICC Rules, Art. 35.6) excluded a right of challenge.

[113] English Arbitration Act 1996, ss 69(1) and 82(1). The underlying policy of the English legislators was related to the long-established tradition of arbitration by non-lawyers in certain commercial sectors, e.g. the construction industry or trading in commodities, and the need for certainty regarding the way in which standard form clauses were to be interpreted.

[114] See, e.g., *AEK v National Basket Association* [2002] 1 All ER (Comm) 70, in which permission to appeal on a point of law under s. 69 was rejected because it related to the arbitrator's application of Greek law.

[115] English Arbitration Act 1996, s. 69(2) and (3). See, e.g., *MRI Trading v Erdenet Mining* [2013] EWCA 156, in which a London Metal Exchange tribunal held that a sale contract was an unenforceable agreement to agree, whilst ignoring the provision requiring that the contract be construed together with a separate settlement agreement, which was the quid pro quo for the sale contract. The Court of Appeal determined that this was obviously wrong as a matter of English law and annulled the award. See also *Martin & ors v Harris* [2019] EWHC 1962 (Ch).

[116] For a comprehensive discussion, see Sutton, Gill, and Gearing (eds) *Russell on Arbitration* (24th edn, Sweet & Maxwell, 2015), paras 8-132–8.170.

[117] English Arbitration Act 1996, s. 69(7).

[118] For example, the English Arbitration Act 1996, s. 69(3)(c)(ii), which provides that one of the requirements for leave to appeal is that the question of law is 'one of general public importance'.

[119] See, e.g., *Edman Controls, Inc.*, 712 F.3d 1021, 1024–1025 (7th Cir. 2013), upholding the district court's judgment that 'neither factual nor legal error is a sufficient ground for vacatur', and adding that the Court 'will not overturn an award because an arbitrator committed serious error' or the decision is 'incorrect or even whacky', quoting *Wise v Wachovia*, 86 F.3d 96, 100 (7th Cir. 1996).

Corporation v Kyocera Corporation,[120] in which the arbitration clause, after providing for arbitration in accordance with the ICC Rules and the Federal Arbitration Act (FAA), went on to say:

> The United States District Court for the Northern District of California may enter judgment upon any award, either by confirming the award or by vacating, modifying or correcting the award. The Court shall vacate, modify or correct any award: (i) based upon any of the grounds referred to in the Federal Arbitration Act, (ii) where the arbitrators' findings of fact are not supported by substantial evidence or (iii) where the arbitrators' conclusions of law are erroneous.

In the district court, Kyocera applied to modify and vacate the award, on the grounds that   **10.75**
there were findings of fact that the evidence did not support and that there were wrong conclusions of law. The court held that its jurisdiction was determined by the FAA and could not be expanded by a private contract.[121] However, the Ninth Circuit overturned this decision and allowed the appeal, holding that this agreement should be enforced. Applying the broader standards of review laid down by the appellate court, the district court nonetheless confirmed the award. This led Kyocera to appeal again. In an *en banc* ruling that has been referred to as 'LaPine II',[122] the Ninth Circuit then chose to revisit the issue of whether expanded review clauses are enforceable and, in so doing, overturned its earlier decision, holding that:

> [A] Federal Court may only review an arbitral decision on the grounds set forth in the [FAA]. Private parties have no power to alter or expand those grounds, and any contractual provision purporting to do so is accordingly legally unenforceable.[123]

For some time, there remained a difference of opinion between different US courts as   **10.76**
to whether or not parties might expand the scope of review.[124] However, in *Hall Street Associates v Mattel*,[125] the US Supreme Court confirmed that parties could not contractually extend the scope of judicial review of an award,[126] because 'the FAA confine[d] its expedited judicial review to the grounds listed in 9 U. S. C. §§10 and 11'. The US Supreme Court added:

> Instead of fighting the text, it makes more sense to see the three provisions, sections 9–11, as substantiating a national policy favoring arbitration with just the limited review needed to maintain arbitration's essential virtue of resolving disputes straightaway. Any other reading opens the door to the full-bore legal and evidentiary appeals that can 'rende[r] informal arbitration merely a prelude to a more cumbersome and time-consuming judicial review process,' *Kyocera*, 341 F.3d, at 998; cf. *Ethyl Corp. v. United Steelworkers of America*, 768 F.2d 180, 184 (C.A.7 1985), and bring arbitration theory to grief in the post-arbitration process.[127]

Other jurisdictions, like Chile, have followed a different approach. For example, the Chilean   **10.77**
Supreme Court has upheld the disputing parties' agreement to allow an appeal and cassation of an international award.[128] In doing so, the Chilean Supreme Court noted that

---

[120]   130 F.3d 884 (9th Cir. 1997).
[121]   *LaPine*, 909 F.Supp. 697 (Cal. 1995).
[122]   *Kyocera Corporation v Prudential-Bache Trade Services Inc.*, 341 F.3d 987 (9th Cir. 2003).
[123]   Ibid., at 988.
[124]   See, e.g., *Gateway Tech. Inc. v MCI Telecomms Corporation*, 64 F.3d 993 (5th Cir. 1995), enforcing a provision requiring the review of arbitral awards for errors of law; *Bowen v Amoco Pipeline Co.*, 254 F.3d 925 (10th Cir. 2001), declining to enforce a provision providing for expanded review. See also Fellas, 'The scope of judicial review of arbitration awards' (2003) 230 New York LJ 1.
[125]   *Hall Street Associates, LLC v Mattel, Inc*, 552 US 576 (2008), at [19].
[126]   Suskin, 'The rejection of contractually expanded judicial review under the Arbitration Act in *Hall Street v Mattel* (06-989)' (2008) 23 Mealey's Intl Arb Rep 1.
[127]   *Hall Street*, at 1405.
[128]   See Case No. 19568-2020, *CCF Sudamérica*, Supreme Court of Chile, 16 January 2020.

consent was the cornerstone of arbitration and that courts should uphold the parties' intent to expand the recourses available against an international award, even if incompatible with the provisions of the applicable law.[129]

(iii) Public policy

10.78   An arbitral award may be set aside if a national court of the place of arbitration finds (on its own initiative) that the award is in conflict with the public policy of its own country. This is particularly true for states adopting the Model Law.[130]

10.79   Each state has its own concept of what is required by its 'public policy' (or *ordre public*, in the civil law terminology).[131] It is possible to envisage, for example, a dispute over the division of gaming profits from a casino. The dispute may be taken to arbitration and an award made. In many states, the underlying transaction that led to the award would be regarded as a normal commercial transaction and the award would be regarded as valid. However, in states that outlaw gambling, the award might well be set aside on the basis that it offends public policy.

10.80   Most developed arbitral jurisdictions have similar conceptions of public policy. According to the Swiss Federal Supreme Court, public policy denotes fundamental legal principles, a departure from which would be incompatible with the Swiss legal and economic system.[132] Similarly, German courts have held that an award will violate public policy (and may thus be set aside) if it conflicts with fundamental notions that regulate the foundations of state or economic life, or if it is in intolerable conflict with German concepts of justice.[133]

---

[129] Ibid. In this case, the arbitration agreement provided for international arbitration seated in Santiago. Once the dispute arose, the parties agreed that the final award could be challenged through appeal and cassation. The losing party appealed the final award before the Appellate Court of Santiago, which dismissed the appeal noting that the only recourse against an international award under Chilean law was annulment. The Supreme Court reversed the lower court's judgment finding that (i) courts should base their decision on the parties' intention with respect to the arbitration agreement; (ii) a party could not oppose the appeal of an award if it had previously agreed that the award would be subject to such appeal; and (iii) laws limiting the recourses available to a disputing party should be interpreted narrowly, thus favouring the disputing parties' rights to appeal over the formalities that limit the available recourses to 'appeal'. Case No. 19568-2020, Supreme Court of Chile, 16 January 2020, at [5–6], [8].

[130] Model Law, Art. 34(2)(b)(ii). Public policy is also discussed in the context of the recognition and enforcement of awards in Chapter 11.

[131] For example, while in the United States, public policy is understood in this context as the 'most basic notions of morality and justice', in Egypt they are the rules aimed at achieving any political, social, or economic public interest, which can be procedural or substantive. See Selim, 'Egyptian public policy as a ground for annulment and refusal of enforcement of arbitral awards' (2016) 3(1) BCDR International Arbitration Review 65. At the other end of the scale is Saudi Arabia, where an award is contrary to public policy if contrary to Islamic law (see Saudi Arbitration Law, art. 50.2) and Japan, where courts have found that procedural irregularities—if serious enough—may amount to violations of public policy. *Heisei 21* (Chu) No. 6, Tokyo District Court (13 June 2011), published in *Hanrei Jiho* No. 2128, at 58. See also *Abnaa Al-Khalaf Co. et al. v Sayed Aghajaved Raza*, Challenge No. 64, Qatari Court of Cassation (2012), setting aside a Qatari award on grounds of public order, since it was not issued in the name of His Highness the Emir of the State of Qatar.

[132] See, e.g., *Özmak Makina Ve Elektrik Anayi AS v Voest Apline Industrieanlagenbau GmBH and anor*, Case No. 4P_143/2001, Decision of the Swiss Federal Supreme Court, 18 September 2001 (2002) 20 ASA Bulletin 311. See also *Francelino da Silva Matuzalem v Fédération Internationale de Football Association (FIFA)*, Case No. 4A_558/2011, Decision of the Swiss Supreme Court, 27 March 2012, in which the Swiss Supreme Court held that the restriction of a person's economic freedom violated public policy. The case involved a FIFA arbitration in which a football player, who had repeatedly violated his FIFA obligations, was banned from participating in any football-related activity until the full amount that he owed the organisation was paid.

[133] Federal Court of Justice, Order of the court dated 25 June 2020, File No. I ZB 108/19 (NJOZ 2020, p 1500, at [13]).

In similar terms, the Superior Court of Justice of Ontario refused to set aside an award ren-   **10.81**
dered by a North American Free Trade Agreement (NAFTA) tribunal, holding that, for an
award to offend public policy, it:

> must fundamentally offend the most basic and explicit principles of justice and fairness
> in Ontario, or evidence intolerable ignorance or corruption on the part of the arbitral
> Tribunal [...] The Applicant must establish that the awards are contrary to the essential
> morality of Ontario.[134]

In 2016, the Santiago Court of Appeals rejected an attempt to set aside an award on public
policy grounds because the arbitrators had not complied with procedural rules of judicial proceedings designed to protect due process. The court held that the concept of public
policy should be understood to reflect basic rules of justice and morality and should not be
assimilated to rules established under domestic judicial proceedings.[135]

Notwithstanding the frequent similarities between the concept of public policy in different   **10.82**
states, there is inevitably a risk that one state may set aside, on grounds of public policy, an
award that other states would regard as valid. Even though many states take a restrictive approach to the application of public policy,[136] the nebulous nature of the concept may be used
by courts in some jurisdictions as a licence to review the merits of a dispute inappropriately.
With this in mind, the concept of 'international public policy' (*ordre public international*)
has been developed to represent a higher obstacle to annulment than purely domestic
public policy. It is embodied in the French Code of Civil Procedure where an international
arbitral award may only be set aside 'if the recognition or enforcement of the award is contrary to *international* public policy'.[137] Other countries have followed this distinction such
as Portugal, Chile, and Colombia.[138]

---

[134] *United Mexican States v Marvin Roy Feldman Karpa*, File No. 03-CV-23500, Ontario Superior Court of
Justice, 3 December 2003, at [87].

[135] See *Ingeniería Proyersa Limitada v Steag GMBH* (Court of Appeals of Santiago) 1 September 2016, Case
2685-2016.

[136] See, e.g., the English courts in *Protech Projects Construction (Pty) Ltd v Al-Kharafi & Sons* [2005] EWHC
2165 (Comm), in which Langley J stressed that s. 68(2)(g) of the English Arbitration Act 1996 would be available only in extreme cases and that the court would not be concerned with the correctness or otherwise of the
award: public policy under English law could be invoked only where the alleged conduct is akin to something 'unconscionable or reprehensible' and where the applicant had suffered 'substantial injustice'.

[137] French Code of Civil Procedure, art. 1520 (emphasis added). In *SA Ancienne Maison Marcel Bauche v
Indagro*, cour d'appel de Paris, 27 September 2016, , Case No. 15/12.614, the court held that it would refuse enforcement of an arbitral award on public policy grounds only where the award violated international public policy
in a 'manifest, effective and concrete' manner. See also *Republic of Kirgizstan v Mr. Valeriy*, cour d'appel de Paris,
21 February 2017, Case No. 15/01.650; *Democratic Republic of Congo v Customs and Tax Consultancy LLC*, cour
d'appel de paris, 16 May 2017, Case No. 15/17.442. French courts have found a violation of international public
policy to exist where the tribunal denied the parties due process by failing to invite comments from them in connection with the award of damages *Commercial Caribbean Niquel v Societe Overseas Mining Investments Ltd*, cour
d'appel de Paris, 25 March 2010, Case No. 08/23901 or where a company has procured a contract for the exploitation of natural resources through fraud: (*MK Group v S.A.R.L. Onix*, cour d'appel de Paris, 16 January 2018, Case
No. 15/21.703) or corruption (*Alstom Transport SA v Alexander Brothers Ltd*, cour d'appel de Paris, 28 May 2019,
Case No. 16/11182; *Sorelec v Lybia*, cour d'appel de Paris, 17 November 2020, Case Nos 18/0737 and 18/02568).

[138] For example, Portugal has a similar provision at the 2013 Code of Civil Procedure, art. 980(f), which refers to
'the principles of international public policy of the Portuguese State'. See also the decision of the Court of Appeals
of Santiago, holding that international arbitral awards rendered in Chile are not subject to all mandatory provisions that are part of domestic public policy. Court of Appeals of Santiago, Docket No. 3390-2017, 5 October 2016.
A similar reasoning is found in the decision of the Colombian Supreme Court in *HM P2, HTM LLC v Fomento de
Catalizadores—FOCA S.A.S.*, SC8453-2016, 24 June 2016, rejecting a challenge because a mandatory rule in the
Colombian Code of Commerce was deemed domestic public policy and not international public policy.

10.83   For arbitrations with a seat within the European Union, the notion of 'EU public policy' is increasingly important. The CJEU has confirmed that EU member states must consider not only their own national public policy, but also EU public policy when reviewing arbitral awards.[139]

10.84   If an internationally acceptable definition of 'international public policy' could be found, it would provide an effective way of preventing an award in an international arbitration from being set aside for purely domestic policy considerations. International public policy would not concern itself with matters of form, or of a purely domestic nature; rather, it would look to the broader public interest of honesty and fair dealing. Despite the efforts of scholars and institutions to develop a widely and accepted definition of a (truly) international public policy, a court's assessment of this concept will typically be influenced by the idiosyncrasies of each country and what each domestic system considers 'international public policy'. Even today, the warning note sounded by an English judge almost 200 years ago still resonates:

> [Public policy is] a very unruly horse, and when once you get astride it you never know where it will carry you. It may lead you from sound law. It is never argued at all, but when other points fail.[140]

(iv) Summary

10.85   This brief review demonstrates that most states are broadly content to restrict the challenge of arbitral awards to excess of jurisdiction and lack of due process. These grounds for challenge are either adopted directly from the Model Law or reflect the policy behind those grounds. In general, the parties are expected to abide by the decision of the tribunal, however disappointed they may be by the outcome. Other states are prepared to offer a limited measure of judicial review on questions of law, if this is what the parties wish—but the possibility of the review of an award on issues of fact is truly rare.[141]

D. Procedures for Bringing a Challenge

10.86   The grounds for bringing a challenge against an international arbitral award are, as we have said, broadly similar in courts across the world. If a challenge is to be brought, it

---

[139] See, e.g., Case C-40/80 *Asturcom Telecomunicaciones SL v Cristina Rodriguez Nogueira* [2009] ECR I–9579; Bermann, 'Navigating EU law and the law of international arbitration' (2012) 28 Arb Intl 397. Also see paragraph 10.39 above for the discussion of the implications of EU public policy on the validity of arbitration agreements in intra-EU investment treaties.

[140] *Richardson v Mellish* (1824) 2 Bing 229, at 252, [1824–34] All ER 258, *per* Burrough J.

[141] A 2016 analysis of industry practitioners confirmed that it is relatively unlikely to succeed in a challenge of an award before the courts of England and Wales, France, Singapore, and the United States. See Carter and Macpherson, 'Arbitral awards—Challenging to challenge' (2016) 1(19) Intl Arb L Rev 89. In the case of England and Wales, e.g., a minute of the Commercial Court User Group Meeting confirmed that 'very few' challenges under the English Arbitration Act 1996 succeeded, with a renowned retired judge 'express[ing] hope that parties were hearing the message that the hurdle for these applications is high'. See Commercial Court User Group Meeting of November 2020. In Switzerland, although successful challenges to awards have increased, they are still low. Between 2008 and December 2015, seventeen challenges were successful as opposed to the thirteen challenges that were successful between 1989 and 2007. Yet, despite this trend, the success rate is still around 7 per cent for non-sports arbitration awards and around 10 per cent for sports awards, for an overall average of 8 per cent as of December 2015. See Dasser and Wójtowicz, 'Challenges of Swiss arbitral awards—Updated and extended statistical data as of 2015' (2016) 34 ASA Bulletin, Swiss Arbitration Association 4–5.

will have to be brought at the 'designated court' (to use the terminology of the Model Law) at the seat of the arbitration. However, since that seat was probably chosen as a 'neutral' place of arbitration, it is possible that the lawyers who acted in the arbitral proceedings are not qualified to bring a challenge before the designated court. For example, a UK practitioner who represents a client in a New York seated arbitration would not be qualified to prepare and argue a challenge before the US District Court for the Southern District of New York. If that is the case, then the party seeking to challenge will have to hire competent local counsel experienced to advise and represent it in the challenge proceedings.[142]

Local counsel will be able to advise on the procedural steps necessary for the challenge. **10.87** Important questions will include:

- the appropriate court before which to bring the application;
- the relevant time limits for such an application to be made;
- the necessary documentation to be filed (and often translations of those documents to the language of the court[143]);
- the grounds upon which an application can be made;
- the form and number of written submissions;
- whether (and in what form) there will be an oral hearing;
- whether an appeal or cassation will be possible and, if so, the scope of such appeal; and
- whether an application to set aside suspends the ability to recognise or enforce the award.[144]

By way of example, in a Paris seated arbitration the challenge is made in the first instance **10.88** to the Paris Court of Appeal.[145] The unsuccessful party may then challenge the decision of the Court of Appeal on limited grounds to the Court of Cassation (the French Supreme Court). However, the Court of Cassation may only annul (in whole or in part) the decision of the Paris Court of Appeal and if it does so, it must remit the case to another section of the Paris Court of Appeal to redecide the challenge in light of its decision.[146] By way of contrast, in the United States, the award is challenged before the federal district court in the district

---

[142] Conscious of the need to provide a 'one stop shop' for clients, some of the larger international arbitration groups of international law firms have built up teams of arbitration specialists who are also experienced litigators in challenge proceedings. This will often involve building multijurisdictional teams across offices.

[143] For example, a recent investment arbitration with a seat in the Hague (*Manuel Garcia Armas v Bolivarian Republic of Venezuela*, PCA Case No. 2016-08) was heard and decided in Spanish. However, challenge proceedings had to be launched before the Dutch courts in the Hague which required the translations of (inter alia) the award.

[144] For the answers to these questions in key arbitral jurisdictions see Rowley (general ed.); Gaillard, Kaiser, and Siino (eds); (Foreword, Redfern) *The Guide to Challenging and Enforcing Arbitration Awards* (2nd edn, Law Business Research Limited, 2021), Part II.

[145] Code of Civil Procedure, art. 1519 (the cour d'appel de Paris which has territorial jurisdiction over the place where the award was rendered).

[146] See, e.g., *Serafin Garcia Armas and ors v Bolivarian Republic of Venezuela* in which the claimants obtained a favourable jurisdictional award in a Paris seated investment arbitration. Venezuela challenged the award before the cour d'appel de Paris (Pole 1 Chambre 1) and obtained a partial annulment (Paris cour d'appel, 25 April 2017). The decision of the cour d'appel de Paris was appealed to the cour de cassation which rendered a judgment on 13 February 2019 overturning the cour d'appel de Paris's decision. The cour de cassation then remitted the case for decision to another section of the cour d'appel de Paris (Pole 5 Chambre 16) which rendered its decision on 3 June 2020. That decision was in turn appealed by the claimants to the cour de cassation which, in a second judgment of 1 December 2021, overturned the judgment of the cour d'appel de Paris. The matter has now been remitted to a new section of the cour d'appel de Paris.

where the award was made.[147] Any decision of the district court may then be appealed to the competent US circuit court of appeals which will usually determine the matter finally (with the very limited exception of a case which seeks and obtains permission to appeal to the US Supreme Court).[148]

E. Effects of Challenge

10.89 The effects of a successful challenge differ depending upon the grounds of the challenge, the relevant law, and the decision of the court that dealt with it. The court's decision may take several forms. The court may decide to confirm the award, refer the award back to the arbitral tribunal for reconsideration, vary the award, or set the award aside, in whole or in part.

10.90 When an award is set aside, it is unenforceable in the country in which it was made, and it will usually be unenforceable elsewhere.[149] In this situation, the party that won the arbitration, but lost the challenge, is in an unenviable position. If, for example, the award has been set aside completely on the basis that the arbitration agreement was null and void, a further resort to arbitration (on the basis of the void agreement) would be out of the question. Resort to litigation might be considered, but there could be problems of statute of limitations, to say nothing of more substantive difficulties.

10.91 If the award has been set aside for procedural defects (e.g. lack of due process), the party who won the arbitration, but lost the challenge, will have to resubmit the dispute to arbitration and the process will start over again. This is a daunting prospect for even the most resilient claimant.

10.92 A successful party does not wish to be deprived of victory because of a procedural failure on the part of the arbitral tribunal. As the practice of international arbitration becomes increasingly litigious, a party that expects to be on the losing side may seek, during the course of the proceedings, to lay the basis for a claim that the hearing was not conducted fairly. This point should be kept well in mind by parties to an arbitration (usually the claimants) who consider that the arbitral tribunal is being too generous to their opponents on procedural questions. In order to minimise the risk of challenges to the award based on the alleged unfair conduct of the hearing, arbitrators often ask the parties to confirm after the last oral hearing whether they have been satisfied with the conduct of the hearing, in order to protect the eventual award from challenge. If a party then declares a concern, there is still time for the tribunal to address it before issuing the final award.

---

[147] 9 U.S.C., § 10.

[148] See, e.g., the case of *BG Group v Argentina*, where the claimant won an investment arbitration with a seat in Washington DC. The respondent, Argentina challenged the award before the competent federal court, the District Court of the District of Columbia. When the District Court affirmed the award (764 F. Supp. 2d 21 (DC 2011)), Argentina appealed to the DC Circuit Court of Appeals and won (665 F.3d 1363 (2012)). BG Group then applied for certiorari (that is, permission to appeal to the US Supreme Court). The application was granted and BG Group subsequently prevailed in the only investment arbitration to be reviewed by the US Supreme Court (572 US 25, 134 S.Ct. 1198 (2014)).

[149] But see fn. 8 above and the discussion in Chapter 11 relating to cases in which an award has been set aside at the seat of the arbitration but has nevertheless been enforced in another country.

F. State Responsibility for Wrongful Setting Aside

If an award is set aside, is that the end of the story for the party seeking annulment? Does **10.93** the winning party have any recourse when an award is vacated for parochial or other inappropriate grounds? What happens where, for example, a state's courts set aside an award against a state-owned company or an otherwise well-connected national of that state? Put another way, if setting-aside applications are governed by national law, does a state have *carte blanche* to determine when and where to annul? In investment arbitration, there are cases that suggest that states may be held responsible under international law for egregious actions by their courts in the setting-aside process and in some instances, claimants have secured awards in international courts and tribunals, granting them damages representing the full amount of their previously annulled arbitral awards.[150]

In one scenario, a decision to set aside an award may constitute a breach of a state's obliga- **10.94** tions under an investment treaty. For example, in *Saipem v Bangladesh*,[151] a case under the ICSID Rules, the respondent was held liable to the claimant for having unlawfully set aside an award by abusing its supervisory jurisdiction over the arbitral process. Bangladesh was thus held responsible for the expropriation of Saipem's ICC award.[152] The investment arbitration tribunal awarded the claimant the full value of its annulled ICC award.

In a second scenario, inappropriate judicial conduct in setting-aside proceedings may **10.95** breach a state's obligations under international human rights treaties. Most notably, the ECHR affords individuals a means of suing signatory states directly before the ECtHR for violation of their rights under the Convention. This is what happened in the case of *BEG SpA v Italy* discussed above where Italy was held liable for its conduct in set-aside proceedings by wrongly upholding an award rendered in breach of the claimant's rights under Article 6 ECHR.[153]

---

[150] King and Moloo, 'Enforcement after the arbitration: Strategic considerations and forum choice', in Ferrari (ed.) *Forum Shopping in the International Commercial Arbitration Context* (Sellier European Law, 2013), pp. 411–412, at 493.

[151] *Saipem SpA v People's Republic of Bangladesh*, ICSID Case No. ARB/05/07, Award, 30 June 2009 (finding Bangladesh liable for its illegal judicial expropriation of Saipem's rights, as crystallised in its award).

[152] Ibid., at [127] finding that '[t]he ICC Award crystallized the parties' rights and obligations under the original contract', thereby constituting an investment for the purposes of both the Italy–Bangladesh BIT and the ICSID Convention.

[153] See *BEG SpA v Italy* (Case 5212/11), Judgment of 20 May 2021 discussed at paragraph 10.54 above.

11

RECOGNITION AND ENFORCEMENT
OF ARBITRAL AWARDS

A. Background

(a) Introduction

11.01 The successful party in an international arbitration expects the award to be performed without delay. This is a reasonable expectation. Unlike mediation and most other methods of alternative dispute resolution (ADR), the purpose of international arbitration is to arrive at a binding decision on the dispute. Once this decision has been made, in the form of a written award, it is an intrinsic element of every arbitration agreement that the parties will carry it out.[1] To put this beyond doubt, it is expressly set out in many of the leading international rules of arbitration. The UNCITRAL Rules provide that the award 'shall be final and binding on the parties', and that 'the parties shall carry out all awards without delay'.[2] The ICC Rules provide that 'the parties undertake to carry out any award without delay'.[3] The LCIA Rules similarly provide that 'every award (including reasons for such award) shall be final and binding on the parties. The parties undertake to carry out any award immediately and without any delay'.[4]

11.02 Such statistics as are available suggest that most arbitral awards in most parts of the world are in fact carried out voluntarily—that is, without the need for enforcement proceedings in national courts.[5] However, in recent years, there is an increasing number of press reports

---

[1] For classic statements of this fundamental element of the agreement to arbitrate see, e.g., Mustill and Boyd, *Commercial Arbitration* (2nd edn, Butterworths, 1989), p. 47; see *Esso/BHP v Plowman* (1995) 11 Arb Intl 282, 283.

[2] UNCITRAL Rules, Art. 34.2. The final and binding nature of the award is further underlined by the optional waiver language contained in the Annex to the UNCITRAL Rules, which states: 'The parties hereby waive their right to any form of recourse against an award to any court or other competent authority, insofar as such waiver can validly be made under the applicable law.'

[3] ICC Rules, Art. 35.6.

[4] LCIA Rules, Art. 26.8.

[5] See Queen Mary University of London, School of International Arbitration, and White & Case LLP, *2018 International Arbitration Survey: The Evolution of International Arbitration*, available online at http://www.arbitration.qmul.ac.uk/media/arbitration/docs/2018-International-Arbitration-Survey-report.pdf, p. 7, which found that 64 per cent of arbitration users consider that 'enforceability of awards' is the most valuable characteristic of

about attempts to attack arbitral awards, or to resist their enforcement.[6] Up-to-date, comprehensive, and reliable statistics about arbitration are not readily available to confirm the state of voluntary compliance with arbitral awards, for two main reasons: first, success stories that do not result in further legal enforcement battles usually do not make the arbitration news; and secondly there is no particular reason why an arbitral tribunal, or indeed an arbitral institution, should ever know whether or not an award has been carried out. Unlike a national court, an arbitral tribunal has no role to play in the enforcement of its decision. When an arbitral tribunal has made a final award, its work is usually done and the tribunal is *functus officio*. As for arbitral institutions, while some of them routinely ask the parties to complete post-proceeding questionnaires that may touch on whether awards have been performed or challenged, few parties go to the trouble of doing so. The most, therefore, that can be said confidently about the rate of voluntary enforcement is that there appear to be relatively few arbitrations that are followed by known enforcement proceedings.

11.03   Although voluntary enforcement therefore appears to be more common than not, it cannot always be relied on. Arbitrations will usually result in a 'winner' and a 'loser', and at least one party to an arbitration is likely to be dissatisfied with the result. In those circumstances, in addition to seeking the annulment of the award (usually in the place of arbitration), the losing party may also resist any attempt by the winning party to obtain recognition or enforcement of the award, in whatever jurisdiction this is sought. The purpose of this chapter is to examine the process by which awards may or may not be recognised and enforced. However, it is appropriate to start by discussing the carrying out, or performance, of awards from a wider perspective, so as to place recognition and enforcement in their proper contexts.

(b) Performance of awards

11.04   As already stated, the majority of awards appear to be performed voluntarily. However, if the losing party fails to carry out an award, the winning party needs to take steps to enforce performance of it. Effectively, only two steps may be taken. The first is to exert some form of pressure, commercial or otherwise, in order to show the losing party that it is in its interests to perform the award voluntarily. The second is to invoke the powers of the state, exercised through its national courts, in order to obtain a hold on the losing party's assets, or in some other way to compel performance of the award.[7]

---

arbitration. See also Queen Mary University of London, School of International Arbitration, and Pricewaterhouse Coopers LLP, *International Arbitration: Corporate Attitudes and Practices 2008*, available online at http://www. pwc.co.uk/en_UK/uk/assets/pdf/pwc-international-arbitration-2008.pdf, pp. 8 and 10, which suggested that in only 11 per cent of cases did participants need to proceed to enforce an award and, in those cases, in less than 20 per cent did enforcing parties encounter difficulties in enforcement.

  [6] See, e.g., 'The Guide to Challenging and Enforcing Arbitration Awards', (2nd edn, 2021) General Editor J. William Rowley Q.C., Law Business Research Ltd., observing at p. xiv that 'in the first three months of 2021, there has not been a day when the news reports have not headlined the attack on, survival of, or a successful or failed attempt to enforce an arbitral award'.
  [7] For instance, by the winding up of a company.

(i) Commercial and other pressures

A successful party may be in a position to exert commercial pressure on a party who fails **11.05** or refuses to perform an award. For example, if a continuing trade relationship exists between the parties, it may well be in the interests of the loser to perform the award, since failure to do so might entail the loss of further profitable business. If a government or state agency is concerned, other pressures may be brought to bear by the diplomatic services of the successful party. It may be pointed out, for instance, that further development loans depend upon the carrying out of existing awards, or that foreign companies may be discouraged from making further investments if outstanding obligations are not honoured.

Pressure may also be exerted by the threat of adverse publicity. This method is sometimes **11.06** adopted by trade associations and has the effect of discouraging other traders in the market from dealing with the defaulting party. The Arbitration Rules of the Grain and Feed Trade Association (GAFTA), for example, contain the following provision:

24. Defaulters
    24.1 In the event of any party to an arbitration or an appeal held under these Rules neglecting or refusing to carry out or abide by a final award of the tribunal or board of appeal made under these Rules, the Council of GAFTA may post on the GAFTA Notice Board, Web-site, and/or circulate amongst Members in any way thought fit notification to that effect. The parties to any such arbitration or appeal shall be deemed to have consented to the Council taking such action as aforesaid.[8]

Before 'posting', GAFTA communicates with the defaulter and asks whether there is anything to be said, for example whether there is an outstanding balance due to him or her from the successful party. However, where GAFTA is satisfied that there is a default, its members are informed. This will naturally make them reluctant to deal with the defaulter unless and until the award has been carried out.

Similarly, but less explicitly, debtor states that end up as losing parties in arbitrations **11.07** under the rules of the International Centre for the Settlement of Investment Disputes (ICSID) may feel (rightly or wrongly) that refusal to perform an award voluntarily may adversely affect their creditworthiness at the World Bank. It may therefore be no coincidence that, to date, the overwhelming majority of ICSID awards have been voluntarily performed.[9] In addition, the successful party may be able to 'monetise' the award without enforcement proceedings, for example, by selling it (potentially at a discount) to a third-party investor, who would then seek to enforce or negotiate with the losing party for payment (or partial payment) of the award.[10]

---

[8] GAFTA Form 125, Arbitration Rules (effective for contracts dated from 1 September 2018 onwards), Art. 24.1.

[9] In recent years, the record of overwhelming voluntary performance has been eroded somewhat. Nevertheless, voluntary performance remains the norm. For a description of the voluntary performance of ICSID awards, see Chapter 8.

[10] For other examples of monetising an arbitral award, see 'The Guide to Challenging and Enforcing Arbitration Awards', 2nd edn, General Editor J. William Rowley Q.C., Law Business Research Ltd., pp. 8–10.

(ii) Arbitrator's duty to render an enforceable award

11.08   Many modern rules of arbitration contain an express provision that the arbitrator shall 'make every effort' to ensure that the award is enforceable.[11] This is an obligation to use best endeavours, rather than an obligation to secure a result. It is difficult to see how it could be otherwise. Even the most conscientious of arbitrators cannot guarantee that the tribunal's award will be enforceable in whatever country enforcement may be sought. The most that can be expected is that the tribunal will do its best to ensure that the appropriate procedure is followed and, above all, that each party is given a fair hearing.

(iii) Enforcement by court proceedings

11.09   The ultimate sanction for non-performance of an award is enforcement by proceedings in a national court. This is something that should be borne in mind from the outset of an arbitration. Sometimes, one of the parties (usually the claimant) urges the arbitral tribunal to run through the proceedings as quickly as possible, so as to obtain a speedy decision. This is understandable—but it is in the interests of the party that stands to gain most from the arbitration (whether by way of claim or counterclaim) to *ensure* that the proper procedures are followed, in case it should become necessary to apply to a national court for enforcement of the award.

11.10   Enforcement of a monetary award usually takes place against assets. This means that as a first step, it is necessary to trace the assets of the losing party (money in a bank account, an aircraft, or a ship, a cargo of oil in transit, or whatever it may be) before applying to the relevant national court for an order against those assets, or, less constructively, for an order that the trade or business of the losing party should be liquidated, if payment of the award continues to be refused.[12] In some jurisdictions, it is possible to enforce against assets held by third parties that are owed to the award debtor. For example, in an enforcement case before the English courts, the successful party in an arbitration sought enforcement against a 'letter of credit' issued by a bank in favour of the losing party in the arbitration. The UK Supreme Court ordered that the funds due under the letter of credit be directed to the award creditor (by way of appointment of a receiver) for satisfaction of the arbitral award.[13]

11.11   There are four ways in which a national legal system might provide for the enforcement of arbitral awards. The first arises when the award is deposited, or registered, with a court or other authority,[14] following which it may be enforced as if it is a judgment of that court. The second arises when the laws of the country of enforcement provide that, with the leave of

---

[11] See, e.g., ICC Rules, Art. 42 ('the Court and the arbitral tribunal shall act in the spirit of the Rules and shall make every effort to make sure that the award is enforceable at law'); LCIA Rules, Art. 32.2 (providing that the tribunal 'shall make every reasonable effort to ensure that any award is legally recognised and enforceable at the arbitral seat'); SIAC Rules, Art. 41.2 (providing that the tribunal 'shall make every reasonable effort to ensure the fair, expeditious and economical conclusion of the arbitration and the enforceability of any Award'); WIPO Rules Arbitration Rules, Art. 64.e (providing that the 'Tribunal may consult the Center with regard to matters of form, particularly to ensure the enforceability of the award').

[12] The successful party may sometimes seek recognition and enforcement of an award in a country in which the losing party may have no assets in order (so to speak) to obtain the *imprimatur* of a respected court upon the award.

[13] *Taurus Petroleum Ltd v State Oil Marketing Co. of the Ministry of Oil, Iraq* [2017] UKSC 64.

[14] As, e.g., under the Swiss Private International Law Act 1987 (Swiss PIL) (as amended in 2021), Ch. 12, s. 193. See also the Egyptian Ministerial Decree, made under s. 47 of the Egyptian Arbitration Law No. 27 of 1994 (as amended in 2017). Further, see also the Italian Code of Civil Procedure (Book 4, Title VIII, 'Arbitration'), art. 825—as amended by Legislative Decree No. 40, 2 February 2006.

the court, the award of an arbitral tribunal may be enforced *directly* without any need for deposit or registration.[15] The third arises when it is necessary to apply to the court for some form of recognition, or *exequatur*, as a preliminary step to enforcement.[16] The fourth is to sue on the award as evidence of a debt, on the basis that the arbitration agreement constitutes a contractual obligation to perform the award. This last method is cumbersome and frequently leaves it open to the losing party to reopen, by way of defence, the issues already determined by the arbitral tribunal. It is therefore to be avoided, unless no other method is available.

The procedures to be followed in any given case vary from country to country and from court to court. It is not possible to lay down detailed procedural guidelines here nor would it be particularly helpful to do so, since if action has to be taken to enforce an award in a particular jurisdiction, it is necessary to obtain competent advice from experienced lawyers who practise in that jurisdiction.   **11.12**

In 2019, in response to the increasing number of arbitrations (and particularly investor–state arbitrations) in which an award was either challenged or simply not carried out, a practical survey to challenging and enforcing international arbitral awards was published.[17]   **11.13**

The survey is in two parts. The first part contains a series of articles by lawyers in law firms around the world on the issues that are likely to be involved in seeking recognition or enforcement of international arbitral awards. The second part, which is likely to be of particular interest to lawyers faced with challenging or enforcing such awards, addresses a series of practical questions to practising lawyers in twenty-nine different states, including Argentina, Austria, Belgium, Canada, England, France, the Czech Republic, Japan, Russia, Singapore, Switzerland, Russia, and elsewhere.[18] These lawyers respond to the questions with practical guidance on, for example, any special local requirements as to the documentation to be filed in support of a request for challenge or enforcement, the local procedural rules that need to be followed, the fees payable, any applicable time limits, the possibilities that exist for making searches as to the existence of assets against which enforcement may be levied, and so forth. Even where recognition or enforcement of an award is sought in a country that is not covered by the survey, it gives a useful indication of the type of questions that will need to be raised with local lawyers when seeking recognition or enforcement of a foreign arbitral award in their jurisdiction.   **11.14**

As already stated, we do not propose to lay down any such procedural guidelines. What follows, therefore, is a review of the general principles underlying recognition and enforcement, including the choice of the appropriate forum (and 'forum shopping'); the role of the international conventions (in particular the New York and ICSID Conventions) in assisting   **11.15**

---

[15] As, e.g., in England, under the English Arbitration Act 1996, s. 66. See also s. 35(2) of the Australian International Arbitration Act 1974, as amended. Further, see also s. 19 of the Singaporean International Arbitration Act 1994, as amended in 2020.

[16] As, e.g., in France, under art. 1487 of the Code of Civil Procedure, as modified by Decree No. 2011-48 of 13 January 2011. See also art. 66(d) of Law No. 30 of 1999 Concerning Arbitration and Alternative Dispute Resolution. Further, see also art. 518 of the Argentinian National Code of Civil and Commercial Procedure (Further Articles).

[17] See 'The Guide to Challenging and Enforcing Arbitration Awards', General Editor J. William Rowley Q.C. (Global Arbitration Review, 2019) Law Business Research Ltd.

[18] The second edition of the Guide includes a useful note on state immunity and responses to questions from lawyers in additional jurisdictions, including China.

recognition and enforcement; and the defences that may be raised, including that of state immunity.

(c) General principles governing recognition and enforcement

11.16   The challenge of an arbitral award, discussed in Chapter 10, is concerned with attacking an award at its source, in the hope of having it modified or set aside in whole or in part. Recognition and enforcement, by contrast, are concerned with giving effect to the award, either in the state in which it was made or in some other state(s).

11.17   A distinction may be drawn at the outset between (a) the enforcement of an award in the state that is the 'seat' of the arbitration, and (b) the enforcement of an award that is regarded as a 'foreign', or 'international', award because it was made *outside* the territory of the state in which recognition or enforcement is sought. Enforcement of an award in the country that is the seat of the arbitration is usually a relatively easy process. It generally involves the same processes as are required for the enforcement of an award in a domestic arbitration.[19] Enforcement of an award that is regarded by the place of enforcement as a 'foreign', or 'international', award is a more complex matter. This chapter is mainly concerned with the recognition and enforcement of such 'foreign' awards.[20]

(d) Difference between recognition and enforcement

11.18   It is necessary to distinguish recognition from enforcement. The terms are sometimes used as though they are inextricably linked. For example, the New York Convention itself speaks of 'recognition *and* enforcement' of foreign arbitral awards.[21] The terms are, however, distinct. On this point, the 1927 Geneva Convention was more precise when it spoke of 'recognition *or* enforcement'.[22] An award may be recognised *without* being enforced.[23] However, if it is enforced, then it is necessarily recognised by the court that orders its enforcement. The precise distinction, in other words, is between 'recognition' and 'recognition and enforcement'.

---

[19] Enforcement provisions in China, similarly, differentiate between purely domestic awards and those awards that have been made in the People's Republic of China (PRC), but have a foreign element, such as (a) a foreign party, (b) the relevant relationship was formed, changed, or terminated in a foreign country, or (c) the subject matter of the dispute is situated outside the PRC.

[20] The New York Convention, the full title of which is the 'Convention on the Recognition and Enforcement of *Foreign* Arbitral Awards' (emphasis added), also applies to arbitral awards that are 'not considered as domestic awards in the State where their recognition and enforcement is sought' (Art. 1(1)). This may lead to an award made in one state being enforced in that same state under the New York Convention, on the basis that it is not regarded as a domestic award.

[21] In Arts I, IV, and V—but Art. V also speaks of 'recognition *or* enforcement' (emphasis added).

[22] The usage is followed in the English Arbitration Act 1996, which distinguishes between the 'recognition' of a New York Convention award (s. 101(1)) and its 'enforcement' (s. 101(2)). The statute also makes this distinction in other relevant sections.

[23] As happened, e.g., in *Dallal v Bank Mellat* [1986] QB 441, in which the English judge held that an award of the Iran–United States Claims Tribunal was not enforceable under the New York Convention, but should nevertheless be *recognised* as the valid judgment of a competent tribunal. The case is also reported in (1986) XI YBCA 547, at 553.

(i) Recognition

Recognition on its own is generally a defensive process.[24] It will usually arise when a court is asked to grant a remedy in respect of a dispute that has been the subject of previous arbitral proceedings. The party in whose favour the award was made will object that the dispute has already been determined. To prove this, it will seek to produce the award to the court, and will ask the court to recognise it as valid and binding upon the parties in respect of the issues with which it dealt. The award may have disposed of *all* of the issues raised in the new court proceedings and so put an end to those new proceedings as *res judicata*—that is, as recognising that the matters in issue between the parties have already been decided. If the award does not dispose of all of the claims or issues raised in the new proceedings, but only some of them, it will need to be recognised for the purposes of 'claim' (or in some jurisdictions, 'issue' estoppel), so as to prevent those claims (or issues) with which it does deal from being raised again. **11.19**

The use of recognition on its own may be illustrated by considering the example of a company that is made a defendant in court proceedings by a foreign supplier for goods sold and delivered, but allegedly not paid for. Suppose that the dispute between the company and the foreign supplier has already been submitted to arbitration, and that an award has been made, in which the foreign supplier's claim was dismissed. In these circumstances, the company will ask the court to *recognise* the award as a valid defence to the foreign supplier's new claim. If the court is prepared to do this, the claim is dismissed. The legal force and effect of the foreign award will have been recognised, but the award itself will not have been enforced. In other circumstances, it may be useful to seek recognition of an award, for example to aid enforcement attempts in other jurisdictions, or because converting an award into a court judgment by recognition may have persuasive value in attempts at post-award settlement. **11.20**

(ii) Enforcement

By contrast, where a court is asked to enforce an award, it is asked not merely to recognise the legal force and effect of the award, but also to ensure that it is carried out, by using such legal sanctions as are available. Enforcement goes a step further than recognition. A court that is prepared to grant enforcement of an award will do so because it recognises the award as validly made and binding upon the parties to it, and therefore suitable for enforcement. In this context, the terms 'recognition' and 'enforcement' do run together: one is a necessary part of the other. **11.21**

(iii) A shield and a sword

The purpose of recognition on its own is generally to act as a shield. Recognition is used to block any attempt to raise in fresh proceedings issues that have already been decided in the arbitration that gave rise to the award of which recognition is sought.[25] By contrast, the purpose of enforcement is to act as a sword. Enforcement of an award means applying legal sanctions to compel the party against whom the award was made to carry it out. Such legal **11.22**

---

[24] Although, in some countries, it may be a necessary step along the way to enforcement.
[25] As expressed in the English Arbitration Act 1996, s. 101(1), the award is recognised 'as binding on the persons as between whom it was made', so that it may accordingly be used by these persons 'by way of defence, set-off or otherwise' in any legal proceedings in England and Wales or Northern Ireland.

sanctions may take many forms. When the defaulting party is an individual, sanctions may include seizure of property and other assets, forfeiture of bank accounts, and even, in extreme cases, imprisonment. Where the defaulting party is a body corporate, enforcement is usually directed primarily against the property and other assets of the corporation, such as its stock-in-trade, bank accounts, trading accounts, and so forth. In certain situations, however, the directors of the company may be held personally liable (for instance on a guarantee). In such cases, the sanctions may be directed against them personally.

(e) Place of recognition and enforcement

11.23   A party who simply seeks *recognition* of an award will generally do so because it needs to rely on the award by way of defence, or set-off, or in some other fashion, in court proceedings to which it is the defendant. For this purpose, the party seeking recognition asks the court concerned to recognise the award as binding on the parties between whom it was made; and the court concerned is not one that is chosen by the party seeking recognition. It must be a court of the place where the proceedings against that party are brought. This fact of itself emphasises how important it is that international arbitral awards should be accepted by courts across the world as truly 'international' in their validity and effect.

11.24   Where the successful party in an arbitration is seeking to *enforce* an award, the position is different. The first step is to determine in which country, or countries, enforcement is to be sought. To reach this decision, it is necessary to locate the state or states in which the losing party has, or is likely to have, assets available to satisfy the award. This usually calls for careful (and possibly difficult) investigative work. If enquiries suggest that assets are likely to be available in only one state, the party seeking enforcement of the award has no choice: for better or worse, he or she must seek enforcement in that state. Where there is a choice, the party seeking enforcement is able to proceed in one or more places as seems appropriate.

11.25   Another factor to be taken into account in selecting a forum for the enforcement of an award is whether, under the New York Convention or some other relevant international convention, the prospective forum recognises and enforces awards rendered at the place of arbitration. A further factor is the attitude of the local courts to requests for recognition and enforcement of foreign awards, and notably whether their outlook is likely to be internationalist or parochial. The attitude that the prospective forum adopts on the question of state immunity[26] is yet another relevant factor if enforcement is being sought against a state or a governmental agency.[27]

(i) Forum shopping
11.26   The need to locate the place(s) in which a defaulting party has assets is not confined to international arbitration. In domestic court proceedings, it may also be necessary to locate the defaulting party's assets in order to enforce a court's judgment or an arbitral tribunal's

---

[26] For a discussion of state immunity, see paragraphs 11.152*ff.*

[27] Local law advice is also necessary to establish whether the local courts will have the necessary jurisdiction over the persons and assets against which enforcement is sought.

award. However, in a domestic dispute, the assets of the losing party are usually situated within the country in which the proceedings take place, since this is normally the country of that party's residence or place of business. In international arbitration, the contrary is likely to be the case. The place of arbitration[28] will usually have been chosen, by or on behalf of the parties, precisely because (inter alia) it is a place with which they have *no* connection. In other words, the place of arbitration has been chosen as a neutral forum. It would be purely fortuitous if the parties happened to have assets situated within this neutral country. When an award has to be enforced, it must generally be enforced in a country other than that in which it was made. As will be further explained later in this chapter,[29] this is why it is important that international awards should be recognised and enforced *internationally*, and not merely in the country in which they are made.

If, as often happens in international commerce, assets are located in different parts of the world, the party seeking enforcement of the award has a choice of country in which to proceed—a chance to go 'forum shopping', as it is sometimes expressed.[30] In looking for the appropriate forum, not merely the location of assets but also the other factors mentioned (such as the attitude of the local courts, the adherence of the target country to the New York Convention, and so on), must be taken into account.   **11.27**

(f) Methods of recognition and enforcement

Internationally, it is generally much easier to obtain recognition and enforcement of an international award than of a foreign court judgment. This is because the network of international and regional treaties providing for the recognition and enforcement of international awards is more widespread and better developed than corresponding provisions for the recognition and enforcement of foreign judgments.   **11.28**

For example, within the European Union (EU), Council Regulation (EC) No. 44/2001 of 22 December 2000 on Jurisdiction and the Recognition and Enforcement of Judgments in Civil and Commercial Matters provides only for the enforcement of European national court judgments solely within Europe.[31] In the global arena, the Hague Conference on Private International Law has been struggling to agree the text of a convention dealing with the recognition and enforcement of foreign judgments in civil and commercial matters. In 2005, the delegates only agreed on the mutual recognition and enforcement of judgments that   **11.29**

---

[28] The chosen place of arbitration is a geographical location in a given country, or more usually, in a given town or city. The arbitration agreement may state e.g. that any arbitration is to take place in Paris, or that it is to take place in New York, or wherever it may be. But, as has been seen in Chapter 3, once chosen, the physical 'place' of arbitration becomes the juridical 'seat' of the arbitration—an event that may have important legal consequences, depending on the *lex arbitri*.

[29] See paragraphs 11.34*ff*.

[30] While the existence of assets within a particular jurisdiction is most commonly used as a basis for enforcement in that jurisdiction, jurisdiction *ratione personae* over a party can sometimes also be used to seize assets outside the jurisdiction in which enforcement is sought. The New York Court of Appeals has held, in *Koehler v Bank of Bermuda Ltd*, 12 NY.3d 533 (2009), that assets located outside New York can be ordered to be brought within the jurisdiction for enforcement purposes, as long as a New York court has jurisdiction over the owner or custodian of those assets: see Friedman, 'Enforcement of international arbitration awards in New York: If you take them there, you can collect from anywhere' (2011) 27 Arb Intl 575.

[31] This Regulation replaces the Brussels Convention of 1968.

were rendered pursuant to exclusive choice of court agreements: the Hague Convention on Choice of Court Agreements of 30 June 2005. Even so, at the time of writing, seventeen years after the 2005 Hague Convention was concluded, it has been ratified only in the EU, Mexico, Montenegro, and Singapore. The text of the Hague Convention on the Recognition and Enforcement of Foreign Judgments in Civil or Commercial Matters of 2 July 2019 (which is aimed at providing mutual recognition and enforcement of foreign judgments on broader civil and commercial matters) has been agreed, but at the time of writing that Convention has not been ratified by any country. It was only signed by Uruguay and Ukraine and it is therefore unlikely to change the enforcement landscape in the near future. These conventions contrast dramatically with the ubiquity of the New York Convention. Indeed, as we have said previously, the widespread recognition and enforceability of arbitral awards is one of the principal advantages of arbitration as a method of resolving international commercial disputes.[32]

11.30 The method of recognition and enforcement to be adopted in any particular case depends on the place where the award was made (that is, whether it qualifies, for example, as a New York Convention award). It also depends on the relevant provisions of the law at the place of intended enforcement (the 'forum state'). On this aspect, it is usually essential (as previously indicated) to obtain advice from experienced lawyers in the forum state.[33]

11.31 Local formalities are bound to be involved, whether or not one of the international conventions is applicable. For example, the original or certified copies of the arbitration agreement and award are usually required. The language of the award may well be different from the language of the court of the forum state, so that a translation is required—and it may be necessary for this to be undertaken with considerable formality (for example by consular attestation in the country of origin).

(g) Time limits

11.32 Time limits for the commencement of proceedings for the recognition and enforcement of an arbitral award are usually laid down in national legislation. Careful attention must be paid to such time limits (and to any other time limits contained in the rules of court of the forum state). In this respect, it would be foolhardy not to consult an experienced local practitioner—and this applies as much to the party seeking recognition or enforcement of an award as it does to the party wishing to challenge an award. In the United States, for instance, time limits vary from state to state and, when it comes to recognition or enforcement of an award, the relevant period may be anything from one year to three years.[34]

---

[32] See Chapter 1.

[33] Recognition and enforcement is likely to be easiest to obtain under an international convention where the forum state is bound by such a convention, but other methods of recognition and enforcement may be available, as discussed at paragraphs 11.139*ff*. The Guide to Challenging and Enforcing Arbitration Awards, referenced in paragraph 11.13, notes any applicable Conventions in the jurisdictions covered in Part II of the Guide.

[34] See also English Limitation Act 1980, s. 7: 'An action to enforce an award, where the submission is not by an instrument under seal, shall not be brought after the expiration of six years from the date on which the cause of action accrued.' For India, the equivalent period is three years under the Limitation Act 1963, Sch. 1, para. 101. The Canadian Supreme Court has concluded that domestic limitation periods are applicable to enforcing awards under the New York Convention: *Yugraneft Corporation v Rexx Management Corporation* [2010] SCC 19.

(h) Consequences of refusal of recognition or enforcement

The immediate consequence of a refusal to enforce an award is that the winning party **11.33**
fails to get what it wants—namely, payment of what it is owed by seizure of the loser's
assets in the place in which enforcement was sought. Although this is a disheartening result for the party seeking enforcement, it should be borne in mind that it will still have an
award that may be enforced in another state in which the losing party *has* assets. Much
depends upon the reason for which enforcement was refused. If, for example, enforcement was refused for local public policy considerations, it may be possible to find another country in which the same considerations do not apply. However, if enforcement
was refused (for example) because of a fundamental failure by the arbitral tribunal to
give the losing party an opportunity to present its case, it may not be possible to enforce
the award elsewhere, since other courts may refuse enforcement for the same reason.[35]
In such an event, the party seeking enforcement may have no option but to recommence
arbitral proceedings, assuming that the right to do so has not been lost by lapse of time.

(i) Role of the international conventions

The dependence of the international arbitral process upon national systems of law is **11.34**
most clearly seen in the context of the recognition and enforcement of international
awards. An arbitral tribunal is limited in the powers that it can exercise—and these
powers, although usually adequate for resolving a particular dispute, fall short of the
coercive powers possessed by national courts. Indeed, a state is generally reluctant to
confer on a private arbitral tribunal the sanctioning powers that it confers on the judges
in its own courts. The power to enforce an award against a reluctant party by such summary methods as the attachment of bank accounts or the sequestration of assets is a
power that forms part of the prerogative of the state. In consequence, the enforcement
of awards must take place via the national court at the place of enforcement, operating
under its own procedural rules. The detailed procedures adopted in these courts will
vary from country to country. However, the effect of the international conventions, cul-
minating in the New York Convention, has been to secure a considerable degree of uniformity in the recognition and enforcement of awards in most of the important trading
countries of the world.

The main international treaties that apply to the recognition and enforcement of inter- **11.35**
national awards are reviewed in the next section. In particular, this chapter includes a discussion of the New York Convention, the ICSID Convention, and a number of regional
conventions.

The New York Convention has the widest scope of application. Subject to two reservations **11.36**
that may restrict its application, the New York Convention facilitates the recognition and
enforcement of foreign arbitral awards in the territories of any of its more than 167 signatory
states, irrespective of the arbitration rules under which the proceedings were conducted.[36]

---

[35] See New York Convention, Art. V(1)(b); Model Law (as amended in 2006), Art. 36(1)(a)(ii).
[36] For example, the ICC Rules, the LCIA Rules, UNCITRAL Rules, or ICSID Additional Facility Rules.

Enshrining as it does a strong pro-enforcement policy, the New York Convention provides for the recognition and enforcement of foreign arbitral awards by national courts, subject to a handful of procedural and substantive grounds for objecting to enforcement that are intended to be limited in scope.

11.37   Similarly, the ICSID Convention (formally described as the 'Washington Convention') provides for the enforcement of those arbitral awards that were rendered in proceedings involving a national of one contracting state and another contracting state. Awards falling under the scope of the ICSID Convention are directly enforceable within the territories of all states parties to ICSID.[37] Like the New York Convention, the ICSID Convention has the vast number of 155 contracting states.

11.38   In this chapter, we also briefly discuss a number of regional conventions. The application of these regional conventions is far more limited than the application of the New York and ICSID Conventions, not least because the New York Convention will apply to almost all disputes, thus superseding those regional conventions.

B. Enforcement under the New York Convention

(a) Introduction

11.39   The origins of the New York Convention have already been described in Chapter 1. The New York Convention replaced the 1927 Geneva Convention as between states that are parties to both Conventions,[38] and was a substantial improvement, since it provides for a simpler and more effective method of obtaining recognition and enforcement of foreign awards. The Convention also replaced the earlier 1923 Geneva Protocol as between states that are bound by both,[39] and again constitutes a substantial improvement, because it gives much wider effect to the validity of arbitration agreements than that given under the Protocol. As a result, the New York Convention has been rightly eulogised as 'the single most important pillar on which the edifice of international arbitration rests',[40] and as a convention that 'perhaps could lay claim to be the most effective instance of international legislation in the entire history of commercial law'.[41] It is for this reason that, for now, many remain reluctant to countenance the possible disruption that would accompany the modernisation of the Convention's existing text.[42]

---

[37] See ICSID Convention, Art. 54.

[38] New York Convention, Art. VII(2).

[39] Ibid.

[40] Wetter, 'The present status of the International Court of Arbitration of the ICC: An appraisal' (1990) 1 Am Rev Intl Arb 91, at 93.

[41] Mustill, 'Arbitration: History and background' (1989) 6 J Intl Arb 43, at 49. See also Schwebel, 'A celebration of the United Nations' New York Convention' (1996) 12 Arb Intl 823.

[42] See van den Berg, 'Hypothetical Draft Convention on the International Enforcement of Arbitration Agreements and Awards: Explanatory Note', Paper prepared for the ICCA Conference, Dublin, 2008, for the last unsuccessful attempt to advocate for such modernisation; available online at https://www.newyorkconvent ion.org/11165/web/files/document/1/6/16015.pdf. See also Gaillard, 'The urgency of not revising the New York Convention', in Albert Jan van den Berg (ed.) *50 Years of the New York Convention: ICCA International Arbitration Conference*, ICCA Congress Series, Vol. 14 (Kluwer Law International, 2009), pp. 689–696.

(i) Enforcing the agreement to arbitrate

Although the title of the New York Convention refers only to the recognition and en- **11.40**
forcement of 'foreign arbitral awards', the Convention also deals with the recognition and
enforcement of arbitration agreements. This has already been discussed in Chapter 1.
In this chapter, the focus is on only the recognition and enforcement of 'foreign arbitral
awards'.

(ii) Enforcing foreign awards

The New York Convention adopts a strikingly internationalist attitude in its opening   **11.41**
statement, despite its title referring to '*foreign* awards' rather than to '*international*
awards' as some proponents at the time, including particularly the ICC, would have
wished. It says:

> This Convention shall apply to the recognition and enforcement of arbitral awards made
> in the territory of a State other than the State where the recognition and enforcement of
> such awards are sought, and arising out of differences between persons, whether physical
> or legal. It shall also apply to arbitral awards not considered as domestic awards in the State
> where their recognition and enforcement are sought.[43]

If this opening statement were to stand without qualification, it would mean that an award
made in any state (even if that state were not a party to the New York Convention) would be
recognised and enforced by any other state that was a party so long as the award satisfied the
basic conditions set down in the Convention. There is, however, a qualification: Article I(3)
of the Convention allows states that adhere to it to make two possible reservations. The first
of these is the 'reciprocity reservation'; the second is the 'commercial reservation', which was
also in the 1923 Geneva Protocol.

(iii) First reservation—reciprocity

Article I(3) of the New York Convention provides that: **11.42**

> When signing, ratifying or acceding to this Convention, or notifying extension under
> Article X hereof, any State may on the basis of reciprocity declare that it will apply the
> Convention to the recognition and enforcement of awards *made only* in the territory of
> another Contracting State.[44]

To the extent that states take advantage of it, the reciprocity reservation has the effect of
narrowing the scope of application of the New York Convention. Instead of applying to
all international arbitral awards wherever they are made, the application of the New York
Convention may be limited to 'Convention awards'—that is, to awards made in a state that
is a party to the New York Convention.[45]

---

[43] New York Convention, Art. I(1).
[44] Emphasis added.
[45] At the time of writing, 167 states had acceded to the New York Convention. Of these, eighty-one had done
so on the basis of the reciprocity reservation. Some countries that had adopted the reciprocity reservation (such
as Germany and Switzerland) have subsequently withdrawn it. See UNCITRAL, 'Status: Convention on the
Recognition and Enforcement of Foreign Arbitral Awards (New York, 1958)', available online at https://uncitral.
un.org/en/texts/arbitration/conventions/foreign_arbitral_awards/status2.

11.43   States that have entered into the New York Convention on the basis of reciprocity have agreed, in effect, that they will recognise and enforce *only* Convention awards. Accordingly, when seeking a suitable state in which to hold an international commercial arbitration, it is advisable to select a state that *has* adopted the New York Convention, so as to improve the chances of securing recognition and enforcement of the award in other Convention countries.

11.44   The limiting effect of the first reservation should not be exaggerated. The number of states that make up the international network for the recognition and enforcement of arbitral awards established by the New York Convention grows year by year. The Convention now links the world's major trading nations: Arab, African, Asian, and Latin American, as well as European and North American. As more countries become Convention countries, the reciprocity reservation becomes less significant. The Model Law, for example, in Articles 35 and 36, requires the recognition and enforcement of an arbitral award '*irrespective* of the country in which it was made'. This reflects the 'dream' of a truly international award, where the place of arbitration is irrelevant and an award has no nationality, rather than the approach of the New York Convention which speaks of 'foreign awards' located in a particular 'place' or 'seat' of arbitration.[46]

(iv) Second reservation—commercial relationships

11.45   Article I(3) of the New York Convention contains a further reservation. This entitles a contracting state to declare that it will apply the Convention only to those differences arising out of legal relationships, whether contractual or not, that are 'considered as commercial under the national law of the state making such declaration'.[47]

11.46   The effect of this reservation, like the reservation as to reciprocity, is to narrow the scope of application of the New York Convention,[48] and the fact that each contracting state may determine for itself what relationships it considers to be 'commercial' has created problems in the application of the New York Convention. Relationships that are regarded as 'commercial' by one state are not necessarily so regarded by others—and this does not assist in obtaining a uniform interpretation of the Convention. Indeed, the commercial reservation has led to difficulties of interpretation even within the same state, as is shown by two cases that arose in India. In the first,[49] the High Court of Bombay (now Mumbai) was asked to stay legal proceedings that had been commenced despite the existence of an arbitration agreement. Under the relevant Indian legislation enacting the New York Convention, the court was obliged to grant such a stay, as long as the arbitration agreement came within the Convention. In ratifying the New York Convention, India had entered the commercial reservation. The court held that whilst the agreement under which the dispute arose was

---

[46]   For further discussion of the role of the Model Law, see Chapter 1, paragraphs 1.109*ff.*

[47]   A similar commercial reservation was permitted in the 1923 Geneva Protocol.

[48]   Of the 167 states that were parties to the Convention by December 2020, fifty-five had applied the commercial reservation. On 12 March 2001, Serbia and Montenegro confirmed Yugoslavia's declaration of 1982 restricting the application of the Convention to 'economic' disputes. Norway's reservation stated that it would not apply the Convention in any disputes if the subject matter were immovable property in Norway or rights in such property.

[49]   *Indian Organic Chemical Ltd v Subsidiary 1 (US), Subsidiary 2 (US), and Chemtex Fibres Inc (Parent Co.) (US)* (1979) IV YBCA 271.

commercial in nature, it could not be considered to be commercial 'under the law in force in India':

> In my opinion, in order to invoke the provisions of [the Convention], it is not enough to establish that an agreement is commercial. It must also be established that it is commercial by virtue of a provision of law or an operative legal principle in force in India.[50]

This decision was subsequently disapproved by the High Court of Gujarat. In this second case,[51] the plaintiffs moved for a stay of legal proceedings that, again, had been commenced despite the existence of an arbitration agreement. The court granted this motion. On the argument as to whether or not the contract was commercial in nature, the judge said that the term 'commerce':   **11.47**

> is a word of the largest import and takes in its sweep all the business and trade transactions in any of their forms, including the transportation, purchase, sale and exchange of commodities between the citizens of different countries.[52]

The judge added:

> It should be noted that the view of the learned single Judge of the Bombay High Court in *Indian Organic Chemical Ltd*'s case has not been approved by the Division Bench of the Bombay High Court. The Division Bench after setting out the view of [the judge] in the aforesaid decision, ultimately disagreed with it [...][53]

This position was confirmed by the Indian Supreme Court in its decision in *RM Investment & Trading Company v Boeing Company*,[54] in which it held that in: **11.48**

> construing the expression 'commercial' in Section 2 of the Act it has to be borne in mind that the 'Act is calculated and designed to subserve the cause of facilitating international trade and promotion thereof by providing for speedy settlement of disputes arising in such trade through arbitration and any expression or phrase occurring [therein] should receive, consistent with its literal and grammatical sense, a liberal construction' [...] The expression 'commercial' should, therefore, be construed broadly having regard to the manifold activities which are an integral part of international trade today.

Nevertheless, the point remains that each national state may decide for itself, under the provisions of the New York Convention, what relationships it considers to be 'commercial' for the purposes of the commercial reservation.[55]   **11.49**

---

[50] Ibid., at 273.
[51] *Union of India and ors v Lief Hoegh Co. (Norway)* (1984) IX YBCA 405.
[52] Ibid., at 407.
[53] Ibid., at 408.
[54] *RM Investment & Trading Company v Boeing Company*, 1994 (4) SCC 541, (1997) XXII Ybk Comm Arb 711.
[55] The Tunisian courts, e.g., have construed the commercial reservation so broadly as to exclude enforcement of an award relating to obligations arising under a contract for professional services. See *Société d'Investissement Kal (Tunisia) v Taieb Haddad (Tunisia) and Hans Barrett* (1998) XXIII YBCA 770. In China, the Supreme People's Court's Circular on Implementing the Convention excludes relationships between 'foreign investors and the host government': Notice of the Supreme People's Court Regarding the Implementation of the Convention on the Recognition and Enforcement of Foreign Arbitral Awards Acceded to by China [1987] *Fa Jing Fa* No. 5, effective from 10 April 1987. At the other end of the spectrum is *Bautista v Star Cruises*, 396 F.3d 1289 (11th Cir. 2005), in

(v) Recognition and enforcement under the New York Convention

11.50   The New York Convention provides for both recognition and enforcement of awards to which the Convention applies. As far as *recognition* is concerned, a state bound by the Convention undertakes to respect the binding effect of awards to which the Convention applies; accordingly, as has been seen, such awards may be relied upon by way of defence or set-off in any legal proceedings. As far as *enforcement* is concerned, a state that is a party to the Convention undertakes to enforce awards to which the Convention applies, in accordance with its local procedural rules. It also undertakes not to impose substantially more onerous conditions, or higher fees or charges, for such enforcement than are imposed in the enforcement of its own domestic awards.[56]

(vi) Formalities

11.51   The formalities required for obtaining recognition and enforcement of awards to which the New York Convention applies are simple.[57] The party seeking such recognition and enforcement is merely required to produce to the relevant court:

> [...]
> (a) The duly authenticated original award or a duly certified copy thereof; [and]
> (b) The original agreement referred to in article II, or a duly certified copy thereof.[58]

11.52   Despite these requirements of Article IV of the Convention, courts in a number of jurisdictions have enforced awards in the absence of an original of the arbitration agreement,[59] or indeed without a written arbitration clause at all.[60]

11.53   If the award and the arbitration agreement are not in the official language of the country in which recognition and enforcement is sought, certified translations are needed.[61] Once the necessary documents have been supplied, the court will grant recognition and enforcement unless one or more of the grounds for refusal, listed in the Convention, are present.

---

which a US court denied the application of an exclusion from arbitration under the Federal Arbitration Act of 1925 (FAA) of the 'contracts of employment of seamen, railroad employees or other class of workers engaged in foreign or interstate commerce' to the commercial reservation. Its rationale was that 'to read industry-specific exceptions into the broad language of the Convention Act would be to hinder the Convention's purpose': ibid., at 1299.

[56] New York Convention, Art. III.
[57] New York Convention, Art. IV. However, see the discussion of the 'writing requirement' in Chapter 2.
[58] Despite this, enforcement fails, from time to time, because these simple formal requirements are not fulfilled: see, e.g., the decisions of the Italian Court of Cassation in *Lampart Vegypary Gepgyar (Hungary) v Srl Campomarzio Impianti (Italy)* (1999) XXIVa YBCA 699; the Bulgarian Supreme Court's decision in *National Electricity Co. AD (Bulgaria) v ECONBERG Ltd (Croatia)* (2000) XXV YBCA 678. Equally, an increasing number of jurisdictions take a liberal and pragmatic approach to the fulfilment of formal requirements. By way of example, a Geneva court recognised a Chinese award that had not been translated into French, noting that the spirit of the Convention was to reduce the obligations for the party seeking recognition and enforcement, and that the burden of proof in respect of any questions relating to the authenticity of the arbitration agreement or the award lay on the party opposing recognition: *R SA v A Ltd* (2001) XXVI YBCA 863.
[59] In *Hewlett-Packard, Inc. v Berg*, 867 F.Supp. 1126, 1130, n. 11 (D. Mass. 1994), the court considered Berg's motion to confirm an arbitral award made in his favour. While noting that the submission of uncertified copies of the arbitral award and arbitration agreement fell short of the requirements in Art. VI of the Convention, the court nevertheless felt able to confirm the arbitral award, in part because neither party had contested the validity of the documents submitted.
[60] See, e.g., *Profura v Blomgren* (T 2863-07, Court of Appeals for Western Sweden), 19 March 2008. Furthermore, under the English Arbitration Act 1996, an oral arbitration agreement is, in some circumstances, capable of enforcement: see the English Arbitration Act 1996, s. 88(1)(b).
[61] New York Convention, Art. IV(2).

(b) Refusal of recognition and enforcement

The various grounds for refusal of recognition and enforcement of an arbitration award that are set out in the New York Convention merit detailed discussion. This is not only because of the importance of the Convention itself, but also (and equally crucially) because the provisions of the Model Law governing recognition and enforcement of awards (in Articles 35 and 36) are almost identical to those set out in the Convention.   **11.54**

First, and fundamentally, neither the New York Convention nor the Model Law permits any review on the merits of an award to which the Convention applies.[62]   **11.55**

Secondly, the grounds for refusal of recognition and enforcement set out in the New York Convention (and in the Model Law) are exhaustive. They are the *only* grounds on which recognition and enforcement may be refused.   **11.56**

Thirdly, the New York Convention sets out five separate grounds on which recognition and enforcement of a Convention award may be refused at the request of the party against whom it is invoked.[63] It is significant that, under both the Convention and the Model Law (which follows the Convention in this respect), the burden of proof is *not* upon the party seeking recognition and enforcement.[64] The remaining two grounds on which recognition and enforcement may be refused, which relate to the public policy of the place of enforcement, are grounds that may be invoked by the enforcing court on its own motion.[65]   **11.57**

Fourthly, even if grounds for refusal of recognition and enforcement of an award are proved to exist, the enforcing court is *not obliged* to refuse enforcement. The opening lines of Article V(1) and (2) of the Convention say that enforcement 'may' be refused; they do not say that it 'must' be refused. The language is permissive, not mandatory.[66] The same is true of the Model Law.[67]   **11.58**

---

[62] This statement, which was made in an earlier edition of this volume, has since been cited with approval by the Supreme Court of India in *Renusagar Power Co. Ltd v General Electric Co.* (1995) XX YBCA 681. The Court added that, in its opinion, 'the scope of enquiry before the court in which the award is sought to be enforced is limited [to the grounds mentioned in the Act] and does not enable a party to the said proceedings to impeach the Award on merits': ibid., at 691.

[63] These grounds are set out in the New York Convention, Art. V.

[64] This represents a major change from the 1927 Geneva Convention.

[65] New York Convention, Art. V(2).

[66] This interpretation of the relevant provision of the Convention seems to be generally accepted, both in court decisions and by experienced commentators: see, e.g., van den Berg, *The New York Arbitration Convention of 1958* (Kluwer Law International, 1981), p. 265; Delaume, 'Enforcement against a foreign state of an arbitral award annulled in the foreign state' (1997) Revue du Droit International des Affaires 254. For a US decision to this effect, see *Chromalloy Aeroservices Inc. v Arab Republic of Egypt*, 939 F.Supp 907, 909 (DDC 1996); for an English decision, see *China Agribusiness Development Corporation v Balli Trading* [1998] 2 Lloyd's Rep 76. See also M. Paulsson, *The 1958 New York Convention in Action* (Kluwer Law International, 2016), pp. 158–160, which analyses the *travaux préparatoires* of the New York Convention and concludes that the word 'may' was intended by the drafters to allow the competent courts to decide whether to refuse enforcement. The suggestion that the French text of the Convention (in contrast to the equally authentic Chinese, English, Spanish, and Russian texts) is mandatory, rather than permissive, is demolished by J. Paulsson, 'May or must under the New York Convention: An exercise in syntax and linguistics' (1998) 14 Arb Intl 227.

[67] The same is true for the grounds for refusal under the English Arbitration Act 1996, although it is not based on the Model Law: see, e.g., *Kanoria v Guinness* [2006] EWCA Civ 222, [2006] Arb LR 513.

11.59   Fifthly, the intention of the New York Convention and of the Model Law is that the grounds for refusing recognition and enforcement of arbitral awards should be applied restrictively. As a leading commentator on the Convention has stated: 'As far as the grounds for refusal for enforcement of the Award as enumerated in Article V are concerned, it means *that they have to be construed narrowly*.'[68]

11.60   Most national courts have recognised this. There has been long-standing approval in the United States, for example, of the 'pro-enforcement bias' of the Convention.[69] However, not all courts follow this internationalist approach. Practitioners of international commercial arbitration are aware, either from their own experience or from the experience of others, of the difficulties that may arise in some places in seeking enforcement of an award under the New York Convention. In particular, the 'public policy' exception[70] enables some states to play the game less fairly than others. Nor is this the only problem.[71] There are states that have ratified the Convention, but have either not brought it into effect or have brought it into effect inadequately. There are states in which the local courts or the local bureaucracy are unfamiliar with international arbitration—and perhaps even suspicious of it. There are also oddities of legislation, such as those provisions of a past law in India (now repealed) stating that where the governing law was that of India, the ensuing award was deemed to be a domestic award, even though the seat of the arbitration was in a foreign state.[72]

11.61   Problems of this kind cannot be ignored, but they should not be exaggerated. The New York Convention *has* proved to be a highly effective international instrument for the enforcement of arbitration agreements and, more importantly in the present context, arbitration awards.[73] The Convention is now somewhat dated,[74] and it is by no means applied consistently by all of the states that have adopted it (or which claim to have done so).[75] However, it has made the greatest single contribution to the internationalisation of commercial arbitration. Even though the Model Law may eventually take its place, decisions under the New York Convention will remain important, since the Model Law's provisions governing recognition and enforcement of arbitral awards are taken directly from that Convention.

---

[68] van den Berg, *The New York Arbitration Convention of 1958* (Kluwer Law International, 1981), pp. 267 and 268 (emphasis added).

[69] *Parsons Whittemore Overseas Co. v Société Générale de L'Industrie de Papier (RAKTA)*, 508 F.2d 969 (2d Cir. 1974); also reported in (1976) I YBCA 205.

[70] See paragraph 11.33.

[71] For further discussion of these problems, see, e.g., Kerr, 'Concord and conflict in international arbitration' (1996) 13 ASA Bulletin 129, paras 1–157 (also published in (1997) 13 Intl Arb 121); Proceedings of the Fourteenth ICCA Congress, Paris, May 1998. See also J. Paulsson, 'Why good arbitration cannot compensate for bad courts' (2013) 30 J Intl Arb 345.

[72] Such an award is normally regarded as a foreign (or international) award under the New York Convention.

[73] See fn. 6.

[74] For instance, in its definition of an 'agreement in writing' as discussed in Chapters 1 and 2.

[75] See, e.g., J. Paulsson, 'The New York Convention in international practice: Problems of assimilation', in Blessing (ed.) *The New York Convention of 1958: A Collection of Reports and Materials Delivered at the ASA Conference Held in Zurich 2 February 1996* (ASA, 1996), pp. 100*ff*; Cheng, 'Celebrating the fiftieth anniversary of the New York Convention' (2009) 14 ICCA Congress Series 679.

(c) Grounds for refusal

Under Article V(1) of the New York Convention, recognition and enforcement of an arbitral award *may* be refused if the opposing party proves that: **11.62**

[...]
(a) The parties to the arbitration agreement [...] were, under the law applicable to them, under some incapacity, or the said agreement is not valid under the law to which the parties have subjected it or, failing any indication thereon, under the law of the country where the award was made; or
(b) The party against whom the award is invoked was not given proper notice of the appointment of the arbitrator or of the arbitration proceedings or was otherwise unable to present his [or her] case; or
(c) The award deals with a difference not contemplated by or not falling within the terms of the submission to arbitration, or it contains decisions on matters beyond the scope of the submission to arbitration, provided that, if the decisions on matters submitted to arbitration can be separated from those not so submitted, that part of the award which contains decisions on matters submitted to arbitration may be recognized and enforced; or
(d) The composition of the arbitral authority or the arbitral procedure was not in accordance with the agreement of the parties, or, failing such agreement, was not in accordance with the law of the country where the arbitration took place; or
(e) The award has not yet become binding on the parties, or has been set aside or suspended by a competent authority of the country in which, or under the law of which, the award was made.

Article V(2) provides: **11.63**

Recognition and enforcement [...] may also be refused if the competent authority in the country where recognition and enforcement is sought finds that:
(a) The subject matter of the difference is not capable of settlement by arbitration under the law of that country; or
(b) The recognition or enforcement of the award would be contrary to the public policy of that country.

These grounds for refusal of recognition and enforcement of foreign arbitral awards are of considerable importance. They represent an internationally accepted standard, not only because of the widespread acceptance of the New York Convention throughout the world, but also because the Model Law adopts the same grounds (although not in precisely the same words) for refusal of recognition and enforcement of an arbitral award, irrespective of the country in which that award was made.[76] In addition, six of these seven grounds for refusal are also set out in the Model Law as grounds for the *setting aside* of an arbitral award by the national court of the place of arbitration.[77]

---

[76] Model Law (as amended in 2006), Art. 36.
[77] Model Law, Art. 34. The ground that is omitted, naturally, is that of the award being set aside by a national court of the place of arbitration.

11.64   In an ideal world, the provisions of the New York Convention and of the Model Law would be interpreted in the same way by courts everywhere. Sadly, this does not happen. There are inconsistent decisions under the New York Convention, just as there may be inconsistent decisions within a national system of law (although the latter may be corrected on appeal). Nevertheless, it is useful to consider how national courts in different parts of the world have applied the different grounds for refusal set out in the New York Convention. Whilst these decisions have no binding authority on national courts in other jurisdictions, they may provide useful guidelines for the interpretation of a particular ground for refusal in a particular case.

(d)   First ground for refusal—incapacity; invalid arbitration agreement

11.65   The first ground for refusal of recognition and enforcement under the New York Convention is set out in Article V(1)(a)[78] as:

(a)   The parties to the agreement [...] were, under the law applicable to them, under some incapacity, or the said agreement is not valid under the law to which the parties have subjected it or, failing any indication thereon, under the law of the country where the award was made [...]

The issue of capacity to enter into an arbitration agreement, which may raise particular difficulties in relation to states and state agencies, has already been discussed in Chapter 2, as have issues as to the validity of the arbitration agreement.

11.66   A classic example of a successful defence to enforcement based on invalidity of the arbitration agreement is provided by the decision of the Administrative Tribunal of Damascus in *Fougerolle SA (France) v Ministry of Defence of the Syrian Arab Republic.*[79] The Tribunal, in its decision of 31 March 1988, refused enforcement of two ICC awards, holding that they were 'non-existent' because they were rendered 'without the preliminary advice on the referral of the dispute to arbitration, which must be given by the competent Committee of the Council of State'.[80]

11.67   A later example of a successful defence to enforcement based on this ground is the decision of the UK Supreme Court in *Dallah Real Estate v Ministry of Religious Affairs.*[81] In *Dallah*, the enforcement in London of an ICC award rendered in Paris against the government of Pakistan was refused by the UK Supreme Court on the grounds that the government was not a party to the arbitration agreement. The agreement containing the arbitration clause had been signed by the government-owned Awami Hajj Trust,[82] which subsequently ceased to exist[83] and was held not to be an organ of the state.[84] In so finding, the Supreme Court reversed the arbitral tribunal's own finding on jurisdiction. Lord Mance emphasised that a

---

[78]   As already noted, this ground for refusal, and the others that follow, also appear in virtually the same terms in the Model Law (as amended in 2006), Art. 36, as grounds for refusing enforcement of arbitral awards wherever made.

[79]   *Fougerolle SA (France) v Ministry of Defence of the Syrian Arab Republic* (1990) XV, YBCA 515.

[80]   Ibid.

[81]   *Dallah Real Estate and Tourism Holding Co. v The Ministry of Religious Affairs, Government of Pakistan* [2010] UKSC 46.

[82]   Ibid., at [2].

[83]   Ibid., at [8].

[84]   Ibid., at [66], [147], [149], [162], and [163].

determination by the arbitral tribunal concerning its own jurisdiction was immaterial to the Court's review:

> The tribunal's own view of its jurisdiction has no legal or evidential value, when the issue is whether the tribunal had any legitimate authority in relation to the Government at all. This is so however full was the evidence before it and however carefully deliberated was its conclusion. It is also so whatever the composition of the tribunal.[85]

11.68 The UK Supreme Court's decision is to be contrasted with the outcome of the application for the annulment of the same award before the Paris Court of Appeal. The Paris court, having fully agreed with the UK Supreme Court on the applicable legal principles, found differently on the facts (it found that, as a matter of fact, the government of Pakistan was a 'true party' to the underlying transaction); and so it reached the opposite conclusion on the question as to whether the government was bound by the arbitration agreement.[86]

(e) Second ground—no proper notice of appointment of arbitrator or of the proceedings; lack of due process

11.69 The second ground for refusal of recognition and enforcement of an award under the New York Convention is set out at Article V(1)(b):

(b) The party against whom the award is invoked was not given proper notice of the appointment of the arbitrator or of the arbitration proceedings or was otherwise unable to present his [or her] case [...]

This is perhaps the most important ground for refusal under the New York Convention (and the Model Law). It is directed at ensuring that the arbitration itself is properly conducted, and in particular that the parties are accorded proper notice and an adequate and fair opportunity to present their case.

11.70 The point as to notice is a matter of formality, but it is important nonetheless. However, the main thrust of this provision of the Convention is directed at ensuring that the requirements of 'due process' are observed and that the parties are given a fair hearing. If parties from different countries are to have confidence in arbitration as a method of dispute resolution, it is essential that the proceedings should be conducted in a manner that *is* fair and which is *seen* to be fair. This is something that should be borne in mind, by parties and arbitrators alike, from the very outset of the arbitration.

11.71 The court of the forum state will naturally have its own concept of what constitutes a 'fair hearing'. In this sense, as was said in a leading case in the United States, the New York Convention 'essentially sanctions the application of the forum state's standards of due process'.[87] This does not mean, however, that the hearing must be conducted as if it were a hearing before a national court in the forum state. It is generally enough if the court is satisfied that the proceedings were conducted with due regard to any agreement between the parties, and

---

[85] Ibid., at [30].

[86] *Gouvernement du Pakistan v Société Dallah Real Estate and Tourism Holding Co.*, Paris Cour d'Appel, 17 February 2011 [2012] Rev Arb 369.

[87] *Parsons Whittemore Overseas Co. Inc. v Société Générale de l'Industrie du Papier (RAKTA)*, 508 F.2d 969, 975 (2d Cir. 1974).

in accordance with the principles of equality of treatment and the right of each party to have a reasonable—rather than exhaustive—opportunity to present its case.

11.72   The national court at the place of enforcement thus has a limited role. Its function is *not* to decide whether or not the award is correct, as a matter of fact and law; its function is simply to decide whether the parties have received a fair hearing. Only a significant and material mistake in the course of the proceedings should be sufficient to lead the court to conclude that there was a denial of 'due process'.

11.73   By way of example, in a case to which reference has already been made,[88] a US corporation, which had been told that there was no need to submit detailed invoices, had its claim rejected by the Iran–United States Claims Tribunal, for failure to submit detailed invoices! The US court— rightly, it is suggested—refused to enforce the award against the US company. In different cir- cumstances, a German court held that an award that was based upon arguments that had not been raised by the parties or the tribunal during the arbitral proceedings, and thus on which the parties had not had an opportunity to comment, violated due process and the right to be heard.[89] In France, in *Overseas Mining Investments*,[90] the successful claimant had not pleaded the grounds on which the arbitral tribunal had found in its favour. In these circumstances, the French Court of Cassation held that the tribunal's failure to invite both the parties to express their views on the grounds in question violated the *principe de la contradiction*, which was essen- tial for the conduct of a fair hearing. Similarly, in *Kanoria and ors v Guinness*,[91] the English Court of Appeal decided that the respondent had not been afforded the chance to present its case when critical legal arguments were made by the claimant at the hearing, which the respondent could not attend because of serious illness. In the circumstances, the Court decided that 'this [was] an extreme case of potential injustice' and resolved not to enforce the arbitral award.

11.74   Examples of unsuccessful 'due process' defences to enforcement are, however, more nu- merous.[92] In *Minmetals Germany v Ferco Steel*,[93] the losing respondent in an arbitration in China opposed enforcement in England on the grounds that the award was founded on evi- dence that the arbitral tribunal had obtained through its own investigations. An English court rejected this defence, on the basis that the respondent was given an opportunity to ask for the disclosure of evidence at issue and to comment on it, but had declined to do so. The court held that the due process defence to enforcement was not intended to accommodate circumstances in which a party had failed to take advantage of an opportunity duly accorded to it.[94]

11.75   A further example of an unsuccessful attempt to rely on this ground is *Gold Reserve Inc v Venezuela*.[95] Following an adverse award against it, Venezuela sought to resist enforcement

---

[88]   *Iran Aircraft Industries v Avco Corporation*, 980 F.2d 141 (2d Cir. 1992). See Chapter 10.

[89]   See the decision of the Stuttgart Court of Appeal, dated 6 October 2001, referred to in Liebscher, *The Healthy Award: Challenge in International Commercial Arbitration* (Kluwer Law International, 2003), p. 406.

[90]   *Société Overseas Mining Investments Ltd v Société Commercial Caribbean Nique*, Cass. Civ., Ch. 1ere, 25 March 2010, Case No. 08-23901l.

[91]   *Kanoria and ors v Guinness* [2006] EWCA Civ 222, [2006] Arb LR 513.

[92]   See Liebscher, *The Healthy Award: Challenge in International Commercial Arbitration* (Kluwer Law International, 2003), ch. VIII, paras 2.2 and 2.3.

[93]   *Minmetals Germany v Ferco Steel* (1999) XXIV YBCA 739.

[94]   Many jurisdictions have taken a similarly restrictive interpretation of the due process defence to enforcement, e.g. German courts have held that a tribunal's refusal to hear evidence can breach the right to be heard only if such evidence is relevant: see Decision of the Bremen Court of Appeal, 30 September 1999, (2001) 4 Intl ALR N-26.

[95]   *Gold Reserve Inc. v Venezuela*, 146 F.Supp.3d 112, 128-29 (DDC 2015).

in the United States by arguing that it had been 'unable to present its case' because Gold Reserve had been allocated more time at the hearing to undertake witness examination. The US District Court for the District of Colombia, having examined the facts, found there to be a good reason for the tribunal's decision to allocate Gold Reserve more time than Venezuela at the hearing: Venezuela itself had requested a condensed hearing and, unlike Gold Reserve, had stated that it did 'not intend to call any of [the opposing party's] witnesses' for cross examination. In dismissing Venezuela's application to resist enforcement, the US District Court emphasised that it was insufficient for Venezuela to show merely that the parties were not afforded equal hearing time. Rather, Venezuela must establish 'exactly what it needed more time for, and how the denial of extra time prevented it from presenting its case', which Venezuela failed to do so in the circumstances.[96]

In recent years, the concern to minimise a 'due process' complaint at the annulment or en-   **11.76**
forcement stage has led some participants in arbitrations (parties and arbitrators alike) to display symptoms of 'due process paranoia'.[97] This can sometimes lead parties or arbitrators to be overly accommodating to procedural objections, procedural obstructions, or dilatory tactics in order to safeguard the enforceability of the award—and thereby, in the process, undermining the equally important procedural expectation of an efficient process.[98] But a right to due process is a right to an adequate and equal opportunity to present a case, not a right to an excessive or unlimited opportunity (which is perhaps better thought of as '*un*due process'). In truth, the description of this concern as a 'paranoia' is apt because it is rarely justified by the actual risk of a successful due process defence to enforcement.[99]

In reality, objections to enforcement are rarely successful on due process grounds. Indeed,   **11.77**
in many jurisdictions, the courts have begun to recognise the negative effect of 'due process paranoia', and have emphasised that arbitrators should not be reluctant to make robust case management decisions. By way of example, in dismissing a due process challenge, the Malaysian High Court observed that '[n]atural justice does not demand that a party is entitled to receive responses to all submissions and arguments presented for only the right to be heard is fundamental'.[100] Similarly, the Singapore Court of Appeal recently observed that the concept of 'due process' does not require tribunals to sacrifice efficiency in order to accommodate unreasonable procedural demands by a party. In sentiments that might be expected from many courts around the world, Singapore's Court of Appeal held that reviewing courts should accord a margin of deference to tribunals in matters of procedure and will not intervene simply because it might have done things differently.[101]

---

[96] Ibid.

[97] This phenomenon is most notably explored by Professor Lucy Reed in the 2016 Freshfields Arbitration Lecture: see Reed, 'Ab(use) of due process: sword vs shield' (2017) 33(3) Arb Intl 361–377.

[98] Queen Mary 2015 International Arbitration Survey: Improvements and Innovations in International Arbitration (which highlights that 'the issue [of "due process paranoia"] was repeatedly raised in responses, including in nearly all the personal interviews').

[99] It has been suggested that the behavioural model known as 'prospect theory', may explain why arbitrators tend to give too much weight to low-probability events (e.g. the successful challenge of an award for 'due process' reasons) in their decision-making when faced with risks and uncertainty: see Metsch and Gerby, 'Prospect Theory and due process paranoia: what behavioral models say about arbitrators' assessment of risk and uncertainty' (2020) 36(2) Arb Intl 233–252.

[100] *Allianz General Insurance Company Malaysia Berhad v Virginia Surety Company Labuan Branch*, Originating Summons No. WA-24NCC(ARB)-13-03/2018, at [31].

[101] *China Machine New Energy Corp v Jaguar Energy Guatemala LLC* [2020] SGCA 12, at [97] and [103].

(f) Third ground—jurisdictional issues

11.78   The third ground for refusal of recognition and enforcement of an award under the New York Convention is set out at Article V(1)(c):

> (c) The award deals with a difference not contemplated by or not falling within the terms of the submission to arbitration, or it contains decisions on matters beyond the scope of the submission to arbitration, provided that, if the decision on matters submitted to arbitration can be separated from those not so submitted, that part of the award which contains decisions on matters submitted to arbitration may be recognised and enforced […]

It is not uncommon for the issue of jurisdiction to be raised as the first line of defence to the enforcement of an arbitral award. The issue may be raised as part of a plea that there was no valid agreement to arbitrate,[102] in which case it would fall under Article V(1)(a) of the New York Convention, or it may be raised under the present heading. Jurisdictional issues as a ground for challenging an award have already been discussed,[103] and it has been noted that the right to raise such an issue may have been lost because of failure to do so at the appropriate time.[104]

11.79   The first part of this ground for refusal of enforcement under the Convention (and under the Model Law) envisages a situation in which the arbitral tribunal is alleged to have exceeded its jurisdiction by going 'beyond what was sought' (that is, *ultra petita*) and dealing with a dispute that was not submitted to it. According to a leading authority on the Convention, courts almost invariably reject this defence.[105] A robust rejection of such a defence comes from the US Court of Appeals for the District of Columbia, in a case in which it was pleaded that the arbitral tribunal had awarded a considerable sum of damages for consequential loss when the contract between the parties clearly excluded this head of damage.[106] The Court stated that, without undertaking an in-depth review of the law of contract, it could not state whether a breach of contract would abrogate a clause that excluded consequential damages. However, 'the standard of review of an arbitration award by an American Court is extremely narrow',[107] and (adopting the words of the US Court of Appeals in the well-known case of *Parsons Whittemore*[108]) the Convention did not sanction 'second-guessing the arbitrators'

---

[102] As in the *Pyramids* arbitration: *The Arab Republic of Egypt v Southern Pacific Properties*, Paris cour d'appel, 12 July 1984, published in English at (1984) 23 ILM 1048. The award of the ICC tribunal in this case was challenged by the Egyptian government on the basis that it was not a party to the relevant agreement and so was not bound by the arbitration clause. The Paris Court of Appeal agreed and the award was set aside. For a discussion of the case, see Redfern, 'Jurisdiction denied: The pyramid collapses' (1986) JBL 15. See also (1984) IX YBCA 113 and (1985) X YBCA 487. The claimants then started fresh arbitration proceedings, under the ICSID Convention. For the rest of the story, see Delaume, 'The pyramids stand: The pharaohs can rest in peace' (1993) 8 ICSID Rev—Foreign Investment LJ 231; J. Paulsson, 'Arbitration without privity' (1995) 10 ICSID Rev—Foreign Investment LJ 232.

[103] See Chapter 10, paragraphs 10.36*ff*.

[104] See Chapter 10, paragraphs 10.25*ff*.

[105] See van den Berg, 'Court decisions on the New York Convention', in Blessing (ed.) *The New York Convention of 1958: A Collection of Reports and Materials Delivered at the ASA Conference Held in Zurich 2 February 1996* (ASA, 1996), p. 86.

[106] *Libyan American Oil Co. (Liamco) v Socialist People's Libyan Arab Yamahirya, formerly Libyan Arab Republic* (1982) VII YBCA 382.

[107] Ibid., at 388. See also *Telenor Mobile Communications AS v Storm LLC*, 584 F.3d 396 (2d Cir. 2009). In this case, the US Court of Appeals for the Second Circuit rejected Storm's contention that the arbitral tribunal acted in 'manifest disregard of the law' by ignoring a Ukrainian court decision that the arbitration clause in dispute was 'null and void'. The Court noted that there is a strong presumption against finding manifest disregard of the law by an arbitral tribunal and upheld the confirmation of the award.

[108] *Parsons Whittemore Overseas Co. Inc. v Société Générale de l'Industrie du Papier (RAKTA)*, 508 F.2d 969 (2d Cir. 1974).

construction of the parties' agreement', nor would it be proper for the court to 'usurp the arbitrators' role'.[109] Accordingly, enforcement was granted.

A further example of an unsuccessful attempt to use this ground to resist enforcement is a decision by the US District Court for the Northern District of Illinois, Eastern Division.[110] The respondents argued that the arbitral tribunal had exceeded its authority by giving a preclusive effect to findings of an English court, rather than holding an evidentiary hearing to make its own findings. The US court held that since the parties' arbitration agreement neither stipulated any specific hearing procedure to be followed nor prohibited the tribunal from deciding on issues of preclusion, these were issues to be decided by the arbitral tribunal.[111]   **11.80**

The second part of this ground for refusal is concerned with the situation in which it is alleged that the tribunal exceeded its jurisdiction in some respects, but not in others. In such a situation, even if the partial excess of authority is proved, that part of the award which concerns matters properly submitted to arbitration *may* be saved and enforcement ordered. For example, in a case that came before the Italian courts, the court examined the award to determine whether or not the arbitral tribunal had exceeded the limits of its jurisdiction.[112] Having done so, the Italian court granted partial enforcement of the award, to the extent that it dealt with matters within the jurisdiction of the arbitral tribunal.   **11.81**

(g) Fourth ground—composition of tribunal or procedure not in accordance with arbitration agreement or the relevant law

The fourth ground for refusal of recognition and enforcement of an award under the New York Convention is set out at Article V(1)(d):   **11.82**

(d) The composition of the arbitral authority or the arbitral procedure was not in accordance with the agreement of the parties, or, failing such agreement, was not in accordance with the law of the country where the arbitration took place [...]

---

[109] *Libyan American Oil Co. (Liamco) v Socialist People's Libyan Arab Yamahirya, formerly Libyan Arab Republic* (1982) VII YBCA 382, at 388.

[110] *Sphere Drake Insurance Ltd v Lincoln National Life Insurance Co. et al.* (2007) XXXII YBCA 857.

[111] A further example of where this ground was unsuccessfully relied upon is *Aloe Vera of America, Inc. (US) v Asianic Food (S) Pte Ltd (Singapore) and anor* (2007) XXXII YBCA 489. One of the defendants argued that he was not a party to the arbitration clause and that, by entering an award against him, the arbitrator went beyond the scope of the submission to arbitration. The Supreme Court of Singapore dismissed this argument and held that the issue of whether the defendant was a party to the arbitration clause did not fall properly under this ground. The Court further held that the defendant had brought no evidence to prove that, under Arizona law, the award contained a decision on a matter beyond the scope of the submission to arbitration. In contrast, and as discussed at paragraph 11.67, the Supreme Court of England and Wales adopted a far less deferential approach, and undertook a full examination of the arbitral tribunal's jurisdiction when presented with a potential breach of jurisdictional issues in *Dallah Real Estate and Tourism Holding Co. v Ministry of Religious Affairs, Government of Pakistan* [2010] UKSC 46. The Court also held that while it can have regard to any statements made by the arbitral tribunal on its own jurisdiction, the Court was neither bound nor restricted by such statements.

[112] *General Organization of Commerce and Industrialisation of Cereals of the Arab Republic of Syria v SpA SIMER (Società delle Industrie Meccaniche di Rovereto) (Italy)* (1983) VIII YBCA 386.

The 1927 Geneva Convention provided that enforcement of an award could be refused if the composition of the arbitral tribunal, or the arbitral procedure, was not in accordance both with the agreement of the parties *and* the law of the place of arbitration. This double requirement meant that if an arbitration was not held in strict accordance with the procedural law of the place of arbitration, the consequent award would not be enforced. Under the New York Convention, the double requirement has been dropped and compliance with the agreement of the parties has become the main area of enquiry.

11.83   In a case that came before the Supreme Court of Hong Kong in 1994, it was argued that enforcement of an award made in China should be refused because the composition of the arbitral tribunal was not in accordance with the agreement of the parties.[113] The arbitrators who had been appointed were on the Shenzhen list of arbitrators, but not (as specified in the arbitration agreement) on the Beijing list.

11.84   Giving judgment, Kaplan J said:

> It is clear therefore that the only grounds upon which enforcement can be refused are those specified [...] and that the burden of proving a ground is upon the defendant. Further, it is clear that even though a ground has been proved, the Court retains a residual discretion.[114]

After considering the facts, the judge said:

> I conclude therefore, somewhat reluctantly, that technically the arbitrators did not have jurisdiction to decide this dispute and that in all the circumstances of this case, the ground specified in the section has been made out. I say technically because the parties did agree to have a CIETAC Arbitration and that is what they got, even though it was held at a place within China not specified in the contract and by arbitrators who apparently were not on the Beijing list.[115]

11.85   Although the ground for refusal of enforcement had been made out, the judge allowed enforcement of the award to go ahead nevertheless on the basis that the party objecting to enforcement had taken part in the arbitration knowing that, technically, the arbitrators were not selected from the correct list. Having done so, it could not now seek to profit from this departure. The judge considered the application of the doctrine of estoppel to other aspects of the New York Convention and said:

> If the doctrine of estoppel can apply to arguments over the written form of the arbitration agreement under Article II(2), then I fail to see why it cannot also apply to the grounds of opposition set out in Article V. It strikes me as quite unfair for a party to appreciate that there might be something wrong with the composition of the tribunal yet not make any formal submission whatsoever to the tribunal about its own jurisdiction, or to the arbitration commission which constituted the tribunal and then to proceed to fight the case on the merits and then two years after the award, attempt to nullify the

---

[113] See *China Nanhai Oil Joint Service Corporation v Gee Tai Holdings Co. Ltd* (1995) XX YBCA 671. Similarly, see *Tongyuan International Trading Group v Uni-Clan* [2001] 4 Intl ALR N-31.
[114] *China Nanhai Oil*, at 672.
[115] Ibid., at 673.

whole proceedings on the grounds that the arbitrators were chosen from the wrong CIETAC list.[116]

He continued:

> [E]ven if a ground of opposition is proved, there is still a residual discretion left in the enforcing court to enforce nonetheless. This shows that the grounds of opposition are not to be inflexibly applied. The residual discretion enables the enforcing court to achieve a just result in all the circumstances […][117]

11.86 Similar problems can arise where the arbitral institution prescribed in the arbitration agreement has subsequently undergone structural changes. In a case before the Indian court in 2018,[118] the arbitration agreement provided for 'arbitration before […] China International Economic and Trade Arbitration Commission (CIETAC) in Shanghai'. When the contract was signed in 2011, CIETAC had two sub-commissions: the Shanghai Sub-Commission and the Shenzhen/South China Sub-Commission. In 2013, however, the two sub-commissions declared independence: The Shanghai Sub-Commission then became the Shanghai International Arbitration Centre (SHIAC), and the Shenzhen/South China sub-commission became the Shenzhen Court of International Arbitration (SCIA). In 2015, following an unsuccessful challenge of a CIETAC award rendered in China, the losing party in the arbitration sought to resist enforcement of the award in India by arguing that the parties had agreed to refer their disputes to the then Shanghai sub-commission (which became SHIAC) and therefore CIETAC had no jurisdiction to hear the dispute at issue. The Delhi High Court rejected this argument, on the basis that the Shanghai sub-commission was not expressly mentioned in the arbitration agreement and that, under the CIETAC Rules effective at the time the arbitration agreement was concluded, in the absence of an agreement between the parties as to which of CIETAC or its sub-commissions would administer the dispute, the final decision was to be made by CIETAC itself.

11.87 In contrast, *Encyclopaedia Universalis SA (Luxembourg) v Encyclopaedia Britannica Inc. (US)*[119] is an example of the successful reliance on this ground before the US Court of Appeals for the Second Circuit. In their contract, the parties had agreed that (a) the two party-appointed arbitrators must attempt to choose a third arbitrator, and (b), upon the failure of the two party-appointed arbitrators to agree on a third, the English Commercial Court would appoint one. The appellant, Encyclopaedia Universalis SA (Luxembourg), sidestepped the first requirement and the Commercial Court nevertheless proceeded to appoint a third arbitrator. In response to a request by Encyclopaedia Britannica Inc. (US) to refuse enforcement of the award rendered against it, the US Court held that:

> [T]he [English court]'s premature appointment of [the third arbitrator] irremediably spoiled the arbitration process […] the issue of how the third arbitrator was to be appointed

---

[116] Ibid., at 677.
[117] Ibid.
[118] *LDK Solar Hi-Tech (Suzhou) Co. Ltd v Hindustan Cleanenergy Limited, ex. parte* 278/2018 in the High Court of Delhi at New Delhi, 4 July 2018.
[119] *Encyclopaedia Universalis SA (Luxembourg) v Encyclopaedia Britannica Inc. (US)* (2005) XXX, YBCA 1136.

is more than a trivial matter of form. Article V(1)(d) of the New York Convention itself suggests the importance of arbitral composition [...][120]

11.88   As described in Chapter 6, it is increasingly common for institutional rules to provide for expedited or emergency arbitration procedure. Parties taking advantage of such procedures, however, may sometimes face difficulty in the enforcement stage. In *Noble Resources International Pte. Ltd v Shanghai Good Credit International Trade Co., Ltd.*,[121] the arbitration agreement provided for a three-member SIAC tribunal. Nobel Resources applied for expedited procedure under the 2013 SIAC Rules and, despite Shanghai Good Credit's objection, the SIAC Court decided to appoint a sole arbitrator to hear the dispute pursuant to the expedited procedure. After the sole arbitrator rendered an award in favour of Nobel Resources, Shanghai Good Credit successfully resisted enforcement of the award in China, on the basis that the appointment of a sole arbitrator was contrary to the parties' agreement for a three-member tribunal, and that the SIAC Court erred in compelling the parties to accept a sole arbitrator in the circumstances.

11.89   Following the Chinese court's decision, SIAC has amended its latest rules (the 2016 SIAC Rules) to prevent the same conflict from arising. Article 5.3 of the 2016 SIAC Rules now provides more explicitly that: '[B]y agreeing to arbitration under these Rules, the parties agree that, where arbitral proceedings are conducted in accordance with the Expedited Procedure under this Rule 5, the rules and procedures set forth in Rule 5.2 shall apply even in cases where the arbitration agreement contains contrary terms'.

(h) Fifth ground—award suspended, or set aside

11.90   The fifth ground for refusal of recognition and enforcement under the New York Convention is set out at Article V(1)(e):

> (e) The award has not yet become binding on the parties, or has been set aside or suspended by a competent authority of the country in which, or under the law of which, that award was made [...]

This fifth ground for refusal of recognition and enforcement of an arbitral award (which, like the others, also appears in the Model Law) has given rise to more controversy than any of the previous grounds. First, there is the reference to an award being 'not binding'. In the 1927 Geneva Convention, the word 'final' was used. This was taken by many to mean that the award had to be declared as 'final' by the court of the place of arbitration and this gave rise to the problem of the double *exequatur*. It was intended that the word 'binding' would avoid this problem, particularly since many international and institutional rules of

---

[120]   Ibid., at [8]–[10]. See also *HSN Capital LLC (US) v Productora y Comercializador de Television, SA de CV (Mexico)* (2007) XXXII YBCA 774, at [3]–[7]. China's Supreme People's Court has more recently gone further still: in *Bunge Agribuss v Guangdong Fengyuan* [2006] *Min Si Ta Zi* No. 41, the designated arbitral institution appointed an arbitrator on behalf of the respondent because of the latter's failure to do so within the permitted time limit. Even though this was entirely consistent with the arbitral rules selected by the parties, the Supreme People's Court held that the failure to consult Fengyuan on the appointment was a valid basis on which to refuse enforcement.

[121]   *Noble Resources International Pte. Ltd v Shanghai Good Credit International Trade Co., Ltd.* (2016) Hu 01 Xie Wai Ren No. 1.

arbitration state in terms that the award of the arbitral tribunal is to be accepted by the parties as final and 'binding' upon them.[122] However, some national courts still consider it necessary to investigate the law applicable to the award to see if it is 'binding' under that law[123]—although the better position appears to be that an award is 'binding' if it is no longer open to an appeal on the merits, either internally (that is, within the relevant rules of arbitration) or by an application to the court.[124]

There are other problems too, with this fifth ground for refusal, which have led to considerable controversy. At first sight, the proposition that an award *may* be refused recognition and enforcement if it has been set aside or suspended by a court at the place (or seat) of the arbitration seems reasonable enough. If, for example, an award has been set aside in Switzerland, it will be unenforceable in that country—and it might be expected that, if only as a matter of international comity, the courts of other states would also regard the award as unenforceable.   **11.91**

This is not necessarily so, however. Courts in other countries may take the view (and indeed, as will be described,[125] in some countries they *have* taken the view) that they will enforce an arbitral award even if it has been set aside by the courts of the seat of the arbitration. This leads to a situation in which an award that has been set aside and so is unenforceable in its country of origin may be refused enforcement under the New York Convention in one country, but granted enforcement in another.   **11.92**

The problem arises because the New York Convention does not in any way restrict the grounds on which an award may be set aside or suspended by the court of the country in which, or under the law of which, that award was made.[126] This is a matter that is left to the domestic law of the country concerned, and this domestic law may impose local requirements (such as the need to initial each page of the award) that judges and lawyers elsewhere would not regard as sufficient to impeach the validity of an *international* arbitral award.   **11.93**

The allowance for local requirements that is made in the New York Convention has been described by a former secretary-general of the ICC Court as: **11.94**

> a hitherto rock-solid rampart against the true internationalisation of arbitration, because in the award's country of origin all means of recourse and all grounds of nullity applicable to purely domestic awards may be used to oppose recognition abroad [...][127]

---

[122] See, e.g., UNCITRAL Rules, Art. 34.2.

[123] van den Berg, 'Court decisions on the New York Convention', in Blessing (ed.) *The New York Convention of 1958: A Collection of Reports and Materials Delivered at the ASA Conference Held in Zurich 2 February 1996* (ASA, 1996), pp. 87 and 88.

[124] Ibid., p. 88. If an appeal is pending, the enforcement court may, if it considers it proper, adjourn the decision on enforcement. It may also order the party against whom enforcement is sought to give security: New York Convention, Art. VI. As to the question of which law determines the 'binding' effect of an award, see *Antilles Cement Corporation (Puerto Rico) v Transficem (Spain)* (2006) XXXI YBCA 846, at [9]–[13], in which the Supreme Court of Spain held, at [13], that whether an award is binding 'is not to be examined in accordance with the law of the State where the award is rendered'.

[125] See paragraph 11.97ff.

[126] Unlike the Model Law (as amended in 2006), which sets out the limited grounds on which an award may be set aside: see Art. 34.

[127] Derains, 'Foreword', in ICC (ed.) *Hommage à Frédéric Eisemann* (ICC, 1978), p. 13, translated in J. Paulsson, 'The case for disregarding local standard annulments under the New York Convention' (1996) 7 Am Rev Intl Arb 99. This is not true of states that have different laws to govern international arbitrations from those that govern domestic arbitrations, but nevertheless the point is a valid one.

Another experienced commentator has referred to the 'anathema of local particularities', which are capable of leading to the setting aside of international awards, and has suggested that 'such local standard annulments' should be given only local effect and should be disregarded internationally.[128]

11.95 The argument in favour of the fifth ground is a familiar one. It is the classic argument that the courts of the place of arbitration should have some control over arbitral proceedings conducted on their territory, if only to guard against lack of due process, fraud, corruption, or other improper conduct on the part of the arbitral tribunal. Perhaps the real argument is: how far should this control go? Should it be limited to the first four grounds of the New York Convention,[129] or should it go further? And if so, how much further? The problem is to strike the correct balance between regulation and laissez-faire.

11.96 Whilst the argument continues, courts in France, Belgium, Austria, the United Kingdom, and the United States have shown themselves prepared on occasion to recognise and enforce arbitral awards even though they have been set aside by the courts at the seat of arbitration.[130] The justification for this is twofold. First, the language of Article V of the New York Convention (as already discussed) is permissive, not mandatory. Specifically, the English language version of the Convention says that the enforcing court *may* refuse recognition and enforcement—not that it *must* do so. Secondly, the New York Convention recognises that there may be more favourable provisions under which an award may be recognised and enforced. The Convention contains the following provision, in Article VII(1):

> The provisions of the present Convention shall not affect the validity of multilateral or bilateral agreements concerning the recognition and enforcement of arbitral awards entered into by the Contracting States nor deprive any interested party of any right he may have to avail himself of the arbitral award in the manner and to the extent allowed by the law or the treaties of the country where such award is sought to be relied upon.

In this way, the New York Convention recognises explicitly that, in any given country, there may be a local law that, whether by treaty or otherwise, is more favourable to the recognition and enforcement of arbitral awards than the Convention itself. The Convention gives its blessing, so to speak, to any party who wishes to take advantage of this more favourable local law.

11.97 The New York Convention has long been regarded as being of fundamental importance to the recognition and enforcement of international arbitral awards. It remains so. However, the possibility of obtaining recognition and enforcement of an award that has been set aside

---

[128] See ibid. In a sense, this comes back to the 'delocalisation' debate, which was a source of lively controversy at the time: see, e.g., J. Paulsson, 'Arbitration unbound: Award detached from the law of its country of origin' (1981) 30 ICLQ 358; J. Paulsson, 'Delocalisation of international commercial arbitration: When and why it matters' (1983) 32 ICLQ 53. See also the discussion in Chapter 3.

[129] As with the European Convention of 1961.

[130] For a comprehensive survey of instances in which national courts have recognised or enforced awards set aside by the courts of the place of arbitration, see Gharavi, *The International Effectiveness of the Annulment of an Arbitral Award* (Kluwer Law International, 2002). The French Code of Civil Procedure, art. 1526 now expressly provides that an application to set aside an arbitral award does not stay the proceedings to enforce the award. For commentary on the rationale behind art. 1526, see Kleiman and Saleh, 'Enforcement of international arbitration awards: Latest developments', available online at https://www.lexology.com/commentary/arbitration-adr/france/freshfields-bruckhaus-deringer-llp/enforcement-of-international-arbitration-awards-latest-developments.

by means of applying a more favourable local law, which does not reflect or rely upon the Convention, should not be overlooked. This approach can be illustrated with some famous examples emanating from the French and US courts. In the French decision of *Hilmarton*,[131] an award rendered by a tribunal in Switzerland in favour of the respondent was later annulled by the Geneva Court of Appeal. In the meantime, however, the respondent had applied to the French courts to enforce the award and was successful at the first instance. On appeal from the enforcement proceedings in France, the French Court of Appeal had to decide whether to uphold the lower court's decision to enforce the award, even though it had been set aside in the country in which it was made. The Court of Appeal decided to let the enforcement proceed. This decision was subsequently confirmed by the French Court of Cassation, which stated that:

> the award rendered in Switzerland is an international award which is not integrated in the legal system of that State, so that it remains in existence even if set aside and its recognition in France is not contrary to international public policy.[132]

In *Chromalloy*,[133] the US Federal Court for the District of Columbia enforced an award **11.98** that had been set aside in Egypt.[134] The Court explicitly contrasted the permissive nature of Article V of the Convention with the mandatory nature of Article VII:

> While Article V provides a discretionary standard, Article VII of the Convention requires that, 'The provisions of the present Convention *shall not* [...] deprive any interested party of any right he may have to avail himself of an arbitral award in the manner and to the extent allowed by the law [...] of the country where such award is sought to be relied on.'[135]

In *Putrabali*,[136] the French courts enforced an award set aside in England. In so doing, the **11.99** Court of Cassation held that:

> [A]n international arbitral award, which does not belong to any state legal system, is an international decision of justice and its validity must be examined according to the applicable rules of the country where its recognition and enforcement are sought.[137]

---

[131] *Hilmarton Ltd v Omnium de Traitement et de Valorisation (OTV)* (1994) Rev Arb 327; English excerpts in (1995) XX YBCA 663.

[132] Ibid., at 664. When a second award in favour of the claimants was subsequently rendered in Switzerland and enforcement was sought in France, the cour de cassation held that the issue was *res judicata* in the French legal order and hence that the award could not be enforced: *Hilmarton Ltd v Omnium de Traitement et de Valorisation (OTV)* (1994) Rev Arb 327; English excerpts in (1997) XXII YBCA 696. The same approach was followed in the recent case of *Egyptian General Petroleum Corporation v National Gas Company*, Cass. Civ., Ch. Civ. 1ere, 13 January 2021, in which the cour de cassation upheld the enforcement of an Egyptian award that had been set aside by the Cairo Court of Appeal.

[133] *Chromalloy Aeroservices Inc. v Arab Republic of Egypt*, 939 F.Supp 907 (DDC 1996).

[134] See paragraphs 11.78*ff*.

[135] *Chromalloy*, at 909–910.

[136] *Société PT Putrabali Adyamulia v Société Rena Holding et Société Mnogutia Est Epices* [2007] Rev Arb 507. The first arbitral award was annulled by the High Court of London and a second award with a directly opposite outcome was issued. Both claimant and respondent sought to enforce the awards in France. In the enforcement proceedings of the first award, the losing party argued that the enforcement of the award would be contrary to international public policy, but the cour de cassation did not follow that reasoning and enforced the annulled first award. The cour de cassation then refused the enforcement of the second award on the basis that *res judicata* attached to the decision enforcing the first award, which was incompatible with the second award.

[137] Ibid.

More recently, in a decision of the US District Court for the Southern District of New York in *COMMISA v Pemex*,[138] a Mexican award was enforced under the 1975 Inter-American Convention on International Commercial Arbitration (the Panama Convention),[139] despite being set aside at the seat. A Mexican court had applied a statute that was not yet in existence at the time the parties entered into the contract, and had set aside the award on the basis that, as a matter of Mexican law, arbitral tribunals lacked the competency to hear and decide cases brought against the Mexican state, or an organ of the state (such as Pemex, Mexico's state-owned oil company). In rejecting the Mexican court's ruling and confirming the award, the US court was careful to explain that it was 'neither deciding, nor reviewing, Mexican law'; rather, its decision was made on the basis that the Mexican court's ruling 'violated basic notions of justice in that it applied a law that was not in existence at the time the parties' contract was formed and left COMMISA without an apparent ability to litigate its claims'.[140]

11.100   Notwithstanding decisions such as *Hilmarton*, *Chromalloy*, *Putrabali*, and *Pemex*, the enforcement of awards that have been set aside by the courts of the place of arbitration remains controversial. With some notable exceptions, courts around the world are more likely than not to decline to enforce annulled awards.[141]

---

[138]   *Corporación Mexicana de Mantenimiento Integral, S. de R.L. de C.V. v PEMEX-Exploración y Producción*, No. 10 Civ 206 (AKH) 2013 WL 4517225 (SDNY, 27 August 2013).

[139]   As will be explained in paragraph 11.144, the grounds for refusal to enforce foreign arbitral awards under the Panama Convention are similar to those under the New York Convention. In particular, Art. 5(e) of the Panama Convention provides that: '[T]he recognition and execution of the decision may be refused, at the request of the party against which it is made, only if such party is able to prove to the competent authority of the State in which recognition and execution are requested [...] that the decision is not yet binding on the parties or has been annulled or suspended by a competent authority of the State in which, or according to the law of which, the decision has been made.'

[140]   *Pemex*, at [14]. See also *Yukos Capital SARL v OJSC Oil Co. Rosneft* [2014] EWHC 2188, in which the English High Court held, as a preliminary issue, that an annulment by the Moscow Arbitrazh Court of arbitral awards rendered in Russia would not prevent the English court from giving effect to the annulled awards (under English common law principles) if it were proven that the annulment offended against basic principles of honesty, natural justice, or English public policy. The awards in question had also previously been enforced by the Amsterdam Appeal Court, despite the local standard annulment in Russia.

[141]   See, e.g., *Baker Marine (Nig.) Ltd v Chevron (Nig.) Ltd*, 191 F.3d 194 (2d Cir. 1999), in which, notwithstanding *Chromalloy*, the US Second Circuit refused to enforce an award that had been set aside by the court of the place of arbitration (in this case, Nigeria). See also *Spier v Tecnica*, 71 F.Supp.2d 279 (SDNY 1999); *TermoRio SA ESP v Electrificadora Del Atlantico SA ESP*, 421 F.Supp.2d 87 (DDC 2006), in which the US court denied the enforcement of a Colombian arbitral award that had been set aside by the Colombian courts on the ground that Colombian law in effect at the date of the agreement did not *expressly* permit the use of ICC procedural rules, which the parties had designated in their arbitration clause. This decision was subsequently upheld by the US appellate court. For a discussion of *Putrabali* and *TermoRio*, see Gaillard, 'Note—29 juin 2007—Cour de Cassation (1re Ch. Civ.)' [2007] Rev Arb 517. In Germany, courts take into account the status of the award in the jurisdiction in which it was rendered. In 1999, the Court of Appeal of Rostock refused to enforce an award rendered by the Moscow Maritime Arbitration Commission that had been set aside in Russia: *Oberlandesgericht Rostock*, 28 October 1999, (2000) XXV YBCA 717, at 719. However, when the Russian Supreme Court overturned the lower courts' decisions setting aside the award, the German Federal Supreme Court similarly reversed the decision of the Court of Appeal of Rostock and deemed it enforceable: *Bundesgerichtshof*, 22 February 2001, (2004) XXIX YBCA 724. A similar approach is taken in Chile: see *EDF Internacional SA v Endesa Internacional SA and YPF SA*, Supreme Court of Chile, 8 September 2011, (2012) 5 Arbitraje: Revista de Arbitraje Comercial y de Inversiones 915, in which the Court held that an Argentinean award set aside at the place of arbitration could not be enforced in Chile. In *Maximov v OJSC Novolipetsky Metallurgichesky Kombinat* [2017] EWHC 1911 (Comm) the English High Court held that for the English courts to enforce awards that had been set aside by the courts in the place of arbitration, the decision to set aside 'must be so wrong as to be evidence of bias, or be such that no court acting in good faith could have arrived at it'. In *Esso Exploration and Production Nigeria Limited v Nigeria National Petroleum Corporation*, 397 F.Supp.3d 323 (SDNY 2019), the US District Court for the Southern District of New York refused to enforce an award that had been annulled in Nigeria, holding that although the US courts can enforce an award that was set aside at the seat if the judgment setting aside the award is contrary to US public policy, this 'public policy exception is narrow and available only in "rare circumstances"', and '[t]he standard is high[] and infrequently met' (at [351]–[354]).

Moreover, it should be noted that the only national court that is competent to suspend or set **11.101** aside an award is the court of the country 'in which, or under the law of which, that award was made'.[142] This court will almost invariably be the national court of the seat of the arbitration. The impracticability of holding an arbitration in country X, but subjecting it to the procedural law of country Y, has already been discussed,[143] and so the prospect of an award being set aside under the procedural law of a state other than that of the seat of arbitration is unlikely. However, an ingenious (but unsuccessful) attempt was made to persuade the US District Court to set aside an award made in Mexico, on the basis that the reference to the law under which that award was made was a reference to the law governing the dispute and not to the procedural law.[144] The US court firmly rejected this argument, stating:

> Decisions of foreign courts under the Convention uniformly support the view that the clause in question means procedural and not substantive (that is, in most cases, contract law) [...]

> Accordingly, we hold that the contested language in Article V(1)(e) of the Convention [...] refers exclusively to procedural and not substantive law, and more precisely to the regimen or scheme of arbitral procedural law under which the arbitration was conducted.[145]

The court went on to hold that since the seat of the arbitration was Mexico, only the Mexican court had jurisdiction to set aside the award.[146]

Courts are not always immune to such creative attempts to resist enforcement. The Indian **11.102** Supreme Court,[147] for example, has in the past accepted that an award rendered in London that was the object of enforcement proceedings in the United States could be set aside in India simply because the parties had chosen Indian law to govern the substance of their dispute.[148] This decision was plainly wrong and the Indian Supreme Court subsequently recognised this. In its decision in *Bharat Aluminium Co. v Kaiser Aluminum Technical Service, Inc.*,[149] the Supreme Court affirmed that Indian courts do not have jurisdiction, in either a supportive or supervisory role, where the seat of the arbitration is outside India.

---

[142] New York Convention, Art. V(1)(e).

[143] See Chapter 3.

[144] *International Standard Electric Corporation (US) v Bridas Sociedad Anonima Petrolera (Argentina)* (1992) VII YBCA 639.

[145] Ibid., at 644 and 645.

[146] Ibid., at 645.

[147] *Venture Global Engineering v Satyam Computer Services* [2008] INSC 40.

[148] *Venture Global Engineering v Satyam Computer Services*, 233 Fed. Appx 517 (6th Cir. 2007). Similar decisions have been rendered by courts in Indonesia and Russia. In *Karaha Bodas Co. LLC (Cayman Islands) v Persusahaan Pertambangan Minyak Dan Gas Bumi Negara aka Pertamina (Indonesia)*, US District Court, Southern District of Texas, Houston Division, 17 April 2003, (2003) XXVIII YBCA 908, the Central Jakarta District Court annulled a Swiss arbitral award applying Indonesian substantive law in favour of Karaha against Pertamina. In Russia, similar arrogations of authority to annul an award have occasionally emerged: see *OAO Stoilensky GOK v Mabetex Project Engineering SA, et al. and Interconstruction Project Management SA v OAO Stoilensky GOK*, Case No. A08-7941/ 02-18, Federal Commercial Court of the Central District, 2 September 2003; *Collective Fishing Farm Krasnoye Znamya v White Arctic Marine Resources Ltd*, Case No. A05-4274/2007, Federal Commercial Court of the North-Western District, 25 July 2007, in which Art. IX(1) of the European Convention of 1961 was used as a basis to set aside awards rendered in Sweden and Norway, respectively, simply because Russian law applied to the substance of the dispute.

[149] *Bharat Aluminium Co. v Kaiser Aluminum Technical Service, Inc.*, Civil Appeal No. 7019 of 2005, Decision of 6 September 2012, given at New Delhi.

11.103   Finally, as described in Chapter 6, it is increasingly common for institutional rules now to provide for emergency arbitration procedures,[150] in addition to endowing arbitral tribunals with the now long-standing power to grant interim measures. The finality for the purposes of enforcement of the awards that result from such emergency procedures, as well as measures that result from applications for interim relief, lead to vastly different decisions across jurisdictions. For example, courts in Australia,[151] Chile,[152] and Russia[153] have considered interim awards generally unenforceable, on the basis that such awards are not yet 'final' or 'binding' on the parties, although it is unclear whether the same approach is extended to emergency awards. In contrast, some courts in the US have held both interim awards and emergency awards to be enforceable provided that the ruling in those awards definitively disposes of a self-contained issue, even if the awards do not themselves resolve part of the dispute.[154] The Supreme Court of India has taken a similar approach.[155] In Hong Kong and Singapore, this question is now settled by national legislation, which expressly provides that both interim and emergency awards are enforceable.[156]

11.104   Given the lack of international consensus on this issue, those invoking an emergency procedure or applying for interim relief should consider closely the particular approach of the likely courts of enforcement before setting off an errand that may not result in an enforceable emergency or interim decision.

11.105   This completes this review of the five grounds for refusal of recognition and enforcement of an arbitral award that are laid down in both the New York Convention and the Model Law,

---

[150] See, e.g. ICC Rules, Art. 29(1) (providing that '[a] party that needs urgent interim or conservatory measures that cannot await the constitution of an arbitral tribunal ('Emergency Measures') may make an application for such measures pursuant to the Emergency Arbitrator Rules […]'); and SCC Rules, Appendix II, Article 1(1) (providing that '[a] party may apply for the appointment of an Emergency Arbitrator until the case has been referred to an Arbitral Tribunal […]').

[151] *Resort Condominiums International Inc. v Ray Bolwell and Resort Condominiums, Pty. Ltd.*, Supreme Court of Queensland, Australia, 29 October 1993, XX Y.B. COM. ARB. 628 (1995).

[152] Supreme Court No. 5468-2009, *Western Technology Services International Inc. (Westech) v a Chilean company, Cauchos Industriales SA (Cainsa)*, 11 May 2010 (case described in UNCITRAL's Case Law on UNCITRAL Texts (CLOUT), dated 23 August 2011 (A/CN.9/SER.C/ABSTRACTS/111), at 5.

[153] *Living Consulting Group AB (Sweden) v OOO Sokotel (Russian Federation)*, Presidium of the Highest Arbitrazh Court, Russian Federation, 5 October 2010, A56-63115/2009, in Albert Jan van den Berg (ed.), XXXVI Yearbook Com. Arb. 317, 318 (Kluwer, 2011): an SCC tribunal rendered an award ordering the respondent to pay the claimant an advance that the claimant had paid on behalf of the respondent earlier in the arbitration proceedings. Although awards of this nature are expressly permitted under the SCC Rules, the Supreme Arbitrazh Court of the Russian Federation declined to enforce the award, citing Art. V(1)(e) of the New York Convention. Specifically, the Russian court considered the award in question to be of an interim nature and therefore unenforceable, noting that the New York Convention is applicable only to final awards on the merits.

[154] *Island Creek Coal Sales Company v City of Gainesville Florida*, 729 F.2d 1046, USCA (6th Cir. 1985); see also *Yahoo! Inc. v Microsoft Corp* [2013] 983 F.Supp 2d 310, 319 (enforcing interim measures rendered by an emergency arbitrator under the AAA-ICDR Rules, holding that 'if an arbitral award of equitable relief based upon a finding of irreparable harm is to have any meaning at all, the parties must be capable of enforcing or vacating it at the time it is made').

[155] *Bharat Aluminium Co v Kaiser Aluminium Technical* [2012] 9 SCC 552; *Future Retail Ltd. v Amazon.com Investment Holdings LLC & ors* [2020] CS(COMM) 493/2020.

[156] Hong Kong Arbitration Ordinance (Cap. 609), s. 22B (providing that '[a]ny emergency relief granted, whether in or outside Hong Kong, by an emergency arbitrator under the relevant arbitration rules is enforceable in the same manner as an order or direction of the Court that has the same effect') and s. 61(5) (providing that 'an interim measure' is 'enforceable in the same manner as an order or direction of the Court that has the same effect'); Singapore International Arbitration Act 1994 (as amended in 2020), s. 2 (providing that the definition of an 'award' expressly includes any 'interim, interlocutory or partial award', and the definition of an 'arbitral tribunal' expressly includes an 'emergency arbitrator').

and which it is for the party resisting enforcement to prove. As already mentioned, there are two further grounds that may be invoked by the enforcement court itself. These concern first, arbitrability and secondly, public policy.

(i) Arbitrability

The New York Convention provides, as does the Model Law, that recognition and enforcement of an arbitral award may be refused: **11.106**

> if the competent authority in the country where recognition and enforcement is sought finds that:
> (a) The subject matter of the difference is not capable of settlement by arbitration under the law of that country [...][157]

Arbitrability has already been discussed in Chapter 2. As indicated, each state has its own   **11.107**
concept of what disputes should be reserved for the courts of law and what disputes that state will allow to be resolved by arbitration. This question may arise both at the beginning of an arbitration ('is this dispute capable of being referred to arbitration?') and at the end ('would this dispute have been capable of settlement by arbitration under the law of the enforcement state?'). When the issue of 'arbitrability' arises as a defence to enforcement under the New York Convention, it becomes an issue for the law of the enforcement state and, being governed principally by considerations of public policy, the decision varies from state to state.

For example, Russian courts used to interpret provisions of the Russian Commercial   **11.108**
Procedure Code stipulating the exclusive jurisdiction of certain Russian courts over corporate governance disputes as precluding the arbitrability of such disputes. In *Maximov v Novolipetsky Metallurgicheskiy Kombinat*,[158] following the entry into an agreement to purchase shares in a Russian-incorporated company, a dispute arose between the seller and buyer over the purchase price. The seller, who alleged that he had not received the price required under the agreement, obtained an arbitral award at the Moscow-based International Commercial Arbitration Court (ICAC). The Supreme Commercial Arbitrazh Court, upholding the decision of a lower court to set aside the award, held that corporate governance disputes are non-arbitrable under Article 225(1) of the Arbitration Procedural Code. However, following a reform of the Russian arbitration law which came into effect in 2017, corporate disputes are now generally arbitrable as a matter of Russian law, subject only to some limited conditions.[159]

---

[157] New York Convention, Art. V(2)(a). See also the discussion of 'public policy' as a ground to challenge an award at Chapter 10, paragraphs 10.78*ff*.

[158] *Maximov v Novolipetsky Metallurgicheskiy Kombinat*, Case No. N VAS-15384/11, Ruling of the Supreme Commercial Arbitrazh Court, 30 January 2012.

[159] For example, in relation to disputes associated with the ownership of shares or participation interests in the authorised capital of Russian companies, the arbitration must be administered by an arbitral institution authorised by the Russian Government: see the Federal Law 'On Arbitration Proceedings in the Russian Federation' No. 382-FZ, Art. 45(7).

11.109   In another example, the Supreme Court of Singapore ruled that whether a person is the alter ego of a company is an issue that does not have a public interest element, so is within the scope of submission to arbitration and is therefore arbitrable.[160] The defendant had argued that the arbitrator could not hold that he was bound by the arbitration clause based on a finding of an alter ego, since the issue of an alter ego was not arbitrable under Arizona law (the governing law of the contract). The Court dismissed this argument, holding that the law of Arizona was irrelevant, since the issue of arbitrability in a Singapore court as a ground for refusing enforcement was to be determined under the law of Singapore.[161]

(j) Public policy

11.110   Recognition and enforcement of an arbitral award may also be refused if it is contrary to the public policy of the enforcement state.[162] It is understandable that a state may wish to have the right to refuse to recognise and enforce an arbitration award that offends its own notions of public policy, and in some jurisdictions an enforcing court is required to examine the possibility of a public policy violation *ex officio*.[163] Yet when reference is made to 'public policy', it is difficult not to recall the sceptical comment of the English judge who said, almost two centuries ago: 'It is never argued at all but where other points fail.'[164]

11.111   Certainly, courts in England are reluctant to excuse an award from enforcement on grounds of public policy. At one time, it was said that 'there is no case in which this exception has been applied by an English court'.[165] Inevitably, of course, the exception then arose and was applied in *Soleimany v Soleimany*.[166] In this case, an English court refused to enforce an award giving effect to a contract between a father and son that involved the illegal smuggling of carpets out of Iran, in breach of Iranian revenue laws and export controls. The father and son had agreed to submit their dispute to arbitration by the Beth Din, the Court of the Chief Rabbi in London, which applied Jewish law. As a matter of the applicable Jewish law, the illegal purpose of the contract had no effect on the rights of the parties and the Beth Din proceeded to make an award enforcing the contract. In declining to enforce the award, the English court held that:

> The Court is in our view concerned to preserve the integrity of its process, and to see that it is not abused. The parties cannot override that concern by private agreement. They cannot by procuring an arbitration conceal that they, or rather one of them, is seeking to enforce an illegal contract. Public policy will not allow it.[167]

---

[160] *Aloe Vera of America, Inc. (US) v Asianic Food (S) Pte Ltd (Singapore) and anor* (2007) XXXII YBCA 489.

[161] Ibid. Similarly, in *Dallah Real Estate & Tourism Holding Co. v Ministry of Religious Affairs, Pakistan* [2010] UKSC 46, the UK Supreme Court held that, in considering jurisdiction over a non-signatory, 'arbitral tribunals are entitled to consider their own jurisdiction, and to do so in the form of an award', but added that 'the last word as to whether or not an alleged arbitral tribunal actually has jurisdiction will lie with the court' (at [86]).

[162] New York Convention, Art. V(2)(b).

[163] See Decision of the Geneva Cour de Justice, 11 December 1997, (1998) XXIII YBCA 764.

[164] *Richardson v Mellish* (1824) 2 Bing 229, at 252 *per* Burrough J, [1824–34] All ER 258.

[165] Kerr, 'Concord and conflict in international arbitration' (1997) 13 Arb Intl 121, at 140.

[166] *Soleimany v Soleimany* [1999] QB 785.

[167] Ibid., at 800.

Apart from rare exceptions such as this, most countries observe the 'pro-enforcement **11.112** bias' of the New York Convention.[168] Indeed, this pro-enforcement bias may itself be considered a matter of public policy, as the English courts confirmed in *Westacre Investments Inc. v Jugoimport-SPDR Holding Co. Ltd.*[169] This dispute arose from a consultancy agreement for the procurement of contracts for the sale of military equipment in Kuwait. Westacre commenced arbitration, claiming payment of its consulting fee. Jugoimport defended the claim on the grounds that, in violation of Kuwaiti law and public policy, the contract involved Westacre bribing various Kuwaitis to exert their influence in favour of entering sales contracts with Jugoimport. The agreement between Westacre and Jugoimport was governed by Swiss law, and provided for arbitration in Switzerland. The arbitral tribunal found that there was no evidence of corruption and that lobbying by private enterprises to obtain public contracts was not illegal under Swiss law. The award was first challenged in the Swiss Federal Court, which rejected the challenge on the basis that allegations of corruption had already been dealt with and rejected by the arbitral tribunal. Attempts to enforce the award were subsequently challenged in the English courts, where Jugoimport filed new affidavit evidence in support of its allegation of corruption.

In decisions that attracted some critical commentary,[170] the English courts rejected the **11.113** challenge to enforcement, both at first instance and in the Court of Appeal, on the grounds that: the arbitral tribunal itself had considered the allegations of bribery and found that they had not been substantiated; 'lobbying' was not, as such, an illegal activity under the governing law chosen by the parties; and the Court was faced with international arbitration awards that had been upheld by the Swiss Federal Tribunal, and therefore had to balance the public policy of discouraging international commercial corruption against the public policy of sustaining international arbitration awards.

It is clear that the 'public policy' referred to in the New York Convention is the public policy **11.114** of the enforcement state.[171] The real question is whether that public policy differentiates between foreign arbitral awards and purely domestic awards.

---

[168] See the discussion of *Parsons Whittemore Overseas Co. Inc. v Société Générale de l'Industrie du Papier (RAKTA)*, 508 F.2d 969 (2d Cir. 1974) at paragraph 11.60. See also the Second Circuit decision in *MGM Productions Group Inc. v Aeroflot Russian Airlines*, WL 234871 (2d Cir. 2004), in which Aeroflot sought to challenge a Stockholm award because it compensated the claimant for Aeroflot's non-performance of an agreement, the provisions of which allegedly violated the United States–Iran Transactions Regulations adopted pursuant to executive orders issued by the President of the United States under the International Emergency Economic Powers Act of 1977. The Second Circuit rejected the challenge, holding, at [3], that: 'Courts construe the public policy limitation in the Convention very narrowly and apply it only when enforcement would violate the forum state's "most basic notions of morality and justice".' In this case, even if the agreement in operation did violate the Iranian Transactions Regulations, which the arbitral tribunal itself had found was not the case, the award would not contravene public policy, because 'a violation of United States foreign policy does not contravene public policy as contemplated in Art V of the Convention': ibid., at [5].

[169] *Westacre Investments Inc. v Jugoimport-SPDR Holding Co. Ltd.* [1999] 2 Lloyd's Rep 65 (CA).

[170] See Rogers and Kaley, 'The impact of public policy in international commercial arbitration' (1999) 65 J CIArb 4.

[171] This is clear from the text of Art. V(2) itself and, accordingly, the Supreme Court of India was right to reject the argument that the references (in the Indian statute that enacted the Convention) to 'public policy', rather than to the 'public policy of India', meant that the words were not restricted to India, but would extend to the laws governing the contract and the place of arbitration: see *Renusagar Power Co. Ltd (India) v General Electric Co. (US)* (1995) XX YBCA 681.

11.115 The approach of the US courts was summarised by the Federal District Court of Massachusetts in *Sonatrach*.[172] The court stated that:

> The line of decisions which conclusively tip the judicial scale in favour of arbitration [are] a line of United States Supreme Court opinions which enthusiastically endorse an inter-nationalist approach towards commercial disputes involving foreign entities. These decisions, The *Bremen v Zapata Offshore Co*[173] (forum selection clauses in international commercial contract enforced); *Scherk v Alberto-Culver Co*[174] (international arbitration clause held enforceable when in conflict with federal securities laws); and most recently *Mitsubishi*[175] (international arbitration clause held enforceable when in conflict with Federal Antitrust laws) eschew the parochial tendencies of domestic tribunals in retaining jurisdiction over international commercial disputes. The Supreme Court powerfully advocates the need for international comity in an increasingly interdependent world. Such respect is especially important, in this Court's view, when parties mutually agree to be bound by freely negotiated contracts.[176]

11.116 A similar line of reasoning is found in the decision of the New York District Court in the well-known case of *Parsons Whittemore Overseas Co. Inc. v Société Générale de l'Industrie du Papier (RAKTA)*.[177] The court was confronted by an argument that recognition and enforcement of an award should be refused on the grounds that diplomatic relations between Egypt (the respondent's state) and the United States had been severed. The court rejected this argument and referred to the 'general pro-enforcement bias' of the New York Convention.[178] It held that the Convention's 'public policy' defence should be construed narrowly, and that enforcement of foreign arbitral awards should be denied on this basis only 'where enforcement would violate the forum state's most basic notions of morality and justice'.[179]

11.117 Courts in other countries have also recognised that, in applying their own public policy to Convention awards, they should give it an international, and not a domestic, dimension. The English Court of Appeal in *RBRG Trading (UK) Ltd v Sinocore International Co. Ltd*,[180] having considered the decisions in both *Soleimany* and *Westacre* discussed above, concluded that 'where, on the facts, there is no illegality under the governing law but there is under English law, public policy will only be engaged where the illegality reflects considerations of international public policy rather than purely English domestic public policy'.[181]

---

[172] *Sonatrach*, 407 US 1 (1972).
[173] *Bremen v Zapata Offshore Co*, 417 US 506 (1974).
[174] *Mitsubishi Motor Corporation v Soler Chrysler-Plymouth Inc.*, 473 US 614, 105 S.Ct. 3346, 87 L.Ed.2d 444 (1985).
[175] *Sonatrach (Algeria) v Distrigas Corporation (United States District Court) Massachusetts*, 80 BR 606, 612 (1987).
[176] *Sonatrach (Algeria) v Distrigas Corporation (United States District Court) Massachusetts*, (1995) XX YBCA 795.
[177] See the discussion of *Parsons Whittemore Overseas Co. Inc. v Société Générale de l'Industrie du Papier (RAKTA)*, 508 F.2d 969 (2d Cir. 1974) at paragraph 11.60.
[178] Ibid., at 973.
[179] Ibid., at 974.
[180] *RBRG Trading (UK) Ltd v Sinocore International Co. Ltd* [2018] EWCA Civ 838.
[181] Ibid, at [25].

Similarly, in India, in a case to which reference has already been made,[182] the Supreme   **11.118**
Court said:

> This raises the question of whether the narrower concept of public policy as applicable in
> the field of public international law should be applied or the wider concept of public policy
> as applicable in the field of municipal law. The Court held that the narrower view should
> prevail and that enforcement would be refused on the public policy ground if such en-
> forcement would be contrary to (i) fundamental policy of Indian law; or (ii) the interests of
> India; or (iii) justice or morality.[183]

French,[184] Swiss,[185] German,[186] and Egyptian[187] courts have made decisions to similar ef-   **11.119**
fect. In addition, the arbitration legislation in some countries makes an express distinction
between domestic and international public policy, limiting the refusal of enforcement to the
latter ground only.[188]

These decisions and legislation, from different parts of the world, show a readiness to limit   **11.120**
(sometimes severely) the public policy defence to enforcement. However, the boundaries
of national public policy are not fixed, and some national courts have historically taken a
broader view of the defence than modern international standards would countenance.[189]

Rather than refer to 'public policy', Chinese law refers to the 'social and public interest',   **11.121**
which is potentially an even more oblique concept. Chinese courts have recognised an obligation to consider, in every case, whether this 'social and public interest' is violated, even if
neither party has raised it.[190] The Supreme People's Court has issued a statement of how to
interpret this 'social and public interest' ground, asking:

> [U]nder what circumstances does the principle of public interest apply? The principle of
> public interest can apply where there are breaches of fundamental principles of Chinese
> law, national sovereignty or national security, or breaches of the principles of social ethics
> and fundamental moral value.[191]

---

[182] *Renusagar Power Co. Ltd (India) v General Electric Co. (US)* (1995) XX YBCA 681.

[183] Ibid., at 702.

[184] See, e.g., *SA Laboratoires Eurosilicone v Société Bez Medizintechnik GmbH* [2004] Rev Arb 133.

[185] (1995) XX YBCA 762.

[186] (1987) XII YBCA 489.

[187] See, e.g., Cases Nos 20, 64/128 and 16, 20, 47/129, 7 April 2013, Cairo Court of Appeal, Commercial
Circuit No. 7.

[188] For example, Art. 814 of the Lebanese Arbitration Provisions provides that 'arbitral awards shall be recognized and granted exequatur [...] if they do not manifestly violate international public policy'.

[189] In a more recent example, the Higher Regional Court of Berlin refused to recognise a foreign arbitral
award to the extent that the award ordered a party to pay penalty interest, on the grounds that the high interest
rate was contrary to German public policy: see Judgment of 7 February 2019, 12 Sch 5/18 (Kammergericht
Berlin). The Saudi Arabian courts often refuse to enforce the interest element included in foreign arbitral
awards since interest is considered a usury (*riba*) under *Shari'ah* rules: *riba* is considered to include any type of
interest. For a more detailed discussion on this subject, see: Emre, 'A refusal reason of recognition and enforcement of foreign arbitral awards: Public policy' (2019) 56(2) Zbornik Radova Pravnog Fakulteta u Splitu 503,
at 510 and Güzeloğlu, 'The role of Shari'a law on the enforcement of arbitral awards in the Kingdom of Saudi
Arabia' (28 January 2016). https://www.lexology.com/library/detail.aspx?g=71e501f7-8552-45fd-8797-077fa
25e88a3.

[190] Peerenboom, 'Seek truth from facts: An empirical study of enforcement of arbitral awards in the PRC' (2001)
49 Am J Comp L 39.

[191] *Explanations on and Answers to Practical Questions in Trial of Foreign-Related Commercial and Maritime
Cases (No. 1)*, Issued by the Supreme People's Court on 8 April 2004, Art. 43.

11.122   Commentators have summarised this position as meaning that in China 'public policy' is broader than 'public morals', and includes 'traditional and societal sentiment'.[192]

11.123   Such broad conceptions of public policy may explain decisions such as that in *Heavy Metal*.[193] In that case, the Supreme People's Court had to decide whether to enforce a foreign-related arbitral award, which directed the respondent to pay compensatory damages to a US heavy metal band, whose performances had been banned by the Chinese Ministry of Culture on the grounds that the artists performed 'outrageous acts' such as drinking, smoking, splashing water, lying on the stage floor while performing, and jumping down from the stage. A CIETAC tribunal awarded damages for the band's lost income. When the band sought enforcement, the Supreme People's Court denied enforcement, on the grounds that the tribunal's findings were in manifest disregard of the underlying facts that the per-formance of heavy metal music was against 'national sentiments', and accordingly contrary to the social and public interests.[194] Whatever one may think of heavy metal music, it is dif-ficult not to reach the conclusion that this amounted to a troublingly broad interpretation of the public policy exception to the enforcement of arbitral awards.

11.124   The requirement that lower courts must obtain leave of the Supreme People's Court to refuse recognition or enforcement has helped to reduce the incidence of overly broad interpret-ations of public policy to deny enforcement of awards in China.[195] According to a speech in 2008 by Deputy Chief Justice Wan E'xiang, of the Supreme People's Court, between 2000 and 2008 the Court did not uphold a single decision by the Chinese lower courts that re-fused to enforce a foreign arbitral award on public policy grounds.[196] Attempts by parties to equate the social and public interest, for example, with a simple violation of Chinese law, or (more worryingly) the interests of state-owned enterprises, have been rejected as falling short of a breach of public policy.[197]

11.125   Russian courts are likewise known for expansive interpretations of the notion of public policy and have declined, for instance, to enforce foreign arbitral awards if the amount of damages awarded was 'punitive' or 'disproportionate to the breach' in the eyes of Russian courts.[198]

11.126   In an attempt at harmonisation, the Committee on International Commercial Arbitration of the International Law Association (ILA) has sought to offer definitions of the concepts of 'public policy', 'international public policy', and 'transnational public policy', and recom-mends that '[t]he finality of awards rendered in the context of international commercial arbitration should be respected save in exceptional circumstances', such exceptional cir-cumstances being the violation of international public policy.[199] The Committee defined

---

[192]   Fei, 'Public policy as a bar to enforcement of international arbitral awards: A review of the Chinese approach' (2010) 26 Arb Intl 301, at 311.

[193]   *Reply of the Supreme People's Court in the matter regarding the request by Beijing First Intermediary People's Court to Refuse Enforcement of Arbitral Award* [1997] Jing Ta 35 ('*Heavy Metal*').

[194]   For further discussion of the topic, see Yeoh, 'Enforcement of dispute outcomes', in Moser (ed.) *Managing Business Disputes in Today's China* (Kluwer Law International, 2007), p. 274.

[195]   *Notice Regarding the Local People's Court Handling Foreign-related Arbitral Awards and Foreign Arbitral Awards*, Issued by the Supreme People's Court on 28 August 1995.

[196]   Chen and Howes, 'Public policy and the enforcement of foreign arbitration awards in China' (2010) 3 Intl News 14.

[197]   Fei, 'Public policy as a bar to enforcement of international arbitral awards: A review of the Chinese approach' (2010) 26 Arb Intl 301, at 305–307.

[198]   See Presidium of Supreme Commercial Arbitrazh Court, Information Letter No. 96, 22 December 2005, s. 29; Presidium of Supreme Commercial Arbitrazh Court, Information Letter No. 156, 26 February 2013, s. 6.

[199]   ILA, *Final Report of the Committee on International Commercial Arbitration on Public Policy* (2004) 1 TDM.

'international public policy' as that 'part of the public policy of a state which, if violated, would prevent a party from invoking a foreign law or foreign judgment or foreign award'.[200]

The application of competition law raises particular issues of public policy that may become **11.127** relevant in both annulment and enforcement proceedings. In *Eco Swiss China Time Ltd v Benetton International NV*,[201] the European Court of Justice (ECJ) held that Article 81 of the Treaty Establishing the European Community, or EC Treaty (now Article 101 of the Treaty on the Functioning of the European Union, or TFEU) constituted a matter of public policy within the meaning of the New York Convention and, on this basis, ruled that:

> [A] national court, to which application is made for annulment of an arbitration award must grant that application if it considers that the award in question is in fact contrary to Article 81 EC (ex Article 85), where its domestic rules of procedure require it to grant an application for annulment founded on failure to observe national rules of public policy.[202]

The French courts (including the French Court of Cassation) have taken a narrow approach **11.128** to the impact of EU competition law on the enforceability of awards, setting aside awards on EU competition law grounds only if they show a 'flagrant, specific and concrete breach' of French international public policy.[203] The Swiss Federal Court has taken an even more restrictive approach. In its decision of 8 March 2006, it held that EU competition law could not be considered as part of the foundation of all legal orders so as to qualify as a matter of public policy and, on that ground, simply dismissed the case.[204] For their part, and in contrast, the Dutch and Belgian courts have shown themselves ready to undertake a substantive review of awards from the perspective of competition law and have not refrained from annulling awards found to be in breach of EU competition law (and in particular Article 81 EC).[205]

In the United States too, the interplay between public policy and the enforcement of **11.129** anti-trust arbitral awards has proved significant. The general approach was set by the US Supreme Court in the case of *Mitsubishi v Soler Chrysler-Plymouth*,[206] in which it confirmed the arbitrability of antitrust claims, but emphasised that US national courts would have the opportunity to have a 'second look' at such arbitral awards at the enforcement stage, in order to ensure that the legitimate interest in the enforcement of anti-trust laws had been addressed by the arbitral tribunal. In practice, however, US appellate courts have demonstrated different views with respect to their power to review an arbitral award *au fond*. For instance, in 2003, a divided Court of Appeal for the Seventh Circuit, considering the enforcement of a domestic award, quoted *Mitsubishi*, stating that a court should confirm only that the arbitral tribunal 'took cognizance of the antitrust claims and actually decided on them'; no further review of the merits had to be carried out.[207] However, one year later, the

---

[200] Ibid. This seems to be a circular definition that is of little assistance. See also *SA Compagnie commercial André v SA Tradigrain France* [2001] Rev Arb 773.

[201] *Eco Swiss China Time Ltd v Benetton International NV,* Case C-126/97 [1999] ECR I–3055.

[202] Ibid., at [49].

[203] See *Thales Air Defence BV v GIE Euromissile et al.,* Paris cour d'appel, 18 November 2004; also the judgment in *SNF SAS v Cytec Industries BV (Holland),* Cass. Civ., Ch. Civ. 1ere, 4 June 2008, in which the cour de cassation explicitly reiterated the narrow approach to the application of public policy.

[204] See *Tensacciai v Terra Armata,* Swiss Federal Court, 8 March 2006.

[205] See *Marketing Displays International Inc. v VR Van Raalte Reclame BV,* Dutch Court of Appeal, The Hague, 24 March 2005; *SNF v Cytec Industries BV,* Brussels Court of First Instance, 8 March 2007.

[206] See the decision of the US Supreme Court in *Mitsubishi v Soler Chrysler-Plymouth,* 473 US 614 (1985).

[207] See *Baxter International v Abbott Laboratories,* 315 F.3d 829 (7th Cir. 2003).

US Court of Appeal for the Fifth Circuit did not refrain from a substantive review of the merits of a domestic antitrust arbitral award.[208]

(k) Other grounds

11.130   Although the grounds for refusal of enforcement listed in Article V of the New York Convention are exhaustive, some courts have refused enforcement on grounds derived from other articles of the Convention. Thus, in the US case *Monegasque de Reassurance SAM (Monde Re) v NAK Naftogart of Ukraine and State of Ukraine*,[209] the Second Circuit refused enforcement of a Moscow award on grounds of *forum non conveniens*—a judicial procedural discretion that exists in the common law world, but is unknown in the civil law world. In so doing, it rejected the contention that Article V sets forth the only grounds for refusing to enforce a foreign arbitral award, and held that Article III made the enforcement of foreign arbitral awards subject to the rules of procedure of the courts where enforcement is sought, which, so it held, included the rule of *forum non conveniens*.

11.131   More recently, the Second Circuit Court of Appeals in *Figueiredo Ferraz E Engenharia de Projeto Ltda v Republic of Peru*[210] reversed, on grounds of *forum non conveniens*, a lower court's confirmation of a Peruvian arbitral award. Figueiredo had obtained an award against the Peruvian government, which the latter began paying out gradually, in accordance with a subsequently enacted Peruvian statute that limits the amount of money that an agency of the Peruvian government may pay annually to satisfy a judgment to 3 per cent of the agency's annual budget. The Second Circuit held that Peru was a more appropriate forum for the enforcement of the award than New York for a number of reasons, including the Peruvian cap statute. Similar to the court in *Monde Re*, the Court in *Figueiredo* held that Article III of the New York Convention and its equivalent Article IV of the Panama Convention, providing for the application of local procedural law at the enforcement stage, allow for the application of *forum non conveniens*. However, Judge Lynch, in a powerful dissent, opined that recognising a *forum non conveniens* defence would undermine the enforceability of arbitral awards in general. Indeed, the very idea of *forum non conveniens* is incompatible with the concept of international enforcement of foreign awards, which takes as its starting point that the places of arbitration and principal performance of the obligation are likely to be different, while the resulting award can be enforced internationally subject to limited grounds for refusal. Almost by definition, there is likely to be another jurisdiction with a closer connection to the underlying dispute than the place of enforcement. Nevertheless, the whole point of enforcement under the New York Convention is to internationalise the enforcement of awards rendered elsewhere, not to constrain a party to enforce in the jurisdiction of origin.

---

[208] See US Court of Appeals for the Fifth Circuit, *American Central Eastern Texas Gas Co. v Union Pacific Resources Group, Inc.*, 93 Fed. Appx. 1, 2004 WL 136091 (5th Cir. 27 Jan. 2004).

[209] *Monegasque de Reassurance SAM (Monde Re) v NAK Naftogart of Ukraine and State of Ukraine*, 311 F.3d 488 (2d Cir. 2002).

[210] *Figueiredo Ferraz E Engenharia de Projeto Ltda v Republic of Peru*, 663 F.4d 384 (2d Cir. 2011).

C. Enforcement under the ICSID Convention

The ICSID Convention is considered in some detail in Chapter 8, and creates its own separate **11.132** enforcement regime. Unless an ICSID award is revised or annulled under ICSID's own internal procedures, each contracting state must recognise an ICSID award as if it were a final judgment of its own national courts and enforce the obligation imposed by that award.[211] To this end, contracting states must designate a competent court or authority, which will deal with any requests for enforcement of an ICSID award.[212]

The special way in which ICSID awards are treated for the purposes of enforcement as com- **11.133** pared with arbitral awards being enforced under the New York Convention is summarised by the English Court of Appeal in the following terms:

> It is an important feature of the ICSID Convention that it does not permit an award to be im-
> pugned or its enforcement to be resisted in national courts even in circumstances where a
> foreign judgment, or even a domestic judgment, could be challenged. Thus, in contrast, for ex-
> ample, to the New York Convention on the Recognition and Enforcement of Foreign Arbitral
> Awards, a contracting state cannot decline to enforce an ICSID award even on the ground
> that its enforcement would be contrary to public policy in that state. Under the scheme of the
> ICSID Convention the only powers to contest the validity or enforceability of an award are
> those contained in the ICSID Convention itself (in Articles 50–52). Subject to those provi-
> sions, enforcement is intended to be automatic.[213]

In particular, under Article 53(1) of the ICSID Convention, ICSID awards 'shall be binding on **11.134** all parties and shall not be subject to any appeal or to any other remedy except those provided for in this Convention'. Article 54(1) of the ICSID Convention requires state parties to 'recognize an award rendered pursuant to [the] Convention as binding and enforce the pecuniary obligations imposed by that award within its territories as if it were a final judgment of a court in that State'.

The remedies mentioned in Article 53(1) are restricted to annulment, revision, or interpret- **11.135** ation of an award, and they can be obtained only through ICSID. Thus only an ICSID annulment committee may annul the award. Setting aside or any other review of ICSID awards by domestic courts is not available.

Article 52(1) contains an exhaustive list of grounds for annulment of ICSID awards, including that (a) the tribunal was not properly constituted;[214] (b) the tribunal has manifestly exceeded its powers;[215] (c) there was corruption on the part of a member of the

---

[211] ICSID Convention, Art. 54.

[212] The courts and authorities designated by each contracting state can be found by clicking into each state listed online in the 'Membership' tab, online at https://icsid.worldbank.org/about/member-states/database-of-member-states. See also ICSID Administrative and Financial Regulations, reg. 23(f).

[213] *Micula v Romania* [2018] EWCA Civ 1801, at [258].

[214] This provision is not intended to be an opportunity to challenge members of the tribunal *de novo*; rather, an ad hoc committee would be able to annul an award under Art. 52(1)(a) only if there had been a failure to comply properly with the procedure for challenging members. See *Azurix Corporation v Argentine Republic*, ICSID Case No. ARB/01/12, Decision on the Application for Annulment of the Argentine Republic, 1 September 2009, at [280], and *EDF International S.A. v Argentine Republic*, ICSID Case No. ARB/03/23, Decision on Annulment, 5 February 2016, at [126].

[215] A tribunal can exercise an 'excess of powers' not only in exercising a jurisdiction that it does not have, but also in failing to exercise a jurisdiction that it does possess: see, e.g., *Compañía de Aguas del Aconquija SA and Vivendi*

tribunal;[216] (d) there was a serious departure from a fundamental rule of procedure;[217] or (e) the award failed to state the reasons on which it is based.[218] There was a period in the early history of ICSID arbitration during which these grounds were interpreted quite broadly, resulting in *de facto* appeals on points of law and fact.[219] However, in recent years, annulment committees have taken a narrower approach,[220] and annulments of ICSID awards have become rarer. The grounds for annulment are considered in further detail in Chapter 8.

11.136   In the face of multiple ICSID claims, several Latin American countries have withdrawn from the Convention—namely, Bolivia, Ecuador, and Venezuela. The possible effects of these withdrawals on the jurisdiction of arbitral tribunals for claims brought under the ICSID Convention are discussed in Chapter 8.

11.137   In a less dramatic, but nevertheless far-reaching, step, Argentina reacted to the growing number of ICSID awards against it by arguing that the enforcement of ICSID awards is not automatic. Specifically, Argentina argued that Article 54 of the Convention requires the claimant party to seek recognition of the award rendered against the respondent state *in that state's national court*. To recall, Article 54 requires each contracting state to enforce 'the pecuniary obligations imposed by that award within its territories as if it were a final judgment of a court in *that* State'. This interpretation has become known as the 'Rosatti doctrine', following its espousal by former Argentine Minister of Justice Dr Horacio Rosatti. However, and perhaps unsurprisingly, it has now been repeatedly rejected by ad hoc annulment

---

Universal (formerly Compagnie Générale des Eaux) v Argentine Republic, ICSID Case No. ARB/97/3, Decision on Annulment, 3 July 2002, at [86]. However, not every 'excess of power' is 'manifest': see, e.g., *Standard Chartered Bank (Hong Kong) Limited v Tanzania Electric Supply Company Limited*, ICSID Case No. ARB/10/20, Decision on Annulment, 22 August 2018, at [181] (holding that an alleged excess of power is 'manifest' only if such excess is 'discernable without the need for an elaborate analysis of the award').

[216] Corruption implies that the arbitrator receives payment except as provided for by the ICSID Convention and as a consequence is biased towards one of the parties. It generally differs from bias and *ex parte* communications. See Schreuer et al., *The ICSID Convention: A Commentary* (2nd edn, Cambridge University Press, 2009), Section 273.

[217] Ad hoc committees have restricted annulment on this ground to violations of those principles that are essential to a fair hearing, observing that a violation of a non-fundamental rule, no matter how serious, would not call into question the validity of an award: see, e.g., *Malicorp Ltd v Arab Republic of Egypt*, ICSID Case No. ARB/08/18, Decision on Annulment, 3 July 2013, at [29]. See also *Tenaris S.A. and Talta—Trading e Marketing Sociedade Unipessoal Lda. v Bolivarian Republic of Venezuela*, ICSID Case No. ARB/11/26, Decision on Annulment, 8 August 2018, at [198] (holding that 'it is not enough for the tribunal to have departed from a rule of procedure, or for the departure to have occurred if it is not serious. Both the serious circumstances of the departure and the fundamental nature of the rule must exist').

[218] This ground of annulment applies only in a clear case in which there has been a failure by the tribunal to give any reasons for its decision on a particular question, and not in a case in which there has merely been a failure by the tribunal to give correct or convincing reasons: see, e.g., *OI European Group B.V. v Bolivarian Republic of Venezuela*, ICSID Case No. ARB/11/25, Decision on Annulment, 6 December 2018, at [321].

[219] See, e.g., the much-criticised *Patrick Mitchell v Democratic Republic of Congo*, ICSID Case No. ARB/99/7, Decision on Annulment, 1 November 2006, in which the ad hoc committee overturned the award on the grounds that the tribunal in the original proceedings had, in its view, incorrectly determined that the claimant held a protected investment within the meaning of the ICSID Convention. The annulment committee deemed that such determination constituted 'manifest excess of powers' under Art. 52(1)(b) of the Convention.

[220] See, e.g., *AES Summit Generation Ltd and AES-Tisza Erömü Kft v Republic of Hungary*, ICSID Case No. ARB/07/22, Decision of the Ad Hoc Committee on the Application for Annulment, 29 June 2012, at [17] ('annulment is an exhaustive, exceptional and narrowly circumscribed remedy and not an appeal'), and *Daimler Financial Services A.G. v Argentine Republic*, ICSID Case No. ARB/05/1, Decision on Annulment, 7 January 2015, at [186] (finding that if the Committee 'were to undertake a careful and detailed analysis of the respective submissions of the parties before the Tribunal […] and annul the Award on the ground that its understanding of facts or interpretation of law or appreciation of evidence is different from that of the Tribunal, it will cross the line that separates annulment from appeal').

committees considering stay of enforcement applications in *Enron v Argentina*[221] and *Compañia Aguas del Aconquija SA and Vivendi Universal v Argentina*.[222]

There are a number of regional conventions that may also have a significant bearing on the recognition and enforcement of foreign arbitral awards. The principal conventions are discussed briefly in turn.   **11.138**

D. Enforcement under Regional Conventions

(a) Middle Eastern and North African Conventions and enforcement regimes

The Riyadh Arab Agreement on Judicial Cooperation, known as the 'Riyadh Convention', entered into force in 1985, has twenty signatory states, and provides for the enforcement in one signatory state of an award rendered in another signatory state.[223] Importantly, however, and unlike the New York Convention, the Riyadh Convention requires that, to enforce an award made in another Arab country, leave to enforce must be obtained in the country in which the award was made.[224] In the same way, the Agreement on the Execution of Rulings, Requests of Legal Assistance and Judicial Notices, entered into by the Gulf Co-operation Council in 1995 and known as the 'GCC Convention',[225] has the same requirement, and while it does not specifically refer to arbitral awards, it is considered applicable to them.[226]   **11.139**

States in this region have also entered into regional investment agreements—notably, the Agreement for Promotion, Protection and Guarantee of Investments, entered into by the Organisation of Islamic Cooperation member states and thus known as the 'OIC Agreement',[227] and the Unified Agreement for the Investment of Arab Capital in the Arab States, entered into by the member states of the Arab League (hence the 'Arab League Investment Agreement').[228] These agreements provide for the settlement of investor–state disputes by international arbitration. If an arbitral award rendered under the Arab League Investment Agreement is not implemented, or if the parties fail to resort to arbitration, or   **11.140**

---

[221] See *Enron Corporation Ponderosa Assets, LP v Argentine Republic*, Decision on the Argentine Republic's Request for a Continued Stay of Enforcement of the Award, 7 October 2008, at [69], [83], and [85].

[222] See *Aguas del Aconquija SA and Vivendi Universal v Argentine Republic*, Decision on the Argentine Republic's Request for a Continued Stay of Enforcement of the Award Rendered on 20 August 2007, 4 November 2008, at [31]–[37] and [45].

[223] The following countries are signatories to the Riyadh Convention: Algeria, Bahrain, Djibouti, Iraq, Jordan, Kuwait, Lebanon, Libya, Mauritania, Morocco, Oman, Palestine, Qatar, Saudi Arabia, Somalia, Sudan, Syria, Tunisia, UAE, and Yemen.

[224] See Riyadh Convention, Art. 37.

[225] The following countries are party to the GCC Convention: Bahrain, Kuwait, Oman, Qatar, Saudi Arabia, and UAE.

[226] GCC Convention, Art. 7.

[227] The following countries have ratified the OIC Agreement: Burkina Faso, Cameroon, Egypt, Gabon, Gambia, Guinea, Indonesia, Iran, Iraq, Jordan, Kuwait, Lebanon, Libya, Mali, Mauritania, Morocco, Oman, Pakistan, Palestine, Qatar, Saudi Arabia, Senegal, Somalia, Sudan, Syria, Tunisia, Turkey, Uganda, and the UAE. The following countries have signed but not yet ratified the OIC Agreement: Afghanistan, Albania, Bangladesh, Benin, Comoros, Cote d'Ivoire, Djibouti, Guinea-Bissau, Malaysia, Niger, Nigeria, Sierra-Leone, Tajikistan, and Yemen.

[228] The following countries are party to the Arab League Agreement: Algeria, Bahrain, Comoros, Djibouti, Egypt, Iraq, Jordan, Kuwait, Lebanon, Libya, Mauritania, Morocco, Oman, Palestine, Qatar, Saudi Arabia, Somalia, Sudan, Syria (temporarily suspended at the time of writing), Tunisia, UAE, and Yemen.

the tribunal fails to render an award within a prescribed period of time, the dispute shall be heard by a permanent Arab Investment Court. The decisions of arbitral tribunals under the OIC Agreement and of the Arab Investment Court under the Arab League Agreement are, like ICSID awards, enforceable as though they were final and enforceable decisions of national courts of the state in which enforcement is sought.[229]

11.141   The enforcement regime in the United Arab Emirates has attracted much attention in recent years. The United Arab Emirates is a civil law jurisdiction, but to promote business it has established two autonomous, English-speaking, common law 'off-shore' jurisdictional enclaves, namely the Dubai International Financial Centre (DIFC) and the Abu Dhabi Global Market (ADGM). These 'off-shore' jurisdictions have their own civil and commercial laws, including their own arbitration laws based on the Model Law. The former Chief Justice of the DIFC courts was a leading Singaporean international arbitrator, Dr Michael Hwang, who described the DIFC as 'a common law island in a civil law ocean'.[230]

11.142   In a notable series of judgments from 2014 to 2016, the DIFC courts held that, under the DIFC arbitration law, the DIFC could be used as a so-called 'conduit jurisdiction' for the enforcement of arbitral awards in the on-shore United Arab Emirates, given the automatic recognition of DIFC judgments in the rest of the United Arab Emirates.[231] This was so even in circumstances where the award debtor had no presence or assets in the DIFC itself. This, in effect, allowed award creditors to bypass the often uncertain and lengthy process of enforcing arbitral awards directly in the on-shore United Arab Emirates, which in turn led to a clash of jurisdictions between the off-shore DIFC courts and the on-shore United Arab Emirates regimes. In light of this, in June 2016, the Ruler of Dubai established the Dubai–DIFC Joint Judicial Committee responsible for determining conflicts of jurisdiction between the on-shore Dubai courts and the DIFC courts.[232] The Joint Judicial Committee, which comprises four on-shore judges and only three DIFC judges, has since handed down a number of decisions that favoured the jurisdiction of the on-shore Dubai courts, thereby gradually curtailing the award creditors' ability to use the DIFC courts as a 'conduit jurisdiction' to enforce arbitral awards in the on-shore United Arab Emirates.[233]

11.143   In addition to the DIFC courts, the DIFC–LCIA Arbitration Centre was established in 2008 as a joint venture between the DIFC and the LCIA to administer arbitration proceedings under its own rules. On 20 September 2021, the Ruler of Dubai issued Decree No. (34) of 2021 dissolving the DIFC–LCIA Arbitration Centre (and the Emirates Maritime Arbitration Centre) and transferring their staff and their assets to the Dubai International

---

[229] OIC Agreement, Art. 17(d); Arab League Agreement, Art. 34(3).

[230] See Hwang, 'The courts of the Dubai International Finance Centre—A common law island in a civil law ocean', in *Selected Essays in Dispute Resolution* (Academy Publishing, 2018), p. 51.

[231] See, e.g., *Banyan Tree Corporate PTE Ltd v Meydan Group LLC* (Claim No: ARB-003-2013) and *DNB Bank ASA v Gulf Eyadah* (Claim No: CA-007-2015).

[232] Dubai Decree No. 19 of 2016, 'Concerning the establishment of a Judicial Tribunal for the Dubai Courts and DIFC Courts'.

[233] See, e.g., *Daman Real Capital Partners Company LLC v Oger Dubai LLC* (Cassation No. 1/2016), where the Joint Judicial Committee ruled that the DIFC courts should 'cease to entertain' an action to enforce an award rendered in on-shore Dubai because of the existence of parallel annulment proceedings in the on-shore Dubai courts. In *Gulf Navigation Holding P.S.C v Jinhai Heavy Industry Co. Limited (Formerly Zhoushan Junhaiwan Shipyard Co Ltd)* (Cassation No. 1/2017), the Joint Judicial Committee went a step further and ordered the DIFC courts to cease entertaining the enforcement of a foreign arbitral award, on the basis that the award creditor had filed a new claim related to the same contract in dispute before the Amicable Settlement of Disputes Centre of the Dubai courts.

Arbitration Centre (DIAC) with a new arbitration court to be established.[234] It remains to be seen whether this and other changes will impact the enforceability of awards in the United Arab Emirates.

(b) Panama Convention

In January 1975, following the Inter-American Conference on Private International Law in Panama, the Panama Convention was signed by twelve South American states.[235] The Convention represented a significant shift away from former Latin American hostility towards international arbitration, as reflected in the Calvo doctrine.[236]   **11.144**

The Panama Convention recognises an agreement to submit existing or future disputes to arbitration,[237] and it also provides for the reciprocal enforcement of arbitral awards in member states as if the award were a judgment of a court in the place of enforcement: **11.145**

> An arbitral decision or award that is not appealable under the applicable law or procedural rules shall have the force of a final judicial judgment. Its execution or recognition may be ordered in the same manner as that of decisions handed down by national or foreign ordinary courts, in accordance with the procedural laws of the country where it is to be executed and the provisions of international treaties.[238]

The Convention speaks of 'execution' of an award rather than 'enforcement', but in practice there is no difference.

Recognition and execution of an award may be refused, at the request of the party against which it is made, only if that party is able to prove to the competent authority of the state in which recognition and execution is sought that one of the five grounds for refusal laid down in Article 5(1) of the Panama Convention applies. Those five grounds closely follow the five grounds set out in Article V(1) of the New York Convention, and include: (i) incapacity, or invalid arbitration agreement; (ii) no proper notice of appointment of arbitrator or of the proceedings, or lack of due process; (iii) lack of jurisdiction; (iv) composition of arbitral tribunal or procedure not in accordance with arbitration agreement or the relevant law; and (v) award not yet binding on the parties, or annulled or suspended at the seat of arbitration.[239] In the same way, and following Article V(2) of the New York Convention, under Article 5(2) of the Panama Convention, recognition and execution of an award may also be refused if the competent authority of the state in which recognition and execution is sought,   **11.146**

---

[234] The Dubai government's media release can be found online at https://mediaoffice.ae/en/news/2021/September/18-09/Mohammed-bin-rashid

[235] The text of the Convention appears in (1978) III YBCA 15 and in (1975) 14 ILM 336. See also Blackaby, Lindsey, and Spinillo (eds) *International Arbitration in Latin America* (Kluwer Law International, 2002), pp. 3–6. The Convention came into effect in the United States on 27 October 1990.

[236] At time of writing, nineteen states had ratified this Convention, including the United States: see online at http://www.oas.org/juridico/english/sigs/b-35.html. For a commentary on US participation, see Lowry, 'The United States joins the Inter-American Arbitration Convention' (1990) 7 J Intl Arb 83.

[237] Panama Convention, Art. 1. Unlike the New York Convention, however, it does not deal with the problem of enforcing an arbitration agreement if one of the parties takes court proceedings notwithstanding the agreement to arbitrate.

[238] Panama Convention, Art. 4.

[239] Panama Convention, Art. 5(1).

finds that: the subject matter of the dispute cannot be settled by arbitration under the law of that state; or that recognition or execution of the decision would be contrary to the public policy ('*ordre public*') of that state.[240]

11.147   Where an application has been made to annul or suspend the award, the authority before which recognition and execution is sought may,[241] under the Panama Convention, postpone its decision; at the request of the party seeking execution, it may also instruct the other party to provide appropriate guarantees.[242]

11.148   It is evident that the Panama Convention was strongly influenced by the provisions of the New York Convention. Indeed, many of the provisions of the former have been copied more or less word for word from the latter. According to one informed commentator, the Panama Convention nevertheless has had 'a tremendous and vital significance'.[243] Certainly, whether because of the Convention or because of other influences—such as the Model Law—arbitration is becoming a more acceptable way of settling disputes in Latin America.

(c) Moscow Convention

11.149   The Moscow Convention was signed on 26 May 1972, the original signatories being those Eastern Bloc states that were grouped together under the leadership of the Soviet Union in the now defunct Council for Mutual Economic Assistance (known in English as the Comecon). Now that the German Democratic Republic has ceased to exist and Poland, the Czech Republic, and Hungary have withdrawn, it applies only to Bulgaria, Cuba, Mongolia, Romania, and Russia, although there is little evidence of any current usage.

11.150   The Convention regulates the settlement by arbitration of disputes 'resulting from economic and scientific-technical cooperation' within the member states. It provides that arbitration awards 'shall be final and binding',[244] and they are to be 'voluntarily' enforced by the parties, failing which they may be enforced in the same way as final decisions made in the courts of the country of enforcement.[245] Enforcement proceedings must be brought within two years of the date of the award, and the three grounds of refusal of enforcement closely parallel those in the New York Convention—namely, lack of jurisdiction, denial of a fair hearing, and when the award has been set aside.[246]

(d) Other regional conventions

11.151   This review of various regional conventions is not intended to be exhaustive. Parties or lawyers who are concerned with the recognition and enforcement of arbitration agreements or

---

[240] Panama Convention, Art. 5(2).
[241] Panama Convention Art. 6.
[242] This provision follows the New York Convention, Art. V(I).
[243] Norberg, 'General introduction to inter-American commercial arbitration' (1978) *III* YBCA 1, at 13.
[244] Moscow Convention, Art. IV(1).
[245] Moscow Convention, Art. IV(2).
[246] Moscow Convention, Art. V(1).

arbitral awards would be well advised to consider whether there are any regional conventions that may be both relevant and helpful.

E. Defence of State Immunity

The defences to recognition and enforcement of an international arbitral award, which are laid down in the New York Convention and the Model Law, have been considered.[247] There is one standard form of defence, however, that is not mentioned in the Convention or the Model Law, but which may be encountered in practice, where the unsuccessful party is either a sovereign state or a state agency. This is the defence of state immunity, or 'sovereign immunity' as it is sometimes known. In essence, the defence means that a sovereign state cannot be compelled to submit to the jurisdiction of the courts of another state:

11.152

> The sovereign was a definable person, to whom allegiance was due. As an integral part of this mystique, the sovereign could not be made subject to the judicial processes of his country. Accordingly, it was only fitting that he could not be sued in foreign courts. The idea of the personal sovereign would undoubtedly have been undermined had courts been able to exercise jurisdiction over foreign sovereigns. This personalisation was gradually replaced by the abstract concept of state sovereignty, but the basic mystique remained. In addition, the independence and equality of states made it philosophically as well as practically difficult to permit municipal courts of one country to manifest their power over foreign sovereign states, without their consent.[248]

State immunity does not prevent a state or state agency from agreeing to submit to the authority of an arbitral tribunal. It is a well-established principle of international law that a sovereign is bound by an agreement to arbitrate contractual disputes,[249] and the ability so to submit may itself be seen as an incident or attribute of sovereignty.

11.153

State immunity exists at two levels. First, at the level of jurisdiction; and secondly, at the level of execution. Accordingly, there may be both immunity from jurisdiction and immunity from execution. In considering state immunity, a distinction will usually need to be made between acts of a state taking place in its capacity as a state (acts *jure imperii*) and those taking place in its commercial capacity (acts *jure gestionis*). As a distinguished Swiss commentator has written, this distinction is clear in theory, but difficult to apply in practice.[250] The distinction is important because some states claim absolute immunity (that is, immunity for all acts carried out by or on behalf of the state) whilst others claim restricted immunity (that is, immunity only for acts *jure imperii*).[251] In *La Générale des Carrières et des*

11.154

---

[247] See paragraphs 11.62ff.

[248] Shaw, *International Law* (6th edn, Cambridge University Press, 2008), p. 698. See also Lauterpacht, 'The problem of jurisdictional immunities of foreign states' (1951) 28 BYIL 220; Higgins, 'Certain unresolved aspects of the law of state immunity' (1982) 29 NILR 265.

[249] This principle of international law is highlighted in the award of 12 April 1977 of Mahmassani, sole arbitrator in *Libyan American Oil Co. (Liamco) v Government of the Libyan Arab Republic* (1982) 62 ILR 140, at 178. It was noted that even UN General Assembly Resolution No. 1803, dated 21 December 1962, which proclaims permanent sovereignty over natural resources, confirms the obligation of states to respect arbitration agreements.

[250] Lalive, 'Quelques observations sur l'immunité d'exécution des états et l'arbitrage international', in Dinstein (ed.) *International Law at a Time of Perplexity* (Brill, 1989), p. 370.

[251] The United Nations Convention on Jurisdictional Immunities of States and their Property attempts to harmonise the approach taken by states. Adopted by the UN General Assembly in December 2004, it will

Mines,[252] the Privy Council of England and Wales considered whether a mining company owned by the Democratic Republic of Congo represented the state in its capacity as a state or in its commercial capacity. In holding to the latter view, the Privy Council observed that where a separate juridical entity is formed by the state for commercial or industrial purposes with its own management and budget, subject to 'quite extreme' circumstances to the contrary, the separate legal personality should be respected.[253]

(a) Jurisdictional immunity

11.155   During the course of arbitration proceedings to which a state is a party, the distinction between absolute and restricted immunity should be of no relevance. The arbitration can proceed validly only on the basis that the state concerned has agreed to arbitrate, and such an agreement is generally held to be a waiver of immunity. This is also taken to extend to the jurisdiction of the relevant court at the seat of the arbitration to supervise the arbitration taking place in its territory.

11.156   The restricted theory of sovereign immunity has been adopted by national courts in many countries,[254] and in some countries the position has been established by legislation. Indeed, it is possible now to state that a majority of states adhere to the doctrine of restricted immunity, although with notable exceptions, such as China, Hong Kong, and some Latin American countries.[255] In the United Kingdom, for example, the State Immunity Act 1978 provides that where a state has agreed in writing to submit existing or future disputes to arbitration, the state is not immune in respect of proceedings in the courts of the United Kingdom that relate to the arbitration.[256] Once again, however, the precise position adopted by a given country can be established only by reference to the law and practice of that country. In the United States, for example, it was not clear under the Foreign Sovereign

---

only come into force once thirty states have ratified it. At time of writing, only twenty-two states had done so (while twenty-eight states have signed the Convention): see online at http://treaties.un.org/Pages/ViewDetails. aspx?src = IND&mtdsg_no = III-13&chapter = 3&lang = en.

[252] *La Générale des Carrières et des Mines v FG Hemisphere Associates LLC* [2012] UKPC 27.

[253] Notwithstanding the robust position on sovereign immunity taken by English courts, the British parliament introduced another obstacle to the enforcement of awards against developing sovereigns, styled 'heavily indebted poor countries' (HIPCs), in the form of the Debt Relief (Developing Countries) Act 2010, which aims to diminish debt in the world's poorest economies, including Africa and Asia. The Act seeks to complement the HIPC initiative and prohibits private creditors from pursuing in English courts any claims against such countries above a limited amount, set by the HIPC Initiative formula: Barratt and Michael, 'Degrees of immunity: A lesson from the Privy Council', in *The European, Middle Eastern and African Arbitration Review* (GAR, 2013), pp. 6–7.

[254] Whilst this position has evolved from case law in many countries, reference must also be had to those countries that have given effect to the 1972 European Convention on State Immunity.

[255] Barratt and Michael, 'Degrees of immunity: A lesson from the Privy Council', in *The European, Middle Eastern and African Arbitration Review* (GAR, 2013), p. 4.

[256] English State Immunity Act 1978, s. 9. See *Svenska Petroleum Exploration AB v Government of the Republic of Lithuania (No. 2)* [2006] EWCA Civ 1529. See also UN Convention on Jurisdictional Immunities of States and their Property 2004, Art. 17, which provides: '[I]f a State enters into an agreement in writing with a foreign natural or juridical person to submit to arbitration differences relating to a commercial transaction, that State cannot invoke immunity from jurisdiction before a court of another State which is otherwise competent in a proceeding which relates to: (a) the validity, interpretation or application of the arbitration agreement; (b) the arbitration procedure; or (c) the confirmation or the setting aside of the award, unless the arbitration agreement otherwise provides.'

Immunities Act of 1976,[257] as enacted, whether a foreign state's agreement to arbitrate could be regarded as a waiver of immunity from the jurisdiction of a US court. Following the *Liamco* case,[258] in which an award made against the Libyan state was recognised, an amendment to the 1976 Act[259] made it clear that the US courts have jurisdiction, inter alia, to confirm an arbitration award made under an agreement to arbitrate where the arbitration takes place, or is authorised to take place, in the United States, or where the award is governed by a treaty to which the United States is a party.[260]

(b) Immunity from execution

Problems are most likely to arise when a winning party attempts to enforce and execute its award against a state or state entity. If the state concerned wishes to evade its obligations,[261] it may do so by claiming immunity from execution.[262] It may be thought inappropriate that a state or state entity can escape its legal obligations in this way, but this is the logical result of conferring immunity upon states. Moreover, whilst the existence of an arbitration agreement is usually held to be a waiver of immunity from jurisdiction, such a waiver is generally not held to extend to immunity from execution. By way of example, statutes in England require separate waivers in respect of execution and jurisdiction.[263]

11.157

Thus, under the ICSID Convention, an ICSID award must be treated by a contracting state as if it were a final judgment of a court of that state. However, this provision for the automatic recognition of such an award does *not* mean that it will be treated as overriding any immunity from *execution* that exists in the contracting state. Indeed, Article 55 of the ICSID Convention states that immunity from execution is a matter of national law. It is surprising that, in a convention that was intended to encourage investment, the state parties did not agree to waive their immunity from execution. It seems, however, that 'abandonment of immunity of execution was mentioned by only one representative and his statement found no echo whatsoever'.[264]

11.158

---

[257] Foreign Sovereign Immunities Act of 1976, Title 28, US Code, § 1605(a)(1). See Kahale, 'New legislation facilitates enforcement of arbitral agreements and awards' (1989) 6 J Intl Arb 57.

[258] *Libyan American Oil Co. (Liamco) v Libyan Arab Republic* (1981) 20 ILM 1.

[259] Section 1605(a)(6), as amended 16 November 1988. For commentary, see Delaume, 'Recognition and enforcement of state contract awards in the United States: A restatement' (1997) 91 Am J Intl L 476.

[260] See, e.g., *Chevron Corporation v Republic of Ecuador* 2013 WL 2449172 (DDC 2013), in which the US District Court for the District of Columbia held that the arbitration exception to sovereign immunity under the Foreign Sovereign Immunities Act of 1976 applied in the case of enforcement of an award under a BIT, which was being enforced under the New York Convention.

[261] If it did not, presumably the question of enforcement would not arise, since it would carry out the award voluntarily.

[262] For a classic discussion of this topic, see van den Berg, 'The enforcement of arbitral awards against a state: The problem of immunity from execution', in Lew (ed.) *Contemporary Problems in International Arbitration* (CCLS/Kluwer, 1986), p. 359.

[263] State Immunity Act 1978, s. 13(3).

[264] See Broches, 'Awards rendered pursuant to the ICSID Convention: Binding force, finality, recognition, enforcement, execution' (1987) 2 ICSID Rev—Foreign Investment LJ 287, at 332. See, e.g., Decision 5A_681/2011 of the Swiss Federal Supreme Court, 23 November 2011, which, in considering the enforcement of an ICSID award rendered against Kyrgyzstan, held that the assets of Kyrgyzaeronavigatsia (a Kyrgyz government agency in charge of aerospace control) were protected by sovereign immunity, since they were used for the exercise of sovereign authority. For a view that the problem of immunity from execution of an ICSID award is more theoretical than real, by reason, inter alia, of the obligation in ICSID Convention, Art. 53, to comply with the award, see Delaume, 'Sovereign immunity and transnational arbitration' (1987) 3 Arb Intl 28, at 43.

11.159   However, courts in some instances have found ways of circumventing this obstacle to the efficacy of the arbitral process. The decision of the French Court of Cassation in *Creighton v Qatar* is a notable example.[265] In 1982, Creighton Ltd, a Cayman Islands corporation with offices in the United States, contracted with the government of Qatar to build a women's hospital in Doha. After obtaining the necessary authorisations, Creighton entered into a contract with the Qatari Ministry of Municipal Affairs and Agriculture on 19 June 1982. In November 1986, Creighton was expelled from the project by the Government of Qatar; in 1987, pursuant to the arbitration clause in the agreement, Creighton commenced ICC arbitration in Paris. In October 1993, final awards were rendered against Qatar.

11.160   After a failed Qatari attempt to challenge the award in France, Creighton sought to enforce the awards against, inter alia, bank accounts held in France by the Qatari ministry. Following Creighton's seizure of those accounts, Qatar initiated proceedings before the Paris Tribunal de Grande Instance to have those seizures lifted, on the grounds of Qatar's immunity from execution. In January 1997, the Paris Tribunal ordered the lifting of the seizures and concluded that the subject matter of the agreement prevented any waiver of Qatar's immunity from execution. Specifically, it held that the construction of a hospital was an activity of a public nature, and therefore subject to state immunity.

11.161   In June 1998, the Paris Court of Appeal confirmed that there was no waiver of immunity from execution. Creighton appealed again, and on 6 July 2000 the Court of Cassation overturned the Paris Court of Appeal's decision. Relying on Article 24 of the then applicable ICC Rules (now reflected in Article 35.6 of the ICC Rules), by which the parties are 'deemed to have undertaken to carry out the resulting award without delay and to have waived their right to any form of appeal insofar as such waiver can validly be made', the Court of Cassation found that, in agreeing to ICC arbitration, a state waives not only its immunity from jurisdiction, but also its immunity from execution.[266] Following *Creighton*, the French courts maintained the position that once a state had waived its immunity from execution, it had opened itself to enforcement against its commercial assets. However, in three simultaneous decisions involving the enforcement of interim measures ordered by a foreign court, the Court of Cassation applied a more exacting test to the waiver of sovereign immunity from execution.[267] All three cases dealt with attachments made by NML Capital on debts owed to Argentina by each of BNP Paribas, Air France, and Total Austral. The Court of Cassation held that waivers can be effective only if made in an express and specific manner, such that the assets or the category of assets over which the waiver is granted are specifically identified.

---

[265] *Creighton Ltd (Cayman Islands) v Minister of Finance and Minister of Internal Affairs and Agriculture of the Government of the State of Qatar*, Cass. Civ., 6 July 2000, (2000) XXV YBCA 458 and [2001] Rev Arb 114; cf. *Yugoslavia v SEEE*, Paris Tribunal de Grande Instance, 6 July 1970, (1970) 65 ILR 47, at 49 ('waiver of jurisdictional immunity does not in any way involve waiver of immunity from execution'); Paris cour d'appel, 21 April 1982, [1983] J du Droit Intl 145.

[266] See Meyer-Fabre, 'Enforcement of arbitral awards against sovereign states: A new milestone' (2000) 15 Mealey's Intl Arb Rep 9, at 48–52. See also Carrier, 'France: Shrinking of immunity from execution and discovery of diplomatic immunity from execution' (2003) 18 Mealey's Intl Arb Rep 1, at 46–50, in which Carrier suggests that the wording of ICC Rules, Art. 24 (now 2012 ICC Rules, Art. 34.6) is not clear enough to deduce such a waiver.

[267] Cass. Civ., Ch. Civ. 1ere, Arrêt No. 395 du 28 mars 2013 (11-10.450), Arrêt No. 395 du 28 mars 2013 (11-10.450), and Arrêt No. 396 du 28 mars 2013 (11-13.323). See Kleiman and Spinelli, '*NML v Argentina*: Supreme Court tightens waiver of sovereign immunity test', available online at http://www.internationallawoffice.com/news letters/

As to the assets over which the immunity from execution can be waived, the position varies. **11.162**
The successful party to an arbitration against a state or state entity is in a better position
where the forum state allows execution against the *commercial* assets of a foreign sovereign.
This is the position, for example, in countries such as Austria, England, France, Germany,
Sweden, and the United States, amongst others. Execution is allowed against funds held
by the defaulting state or state entity *for commercial purposes*. Care must be taken to ascertain whether all commercial property of the foreign state is subject to execution (such as in
England), or merely that property which is (or was) used for the commercial activity upon
which the claim is based.[268]

However, even where execution against state assets is allowed, national legislation and na- **11.163**
tional courts have traditionally tended to show considerable respect for foreign states. In the
United Kingdom, for example, the State Immunity Act 1978 provides that a certificate from
the head of a state's diplomatic mission that certain property is not used for commercial
purposes is sufficient evidence of that fact unless the contrary is proved.[269] Consequently, in
1984, the highest appellate court in England decided that a declaration by the ambassador
of a foreign state that its account with a London bank was *not* held for commercial purposes
should be accepted as sufficient evidence of this fact, unless the contrary could be proved
by showing that the account *was* used almost exclusively for commercial purposes.[270] In
reaching this decision, the court was strongly influenced by a decision of the Constitutional
Court of the Federal Republic of Germany in the *Philippine Republic* case,[271] in which a
similar dispute was decided according to principles of public international law. In recent
years, however, courts in some jurisdictions have broadened the scope of government assets
that are considered commercial.[272]

Other important targets in the execution of awards against states are assets held by foreign **11.164**
central banks or monetary authorities. The English State Immunity Act 1978, as one example, affords those assets complete immunity irrespective of the purposes for which they
are used.[273]

In the United States, the Liberian Eastern Timber Company (Letco), a company regis- **11.165**
tered in France, failed in its attempt to enforce an ICSID award[274] against those assets of

---

[268] See J. Paulsson, 'Sovereign immunity from jurisdiction: French case law revisited' (1985) 19 Intl Lawyer 277.
[269] State Immunity Act 1978, s. 13(5).
[270] *Alcom Ltd v Republic of Colombia* [1984] AC 580 (HL). See also *SerVaas Incorporated v Rafidain Bank & Republic of Iraq and ors* [2012] UKSC 40, in which a certificate issued by the Iraqi head of mission was held sufficient to prove that the funds in question were earmarked for the restructuring of Iraq's sovereign debt and, as such,
protected by sovereign immunity.
[271] BVerfGE 46, 342 2 BvM 1/76 '*Philippine Embassy*'.
[272] See, e.g., *Orascom Telecom Holding SAE v Republic of Chad and anor* [2008] 2 Lloyd's Rep 396, at [23], in
which enforcement of an ICC award was allowed against Chad's Citibank account, which was set up and operated
so as 'to receive the proceeds of a contract for the supply of goods or services, and/or to be part of a system specifically established for the purposes of repayment of the loans by the World Bank etc to Chad'. See also *Russian
Federation v Franz J. Sedelmayer*, Case No. ö 170-10, Swedish Supreme Court, 1 July 2011, in which the Court held
that an arbitral award could be enforced against a block of flats in Stockholm owned by the Russian government,
which was partially used by the Russian Federation to house diplomats, partly for non-commercial (but non-
official) purposes and partly for commercial purposes.
[273] State Immunity Act 1978, s. 14(4); *AIG Capital Partners Inc. v Kazakhstan* [2005] App LR 10/20. See also
the US Foreign Sovereign Immunities Act of 1976, § 1611(b)(1), which also provides that the immunity of central
banks or monetary authorities can be waived: see *LNC Investments Inc. v Republic of Nicaragua*, 115 F.Supp.2d 358
(SDNY 2000) for a restrictive approach to waivers of immunity.
[274] One of the authors was a member of the tribunal.

the government of Liberia that were in the United States. There were a series of proceedings in the courts and Letco was permitted to enter judgment against the Liberian government. However, because of state immunity, Letco was refused leave to execute this judgment, first against shipping fees due to the Liberian government, and secondly (and more predictably), against Liberian embassy bank accounts.[275]

11.166   In France, the Compagnie NOGA d'Importation et d'Exportation SA, a Swiss company, was frustrated in its attempt to enforce an ICC award rendered in Stockholm against assets of the Russian Federation. In March 2000, the Paris Tribunal de Grande Instance granted *exequatur* of the award; in May 2000, NOGA proceeded, inter alia, to seize bank accounts opened in the names of the embassy of the Russian Federation in France, the commercial delegation of the Russian Federation, and the permanent delegation of the Russian Federation at the United Nations Educational, Scientific and Cultural Organization (UNESCO). Following Russia's failed attempt to have the seizures lifted by the Paris Tribunal, Russia appealed to the Paris Court of Appeal. Notwithstanding explicit contractual waivers of immunity from execution in the underlying agreements, the Court of Appeal held that Russia had not waived its diplomatic immunity, which is governed by the distinct regime of the 1961 Vienna Convention on Diplomatic Relations. A general waiver of immunity from execution therefore did not extend to diplomatic assets.[276] The Paris Court of Appeal based its decision on Articles 22(3) and 25 of the Vienna Convention, and concluded that all of the accounts that had been seized by NOGA were held by Russian diplomatic bodies and, as such, could not be part of Russia's waiver of immunity from execution.[277] Following failed attempts to enforce its Stockholm award in France against a Russian ship in the port of Brest and Russian Mig fighter jets participating in an air show outside of Paris, NOGA sought to enforce the award in Switzerland, inter alia, against bank accounts of the Russian central bank.[278] However, the Swiss Federal Supreme Court went on to refuse NOGA's attempt to block an award subsequently rendered in Paris in the Russian Federation's favour, which declared that the claim underlying the debt collection proceedings did not exist.[279]

11.167   However, the French Court of Cassation in *Commissions Import Export SA. v The Republic of the Congo*[280] did not adopt the approach taken by the Paris Court of Appeal in *NOGA*. In the *Commissions* case, Congo entered into an arbitration agreement by which it expressly waived its right to 'invoke, in the context of the settlement of a dispute relating to

---

[275] *Liberian Eastern Timber Co. (Letco) v Government of the Republic of Liberia*, 650 F.Supp. 73 (SDNY 1986), 659 F.Supp. 606 (DDC 1987) (embassy bank accounts). For a commentary, see Broches, 'Awards rendered pursuant to the ICSID Convention: Binding force, finality, recognition, enforcement, execution' (1987) 2 ICSID Rev—Foreign Investment LJ 287.

[276] *Ambassade de la Féderation de Russie en France v Compagnie NOGA d'Importation et d'Exportation SA*, Paris cour d'appel, Ch. 1ere A, 10 August 2000, [2001] Rev Arb 114; for excerpts in English, see also (2001) XXVI YBCA 273. Although the cour de cassation subsequently overturned the Court of Appeal's decision on 12 May 2004, it did not impugn the Court of Appeal's reasoning on the relationship between a waiver of immunity from execution and diplomatic immunity. See also Gaillard, 'La jurisprudence de la Cour de Cassation en matiere d'arbitrage international' (2007) 4 Rev Arb 697, at 716–720.

[277] Separately, in February 2000, the Brussels Court of Appeal followed the decision of the Paris Court of Appeal in *NOGA* (whilst basing its reasoning solely on Art. 25 of the Vienna Convention) and found the Embassy of Iraq's bank accounts to be immune from execution.

[278] See, e.g., *Fédération de Russie v BNP Paribas (Suisse) SA Compagnie NOGA d'Importation et d'Exportation SA*, Decision 5A_618/2007, Swiss Federal Supreme Court, 10 January 2008.

[279] Decision 4A_403/2008, Federal Supreme Court of Switzerland, 9 December 2008.

[280] *Commissions Import Export SA. v The Republic of the Congo*, Cass. Civ., Chambre civile 1, no. 13-17751.

the undertakings which are the subject of this letter, any immunity of jurisdiction as well as any immunity of execution'. Following an award rendered against the Congo, Commissions sought to enforce the award by seizing the bank accounts held in the name of the Congo's diplomatic mission as well as those held in the name of the Congo's delegation to UNESCO in Paris. In a marked departure from the precedent set in the *NOGA* case, the Court of Cassation held that, based on a proper interpretation of the Vienna Convention, diplomatic missions of foreign states do not enjoy an independent form of immunity and therefore the bank accounts at issue were subject to Congo's waiver in the arbitration agreement.[281]

---

[281] Ibid, at the *dispositif* section.

APPENDICES

APPENDIX A

UNCITRAL Model Law on International Commercial Arbitration 1985

(As adopted by the United Nations Commission on International Trade Law on 21 June 1985 and amended by the United Nations Commission on International Trade Law on 7 July 2006)

CHAPTER I. GENERAL PROVISIONS

Article 1. Scope of application[1]

(1) This Law applies to international commercial[2] arbitration, subject to any agreement in force between this State and any other State or States.

(2) The provisions of this Law, except articles 8, 9, 17 H, 17 I, 17 J, 35 and 36, apply only if the place of arbitration is in the territory of this State.
(Article 1(2) has been amended by the Commission at its thirty-ninth session, in 2006)

(3) An arbitration is international if:
  (a) the parties to an arbitration agreement have, at the time of the conclusion of that agreement, their places of business in different States; or
  (b) one of the following places is situated outside the State in which the parties have their places of business:
    (i) the place of arbitration if determined in, or pursuant to, the arbitration agreement;
    (ii) any place where a substantial part of the obligations of the commercial relationship is to be performed or the place with which the subject-matter of the dispute is most closely connected; or
  (c) the parties have expressly agreed that the subject matter of the arbitration agreement relates to more than one country.

(4) For the purposes of paragraph (3) of this article:
  (a) if a party has more than one place of business, the place of business is that which has the closest relationship to the arbitration agreement;
  (b) if a party does not have a place of business, reference is to be made to his habitual residence.

(5) This Law shall not affect any other law of this State by virtue of which certain disputes may not be submitted to arbitration or may be submitted to arbitration only according to provisions other than those of this Law.

---

[1] Article headings are for reference purposes only and are not to be used for purposes of interpretation.
[2] The term 'commercial' should be given a wide interpretation so as to cover matters arising from all relationships of a commercial nature, whether contractual or not. Relationships of a commercial nature include, but are not limited to, the following transactions: any trade transaction for the supply or exchange of goods or services; distribution agreement; commercial representation or agency; factoring; leasing; construction of works; consulting; engineering; licensing; investment; financing; banking; insurance; exploitation agreement or concession; joint venture and other forms of industrial or business cooperation; carriage of goods or passengers by air, sea, rail or road.

Article 2. Definitions and rules of interpretation

For the purposes of this Law:

(a) 'arbitration' means any arbitration whether or not administered by a permanent arbitral institution;

(b) 'arbitral tribunal' means a sole arbitrator or a panel of arbitrators;

(c) 'court' means a body or organ of the judicial system of a State;

(d) where a provision of this Law, except article 28, leaves the parties free to determine a certain issue, such freedom includes the right of the parties to authorize a third party, including an institution, to make that determination;

(e) where a provision of this Law refers to the fact that the parties have agreed or that they may agree or in any other way refers to an agreement of the parties, such agreement includes any arbitration rules referred to in that agreement;

(f) where a provision of this Law, other than in articles 25(a) and 32(2) (a), refers to a claim, it also applies to a counter-claim, and where it refers to a defence, it also applies to a defence to such counter-claim.

Article 2A. International origin and general principles

(As adopted by the Commission at its thirty-ninth session, in 2006)

(1) In the interpretation of this Law, regard is to be had to its international origin and to the need to promote uniformity in its application and the observance of good faith.

(2) Questions concerning matters governed by this Law which are not expressly settled in it are to be settled in conformity with the general principles on which this Law is based.

Article 3. Receipt of written communications

(1) Unless otherwise agreed by the parties:

(a) any written communication is deemed to have been received if it is delivered to the addressee personally or if it is delivered at his place of business, habitual residence or mailing address; if none of these can be found after making a reasonable inquiry, a written communication is deemed to have been received if it is sent to the addressee's last-known place of business, habitual residence or mailing address by registered letter or any other means which provides a record of the attempt to deliver it;

(b) the communication is deemed to have been received on the day it is so delivered.

(2) The provisions of this article do not apply to communications in court proceedings.

Article 4. Waiver of right to object

A party who knows that any provision of this Law from which the parties may derogate or any requirement under the arbitration agreement has not been complied with and yet proceeds with the arbitration without stating his objection to such non-compliance without undue delay or, if a time-limit is provided therefore, within such period of time, shall be deemed to have waived his right to object.

Article 5. Extent of court intervention

In matters governed by this Law, no court shall intervene except where so provided in this Law.

Article 6. Court or other authority for certain functions of arbitration assistance and supervision

The functions referred to in articles 11(3), 11(4), 13(3), 14, 16(3) and 34(2) shall be performed by ... [Each State enacting this model law specifies the court, courts or, where referred to therein, other authority competent to perform these functions.]

CHAPTER II. ARBITRATION AGREEMENT

Option I

Article 7. Definition and form of arbitration agreement

(As adopted by the Commission at its thirty-ninth session, in 2006)

(1) 'Arbitration agreement' is an agreement by the parties to submit to arbitration all or certain disputes which have arisen or which may arise between them in respect of a defined legal relationship, whether contractual or not. An arbitration agreement may be in the form of an arbitration clause in a contract or in the form of a separate agreement.

(2) The arbitration agreement shall be in writing.

(3) An arbitration agreement is in writing if its content is recorded in any form, whether or not the arbitration agreement or contract has been concluded orally, by conduct, or by other means.

(4) The requirement that an arbitration agreement be in writing is met by an electronic communication if the information contained therein is accessible so as to be useable for subsequent reference; 'electronic communication' means any communication that the parties make by means of data messages; 'data message' means information generated, sent, received or stored by electronic, magnetic, optical or similar means, including, but not limited to, electronic data interchange (EDI), electronic mail, telegram, telex or telecopy.

(5) Furthermore, an arbitration agreement is in writing if it is contained in an exchange of statements of claim and defence in which the existence of an agreement is alleged by one party and not denied by the other.

(6) The reference in a contract to any document containing an arbitration clause constitutes an arbitration agreement in writing, provided that the reference is such as to make that clause part of the contract.

Option II

Article 7. Definition of arbitration agreement

(As adopted by the Commission at its thirty-ninth session, in 2006)

'Arbitration agreement' is an agreement by the parties to submit to arbitration all or certain disputes which have arisen or which may arise between them in respect of a defined legal relationship, whether contractual or not.

Article 8. Arbitration agreement and substantive claim before court

(1) A court before which an action is brought in a matter which is the subject of an arbitration agreement shall, if a party so requests not later than when submitting his first statement on the substance of the dispute, refer the parties to arbitration unless it finds that the agreement is null and void, inoperative or incapable of being performed.

(2) Where an action referred to in paragraph (1) of this article has been brought, arbitral proceedings may nevertheless be commenced or continued, and an award may be made, while the issue is pending before the court.

Article 9. Arbitration agreement and interim measures by court

It is not incompatible with an arbitration agreement for a party to request, before or during arbitral proceedings, from a court an interim measure of protection and for a court to grant such measure.

CHAPTER III. COMPOSITION OF ARBITRAL TRIBUNAL

Article 10. Number of arbitrators

(1) The parties are free to determine the number of arbitrators.
(2) Failing such determination, the number of arbitrators shall be three.

Article 11. Appointment of arbitrators

(1) No person shall be precluded by reason of his nationality from acting as an arbitrator, unless otherwise agreed by the parties.
(2) The parties are free to agree on a procedure of appointing the arbitrator or arbitrators, subject to the provisions of paragraphs (4) and (5) of this article.
(3) Failing such agreement,
  (a) in an arbitration with three arbitrators, each party shall appoint one arbitrator, and the two arbitrators thus appointed shall appoint the third arbitrator; if a party fails to appoint the arbitrator within thirty days of receipt of a request to do so from the other party, or if the two arbitrators fail to agree on the third arbitrator within thirty days of their appointment, the appointment shall be made, upon request of a party, by the court or other authority specified in article 6;
  (b) in an arbitration with a sole arbitrator, if the parties are unable to agree on the arbitrator, he shall be appointed, upon request of a party, by the court or other authority specified in article 6.
(4) Where, under an appointment procedure agreed upon by the parties,
  (a) a party fails to act as required under such procedure, or
  (b) the parties, or two arbitrators, are unable to reach an agreement expected of them under such procedure, or
  (c) a third party, including an institution, fails to perform any function entrusted to it under such procedure, any party may request the court or other authority specified in article 6 to take the necessary measure, unless the agreement on the appointment procedure provides other means for securing the appointment.
(5) A decision on a matter entrusted by paragraph (3) or (4) of this article to the court or other authority specified in article 6 shall be subject to no appeal. The court or other authority, in appointing an arbitrator, shall have due regard to any qualifications required of the arbitrator by the agreement of the parties and to such considerations as are likely to secure the appointment of an independent and impartial arbitrator and, in the case of a sole or third arbitrator, shall take into account as well the advisability of appointing an arbitrator of a nationality other than those of the parties.

Article 12. Grounds for challenge

(1) When a person is approached in connection with his possible appointment as an arbitrator, he shall disclose any circumstances likely to give rise to justifiable doubts as to his impartiality or independence. An arbitrator, from the time of his appointment and throughout the arbitral proceedings, shall without delay disclose any such circumstances to the parties unless they have already been informed of them by him.

(2) An arbitrator may be challenged only if circumstances exist that give rise to justifiable doubts as to his impartiality or independence, or if he does not possess qualifications agreed to by the parties. A party may challenge an arbitrator appointed by him, or in whose appointment he has participated, only for reasons of which he becomes aware after the appointment has been made.

Article 13. Challenge procedure

(1) The parties are free to agree on a procedure for challenging an arbitrator, subject to the provisions of paragraph (3) of this article.

(2) Failing such agreement, a party who intends to challenge an arbitrator shall, within fifteen days after becoming aware of the constitution of the arbitral tribunal or after becoming aware of any circumstance referred to in article 12(2), send a written statement of the reasons for the challenge to the arbitral tribunal. Unless the challenged arbitrator withdraws from his office or the other party agrees to the challenge, the arbitral tribunal shall decide on the challenge.

(3) If a challenge under any procedure agreed upon by the parties or under the procedure of paragraph (2) of this article is not successful, the challenging party may request, within thirty days after having received notice of the decision rejecting the challenge, the court or other authority specified in article 6 to decide on the challenge, which decision shall be subject to no appeal; while such a request is pending, the arbitral tribunal, including the challenged arbitrator, may continue the arbitral proceedings and make an award.

Article 14. Failure or impossibility to act

(1) If an arbitrator becomes *de jure* or *de facto* unable to perform his functions or for other reasons fails to act without undue delay, his mandate terminates if he withdraws from his office or if the parties agree on the termination. Otherwise, if a controversy remains concerning any of these grounds, any party may request the court or other authority specified in article 6 to decide on the termination of the mandate, which decision shall be subject to no appeal.

(2) If, under this article or article 13(2), an arbitrator withdraws from his office or a party agrees to the termination of the mandate of an arbitrator, this does not imply acceptance of the validity of any ground referred to in this article or article 12(2).

Article 15. Appointment of substitute arbitrator

Where the mandate of an arbitrator terminates under article 13 or 14 or because of his withdrawal from office for any other reason or because of the revocation of his mandate by agreement of the parties or in any other case of termination of his mandate, a substitute arbitrator shall be appointed according to the rules that were applicable to the appointment of the arbitrator being replaced.

CHAPTER IV. JURISDICTION OF ARBITRAL TRIBUNAL

Article 16. Competence of arbitral tribunal to rule on its jurisdiction

(1) The arbitral tribunal may rule on its own jurisdiction, including any objections with respect to the existence or validity of the arbitration agreement. For that purpose, an arbitration clause which forms part of a contract shall be treated as an agreement independent of the other terms of the contract. A decision by the arbitral tribunal that the contract is null and void shall not entail *ipso jure* the invalidity of the arbitration clause.

(2) A plea that the arbitral tribunal does not have jurisdiction shall be raised not later than the submission of the statement of defence. A party is not precluded from raising such a plea by the fact that he has appointed, or participated in the appointment of, an arbitrator. A plea that the arbitral tribunal is exceeding the scope of its authority shall be raised as soon as the matter alleged to be beyond the scope of its authority is raised during the arbitral proceedings. The arbitral tribunal may, in either case, admit a later plea if it considers the delay justified.

(3) The arbitral tribunal may rule on a plea referred to in paragraph (2) of this article either as a preliminary question or in an award on the merits. If the arbitral tribunal rules as a preliminary question that it has jurisdiction, any party may request, within thirty days after having received notice of that ruling, the court specified in article 6 to decide the matter, which decision shall be subject to no appeal; while such a request is pending, the arbitral tribunal may continue the arbitral proceedings and make an award.

CHAPTER IV A. INTERIM MEASURES AND PRELIMINARY ORDERS

(As adopted by the Commission at its thirty-ninth session, in 2006)

Section 1. Interim measures

Article 17. Power of arbitral tribunal to order interim measures

(1) Unless otherwise agreed by the parties, the arbitral tribunal may, at the request of a party, grant interim measures.

(2) An interim measure is any temporary measure, whether in the form of an award or in another form, by which, at any time prior to the issuance of the award by which the dispute is finally decided, the arbitral tribunal orders a party to:

  (a) Maintain or restore the status quo pending determination of the dispute;

  (b) Take action that would prevent, or refrain from taking action that is likely to cause, current or imminent harm or prejudice to the arbitral process itself;

  (c) Provide a means of preserving assets out of which a subsequent award may be satisfied; or

  (d) Preserve evidence that may be relevant and material to the resolution of the dispute.

Article 17A. Conditions for granting interim measures

(1) The party requesting an interim measure under article 17(2)*(a)*, *(b)* and *(c)* shall satisfy the arbitral tribunal that:

  (a) Harm not adequately reparable by an award of damages is likely to result if the measure is not ordered, and such harm substantially outweighs the harm that is likely to result to the party against whom the measure is directed if the measure is granted; and

(b) There is a reasonable possibility that the requesting party will succeed on the merits of the claim. The determination on this possibility shall not affect the discretion of the arbitral tribunal in making any subsequent determination.

(2) With regard to a request for an interim measure under article 17(2)(d), the requirements in paragraphs (1)(a) and (b) of this article shall apply only to the extent the arbitral tribunal considers appropriate.

Section 2. Preliminary orders

Article 17B. Applications for preliminary orders and conditions for granting preliminary orders

(1) Unless otherwise agreed by the parties, a party may, without notice to any other party, make a request for an interim measure together with an application for a preliminary order directing a party not to frustrate the purpose of the interim measure requested.

(2) The arbitral tribunal may grant a preliminary order provided it considers that prior disclosure of the request for the interim measure to the party against whom it is directed risks frustrating the purpose of the measure.

(3) The conditions defined under article 17A apply to any preliminary order, provided that the harm to be assessed under article 17A(1)(a), is the harm likely to result from the order being granted or not.

Article 17C. Specific regime for preliminary orders

(1) Immediately after the arbitral tribunal has made a determination in respect of an application for a preliminary order, the arbitral tribunal shall give notice to all parties of the request for the interim measure, the application for the preliminary order, the preliminary order, if any, and all other communications, including by indicating the content of any oral communication, between any party and the arbitral tribunal in relation thereto.

(2) At the same time, the arbitral tribunal shall give an opportunity to any party against whom a preliminary order is directed to present its case at the earliest practicable time.

(3) The arbitral tribunal shall decide promptly on any objection to the preliminary order.

(4) A preliminary order shall expire after twenty days from the date on which it was issued by the arbitral tribunal. However, the arbitral tribunal may issue an interim measure adopting or modifying the preliminary order, after the party against whom the preliminary order is directed has been given notice and an opportunity to present its case.

(5) A preliminary order shall be binding on the parties but shall not be subject to enforcement by a court. Such a preliminary order does not constitute an award.

Section 3. Provisions applicable to interim measures and preliminary orders

Article 17D. Modification, suspension, termination

The arbitral tribunal may modify, suspend or terminate an interim measure or a preliminary order it has granted, upon application of any party or, in exceptional circumstances and upon prior notice to the parties, on the arbitral tribunal's own initiative.

Article 17E. Provision of security

(1) The arbitral tribunal may require the party requesting an interim measure to provide appropriate security in connection with the measure.
(2) The arbitral tribunal shall require the party applying for a preliminary order to provide security in connection with the order unless the arbitral tribunal considers it inappropriate or unnecessary to do so.

Article 17F. Disclosure

(1) The arbitral tribunal may require any party promptly to disclose any material change in the circumstances on the basis of which the measure was requested or granted.
(2) The party applying for a preliminary order shall disclose to the arbitral tribunal all circumstances that are likely to be relevant to the arbitral tribunal's determination whether to grant or maintain the order, and such obligation shall continue until the party against whom the order has been requested has had an opportunity to present its case. Thereafter, paragraph (1) of this article shall apply.

Article 17G. Costs and damages

The party requesting an interim measure or applying for a preliminary order shall be liable for any costs and damages caused by the measure or the order to any party if the arbitral tribunal later determines that, in the circumstances, the measure or the order should not have been granted. The arbitral tribunal may award such costs and damages at any point during the proceedings.

Section 4. Recognition and enforcement of interim measures

Article 17H. Recognition and enforcement

(1) An interim measure issued by an arbitral tribunal shall be recognized as binding and, unless otherwise provided by the arbitral tribunal, enforced upon application to the competent court, irrespective of the country in which it was issued, subject to the provisions of article 17 I.
(2) The party who is seeking or has obtained recognition or enforcement of an interim measure shall promptly inform the court of any termination, suspension or modification of that interim measure.
(3) The court of the State where recognition or enforcement is sought may, if it considers it proper, order the requesting party to provide appropriate security if the arbitral tribunal has not already made a determination with respect to security or where such a decision is necessary to protect the rights of third parties.

Article 17I. Grounds for refusing recognition or enforcement[3]

(1) Recognition or enforcement of an interim measure may be refused only:
   (a) At the request of the party against whom it is invoked if the court is satisfied that:

---

[3] The conditions set forth in article 17I are intended to limit the number of circumstances in which the court may refuse to enforce an interim measure. It would not be contrary to the level of harmonization sought to be achieved by these model provisions if a State were to adopt fewer circumstances in which enforcement may be refused.

(i) Such refusal is warranted on the grounds set forth in article 36(1)(*a*)(i), (ii), (iii) or (iv); or

(ii) The arbitral tribunal's decision with respect to the provision of security in connection with the interim measure issued by the arbitral tribunal has not been complied with; or

(iii) The interim measure has been terminated or suspended by the arbitral tribunal or, where so empowered, by the court of the State in which the arbitration takes place or under the law of which that interim measure was granted; or

(*b*) If the court finds that:

(i) The interim measure is incompatible with the powers conferred upon the court unless the court decides to reformulate the interim measure to the extent necessary to adapt it to its own powers and procedures for the purposes of enforcing that interim measure and without modifying its substance; or

(ii) Any of the grounds set forth in article 36(1)(*b*)(i) or (ii), apply to the recognition and enforcement of the interim measure.

(2) Any determination made by the court on any ground in paragraph (1) of this article shall be effective only for the purposes of the application to recognize and enforce the interim measure. The court where recognition or enforcement is sought shall not, in making that determination, undertake a review of the substance of the interim measure.

Section 5. Court-ordered interim measures

Article 17J. Court-ordered interim measures

A court shall have the same power of issuing an interim measure in relation to arbitration proceedings, irrespective of whether their place is in the territory of this State, as it has in relation to proceedings in courts. The court shall exercise such power in accordance with its own procedures in consideration of the specific features of international arbitration.

CHAPTER V. CONDUCT OF ARBITRAL PROCEEDINGS

Article 18. Equal treatment of parties

The parties shall be treated with equality and each party shall be given a full opportunity of presenting his case.

Article 19. Determination of rules of procedure

(1) Subject to the provisions of this Law, the parties are free to agree on the procedure to be followed by the arbitral tribunal in conducting the proceedings.

(2) Failing such agreement, the arbitral tribunal may, subject to the provisions of this Law, conduct the arbitration in such manner as it considers appropriate. The power conferred upon the arbitral tribunal includes the power to determine the admissibility, relevance, materiality and weight of any evidence.

Article 20. Place of arbitration

(1) The parties are free to agree on the place of arbitration. Failing such agreement, the place of arbitration shall be determined by the arbitral tribunal having regard to the circumstances of the case, including the convenience of the parties.

(2) Notwithstanding the provisions of paragraph (1) of this article, the arbitral tribunal may, unless otherwise agreed by the parties, meet at any place it considers appropriate for consultation among its members, for hearing witnesses, experts or the parties, or for inspection of goods, other property or documents.

Article 21. Commencement of arbitral proceedings

Unless otherwise agreed by the parties, the arbitral proceedings in respect of a particular dispute commence on the date on which a request for that dispute to be referred to arbitration is received by the respondent.

Article 22. Language

(1) The parties are free to agree on the language or languages to be used in the arbitral proceedings. Failing such agreement, the arbitral tribunal shall determine the language or languages to be used in the proceedings. This agreement or determination, unless otherwise specified therein, shall apply to any written statement by a party, any hearing and any award, decision or other communication by the arbitral tribunal.

(2) The arbitral tribunal may order that any documentary evidence shall be accompanied by a translation into the language or languages agreed upon by the parties or determined by the arbitral tribunal.

Article 23. Statements of claim and defence

(1) Within the period of time agreed by the parties or determined by the arbitral tribunal, the claimant shall state the facts supporting his claim, the points at issue and the relief or remedy sought, and the respondent shall state his defence in respect of these particulars, unless the parties have otherwise agreed as to the required elements of such statements. The parties may submit with their statements all documents they consider to be relevant or may add a reference to the documents or other evidence they will submit.

(2) Unless otherwise agreed by the parties, either party may amend or supplement his claim or defence during the course of the arbitral proceedings, unless the arbitral tribunal considers it inappropriate to allow such amendment having regard to the delay in making it.

Article 24. Hearings and written proceedings

(1) Subject to any contrary agreement by the parties, the arbitral tribunal shall decide whether to hold oral hearings for the presentation of evidence or for oral argument, or whether the proceedings shall be conducted on the basis of documents and other materials. However, unless the parties have agreed that no hearings shall be held, the arbitral tribunal shall hold such hearings at an appropriate stage of the proceedings, if so requested by a party.

(2) The parties shall be given sufficient advance notice of any hearing and of any meeting of the arbitral tribunal for the purposes of inspection of goods, other property or documents.

(3) All statements, documents or other information supplied to the arbitral tribunal by one party shall be communicated to the other party. Also any expert report or evidentiary document on which the arbitral tribunal may rely in making its decision shall be communicated to the parties.

Article 25. Default of a party

Unless otherwise agreed by the parties, if, without showing sufficient cause,

(*a*) the claimant fails to communicate his statement of claim in accordance with article 23(1), the arbitral tribunal shall terminate the proceedings;

(*b*) the respondent fails to communicate his statement of defence in accordance with article 23(1), the arbitral tribunal shall continue the proceedings without treating such failure in itself as an admission of the claimant's allegations;

(*c*) any party fails to appear at a hearing or to produce documentary evidence, the arbitral tribunal may continue the proceedings and make the award on the evidence before it.

Article 26. Expert appointed by arbitral tribunal

(1) Unless otherwise agreed by the parties, the arbitral tribunal
  (*a*) may appoint one or more experts to report to it on specific issues to be determined by the arbitral tribunal;
  (*b*) may require a party to give the expert any relevant information or to produce, or to provide access to, any relevant documents, goods or other property for his inspection.
(2) Unless otherwise agreed by the parties, if a party so requests or if the arbitral tribunal considers it necessary, the expert shall, after delivery of his written or oral report, participate in a hearing where the parties have the opportunity to put questions to him and to present expert witnesses in order to testify on the points at issue.

Article 27. Court assistance in taking evidence

The arbitral tribunal or a party with the approval of the arbitral tribunal may request from a competent court of this State assistance in taking evidence.

The court may execute the request within its competence and according to its rules on taking evidence.

CHAPTER VI. MAKING OF AWARD AND TERMINATION OF PROCEEDINGS

Article 28. Rules applicable to substance of dispute

(1) The arbitral tribunal shall decide the dispute in accordance with such rules of law as are chosen by the parties as applicable to the substance of the dispute. Any designation of the law or legal system of a given State shall be construed, unless otherwise expressed, as directly referring to the substantive law of that State and not to its conflict of laws rules.
(2) Failing any designation by the parties, the arbitral tribunal shall apply the law determined by the conflict of laws rules which it considers applicable.
(3) The arbitral tribunal shall decide *ex aequo et bono* or as *amiable compositeur* only if the parties have expressly authorized it to do so.
(4) In all cases, the arbitral tribunal shall decide in accordance with the terms of the contract and shall take into account the usages of the trade applicable to the transaction.

Article 29. Decision-making by panel of arbitrators

In arbitral proceedings with more than one arbitrator, any decision of the arbitral tribunal shall be made, unless otherwise agreed by the parties, by a majority of all its members. However, questions of procedure may be decided by a presiding arbitrator, if so authorized by the parties or all members of the arbitral tribunal.

Article 30. Settlement

(1) If, during arbitral proceedings, the parties settle the dispute, the arbitral tribunal shall terminate the proceedings and, if requested by the parties and not objected to by the arbitral tribunal, record the settlement in the form of an arbitral award on agreed terms.

(2) An award on agreed terms shall be made in accordance with the provisions of article 31 and shall state that it is an award. Such an award has the same status and effect as any other award on the merits of the case.

Article 31. Form and contents of award

(1) The award shall be made in writing and shall be signed by the arbitrator or arbitrators. In arbitral proceedings with more than one arbitrator, the signatures of the majority of all members of the arbitral tribunal shall suffice, provided that the reason for any omitted signature is stated.

(2) The award shall state the reasons upon which it is based, unless the parties have agreed that no reasons are to be given or the award is an award on agreed terms under article 30.

(3) The award shall state its date and the place of arbitration as determined in accordance with article 20(1). The award shall be deemed to have been made at that place.

(4) After the award is made, a copy signed by the arbitrators in accordance with paragraph (1) of this article shall be delivered to each party.

Article 32. Termination of proceedings

(1) The arbitral proceedings are terminated by the final award or by an order of the arbitral tribunal in accordance with paragraph (2) of this article.

(2) The arbitral tribunal shall issue an order for the termination of the arbitral proceedings when:
   (a) the claimant withdraws his claim, unless the respondent objects thereto and the arbitral tribunal recognizes a legitimate interest on his part in obtaining a final settlement of the dispute;
   (b) the parties agree on the termination of the proceedings;
   (c) the arbitral tribunal finds that the continuation of the proceedings has for any other reason become unnecessary or impossible.

(3) The mandate of the arbitral tribunal terminates with the termination of the arbitral proceedings, subject to the provisions of articles 33 and 34(4).

Article 33. Correction and interpretation of award; additional award

(1) Within thirty days of receipt of the award, unless another period of time has been agreed upon by the parties:
   (a) a party, with notice to the other party, may request the arbitral tribunal to correct in the award any errors in computation, any clerical or typographical errors or any errors of similar nature;

(b) if so agreed by the parties, a party, with notice to the other party, may request the arbitral tribunal to give an interpretation of a specific point or part of the award.

If the arbitral tribunal considers the request to be justified, it shall make the correction or give the interpretation within thirty days of receipt of the request. The interpretation shall form part of the award.

(2) The arbitral tribunal may correct any error of the type referred to in paragraph (1)(a) of this article on its own initiative within thirty days of the date of the award.

(3) Unless otherwise agreed by the parties, a party, with notice to the other party, may request, within thirty days of receipt of the award, the arbitral tribunal to make an additional award as to claims presented in the arbitral proceedings but omitted from the award. If the arbitral tribunal considers the request to be justified, it shall make the additional award within sixty days.

(4) The arbitral tribunal may extend, if necessary, the period of time within which it shall make a correction, interpretation or an additional award under paragraph (1) or (3) of this article.

(5) The provisions of article 31 shall apply to a correction or interpretation of the award or to an additional award.

CHAPTER VII. RECOURSE AGAINST AWARD

Article 34. Application for setting aside as exclusive recourse against arbitral award

(1) Recourse to a court against an arbitral award may be made only by an application for setting aside in accordance with paragraphs (2) and (3) of this article.

(2) An arbitral award may be set aside by the court specified in article 6 only if:

(a) the party making the application furnishes proof that:

(i) a party to the arbitration agreement referred to in article 7 was under some incapacity; or the said agreement is not valid under the law to which the parties have subjected it or, failing any indication thereon, under the law of this State; or

(ii) the party making the application was not given proper notice of the appointment of an arbitrator or of the arbitral proceedings or was otherwise unable to present his case; or

(iii) the award deals with a dispute not contemplated by or not falling within the terms of the submission to arbitration, or contains decisions on matters beyond the scope of the submission to arbitration, provided that, if the decisions on matters submitted to arbitration can be separated from those not so submitted, only that part of the award which contains decisions on matters not submitted to arbitration may be set aside; or

(iv) the composition of the arbitral tribunal or the arbitral procedure was not in accordance with the agreement of the parties, unless such agreement was in conflict with a provision of this Law from which the parties cannot derogate, or, failing such agreement, was not in accordance with this Law; or

(b) the court finds that:

(i) the subject-matter of the dispute is not capable of settlement by arbitration under the law of this State; or

(ii) the award is in conflict with the public policy of this State.

(3) An application for setting aside may not be made after three months have elapsed from the date on which the party making that application had received the award or, if a request had been made under article 33, from the date on which that request had been disposed of by the arbitral tribunal.

(4) The court, when asked to set aside an award, may, where appropriate and so requested by a party, suspend the setting aside proceedings for a period of time determined by it in order to give the arbitral tribunal an opportunity to resume the arbitral proceedings or to take such other action as in the arbitral tribunal's opinion will eliminate the grounds for setting aside.

CHAPTER VIII. RECOGNITION AND ENFORCEMENT OF AWARDS

Article 35. Recognition and enforcement

(1) An arbitral award, irrespective of the country in which it was made, shall be recognized as binding and, upon application in writing to the competent court, shall be enforced subject to the provisions of this article and of article 36.

(2) The party relying on an award or applying for its enforcement shall supply the original award or a copy thereof. If the award is not made in an official language of this State, the court may request the party to supply a translation thereof into such language.[4]

(Article 35(2) has been amended by the Commission at its thirty-ninth session, in 2006)

Article 36. Grounds for refusing recognition or enforcement

(1) Recognition or enforcement of an arbitral award, irrespective of the country in which it was made, may be refused only:

    (a) at the request of the party against whom it is invoked, if that party furnishes to the competent court where recognition or enforcement is sought proof that:

        (i) a party to the arbitration agreement referred to in article 7 was under some incapacity; or the said agreement is not valid under the law to which the parties have subjected it or, failing any indication thereon, under the law of the country where the award was made; or

        (ii) the party against whom the award is invoked was not given proper notice of the appointment of an arbitrator or of the arbitral proceedings or was otherwise unable to present his case; or

        (iii) the award deals with a dispute not contemplated by or not falling within the terms of the submission to arbitration, or it contains decisions on matters beyond the scope of the submission to arbitration, provided that, if the decisions on matters submitted to arbitration can be separated from those not so submitted, that part of the award which contains decisions on matters submitted to arbitration may be recognized and enforced; or

        (iv) the composition of the arbitral tribunal or the arbitral procedure was not in accordance with the agreement of the parties or, failing such agreement, was not in accordance with the law of the country where the arbitration took place; or

        (v) the award has not yet become binding on the parties or has been set aside or suspended by a court of the country in which, or under the law of which, that award was made; or

    (b) if the court finds that:

        (i) the subject-matter of the dispute is not capable of settlement by arbitration under the law of this State; or

        (ii) the recognition or enforcement of the award would be contrary to the public policy of this State.

(2) If an application for setting aside or suspension of an award has been made to a court referred to in paragraph (1)(a)(v) of this article, the court where recognition or enforcement is sought may, if it considers it proper, adjourn its decision and may also, on the application of the party claiming recognition or enforcement of the award, order the other party to provide appropriate security.

---

[4] The conditions set forth in this paragraph are intended to set maximum standards. It would, thus, not be contrary to the harmonization to be achieved by the model law if a State retained even less onerous conditions.

New York Convention on the Recognition and Enforcement of Foreign Arbitral Awards 1958

Article I

1. This Convention shall apply to the recognition and enforcement of arbitral awards made in the territory of a State other than the State where the recognition and enforcement of such awards are sought, and arising out of differences between persons, whether physical or legal. It shall also apply to arbitral awards not considered as domestic awards in the State where their recognition and enforcement are sought.
2. The term 'arbitral awards' shall include not only awards made by arbitrators appointed for each case but also those made by permanent arbitral bodies to which the parties have submitted.
3. When signing, ratifying or acceding to this Convention, or notifying extension under article X hereof, any State may on the basis of reciprocity declare that it will apply the Convention to the recognition and enforcement of awards made only in the territory of another Contracting State. It may also declare that it will apply the Convention only to differences arising out of legal relationships, whether contractual or not, which are considered as commercial under the national law of the State making such declaration.

Article II

1. Each Contracting State shall recognize an agreement in writing under which the parties undertake to submit to arbitration all or any differences which have arisen or which may arise between them in respect of a defined legal relationship, whether contractual or not, concerning a subject matter capable of settlement by arbitration.
2. The term 'agreement in writing' shall include an arbitral clause in a contract or an arbitration agreement, signed by the parties or contained in an exchange of letters or telegrams.
3. The court of a Contracting State, when seized of an action in a matter in respect of which the parties have made an agreement within the meaning of this article, shall, at the request of one of the parties, refer the parties to arbitration, unless it finds that the said agreement is null and void, inoperative or incapable of being performed.

Article III

Each Contracting State shall recognize arbitral awards as binding and enforce them in accordance with the rules of procedure of the territory where the award is relied upon, under the conditions laid down in the following articles. There shall not be imposed substantially more onerous conditions or higher fees or charges on the recognition or enforcement of arbitral awards to which this Convention applies than are imposed on the recognition or enforcement of domestic arbitral awards.

Article IV

1. To obtain the recognition and enforcement mentioned in the preceding article, the party applying for recognition and enforcement shall, at the time of the application, supply:
   (a) The duly authenticated original award or a duly certified copy thereof;
   (b) The original agreement referred to in article II or a duly certified copy thereof.
2. If the said award or agreement is not made in an official language of the country in which the award is relied upon, the party applying for recognition and enforcement of the award shall produce a translation of these documents into such language. The translation shall be certified by an official or sworn translator or by a diplomatic or consular agent.

Article V

1. Recognition and enforcement of the award may be refused, at the request of the party against whom it is invoked, only if that party furnishes to the competent authority where the recognition and enforcement is sought, proof that:
   (a) The parties to the agreement referred to in article II were, under the law applicable to them, under some incapacity, or the said agreement is not valid under the law to which the parties have subjected it or, failing any indication thereon, under the law of the country where the award was made; or
   (b) The party against whom the award is invoked was not given proper notice of the appointment of the arbitrator or of the arbitration proceedings or was otherwise unable to present his case; or
   (c) The award deals with a difference not contemplated by or not falling within the terms of the submission to arbitration, or it contains decisions on matters beyond the scope of the submission to arbitration, provided that, if the decisions on matters submitted to arbitration can be separated from those not so submitted, that part of the award which contains decisions on matters submitted to arbitration may be recognized and enforced; or
   (d) The composition of the arbitral authority or the arbitral procedure was not in accordance with the agreement of the parties, or, failing such agreement, was not in accordance with the law of the country where the arbitration took place; or
   (e) The award has not yet become binding on the parties, or has been set aside or suspended by a competent authority of the country in which, or under the law of which, that award was made.
2. Recognition and enforcement of an arbitral award may also be refused if the competent authority in the country where recognition and enforcement is sought finds that:
   (a) The subject matter of the difference is not capable of settlement by arbitration under the law of that country; or
   (b) The recognition or enforcement of the award would be contrary to the public policy of that country.

Article VI

If an application for the setting aside or suspension of the award has been made to a competent authority referred to in article V (1) *(e)*, the authority before which the award is sought to be relied upon may, if it considers it proper, adjourn the decision on the enforcement of the award and may also, on the application of the party claiming enforcement of the award, order the other party to give suitable security.

Article VII

1. The provisions of the present Convention shall not affect the validity of multilateral or bilateral agreements concerning the recognition and enforcement of arbitral awards entered into by the Contracting States nor deprive any interested party of any right he may have to avail himself of an arbitral award in the manner and to the extent allowed by the law or the treaties of the country where such award is sought to be relied upon.
2. The Geneva Protocol on Arbitration Clauses of 1923 and the Geneva Convention on the Execution of Foreign Arbitral Awards of 1927 shall cease to have effect between Contracting States on their becoming bound and to the extent that they become bound, by this Convention.

Article VIII

1. This Convention shall be open until 31 December 1958 for signature on behalf of any Member of the United Nations and also on behalf of any other State which is or hereafter becomes a member of any specialized agency of the United Nations, or which is or hereafter becomes a party to the Statute of the International Court of Justice, or any other State to which an invitation has been addressed by the General Assembly of the United Nations.
2. This Convention shall be ratified and the instrument of ratification shall be deposited with the Secretary-General of the United Nations.

Article IX

1. This Convention shall be open for accession to all States referred to in article VIII.
2. Accession shall be effected by the deposit of an instrument of accession with the Secretary-General of the United Nations.

Article X

1. Any State may, at the time of signature, ratification or accession, declare that this Convention shall extend to all or any of the territories for the international relations of which it is responsible. Such a declaration shall take effect when the Convention enters into force for the State concerned.
2. At any time thereafter any such extension shall be made by notification addressed to the Secretary-General of the United Nations and shall take effect as from the ninetieth day after the day of receipt by the Secretary-General of the United Nations of this notification, or as from the date of entry into force of the Convention for the State concerned, whichever is the later.
3. With respect to those territories to which this Convention is not extended at the time of signature, ratification or accession, each State concerned shall consider the possibility of taking the necessary steps in order to extend the application of this Convention to such territories, subject, where necessary for constitutional reasons, to the consent of the Governments of such territories.

Article XI

In the case of a federal or non-unitary State, the following provisions shall apply:

(a) With respect to those articles of this Convention that come within the legislative jurisdiction of the federal authority, the obligations of the federal Government shall to this extent be the same as those of Contracting States which are not federal States;

(b) With respect to those articles of this Convention that come within the legislative jurisdiction of constituent states or provinces which are not, under the constitutional system of the federation, bound to take legislative action, the federal Government shall bring such articles with a favourable recommendation to the notice of the appropriate authorities of constituent states or provinces at the earliest possible moment;

(c) A federal State Party to this Convention shall, at the request of any other Contracting State transmitted through the Secretary-General of the United Nations, supply a statement of the law and practice of the federation and its constituent units in regard to any particular provision of this Convention, showing the extent to which effect has been given to that provision by legislative or other action.

Article XII

1. This Convention shall come into force on the ninetieth day following the date of deposit of the third instrument of ratification or accession.
2. For each State ratifying or acceding to this Convention after the deposit of the third instrument of ratification or accession, this Convention shall enter into force on the ninetieth day after deposit by such State of its instrument of ratification or accession.

Article XIII

1. Any Contracting State may denounce this Convention by a written notification to the Secretary-General of the United Nations. Denunciation shall take effect one year after the date of receipt of the notification by the Secretary-General.
2. Any State which has made a declaration or notification under article X may, at any time thereafter, by notification to the Secretary-General of the United Nations, declare that this Convention shall cease to extend to the territory concerned one year after the date of the receipt of the notification by the Secretary-General.
3. This Convention shall continue to be applicable to arbitral awards in respect of which recognition or enforcement proceedings have been instituted before the denunciation takes effect.

Article XIV

A Contracting State shall not be entitled to avail itself of the present Convention against other Contracting States except to the extent that it is itself bound to apply the Convention.

Article XV

The Secretary-General of the United Nations shall notify the States contemplated in article VIII of the following:

(a) Signatures and ratifications in accordance with article VIII;
(b) Accessions in accordance with article IX;
(c) Declarations and notifications under articles I, X and XI;
(d) The date upon which this Convention enters into force in accordance with article XII;
(e) Denunciations and notifications in accordance with article XIII.

Article XVI

1. This Convention, of which the Chinese, English, French, Russian and Spanish texts shall be equally authentic, shall be deposited in the archives of the United Nations.
2. The Secretary-General of the United Nations shall transmit a certified copy of this Convention to the States contemplated in article VIII.

ANNEX II

Recommendation regarding the interpretation of article II, paragraph 2, and article VII, paragraph 1, of the Convention on the Recognition and Enforcement of Foreign Arbitral Awards, done in New York, 10 June 1958, adopted by the United Nations Commission on International Trade Law on 7 July 2006 at its thirty-ninth session

The United Nations Commission on International Trade Law,
[...]

1. *Recommends* that article II, paragraph 2, of the Convention on the Recognition and Enforcement of Foreign Arbitral Awards, done in New York, 10 June 1958, be applied recognizing that the circumstances described therein are not exhaustive;
2. *Recommends also* that article VII, paragraph 1, of the Convention on the Recognition and Enforcement of Foreign Arbitral Awards, done in New York, 10 June 1958, should be applied to allow any interested party to avail itself of rights it may *have*, under the law or treaties of the country where an arbitration agreement is sought to be relied upon, to seek recognition of the validity of such an arbitration agreement.

Convention on the Settlement of Investment Disputes between States and Nationals of Other States 1965 ('Washington Convention') (excerpts)

CHAPTER I. INTERNATIONAL CENTRE FOR SETTLEMENT OF INVESTMENT DISPUTES

[…]

Section 4 The Panels

[…]

Article 14

(1) Persons designated to serve on the Panels shall be persons of high moral character and recognized competence in the fields of law, commerce, industry or finance, who may be relied upon to exercise independent judgment. Competence in the field of law shall be of particular importance in the case of persons on the Panel of Arbitrators.
(2) The Chairman, in designating persons to serve on the Panels, shall in addition pay due regard to the importance of assuring representation on the Panels of the principal legal systems of the world and of the main forms of economic activity.

[…]

CHAPTER II. JURISDICTION OF THE CENTRE

Article 25

(1) The jurisdiction of the Centre shall extend to any legal dispute arising directly out of an investment, between a Contracting State (or any constituent subdivision or agency of a Contracting State designated to the Centre by that State) and a national of another Contracting State, which the parties to the dispute consent in writing to submit to the Centre. When the parties have given their consent, no party may withdraw its consent unilaterally.
(2) 'National of another Contracting State' means:
   (a) any natural person who had the nationality of a Contracting State other than the State party to the dispute on the date on which the parties consented to submit such dispute to conciliation or arbitration as well as on the date on which the request was registered pursuant to paragraph (3) of Article 28 or paragraph (3) of Article 36, but does not include any person who on either date also had the nationality of the Contracting State party to the dispute; and
   (b) any juridical person which had the nationality of a Contracting State other than the State party to the dispute on the date on which the parties consented to submit such dispute to conciliation or arbitration and any juridical person which had the nationality of the Contracting

State party to the dispute on that date and which, because of foreign control, the parties have agreed should be treated as a national of another Contracting State for the purposes of this Convention.

(3) Consent by a constituent subdivision or agency of a Contracting State shall require the approval of that State unless that State notifies the Centre that no such approval is required.

(4) Any Contracting State may, at the time of ratification, acceptance or approval of this Convention or at any time thereafter, notify the Centre of the class or classes of disputes which it would or would not consider submitting to the jurisdiction of the Centre. The Secretary-General shall forthwith transmit such notification to all Contracting States. Such notification shall not constitute the consent required by paragraph (1).

Article 26

Consent of the parties to arbitration under this Convention shall, unless otherwise stated, be deemed consent to such arbitration to the exclusion of any other remedy. A Contracting State may require the exhaustion of local administrative or judicial remedies as a condition of its consent to arbitration under this Convention.

Article 27

(1) No Contracting State shall give diplomatic protection, or bring an international claim, in respect of a dispute which one of its nationals and another Contracting State shall have consented to submit or shall have submitted to arbitration under this Convention, unless such other Contracting State shall have failed to abide by and comply with the award rendered in such dispute.

(2) Diplomatic protection, for the purposes of paragraph (1), shall not include informal diplomatic exchanges for the sole purpose of facilitating a settlement of the dispute.

[…]

CHAPTER IV. ARBITRATION

[…]

Section 2 Constitution of the Tribunal

[…]

Article 39

The majority of the arbitrators shall be nationals of States other than the Contracting State party to the dispute and the Contracting State whose national is a party to the dispute; provided, however, that the foregoing provisions of this Article shall not apply if the sole arbitrator or each individual member of the Tribunal has been appointed by agreement of the parties.

Article 40

(1) Arbitrators may be appointed from outside the Panel of Arbitrators, except in the case of appointments by the Chairman pursuant to Article 38.

(2) Arbitrators appointed from outside the Panel of Arbitrators shall possess the qualities stated in paragraph (1) of Article 14.

Section 3 Powers and Functions of the Tribunal

[...]

Article 42

(1) The Tribunal shall decide a dispute in accordance with such rules of law as may be agreed by the parties. In the absence of such agreement, the Tribunal shall apply the law of the Contracting State party to the dispute (including its rules on the conflict of laws) and such rules of international law as may be applicable.

(2) The Tribunal may not bring in a finding of *non liquet* on the ground of silence or obscurity of the law.

(3) The provisions of paragraphs (1) and (2) shall not prejudice the power of the Tribunal to decide a dispute *ex aequo et bono* if the parties so agree.

[...]

Article 47

Except as the parties otherwise agree, the Tribunal may, if it considers that the circumstances so require, recommend any provisional measures which should be taken to preserve the respective rights of either party.
   [...]

Section 5 Interpretation, Revision and Annulment of the Award

Article 50

(1) If any dispute shall arise between the parties as to the meaning or scope of an award, either party may request interpretation of the award by an application in writing addressed to the Secretary-General.

(2) The request shall, if possible, be submitted to the Tribunal which rendered the award. If this shall not be possible, a new Tribunal shall be constituted in accordance with Section 2 of this Chapter. The Tribunal may, if it considers that the circumstances so require, stay enforcement of the award pending its decision.

Article 51

(1) Either party may request revision of the award by an application in writing addressed to the Secretary-General on the ground of discovery of some fact of such a nature as decisively to affect the award, provided that when the award was rendered that fact was unknown to the Tribunal and to the applicant and that the applicant's ignorance of that fact was not due to negligence.

(2) The application shall be made within 90 days after the discovery of such fact and in any event within three years after the date on which the award was rendered.

(3) The request shall, if possible, be submitted to the Tribunal which rendered the award. If this shall not be possible, a new Tribunal shall be constituted in accordance with Section 2 of this Chapter.

(4) The Tribunal may, if it considers that the circumstances so require, stay enforcement of the award pending its decision. If the applicant requests a stay of enforcement of the award in his application, enforcement shall be stayed provisionally until the Tribunal rules on such request.

Article 52

(1) Either party may request annulment of the award by an application in writing addressed to the Secretary-General on one or more of the following grounds:
   (*a*) that the Tribunal was not properly constituted;
   (*b*) that the Tribunal has manifestly exceeded its powers;
   (*c*) that there was corruption on the part of a member of the Tribunal;
   (*d*) that there has been a serious departure from a fundamental rule of procedure; or
   (*e*) that the award has failed to state the reasons on which it is based.
(2) The application shall be made within 120 days after the date on which the award was rendered except that when annulment is requested on the ground of corruption such application shall be made within 120 days after discovery of the corruption and in any event within three years after the date on which the award was rendered.
(3) On receipt of the request the Chairman shall forthwith appoint from the Panel of Arbitrators an *ad hoc* Committee of three persons. None of the members of the Committee shall have been a member of the Tribunal which rendered the award, shall be of the same nationality as any such member, shall be a national of the State party to the dispute or of the State whose national is a party to the dispute, shall have been designated to the Panel of Arbitrators by either of those States, or shall have acted as a conciliator in the same dispute. The Committee shall have the authority to annul the award or any part thereof on any of the grounds set forth in paragraph (1).
(4) The provisions of Articles 41-45, 48, 49, 53 and 54, and of Chapters VI and VII shall apply *mutatis mutandis* to proceedings before the Committee.
(5) The Committee may, if it considers that the circumstances so require, stay enforcement of the award pending its decision. If the applicant requests a stay of enforcement of the award in his application, enforcement shall be stayed provisionally until the Committee rules on such request.
(6) If the award is annulled the dispute shall, at the request of either party, be submitted to a new Tribunal constituted in accordance with Section 2 of this Chapter.
   [...]

UNCITRAL Arbitration Rules (as revised in 2021)

Resolution adopted by the General Assembly on 9 December 2021

76/108. *Expedited Arbitration Rules of the United Nations Commission on International Trade Law*

The General Assembly,

Recalling its resolution 2205 (XXI) of 17 December 1966, by which it established the United Nations Commission on International Trade Law with a mandate to further the progressive harmonization and unification of the law of international trade and in that respect to bear in mind the interests of all peoples, in particular those of developing countries, in the extensive development of international trade,

Recalling also its resolution 31/98 of 15 December 1976 recommending the use of the Arbitration Rules of the United Nations Commission on International Trade Law[1] and its resolution 65/22 of 6 December 2010 recommending the use of the Arbitration Rules as revised in 2010,[2]

Mindful of the value of arbitration as a method of settling disputes that may arise in the context of international commercial relations,

Noting the value of expedited arbitration as a streamlined and simplified procedure for settling disputes that arise in the context of international commercial relations within a shortened time frame, and its increased use in international and domestic commercial practice for parties to reach a final resolution of the dispute in a cost- and time-effective manner,

Aware of the need to balance the efficiency of the arbitral proceedings and the rights of the disputing parties to due process and fair treatment,

Noting that the preparation of the UNCITRAL Expedited Arbitration Rules and the accompanying explanatory note benefited greatly from consultations with Governments and interested intergovernmental and international non-governmental organizations,

Noting also that the Expedited Arbitration Rules were adopted by the United Nations Commission on International Trade Law at its fifty-fourth session, after due deliberations,[3]

1. *Expresses its appreciation* to the United Nations Commission on International Trade Law for having formulated and adopted the Expedited Arbitration Rules, the text of which is contained in annex IV to the report of the United Nations Commission on International Trade Law on the work of its fifty-fourth session[4] and which came into effect on 19 September 2021;
2. *Recommends* the use of the UNCITRAL Expedited Arbitration Rules in the settlement of disputes arising in the context of international commercial relations;
3. *Requests* the Secretary-General to make all efforts to ensure that the UNCITRAL Expedited Arbitration Rules become generally known and available.

---

[1] *Official Records of the General Assembly, Thirty-first Session, Supplement No. 17* (A/31/17), chap. V, sect. C.
[2] Ibid., *Sixty-fifth Session, Supplement No. 17* (A/65/17), annex I.
[3] Ibid., *Seventy-sixth Session, Supplement No. 17* (A/76/17), chap. VII.
[4] Ibid., annex IV.

UNCITRAL Arbitration Rules

(with article 1, paragraph 4, as adopted in 2013 and article 1, paragraph 5, as adopted in 2021)

SECTION I.   INTRODUCTORY RULES

Scope of application*

Article 1

1. Where parties have agreed that disputes between them in respect of a defined legal relationship, whether contractual or not, shall be referred to arbitration under the UNCITRAL Arbitration Rules, then such disputes shall be settled in accordance with these Rules subject to such modification as the parties may agree.
2. The parties to an arbitration agreement concluded after 15 August 2010 shall be presumed to have referred to the Rules in effect on the date of commencement of the arbitration, unless the parties have agreed to apply a particular version of the Rules. That presumption does not apply where the arbitration agreement has been concluded by accepting after 15 August 2010 an offer made before that date.
3. These Rules shall govern the arbitration except that where any of these Rules is in conflict with a provision of the law applicable to the arbitration from which the parties cannot derogate, that provision shall prevail.
4. For investor-State arbitration initiated pursuant to a treaty providing for the protection of investments or investors, these Rules include the UNCITRAL Rules on Transparency in Treaty-based Investor-State Arbitration ("Rules on Transparency"), subject to article 1 of the Rules on Transparency.
5. The Expedited Arbitration Rules in the appendix shall apply to the arbitration where the parties so agree.

Notice and calculation of periods of time

Article 2

1. A notice, including a notification, communication or proposal, may be transmitted by any means of communication that provides or allows for a record of its transmission.
2. If an address has been designated by a party specifically for this purpose or authorized by the arbitral tribunal, any notice shall be delivered to that party at that address, and if so delivered shall be deemed to have been received. Delivery by electronic means such as facsimile or e-mail may only be made to an address so designated or authorized.
3. In the absence of such designation or authorization, a notice is:
   (a) Received if it is physically delivered to the addressee;
   or
   (b) Deemed to have been received if it is delivered at the place of business, habitual residence or mailing address of the addressee.
4. If, after reasonable efforts, delivery cannot be effected in accordance with paragraphs 2 or 3, a notice is deemed to have been received if it is sent to the addressee's last-known place of business, habitual residence or mailing address by registered letter or any other means that provides a record of delivery or of attempted delivery.
5. A notice shall be deemed to have been received on the day it is delivered in accordance with paragraphs 2, 3 or 4, or attempted to be delivered in accordance with paragraph 4. A notice transmitted

---

* A model arbitration clause for contracts can be found in the annex to the Rules.

by electronic means is deemed to have been received on the day it is sent, except that a notice of arbitration so transmitted is only deemed to have been received on the day when it reaches the addressee's electronic address.

6. For the purpose of calculating a period of time under these Rules, such period shall begin to run on the day following the day when a notice is received. If the last day of such period is an official holiday or a non-business day at the residence or place of business of the addressee, the period is extended until the first business day which follows. Official holidays or non-business days occurring during the running of the period of time are included in calculating the period.

Notice of arbitration

Article 3

1. The party or parties initiating recourse to arbitration (hereinafter called the "claimant") shall communicate to the other party or parties (hereinafter called the "respondent") a notice of arbitration.
2. Arbitral proceedings shall be deemed to commence on the date on which the notice of arbitration is received by the respondent.
3. The notice of arbitration shall include the following:
   (a) A demand that the dispute be referred to arbitration;
   (b) The names and contact details of the parties;
   (c) Identification of the arbitration agreement that is invoked;
   (d) Identification of any contract or other legal instrument out of or in relation to which the dispute arises or, in the absence of such contract or instrument, a brief description of the relevant relationship;
   (e) A brief description of the claim and an indication of the amount involved, if any;
   (f) The relief or remedy sought;
   (g) A proposal as to the number of arbitrators, language and place of arbitration, if the parties have not previously agreed thereon.
4. The notice of arbitration may also include:
   (a) A proposal for the designation of an appointing authority referred to in article 6, paragraph 1;
   (b) A proposal for the appointment of a sole arbitrator referred to in article 8, paragraph 1;
   (c) Notification of the appointment of an arbitrator referred to in article 9 or 10.
5. The constitution of the arbitral tribunal shall not be hindered by any controversy with respect to the sufficiency of the notice of arbitration, which shall be finally resolved by the arbitral tribunal.

Response to the notice of arbitration

Article 4

1. Within 30 days of the receipt of the notice of arbitration, the respondent shall communicate to the claimant a response to the notice of arbitration, which shall include:
   (a) The name and contact details of each respondent;
   (b) A response to the information set forth in the notice of arbitration, pursuant to article 3, paragraphs 3 (c) to (g).
2. The response to the notice of arbitration may also include:
   (a) Any plea that an arbitral tribunal to be constituted under these Rules lacks jurisdiction;
   (b) A proposal for the designation of an appointing authority referred to in article 6, paragraph 1;
   (c) A proposal for the appointment of a sole arbitrator referred to in article 8, paragraph 1;
   (d) Notification of the appointment of an arbitrator referred to in article 9 or 10;

  (e) A brief description of counterclaims or claims for the purpose of a set-off, if any, including where relevant, an indication of the amounts involved, and the relief or remedy sought;

  (f) A notice of arbitration in accordance with article 3 in case the respondent formulates a claim against a party to the arbitration agreement other than the claimant.

3. The constitution of the arbitral tribunal shall not be hindered by any controversy with respect to the respondent's failure to communicate a response to the notice of arbitration, or an incomplete or late response to the notice of arbitration, which shall be finally resolved by the arbitral tribunal.

Representation and assistance

Article 5

Each party may be represented or assisted by persons chosen by it. The names and addresses of such persons must be communicated to all parties and to the arbitral tribunal. Such communication must specify whether the appointment is being made for purposes of representation or assistance. Where a person is to act as a representative of a party, the arbitral tribunal, on its own initiative or at the request of any party, may at any time require proof of authority granted to the representative in such a form as the arbitral tribunal may determine.

Designating and appointing authorities

Article 6

1. Unless the parties have already agreed on the choice of an appointing authority, a party may at any time propose the name or names of one or more institutions or persons, including the Secretary-General of the Permanent Court of Arbitration at The Hague (hereinafter called the "PCA"), one of whom would serve as appointing authority.

2. If all parties have not agreed on the choice of an appointing authority within 30 days after a proposal made in accordance with paragraph 1 has been received by all other parties, any party may request the Secretary-General of the PCA to designate the appointing authority.

3. Where these Rules provide for a period of time within which a party must refer a matter to an appointing authority and no appointing authority has been agreed on or designated, the period is suspended from the date on which a party initiates the procedure for agreeing on or designating an appointing authority until the date of such agreement or designation.

4. Except as referred to in article 41, paragraph 4, if the appointing authority refuses to act, or if it fails to appoint an arbitrator within 30 days after it receives a party's request to do so, fails to act within any other period provided by these Rules, or fails to decide on a challenge to an arbitrator within a reasonable time after receiving a party's request to do so, any party may request the Secretary-General of the PCA to designate a substitute appointing authority.

5. In exercising their functions under these Rules, the appointing authority and the Secretary-General of the PCA may require from any party and the arbitrators the information they deem necessary and they shall give the parties and, where appropriate, the arbitrators, an opportunity to present their views in any manner they consider appropriate. All such communications to and from the appointing authority and the Secretary-General of the PCA shall also be provided by the sender to all other parties.

6. When the appointing authority is requested to appoint an arbitrator pursuant to articles 8, 9, 10 or 14, the party making the request shall send to the appointing authority copies of the notice of arbitration and, if it exists, any response to the notice of arbitration.

7. The appointing authority shall have regard to such considerations as are likely to secure the appointment of an independent and impartial arbitrator and shall take into account the advisability of appointing an arbitrator of a nationality other than the nationalities of the parties.

SECTION II.   COMPOSITION OF THE ARBITRAL TRIBUNAL

Number of arbitrators

Article 7

1. If the parties have not previously agreed on the number of arbitrators, and if within 30 days after the receipt by the respondent of the notice of arbitration the parties have not agreed that there shall be only one arbitrator, three arbitrators shall be appointed.
2. Notwithstanding paragraph 1, if no other parties have responded to a party's proposal to appoint a sole arbitrator within the time limit provided for in paragraph 1 and the party or parties concerned have failed to appoint a second arbitrator in accordance with article 9 or 10, the appointing authority may, at the request of a party, appoint a sole arbitrator pursuant to the procedure provided for in article 8, paragraph 2, if it determines that, in view of the circumstances of the case, this is more appropriate.

Appointment of arbitrators (articles 8 to 10)

Article 8

1. If the parties have agreed that a sole arbitrator is to be appointed and if within 30 days after receipt by all other parties of a proposal for the appointment of a sole arbitrator the parties have not reached agreement thereon, a sole arbitrator shall, at the request of a party, be appointed by the appointing authority.
2. The appointing authority shall appoint the sole arbitrator as promptly as possible. In making the appointment, the appointing authority shall use the following list-procedure, unless the parties agree that the list-procedure should not be used or unless the appointing authority determines in its discretion that the use of the list-procedure is not appropriate for the case:

   (a) The appointing authority shall communicate to each of the parties an identical list containing at least three names;
   (b) Within 15 days after the receipt of this list, each party may return the list to the appointing authority after having deleted the name or names to which it objects and numbered the remaining names on the list in the order of its preference;
   (c) After the expiration of the above period of time the appointing authority shall appoint the sole arbitrator from among the names approved on the lists returned to it and in accordance with the order of preference indicated by the parties;
   (d) If for any reason the appointment cannot be made according to this procedure, the appointing authority may exercise its discretion in appointing the sole arbitrator.

Article 9

1. If three arbitrators are to be appointed, each party shall appoint one arbitrator. The two arbitrators thus appointed shall choose the third arbitrator who will act as the presiding arbitrator of the arbitral tribunal.
2. If within 30 days after the receipt of a party's notification of the appointment of an arbitrator the other party has not notified the first party of the arbitrator it has appointed, the first party may request the appointing authority to appoint the second arbitrator.
3. If within 30 days after the appointment of the second arbitrator the two arbitrators have not agreed on the choice of the presiding arbitrator, the presiding arbitrator shall be appointed by the appointing authority in the same way as a sole arbitrator would be appointed under article 8.

Article 10

1. For the purposes of article 9, paragraph 1, where three arbitrators are to be appointed and there are multiple parties as claimant or as respondent, unless the parties have agreed to another method of

appointment of arbitrators, the multiple parties jointly, whether as claimant or as respondent, shall appoint an arbitrator.

2. If the parties have agreed that the arbitral tribunal is to be composed of a number of arbitrators other than one or three, the arbitrators shall be appointed according to the method agreed upon by the parties.

3. In the event of any failure to constitute the arbitral tribunal under these Rules, the appointing authority shall, at the request of any party, constitute the arbitral tribunal and, in doing so, may revoke any appointment already made and appoint or reappoint each of the arbitrators and designate one of them as the presiding arbitrator.

Disclosures by and challenge of arbitrators ** *(articles 11 to 13)*

Article 11

When a person is approached in connection with his or her possible appointment as an arbitrator, he or she shall disclose any circumstances likely to give rise to justifiable doubts as to his or her impartiality or independence. An arbitrator, from the time of his or her appointment and throughout the arbitral proceedings, shall without delay disclose any such circumstances to the parties and the other arbitrators unless they have already been informed by him or her of these circumstances.

Article 12

1. Any arbitrator may be challenged if circumstances exist that give rise to justifiable doubts as to the arbitrator's impartiality or independence.

2. A party may challenge the arbitrator appointed by it only for reasons of which it becomes aware after the appointment has been made.

3. In the event that an arbitrator fails to act or in the event of the de jure or de facto impossibility of his or her performing his or her functions, the procedure in respect of the challenge of an arbitrator as provided in article 13 shall apply.

Article 13

1. A party that intends to challenge an arbitrator shall send notice of its challenge within 15 days after it has been notified of the appointment of the challenged arbitrator, or within 15 days after the circumstances mentioned in articles 11 and 12 became known to that party.

2. The notice of challenge shall be communicated to all other parties, to the arbitrator who is challenged and to the other arbitrators. The notice of challenge shall state the reasons for the challenge.

3. When an arbitrator has been challenged by a party, all parties may agree to the challenge. The arbitrator may also, after the challenge, withdraw from his or her office. In neither case does this imply acceptance of the validity of the grounds for the challenge.

4. If, within 15 days from the date of the notice of challenge, all parties do not agree to the challenge or the challenged arbitrator does not withdraw, the party making the challenge may elect to pursue it. In that case, within 30 days from the date of the notice of challenge, it shall seek a decision on the challenge by the appointing authority.

Replacement of an arbitrator

Article 14

1. Subject to paragraph 2, in any event where an arbitrator has to be replaced during the course of the arbitral proceedings, a substitute arbitrator shall be appointed or chosen pursuant to the

---

** Model statements of independence pursuant to article 11 can be found in the annex to the Rules.

procedure provided for in articles 8 to 11 that was applicable to the appointment or choice of the arbitrator being replaced. This procedure shall apply even if during the process of appointing the arbitrator to be replaced, a party had failed to exercise its right to appoint or to participate in the appointment.

2. If, at the request of a party, the appointing authority determines that, in view of the exceptional circumstances of the case, it would be justified for a party to be deprived of its right to appoint a substitute arbitrator, the appointing authority may, after giving an opportunity to the parties and the remaining arbitrators to express their views: *(a)* appoint the substitute arbitrator; or *(b)* after the closure of the hearings, authorize the other arbitrators to proceed with the arbitration and make any decision or award.

Repetition of hearings in the event of the replacement of an arbitrator

Article 15

If an arbitrator is replaced, the proceedings shall resume at the stage where the arbitrator who was replaced ceased to perform his or her functions, unless the arbitral tribunal decides otherwise.

Exclusion of liability

Article 16

Save for intentional wrongdoing, the parties waive, to the fullest extent permitted under the applicable law, any claim against the arbitrators, the appointing authority and any person appointed by the arbitral tribunal based on any act or omission in connection with the arbitration.

SECTION III.   ARBITRAL PROCEEDINGS

General provisions

Article 17

1. Subject to these Rules, the arbitral tribunal may conduct the arbitration in such manner as it considers appropriate, provided that the parties are treated with equality and that at an appropriate stage of the proceedings each party is given a reasonable opportunity of presenting its case. The arbitral tribunal, in exercising its discretion, shall conduct the proceedings so as to avoid unnecessary delay and expense and to provide a fair and efficient process for resolving the parties' dispute.

2. As soon as practicable after its constitution and after inviting the parties to express their views, the arbitral tribunal shall establish the provisional timetable of the arbitration. The arbitral tribunal may, at any time, after inviting the parties to express their views, extend or abridge any period of time prescribed under these Rules or agreed by the parties.

3. If at an appropriate stage of the proceedings any party so requests, the arbitral tribunal shall hold hearings for the presentation of evidence by witnesses, including expert witnesses, or for oral argument. In the absence of such a request, the arbitral tribunal shall decide whether to hold such hearings or whether the proceedings shall be conducted on the basis of documents and other materials.

4. All communications to the arbitral tribunal by one party shall be communicated by that party to all other parties. Such communications shall be made at the same time, except as otherwise permitted by the arbitral tribunal if it may do so under applicable law.

5. The arbitral tribunal may, at the request of any party, allow one or more third persons to be joined in the arbitration as a party provided such person is a party to the arbitration agreement, unless the arbitral tribunal finds, after giving all parties, including the person or persons to be joined, the opportunity to be heard, that joinder should not be permitted because of prejudice to any of those

parties. The arbitral tribunal may make a single award or several awards in respect of all parties so involved in the arbitration.

Place of arbitration

Article 18

1. If the parties have not previously agreed on the place of arbitration, the place of arbitration shall be determined by the arbitral tribunal having regard to the circumstances of the case. The award shall be deemed to have been made at the place of arbitration.
2. The arbitral tribunal may meet at any location it considers appropriate for deliberations. Unless otherwise agreed by the parties, the arbitral tribunal may also meet at any location it considers appropriate for any other purpose, including hearings.

Language

Article 19

1. Subject to an agreement by the parties, the arbitral tribunal shall, promptly after its appointment, determine the language or languages to be used in the proceedings. This determination shall apply to the statement of claim, the statement of defence, and any further written statements and, if oral hearings take place, to the language or languages to be used in such hearings.
2. The arbitral tribunal may order that any documents annexed to the statement of claim or statement of defence, and any supplementary documents or exhibits submitted in the course of the proceedings, delivered in their original language, shall be accompanied by a translation into the language or languages agreed upon by the parties or determined by the arbitral tribunal.

Statement of claim

Article 20

1. The claimant shall communicate its statement of claim in writing to the respondent and to each of the arbitrators within a period of time to be determined by the arbitral tribunal. The claimant may elect to treat its notice of arbitration referred to in article 3 as a statement of claim, provided that the notice of arbitration also complies with the requirements of paragraphs 2 to 4 of this article.
2. The statement of claim shall include the following particulars:
   (a) The names and contact details of the parties;
   (b) A statement of the facts supporting the claim;
   (c) The points at issue;
   (d) The relief or remedy sought;
   (e) The legal grounds or arguments supporting the claim.
3. A copy of any contract or other legal instrument out of or in relation to which the dispute arises and of the arbitration agreement shall be annexed to the statement of claim.
4. The statement of claim should, as far as possible, be accompanied by all documents and other evidence relied upon by the claimant, or contain references to them.

Statement of defence

Article 21

1. The respondent shall communicate its statement of defence in writing to the claimant and to each of the arbitrators within a period of time to be determined by the arbitral tribunal. The respondent

may elect to treat its response to the notice of arbitration referred to in article 4 as a statement of defence, provided that the response to the notice of arbitration also complies with the requirements of paragraph 2 of this article.

2. The statement of defence shall reply to the particulars *(b)* to *(e)* of the statement of claim (art. 20, para. 2). The statement of defence should, as far as possible, be accompanied by all documents and other evidence relied upon by the respondent, or contain references to them.

3. In its statement of defence, or at a later stage in the arbitral proceedings if the arbitral tribunal decides that the delay was justified under the circumstances, the respondent may make a counterclaim or rely on a claim for the purpose of a set-off provided that the arbitral tribunal has jurisdiction over it.

4. The provisions of article 20, paragraphs 2 to 4, shall apply to a counterclaim, a claim under article 4, paragraph 2 *(f)*, and a claim relied on for the purpose of a set-off.

Amendments to the claim or defence

Article 22

During the course of the arbitral proceedings, a party may amend or supplement its claim or defence, including a counterclaim or a claim for the purpose of a set-off, unless the arbitral tribunal considers it inappropriate to allow such amendment or supplement having regard to the delay in making it or prejudice to other parties or any other circumstances. However, a claim or defence, including a counterclaim or a claim for the purpose of a set-off, may not be amended or supplemented in such a manner that the amended or supplemented claim or defence falls outside the jurisdiction of the arbitral tribunal.

Pleas as to the jurisdiction of the arbitral tribunal

Article 23

1. The arbitral tribunal shall have the power to rule on its own jurisdiction, including any objections with respect to the existence or validity of the arbitration agreement. For that purpose, an arbitration clause that forms part of a contract shall be treated as an agreement independent of the other terms of the contract. A decision by the arbitral tribunal that the contract is null shall not entail automatically the invalidity of the arbitration clause.

2. A plea that the arbitral tribunal does not have jurisdiction shall be raised no later than in the statement of defence or, with respect to a counterclaim or a claim for the purpose of a set-off, in the reply to the counterclaim or to the claim for the purpose of a set-off. A party is not precluded from raising such a plea by the fact that it has appointed, or participated in the appointment of, an arbitrator. A plea that the arbitral tribunal is exceeding the scope of its authority shall be raised as soon as the matter alleged to be beyond the scope of its authority is raised during the arbitral proceedings. The arbitral tribunal may, in either case, admit a later plea if it considers the delay justified.

3. The arbitral tribunal may rule on a plea referred to in paragraph 2 either as a preliminary question or in an award on the merits. The arbitral tribunal may continue the arbitral proceedings and make an award, notwithstanding any pending challenge to its jurisdiction before a court.

Further written statements

Article 24

The arbitral tribunal shall decide which further written statements, in addition to the statement of claim and the statement of defence, shall be required from the parties or may be presented by them and shall fix the periods of time for communicating such statements.

Periods of time

Article 25

The periods of time fixed by the arbitral tribunal for the communication of written statements (including the statement of claim and statement of defence) should not exceed 45 days. However, the arbitral tribunal may extend the time limits if it concludes that an extension is justified.

Interim measures

Article 26

1. The arbitral tribunal may, at the request of a party, grant interim measures.
2. An interim measure is any temporary measure by which, at any time prior to the issuance of the award by which the dispute is finally decided, the arbitral tribunal orders a party, for example and without limitation, to:
   (a) Maintain or restore the status quo pending determination of the dispute;
   (b) Take action that would prevent, or refrain from taking action that is likely to cause, (i) current or imminent harm or (ii) prejudice to the arbitral process itself;
   (c) Provide a means of preserving assets out of which a subsequent award may be satisfied; or
   (d) Preserve evidence that may be relevant and material to the resolution of the dispute.
3. The party requesting an interim measure under paragraphs 2 *(a)* to *(c)* shall satisfy the arbitral tribunal that:
   (a) Harm not adequately reparable by an award of damages is likely to result if the measure is not ordered, and such harm substantially outweighs the harm that is likely to result to the party against whom the measure is directed if the measure is granted; and
   (b) There is a reasonable possibility that the requesting party will succeed on the merits of the claim. The determination on this possibility shall not affect the discretion of the arbitral tribunal in making any subsequent determination.
4. With regard to a request for an interim measure under paragraph 2 *(d)*, the requirements in paragraphs 3 *(a)* and *(b)* shall apply only to the extent the arbitral tribunal considers appropriate.
5. The arbitral tribunal may modify, suspend or terminate an interim measure it has granted, upon application of any party or, in exceptional circumstances and upon prior notice to the parties, on the arbitral tribunal's own initiative.
6. The arbitral tribunal may require the party requesting an interim measure to provide appropriate security in connection with the measure.
7. The arbitral tribunal may require any party promptly to disclose any material change in the circumstances on the basis of which the interim measure was requested or granted.
8. The party requesting an interim measure may be liable for any costs and damages caused by the measure to any party if the arbitral tribunal later determines that, in the circumstances then prevailing, the measure should not have been granted. The arbitral tribunal may award such costs and damages at any point during the proceedings.
9. A request for interim measures addressed by any party to a judicial authority shall not be deemed incompatible with the agreement to arbitrate, or as a waiver of that agreement.

Evidence

Article 27

1. Each party shall have the burden of proving the facts relied on to support its claim or defence.
2. Witnesses, including expert witnesses, who are presented by the parties to testify to the arbitral tribunal on any issue of fact or expertise may be any individual, notwithstanding that the individual is a party to the arbitration or in any way related to a party. Unless otherwise directed by the

arbitral tribunal, statements by witnesses, including expert witnesses, may be presented in writing and signed by them.

3. At any time during the arbitral proceedings the arbitral tribunal may require the parties to produce documents, exhibits or other evidence within such a period of time as the arbitral tribunal shall determine.

4. The arbitral tribunal shall determine the admissibility, relevance, materiality and weight of the evidence offered.

Hearings

Article 28

1. In the event of an oral hearing, the arbitral tribunal shall give the parties adequate advance notice of the date, time and place thereof.

2. Witnesses, including expert witnesses, may be heard under the conditions and examined in the manner set by the arbitral tribunal.

3. Hearings shall be held in camera unless the parties agree otherwise. The arbitral tribunal may require the retirement of any witness or witnesses, including expert witnesses, during the testimony of such other witnesses, except that a witness, including an expert witness, who is a party to the arbitration shall not, in principle, be asked to retire.

4. The arbitral tribunal may direct that witnesses, including expert witnesses, be examined through means of telecommunication that do not require their physical presence at the hearing (such as videoconference).

Experts appointed by the arbitral tribunal

Article 29

1. After consultation with the parties, the arbitral tribunal may appoint one or more independent experts to report to it, in writing, on specific issues to be determined by the arbitral tribunal. A copy of the expert's terms of reference, established by the arbitral tribunal, shall be communicated to the parties.

2. The expert shall, in principle before accepting appointment, submit to the arbitral tribunal and to the parties a description of his or her qualifications and a statement of his or her impartiality and independence. Within the time ordered by the arbitral tribunal, the parties shall inform the arbitral tribunal whether they have any objections as to the expert's qualifications, impartiality or independence. The arbitral tribunal shall decide promptly whether to accept any such objections. After an expert's appointment, a party may object to the expert's qualifications, impartiality or independence only if the objection is for reasons of which the party becomes aware after the appointment has been made. The arbitral tribunal shall decide promptly what, if any, action to take.

3. The parties shall give the expert any relevant information or produce for his or her inspection any relevant documents or goods that he or she may require of them. Any dispute between a party and such expert as to the relevance of the required information or production shall be referred to the arbitral tribunal for decision.

4. Upon receipt of the expert's report, the arbitral tribunal shall communicate a copy of the report to the parties, which shall be given the opportunity to express, in writing, their opinion on the report. A party shall be entitled to examine any document on which the expert has relied in his or her report.

5. At the request of any party, the expert, after delivery of the report, may be heard at a hearing where the parties shall have the opportunity to be present and to interrogate the expert. At this hearing, any party may present expert witnesses in order to testify on the points at issue. The provisions of article 28 shall be applicable to such proceedings.

Default

Article 30

1. If, within the period of time fixed by these Rules or the arbitral tribunal, without showing sufficient cause:
   (a) The claimant has failed to communicate its statement of claim, the arbitral tribunal shall issue an order for the termination of the arbitral proceedings, unless there are remaining matters that may need to be decided and the arbitral tribunal considers it appropriate to do so;
   (b) The respondent has failed to communicate its response to the notice of arbitration or its statement of defence, the arbitral tribunal shall order that the proceedings continue, without treating such failure in itself as an admission of the claimant's allegations; the provisions of this subparagraph also apply to a claimant's failure to submit a defence to a counterclaim or to a claim for the purpose of a set-off.
2. If a party, duly notified under these Rules, fails to appear at a hearing, without showing sufficient cause for such failure, the arbitral tribunal may proceed with the arbitration.
3. If a party, duly invited by the arbitral tribunal to produce documents, exhibits or other evidence, fails to do so within the established period of time, without showing sufficient cause for such failure, the arbitral tribunal may make the award on the evidence before it.

Closure of hearings

Article 31

1. The arbitral tribunal may inquire of the parties if they have any further proof to offer or witnesses to be heard or submissions to make and, if there are none, it may declare the hearings closed.
2. The arbitral tribunal may, if it considers it necessary owing to exceptional circumstances, decide, on its own initiative or upon application of a party, to reopen the hearings at any time before the award is made.

Waiver of right to object

Article 32

A failure by any party to object promptly to any non-compliance with these Rules or with any requirement of the arbitration agreement shall be deemed to be a waiver of the right of such party to make such an objection, unless such party can show that, under the circumstances, its failure to object was justified.

SECTION IV.   THE AWARD

Decisions

Article 33

1. When there is more than one arbitrator, any award or other decision of the arbitral tribunal shall be made by a majority of the arbitrators.
2. In the case of questions of procedure, when there is no majority or when the arbitral tribunal so authorizes, the presiding arbitrator may decide alone, subject to revision, if any, by the arbitral tribunal.

Form and effect of the award

Article 34

1. The arbitral tribunal may make separate awards on different issues at different times.

2. All awards shall be made in writing and shall be final and binding on the parties. The parties shall carry out all awards without delay.
3. The arbitral tribunal shall state the reasons upon which the award is based, unless the parties have agreed that no reasons are to be given.
4. An award shall be signed by the arbitrators and it shall contain the date on which the award was made and indicate the place of arbitration. Where there is more than one arbitrator and any of them fails to sign, the award shall state the reason for the absence of the signature.
5. An award may be made public with the consent of all parties or where and to the extent disclosure is required of a party by legal duty, to protect or pursue a legal right or in relation to legal proceedings before a court or other competent authority.
6. Copies of the award signed by the arbitrators shall be communicated to the parties by the arbitral tribunal.

Applicable law, amiable compositeur

Article 35

1. The arbitral tribunal shall apply the rules of law designated by the parties as applicable to the substance of the dispute. Failing such designation by the parties, the arbitral tribunal shall apply the law which it determines to be appropriate.
2. The arbitral tribunal shall decide as amiable compositeur or ex aequo et bono only if the parties have expressly authorized the arbitral tribunal to do so.
3. In all cases, the arbitral tribunal shall decide in accordance with the terms of the contract, if any, and shall take into account any usage of trade applicable to the transaction.

Settlement or other grounds for termination

Article 36

1. If, before the award is made, the parties agree on a settlement of the dispute, the arbitral tribunal shall either issue an order for the termination of the arbitral proceedings or, if requested by the parties and accepted by the arbitral tribunal, record the settlement in the form of an arbitral award on agreed terms. The arbitral tribunal is not obliged to give reasons for such an award.
2. If, before the award is made, the continuation of the arbitral proceedings becomes unnecessary or impossible for any reason not mentioned in paragraph 1, the arbitral tribunal shall inform the parties of its intention to issue an order for the termination of the proceedings. The arbitral tribunal shall have the power to issue such an order unless there are remaining matters that may need to be decided and the arbitral tribunal considers it appropriate to do so.
3. Copies of the order for termination of the arbitral proceedings or of the arbitral award on agreed terms, signed by the arbitrators, shall be communicated by the arbitral tribunal to the parties. Where an arbitral award on agreed terms is made, the provisions of article 34, paragraphs 2, 4 and 5, shall apply.

Interpretation of the award

Article 37

1. Within 30 days after the receipt of the award, a party, with notice to the other parties, may request that the arbitral tribunal give an interpretation of the award.
2. The interpretation shall be given in writing within 45 days after the receipt of the request. The interpretation shall form part of the award and the provisions of article 34, paragraphs 2 to 6, shall apply.

Correction of the award

Article 38

1. Within 30 days after the receipt of the award, a party, with notice to the other parties, may request the arbitral tribunal to correct in the award any error in computation, any clerical or typographical error, or any error or omission of a similar nature. If the arbitral tribunal considers that the request is justified, it shall make the correction within 45 days of receipt of the request.
2. The arbitral tribunal may within 30 days after the communication of the award make such corrections on its own initiative.
3. Such corrections shall be in writing and shall form part of the award. The provisions of article 34, paragraphs 2 to 6, shall apply.

Additional award

Article 39

1. Within 30 days after the receipt of the termination order or the award, a party, with notice to the other parties, may request the arbitral tribunal to make an award or an additional award as to claims presented in the arbitral proceedings but not decided by the arbitral tribunal.
2. If the arbitral tribunal considers the request for an award or additional award to be justified, it shall render or complete its award within 60 days after the receipt of the request. The arbitral tribunal may extend, if necessary, the period of time within which it shall make the award.
3. When such an award or additional award is made, the provisions of article 34, paragraphs 2 to 6, shall apply.

Definition of costs

Article 40

1. The arbitral tribunal shall fix the costs of arbitration in the final award and, if it deems appropriate, in another decision.
2. The term "costs" includes only:
   (a) The fees of the arbitral tribunal to be stated separately as to each arbitrator and to be fixed by the tribunal itself in accordance with article 41;
   (b) The reasonable travel and other expenses incurred by the arbitrators;
   (c) The reasonable costs of expert advice and of other assistance required by the arbitral tribunal;
   (d) The reasonable travel and other expenses of witnesses to the extent such expenses are approved by the arbitral tribunal;
   (e) The legal and other costs incurred by the parties in relation to the arbitration to the extent that the arbitral tribunal determines that the amount of such costs is reasonable;
   (f) Any fees and expenses of the appointing authority as well as the fees and expenses of the Secretary-General of the PCA.
3. In relation to interpretation, correction or completion of any award under articles 37 to 39, the arbitral tribunal may charge the costs referred to in paragraphs 2 (b) to (f), but no additional fees.

Fees and expenses of arbitrators

Article 41

1. The fees and expenses of the arbitrators shall be reasonable in amount, taking into account the amount in dispute, the complexity of the subject matter, the time spent by the arbitrators and any other relevant circumstances of the case.

2. If there is an appointing authority and it applies or has stated that it will apply a schedule or particular method for determining the fees for arbitrators in international cases, the arbitral tribunal in fixing its fees shall take that schedule or method into account to the extent that it considers appropriate in the circumstances of the case.

3. Promptly after its constitution, the arbitral tribunal shall inform the parties as to how it proposes to determine its fees and expenses, including any rates it intends to apply. Within 15 days of receiving that proposal, any party may refer the proposal to the appointing authority for review. If, within 45 days of receipt of such a referral, the appointing authority finds that the proposal of the arbitral tribunal is inconsistent with paragraph 1, it shall make any necessary adjustments thereto, which shall be binding upon the arbitral tribunal.

4. *(a)* When informing the parties of the arbitrators' fees and expenses that have been fixed pursuant to article 40, paragraphs 2 *(a)* and *(b)*, the arbitral tribunal shall also explain the manner in which the corresponding amounts have been calculated;

   (b) Within 15 days of receiving the arbitral tribunal's determination of fees and expenses, any party may refer for review such determination to the appointing authority. If no appointing authority has been agreed upon or designated, or if the appointing authority fails to act within the time specified in these Rules, then the review shall be made by the Secretary-General of the PCA;

   (c) If the appointing authority or the Secretary-General of the PCA finds that the arbitral tribunal's determination is inconsistent with the arbitral tribunal's proposal (and any adjustment thereto) under paragraph 3 or is otherwise manifestly excessive, it shall, within 45 days of receiving such a referral, make any adjustments to the arbitral tribunal's determination that are necessary to satisfy the criteria in paragraph 1. Any such adjustments shall be binding upon the arbitral tribunal;

   (d) Any such adjustments shall either be included by the arbitral tribunal in its award or, if the award has already been issued, be implemented in a correction to the award, to which the procedure of article 38, paragraph 3, shall apply.

5. Throughout the procedure under paragraphs 3 and 4, the arbitral tribunal shall proceed with the arbitration, in accordance with article 17, paragraph 1.

6. A referral under paragraph 4 shall not affect any determination in the award other than the arbitral tribunal's fees and expenses; nor shall it delay the recognition and enforcement of all parts of the award other than those relating to the determination of the arbitral tribunal's fees and expenses.

Allocation of costs

Article 42

1. The costs of the arbitration shall in principle be borne by the unsuccessful party or parties. However, the arbitral tribunal may apportion each of such costs between the parties if it determines that apportionment is reasonable, taking into account the circumstances of the case.

2. The arbitral tribunal shall in the final award or, if it deems appropriate, in any other award, determine any amount that a party may have to pay to another party as a result of the decision on allocation of costs.

Deposit of costs

Article 43

1. The arbitral tribunal, on its establishment, may request the parties to deposit an equal amount as an advance for the costs referred to in article 40, paragraphs 2 *(a)* to *(c)*.

2. During the course of the arbitral proceedings the arbitral tribunal may request supplementary deposits from the parties.

3. If an appointing authority has been agreed upon or designated, and when a party so requests and the appointing authority consents to perform the function, the arbitral tribunal shall fix the amounts of any deposits or supplementary deposits only after consultation with the appointing authority, which may make any comments to the arbitral tribunal that it deems appropriate concerning the amount of such deposits and supplementary deposits.

4. If the required deposits are not paid in full within 30 days after the receipt of the request, the arbitral tribunal shall so inform the parties in order that one or more of them may make the required payment. If such payment is not made, the arbitral tribunal may order the suspension or termination of the arbitral proceedings.

5. After a termination order or final award has been made, the arbitral tribunal shall render an accounting to the parties of the deposits received and return any unexpended balance to the parties.

Annex

Model arbitration clause for contracts

Any dispute, controversy or claim arising out of or relating to this contract, or the breach, termination or invalidity thereof, shall be settled by arbitration in accordance with the UNCITRAL Arbitration Rules.

> *Note. Parties should consider adding:*
> *(a)* The appointing authority shall be ... [name of institution or person];
> *(b)* The number of arbitrators shall be .... [one or three];
> *(c)* The place of arbitration shall be ... [town and country];
> *(d)* The language to be used in the arbitral proceedings shall be ....

Possible waiver statement

> *Note. If the parties wish to exclude recourse against the arbitral award that may be available under the applicable law, they may consider adding a provision to that effect as suggested below, considering, however, that the effectiveness and conditions of such an exclusion depend on the applicable law.*

Waiver

The parties hereby waive their right to any form of recourse against an award to any court or other competent authority, insofar as such waiver can validly be made under the applicable law.

Model statements of independence pursuant to article 11 of the Rules

No circumstances to disclose

I am impartial and independent of each of the parties and intend to remain so. To the best of my knowledge, there are no circumstances, past or present, likely to give rise to justifiable doubts as to my impartiality or independence. I shall promptly notify the parties and the other arbitrators of any such circumstances that may subsequently come to my attention during this arbitration.

Circumstances to disclose

I am impartial and independent of each of the parties and intend to remain so. Attached is a statement made pursuant to article 11 of the UNCITRAL Arbitration Rules of *(a)* my past and present professional, business and other relationships with the parties and *(b)* any other relevant circumstances. [Include statement.] I confirm that those circumstances do not affect my independence and impartiality. I shall promptly notify the parties and the other arbitrators of any such further relationships or circumstances that may subsequently come to my attention during this arbitration.

Note. Any party may consider requesting from the arbitrator the following addition to the statement of independence:

I confirm, on the basis of the information presently available to me, that I can devote the time necessary to conduct this arbitration diligently, efficiently and in accordance with the time limits in the Rules.

IBA Rules on the Taking of Evidence in International Commercial Arbitration

(Adopted by a resolution of the IBA Council on 17 December 2020)

The Rules

Preamble

1. These IBA Rules on the Taking of Evidence in International Arbitration are intended to provide an efficient, economical and fair process for the taking of evidence in international arbitrations, particularly those between Parties from different legal traditions. They are designed to supplement the legal provisions and the institutional, ad hoc or other rules that apply to the conduct of the arbitration.
2. Parties and Arbitral Tribunals may adopt the IBA Rules of Evidence, in whole or in part, to govern arbitration proceedings, or they may vary them or use them as guidelines in developing their own procedures. The Rules are not intended to limit the flexibility that is inherent in, and an advantage of, international arbitration, and Parties and Arbitral Tribunals are free to adapt them to the particular circumstances of each arbitration.
3. The taking of evidence shall be conducted on the principles that each Party shall act in good faith and be entitled to know, reasonably in advance of any Evidentiary Hearing or any fact or merits determination, the evidence on which the other Parties rely.

Definitions

In the IBA Rules of Evidence:

'Arbitral Tribunal' means a sole arbitrator or a panel of arbitrators;

'Claimant' means the Party or Parties who commenced the arbitration and any Party who, through joinder or otherwise, becomes aligned with such Party or Parties;

'Document' means a writing, communication, picture, drawing, program or data of any kind, whether recorded or maintained on paper or by electronic, audio, visual or any other means;

'Evidentiary Hearing' means any hearing, whether or not held on consecutive days, at which the Arbitral Tribunal, whether in person, by teleconference, videoconference or other method, receives oral or other evidence;

'Expert Report' means a written statement by a Tribunal-Appointed Expert or a Party-Appointed Expert;

'General Rules' mean the institutional, ad hoc or other rules that apply to the conduct of the arbitration;

'IBA Rules of Evidence' or *'Rules'* means these IBA Rules on the Taking of Evidence in International Arbitration, as they may be revised or amended from time to time;

'Party' means a party to the arbitration;

'Party-Appointed Expert' means a person or organisation appointed by a Party in order to report on specific issues determined by the Party;

'Remote Hearing' means a hearing conducted, for the entire hearing or parts thereof, or only with respect to certain participants, using teleconference, videoconference or other communication technology by which persons in more than one location simultaneously participate;

'Request to Produce' means a written request by a Party that another Party produce Documents;

'Respondent' means the Party or Parties against whom the Claimant made its claim, and any Party who, through joinder or otherwise, becomes aligned with such Party or Parties, and includes a Respondent making a counterclaim;

'Tribunal-Appointed Expert' means a person or organisation appointed by the Arbitral Tribunal in order to report to it on specific issues determined by the Arbitral Tribunal; and

'Witness Statement' means a written statement of testimony by a witness of fact.

Article 1 Scope of Application

1. Whenever the Parties have agreed or the Arbitral Tribunal has determined to apply the IBA Rules of Evidence, the Rules shall govern the taking of evidence, except to the extent that any specific provision of them may be found to be in conflict with any mandatory provision of law determined to be applicable to the case by the Parties or by the Arbitral Tribunal.
2. Where the Parties have agreed to apply the IBA Rules of Evidence, in whole or in part, they shall be deemed to have agreed, in the absence of a contrary indication, to the version as current on the date of such agreement.
3. In case of conflict between any provisions of the IBA Rules of Evidence and the General Rules, the Arbitral Tribunal shall apply the IBA Rules of Evidence in the manner that it determines best in order to accomplish, to the extent possible, the purposes of both the General Rules and the IBA Rules of Evidence, unless the Parties agree to the contrary.
4. In the event of any dispute regarding the meaning of the IBA Rules of Evidence, the Arbitral Tribunal shall interpret them according to their purpose and in the manner most appropriate for the particular arbitration.
5. Insofar as the IBA Rules of Evidence and the General Rules are silent on any matter concerning the taking of evidence and the Parties have not agreed otherwise, the Arbitral Tribunal shall conduct the taking of evidence as it deems appropriate, in accordance with the general principles of the IBA Rules of Evidence.

Article 2 Consultation on Evidentiary Issues

1. The Arbitral Tribunal shall consult the Parties at the earliest appropriate time in the proceedings and invite them to consult each other with a view to agreeing on an efficient, economical and fair process for the taking of evidence.
2. The consultation on evidentiary issues may address the scope, timing and manner of the taking of evidence, including, to the extent applicable:
   (a) the preparation and submission of Witness Statements and Expert Reports;
   (b) the taking of oral testimony at any Evidentiary Hearing;
   (c) the requirements, procedure and format applicable to the production of Documents;
   (d) the level of confidentiality protection to be afforded to evidence in the arbitration;
   (e) the treatment of any issues of cybersecurity and data protection; and
   (f) the promotion of efficiency, economy and conservation of resources in connection with the taking of evidence.
3. The Arbitral Tribunal is encouraged to identify to the Parties, as soon as it considers it to be appropriate, any issues:

(a) that the Arbitral Tribunal may regard as relevant to the case and material to its outcome; and/ or

(b) for which a preliminary determination may be appropriate.

Article 3 Documents

1. Within the time ordered by the Arbitral Tribunal, each Party shall submit to the Arbitral Tribunal and to the other Parties all Documents available to it on which it relies, including public Documents and those in the public domain, except for any Documents that have already been submitted by another Party.

2. Within the time ordered by the Arbitral Tribunal, any Party may submit to the Arbitral Tribunal and to the other Parties a Request to Produce.

3. A Request to Produce shall contain:
   (a) *(i)* a description of each requested Document sufficient to identify it, or
       (ii) a description in sufficient detail (including subject matter) of a narrow and specific requested category of Documents that are reasonably believed to exist; in the case of Documents maintained in electronic form, the requesting Party may, or the Arbitral Tribunal may order that it shall be required to, identify specific files, search terms, individuals or other means of searching for such Documents in an efficient and economical manner;
   (b) a statement as to how the Documents requested are relevant to the case and material to its outcome; and
   (c) *(i)* a statement that the Documents requested are not in the possession, custody or control of the requesting Party or a statement of the reasons why it would be unreasonably burdensome for the requesting Party to produce such Documents, and
       (ii) a statement of the reasons why the requesting Party assumes the Documents requested are in the possession, custody or control of another Party.

4. Within the time ordered by the Arbitral Tribunal, the Party to whom the Request to Produce is addressed shall produce to the other Parties and, if the Arbitral Tribunal so orders, to it, all the Documents requested in its possession, custody or control as to which it makes no objection.

5. If the Party to whom the Request to Produce is addressed has an objection to some or all of the Documents requested, it shall state the objection in writing to the Arbitral Tribunal and the other Parties within the time ordered by the Arbitral Tribunal. The reasons for such objection shall be any of those set forth in Articles 9.2 or 9.3, or a failure to satisfy any of the requirements of Article 3.3. If so directed by the Arbitral Tribunal, and within the time so ordered, the requesting party may respond to the objection.

6. Upon receipt of any such objection and response, the Arbitral Tribunal may invite the relevant Parties to consult with each other with a view to resolving the objection.

7. Either Party may, within the time ordered by the Arbitral Tribunal, request the Arbitral Tribunal to rule on the objection. The Arbitral Tribunal shall then, in timely fashion, consider the Request to Produce, the objection and any response thereto. The Arbitral Tribunal may order the Party to whom such Request is addressed to produce any requested Document in its possession, custody or control as to which the Arbitral Tribunal determines that *(i)* the issues that the requesting Party wishes to prove are relevant to the case and material to its outcome; *(ii)* none of the reasons for objection set forth in Articles 9.2 or 9.3 applies; and *(iii)* the requirements of Article 3.3 have been satisfied. Any such Document shall be produced to the other Parties and, if the Arbitral Tribunal so orders, to it.

8. In exceptional circumstances, if the propriety of an objection can be determined only by review of the Document, the Arbitral Tribunal may determine that it should not review the Document. In that event, the Arbitral Tribunal may, after consultation with the Parties, appoint an independent and impartial expert, bound to confidentiality, to review any such Document and to report on the

objection. To the extent that the objection is upheld by the Arbitral Tribunal, the expert shall not disclose to the Arbitral Tribunal and to the other Parties the contents of the Document reviewed.

9. If a Party wishes to obtain the production of Documents from a person or organisation who is not a Party to the arbitration and from whom the Party cannot obtain the Documents on its own, the Party may, within the time ordered by the Arbitral Tribunal, ask it to take whatever steps are legally available to obtain the requested Documents, or seek leave from the Arbitral Tribunal to take such steps itself. The Party shall submit such request to the Arbitral Tribunal and to the other Parties in writing, and the request shall contain the particulars set forth in Article 3.3, as applicable. The Arbitral Tribunal shall decide on this request and shall take, authorize the requesting Party to take, or order any other Party to take, such steps as the Arbitral Tribunal considers appropriate if, in its discretion, it determines that *(i)* the Documents would be relevant to the case and material to its outcome, *(ii)* the requirements of Article 3.3, as applicable, have been satisfied and *(iii)* none of the reasons for objection set forth in Articles 9.2 or 9.3 applies.

10. At any time before the arbitration is concluded, the Arbitral Tribunal may *(i)* request any Party to produce Documents, *(ii)* request any Party to use its best efforts to take or *(iii)* itself take, any step that it considers appropriate to obtain Documents from any person or organisation. Any Party may object to the request for any of the reasons set forth in Articles 9.2 or 9.3. In such cases, Article 3.4 to Article 3.8 shall apply correspondingly.

11. Within the time ordered by the Arbitral Tribunal, the Parties may submit to the Arbitral Tribunal and to the other Parties any additional Documents on which they intend to rely or which they believe have become relevant to the case and material to its outcome as a consequence of the issues raised in Documents, Witness Statements or Expert Reports submitted or produced, or in other submissions of the Parties.

12. With respect to the form of submission or production of Documents, unless the Parties agree otherwise or, in the absence of such agreement, the Arbitral Tribunal decides otherwise:
    (a) copies of Documents shall conform to the originals and, at the request of the Arbitral Tribunal, any original shall be presented for inspection;
    (b) Documents that a Party maintains in electronic form shall be submitted or produced in the form most convenient or economical to it that is reasonably usable by the recipients;
    (c) a Party is not obligated to produce multiple copies of Documents which are essentially identical;
    (d) Documents to be produced in response to a Request to Produce need not be translated; and
    (e) Documents in a language other than the language of the arbitration that are submitted to the Arbitral Tribunal shall be accompanied by translations marked as such.

13. Any Document submitted or produced by a Party or non-Party in the arbitration and not otherwise in the public domain shall be kept confidential by the Arbitral Tribunal and the other Parties, and shall be used only in connection with the arbitration. This requirement shall apply except and to the extent that disclosure may be required of a Party to fulfil a legal duty, protect or pursue a legal right, or enforce or challenge an award in bona fide legal proceedings before a state court or other judicial authority. The Arbitral Tribunal may issue orders to set forth the terms of this confidentiality. This requirement shall be without prejudice to all other obligations of confidentiality in the arbitration.

14. If the arbitration is organised into separate issues or phases (such as jurisdiction, preliminary determinations, liability or damages), the Arbitral Tribunal may, after consultation with the Parties, schedule the submission of Documents and Requests to Produce separately for each issue or phase.

Article 4 Witnesses of Fact

1. Within the time ordered by the Arbitral Tribunal, each Party shall identify the witnesses on whose testimony it intends to rely and the subject matter of that testimony.

2. Any person may present evidence as a witness, including a Party or a Party's officer, employee or other representative.

3. It shall not be improper for a Party, its officers, employees, legal advisors or other representatives to interview its witnesses or potential witnesses and to discuss their prospective testimony with them.

4. The Arbitral Tribunal may order each Party to submit within a specified time to the Arbitral Tribunal and to the other Parties Witness Statements by each witness on whose testimony it intends to rely, except for those witnesses whose testimony is sought pursuant to Articles 4.9 or 4.10. If Evidentiary Hearings are organised into separate issues or phases (such as jurisdiction, preliminary determinations, liability or damages), the Arbitral Tribunal or the Parties by agreement may schedule the submission of Witness Statements separately for each issue or phase.

5. Each Witness Statement shall contain:
   (a) the full name and address of the witness, a statement regarding his or her present and past relationship (if any) with any of the Parties, and a description of his or her background, qualifications, training and experience, if such a description may be relevant to the dispute or to the contents of the statement;
   (b) a full and detailed description of the facts, and the source of the witness's information as to those facts, sufficient to serve as that witness's evidence in the matter in dispute. Documents on which the witness relies that have not already been submitted shall be provided;
   (c) a statement as to the language in which the Witness Statement was originally prepared and the language in which the witness anticipates giving testimony at the Evidentiary Hearing;
   (d) an affirmation of the truth of the Witness Statement; and
   (e) the signature of the witness and its date and place.

6. If Witness Statements are submitted, any Party may, within the time ordered by the Arbitral Tribunal, submit to the Arbitral Tribunal and to the other Parties revised or additional Witness Statements, including statements from persons not previously named as witnesses, so long as any such revisions or additions respond only to:
   (a) matters contained in another Party's Witness Statements, Expert Reports or other submissions that have not been previously presented in the arbitration; or
   (b) new factual developments that could not have been addressed in a previous Witness Statement.

7. If a witness whose appearance has been requested pursuant to Article 8.1 fails without a valid reason to appear for testimony at an Evidentiary Hearing, the Arbitral Tribunal shall disregard any Witness Statement related to that Evidentiary Hearing by that witness unless, in exceptional circumstances, the Arbitral Tribunal decides otherwise.

8. If the appearance of a witness has not been requested pursuant to Article 8.1, none of the other Parties shall be deemed to have agreed to the correctness of the content of the Witness Statement.

9. If a Party wishes to present evidence from a person who will not appear voluntarily at its request, the Party may, within the time ordered by the Arbitral Tribunal, ask it to take whatever steps are legally available to obtain the testimony of that person, or seek leave from the Arbitral Tribunal to take such steps itself. In the case of a request to the Arbitral Tribunal, the Party shall identify the intended witness, shall describe the subjects on which the witness's testimony is sought and shall state why such subjects are relevant to the case and material to its outcome. The Arbitral Tribunal shall decide on this request and shall take, authorize the requesting Party to take or order any other Party to take, such steps as the Arbitral Tribunal considers appropriate if, in its discretion, it determines that the testimony of that witness would be relevant to the case and material to its outcome.

10. At any time before the arbitration is concluded, the Arbitral Tribunal may order any Party to provide for, or to use its best efforts to provide for, the appearance for testimony at an Evidentiary Hearing of any person, including one whose testimony has not yet been offered. Any Party may object for any of the reasons set forth in Articles 9.2 or 9.3.

Article 5 Party-Appointed Experts

1. A Party may rely on a Party-Appointed Expert as a means of evidence on specific issues. Within the time ordered by the Arbitral Tribunal, (i) each Party shall identify any Party-Appointed Expert on whose testimony it intends to rely and the subject-matter of such testimony; and (ii) the Party-Appointed Expert shall submit an Expert Report.
2. The Expert Report shall contain:
   (a) the full name and address of the Party-Appointed Expert, a statement regarding his or her present and past relationship (if any) with any of the Parties, their legal advisors and the Arbitral Tribunal, and a description of his or her background, qualifications, training and experience;
   (b) a description of the instructions pursuant to which he or she is providing his or her opinions and conclusions;
   (c) a statement of his or her independence from the Parties, their legal advisors and the Arbitral Tribunal;
   (d) a statement of the facts on which he or she is basing his or her expert opinions and conclusions;
   (e) his or her expert opinions and conclusions, including a description of the methods, evidence and information used in arriving at the conclusions. Documents on which the Party-Appointed Expert relies that have not already been submitted shall be provided;
   (f) if the Expert Report has been translated, a statement as to the language in which it was originally prepared, and the language in which the Party-Appointed Expert anticipates giving testimony at the Evidentiary Hearing;
   (g) an affirmation of his or her genuine belief in the opinions expressed in the Expert Report;
   (h) the signature of the Party-Appointed Expert and its date and place; and
   (i) if the Expert Report has been signed by more than one person, an attribution of the entirety or specific parts of the Expert Report to each author.
3. If Expert Reports are submitted, any Party may, within the time ordered by the Arbitral Tribunal, submit to the Arbitral Tribunal and to the other Parties revised or additional Expert Reports, including reports or statements from persons not previously identified as Party-Appointed Experts, so long as any such revisions or additions respond only to:
   (a) matters contained in another Party's Witness Statements, Expert Reports or other submissions that have not been previously presented in the arbitration; or
   (b) new developments that could not have been addressed in a previous Expert Report.
4. The Arbitral Tribunal in its discretion may order that any Party-Appointed Experts who will submit or who have submitted Expert Reports on the same or related issues meet and confer on such issues. At such meeting, the Party-Appointed Experts shall attempt to reach agreement on the issues within the scope of their Expert Reports, and they shall record in writing any such issues on which they reach agreement, any remaining areas of disagreement and the reasons therefor.
5. If a Party-Appointed Expert whose appearance has been requested pursuant to Article 8.1 fails without a valid reason to appear for testimony at an Evidentiary Hearing, the Arbitral Tribunal shall disregard any Expert Report by that Party-Appointed Expert related to that Evidentiary Hearing unless, in exceptional circumstances, the Arbitral Tribunal decides otherwise.
6. If the appearance of a Party-Appointed Expert has not been requested pursuant to Article 8.1, none of the other Parties shall be deemed to have agreed to the correctness of the content of the Expert Report.

Article 6 Tribunal-Appointed Experts

1. The Arbitral Tribunal, after consulting with the Parties, may appoint one or more independent Tribunal-Appointed Experts to report to it on specific issues designated by the Arbitral Tribunal. The Arbitral Tribunal shall establish the terms of reference for any Tribunal-Appointed Expert Report after consulting with the Parties. A copy of the final terms of reference shall be sent by the Arbitral Tribunal to the Parties.

2. The Tribunal-Appointed Expert shall, before accepting appointment, submit to the Arbitral Tribunal and to the Parties a description of his or her qualifications and a statement of his or her independence from the Parties, their legal advisors and the Arbitral Tribunal. Within the time ordered by the Arbitral Tribunal, the Parties shall inform the Arbitral Tribunal whether they have any objections as to the Tribunal-Appointed Expert's qualifications and independence. The Arbitral Tribunal shall decide promptly whether to accept any such objection. After the appointment of a Tribunal-Appointed Expert, a Party may object to the expert's qualifications or independence only if the objection is for reasons of which the Party becomes aware after the appointment has been made. The Arbitral Tribunal shall decide promptly what, if any, action to take.

3. Subject to the provisions of Articles 9.2 and 9.3, the Tribunal-Appointed Expert may request a Party to provide any information or to provide access to any Documents, goods, samples, property, machinery, systems, processes or site for inspection, to the extent relevant to the case and material to its outcome. The Parties and their representatives shall have the right to receive any such information and to attend any such inspection. Any disagreement between a Tribunal-Appointed Expert and a Party as to the relevance, materiality or appropriateness of such a request shall be decided by the Arbitral Tribunal, in the manner provided in Articles 3.5 through 3.8. The Tribunal-Appointed Expert shall record in the Expert Report any non-compliance by a Party with an appropriate request or decision by the Arbitral Tribunal and shall describe its effects on the determination of the specific issue.

4. The Tribunal-Appointed Expert shall report in writing to the Arbitral Tribunal in an Expert Report. The Expert Report shall contain:
    (a) the full name and address of the Tribunal-Appointed Expert, and a description of his or her background, qualifications, training and experience;
    (b) a statement of the facts on which he or she is basing his or her expert opinions and conclusions;
    (c) his or her expert opinions and conclusions, including a description of the methods, evidence and information used in arriving at the conclusions. Documents on which the Tribunal-Appointed Expert relies that have not already been submitted shall be provided;
    (d) if the Expert Report has been translated, a statement as to the language in which it was originally prepared, and the language in which the Tribunal-Appointed Expert anticipates giving testimony at the Evidentiary Hearing;
    (e) an affirmation of his or her genuine belief in the opinions expressed in the Expert Report;
    (f) the signature of the Tribunal-Appointed Expert and its date and place; and
    (g) if the Expert Report has been signed by more than one person, an attribution of the entirety or specific parts of the Expert Report to each author.

5. The Arbitral Tribunal shall send a copy of such Expert Report to the Parties. The Parties may examine any information, Documents, goods, samples, property, machinery, systems, processes or site for inspection that the Tribunal-Appointed Expert has examined and any correspondence between the Arbitral Tribunal and the Tribunal-Appointed Expert. Within the time ordered by the Arbitral Tribunal, any Party shall have the opportunity to respond to the Expert Report in a submission by the Party or through a Witness Statement or an Expert Report by a Party-Appointed Expert. The Arbitral Tribunal shall send the submission, Witness Statement or Expert Report to the Tribunal-Appointed Expert and to the other Parties.

6. At the request of a Party or of the Arbitral Tribunal, the Tribunal-Appointed Expert shall be present at an Evidentiary Hearing. The Arbitral Tribunal may question the Tribunal-Appointed Expert, and he or she may be questioned by the Parties or by any Party-Appointed Expert on issues raised in his or her Expert Report, the Parties' submissions or Witness Statement or the Expert Reports made by the Party-Appointed Experts pursuant to Article 6.5.

7. Any Expert Report made by a Tribunal-Appointed Expert and its conclusions shall be assessed by the Arbitral Tribunal with due regard to all circumstances of the case.

8. The fees and expenses of a Tribunal-Appointed Expert, to be funded in a manner determined by the Arbitral Tribunal, shall form part of the costs of the arbitration.

Article 7 Inspection

Subject to the provisions of Articles 9.2 and 9.3, the Arbitral Tribunal may, at the request of a Party or on its own motion, inspect or require the inspection by a Tribunal-Appointed Expert or a Party-Appointed Expert of any site, property, machinery or any other goods, samples, systems, processes or Documents, as it deems appropriate. The Arbitral Tribunal shall, in consultation with the Parties, determine the timing and arrangements for the inspection. The Parties and their representatives shall have the right to attend any such inspection.

Article 8 Evidentiary Hearing

1. Within the time ordered by the Arbitral Tribunal, each Party shall inform the Arbitral Tribunal and the other Parties of the witnesses whose appearance it requests. Each witness (which term includes, for the purposes of this Article, witnesses of fact and any experts) shall, subject to Article 8.3, appear for testimony at the Evidentiary Hearing if such person's appearance has been requested by any Party or by the Arbitral Tribunal.
2. At the request of a Party or on its own motion, the Arbitral Tribunal may, after consultation with the Parties, order that the Evidentiary Hearing be conducted as a Remote Hearing. In that event, the Arbitral Tribunal shall consult with the Parties with a view to establishing a Remote Hearing protocol to conduct the Remote Hearing efficiently, fairly and, to the extent possible, without unintended interruptions. The protocol may address:
   (a) the technology to be used;
   (b) advance testing of the technology or training in use of the technology;
   (c) the starting and ending times considering, in particular, the time zones in which participants will be located;
   (d) how Documents may be placed before a witness or the Arbitral Tribunal; and
   (e) measures to ensure that witnesses giving oral testimony are not improperly influenced or distracted.
3. The Arbitral Tribunal shall at all times have complete control over the Evidentiary Hearing. The Arbitral Tribunal may limit or exclude any question to, answer by or appearance of a witness, if it considers such question, answer or appearance to be irrelevant, immaterial, unreasonably burdensome, duplicative or otherwise covered by a reason for objection set forth in Articles 9.2 or 9.3. Questions to a witness during direct and re-direct testimony may not be unreasonably leading.
4. With respect to oral testimony at an Evidentiary Hearing:
   (a) the Claimant shall ordinarily first present the testimony of its witnesses, followed by the Respondent presenting the testimony of its witnesses;
   (b) following direct testimony, any other Party may question such witness, in an order to be determined by the Arbitral Tribunal. The Party who initially presented the witness shall subsequently have the opportunity to ask additional questions on the matters raised in the other Parties' questioning;
   (c) thereafter, the Claimant shall ordinarily first present the testimony of its Party-Appointed Experts, followed by the Respondent presenting the testimony of its Party-Appointed Experts. The Party who initially presented the Party-Appointed Expert shall subsequently have the opportunity to ask additional questions on the matters raised in the other Parties' questioning;
   (d) the Arbitral Tribunal may question a Tribunal-Appointed Expert, and he or she may be questioned by the Parties or by any Party-Appointed Expert, on issues raised in the Tribunal-Appointed Expert Report, in the Parties' submissions or in the Expert Reports made by the Party-Appointed Experts;
   (e) if the arbitration is organised into separate issues or phases (such as jurisdiction, preliminary determinations, liability and damages), the Parties may agree or the Arbitral Tribunal may order the scheduling of testimony separately for each issue or phase;
   (f) the Arbitral Tribunal, upon request of a Party or on its own motion, may vary this order of proceeding, including the arrangement of testimony by particular issues or in such a manner

that witnesses be questioned at the same time and in confrontation with each other (witness conferencing);

(g) the Arbitral Tribunal may ask questions to a witness at any time.

5. A witness of fact providing testimony shall first affirm, in a manner determined appropriate by the Arbitral Tribunal, that he or she commits to tell the truth or, in the case of an expert witness, his or her genuine belief in the opinions to be expressed at the Evidentiary Hearing. If the witness has submitted a Witness Statement or an Expert Report, the witness shall confirm it. The Parties may agree or the Arbitral Tribunal may order that the Witness Statement or Expert Report shall serve as that witness's direct testimony, in which event the Arbitral Tribunal may nevertheless permit further oral direct testimony.

6. Subject to the provisions of Articles 9.2 and 9.3, the Arbitral Tribunal may request any person to give oral or written evidence on any issue that the Arbitral Tribunal considers to be relevant to the case and material to its outcome. Any witness called and questioned by the Arbitral Tribunal may also be questioned by the Parties.

Article 9 Admissibility and Assessment of Evidence

1. The Arbitral Tribunal shall determine the admissibility, relevance, materiality and weight of evidence.

2. The Arbitral Tribunal shall, at the request of a Party or on its own motion, exclude from evidence or production any Document, statement, oral testimony or inspection, in whole or in part, for any of the following reasons:

   (a) lack of sufficient relevance to the case or materiality to its outcome;

   (b) legal impediment or privilege under the legal or ethical rules determined by the Arbitral Tribunal to be applicable (see Article 9.4 below);

   (c) unreasonable burden to produce the requested evidence;

   (d) loss or destruction of the Document that has been shown with reasonable likelihood to have occurred;

   (e) grounds of commercial or technical confidentiality that the Arbitral Tribunal determines to be compelling;

   (f) grounds of special political or institutional sensitivity (including evidence that has been classified as secret by a government or a public international institution) that the Arbitral Tribunal determines to be compelling; or

   (g) considerations of procedural economy, proportionality, fairness or equality of the Parties that the Arbitral Tribunal determines to be compelling.

3. The Arbitral Tribunal may, at the request of a Party or on its own motion, exclude evidence obtained illegally.

4. In considering issues of legal impediment or privilege under Article 9.2(b), and insofar as permitted by any mandatory legal or ethical rules that are determined by it to be applicable, the Arbitral Tribunal may take into account:

   (a) any need to protect the confidentiality of a Document created or statement or oral communication made in connection with and for the purpose of providing or obtaining legal advice;

   (b) any need to protect the confidentiality of a Document created or statement or oral communication made in connection with and for the purpose of settlement negotiations;

   (c) the expectations of the Parties and their advisors at the time the legal impediment or privilege is said to have arisen;

   (d) any possible waiver of any applicable legal impediment or privilege by virtue of consent, earlier disclosure, affirmative use of the Document, statement, oral communication or advice contained therein, or otherwise; and

   (e) the need to maintain fairness and equality as between the Parties, particularly if they are subject to different legal or ethical rules.

5. The Arbitral Tribunal may, where appropriate, make necessary arrangements to permit Documents to be produced, and evidence to be presented or considered subject to suitable confidentiality protection.

6. If a Party fails without satisfactory explanation to produce any Document requested in a Request to Produce to which it has not objected in due time or fails to produce any Document ordered to be produced by the Arbitral Tribunal, the Arbitral Tribunal may infer that such document would be adverse to the interests of that Party.

7. If a Party fails without satisfactory explanation to make available any other relevant evidence, including testimony, sought by one Party to which the Party to whom the request was addressed has not objected in due time or fails to make available any evidence, including testimony, ordered by the Arbitral Tribunal to be produced, the Arbitral Tribunal may infer that such evidence would be adverse to the interests of that Party.

8. If the Arbitral Tribunal determines that a Party has failed to conduct itself in good faith in the taking of evidence, the Arbitral Tribunal may, in addition to any other measures available under these Rules, take such failure into account in its assignment of the costs of the arbitration, including costs arising out of or in connection with the taking of evidence.

IBA Guidelines on Conflicts of Interest in International Arbitration

(Adopted by resolution of the IBA Council on Thursday 23 October 2014)

INTRODUCTION

1. Arbitrators and party representatives are often unsure about the scope of their disclosure obligations. The growth of international business, including larger corporate groups and international law firms, has generated more disclosures and resulted in increased complexity in the analysis of disclosure and conflict of interest issues. Parties have more opportunities to use challenges of arbitrators to delay arbitrations, or to deny the opposing party the arbitrator of its choice. Disclosure of any relationship, no matter how minor or serious, may lead to unwarranted or frivolous challenges. At the same time, it is important that more information be made available to the parties, so as to protect awards against challenges based upon alleged failures to disclose, and to promote a level playing field among parties and among counsel engaged in international arbitration.

2. Parties, arbitrators, institutions and courts face complex decisions about the information that arbitrators should disclose and the standards to apply to disclosure. In addition, institutions and courts face difficult decisions when an objection or a challenge is made after a disclosure. There is a tension between, on the one hand, the parties' right to disclosure of circumstances that may call into question an arbitrator's impartiality or independence in order to protect the parties' right to a fair hearing, and, on the other hand, the need to avoid unnecessary challenges against arbitrators in order to protect the parties' ability to select arbitrators of their choosing.

3. It is in the interest of the international arbitration community that arbitration proceedings are not hindered by ill-founded challenges against arbitrators and that the legitimacy of the process is not affected by uncertainty and a lack of uniformity in the applicable standards for disclosures, objections and challenges. The 2004 Guidelines reflected the view that the standards existing at the time lacked sufficient clarity and uniformity in their application. The Guidelines, therefore, set forth some 'General Standards and Explanatory Notes on the Standards'. Moreover, in order to promote greater consistency and to avoid unnecessary challenges and arbitrator withdrawals and removals, the Guidelines list specific situations indicating whether they warrant disclosure or disqualification of an arbitrator. Such lists, designated 'Red', 'Orange' and 'Green' (the 'Application Lists'), have been updated and appear at the end of these revised Guidelines.

4. The Guidelines reflect the understanding of the IBA Arbitration Committee as to the best current international practice, firmly rooted in the principles expressed in the General Standards below. The General Standards and the Application Lists are based upon statutes and case law in a cross-section of jurisdictions, and upon the judgement and experience of practitioners involved in international arbitration. In reviewing the 2004 Guidelines, the IBA Arbitration Committee updated its analysis of the laws and practices in a number of jurisdictions. The Guidelines seek to balance the various interests of parties, representatives, arbitrators and arbitration institutions, all of whom have a responsibility for ensuring the integrity, reputation and efficiency of international arbitration. Both the 2004 Working Group and the Subcommittee in 2012/2014 have sought and considered the views of leading arbitration institutions, corporate counsel and other persons involved in international arbitration through public consultations at IBA annual meetings, and at meetings with arbitrators and practitioners. The comments received were reviewed in detail and many were adopted. The IBA Arbitration Committee is grateful for the serious consideration given to its proposals by so many institutions and individuals.

5. The Guidelines apply to international commercial arbitration and investment arbitration, whether the representation of the parties is carried out by lawyers or non-lawyers, and irrespective of whether or not non-legal professionals serve as arbitrators.

6. These Guidelines are not legal provisions and do not override any applicable national law or arbitral rules chosen by the parties. However, it is hoped that, as was the case for the 2004 Guidelines and other sets of rules and guidelines of the IBA Arbitration Committee, the revised Guidelines will find broad acceptance within the international arbitration community, and that they will assist parties, practitioners, arbitrators, institutions and courts in dealing with these important questions of impartiality and independence. The IBA Arbitration Committee trusts that the Guidelines will be applied with robust common sense and without unduly formalistic interpretation.

7. The Application Lists cover many of the varied situations that commonly arise in practice, but they do not purport to be exhaustive, nor could they be. Nevertheless, the IBA Arbitration Committee is confident that the Application Lists provide concrete guidance that is useful in applying the General Standards. The IBA Arbitration Committee will continue to study the actual use of the Guidelines with a view to furthering their improvement.

8. In 1987, the IBA published *Rules of Ethics for International Arbitrators*. Those Rules cover more topics than these Guidelines, and they remain in effect as to subjects that are not discussed in the Guidelines. The Guidelines supersede the *Rules of Ethics* as to the matters treated here.

PART I: GENERAL STANDARDS REGARDING IMPARTIALITY, INDEPENDENCE AND DISCLOSURE

(1) General Principle

Every arbitrator shall be impartial and independent of the parties at the time of accepting an appointment to serve and shall remain so until the final award has been rendered or the proceedings have otherwise finally terminated.

Explanation to General Standard 1:

A fundamental principle underlying these Guidelines is that each arbitrator must be impartial and independent of the parties at the time he or she accepts an appointment to act as arbitrator, and must remain so during the entire course of the arbitration proceeding, including the time period for the correction or interpretation of a final award under the relevant rules, assuming such time period is known or readily ascertainable.

The question has arisen as to whether this obligation should extend to the period during which the award may be challenged before the relevant courts. The decision taken is that this obligation should not extend in this manner, unless the final award may be referred back to the original Arbitral Tribunal under the relevant applicable law or relevant institutional rules. Thus, the arbitrator's obligation in this regard ends when the Arbitral Tribunal has rendered the final award, and any correction or interpretation as may be permitted under the relevant rules has been issued, or the time for seeking the same has elapsed, the proceedings have been finally terminated (for example, because of a settlement), or the arbitrator otherwise no longer has jurisdiction. If, after setting aside or other proceedings, the dispute is referred back to the same Arbitral Tribunal, a fresh round of disclosure and review of potential conflicts of interests may be necessary.

(2) Conflicts of Interest

(a) An arbitrator shall decline to accept an appointment or, if the arbitration has already been commenced, refuse to continue to act as an arbitrator, if he or she has any doubt as to his or her ability to be impartial or independent.

(b) The same principle applies if facts or circumstances exist, or have arisen since the appointment, which, from the point of view of a reasonable third person having knowledge of the relevant facts and circumstances, would give rise to justifiable doubts as to the arbitrator's impartiality or independence, unless the parties have accepted the arbitrator in accordance with the requirements set out in General Standard 4.

(c) Doubts are justifiable if a reasonable third person, having knowledge of the relevant facts and circumstances, would reach the conclusion that there is a likelihood that the arbitrator may be influenced by factors other than the merits of the case as presented by the parties in reaching his or her decision.

(d) Justifiable doubts necessarily exist as to the arbitrator's impartiality or independence in any of the situations described in the Non-Waivable Red List.

Explanation to General Standard 2:

(a) If the arbitrator has doubts as to his or her ability to be impartial and independent, the arbitrator must decline the appointment. This standard should apply regardless of the stage of the proceedings. This is a basic principle that is spelled out in these Guidelines in order to avoid confusion and to foster confidence in the arbitral process.

(b) In order for standards to be applied as consistently as possible, the test for disqualification is an objective one. The wording 'impartiality or independence' derives from the widely adopted Article 12 of the United Nations Commission on International Trade Law (UNCITRAL) Model Law, and the use of an appearance test based on justifiable doubts as to the impartiality or independence of the arbitrator, as provided in Article 12(2) of the UNCITRAL Model Law, is to be applied objectively (a 'reasonable third person test'). Again, as described in the Explanation to General Standard 3(e), this standard applies regardless of the stage of the proceedings.

(c) Laws and rules that rely on the standard of justifiable doubts often do not define that standard. This General Standard is intended to provide some context for making this determination.

(d) The Non-Waivable Red List describes circumstances that necessarily raise justifiable doubts as to the arbitrator's impartiality or independence. For example, because no one is allowed to be his or her own judge, there cannot be identity between an arbitrator and a party. The parties, therefore, cannot waive the conflict of interest arising in such a situation.

(3) Disclosure by the Arbitrator

(a) If facts or circumstances exist that may, in the eyes of the parties, give rise to doubts as to the arbitrator's impartiality or independence, the arbitrator shall disclose such facts or circumstances to the parties, the arbitration institution or other appointing authority (if any, and if so required by the applicable institutional rules) and the co-arbitrators, if any, prior to accepting his or her appointment or, if thereafter, as soon as he or she learns of them.

(b) An advance declaration or waiver in relation to possible conflicts of interest arising from facts and circumstances that may arise in the future does not discharge the arbitrator's ongoing duty of disclosure under General Standard 3(a).

(c) It follows from General Standards 1 and 2(a) that an arbitrator who has made a disclosure considers himself or herself to be impartial and independent of the parties, despite the disclosed facts, and, therefore, capable of performing his or her duties as arbitrator. Otherwise, he or she would have declined the nomination or appointment at the outset, or resigned.

(d) Any doubt as to whether an arbitrator should disclose certain facts or circumstances should be resolved in favour of disclosure.

(e) When considering whether facts or circumstances exist that should be disclosed, the arbitrator shall not take into account whether the arbitration is at the beginning or at a later stage.

Explanation to General Standard 3:

(a) The arbitrator's duty to disclose under General Standard 3(a) rests on the principle that the parties have an interest in being fully informed of any facts or circumstances that may be relevant in their view. Accordingly, General Standard 3(d) provides that any doubt as to whether certain facts or circumstances should be disclosed should be resolved in favour of disclosure. However, situations that, such as those set out in the Green List, could never lead to disqualification under the objective test set out in General Standard 2, need not be disclosed. As reflected in General Standard 3(c), a disclosure does not imply that the disclosed facts are such as to disqualify the arbitrator under General Standard 2. The duty of disclosure under General Standard 3(a) is ongoing in nature.

(b) The IBA Arbitration Committee has considered the increasing use by prospective arbitrators of declarations in respect of facts or circumstances that may arise in the future, and the possible conflicts of interest that may result, sometimes referred to as 'advance waivers'. Such declarations do not discharge the arbitrator's ongoing duty of disclosure under General Standard 3(a). The Guidelines, however, do not otherwise take a position as to the validity and effect of advance declarations or waivers, because the validity and effect of any advance declaration or waiver must be assessed in view of the specific text of the advance declaration or waiver, the particular circumstances at hand and the applicable law.

(c) A disclosure does not imply the existence of a conflict of interest. An arbitrator who has made a disclosure to the parties considers himself or herself to be impartial and independent of the parties, despite the disclosed facts, or else he or she would have declined the nomination, or resigned. An arbitrator making a disclosure thus feels capable of performing his or her duties. It is the purpose of disclosure to allow the parties to judge whether they agree with the evaluation of the arbitrator and, if they so wish, to explore the situation further. It is hoped that the promulgation of this General Standard will eliminate the misconception that disclosure itself implies doubts sufficient to disqualify the arbitrator, or even creates a presumption in favour of disqualification. Instead, any challenge should only be successful if an objective test, as set forth in General Standard 2 above, is met. Under Comment 5 of the Practical Application of the General Standards, a failure to disclose certain facts and circumstances that may, in the eyes of the parties, give rise to doubts as to the arbitrator's impartiality or independence, does not necessarily mean that a conflict of interest exists, or that a disqualification should ensue.

(d) In determining which facts should be disclosed, an arbitrator should take into account all circumstances known to him or her. If the arbitrator finds that he or she should make a disclosure, but that professional secrecy rules or other rules of practice or professional conduct prevent such disclosure, he or she should not accept the appointment, or should resign.

(e) Disclosure or disqualification (as set out in General Standards 2 and 3) should not depend on the particular stage of the arbitration. In order to determine whether the arbitrator should disclose, decline the appointment or refuse to continue to act, the facts and circumstances alone are relevant, not the current stage of the proceedings, or the consequences of the withdrawal. As a practical matter, arbitration institutions may make a distinction depending on the stage of the arbitration. Courts may likewise apply different standards. Nevertheless, no distinction is made by these Guidelines depending on the stage of the arbitral proceedings. While there are practical concerns, if an arbitrator must withdraw after the arbitration has commenced, a distinction based on the stage of the arbitration would be inconsistent with the General Standards.

(4) Waiver by the Parties

(a) If, within 30 days after the receipt of any disclosure by the arbitrator, or after a party otherwise learns of facts or circumstances that could constitute a potential conflict of interest for an arbitrator, a party does not raise an express objection with regard to that arbitrator, subject to paragraphs (b) and (c) of this General Standard, the party is deemed to have waived any potential conflict of interest in respect of the arbitrator based on such facts or circumstances and may not raise any objection based on such facts or circumstances at a later stage.

(b) However, if facts or circumstances exist as described in the Non-Waivable Red List, any waiver by a party (including any declaration or advance waiver, such as that contemplated in General Standard 3(b)), or any agreement by the parties to have such a person serve as arbitrator, shall be regarded as invalid.

(c) A person should not serve as an arbitrator when a conflict of interest, such as those exemplified in the Waivable Red List, exists. Nevertheless, such a person may accept appointment as arbitrator, or continue to act as an arbitrator, if the following conditions are met:

    (i) all parties, all arbitrators and the arbitration institution, or other appointing authority (if any), have full knowledge of the conflict of interest; and

    (ii) all parties expressly agree that such a person may serve as arbitrator, despite the conflict of interest.

(d) An arbitrator may assist the parties in reaching a settlement of the dispute, through conciliation, mediation or otherwise, at any stage of the proceedings. However, before doing so, the arbitrator should receive an express agreement by the parties that acting in such a manner shall not disqualify the arbitrator from continuing to serve as arbitrator. Such express agreement shall be considered to be an effective waiver of any potential conflict of interest that may arise from the arbitrator's participation in such a process, or from information that the arbitrator may learn in the process. If the assistance by the arbitrator does not lead to the final settlement of the case, the parties remain bound by their waiver. However, consistent with General Standard 2(a) and notwithstanding such agreement, the arbitrator shall resign if, as a consequence of his or her involvement in the settlement process, the arbitrator develops doubts as to his or her ability to remain impartial or independent in the future course of the arbitration.

Explanation to General Standard 4:

(a) Under General Standard 4(a), a party is deemed to have waived any potential conflict of interest, if such party has not raised an objection in respect of such conflict of interest within 30 days. This time limit should run from the date on which the party learns of the relevant facts or circumstances, including through the disclosure process.

(b) General Standard 4(b) serves to exclude from the scope of General Standard 4(a) the facts and circumstances described in the Non-Waivable Red List. Some arbitrators make declarations that seek waivers from the parties with respect to facts or circumstances that may arise in the future. Irrespective of any such waiver sought by the arbitrator, as provided in General Standard 3(b), facts and circumstances arising in the course of the arbitration should be disclosed to the parties by virtue of the arbitrator's ongoing duty of disclosure.

(c) Notwithstanding a serious conflict of interest, such as those that are described by way of example in the Waivable Red List, the parties may wish to engage such a person as an arbitrator. Here, party autonomy and the desire to have only impartial and independent arbitrators must be balanced. Persons with a serious conflict of interest, such as those that are described by way of example in the Waivable Red List, may serve as arbitrators only if the parties make fully informed, explicit waivers.

(d) The concept of the Arbitral Tribunal assisting the parties in reaching a settlement of their dispute in the course of the arbitration proceedings is well-established in some jurisdictions, but not in others. Informed consent by the parties to such a process prior to its beginning should be regarded as an effective waiver of a potential conflict of interest. Certain jurisdictions may require such consent to be in writing and signed by the parties. Subject to any requirements of applicable law, express consent may be sufficient and may be given at a hearing and reflected in the minutes or transcript of the proceeding. In addition, in order to avoid parties using an arbitrator as mediator as a means of disqualifying the arbitrator, the General Standard makes clear that the waiver should remain effective, if the mediation is unsuccessful. In giving their express consent, the parties should realise the consequences of the arbitrator assisting them in a settlement process, including the risk of the resignation of the arbitrator.

(5) Scope

(a) These Guidelines apply equally to tribunal chairs, sole arbitrators and co-arbitrators, howsoever appointed.
(b) Arbitral or administrative secretaries and assistants, to an individual arbitrator or the Arbitral Tribunal, are bound by the same duty of independence and impartiality as arbitrators, and it is the responsibility of the Arbitral Tribunal to ensure that such duty is respected at all stages of the arbitration.

Explanation to General Standard 5:

(a) Because each member of an Arbitral Tribunal has an obligation to be impartial and independent, the General Standards do not distinguish between sole arbitrators, tribunal chairs, party-appointed arbitrators or arbitrators appointed by an institution.
(b) Some arbitration institutions require arbitral or administrative secretaries and assistants to sign a declaration of independence and impartiality. Whether or not such a requirement exists, arbitral or administrative secretaries and assistants to the Arbitral Tribunal are bound by the same duty of independence and impartiality (including the duty of disclosure) as arbitrators, and it is the responsibility of the Arbitral Tribunal to ensure that such duty is respected at all stages of the arbitration. Furthermore, this duty applies to arbitral or administrative secretaries and assistants to either the Arbitral Tribunal or individual members of the Arbitral Tribunal.

(6) Relationships

(a) The arbitrator is in principle considered to bear the identity of his or her law firm, but when considering the relevance of facts or circumstances to determine whether a potential conflict of interest exists, or whether disclosure should be made, the activities of an arbitrator's law firm, if any, and the relationship of the arbitrator with the law firm, should be considered in each individual case. The fact that the activities of the arbitrator's firm involve one of the parties shall not necessarily constitute a source of such conflict, or a reason for disclosure. Similarly, if one of the parties is a member of a group with which the arbitrator's firm has a relationship, such fact should be considered in each individual case, but shall not necessarily constitute by itself a source of a conflict of interest, or a reason for disclosure.
(b) If one of the parties is a legal entity, any legal or physical person having a controlling influence on the legal entity, or a direct economic interest in, or a duty to indemnify a party for, the award to be rendered in the arbitration, may be considered to bear the identity of such party.

Explanation to General Standard 6:

(a) The growing size of law firms should be taken into account as part of today's reality in international arbitration. There is a need to balance the interests of a party to appoint the arbitrator of its choice, who may be a partner at a large law firm, and the importance of maintaining confidence in the impartiality and independence of international arbitrators. The arbitrator must, in principle, be considered to bear the identity of his or her law firm, but the activities of the arbitrator's firm should not automatically create a conflict of interest. The relevance of the activities of the arbitrator's firm, such as the nature, timing and scope of the work by the law firm, and the relationship of the arbitrator with the law firm, should be considered in each case. General Standard 6(a) uses the term 'involve' rather than 'acting for' because the relevant connections with a party may include activities other than representation on a legal matter. Although barristers' chambers should not be equated with law firms for the purposes of conflicts, and no general standard is proffered for barristers' chambers, disclosure may be warranted in view of the relationships among barristers, parties or counsel. When a party to an arbitration is a member of a group of companies, special questions regarding conflicts of interest arise. Because individual corporate structure arrangements vary widely, a catch-all rule is not appropriate. Instead, the particular circumstances of an affiliation with another entity within the same group of companies, and the relationship of that entity with the arbitrator's law firm, should be considered in each individual case.

(b) When a party in international arbitration is a legal entity, other legal and physical persons may have a controlling influence on this legal entity, or a direct economic interest in, or a duty to indemnify a party for, the award to be rendered in the arbitration. Each situation should be assessed individually, and General Standard 6(b) clarifies that such legal persons and individuals may be considered effectively to be that party. Third-party funders and insurers in relation to the dispute may have a direct economic interest in the award, and as such may be considered to be the equivalent of the party. For these purposes, the terms 'third-party funder' and 'insurer' refer to any person or entity that is contributing funds, or other material support, to the prosecution or defence of the case and that has a direct economic interest in, or a duty to indemnify a party for, the award to be rendered in the arbitration.

(7) Duty of the Parties and the Arbitrator

(a) A party shall inform an arbitrator, the Arbitral Tribunal, the other parties and the arbitration institution or other appointing authority (if any) of any relationship, direct or indirect, between the arbitrator and the party (or another company of the same group of companies, or an individual having a controlling influence on the party in the arbitration), or between the arbitrator and any person or entity with a direct economic interest in, or a duty to indemnify a party for, the award to be rendered in the arbitration. The party shall do so on its own initiative at the earliest opportunity.

(b) A party shall inform an arbitrator, the Arbitral Tribunal, the other parties and the arbitration institution or other appointing authority (if any) of the identity of its counsel appearing in the arbitration, as well as of any relationship, including membership of the same barristers' chambers, between its counsel and the arbitrator. The party shall do so on its own initiative at the earliest opportunity, and upon any change in its counsel team.

(c) In order to comply with General Standard 7(a), a party shall perform reasonable enquiries and provide any relevant information available to it.

(d) An arbitrator is under a duty to make reasonable enquiries to identify any conflict of interest, as well as any facts or circumstances that may reasonably give rise to doubts as to his or her impartiality or independence. Failure to disclose a conflict is not excused by lack of knowledge, if the arbitrator does not perform such reasonable enquiries.

Explanation to General Standard 7:

(a) The parties are required to disclose any relationship with the arbitrator. Disclosure of such relationships should reduce the risk of an unmeritorious challenge of an arbitrator's impartiality or independence based on information learned after the appointment. The parties' duty of disclosure of any relationship, direct or indirect, between the arbitrator and the party (or another company of the same group of companies, or an individual having a controlling influence on the party in the arbitration) has been extended to relationships with persons or entities having a direct economic interest in the award to be rendered in the arbitration, such as an entity providing funding for the arbitration, or having a duty to indemnify a party for the award.

(b) Counsel appearing in the arbitration, namely the persons involved in the representation of the parties in the arbitration, must be identified by the parties at the earliest opportunity. A party's duty to disclose the identity of counsel appearing in the arbitration extends to all members of that party's counsel team and arises from the outset of the proceedings.

(c) In order to satisfy their duty of disclosure, the parties are required to investigate any relevant information that is reasonably available to them. In addition, any party to an arbitration is required, at the outset and on an ongoing basis during the entirety of the proceedings, to make a reasonable effort to ascertain and to disclose available information that, applying the general standard, might affect the arbitrator's impartiality or independence.

(d) In order to satisfy their duty of disclosure under the Guidelines, arbitrators are required to investigate any relevant information that is reasonably available to them.

PART II: PRACTICAL APPLICATION OF THE GENERAL STANDARDS

1. If the Guidelines are to have an important practical influence, they should address situations that are likely to occur in today's arbitration practice and should provide specific guidance to arbitrators, parties, institutions and courts as to which situations do or do not constitute conflicts of interest, or should or should not be disclosed. For this purpose, the Guidelines categorise situations that may occur in the following Application Lists. These lists cannot cover every situation. In all cases, the General Standards should control the outcome.

2. The Red List consists of two parts: 'a Non-Waivable Red List' (see General Standards 2(d) and 4(b)); and 'a Waivable Red List' (see General Standard 4(c)). These lists are non-exhaustive and detail specific situations that, depending on the facts of a given case, give rise to justifiable doubts as to the arbitrator's impartiality and independence. That is, in these circumstances, an objective conflict of interest exists from the point of view of a reasonable third person having knowledge of the relevant facts and circumstances (see General Standard 2(b)). The Non-Waivable Red List includes situations deriving from the overriding principle that no person can be his or her own judge. Therefore, acceptance of such a situation cannot cure the conflict. The Waivable Red List covers situations that are serious but not as severe. Because of their seriousness, unlike circumstances described in the Orange List, these situations should be considered waivable, but only if and when the parties, being aware of the conflict of interest situation, expressly state their willingness to have such a person act as arbitrator, as set forth in General Standard 4(c).

3. The Orange List is a non-exhaustive list of specific situations that, depending on the facts of a given case, may, in the eyes of the parties, give rise to doubts as to the arbitrator's impartiality or independence. The Orange List thus reflects situations that would fall under General Standard 3(a), with the consequence that the arbitrator has a duty to disclose such situations. In all these situations, the parties are deemed to have accepted the arbitrator if, after disclosure, no timely objection is made, as established in General Standard 4(a).

4. Disclosure does not imply the existence of a conflict of interest; nor should it by itself result either in a disqualification of the arbitrator, or in a presumption regarding disqualification. The purpose of the disclosure is to inform the parties of a situation that they may wish to explore further in order to determine whether objectively—that is, from the point of view of a reasonable third person having knowledge of the relevant facts and circumstances—there are justifiable doubts as to the arbitrator's impartiality or independence. If the conclusion is that there are no justifiable doubts, the arbitrator can act. Apart from the situations covered by the Non-Waivable Red List, he or she can also act if there is no timely objection by the parties or, in situations covered by the Waivable Red List, if there is a specific acceptance by the parties in accordance with General Standard 4(c). If a party challenges the arbitrator, he or she can nevertheless act, if the authority that rules on the challenge decides that the challenge does not meet the objective test for disqualification.

5. A later challenge based on the fact that an arbitrator did not disclose such facts or circumstances should not result automatically in non-appointment, later disqualification or a successful challenge to any award. Nondisclosure cannot by itself make an arbitrator partial or lacking independence: only the facts or circumstances that he or she failed to disclose can do so.

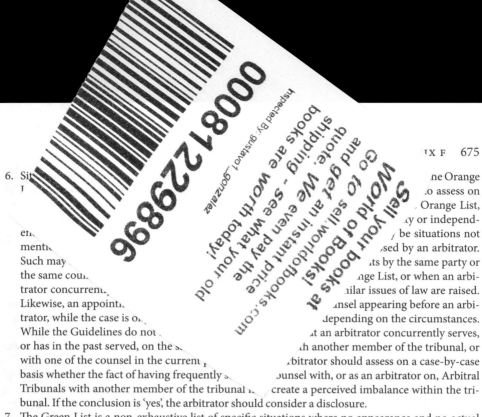

6. Sit _____ ne Orange
ɪ _____ o assess on
_____ Orange List,
_____ ty or independ-
en _____ be situations not
menti _____ sed by an arbitrator.
Such may _____ ts by the same party or
the same cou _____ nge List, or when an arbitrator concurren _____ ilar issues of law are raised.
Likewise, an appoint _____ unsel appearing before an arbitrator, while the case is o _____ depending on the circumstances.
While the Guidelines do not _____ t an arbitrator concurrently serves,
or has in the past served, on the _____ h another member of the tribunal, or
with one of the counsel in the current _____ bitrator should assess on a case-by-case
basis whether the fact of having frequently _____ ounsel with, or as an arbitrator on, Arbitral
Tribunals with another member of the tribunal _____ create a perceived imbalance within the tribunal. If the conclusion is 'yes', the arbitrator should consider a disclosure.

7. The Green List is a non-exhaustive list of specific situations where no appearance and no actual conflict of interest exists from an objective point of view. Thus, the arbitrator has no duty to disclose situations falling within the Green List. As stated in the Explanation to General Standard 3(a), there should be a limit to disclosure, based on reasonableness; in some situations, an objective test should prevail over the purely subjective test of 'the eyes' of the parties.

8. The borderline between the categories that comprise the Lists can be thin. It can be debated whether a certain situation should be on one List instead of another. Also, the Lists contain, for various situations, general terms such as 'significant' and 'relevant'. The Lists reflect international principles and best practices to the extent possible. Further definition of the norms, which are to be interpreted reasonably in light of the facts and circumstances in each case, would be counterproductive.

1.   Non-Waivable Red List

1.1 There is an identity between a party and the arbitrator, or the arbitrator is a legal representative or employee of an entity that is a party in the arbitration.

1.2 The arbitrator is a manager, director or member of the supervisory board, or has a controlling influence on one of the parties or an entity that has a direct economic interest in the award to be rendered in the arbitration.

1.3 The arbitrator has a significant financial or personal interest in one of the parties, or the outcome of the case.

1.4 The arbitrator or his or her firm regularly advises the party, or an affiliate of the party, and the arbitrator or his or her firm derives significant financial income therefrom.

2.   Waivable Red List

2.1 Relationship of the arbitrator to the dispute
  2.1.1 The arbitrator has given legal advice, or provided an expert opinion, on the dispute to a party or an affiliate of one of the parties.
  2.1.2 The arbitrator had a prior involvement in the dispute.

2.2 Arbitrator's direct or indirect interest in the dispute
  2.2.1 The arbitrator holds shares, either directly or indirectly, in one of the parties, or an affiliate of one of the parties, this party or an affiliate being privately held.
  2.2.2 A close family member of the arbitrator has a significant financial interest in the outcome of the dispute.

2.2.3 The arbitrator, or a close family member[1] of the arbitrator, has a close relationship with a non-party who may be liable to recourse on the part of the unsuccessful party in the dispute.

2.3 Arbitrator's relationship with the parties or counsel

2.3.1 The arbitrator currently represents or advises one of the parties, or an affiliate of one of the parties.

2.3.2 The arbitrator currently represents or advises the lawyer or law firm acting as counsel for one of the parties.

2.3.3 The arbitrator is a lawyer in the same law firm as the counsel to one of the parties.

2.3.4 The arbitrator is a manager, director or member of the supervisory board, or has a controlling influence in an affiliate[2] of one of the parties, if the affiliate is directly involved in the matters in dispute in the arbitration.

2.3.5 The arbitrator's law firm had a previous but terminated involvement in the case without the arbitrator being involved himself or herself.

2.3.6 The arbitrator's law firm currently has a significant commercial relationship with one of the parties, or an affiliate of one of the parties.

2.3.7 The arbitrator regularly advises one of the parties, or an affiliate of one of the parties, but neither the arbitrator nor his or her firm derives a significant financial income therefrom.

2.3.8 The arbitrator has a close family relationship with one of the parties, or with a manager, director or member of the supervisory board, or any person having a controlling influence in one of the parties, or an affiliate of one of the parties, or with a counsel representing a party.

2.3.9 A close family member of the arbitrator has a significant financial or personal interest in one of the parties, or an affiliate of one of the parties.

3. Orange List

3.1 Previous services for one of the parties or other involvement in the case

3.1.1 The arbitrator has, within the past three years, served as counsel for one of the parties, or an affiliate of one of the parties, or has previously advised or been consulted by the party, or an affiliate of the party, making the appointment in an unrelated matter, but the arbitrator and the party, or the affiliate of the party, have no ongoing relationship.

3.1.2 The arbitrator has, within the past three years, served as counsel against one of the parties, or an affiliate of one of the parties, in an unrelated matter.

3.1.3 The arbitrator has, within the past three years, been appointed as arbitrator on two or more occasions by one of the parties, or an affiliate of one of the parties.[3]

3.1.4 The arbitrator's law firm has, within the past three years, acted for or against one of the parties, or an affiliate of one of the parties, in an unrelated matter without the involvement of the arbitrator.

3.1.5 The arbitrator currently serves, or has served within the past three years, as arbitrator in another arbitration involving one of the parties, or an affiliate of one of the parties.

---

[1] Throughout the Application Lists, the term 'close family member' refers to a: spouse, sibling, child, parent or life partner, in addition to any other family member with whom a close relationship exists.

[2] Throughout the Application Lists, the term 'affiliate' encompasses all companies in a group of companies, including the parent company.

[3] It may be the practice in certain types of arbitration, such as maritime, sports or commodities arbitration, to draw arbitrators from a smaller or specialised pool of individuals. If in such fields it is the custom and practice for parties to frequently appoint the same arbitrator in different cases, no disclosure of this fact is required, where all parties in the arbitration should be familiar with such custom and practice.

3.2 Current services for one of the parties
- 3.2.1 The arbitrator's law firm is currently rendering services to one of the parties, or to an affiliate of one of the parties, without creating a significant commercial relationship for the law firm and without the involvement of the arbitrator.
- 3.2.2 A law firm or other legal organisation that shares significant fees or other revenues with the arbitrator's law firm renders services to one of the parties, or an affiliate of one of the parties, before the Arbitral Tribunal.
- 3.2.3 The arbitrator or his or her firm represents a party, or an affiliate of one of the parties to the arbitration, on a regular basis, but such representation does not concern the current dispute.

3.3 Relationship between an arbitrator and another arbitrator or counsel
- 3.3.1 The arbitrator and another arbitrator are lawyers in the same law firm.
- 3.3.2 The arbitrator and another arbitrator, or the counsel for one of the parties, are members of the same barristers' chambers.
- 3.3.3 The arbitrator was, within the past three years, a partner of, or otherwise affiliated with, another arbitrator or any of the counsel in the arbitration.
- 3.3.4 A lawyer in the arbitrator's law firm is an arbitrator in another dispute involving the same party or parties, or an affiliate of one of the parties.
- 3.3.5 A close family member of the arbitrator is a partner or employee of the law firm representing one of the parties, but is not assisting with the dispute.
- 3.3.6 A close personal friendship exists between an arbitrator and a counsel of a party.
- 3.3.7 Enmity exists between an arbitrator and counsel appearing in the arbitration.
- 3.3.8 The arbitrator has, within the past three years, been appointed on more than three occasions by the same counsel, or the same law firm.
- 3.3.9 The arbitrator and another arbitrator, or counsel for one of the parties in the arbitration, currently act or have acted together within the past three years as cocounsel.

3.4 Relationship between arbitrator and party and others involved in the arbitration
- 3.4.1 The arbitrator's law firm is currently acting adversely to one of the parties, or an affiliate of one of the parties.
- 3.4.2 The arbitrator has been associated with a party, or an affiliate of one of the parties, in a professional capacity, such as a former employee or partner.
- 3.4.3 A close personal friendship exists between an arbitrator and a manager or director or a member of the supervisory board of: a party; an entity that has a direct economic interest in the award to be rendered in the arbitration; or any person having a controlling influence, such as a controlling shareholder interest, on one of the parties or an affiliate of one of the parties or a witness or expert.
- 3.4.4 Enmity exists between an arbitrator and a manager or director or a member of the supervisory board of: a party; an entity that has a direct economic interest in the award; or any person having a controlling influence in one of the parties or an affiliate of one of the parties or a witness or expert.
- 3.4.5 If the arbitrator is a former judge, he or she has, within the past three years, heard a significant case involving one of the parties, or an affiliate of one of the parties.

3.5 Other circumstances
- 3.5.1 The arbitrator holds shares, either directly or indirectly, that by reason of number or denomination constitute a material holding in one of the parties, or an affiliate of one of the parties, this party or affiliate being publicly listed.
- 3.5.2 The arbitrator has publicly advocated a position on the case, whether in a published paper, or speech, or otherwise.
- 3.5.3 The arbitrator holds a position with the appointing authority with respect to the dispute.
- 3.5.4 The arbitrator is a manager, director or member of the supervisory board, or has a controlling influence on an affiliate of one of the parties, where the affiliate is not directly involved in the matters in dispute in the arbitration.

4. Green List

4.1 Previously expressed legal opinions

    4.1.1 The arbitrator has previously expressed a legal opinion (such as in a law review article or public lecture) concerning an issue that also arises in the arbitration (but this opinion is not focused on the case).

4.2 Current services for one of the parties

    4.2.1 A firm, in association or in alliance with the arbitrator's law firm, but that does not share significant fees or other revenues with the arbitrator's law firm, renders services to one of the parties, or an affiliate of one of the parties, in an unrelated matter.

4.3 Contacts with another arbitrator, or with counsel for one of the parties

    4.3.1 The arbitrator has a relationship with another arbitrator, or with the counsel for one of the parties, through membership in the same professional association, or social or charitable organisation, or through a social media network.

    4.3.2 The arbitrator and counsel for one of the parties have previously served together as arbitrators.

    4.3.3 The arbitrator teaches in the same faculty or school as another arbitrator or counsel to one of the parties, or serves as an officer of a professional association or social or charitable organisation with another arbitrator or counsel for one of the parties.

    4.3.4 The arbitrator was a speaker, moderator or organiser in one or more conferences, or participated in seminars or working parties of a professional, social or charitable organisation, with another arbitrator or counsel to the parties.

4.4 Contacts between the arbitrator and one of the parties

    4.4.1 The arbitrator has had an initial contact with a party, or an affiliate of a party (or their counsel) prior to appointment, if this contact is limited to the arbitrator's availability and qualifications to serve, or to the names of possible candidates for a chairperson, and did not address the merits or procedural aspects of the dispute, other than to provide the arbitrator with a basic understanding of the case.

    4.4.2 The arbitrator holds an insignificant amount of shares in one of the parties, or an affiliate of one of the parties, which is publicly listed.

    4.4.3 The arbitrator and a manager, director or member of the supervisory board, or any person having a controlling influence on one of the parties, or an affiliate of one of the parties, have worked together as joint experts, or in another professional capacity, including as arbitrators in the same case.

    4.4.4 The arbitrator has a relationship with one of the parties or its affiliates through a social media network.

Index

Note: please see under entries for individual countries and institutions/tribunals for specific topics relating to that country or institution/tribunal